Lecture Notes in Computer Science 1709

Edited by G. Goos, J. Hartmanis and J. van Leeuwen

Springer

Berlin
Heidelberg
New York
Barcelona
Hong Kong
London
Milan
Paris
Singapore
Tokyo

Jeannette M. Wing   Jim Woodcock
Jim Davies (Eds.)

FM'99 –
Formal Methods

World Congress on Formal Methods
in the Development of Computing Systems
Toulouse, France, September 20-24, 1999
Proceedings, Volume II

 Springer

Series Editors

Gerhard Goos, Karlsruhe University, Germany
Juris Hartmanis, Cornell University, NY, USA
Jan van Leeuwen, Utrecht University, The Netherlands

Volume Editors

Jeannette M. Wing
Carnegie Mellon University, Computer Science Department
5000 Forbes Avenue, Pittsburgh, PA 15213, USA
E-mail: wing@cs.cmu.edu

Jim Woodcock
Jim Davies
Oxford University Computing Laboratory
Software Engineering Programme
Wolfson Building, Parks Road, Oxford OX1 3QD, UK
E-mail: {jim.woodcock, jim.davies}@ comlab.ox.ac.uk

Cataloging-in-Publication data applied for

Die Deutsche Bibliothek - CIP-Einheitsaufnahme

Formal methods : proceedings / FM '99, World Congress on Formal Methods in the
Development of Computing Systems, Toulouse, France, September 20 - 24, 1999 /
Jeannette M. Wing ... (ed.). - Berlin ; Heidelberg ; New York ; Barcelona ;
Hong Kong ; London ; Milan ; Paris ; Singapore ; Tokyo : Springer

Vol. 2. - (1999)
 (Lecture notes in computer science ; Vol. 1709)
 ISBN 3-540-66588-9

CR Subject Classification (1998): F.3, D.2, F.4.1, D.3, D.1, C.2, C.3, I.2.3, B,
J.2

ISSN 0302-9743
ISBN 3-540-66588-9 Springer-Verlag Berlin Heidelberg New York

© Springer-Verlag Berlin Heidelberg 1999
Printed in Germany

Typesetting: Camera-ready by author
SPIN: 10705018   06/3142 – 5 4 3 2 1 0   Printed on acid-free paper

Preface

Formal methods are coming of age. Mathematical techniques and tools are now regarded as an important part of the development process in a wide range of industrial and governmental organisations. A transfer of technology into the mainstream of systems development is slowly, but surely, taking place.

FM'99, the First World Congress on Formal Methods in the Development of Computing Systems, is a result, and a measure, of this new-found maturity. It brings an impressive array of industrial and applications-oriented papers that show how formal methods have been used to tackle real problems.

These proceedings are a record of the technical symposium of *FM'99*: alongside the papers describing applications of formal methods, you will find technical reports, papers, and abstracts detailing new advances in formal techniques, from mathematical foundations to practical tools.

The World Congress is the successor to the four Formal Methods Europe Symposia, which in turn succeeded the four VDM Europe Symposia. This succession reflects an increasing openness within the international community of researchers and practitioners: papers were submitted covering a wide variety of formal methods and application areas.

The programme committee reflects the Congress's international nature, with a membership of 84 leading researchers from 38 different countries. The committee was divided into 19 tracks, each with its own chair to oversee the reviewing process. Our collective task was a difficult one: there were 259 high-quality submissions from 35 different countries.

Each paper was reviewed within a track, the track chairs resolved conflicts between reviewers, and the recommendations of each track chair were considered by the executive programme committee. This resulted in 92 papers being accepted, along with 15 abstracts describing work in progress and industrial applications.

We thank all those members of the programme and organising committees for their hard work, carried out under necessarily short deadlines. Thanks are due also to our able administrators, Maureen York and Anna Curtis; they did an excellent job and they deserve our gratitude for their contribution.

Finally, thanks to all those who submitted papers and attended the Congress: it is your hard work that has made it such a timely and important event.

July 1999

Jeannette Wing
Jim Woodcock
Jim Davies

Technical Tracks

The tracks that structure the technical symposium may be divided into three groups. First, there are application areas:

- Avionics
- Co-design
- Open information systems

- Safety
- Security
- Telecommunications

Second, there are processes and techniques:

- Composition and synthesis
- Integration
- Model checking
- Software architecture

- Object orientation
- Program verification
- Refinement
- Testing

Finally, there are groups of users and researchers:

- European Association for Theoretical Computer Science
- Foundations of System Specification
- Formal Description of Programming Concepts
- Abstract State Machines

- European Theory and Practice of Software
- Algebraic Methods in Software Technology
- OBJ / CafeOBJ / Maude
- The B method

Our five distinguished invited speakers are Tony Hoare of the University of Oxford, Cliff Jones of the University of Manchester, Amir Pnueli of the Weizmann Institute, Joseph Sifakis of Verimag, John Rushby of SRI International, and Michael Jackson, independent consultant.

Symposium Committee

Keijiro Araki, Japan
Egidio Astesiano, Italy
Albert Benveniste, France
Didier Bert, France
Dines Bjørner, Denmark
Robin Bloomfield, UK
Dominique Bolignano, France
Egon Börger, Italy
Jonathan Bowen, UK
Wilfried Brauer, Germany
Ed Brinksma, NL
Manfred Broy, Germany
Andrew Butterfield, Ireland
Jacques Cazin, France
Edmund Clarke, USA
Dan Craigen, Canada
Jorge Cuéllar, Germany
Aristides Dasso, Argentina
Jim Davies, UK
Tim Denvir, UK
Jin Song Dong, Singapore
Steve Dunne, UK
Hartmut Ehrig, Germany
John Fitzgerald, UK
Laure Pauline Fotso, Cameroon
Birgitte Fröhlich, Austria
Kokichi Futatsugi, Japan
David Garlan, USA
Marie-Claude Gaudel, France
Chris George, Macau
David Gries, USA
Henri Habrias, France
Armando Haeberer, Brazil
Nicolas Halbwachs, France
Kirsten Mark Hansen, Denmark
Anne Haxthausen, Denmark
Ian Hayes, Australia
Rick Hehner, Canada
Valérie Issarny, France
Rene Jacquart, France
Randolph Johnson, USA
Bengt Jonsson, Sweden
Leonid Kalinichenko, Russia
Kanchana Kanchanasut, Thailand

Kyo Chul Kang, Korea
Marite Kirikova, Latvia
Derrick Kourie, South Africa
Souleymane Koussoube, Burkina Faso
Reino Kurki-Suonio, Finland
Axel van Lamsweerde, Belgium
Jean-Claude Laprie, France
Peter Gorm Larsen, Denmark
Shaoying Liu, Japan
Peter Lucas, Austria
Micheal Mac an Airchinnigh, Ireland
Tom Maibaum, UK
Zohar Manna, USA
Lynn Marshall, Canada
Kees Middelburg, NL
Markus Montigel, Austria
Peter Mosses, Denmark
Friederike Nickl, Germany
Nikolai Nikitchenko, Ukraine
Roger Noussi, Gabon
Ernst-Rüdiger Olderog, Germany
José Nuno Oliveira, Portugal
Fernando Orejas, Spain
Paritosh Pandya, India
Jan Peleska, Germany
Frantisek Plásil, Czech Republic
Igor Prívara, Slovakia
Hans Rischel, Denmark
Ken Robinson, Australia
Teodor Rus, USA
Augusto Sampaio, Brazil
Georgy Satchock, Belarus
Kaisa Sere, Finland
Natarajan Shankar, USA
Joseph Sifakis, France
Doug Smith, USA
Radu Soricut, Rumania
Andrzej Tarlecki, Poland
T.H. Tse, Hong Kong
Bogdan Warinski, Rumania
Jeannette Wing, USA
Jim Woodcock, UK
Pamela Zave, USA
Zhou Chaochen, Macau

Congress General Chair
  Dines Bjørner

Programme Committee Co-chairs
  Jeannette Wing and Jim Woodcock

Organisation Committee Chair
  Rene Jacquart

Local Organisation and Publicity
  Jacques Cazin

Congress Public Relations Officer
  Jonathan Bowen

Congress Sponsors

AMAST	France Telecom
Aérospatiale Airbus	IFIP
Alcatel Space	INRIA
CCIT	IPSJ
CEPIS	IRIT
CNES	JSSST
CNRS	LAAS
Cap Gemini	Mairie de Toulouse
Carnegie-Mellon University	Matra Marconi Space
Conseil Regional Midi-Pyrenees	ONERA
DGA	Technical University of Delft
EATCS	Technical University of Denmark
ESA	Technical University of Graz
ETAPS	Translimina
European Union	University of Oxford
FACS	University of Reading
FME	

Table of Contents

Refinement

Safety

Works-in-Progress

Industrial Experience

Table of Contents, Volume I

Composition and Synthesis

Telecommunications

From Informal Requirements to COOP:
A Concurrent Automata Approach

Pascal Poizat[1], Christine Choppy[2], and Jean-Claude Royer[1]

[1] IRIN, Université de Nantes & Ecole Centrale
2 rue de la Houssinière, B.P. 92208, F-44322 Nantes cedex 3, France
{Poizat, Royer}@irin.univ-nantes.fr
http://www.sciences.univ-nantes.fr/info/perso/permanents/poizat/
phone: +33 2 51 12 58 22 — fax: +33 2 51 12 58 12
[2] LIPN, Institut Galilée - Université Paris XIII,
Avenue Jean-Baptiste Clément, F-93430 Villetaneuse, France
Christine.Choppy@lipn.univ-paris13.fr

Abstract. Methods are needed to help using formal specifications in a practical way. We herein present a method for the development of mixed systems, i.e. systems with both a static and a dynamic part. Our method helps the specifier providing means to structure the system in terms of communicating subcomponents and to give the sequential components using a semi-automatic concurrent automata generation with associated algebraic data types. These components and the whole system may be verified using common set of tools for transition systems or algebraic specifications. Furthermore, our method is equipped with object oriented code generation in Java, to be used for prototyping concerns. In this paper, we present our method on a small example: a transit node component in a communication network.
Keywords: Concurrent systems, specification method, automata, object oriented (Java) code generation.

Stream: Foundations and Methodology
Mini-Track: FoSS (Foundations of Software Specifications)

1 Introduction

The use of formal specifications is now widely accepted in software development. Formal specifications are mainly useful to provide an abstract, rigorous and complete description of a system. They are also essential to prove properties, to prototype the system and to generate tests. The need for a method that helps and guides the specifier is another well-known fact. A last point is the need for mixed specifications: *i.e.* specifications able to describe both the dynamic (process control) and the static aspects (data types). We think that mixed specifications also enable, at a specification level, to have a clear separation of concerns between these two aspects of systems that should be orthogonal as

J. Wing, J. Woodcock, J. Davies (Eds.): FM'99, Vol. II, LNCS 1709, pp. 939–962, 1999.
© Springer-Verlag Berlin Heidelberg 1999

advocated (at the implementation level) by recent Concurrent Object Oriented Programming (COOP) research.

We herein present a method based on LOTOS [7, 20] and SDL[1] [11] experiences [25, 24]. Our method was first presented in [26] and is here elaborated in terms of *agenda* and extended to Java code generation. We chose to describe our method in terms of the *agenda* concept [17, 16] because it describes a list of activities for solving a task in software engineering, and is developed to provide guidance and support for the application of formal specification techniques. Our method mixes constraint-oriented and state oriented specification styles [33] and produces a modular description with a dynamic behaviour and its associated data type.

The dynamic behaviour extraction is based on a guarded automaton that is progressively and rigorously built from requirements. Type information and operation preconditions are used to define states and transitions. The dynamic behaviour is computed from the automaton using some standard patterns. The last improvement is the assisted computation of the functional part. Our method reuses a technique [3] which allows one to get an abstract data type from an automaton. This technique extracts a signature and generators from the automaton. Furthermore, the automaton drives the axiom writing so that the specifier has only to provide the axioms right hand sides.

Our method is extended here to code generation. Code generation is a really useful tool from a practical point of view. It allows to generate from a specification a prototype which may be used as the basis for the future system, to validate client requirements or to test the system. We use Java [15] as a target language for the static part and we focus on the dialect ActiveJava [1] for the dynamic part.

The paper is structured as follows. We briefly present the case study: a transit node case in a telecommunications network [5]. In Section 3, the general process of our method is given. Section 4 is devoted to code generation, namely it consists in two subsections: the static generation part in Java and the dynamic generation part in ActiveJava. The conclusion summarizes the main points of our method.

2   Case-Study Presentation

This case study was adapted within the VTT project [5] from one defined in the RACE project 2039 (SPECS : Specification Environment for Communication Software). It consists of a simple transit node where messages arrive, are routed, and leave the node. The informal specification reads as follows:

clause 1 The system to be specified consists of a transit node with: one *Control Port-In,* one *Control Port-Out,* N *Data Ports-In,* N *Data Ports-Out,* M *Routes Through.* The limits of *N* and *M* are not specified.

---

[1] Both are used for the specification of distributed systems and are mixed specification languages.

clause 2 (a) Each port is serialized. (b) All ports are concurrent to all others. The ports should be specified as separate, concurrent entities. (c) Messages arrive from the environment only when a *Port-In* is able to treat them.

clause 3 The node is "fair". All messages are equally likely to be treated, when a selection must be made,

clause 4 and all data messages will eventually transit the node, or become faulty.

clause 5 *Initial State :* one *Control Port-In,* one *Control Port-Out.*

clause 6 The *Control Port-In* accepts and treats the following three messages:

(a) *Add-Data-Port-In-&-Out(n)* gives the node knowledge of a new *Port-In(n)* and a new *Port-Out(n).* The node commences to accept and treat messages sent to the *Port-In,* as indicated below on *Data Port-In.*
(b) *Add-Route(m,n_i)* , associates route m with *Data-Port-Out(n_i).*
(c) *Send-Faults* routes some messages in the faulty collection, if any, to *Control Port-Out.* The order in which the faulty messages are transmitted is not specified.

clause 7 A *Data Port-In* accepts only messages of the type : *Route(m).Data.*

(a) The *Port-In* routes the message, unchanged, to any one (non determinate) of the open *Data Ports-Out* associated with route m. If no such port exists, the message is put in the faulty collection.
(b) (Note that a *Data Port-Out* is serialized – the message has to be buffered until the *Data Port-Out* can process it).
(c) The message becomes a faulty message if its transit time through the node (from initial receipt by a *Data Port-In* to transmission by a *Data Port-Out*) is greater than a constant time T.

clause 8 *Data Ports-Out* and *Control Port-Out* accept messages of any type and will transmit the message out of the node. Messages may leave the node in any order.

clause 9 All faulty messages are eventually placed in the faulty collection where they stay until a *Send-Faults* command message causes them to be routed to *Control Port-Out.*

clause 10 Faulty messages are (a) messages on the *Control Port-In* that are not one of the three commands listed, (b) messages on a *Data Port-In* that indicate an unknown route, or (c) messages whose transit time through the node is greater than T.

clause 11 (a) Messages that exceed the transit time of T become faulty as soon as the time T is exceeded.

(b) It is permissible for a faulty message not to be routed to *Control Port-Out* by a *Send-Faults* command (because, for example, it has just become faulty, but has not yet been placed in a faulty message collection),

(c) but all faulty messages must eventually be sent to *Control Port-Out* with a succession of *Send-Faults* commands.

clause 12 It may be assumed that a source of time (time-of-day or a signal each time interval) is available in the environment and need not be modeled within the specification.

3   A New Specification Method

Overall Presentation

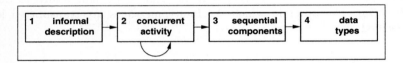

Fig. 1. The step dependencies at the overall level

Our method is composed of four steps for obtaining the specification (cf. Fig. 1): the **informal description** of the system to be specified, the **concurrent activity** description, the **sequential component** descriptions by an automaton, the **data type** specifications. Two validation steps may also be associated to the specification steps but they are not detailed here. Each step is described below with a proper agenda and is briefly described. A more complete presentation of our method may be found in [25] and the whole application to the case study in [24].

Step 1: Informal description (Fig. 2)

step	expression / schema	validation conditions
1.1: system functionalities	F_i: text	o no redundancy
1.2: system constraints	C_i: text	o consistency
1.3: system data	D_i: sort	

Fig. 2. Informal description agenda

The aim of this first step is to sketch out the system characteristics.

Step 1.1: Description of the system functionalities. In this substep all possible operations are inventoried, given a name (F_i in Fig. 2) and described. For instance, in our example, some operations are given by clauses 6 and 7:

- at the Control Port In: the reception of a command message (`in_cmde`)
- at the Data Ports In: the reception of a data message (`in_data`).

Step 1.2: System constraints description. The system constraints relative to orders, operations ordering, size limits, ... are expressed here and should be consistent, *i.e.* without contradiction.

Step 1.3: System data description. The point of view is very abstract here. The system data are given a name (and a sort name).

The transit node data are a list of open ports numbers (clause 6a), a list of routes (clauses 6b and 7a) and a list of faulty messages (clauses 4, 6c, 7a and 9).

Step 2: Concurrent activity

In this step the components that are executed in parallel are identified. Each one is modeled by a process. The process decomposition into subprocesses is inspired by the constraint-oriented and the resource-oriented specification styles [32, 33]. For each process there is a control part (dynamic part). Moreover, a data type (static part) may be associated with sequential processes and a variable of this type used as a formal parameter for the process. This unifies with the object-oriented encapsulation concept used later on. This step is decomposed in the following way: 2.1 communications, 2.2 decomposition and distribution, 2.3 parallel composition. As shown in Fig. 3, the substeps 2.2 and 2.3 may be iterated.

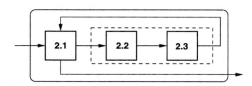

Fig. 3. Step dependencies for the concurrent activity

Step 2.1: Communications.

step 2.1.1: communication ports and data. The components interactions are modeled by communications on formal ports that represent the component services. Both communication ports and data are given by the informal description (step 1) or a previous decomposition (step 2).

step	expression / schema	validation conditions
2.1.1: communication ports and data	**PROCESS** D_i : sort ... F_i ...	○ no omission: the F_i and D_i from 1.1 and 1.3 are all taken into account
2.1.2: communications typing	F_i: ?x_j:s_j !x_k:s_k	○ no omission: the F_i from 1.1 are all taken into account ○ emission sorts are *available*

Fig. 4. Communications agenda

step 2.1.2: communications typing. The data that are either emitted (denoted by !x:T) or received (denoted by ?x:T) on the ports are typed. The communication typing is used to describe the processes interface, and also to specify the static part.

A validation criteria is to make sure that the emission sorts of a process are "available". A sort s is *available* for a process when:

— either it is directly available, that is predefined and imported, defined within the process, or received by the process
— or there exists an imported operation f : $d^* \rightarrow s$ such that all sorts in d^* are available. Since the data specification is achieved at step 4 this criteria validation may not be completed at this level.

We use a type Msg as an abstraction to represent the different messages in the transit node:

— reception of a command message: in_cmde : ?m:Msg
— reception of a data message: in_data : !id:PortNumber ?m:Msg ?r: RouteNumber
— emission of a list of faulty messages: out_cmde : !l:List[Msg]
— emission of a data message: out_data : !m:Msg

Step 2.2: Decomposition and distribution. The process decomposition into subprocesses is done using pieces of information (constraints) from the informal description (or a previous decomposition), using the data and/or functionalities. The decomposition may be done in such a way that already specified components may be reused.

Clause 1 leads to consider four components in the transit node: the Control Port In (CPI), the Data Ports In (DPI), the Control Port Out (CPO) and the Data Ports Out (DPO). The CPI manages the declared routes and the open ports (clause 6). The DPI needs access to information about which ports are related to which routes (clause 2a). Given the pieces of information collected from the preceding steps, the system may be represented as in Fig. 6 (see also Fig. 8).

step	expression / schema	validation conditions
2.2.1: data distribution	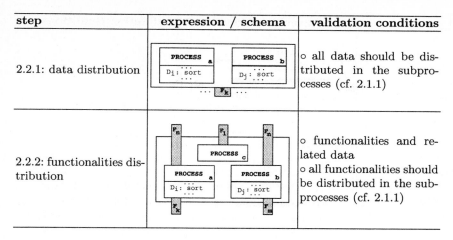	o all data should be distributed in the subprocesses (cf. 2.1.1)
2.2.2: functionalities distribution		o functionalities and related data o all functionalities should be distributed in the subprocesses (cf. 2.1.1)

Fig. 5. Decomposition and distribution agenda

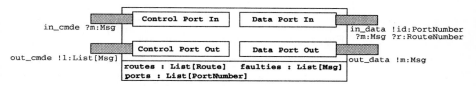

Fig. 6. Transit node external view (from Step 2.2)

Step 2.3: Parallel composition (Fig. 7). Processes composition often follows already known patterns, such as the synchronization schemata or the architectural styles given in [21, 18, 31]. Therefore we suggest to use a library of "composition schemata" that may be extended as needed. The specification of the subprocesses parallel composition may be derived from the set of the composition schemata using language specific features such as LOTOS operators [25] or SDL block structure and channels [24].

The process composition may lead to create new (internal) communications and possibly new data that have to be specified. Let us note that the process parallel composition is a way to express some constraints between the processes. Thus, clause 2b leads to a constraint on the parallel composition between the different ports. In order to take this into account, the DPI (resp. DPO) should be rather composed by interleaving than by synchronization.

Faulty messages. They are saved in the CPO collection (clause 9). They are (clause 10) either incorrect command messages (wrong_cmde, received by the CPI), or data messages with an unknown route (wrong_route, received by a DPI), or obsolete messages (timeout, from a DPO).

Information on routes. The DPI needs information on the transit node routes (whether a route is declared, and what are its associated ports). These pieces of information are held by the CPI, and will be transmitted to the DPI through

step	expression / schema	validation conditions
2.3.1: composition schema choice	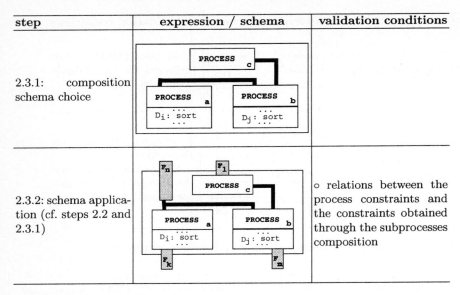	
2.3.2: schema application (cf. steps 2.2 and 2.3.1)		o relations between the process constraints and the constraints obtained through the subprocesses composition

Fig. 7. Parallel composition agenda

question/answer communications between the DPI and the CPI (ask_route and reply_route).

Message routing. When the data message route is correct, the message is routed (**correct** communication) by the DPI to one of the corresponding DPOs (clause 7a).

New ports. When the CPI receives the *Add-Data-Port-In-&-Out* command, it creates the corresponding ports (clause 6). In our modelization, this is taken into account by the fact that the Data Ports are enabled (**enable** communication) by the CPI on reception of this command.

New data. New data may arise from decomposition (or recomposition). Here, the DPOs are serialized (clause 7b) and have a buffer for messages. The Data Ports have an identifier used in enabling and routing communications.

Step 2 was iterated until obtaining the Fig. 8 schema. In the sequel, we shall focus on the DPI communication typing which is the following:

```
correct : !ident:PortNumber !m:Msg        ask_route : !r:RouteNumber
wrong_route : !m:Msg                      enable : !ident:PortNumber
reply_route : !r:RouteNumber ?l:List[PortNumber]
in_data : !id:PortNumber ?m:Msg ?r:RouteNumber
```

Step 3: Sequential components (Fig. 9)

Each sequential component is described by a guarded finite state automaton.

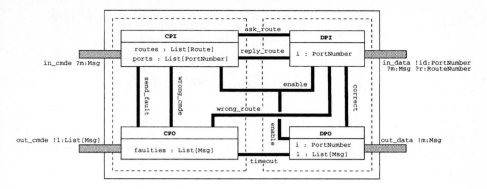

Fig. 8. Transit node internal view (from Step 2.3)

Steps 3.1 to 3.4: Conditions. The ports are put in four disjoint sets depending on whether they modify (C and CC) or not (O and OC) the state of the process and whether they are conditioned (CC and OC) or not (C and O). The names stand for *Constructor* (C), *Conditioned Constructor* (CC), *Observer* (O) and *Conditioned Observer* (OC).

The term "condition" refers to preconditions required for a communication to take place, and also to conditions that affect the behaviour when a communication takes place.

It should be checked that all conditions mentioned in step 1.2 are taken into account. However, some of them will be taken into account when dealing with the parallel composition of processes (step 2.3).

Applying the steps 3.1 and 3.2 to the DPI leads to identify the following conditions: `enabled` (the port is enabled), `received` (a message is received and not yet routed), `requested` (routing information was requested), `answered` (the answer on routing information is received), and `routeErr`[2] (routing error).

For instance, the `wrong_route` operation in CC has the following conditions: `enabled` $\land$ `received` $\land$ `requested` $\land$ `answered` $\land$ `¬routeErr`.

Relationships between conditions are expressed by formulas $(\vdash \phi_i(C_j))$. The relationship formula have to be consistent and may lead to simplify some conditions (possibly eliminating some).

In the DPI example, we have: `answered` $\Rightarrow$ `requested`, `requested` $\Rightarrow$ `received`, `received` $\Rightarrow$ `enabled`. This is consistent and leads to: `answered` $\land$ `¬routeErr` when applied to the condition on `wrong_route`.

Steps 3.5 to 3.7: States retrieval. Whether a process may perform a service (through a communication on a port) depends on which abstract state the process is in. The states are thus retrieved by composition of the communications conditions (these conditions were identified in steps 3.2 to 3.4, and a truth table is constructed in 3.5). The formulas $(\phi_i(C_j))$ expressing relationships between

---

[2] The `routeErr` condition bears on the value of the variable l of `reply_route` after the communication took place (see the communication typing at the end of step 2).

step	expression / schema	validation conditions
3.1: obtaining ports of O, OC, C, CC	O, OC, C, CC	∘ disjoint sets
3.2: conditions on ports of OC or CC category: precondition or behaviour	F_i : C_j (category)	∘ 1.2 (cf also 2.3)
3.3: relationships between conditions	$\vdash \phi_i(C_j)$	$\vdash_\lambda$ consistency: $\vdash \wedge_i \phi_i(C_j)$
3.4: simplification of conditions		$\vdash_\lambda$ simplifications
3.5: creating the conditions table	[... C_i ... | interpretation | reference]	
3.6: elimination of impossible cases	[... C_i ... | interpretation | reference]	$\vdash_\lambda \phi_i(C_j)$ (3.3)
3.7: states	$\mathcal{E}_i = <...,v(C_j),...>$ $v(C_j) \in \{T,F\}$	
3.8: operations preconditions	$\mathcal{P}_k = <...,v(C_j),...>$ $v(C_j) \in \{T,F,\forall\}$	$\vdash_\lambda$ consistency of preconditions w.r.t. $\phi_i(C_j)$ $\vdash$ correction w.r.t. 3.2
3.9: operations postconditions	$\mathcal{Q}_k = <...,\Phi_i(C'_j),...>$	C' : C + new conditions
3.10: relationships between conditions	$\vdash \phi_i(C'_j)$	$\vdash_\lambda$ consistency: $\vdash \wedge_i \phi_i(C'_j)$ $\vdash_\lambda$ consistency of postconditions w.r.t. $\phi_i(C'_j)$
3.11: computing the transitions	$\mathcal{T} = f(\mathcal{E},\mathcal{P},\mathcal{Q})$	
3.12: choice of an initial state from possible (O_i) and impossible $(\overline{O_j})$ operations	$\mathcal{E}_{init}$	$\vdash_\lambda$ consistency of $\wedge_i \mathcal{P}_{O_i} \wedge_j \neg \mathcal{P}_{\overline{O_j}}$ $\vdash_\lambda$ only one initial state
3.13: automaton simplifications		$\vdash$ equivalences
3.14: translating the automaton to the target language		$\vdash$ automaton / specification
3.15: simplifying the specification		$\vdash$ correct simplifications

Fig. 9. Sequential components agenda

these conditions are used to eliminate incoherent states (3.6). Table 1 gives the DPI coherent states.

Table 1. State conditions table for the Data Port In

enabled	received	requested	answered	routeERR	state
T	T	T	T	T	IR (Incorrect Route)
T	T	T	T	F	CR (Correct Route)
T	T	T	F	F	WA (Waiting for Answer)
T	T	F	F	F	RfR (Ready for Request)
T	F	F	F	F	RfI (Ready for Input)
F	F	F	F	F	NA (Not Authorized)

Steps 3.8 to 3.11: Transitions retrieval. To retrieve the transitions, we shall define each operation in terms of possible source states (preconditions) and corresponding target states (postconditions). Therefore, preconditions ($\mathcal{P}$, 3.8) and postconditions ($\mathcal{Q}$, 3.9) are expressed in terms of the conditions values, respectively before and after the communications take place. The case where the condition value is not relevant is denoted by $\forall$, and $=$ denotes the case where the value is not modified after the communication. Verifications and simplifications may be achieved on both preconditions and postconditions [25].

Examples of preconditions and postconditions for some DPI operations are given below with the following notation: en for **enabled**, rec for **received**, req for **requested**, rep for **answered**, and **rerr** for routeErr.

ask_route	en rec req rep rerr
$\mathcal{P}$	T T $\forall$ F $\forall$
$\mathcal{Q}$	= = T = =

reply_route	en rec req rep rerr
$\mathcal{P}$	T T T F $\forall$
$\mathcal{Q}$	= = = T l=[]

There are generally *critical cases* [25] and some postconditions may not be expressed using only state conditions. It is thus necessary to use new conditions to check whether the process data type is in a critical state. Informally, critical state conditions act as transition guards to avoid infinite state automata.

Operationally to retrieve the transitions, and for each operation:

− start from a given state e (a condition boolean tuple)
− if this tuple yields the operation precondition, find the tuple for the corresponding postcondition and the associated state f
− there is therefore a transition from e to f
− start over with another state.

Some improvements of this operational method are given in [25]. This automatic method leads to deal with cases that might not have been detected otherwise, as the critical cases.

Step 3.12: Initial state. In order to determine the *initial state*, it is necessary to identify the services (associated to some ports) the process should give or not in that state (constraints). It is a requirement based choice. The potential initial states are found from the ports preconditions and the state table. If no initial state is found, this means that the specifier gave inconsistent constraints for it. In order to be able to generate code, a single initial state is needed. When several potential initial states are found, it possible to choose one of them arbitrarily or by adding some constraint on the services. The DPI automaton is given in Fig. 10.

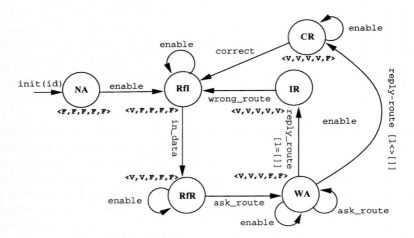

Fig. 10. Data Port In automaton

Steps 3.13 to 3.15: Simplifications and translation. It is possible to translate the automaton to various specification languages by applying translation schemata. This technique was applied to LOTOS [25] and to SDL [24]. Whenever the translation is not optimal, some simplifications may possibly be applied [25, 24]. The automaton may also be simplified before the translation, for instance by hierarchical grouping of states achieved using the conditions [24].

Step 4: Data types

The last step is the specification of the abstract data types associated to each process, and of the data types used within the processes. As regards the data types associated to each process, the work achieved in the preceding steps yields most of the signature (cf. [25] from a description of the automatic processing). Thus, the operations names and profiles are retrieved automatically from the communication typing, and from the conditions identified upon building the automata. Let us note that with each communication m, one or several algebraic operations may be associated (Fig. 11).

Some additional operations may be needed to express the axioms. Most of the axioms are written in a "constructive" style which requires to identify the generators. [3] describes a method to retrieve the data type associated to an automaton and to compute a minimal set of operations necessary to reach all states.

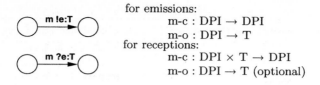

for emissions:

$$\text{m-c} : \text{DPI} \to \text{DPI}$$
$$\text{m-o} : \text{DPI} \to \text{T}$$

for receptions:

$$\text{m-c} : \text{DPI} \times \text{T} \to \text{DPI}$$
$$\text{m-o} : \text{DPI} \to \text{T (optional)}$$

Fig. 11. Correspondence between communications and algebraic operations

In our example, this set is `init, enable, in_data, ask_route, reply_route`. [3] uses Ω-derivation [6] to write the axioms (conditional equations). In order to extract the axioms describing the properties of the operation `op(dpi:DPI)`, the states where this operation is allowed should be identified together with the generators to reach these states, thus yielding the premises and the axioms left hand sides.

Part of this automatic processing is shown here for the axioms of the `correct_c` operation, the internal operation associated with the `correct` transition. The premises express conditions on the source states and on the `l` variable.

```
% correct-c : DPI -> DPI
CR(dpi) => correct-c(enable-c(dpi)) = correct-c(dpi)
WA(dpi) /\ not(l=[]) => correct-c(reply-route-c(ask-route-c(dpi),l)) =
    correct-c(reply-route-c(dpi,l))
WA(dpi) /\ not(l=[]) => correct-c(reply-route-c(enable-c(dpi),l)) =
    correct-c(reply-route-c(dpi,l))
RfR(dpi) /\ not(l=[]) =>
    correct-c(reply-route-c(ask-route-c(enable-c(dpi)),l)) =
        correct-c(reply-route-c(ask-route-c(dpi),l))
RfI(dpi) /\ not(l=[]) =>
    correct-c(reply-route-c(ask-route-c(in-data-c(dpi,m,r)),l)) = dpi
```

The algebraic specification may then be used for proving properties needed for the specification verification and validation.

4   Code Generation

Once we get a formal specification it is not necessarily executable. Often the dynamic part is executable because it is based on operational models (state transition diagrams). This is not always true for the static part (algebraic abstract data type).

We will illustrate assisted code generation in Java, however the method is suitable for other object-oriented languages.

The general method is depicted on Fig. 12 and is split in two parts: the static part (on the right of Fig. 12) and the dynamic part (on the left of Fig. 12).

4.1   Static Part Generation

Java classes are generated for each abstract data type in the specification, and this process is achieved by four intermediate steps (cf. Fig. 12). The translations

Formal Specification

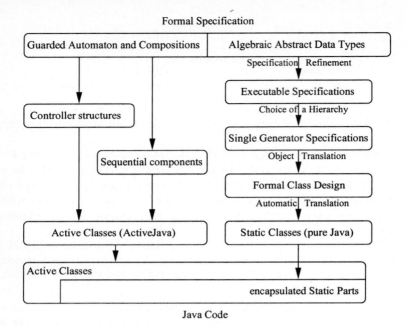

Java Code

Fig. 12. Object code generation scheme

are partly automatic, for instance to get a simpler or a more efficient result may require some specifier (or programmer) interaction. The first step is to obtain an executable specification (possibly through refinements). Then, code generation is decomposed into (i) the choice of a hierarchy for representing the specification generators, (ii) the translation into formal classes (i.e. abstractions of classes in object-oriented languages), from which (iii) a generation in a given language (e.g. Java) may be done.

Executable Specification. The "constructive" style adopted for the specifications associated with the automatons is likely to yield executable specifications (e.g. through rewriting, where tools, e.g. [14], may be used to check the convergence). However, other specification modules may be introduced (e.g. for the data managed by the processes) with other specification styles (e.g. observational style). A refinement process (abstract implementation [12]) is then needed to add elements for executability such as algorithmic choices, etc.

Single Generator Specifications. In object-oriented languages, classes have a single generation operation called for instance "new" (or the class name), while algebraic specifications allow several generators. The problem addressed here is how to represent these generators within classes, or more precisely how to transform (e.g. by abstract implementation) the original algebraic specifications into single generator specifications from which classes may be derived. We propose several solutions to this issue. A first solution is to associate to the several generators of the algebraic specification a single generator with a "switch" (to each original generator), we refer to this solution as the "flat organization". Another solution is to use the associated class as an interface to subclasses, where each subclass is associated to one generator of the original specification, this will be denoted as the "two level hierarchy organization". Then, of course, it is possible to mix these two solutions as appropriate.

Several frameworks are available for abstract implementation [12], a first sketch is to follow the general framework of Hoare's representation [19]. It consists into defining an abstraction function, to prove it is an onto function and to prove the implementation of operations. These aspects are not detailed here.

In the following, we present the alternative organizations for single generator specifications. When the abstract data type has only one generator we directly apply the simple representation described below to get a class.

Flat Organization. In this organization, a specification module with several generators is transformed into a single generator specification module with a "switch" to each original generator. For example, in the DPI specification module, the generators are init, enable, in_data, ask_route, reply_route. We define SwitchDPI = {init, enable, in_data, ask_route, reply_route} and the single generator newSDPI (SDPI stands for Switch DPI) with the profile newSDPI : Switch PortNumber Msg RouteNumber List SDPI -> SDPI (note that this profile may be easily computed from the DPI generators profiles). The abstraction function Abs is defined as usual, e.g.:
Abs(newSDPI(reply_route, Bport, Bmsg, Broute, Z, T)) == reply_route_c(T, Z)...
Terms beginning by B are don't care values. We also introduce selectors associated to relevant arguments occurring in the single generator, e.g.:
switch(newSDPI(S, X, Y, R, Z, T)) = S
(S = reply_route ∧ WA(T)) => selRoutes(newSDPI(S, X, Y, R, Z, T)) = Z...
The axioms are then transformed within this framework to complete the specification.

Two Level Hierarchy Organization. In this approach, several specification modules are associated with the original specification module: one module that is just an interface to modules that introduce (each) one of the original generators together with the appropriate subsort. Clearly, this approach may yield semantics issues (depending on the framework adopted), and may not be as practical and straightforward as the previous one. However, in some cases the specification style may be more legible.

Mixed Organization. Of course between these two previous extrema there are many other ways to transform the type depending of the chosen hierarchy. We studied in [2] how to get a better hierarchy and we presented a general process for it. However some important problems remain: metrics to define a best hierarchy and problems linked with inheritance of properties.

In case of abstract data types with less than five generators, the flat organization is acceptable but with more complex ones this will not be the case.

Another way to solve this problem is to introduce a kind of inheritance or subsort (OBJ subsort) in the method. This problem is known to be difficult in itself and rather complex with concurrent systems.

Formal Class Design: The Model. This model [4] defines the notion of *formal class* as an abstraction of a concrete class in languages like C++, Eiffel, Java or Smalltalk. A formal class is an algebraic specification (as abstract data type) with an object-orientation. This general model is functional and unifies the major concepts of object-oriented programming. It can be used both to build formal specifications and to design a system. An abstract operational semantics [4] was given to this model using conditional term rewriting [10].

Figure 13 shows a formal class example associated to the SDPI specification module obtained with the flat organization.

```
                                 FCDPI

field selectors
    switch    : FCDPI ⟶ Switch
    ident     : FCDPI ⟶ PortNumber
        requires: switch(Self) = init
    selRoutes : FCDPI ⟶ List
        requires: switch(Self) = reply_route ∧ WA(previous(Self))
    ...

methods
correct_c : FCDPI ⟶ FCDPI
;; correct_c : internal operation associated to a correct route
        (switch(Self) = enable ∧ CR(previous(Self))) =>
        correct_c(Self) = correct_c(previous(Self))
        (switch(Self) = reply_route ∧ switch(previous(Self)) = ask_route
        ∧ WA(previous(Self)) ∧ is_empty(list(Self))) =>
        correct_c(Self) = correct_c(new(reply_route, Bport, Bmsg, Broute,
                                selRoutes(Self), previous(previous(Self))))
    ...
```

Fig. 13. Formal Class FCDPI

The translation into (purely functional) Java code is straightforward. A formal class is translated to an interface (corresponding to the signature) and an implementation class. We use abstract methods and classes when needed (depending on the chosen organization). The structure is represented by private instance variables. Fields selectors are coded by a public accessor to the corresponding instance variable with a condition corresponding to the precondition.

A tool to generate Java classes is not available yet, but experimental tools have been done for Eiffel and Smalltalk.

Formal Class Design: A Simple Representation. The simple representation allows one to translate a single generator type into a formal class, denoted by FCADT. This generator will be the newFCADT instantiation function of the object model. We must identify selectors, *i.e.* operations sel_i such that $sel_i(new(X_1, \ldots, X_n)) = X_i$. These field selectors yield the instance variables of the class. We assume that the specification (axioms and preconditions) has no variable named Self. A term is said to be in a receiver position if it appears at first position in an operation different from the generator. If a variable appears in a receiver position in the left conclusion term then it will be replaced by Self. In our model this variable denotes the object receiver. An important translation rule is to replace newSADT(e_1, $\ldots$, e_n) by V with V : FCADT. This leads to a set of equations: $sel_i(V) = e_i$.

1. This rule is applied on every newSADT occurrence in a receiver position in the left conclusion term, where V is named Self. If e_i is a variable then it is replaced by sel_i(Self) in axioms. If e_i is neither a variable nor a don't care term, the equation sel_i(Self) = e_i is added to the axiom condition.
2. This rule is applied on all other occurrences in the left conclusion term with any variable other than Self.

This representation was processed over the single generator specification SDPI and the result is the above formal class (Fig. 13).

4.2 Dynamic Part Generation

This part deals with the code generation for the dynamic part in an object oriented language. The language we aim at is ActiveJava [1], a Java dialect (pre-processed into pure Java) based on ATOM [23].

The ActiveJava model defines abstract states, state predicates, methods activation conditions and state notification. Its main advantages are that: (i) its syntax is defined as a Java extension, (ii) it permits to model both inter and intra-object concurrency, and (iii) it supports both asynchronous and synchronous message passing. ActiveJava presents a good adequation between reusability of components (through separation of concerns into a dynamic and a static part) and expressivity.

The dynamic part generation is build upon (i) coding subsystems structuration and LOTOS-like communication semantics, (ii) coding sequential automata, and (iii) integrating dynamic and static parts.

Structuration and Communication Semantics. LOTOS communication semantics is more strict than the ActiveJava (object oriented) one. For this purpose and for better structuration matters, we choose to model each subsystem structuration with a *controller*. This approach is close to Coordinated Roles [22] and aims at the same properties: a better structuration and reusability of composition patterns.

The system specification is taken as a tree with sequential components at the leaves and controllers at the nodes where the LOTOS structuring mechanisms are encoded. The subtrees under a given controller will be called its *sons*. Structuration for the transit node is given in Fig. 14 where coordinators are drawn as square boxes and sequential components as round boxes. This is another representation of Fig. 8.

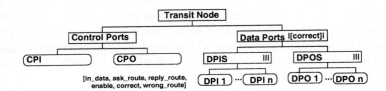

Fig. 14. Sketch of structuration and coordinators of the transit node

We have three main communication mechanisms for structuration: interleaving, synchronization and hidden synchronization.

Common mechanisms. The communication is achieved in three phases as shown in Fig. 15. In the *run phase*, controllers dispatch calls to a *run method* to their non waiting sons. Thus, in Fig. 15-1, C sends a run method to P but not to E. When these calls reach non controller components (i.e. the leaves, as P in Fig. 15-1) or controller with all sons blocked, then the second phase, *return phase* begins.

In this return phase, sons return the communications they are ready to get involved with in a *runnable list*: a list of tuples containing the communication name and its arguments, with values for emission arguments and a special indicator (_) for reception arguments. P returns [(''m'',_,4),(''n'',3)] to assess it is ready for a m or n communication (Fig. 15-2). The controller then computes a *common intersection* of the runnable lists and sends it up. Here, n from P does not match with anything from E whereas two m elements match to make the intersection that C sends upwards. Since some E and P runnable lists elements are in the common intersection, E and P are called *participants*. Elements with the same communication name have to match in the same way LOTOS offers match. Matching cases are given in Table. 2. All other cases mismatch.

The second phase ends when there is no intersection (this yields a blocking status) or at the root where a final intersection in computed. The controller where the second phase ends is called *temporary root*.

In the third phase (Fig. 15-3), the temporary root sends down the message corresponding to the final intersection it has previously computed. This message has to be unique, and non determinism (whether a received value has not been bound or there is communication non determinism) is solved by the temporary

Table 2. Matching elements and intersections

element 1	element 2	common intersection
("m",_:T)	("m",value:T)	("m",value:T)
("m",value:T)	("m",_:T)	("m",value:T)
("m",value:T)	("m",value:T)	("m",value:T) – same values
("m",_:T)	("m",_:T)	("m",_:T)

root controller [27]. Controllers send the message only to *participants* (both P and E for C) and then erase their table entry. Non participant sons are left waiting. To end, the temporary root controller relaunches the first phase by sending again the run method to its non waiting sons.

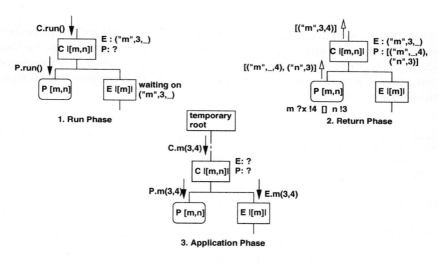

Fig. 15. A communication scheme example

Interleaving. As soon as a controller receives a non synchronized element in a runnable list, it transmits it up.

Synchronization. When two sons are composed in order to synchronize on a given method, their parent controller will transmit the corresponding element in runnable lists only if it has received this element in both sons runnable lists.

Hidden synchronization. In the return phase, when the runnable lists reach a node, elements referring to hidden messages are not returned upwards but are kept at this node level. When only hidden messages reach a controller which has to block them, this controller acts as the temporary root controller. If there are also non hidden messages, the controller chooses whether to transmit them upwards or to act as the temporary root (this choice simulates non determinism).

Coding the Automata in ActiveJava. The precondition and postcondition tables are used to code the automaton. But this has to be slightly modified to take into account run message receptions. The schema given in Fig. 16 is applied to each state.

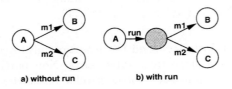

a) without run   b) with run

Fig. 16. Adding run in the automata

Operation preconditions are defined as "activation conditions" in ActiveJava. Optionally, condition variables may be set (postconditions) in the "post actions" methods of ActiveJava. In the class constructor, initial values for the conditions are set according to the automaton initial state. Fig. 17 illustrates this on a part of the DPI example.

```
active class DPI(CPI cpi, FC fc, DPO dpo) {
    boolean v_a, v_r, v_d, v_rep, v_rerr;
    PortNumberList received_l; ...

abstract state definitions {a as is_a(); ...}

activations conditions {
    reply_route(RouteNumber r, PortNumberList l)
        with reply_route_precondition(); ...}

synchronization actions {
    reply_route(RouteNumber r, PortNumberList l) with
        post_actions reply_route_postcondition(); ...}

implement synchronization {
    boolean is_a() {return v_a;}
    ...
    boolean reply_route_precondition() {
        return v_a==TRUE && v_r==TRUE && v_d==TRUE && v_rep==FALSE;}
    ...
    void reply_route_postcondition() {
        v_rep=TRUE; v_rerr=received_l.isEmpty();}
    ...
}}
```

Fig. 17. (Part of) Active Class for DPI

Integrating the Static and the Dynamic Parts The integration of the static and the dynamic part is done using encapsulation of a static class instance into the dynamic class with static methods called into dynamic methods bodies (Fig. 18). Observers are called in the run method to compute some of the run list elements arguments. Statics methods are also called in each corresponding dynamic method.

```
import StaticClass;

active class DynamicClass {
    StaticClass nested;
    < ActiveClass part >
    public methods {
        public DynamicClass( < arguments > ) {
            nested = new StaticClass( < arguments > );
            < dynamic initialization (initial state) >
        }
        public RunnableList run() {
        // uses nested.observers return values in runnable list
        }
        public void otherMethod( < arguments > ) {
            nested.otherMethod( < arguments > );
        }}}
```

Fig. 18. Integration of static and dynamic parts

5   Conclusion

While there are good motivations for the use of formal specifications in software development, the lack of methods may restrict it to "few experts". There are several points which may cause problems: the use of formal notation, the structure of the system, the proofs of properties and the code generation (or refinement for others) are some of the most important. In this paper, we address a specification method for systems where both concurrency and data types issues have to be taken into account. One important feature is the help provided to the user: help to build dynamic behaviours, help to decompose the system, help to extract the data types and help to generate code. Our method takes advantage of both the constraint and state oriented approaches that are used for LOTOS or SDL specifications. The system is described in terms of parallel components with well defined external interfaces (the gates and communication typing). The behaviour of the component is described by a sequential process associated with an internal data type. The study of the communications and their effect on this data type allows one to build, in a semi-automatic way, an automaton describing the process internal behaviour. The automaton is then translated into a specification language (LOTOS or SDL). The data type is extracted by a semi-automatic method from this automaton.

The components and the whole system may then be verified using common set of tools for transition systems [13] or algebraic specifications [14].

Our specification method is equipped with a prototype generation. Object-oriented languages are another major phenomenon in software engineering. One cannot ignore the qualities of such code, however writing such code may be a hard task. We choose to generate Java code but our method may be applied to other object oriented languages. This code generation is mainly automatic and modular. We plan to experiment code generation on other frameworks for concurrent object oriented programming such as [8].

One future research direction is the extension of this approach to other specification languages, like Raise [30] or Object-Z [28]. Other connected areas of research are about object-oriented analysis and design methods. We currently work on the use of UML [29] diagrams to improve system architecture and to validate the automaton behaviour (with communication diagrams for instance). Therefore, we plan to provide our specification model with inheritance, more complete communication (experimenting new controller semantics) and structuration mechanisms as in related models [9].

References

[1] Luis A. Álvarez, Juan M. Murillo, Fernando Sánchez, and Juan Hernández. ActiveJava, un modelo de programación concurrente orientado a objeto. In *III Jornadas de Ingenería del Software, Murcia, Spain*, 1998.

[2] Pascal André. *Méthodes formelles et à objets pour le développement du logiciel : Etudes et propositions.* PhD Thesis, Université de Rennes I (Institut de Recherche en Informatique de Nantes), Juillet 1995.

[3] Pascal André and Jean-Claude Royer. How To Easily Extract an Abstract Data Type From a Dynamic Description. Research Report 159, Institut de Recherche en Informatique de Nantes, September 1997.

[4] Pascal André, Dan Chiorean, and Jean-Claude Royer. The formal class model. In *Joint Modular Languages Conference*, pages 59–78, Ulm, Germany, 1994. GI, SIG and BCS.

[5] M. Bidoit, C. Choppy, and F. Voisin. Validation d'une spécification algébrique du "Transit-node" par prototypage et démonstration de théorèmes. Chapitre du Rapport final de l'Opération VTT, Validation et vérification de propriétés Temporelles et de Types de données (commune aux PRC PAOIA et C3), LaBRI, Bordeaux, 1994.

[6] Michel Bidoit. Types abstraits algébriques : spécifications structurées et présentations gracieuses. In *Colloque AFCET, Les mathématiques de l'informatique*, pages 347–357, Mars 1982.

[7] Tommaso Bolognesi and Ed Brinksma. Introduction to the ISO Specification Language LOTOS. *Computer Networks and ISDN Systems*, 14(1):25–29, January 1988.

[8] D. Caromel and J. Vayssière. A Java Framework for Seamless Sequential, Multi-threaded, and Distributed Programming. In *ACM Workshop "Java for High-*

Performance Network Computing", pages 141–150, Stanford University, Palo Alto, California, 1998.

[9] Eva Coscia and Gianna Reggio. JTN: A Java-Targeted Graphic Formal Notation for Reactive and Concurrent Systems. In Jean-Pierre Finance, editor, *Fundamental Approaches to Software Engineering (FASE'99)*, volume 1577 of *Lecture Notes in Computer Science*, pages 77–97. Springer-Verlag, 1999.

[10] Nachum Dershowitz and Jean-Pierre Jouannaud. *Rewrite Systems*, volume B of *Handbook of Theoretical Computer Science*, chapter 6, pages 243–320. Elsevier, 1990. Jan Van Leeuwen, Editor.

[11] Jan Ellsberger, Dieter Hogrefe, and Amardeo Sarma. *SDL : Formal Object-oriented Language for Communicating Systems*. Prentice-Hall, 1997.

[12] M. Navarro F. Orejas and A. Sanchez. Implementation and behavioural equivalence: a survey. In M. Bidoit and C. Choppy (Eds.), editors, *Recent Trends in data Type Specification*, volume 655 of *Lecture Notes in Computer Science*, pages 93–125. Springer-Verlag, August 1993.

[13] Jean-Claude Fernandez, Hubert Garavel, Alain Kerbrat, Radu Mateescu, Laurent Mounier, and Mihaela Sighireanu. CADP: A Protocol Validation and Verification Toolbox. In *8th Conference on Computer-Aided Verification*, pages 437–440, New Brunswick, New Jersey, USA, 1996.

[14] S. Garland and J. Guttag. An overview of LP, the Larch Prover. In *Proc. of the Third International Conference on Rewriting Techniques and Applications*, volume 355 of *Lecture Notes in Computer Science*, pages 137–151. Springer-Verlag, 1989.

[15] Gosling, Joy, and Steele. *The Java Language Specification*. Addison Wesley, 1996.

[16] Wolfgang Grieskamp, Maritta Heisel, and Heiko Dörr. Specifying Embedded Systems with Statecharts and Z: An Agenda for Cyclic Software Components. In Egidio Astesiano, editor, *FASE'98*, volume 1382 of *Lecture Notes in Computer Science*, pages 88–106. Springer-Verlag, 1998.

[17] Maritta Heisel. Agendas – A Concept to Guide Software Development Activities. In R. N. Horspool, editor, *Proceedings Systems Implementation 2000*, pages 19–32. Chapman & Hall, 1998.

[18] Maritta Heisel and Nicole Lévy. Using LOTOS Patterns to Characterize Architectural Styles. In Michel Bidoit and Max Dauchet, editors, *TAPSOFT'97 (FASE'97)*, volume 1214 of *Lecture Notes in Computer Science*, pages 818–832, 1997.

[19] C.A.R. Hoare. Proof of Correctness of Data Representations. *Acta Informatica*, 1:271–281, 1972.

[20] ISO/IEC. LOTOS: A Formal Description Technique based on the Temporal Ordering of Observational Behaviour. ISO/IEC 8807, International Organization for Standardization, 1989.

[21] Thomas Lambolais, Nicole Lévy, and Jeanine Souquières. Assistance au développement de spécifications de protocoles de communication. In *AFADL'97 Approches Formelles dans l'Assistance au Développement de Logiciel*, pages 73–84, 1997.

[22] Juan M. Murillo, Juan Hernández, Fernando Sánchez, and Luis A. Álvarez. Coordinated Roles: Promoting Re-usability of Coordinated Active Objects Using Event Notification Protocols. In Paolo Ciancarini and Alexander L. Wolf, editors, *Third International Conference, COORDINATION'99*, volume 1594 of *Lecture Notes in Computer Science*, Amsterdam, The Nederlands, April 1999. Springer-Verlag.

[23] M. Papathomas, J. Hernàndez, J. M. Murillo, and F. Sànchez. Inheritance and expressive power in concurrent object-oriented programming. In *LMO'97 Langages et Modèles à Objets*, pages 45–60, 1997.

[24] Pascal Poizat, Christine Choppy, and Jean-Claude Royer. Un support méthodologique pour la spécification de systèmes "mixtes". Research Report 180, Institut de Recherche en Informatique de Nantes, Novembre 1998. /papers/rr180.ps.gz in Poizat's web page.

[25] Pascal Poizat, Christine Choppy, and Jean-Claude Royer. Une nouvelle méthode pour la spécification en LOTOS. Research Report 170, Institut de Recherche en Informatique de Nantes, Février 1998. /papers/rr170.ps.gz in Poizat's web page.

[26] Pascal Poizat, Christine Choppy, and Jean-Claude Royer. Concurrency and Data Types: A Specification Method. An Example with LOTOS. In J. Fiadeiro, editor, *Recent Trends in Algebraic Development Techniques, Selected Papers of the 13th International Workshop on Algebraic Development Techniques WADT'98*, volume 1589 of *Lecture Notes in Computer Science*, pages 276–291, Lisbon, Portugal, 1999. Springer-Verlag.

[27] Pascal Poizat, Christine Choppy, and Jean-Claude Royer. From Informal Requirements to Object Oriented Code using Structured Concurrent Sequential Communicating Automata. Research Report, Institut de Recherche en Informatique de Nantes, 1999.

[28] Graeme Smith. A Fully-Abstract Semantics of Classes for Object-Z. *Formal Aspects of Computing*, 7(E):30–65, 1995.

[29] Rational Software and al. Unified Modeling Language, Version 1.1. Technical report, Rational Software Corp, http://www.rational.com/uml, September 1997.

[30] The Raise Method Group. *The RAISE Development Method*. The Practitioner Series. Prentice-Hall, 1995.

[31] K. Turner. Relating architecture and specification. *Computer Networks and ISDN Systems*, 29(4):437–456, 1997.

[32] Kenneth J. Turner, editor. *Using Formal Description Techniques, An introduction to Estelle, Lotos and SDL*. Wiley, 1993.

[33] C.A. Vissers, G. Scollo, M. Van Sinderen, and E. Brinksma. Specification styles in distributed systems design and verification. *Theoretical Computer Science*, (89):179–206, 1991.

A Framework for Defining Object-Calculi
Extended Abstract

Frédéric Lang, Pierre Lescanne, and Luigi Liquori

École Normale Supérieure de Lyon
Laboratoire de l'Informatique du Parallélisme
46, Allée d'Italie, F–69364 Lyon Cedex 07, FRANCE
E-mail: {flang,plescann,lliquori}@ens-lyon.fr

Abstract. In this paper, we give a general framework for the foundation of an operational (small step) semantics of object-based languages with an emphasis on functional and imperative issues. The framework allows classifying very naturally many object-based calculi according to their main implementation techniques of inheritance, namely *delegation* and *embedding*, and their particular strategies. This distinction comes easily from a choice in the rules. Our framework is founded on two previous works: λObj^+, a version of the *Lambda Calculus of Objects* of Fischer, Honsell, and Mitchell, for the object aspects, and $\lambda \sigma_w^a$ of Benaissa, Lescanne, and Rose, for the description of the operational semantics and sharing. The former is the formalization of a small delegation-based language which contains both lambda calculus and object primitives to create, update, and send messages to objects, while the latter is designed to provide a generic description of functional language implementations and is based on a calculus of explicit substitution extended with *addresses* to deal with memory management. The framework is presented as a set of *modules*, each of which captures a particular aspect of object-calculi (functional *vs.* imperative, delegation *vs.* embedding, and any combination of them). Above all, it introduces and illustrates a new promising approach to formally reason about the operational semantics of languages with (possibly) mutable states.

Keywords. Design of functional and imperative object-oriented languages, operational semantics, implementation issues, memory management.

1 Introduction

An (operational) semantics for a programming language is aimed to help the programmer and the designer of a compiler to better understand her (his) work and possibly to prove mathematically that what she (he) does is correct. For instance, the designers of Java proposed a description of an operational semantics of the Java Virtual Machine [16], but unfortunately its informal character does not fulfill the above aim. In this paper, we set the foundation for a formal description of the operational semantics (small step) of object-based languages. One main characteristic of our framework, called λObj^{+a}, is that it induces an easy *classification* of the object-based languages and their semantics, making a clear distinction between functional and imperative languages. Moreover, the present formal system is *generic*, which means that it presents

J. Wing, J. Woodcock, J. Davies (Eds.): FM'99, Vol. II, LNCS 1709, pp. 963–982, 1999.

many semantics in one framework which can be instantiated to conform to specific wishes. For this, it proposes a set of several *modules*, each of which captures a particular aspect of object-calculi (functional *vs.* imperative[1], delegation *vs.* embedding, and any combination of them). Genericity comes also from a total *independence from the strategy*, the latter being sometimes crucial when dealing with imperative semantics.

The framework $\lambda\mathcal{O}bj^{+a}$ describes both static and dynamic aspects of object-oriented languages. *Static* aspects are the concepts related to the program, namely its syntax, including variable scoping, and above all its type system. The type system (not presented in this paper for obvious lack of space) avoids the unfortunate run-time error `message-not-understood`, obtained when one sends a message, say m, to an object which has no m in its protocol. *Dynamic* aspects are related to its behavior at run-time *i.e.*, its operational semantics, also known as the implementation choices. In addition, this paper introduces in the world of the formal operational semantics of object-based languages, the concepts of *addresses* and *simultaneous rewriting*, which differ from the classical *match and replace* technique of rewriting.

"Road Map". Section 2 sets the context of the framework $\lambda\mathcal{O}bj^{+a}$. Section 3 addresses mostly the implementation aspects of object-based languages. Section 4 introduces ancestors of $\lambda\mathcal{O}bj^{+a}$, namely $\lambda\mathcal{O}bj^{+}$, a slightly modified version of the Lambda Calculus of Objects, and $\lambda\sigma_w^a$, a weak lambda-calculus with explicit substitution and addresses. Section 5 is the real core of the paper as it details the notion of simultaneous rewriting, and presents $\lambda\mathcal{O}bj^{+a}$ through its four modules L, C, F, and I. Section 6 gives some examples motivating our framework. Finally, Section 7 compares our framework with some related works.

A richer version of this paper (containing some open problems) can be found in [14].

2   The Context of $\lambda\mathcal{O}bj^{+a}$

The framework $\lambda\mathcal{O}bj^{+a}$ is founded on an *object-based calculus*, enriched with *explicit substitution* and *addresses*. We explain this in the current section.

2.1   Object-Based Calculi

The last few years have addressed the foundation of object-oriented languages. The main goal of this research was twofold: to understand the operational behaviour of object-oriented languages and to build *safe and flexible* type systems which analyze the program text before execution. In addition (and not in contrast) to the traditional class-based view, where *classes* are seen as the primitive notion to build object instances, recent years have seen the development of the, so called, *object-based* (or *prototype-based*) languages. Object-based languages can be either viewed as a novel object-oriented style of programming (such as in Self [22], Obliq [6], Kevo [19], Cecil

---

[1] The terminology "functional" and "imperative" seems to be more or less classical in the scientific object-oriented community. However, we could use "calculi of non-mutable (resp. mutable) objects" as synonymous for functional (resp. imperative) calculi.

[7], O-{1,2,3} [1]) or simply as a way to implement the more traditional class-based languages. In object-based languages there is no notion of class: the inheritance takes place at the object level. Objects are built "from scratch" or by inheriting the methods and fields from other objects (sometimes called *prototypes*). Most of the theoretical papers on object-based calculi address the study of *functional object-calculi*; nevertheless, it is well-known that object-oriented programming is inherently "imperative" since it is based on a notion of "mutable state". However, those papers are not a simple exercise of style, since, as stated in [1, 5], it may happen that a type system designed for a functional calculus can be "well fitted" for an imperative one. Among the proposals firmly setting the theoretical foundation of object-oriented languages, two of them have spurred on an intense research.

The Object Calculus of Abadi and Cardelli [1], is a calculus of *typed objects* of *fixed size* in order to give an account of a standard notion of subtyping. The operations allowed on objects are method invocation and method update. The calculus is computationally complete since the lambda calculus can be encoded via suitable objects. The calculus has both functional and imperative versions, the latter being obtained by simply modifying (with the help of a strategy and suitable data structures) the dynamic semantics of the former. Classes can be implemented using the well-known *record-of-premethods* approach: a class A is an object which has a method called new creating an instance a of the class and a set of "premethods" which become real methods when embedded (*i.e.*, installed) into a. Class inheritance can be treated by "reusing" the premethods of the superclass.

The Lambda Calculus of Objects λObj of Fisher, Honsell, and Mitchell [11] is an untyped lambda calculus enriched with object primitives. Objects are *untyped* and a new object can be created by modifying and/or extending an existing prototype object. The result is a new object which inherits all the methods and fields of the prototype. This calculus is also (trivially) computationally complete, since the lambda calculus is built in the calculus itself. Classes can also be implemented in λObj: in a simplified view, a class A has a method new which first creates an instance b of the superclass B of A and then adds (or updates) this instance with all the fields/methods declared in A. In [5], an imperative version of λObj featuring an encapsulation mechanism obtained via abstract data types, was introduced. In [9], a modified version of λObj, called λObj^+ (see Subsection 4.1), was introduced together with a more powerful type system.

2.2 Explicit Substitution Calculi and Addresses

Explicit Substitution Calculi (see for instance [2, 15]) were invented in order to give a finer description of operational semantics of the functional programming languages. Roughly speaking, an explicit substitution calculus fully includes the *meta substitution* operation as part of the syntax, adding suitable rewriting rules to deal with it. These calculi give a good description of implementations by modeling the concept of *closure*, but do not give an account of the *sharing* needed in lazy functional languages implementations. In [8], a *weak* lambda-calculus of explicit substitution, called $\lambda \sigma_w$, was introduced; here *weak* means a calculus in which one can not compute inside abstractions. In [4], an extension of $\lambda\sigma_w$, called $\lambda\sigma_w^a$, was presented (see Subsection 4.2); this calculus added the notion of *address* and *simultaneous rewriting*, introduced by Rose in his thesis [18]. Addresses are global annotations on terms, which allow to handle sharing of arguments.

2.3 The Framework

The framework $\lambda\mathcal{O}bj^{+a}$ is founded on $\lambda\mathcal{O}bj^{+}$ for the object aspects, to which we add addresses and explicit substitution, following the lines of $\lambda\sigma_w^a$. The reason why we are interested in addresses in the context of an object-based calculus is not only their ability to express sharing of arguments, as in lazy languages, but much more because objects are typical structures which need to be shared in a memory, independently of the chosen strategy.

The framework $\lambda\mathcal{O}bj^{+a}$ deals also with graphs. As a positive consequence of having addresses, the technique of "stack and store" used to design static and dynamic features of imperative languages [10, 20, 24, 1, 5] is substituted in our framework by a technique of graphs (directed and possibly cyclic) which can undergo *destructive updates* through mutation of objects. This makes our framework more abstract, as it involves no particular structure for computing. Moreover it provides a small step semantics of object mutation. This is in fact a generalization of Wadsworth's graph reduction technique of implementation of functional languages [23, 21], which, by essence, forbids destructive updates. Moreover, our graphs are represented as special terms, called *addressed terms*, exploiting the idea of *simultaneous rewriting*, already mentioned in [18, 4], and slightly generalized in this paper (see [13]).

The framework $\lambda\mathcal{O}bj^{+a}$ is much more than a simple calculus. One of the consequences of this abstraction is that $\lambda\mathcal{O}bj^{+a}$ allows to define many calculi. A specific calculus is therefore a combination of *modules plus a suitable strategy*. Hence, what makes our approach original are the following features: genericity, independence of the strategy, and capture of both dynamic and static aspects of a given language. Thanks to these features, our framework handles in a unified way and with a large flexibility, functional and imperative object-oriented languages, using both embedding- and delegation-based inheritance techniques, and many different evaluation strategies.

3 Implementation of Object-Based Languages

While issues related to the soundness of the various type systems of object-calculi are widely studied in the literature, a few papers address how to build formally a general framework to study and implement inheritance in the setting of object-based calculi. Among the two main categories of object-based calculi (*i.e.*, functional and imperative ones, or with non-mutable and with mutable objects) there are two different techniques of implementation of inheritance, namely the *embedding-based* and the *delegation-based* ones, studied in this section.

The following schematic example will be useful to understand how inheritance can be implemented using the embedding-based and the delegation-based techniques.

Example 1. Consider the following (untyped) definition of a "pixel" prototype.

```
object pixel is
  x:=0; y:=0; onoff:=true;
  set(a,b,c){(((self.x:=a).y:=b).onoff:=c}
end
```

Consider the following piece of code.

```
let p=clone(pixel) in
 let q=p.set(a,b,c):={(((self.x:=self.x*a).y:=self.y*b).onoff:=c}
  in let r=q.switch():={self.onoff:=not(self.onoff)}
```

where : = denotes both a method override and an object extension.

In the following we discuss the two models of implementation of inheritance and we highlight the differences between functional versus imperative models of object-calculi. Before we start, we explain (rather informally) the semantics of the `clone` operator, present in many real object-oriented programming languages.

3.1 The `clone` Operator

The semantics of the `clone` operator changes depending on the delegation-based or embedding-based technique of inheritance, and is *orthogonal* to the functional or imperative features of the framework. In delegation-based inheritance, a `clone` operation produces a "shallow" copy of the prototype *i.e.*, another object-identity which shares the *same* object-structure as the prototype itself. On the contrary, in embedding-based inheritance, a `clone` operation produces a "hard copy" of the prototype, with a proper object-identity and a proper object-structure obtained by "shallowing" and "refreshing" the object-structure of the prototype. This difference will be clear in the next subsections which show possible implementations of the program of Example 1.

3.2 Functional Object-Calculi

As known, functional calculi lack a notion of *mutable state*. Although people feel that object-calculi have only little sense in functional setting, we will show in this paper that they are worth studying and that it may be possible to include an object calculus in a pure functional language, like Haskell [17], with much of the interesting features of objects.

Delegation-based Inheritance. The main notion is this of object since there are no classes. Some objects are taken as *prototypical* in order to build other objects. An "update" operation (indicated in the example as : =) can either override or extend an object with some fields or methods. A functional update always produces another object, which owns a proper "object-identity" (*i.e.*, a memory location containing a reference to the object-structure, represented as a small square in figures). The result of an update is a "new" object, with a proper object-identity, which shares all the methods of the prototype except the one affected by the update operation. A `clone` operator builds another object with a proper object-identity which shares the structure of the prototype. By looking at Figure 1, one sees how Example 1 can be implemented using a delegation-based technique.

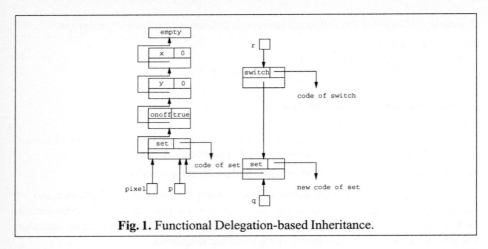

Fig. 1. Functional Delegation-based Inheritance.

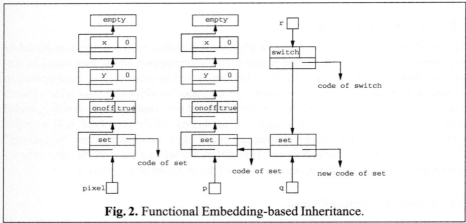

Fig. 2. Functional Embedding-based Inheritance.

Embedding-based Inheritance. In embedding-based inheritance a new object is built by a "hard copy" of the prototype; in fact, `clone` really builds another object with a proper object-identity and a proper copy of the object-structure of the prototype. By looking at Figure 2 one can see how Example 1 can be implemented using an embedding-based technique.

3.3   Imperative Object-Calculi

Imperative object-calculi have been shown to be fundamental in describing implementations of class-based languages like Smalltalk and Java. They are also essential as foundations of object-based programming languages like Obliq and Self. The main goal when one tries to define the semantics of an imperative object-based language is to say how an object can be modified while maintaining its object-identity. Particular attention must be paid to this when dealing with object extension. This makes the semantics

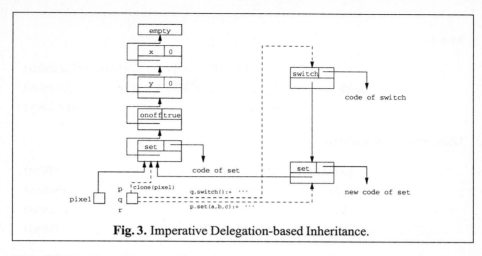

Fig. 3. Imperative Delegation-based Inheritance.

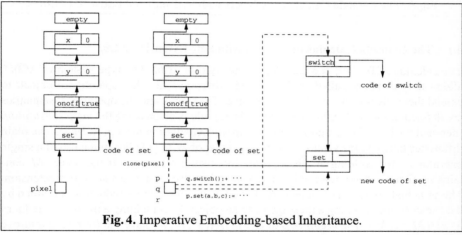

Fig. 4. Imperative Embedding-based Inheritance.

of the imperative update operation subtle because of side effects. Figure 3 shows the implementation of Example 1 with delegation-based inheritance, and Figure 4 with embedding-based inheritance. Dashed lines represent pointers due to the evaluation of some expression indicated as annotation. Each dashed line cancels the others *i.e.*, there is only one dashed line at each moment. In both cases, observe how the override of the set method and the addition of the switch method change the object structure of p (later on also called q, r) without changing its object-identity.

4   Some Ancestors of $\lambda \mathcal{O}bj^{+a}$

In this section we give a gentle introduction to calculi which inspired our framework, namely $\lambda \mathcal{O}bj^{+}$ and $\lambda \sigma_w^a$.

Syntax.

$$M, N ::= \lambda x.M \mid MN \mid x \mid c \qquad \text{(Lambda Calculus)}$$
$$\mid \langle \rangle \mid \langle M \leftarrow m = N \rangle \mid M \Leftarrow m \qquad \text{(Objects)}$$
$$\mid Sel(M, m, N) \qquad \text{(Auxiliary)}$$

Operational Semantics.

$$(\lambda x.M)\, N \rightarrow M\{N/x\} \qquad \text{(Beta)}$$
$$M \Leftarrow m \rightarrow Sel(M, m, M) \qquad \text{(Select)}$$
$$Sel(\langle M \leftarrow m = N \rangle, m, P) \rightarrow NP \qquad \text{(Success)}$$
$$Sel(\langle M \leftarrow n = N \rangle, m, P) \rightarrow Sel(M, m, P) \quad m \neq n \qquad \text{(Next)}$$

Fig. 5. The Lambda Calculus of Objects with Self-inflicted Extension $\lambda \mathcal{O}bj^+$.

4.1 The Lambda Calculus of Objects with Self-Extension $\lambda \mathcal{O}bj^+$

The calculus $\lambda \mathcal{O}bj^+$ [9] is a calculus in the style of $\lambda \mathcal{O}bj$. The type system of $\lambda \mathcal{O}bj^+$ allows to type the, so called, "self-inflicted extensions" *i.e.*, the capability of objects to extend themselves upon receiving a message. The syntax and the operational semantics are defined in Figure 5. Observe that the (Beta) rule is given using the *meta substitution* (denoted by $\{N/x\}$), as opposed to the *explicit substitution* used in $\lambda \mathcal{O}bj^{+a}$. The main difference between the syntax of $\lambda \mathcal{O}bj^+$ and that of $\lambda \mathcal{O}bj$ [11] lies in the use of a single operator $\leftarrow$ for building an object from an existing prototype. If the object M contains m, then $\leftarrow$ denotes an object override, otherwise $\leftarrow$ denotes an object extension. The principal operation on objects is method invocation, whose reduction is defined by the (Select) rule. Sending a message m to an object M containing a method m reduces to $Sel(M, m, M)$. The arguments of Sel in $Sel(M, m, P)$ have the following intuitive meaning (in reverse order):

- P is the receiver (or recipient) of the message;
- m is the message we want to send to the receiver of the message;
- M is (or reduces to) a proper sub-object of the receiver of the message.

By looking at the last two rewrite rules, one may note that the Sel function "scans" the recipient of the message until it finds the definition of the method we want to use. When it finds the body of the method, it applies this body to the recipient of the message.

Example 2 (An object with "self-inflicted extension"). Consider the object self_ext defined as follows: $\text{self\_ext} \triangleq \langle \langle \rangle \leftarrow \text{add\_n} = \lambda \text{self}.\langle \text{self} \leftarrow \text{n} = \lambda \text{s}.1 \rangle \rangle$. If we send the message add_n to self_ext, then we get the following computation:

$$\text{self\_ext} \Leftarrow \text{add\_n} \longrightarrow Sel(\text{self\_ext}, \text{add\_n}, \text{self\_ext})$$
$$\longrightarrow (\lambda \text{self}.\langle \text{self} \leftarrow \text{n} = \lambda \text{s}.1 \rangle)\, \text{self\_ext}$$
$$\longrightarrow \langle \text{self\_ext} \leftarrow \text{n} = \lambda \text{s}.1 \rangle,$$

Terms.

$$M, N ::= \lambda x.M \mid MN \mid x \mid c \qquad \text{(Lambda Calculus)}$$
$$U, V, E^a ::= M[s]^a \mid (UV)^a \qquad \text{(Evaluation Contexts)}$$
$$s ::= U/x; s \mid id \qquad \text{(Substitution)}$$

where a ranges over an infinite set of *addresses*.

Rules.

$$\left((\lambda x.M)[s]^b \, U\right)^a \to M[U/x; s]^a \qquad\qquad\qquad \text{(B)}$$
$$(MN)[s]^a \to (M[s]^b \, N[s]^c)^a \qquad b, c \text{ fresh} \qquad \text{(App)}$$
$$x[E^b/x; s]^a \to E^b \qquad\qquad\qquad \text{(FVarG)}$$
$$x[E^b/x; s]^a \to E^a \qquad\qquad\qquad \text{(FVarE)}$$
$$x[U/y; s]^a \to x[s]^a \qquad\qquad x \not\equiv y \qquad \text{(RVar)}$$

Fig. 6. The Weak Lambda Calculus with Explicit Substitution and Addresses $\lambda\sigma_w^a$.

resulting in the method n being added to self_ext. On the other hand, if we send the message add_n twice to self_ext instead, the method n is only overridden with the same body; hence we obtain an object which is "operationally equivalent" to the previous one.

4.2   The Weak Lambda Calculus with Explicit Substitution and Addresses $\lambda\sigma_w^a$

We introduce the weak lambda calculus with explicit substitution and addresses $\lambda\sigma_w^a$ [4], where for the sake of simplicity, and in the style of Rose [18], we replace de Bruijn indexes with variable names. By "weak", we mean a lambda calculus in which reductions may not occur under abstractions, as standard in many programming languages. The syntax and the rules of this calculus are given in Figure 6. The explicit substitution gives an account of the concept of closure, while addresses give an account of sharing. Both are essential in efficient implementations of functional languages.

There are three levels of expressions. The first level is static. It gives the syntax of programs *code* (terms written $M, N, \dots$), and it contains no address. The second and third levels are dynamic. They contain addresses and they are the level of *evaluation contexts*, and the level of *substitutions*. Evaluation contexts (terms written $U, V, \dots$) model states of abstract machines. An evaluation context contains the temporary structure needed to compute the result of an operation. It denotes a term closed by a list of bindings also called substitution. There is an evaluation context associated with each construct of the language. Addresses (denoted by $a, b, \dots$) label evaluation contexts. Intuitively, an address a models a reference to a unique term graph which is denoted as a standard term by simply unraveling it. The sharing information is kept through addresses, as superscripts of terms. This leads to two associated notions, namely *admissible terms* and *simultaneous rewriting*. An *admissible term* is a term in which there is not two different subterms at the same address. In the following, we only deal with admissible terms. A *simultaneous rewriting* (see also Subsection 5.1) means that, if a subterm U at address a is reduced to a term V, then all the subterms at the same address a are reduced in the same step to V. In other words, the simultaneous rewriting is a rewriting relation meant to preserve admissibility.

To be seen as a program *i.e.*, to enable a computation, a closed lambda term M must be given a substitution s (also called *environment*), initially the empty substitution *id*, and a location a to form an evaluation context called *addressed closure* $M[s]^a$. The environment s is the list of bindings of the variables free in M. To reduce terms, environments have to be distributed inside applications (App) until reaching a function or a variable. Hence, applications of weak lambda terms are also evaluation contexts. In this step of distributing the environment, "fresh" addresses are provided to evaluation contexts. A fresh address is an address unused in the global term. Intuitively, the address of an evaluation context is the address where the result of the computation will be stored. Since in a *closure* $M[s]^a$, the terms in s are also addressed terms, it follows that the duplication of s in (App) induces duplications of lists of pointers. Not only a duplication does not loose sharing, but it increases it.

When an abstraction is reached by a substitution, one gets a redex $((\lambda x.M)[s]^b U)^a$ (provided there is an argument U), hence one can apply the rule (B). This redex is reduced locally *i.e.*, U is not propagated to the occurrences of x, but the environment is just enlarged with the new pair U/x. Moreover, the result of the reduction is put at the same location as this of the redex in the left hand side, namely a. As a matter of fact, the result of the rewriting step is *shared* by all the subterms that occur at address a.

When a variable x is reached, and the environment scanned by several steps of rule (RVar), x has eventually to be replaced by the evaluation context it refers to. The calculus $\lambda\sigma_w^a$ proposes two rules to do this, namely (FVarG), and (FVarE). The reason is that a choice has to be made on the address where to "store" the right hand side: it may be either the address of the evaluation context bound to x (FVarG), or the address of the main evaluation context (FVarE). In the first case, a redirection of the pointer which refers to the address a is performed toward the address b (where the term E lies), whereas in the latter case a copy of the part of the term E from address b to address a is made. In both cases, the result of the rewriting step is shared.

In the case of a copy, further sharing between the original node and the copied node will not be possible, but this has no influence on efficiency if the copied node denoted a value *i.e.*, a term of the form $(\lambda x.M)[s]^a$ or $c[s]^a$, because there may be no more further reductions on them.

A detailed discussion on this choice of rules can be found in [3, 4].

Example 3. The term $((V U)^a U)^b$ where $U \equiv ((\lambda x.x)[id]^c true[id]^d)^e$ and V is any evaluation context, may reduce in one step by rule (B) of Figure 6 to

$$((V \, x[true[id]^d/x; id]^e)^a \, x[true[id]^d/x; id]^e)^b,$$

but not to *e.g.*, $((V\ \underline{x[true[id]^d/x;\ id]^e})^a\ (\underline{(\lambda x.x)[id]^c\ true[id]^d)^e})^b$ since the two distinct underlined subterms have a same address, namely e.

If we set V to $(\lambda y.\lambda z.y)[id]^f$, then the computation may proceed as follows:

$$(((\lambda y.\lambda z.y)[id]^f\ x[true[id]^d/x;\ id]^e)^a\ x[true[id]^d/x;\ id]^e)^b$$

$$\xrightarrow{*} y[x[true[id]^d/x;\ id]^e/z;\ x[true[id]^d/x;\ id]^e/y;\ id]^b \qquad \text{(B+B)}$$

$$\to y[x[true[id]^d/x;\ id]^e/y;\ id]^b \qquad \text{(RVar)}$$

$$\to x[true[id]^d/x;\ id]^e \qquad \text{(FVarG)}$$

$$\to true[id]^e, \qquad \text{(FVarE)}$$

where we chose to use both (FVarG) and (FVarE) for the sake of illustration.

All along this paper, we use the helpful intuition that an address corresponds to a location in a physical memory. However, we warn the reader that this intuition may be error prone. Access and allocation in a physical memory are expensive and often avoidable. Since a fresh address is given to every new evaluation context, the reader may think that we are not aware of this cost and have in mind an implementation which overuse locations. In fact, addresses capture more than locations. This has been shown in [12] where the states of an environment machine (with code, environment, stacks, and heap) are translated into $\lambda\sigma_w^a$. This translation showed that many addresses are *artificial i.e.*, do not have a physical reality in the heap, but correspond to components of states. It was also shown that the abstraction of sharing with addresses fits well with the environment machine, because it captures the strategy of the machine. The moral is that *everything which could have a physical location, in a particular implementation, has an address in the framework.*

5   The Syntax and the Operational Semantics of $\lambda\mathcal{O}bj^{+a}$

This section presents our framework. It is split into separated modules, namely L for the lambda calculus, C for the common operations on objects, F for the functional object part, and I for the imperative object part. All these modules can be combined, giving the whole $\lambda\mathcal{O}bj^{+a}$. The union of modules L, C, and F can be understood as the *the functional fragment of* $\lambda\mathcal{O}bj^{+a}$. As described in Figure 7, we find in $\lambda\mathcal{O}bj^{+a}$ the same levels as in $\lambda\sigma_w^a$, plus a dynamic level of *internal structures of objects* (or simply *object-structures*).

To the static level, we add some constructs: constructors of objects, method invocations, and explicit duplicators. There are operations to modify objects: the functional update, denoted by $\leftarrow$, and the imperative update, denoted by $\leftarrow:$. An informal semantics of these operators has been given in Section 3. As in [9], these operators can be understood as extension as well as override operators, since an extension is handled as a particular case of an override. One has also two imperative primitives for "copying" objects: shallow(x) is an operator which gives a new object-identity to the object pointed by x but still shares the same object-structure as the object x itself; refresh(x)

Code

$$M, N ::= \lambda x.M \mid MN \mid x \mid c \qquad \text{(Lambda Calculus)}$$
$$\mid M \Leftarrow m \qquad \text{(Message Sending)}$$
$$\mid \langle \rangle \qquad \text{(Object Initialization)}$$
$$\mid \langle M \leftarrow m = N \rangle \mid \langle M \leftarrow: m = N \rangle \qquad \text{(Object Updates)}$$
$$\mid \mathsf{shallow}(x) \mid \mathsf{refresh}(x) \qquad \text{(Duplication Primitives)}$$

where x ranges over variables, c ranges over constants and m ranges over methods.

Evaluation Contexts

$$U, V ::= M[s]^a \qquad \text{(Closure)}$$
$$\mid (UV)^a \qquad \text{(Application)}$$
$$\mid (U \Leftarrow m)^a \qquad \text{(Message Sending)}$$
$$\mid \langle U \leftarrow m = V \rangle^a \mid \langle U \leftarrow: m = V \rangle^a \qquad \text{(Object Updates)}$$
$$\mid \lceil O \rceil^a \mid \bullet^a \qquad \text{(Objects)}$$
$$\mid Sel^a(O, m, U) \qquad \text{(Lookup)}$$

where a ranges over an infinite set of *addresses*.

Object-structures

$$O ::= \langle \rangle^a \mid \langle O \leftarrow m = V \rangle^a \mid \bullet^a \qquad \text{(Internal Objects)}$$
$$\mid \mathsf{copy}(O)^a \qquad \text{(Duplicator)}$$

Environments

$$s ::= U/x; s \mid id \qquad \text{(Substitution)}$$

Fig. 7. The Syntax of $\lambda \mathcal{O}bj^{+a}$.

is a kind of *dual* to shallow(x) as it makes a "hard copy" of the object-structure of x, and reassigns this structure to x. Therefore, the object-identity of x is not affected.

Similarly, some constructs are added as evaluation contexts. The evaluation context $\lceil O \rceil^a$ represents an object whose *internal* object-structure is O and whose object-identity is $\lceil\ \rceil^a$. In other words, the address a plays the rôle of an *entry point* of the object-structure O. An expression like $Sel^a(O, m, \lceil O \rceil^b)$ is an evaluation context (at address a). It looks up in the object-structure O of the receiver (represented by an evaluation context $\lceil O \rceil^b$), gets the method body and applies it to the receiver itself. The term $\bullet^a$ is a *back pointer* [18], its rôle is explained in Subsection 5.5 when we deal with the cyclic aspects of objects *i.e.*, the possibility to create "loops in the store". Only $\bullet^a$ can occur inside a term having the same address a, therefore generalizing our informal notion of admissible term and simultaneous rewriting.

Internal objects O model the object-structures in memory. They are permanent structures which may only be accessed through the address of an object (denoted by a in $\lceil O \rceil^a$), and are never destroyed nor modified (but by the garbage collector, if there is one). Our calculus being inherently delegation-based, objects are implemented as linked lists (of fields/methods). Embedding-based inheritance can however be simulated thanks to the refresh(x) and shallow(x) operators. In particular, refresh(x) is defined in terms of an auxiliary operator called copy(O) which makes a copy of the object-structure. Again, because of imperative traits, object-structures can contain occurrences of $\bullet^a$.

5.1   The Simultaneous Rewriting

Simultaneous rewriting [18, 3] is a key concept in this paper and we would like to warn the reader not to take it as just a slight variant of the usual term rewriting. Actually, due mostly to imperative features introduced in module I, simultaneous rewriting goes much beyond the classical *match and replace* paradigm of the traditional first order rewriting and must be defined extremely carefully in order to preserve:

Horizontal Admissibility, *i.e.*, all the subterms at the same address should be equal and rewritten together, as shown in Example 3.

Vertical Admissibility, *i.e.*, a term can contain its own address a as the address of one of its proper subterms, only if this subterm is a $\bullet^a$. This ensures that back-pointers for terms at address a are only denoted by the term $\bullet^a$.

Roughly speaking, in order to maintain these requirements the definition proceeds as follows to rewrite a term U into V.

1. Match a subterm of U at address say a with a left hand side of a rule, compute the corresponding right hand side and create the new fresh addresses (if required), then replace all the subterms of U at address a with the obtained right hand side.
2. Replace some subterms by back-pointers (a *fold* operation), or some back-pointers by particular terms (an *unfold* operation), following some specific techniques (see [13]), so that the result is a vertically admissible term.

Instantiation

$$\langle\,\rangle[s]^a \to \lceil\langle\,\rangle^b\rceil^a \qquad\qquad b \text{ fresh} \qquad \text{(OI)}$$

Message Sending

$$(M \Leftarrow m)[s]^a \to (M[s]^b \Leftarrow m)^a \qquad b \text{ fresh} \qquad \text{(CP)}$$

$$(\lceil O\rceil^b \Leftarrow m)^a \to Sel^a(O, m, \lceil O\rceil^b) \qquad\qquad \text{(SE)}$$

$$Sel^a(\langle O \leftarrow m = V\rangle^b, m, U) \to (VU)^a \qquad\qquad \text{(SU)}$$

$$Sel^a(\langle O \leftarrow n = V\rangle^b, m, U) \to Sel^a(O, m, U) \qquad\qquad \text{(NE)}$$

Fig. 8. The Common Object Module C.

5.2 The Module L

The module L is the calculus $\lambda\sigma_w^a$, and needs no comments.

5.3 The Common Object Module C

The Common Object module is shown in Figure 8. It handles object instantiation and message sending. *Object instantiation* is characterized by the rule (OI) where an empty object is given an object-identity. More sophisticated objects may then be obtained by functional or imperative update. *Message sending* is formalized by the four remaining rules. The rule (CP) which propagates a given substitution into the receiver of the message; apply this rule means to "install" the evaluation context needed to actually proceed. The meaning of the remaining rules is quite intuitive: (SE) performs message sending, while (SU), and (NE) perform the method-lookup. We can observe here the similarity with the operational semantics of λObj^+.

Functional Update

$$\langle M \leftarrow m = N\rangle[s]^a \to \langle M[s]^b \leftarrow m = N[s]^c\rangle^a \qquad b, c \text{ fresh} \qquad \text{(FP)}$$

$$\langle\lceil O\rceil^b \leftarrow m = V\rangle^a \to \lceil\langle O \leftarrow m = V\rangle^c\rceil^a \qquad c \text{ fresh} \qquad \text{(FC)}$$

Fig. 9. The Functional Object Module F.

5.4   The Functional Object Module **F**

The Functional Object module gives the operational semantics of a calculus of non mutable objects. It contains only two rules (Figure 9). Rule (FP) "pre-computes" the functional update, installing the evaluation context needed to actually proceed. Rule (FC) describes the actual update of an object of identity b. The update is not made in place and no mutation is performed, but the result is a new object (with a different object-identity). This is why we call this operator "functional" or "non mutating".

Imperative Update

$$\langle M \leftarrow: m = N\rangle[s]^a \to \langle M[s]^b \leftarrow: m = N[s]^c\rangle^a \qquad b, c \text{ fresh} \qquad \text{(IP)}$$

$$\langle \lceil O\rceil^b \leftarrow: m = V\rangle^a \to \lceil\langle O \leftarrow m = V\rangle^c\rceil^b \qquad c \text{ fresh} \qquad \text{(IC)}$$

Cloning Primitives

$$\mathsf{shallow}(x)[U/y; s]^a \to \mathsf{shallow}(x)[s]^a \qquad x \not\equiv y \qquad \text{(VS)}$$

$$\mathsf{shallow}(x)[\lceil O\rceil^b/x; s]^a \to \lceil O\rceil^a \qquad \text{(SC)}$$

$$\mathsf{refresh}(x)[U/y; s]^a \to \mathsf{refresh}(x)[s]^a \qquad x \not\equiv y \qquad \text{(RS)}$$

$$\mathsf{refresh}(x)[\lceil O\rceil^b/x; s]^a \to \lceil\mathsf{copy}(O)^c\rceil^b \qquad c \text{ fresh} \qquad \text{(RE)}$$

$$\mathsf{copy}(\langle\,\rangle^b)^a \to \langle\,\rangle^a \qquad \text{(CE)}$$

$$\mathsf{copy}(\langle O \leftarrow m = V\rangle^b)^a \to \langle\mathsf{copy}(O)^c \leftarrow m = V\rangle^a \qquad c \text{ fresh} \qquad \text{(CO)}$$

Fig. 10. The Imperative Object Module I.

5.5   The Imperative Object Module **I**

The Imperative Object module (Figure 10) contains rules for the mutation of objects (imperative update) and cloning primitives. Imperative update is formalized in a way close to the functional update. Rules (IP) and (IC) are much like (FP) and (FC); they differ in address management and they are self-explaining. Indeed let us look at the address b in rule (IC). In the left hand side, b is the identity of an object $\lceil O\rceil$, when in the right hand side it is the identity of the whole object modified by the rule. Since b may be shared from anywhere in the context of evaluation, this modification is observable non locally, hence a mutation is performed.

It is worth to note that the rule (IC) may create cycles and therefore back pointers. Intuitively, when we deal with imperative traits, we can create non admissible terms because of cyclic references. Every reference to $\lceil O\rceil^b$ in V must be replaced by $\bullet^b$ to avoid $\lceil\langle O \leftarrow m = V\rangle\rceil^b$ to contain itself.

The primitives for cloning are shallow(x) and refresh(x).

- A shallow(x) creates an object-identity for an object, but x and shallow(x) share the same object-structure. The rule (SC) can be seen as the imperative counterpart of the rule (FVarE) of module L in case $E^b \equiv \lceil O \rceil^b$, for a given b.
- A refresh(x) creates for x a new object-structure isomorphic to the previous one. A refresh(x) calls, through the rule (RE), an auxiliary operator named copy. A copy(O) recursively performs a copy of the linked list, via the rules (CE), and (CO).

An intuitive representation of the behaviour of those operators is given in Figure 11.

6   Understanding $\lambda \mathcal{O}bj^{+a}$

6.1   Examples of Terms

Example 4. The term $\langle \lceil \langle \rangle^a \rceil^b \leftarrow: \mathtt{m} = (\lambda \mathtt{self}.\mathtt{x})[\lceil \langle \rangle^a \rceil^b / \mathtt{x}; id]^c \rangle^d$ does not reduce to

$$\lceil \langle \langle \rangle^a \leftarrow \mathtt{m} = (\lambda \mathtt{self}.\mathtt{x})[\lceil \langle \rangle^a \rceil^b / \mathtt{x}; id]^c \rangle^d \rceil^b$$

(which is a non admissible term) but instead to

$$\langle \lceil \langle \rangle^a \leftarrow \mathtt{m} = (\lambda \mathtt{self}.\mathtt{x})[\bullet^b / \mathtt{x}; id]^c \rangle^d \rceil^b.$$

It is crucial to note that the sense of the two terms is essentially different, since the latter expresses a loop in the store whereas the former does not mean anything consistent, since two semantically distinct subterms have the same address b.

Example 5. The term $\langle \lceil \langle \langle \rangle^a \leftarrow \mathtt{m} = M[\bullet^d / \mathtt{x}; id]^b \rangle^c \rceil^d \leftarrow \mathtt{n} = N[id]^e \rangle^f$ does not reduce to

$$\lceil \langle \langle \langle \rangle^a \leftarrow \mathtt{m} = M[\bullet^d / \mathtt{x}; id]^b \rangle^c \leftarrow \mathtt{n} = N[id]^e \rangle^g \rceil^f$$

(which is not admissible) but instead to

$$\lceil \langle \langle \langle \rangle^a \leftarrow \mathtt{m} = M[\lceil \bullet^c \rceil^d / \mathtt{x}; id]^b \rangle^c \leftarrow \mathtt{n} = N[id]^e \rangle^g \rceil^f.$$

In this last term, the back pointer $\bullet^d$ has been *unfolded* following the definition of simultaneous rewriting *i.e.*, replaced by the term it refers to, namely $\lceil \bullet^c \rceil^d$ (c is still in the context of the subterm, and therefore $\bullet^c$ is not unfolded). This unfolding is due to the removal of the surrounding address d, which otherwise could lead to a loss of information on the shape of the term associated to the address d.

6.2   Examples of Derivations

Example 6. Let `self_ext` be the term defined in Example 2, and N denote the subterm $\lambda\texttt{self}.\langle\texttt{self} \leftarrow \texttt{n} = \lambda\texttt{s}.1\rangle$.

$$(\texttt{self\_ext} \Leftarrow \texttt{add\_n})[id]^a \xrightarrow{*} (\langle\langle\langle\rangle[id]^d \leftarrow \texttt{add\_n} = N[id]^c\rangle^b \Leftarrow \texttt{add\_n})^a \tag{1}$$

$$\rightarrow (\langle\langle\lceil\langle\rangle^e\rceil^d \leftarrow \texttt{add\_n} = N[id]^c\rangle^b \Leftarrow \texttt{add\_n})^a \tag{2}$$

$$\rightarrow (\lceil \underbrace{\langle\langle\rangle^e \leftarrow \texttt{add\_n} = N[id]^c\rangle^f}_{O} \rceil^b \Leftarrow \texttt{add\_n})^a \tag{3}$$

$$\rightarrow Sel^a(O, \texttt{add\_n}, \lceil O\rceil^b) \tag{4}$$

$$\rightarrow ((\lambda\texttt{self}.\langle\texttt{self} \leftarrow \texttt{n} = \lambda\texttt{s}.1\rangle)[id]^c \lceil O\rceil^b)^a \tag{5}$$

$$\rightarrow \langle\texttt{self} \leftarrow \texttt{n} = \lambda\texttt{s}.1\rangle[\lceil O\rceil^b/\texttt{self}; id]^a \tag{6}$$

$$\xrightarrow{*} \langle\lceil O\rceil^b \leftarrow \texttt{n} = \lambda\texttt{s}.1[\lceil O\rceil^b/\texttt{self}; id]^g\rangle^a \tag{7}$$

$$\rightarrow \lceil\langle O \leftarrow \texttt{n} = \lambda\texttt{s}.1[\lceil O\rceil^b/\texttt{self}; id]^g\rangle^h\rceil^a \tag{8}$$

In (1,2), two steps are performed to distribute the environment inside the expression by rules (CP) and (FP), then the empty object is given an object-structure and an object identity (OI). In (3), this new object is functionally extended (FC), hence it shares the structure of the former object but has a different object-identity. In (4,5), two steps are performed to look-up the method `add_n` (rules (NE) and (SU)). Step (6) is an application of (B). In (7), the environment is distributed inside the functional extension (FP), and then `self` is replaced by the object it refers (FVarG). Step (8) is simply an application of rule (FC) *i.e.*, the proceeding of a functional extension. The final term contains some sharing, as the object-structure denoted by O and rooted at address b occurs twice.

Example 7. We give a similar example, where a functional update is replaced by an imperative one. Let `self_ext'` denote the term $\langle\langle\rangle \leftarrow \texttt{add\_n} = N'\rangle$, where N' is $\lambda\texttt{self}.\langle\texttt{self} \leftarrow: \texttt{n} = \lambda\texttt{s}.1\rangle$.

$$(\texttt{self\_ext'} \Leftarrow \texttt{add\_n})[id]^a \xrightarrow{*} (\lceil \underbrace{\langle\langle\rangle^e \leftarrow \texttt{add\_n} = N'[id]^c\rangle^f}_{O'} \rceil^b \Leftarrow \texttt{add\_n})^a \tag{1}$$

$$\xrightarrow{*} \langle\lceil O'\rceil^b \leftarrow: \texttt{n} = \lambda\texttt{s}.1[\lceil O'\rceil^b/\texttt{self}; id]^g\rangle^a \tag{2}$$

$$\rightarrow \lceil\langle O' \leftarrow \texttt{n} = \lambda\texttt{s}.1[\bullet^b/\texttt{self}; id]^g\rangle^h\rceil^b \tag{3}$$

The first steps (1,2) are similar to the first steps (1 to 7) of the previous example. In (3), the imperative extension is performed (IC), and a subterm replaced by $\bullet^b$ to denote the loop to the root, since the object in the environment has the same identity as the object the environment belongs to.

6.3   Functional *vs.* Imperative (Non Mutable *vs.* Mutable)

The functional module F can be simulated by the imperative one I. This can be simply done by combining the shallow(x) operation with an imperative update. Indeed, a functional object obtained by inheriting the properties of a prototype can be encoded by a shallow followed by an imperative method update. This proves the fact that $F \subseteq I$. The encoding of $\langle M \leftarrow m = N \rangle$ is $(\lambda x.\langle \text{shallow}(x) \leftarrow: m = N \rangle)\, M$.

6.4   Cloning

It is possible, using the Imperative Object module, to define a clone operation. The clone used in Figures 2 and 4, whose intuitive semantics is illustrated in Figure 11, is defined as follows: clone$(x) \triangleq (\text{refresh} \circ \text{shallow})(x) \triangleq (\lambda y.\text{refresh}(y))\, \text{shallow}(x)$. The clone used in Figures 1 and 3, instead, is defined as follows: clone$(x) \triangleq \text{shallow}(x)$.

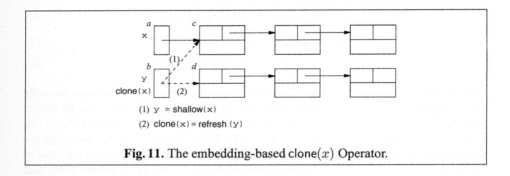

(1) y = shallow(x)
(2) clone(x) = refresh (y)

Fig. 11. The embedding-based clone(x) Operator.

Since $\lambda\mathcal{O}bj^{+}$ is inherently delegation-based, it follows that an embedding-based technique of inheritance can be encoded using the Imperative Object module I. Other interesting operators can be defined by combining the different features of $\lambda\mathcal{O}bj^{+a}$.

7   Related Work

– The framework $\lambda\mathcal{O}bj^{+a}$ generalizes a novel technique to implement programming languages: we call this technique *address-based*. Addresses are attached to every entities of our framework. The graph-based implementation technique à la Wadsworth, as well as others, can be subsumed within our framework. A type system can be defined quite easily by adding in the "context soup" also the type of addresses. As such, a type soundness result can be proved relatively simply, if we compare it with the traditional approaches of stack (a function from variables to results) and store (a function from store locations to "closures"). It is worth to note that the choice of the target calculus (an object based one) is not important; the address-based technique can be used, in principle, to implement other calculi, but it fits well to object-calculi.

– The framework λObj^{+a} performs an *imperative object extension*: an imperative (mutable) object is a "functional (non-mutable) internal object-structure" pointed by an object-identity. To extend an imperative object means to functionally extend its object-structure while keeping its object-identity. Note that the same mechanism is used to implement method override.

Among the many imperative object calculi presented in the literature, the closest are the one described in [1] (Chapter 10-11), and [5]. The first is the ς_{imp} calculus of Abadi and Cardelli, while the second is the imperative version of λObj of Fisher, Honsell, and Mitchell. Both calculi use a stack and store technique to present the semantics of the calculus and to prove type soundness. Both calculi have an imperative override that (in contrast to our approach) *substitutes* the old body of a field/method with the new one. Both calculi adopt a *call-by-value* strategy. In addition, the calculus presented in [5] have a *functional object extension*. The divergence from those calculi is shown in the following table, where s&s stands for stack and store, addr. for address-based, and c.b.v. for call-by-value:

	model	override	extension	self-infliction	strategies
[1]	s&s	imperative	no	no	c.b.v.
[5]	s&s	imperative	functional	no	c.b.v.
λObj^{+a}	addr.	funct./imp.	funct./imp.	yes	many

Less specifically, a work is in progress [13] to formalize in a general setting all the notions of sharing, cycles, and mutation, mentioned in this paper.

8 Conclusions

We have defined λObj^{+a}, a framework for object calculi which is intended to give a firm foundation for the operational semantics of object oriented languages. Future works will focus on specific calculi as combination of modules and strategies *e.g.*, the functional fragment with embedding and call-by-need, or the imperative fragment with delegation and call-by-value. It should also be interesting to study specific aspects like typing, strategies (see [14]) and distribution of objects across networks. Other useful extensions of this framework should be studied, such as providing an imperative override of fields in the style of [1, 5] *i.e.*, a *field look up and replacement*. To this aim, a distinction has to be made between fields (and may be more generally procedures or functions that do not have a self-reference) and methods. The formalism used to describe λObj^{+a} provides the suited tools for such an extension.

Acknowledgement. The authors are grateful to Zine-El-Abidine Benaissa, Furio Honsell, and Kristoffer Høgsbro Rose for their useful comments on this work.

References

[1] M. Abadi and L. Cardelli. *A Theory of Objects*. Springer-Verlag, 1996.
[2] M. Abadi, L. Cardelli, P.-L. Curien, and J.-J. Lévy. Explicit substitutions. *Journal of Functional Programming*, 1(4):375–416, 1991.

[3] Z.-E.-A. Benaissa. *Les calculs de substitutions explicites comme fondement de l'implantation des langages fonctionnels*. PhD thesis, Université Henri Poincaré Nancy 1, 1997. In french.

[4] Z.-E.-A. Benaissa, K.H. Rose, and P. Lescanne. Modeling sharing and recursion for weak reduction strategies using explicit substitution. In *Proc. of PLILP*, number 1140 in Lecture Notes in Computer Science, pages 393–407. Springer-Verlag, 1996.

[5] V. Bono and K. Fisher. An imperative first-order calculus with object extension. In *Proc. of ECOOP*, volume 1445 of *Lecture Notes in Computer Science*, pages 462–497. Springer-Verlag, 1998.

[6] L. Cardelli. A language with distributed scope. *Computing Systems*, 8(1):27–59, 1995.

[7] C. Chambers. The Cecil language specification, and rationale. Technical Report 93-03-05, University of Washington, Department of Computer Science and Engineering, 1993.

[8] P.-L. Curien, T. Hardin, and J.-J. Lévy. Confluence properties of weak and strong calculi of explicit substitutions. *Journal of the ACM*, 43(2):362–397, 1996.

[9] P. Di Gianantonio, F. Honsell, and L. Liquori. A lambda calculus of objects with self-inflicted extension. In *Proc. of OOPSLA*, pages 166–178. The ACM Press, 1998.

[10] M. Felleisen and R. Hieb. The revised report on the syntactic theories of sequential control and state. *Theoretical Computer Science*, 102, 1992.

[11] K. Fisher, F. Honsell, and J. C. Mitchell. A lambda calculus of objects and method specialization. *Nordic Journal of Computing*, 1(1):3–37, 1994.

[12] F. Lang. *Modèles de la β-réduction pour les implantations*. PhD thesis, École Normale Supérieure de Lyon, 1998. In french.

[13] F. Lang, D. Dougherty, P. Lescanne, and K. H. Rose. Addressed term rewriting systems. Research Report RR 1999-30, Laboratoire de l'Informatique du Parallélisme, École Normale Supérieure de Lyon, 1999.

[14] F. Lang, P. Lescanne, and L. Liquori. A framework for defining object calculi. Research Report RR 1998-51, Laboratoire de l'Informatique du Parallélisme, École Normale Supérieure de Lyon, 1998.

[15] P. Lescanne. From $\lambda\sigma$ to $\lambda\upsilon$, a journey through calculi of explicit substitutions. In *Proc. of POPL*, pages 60–69, 1994.

[16] T. Lindholm and F. Yellin. *The Java Virtual Machine specification*. Addison-Wesley Publishing Company, 1996.

[17] J. Peterson, K. Hammond, L. Augustsson, B. Boutel, W. Burton, J. Fasel, A. Gordon, J. Hughes, P. Hudak, T. Johnsson, M. Jones, E. Meijer, S. Peyton Jones, A. Reid, and P. Wadler. *Haskell 1.4, a non strict purely functional language*, 1997.

[18] K. H. Rose. *Operational reduction models for functional programming languages*. PhD thesis, DIKU, København, 1996.

[19] A. Tailvalsaari. Kevo, a prototype-based object-oriented language based on concatenation and modules operations. Technical Report LACIR 92-02, University of Victoria, 1992.

[20] M. Tofte. Type inference for polymorphic references. *Information and Computation*, 89(1):1–34, 1990.

[21] D. A. Turner. A new implementation technique for applicative languages. *Software Practice and Experience*, 9:31–49, 1979.

[22] D. Ungar and B. Smith, R. Self: the power of simplicity. In *Proc. of OOPSLA*, pages 227–241. The ACM Press, 1987.

[23] C. P. Wadsworth. *Semantics and pragmatics of the lambda calculus*. PhD thesis, Oxford, 1971.

[24] A. K. Wright and M. Felleisen. A syntactic approach to type soundness. *Information and Computation*, 115(1):38–94, 1994.

A Translation of Statecharts to Esterel

S.A. Seshia[1]*, R.K. Shyamasundar[1], A.K. Bhattacharjee[2], and
S.D. Dhodapkar[2]

[1] School of Technology & Computer Science,
Tata Institute of Fundamental Research, Mumbai 400 005, India
`shyam@tcs.tifr.res.in`
[2] Reactor Control Division, Bhabha Atomic Research Centre, Mumbai 400 025, India
`{anup,sdd}@magnum.barc.ernet.in`

Abstract. Statecharts and ESTEREL are two formalisms that have been
widely used in the development of reactive systems. Statecharts are a
powerful graphical formalism for system specification. ESTEREL is a rich
synchronous programming language with supporting tools for formal
verification. In this paper, we propose a translation of Statecharts to
ESTEREL and discuss such an implementation. A characteristic feature
of the translation is that deterministic Statechart programs can be effectively translated to ESTEREL and hence, the tools of verification of
ESTEREL can be used for verifying Statechart programs as well. The
translation serves as a diagnostic tool for checking nondeterminism. The
translation is syntax-directed and is applicable for synchronous and asynchronous (referred to as the superstep model) models. In the paper, we
shall describe the main algorithms for translation and implementation
and illustrate the same with examples. We have built a prototype system based on the translation. It has the advantages of the visual power
usually liked by engineers reflected in Statecharts and of a language that
has a good semantic and implementation basis such as ESTEREL that can
be gainfully exploited in the design of reliable reactive systems.

1 Introduction

Significant amount of research has been done in the last decade in the design
and development of reactive systems. The class of synchronous languages and
various visual formalisms are two approaches that have been widely used in the
study of reactive systems. The family of synchronous languages has based on
perfect synchrony hypothesis which can be interpreted to mean that the program
reacts rapidly enough to perceive all the external events in a suitable order and
produces the output reactions before reacting to a new input event set. Embedded controllers can be abstracted in this way. Some of the prominent languages
of the family include ESTEREL, Lustre, Signal etc. These languages are also being used widely in industry. Significant advantages of the family of synchronous

---

* Current address:School of Computer Science, Carnegie Mellon University, Pittsburgh,PA 15217, USA, email: Sanjit.Seshia@cs.cmu.edu

J. Wing, J. Woodcock, J. Davies (Eds.): FM'99, Vol. II, LNCS 1709, pp. 983–1007, 1999.
© Springer-Verlag Berlin Heidelberg 1999

languages include the availability of idealized primitives for concurrency, communication and preemption, a clean rigorous semantics, a powerful programming environment with the capability of formal verification. The advantages of these languages are nicely paraphrased by Gerard Berry, the inventor of ESTEREL, as follows: *What you prove is what you execute.*

Statecharts is a visual formalism which can be seen as a generalization of the conventional finite automata to include features such as hierarchy, orthogonality and broadcast communication between system components. Being a formalism rather than a language, there is no unique semantics in the various implementations and further Statechart specifications can be nondeterministic. For these reasons, even though there are powerful programming environments for Statecharts such as STATEMATE[1] (which includes simulators), environments lack formal verification tools.

Textual and graphical formalisms have their own intrinsic merits and demerits. For instance consider the following reactive system design:

> Consider the specification of control flow (switching of tasks) among various computing tasks and interrupt service tasks in a control software. The computing tasks switch from one to another in cyclic fashion and are shown as substates of `compute_proc`. The interrupt service tasks are entered as a result of the occurrence of interrupt events. The history notation has been used to indicate that on return from interrupt tasks, the system returns to last executing compute task (except when event 100 ms occurs, the control returns to `compute task hpt`). The event `wdt_int` occurs on system failure and it can be verified that when `wdt_isr` is entered, the system will toggle between states `wdt_isr` and `nmi_isr`, which is the intended behavior.

Such systems can be specified using graphical formalisms easily. The statechart for the above system is shown in Figure 1. Arguing the formal correctness from such descriptions, however, is not easy. Our work is concerned with methods that will combine advantages of using graphical formalisms for the design of reactive systems with that of using formal verification tools in textual formalisms.

In this paper, we study a method of translating Statechart formalisms into ESTEREL with the idea that the powerful verification tools and code optimization tools of ESTEREL can be applied for Statechart programs. Our aim has been to provide a clean formally verifiable code for Statechart programs rather than yet another attempt to define the semantics of Statecharts. For this reason, we stick to using the STATEMATE semantics (refer [7]), which is an industrial strength version of Statecharts. It must be noted that ESTEREL is deterministic and hence, our study will confine to the deterministic class of Statecharts. However, it may be noted that the translation procedure will detect the underlying nondeterminism if any.

We discuss algorithms of translation and discuss the implementations and also compare our study with respect to other similar translations of Statecharts.

---

[1] STATEMATE is a registered trademark of I-Logix Inc.

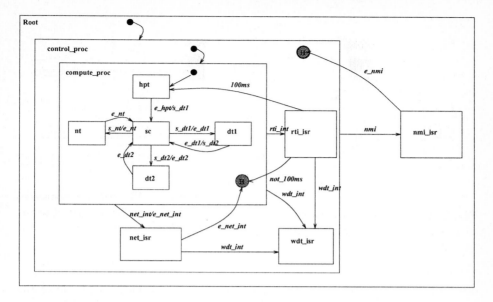

Fig. 1. Example of Switching Interrupts

The main advantage of our translation is that the code generated is verifiable and also, ESTEREL optimizers can used for efficient code generation. We are currently in the process of evaluating the quality of code generated vis-a-vis other Statechart code generators.

The rest of the paper is organized as follows: Section 2 briefly introduces Statecharts, ESTEREL and the STATEMATE semantics. In section 3, we discuss how we abstract out the essential details of the Statechart and the core ideas in the translation process, along with illustrative examples. Section 4 sums up the work along with comparisons to other works.

2   Background

2.1   Statecharts

In this section, we present a brief overview of Statecharts (see [6] for complete details). Statechart shown in Figure 2 (derived from the example in [6]) is used for illustrative purposes.

Components of a Statechart:
States: These are of three types: *basic states, and states* and *or states*. Basic States are those states which do not contain any other state, e.g. *lap* is a basic state.

An Or-state is a compound state containing two or more other states. To be in a Or-state is to be in one of its component states. In this paper, we will

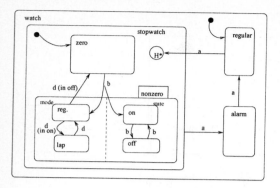

Fig. 2. Statechart of stopwatch within a wristwatch - with deep history

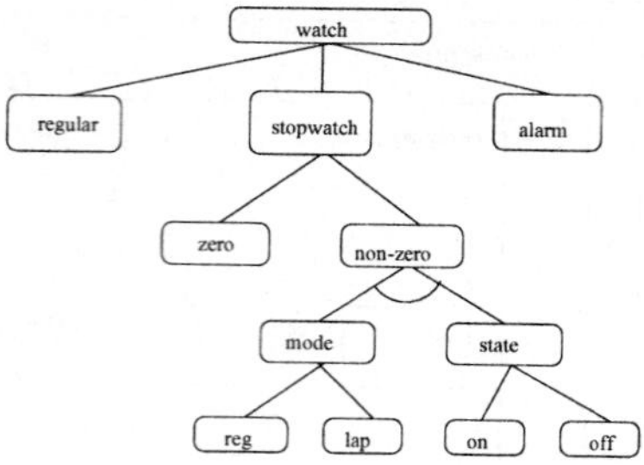

Fig. 3. AND-OR tree representation of the Statechart of wristwatch

use Or-State synonymously with XOR-state, i.e. we can be in only one of the component states at a given time. An example of an Or-state in Figure 2 is *stopwatch*.

An And-state is also a compound state and staying in an And-state implies staying in each one of its substates. These are provided to model concurrency. The substates of an And-state may contain transitions which may be executed simultaneously. *nonzero* shown in Figure 2 is an And-state.

Transitions: A Transition in the Statechart is a five-tuple (*source, target, event, action, condition*). The arrow on the Statechart goes from source to target and is labelled as **e[C]/a**, meaning that event **e** triggered the transition when condition **C** was valid and action **a** was carried out when the transition was taken. In general, **a** could be a list of actions to be taken.

History and Defaults: Statecharts incorporates the idea of a *history* state in a OR-State. The history state keeps track of the substate most recently visited. This is denoted by **H** in a Or-state, as in the or-state stopwatch in Figure 2. A *default* state, marked by a shaded circle, is a substate of an or-state such that if a transition is made to the or-state and no other condition (e.g. enter-by-history) is specified, then that substate must be entered by default. e.g. *regular* is the default substate for the *watch*. In Figure 2, we have a *deep-history* state, which means that a transition to that state implies being in the maximal most recent set of basic substates. This can be represented by history states in each one of the Or-substates.

2.2   STATEMATE

The informal semantics of the STATEMATE version of Statecharts is provided through rules describing the semantics of a step. The main rules are listed below. For detailed discussions, the reader is referred to [7].

1. Reactions to external/internal events and changes that occur in a step can be sensed only after completion of the step.
2. Events are "live" for the duration of the step following the one in which they occur only.
3. Calculations in a step are based on the situation at the beginning of the step
4. If two transitions are in conflict, then priority is given to that transition whose scope is higher in the hierarchy. The scope as defined in [7] is: The scope of a transition *tr* is the lowest Or-state in the hierarchy of states that is a proper common ancestor of all sources or targets of *tr*, including nonbasic states that are explicit sources or targets of transition arrows appearing in *tr*.
5. Each step follows the Basic Step Algorithm as described in [7].

2.3   ESTEREL

The basic object of ESTEREL without value passing (referred to as Pure ES-TEREL) is the signal. Signals are used for communication with the environment as well as for internal communication.

The programming unit is the module. A module has an interface that defines its input and output signals and a body that is an executable statement:

```
module M:
    input I1, I2;
    output O1, O2;
    input relations
    statement
end module
```

Input relations can be used to restrict input events and a typical exclusion relation is declared as

```
relation I1 # I2;
```

Such a relation states that input events cannot contain I1 and I2 together. That is, it is an assertion on the behavior of the asynchronous environment.

At execution time, a module is activated by repeatedly giving it an input event consisting of a possibly empty set of input signals assumed to be present and satisfying the input relations. The module reacts by executing its body and outputs the emitted output signals. We assume that the reaction is *instantaneous* or *perfectly synchronous* in the sense that the outputs are produced in no time. Hence, all necessary computations are also done in no time. In Pure ESTEREL these computations are either signal emissions or control transmissions between statements; in full ESTEREL they can be value computations and variable updates as well. The only statements that consume time are the ones explicitly requested to do so. The reaction is also required to be deterministic: for any state of the program and any input event, there is exactly one possible output event. In perfectly synchronous languages, a *reaction* is also called an *instant*. There is one predefined signal, the *tick*, which represents the activation clock of the reactive program.

Statements: ESTEREL has two kinds of statements: the kernel statements, and the derived statements (those that can be expanded by macro-expansions) to make the language user-friendly. The list of kernel statements is:

```
nothing
halt
emit S
stat1; stat2
loop stat end
present S then stat1 else stat2 end
do stat watching S
stat1 || stat2
trap T in stat end
exit T
signal S in stat end
```

Kernel statements are imperative in nature, and most of them are classical in appearance. The `trap-exit` constructs form an exception mechanism fully compatible with parallelism. Traps are lexically scoped. The local signal declaration "`signal in` *stat* `end`" declares a lexically scoped signal S that can be used for internal broadcast communication within stat. The `then` and `else` parts are optional in a present statement. If omitted, they are supposed to be `nothing`. Informal semantics of the kernel constructs are given in Appendix C.

3   The Translation

A Statechart basically denotes a network of automata with hierarchy and other properties. The crux of the translation lies in

(A) Extracting the hierarchy of states and transitions,
(B) Resolving the conflict in the transitions as per the STATEMATE semantics,
(C) Generating the code corresponding to the transitions between states,
(D) Generating code that models system state between transitions, and,
(E) Generating code that supports communication via events and actions.

In the following, we shall highlight the underlying issues of representation, resolution of conflicts and code generation. Note that we refer to signals in the Statechart as *actions* or *events*, while those in ESTEREL are referred to simply as *signals*. We first present the underlying ideas and the full code generation algorithm is presented at the end.

3.1   AND-OR Tree Representation of Statecharts

The Statechart can be represented as an AND-OR tree: being in an AND-node meaning that the system is in each of its child nodes, while being in an OR-node means that we are in exactly one of its child nodes. Such a representation allows us to express the hierarchy of states of the Statecharts in a convenient manner to trace the path of arbitrary transitions. This also allows us to resolve conflicts between enabled transitions, by calculating the *scope*(refer to section 2.2).

For purposes of code generation, we actually use an annotated representation of AND-OR tree described in the following section. An AND-OR tree representation of the Statechart of Figure 2 is shown in Figure 3.

Annotated AND-OR Tree Representation: The annotated AND-OR tree keeps track of information about the Statechart pertinent for the translation, such as (i) the states and their types, (ii) hierarchy of States, and (iii) Transitions between states, which includes Entry and Exit points for each transition & Inner states that need to be hidden (signals suppressed) during a transition that exits a state.

Each node A of the AND-OR tree is represented as a seven-tuple[2]:

$$(Name, Type, T_{entry}, T_{exit}, T_{loop}, T_{default}, T_{history}), \text{ where,}$$

$Name$: Name of the state, viz. A.
$Type$: AND, OR or BASIC.
T_{entry}: The set of all transitions that enter A.
T_{exit}: The set of all transitions that exit A.
T_{loop}: The set of all transitions that exit one of A's immediate child states and enters another(possibly same) child state.
$T_{default}$: The single transition to an immediate child state from A.
$T_{history}$: The set of transitions to the history state of A.

For translating Statecharts, we need to keep track of the Entry and Exit Point Information so that the transitions including the inter-level transitions can be enabled in the translated ESTEREL code preserving the STATEMATE semantics. The actual information we need to keep track of will be clear by considering the states between which the transition takes place. Transitions in Statecharts can be broadly classified as:

T1: Between child states of the same parent.
T2: From a parent state to its (not necessarily immediate) child state.
T3: From a child state to its (not necessarily immediate) parent state.
T4: Any transition that is not of type T1, T2 or T3.

Note that all of these transitions may not occur in a given Statechart. In particular, types T2 and T3 may not occur, but the way they are translated forms part of the translation for type T4. The book keeping of the above classes of transitions is achieved through the Node-Labelling Algorithm by keeping the appropriate entry and exit information in each node of the AND-OR tree.

Node-Labelling Algorithm: Assuming levels of the nodes in the tree have already been computed (with root node having level 0, and increasing level for its child nodes), for each transition in the set Tr of transitions, the algorithm

---

[2] We shall use *node* synonymously with *state* and vice-versa.

traverses the path from source node n_1 to target node n_2, labelling these two nodes as well as intermediate nodes with: (i) name of the transition, (ii) type of the transition, viz. T1, T2, T3 or T4 and (iii) the fact whether the transition is entering that node or exiting it. This information is used to generate code in the translation.

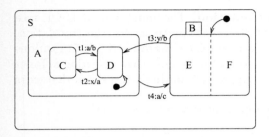

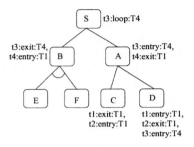

Fig. 4. Example Statechart

Fig. 5. Corresponding Node-labelled AND-OR tree

3.2   Labelling for Transition Conflict Resolution

As per STATEMATE semantics, two transitions are in conflict if they exit a common state A. Further, conflict resolution is based on the following: Transition t_1 has priority over transition t_2 if the lowest[3] Or-state exited by t_1 is lower than the lowest Or-state exited by t_2.

Given this, if trigger events for t_1 and t_2 occur simultaneously then, we must ensure that t_2 is not taken along with its actions. This is done by a signal $hide\_A$. On taking t_1, $hide\_A$ will be emitted. Therefore, before t_2 is taken, a check must be made for the presence of signal $hide\_A$.

This is indicated in the AND-OR tree by traversing the tree top-down, maintaining a list of *"hide-signals"* that we need to label the nodes with. At a node, which has *at least* one transition that exits it, and which is either the source of that transition, or the last state exited by it, we label all of its children with $hide\_A$. This is to ensure that while translating, a statement to check for the presence of $hide\_A$ is executed before any transition is taken. This will perform the job of hiding internal signals. The algorithm to implement hide-signal labeling is omitted here for brevity.

3.3   Code-Generation

The Code-Generation is done in a top down manner traversing the AND-OR tree. In short, the process is as follows : (1) Declare all necessary signals, (2) generate code for states and transitions between states, (3) generate code to

---

[3] Lowest means closest to the root node.

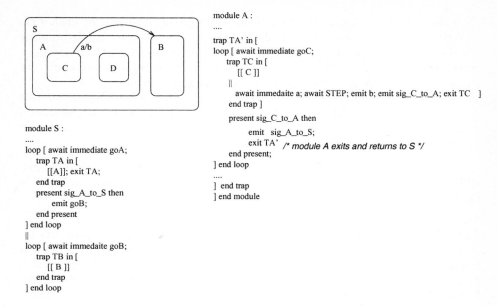

Fig. 6. Translation of a transition of type T4

do communication within the Statechart, (4) generate code to deal with special constructs such as history substates.

Declarations: Information about the following kinds of signals is stored in the annotated AND-OR tree and these are declared at each node while generating code for the module corresponding to that node.

1. External Input signals.
2. Internal Input events generated during transitions out of substates of parent node A.
3. Internal Output events(actions) generated during transitions out of substates of parent node A.
4. If A is a substate of an Or-state with history, then a valued signal *new_history_A* is used so that the history can be changed appropriately whenever transition to a substate A_i of A takes place.
5. Dummy signals for T2 or T4 transitions that enter A: In this case signals of the form *sig_BtoA* or *sig_AtoB* would be needed, where B is either an immediate parent or an immediate child of A. This list is built up for each such node A, during the *Node -Labelling* Algorithm. These signals are used to build a chain of signals that trigger transitions between immediate parent-child states, and the whole chain generates the entire transition.
6. Dummy signals for T3 or T4 transitions that exit A. Similar to 5 above.

7. Valued History signals for all Or-sub-states having history; for each such OR-state these store the value of the most recent substate. While building the AND-OR tree we can maintain a list of Or-states which have history.
8. Signals that indicate transition to a history[4] substate of a substate of A, or if A is an Or-state, to indicate transition to history substate of A.
9. Characteristic signals (in, enter, exit) for each substate of A. To generate this list, traverse the AND-OR tree bottom-up (postorder) and at each node, add to a list of child nodes. Then while generating code for node A, declare all characteristic signals for each of its child nodes as listed.

We have a new module only for each OR-node, therefore, we need not keep a list of all nine types of signals with an AND-node or BASIC-node unless it is the ROOT node.

The *STEP* Signal: In the ESTEREL code generated, each step occurs on receipt of an external signal called *STEP*. This signal is needed to provide a tick on which transitions can be made even when there are no input signals from the environment (i.e. when all triggering events are internally generated). Use of STEP is necessary to implement the super-step semantics of STATEMATE, wherein several steps are executed starting with some initial triggering events, till the system reaches a set of stable states (i.e., states with no enabled transitions out of them).

Transitions: Consider code generation for the translation for a transition t of type T, with source state A and target state B.

In brief, the translation involves the following : (1) Generate code to await the occurrence of the triggering event, and, (2) on occurrence of the STEP (as in STATEMATE semantics), if the triggering condition is true and no transition pre-empts t, emit : (a) a signal to activate the next state (called a "go" signal), (b) a signal to activate a chain of transitions (for types T2 through T4), (c) signals to exit the current state, i.e., to terminate emission of signals that depict the current state as active.

Figure 6 illustrates translations with respect to T4 transition.

The complete procedure `translate-transition` is given in Appendix A. The parameter curr_node is the node for which we are generating code.

Note: For lack of space, we give only snippets of the most essential parts of the ESTEREL code. The full code generated is well formed and syntactically correct.

Code-Generation Algorithm: In the following, we describe the basic-code generation algorithm. Code to be emitted for immediate states like *history* and special actions are omitted for brevity.

Notation: In the code-generation algorithms, algorithm details are in Roman font while the code is boxed in `Typewriter font`.

---

[4] We have implemented *deep-history* as a sequence of transitions between history states. Such signals are used to make ϵ transitions between history states.

Algorithm 1 *Basic Code-Generation Algorithm: The main algorithmic steps are sketched below.*

1. Traverse the AND-OR tree top-down. (in preorder)
2. For each node A do
   - If A is an OR-node:
   (a) Begin a new module, and declare all signals that occur A's signal list, or in the signal list of child nodes of A, till the first child Or-node is encountered.
   (b) Generate code for each block representing the substate of A. Let A_1, A_2, ..., A_n be the immediate child nodes of node A. Let e_{i1}, e_{i2}, ... e_{im} be the external or internal events on which transitions are made out of the A_i. Let the corresponding actions be act_{i1} to act_{im}. Further, let the conditions under which the transitions are to be taken be C_{i1} to C_{im}. Let the list of *hide* signals for the nodes $A_i, \forall\ i$ be $hide_1$ to $hide_t$. $STEP$ is a signal that indicates that the next step must be performed. It is an external signal. Steps of the translation are described below:

   Step 1. Emit *preamble* code. If A is a substate of an OR-state B with history, then appropriate *newhist* signals are emitted to update history. Code to be emitted *from this step* is given below:

   ```
   emit enter_A;
   [ trap T'_A in [
                   sustain in_A;
           ‖ [ await tick; emit newhistB(A); ]
           ‖ [ signal goA_1, goA_2, ..., goA_n in [
                 ··· % to be completed in other steps
   ```

   Step 2. Emit code to check for T2 and T4 transitions, or for transitions to the history substate of A. If none of these are true then default state is entered. Code *from this step* is given below:

   ```
   present
       case sig_AtoA_j do
               emit goA_j % This is repeated for each sig_AtoA_j%
       case enterhist_A do
           [ if histA = 1 then
                       emit goA_1 %  Check for each i%
               elseif histA = 2 then
                       emit goA_2
               else emit goA_k % A_k is the default substate
                               for A%
               end if
       end present;
   ```

   Step 3. For each i, emit code to handle transitions out of A_i and also the refinement of A_i. The code for each of the i are composed in parallel. The respective codes *to be emitted* are given in the substeps below:

Substep 1. Preamble code for A_i.

```
            [ loop [
                      await immediate goAi;
                      trap TAi in
                         ··· % Subsequent codes will be completed by other
steps %
```

Substep 2. Emit code corresponding to the refinement of A_i. We indicate the refinement of A_i by $<< A_i >>$. If A_i is an AND-node or BASIC-node then this is the block for A_i. If A_i is an Or-node, then this is a "run A_i" statement. In this case, add it to a queue[5] of Or-nodes Q_{nodes}, so that we emit code for it and its child nodes later. When the node is visited during the preorder tree traversal, the entire subtree under that node A_i is skipped to be processed later.

```
            [ << Ai >>; exit TAi;
            || ··· % subsequent codes will be completed by other steps %
```

Substep 3. Emit code for each transition triggered by e_{ij}, j = 1..m, and compose in parallel with the above code. i.e., [6] $\forall\ t_i\ \in\ T^i_{exit}$,

```
        call translate-transition(ti,TYPE_of_ti,Ai);
        end trap % TAi
```

Substep 4. Code emitted in case there are transitions of type T3 or T4. Thus, for all transitions t of type T3 or T4 which exit state A_i we would have:

```
        call exit-code-trans(t,TYPE_of_t,Ai);
```

Substep 5. Postamble code for the substate A_i is given below:

```
              ] end loop
              ]
```

Step 4. The postamble code to be emitted is given below:

```
              end signal
           ]
         end trap % T'A
       ]
    end module
```

- If A is an AND-node:
- (a) Generate code to emit enter and in signals for A, or for updating history, as in preamble code above.
- (b) Generate code for each one of A's child nodes, A_i, and compose these in parallel.

---

[5] Note that queue is implicit in the underlying tree traversal algorithm.

[6] For two transitions out of the same state with the same priority, we assume some priority order known in advance and instead of composing code for these transitions in parallel, we use the **await case .. end await** construct of ESTEREL.

(c) Generate code for each transition that quits a child node of A and compose each in parallel with that in item 2 above. The translation for the individual transitions is exactly as for an Or-node. There are no looping transitions of type T4 for an AND-node.

- If A is an BASIC-node:

Generate code to emit enter and in signals for A, or for updating history of its parent state, just as was done for the Or-state. Also generate code to *begin*, *await* a return signal from or *end* an activity.

3. Generate code for each of the Or-nodes in the queue Q_{nodes} till no more Or-nodes remain in the queue.

Note: Algorithm 1 preserves the priority structure of transitions based on *scope* by appropriately nesting the *trap*s and using the ESTEREL semantics of nesting of *trap*s.

Generation of $STEP$ Signal: In the above Algorithm 1, each step occurs on receipt of an artificially created external signal called $STEP$.

Clearly, this $STEP$ signal cannot be generated internally, as it will not generate a tick then. Further, $STEP$ must be given to the state machine (system) as long as there are enabled transitions (enabled on internally generated signals). In our translation, this indication is obtained from the *enter* and *exit* signals emitted.

We define a new signal "*give_step*" which is emitted whenever an *enter* or *exit* signal is emitted. Thus, whenever *give_step* is emitted, a $STEP$ signal must be emitted. Additionally, $STEP$ must be emitted on occurrence of an external input. The state machine generated by the ESTEREL compiler must interface with the environment through a *driver routine*. The driver routine executes the state machine whenever there is an input from the external environment. Thus, our problem is to execute the state machine under certain conditions(namely when *give_step* is emitted) even when there is no external input. The trick here (as in [11]) is to set a bit for every occurrence of *give_step* that is checked by the driver routine; the bit indicates that the driver routine must generate a tick (and supply a $STEP$)[7]. Thus, due to the presence of "await STEP" in the translation for transitions, although the actions are "activated" in the current step, they take effect only in the next step. This is in accordance with the STATEMATE semantics.

Our translation faithfully represents all behaviors of the STATEMATE Statecharts, in both the *Step* and *Superstep* time models. In our translation, the STEP of Statecharts is mapped to the *tick* of ESTEREL. Time instants are indicated by a separate TIME signal. In the *Superstep* time model, the STEP and TIME signals are distinct, while in the *Step* model they always occur together. As noted in [7], a Statechart using the *Superstep* time model can have possible infinite loops in the same TIME instant. This can also happen in our ESTEREL translation, and cannot be detected using the present ESTEREL tools.

---

[7] During simulation with the standard ESTEREL tool **xes**, we supply $STEP$ as an external input in much the same way as a tick is supplied.

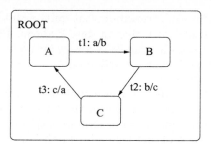

Fig. 7. Statechart with cycle

Let us consider the Statechart shown in fig. 7. Following are the steps executed when the event a occurs.

- STEP 1: Transition t1 is enabled because of occurrence of a and the system goes from the configuration {R,A} to {R,B} and the event b is generated in the system.
- STEP 2: In this step since event b is available, transition t2 is enabled and the system leaves the configuration {R,B} and goes to {R,C} and the event c is generated.
- STEP 3: In this step since event c is available, transition t3 is enabled

In the asynchronous time model [7], all these steps will constitute one superstep and be executed in one time instant. Each of these steps is executed when the external signal STEP is given.

It is possible to detect such loops, however, we shall not discuss it here.

3.4   History

As noted in [7], history states can occur only within Or-states. History is implemented using valued *history* signals for each Or-state having history. The value 0 corresponds to the default state, i.e. no history. The emission of the history signal for a state S, *histS* is done only by the root module ROOT, of the entire Statechart. When a new state is entered within an Or-state S, the module corresponding to that state emits a *newhistS* signal which is captured by ROOT which in turn updates *histS*. The history itself is maintained as a integer valued signal[8], the integer indicating which substate of the Or-state is the most recent one. Below, we show the code part of ROOT which updates the history values.
```
module ROOT :
...
var x in
[ % the below block exists for each Or-state with history
```

---

[8] However, if we use a shared variable for keeping track of the history, there will be no need to *sustain* the integer valued signal used for that purpose.

```
every immediate newhistS
   x := ?newhistS ;
   sustain histS(x) ;
end
|| ...
] ...
end module
```

3.5   Illustrative Examples

Here, we shall discuss two examples developed and verified using the above system.

Example 1. Figure 8 shows an example of the Priority Inversion problem arising due to nondeterministic behavior of the Statechart. Processes P1, P2 and P3 have priorities 1,2 and 3 respectively, and P1 and P3 share a common resource, access through which is controlled by a mutex.

It can be shown (by automata reduction) that the configuration (Root, Sys, P1blocked, P2run, P3premp) is a case of priority inversion and the system is deadlocked because of the following sequence : P3 enters critical region, P1 blocks on mutex, P2 pre-empts P3 with P1 and P3 now blocked, and thus priority of P1 and P2 has been inverted. It has been verified that this will always lead to the configuration (Root,Error). To overcome deadlock, we can add one transition between the states Error and Sys, which will again bring the system to default configuration and normal operation can resume.

A sample snippet of the ESTEREL code generated by our system is given in the Appendix. Note that the actual code generator slightly deviates from the abstract algorithms as it uses some implementation optimizations.

Example 2. This is the example of switching interrupts described in section 1 depicted by the Statechart shown in Figure 1.

Our translation described earlier has been applied to the Statechart shown in Figure 1 and the ESTEREL code obtained, tested, simulated and verified (using the Auto/Autograph tools). Some of specific properties that have been verified are: Event wdt_int occurs on system failure and when wdt_isr is entered, the system will toggle between states wdt_isr and nmi_isr, which is the intended behaviour. The actual code is not given for brevity.

4   Conclusions and Related Work

In this paper, we have proposed a translation from Statecharts to ESTEREL, and have applied this translation to successfully model and analyze some systems that might occur in real world problems. The translation is syntax-directed so that the translation of the entire Statecharts specification can be put together from the translation of its individual components. We have only sketched some of the algorithms for lack of space.

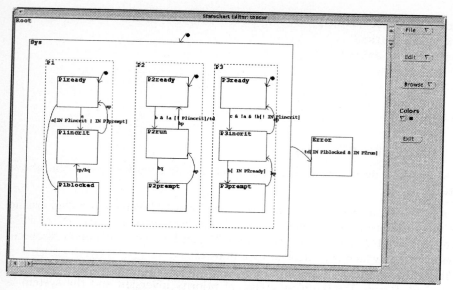

Fig. 8. Priority Inversion Example

4.1   Related Work

An early attempt towards a graphical formalism avoiding the anomalies of Statecharts was the definition of *Argos* (see [8]). Very recently efforts have also been reported in combining *Argos* and the synchronous languages ESTERELdescribed in [5]. Another effort of translating STATEMATE Statecharts to *Signal* has been reported in [3] where the aim has been to use *Signal* (another synchronous language) and its environment for formal verification purposes. *Signal* and ESTEREL are quite different considered from the point of view of verification basis and flexibility. Our approach provides the possibility of using various automata-based/temporal logic based tools for verification in a fairly natural way.

A recent approach is that of Mikk et al.[9], in which the authors discuss the translation of Statecharts into another graphical formalism called *Extended Hierarchical Automata*(EHA). In this formulation, the inter-level transitions are eliminated, by extending the labels to include *source_restriction* and *target_determinator* sets. Our translation does something similar to the one that is resorted to for EHAs, in that we use dummy signals to make interlevel transitions, one for each level transcended. It must be noted that the translation in [9] is from one graphical language to another, ours is from a graphical language to a textual language. In a subsequent work [10], which is of a similar flavour as ours, Mikk et al. have translated EHAs into Promela for use with the model checker SPIN. This enables them to do LTL model checking on Statecharts. With our translation, we are able to use ESTEREL tools such as *FC2Tools* to do equivalence checking, checking for deadlock, livelock and divergent states; and

Hurricane, which does verification of LTL safety properties. We also support special Statechart features such as timing primitives and history.

Another approach taken with the spirit of providing an integration of *Argos* and ESTEREL has been the work on *SyncCharts* reported in [1] and [2]. SyncCharts have a precise semantics, and is translatable to ESTEREL. It does not allow for inter-level transitions, and history, which are very useful features of Statecharts, and which are part of STATEMATE Statecharts (which we have worked with). SyncCharts however has explicit syntactic constructs for preemption such as suspension, weak abortion, and strong abortion, much like ESTEREL. The semantics of these constructs is the same as that of corresponding constructs in ESTEREL. Unlike such an approach of having another language, our aim has been to translate the existing Statecharts that is pragmatically very attractive and used widely, into an existing framework that permits formal verification. We have illustrated how the behaviours of a large class of Statecharts can be captured through the use of the unifying threads that run through the semantics of synchronous languages, both textual and graphical. Also, our aim has not been to define yet another semantics of Statecharts. Our goal has been to show how a class of Statecharts which have constructs like inter-level transitions and global communication of events, and which is used in the industrial strength tool STATEMATE, can be translated to a textual synchronous language and formally verified.

4.2   Summary of Work

We have translated Statecharts to ESTEREL version 5.10 described in [4] and a prototype system is in use. We have been using the tools of ESTEREL verification such as *FC2tools* based on bisimulation and *Hurricane* (from INRIA/CMA); we are also working on integrating the system with a tool being developed here by Paritosh Pandya on generating synchronous observers from DC specification of properties. A spectrum of industrial scale examples have been verified using ESTEREL and our translation will help combine ease of specification with this advantage of verification. The system implemented has shown that it is possible to integrate the advantages of Statecharts and ESTEREL in the design of reactive systems. While it is true that STATEMATE Statecharts and ESTEREL have different semantics, our translation works for a subset of deterministic Statecharts, and using a subset of ESTEREL constructs in a limited manner. We have thus maintained STATEMATE semantics while restricting the class of Statecharts we translate. The current translation also considers only simple events and actions; work is in progress to extend this to more general events and actions.

To sum up, this work is interesting from many standpoints. Considered from view of Statecharts, we have found it useful as a way to incorporate formal verification and as a diagnostic tool for detecting nondeterminism. From the point of view of ESTEREL, it provides an integration of textual and graphical formalisms. From a practical perspective, it is possible to use heterogeneous systems such as Statecharts and ESTEREL together in the development of reactive systems and the use of the industrial strength STATEMATE shows this work has potential worth in industrial system verification. There has been a large effort in integrating synchronous languages such as ESTEREL, Lustre and Signal. This work has attempted to bring Statecharts in a restricted way under this umbrella. The prototype has been built and found to be effective in the design of small-scale reactive systems. Experiments are going on in the development of large complex systems using the system.

Acknowledgments

We thank the anonymous referees for their valuable suggestions and comments. The work was initiated while Sanjit Seshia was with I.I.T., Bombay working on a summer project with R.K. Shyamasundar at TIFR, Bombay. He thanks I.I.T. Bombay, TIFR and CMU for their support. R.K. Shyamasundar thanks IFCPAR, New Delhi for the partial support under the project 2202-1.

References

[1] ANDRÉ, C. SyncCharts: A Visual Representation of Reactive Behaviors. Tech. Rep. RR 95-52, I3S, Sophia-Antipolis, France, 1995.

[2] ANDRÉ, C. Representation and Analysis of Reactive Behaviors: A Synchronous Approach. Tech. Rep. 96-28, Université de Nice, Sophia-Antipolis, France, 1996.

[3] BEAUVAIS, J.-R. ET AL. A Translation of Statecharts to Signal/DC+. Tech. rep., IRISA, 1997.

[4] BERRY, G. A Quick Guide to Esterel Version 5.10, release 1.0. Tech. rep., Ecole des Mines and INRIA, February 1997.

[5] BERRY, G., HALBWACHS, N., AND MARANINCHI, F. Unpublished note on Esterel and Argos. 1995.

[6] HAREL, D. Statecharts: A Visual Formalism for Complex Systems. *Science of Computer Programming 8* (1987), 231–274.

[7] HAREL, D., AND NAAMAD, A. The STATEMATE Semantics of StateCharts. *ACM Transactions on Software Engineering and Methodology 5*, 4 (October 1996).

[8] LEGUERNIC, P. ET AL. Programming Real-time applications with Signal. *Proceedings of the IEEE 79*, 9 (September 1991), 1321–1336.

[9] MIKK, E., LAKHNECH, Y., AND SIEGEL, M. Hierarchical automata as model for statecharts. In *LNCS* (Dec. 1997), 1345, pp. 181–197.

[10] MIKK, E., LAKHNECH, Y., SIEGEL, M., AND HOLZMANN, G. Implementing Statecharts in Promela/SPIN. In *Proc. of the 2nd IEEE Workshop on Industrial-Strength Formal Specification Techniques* (1999), IEEE Computer Society.

[11] PUCHOL, C. ET AL. A Formal Approach to Reactive Systems Software: A Telecommunications Application in Esterel. In *Proc. of the Workshop on Industrial Strength Formal Specification Techniques* (April 1995).

Appendix A: Code Generation for Transitions

This procedure gives the translation for a transition t of type T, with source
state A and target state B. curr_node is the node which we are generating code
for. As mentioned before, the algorithm details are in Roman font while the
emitted code is boxed and in typewriter font.

> *procedure* **translate-transition**
>   **(t,T,curr_node)**
> begin
>   A := source(t);   B := target(t);
> e_t := event(t); a_t := action(t);
> C_t := condition(t);
> /* Let hideS be signal corresponding to transition t which hides other transitions
> of scope less than that of t. let t be hidden by signals $hide_1$, $hide_2$, ..., $hide_n$.*/
>   if (A = curr_node) then
>   begin
>   EMIT :-

```
loop
  await (immediate) e_t;
  (await STEP;)
  if C_t then [
    present hide_1 else
     present hide_2 else
       . . .
      present hide_n else
        emit hideS;
        emit a_t; emit exit_A;
```

>   if (T = T1) then
>   begin
>   EMIT :-

```
        emit goB; exit T_A;
```

>   end
>   if (T = T2 OR T = T4) then
>   begin
> /* Let S_1, S_2, ..., S_n be intermediate states between A and B. */
>   EMIT :-

```
        emit sig_AtoS_1;
        exit T_A; % exit trap
```

>   end
>   EMIT :-

/* Complete all **present** statements */

```
      end present
      ...
   end present
] end if ]
end loop
```

    end /* if A==curr_node */
    else /* if A $\neq$ curr_node, i.e., t of type T2 or T4 */
    begin
        EMIT :-
/* Let A_1 and A_2 be the two immediate child nodes of A */

```
present sig_AtoA_1 then
   emit sig_A_1toA_2;
end present;
```

        end
end procedure

Note: Above, we have assumed that the condition is a boolean expression, as in ESTEREL syntax. If the condition is the test of presence of a signal it must be replaced by a

```
present SIG then ...
   else ...
end present
```

translation. If the condition involves testing values of shared valued signals, which could possibly change value "simultaneously", then we need to ensure that the value tested is the one at the time of occurrence of the triggering event. This code is omitted for brevity.

Further, for transitions of type *T3* and *T4*, on exiting a state, code must be emitted for continuing the chain of transitions. This code generates signals that trigger transitions in child states. The code generation routine for this is referred to in Algorithm 1 as *procedure* exit-code-trans (trans, Type-of-transition, States). We omit the detailed description of this routine in this paper.

Appendix B: Esterel Code : Priority Inversion Problem

Below we attach code snippets for the states P1 and P1ready.

```
module P1ready:
% Signal Declarations
output EnterP1ready, InP1ready,
ExitP1ready;

% Program Body --------------
emit EnterP1ready;
do sustain InP1ready watching
ExitP1ready;
end module
%----------------------------
module P1:

% Declarations deleted for brevity

signal goP1ready, goP1incrit,
goP1blocked, goP1, goP2ready,
goP2run, goP2prempt, goP2,
goP3ready, goP3incrit, goP3prempt,
goP3,goSys in [

% Program Body --------------
emit goP1ready;

emit EnterP1;
do sustain InP1 watching ExitP1;
||
loop
await immediate goP1ready;
 trap outP1ready in
    run P1ready;
 ||
 loop
   await % Exit
    case immediate [a] do
      present InP3incrit or InP3prempt
      then [
      % Testing condition
        present HideSys then
         await STEP
         else [
         await STEP;emit ExitP1ready;
```

```
          emit goP1blocked;
          exit outP1ready;]
        end ]
     else [
        present HideSys then await STEP
        else [
          await STEP; emit ExitP1ready;
          emit goP1incrit;
          exit outP1ready ]
        end % end present
        ]
     end % end present
   end % end await
 end % end loop
end % end trap
end % end loop
||
loop
await immediate goP1incrit;
trap outP1incrit in
run P1incrit;
||
loop
 await % Exit
 case immediate [ap] do
  present HideSys then await STEP else [
    await STEP; emit ExitP1incrit;
    emit goP1ready; exit outP1incrit ]
  end % end present
 end % end await
end % end loop
end % end trap
end % end loop
||
loop
await immediate goP1blocked;
trap outP1blocked in
run P1blocked;
||
loop
 await % Exit
 case immediate [cp] do
  present HideSys then await STEP else [
    await STEP; emit bq; emit ExitP1blocked;
    emit goP1incrit; exit outP1blocked; ]
```

```
  end % end present
 end % end await
end % end loop
end % end trap
end % end loop
] end % end signal
end module
```

Appendix C: Intuitive Semantics of ESTEREL

At each instant, each interface or local signal is consistently seen as present or absent by all statement, ensuring determinism. By default, signals are absent; a signal is present if and only if it is an input signal emitted by the environment or a signal internally broadcast by executing an `emit` statement.

To explain how control propagates, consider first examples using the simplest derived statement that takes time: the waiting statement "`await S`", whose kernel expansion "`do halt watching S`" will be explained later. When it starts executing, this statement simply retains the control up to the first future instant where S is present. If such an instant exists, the `await` statement terminates immediately; that is the control is released instantaneously; If no such instant exists, then the `await` statements waits forever and never terminates. If two `await` statements are put in sequence, as in "`await S1; await S2`", one just waits for S1 and S2 in sequence: control transmission by the sequencing operator ';' takes no time by itself. In the parallel construct "`await S1 || await S2`", both await statements are started simultaneously right away when the parallel construct is started. The parallel statement terminates exactly when its two branches are terminated, i.e. when the last of S1 and S2 occurs. Again, the "||" operator takes no time by itself.

Instantaneous control transmission appears everywhere. The nothing statement is purely transparent: it terminates immediately when started. An " `emit S` " statement is instantaneous: it broadcasts S and terminates right away, making the emission of S transient. In "`emit S1; emit S2`", the signals S1 and S2 are emitted simultaneously. In a signal-presence test such as "`present S ...`", the presence of S is tested for right away and the `then` or `else` branch is immediately started accordingly. In a "`loop stat end`" statement, the body stat starts immediately when the loop statement starts, and whenever *stat* terminates it is instantaneously restarted afresh (to avoid infinite instantaneous looping, the body of a loop is required not to terminate instantaneously when started).

The `watching` and `trap-exit` statements deal with behavior preemption, which is the most important feature of Esterel. In the watchdog statement "`do state watching S`", the statement stat is executed normally up to proper termination or up to future occurrence of the signal S, which is called the guard. If *stat* terminates strictly before S occurs, so does the whole `watching` statement; then the guard has no action. Otherwise, the occurrence of S provokes immediate preemption of the body *stat* and immediate termination of the whole watching statement. Consider for example the statement

```
do
    do
        await I1; emit 01
    watching I2;
    emit 02
watching I3
```

If I1 occurs strictly before I2 and I3, then the internal `await` statement terminates normally; 01 is emitted, the internal watching terminates since its body terminates, 02 is emitted, and the external watching also terminates since its body does. If I2 occurs before I1 or at the same time as it, but strictly before I3, then the internal watching preempts the await statement that should otherwise terminate, 01 is not emitted, 02 is emitted, and the external watching instantaneously terminates. If I3 occurs before I1 and I2 or at the same time as then, then the external watching preempts its body and terminates instantaneously, no signal being emitted. Notice how nesting watching statements provides for priorities.

Now the translation of "await S" as "do halt watching S" will be clear. The semantics of halt is simple: it keeps the control forever and never terminates. When S occurs, `halt` is preempted and the whole construct terminates. Note that `halt` is the only kernel statement that takes time by itself.

The trap-exit construct is similar to an exception handling mechanism, but with purely static scoping and concurrency handling. In `trap T in stat end`, the body `stat` is run normally until it executes an `exit T` statement. Then execution of `stat` is preempted and the whole construct terminates. The body of a `trap` statement can contain parallel components; the `trap` is exited as soon as one of the components executes an `exit T` statement, the other components being preempted. However, `exit` preemption is weaker than `watching` preemption, in the sense that concurrent components execute for a last time when `exit` occurs. Consider for example the statement

```
trap T in
    await I1; emit 01
        ||
    await I2; exit T
end
```

If I1 occurs before I2, then 01 is emitted and one waits for I2 to terminate. If I2 occurs before I1, then the first branch is preempted, the whole statement terminates instantaneously, and 01 will never be emitted. If I1 and I2 occur simultaneously, then both branches do execute and 01 is emitted. Preemption occurs only after execution at the concerned instant: by exiting a `trap`, a statement can preempt a concurrent statement, but it does leave it its "last wills". The rule for exiting from nested traps is simple: *only the outermost trap matters, the other ones being discarded.* For example, in

```
trap T1 in
        trap T2 in
            exit T1
            ||
            exit T2
        end;
        emit O
end
```

traps T1 and T2 are exited simultaneously, the internal trap T2 is discarded
and O is not emitted. Traps also provide a way of breaking loops, which would
otherwise never terminate as reflected by:

```
trap T in
    loop ... exit T ... end
end
```

One can declare local variables by the statement

```
var X in stat end
```

Variables deeply differ from signals by the fact that they cannot be shared by
concurrent statements. Variables are updated by instantaneous assignments
"X:=exp" or by instantaneous side effect procedure calls "call P(...)",
where a procedure P is an external host language piece of code that receives both
value and reference arguments.

An Operational Semantics for Timed RAISE

Xia Yong and Chris George

United Nations University/International Institute for Software Technology,
P.O.Box 3058, Macau
{xy,cwg}@iist.unu.edu
http://www.iist.unu.edu/{~xy,~cwg}

Abstract. The reliability of software is an increasingly important demand, especially for safety critical systems. RAISE is a mathematically based method which has been shown to be useful in the development of many kinds of software systems. However, RAISE has no particular features for specifying real-time requirements, which often occur in safety critical systems. Adding timing features to RAISE makes a new specification language, Timed RAISE Specification Language (TRSL), and gives it the power of specifying real-time applications. We then have to find a theoretical foundation for TRSL. In this paper, an operational semantics of TRSL is first introduced. Then we define a pre-order and test equivalence relation for TRSL. Some proof rules for TRSL are listed, and their soundness corresponding to our operational model is also explained.

1 Introduction

The reliability of software is an increasingly important demand, especially for critical systems like train control systems or banking systems, for which failures may have very severe consequences. Mathematically based "formal" methods for specification and stepwise development of software have been invented in order to increase the reliability of software. Some of these languages provide facilities to specify concurrent systems, and therefore, they can capture various *qualitative* aspects of system behaviour, such as deadlock, synchronisation and safety. However, in a real-time system we may be concerned with the timing of events. We might want not merely to say that an event occurs, but to say that it occurs within a particular time interval.

RAISE is a mathematically based method which has been shown to be useful in the development of many kinds of software systems. However, RAISE has no particular features for specifying such real-time requirements. Adding real-time features to RAISE Specification Language (RSL) is not only an interesting topic for theoretical computer science research, but also a requirement of some RAISE users.

Integrating RSL with a real-time logic, the Duration Calculus (DC) [ZHR91], seems a good choice to achieve the above aim. RAISE has good features (in particular modularity) for describing large systems, while DC is concerned only with timing properties. The degree of overlap between the two languages is therefore very small.

J. Wing, J. Woodcock, J. Davies (Eds.): FM'99, Vol. II, LNCS 1709, pp. 1008–1027, 1999.
© Springer-Verlag Berlin Heidelberg 1999

We do not wish to perform a syntactic integration of RSL and DC. This would create a large language and probably cause the added complications of time to permeate much of RSL. Instead we note that adding time to a description can be seen as a design step. For example, going from "B must follow A" to "B must follow A within 3 time units" adds an extra constraint, a design decision. It therefore seems reasonable to add time within the part of RSL that is used later in design. The idea is then to be able to (partially) *interpret* TRSL descriptions in terms of DC formulae, and show that these formulae satisfy the timing requirements, also written in DC.

So we have two tasks. The first is extending original RSL to Timed RSL (TRSL) by introducing some real-time constructs. The second step is relating TRSL to DC. This paper concentrates on the first of these.

The proposed TRSL, the syntactic extension to RSL, can be found in [GX98]. Section 2 summarises the proposed extension and discusses its effect on the existing language and its proof system.

After syntactically proposing TRSL, we should establish a theoretical foundation for this new specification language. The theoretical foundation we need is the proof system, the collection of rules that enable us to reason about specifications. In this paper we propose an operational semantics and show how it can be used to establish validity of proof rules. We give an operational semantics of TRSL in Section 3, define an equivalence relation among TRSL expressions in Section 4, and apply it to the proof of soundness of TRSL proof rules in Section 5. Section 6 considers future and related work.

2   Adding Time to RSL

We would like the addition of time to RSL to be the smallest extension that gives us a useful language, and if possible for it to be a conservative extension, i.e. for it to leave the existing proof rules unchanged. By "useful" we mean expressive and convenient for establishing properties. The latter implies an intuitive and simple proof system, which in turn suggests a simple semantics.

The simplest extension to RSL to include time would seem to be to add a **wait** expression. Since we want eventually to relate timed RSL (TRSL) to DC we will make the parameter type of **wait** non-negative reals, which we will define as the type **Time**. For convenience, we allow natural numbers as arguments of **wait** by overloading it. A **Nat** argument is converted to **Time** by the existing RSL prefix operator **real**. For example, **wait** 1 is equivalent to **wait** 1.0.

If we need a parallel expansion rule, it seems necessary also to add a new construct, "time dependence", to input and output. An input, as well as returning the value input, will also return a time value representing the time elapsed between the input being ready and the the communication taking place. Similarly, an output will return the time elapsed between the output being ready and the the communication taking place.

The extension defined here owes much to the work of Wang Yi [Wang91]. He in particular introduced time dependence. We also follow him in making only

wait expressions, and input and output, cause or allow time to elapse. All other evolutions of expressions are regarded as instantaneous.

We also follow Wang Yi in adopting the *maximal progress* assumption. This means that the time between an input or output being ready and the communication taking place is minimised. In other words, when an expression can evolve without waiting for the environment, it will not wait.

This raises a question of what we mean by an internal (non-deterministic) choice like

e1 $\lceil\rceil$ **wait** 1 ; e2

where *e1* and *e2* do not initially wait. Blindly applying the maximum progress assumption leads to this expression evolving only to *e1*. But this would remove the possibility of specifying an expression that might immediately perform *e1*, or might (non-deterministically) wait for one time unit and then perform *e2*. We want to allow this possibility in specification. This leads to the need for a new operator to replace internal choice in the parallel and interlock expansion rules, where we need the "maximal progress" version of internal choice. But this is no more than the addition of another special function internal to the proof rules: it is not needed in the language.

To see how **wait** can be used in parallel or interlocked composition, consider

c? ; normal() $\lceil\rceil$ **wait** 1 ; time_out()

The intention is that this expression initially waits for its environment to offer an output on channel *c*. If this output on channel *c* is available within 1 time unit then the communication should be accepted and *normal()* is executed. If the output is not available within 1 time unit then it should instead execute *time_out()*. We can specify these behaviours using the RSL interlock operator ‖. Interlocked composition is like parallel composition in that the expressions evolve concurrently, but more aggressive: it forces them to communicate only with each other until one of them terminates. We expect the following equivalences to hold for any strictly positive k, assuming that *time_out()* can not itself initially wait:

(c? ; normal() $\lceil\rceil$ **wait** 1 ; time_out()) ‖ (**wait**$(1-k)$; c!()) $\equiv$
  wait$(1-k)$; normal()

(c? ; normal() $\lceil\rceil$ **wait** 1 ; time_out()) ‖ **wait**$(1+k)$ $\equiv$
  wait 1 ; (time_out() ‖ **wait** k)

2.1   Conservative Extension

Conservative extension of RSL to make TRSL, i.e. all existing RSL proof rules being unchanged, would be ideal but does not seem to be achievable. There are two problems.

First, introducing time can reduce non-determinacy. For example, specifying an expression like the one we considered earlier, that will take a special action (time-out) if some event does not occur within a specified period, can only be specified without time as a non-deterministic choice between the normal and time-out behaviour. When time is included we may be able to calculate which behaviour will be taken; the non-determinacy may be reduced.

Secondly, there are are some rules in RSL that we expect not to hold because of the kind of properties we are interested in when we want to relate TRSL to DC. DC is concerned with the duration of states, i.e. for how long properties hold. We expect properties to be reflected in the values of imperative variables in RSL. Now consider the following equivalence that is valid in RSL, provided the expression e does not involve input or output and is convergent:

$$c? \; ; \; v := e \equiv v := e \; ; \; c?$$

The assignment and the input can be commuted. In TRSL in general we have to introduce a let expression for the time dependence. We would expect from the RSL proof rules, provided again e does not involve input or output and is convergent, and provided also that t is not free in e, to be able to derive the following:

let $t = c?$ **in** $v := e$ **end**

$\equiv$

let $t = v := e \; ; \; c?$ **in skip end**

$\equiv$

$v := e \; ;$ **let** $t = c?$ **in skip end**

It is not immediately clear what the meaning of the second expression should be, but it is clear that the last would differ from the first in changing the duration of the state in which v has the value e; the possible wait for the communication on c shifts from before the assignment to after it. So this derivation cannot be allowed in TRSL.

These two examples, of reduced non-determinism and restrictions on commuting expressions, do seem, however, to encompass the problems. It also seems likely (though this is the subject of further work) that there is a reduction from TRSL to RSL (just throwing away the timing information) that is consistent with a "more deterministic" ordering: the ordering derived later in in Section 4.2. That is, any behaviour of a timed specification will be a possible behaviour of its reduction to an untimed one. The second problem involves the strengthening of applicability conditions for commuting sequential expressions.

3   Operational Semantics

For the sake of clarity, we follow the approach of [HI93, BD93, Deb94]: the operational semantics in this paper for untimed part of TRSL is closely based on them, and we only consider a core syntax of TRSL. Our operational semantics can be viewed as a version of Timed CCS [Wang91] without τs.

3.1   The Core Syntax

For simplicity we restrict the types of expressions to be **Unit**, **Bool** and **Real**. The set of allowed expressions includes:

- As constants the reals, the booleans **true** and **false**, the **Unit** value (). The basic expression **skip** is an expression that immediately terminates successfully. We consider also the basic expression **stop** which represents deadlock and the basic expression **chaos** which stands for the divergent process.
- Three binding operators that are the abstraction, the recursion and the let definition (λ, **rec**, **let**). The reader should notice that the **rec** is not an RSL binding operator: RSL does not syntactically distinguish recursion. In the core syntax, it is convenient to indicate where recursion may occur.
- Imperative aspects are supported through the notion of variables and assignment.
- We have the following combinators:
  - $_-\lceil\rceil_-$: Nondeterministic choice between two expressions (also called internal choice). One of the two expressions is selected nondeterministically for evaluation.
  - $_-\lceil\rceil_-$: External choice between two expressions. The choice is context dependent, i.e. the environment influences the choice between the two expressions.
  - $_-\|_-$: Parallel composition of two expressions.
  - $_-\#_-$: The interlock operator. It is similar to the parallel operator, but more aggressive. In other words, two interlocked expressions will communicate if they are able to communicate with one another. If they are able to communicate with other concurrently executing value expressions but not with each other, they deadlock unless one of them can terminate. The interlock operator is the main novelty in the RSL process algebra. It has been devised mainly to allow implicit specification of concurrency.
  - $_-;_-$: Sequencing operator.

The above operators in TRSL have the same meanings as those in RSL. We also have the extensions to be included:

- TRSL is essentially independent of the time domain. For simplicity, in our core syntax of TRSL, we just assume the time Domain to be Real^{+0}.
- The expression **wait** E means we first evaluate the expression E, get the result d, then delay exactly d units of time.
- Expressions may communicate through unidirectional channels. The expression **let** t = c!E1 **in** E2 means: evaluate E1, send the result (when possible) on the channel c, and then evaluate E2. t records the time between the communication on c being ready and it occurring. The expression **let** t = c?x **in** E means: assign any value received on the channel c to variable x, and then evaluate E. Again, t records the time between the communication on c being ready and it occurring.

More formally the BNF syntax of our language is:

Syntactic Categories:

- E in Expressions
- x in Variables
- t, id in Identifiers
- c in Channels
- r in Reals
- T in Time
- τ in Types
- V in ValueDefinitions

Expression The BNF grammar of expressions is:

V ::= id : τ | id : τ, V
E ::= () | **true** | **false** | r | T | id | x | **skip** | **stop** | **chaos** |
    x := E | **if** E **then** E **else** E | **let** id = E **in** E |
    wait E | **let** t = c?x **in** E | **let** t = c!E **in** E |
    E $\sqcap$ E | E $\square$ E | E $\parallel$ E | E $\#$ E | E ; E |
    λ id : τ $\bullet$ E | E E | **rec** id : τ $\bullet$ E |

In fact E ; E$'$ is equivalent to **let** id = E **in** E$'$ provided id is chosen so as not to be free in E$'$. We include E ; E to give a conventional presentation.

3.2 Definition

Store A store s is a finite map from variables (noted x) to values (noted v):
$s = [x \mapsto v, ...]$

Environment An environment ρ is a finite map from identifiers (noted id) to values (noted v):
$\rho = [\text{id} \mapsto \text{v}, ...]$

Closures A closure, $[\![\lambda \text{ id} : \tau \bullet \text{E}, \rho]\!]$, is a pair made of

- a lambda expression : λ id : τ $\bullet$ E
- an environment : ρ

Computable Values $\mathcal{V}$ is the least set which satisfies:

- $\mathcal{V}$ contains values from our types: (), **true, false**, ... , -1, ..., 0, ..., 1, ...
- if ρ is an environment, then $\mathcal{V}$ contains $[\![\lambda \text{ id} : \tau \bullet \text{E}, \rho]\!]$

Expressions and Computable Values The set $\mathcal{EV}$ of expressions and computable values is defined as
$\mathcal{EV} = \mathcal{E} \cup \mathcal{V}$

Events "$\diamond$" denotes any event;
"$\triangle$" denotes visible events and silent events.

Visible events

Visible events a consist of :
- input events : $c?v$
- output events : $c!v$

where c is a channel and v is a value in $\mathcal{V}$.
$\bar{a}$ denotes the complement action of a (e.g. : $\overline{c?v} = c!v$).

Time-measurable events

$\varepsilon(d)$ denotes waiting d unit of time, where d is a value from the time domain and $d > 0$.

Silent events

ε denotes internal moves, including internal behaviours of communication (which is denoted as "τ" in CCS).

Time Model We assume that all silent events can perform instantaneously and will never wait unnecessarily. Once both sides of a channel are ready for communication, the communication will happen without any delay (unless some other visible event or silent event happens instead) and the communication takes no time.

The above assumptions are conventional and the reason for adopting them is just to make proof theory easier.

Notations We introduce some notations that are used later.

1. $v, v', \ldots$ represent values drawn from $\mathcal{V}$
2. $d, d', \ldots$ represent values drawn from the **Time** domain.
3. $ev, ev', \ldots$ represent values drawn from $\mathcal{EV}$,
4. $a, \bar{a}, \varepsilon(d), \varepsilon, \triangle, \diamond \ldots$ represent events,
5. $E, E_i, \ldots$ represent expressions.
6. $x, y, \ldots$ represent variables.
7. $s, s', s'', \ldots$ represent stores.

Configurations Our operational semantics is based on the evolution of configurations.

The set of basic configurations $\mathcal{BC}$ is defined as:

$$\mathcal{BC} = \{< ev, s > \mid ev \in \mathcal{EV} \wedge s \in Store\}$$

The set of configurations, $\mathcal{C}$, is the least set which satisfies:

1. $\mathcal{BC} \subset \mathcal{C}$
2. $\alpha, \beta \in \mathcal{C}$ implies $\alpha \; op \; \beta \in \mathcal{C}$ where: $op = \sqcap, [], \|, \|\!\|$
3. $\alpha, \beta \in \mathcal{C}$ implies $\alpha \; op \; s \; op \; \beta \in \mathcal{C}$ where: $op = \|, \|\!\|$
4. $\alpha \in \mathcal{C}$ implies $\alpha \; ; \; E, wait \; \alpha, x := \alpha, (\alpha \; E) \in \mathcal{C}$

5. $\alpha \in \mathcal{C}$ implies $\alpha v \in \mathcal{C}$
6. $\alpha \in \mathcal{C}$ implies :
   (a) $[\![\lambda \text{ id} : \tau \bullet \alpha, \rho]\!] \, v \in \mathcal{C}$
   (b) $[\![\lambda \text{ id} : \tau \bullet E, \rho]\!] \, \alpha \in \mathcal{C}$
7. $\alpha \in \mathcal{C}$ implies :
   (a) **let** $id = \alpha$ **in** $E \in \mathcal{C}$
   (b) **if** α **then** E_1 **else** $E_2 \in \mathcal{C}$
   (c) **let** $t = c!$ α **in** $E \in \mathcal{C}$

3.3 Operational Rules

The operational rules are given in Figure 1 and Figure 2. Each rule is divided into two parts: the lower part describes the possible evolution of the configurations, and the upper part presents the precondition of that evolution. □ indicates that there is no precondition.

We use the standard notation $E[v/t]$ to describe the substitution of v for all free occurrences of the identifier t in E.

3.4 Semantic Function : Merge

$$\text{merge}(s, s', s'') = s' \dagger [\, x \mapsto s''(x) \mid x \in \mathbf{dom}(s'') \cap \mathbf{dom}(s) \bullet s(x) \neq s''(x) \,]$$

3.5 Meaning of "$Sort_d$" and "$SORT_d$"

$Sort_d$ $Sort_d(\alpha)$ is a set of ports (channel names tagged as input or output), whose intuitive meaning is the possible (input or output) visible events that α can evolve to within the next d units of time. We define "$Sort_d$" inductively according to configuration structures.

We find that there are three kinds of configuration that can evolve with $\varepsilon(d)$: **wait**, input and output. So, they are named "Basic Forms". There are some other kinds of configurations that can evolve with $\varepsilon(d)$, if their components are in Basic Forms. They are named "Extended Forms".

BASIC FORMS:

- $Sort_0(\alpha) = \emptyset$ for $\alpha \in \mathcal{C}$
- $Sort_d(c?) = \overline{Sort_d(c!)}$ and $Sort_d(c!) = \overline{Sort_d(c?)}$ for any channel c
- $Sort_d(\textbf{ wait } < (d + d'), \, s >) = \emptyset$
- $Sort_d(\, < \textbf{let } t = c?x \textbf{ in } E \, , s >) = \{c?\}$
- $Sort_d(\textbf{ let } t = c! < v, s > \textbf{ in } E = \{c!\}$

EXTENDED FORMS:
Assume that α and β are one of the Basic Forms.

- $Sort_{d+d'}(\textbf{wait} d; E) = Sort_{d'}(E)$
- $Sort_d(\alpha \, ; \, E) = Sort_d(\alpha)$

Basic Expressions

$$\frac{\square}{\rho \vdash\; <\textbf{skip}, s> \xrightarrow{\varepsilon} <(), s>}$$

$$\frac{\square}{\rho \vdash\; <\textbf{stop}, s> \xrightarrow{\varepsilon(d)} <\textbf{stop}, s>}$$

$$\frac{\square}{\rho \vdash\; <\textbf{chaos}, s> \xrightarrow{\varepsilon} <\textbf{chaos}, s>}$$

Configuration Fork

$$\frac{\square}{\rho \vdash\; <E_1\ op\ E_2, s> \xrightarrow{\varepsilon} <E_1, s>\ op\ <E_2, s>}$$

where op = $\sqcap$, $\parallel$

Look Up

$$\frac{\square}{\rho \dagger [id \mapsto v] \vdash\; <id, s> \xrightarrow{\varepsilon} <v, s>}$$

$$\frac{\square}{\rho \vdash\; <id, s \dagger [id \mapsto v]> \xrightarrow{\varepsilon} <v, s \dagger [id \mapsto v]>}$$

Sequencing

$$\frac{\square}{\rho \vdash\; <E_1\ ;\ E_2, s> \xrightarrow{\varepsilon} <E_1, s>\ ;\ E_2}$$

$$\frac{\rho \vdash \alpha \xrightarrow{\diamond} \alpha'}{\rho \vdash \alpha\ ;\ E \xrightarrow{\diamond} \alpha'\ ;\ E}$$

$$\frac{\square}{\rho \vdash\; <v, s>;\ E \xrightarrow{\varepsilon} <E, s>}$$

Assignment

$$\frac{\square}{\rho \vdash\; <x := E, s> \xrightarrow{\varepsilon} x := <E, s>}$$

$$\frac{\rho \vdash \alpha \xrightarrow{\diamond} \alpha'}{\rho \vdash x := \alpha \xrightarrow{\diamond} x := \alpha'}$$

$$\frac{\square}{\rho \vdash x := <v, s> \xrightarrow{\varepsilon} <(), s \dagger [x \mapsto v]>}$$

Waiting

$$\frac{\square}{\rho \vdash\; <\textbf{wait } E,\ s> \xrightarrow{\varepsilon} \textbf{wait } <E,\ s>}$$

$$\frac{\rho \vdash \alpha \xrightarrow{\diamond} \alpha'}{\rho \vdash \textbf{wait } \alpha \xrightarrow{\diamond} \textbf{wait } \alpha'}$$

$$\frac{\square}{\rho \vdash \textbf{wait} <(d + d'),\ s> \xrightarrow{\varepsilon(d)} \textbf{wait} <d',\ s>}$$

when $\{\ d > 0\ \}$

$$\frac{\square}{\rho \vdash \textbf{wait} <(0),\ s> \xrightarrow{\varepsilon} <(),\ s>}$$

Input

$$\frac{\square}{\rho \vdash\; <\textbf{let } t = c?x \textbf{ in } E, s> \xrightarrow{c?v} <E[0/t], s \dagger [x \mapsto v]>}$$

$$\frac{\square}{\rho \vdash\; <\textbf{let } t = c?x \textbf{ in } E, s> \xrightarrow{\varepsilon(d)} <\textbf{let } t = c?x \textbf{ in } E[t + d/t], s>}$$

Output

$$\frac{\square}{\rho \vdash\; <\textbf{let } t = c\ !\ E \textbf{ in } E, s> \xrightarrow{\varepsilon} \textbf{let } t = c\ ! <E,\ s> \textbf{ in } E}$$

$$\frac{\rho \vdash \alpha \xrightarrow{\diamond} \alpha'}{\rho \vdash \textbf{let } t = c\ !\ \alpha \textbf{ in } E \xrightarrow{\diamond} \textbf{let } t = c\ !\ \alpha' \textbf{ in } E}$$

$$\frac{\square}{\rho \vdash \textbf{let } t = c\ ! <v, s> \textbf{ in } E \xrightarrow{c!v} <E[0/t], s>}$$

$$\frac{\square}{\rho \vdash \textbf{let } t = c\ ! <v, s> \textbf{ in } E \xrightarrow{\varepsilon(d)} \textbf{let } t = c\ ! <v, s> \textbf{ in } E[t + d/t]}$$

Internal Choice

$$\frac{\square}{\rho \vdash \alpha \sqcap \beta \xrightarrow{\varepsilon} \alpha \; \xrightarrow{\varepsilon} \beta}$$

External Choice

$$\frac{\rho \vdash \alpha \xrightarrow{a} \alpha'}{\rho \vdash \alpha \parallel \beta \xrightarrow{a} \alpha' \quad \beta \parallel \alpha \xrightarrow{a} \alpha'}$$

$$\frac{\rho \vdash \alpha \xrightarrow{\varepsilon(d)} \alpha' ,\ \rho \vdash \beta \xrightarrow{\varepsilon(d)} \beta'}{\rho \vdash \alpha \parallel \beta \xrightarrow{\varepsilon(d)} \alpha' \parallel \beta' \quad \beta \parallel \alpha \xrightarrow{\varepsilon(d)} \beta' \parallel \alpha'}$$

$$\frac{\rho \vdash \alpha \xrightarrow{\varepsilon} \alpha'}{\rho \vdash \alpha \parallel \beta \xrightarrow{\varepsilon} \alpha' \parallel \beta \quad \beta \parallel \alpha \xrightarrow{\varepsilon} \beta \parallel \alpha'}$$

$$\frac{\square}{\rho \vdash\; <v, s> \parallel \alpha \xrightarrow{\varepsilon} <v, s> \quad \alpha \parallel <v, s> \xrightarrow{\varepsilon} <v, s>}$$

Fig. 1. Operational Rules for TRSL : Part 1

Parallel Combinator

$$\frac{\Box}{\rho \vdash < E_1 \parallel E_2, s > \xrightarrow{\varepsilon} < E_1, s > \parallel s \parallel < E_2, s >}$$

$$\frac{\rho \vdash \alpha \xrightarrow{a} \alpha' , \rho \vdash \beta \xrightarrow{\bar{a}} \beta'}{\begin{array}{c}\rho \vdash \alpha \parallel s \parallel \beta \xrightarrow{\varepsilon} \alpha' \parallel s \parallel \beta' \\ \beta \parallel s \parallel \alpha \xrightarrow{\varepsilon} \beta' \parallel s \parallel \alpha'\end{array}}$$

$$\frac{\rho \vdash \alpha \xrightarrow{\triangle} \alpha'}{\begin{array}{c}\rho \vdash \alpha \parallel s \parallel \beta \xrightarrow{\triangle} \alpha' \parallel s \parallel \beta \\ \beta \parallel s \parallel \alpha \xrightarrow{\triangle} \beta \parallel s \parallel \alpha'\end{array}}$$

$$\frac{\rho \vdash \alpha \xrightarrow{\varepsilon(d)} \alpha' , \rho \vdash \beta \xrightarrow{\varepsilon(d)} \beta'}{\begin{array}{c}\rho \vdash \alpha \parallel s \parallel \beta \xrightarrow{\varepsilon(d)} \alpha' \parallel s \parallel \beta' \\ \beta \parallel s \parallel \alpha \xrightarrow{\varepsilon(d)} \beta' \parallel s \parallel \alpha'\end{array}}$$

$$when \left\{ \begin{array}{c} [\; Sort_d(\alpha) \cap \overline{Sort_d(\beta)} = \emptyset \; ; \\ Sort_d(\alpha) \cap \overline{SORT_d} = \emptyset \; ; \\ Sort_d(\beta) \cap \overline{SORT_d} = \emptyset \;] \end{array} \right\}$$

$$\frac{\Box}{\begin{array}{c}\rho \vdash \alpha \parallel s \parallel < v, s' > \xrightarrow{\varepsilon} \alpha \parallel s \parallel s' \\ < v, s' > \parallel s \parallel \alpha \xrightarrow{\varepsilon} s' \parallel s \parallel \alpha\end{array}}$$

$$\frac{\rho \vdash \alpha \xrightarrow{\Diamond} \alpha'}{\begin{array}{c}\rho \vdash \alpha \parallel s \parallel s' \xrightarrow{\Diamond} \alpha' \parallel s \parallel s' \\ s' \parallel s \parallel \alpha \xrightarrow{\Diamond} s' \parallel s \parallel \alpha'\end{array}}$$

$$\frac{\Box}{\begin{array}{c}\rho \vdash < v, s'' > \parallel s \parallel s' \xrightarrow{\varepsilon} < v, merge(s, s', s'') > \\ s' \parallel s \parallel < v, s'' > \xrightarrow{\varepsilon} < v, merge(s, s', s'') > \end{array}}$$

Interlocking

$$\frac{\Box}{\rho \vdash < E_1 \mathrel{\#} E_2, s > \xrightarrow{\varepsilon} < E_1, s > \mathrel{\#} s \mathrel{\#} < E_2, s >}$$

$$\frac{\rho \vdash \alpha \xrightarrow{a} \alpha' , \rho \vdash \beta \xrightarrow{\bar{a}} \beta'}{\begin{array}{c}\rho \vdash \alpha \mathrel{\#} s \mathrel{\#} \beta \xrightarrow{\varepsilon} \alpha' \mathrel{\#} s \mathrel{\#} \beta' \\ \beta \mathrel{\#} s \mathrel{\#} \alpha \xrightarrow{\varepsilon} \beta' \mathrel{\#} s \mathrel{\#} \alpha'\end{array}}$$

$$\frac{\rho \vdash \alpha \xrightarrow{\varepsilon} \alpha'}{\begin{array}{c}\rho \vdash \alpha \mathrel{\#} s \mathrel{\#} \beta \xrightarrow{\varepsilon} \alpha' \mathrel{\#} s \mathrel{\#} \beta \\ \beta \mathrel{\#} s \mathrel{\#} \alpha \xrightarrow{\varepsilon} \beta \mathrel{\#} s \mathrel{\#} \alpha'\end{array}}$$

$$\frac{\rho \vdash \alpha \xrightarrow{\varepsilon(d)} \alpha' , \rho \vdash \beta \xrightarrow{\varepsilon(d)} \beta'}{\begin{array}{c}\rho \vdash \alpha \mathrel{\#} s \mathrel{\#} \beta \xrightarrow{\varepsilon(d)} \alpha' \mathrel{\#} s \mathrel{\#} \beta' \\ \beta \mathrel{\#} s \mathrel{\#} \alpha \xrightarrow{\varepsilon(d)} \beta' \mathrel{\#} s \mathrel{\#} \alpha'\end{array}}$$

$$when \{ \; Sort_d(\alpha) \cap \overline{Sort_d(\beta)} = \emptyset \}$$

$$\frac{\Box}{\begin{array}{c}\rho \vdash \alpha \mathrel{\#} s \mathrel{\#} < v, s' > \xrightarrow{\varepsilon} \alpha \mathrel{\#} s \mathrel{\#} s' \\ < v, s' > \mathrel{\#} s \mathrel{\#} \alpha \xrightarrow{\varepsilon} s' \mathrel{\#} s \mathrel{\#} \alpha\end{array}}$$

$$\frac{\rho \vdash \alpha \xrightarrow{\Diamond} \alpha'}{\begin{array}{c}\rho \vdash \alpha \mathrel{\#} s \mathrel{\#} s' \xrightarrow{\Diamond} \alpha' \mathrel{\#} s \mathrel{\#} s' \\ s' \mathrel{\#} s \mathrel{\#} \alpha \xrightarrow{\Diamond} s' \mathrel{\#} s \mathrel{\#} \alpha'\end{array}}$$

$$\frac{\Box}{\rho \vdash < v, s'' > \mathrel{\#} s \mathrel{\#} s' \xrightarrow{\varepsilon} < v, merge(s, s', s'') > \\ s' \mathrel{\#} s \mathrel{\#} < v, s'' > \xrightarrow{\varepsilon} < v, merge(s, s', s'') >}$$

Function

$$\frac{\Box}{\rho \vdash < E_1 \; E_2, s > \xrightarrow{\varepsilon} < E_1, s > \; E_2}$$

$$\frac{\rho \vdash \alpha \xrightarrow{\Diamond} \alpha'}{\rho \vdash \alpha \; E \xrightarrow{\Diamond} \alpha' \; E}$$

$$\frac{\Box}{\rho \vdash < \lambda \; id : \tau \bullet E, s > \xrightarrow{\varepsilon} < [\lambda \; id : \tau \bullet E, \rho \,], s >}$$

$$\frac{\Box}{\rho \vdash < [\lambda \; id : \tau \bullet E_1, \rho_1 \,], s > \; E_2 \xrightarrow{\varepsilon} [\lambda \; id : \tau \bullet E_1, \rho_1] \; < E_2, s >}$$

$$\frac{\rho \vdash \alpha \xrightarrow{\Diamond} \alpha'}{\rho \vdash [\lambda \; id : \tau \bullet E, \rho_1 \,] \; \alpha \xrightarrow{\Diamond} [\lambda \; id : \tau \bullet E, \rho_1 \,] \; \alpha'}$$

$$\frac{\Box}{\rho \vdash [\lambda \; id : \tau \bullet E, \rho_1 \,] \; < v, s > \xrightarrow{\Diamond} [\lambda \; id : \tau \bullet < E, s >, \rho_1 \,] \; v}$$

$$\frac{\rho_1 \dagger [id \mapsto v] \vdash \alpha \xrightarrow{\Diamond} \alpha'}{\rho \vdash [\lambda \; id : \tau \bullet \alpha, \rho_1 \,] \; v \xrightarrow{\Diamond} [\lambda \; id : \tau \bullet \alpha', \rho_1 \,] \; v}$$

$$\frac{\rho_1 \dagger [id \mapsto v] \vdash \alpha \xrightarrow{\Diamond} < v', s >}{\rho \vdash [\lambda \; id : \tau \bullet \alpha, \rho_1 \,] \; v \xrightarrow{\Diamond} < v', s >}$$

Let Expression

$$\frac{\Box}{\rho \vdash < let \; id = E_1 \; in \; E_2, s > \xrightarrow{\varepsilon} let \; id = < E_1, s > \; in \; E_2}$$

$$\frac{\rho \vdash \alpha \xrightarrow{\Diamond} \alpha'}{\rho \vdash let \; id = \alpha \; in \; E \xrightarrow{\Diamond} let \; id = \alpha' \; in \; E}$$

$$\frac{\Box}{\rho \vdash let \; id = \; < v, s > \; in \; E \xrightarrow{\varepsilon} \; < E[v/id], s >}$$

If Expression

$$\frac{\Box}{\rho \vdash < if \; E \; then \; E_1 \; else \; E_2, s > \xrightarrow{\varepsilon} if < E, s > then \; E_1 else \; E_2}$$

$$\frac{\rho \vdash \alpha \xrightarrow{\Diamond} \alpha'}{\rho \vdash if \; \alpha \; then \; E_1 \; else \; E_2 \xrightarrow{\Diamond} if \; \alpha' \; then \; E_1 \; else \; E_2}$$

$$\frac{\Box}{\rho \vdash if \; < true, s > \; then \; E_1 \; else \; E_2 \xrightarrow{\varepsilon} \; < E_1, s >}$$

$$\frac{\Box}{\rho \vdash if \; < false, s > \; then \; E_1 \; else \; E_2 \xrightarrow{\varepsilon} \; < E_2, s >}$$

Recursion

$$\frac{\Box}{\rho \vdash < rec \; id : \tau \bullet E, s > \xrightarrow{\varepsilon} < E[rec \; id : \tau \bullet E/id], s >}$$

Fig. 2. Operational Rules for TRSL : Part 2

- $\text{Sort}_d(x := \alpha) = \text{Sort}_d(\alpha)$
- $\text{Sort}_d(\textbf{wait } \alpha) = \text{Sort}_d(\alpha)$
- $\text{Sort}_d(\textbf{let } t = c! \, \alpha \textbf{ in } E) = \text{Sort}_d(\alpha)$
- $\text{Sort}_d(\alpha \parallel s \parallel s') = \text{Sort}_d(s' \parallel s \parallel \alpha) = \mathit{Sort}_d(\alpha)$
- $\text{Sort}_d(\alpha \between s \between s') = \text{Sort}_d(s' \between s \between \alpha) = \mathit{Sort}_d(\alpha)$
- $\text{Sort}_d(\alpha \text{ E}) = \text{Sort}_d(\alpha)$
- $\text{Sort}_d(\alpha \text{ v}) = \text{Sort}_d(\alpha)$
- $\text{Sort}_d([\![\lambda \; id \, : \, \tau \bullet \alpha, \; \rho]\!] \, v) = \text{Sort}_d(\alpha)$
- $\text{Sort}_d(\textbf{let } id = \alpha \textbf{ in } E) = \text{Sort}_d(\alpha)$
- $\text{Sort}_d(\textbf{if } \alpha \textbf{ then } E_1 \textbf{ else } E_2) = \text{Sort}_d(\alpha)$
- $\text{Sort}_d(\alpha \; op \; \beta) = \text{Sort}_d(\alpha) \cup \text{Sort}_d(\beta)$ where op = "$[\!]$", "$\parallel$"

SORT$_d$ SORT$_d$ is a set of ports. Its definition is just same as Sort$_d$, but can only be calculated if we know what the environment expressions are. I.e. port c? (c!) $\in$ SORT$_d$ means that within d units of time, there are some other processes that will be ready for complementary communication, c! (c?), on channel c.

3.6 Commentary on Operational Rules

The transition relation is defined as the smallest relation satisfying the axioms and rules given in our operational rules. We note in particular:

Time-measurable event A configuration can evolve with a time-measurable event only if all its sub-configurations on both sides of combinators $[\!]$, $\parallel$ and $\between$, can evolve with this same time-measurable event.

Maximal progress Maximal progress in RSL means that once a communication on a channel is ready, it will never wait. In the rules for interlocking, the semantic function, Sort$_d$, is used to specify that only if no pair of complementary actions, one from each side of the combinator, is ready for communication, can this configuration evolve with a time-measurable event. In the rules for parallel combinator, the condition is stronger: a configuration can evolve with a time-measurable event only when no communication is possible, either internal (between the parallel expressions) or external (between one of them and the environment). (c.f. Section 2). Using "Sort (SORT)" to guarantee that the composite processes satisfy maximal progress was first proposed by Wang Yi in his work on Timed CCS [Wang91].

4   Time Test Equivalence

4.1   Definitions

- Let l be a sequence of events, α, β two configurations in $\mathcal{C}$, d $\in$ **Time** and d > 0. We define $\alpha \overset{l}{\Rightarrow} \beta$ by:
  1. $\alpha \overset{<>}{\Longrightarrow} \beta$ if $\alpha \, (\overset{\varepsilon}{\rightarrow})^* \, \beta$.

2. $\alpha \overset{al'}{\Longrightarrow} \beta$ if for some α, α', α'' we have : $\alpha \overset{<>}{\Longrightarrow} \alpha'$, $\alpha' \overset{a}{\rightarrow} \alpha''$, and $\alpha'' \overset{l'}{\Longrightarrow} \beta$.

3. $\alpha \overset{\varepsilon(d)l'}{\Longrightarrow} \beta$ if for some α, α', α'' we have : $\alpha \overset{<>}{\Longrightarrow} \alpha'$, $\alpha' \overset{\varepsilon(d)}{\longrightarrow} \alpha''$, and $\alpha'' \overset{l'}{\Longrightarrow} \beta$.

where $<>$ stands for the empty sequence. Moreover, we merge successive time-measurable events by treating the sequence $\varepsilon(d_1)\varepsilon(d_2)...\varepsilon(d_n)$ as the event $\varepsilon(d_1 + d_2 + ... + d_n)$.

- Let L be set of traces of a configuration, defined as :

$$L(\alpha) = \{l \mid for \ some \ \beta \ , \ \alpha \overset{l}{\Longrightarrow} \beta\}$$

- We define the following convergence predicates:
  1. We write $\alpha \downarrow$ if there is no infinite sequence of internal moves:

$$\alpha \ = \ \alpha_0 \overset{\varepsilon}{\rightarrow} \alpha_1 \overset{\varepsilon}{\rightarrow} ...$$

  2. $\alpha \downarrow <>$ if $\alpha \downarrow$
  3. $\alpha \downarrow \ al'$ if $\alpha \downarrow$ and for all α' if $\alpha \overset{a}{\Rightarrow} \alpha'$ then $\alpha' \downarrow l'$
  4. $\alpha \downarrow \ \varepsilon(d)l'$ if $\alpha \downarrow$ and for all α' if $\alpha \overset{\varepsilon(d)}{\Longrightarrow} \alpha'$ then $\alpha' \downarrow l'$
  5. $\alpha \uparrow$ if $\alpha \downarrow$ is false and $\alpha \uparrow l$ if $\alpha \downarrow l$ is false.

- We define the set S(α) of the next possible moves of the configuration α by:

$$S(\alpha) = \{c? \mid for \ some \ v \ and \ \beta, \ \alpha \overset{c?v}{\Longrightarrow} \beta\} \ \cup$$
$$\{c! \mid for \ some \ v \ and \ \beta, \ \alpha \overset{c!v}{\Longrightarrow} \beta\}$$

- We define A(α, l), the acceptance set of events of α after performing the events in the sequence l by :

$$A(\alpha, \ l) \ = \ \{S(\alpha') \mid \alpha \overset{l}{\Longrightarrow} \alpha'\}$$

- We define : $T(\alpha) = \pi_2(\alpha)$, if for some d > 0 and $\alpha \overset{\varepsilon(d)}{\longrightarrow}$ (i.e. α can evolve an event of $\varepsilon(d)$ in the next step). Otherwise T(α) is defined as $\emptyset$.

π_2 is a "projection" function, which returns the set of stores in a configuration that can perform a time-measurable event:
  - For basic configurations: $\pi_2(<ev, s>) = \{s\}$
  - For configurations, $\alpha \ op \ \beta$ where $op = \|, \#: \pi_2(\alpha \ op \ \beta) = \pi_2(\alpha) \bigtriangledown \pi_2(\beta)$
  - For configurations: $\pi_2(\alpha \ [] \ \beta) = \pi_2(\alpha) \cup \pi_2(\beta)$
  - For other configurations, e.g. $\pi_2(\alpha \ ; \ E) = \pi_2(\alpha)$

The function "$\bigtriangledown$" is defined by

$$\{s_1, ..., s_{n1}\} \bigtriangledown \{t_1, ..., t_{n2}\} = \bigcup_{\substack{i = 1...n1 \\ j = 1...n2}} \{s_i \cup t_j\}$$

- We define $W(\alpha, l)$, the store set of events of α after performing the events in the sequence l by :

$$W(\alpha, l) \ = \ \{T(\alpha') \mid \alpha \overset{l}{\Longrightarrow} \alpha'\}$$

- We define also $R(\alpha, l)$, the set of possible returned pairs (of values and stores) after l:

$$R(\alpha, l) \ = \ \{(v, s) \mid \alpha \overset{l}{\Longrightarrow} < v, s >\}$$

4.2   Equivalence of TRSL Expressions

We first define a pre-order between TRSL configurations.

Definition. For α, β in $\mathcal{C}$, $\alpha \ll_{SOS} \beta$ if for every l and for any given ρ:

$$\alpha \downarrow l \Rightarrow a) \ \beta \downarrow l$$
$$ b) \ A(\beta, l) \ \subset\subset \ A(\alpha, l)$$
$$ c) \ W(\beta, l) \ \subset\subset \ W(\alpha, l)$$
$$ d) \ R(\beta, l) \ \subseteq \ R(\alpha, l)$$

where:

$\mathcal{A} \ \subset\subset \ \mathcal{B}$ is defined by: $\forall \ X \ \in \mathcal{A} \bullet \exists \ Y \ \in \mathcal{B} \bullet \ Y \ \subseteq \ X$

Now, we begin to define the equivalence between TRSL expressions through their operational semantics.

Actually, the equivalence between TRSL configurations: α , β, can be defined as : $\alpha \ll_{SOS} \beta$ and $\beta \ll_{SOS} \alpha$. For simplicity of future proof, we rewrite that equivalence definition as follows.

- $\alpha \uparrow l$ iff $\beta \uparrow l$
- if $\alpha \downarrow l$ and $\beta \downarrow l$ then
  1. $A(\alpha, l) \subset\subset A(\beta, l)$ and $A(\beta, l) \subset\subset A(\alpha, l)$
  2. $W(\alpha, l) \subset\subset W(\beta, l)$ and $W(\beta, l) \subset\subset W(\alpha, l)$
  3. $R(\alpha, l) = R(\beta, l)$

Definition. For any TRSL expressions: P and Q, P $=$ Q iff for any s and for any given ρ, $<P, s> = <Q, s>$

4.3   Commentary and Examples

Pre-order Our definition of the pre-order relation on two configuration : $\alpha \ll_{SOS} \beta$ stands for

1. α is more general than β, or
2. α is more nondeterministic than β, or
3. α is implemented by β, or
4. α is more unstable than β, ...

Therefore, in order to guarantee the condition 2, we ask $A(\beta, l) \subset\subset A(\alpha, l)$ to hold; and to guarantee the condition 4, we ask $W(\beta, l) \subset\subset W(\alpha, l)$ to hold.

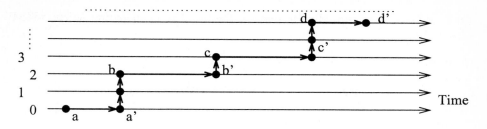

Fig. 3. A Trajectory in Two-dimension Time Space

Time Model We view processes under a super-dense model [MP93] as a trajectory in a two dimensional time space [ZH96, PD97, QZ97]. We suppose there are countably infinite time axes, indexed by natural numbers. Events and processes happen and evolve in this space. A process starts at some time on a time axis. When the process executes a time-measurable event, time progresses horizontally, and the process stays on the same time axis. When the process executes visible and silent events, it jumps vertically up to another time axis, and may have a new state there. A trajectory of a super-dense behaviour is shown in Figure 3.

There are two types of turning point. One is called a start_turning_point (points a, b, c, d in Figure 3), from which the process will execute a time-measurable event. The other is called an end_turning_point (points a', b', c', d' in Figure 3), from which the process will execute a visible or silent event.

The super-dense model distinguishes clearly between time measurable events like delays and waits for synchronisation, and visible and silent events like synchronisation and assignments. It allows arbitrary numbers of the latter to occur instantaneously but in some order, which matches well with the interleaving semantics of concurrency in (T)RSL.

In our time test equivalence definition, for two equivalent processes (expressions), α and β, demanding $A(\alpha, l) = A(\beta, l)$ guarantees the same possible temporal order of visible events and time-measurable events of the two processes.

Demanding $W(\alpha, l) = W(\beta, l)$ guarantees that the stores (variable states) of two processes (expressions) on every start_turning_point are the same.

Demanding $R(\alpha, l) = R(\beta, l)$ guarantees that two expressions, if they terminate, can return the same sets of possible values and final stores.

5   Soundness of Proof Rules

5.1   Proof Rules of TRSL

One of the major reasons for expressing specifications in a formal language like (T)RSL is to prove properties of specification. Therefore, a proof system for

TRSL should be set up. We list some of the proof rules involving newly added time constructs.

[wait_annihilation]
   wait $0.0 \simeq$ **skip**

[wait_plus]
   wait er ; **wait** er$' \simeq$ **wait**(er $\dot{+}$ er$'$)

[wait_introduction]
   e $\simeq$ **wait** er ; **shift**(e, er)
   when pure(er) $\wedge$ **convergent**(er) $\wedge$ er $\geq 0.0 \wedge$ **must_wait**(e, er)

The complete set of proof rules can be found in [GX98]. The original "special functions" **convergent**, **pure**, **express**,etc. are defined in [RMG95]. New special functions **must_wait**, **shift**, etc. are defined in [GX98]. The parallel expansion rule is changed to:

eu $\parallel$ eu$' \simeq$
   if parallel_ints(eu, eu$'$) $\equiv$ **swap**
   then parallel_exts(eu, eu$'$) $[]$ **parallel_exts**(eu$'$, eu)
   else
      (**parallel_exts**(eu, eu$'$) $[]$ **parallel_exts**(eu$'$, eu) $[]$ **parallel_ints**(eu, eu$'$))$\sqcap$
      parallel_ints(eu, eu$'$)
   end
      when isin_standard_form(eu) $\wedge$ **isin_standard_form**(eu$'$) $\wedge$
      ($\square$ **assignment_disjoint**(eu, eu$'$))

where the operator "$\sqcap$" is the "maximal progress" version of the internal choice operator mentioned in Section 2 and defined in [GX98]. The other "dotted" operators like "$\dot{+}$" are simple extensions of the standard arithmetic operators, returning zero if the result would otherwise be negative.

The revised definitions of **parallel_exts**, **parallel_ints**, and **interlock_ints** are (showing just one case of each):

parallel_exts(**wait** er ; **let** (b,t) = c? **in** eu **end**, eu$'$) $\simeq$
   wait er ; **let** (b,t) = c? **in** eu $\parallel$ **shift**(eu$'$, er $\dot{+}$ t) **end**
      when no_capture(b, eu$'$) $\wedge$ **no_capture**(t, eu$'$) $\wedge$
      no_capture(b, er) $\wedge$ **no_capture**(t, er)

parallel_ints(**wait** er ; **let** (b,t) = c? **in** eu **end**,
               wait er$'$; **let** t$' = $ c!e **in** eu$'$ **end**) $\simeq$
   wait máx(er,er$'$) ;
   let b = e **in subst_expr**(er$' \dot{-}$ er,t,eu) $\parallel$ **subst_expr**(er $\dot{-}$ er$'$,t$'$,eu$'$) **end**
      when no_capture(b, eu$'$) $\wedge$ **no_capture**(b, er) $\wedge$ **no_capture**(b, er$'$)

interlock_ints(wait er ; **let** (b,t) = c? **in** eu **end,**
          wait er′ ; **let** t′ = c!e **in** eu′ **end)** ≃
  wait màx(er,er′) ;
  let b = e **in subst_expr**(er′ $\dot{-}$ er,t,eu) $\parallel$ **subst_expr**(er $\dot{-}$ er′,t′,eu′) **end**
    when no_capture(b, eu′) ∧ **no_capture**(b, er) ∧ **no_capture**(b, er′)

5.2   Soundness

We would like to show that

- The original RSL Proof Rules for the TRSL expressions not involving time
  (e.g. *simple* assignment expressions) still hold in our semantic model.
- Most of the original RSL Proof Rules for TRSL expressions involving time
  (e.g. input expressions, output expressions) with newly added side conditions
  hold in our semantic model.
- New rules applied to extended operators are sound with respect to our operational semantics
- In our semantic model, no new rules for the original RSL syntax are generated.

As mentioned in Section 2.1, not all the original RSL proof rules are sound
with respect to our semantic model.

However, it is trivial to prove that all the original proof rules for TRSL expressions not involving time-measurable events still hold in our semantic model,
because our semantics and the definition of equivalence are just the same as the
original one, if we ignore the "$\varepsilon(d)$" transitions.

For the same reason, it is clear that no new rules for the original RSL syntax
are generated in our semantic model.

We need to add side conditions to some of the proof rules for TRSL expressions involving time-measurable events. We are interested in proving the
soundness of these rules with respect to our semantic model. Most of the rules
that we need to study are listed on page 457 of [RMG95].

Of course we should also prove the soundness of rules for the extended operators too. above recommendations.

Proof
Here we just show one example. Other detailed proofs can be seen in [GX98]

[ext_choice_replacement]
    e $[]$ e′ ≃ e″ $[]$ e‴
      when (e ≡ e″) ∧ (e′ ≡ e‴)

Proof for any s, for any given ρ,

- For Divergence: if one of the configuration is divergent, w.l.g. suppose $<e,s>\uparrow\ l$, because $e \equiv e''$, we have $<e'',s>\uparrow\ l$ too. then from the 3rd rule in External Choice (c.f. Section **??**), we know $<e\ [] \ e', s>\uparrow\ l$ and $<e''\ [] \ e''', s>\uparrow\ l$
- if none of configurations are divergent, we would like to prove
  1. for any l, we have $A(<e\ [] \ e', s>, l) = A(<e''\ [] \ e''', s>, l)$:

     For visible action, one branch will be selected. For silent action either e or e' will evolve to next configuration. For time-measurable action, both of them will evolve. So for any possible sequence of action, $A(<e\ [] \ e', s >, l) \subseteq A(<e, s>, l) \cup A(<e', s>, l)$. On the other hand, for any possible sequence, from semantics, it is clear $A(<e\ [] \ e', s >, l) \supseteq A(<e, s>, l)$ and $A(<e\ [] \ e', s >, l) \supseteq A(<e', s>, l)$. So $A(<e\ [] \ e'>, l) = A(<e, s>, l) \cup A(<e', s>, l)$. For the same reason, we know $A(<e''\ [] \ e''', s>, l) = A(<e'', s>, l) \cup A(<e''', s>, l)$. Because $e \equiv e''$ and $e' \equiv e'''$, $A(<e, s>, l) = A(<e'',s>, l)$ and $A(<e', s>, l) = A(<e''', s>, l)$. So $A(<e\ [] \ e', s>, l) = A(<e''\ [] \ e''', s>, l)$.
  2. for any l, we have $W(<e\ [] \ e', s>, l) = W(<e''\ [] \ e''', s>, l)$:

     From the definition of "π_2" function : $\pi_2(\alpha\ [] \ \beta) = \pi_2(\alpha) \cup \pi_2(\beta)$, we can conclude trivially that $W(<e\ [] \ e'>, l) = W(<e, s>, l) \cup W(<e', s>, l)$ and $W(<e''\ [] \ e''', s>, l) = W(<e'', s>, l) \cup W(<e''', s>, l)$. Because $e \equiv e''$ and $e' \equiv e'''$, $W(<e, s>, l) = W(<e'',s>, l)$ and $W(<e', s>, l) = W(<e''', s>, l)$.
     So, we get $W(<e\ [] \ e', s>, l) = W(<e''\ [] \ e''', s>, l)$.
  3. for any l, we have $R(<e\ [] \ e', s>, l) = R(<e''\ [] \ e''', s>, l)$:

     From semantics, we know only one branch of the choice can be selected and evolve to its end. So $R(<e\ [] \ e', s>, l) = R(<e, s>, l) \cup R(<e', s>, l)$ and $R(<e''\ [] \ e''', s>, l) = R(<e'', s>, l) \cup R(<e''', s>, l)$. because $e \equiv e''$ and $e' \equiv e'''$, $R(<e, s>, l) = R(<e'',s>, l)$ and $R(<e', s>, l) = R(<e''', s>, l)$.
     We get $R(<e\ [] \ e', s>, l) = R(<e''\ [] \ e''', s>, l)$ at last.

This completes the proof.

6   Discussion

6.1   Future Work

This paper gives a set of proof rules and an operational semantics for TRSL. A denotational semantics and its formal interrelations with proof rules (axiomatic semantics) and operational semantics needs to be further investigated. What is more, a formal relation between an event-based process algebra and a state-based logic like the Duration Calculus is a non-trivial research topic [Rav94,

PG96]. Actually, [LH99] gives a denotational DC semantics of TRSL, and an "operational semantics with behaviour", which relates TRSL with DC, has been proposed in [HX99]. We need more time to give further results.

The method for developing timed RSL specifications is also an important research direction for TRSL. Some initial results can be seen in [LH99].

6.2   Related Work

Over the past decade, a number of formal calculi (also called process algebras) for real-time, concurrent systems have been developed; examples are TCCS [Wang91] and TCSP [Dav93]. These calculi are suitable specification languages to describe real-time system requirements. They give us ideas for our construction of Timed RSL and its operational semantics.

However, if one uses those specification languages, the design part of the program has to be given in another language. Using TRSL, we can stay with the same language in all steps of development. This is a major motivation for us to add real-time features to RSL.

There are other approaches to adding real time features to a specification language. [F92] represents RTL formulae in Z and [FHM98] directly introduces the differential and integral calculus operators into the Z notation. They are essentially encodings of time using facilities already in Z. As such they add no power to the language. In addition they allow all variables to be functions of time and so permeate the language. For example, notions of refinement become more complicated. [HX98] embeds DC into RSL using high order logic and also proposes an extension of RSL syntax with DC constructs. But again this is an encoding and the power of the language is not changed.

These notational extensions are also at the abstract specification level. They provide no explicit assistance with implementation.

Our aim is rather different. The addition of the **wait** construct adds to the power of RSL. Further, it allows both the abstract specification of timing features in a DC notation and also the concrete specification of particular timed algorithms that can be readily expressed in suitable programming languages.

The *super-dense computation* model is an important abstract model of real-time systems [MP93]. Some industrially applicable programming languages, such as Esterel, adopt similar models.

[ZH96, PD97, QZ97] use (Extended) Duration Calculus to give a denotational semantics to an OCCAM-like programming language under the super-dense computation model.

Acknowledgements

The authors thank Zhou Chaochen for his advice and guidance while doing this research work, Anne Haxthausen for her ideas and comments on Timed RAISE, and He Jifeng for his comments on a draft of this paper. Anonymous reviewers also provided useful comments.

References

[BD93]   D.Bolignano, and M.Debabi.   *RSL: An Integration of Concurrent, Functional and Imperative Paradigms.*   Technical Report LA-COS/BULL/MD/3/V12.48, 1993.

[Dav93]   Jim Davies. *Specification and Proof in Real-Time CSP.* Distinguished Dissertation Series. Cambridge University Press, 1993.

[Deb94]   M.Debabi. *Intégration des paradigmes de programmation parallèle, fonctionnelle et impérative : fondements sémantiques.* Ph.D. Thesis (Thèse de Doctorat en Informatique), Université Paris XI, Centre d'Orsay, July 1994.

[F92]   C. J. Fidge Specification and verification of Real-Time Behaviour Using Z and RTL in J. Vytopil (ed.), Proc FME'92, LNCS571 (Springer), 1992.

[FHM98]   C. J. Fidge, I. J. Hayes and B. P. Mahony, *Defining Differentiation and Integration in Z,* Technical report 98-09, Software Verification Research Centre, School of Information Technology, The University of Queensland, September 1998.

[GX98]   Chris George and Xia Yong *An Operational Semantics for Timed RAISE* Technical Report No. 149, United Nations University/International Institute for Software Technology, November 1998.

[HI93]   M. Hennessy and A. Ingólfsdóttir. *Communicating Process with Value-passing and Assignments.* In *Formal Aspects of Computing*, 1993.

[HX98]   Anne Haxthausen and Xia Yong *A RAISE Specification Framework and Justification Assistant for the Duration Calculus.* In *ESSLLI-98 Workshop on Duration Calculus*, August 1998.

[HX99]   Anne Haxthausen and Xia Yong. *Linking DC together with TRSL.* Research Report, Department of Information Technology, Technical University of Denmark, April 1999.

[LH99]   Li Li and He Jifeng *Towards a Denotational Semantics of Timed RSL using Duration Calculus* Technical Report No. 161, United Nations University/International Institute for Software Technology, April 1999.

[MP93]   Z. Manna and A. Pnueli. *Models of reactivity.* In *Acta Informatica*. 30(7), 609–678, Springer-Verlag, 1993.

[Rav94]   Anders P. Ravn. *Design of Embedded Real Time Computing Systems.* PhD thesis, Department of Computer Science, Technical University of Denmark, Denmark, September 1994.

[RLG92]   The RAISE Language Group. *The RAISE Specification Language.* The BCS Practitioners Series. Prentice Hall Int., 1992.

[RMG95]   The RAISE Method Group. *The RAISE Development Method.* The BCS Practitioners Series. Prentice Hall Int., 1995.

[PD97]   Paritosh K. Pandya and Dang Van Hung. *Duration Calculus of weakly monotonic time.* Technical Report No. 122, United Nations University/International Institute for Software Technology, September 1997.

[PG96]   Jifeng He, C.A.R. Hoare, Markus Müller-Olm, Ernst-Rüdiger Olderog, Michael Schenke, Michael R. Hansen, Anders P. Ravn, and Hans Rischel. The ProCoS Approach to the Design of Real-Time Systems: Linking Different Formalisms. In *Formal Methods Europe 96*, Oxford, UK, March 1996. Tutorial Material.

[QZ97]   Qiu Zhongyan and Zhou Chaochen *A Combination of Interval Logic and Linear Temporal Logic* Technical Report No. 123, United Nations University/International Institute for Software Technology, September 1997.

[Wang91]   Wang Yi. *A Calculus of Real Time Systems*. PhD thesis, Department of
             Computer Sciences, Chalmers University of Technology, Göterborg, Swe-
             den, 1991
[ZH96]   Zhou Chaochen and Michael R. Hansen. *Chopping a point*. In J. F. He *et
             al* (Eds.), *BCS-FACS 7th Refinement Workshop*, Electronic Workshops in
             Computing, Springer-Verlag, 1996.
[ZHR91]   Zhou Chaochen, C.A.R. Hoare and A.P. Ravn. A Calculus of Durations.
             Information Processing Letters, 40(5):269–276, 1991. Revised June 3, 1992.

Data Abstraction for CSP-OZ*

Heike Wehrheim

Universität Oldenburg
Fachbereich Informatik
Postfach 2503, D–26111 Oldenburg, Germany
`wehrheim@informatik.uni-oldenburg.de`

Abstract. CSP-OZ is an integrated formal method which combines the state-oriented method Object-Z with the process algebra CSP, thereby allowing a description of static as well as dynamic aspects of a system. Checking correctness of CSP-OZ specifications can be done via a *translation* into (FDR-)CSP, on which automatic verification can be performed with the tool FDR *if* the resulting CSP process is not too large to be processed. This paper investigates how *data abstraction* techniques can be used to bring a translated specification within range of automatic verification.

1 Introduction

Recently, there is an emerging interest in specification techniques that combine specification methods for different views on a system. In particular, methods integrating static aspects (data) and dynamic aspects (behaviour) are investigated (see for example [17, 10, 22, 20]). CSP-OZ [7] is a formal method that combines a method for the description of static aspects of systems, Object-Z [6] (an object-oriented extension of Z [21, 24]), with a method for the specification of dynamic behaviour, the process algebra CSP [11, 18]. The general idea behind this integration is to augment the state-oriented Object-Z specification with the specification of behaviour in the style of CSP while maintaining a clear separation of the issues of data and behaviour. The combination has a uniform formal semantics in the style of CSP failures and divergences.

In this paper, we will be concerned with verifying CSP-OZ specifications. The first step in the verification of a given CSP-OZ specification will be a translation into CSP[1], to be precise, into the CSP dialect of the model checker FDR (Failure-Divergence-Refinement [9]). This technique has been proposed in [8], extending previous ideas of [16, 19] to use FDR to check properties of (CSP-)Z specifications. FDR-CSP is a combination of CSP with a functional language in the style of Haskell and Miranda. The functional language can be used to encode the Z data descriptions. Due to the possibly large data domain specified in the

---

* This work was partially funded by the Leibniz Programme of the German Research Council (DFG) under grant Ol 98/1-1.

[1] The translation is possible for a large subset of CSP-OZ, but cannot treat all Z features.

J. Wing, J. Woodcock, J. Davies (Eds.): FM'99, Vol. II, LNCS 1709, pp. 1028–1047, 1999.
© Springer-Verlag Berlin Heidelberg 1999

Object-Z part of a CSP-OZ specification, the resulting CSP process may however be too complex to be processed by FDR. This paper investigates the usefulness of data abstraction techniques to reduce the complexity of property checking on CSP-OZ specifications. The general idea is to apply the framework of *abstract interpretation* [4] in the specific setting of CSP-OZ. The use of abstraction techniques for verification has already been investigated for temporal-logic model checking [5, 1, 14] and is based on abstracting transition systems (the models for various specification formalisms) while preserving properties formulated in temporal logic. Techniques for directly constructing abstract transition systems from specifications are given to avoid the construction of the (possibly large) concrete transition system at all. These techniques most often rely on choosing some abstract data domain and abstractly interpreting the operators in the program on this domain. Another application of abstract interpretation in verification is the construction of models from real software written in a programming language [3].

The work most closest to us is [2] which gives abstract interpretations for value-passing CCS where the correctness checks are based on the notion of *testing*. However, their abstraction results are formulated within the framework of Galois connections on transition systems, the semantic models of CCS. For a designer having written a specification in CCS, it is hard to understand the practical meaning of the result, it is formulated completely different than his specification. Furthermore, the obtained abstraction result cannot be the basis for further process algebraic manipulation. In the approach we present here, specifications, correctness checks and abstraction results are formulated in the process algebra theory of CSP. Thus we have a *uniform* formalism for specification and verification. A designer using the abstraction technique does not have to understand the "lower" semantic level of transition systems. Since the abstraction results are formulated within CSP theory, they can for instance be further combined (compositionality) or projected down to the concrete level. Furthermore, due to the clear separation of data and behaviour in a CSP-OZ specification, data abstraction only requires *local* changes of the CSP-OZ specification (or directly of the CSP process obtained by translation): changing the Z part by replacing concrete data domains/operations by abstract ones. We neither change the structure of the process, nor the interpretation of CSP operators. This enables us to use FDR without any additional modifications to the program or the model checking algorithm.

The paper is structured as follows: we start with a brief introduction of CSP-OZ and the translation into CSP. The translation maintains the separation into data and behaviour. Hence the resulting CSP processes have a quite specific structure, which we call *CSP-OZ form*. Section 3 discusses data abstraction for CSP processes in CSP-OZ form and Section 4 gives a first example. The next section presents compositionality results for data abstraction and illustrates the applicability of the results by means of the verification of a router. The conclusion discusses further related work, especially that of Roscoe, whose book

[18] contains a great variety of techniques to overcome the problem of state space complexity, and we discuss the issue of *data independence*.

2   Prerequisites

We start with a brief description of CSP-OZ and the specific structure of the translated specifications. The data abstraction techniques we suggest are tailored towards this specific structure. The translation will be explained through an example, details can be found in [8]. Afterwards we briefly describe the semantics underlying the process algebra CSP. A summary of CSP operators can be found in the appendix, a more detailed introduction in [11].

2.1   CSP-OZ

CSP-OZ is an integrated formal method that allows for a description of static aspects (by means of Object-Z) as well as dynamic aspects (by means of the process algebra CSP). A CSP-OZ specification describes a system as a collection of interacting objects, each of which has a prescribed structure and behaviour. Communication takes place via *channels* in the style of CSP. In general, a CSP-OZ specification consists of a number of paragraphs, introducing classes, global variables, functions and types. CSP-OZ classes can be combined using the CSP operators parallel composition, external and internal choice and hiding; thus overriding the corresponding operators in Object-Z. In this paper, we will mainly be concerned with CSP-OZ classes, to be precise, with CSP processes which are translations of CSP-OZ classes. The specific structure of these programs can best be understood with the original CSP-OZ class structure in mind, which is as follows:

```
┌─ Name ──────────────────────────────────────────
│  channel definitions
│  CSP − Part
│
│  type and constant definitions
│  state schema
│  initial state schema
│  operations
└──────────────────────────────────────────────────
```

We explain the different parts of a CSP-OZ class through a simple example, the specification of a pool. The pool simply stores elements out of some element set *Elem*,

$$Elem == 0..10$$

and allows to input and output elements. Every input is signalled to the environment.

─── *Pool* ──
  channel *signal*
  channel *in* : $[\, el : Elem \,]$
  channel *out* : $[\, el : Elem \,]$
  $\mathtt{main} = in?x \rightarrow signal \rightarrow \mathtt{main} \; \square \; out?x \rightarrow \mathtt{main}$

  ──────────────────────────   ─── Init ────────────────
  │ *pool* : $\mathbb{P}\, Elem$ │ *pool* = $\varnothing$

  ─── enable_*out* ──────────   ─── effect_*out* ────────────
  │ *pool* $\neq \varnothing$ │ $\Delta(pool)$
                                       │ *el*! : *Elem*
                                       ────────────────────
                                       │ $el \in pool$
                                       │ $pool' = pool \setminus \{el\}$

  ─── effect_*in* ──────────────────────────────────────
  │ $\Delta(pool)$
  │ *el*? : *Elem*
  ────────────────────
  │ $pool' = pool \cup \{el\}$
───

The first part defines the syntactic interface of the class, i.e. the channels which can be used for communication with the environment. The second part contains all CSP-declarations, defining the dynamic behaviour of the class; for our pool: it may either input some new elements after which this has to be signalled to the environment or ($\square$) output some elements. No reference to data in any kind occurs in the CSP part; all communications are of the form ch?x (a communication of the form ch!e would refer to some concrete data value). Thus also the output of our pool has the form out?x.

The remaining part of the class definition contains Object-Z-declarations. The main part is the declaration of the state schema (here the state variable *pool*), the initial state schema (its initial value), and operation schemas. The definition of an operation has to be divided into an (optional) enabling and an effect schema. The enabling schema (e.g. enable_*out*) is a predicate over the state variables of the class, and describes the states in which the operation can be executed (e.g. outputs are only possible when the pool is non-empty). Enable schemas are thus used to describe *data-dependent behaviour*. The effect schema (a predicate over the state variables and input parameters) describes the effect of an operation on the state space and the values of possible output parameters (the primed variables are used to describe the value of a variable in the next state, the Δ-list lists all variables which are changed by the operation).

2.2   Structure of Translated CSP-OZ Specifications

For the verification, every class of a CSP-OZ specification is translated into the definition of a CSP process. When using such a definition, we will also refer to this as the CSP process of an *object*, a particular instance of a class.

The translation preserves the clear separation between data and behaviour. The CSP part of the CSP-OZ specification remains unchanged while the Z part has to be translated into CSP. Intuitively, the behaviour of the Z part is as follows: in every state (specific values of the state variables) one of the enabled operations may be taken and the resulting state is determined by the effect of the operation. Thus the CSP translation of the Z part is an *external choice* over all class operations with their enabling conditions as guards. The effect schemas, which are predicates in the CSP-OZ specification, are translated into functions from state space and input parameters to sets of possible new states and values of output parameters. The resulting new state and the values for output parameters are nondeterministically chosen out of this effect set of an operation.

Assume that we are given a CSP-OZ class specification *CLS* with state variables $v_1, \ldots, v_n$ in the state schema, initial values $ini(v_i)$ $(1 \le i \le n)$ and set of operations *Ops*, and that we may derive a function *In* assigning to every channel $ch \in Ops$ its possible values of input variables (derived from the type of the channel), then the translated specification has the following form (using partly FDR-CSP and CSP syntax to improve readability; for a description of FDR-CSP see appendix):

```
CLS =
  let
     -- CSP part
     main = ...
       ⋮
     -- Z part
     Z_PART(v_1, ..., v_n) =
       [] ch: Ops @                          --  for every channel
          enable_ch(v_1, ...,v_n) &          --  if enabled
          [] in:In(ch) @                     --  for every input value
             |~|DIV(out,v_1',...,v_n'):effect_ch(v_1,...,v_n,in) @
                      --  choose new state and output
                   ch.in.out -> Z_PART(v_1',...,v_n') --  event
  within Z_PART(ini(v_1), ...,ini(v_n)) ||α(main) main
```

The abbreviation $\alpha(\texttt{main})$ stands for the alphabet of the process **main** (the set of channel names occurring in it) and $|\tilde{\ }|_{\text{DIV}}$ is a special internal choice operator capturing the case that the index set of the iterated $|\tilde{\ }|$ is empty, in this case the process diverges. The intuition behind the use of this operator is the following: if an operation is enabled but its effect is not defined for the current state (yielding an empty effect set), the process behaves as completely undetermined, it diverges.

The structure of the translated class can be further simplified when there are no input or no output parameters of a channel, or when the effect of an

operation is deterministic, i.e. the effect set contains a single value. None of our examples will use the general structure, most often the Z part is simply of the form `guard1 & ch_1 -> Z(...) [] guard2 & ch_2 -> Z(...) ....`
The translation of the class *Pool* given above is:

```
Elem = {0..10}
channel signal
channel in, out: Elem

POOL = let
        -- CSP part
        main = in?x -> signal -> main [] out?x -> main
        -- Z part
        Z_PART(pool) =
                (true & signal -> Z_PART(pool))
            [] (true & in?x -> Z_PART(union(pool,{x})))
            [] (not(empty(pool)) &
                    |~| el:pool @ out.el -> Z_PART(diff(pool,{el})))
    within Z_PART({}) [| {| signal,in,out |} |] main
```

2.3   CSP Semantics

The standard semantic model of CSP is the failure-divergence model. The same model has been used in [7] to give a semantics to CSP-OZ, by defining a failure-divergence semantics for the Z part. Thus a uniform semantics is achieved. An alternative weaker semantic model which is also supported by FDR is the trace model. We will use both models here. The trace model is sufficient for studying *safety* properties, while for *liveness* properties (e.g. deadlock or livelock freedom) a more discriminating semantics has to be chosen. Traces record the possible runs of a process, failures additionally give sets of events that are refused after some run, and divergences describe the set of traces after which the process may diverge, i.e. perform an infinite number of internal events. Thus, given a set of events Σ (typically of the form $ch.v$, where ch is a channel name and v a value), we have

$$traces(P) \subseteq \mathbf{2}^{\Sigma^*}$$
$$failures(P) \subseteq \mathbf{2}^{\Sigma^* \times \mathbf{2}^{\Sigma}}$$
$$divergences(P) \subseteq \mathbf{2}^{\Sigma^*}$$

These semantic models are used to compare processes and check properties on them. The most important comparison concept in CSP theory is *refinement*:

Definition 1. *A CSP process P_1 is a* failure-divergence refinement *of a process P_2 (denoted $P_2 \sqsubseteq_{\mathcal{F}} P_1$) if*

$$failures(P_2) \supseteq failures(P_1) \text{ and } divergences(P_2) \supseteq divergences(P_1).$$

They are failure-divergence equivalent *($P_1 =_{\mathcal{F}} P_2$) if $P_1 \sqsubseteq_{\mathcal{F}} P_2$ and $P_2 \sqsubseteq_{\mathcal{F}} P_1$.*

If P_1 is a refinement of P_2, it can be seen as an *implementation* of P_2 since it is more deterministic than P_2. A weaker refinement notion is obtained when only the traces are used for comparison:

Definition 2. *A CSP process P_1 is a* trace refinement *of a process P_2 (denoted $P_2 \sqsubseteq_T P_1$) if $traces(P_2) \supseteq traces(P_1)$.*

Both refinement notions are *compositional* (or *monotone*): given two processes P_1, P_2 and a CSP context $C[\cdot]$, then $P_1 \sqsubseteq P_2 \Rightarrow C[P_1] \sqsubseteq C[P_2]$, where $\sqsubseteq \in \{\sqsubseteq_T, \sqsubseteq_\mathcal{F}\}$.

There are two possibilities for deriving the semantics of a CSP process: by a *denotational* semantics which compositionally computes traces, failures and divergences, or via a structured *operational* semantics which constructs a transition system for a process, from which traces, failures and divergences are computed. Both semantics are consistent: they compute the same traces, failures and divergences of a process. We refer to [18]) for details. A summary of CSP operators in FDR syntax can be found in the appendix. The two operators which will be used in our results are

- parallel composition with sychronisation on some set of events A: $\|_A$, and
- renaming: $[R]$, which renames all events according to the renaming relation R.

We use general renaming relations, not just injective functions. As an example for a CSP process with renaming: Let $P = a \to SKIP$ and $R = \{(a, b), (a, c)\}$, then $P[R]$ is equal to $b \to SKIP \; \Box \; c \to SKIP$.

3 Data Abstraction

Since CSP-OZ specifications may contain rather large amounts of data, the state space of the resulting CSP process can often be too large to be processed by FDR. Several techniques have already been proposed to overcome this problem; especially in the book of Roscoe [18] several methods can be found together with various application examples.

The technique we propose here is based on *abstract interpretation* of programs [4] and can be seen as complementing the other techniques. Abstract interpretation is a technique for program analysis which is often used in compiler design for static analysis (e.g. data-flow analysis, strictness analysis, etc.). The results of an abstract interpretation can for instance be used in type checking or optimisation. The idea of abstract interpretation is to interpret a program in an abstract domain using abstract operations. The main advantage is that the concrete program does not have to be executed while still being able to obtain information about its real execution. For verification of formal specifications, the basis of abstract interpretation is to construct an *abstract model* of the specification on which abstract properties can be proven which give information on the concrete model [5, 1, 14]. For this, the data domain of the concrete program has to be abstracted and operations of the program are abstractly interpreted on the new data domain.

In order to apply data abstraction techniques to CSP-OZ, we first have to make clear what the *data* is we want to abstract, and what the *operations* are we want to interpret abstractly. Since the goal is to use FDR for automatic verification of properties on the abstracted systems, we certainly cannot change the semantics of CSP operators in any way. What may be interpreted abstractly are the enable and effect operations coming from the Z part of the CSP-OZ specification. The relevant data domains to be abstracted are the domains of the state variables: $D_1, \ldots, D_n$ for variables $v_1, \ldots, v_n$, and the domains of the channels: $M_1, \ldots, M_k$ for channels $ch_1, \ldots, ch_k$. We assume that a domain of a channel ch_i is split into a domain for input parameters M_i^{in} and for output parameters M_i^{out}. Then the enable and effect operations have the following signature (we will refer to this concrete semantics of enable and effect by using the semantic brackets $[\![\cdot]\!]$):

$$[\![enable\_ch_i]\!] : D_1 \times \ldots \times D_n \qquad \rightarrow \mathbb{B}$$
$$[\![effect\_ch_i]\!] \; : (D_1 \times \ldots \times D_n \times M_i^{in}) \rightarrow 2^{M_i^{out} \times D_1 \times \ldots \times D_n}$$

Instead of interpreting the CSP program on these concrete data domains with the concrete meaning of enable and effect operations, we use abstract data domains and abstract interpretations of enable and effect. For this, we first choose abstract data domains D_i^A and M_j^A and *abstraction functions*:

$$h_i : D_i \rightarrow D_i^A$$
$$g_j : M_j \rightarrow M_j{}^A$$

We define $h(d_1, \ldots d_n) := (h_1(d_1), \ldots, h_n(d_n))$ and let $(h, g)(d_1, \ldots, d_n, m)$ stand for $(h_1(d_1), \ldots, h_n(d_n), g(m))$. In the following, we will abbreviate $(d_1, \ldots, d_n)$ simply by d. For a given abstraction function g of channel values, we let G denote the corresponding renaming function on events: $G(ch_i.w) = ch_i.g(w)$.

An abstract interpretation $[\![\cdot]\!]^A$ of enable and effect operations operates on abstract data domains:

$$[\![enable\_ch_i]\!]^A : D_1^A \times \ldots \times D_n^A \qquad \rightarrow \mathbb{B}$$
$$[\![effect\_ch_i]\!]^A \; : (D_1^A \times \ldots \times D_n^A \times M_i^{in\,A}) \rightarrow 2^{M_i^{out\,A} \times D_1^A \times \ldots \times D_n^A}$$

In order to use FDR as a model-checker on abstracted systems, we have to replace the concrete enable and effect predicates by abstract predicates $enable^A$ and $effect^A$ such that $[\![enable_{ch_i}^A]\!] = [\![enable_{ch_i}]\!]^A$ and $[\![effect_{ch_i}^A]\!] = [\![effect_{ch_i}]\!]^A$ holds, i.e. the concrete semantics of the new enable and effects must equal the abstract semantics of the old ones. Furthermore channels have to be declared over the abstract domains. These changes can already be done in the CSP-OZ specification, the designer does not have to look at the CSP code at all.

So far, we are free to use whatever abstract interpretation we want. Of course, the abstracted system should somehow reflect the behaviour of the concrete system: we want to abstractly observe the events of the concrete system. To ensure this, we have to impose conditions on the abstract interpretations. We consider two types of abstract interpretations: *safe* and *optimal* interpretations.

Definition 3. *An abstract interpretation* $[\cdot]^{\mathcal{S}}$ *of enable and effect predicates is safe with respect to abstraction functions* h *and* g *iff*

$$\forall\, d \in D^A : [\![enable\_ch_i]\!]^{\mathcal{S}}(d^A) \Leftrightarrow \exists\, d \in D : h(d) = d^A \land [\![enable\_ch_i]\!](d)$$

and

$$\forall\, d \in D^A, m \in M^A :$$
$$[\![effect\_ch_i]\!]^{\mathcal{S}}(d^A, m^A) = \bigcup_{\substack{(d,m)\in D\times M \\ h(d)=d^A, g_i(m)=m^A}} (h, g_i^{out})([\![effect\_ch_i]\!](d, m))$$

A safe abstract interpretation guarantees that in a state of the abstract system a communication over some channel is possible whenever there is some corresponding concrete state in which this communication is enabled. The result of a safe abstraction is an abstract system that allows *more* moves than the concrete system. An abstraction which more faithfully represents the concrete system, is an optimal abstraction.

Definition 4. *An abstract interpretation* $[\cdot]^{\mathcal{O}}$ *of enable and effect predicates is optimal with respect to abtraction functions* h *and* g *iff*

$$\forall\, d \in D^A : [\![enable\_ch_i]\!]^{\mathcal{O}}(h(d)) \Leftrightarrow [\![enable\_ch_i]\!](d) \qquad and$$
$$\forall\, d \in D^A, m \in M^A : [\![effect\_ch_i]\!]^{\mathcal{O}}(h(d), g_i(m)) = (h, g_i^{out})([\![effect\_ch_i]\!](d, m))$$

An optimal abstracted system exactly mimics the behaviour of the concrete system, only the precise values of communication cannot be observed anymore. Depending on the choice of abstraction functions, it may not be possible to find an optimal abstract interpretation. Optimality requires abstraction functions which guarantee that all concrete states which are abstracted into the same abstract state abstractly behave "the same". Note that every optimal abstraction is safe. Tool support for proving optimality or safety of interpretations is available in the form of theorem provers for Z [13, 15].

Given a specification S, we let $S^{\mathcal{S}}$ refer to a safe and $S^{\mathcal{O}}$ to an optimal abstraction of S.

What is now the relationship between the behaviour of the abstracted and the concrete system? Our goal is to express this relationship completely in terms of process algebra notions. This enables us to use all of the process algebra theory for further manipulation of the result. In the abstracted system we can, of course, only observe communications with abstract values. This is the nature of abstract interpretation, we have lost some information about the concrete system, in our case the concrete values of communication. Thus we can only compare the abstracted system with the *renamed* concrete system:

Theorem 1. *Let S be a CSP process in CSP-OZ form, g_1, h_1 abstraction functions for a safe and g_2, h_2 for an optimal interpretation. Then the following holds:*

$$S^S \sqsubseteq_T S[G_1] \qquad and$$
$$S[G_2] =_F S^O \ .$$

The proof can be found in the appendix. This result can be the basis for further process algebraic computations; for instance compositionality of trace refinement immediately gives us $(S^S)[G^{-1}] \sqsubseteq_T (S[G])[G^{-1}]$. The latter is equal to $S[G \circ G^{-1}]$ which itself can easily be shown to be trace refined by S: $S[G \circ G^{-1}] \sqsubseteq_T S$. All in one, we therefore get:

$$(S^S)[G^{-1}] \sqsubseteq_T S$$

This result refers directly to the concrete system S. With the help of this abstraction theorem, we are now able to proof properties of a CSP-OZ class S in the following way:

- construct an *abstract* class specification: choose abstract domains, abstraction functions and abstract enable and effect predicates,
- show safety/optimality of abstraction (supported by some theorem prover extension for Z),
- translate the abstract specification into FDR-CSP (in future automatic),
- show property for S^S/S^O (FDR),
  e.g. *Prop* $\sqsubseteq_T S^S$,
- conclude the holding of a concretised property for S (abstraction theorem),
  e.g. *Prop*$[G^{-1}] \sqsubseteq_T S$.

Most of these steps in the verification are tool-supported or even automatic. Nevertheless, the crucial part of abstraction, finding good abstract domains and abstraction functions, is still left to the user. [1] gives some heuristics for the choice of abstraction functions.

4   First Example: An Optimal Abstraction

The following example gives a first impression of data abstractions for CSP-OZ. It is an optimal abstraction, that reduces an equivalence check between an infinite state and a finite state specification to an equivalence check between two finite state systems. Although both systems are very simple, this already shows the potential of abstract interpretation.

Both specifications describe a simple clock with alternating *tick* and *tock* events. While in the first clock the alternation is encoded by the usage of enabling predicates (the Z part uses a counter),

```
Clock1 = let
            -- empty CSP part
```

```
main = SKIP
-- Z part
Z_PART(n) = odd(n) & tock -> Z_PART(n+1)
          [] even(n) & tick  -> Z_PART(n+1)
within Z_PART(0) ||| main
```

the second clock encodes alternation in the CSP part.

```
Clock2 = let
         -- CSP part
         main = tick -> tock -> main
         -- Z part
         Z_PART = true & tick -> Z_PART
                [] true & tock -> Z_PART
         within Z_PART [| tick,tock |] main
```

Hence an equivalence proof of both clocks by separate data and process refinement proofs is not possible. FDR can also not be used since the state space of the first clock is infinite.

We now apply the following abstraction function h to the first clock

$$h : k \mapsto \begin{cases} 0 & \text{if } even(k) \\ 1 & \text{if } odd(k) \end{cases}$$

and replace the enabling and effect operations by their following abstract versions: $(+1)^A(k) := (+1)(k)mod2$, $even^A(k) := even(k)$, $odd^A(k) := odd(k)$. This is an optimal abstract interpretation for Clock1 with respect to h. Note that in this case no abstraction function for channel values is needed and thus the renaming function G of Theorem 1 is empty. Thus we get the first result: $Clock1^{\mathcal{O}} =_{\mathcal{F}} Clock1$. The abstracted clock is now finite state, thus we can use FDR for checking whether $Clock1^{\mathcal{O}} =_{\mathcal{F}} Clock2$ (the answer is yes), and this implies $Clock1 =_{\mathcal{F}} Clock2$.

This rather simple example (without input and output parameters) also reveals close similarities between data abstraction and *data refinement* (which is the standard refinement notion within Z). The data abstraction we have used here is in fact also a valid data refinement (from $Clock1$ to $Clock1^{\mathcal{O}}$ and vice versa). In general, in our setting every optimal data abstraction can also be seen as a data refinement plus a renaming.

5 Compositionality

In this section, we will be concerned with the issue of *compositionality* of data abstractions. Two aspects will be considered here:

- combining abstraction results for different objects of a system, and
- combining different abstractions of the same object.

The results we get here are formulated within the traces model, thus we only deal with safety properties.

5.1   Composing Objects

In general, we will not be interested in a single object alone, but in a system which is composed out of a number of objects operating in parallel. Thus we have to extend our abstraction theorem to parallel compositions of objects. Two aspects are helpful for this extension: the first is the fact that the abstraction theorem for objects is completely formulated within process algebra theory, and the second is the compositionality (monotonicity) of both trace and failure refinement.

Consider a system S composed out of two objects S_1 and S_2 operating in parallel with synchronisation on some set $A \subseteq \Sigma$: $S = S_1 \parallel_A S_2$. So far, we are able to prove properties of S_1 and S_2 alone by for instance using some safe abstraction with respect to abstraction functions h_1, g_1, h_2, g_2 respectively. By our abstraction theorem, we know that $S_1^{\mathcal{S}} \sqsubseteq_{\mathcal{T}} S_1[G_1]$ and $S_2^{\mathcal{S}} \sqsubseteq_{\mathcal{T}} S_2[G_2]$. The first prerequisite for a combination of the abstracted objects is the preservation of their communication ability: the abstraction functions for the channel values have to agree on joint channels.

Definition 5. *Let g_1, g_2 be abstraction functions for S_1's and S_2's channel values and let $A = \alpha(S_1) \cap \alpha(S_2)$ be the set of joint events, with channel names Ch in A. g_1 and g_2 agree on A iff for all $ch \in Ch$, $v \in D_{ch}$, $g_{1,ch}(v) = g_{2,ch}(v)$.*

When the abstraction functions of the components agree on the joint events of the components, we can look at the abstracted system as $S^{\mathcal{S}} = S_1^{\mathcal{S}} \parallel_{G_1(A)} S_2^{\mathcal{S}}$. Compositionality of trace refinement already gives us the following result:

$$S_1^{\mathcal{S}} \parallel_{G_1(A)} S_2^{\mathcal{S}} \sqsubseteq_{\mathcal{T}} S_1[G_1] \parallel_{G_1(A)} S_2[G_2]$$

However, the left hand side is not the system we are actually interested in, namely $S_1 \parallel_A S_2$. The next proposition helps us towards this goal.

Proposition 1. *Let $f : \Sigma \to \Sigma$ be a renaming function and $A \subseteq \Sigma$ a set of events such that $a \in A \Leftrightarrow f(a) \in f(A)$ holds; let P_1, P_2 be CSP processes. Then*

$$P_1[f] \parallel_{f(A)} P_2[f] \sqsubseteq_{\mathcal{T}} (P_1 \parallel_A P_2)[f]$$

All renaming functions G generated by some abstraction function g have the above stated property, thus we immediately get:

$$S_1[G_1] \parallel_{G_1(A)} S_2[G_2] \sqsubseteq_{\mathcal{T}} (S_1 \parallel_A S_2)[G_1 \cup G_2]$$

Combining these two parts, we get the following compositionality result:

Corollary 1. *Let S_1, S_2 be CSP processes in CSP-OZ form, g_1, g_2 abstraction functions which agree on joint events of S_1 and S_2. Then*

$$S_1^{\mathcal{S}} \parallel_{G_1(A)} S_2^{\mathcal{S}} \sqsubseteq_{\mathcal{T}} (S_1 \parallel_A S_2)[G_1 \cup G_2] \ .$$

Thus we have extended our abstraction theorem for safe abstractions to parallel compositions of objects. Unfortunately, this result cannot be extended to optimal abstractions in the sense, that we may replace trace refinement by failures equivalence. Proposition 1 does not even hold for trace equivalence since the concrete components may fail to synchronise while their abstractions communicate.

5.2 Combining Abstractions

Besides compositions of objects, we are also interested in composing *different* abstraction results of the *same* object. The idea is to use different abstractions to prove different properties of an object and afterwards combine these abstractions to show that also their combination holds.

Consider an object S and two different safe abstractions wrt. h_1, g_1 and wrt. h_2, g_2. We prove two properties of the object via abstractions, using FDR to show $Prop_1 \sqsubseteq_T S^{S_1}$ and $Prop_2 \sqsubseteq_T S^{S_2}$. With the abstraction theorem and monotonicity of trace refinement we get $Prop_1[G_1^{-1}] \sqsubseteq_T S$ and $Prop_2[G_2^{-1}] \sqsubseteq_T S$ which can again be combined to give

$$Prop_1[G_1^{-1}] \|_{\alpha(S)} Prop_2[G_2^{-1}] \sqsubseteq_T S \|_{\alpha(S)} S$$

Furthermore, $S \|_{\alpha(S)} S =_T S$. Combining these two parts, we obtain as a corollary:

Corollary 2. *Let S be a CSP process in CSP-OZ form, g_1, g_2 abstraction functions for its channels, $Prop_1, Prop_2$ arbitrary CSP processes. Then*

$$Prop_1[G_1^{-1}] \|_{\alpha(S)} Prop_2[G_2^{-1}] \sqsubseteq_T S .$$

Afterwards we can use process algebra theory to compute the overall property $Prop = Prop_1[G_1^{-1}]\|_{\alpha(S)} Prop_2[G_2^{-1}]$. When the abstractions have been carefully chosen (and when they fit together well), *Prop* might indeed be the property of interest. The following example demonstrates the use of both kinds of compositionality results.

5.3 Illustrating Example

The example is a 1-to-2^n router with n stages (Figure 1 shows a router with two stages). Stage i contains 2^i switches which one input (*in*) and two outputs (*out0*, *out1*) each.

The messages which are send through the router consist of an address (a binary number of length n) and a data part. The address is used for routing: a switch at stage i looks at the i-th bit of the address; when it is 0 it sends the message to the upper channel (*out0*), otherwise to the

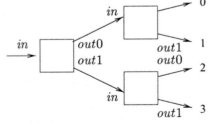

Fig. 1. A 1-to-2^n router

lower channel (*out1*). Receipt of messages is acknowledged (*ack*) and the switches delay the next input until an acknowledge has been received (*rack*). Thus the router contains at most one message. The following CSP specification in CSP-OZ form describes a router with 2 stages.

```
Adr = {<x1,x2>|x1<-{0,1},x2<-{0,1}}
Data = {0..100}

channel ack,ack0,ack1,rack0,rack1        -- channel declarations
channel in,in0,in1           : Adr.Data
channel out0,out1,out2,out3 : Adr.Data

SWITCH(i) = let                          -- a switch at stage i
        -- CSP Part
        main = in?x -> (out0?x -> rack0 -> SKIP
                        [] out1?x -> rack1 -> SKIP);
                       ack -> main
        -- Z Part
        Z_Part(adr,msg) =
                (true & in?a?d -> Z_Part(a,d))
            [] (nth(adr,i) == 0 &
                        out0.adr.msg -> Z_Part(adr,msg))
            [] (nth(adr,i) == 1 &
                        out1.adr.msg -> Z_Part(adr,msg))
    within
        Z_Part(<0,1>,0) [| {| in,out0,out1 |} |] main

ROUTER = (         SWITCH(1)                  -- the router
    [out0 <-> in0, out1 <-> in1, rack0 <-> ack0, rack1 <-> ack1]
        (SWITCH(2)[[in <- in0, ack <- ack0]]
                    |||
        SWITCH(2)[[in <- in1, ack <-ack1,
                    out0 <- out2, out1 <- out3 ]]))
              \{ack,rack0,rack1}
```

The routing within a switch is encoded in the enabling conditions of output communications *out0* and *out1*. The ordering of events (first input, then output, receive acknowledge and acknowledge itself) is encoded in the CSP process main. The switches are combined into router by renaming the corresponding ports appropriately and synchronising on them[2]. The output ports of the second stage are renamed into *out0*, *out1*, *out2* and *out3*.

The property to be verified is a safety property: every message input to the router with address a and data d is, if it is delivered at all, correctly delivered at output port $num(a)$ (the number with binary encoding a). Formulated within CSP: we would like to show that BUF $\sqsubseteq_T$ ROUTER, where BUF is defined as

```
BUF = in?x?y -> OUT(x,y)
OUT(adr,d) = (adr == <0,0> &
```

---

[2] The composition operators used in ROUTER also involve hiding (linked parallel), for which we have not established a compositionality result. However, hiding of channels commutes with renaming of channel values, i.e. $(S \setminus a)[G] = S[G] \setminus a$.

```
            out0.adr.d -> BUF)
    [] (adr == <0,1> &
            out1.adr.d -> BUF)
    [] (adr == <1,0> &
            out2.adr.d -> BUF)
    [] (adr == <1,1> &
            out3.adr.d -> BUF)
```

However, it may not be possible to use FDR to prove this property since the router may be too large to be processed with FDR when the domain of Data is large.

Two abstractions are possible: abstracting from the data, i.e. mapping all different data values onto one single value (functions h_1, g_1), or abstracting from the address, mapping all addresses onto a single one (functions h_2, g_2). The first abstraction allows for an optimal abstract interpretation of enable and effects (the enabling conditions are independent of the data), the latter only for a safe abstraction. For the optimal abstraction the only change in the CSP code is a change of the definition of Data, for the safe abstraction we have to change Adr (to a single-value type <0>) and the enabling conditions for $out0$ and $out1$ which are now both true. We now separately prove two properties:

- if a message with address a is received, the next message is delivered at port $num(a)$, and
- if a message with data d is received, the next delivered message contains data d.

The formulation of these two properties in CSP is:

```
ACBUF = in?x?y -> OUTA(x)          DCBUF = in?x?y -> OUTD(y)
OUTA(adr) =                        OUTD(d) =
    (adr == <0,0> &                    out0.<0>.d -> DCBUF
        out0.adr.0 -> ACBUF)       [] out1.<0>.d -> DCBUF
    [] (adr == <0,1> &             [] out2.<0>.d -> DCBUF
        out1.adr.0 -> ACBUF)       [] out3.<0>.d -> DCBUF
    [] (adr == <1,0> &
        out2.adr.0 -> ACBUF)
    [] (adr == <1,1> &
        out3.adr.0 -> ACBUF)
```

and we ask FDR whether the following two assertions are valid (a check for trace refinement):

```
    assert ACBUF [T= ROUTERA1
    assert DCBUF [T= ROUTERA2
```

The answer is yes. This so far proves that $\text{ACBUF}[G_1^{-1}] \sqsubseteq_T \text{ROUTER}$ and $\text{DCBUF}[G_2^{-1}] \sqsubseteq_T \text{ROUTER}$. Combining these two abstractions we get:

$$\text{ACBUF}[G_1^{-1}] \,\|_{\alpha(\text{ROUTER})}\, \text{DCBUF}[G_2^{-1}] \sqsubseteq_T \text{ROUTER}$$

It is easy to prove within process algebra theory (by giving a divergence respecting bisimulation relation) that $\mathtt{ACBUF}[G_1^{-1}] \parallel_{\alpha(\mathtt{ROUTER})} \mathtt{DCBUF}[G_2^{-1}]$ is failures equivalent to BUF. Thus we have proven the desired property: $\mathtt{BUF} \sqsubseteq_\mathcal{T} \mathtt{ROUTER}$. For the here chosen domain for Data, the refinement check is still possible for FDR; nevertheless the abstraction reduces a check of 16975474 states in about 170 minutes (on a SUN Ultra 2C with two processors at 300 MHZ each and 896 MB) to one of 1152511 states in 5 minutes.

6   Conclusion

In this paper we have proposed a data abstraction technique for CSP-OZ, which was based on the idea of abstract interpretation of specifications. We have shown how properties of concrete specifications are preserved by abstraction by relating the abstract to the renamed concrete specification. We studied compositionality of class abstractions and showed how abstraction results can be combined to give more information about the concrete system. The advantage of our method is that it is both simple to carry out (abstraction requires only small local changes in the CSP-OZ specification) and the results are easy to interpret. Specification, verification *and* abstraction is formulated within the CSP setting.

So far, the object-oriented nature of the specification language has played no role in the verification. We intend to further investigate how the object-oriented structuring of specifications can be exploited to facilitate verification.

Related work. Besides the work already discussed in the introduction, we want to further comment on some related work, especially on the work of Roscoe, both because it deals with CSP and because of its great variety of techniques. The book [18] presents several methods that can be used to analyse CSP programs which are per se too large to be processed with FDR. These techniques include

- abstraction techniques based on *hiding*,
- *local* deadlock analysis and
- *data independent* property checks.

Especially the last point is of interest for data abstraction: data independence (first studied by Wolper [23]) is concerned with the behaviour of programs independent of some of their parameters. For instance, one might be interested in knowing whether a buffer specification works like a buffer independently of the stored elements. Roscoe [18] reports on some work (together with Lasic) that allows to *compute* thresholds on the size of data domains used for particular parameters, such that it is sufficient to check a property on a given program with parameters instantiated with a domain of this size and *conclude* correctness for all instantiations with larger domains. This could very much facilitate correctness checks for CSP programs, since it is to be expected that usually a data independent program with a small data domain already exhibits all the "relevant" behaviour. The router example could profit from this technique; it is possibly sufficient to check the trace refinement on a domain of Data of size 2.

The clock example is, however, not amenable to such techniques since it is not data independent: it contains tests on data values (*even*, *odd*).

Data independence has also been an issue in other work on verification; a very interesting approach in a process algebraic setting is [12]. Jonsson and Parrow study programs which are completely data independent (no modification on data, no testing of values) and show that bisimulation is decidable on this class of systems, even when the data domain is infinite. Their idea could possibily also be used for refinement, but is limited to this restricted class.

Acknowledgements. Many thanks to E.-R.Olderog, C.Fischer, H.Dierks and J.Bredereke for discussions on the paper.

References

[1] E.M. Clarke, O. Grumberg, and D.E. Long. Model checking and abstraction. In *19th ACM POPL*, 1992.

[2] R. Cleaveland and J. Riely. Testing-based abstractions for value-passing systems. In B. Jonsson and J. Parrow, editors, *CONCUR'94*, volume 836 of *Lecture Notes in Computer Science*, pages 417–432, 1994.

[3] J. Corbett. Constructing abstract models for concurrent real time software. In *International Symposium on Software Testing and Analysis*, 1996.

[4] P. Cousot and R. Cousot. Abstract interpretation: A unified lattice model for static analysis of programs by construction or approximation of fixpoints. In *4th ACM POPL*, 1977.

[5] D. Dams, O. Grumberg, and R. Gerth. Abstract interpretation of reactive systems: Abstractions preserving $\forall CTL^*$, $\exists CTL^*$ and CTL^*. In E.-R. Olderog, editor, *Programming concepts, methods and calculi*, volume A-56, pages 573–592. Elsevier, 1994.

[6] R. Duke, G. Rose, and G. Smith. Object-Z: A specification language advocated for the description of standards. *Computer Standards and Interfaces*, 17:511–533, 1995.

[7] C. Fischer. CSP-OZ: A combination of Object-Z and CSP. In H. Bowman and J. Derrick, editors, *Formal Methods for Open Object-Based Distributed Systems (FMOODS '97)*, volume 2, pages 423–438. Chapman & Hall, 1997.

[8] C. Fischer and H. Wehrheim. Model-checking CSP-OZ specifications with FDR. In *IFM '99: International Workshop on Integrated Formal Methods*, Workshops in Computing. Springer, 1999.

[9] Formal Systems (Europe) Ltd. *Failures-Divergence Refinement: FDR2 User Manual*, Oct 1997.

[10] J.F. Groote and A. Ponse. Proof theory for μ-CRL: A language for processes with data. In *Semantics of specification languages*, Workshops in Computing. Springer, 1993.

[11] C. A. R. Hoare. *Communicating Sequential Processes*. Prentice-Hall, 1985.

[12] B. Jonsson and J. Parrow. Deciding bisimulation equivalence for a class of non-finite state programs. *Information and Computation*, pages 272–302, 1993.

[13] Kolyang, T. Santen, and B. Wolff. A structure preserving encoding of Z in Isabelle/HOL. In J. von Wright, J. Grundy, and J. Harrison, editors, *Theorem Proving in Higher Order Logics*, LNCS 1125, pages 283–298. Springer Verlag, 1996.

[14] C. Loiseaux, S. Graf, J. Sifakis, A. Bouajjani, and S. Bensalem. Property preserving abstractions for the verification of concurrent systems. *Formal methods
in system design*, 6:1–35, 1995.

[15] I. Meisels and M. Saaltink. *The Z/EVES Reference Manual*. ORA Canada, 1997.
http://www.ora.on.ca/z-eves/.

[16] A. Mota and A. Sampaio. Model-checking CSP-Z. In *Proceedings of the European
Joint Conference on Theory and Practice of Software*, volume 1382 of *LNCS*,
pages 205–220, 1998.

[17] J. Quemada, editor. *Revised working draft on enhancements to LOTOS (V4)*.
1996.

[18] A. W. Roscoe. *The Theory and Practice of Concurrency*. Prentice-Hall, 1997.

[19] A. W. Roscoe, J. C. P. Woodcock, and L. Wulf. Non-interference through determinism. In D. Gollmann, editor, *ESORICS 94*, volume 875 of *LNCS*, pages
33–54. Springer-Verlag, 1994.

[20] G. Smith. A semantic integration of Object-Z and CSP for the specification of concurrent systems. In J. Fitzgerald, C. B. Jones, and P. Lucas, editors, *Proceedings
of FME 1997*, volume 1313 of *LNCS*, pages 62–81. Springer, 1997.

[21] J. M. Spivey. *The Z Notation: A Reference Manual*. Prentice-Hall International
Series in Computer Science, 2nd edition, 1992.

[22] K. Taguchi and K. Araki. Specifying concurrent systems by Z + CCS. In *International Symposium on Future Software Technology (ISFST)*, pages 101–108,
1997.

[23] P. Wolper. Expressing interesting properties of programs in propositional temporal logic. In *ACM POPL*, pages 184–193, 1986.

[24] J. Woodcock and J. Davies. *Using Z*. Prentice-Hall International, 1996.

A   Brief Introduction to CSP Operators

We briefly describe the main CSP operators in the syntax that FDR uses.

- SKIP, STOP: empty processes with successful/unsuccessful termination,
- a -> P: action prefix, first a and then P,
- c?x -> P: complex prefix, first communication on c with input value v
  bound to x, then $P[v/x]$,
- P;Q: sequential composition,
- P\a: hiding,
- P[[c <- c']]: renaming, c "becomes" c',
- P[]Q: external choice,
- P|~|Q: internal nondeterministic choice,
- b&P: boolean guard, execute P if b evaluates to true,
- P|||Q: interleaving,
- P[| a |]Q: parallel composition with synchronisation on a,
- P[c <-> c']Q: linked parallel, parallel composition with synchronisation of
  c and c', hiding both channels.

Furthermore most binary operators have an iterated version of the following
form (here for []): []x:a @ P(x) stands for $\Box_{x \in a} P(x)$.

B   Proof of Theorem 1

The proof proceeds via the operational semantics of CSP, i.e. via the generated transition systems and their traces, failures and divergences. We let Σ denote a set of visible actions, τ a distinguished *internal* action such that $\tau \notin \Sigma$.

Definition 6. *A* labelled transition system *(LTS) is a tuple* $T = \langle Q, \rightarrow, q_{in} \rangle$, *where* Q *is a set of states,* $\rightarrow \subseteq Q \times \Sigma \times Q$ *a transition relation and* $q_{in} \in Q$ *an initial state.*

We write $q \xrightarrow{a} q'$ if $(q, a, q') \in \rightarrow$, $q \xrightarrow{a_1 \cdots a_n} q'$ if there are states $q_0, q_1, \ldots q_n$ such that $q = q_0$, $q_i \xrightarrow{a_{i+1}} q_{i+1}$ and $q_n = q'$, and $q \xRightarrow{a} q'$ iff $q \xrightarrow{\tau^*} \xrightarrow{a} q'$ and $a \in \Sigma$. A state $q \in Q$ *diverges* $(q\uparrow)$ if there are states $q_1, q_2, \ldots$ such that for all $n \in \mathbb{N}$, $q_n \xrightarrow{\tau} q_{n+1}$ and $q = q_1$.

We prove an even stronger result than Theorem 1, replacing trace refinement by simulation and equivalence by bisimulation. Most results in the area of abstract interpretation for model checking are also based on showing (bi-)similarity of abstract and concrete system. In order to take care about divergences and refusals, we need a special form of bisimulation:

Definition 7. *Let* T_1, T_2 *be transition systems. A relation* $\rho \subseteq Q_1 \times Q_2$ *is a* simulation *between* T_1 *and* T_2 *if* $(q_{01}, q_{02}) \in \rho$ *and for all* $(q_1, q_2) \in \rho$, $a \in \Sigma$:

- $q_2 \xRightarrow{a} q_2'$ *implies* $\exists q_1' : q_1 \xRightarrow{a} q_1'$ *and* $(q_1', q_2') \in \rho$.

The relation $\rho \subseteq Q_1 \times Q_2$ *is a* divergence-respecting bisimulation *between* T_1 *and* T_2 *if* $(q_{01}, q_{02}) \in \rho$ *and for all* $(q_1, q_2) \in \rho$, $a \in \Sigma \cup \{\tau\}$:

- $q_1 \xrightarrow{a} q_1'$ *implies* $\exists q_2' : q_2 \xrightarrow{a} q_2'$ *and* $(q_1', q_2') \in \rho$, *and vice versa,*
- $q_2 \xrightarrow{a} q_2'$ *implies* $\exists q_1' : q_1 \xrightarrow{a} q_1'$ *and* $(q_1', q_2') \in \rho$, *and*
- $q_1\uparrow \Longleftrightarrow q_2\uparrow$.

T_1 *can simulate* T_2 *(denoted* $T_1 \succeq T_2$*) if there is a simulation from* T_1 *to* T_2; T_1 *is d-bisimilar to* T_2 *(denoted* $T_1 \approx_d T_2$*) if there is divergence-respecting bisimulation between* T_1 *and* T_2.

Note the different transition relations used in the definition. A relation ρ is thus not necessarily a bisimulation if both ρ and ρ^{-1} are simulations. The unusual definition of $\xRightarrow{}$ (no further invisible actions after a) allows for a more convenient proof, we just have to consider the states after one visible step and no further internal moves. This is sufficient for trace refinement.

Proposition 2. *Let* T_1, T_2 *be two transition systems. Then*

- $T_1 \succeq T_2 \Rightarrow T_1 \sqsubseteq_{\mathcal{T}} T_2$.
- $T_1 \approx_d T_2 \Rightarrow T_1 =_{\mathcal{F}} T_2$.

Proof of Theorem 1: In the following, we let Z stand for Z_PART and $\|_{\alpha(main)}$ stand for $[| \ \alpha(main) \ |]$. For some given term Z, $h(Z)$ is obtained by replacing in Z all d by $h(d)$ and all enable predicates and effect functions by their abstracted versions. The following general observation is used in all three proofs: for some data-free CSP term P, we have: if $P \xrightarrow{ch.d_1.d_2} P'$ then $P \xrightarrow{ch.d_1'.d_2'} P'$ for all d_1', d_2' in the data domain of the channel ch. This holds since P only contains communication operations $ch?x$, thus P can either make any communication over a channel or none.

- The relation proving simulation of $S[G]$ by $S^{\mathcal{S}}$ is

$$\rho = \{(Z(h(d)) \ \|_{\alpha(main)} \ P, (Z(d) \ \|_{\alpha(main)} \ P)[G]) \mid main \rightarrow^* P, d \in D\} \ .$$

Assume that $(Z(d) \ \|_{\alpha(main)} \ P)[G] \xrightarrow{ch_i.w_1.w_2} (Z(d') \ \|_{\alpha(main)} \ P')[G]$. Then $Z(d) \ \|_{\alpha(main)} \ P \xrightarrow{ch_i.m_1.m_2}$ for some m_1, m_2 such that $g_i(m_1) = w_1$ and $g_i(m_2) = w_2$. Hence $enable_{ch_i}(d) = true$. By definition of safe abstraction, then $enable_{ch_i}^A(h(d)) = true$. Furthermore, $m_1 \in In(ch_i)$ and $(m_2, d') \in effect_{ch_i}(d, m_1)$. Again by definition of safe abstraction we get: $g_i(m_1) \in In^A(ch_i)$ and $(g_i(m_2), h(d')) \in effect_{ch_i}^A(h(d)), g_i(m_1))$. Hence $Z(h(d)) \ \|_{\alpha(main)} \ P \xrightarrow{ch_i.w_1.w_2} Z(h(d')) \ \|_{\alpha(main)} \ P'$.

- The relation proving divergence-respecting bisimulation between $S^{\mathcal{O}}$ and $S[G]$ is

$$\rho = \{(h(Y) \ \|_{\alpha(main)} \ P, (Y \ \|_{\alpha(main)} \ P)[G]) \mid main \rightarrow^* P, d \in D\} \ ,$$

where Y is either of the form $Z(d)$ or $Y = \square_{ch:Ops} \ enable_{ch}(d) \& \ \square_{in:In(ch)} X(ch, in)$, and $X(ch, in)$ may either be $\sqcap_{DIV(out,d'):effect_{ch}(d,in)} \ ch.in.out \rightarrow Z(d')$ or DIV or $ch.in.out \rightarrow Z(d')$ such that $(out, d') \in effect_{ch}(d, in)$. Some of the internal choices may have already been resolved (in case of an empty effect set, this might also lead to divergence), while others are not yet taken.

The proof is similar to the above proof, with the difference that we now have to consider single steps (therefore we get all the above terms in our bisimulation relation), and that now the abstract interpretation of the enable and effect predicates match exactly the concrete interpretations. A τ transition can either be 1) taking an internal choice (resolving $\sqcap$) or 2) a divergence. For the divergence we have: $effect_{ch_i(d,m)}$ is empty if and only if $effect_{ch_i^A(h(d),g_i(m))}$ is empty. Concerning the resolution of choices: assume that the τ resolves the choice over all possible values in the effect set of some channel ch_i in the concrete system. Then ch_i is enabled in the current abstract as well as concrete state. Hence the τ event occurs in both systems and the resulting processes are in ρ again. $\square$

Systems Development Using Z Generics

Fiona Polack[1] and Susan Stepney[2]

[1] Department of Computer Science, University of York, UK.
fiona@cs.york.ac.uk, (tel +44 1904 432722)
[2] Logica UK Ltd, Betjeman House, 104 Hills Road, Cambridge, CB2 1LQ, UK.
stepneys@logica.com

1 Introduction

In this paper we present a method for using generic components in formal specifications. This approach results in a flexible generic system description that separates the concerns of structure and data types. The generic specification can be extended and modified in a natural manner, to track requirements as they inevitably evolve during the development process. In addition, the specification can readily be specialised to use more concrete data types without the need for a formal refinement, using explicit generic instantiation. Such generic instantiation also allows operation preconditions to be *strengthened*; this is not allowed by classic refinement, but it permits a separation of concerns by allowing preconditions relevant to specialised data types to be added only when they become relevant.

Here we use the Z specification language and a simple entity-relationship form as demonstration notations. No new notation or theory is presented; rather it is the use of Z's generic schemas to structure and specialise a specification that is somewhat different from the classical Z specification style described in much of the literature. We believe that this approach could also be applicable to other formal methods.

2 The Case for Z, and Z Generics

Z is similar to many model based notations: it applies typed set theory and predicate logic to system description; it permits rigorous analysis and proof of system properties; it expresses a system description in precise terms.

Z's most recognisable feature is the *schema box*, used to help structure specifications by grouping together definitions. Z also allows *generic definitions* that may be instantiated on use with any set of any type; schemas may themselves be generic. Most Z specifiers confine their use of generics to global toolkit-style constants used with implicit instantiation; few fully exploit the possibility of generic schemas with explicit instantiation.

J. Wing, J. Woodcock, J. Davies (Eds.): FM'99, Vol. II, LNCS 1709, pp. 1048–1067, 1999.
© Springer-Verlag Berlin Heidelberg 1999

2.1   Generic Definitions in Defining Z Toolkits

Z has used generic definitions from its earliest public appearances. In his definitive Z Reference Manual [1] Spivey gives a generic *Mathematical Toolkit* for the Z language. All Z text books (for example [2, 3, 4]) demonstrate generic definitions of operations on sets, sequences and bags, as well as more customised operations.

An example of such a generic definition (used in our case study below) is a generic optionality definition [5].

$$optional[X] == \{\, a : \mathbb{F}\, X \mid \#a \leq 1 \,\}$$

This can be used to model an item that may be present or absent. If y is declared to be $y : optional[Y]$, then y is a set that is either empty (absent) or a singleton (containing a single element of the actual parameter set Y). The type of the set is controlled by the type of the parameter Y.

It may be tempting to see this basic use of Z generic definitions as fulfilling the dream of 1980s programmers, regarding generic data types. Although fundamental to the use of the Z notation, however, these generic definitions do not contribute to the process of developing systems.

2.2   Generics for Secondary Toolkits

The widespread development of formal/structured integrations in the 1990s (see summary papers [6, 7]) has seen the use of Z generic schemas to define representations of structured model components. For example, the SAZ Method [8, 9, 10] includes generic representations of entities and the various forms of relationship encountered in its data modelling notation.

SAZ is an *interpretive* method (guidelines are used to convert a structured specification in to a formal notation), rather than a formal *translation* approach; the SAZ generics form a toolkit that is imported in to the formal document environment, giving a uniform appearance to the formal description.

SAZ generic toolkit definitions have advantages and disadvantages.

On the plus side, they reduce the tedium of transliteration, and provide recognisable components for a reviewer of the formal description. There is little doubt, for example, that the component

$$CustomerSet == EntitySet[CID, Customer]$$

represents a set of entity instances. In addition, such generics conceal or defer low-level decisions about details of components, such as an implementation type for *Customer*.

On the other hand, the component generic definitions become extremely complex, so the simplicity gained in the system description merely masks, rather than removes, a complexity of meaning. For example, the various SAZ relationship generics have formal parameters that are instantiated implicitly in both the declaration and predicate parts. Current Z tool support often fails to expand these generics fully, and then cannot assist in proof of many properties of systems that use them.

Again, these generic usages simply help to express systems; they do not offer any real contribution to the *system development process*.

2.3   Generic Systems

The approach advocated here is to use generic definition at the *system level*. This approach has some well-known precursors, although neither has the simplicity or applicability of the approach demonstrated below.

One example is Flinn and Sørensen's CAVIAR case study [11, chapter 5]. This includes generic modules, providing a super-structure for the specification, and promotes the development of generic specification libraries, as the authors advocate. The module concept is very similar to the use below, but uses an extension to the Z notation to bring this about.

Another example is a proof of compliance to a security policy model, summarised in [2, chapter 4]. Here, a generic top level specification is defined, and it is demonstrated that this has the generic security properties. The specification is instantiated with suitable parameters (input structures, output structures, states), without need to re-prove the high level properties. Again, the approach is closely related to that demonstrated below. The entire specification is cast as an axiomatic state transition relation, however.

3   System Development in Z

Literature on system development in Z concentrates on *formal refinement* [23, 2, 4], neglecting simpler or more intuitive development options. Formal refinement in Z as part of the development of commercial applications is a reality (for example, [12, 13]), but it requires considerable effort, and can still justify its costs only for critical applications. Limitations of refinement (in addition to the difficulty of performing them) are also being recognised among the academic formal methods community [14, 15].

Here we explore the use of generic instantiation rather than refinement as the formal process for developing a system. The development process can be seen as a progressive reduction in options, as the detail in the system description increases and becomes more targeted to specific implementation media [16, 17]. We use a simple development lifecycle to illustrate possible development paths. Although this is not taken forward to implementation, the techniques demonstrated can be reiterated until the required level of specialisation is attained.

4   Entity-Relationship Description of the Case Study

To illustrate our approach, we use a simple case study derived from the SAZ project [9, 10].

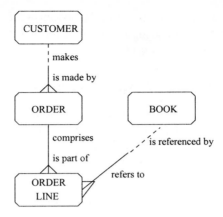

Fig. 1. The data model for the case study, using SSADM v4 notation [18].

In this section we give an informal description of the system. In the next section we formalise the system state and some sample operations as a generic Z specification. In section 6 we perform a first specialisation, by defining the objects in the data-dictionary, and instantiating the specification with them. In section 7 we describe how the generic structure of the specification makes it relatively easy to extend and modify both the structure and the components seperately.

4.1   Scenario

A publishing company accepts orders for books. An order must be placed by a customer; details of customers placing orders are kept on file. The company processes orders and notes whether each order line is met in full.

4.2   Data Model

A data structure to support this system is given in figure 1, as an Entity-Relationship Diagram (ERD).

4.3   Events and Processing

The system receives events to create, modify and delete elements of the data structure. These could be modelled dynamically, using entity life histories or state charts; here they are simply described.

Receiving an Order: Receipt of an order from a new customer triggers the creation of a new customer instance. Receipt of any order triggers the creation of an order instance, and of a set of instances of order line. The processing includes validation checks to determine whether the customer is known or new, and on the composition of order lines.

Customer and Order Modifications: Customer details, especially addresses, may be changed at any time. Order details are never changed; a reorder would be a new instance. However, additional lines might be added to an existing order. Customers are deleted from the records if they have not placed an order for 5 years. Orders are deleted from the records when the customer is deleted, or after 10 years if this is sooner.

Processing an Order and Its Component Order Lines: An order instance is processed by first processing each of its order lines. The details of the processing are not included here, but involve checking that at least some of the order lines can be met and that an order line is not for the same book as another order line on the same order.

If an order has no order lines that can be met (that is, all supplied stock entries are zero), the order is required to be returned to the customer marked "unmet", with some suitable covering letter; the order instance is deleted, but the customer information is retained. Again, the detail is not pursued here.

5   Top-Level Generic Specification

This section presents a top-level Z specification, such as may be used to derive and clarify requirements. It demonstrates the scope of the system and outlines its structure. The Z description focuses on the state and operations of the system. It excludes low-level information, such as attributes and detailed operation pre- and post-conditions. The approach is derived from the SAZ method, in that the starting point is a data model and the formal description expresses the entities and relationships from that model[1].

Even with a predetermined approach and style, there are a number of possible representations in Z for the system described. One approach might be to represent each entity such as *Order* as a set of instances, and each relationship as a relation between the instances of the entities involved. Here, a less abstract but more intuitive approach is used: we model each entitiy as a mapping from identifier to instance. This removes the need to modify the underlying structure using a formal refinement of the specification.

In most published Z case studies, *given sets* are used to achieve the required level of abstraction. A given set provides a pool of elements with no internal structure, and is a suitable model in a specification that abstracts away from

---

[1] There is no attempt to check that the formal and informal descriptions are equivalent, since it is the formal development that is of interest here. A true development method would need to document the extent of equivalence of the descriptions in the different notation and levels of abstraction.

such internal structure. However, in the development of a system, the high-level description needs to be capable of elaboration as further information about the data and processing structures emerges during development. The traditional approach is to refine a given set to a set of structured elements with the desired low-level properties. Such a refinement requires a proof to show that it has been performed correctly, which in turn constrains the kind of instantiations that can be made. Instead of using given sets to model entities, we present a description made up almost entirely of generic schemas.

5.1   Unique Identifiers

In our high level Z representation, the data model entities that make up the state are modelled as functions from some unique identifier to the instance. Although these identifiers could be introduced as generic parameters, they are in fact genuinely uninteresting. They have but one role: to provide a unique identity for otherwise potentially identical instances of an entity. The only interest in an identifier arises at implementation, when uniqueness must be guaranteed. We do not consider implementation here, so we model these identifiers with given sets[2].

$$[CID, OID, OLID]$$

CID are customer identifiers, OID are order identifiers, $OLID$ are order line identifiers. (We choose not to specify the $BOOK$ component yet: that is introduced to illustrate system extension in section 7.2.)

5.2   System State

Rather than specify the entire state space in one chunk, we split it into logically separate components [2, chapter 11]. Dotted lines (optional relationships) on the ERD are good places to think about splitting the state.

The customer entity is independent of the others. We model it using a simple schema, mapping customer identifiers to customer instances, generic in the type of those instances[3].

$$\begin{array}{l} \underline{\quad CustomerBase[CUST]\quad\rule{8cm}{0pt}} \\ \quad customer : CID \nrightarrow CUST \\ \rule{10cm}{0pt} \end{array}$$

---

[2] In Z, given sets are disjoint. This may constrain their use to some extent, requiring the specification of a given set as a super set, and then more detailed subsetting. For any particular given set, such subsetting can be achieved using a free type. Z does not support generic free types, however.

[3] One difference in style between the use of generic definitions and generic schemas is the naming of the generic formal parameters. In the former, a parameter tends to be a single letter; in the latter it tends to be a short word indicating its role. The longer names lead to formatting problems in the case of multiple parameters.

As described in the ERD and text, an order must have some order lines; an order line must be related to one order. The order and order line entities are thus dependent, as defined by the required relationship *isPartOf* between the respective identifiers.

$$
\begin{array}{l}
\_\ OrderBase[ORDER, OLINE] _____ \\
\quad order : OID \twoheadrightarrow ORDER \\
\quad orderLine : OLID \twoheadrightarrow OLINE \\
\quad isPartOf : OLID \leftrightarrow OID \\
\rule{4cm}{0.4pt} \\
\quad isPartOf \in (\mathrm{dom}\ orderLine) \twoheadrightarrow (\mathrm{dom}\ order)
\end{array}
$$

To capture the meaning of the 'crows foot' on the *isPartOf* relationship, we constrain the Z relation to be a total surjection (an order line instance is related to no more than one order instance, hence functional; each order line instance is related to an order instance, hence total; each order instance is related to at least one order line, hence surjective).

The full system state includes these two substate components, and the *isMadeBy* relationship between them.

$$
\begin{array}{l}
\_\ OrderingSystem[CUST, ORDER, OLINE] _____ \\
\quad CustomerBase[CUST] \\
\quad OrderBase[ORDER, OLINE] \\
\quad isMadeBy : OID \leftrightarrow CID \\
\rule{4cm}{0.4pt} \\
\quad isMadeBy \in (\mathrm{dom}\ order) \to (\mathrm{dom}\ customer)
\end{array}
$$

The *isMadeBy* relation is constrained to be a total function (each order instance is related to precisely one customer instance, hence functional and total; but not necessarily all customer instances take part, hence not surjective).

5.3   Sample Operations

The events that affect this small system are the receipt and deletion of orders, and the creation, modification and deletion of customers. (The processing of an order is not described, because the book description has been omitted.) Generic operations are defined to model these events. (In the examples below, we omit the error case schemas, for brevity.)

Having specified the state as independent substates, it is useful to define schemas for updating just these substates [2, chapter 10]. When we update on the customer substate, we do not change the *isMadeBy* relation; when we update the order part, we may change this relation.

$$
\begin{array}{l}
\_\ \Delta CustomerBase[CUST, ORDER, OLINE] _____ \\
\quad \Delta OrderingSystem[CUST, ORDER, OLINE] \\
\quad \Xi OrderBase[ORDER, OLINE] \\
\rule{4cm}{0.4pt} \\
\quad isMadeBy' = isMadeBy
\end{array}
$$

```
┌─ ΔOrderBase[CUST, ORDER, OLINE] ──────────────────────────
│ ΔOrderingSystem[CUST, ORDER, OLINE]
│ Ξ CustomerBase[CUST]
└────────────────────────────────────────────────────────────
```

Customer creation is straightforward. The customer details (for the moment simply a generic parameter) are input, and the new customer identifier is output.

```
┌─ CreateCustomer[CUST, ORDER, OLINE] ──────────────────────
│ ΔCustomerBase[CUST, ORDER, OLINE]
│ cust? : CUST
│ cid! : CID
├────────────────────────────────────────────────────────────
│ cid! ∉ dom customer
│ customer' = customer ∪ {cid! ↦ cust?}
└────────────────────────────────────────────────────────────
```

When an order is created, the appropriate order and order line entity instances are created, and the relationship between their identifiers, and between the order identifier and the identifier of the customer placing the order, are updated. This could all be specified in a single operation, say by having the input include a sequence of the order lines that comprise the order. However, that leads to a relatively complicated definition that is not reusable for the purpose of adding a single order line. So we model the effect of the complete operation in two parts. The first creates an order with one attached order line[4]. The second adds an order line to an existing order.

```
┌─ CreateOrder[CUST, ORDER, OLINE] ─────────────────────────
│ ΔOrderBase[CUST, ORDER, OLINE]
│ orderLine? : OLINE
│ order? : ORDER
│ cid? : CID
│ olid! : OLID
│ oid! : OID
├────────────────────────────────────────────────────────────
│ cid? ∈ dom customer
│ oid! ∉ dom order
│ olid! ∉ dom orderLine
│ order' = order ∪ {oid! ↦ order?}
│ orderLine' = orderLine ∪ {olid! ↦ orderLine?}
│ isPartOf' = isPartOf ∪ {olid! ↦ oid!}
│ isMadeBy' = isMadeBy ∪ {oid! ↦ cid?}
└────────────────────────────────────────────────────────────
```

---

[4] We cannot create an order with no order lines, because of the surjectivity requirement. Now would be a good time to check if that requirement is too strong.

$\underline{\quad AddOrderLine[CUST, ORDER, OLINE]}$

$\Delta OrderBase[CUST, ORDER, OLINE]$
$orderLine? : OLINE$
$oid? : OID$
$olid! : OLID$

$\rule{7cm}{0.4pt}$

$oid? \in \mathrm{dom}\ order$
$olid! \notin \mathrm{dom}\ orderLine$
$order' = order$
$orderLine' = orderLine \cup \{olid! \mapsto orderLine?\}$
$isPartOf' = isPartOf \cup \{olid! \mapsto oid?\}$
$isMadeBy' = isMadeBy$

There are several operations to change the details of entity instances. These include an operation to select a specific customer (by identifier) and change the value of the instance that it identifies, and an operation to change the value of an instance of customer however many identifiers it has linked to it. The former is illustrated. The customer's relationships do not change.

$\underline{\quad ChangeCustomer[CUST, ORDER, OLINE]}$

$\Delta CustomerBase[CUST, ORDER, OLINE]$
$cust? : CUST$
$cid? : CID$

$\rule{7cm}{0.4pt}$

$cid? \in \mathrm{dom}\ customer$
$cid? \mapsto cust? \notin customer$
$customer' = customer \oplus \{cid? \mapsto cust?\}$

Deletion is similar to modification, with the stronger precondition that a customer instance cannot be deleted if there are still orders for that customer.

$\underline{\quad DeleteCustomer[CUST, ORDER, OLINE]}$

$\Delta CustomerBase[CUST, ORDER, OLINE]$
$cid? : CID$

$\rule{7cm}{0.4pt}$

$cid? \in \mathrm{dom}\ customer \setminus \mathrm{ran}\ isMadeBy$
$customer' = \{cid?\} \lhd customer$

Similar operations can be defined for the other entities.

5.4   Discussion

The above Z specification is a simple, but precise, account of (part of) an abstract ordering system. It captures the essential relationships between entities without discussing any internal structure of those entities. (It captures the ERD, but no details from the underlying Data Dictionary.) It specifies how those relationships may be modified, incorporating all constraints that can be expressed without reference to internal entity structure.

Such a specification can be used as a starting point for discussion with customers, for example in a discussion of business rules or operational details for the system. Additional information is added in the next development phase, which is at a lower level of abstraction.

This first Z document has many possible instantiations, representing different development scenarios and customer requirements. Although it could be instantiated at this stage, there is nothing to be gained by doing so; the abstraction level requires no extra details, and the instantiation would simply use given sets for the actual parameters.

6   Design by Instantiation

The full development process is likely to be iterative; this case study merely captures one step in the development.

The objective of this design is to record the logical details of data and processing. When considering a formal development, the static and dynamic constraints are an area of particular interest. This is where formal approaches add most value for limited effort, compared to the traditional diagram-and-text models, which are generally poor at recording and exploring these system rules [19, 20].

The system description is constrained only in so far as the development outcomes are genuinely determined at this phase of the development. The specification of data must capture known client requirements. It is a matter of policy as to how such a specification captures additional data formatting and constraints; managers of development projects should determine whether requirements in this area are to be expressed at this stage.

As noted earlier, traditional Z development uses given sets for data that has not yet been fully defined. When the data types are elaborated, a refinement is required to move from given sets to the new types. Here we show how instead our generic formulation can be instantiated, to provide a first specialisation of these data types. In section 6.1 we illustrate the instantiation process by giving a 'traditional'-style given sets instantiation of the *CustomerBase*. In section 6.3 we show how the generic approach may be used at each level.

6.1   Traditional Specification of the Customer Entity

The Data Dictionary says that a customer has a name, an address, the date when they become a customer, and a credit limit. The credit limit must be within some globally imposed limit. An address, in turn, comprises a house identifier, a street, a town, and a postcode. Furthermore, a house identifier may be a number or a house name.

First we specify the house identifier, using a free type. Simple free types, enumerated types, allow the specifier to make clear the specific values that an attribute can take, for example for status-check attributes, and for use in the processing specification. This is a step that is often overlooked in structured method developments, where the specifier may concentrate too early on the potential implementations of enumerated attribute domains. Enumerated types are often modified in the course of the development, as more or fewer statuses become necessary[5].

$$[HOUSENAME]$$

$$HOUSE ::= number \langle\!\langle \mathbb{N} \rangle\!\rangle \mid name \langle\!\langle HOUSENAME \rangle\!\rangle$$

Where a domain for a particular attribute is a subset of a wider set, it is given a specific domain name as an abbreviation for the wider. This acts as a reminder that there may need to be more detailed specification of constraints on the domain. So we introduce *limit*, which may need to be further constrained, for example, to be within some global limit.

$$limit == \mathbb{N}_1$$

$$\mid maxLim : limit$$

Schema types are used where some structural information is already known about a type. A typical example concerns the format of an address.

$$[STREET, TOWN, POSTCODE]$$

```
__ Address0 _____
  house : HOUSE
  street : STREET
  town : TOWN
  postcode : POSTCODE
```

We are now in a position to specify the customer entity.

$$[DATE, NAME]$$

```
__ Customer0 _____
  name : NAME
  address : Address0
  creditLimit : limit
  registeredDate : DATE
  _____
  creditLimit ≤ maxLim
```

[5] In Z, enumerated types must have unique values; thus, a value such as *notFound* cannot be part of more than one enumerated type. This can cause frustration in large specifications; however, the bonus is that, in complex operations, the status or message information is clearly readable.

The traditional Z style would then instantiate the customer substate as follows, but would eventually require the elaboration of most of its component types.

$$TradCustomerBase == CustomerBase[Customer0]$$

One advantage of this specification is that the Z toolkit operators for integers can be used when putting constraints on credit limits. The main disadvantage is that types become established, and developers are not prompted to consider how best features such as limits and maxima should be implemented.

6.2   Operator Definition

In what follows, we use generic types to represent quantities such as credit limit. We still want to be able to specify that the limit must be less than some global maximum. So we generically specify the set of all total orders (that is, reflexive, antisymmetric, transitive and total), and we specify our generic comparison operator to be one such total order[6] [7].

relation $(\_ \preccurlyeq \_)$

$$
\begin{array}{l}
=[X]============================\\
\_ \preccurlyeq \_ : \{\, r : X \leftrightarrow X \mid \text{id}\,X \subseteq r \wedge r \cap r^{\sim} \subseteq \text{id}\,X \\
\qquad\qquad\qquad \wedge\ r \,\mathbin{\substack{\circ\\\circ}}\, r \subseteq r \wedge r \cup r^{\sim} = X \times X \,\}
\end{array}
$$

The use of a defined order avoids the use of meaning-free type operators that rely on the semantic understanding of the operator name[8], or the completely unacceptable provision of general purpose type operators (for example, a general *dateComparison* operator).

6.3   Generic Specification of the Customer Entity

Continuing our style of using generics to model as yet unelaborated data types, we can use generic parameters in place of many of the above data types, depending on the extent to which type details are determined by the developers and clients.

---

[6] Note that this is a loose generic definition. Spivey Z has a proof obligation that a generic definition is uniquely determined for all possible instantiations. Standard Z permits loose generics; the proof obligation is that the definition is well formed at each point of instantiation.

[7] This may all seem a little over-complicated. But consider the case of dates or times. We do not want to be forced to model a date as a simple number, neither do we want to be forced to model it as a complicated structure yet. But we certainly want to be able to say one date is before another. Using a generic order, and requiring date to be ordered, solves the problem.

[8] The problem has not been solved entirely, however. An unwanted instantiation of X and $\_ \preccurlyeq \_$ is $\mathbb{N}$ and $\_ \geqslant \_$. A validation process is always required at instantiation.

Assuming that the address structure is accepted, this can be re-expressed as

$$
\begin{array}{|l}
\_\_Address[HOUSE, STREET, TOWN, POSTCODE]_____ \\
house : HOUSE \\
street : STREET \\
town : TOWN \\
postcode : POSTCODE \\
\hline
\end{array}
$$

A generic limit is defined.

$$
\begin{array}{|l}
=[LIMIT]================================ \\
maxLimit : LIMIT \\
\hline
\end{array}
$$

The customer type is defined as a generic, incorporating elaborated types[9].

$$
\begin{array}{|l}
\_\_Customer[NAME, HOUSE, STREET, TOWN, POSTCODE,_____ \\
\qquad\qquad\qquad\qquad\qquad\qquad\qquad LIMIT, DATE] \\
name : NAME \\
address : Address[HOUSE, STREET, TOWN, POSTCODE] \\
creditLimit : LIMIT \\
registeredDate : DATE \\
\hline
creditLimit \preccurlyeq maxLimit \\
\hline
\end{array}
$$

The order and order line entities can be similarly defined.

$$
\begin{array}{|l}
\_\_Order[DATE]_____ \\
orderDate : DATE \\
\hline
\end{array}
$$

$$
\begin{array}{|l}
=[AMOUNT]=============================== \\
minAmount : AMOUNT \\
\hline
\end{array}
$$

$$
\begin{array}{|l}
\_\_OrderLine[AMOUNT, NOTE]_____ \\
quantity, supplied : AMOUNT \\
note : NOTE \\
\hline
minAmount \preccurlyeq quantity \\
supplied \preccurlyeq quantity \\
\hline
\end{array}
$$

---

[9] It would be nice if Z had some support for grouping the generic parameters, to highlight the fact that some are relevant only to the further instantiation of *Address*, for example.

6.4 Instantiating the State

The instantiation uses the entity types to define all necessary sets and relationships. The full state includes the full list of generic parameters.

$$SystemI[NAME, HOUSE, STREET, TOWN, POSTCODE, LIMIT,$$
$$DATE, AMOUNT, NOTE] ==$$
$$OrderingSystem[Customer[NAME, HOUSE, STREET, TOWN,$$
$$POSTCODE, LIMIT, DATE],$$
$$Order[DATE], OrderLine[AMOUNT, NOTE]]$$

Substates may also be defined by instantiation, and constraints can be added if necessary. Although the quantity of generic parameters in this expression is unwieldy, this has an advantage in terms of traceability. Since the innards of the system types are explicit, it is clear what needs elaborating at a later stage, and where each component is used in the substates. This is analogous to an automatic, in-line indexing, which could form the basis for a development documentation tool.

6.5 Operations

Operations are also specified by instantiation, both of state components, and of the operations. However, most operations require elaboration of pre- and post-conditions, taking account of the greater state information, and research into business rules. A developer seeking additional predicates should, for example, be encouraged to check the attributes of all the entities in the specification, looking for range constraints, default entry values, derivation formulae, and relationships to the values of other attributes in the system.

The specification of an operation is illustrated for the creation of a customer.

$$\_\_CreateCustomerI[NAME, HOUSE, STREET, TOWN, POSTCODE,$$
$$LIMIT, DATE, AMOUNT, NOTE]$$
$$CreateCustomer[Customer[NAME, HOUSE, STREET, TOWN,$$
$$POSTCODE, LIMIT, DATE],$$
$$Order[DATE], OrderLine[AMOUNT, NOTE]]$$
$$today? : DATE$$

$$cust?.registeredDate = today?$$
"Additional predicates to enforce state invariants"
$$cust?.creditLimit \preccurlyeq maxLimit$$

Notice that this operation has additional preconditions. So some attempted uses of the operation for certain values of *Customer* will fail, where the abstract operation succeeds for any value of generic *CUST*. Along with elaborating the data type, we have *strengthened the precondition*, and so we do not have a formal refinement (which permits only weakening the precondition). Generic instantiation has allowed us to separate concerns. The preconditions that depend on details of the entity structure are omitted until that entity is elaborated: a different elaboration could result in a different precondition. This permits a more abstract top-level specification, where the concrete instantiations are not classic refinements.

6.6   Discussion

The abstraction level of the specification presented here is similar to the level of abstraction achieved in published case studies that use integrations of Z with a structured technique or method. In the integrated methods area, it has generally been the case that the formal system description has been derived once, from data models (with dynamic and/or process models as relevant) with low-level documentation[10].

There are intuitive or aesthetic arguments in favour of specification by instantiation. There is a clear separation of concerns; the developer is encouraged to think abstractly and not to make premature decisions about implementation or design features.

However, the utility of the approach comes down to an argument between readability, or adaptability of formal descriptions, and simplicity in the formal structures used. The use of generics increases the complexity of the Z descriptions. Indeed, the assistance provided by support tools has, in the authors' experience, been jeopardised where proofs are required of features of descriptions that contain such nested generic instantiations.

7   Reusing and Elaborating through Instantiation

There would seem to be a number of advantages to arriving at this level of description via instantiation.

- It is easy to modify the initial analysis-derived description, for example to amend the scope of the system developed, since the essential data and processing structures are not lost among lower-level details.
- It is easy to modify the data domains where a client corrects the analysts' interpretation or changes their mind about domains, or where a developer is required to produce another system with a similar structure but different details. Processing descriptions can be modified to include pre- and post-conditions, not as a refinement, but as a description of a different specification that can be derived from the analysis.

These advantages are further illustrated by changing the detail of the instantiation, both in terms of the data dictionary, and in terms of the static structure of the system.

---

[10] See for example, SAZ case studies [8, 19, 10], Semmens et al [21], Josephs et al [22].

7.1   Data Dictionary Modifications

The most common changes to a specification during the development of a system concern the details of data and constraints. In structured modelling, these are generally held in some form of textual data dictionary, and support the diagrammatic models. Formal specification is particularly clear in the areas of data domains and static and dynamic constraints; the generic form can easily adapt to capture alterations made. The problem reduces to a versioning issue, which is beyond the scope of this paper.

To illustrate the accommodation of such changes, consider the modifications,

- there are no more than n customers in the system;
- orders met in full have a marker attribute set.

These changes do not affect the high-level generic state, which captures the structure of the system (section 5); they affect only the details of the first instantiation of the structure, section 6.

First, the order entity type is modified to add the new attribute.

$$
\begin{array}{|l}
\_\ RevOrder[DATE, MARKER]\ \rule{0pt}{0pt}\underline{\hspace{5cm}} \\
\quad orderDate : DATE \\
\quad metInFull : MARKER \\
\hline
\end{array}
$$

This specification replaces *Order* in subsequent instantiations. None of the operations on order need modifying, since none makes explicit reference to the component data attributes of the order. In general, however, an operation that made explicit reference to the component data attributes of a changed entity would require modification.

The constraint on the number of customers can be introduced as an elaboration to the state schema.

$$
\begin{array}{|l}
customerLimit : \mathbb{N}_1 \\
\end{array}
$$

$$
\begin{array}{|l}
\_\ RevOrderSystem[NAME, HOUSE, STREET, TOWN, POSTCODE,\_ \\
\qquad\qquad\qquad\qquad LIMIT, DATE, AMOUNT, NOTE] \\
\quad OrderingSystem[Customer[NAME, HOUSE, STREET, TOWN, \\
\qquad\qquad\qquad POSTCODE, LIMIT, DATE], \\
\qquad\quad Order[DATE], OrderLine[AMOUNT, NOTE]] \\
\hline
\quad \#customer \le customerLimit \\
\hline
\end{array}
$$

Since the signature of the schema is unchanged, there are no knock-on effects in the operations. However, there is a new pre-condition in *AddCustomer*: a new customer cannot be added if it would take the system over the newly-imposed limit. It is a matter of style whether this pre-condition is left implicit or made explicit.

7.2 Structural Modifications

During development of a system, it may be necessary to perform some extension or specialisation. The most obvious illustrations of this are the addition of an entity, and the subtyping of an entity in the system data model or state. Although fundamental changes to the data structure would require respecification, specialisation and extension to the model can generally be accommodated more simply. This promotes the reuse of formal descriptions.

Extending the State: The scenario data model (figure 1) shows an additional entity, *BOOK*. This can be defined generically and added to the system state. Side issues are the addition of the relationship with existing entities and the expression of any new constraints on the structure.

$[BID]$

$$
\begin{array}{l}
\_\_BookState[BOOK]_____ \\
\quad book : BID \rightarrowtail BOOK \\
\end{array}
$$

$$
\begin{array}{l}
\_\_BookOrderSystem[CUST, ORDER, OLINE, BOOK]_____ \\
\quad OrderingSystem[CUST, ORDER, OLINE] \\
\quad BookState[BOOK] \\
\quad refersTo : OLID \leftrightarrow BID \\
\hline
\quad refersTo \in (\mathrm{dom}\ orderLine) \rightarrow (\mathrm{dom}\ book) \\
\quad \forall\, o : \mathrm{ran}\ isPartOf \bullet (isPartOf^\sim)(\!|\ \{o\}\ |\!) \lhd refersTo \in OLID \rightarrowtail BID \\
\end{array}
$$

The additional predicate state that no two order lines of an order may refer to the same book. Operation schemas need amending accordingly.

Specialising Entities: Specialisation is illustrated by subtyping the customer entity to express two different kinds of customer:

$$
\begin{array}{l}
\_\_Corporate[HOUSE, STREET, TOWN, POSTCODE]\_\_\_\_\_ \\
\quad invoiceAddress : Address[HOUSE, STREET, TOWN, POSTCODE] \\
\end{array}
$$

$$
\begin{array}{l}
\_\_[RATING]_____ \\
\quad minRating : RATING \\
\end{array}
$$

$$
\begin{array}{l}
\_\_Private[RATING]_____ \\
\quad creditRating : RATING \\
\hline
\quad minRating \preccurlyeq creditRating \\
\end{array}
$$

The customer type is now composed of the common elements (defined in the original specification), and optional components of these types[11]. A predicate can require that a customer is of one subtype only. (The optionality mechanism is defined in section 2.1.)

$$
\begin{array}{l}
\_SpecialCustomerSpec[NAME, HOUSE, STREET, TOWN, POSTCODE, \\
\qquad\qquad\qquad\qquad CREDITLIMIT, DATE, RATING] \\
Customer[NAME, HOUSE, STREET, TOWN, POSTCODE, \\
\qquad\qquad CREDITLIMIT, DATE] \\
private : optional[Private[RATING]] \\
corporate : optional[Corporate[HOUSE, STREET, TOWN, POSTCODE]] \\
\hline
\#private = 1 \Leftrightarrow \#corporate = 0
\end{array}
$$

Selectors for private and corporate customers can be written [5]. Again, operations need extending and modifying accordingly.

8   Discussion

Traditional Z development uses given sets for initially unstructured data types that can be elaborated during the development. It relies on formal development methods such as refinement to move towards an implementation goal.

In contrast, we describe an approach that uses generic specification with elaboration by instantiation. It has the following properties:

- Separation of data and relationships. The abstract specification captures relationships between entities as captured by the ERD; the generic parameters are instantiated with structures defined from the data dictionary. Each can be modified independently of the other.
- Elaboration by instantiation. No proof obligations are generated by the instantiation. Different instantiations of the same specification can be used to produce different systems. Preconditions on operations can be introduced at the appropriate level of abstraction; development remains valid even though such precondition strengthening does not follow the formal refinement relationship.

It is notoriously difficult to document a development. Features that are developed successively to an implementation are scattered across models and within models, and traceability becomes a major problem. Whilst the generic development presented does not contribute any large-scale improvement in this area, the inclusion of all the required types in the headings of the generic schemas at least ensures that these are all available to the developer without searching the document for given sets and other type instantiations.

---

[11] This slightly clumsy formulation, or something equivalent, is needed in the absence of generic free types.

The case study example is small, and although we assert that the approach scales, it is not entirely clear how the levels of complexity introduced affect the readability and usability of the development products. The approach would definitely be improved by better Z support for

- formatting long lists of generic formal parameters
- grouping generic parameters
- generic free types

A tool to support a rigorous development following the approach described here (as opposed to a tool to support the formal descriptions and proofs) might be expected to have at least the following characteristics:

- discrimination between levels of detail in the development descriptions, encouraging the developer to work consistently through lower levels of abstraction (but, to support practical working, not necessarily requiring the developer to complete one level of abstraction before attempting a lower level);
- good visualisation and expansion of generic structures and generic instantiations, allowing the developer to explore structures, construct proofs and so on, without resorting to a complete expansion of all schemas;
- support for the development and use of templates, where a design follows the outline of the specification but with different structural details, or where routine structures such as entity sets, refinement retrievals, and structural proof conjectures, are required.

Support tools might also take design on to generation of, for example, relations for a relational database, or, at a less specific level, might provide guidance on the form of design and specification specialisation needed for different media (programming or database paradigms).

Acknowledgements

The work described in this paper derives in part from work undertaken during and as a result of the SAZ project, 1990–94, EPSRC grants (GR/J81655) and (GR/F98642).

We would like to thank Sam Valentine and Ian Toyn for helpful discussions.

References

[1] J. M. Spivey. *The Z Notation: A Reference Manual*. Prentice Hall, 2nd Edition, 1992.
[2] R. Barden, S. Stepney, D. Cooper. *Z In Practice*. Prentice Hall, 1994.
[3] B. Potter, J. Sinclair, and D. Till. *An Introduction to Formal Specification and Z*. Prentice Hall, 2nd Edition, 1996.
[4] J. C. P. Woodcock and J. Davies. *Using Z: Specification, Refinement, and Proof*. Prentice Hall, 1996.

[5] M. d'Inverno and M. Priestley. Structuring Specification in Z to Build a Unifying Framework for Hypertext Systems. *ZUM'95: The Z Formal Specification Notation; Proceedings of Ninth International Conference of Z Users, Limerick, Ireland, September 1995*, pp83–102. LNCS 967. Springer Verlag, 1995.

[6] L. T. Semmens, R. B. France, and T. W. G. Docker. Integrated Structured Analysis and Formal Specification Techniques. *The Computer Journal*, vol 35, no 6, 1992.

[7] R. B. France and M. M. Larrondo-Petrie. A Two-Dimensional View of Integrated Formal and Informal Specification Techniques. *ZUM'95: The Z Formal Specification Notation; Proceedings of Ninth International Conference of Z Users, Limerick, Ireland, September 1995*, pp434-448. LNCS 967. Springer Verlag, 1995.

[8] F. A. C. Polack, M. Whiston, and P. Hitchcock. Structured Analysis – A Draft Method for Writing Z Specifications. *Proceedings of Sixth Annual Z User Meeting, York, Dec 1991*. Springer Verlag, 1992.

[9] F. Polack, M. Whiston, and K.C. Mander. The SAZ Project: Integrating SSADM and Z. *Proceedings, FME'93 : Industrial Strength Formal Methods, Odense, Denmark, April 1993*. LNCS 670. Springer Verlag, 1993

[10] F. Polack, M. Whiston, and K. C. Mander. *The SAZ Method Version 1.1*. York, YCS 207, Jan 1994.

[11] I. Hayes. *Specification Case Studies*. Prentice Hall, 2nd Edition, 1992.

[12] S. Stepney. A Tale of Two Proofs. *Proceedings, 3rd Northern Formal Methods Workshop, Ilkley, Sept 1998*. BCS-FACS, 1998.

[13] S. Stepney, D. Cooper, and J. C. P. Woodcock. More Powerful Z Data Refinement: Pushing the State of the Art in Industrial Refinement. *ZUM'98 : 11th international conference of Z Users, Berlin*. LNCS 1493. Springer Verlag, 1998.

[14] E. Boiten and J. Derrick. IO-Refinement in Z. *Proceedings, 3rd Northern Formal Methods Workshop, Ilkley, Sept 1998*. BCS-FACS, 1998.

[15] R. Banach and M. Poppleton. Retrenchment: An Engineering Variation on Refinement. *Proceedings, B98, Montpellier, France*. LNCS 1393. Springer Verlag, 1998.

[16] I. Hayes. Specification Models. *Z Twenty Years On: What Is Its Future?, Nantes, France, October 1995*. 1995.

[17] I. J. Hayes and M. Utting. Coercing real-time refinement: A transmitter *Northern Formal Methods Workshop, Ilkley, UK, September 1995*. 1995.

[18] CCTA. *SSADM Version 4 Reference Manual*. NCC Blackwell Ltd, 1990.

[19] H. E. D. Parker, F. Polack, and K. C. Mander The Industrial Trial of SAZ: Reflections on the Use of an Integrated Specification Method. *Z Twenty Years On: What Is Its Future?, Nantes, France, October 1995*.

[20] F. A. C. Polack and K. C. Mander. Software Quality Assurance Using the SAZ Method. *Proceedings of Eighth Annual Z User Meeting, Cambridge, June 1994*. Springer Verlag, 1994.

[21] L. Semmens and P. Allen. Using Yourdon and Z: an Approach to Formal Specification. *Proceedings of Fifth Annual Z User Meeting, Oxford, Dec 1990*. Springer-Verlag, 1991.

[22] D. Redmond-Pyle and M. Josephs. Enriching a Structured Method with Z. *Workshop on Methods Integration, 26 September 1991, Leeds*, (unpublished)

[23] C. Morgan. *Programming from Specifications*. Prentice-Hall, 2nd edition, 1994.

A Brief Summary of VSPEC⋆

Perry Alexander[1], Murali Rangarajan[1], and Phillip Baraona[2]

[1] Department of Electrical & Computer Engineering
and Computer Science
PO Box 210030
The University of Cincinnati
Cincinnati, OH
{alex,rmurali}@ececs.uc.edu
[2] Chrysalis Symbolic Design, Inc.
101 Billerica Ave
5 Billerica Park
Billerica, MA 01862
phil@chrysalis.com

Abstract. This paper provides an overview of the VSPEC behavioral interface specification language for VHDL. Although operational specification language such as VHDL provide exceptional specification capabilities, at the systems requirements level the operational style is a hindrance. VSPEC provides VHDL users with a declarative mechanism for defining functional requirements and performance constraints. In the tradition of behavioral interface specification languages, VSPEC adds clauses to the VHDL entity construct allowing axiomatic specification of functional requirements. Because system constraints play an ever increasing role in systems design, VSPEC also provides performance constraint specification capability. This paper presents the basics of VSPEC, its semantics, semantic analysis, and briefly describes current and future applications.

Keywords: systems level design, notations, languages, VHDL, Larch

1 Introduction

Requirements analysis is a critical activity in any systems design process. However, it is poorly supported by tools and languages. Although operational, simulation centered, hardware description languages such as VHDL [1] provide excellent support for design, they are less appropriate for requirements analysis. The operational style tends to introduce implementation bias into requirements. Furthermore, simulation-based analysis is not always appropriate for evaluating highly declarative, frequently incomplete requirements. To address such problems, VSPEC [2, 3, 4, 5] augments VHDL to provide a declarative requirements specification capability that support rigorous, formal analysis.

⋆ Support for this work was provided in part by the Advanced Research Projects Agency and monitored by Wright Labs under the RASSP Technology Program, contract number F33615-93-C-1316 and by Air Force MANTECH, contract number F33615-93-C-4303

J. Wing, J. Woodcock, J. Davies (Eds.): FM'99, Vol. II, LNCS 1709, pp. 1068–1086, 1999.
© Springer-Verlag Berlin Heidelberg 1999

VSPEC is a Larch interface language [6, 7] for VHDL. The Larch family of specification languages supports a two-tiered, model-based approach to specifying software. A Larch specification is written in two languages: a Larch Interface Language (LIL) and the Larch Shared Language (LSL). Larch Interface Language definitions specify the inputs and outputs of a program component and the component's observable behavior. Typically, input and output parameters are defined in the host programming language. Then, first order predicates define component behavior using a traditional axiomatic style. Larch Interface Languages exist for a variety of programming languages, including C [8, 9], C++ [10] and Ada [11].

LSL is a formal algebraic language that defines the underlying sorts and operators used in interface language definitions. As the name implies, LSL is common among all Larch Interface Languages. Specifiers use LSL to define reusable domain theories for specification activities and to define semantics for interface languages.

VSPEC describes the requirements of a digital system using the canonical Larch approach. Each VHDL entity is annotated with a pre- and post-condition to indicate the component's functional requirements. The operators used in a VSPEC description are defined with LSL. VSPEC also allows a designer to describe non-functional requirements and the internal state of a device. VSPEC semantics is defined by providing a translation of VSPEC language constructs and VHDL types into LSL enabling formal verification using Larch tools.

VSPEC-annotated components can be connected together to form an abstract architecture. An abstract architecture is an inter-connected collection of components where the requirements of each component are specified without defining their implementation. This describes a class of solutions with a common structure. A standard VHDL structural architecture referencing VSPEC annotated entities defines an abstract architecture. The VHDL architecture indicates interconnection in the traditional manner, but the requirements of each component are defined instead of their implementations.

Abstract architectures specified with VSPEC present a problem that other Larch interface languages do not have to address: when is a component in an abstract architecture active? In traditional sequential programming languages, a language construct executes after the construct immediately preceding it terminates. For correct execution, a construct's pre-condition must be satisfied when the preceding construct terminates. In a VSPEC abstract architecture, each of the components behave as independent processes. There is no predefined execution order so there is no means of determining when a component's pre-condition should hold. VSPEC solves this problem by allowing a user to define an activation condition for a component. The activation condition defines what causes the component to begin processing its inputs. When the component state changes to one that satisfies the activation condition, the pre-condition must hold and the component performs its specified transformation.

This paper describes the semantics of VSPEC, concentrating on the language's facilities for describing abstract architectures. The opening section provides a brief summary of the VSPEC language. Section 3 describes VSPEC abstract architectures, including a definition of the VSPEC state model and a description of how a process algebra (CSP) [12] is used to provide a semantics for the VSPEC activation condition. Section 5 discusses how these semantics can be used verify that an abstract architecture satisfies the specification of the entity. Finally, the paper concludes with a discussion of VSPEC applications and some related work.

2   The VSPEC Language

VSPEC's declarative specification style complements the traditional VHDL operational style by providing a requirements specification capability. As a requirements specification language, VSPEC is used very early in the design process to describe "what" a system should do. The operational style of VHDL makes VHDL alone ill-suited for requirements specification. It forces a designer to describe a system by defining a specific design artifact that describes "how" the system behaves. When attempting to use VHDL as a requirements specification language, this forces a designer to deal with unnecessary detail at a very early point in the design process. In contrast to VHDL's operational style, VSPEC allows a designer to declaratively describe a component. Together, VSPEC and VHDL support modeling from requirements acquisition through verification and synthesis.

As a working example, a VSPEC description of a sorting component is shown in Figure 1. Three basic clauses define functional requirements for an entity: (i) the **requires** clause defines the component precondition; (ii) the **ensures** clause defines the component postcondition; and (iii) the **sensitive to** clause defines the component activation condition. Effectively, the **requires** and **ensures** clauses define component function while the **sensitive to** clause defines component control.

The **requires** and **ensures** clauses are used to define an axiomatic relationship between current and the next state. Specifically, they specify the pre- and post-conditions of the component. Any component that makes the postcondition true in the next state given that the precondition is true in the current state is a valid implementation of these requirements. More precisely, given a component with **requires** clause $I(St)$ and **ensures** clause $O(St, St'post)$[1], $f(St)$ is a correct implementation of the requirements if the following condition holds:

$$\forall s \cdot I(St) \Rightarrow O(St, f(St)) \tag{1}$$

The **sensitive to** clause plays the same role in a VSPEC definition that sensitivity lists and wait statements play in a VHDL description. It defines when a component is active. The **sensitive to** clause for **sort** in Figure 1 states that the entity activates (and sorts its input) whenever the input changes. The **sensitive to** clause contains a predicate indicating when an entity should begin

---

[1] The $St'post$ notation references the value of St in the state after the transformation described by the entity is performed. This is analogous to the *variable'* notation of LCL [8, 9]

```
entity sort is port
  (input: in integer_array;
   output: out integer_array);
  includes sort;
  modifies output;
  sensitive to input'event;
  requires true;
  ensures
    permutation(output'post, input)
    and inorder(output'post);
  constrained by
    power <= 5 mW and
    size <= 3 um * 5 um and
    heat <= 10 mW and
    clock <= 50 MHz and
    input<->output <= 5 Ms;
end sort;
```

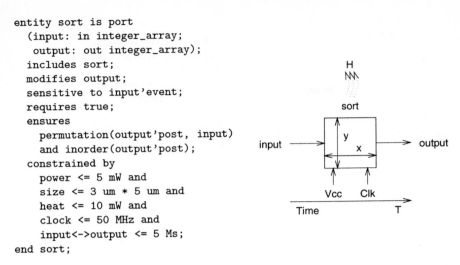

Fig. 1. VSPEC description of a sorting component.

executing and the next section contains a more precise definition of the meaning of the **sensitive to** predicate.

In the example specification from Figure 1, the SORT component is defined to operate correctly in any initial state whenever its input changes and produce an output that is ordered and a permutation of the input. The **requires** clause defines a precondition of true. As true holds in any state, the component must execute starting in any state. The **ensures** clause defines a postcondition of **permutation(input,output'post)** and **ordered(output'post)** requiring that after execution the output should be an ordered permutation of the input. Note that *ordered* and *permutation* are defined in the included trait sort. The **sensitive to** clause defines an activation condition of **input'event**. Event is a predefined VSPEC predicate that is true whenever its associated signal changed values in the previous state change.

In addition to allowing a designer to describe functional requirements, VSPEC also allows specification of performance constraints. The VSPEC **constrained by** clause is used for this purpose. As shown in Figure 1, this clause defines relations over constraint variables. Currently, the defined constraint variables include power consumption, layout area (expressed as a bounding box), heat dissipation, clock speed and pin to pin timing. Constraint theories written in LSL define each constraint type. Users may define their own constraints and theories if desired.[2]

The **state** clause contains a list of variable declarations that define the internal state of a component. These variables maintain state information that is not

---

[2] VSPEC constraint specification is not presented in detail in this paper. For further exposition, please see the Language Reference Manual [13].

```
entity find is port
  (input: in element_array;
   k: in keytype;
   output: out element);
  includes
    Element(element,keytype,
            element_array);
  modifies output;
  requires true;
  ensures forall (e : element)
   (output = e implies
     (e.key = k
      and elem_of(e,input)));
  constrained by
    power <= 5 mW
    and size <= 3 um * 5 um
    and k<->output <= 5 Ms
    and heat <= 10 mW
    and clock <= 50 MHz;
end search;
```

(a.)

```
entity bin_search is port
  (input: in element_array;
   k: in integer;
   value: out element);
  modifies value;
  sensitive to
    k'event or input'event;
  requires
    sorted(input);
  ensures
    output = e iff
     (e.key=k and
       element_of(e,input));
  constrained by
    power <= 1 mW and
    size <= 1 um * 2 um;
end bin_search;
```

(b.)

Fig. 2. VSPEC descriptions of find and binary search components.

visible outside the component. A state clause is not needed in the specification of a sorting component in Figure 1 as no internal state is stored.

The modifies clause lists variables, ports and signals whose values may be changed by the entity. Most other Larch interface languages contain a modifies clause, and the definition of VSPEC modifies clause is very similar to the definitions found in these languages [8, 9, 10].

The includes clause is used to include Larch Shared Language definitions in a VSPEC description. The sorts and operators defined in the LSL trait named by the includes clause can be used in the VSPEC definition.

3   Abstract Architectures

VHDL structural architectures composed only of VSPEC annotated components specify abstract architectures. The VHDL architecture syntax remains unchanged indicating component instantiation and connections. However, the configuration does not assign an entity/architecture pair to each component instance in the architecture. Instead, the configuration defines that each component references an entity with an architecture called VSPEC. This signifies that at the current point in the design, the requirements of this component are known (via the VSPEC description) but no implementation has been defined.

Consider the VSPEC description of a find component shown in Figure 2a. The output of find is the element from the input array with the same key as

```
architecture structure of find is   configuration test_vspec of find is
   component sort port                    for structure
      (input: in element_array;             for b1:sort use entity
       output: out element_array);            work.sort(VSPEC);
   end component;                            end for;
   component search port                   for b2:search use entity
      (input: in element_array;              work.bin_search(VSPEC);
       key: in integer;                     end for;
       value: out element);                end for;
   end component;                        end test_struct;
   signal y: element_array;
begin
   b1: sort port map(input,y);
   b2: search port map(y,k,output);
end structure;
```

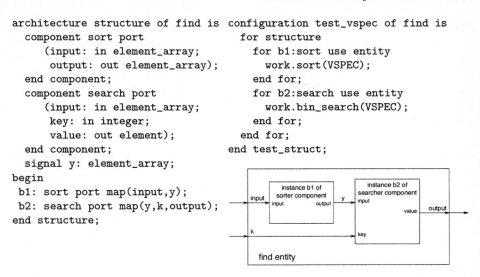

Fig. 3. A VSPEC abstract architecture representation of the find component.

the k input. This requirement is represented by find's **ensures** clause predicate. One possible way to meet this requirement is to connect the output of a sorting component to a binary search component as shown in Figure 3. The specification for sort is the same as the one in in Section 2, while the bin_search specification is shown in Figure 2b. The only difference between this structural description of find and a VHDL structural description of find is that the configuration specifies that the VSPEC descriptions of sort and bin_search should be used instead of a specific architecture for these two entities. This configuration describes an abstract architecture for the find component. Any implementation satisfying the VSPEC requirements of sort and bin_search may be associated with the **entity** definitions. This abstract architecture for find actually defines a class of solutions with a common structure.

Although a VHDL architecture referencing VSPEC definitions defines components and interconnections, additional information must be added to specify when the VSPEC components activate. In traditional sequential programming, a language construct "executes" following termination of the construct preceding it. For correct execution, a construct's pre-condition must be satisfied when the preceding construct terminates. In hardware systems, components exist simultaneously and behave as independent processes. No predefined execution order exists so there is no means of implicitly determining when a component's pre-condition should hold. Consider the find example. The pre-condition of bin_search must hold only when sort has completed its transformation. At all other times, bin_search need only maintain its state.

VHDL provides sensitivity lists and **wait** statements to synchronize entity execution and define when a component in a structural architecture is active. VSPEC achieves the same end using the **sensitive to** clause. The **sensitive to** clause contains a predicate called the activation condition that indicates when an entity should begin executing. Effectively, this activation condition defines when a VSPEC annotated entity's precondition must hold. When the `sensitive to` predicate is true, the pre-condition must hold and the implementation must satisfy the post-condition. When the `sensitive to` predicate is false, the entity makes no contribution to the state of the system. In the `find` example, both components activate when any of their input signals change.

Formally, the contribution of the `sensitive to` clause to the transformation specified by VSPEC is easily represented using a traditional process algebra such as CSP [12]. Components become processes and events are defined as the states the entity enters. Thus, any VSPEC component can be described by a process that consumes states and generates a process in a new state. To define such state changes, a component state is defined along with a means for combining component states into an architecture state.

The formal VSPEC model of the state of a component is based on Chalin's state model [8, Chapter 6] for LCL. This model partitions the computational state of an LCL description into an environment and a store [14]. The environment maps (variable) identifiers into objects and the store binds objects to the values they contain:

```
Env: Id -> Obj
Store: Obj -> Value
```

Separating the environment and the store is common among formal models of programming language semantics. In a language such as LCL, one of the motivating factors for this is to allow multiple names for the same element of memory. For example, two C pointers can obviously reference the same memory location. The program state model above represents this situation by mapping each of these pointers to the same object in the *Env* map.

This partitioning of the state of a component is used in the VSPEC semantics to model component communication. For a single VSPEC-specified component, *Env* contains a map from each port and state variable in the VSPEC description to an object. *Store* maps each of these objects to their current value. We call this the *abstract state* of the VSPEC component. When VSPEC components are connected together to form an abstract architecture, the elements of *Env* and *Store* are slightly different. The *Store* contains objects for each port in the architecture's entity, for each signal in the architecture and for the state variables of each component in the architecture. The *Env* maps each of these three types of elements to the proper object, but it also maps the ports of each architecture component to the object that represents the architecture signal the port is connected to. We call the state model of an abstract architecture the *concrete state* of the component.

In the simple two component example of Figure 4, the abstract state of `system`, A and B are:

```
entity A is port                architecture struct of system is
  (x : in integer;              component A
   y : out integer);              port (x : in integer;
  requires IA(x);                            y : out integer);
  ensures OA(x,y'post);         end component;
  modifies y;                   component B
end A;                            port (w : in integer;
                                           z : out integer);
entity B is port                end component;
  (w : in integer;              signal c;
   z : out integer);
  requires IB(w);               begin
  ensures OB(w,z'post);           c1: A port map(sys_in,c);
  modifies z;                     c2: B port map(c,sys_out);
end B;                          end struct;

entity system is port
  (sys_in : in integer;
   sys_out : out integer);
end system;
```

Fig. 4. Example of two entities connected serially.

$$Env_{system} = \{sys\_in \mapsto obj_{sys\_in}, sys\_out \mapsto obj_{sys\_out}\}$$
$$Store_{system} = \{obj_{sys\_in} \mapsto v_{sys\_in}, obj_{sys\_out} \mapsto v_{sys\_out}\}$$
$$Env_A = \{x \mapsto obj_x, y \mapsto obj_y\}$$
$$Store_A = \{obj_x \mapsto v_x, obj_y \mapsto v_y\}$$
$$Env_B = \{w \mapsto obj_w, z \mapsto obj_z\}$$
$$Store_B = \{obj_w \mapsto v_w, obj_z \mapsto v_z\}$$

The concrete state of the **struct** architecture is:

$$Env_{struct_{system}} = \{sys\_in \mapsto obj_{sys\_in}, sys\_out \mapsto obj_{sys\_out}, c \mapsto obj_c,$$
$$x \mapsto obj_{sys\_in}, y \mapsto obj_c, w \mapsto obj_c, z \mapsto obj_{sys\_out}\}$$
$$Store_{struct_{system}} = \{obj_{sys\_in} \mapsto v_{sys\_in}, obj_{sys\_out} \mapsto v_{sys\_out}, obj_c \mapsto v_c\}$$

Notice that x, y, w and z now map to the objects that contain the values of the signals that these component ports are connected to in the architecture.

Using a component's state, its semantics are defined using a CSP process and its **requires** and **ensures** clauses. Let $f(St)$ be a function between two states of entity C that implements the requirements specified in C's **requires** and **ensures** clauses (i.e. $f(St)$ satisfies Equation 1). The process defining entity C with a **sensitive** to predicate $S(St)$ in any state r is:

$$C_r = r : \Psi \to C_{f(r)} \tag{2}$$

where Ψ is the set of states that satisfy C's activation condition: $\Psi = \{t : T_C \mid S(t)\}$.

The traces of the process defined by a VSPEC entity is a sequence of abstract states the entity enters. When the abstract state changes to an abstract state that satisfies the entity's activation condition (r in Equation 2), the transformation defined by the **requires** and **ensures** predicates ($f(St)$) is applied to r. This generates a new abstract state and the entity behaves like the process defined by $C_{f(r)}$. The abstract states that satisfy C's activation condition form the alphabet of C. Thus, every trace of C contains only elements from Ψ.

CSP's concurrency operator ($\parallel$) combines component processes to define the behavior of a VSPEC architecture. Let $C_1, C_2, ..., C_n$ be the processes represented by Equation 2 for the set of VSPEC component instances in architecture $\mathcal{A}$. The process representing architecture $\mathcal{A}$ is:

$$\mathcal{A} = C_1 \parallel C_2 \parallel ... \parallel C_n \tag{3}$$

When a state change occurs that satisfies some component's activation condition, the component performs its specified transformation to its abstract state. This change is propagated to the concrete state of the architecture where the activation condition of another component may be satisfied. This causes the process to repeat until the system changes to a concrete state where no component's activation condition is satisfied. The system then waits until some external device changes the concrete state to one that activates some component in the architecture to start the process again.

In the CSP model of a VSPEC process, this notion can be understood by examining the possible traces of $\mathcal{A}$ from Equation 3. Hoare [12] defines traces over parallel composition, $traces(C_1 \parallel C_2)$, as:

$$\{t \mid (t \uparrow \alpha C_1) \in traces(C_1) \wedge (t \uparrow \alpha C_2) \in traces(C_2) \wedge t \in (\alpha C_1 \cup \alpha C_2)^*\} \tag{4}$$

Recall that in CSP [12], $t \uparrow \alpha P$ restricts the trace t to contain only events that appear in the alphabet of P. Thus, the traces of a parallel composition of components are all traces that when restricted to the alphabet of each component yield a trace of that component. Furthermore, traces of $C_1 \parallel C_2$ only contain events from the alphabet of the two components. This means that every trace of $\mathcal{A}$ contains only elements that satisfy the activation condition of at least one component in $\mathcal{A}$.

4   Generating Semantic Models

VSPEC semantics are used to verify requirements by transforming VSPEC into Larch Shared Language equivalent representations and using the Larch Prover. The SAVANT VHDL parser [15] has been extended to recognize VSPEC components and generate LSL representations. To support translation, background theories representing: (i) VHDL data types; (ii) the store model; and (iii) the CSP semantics were implemented to provide underlying semantics. The resulting LSL models are suitable for various verification activities using the Larch Prover.

Extending the SAVANT parser to recognize VSPEC and generate LSL required extending the language recognizer and the AIRE intermediate form. The parser was extended in the canonical fashion to recognize and type check VSPEC components. To generate LSL representations, the AIRE intermediate form has been extended to include: (i) VSPEC constructs; and (ii) "publish" methods to generate LSL traits representing components and architectures.

Generating LSL representations for VHDL data types, the store model and CSP functions involves defining LSL theories for each construct. For each VHDL type, a parameterized trait was developed. When the associated type is used in a specification, the appropriate trait is included to provide a theory for that type in the LSL model. Similar techniques are used for the store and CSP models. LSL traits defined by Chalin [8] were reused here after some modification and reverification. For CSP functions, the CSP axiomatization developed by Camilleri [16] is adapted. Camilleri's original theories were developed in HOL [17], thus requiring translation to LSL and verification.

The only challenging task associated with translating Camilleri's CSP axiomatization involved moving from a higher order logic representation to a first order representation. Specifically, the CSP choice operation plays a major role in the VSPEC definition. In the HOL axiomatization, choice is parameterized over a choice operation. In LSL, this is achieved using a parameterized trait with the choice function as a parameter. The instantiation of the trait parameter is achieved at parse time requiring a new version of the choice trait to be instantiated for each instance of choice. The higher order representation allows instantiation of the choice function at proof time making for dramatically simpler proof activities.

Each VSPEC component is translated into an associated LSL trait. Brevity prevents the expansion of a component in this paper, however these traits share a common structure centering on: (i) the pre- and post-conditions; and (ii) the CSP choice operator. Specifically, the choice operator is specialized by specifying a choice function and an alphabet. The alphabet specifies what states can occur next and was defined as Ψ earlier. The choice function generates the next state and is defined using the pre- and post-condition of the component.

Figure 5 shows the template used to generate LSL traits for each system component. The trait is instantiated using the table shown in Table 1. In the template, operations I(pre) and O(pre,post) are instantiated with the VSPEC component's **requires** and **ensures** clauses respectively. The **sensitive to** clause is incorporated in the alphabet of the CSP process associated with each component. Recall that the alphabet of the component is defined to be the set of states satisfying the activation condition. Note that the **constrained by** clause is not involved in the definition. Performance constraints are evaluated using PDL as described in a later section.

```
trait_name (
  port_list %% Port symbols from entity
  state_variable_list %% State symbols from state clause
  I, O, modSet, modSet_event, input_event, Psi, InitStates,
  maintain_state, F, well_def_alpha, choice_F, choice_traces,
  choice, entity_process) : trait
includes
  OneComponent
includes
  includes_list %% Traits explicitly included by the entity
includes
  type_trait_list %% Traits included to define VHDL types
includes
  program_store_list %% Traits representing program store
introduces
  port_declaration_list %% Declaration of ports
  state_variable_declaration_list %% Declaration of state variables
asserts
  ∀ pre, post, any: Store
    InitStates_predicate;
  %% Value of outputs and state does not change from post state of
  %% one element of trace top the next element of the trace
    maintain_state(post,any) == maintain_state_predicate;
  %% Sensitive to clause defines Psi
    pre ∈ Psi == modified_sensitive_to_predicate;
  %% requires clause defines I
    I(pre) == modified_requires_predicate;
  %% ensures clause defines O
    O(pre,post) == modified_ensures_predicate;
  %% modifies clause defines modSet
    modSet == ({} \ins modifies_list);
    modSet_event(any) == modifies_event_list;
  %% True when an event occurs on an input signal
    input_event_assertion;
  %% All objects are active objects in store model
    active_objects_assertions;
  %% All objects above are independent of one another
    indep(empty \apd independent_objects_list);
    independent_objects_assertions;
```

Fig. 5. Template specialized to generate traits for single components.

5   Verification

Correctness checks in VSPEC take three fundamental forms: (i) component verification; (ii) interconnection verification; and (iii) bisimulation. Component and
interconnection verification represent partial correctness checks used to quickly
assess the quality of a specification. Bisimulation precisely defines the relationship between a VSPEC architecture and an associated system specification. Although component and interconnection verification only verify specific system
properties, they are frequently simpler to prove than bisimulation relationships.

Component verification allows users to specify properties of a single component using LSL. The component is transformed into an LSL trait and the Larch
Prover called with the property as a theorem. Component interconnections are
not considered and typically only the precondition, postcondition and activation
condition are included the verification. This is the simplest verification activity
and is used simply to verify properties of single VSPEC components.

Name from Template	Description
trait_name	*entity_name*_trait
port_list	Comma-separated list of all entity port names.
state_variable_list	Comma-separated list of all entity state variable names.
includes_list	Comma-separated list of names of all traits explicitly included in the entity.
type_trait_list	Comma-separated list of trait names that define the VHDL types needed in this entity.
program_store_list	Comma-separated list of sorted projections of the program store (SProjStore) needed in this trait.
port_declaration_list	LSL constant declaration for each port signal in the entity.
state_variable_declaration_list	LSL constant declaration for each state variable in the entity.
InitStates_predicate	Predicate to define initial Stores an entity can enter. Takes into account the initial value of all entity state variables.
maintain_state_predicate	Assertion that the value of all outputs and state variables does not change from Store post to Store any.
modified_sensitive_to_predicate	Entity's **sensitive** to clause predicate converted to LSL format with all port and state variable references replaced with call to Chalin's **val** operator for the proper Store (**pre** or **post**).
modified_requires_predicate	Entity's **requires** clause predicated converted to LSL format with all port and state variable references replaced with call to Chalin's **val** operator for the proper Store (**pre** or **post**).
modified_ensures_predicate	Entity's **ensures** clause predicated converted to LSL format with all port and state variable references replaced with call to Chalin's **val** operator for the proper Store (**pre** or **post**).
modifies_list	List of all modified port signals and state variables (including "implicitly" modified ones). The \ins operator separates each element in this list.
modifies_event_list	Assertion there is an event on the value of at least one modified object in Store any.
input_event_assertion	Disjunction of statements that an event occurred on an input signal in state any.
active_objects_assertions	Assertion of the form X \in activeObjs(any) for every object X (i.e. each signal and state variable) in the entity.
independent_objects_list	List of all objects in the entity. The \apd operator separates each element in this list.
independent_objects_assertions	One commented out assertion of the form ~depOn(dwn(x), dwn(y)) for every possible combination of port signals and state variables x and y.

Table 1. Summary of substitutions to create a trait for an associate entity using the entity template.

Interconnection verification examines specific relationships between components. As the name implies, interconnection verification centers primarily on properties of interconnected ports. In most cases, users select from pre-defined conditions. Proof obligations are generated and verified automatically in most cases. Specific examples of interconnection verifications include proving: (i) all outputs from a component are legal inputs to another; (ii) some output from a component will activate another; and (iii) all inputs activating a component are legal component inputs. Many similar, additional obligations can be generated and discharged automatically.

Bisimulation allows a user to verify that an abstract architecture correctly implements its requirements. This verification obligation is generated automatically by the VSPEC parser and is based on weak bisimulation [18]. A weak bisimulation (or simply bisimulation) condition holds when a sequence of states in the architecture (or concrete) model produces the desired single state change specified by the system level (or abstract) model (see Figure 6). Only the first and last state of the concrete state sequence are significant. The specific state sequence leading from the initial concrete state to the final concrete state is ignored.

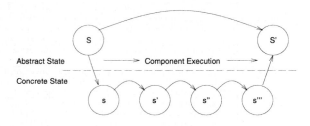

Fig. 6. Concrete state changes associated with a single abstract state change.

Equation 5 is a weak bisimulation correctness obligation for showing abstract architecture $\mathcal{A}$ satisfies a single abstract state change. Here, $\Psi_{\mathcal{A}}$ is the set of concrete states where the activation condition of at least one component in $\mathcal{A}$ is true. The obligation states that for all traces of the concrete state starting in a state whose abstract projection satisfies the abstract specification's pre-condition, either the resulting process state satisfies the component postcondition or the process can consume the state and continue.

$$\forall \tau : traces(\mathcal{A}) \cdot I(abs(\tau_0)) \wedge \mathcal{A}/\tau = \mathcal{A}_s \Rightarrow (O(abs(\tau_0), abs(s)) \vee s \in \Psi_{\mathcal{A}}) \quad (5)$$

In addition to functional verification, the current VSPEC tool suite supports constraint verification using The Performance Description Language (PDL) [19]. The semantics of constraints is defined using LSL in a fashion similar to the other VSPEC clauses. However, constraint evaluation requires significant manipulation of intervals. This activity proved to be exceptionally difficult in the Larch toolset.

PDL is a language designed explicitly for representing and evaluating constraint information. Specifically, PDL provides a mechanism for representing and evaluating interval mathematics representations. In PDL, designers define models for various constraint types. These models are then used to instantiate architectures of components. Each interconnected component is assigned one model for each constraint to be evaluated.

VSPEC constraint evaluation allows the user compare a systems level constraint description to an architectural description. For each VSPEC constraint, a PDL model has been defined. Each model minimally defines the data type associated with the constraint, and a function to combine two constraint values. An architecture is derived from the VHDL architecture and populated with the various constraint models. Using the PDL evaluator and the combine operators associated with each constraint, a system level constraint value is calculated. This value is then compared with the system level specification to determine if the architecture meets its associated systems level performance requirements.

6   VSPEC in Practice

VSPEC has been evaluated in both academic and industrial settings. Many example specifications have been written in the research setting. Two of which, the Move Machine and Find, represent significant milestones in the VSPEC life-cyle. More recently, TRW has used VSPEC to specify two significant avionics components.

6.1   The Move Machine

The first significant specification developed using VSPEC was done by Baraona [4]. The Move Machine is a simple CPU specification where operations are mapped to memory locations. The only operations performed by the Move Machine move data from one memory location to another. The Move Machine was specified as an instruction interpreter and at the register transfer level. Specifications were written, however no analysis was performed. The Move Machine exercise served to shake out initial problems in the VSPEC semantics. Although no verification was performed, the exercise represented the first actual VSPEC usage example. Furthermore, the example represents a common class of systems and provided an excellent usage example for early users.

6.2   Find

The Find system and architecture specifications presented in Figure 2 represent the first complete bisimulation verification activity performed using VSPEC. Like the Move Machine, Find was developed as a synthesis benchmark and exhibits some interesting modeling capabilities. Specifically, the use of activation conditions to model data caching. The Find architecture decomposes the problem into two components: (i) a sorting component; and (ii) a binary search component. The architecture is specified to cache the results of sorting so that if the input array does not change, it is not resorted. The result is a more efficient search.

Specifications similar to those presented in Figure 2 were written and parsed by the original VSPEC parser. Formal models were generated by the parser and the Larch Prover was used to perform the verification. For this example, the proof obligations necessary to show the bisimulation relationship were written by hand. Although the verification was completed successfully, this activity demonstrated limitations in using LSL and the Larch Prover for verifications of this size. The fundamental problem was the first order nature of LSL and the mechanisms used to specify the basic CSP theories.

6.3   Pulse Interval Processor

In an initial technology transfer effort, VSPEC was used jointly by TRW and The University of Cincinnati to model the Pulse Interval Processing (PIP) section of an Interrogate Friend or Foe (IFF) transponder. The IFF transponder redesign represents a real Digital Signal Processing (DSP) product being designed and fielded by TRW. Although VSPEC was not used in the actual design flow, we were given access to specifications and worked with engineers designing the system. Unfortunately the PIP architecture is proprietary to TRW and details of the specification cannot be presented here. However, several important results are presented.

The PIP is an interesting challenge problem because of its means of encoding information. The PIP's function is to: (i) receive pulses from a digital signal processing system; (ii) transform pulse trains into commands; and (ii) produce appropriate output in response to those commands. Commands are used by other aircraft and air traffic control systems to gather information about an aircraft's altitude, position, mission and origin. The PIP is a particularly interesting model because information is encoded in the time difference between received pulses. This presented an interesting specification challenge as VSPEC does not use a temporal logic.

The specification was written using LSL to represent pulse times and their associated receive times. Pulse streams are processed by examining each pulse with respect to the PIP state and receive time of the last pulse. When a pulse is received its receive time is stored in the PIP state. When a second pulse is received, the difference between its receive time and the stored receive time determines the command issued. The VSPEC state clause is used to maintain the last pulse received and a nested IF-THEN-ELSE statement is used to represent various processing cases.

The PIP specification was partially verified by automatically generating interconnect and component proof obligations. We were able to verify several interconnect conditions and TRW found one type error that had not been caught in the actual design flow. This error was not significant and would likely have been caught during design inspection or testing. No bisimulation relationships were specified or verified as the PIP architecture was established before beginning this specification task. As an extensive design activity for PIP preceded our efforts and this represented a redesign of a well understood system, the use of VSPEC did not seriously impact the actual design flow. However, design engineers commented that writing VSPEC made specification of test vectors much simpler. This represents an interesting and somewhat unexpected result.

6.4   Real Time Monitor

The Real Time Monitor (RTM) is a proprietary special purpose signal processor used in military aircraft avionics subsystems. It is similar to the PIP except it contains programmability features allowing it to process multiple pulse streams and recognize multiple protocols. The RTM processor was specified by TRW exclusively with only VSPEC language assistance from the developers. Little verification was performed due to time restraints on the overall project.

Although details of the activity are considered proprietary, TRW acknowledges that using VSPEC played a key role in reducing estimated product costs by 25%. They observed that although VSPEC increased cost and development time during requirements analysis and representation, early mitigation of errors, precise requirements capture and ease of test vector generation compensated for initial costs. Specifically, they reported that the result of the VSPEC specification activity resulted in much more precise and complete specifications. Even without extensive verification, they reported discovering and mitigating ambiguities in the specifications. Although only one legitimate error was discovered, using VSPEC forced them to be more precise in their specification activities. However, it should be noted that the primary motivation for writing VSPEC was a promise for automated verification, not more precise specifications.

An unexpected result was TRW's engineer's belief that having VSPEC specifications made defining and generating test vectors an easier task. In the design and implementation of avionics systems such as those developed by TRW, test vector generation and maintenance is a resource intensive task. TRW engineers reported that having VSPEC specifications made identification of test cases and definition of test vectors easier. Although unexpected, careful analysis indicates this result is not surprising. It should be the case that test vectors correspond with requirements and ultimately that is what they are designed to test. This result is being explored in a follow on effort to determine if VSPEC can systematically impact the testing process.

TRW commented further that mature tools integrated into VHDL design environments would contribute to potential cost savings. Although this represents a development task, it does indicate the importance of integrating formal methods into traditional design flows.

6.5   Evaluation Summary

The VSPEC language and tools were evaluated with respect to two internal and two industrial examples. Internal examples were evaluated by students at The University of Cincinnati. The first industrial example was evaluated jointly with TRW and the second evaluated solely by TRW. Table 2 represents specification and verification operations performed in each example. Each evaluation was completed to a large degree of success. Although language semantics and tool problems were certainly found, TRW is continuing to actively use VSPEC and continues to support tool development activities.

7   Related Work

Odyssey Research Associates (ORA) has developed Larch/VHDL, an alternative Larch interface language for VHDL [20]. Larch/VHDL is targeted for formal analysis of a VHDL description and ORA is defining a formal semantics for VHDL

Example	System Spec	Architecture Spec	Interconnect Verification	Bisimulation Verification
Move Machine	X	X		
Find	X	X	X	X
PIP		X	X	
RTM		X		

Table 2. Major VSPEC evaluation activities.

using LSL. The LSL representations are used in a traditional theorem prover to verify system correctness. Larch/VHDL annotations are added to a specific VHDL description to represent proof obligations for the verification process. This differs from VSPEC's purpose of representing requirements and design decisions at high levels of abstraction.

Augustin et al.'s VAL [21] is another attempt to annotate VHDL. The purpose of a VAL annotation to a VHDL description is to document the design for verification. VAL provides mechanisms for mapping a behavioral description to a structural description. Two VAL/VHDL descriptions of a design can be transformed into a self-checking VHDL program that is simulated to verify that the two descriptions implement the same function. This is once again slightly different than VSPEC's purpose of high level requirements representation.

The abstract architecture representation capabilities of VSPEC are also fairly closely related to several architecture description languages that have been developed to describe software architectures [22]. Some of the more well known architecture description are UniCon [23], WRIGHT [24, 25] and RAPIDE [26, 27]. Each of these languages allow the definition of components and connectors to define a software architecture. This is very similar to the VHDL notion of a structural architecture.

Allen and Garlan's WRIGHT language is of particular interest when discussing VSPEC because a WRIGHT component is defined with a variant of CSP. Unlike VSPEC's use of CSP to define component synchronization, WRIGHT uses CSP to define component behavior as well. A WRIGHT description consists of a collection of components interacting via instances of connector types. WRIGHT's CSP descriptions define the sequence of events a component or connector participates in.

8   Conclusions and Current Status

Several problems and complexities of the Larch-based semantics were discovered in our prototyping activities. In an effort to eliminate difficulties, the VSPEC semantics have been transformed into PVS [28] form. The use of higher order logic substantially simplifies the specification and verification of CSP properties. The VSPEC parser has been re-implemented in Java and generates PVS models in place of Larch. The higher order nature of PVS and maturity of its associate toolset will dramatically improve verification efficiency.

VSPEC is currently involved in several commercialization efforts. First, under Air Force and TRW sponsorship, the VSPEC toolset is being integrated with Mentor Graphics' Renoir development environment. This integration will allow VSPEC to be evaluated by engineers in their traditional design cycle. Second, under DARPA and EDAptive Computing sponsorship, VSPEC is being used to facilitate component retrieval by comparing component requirements with available components described by VSPEC. Comparing requirements with components formally supports high assurance in the quality of the match. Finally, under TRW sponsorship we have begun an effort to generate test vectors from VSPEC specifications.

This paper briefly presented the VSPEC language and its associated semantics. The semantics of single components were defined using a canonical axiomatic approach. Activation conditions were described and a CSP-base semantics provided. The use of VHDL architectures to describe abstract architectures was then discussed. The paper concluded with a presentation of examples used to evaluate the system and results of those activities.

References

[1] *IEEE Standard VHDL Language Reference Manual.* New York, NY, 1993.

[2] P. Alexander, P. Baraona, and J. Penix. Using Declarative Specifications and Case-Based Planning for System Synthesis. *Concurrent Engineering: Research and Applications*, 2(4), 1994.

[3] P. Alexander, P. Baraona, and J. Penix. Application of Software Synthesis Techniques to Composite Systems. In *Computers in Engineering Symposisum of the ASME ETCE*, Houston, TX, January 1995.

[4] P. Baraona, J. Penix, and P. Alexander. VSPEC: A Declarative Requirements Specification Language for VHDL. In Jean-Michel Berge, Oz Levia, and Jacques Rouillard, editors, *High-Level System Modeling: Specification Languages*, volume 3 of *Current Issues in Electronic Modeling*, chapter 3, pages 51–75. Kluwer Academic Publishers, Boston, MA, 1995.

[5] Phillip Baraona and Perry Alexander. Abstract architecture representation using VSPEC. *VLSI Design*, 9(2):181–201, 1999.

[6] J. Guttag, J. Horning, and J. Wing. The Larch Family of Specification Languages. *IEEE Software*, 2(5):24–36, 1985.

[7] John V. Guttag and James J. Horning. *Larch: Languages and Tools for Formal Specification.* Springer-Verlag, New York, NY, 1993.

[8] Patrice Chalin. *On the Language Design and Semantic Foundation of LCL, a Larch/C Interface Specification Language.* PhD thesis, Concordia University, Department of Computer Science, Montreal, Quebec, Canada, December 1995.

[9] John V. Guttag and James J. Horning. Introduction to LCL, A Larch/C Interface Language. Technical Report 74, Digital Equipment Corporation Systems Research Center, 130 Lytton Avenue, Palo Alto, CA 94301, July 1991.

[10] Gary T. Leavens. Larch/C++ Reference Manual. Available at: ftp://ftp.cs.iastate.edu/pub/larchc++/lcpp.ps.gz, 1995.

[11] David Guaspari, Carla Marceau, and Wolfgang Polak. Formal Verification of Ada Programs. *IEEE Transactions on Software Engineering*, 16(9):1058–1075, September 1990.

[12] C. A. R. Hoare. *Communicating Sequential Processes*. Prentice-Hall, Englewood Cliffs, 1985.

[13] Knowledge Based Software Engineering Laboratory, University of Cincinnati. *VSPEC Language Reference Manual*, 1996.

[14] R.D. Tennent. *Principles of Programming Languages*. Computer Science Series. Prentice-Hall International, 1981.

[15] P. A. Wilsey, D. E. Martin, and K. Subramani. Savant/tyvis/warped: Components for the analysis and simulation of vhdl. In *VHDL Users' Group Spring 1998 Conference*, pages 195–201, 1998.

[16] Albert John Camilleri. Mechanizing CSP trace theory in higher order logic. *IEEE Transactions on Software Engineering*, 16(9):993–1004, September 1990.

[17] M. J. C. Gordon. HOL: A proof generating system for higher-order logic. In G. Birtwistle and P. A. Subrahmanyam, editors, *Current Trends in Hardware Verification and Automated Theorem Proving*, pages 73–128. Springer-Verlag, 1989.

[18] Robin Milner. *A Calculus of Communicating Systems*, volume 92 of *Lecture Notes in Computer Science*. Springer-Verlag, Berlin, 1980.

[19] Ranga Vemuri, Ram Mandayam, and Vijay Meduri. Performance modeling using PDL. *Computer*, 29(4):44–53, April 1996.

[20] D. Jamsek and M. Bickford. Formal Verification of VHDL Models. Technical Report RL-TR-94-3, Rome Laboratory, Griffiss Air Force Base, NY, March 1994.

[21] L. Augustin, D. Luckham, B. Gennart, Y. Huh, and A. Stanculescu. *Hardware Design and Simulation in VAL/VHDL*. Kluwer Academic Publishers, Boston, MA, 1991.

[22] D. Garlan and M. Shaw. An Introduction to Software Architecture. In V. Ambriola and G. Tortora, editors, *Advances in Software Eng. and Knowledge Eng.*, volume 2, pages 1–39. World Scientific, New York, 1993.

[23] M. Shaw, R. DeLine, D. Klein, T. Ross, D. Young, and G. Zelesnik. Abstractions for Software Architecture and Tools to Support Them. *IEEE Transactions on Software Engineering*, 21(4):314–335, April 1995.

[24] R. Allen and D. Garlan. Formalizing Architectural Connection. In *Proc. Sixteenth International Conference on Software Engineering*, pages 71–80, May 1994.

[25] R. Allen and D. Garlan. A Case Study in Architectural Modelling: The AEGIS System. In *Proceedings of the 8th International Workshop on Software Specification and Design*, March 1996.

[26] D. Luckham, J. Kenney, L. Augustin, J. Vera, D. Bryan, and W. Mann. Specification and Analysis of System Architecture Using Rapide. *IEEE Transactions on Software Engineering*, 21(4):315–355, April 1995.

[27] D. Luckham and J. Vera. An Event-Based Architecture Definition Language. *IEEE Transactions on Software Engineering*, 21(9):717–734, September 1995.

[28] Judy Crow, John Rushby, Natarajan Shankar, and Mandayan Srivas. *A Tutorial Introduction to PVS*. SRI International, Menlo Park, CA, June 1995. Presented at WIFT'95.

Enhancing the Pre- and Postcondition Technique for More Expressive Specifications

Gary T. Leavens and Albert L. Baker

Department of Computer Science, Iowa State University
226 Atanasoff Hall, Ames, Iowa 50011-1040 USA
phone: +1 515 294 1580, fax: +1 515 294 1580
http://www.cs.iastate.edu/~leavens/index.html
http://www.cs.iastate.edu/~baker/baker.html
leavens@cs.iastate.edu and baker@cs.iastate.edu

Abstract. We describe enhancements to the pre- and postcondition technique that help specifications convey information more effectively. Some enhancements allow one to specify redundant information that can be used in "debugging" specifications. For instance, adding examples to a specification gives redundant information that may aid some readers, and can also be used to help ensure that the specification says what is intended. Other enhancements allow improvements in frame axioms for object-oriented (OO) procedures, better treatments of exceptions and inheritance, and improved support for incompletely-specified types.

Many of these enhancements were invented by other authors, but are not widely known. They have all been integrated into Larch/C++, a Larch-style behavioral interface specification language for C++. However, such enhancements could also be used to make other specification languages more effective tools for communication.

Keywords: specification language design, expressiveness, liberal specification, redundancy, debugging, history constraint, Larch.

1 Introduction

1.1 Background and Motivation

The pre- and postcondition technique was described by Hoare in his classic article [26]. This technique forms the basis of most contemporary specification languages for sequential systems [1, 15, 16, 18, 23, 28, 31, 41, 40, 42, 43, 47, 50, 51]. (However, Z [24, 52] is an exception, as Z preconditions are not explicitly stated, but instead are calculated from the specification given [60, Chapter 14].)

We take as our starting point an excellent article by Jonkers [30], which, like this paper, is addressed to specification language designers. Jonkers says (page 428):

J. Wing, J. Woodcock, J. Davies (Eds.): FM'99, Vol. II, LNCS 1709, pp. 1087–1106, 1999.
© Springer-Verlag Berlin Heidelberg 1999

"Nowadays the pre- and postcondition technique is considered a standard technique in software development as it is being taught in almost every basic software engineering course. This gives the impression that the technique has fully matured and that it can be applied everyday in software development practice. The fact that this is not really the case is camouflaged by the sloppy and informal way pre- and postconditions are generally used in practice."

Besides reconstructing the pre- and postcondition technique, Jonkers describes several enhancements. These enhancements are found in the specification language COLD-1 [15]. The following briefly summarizes the enhancements COLD-1 makes over previous specification languages, such as VDM [1, 16, 28] and other languages in the Larch family [23]:

- Dependent variables, the declaration of which allows the dependent variable to be modified whenever the variables it depends on are modified. Dependent variables can be specified either directly, or indirectly using pre- and postconditions. (See also Leino's work on dependencies [37].)
- Fine-grained frame axioms using wild cards and expressions, which allow one to specify the variables that can be changed more concisely and precisely.
- Let clauses, which allow the introduction of local named abbreviations.
- Some extensions for the specification of reactive systems.

1.2   Contribution

Our work extends Jonker's work in that all the extensions we discuss in this paper are new with respect to COLD-1. Many enhancements that we describe are the work of other authors. Except for the ideas of user-selectable partial vs. total correctness, and certain forms of redundancy, it is not our intention to claim the other enhancements as our own. Instead we wish to highlight them so that they might become more widely known and used in specification language design.

We show how all these enhancements are integrated in Larch/C++ [32, 33], a Larch-style behavioral interface specification language for C++. Larch/C++ adopts most of the COLD-1 extensions, except for the technical ideas for fine-grained frame axioms and the extensions for the specification of reactive systems, and includes the enhancements discussed below. This integration enhances the rhetorical effectiveness and utility of Larch/C++.

Nevertheless, the enhancements we discuss would apply equally well to other specification languages, including those outside the Larch family. That is, the ideas themselves are not specific to Larch/C++ or even to Larch, but to the pre- and postcondition technique generally.

We believe that specifications written using these enhancements provide more precise and more easily understandable contracts. Briefly, we hope that our enhancements make specifications more expressive.

By *more expressive* we mean that the specifications convey information more immediately to the reader. That is, in this paper we care not so much about what can be expressed, but how easy it is to express and understand.

It is beyond the scope of this paper to experimentally validate our hopes for increased expressiveness. Instead, we claim just to demonstrate the plausibility of increased expressiveness by showing suggestive examples, and leave for later experiential or experimental validation. What we present is a necessary first step. Furthermore, we believe that too little attention is paid to the expressiveness of specifications in the formal methods and reuse communities. We believe that it would be interesting to investigate the degree to which the expressiveness of formal methods affects their use and cost-effectiveness.

We also claim that some of the enhancements we describe can increase the quality of specifications. This is particularly true of the redundancy enhancements described in Section 5, which can be used to check that the specification says what is intended [55, 54, 56].

1.3   Overview

In Section 2 below we show how to allow the specifier to choose either total or partial correctness specifications. In Section 3, we describe a syntactic sugar, "case analysis," that helps break specifications up into more easily understood pieces. In Section 4, we describe some improvements to frame axioms. In Section 5, we describe how to add redundancy, including examples, to specifications. In Section 6, we describe "history constraints" that can constrain how states can change. Finally, we offer some conclusions.

2   Liberal Specifications

Most pre- and postcondition-based specification languages have a *total correctness* [13] semantics. That is, a specification such as Figure 1 must always terminate if the precondition is satisfied.

```
extern void inc(int& i) throw();
//@ behavior {
//@   requires assigned(i, pre) /\ i^ < INT_MAX;
//@   modifies i;
//@   ensures i' = i^ + 1;
//@ }
```

Fig. 1. The Larch/C++ specification of the C++ function inc.

(In Figure 1, the first line gives the C++ function's interface. It says that inc takes an integer argument passed by reference, returns nothing, and may not throw exceptions. The behavior of inc is specified in the remaining lines. The precondition starts with the keyword requires, and the postcondition with the keyword ensures. The notation i^ is the pre-state value of the variable i, and i' is its post-state value. The notation assigned(i, pre) means that i has been assigned a proper value in the pre-state; /\ means "and". The modifies clause is a frame axiom, which says that only the object i can have its value changed.)

A *partial correctness*, or *liberal*, semantics means that when the precondition is satisfied, then if the procedure terminates, the postcondition must hold. However, termination is not required. By termination, we mean return to the caller of a procedure, either normally or by throwing an exception. Infinite loops, jumps to other parts of the program, and program abortion are not termination.

In Larch/C++, users can specify procedures using either the total or partial correctness semantics. Specifications that use just the keyword ensures have a total correctness semantics, and those that use ensures liberally have a partial correctness semantics. (The keyword liberally is inspired by Dijkstra's terminology [13]; it has been suggested that on exit might be better.)

One use for partial correctness specifications, as in Hoare's original work [26], is to avoid finiteness issues. For example, instead of specifying inc as in Figure 1, one could drop the precondition conjunct i^ < INT_MAX and use ensures liberally in the postcondition. In this altered specification, the postcondition would only need to be satisfied if the procedure terminated; for example, a correct implementation could abort the program if the result could not be represented. As a contract this is less precise since no call need terminate, but it is shorter.

Such finiteness issues often arise in allocation routines, such as C++ constructors. For example, if an implementation of a constructor might plausibly need to allocate some memory from the heap, a total correctness specification would have to describe the circumstances in which there is enough memory available. Not only would such a specification be tedious and longer, but it might also overly constrain implementations. The problem is that there is no way to know how much memory all possible implementations might need.

Although one might specify that a very generous amount of memory is required for termination, doing so with just a total correctness specification would impose no obligation at all on implementations when the very generous amount was not available. In Larch/C++, one can combine total and partial correctness specifications for the same procedure, and thus more precisely specify both when a call must terminate and what must be true on termination. The semantics of such combinations uses the ideas of Dijkstra and others [13, 46, 25].

Another way out of the difficulty with allocation routines would be to change the meaning of total correctness. For example, one could use a variation on Poetzsch-Heffter's semantics [49, page 48] and require termination only if no memory allocation errors occur.

However, there are other uses for partial correctness. A prime use is in specifying when a procedure must not terminate. A simple example is the C++ **abort** procedure, which can be specified as in Figure 2. This procedure can always be called, but when called must abort program execution instead of terminating, and hence cannot be specified with a total correctness semantics.

```
void abort();
//@ behavior {
//@    ensures liberally false;
//@ }
```

Fig. 2. Specification of `abort`.

The use of partial correctness, together with case analysis (see below), allows one to specify exactly under what conditions a procedure must not terminate. This technique is useful in precisely specifying contracts for procedures written for languages (or compilers) without exception handling. This idea appears in sugared form in the LCL `checks` clause [23, 55, 54, 56].

Partial correctness is also useful for specifying procedures for which there is no known totally-correct implementation. Interpreters for Turing-complete languages are examples.

3   Case Analysis

A simple syntactic sugar, which we call *case analysis*, is helpful in breaking up specifications into more manageable chunks, and in specifying procedures that can throw exceptions. Its advantage over special-purpose notations for exceptions (as in LM3 [29, 23], to cite just one example) is that it is also useful for other kinds of case analysis This sugar was pioneered by Wing [59, Section 4.1.4]. The idea is that a specification can be split into several cases, all of which must be satisfied by a correct implementation. This concept was independently reinvented by Wills [57]. Wills called specification cases "capsules", and used them effectively in OO specifications.

In Larch/C++, specification cases are separated by the keyword **also**. Consider the example of Figure 3. This example shows a specification with two cases. The first case specifies an exception, the second the function's "normal" behavior, which is to set each element of the argument array to zero. (The notation \A means "for all".)

The desugaring of a specification with case analysis turns it into a specification with a single total correctness and a single partial correctness case. Each

```
#include "BadSize.h"
extern void ZeroArray(double x[], int n) throw(BadSize);
//@ behavior {
//@     requires n <= 0;
//@     ensures throws(BadSize);
//@   also
//@     requires 0 < n /\ n <= size(x) /\ allocated(x, pre);
//@     modifies x;
//@     ensures returns
//@            /\ (\A i: int ((0 <= i /\ i < n) => x'[i] = 0.0));
//@ }
```

Fig. 3. Specification of the C++ function `ZeroArray`. The predicate `throws(BadSize)` is true when the function terminates and throws the named exception; `returns` is true when the function terminates normally. The predicate `allocated(x, pre)` is true when `x` is allocated in the pre-state.

such desugared case has as its precondition the disjunction (written \/) of the preconditions of each corresponding case, and as its postcondition a conjunction of implications, with each precondition implying (written =>) the corresponding postcondition. For example, the specification in Figure 4 is the desugaring of the specification in Figure 3. We think that Figure 3 is significantly easier to understand.

The interaction of frame axioms with this desugaring is subtle. The frame for the desugared specification has to allow all modifications permitted in each original case, since that permission is needed by the whole procedure. To keep the original meaning, however, the operator **unchanged** is used as needed in each case. For example, in Figure 4, `unchanged(x)` is conjoined to the original first case's postcondition.

With just this sugar, however, precondition conjuncts that are shared among cases would have to be repeated in each case. To avoid such repetition, cases in Larch/C++ can be put in the scope of a precondition (and can also be nested). For example, in Figure 5, the precondition `assigned(s, pre)` applies to both cases. The desugaring first conjoins the outer precondition to each of the inner ones, and applies the previous desugaring. Extracting common parts of preconditions like this also highlights them for the reader. (We attach no special semantics to such common preconditions, unlike Poetzsch-Heffter [49, pages 96-97].)

For OO specification languages, Wills pointed out that one can understand inheritance of specifications as meaning that subtype objects must satisfy the cases specified for them explicitly, as well as those of their supertypes. This ensures that subtyping is behavioral [11, 42]; that is, subtype objects can be reused according to their supertypes' contracts.

```
#include "BadSize.h"
extern void ZeroArray(double x[], int n) throw(BadSize);
//@ behavior {
//@    requires n <= 0 \/ (0 < n /\ n <= size(x) /\ allocated(x, pre));
//@    modifies x;
//@    ensures ((n <= 0) => (throws(BadSize) /\ unchanged(x)))
//@           /\ ((0 < n /\ n <= size(x) /\ allocated(x, pre))
//@                => (returns
//@                     /\ \A i: int ((0 <= i /\ i < n) => x'[i] = 0.0)));
//@ }
```

Fig. 4. Desugared specification of `ZeroArray`.

4 Framing

A frame axiom in a procedure specification says that "nothing else changes" [5]. VDM and Z both have features to permit the specification of frame axioms (write permissions in VDM, and Δ in Z). In the Larch family, interface specifications languages have followed Wing's design for Larch/CLU [58] in using the `modifies` clause to say that only the objects listed may have their abstract values changed.

In Larch/C++, the meaning of the `modifies` clause "`modifies i;`" is translated by a predicate like the following (see [33, Section 6.2.3.4] for exact details), which can be thought of as conjoined to the postcondition.

   `ModifiedObjects(pre, post) \subseteq {i, residue_i}`

In the above, the term `ModifiedObjects(pre, post)` denotes the set of all objects modified in the transition from the pre-state to the post-state, and `\subseteq` is a subset operator. The object `residue_i` stands for whatever objects i may depend on that are not in scope [37, Section 11.3]. The `modifies` clause gives considerable notational abbreviation, because it asserts that all objects not mentioned retain their values.

4.1 Trashing

In the Larch family, predicates use the logic of the Larch Shared Language, which is a logic of total functions [21, 35]. In such a logic, the pre- and post-states, which are modeled by functions, will return proper values for objects that are not allocated or that are not assigned a proper value. To avoid ill-defined specifications, it is important that a specification written in such a logic ensures that whenever an object's value is mentioned in a given state, the object is allocated (i.e., found in the domain of the state function), and assigned (i.e., given a proper value). If this is not done, then logical problems may occur [8, 27, 36].

```
#include "Stack.h"
#include "BadSize.h"
extern void pop2(Stack & s) throw(BadSize);
//@ behavior {
//@   requires assigned(s, pre);
//@   {
//@      requires size(s^) < 2;
//@      ensures throws(BadSize);
//@   also
//@      requires size(s^) >= 2;
//@      modifies s;
//@      ensures returns /\ s' = pop(pop(s));
//@      ensures redundantly size(s') = size(s^) - 2;
//@   }
//@ }
```

Fig. 5. Specification of `pop2`. The `ensures redundantly` clause is explained below.

To avoid such problems in the semantics of the `modifies` clause, the set `ModifiedObjects(pre, post)` can only include objects that are assigned values in both the pre- and post-states and change their values, or that are allocated in the pre-state and become assigned in the post-state.

However, in C++ and other languages without garbage collection, procedures can *trash* an object, either by deallocating it or by making it unassigned (for example, by "uninitializing" it from an unassigned variable). Since these actions are not considered modifications, they are not covered by the `modifies` clause. However, without additional support from the specification language, specifiers would have to make assertions about which objects remain allocated and assigned in each postcondition [7], which would be inconvenient and verbose.

To avoid having users write in postconditions assertions about what is not trashed, Chalin [7] argued for a second part to the frame axiom in Larch interface specifications. In Larch/C++ this is called the `trashes` clause. Only the objects listed in the `trashes` clause may be trashed; hence all objects not mentioned must remain assigned and allocated if they were in the pre-state, and an omitted `trashes` clause means that nothing may be trashed.

As with the `modifies` clause, the `trashes` clause is a permission, not a requirement to trash the objects mentioned. Consider the example in Figure 6 [33, Section 6.3.2.1]. The object pointed to by `cp` may be trashed, since it is mentioned in the `trashes` clause. The postcondition says that it must be trashed when the value of `ref_count` drops to 0, but may not be otherwise.

```
extern void dec_ref(char *cp, int & ref_count) throw();
//@ behavior {
//@    requires allocated(cp, pre) /\ assigned(ref_count, pre)
//@        /\ ref_count^ >= 1;
//@    modifies ref_count;
//@    trashes *cp;
//@    ensures ref_count' = ref_count^ - 1
//@        /\ (if ref_count' = 0 then trashed(*cp) else ~trashed(*cp));
//@    ensures redundantly ref_count^ > 1 => ~trashed(*cp);
//@    example ref_count^ = 1 /\ ref_count' = 0 /\ trashed(*cp);
//@ }
```

Fig. 6. Specification of the C++ function dec_ref. The ensures redundantly and example clauses are explained below.

In Larch/C++, the meaning of the trashes clause "trashes *cp;" is translated by a predicate like the following (see [33, Section 6.2.3.4] for details), which can be thought of as conjoined to the postcondition.

TrashedObjects(pre, post) \subseteq {*cp, residue_star_cp}

As above, the object residue_star_cp stands for whatever objects *cp may depend on that are not in scope [37, Section 11.3].

5   Redundancy

A *redundant* part of a specification does not itself form part of the contract, but instead is a formalized commentary on it. By allowing a specifier to state redundant properties explicitly, a specification language becomes more expressive. First, it allows specifiers to state properties that are important for readers, without cluttering up the main parts of the specification. More importantly, redundant parts, since they are marked as redundant, allow checking of the main parts of the specification. One important benefit is that the reader can check his or her understanding of the main parts against the redundant parts. Another benefit is that the specifier can record more of the thinking that went into the specification; for example, various examples or properties of the specification may be thought of first, and these do not have to be dropped when a more general form is discovered.

The Larch family has emphasized the benefit of checking how well a specification captures the specifier's intuition by comparing the redundant parts against the main parts; such checking is called "debugging" a specification [17]. For example, the Larch Shared Language incorporates features that can be used to state redundant claims about theories [23, Chapter 7].

5.1   Redundant Postconditions

Tan's work on LCL introduced redundancy into a specification language with
pre- and postconditions [55, 54, 56]. Of particular relevance here are Tan's "procedure claims," which state redundant properties that follow from the main part
of a specification. In Larch/C++, one can use an ensures redundantly clause
to state procedure claims. For example, in Figure 5 the ensures redundantly
clause in the second specification case highlights a property of that case; it says
that the stack's size decreases by two. Another example occurs in Fig 6.

To use redundant postconditions in debugging a specification, for each such
redundancy claim, one would try to prove the following, where *Pre* is the case's
precondition, *Frame* is the predicate that translates its frame axioms, *Post* is its
postcondition, and *RedunPost* is the claimed redundant postcondition [55, 54, 56]
[33, Section 6.8]. (All of these should be in their desugared forms.)

$$Pre \land Frame \land Post \Rightarrow RedunPost \tag{1}$$

5.2   Examples

When we give problem statements to students, we observe that many students
primarily focus on examples. By adding examples as another form of redundancy
to specifications one gains the benefits of additional redundancy as well as the
ability to convey more clearly what is to be done. (Examples as part of interface
specifications first appeared in Larch/C++ [32].) For instance, in Figure 7, examples are used to show that isqrt is underspecified; the two examples given
show different approximations that may be returned for the square root of 31.

```
extern unsigned int isqrt(unsigned int & x) throw();
//@ behavior {
//@    requires assigned(x, pre);
//@    ensures (result-1)*(result-1) < x^ /\ x^ < (result+1)*(result+1);
//@    example x^ = 31 /\ result = 6;
//@    example x^ = 31 /\ result = 5;
//@ }
```

Fig. 7. Specification of the C++ function isqrt.

One might wonder whether examples are needed when one has case analysis;
for example, why not specify isqrt as in Figure 8? One reason is that this style
of specifying examples would not mark the examples as redundant for the reader.
Worse, the specification in Figure 8 is inconsistent, because it says that when x
is 31, the result must be both 5 and 6.

```
extern unsigned int isqrt(unsigned int & x) throw();
//@ behavior {
//@  requires assigned(x, pre);
//@  {
//@     ensures (result-1)*(result-1) < x^ /\ x^ < (result+1)*(result+1);
//@  also
//@     requires x^ = 31;
//@     ensures result = 6;
//@  also
//@     requires x^ = 31;
//@     ensures result = 5;
//@  }
//@ }
```

Fig. 8. A bad (inconsistent) specification of isqrt; this shows how examples are different than specification cases.

Examples can also be used to help debug specifications. What should be checked is that an example, together with the frame, describes a pair of states that are in the relation specified by the specification's main parts. In terms of predicates, this means that for each example, one should prove the following, where *Example* is the example predicate, and *Pre*, *Frame*, and *Post* are as before.

$$(Example \land Frame) \Rightarrow (Pre \Rightarrow (Frame \land Post)) \qquad (2)$$

By predicate calculus, this is the same as the following.

$$(Example \land Frame \land Pre) \Rightarrow Post \qquad (3)$$

We believe that it is best to give examples that do not contradict the precondition of a specification; hence it is also worthwhile to check that the conjunction of the example predicate, frame, and precondition is consistent.

The reason why the frame is conjoined to the example predicate in Formula 2 is to avoid forcing the specifier to state what objects are not modified in examples. For instance, in Figure 7, if the frame axiom were not conjoined to the example predicate, then there would be no way to prove that the example and the precondition imply the frame and the postcondition for that example, since the example predicate says nothing about the value of x in the post-state.

5.3   Redundant Preconditions

One can also apply the idea of redundancy to the precondition. The **requires redundantly** clause in Larch/C++ is the analog of the **ensures redundantly** clause for the precondition. It allows one to state redundant preconditions. Redundant preconditions are sometimes useful for pointing out to the reader properties that follow from the semantics of the specification language, such as that certain objects are allocated or assigned. For example, in Figure 9, the requires redundantly clause highlights the fact that reference arguments are implicitly required to be allocated, and that unsigned integers are non-negative.

```
extern unsigned int isqrt(unsigned int & x) throw();
//@ behavior {
//@    requires assigned(x, pre);
//@    requires redundantly allocated(x, pre) /\ x^ >= 0;
//@    ensures (result-1)*(result-1) < x^ /\ x^ < (result+1)*(result+1);
//@    example x^ = 31 /\ result = 6;
//@    example x^ = 31 /\ result = 5;
//@ }
```

Fig. 9. A specification of isqrt that shows the use of requires redundantly.

To use the requires redundantly clause in debugging a specification, one would prove the following, where again *Pre* is the desugared precondition, and *RedunPre* is the redundant precondition.

$$Pre \Rightarrow RedunPre \tag{4}$$

It would be possible to have an analog of the example clause for preconditions, say with an example input clause. The example input predicates would be used in debugging the specification by checking that they are consistent with the precondition. Example inputs are not included in the current version of Larch/C++ [33], because we have not found a great need for them.

5.4   Redundant Frames

Larch/C++ was also the first interface specification language to extend the idea of redundancy to the modifies and trashes clauses. In Larch/C++, one can use modifies redundantly and trashes redundantly clauses. One use for such clauses is to highlight objects that are implicitly allowed to be modified or trashed because some explicitly named object has been declared to depend on them [37]. The debugging of redundant frames is analogous to that used for redundant preconditions; that is, one would prove that the permissions that are claimed to be redundant follow from the language's semantics and the explicit permissions.

5.5   An Alternative Design for Redundancy

We now briefly describe an alternative design for redundancy that has been considered for Larch/C++, but never adopted. We are experimenting with it in our specification language for Java [34], and it may be of interest to other specification language designers.

The idea is that instead of having clauses that allow the specification of redundancy, that one label entire specification cases as redundant or examples. For example, one might write the specification of Figure 6 as in Figure 10.

```
extern void dec_ref(char *cp, int & ref_count) throw();
//@ behavior {
//@    requires allocated(cp, pre) /\ assigned(ref_count, pre)
//@        /\ ref_count^ >= 1;
//@    modifies ref_count;
//@    trashes *cp;
//@    ensures ref_count' = ref_count^ - 1
//@        /\ (if ref_count' = 0 then trashed(*cp) else ~trashed(*cp));
//@ }
//@ behavior redundantly {
//@    requires allocated(cp, pre) /\ assigned(ref_count, pre)
//@        /\ ref_count^ > 0;
//@    modifies ref_count;
//@    trashes *cp;
//@    ensures ref_count^ > 1 => ~trashed(*cp);
//@ }
//@ example {
//@    requires ref_count^ = 1;
//@    modifies ref_count;
//@    trashes *cp
//@    ensures ref_count' = 0 /\ trashed(*cp);
//@ }
```

Fig. 10. An alternative style for writing redundancy into specifications. This is not part of Larch/C++, but given in a Larch/C++ style.

One advantage of this style is that it more cleanly separates the redundant parts of a specification from the main parts. Also, examples seem clearer, because the descriptions of the pre- and post-states are separated into the requires and ensures clauses of the example.

The disadvantage of this style is that the specifications become somewhat more verbose. In a `behavior redundantly` clause, one must repeat the precondition and frame, which is not necessary with `ensures redundantly`. While an example clause does not need to repeat the precondition, it does seem necessary to repeat the frame in examples, because this keeps the semantics of an omitted modifies or trashes clause uniform. However, there might be ways of making this more palatable.

6   History Constraints

Many specification languages allow one to state invariants for the values of an abstract data type (ADT). An invariant property is one that must be true of each object of the ADT in all visible states. A *visible* state is one that can be observed by clients of the ADT. Such invariants can be seen as an expressive way to state properties that would otherwise have to be repeated in every operation's pre- and postcondition. However, invariants are not mere notational abbreviations, because they apply to all operations, even when new ones are added to an ADT.

Liskov and Wing introduced a similar idea as an aid to specifying OO programs that use behavioral subtyping [39, 38]. A *history constraint* for a type describes a property of objects of that type (and all subtypes) that must hold for any ordered pair of visible states in a computation, where the first state occurs before the second. To make sense, such a property must describe a reflexive and transitive relation on states. History constraints, if not stated as such, would otherwise have to be repeated in every operation's postcondition. However, history constraints are not mere notational abbreviations, because they apply to all operations, even new ones added in subtypes.

A simple example is the constraint that some field of an object never changes its value, once initialized. For instance, in the specification of a BoundedStack class in Larch/C++, one might write the following history constraint, to state that a Stack's field max_size never changes.

```
//@ constraint max_size^ = max_size';
```

The max_size field is allowed to be initialized, because history constraints do not apply to constructors, as the pre-state value of the object is not visible. (Technically, in Larch/C++ this is because the field has not yet been assigned a proper value upon entry to a constructor.) For analogous reasons history constraints do not apply to destructors. However, the example constraint does say that one *cannot* list make_size in a modifies clause for a normal operation (C++ member function) of the type BoundedStack. It thus collects information that would otherwise be spread out in all the modifies clauses of all the operations. Furthermore, the immutability of a field like this would only be written negatively, by not being listed in all these modifies clauses. Finally, the immutability of a field could be changed by new operations or by subtypes if it were not listed in the history constraint.

History constraints can also be used to succinctly express monotonic relationships between pre- and post-states. For example, the Larch/C++ manual's specification of a class Person [33, Section 7.1.1], includes the following history constraint, which expresses the inexorable arrow of time.

```
//@ constraint age^ <= age';
```

To allow debugging of invariants and history constraints, Larch/C++ also allows one to state redundant invariants and history constraints, using `invariant redundantly` and `constraint redundantly` clauses.

An innovation in Larch/C++ is that one can limit a history constraint so that it only applies to various named operations [11] [33, Section 7.4]. This can be used to collect common, monotonic, parts of the postconditions of several operations in one place. A more general version of this idea was advocated by Borgida *et al.* as an approach to dealing with frame axioms [5]. The form found in Larch/C++ is useful in specifying history constraints for types that are intended as supertypes of weak behavioral subtypes [11, 10] [33, Section 7.8]. However, an explanation of weak behavioral subtyping is outside the scope of this paper.

7   Other Related Work

Our goal of making pre- and postcondition specifications more expressive is also served by the refinement calculus [2, 3, 4, 43, 44, 45]. The major extension in the refinement calculus is the use of abstract programs as specifications. These are programs that may include specification statements (and other kinds of nonconstructive statements). This makes it possible to specify higher-order procedures conveniently, and is particularly useful in component-based or event-driven settings [6]. However, this extension is orthogonal to the techniques we have discussed.

The work of Perry on Inscape [48] also has as one of its goals making pre- and postcondition specifications more practical. It adds to postconditions the notion of an obligation, which clients are expected to satisfy eventually. Again, this extension is orthogonal to those discussed in this paper. Inscape also splits preconditions up into three kinds, although none of them are redundant and thus cannot be used for debugging specifications. Perry's Instress tool uses static analysis to help debug programs, not specifications.

The Extended Static Checker from Compaq SRC [9] carries on this tradition of static analysis using specifications to help debug programs; again the work is not aimed at helping debug specifications. The specifications used in this checker do, however, have some additional constructs for more expressive framing than what is described in this paper.

Our emphasis on expressiveness in specifications can be seen as following the emphasis on expressive notation in the "calculational school" of Dijkstra, Gries, and others (see, e.g., [12, 14, 19, 20]). These authors have considerably adapted standard mathematical notations to be more consistent and communicative. However, they have not directed much attention to the pre- and postcondition technique itself. Similarly, the specification language Z has a great variety of notational refinements, but these refinements are not aimed at the pre- and postcondition technique.

8   Conclusions

In this paper we have described several enhancements to the pre- and postcondition technique for specifications. These enhancements contribute to the expressiveness of Larch/C++, and could be adapted to other specification languages. We have suggested how the enhancements help the specifier communicate more effectively with potential clients and implementors. Moreover, they do not result in any loss of formal rigor.

In our experience, the most significant of these enhancements is the ability to add redundant examples to specifications. In addition to their potential use in debugging specifications, we have found that they can help make specifications clearer. We are also excited about their potential for automated testing [22].

Besides examples, the enhancement we use most often is case analysis [59, Section 4.1.4] [57]. This is helpful in stating specifications of procedures that may throw exceptions. However, since it is more general than a special-purposed notation for exceptions, it is also useful in breaking up the logic of a specification into more easily understood parts.

Even if specification language designers do not like our syntax, we hope they will address the issues we have raised and go beyond them. We also look forward to experimental tests of the expressiveness of these enhancements, and the eventual refinement of our ideas by that research.

Acknowledgments

Thanks to Yoonsik Cheon, Krishna Kishore Dhara, Matt Markland, and Clyde Ruby for their work on Larch/C++. Thanks to Patrice Chalin, Peter Müller, and Rustan Leino for several discussions about the semantics of Larch/C++. Thanks to Kishore, Peter, Rustan, and Arnd Poetzsch-Heffter, for many helpful suggestions about an earlier draft of this paper.

The work of both authors was supported in part by the National Science Foundation under Grant CCR-9803843. Leavens's work was also supported in part under Grant CCR-9503168.

References

[1] Derek Andrews. *A Theory and Practice of Program Development*. FACIT. Springer-Verlag, London, UK, 1997.
[2] R. J. R. Back. A calculus of refinements for program derivations. *Acta Informatica*, 25(6):593–624, August 1988.
[3] R. J. R. Back and J. von Wright. Combining angels, deamons and miracles in program specifications. *Theoretical Computer Science*, 100(2):365–383, June 1992.
[4] Ralph-Johan Back and Joakim von Wright. *Refinement Calculus: A Systematic Introduction*. Springer-Verlag, 1998.
[5] Alex Borgida, John Mylopoulos, and Raymond Reiter. '... and nothing else changes': The frame problem in procedure specification. In *Proceedings Fifteenth International Conference on Software Engineering, Baltimore*, May 1993. Preliminary version obtained from the authors.

[6] Martin Büchi and Emil Sekerinski.   Formal methods for component software: The refinement calculus perspective.   In *Proceedings of the Second Workshop on Component-Oriented Programming (WCOP)*, June 1997. ftp://ftp.abo.fi/pub/cs/papers/mbuechi/FMforCS.ps.gz.

[7] Patrice Chalin.   *On the Language Design and Semantic Foundation of LCL, a Larch/C Interface Specification Language.*   PhD thesis, Concordia University, 1455 de Maisonneuve Blvd. West, Montreal, Quebec, Canada, October 1995.   Available as CU/DCS TR 95-12, from the URL ftp://ftp.cs.concordia.ca/pub/chalin/tr.ps.Z.

[8] Patrice Chalin, Peter Grogono, and T. Radhakrishnan. Identification of and solutions to shortcomings of LCL, a Larch/C interface specification language. In Marie-Claude Gaudel and James Woodcock, editors, *FME '96: Industrial Benefit and Advances in Formal Methods*, volume 1051 of *Lecture Notes in Computer Science*, pages 385–404, New York, N.Y., March 1996. Springer-Verlag.

[9] David L. Detlefs, K. Rustan M. Leino, Greg Nelson, and James B. Saxe. Extended static checking. SRC Research Report 159, Compaq Systems Research Center, 130 Lytton Ave., Palo Alto, Dec 1998.

[10] Krishna Kishore Dhara. Behavioral subtyping in object-oriented languages. Technical Report TR97-09, Department of Computer Science, Iowa State University, 226 Atanasoff Hall, Ames IA 50011-1040, May 1997. The author's Ph.D. dissertation.

[11] Krishna Kishore Dhara and Gary T. Leavens.   Forcing behavioral subtyping through specification inheritance. In *Proceedings of the 18th International Conference on Software Engineering, Berlin, Germany*, pages 258–267. IEEE Computer Society Press, March 1996. A corrected version is Iowa State University, Dept. of Computer Science TR #95-20c.

[12] E. W. Dijkstra, editor. *Formal Development of Programs and Proofs.* University of Texas at Austin Year of Programming series. Addison-Wesley Publishing Co., 1990.

[13] Edsger W. Dijkstra. *A Discipline of Programming.* Prentice-Hall, Inc., Englewood Cliffs, N.J., 1976.

[14] Edsger W. Dijkstra and Carel S. Scholten. *Predicate Calculus and program semantics.* Springer-Verlag, NY, 1990.

[15] L. M. G. Feijs and H. B. M. Jonkers. *Formal Specification and Design*, volume 35 of *Cambridge Tracts in Theoretical Computer Science.* Cambridge University Press, Cambridge, UK, 1992.

[16] John Fitzgerald and Peter Gorm Larsen. *Modelling Systems: Practical Tools in Software Development.* Cambridge, Cambridge, UK, 1998.

[17] Stephen J. Garland, John V. Guttag, and James J. Horning. Debugging Larch Shared Language specifications. *IEEE Transactions on Software Engineering*, 16(6):1044–1057, September 1990.

[18] M. Gogolla, S. Conrad, G. Denker, R. Herzig, N. Vlachantonis, and H. Ehrig. TROLL *light* — the language and its development environment. In Manfred Broy and Stefan Jähnichen, editors, *KORSO: Methods, Languages and Tools for the Construction of Correct Software*, volume 1009 of *Lecture Notes in Computer Science*, pages 205–220. Springer-Verlag, New York, N.Y., 1995.

[19] David Gries. Teaching calculation and discrimination: A more effective curriculum. *Communications of the ACM*, 34(3):44–55, March 1991.

[20] David Gries and Fred B. Schneider. *A Logical Approach to Discrete Math.* Texts and Monographs in Computer Science. Springer-Verlag, New York, N.Y., 1994.

[21] David Gries and Fred B. Schneider. Avoiding the undefined by underspecification. In Jan van Leeuwen, editor, *Computer Science Today: Recent Trends and Developments*, number 1000 in Lecture Notes in Computer Science, pages 366–373. Springer-Verlag, New York, N.Y., 1995.

[22] M. Gurski and A. L. Baker. Testing SPECS-C++: A first step in validating distributed systems. In *Intellegent Information Management Systems*, pages 105–108, Anaheim, 1994. The International Society for Mini and Microcomputers - ISMM.

[23] John V. Guttag, James J. Horning, S.J. Garland, K.D. Jones, A. Modet, and J.M. Wing. *Larch: Languages and Tools for Formal Specification.* Springer-Verlag, New York, N.Y., 1993.

[24] I. Hayes, editor. *Specification Case Studies.* International Series in Computer Science. Prentice-Hall, Inc., second edition, 1993.

[25] Wim H. Hesselink. *Programs, Recursion, and Unbounded Choice*, volume 27 of *Cambridge Tracts in Theoretical Computer Science.* Cambridge University Press, New York, N.Y., 1992.

[26] C. A. R. Hoare. An axiomatic basis for computer programming. *Communications of the ACM*, 12(10):576–583, October 1969.

[27] C.B. Jones. Partial functions and logics: A warning. *Information Processing Letters*, 54(2):65–67, 1995.

[28] Cliff B. Jones. *Systematic Software Development Using VDM.* International Series in Computer Science. Prentice Hall, Englewood Cliffs, N.J., second edition, 1990.

[29] Kevin D. Jones. LM3: A Larch interface language for Modula-3: A definition and introduction: Version 1.0. Technical Report 72, Digital Equipment Corporation, Systems Research Center, 130 Lytton Avenue Palo Alto, CA 94301, June 1991. Order from src-report@src.dec.com.

[30] H. B. M. Jonkers. Upgrading the pre- and postcondition technique. In S. Prehn and W. J. Toetenel, editors, *VDM '91 Formal Software Development Methods 4th International Symposium of VDM Europe Noordwijkerhout, The Netherlands, Volume 1: Conference Contributions*, volume 551 of *Lecture Notes in Computer Science*, pages 428–456. Springer-Verlag, New York, N.Y., October 1991.

[31] Kevin Lano. *The B Language and Method: A guide to Practical Formal Development.* Formal Appoaches to Computing and Information Technology. Springer-Verlag, London, UK, 1996.

[32] Gary T. Leavens. An overview of Larch/C++: Behavioral specifications for C++ modules. In Haim Kilov and William Harvey, editors, *Specification of Behavioral Semantics in Object-Oriented Information Modeling*, chapter 8, pages 121–142. Kluwer Academic Publishers, Boston, 1996. An extended version is TR #96-01d, Department of Computer Science, Iowa State University, Ames, Iowa, 50011.

[33] Gary T. Leavens. Larch/C++ Reference Manual. Version 5.41. Available in ftp://ftp.cs.iastate.edu/pub/larchc++/lcpp.ps.gz or on the World Wide Web at the URL http://www.cs.iastate.edu/~leavens/larchc++.html, April 1999.

[34] Gary T. Leavens, Albert L. Baker, and Clyde Ruby. Preliminary design of JML: A behavioral interface specification language for Java. Technical Report 98-06e, Iowa State University, Department of Computer Science, June 1999.

[35] Gary T. Leavens and Jeannette M. Wing. Protective interface specifications. In Michel Bidoit and Max Dauchet, editors, *TAPSOFT '97: Theory and Practice of Software Development, 7th International Joint Conference CAAP/FASE, Lille, France*, volume 1214 of *Lecture Notes in Computer Science*, pages 520–534. Springer-Verlag, New York, N.Y., 1997.

[36] Gary T. Leavens and Jeannette M. Wing. Protective interface specifications. *Formal Aspects of Computing*, 10:59–75, 1998.

[37] K. Rustan M. Leino. *Toward Reliable Modular Programs*. PhD thesis, California Institute of Technology, 1995. Available as Technical Report Caltech-CS-TR-95-03.

[38] Barbara Liskov and Jeannette Wing. A behavioral notion of subtyping. *ACM Transactions on Programming Languages and Systems*, 16(6):1811–1841, November 1994.

[39] Barbara Liskov and Jeannette M. Wing. Specifications and their use in defining subtypes. *ACM SIGPLAN Notices*, 28(10):16–28, October 1993. *OOPSLA '93 Proceedings*, Andreas Paepcke (editor).

[40] David Luckham. *Programming with Specifications: An Introduction to Anna, A Language for Specifying Ada Programs*. Texts and Monographs in Computer Science. Springer-Verlag, New York, N.Y., 1990.

[41] David Luckham and Friedrich W. von Henke. An overview of anna - a specification language for Ada. *IEEE Software*, 2(2):9–23, March 1985.

[42] Bertrand Meyer. *Object-oriented Software Construction*. Prentice Hall, New York, N.Y., second edition, 1997.

[43] Carroll Morgan. *Programming from Specifications: Second Edition*. Prentice Hall International, Hempstead, UK, 1994.

[44] Carroll Morgan and Trevor Vickers, editors. *On the refinement calculus*. Formal approaches of computing and information technology series. Springer-Verlag, New York, N.Y., 1994.

[45] Joseph M. Morris. A theoretical basis for stepwise refinement and the programming calculus. *Science of Computer Programming*, 9(3):287–306, December 1987.

[46] Greg Nelson. A generalization of Dijkstra's calculus. *ACM Transactions on Programming Languages and Systems*, 11(4):517–561, October 1989.

[47] William F. Ogden, Murali Sitaraman, Bruce W. Weide, and Stuart H. Zweben. Part I: The RESOLVE framework and discipline — a research synopsis. *ACM SIGSOFT Software Engineering Notes*, 19(4):23–28, Oct 1994.

[48] D. E. Perry. The Inscape environment. In *Proceedings of the 11th International Conference on Software Engineering*, pages 2–12, May 1989.

[49] Arnd Poetzsch-Heffter. Specification and verification of object-oriented programs. Habilitation thesis, Technical University of Munich, January 1997.

[50] David S. Rosenblum. A practical approach to programming with assertions. *IEEE Transactions on Software Engineering*, 21(1):19–31, January 1995.

[51] Murali Sitaraman, Lonnie R. Welch, and Douglas E. Harms. On specification of reusable software components. *International Journal of Software Engineering and Knowledege Engineering*, 3(2):207–229, 1993.

[52] J. Michael Spivey. *The Z Notation: A Reference Manual*. International Series in Computer Science. Prentice-Hall, New York, N.Y., second edition, 1992.

[53] Susan Stepney, Rosalind Barden, and David Cooper, editors. *Object Orientation in Z*. Workshops in Computing. Springer-Verlag, Cambridge CB2 1LQ, UK, 1992.

[54] Yang Meng Tan. Formal specification techniques for promoting software modularity, enhancing documentation, and testing specifications. Technical Report 619, Massachusetts Institute of Technology, Laboratory for Computer Science, 545 Technology Square, Cambridge, Mass., June 1994.

[55] Yang Meng Tan. Interface language for supporting programming styles. *ACM SIGPLAN Notices*, 29(8):74–83, August 1994. Proceedings of the Workshop on Interface Definition Languages.

[56] Yang Meng Tan. *Formal Specification Techniques for Engineering Modular C Programs*, volume 1 of *Kluwer International Series in Software Engineering*. Kluwer Academic Publishers, Boston, 1995.

[57] Alan Wills. Specification in Fresco. In Stepney et al. [53], chapter 11, pages 127–135.

[58] Jeannette M. Wing. Writing Larch interface language specifications. *ACM Transactions on Programming Languages and Systems*, 9(1):1–24, January 1987.

[59] Jeannette Marie Wing. A two-tiered approach to specifying programs. Technical Report TR-299, Massachusetts Institute of Technology, Laboratory for Computer Science, 1983.

[60] Jim Woodcock and Jim Davies. *Using Z: Specification, Refinement, and Proof.* Prentice Hall International Series in Computer Science, 1996.

On Excusable and Inexcusable Failures
Towards an Adequate Notion of Translation Correctness

Markus Müller-Olm and Andreas Wolf*

[1] Fachbereich Informatik, LS V, Universität Dortmund, 44221 Dortmund, Germany
mmo@ls5.cs.uni-dortmund.de
[2] Institut für Informatik und Praktische Mathematik,
Christian-Albrechts-Universität, 24105 Kiel, Germany
awo@informatik.uni-kiel.de

Abstract. The classical concepts of partial and total correctness identify all types of runtime errors and divergence. We argue that the associated notions of translation correctness cannot cope adequately with
practical questions like optimizations and finiteness of machines. As a
step towards a solution we propose more fine-grained correctness notions, which are parameterized in sets of acceptable failure outcomes,
and study a corresponding family of predicate transformers that generalize the well-known wp and wlp transformers. We also discuss the utility
of the resulting setup for answering compiler correctness questions.

Keywords: compiler, correctness, divergence, refinement, runtime-error,
predicate transformer, verification

1   Introduction

Compilers are ubiquitous in today's computing environments. Their use ranges
from the traditional translation of higher programming languages to conversions
between data formats of a large variety. The rather inconspicuous use of compilers helps to get rid of architecture or system specific representations and allows
thus to handle data or algorithms in a more convenient abstract form.

There is a standard theory for the syntactic aspects of compiler construction
which is well-understood and documented in a number of text books (e.g. [1,
24, 25, 26]). It is applied easily in practice via automated tools like scanner
and parser generators. This has made the construction of the syntactic phases
of compilers, which has been a challenge back in the sixties, to a routine task
nowadays.

This is different for the semantic phases concerned with the question, which
output is to be generated for a given input. In this respect every translation task
requires rather specific considerations and, due to the wide range of applications sketched above, no general approach is available or to be expected for this
problem. Even if one restricts attention to a more narrow task, the translation
of imperative programming languages considered in this paper, there is still no

---

* The work of the second author is supported by DFG grant La 426/15-1,2.

J. Wing, J. Woodcock, J. Davies (Eds.): FM'99, Vol. II, LNCS 1709, pp. 1107–1127, 1999.

generally followed approach, although some well-studied frameworks like, e.g., action semantics [19] exist. Of course much is known on efficient (and presumably correct) translation schemes and runtime environments and there is also a vast amount of literature on optimizations (a recent textbook is [20]). But these considerations do not build on a consistent, widely accepted semantic basis. As a consequence, subtle errors are present in generated code and it is difficult to fully understand which properties are guaranteed to transfer from source to target programs, in particular if aggressive optimization levels are employed in the compiler. This is exemplified by the surprising results experienced by many compiler users every now and then when running generated code.

In many applications errors and uncertainties, although annoying, can be tolerated. When compilers are used to construct software for safety-critical systems the matter changes dramatically. The mistrust in compilers is one of the reasons why such code often is certified on the level of machine- or assembler-code [15, 23]. Trusted and fully-understood compilers would permit a certification on the source language level. This would be less time-consuming, cheaper, and more reliable. From a practical point of view, the ultimate goal of compiler verification [4, 6, 12, 14, 16, 21, 22] should be to improve on this state of affairs.

Every compiler proof is in danger of burying the essential considerations under a mountain of technicalities, which could seriously affect the credibility of the established correctness claim. Thus a compiler proof should be based on a semantic definition in an abstract style. On the other hand, it is important that the semantic description is rather close to the intuition of the average programmer in order to avoid errors resulting from misunderstandings of or, seen from the perspective of the programmer, errors in the formal semantics definition. As most people have a rather concrete, operational intuition about the behavior of (imperative) programs, the ultimate reference point should thus be a rather concrete, operational semantics.

How can we resolve the obvious conflict between the requirements of using an operational as well as an abstract kind of semantics? We envision the following approach: The operational semantics is defined first and provides the ultimate reference. In particular, the correctness property to be established for the translation is interpreted in terms of the operational semantics. From the operational semantics, the more abstract semantics to be used in the compiler proof is derived. This involves defining the objects handled by the abstract semantics in terms of the operational semantics. Afterwards sufficiently strong properties of the abstract semantics are established that allow to reason in the compiler proof on the abstract level without directly recurring to its operational definition.

A particular benefit of this approach is that the abstract semantics can be suited to the specific correctness property to be established. We shall argue later in this paper (see Sect. 2) that there is no single universal notion of correct translation even in the simplified setting considered here. Instead there is a whole range of sensible notions and the abstract semantics can specifically be constructed to accommodate reasoning w.r.t. the chosen one.

So much for the context of this paper; let us now become a bit more concrete about our contribution. On the one hand, we are looking for a realistic, yet tractable, notion of translation correctness and, on the other hand, for abstract semantics suited to reasoning about it. We argue that common code-optimizing transformations and the limitations of finite machines give rise to different expectations about the relationship of the behavior of source and target code. We show that the notions of translation correctness that derive in a natural way from the classic idealized notions of partial and total correctness are not able to cope adequately with these topics. The problem results from the traditional identification of runtime errors and divergence. As a step towards a solution we propose relativized correctness notions that are parameterized in sets of acceptable failures. In order to facilitate compiler correctness proofs we also study relativized versions of the well-known wp and wlp predicate transformers and discuss the utility of the resulting setup. The aim of this line of research is to preserve as much as possible from the elegant appeal of the traditional idealized setting, while being able to cope with the more practical problems.

The remainder of this article is organized as follows. Section 2 discusses by means of small examples some pitfalls in defining semantic correctness conditions for practical compilers. The classical concepts of partial and total correctness and the associated notions of correct translation are revisited in Sect. 3 before we introduce the proposed relativized notions in Sect. 4. In particular we introduce a generalization of the classic wp and wlp predicate transformers [8, 11] called wrp (weakest relativized predicate transformer) and discuss its relationship to the classic transformers and its basic properties. In Sect. 6 we study wrp for the commands of a simple imperative programming language. These commands are applied to an example in Sect. 7 in order to indicate the utility of the proposed framework for answering translation correctness questions. We finish the paper with a number of concluding remarks.

2   On Correctness of Translations

Let us first of all set the stage for the technical discussion. We assume given a set Π of programs π. The reader should imagine imperative programs intended to compute on a certain non-empty set of states Σ. Computations of π start in a state $s \in \Sigma$; s represents the input to the program. There are three different types of computations: a computation may terminate regularly in a state $s' \in \Sigma$; it may end up in an error state; or it may diverge, i.e. run forever. Programs can be non-deterministic, i.e. there may be more than one computation from a given initial state s.

The details of program execution are not of interest for our purpose; we are only interested in the final outcomes of computations. Therefore, we assume that each program π is furnished with a relation $R(\pi) \subseteq \Sigma \times (\Sigma \cup \Omega)$. Here Ω is a non-empty set of *failure (or irregular) outcomes* disjoint from Σ. Intuitively, Ω contains the error states mentioned above and a special symbol ∞ representing divergence. Examples of error states are, e.g., 'div-by-zero', 'arithmetic overflow' etc. We call π *deterministic* if $R(\pi)$ is a function, i.e. if for any $s \in \Sigma$ there is at most one σ such that $(s,\sigma) \in R(\pi)$. As any practical program has at least one computation from a given initial state, we may safely assume that $R(\pi)$ is *total*, i.e. that there is an outcome σ with $(s,\sigma) \in R(\pi)$ for any $s \in \Sigma$. Unless otherwise stated this assumption is, however, not needed in this article.

We use the following conventions for the naming of variables: Σ is ranged over by s, Ω by ω, and $\Sigma \cup \Omega$ by σ. We also use the letter o to range over $\Omega - \{\infty\}$.

Intuitively, $(s,s') \in R(\pi)$ records that s' is a possible regular result of π from initial state s, $(s,o) \in R(\pi)$ means that error state o can be reached from s, and $(s,\infty) \in R(\pi)$ that π may diverge from s. $R(\pi)$ can be thought to be derived from an operational or denotational semantics. Relational definitions for familiar programming operators can be found in Sect. 6.

After these preparations, let us discuss what correctness properties we reasonably can expect from translations. Assume for the purpose of this discussion that π is a source program that has been translated to a target program π'. We will freely use various features and representations of imperative programs in the illustrating examples. For simplicity we assume that π and π' operate on the same state space.

If π' is to be a correct implementation of π, we clearly expect that the computations of π' are related to the computations of π in some sense. Usually, we are not interested in the intermediate states occurring in computations but just in the final outcomes produced.[1] Therefore, a relational semantics like the above introduced $R(\pi)$, which provides an abstraction of the possible computations of π to possible outcomes, is appropriate for defining correctness of translation.

At first glance, we might require that π' has the same outcomes as π for any given initial state, i.e. that $R(\pi') = R(\pi)$. But this requirement is far too strong. One of the reasons is that non-determinism in π might be resolved in a specific way in π'. Assume, e.g., that π contains an un-initialized local variable and that the result of π depends on the (arbitrary) initial value of this local variable, like in the following program.

```
BEGIN
  int y: y := 17
END;
BEGIN
  int z: x := z
END
```

The final value of x is arbitrary, i.e. we have $R(\pi) = \{(s,s[x \mapsto n]) \mid n \in \mathbb{Z}\}$ where $s[x \mapsto n]$ denotes the substitution of value n for the variable x in state s. The generated code π', on the other hand, might well provide the deterministic

---

[1] Of course, for programs with input/output instructions we are also interested in relating the communicated values. And even for strictly transformational programs, we might occasionally want to relate intermediate states; for example when we are interested in correctness of debuggers. But this is beyond the scope of this paper.

result 17, as it allocates for z the memory location used previously for y, which still contains y's old value. No sensible means can enforce full non-determinism in the target code and we should thus expect at most $R(\pi') \subseteq R(\pi)$: every outcome produced by the target code is a possible outcome of the source code. This is the very idea of *refinement*.

However, reality is not that simple: for various reasons, even $R(\pi') \subseteq R(\pi)$ is a too strong requirement. A realistic notion of correctness must also accommodate limitations of the execution mechanism and optimizations. Let us discuss each of these in turn.

Limited abilities of the implementation might give rise to failure outcomes of the target program that are not possible for the source program. Full implementation of recursion, e.g., requires stacks of unbounded size. Actual computers, however, provide only a finite amount of memory; we must thus be prepared to accept the outcome 'stack-overflow' or 'out-of-memory' every now and then when executing programs from languages with unrestricted use of recursion. Another example is restricted arithmetic. If the source language provides e.g. the full set of integers as a data type but the executing processor just uses, e.g., 32-bit representations, the outcome 'arithmetic overflow' will occur occasionally.

Such limitations could be handled in various ways. Firstly, we could try to model the limitations precisely in the source language semantics. This approach is often applied for restricted arithmetic (consider e.g. the ANSI/IEEE 754 standard for representation of the reals) but is generally impractical for e.g. bounded stack sizes as it would require very specific knowledge on the implementation when defining semantics of the source language. Secondly, we could simply enrich the source language semantics by the error outcomes which would allow them as possible results of the implementation. This would amount to considering

$$R(\pi) \cup \{(s, error) \mid error \text{ is an outcome reflecting a limitation}\}$$

the semantics of π. Thirdly, we could try to handle limitations as part of the relationship between $R(\pi)$ and $R(\pi')$. The latter is perhaps the most natural approach but it leads to complicated formalizations in practice. The predicate transformer semantics solution proposed below will somehow have the flavor of the second approach but avoids its somewhat unhandy nature.

Optimizations can replace error outcomes by arbitrary outcomes. As a first example consider the innocuously looking transformation pictured in Fig. 1, an instance of what is called *dead-code elimination* [20]. The justification for this transformation is that the value of e assigned to x in the initial assignment is never needed, as any path through the program overwrites x's value before using it by either the assignment $x := 12$ or $x := 42$. Hence it should not be necessary to perform the evaluation of e and the assignment $x := e$ at all. But suppose that e is the expression $1/0$. Then the left program is guaranteed to produce the error outcome 'div-by-zero' while the right program can have, depending on P, whatever outcomes you want! (Note, that it is not always as obvious as in this example that evaluation of an expression at a certain point in a program might lead to a run-time error; in general this is undecidable.)

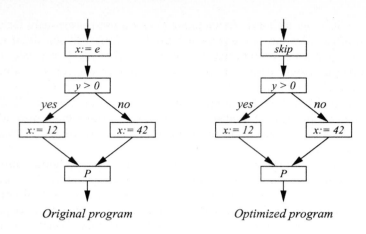

Original program   Optimized program

Fig. 1. Elimination of dead code.

As a second example of an optimization consider the *code motion transformation* [20] in Fig. 2 where b, e and f are assumed not to contain y, and g is assumed not to contain x. In the optimized program the assignment $y := g$ appearing in both branches is moved to the start of the program in order to save code. The reasoning is that g can safely be evaluated before the branching, as it is evaluated on each path anyhow (in traditional parlance one says g is 'very busy' or 'downward safe' at the initial node). Assume now that evaluation of e, f and g can lead to different error outcomes, say g to an arithmetic overflow and e, f to a division by zero. Then the left program produces a 'division-by-zero' outcome while the optimized right program produces an arithmetic overflow. The reason is that the notion of downward safety, disregards the possibility of errors.

In summary, many common optimizing transformations can replace certain error outcomes by different regular and irregular outcomes. Some optimizations can even introduce new errors into regularly terminating programs because they compute intermediate values that are not computed by the original program. Examples are strength reduction transformations and naive code motion transformations that move loop-invariant pieces of code out of loops.

Should optimizations be banned from verified compilers for these reasons? No, this would throw out the baby with the bath water in our opinion. Optimizations play a very important role in increasing the efficiency of program execution and in many applications effects like the above can be tolerated. But the possible effects should be precisely understood and documented. A user should thus be enabled to judge which optimizations are permissible for his particular application and to select just these (e.g. by means of compiler switches).

As a curiosity, we mention that common efficiency-improving compiler options can even lead to a translation of terminating programs into non-terminating ones in rare cases. The Modula-2 loop for $i := 0$ to maxcard do..., for instance,

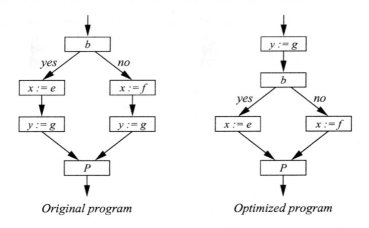

Fig. 2. A code motion transformation.

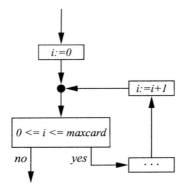

Fig. 3. Prototypical implementation of a for-loop.

obviously is terminating. A typical implementation is the following: i is initialized with the value 0; each iteration starts with a check whether i is still in the range $0 \leq i \leq$ maxcard; at the end of each iteration i is incremented. This is illustrated in Fig 3. Now suppose an implementation disregards arithmetic overflows in order to increase the performance. Then the incrementation of i at the end of the iteration $i =$ maxcard effectively sets i to 0 due to the representation of numbers. It also sets the carry-flag but sadly this is ignored. Now the test whether i is still in the range $0 \leq i \leq$ maxcard succeeds! Thus, this implementation of the loop, which is actually found in practice, will not terminate in contrast to the original program.

It should have become clear that there is no single universal notion of correct translation but that different applications and translation schemes preserve a different amount from the behavior of programs. For a specific translation scheme the set $\Sigma \cup \Omega$ of (regular and irregular) outcomes can be partitioned into three sets:

- a set PO ('*preserved outcomes*') of outcomes that has to be preserved literally;
- a set AO ('*accepted outcomes*') of outcomes that may arise as result of target program executions even if not present in the source program's semantics (e.g. 'stack-overflow' or 'out-of-memory'); and
- a set CO ('*chaotic outcomes*') of outcomes of source programs that might lead to arbitrary outcomes in the target program (e.g. arithmetic errors in connection with dead code elimination).

Typically the regular outcomes belong to the set PO but also irregular outcomes may, e.g. 'division-by-zero', for debugging purposes.

Now suppose given a partition of $\Sigma \cup \Omega$ as described above. We call π' a *correct implementation* of π *w.r.t. preserved outcomes PO, accepted outcomes AO, and chaotic outcomes CO* if for all $(s, \sigma) \in R(\pi')$ (at least) one of the following is valid:

(a) σ is a preserved outcome of a computation of π from s, i.e. $\sigma \in PO \wedge (s, \sigma) \in R(\pi)$,
(b) σ is an accepted outcome, i.e. $\sigma \in AO$, or
(c) there is a chaotic outcome of a source program computation from s, i.e. $\exists \sigma' \in CO : (s, \sigma') \in R(\pi)$.

There are various ways of characterizing this property as an inclusion between relations derived from $R(\pi)$ and $R(\pi')$. One of them is the following that we are going to take as a definition.

Definition 1 (Correct implementation). *π' implements π w.r.t. preserved outcomes PO, accepted outcomes AO, and chaotic outcomes CO if and only if*

$$R(\pi') \subseteq R(\pi) \cup \{(s, \sigma) \mid \sigma \in AO \vee \exists \sigma' \in CO : (s, \sigma') \in R(\pi)\} \ .$$

Often divergence and runtime-errors are identified in simplified semantic treatments of programming languages. This has proved very helpful in establishing a rich and useful theory of program verification [2, 7, 13] and program refinement [3, 17, 18].[2] However, this idealization does not lead to a realistic notion of correct implementation: on the one hand, the single irregular outcome must be treated as chaotic, in order to accommodate the effect of optimizations like dead

---

[2] We should mention that Apt and Olderog [2] do consider different irregular outcomes of programs: divergence, failure, and deadlock. In their proof theories divergence and failure are identified, but in Chaps. 7 and 8 they introduce a notion of *weak total correctness* that reflects the distinction between divergence and deadlock. Weak total correctness is an instance of our relative correctness notion (Sect. 4). It is introduced in [2] in order to justify proof rules for total correctness and is said to be not of interest in itself. In contrast, we emphasize here that relative correctness is indeed often of independent interest.

code elimination, because dead code elimination can change the single irregular outcome (which could represent e.g. 'div-by-zero' in this case) to an arbitrary outcome. On the other hand, it must be treated as acceptable, as it could also report on a limitation of the execution mechanisms at hand (e.g. standing for 'out-of-memory').

We propose more fine-grained notions of program correctness and refinement intended to allow an adequate treatment of these more practical questions, while preserving as much as possible from the idealized setup. Before doing so let us have a more careful look at the classical treatment of program correctness and the notions of translation correctness to which they give rise, because our proposal is modeled on this.

3   The Classical Setup

3.1   Program Verification and Predicate Transformers

In Hoare-style program verification one is interested in proving programs partially or totally correct w.r.t. pre- and postconditions on the set of regular states. For the purpose of this paper a predicate is identified with the set of states for which it is valid. Thus, the set of predicates is $Pred = 2^{\Sigma}$; we range over $Pred$ by the letters ϕ and ψ. $Pred$, ordered by set-inclusion $\subseteq$, is a standard example of a complete Boolean lattice. The meet and join operations are $\cap$ and $\cup$; they represent conjunction and disjunction respectively, $\neg\phi$ is the complement of predicate ϕ, i.e. $\neg\phi = \Sigma - \phi$, the strongest (the smallest) and the weakest (the greatest) predicate w.r.t. this order is $\emptyset$ and Σ. We denote the latter also by `false` and `true`.

The classic literature on Hoare-style program verification and the refinement calculus identifies, for the sake of simplicity, divergence and failure outcomes or fully ignores failures. In our setting this amounts to assuming that Ω contains just one symbol, $\bot$, which represents any kind of irregular outcomes, divergence and failures, $R(\pi)$ is then a subset of $\Sigma \times (\Sigma \cup \{\bot\})$. For the purpose of the later discussion it is, however, more convenient to stay with the distinction between different irregular outcomes in the relational semantics. The definitions of total and partial correctness below treat all irregular outcomes as if they were identified and can thus equivalently be read in both models.

Partial correctness of a program π w.r.t. a precondition ϕ and postcondition ψ, denoted by $\{\phi\}\pi\{\psi\}$ can be defined as follows.

$$\{\phi\}\pi\{\psi\} \quad \text{iff} \quad \forall s, \sigma : s \in \phi \wedge (s, \sigma) \in R(\pi) \Rightarrow \sigma \in \psi \cup \Omega .$$

Intuitively, π is partially correct if each regularly terminating computation from a state in ϕ results in a state in ψ. Note, how the restriction to regular results is expressed by allowing all outcomes in Ω.

Total correctness of π w.r.t. precondition ϕ and postcondition ψ, denoted by $[\phi]\pi[\psi]$ additionally requires that there are no irregular computations from states in ϕ. This can be expressed nicely by *not* allowing outcomes in Ω.

$$[\phi]\pi[\psi] \quad \text{iff} \quad \forall s, \sigma : s \in \phi \wedge (s, \sigma) \in R(\pi) \Rightarrow \sigma \in \psi .$$

An elegant way of expressing partial and total correctness is by means of predicate transformers, i.e. mappings on the space of predicates. Dijkstra [8, 9] considers two predicate transformers. The *weakest liberal precondition* transformer wlp is suited to partial correctness and the *weakest precondition* transformer wp to total correctness.

A few words on notation: it is convenient and customary in connection with predicate transformers to denote function application by an infix dot, i.e. writing $f.x$ instead of the more familiar $f(x)$. Moreover, we adopt the usual convention that function application associates to the left, i.e. $f.x.y$ means $(f.x).y$.

For a program π, both wlp.π and wp.π are of type $2^\Sigma \to 2^\Sigma$. As their name suggests wlp.$\pi.\psi$ (wp.$\pi.\psi$) is the weakest predicate ϕ satisfying the Hoare-triple $\{\phi\}\pi\{\psi\}$ (resp. $[\phi]\pi[\psi]$) (see (1) and (2) below).

Based on the relational semantics $R(\pi)$ of a program π the predicate transformers wlp.π and wp.π can be defined as follows.

$$\text{wlp.}\pi.\psi = \{s \in \Sigma \mid \forall \sigma : (s, \sigma) \in R(\pi) \Rightarrow \sigma \in \psi \cup \Omega\}$$
$$\text{wp.}\pi.\psi = \{s \in \Sigma \mid \forall \sigma : (s, \sigma) \in R(\pi) \Rightarrow \sigma \in \psi\} .$$

Their relationship to partial and total correctness is captured by the following equivalences, the proof of which is straightforward. These equivalences could also serve as the definition of wlp and wp.

$$\phi \subseteq \text{wlp.}\pi.\psi \quad \text{iff} \quad \{\phi\}\pi\{\psi\} . \tag{1}$$
$$\phi \subseteq \text{wp.}\pi.\psi \quad \text{iff} \quad [\phi]\pi[\psi] . \tag{2}$$

wlp.π and wp.π provide abstractions of $R(\pi)$ suited to partial and total correctness. Both carry less information than $R(\pi)$. This can be seen from the following examples in which we use | to denote (demonic) nondeterministic choice.[3]

$$\pi \stackrel{\text{def.}}{=} \quad x := e \mid \text{while true do skip od}$$
$$\pi' \stackrel{\text{def.}}{=} \quad x := e$$

Here wlp.π equals wlp.π' because the two programs yield the same result, if they terminate. On the other hand, for

$$\pi \stackrel{\text{def.}}{=} \quad x := 12 \mid \text{while true do skip od}$$
$$\pi' \stackrel{\text{def.}}{=} \quad x := 42 \mid \text{while true do skip od}$$

wp.π equals wp.π' because both programs may diverge. Obviously, in both examples $R(\pi)$ and $R(\pi')$ differ.

It is interesting to note that in the traditional model where $|\Omega| = 1$, $R(\pi)$ can be reconstructed from wp.π *together* with wlp.π. More specifically,

$$R(\pi) = \quad \{(s, s') \mid s \notin \text{wlp.}\pi.(\Sigma - \{s'\})\}$$
$$\cup \{(s, \perp) \mid s \notin \text{wp.}\pi.\text{true}\} .$$

---

[3] Semantics of | is characterized by the identity $R(\pi \mid \pi') = R(\pi) \cup R(\pi')$.

This is no longer true if $|\Omega| > 1$, as, intuitively speaking, the information about the different causes of failures is not recorded in the predicate transformers.

3.2   Implementation Correctness

There are three natural ways to approach translation correctness. First, one can focus on *properties* that transfer from source to target programs. This point of view is particularly adequate if one is interested mainly in program proving. Second, one might focus on the *outcomes* produced by the source and target program, if one has a particular interest in actually interpreting results of program execution. Finally, one might look for a formulation in terms of *refinement*. The latter is of particular importance when *proving* correctness of translations. Fortunately, there are natural notions of implementation correctness that accommodate all three points of view as we will see in a moment.

The idea of the property-oriented point of view is to consider a program π' a correct implementation of a program π if validity of all properties from a certain class of interest transfers from π to π'. Two natural notions of this kind are preservation of partial and total correctness.

Definition 2 (Preservation of partial and total correctness).

1. *A program π' implements π w.r.t. preservation of partial correctness (PPC) if the following holds:* $\forall \phi, \psi : \{\phi\}\pi\{\psi\} \Rightarrow \{\phi\}\pi'\{\psi\}$.
2. *π' implements π w.r.t. preservation of total correctness (PTC) if the following holds:* $\forall \phi, \psi : [\phi]\pi[\psi] \Rightarrow [\phi]\pi'[\psi]$.

Note that, while total correctness implies partial correctness, the corresponding preservation properties are unrelated. Neither does PPC imply PTC nor vice versa.

If one concentrates on outcomes one wants to know which outcomes of the source program can result in which outcomes of the target program. This point of view was taken in Sect. 2 and we resort in the theorem below to the notion of correct implementation introduced in Def. 1. The theorem shows that we can interpret PPC and PTC also in terms of outcomes in a natural way.

Theorem 3 (Outcome interpretation of PPC and PTC).

1. *π' implements π w.r.t. PPC iff π' implements π w.r.t. preserved outcomes Σ, accepted outcomes Ω, and chaotic outcomes $\emptyset$.*
2. *π' implements π w.r.t. PTC iff π' implements π w.r.t. preserved outcomes Σ, accepted outcomes $\emptyset$, and chaotic outcomes Ω.*

Hence for PPC we have to choose $AO = \Omega$ and $CO = \emptyset$ and for PTC, just to the opposite, $AO = \emptyset$ and $CO = \Omega$; in both cases we take $PO = \Sigma$.

The goal of the refinement-oriented view is to devise a semantic model of programs that accommodates reasoning about implementation relationships. More specifically, one is looking for an interpretation of programs in a semantic space that is equipped with an ordering; π' should implement π iff its interpretation in the model is related to π's by the order.

For PPC and PTC adequate interpretations are well-known: they are given by wlp and wp. The semantic space is the set of monotonic predicate transformers $2^\Sigma \to 2^\Sigma$. It is ordered by the pointwise extensions $\leq$ of the inclusion relation on 2^Σ, which is defined by $f \leq g$ iff $\forall \psi : f.\psi \subseteq g.\psi$: a predicate transformer g is considered a refinement of another predicate transformer f if it establishes all postconditions from weaker preconditions. Restricting attention to *monotonic* predicate transformers (i.e. those transformers for which $f.\psi \subseteq f.\phi$ if $\psi \subseteq \phi$) makes functional composition monotonic.

As indicated, refinement in the space of predicate transformers corresponds to PPC and PTC.

Theorem 4 (Refinement characterization of PPC and PTC).

1. π' *implements* π *w.r.t. PPC iff* $\mathsf{wlp}.\pi \leq \mathsf{wlp}.\pi'$.
2. π' *implements* π *w.r.t. PTC iff* $\mathsf{wp}.\pi \leq \mathsf{wp}.\pi'$.

In the traditional setup, where $|\Omega| = 1$, the idealized notion of implementation correctness $R(\pi') \subseteq R(\pi)$ can be regained from wlp and wp. In this case,

$$R(\pi') \subseteq R(\pi) \quad \text{iff} \quad \mathsf{wlp}.\pi \leq \mathsf{wlp}.\pi' \wedge \mathsf{wp}.\pi \leq \mathsf{wp}.\pi' \;. \tag{3}$$

Again, this is no longer true if $|\Omega| > 1$.

It follows from (3) that for the translations discussed in Sect. 2 refinement w.r.t. either PPC or PTC does not hold, as they did not satisfy $R(\pi') \subseteq R(\pi)$. Thus, many practical compilers are either incorrect in the sense of PPC or PTC. A little further reflection unveils that the situation is as worse as it could be: reported limitations of the execution mechanism prohibit PTC, optimizations prohibit PPC. Consequently, most practical compilers preserve neither partial nor total correctness!

However, not the compilers are to be blamed for this sad state of affairs but the restricted selectivity of the notions of partial and total correctness, particularly their indiscriminate identification of any kind of run-time errors and divergence. We, therefore, establish a finer framework in the next section.

4   The Relativized Setup

4.1   Relative Correctness and Relativized Predicate Transformers

For evaluating partial correctness assertions all irregular outcomes of programs are disregarded; in contrast in total correctness assertions all irregular outcomes are taken as disproof. The correctness concept we are going to elaborate now is built around the idea of *parameterizing* assertions w.r.t. the set of accepted outcomes. The irregular outcomes that are not accepted are taken as disproof.

Suppose given a set $A \subseteq \Omega$ of outcomes to be accepted. We introduce the notion of a program π being *relatively correct* w.r.t. a precondition ϕ, a postcondition ψ, and the set A of accepted outcomes, denoted by $\langle \phi \rangle \pi \langle \psi \rangle_A$ for short. It is defined as follows:

$$\langle \phi \rangle \pi \langle \psi \rangle_A \quad \text{iff} \quad \forall s, \sigma : s \in \phi \wedge (s, \sigma) \in R(\pi) \Rightarrow \sigma \in \psi \cup A .$$

Intuitively, a program π is relatively correct if the following holds.

Whenever π is started in a state contained in ϕ we can be sure that either π terminates regularly in a state contained in ψ, irregularly with a failure in A, or, if $\infty \in A$, diverges.

We can also define a corresponding predicate transformer along the lines of wlp and wp. It is called the *weakest relativized precondition* transformer $\mathsf{wrp}_A.\pi :$ $Pred \to Pred.$ [4]

$$\mathsf{wrp}_A.\pi.\psi = \{ s \in \Sigma \mid \forall \sigma : (s, \sigma) \in R(\pi) \Rightarrow \sigma \in \psi \cup A \} .$$

Again, we have the following equivalence, that shows that $\mathsf{wrp}_A.\pi$ indeed deserves the name weakest relativized precondition transformer.

$$\phi \subseteq \mathsf{wrp}_A.\pi.\psi \quad \text{iff} \quad \langle \phi \rangle \pi \langle \psi \rangle_A .$$

These relativized notions generalize the classical ones. It is easy to see that partial and total correctness are just the border cases of relative correctness for the sets $A = \Omega$ and $A = \emptyset$. Similarly we have for wlp and wp:

$$\mathsf{wlp}.\pi = \mathsf{wrp}_\Omega.\pi \quad \text{and} \quad \mathsf{wp}.\pi = \mathsf{wrp}_\emptyset.\pi ,$$

so wp and wlp are just the extreme relativized predicate transformers.

4.2   Implementation Correctness

Each set $A \subseteq \Omega$ now gives rise to a notion of translation correctness relatively to A. As in the classic case it can be characterized in terms of preservation, refinement, and outcomes. More precisely, we have the following theorem, where we again refer to the notion introduced in Def. 1.

Theorem 5 (Preservation of relative correctness). *For all programs π, π' and accepted sets of outcomes $A \subseteq \Omega$, the following three conditions are equivalent.*

---

[4] If we would allow error outcomes in postconditions, we could have defined $\mathsf{wrp}_A.\pi.\psi = \mathsf{wp}.\pi.(\psi \cup A)$. But this would destroy the homogeneity of pre- and postconditions, and lead to a more complicated definition of sequential composition of predicate transformers.

1. *(Preservation)* $\forall \phi, \psi : \langle \phi \rangle \pi \langle \psi \rangle_A \Rightarrow \langle \phi \rangle \pi' \langle \psi \rangle_A$.
2. *(Refinement)* $\mathsf{wrp}_A.\pi \leq \mathsf{wrp}_A.\pi'$.
3. *(Outcomes)* π' *is a correct implementation of* π *w.r.t. preserved outcomes* Σ, *accepted outcomes* A, *and chaotic outcomes* $\Omega - A$.

The intuitive interpretation of these conditions is as follows. There is no restriction for the behavior of the target program from initial states for which the source program has a failure outcome in $\Omega - A$; otherwise, we don't care about the accepted outcomes in A, and every other outcome of the target program must also be possible for the source program.

This looks fine, but it is not as general as the aspired notion of correct implementation from Def. 1, where we assumed that the set of outcomes $\Sigma \cup \Omega$ is partitioned into preserved, accepted and chaotic outcomes PO, AO and CO. From the definition of wrp it is clear that each element of the set A that we carry in wrp's index is just accepted, not preserved; and the outcomes in $\Omega - A$ are treated chaotically. What about those failure outcomes we really want to preserve? A compiler user, for instance, might require that an observed outcome 'div-by-zero' indeed is caused by a division by zero on the source level. Roughly speaking we have to treat those outcomes twice, firstly as accepted, and secondly as chaotic. If we can prove refinement for each of these choices, we have proved that it is preserved. More formally, we have the following result.

Theorem 6. π' *implements* π *w.r.t. preserved outcomes* PO, *accepted outcomes* AO, *and chaotic outcomes* CO *iff, for all* A *with* $AO \subseteq A \subseteq AO \cup (PO \cap \Omega)$, $\mathsf{wrp}_A.\pi \leq \mathsf{wrp}_A.\pi'$.

Thus, although the notion of correct implementation from Def. 1 is not accommodated by refinement reasoning w.r.t. a single fixed set A, it can still be established by refinement arguments that are appropriately parameterized in A.

As a corollary to Theorem 6, the relational inclusion $R(\pi') \subseteq R(\pi)$ can also be established with wrp-based reasoning. To see this, just choose $PO = \Sigma \cup \Omega$ and $AO = CO = \emptyset$ and observe that the notion of correctness of implementations degenerates to the relational inclusion $R(\pi') \subseteq R(\pi)$ with this choice.

Corollary 7. $R(\pi') \subseteq R(\pi)$ *iff* $\mathsf{wrp}_A.\pi \leq \mathsf{wrp}_A.\pi'$ *for all* $A \subseteq \Omega$.

Relativized refinement enables us hence to be as fine-grained w.r.t. outcomes as on the relational level, if desired.

5   Properties of wrp

In the next lemma we collect some basic properties enjoyed by the family of wrp-transformers. Validity of 4, 7, and 8 depends on the program relation $R(\pi)$ being *total*.

Lemma 8. *Suppose* π *is a program,* ψ *a predicate, and* $A, B \subseteq \Omega$ *are sets of irregular outcomes.*

1. $\mathrm{wrp}_{A \cap B}.\pi = \mathrm{wrp}_A.\pi \wedge \mathrm{wrp}_B.\pi$.
2. $\mathrm{wrp}_A.\pi \leq \mathrm{wrp}_B.\pi$, if $A \subseteq B$.
3. $\mathrm{wrp}_A.\pi.\psi = \mathrm{wrp}_B.\pi.\psi \cap \mathrm{wrp}_A.\pi.\mathtt{true}$, if $A \subseteq B$.
4. $\mathrm{wrp}_\emptyset.\pi.\mathtt{false} = \mathtt{false}$.
5. $\mathrm{wrp}_A.\pi$ is positively conjunctive, i.e. distributes over every non-empty conjunction of predicates.
6. $\mathrm{wrp}_\Omega.\pi$ is universally conjunctive, i.e. distributes over every, even the empty conjunction of predicates.
7. $\mathrm{wrp}_A.\pi.\psi \subseteq \neg(\mathrm{wrp}_{\Omega-A}.\pi.\neg\psi)$.
8. $\mathrm{wrp}_A.\pi.\psi = \neg(\mathrm{wrp}_{\Omega-A}.\pi.\neg\psi)$ iff π is deterministic.

Dijkstra and Scholten [9] discuss so-called *healthiness conditions* of wp and wlp. In our notation they look as follows.

- $\mathrm{wp}.\pi.\psi = \mathrm{wlp}.\pi.\psi \cap \mathrm{wp}.\pi.\mathtt{true}$ (Pairing condition).
- $\mathrm{wp}.\pi.\mathtt{false} = \mathtt{false}$ (Excluded miracle).
- wp is positively conjunctive.
- wlp is universally conjunctive.

In the sense of [9] these properties have to be satisfied by a pair of predicate transformers to model an adequate semantics of implementable programs. The items 3–6 of Lemma 8 show how the healthiness conditions generalize to the family of wrp-transformers. Note that in our framework they are derived properties and not postulates as in [9], due to our point of view that predicate transformer semantics is derived from an underlying, more concrete operationally-based semantics. Property 8 generalizes the equivalence

- $\mathrm{wp}.\pi.\psi = \neg\mathrm{wlp}.\pi.\neg\psi$ iff π is deterministic

that is used as the definition of deterministic programs in [9].

6   Programming Operators

In this section we discuss briefly the wrp characterizations of typical commands of an imperative programming language. More specifically, we consider assignments $x := e$, conditionals if b then π_1 else π_2, while-loops while b do π od, and sequential composition. We would like to show that wrp enjoys similar, and only slightly more complicated characterizations as the classic predicate transformers. Reasoning in terms of wrp seems obviously to be more tractable than reasoning in terms of an operational or relational semantics.

We suppose given three additional sets of syntactic objects: variables x, expressions e and Boolean expressions b. The set of variables is denoted by *Var*. We assume interpretation functions for expressions and Boolean expressions $\mathcal{E}(e) : \Sigma \rightarrow (Val \cup \Omega)$ and $\mathcal{B}(b) : \Sigma \rightarrow (\mathbb{B} \cup \Omega)$. Here *Val* is the value set of variables; we range over *Val* by the letter v. The set $\mathbb{B} = \{\mathtt{tt}, \mathtt{ff}\}$ represents the truth values. For the purpose of this section, states are valuations of variables, i.e. $\Sigma = (Var \rightarrow Val)$. As usual $s[x \mapsto v]$ denotes the substitution of value

v for the variable x in state s. Intuitively, results $\mathcal{E}(e)(s), \mathcal{B}(b)(s) \in \Omega$ represent failures during evaluation of (Boolean) expressions. Such failures are assumed to propagate to the statement level.

For simplicity we identify syntax and semantics when writing concrete predicates. In order to deal with partially defined expressions we assume special types of basic predicates: $\mathsf{def}(e)$ and $\mathsf{in}_A(e)$ for expressions e and $A \subseteq \Omega$, and $\mathsf{def}(b)$, $\mathsf{in}_A(b)$, $b = \mathsf{tt}$, and $b = \mathsf{ff}$ for Boolean expressions b. They are interpreted as follows: $\mathsf{def}(e) \stackrel{\text{def.}}{=} \{s \mid \mathcal{E}(e)(s) \in \mathit{Val}\}$, $\mathsf{in}_A(e) \stackrel{\text{def.}}{=} \{s \mid \mathcal{E}(e)(s) \in A\}$, $b = \mathsf{tt} \stackrel{\text{def.}}{=} \{s \mid \mathcal{B}(b)(s) = \mathsf{tt}\}$. The interpretation of the remaining predicates is obvious. Note that Boolean expressions can have 'undefined' failure results while predicates cannot.

Let us first consider assignments, conditionals, and the sequential composition operator. Their relational semantics reads as follows, where we rely on the convention (from Sect. 2) that s ranges over Σ and ω over Ω.

$$
\begin{aligned}
R(x := e) = \quad & \{(s, s[x \mapsto v]) \mid \mathcal{E}(e)(s) = v\} \\
\cup \; & \{(s, \omega) \mid \mathcal{E}(e)(s) = \omega\} \\[4pt]
R(\text{if } b \text{ then } \pi_1 \text{ else } \pi_2) = \quad & \{(s, \sigma) \mid \mathcal{B}(b)(s) = \mathsf{tt} \wedge (s, \sigma) \in R(\pi_1)\} \\
\cup \; & \{(s, \sigma) \mid \mathcal{B}(b)(s) = \mathsf{ff} \wedge (s, \sigma) \in R(\pi_2)\} \\
\cup \; & \{(s, \omega) \mid \mathcal{B}(b)(s) = \omega\} \\[4pt]
R(\pi_1; \pi_2) = \quad & \{(s, \sigma) \mid \exists s' \in \Sigma : (s, s') \in R(\pi_1) \wedge (s', \sigma) \in R(\pi_2)\} \\
\cup \; & \{(s, \omega) \mid (s, \omega) \in R(\pi_1)\}
\end{aligned}
$$

Note how the last set in the clauses for assignments and conditionals expresses that failures propagate from the expression level to the statement level.

From these relational definitions the following characterizations for the weakest relativized predicate transformer can be derived. The proofs are easy but a bit tedious and hence omitted.

$$
\mathsf{wrp}_A.x := e.\psi = \mathsf{in}_A(e) \vee (\mathsf{def}(e) \wedge \psi[e/x])
$$
$$
\mathsf{wrp}_A.\text{if } b \text{ then } \pi_1 \text{ else } \pi_2.\psi = \mathsf{in}_A(b) \vee (b{=}\mathsf{tt} \wedge \mathsf{wrp}_A.\pi_1.\psi) \vee (b{=}\mathsf{ff} \wedge \mathsf{wrp}_A.\pi_2.\psi)
$$
$$
\mathsf{wrp}_A.\pi_1; \pi_2.\psi = \mathsf{wrp}_A.\pi_1.(\mathsf{wrp}_A.\pi_2.\psi)
$$

Note how the disjuncts $\mathsf{in}_A(e)$ and $\mathsf{in}_A(b)$ handle the case of an acceptable failure. As for wp and wlp, sequential composition corresponds to functional composition of predicate transformers.

Loop. The situation gets more interesting for loops. The semantics of a while loop while b do π od can be captured in an intuitive way in terms of the following notion of a (b, π)-path [21]: A (b, π)-path is a finite or infinite sequence $p = s_1, s_2, \ldots$ of states in Σ, such that the following conditions are valid.

- Progression: each state in p, except for the last one in the finite case, satisfies b, i.e. $\mathcal{B}(b)(s_i) = \mathsf{tt}$ for all $1 \le i < |p|$, and
- Succession: successive state are related by $R(\pi)$, i.e. $(s_i, s_{i+1}) \in R(\pi)$ for all $1 \le i < |p|$.

Here the *length* $|p|$ of (b, π)-path is the number of states in p in the finite case and ∞ in the infinite case. A finite (b, π)-path is said to go from s to s' if s and s' are its first and last state respectively. Intuitively, the states in a (b, π)-path represent the intermediate states at the beginning of the loop in a prefix of a computation with $|p| - 1$ iterations of the body.

The relational semantics of a while loop while b do π od can now be defined as follows.

$R(\text{while } b \text{ do } \pi \text{ od}) =$

$\qquad \{(s, s') \mid \text{there is a finite } (b, \pi)\text{-path from } s \text{ to } s' \text{ with } \mathcal{B}(b)(s') = \text{ff}\}$

$\qquad \cup \, \{(s, \omega) \mid \text{there is a finite } (b, \pi)\text{-path from } s \text{ to } s' \text{ with } \mathcal{B}(b)(s') = \omega\}$

$\qquad \cup \, \{(s, \omega) \mid \text{there is a finite } (b, \pi)\text{-path from } s \text{ to } s' \text{ with } \mathcal{B}(b)(s') = \text{tt}$
$\qquad\qquad\qquad\qquad\qquad\qquad\qquad\qquad\qquad \text{and } (s', \omega) \in R(\pi)\}$

$\qquad \cup \, \{(s, \infty) \mid \text{there is an infinite } (b, \pi)\text{-path starting in } s\}$

The first set describes the case of regular termination; the other three sets are concerned with the different causes for failures of loops. First, evaluation of the guard could fail; second, the evaluation of the body could fail; and, finally, the loop may diverge.

$\text{wrp}_A.\text{while } b \text{ do } \pi$ can be characterized as a (semantic) fixpoint of the equation

$$X = \text{if } b \text{ then } \pi; X \text{ else skip od} \,.$$

Not surprisingly, the cases whether divergence is an accepted outcome or not, differ substantially. We have to take the greatest fixpoint w.r.t. $\leq$, if $\infty \in A$, and the smallest fixpoint if $\infty \notin A$.

Alternatively, the relativized predicate transformer of a loop can be characterized by a recurrence on the predicate level. This generalizes and justifies the well-known postulates from [9].

Theorem 9. *Suppose $A \subseteq \Omega$ and $\psi \in \text{Pred}$. Then $\text{wrp}_A.\text{while } b \text{ do } \pi.\psi$ is the greatest (weakest) solution of the predicate equation*

$$\phi = \text{in}_A(b) \vee (b = \text{tt} \wedge \text{wrp}_A.\pi.\phi) \vee (b = \text{ff} \wedge \psi)$$

if $\infty \in A$, and the smallest (strongest) solution otherwise.

Due to lack of space, we cannot give the full proof. Let us for explanation just mention that, if we accept diverging loops, i.e. $\infty \in A$, then there are more initial states from which all outgoing computations either satisfy postcondition ψ or have an outcome contained in A. Thus, the solution must have a greater cardinality in this case. This makes it plausible that indeed the weakest solution is the right one.

7   An Application

In order to show the utility of the relativized setup, let us recall one of our examples from Sect. 2. We are going to study a question of the kind 'Is a given transformation (translation) permitted w.r.t. some set of accepted outcomes?'. We consider a simplified version of the dead-code elimination example (Fig. 1). Suppose π and π' are the following programs:

$$\pi \stackrel{\text{def.}}{=} x := e \; ; x := f \; ; P \qquad\qquad \pi' \stackrel{\text{def.}}{=} x := f \; ; P$$

The expression f is assumed not to contain x; intuitively, it should thus safely be possible to remove $x := e$ from π as the value of x is over-written immediately. Let us see whether we can justify the transformation from π to π' with the relativized predicate transformers. Note that π can be written in the form $x := e \; ; \pi'$.

Using the identities from the previous section we obtain the following.

$$\text{wrp}_A.\pi.\psi \quad = \quad \text{in}_A(e) \vee (\text{def}(e) \wedge (\text{wrp}.\pi'.\psi)[e/x])$$
$$\text{wrp}_A.\pi'.\psi \quad = \quad \text{in}_A(f) \vee (\text{def}(f) \wedge (\text{wrp}.P.\psi)[f/x])$$

From the assumption that f does not contain x it follows by standard logical arguments that the substitution $[e/x]$ has no effect when applied to $\text{wrp}_A.\pi'.\psi$. Thus, the identity for $\text{wrp}_A.\pi.\psi$ can be simplified.

$$\text{wrp}_A.\pi.\psi \quad = \quad \text{in}_A(e) \vee (\text{def}(e) \wedge (\text{wrp}.\pi'.\psi))$$

Now, deciding whether π' implements π amounts to checking whether $\text{wrp}_A.\pi.\psi$ implies $\text{wrp}_A.\pi'.\psi$ for all predicates ψ. This is certainly the case if $\text{in}_A(e)$ is equivalent to `false`, i.e. does not hold for any state. Indeed in the absence of any further knowledge about e, f and P this is the only safe statement we can make.

What does this mean intuitively? The transformation from π to π' is permissible, if we can be sure that none of the failures potentially produced by e belong to the accepted failures in A. This is in particular the case if A does not contain any arithmetic error, i.e. none of the errors produced by arithmetic expressions.[5] For a more far-reaching conclusion we would need more specific knowledge about e. For example, we might conclude from the fact that e does not contain a division that A might contain the 'div-by-zero' failure.

It is interesting to discuss also the border cases for this example. In the PTC-case we have $A = \emptyset$; then $\text{in}_A(e)$ is equivalent to `false` for trivial reasons. Thus, π' indeed implements π w.r.t. PTC. In the PPC-case, on the other hand we have $A = \Omega$. Then $\text{in}_A(e)$ might be valid for some state if evaluation of e might fail. Thus, the transformation might be invalid in the sense of PPC, depending on the shape of e. So, the formal framework confirms the informal reasoning from Sect. 2.

A similar analysis might be performed for the other examples from that section.

---

[5] Formally, we call an error ω an *arithmetic error* if there is an expression e and a state s such that $\mathcal{E}(e)(s) = \omega$.

8   Conclusion

In this paper we suggested a semantic framework for performing compiler correctness or refinement proofs in scenarios where optimizations and finiteness of machines are allowed for. The proposed notions of weakest relativized preconditions and the corresponding predicate transformers permit to abandon the irregular outcomes from the scene in which we actually are working. We have to take them into account only when interpreting the programs in question. Afterwards the actual reasoning can take place in the familiar complete Boolean lattices of predicates and predicate transformers. Nevertheless the obtained correctness results can immediately be interpreted in terms of the more concrete objects of our operational intuition. We see our work as a step towards bridging a gap between elegant theory and practical needs.

This paper draws its motivation partly from work performed in the Verifix project [10] funded by the German DFG (Deutsche Forschungsgemeinschaft), which aims at a fully verified and correctly implemented compiler. Its roots also lie in the ProCoS project [5] in which we pursued a rather comprehensive compiler proof [21] for a prototypic real-time programming language to Transputer code. In that proof monotonic predicate transformers proved to provide a very convenient space that facilitates achieving modularity in the correct construction of the compiling mapping. Modularity is a very important requirement for such an undertaking as otherwise things might easily become unmanageable and untrustworthy. wrp is intended to permit an elegant treatment of runtime errors and finiteness of machines while staying in the familiar and well-studied realm of predicates and predicate transformers. No new theory about predicate transformers is necessary; wrp just provides a different interpretation of programs than wlp and wp, but by objects of the same kind.

For simplicity we have assumed that source and target programs act on the same state space. Of course this is an unrealistic assumption, from a practical point of view. It is, however, a useful idealization if one is mainly interested in considerations concerning control flow implementation. The more realistic situation of different state spaces can be handled with data refinement techniques and Galois connections. For more information on this topic and corresponding references see [21].

Future work includes a more thorough study of wrp and its utility for compiler correctness proofs. More specifically, we are currently investigating the use of wrp for proving the correctness of the translation of nested parameterless procedures to machines with bounded stacks.

Acknowledgments. We are grateful to our colleagues from the ProCoS and Verifix project for many discussions that shaped our view of compiler correctness and verification; a special thank goes to Hans Langmaack for encouraging us to write this paper. The funny example of the MODULA 2 loop was communicated by Gerhard Goos. We also thank Jens Knoop, Hans Langmaack, and an anonymous referee of FM'99 for comments that helped to improve on a draft version.

References

[1] A. V. Aho, R. Sethi, and J. D. Ullman. *Compilers: Principles, Techniques, and Tools*. Addison-Wesley, 1986.

[2] K.-R. Apt and E.-R. Olderog. *Verification of Sequential and Concurrent Programs*. Springer-Verlag, 2nd edition, 1997.

[3] R.-J. Back and J. von Wright. *Refinement Calculus: A Systematic Introduction*. Springer, 1998.

[4] E. Börger and I. Durdanović. Correctness of compiling Occam to transputer code. *The Computer Journal*, 39(1), 1996.

[5] J. P. Bowen et al. A ProCoS II project description: ESPRIT Basic Research project 7071. *Bulletin of the EATCS*, 50:128–137, June 1993.

[6] L. M. Chirica and D. F. Martin. Towards compiler implementation correctness proofs. *ACM Transactions on Programming Languages and Systems*, 8(2):185–214, April 1986.

[7] J. W. de Bakker. *Mathematical Theory of Program Correctness*. Prentice-Hall, 1980.

[8] E. W. Dijkstra. *A Discipline of Programming*. Prentice-Hall, 1976.

[9] E. W. Dijkstra and C. S. Scholten. *Predicate Calculus and Program Semantics*. Texts and Monographs in Computer Science. Springer-Verlag, 1990.

[10] W. Goerigk, A. Dold, T. Gaul, G. Goos, A. Heberle, F. Henke, U. Hoffmann, H. Langmaack, H. Pfeifer, H. Ruess, and W. Zimmermann. Compiler correctness and implementation verification: The Verifix approach. In P. Fritzson, editor, *Proc. Poster Session CC'96*, pages 65 – 73, IDA Technical Report LiTH-IDA-R-96-12, Linköping, Sweden, 1996.

[11] D. Gries. *The Science of Programming*. Springer-Verlag, 1981.

[12] J. D. Guttman, J. D. Ramsdell, and M. Wand. VLISP: A verified implementation of Scheme. *Lisp and Symbolic Computation*, 8:5–32, 1995.

[13] C. A. R. Hoare. An axiomatic basis for computer programming. *Communications of the ACM*, 12(10):576–583, 1969.

[14] C. A. R. Hoare, H. Jifeng, and A. Sampaio. Normal form approach to compiler design. *Acta Informatica*, 30:701–739, 1993.

[15] H. Langmaack. Software engineering for certification of systems: Specification, implementation, and compiler correctness (in German). *Informationstechnik und Technische Informatik*, 39(3):41–47, 1997.

[16] J. S. Moore. *Piton, A Mechanically Verified Assembly-Level Language*. Kluwer Academic Publishers, 1996.

[17] C. Morgan and T. Vickers, editors. *On the Refinement Calculus*. Springer-Verlag, 1994.

[18] J. M. Morris. A theoretical basis for stepwise refinement and the programming calculus. *Science of Computer Programming*, 9:287–306, 1987.

[19] P. D. Mosses. *Action Semantics*. Cambridge University Press, 1992.

[20] S. S. Muchnick. *Advanced compiler design implementation*. Morgan Kaufmann Publishers, San Francisco, California, 1997.

[21] M. Müller-Olm. *Modular Compiler Verification: A Refinement-Algebraic Approach Advocating Stepwise Abstraction*, LNCS 1283. Springer-Verlag, 1997.

[22] T. S. Norvell. Machine code programs are predicates too. In D. Till, editor, *6th Refinement Workshop*, Workshops in Computing. Springer-Verlag and British Computer Society, 1994.

[23] E. Pofahl. Methods used for inspecting safety relevant software. In W. J. Cullyer, W. A. Halang, and B. J. Krämer, editors, *High Integrity Programmable Electronics*, pages 13–14. Dagstuhl-Sem.-Rep. 107, 1995.

[24] S. Sippu and E. Soisalon-Soininen. *Parsing Theory Vol. I.* Springer-Verlag, 1988.

[25] W. M. Waite and G. Goos. *Compiler Construction.* Springer-Verlag, 1984.

[26] R. Wilhelm and D. Maurer. *Übersetzerbau.* Springer, 1992.

Interfacing Program Construction and Verification

Richard Verhoeven* and Roland Backhouse

Department of Mathematics and Computing Science, Eindhoven University of
Technology, PO Box 513, 5600 MB Eindhoven, The Netherlands
{river,rolandb}@win.tue.nl

Abstract. Math∫pad is a document preparation system designed and
developed by the authors and oriented towards the calculational construction of programs. PVS (Prototype Verification System) is a theorem checker developed at SRI that has been extensively used for verifying software, in particular in safety-critical applications. This paper
describes how these two systems have been combined into one. We discuss the potential benefits of the combination seen from the viewpoint
of someone wanting to use formal methods for the construction of computer programs, and we discuss the architecture of the combined system
for the benefit of anyone wanting to investigate combining the Math∫pad
system with other programming tools.

1 Introduction

Math∫pad [5] is a document preparation system designed and implemented by
the first author under the direction of the second author, initially with the help
of Olaf Weber. The almost-WYSIWYG nature and flexibility of Math∫pad means
that it can be used for on-screen mathematical calculation (in any formal system) and, in particular, for the calculational construction and documentation
of programs, this being indeed the purpose for which the system was originally
designed. The system has now been stable for several years and has been used
to write a number of Ph.D. and M.Sc. theses and articles in the area of the
mathematics of program construction [3] and program specification using Z [8],
as well as the on-line documentation of the system itself [6].

PVS (Prototype Verification System) is a theorem checker developed at SRI
that has been extensively used for verifying software, in particular in safety-
critical applications. A description of PVS is given on the "What is PVS?" page
at SRI [17]:

> PVS is a verification system: that is, a specification language inte-
> grated with support tools and a theorem prover. It is intended to capture
> the state-of-the-art in mechanized formal methods and to be sufficiently

* Research supported by the Dutch Organisation for Scientific Research (NWO) under
contract SION 612–14–001

J. Wing, J. Woodcock, J. Davies (Eds.): FM'99, Vol. II, LNCS 1709, pp. 1128–1146, 1999.
© Springer-Verlag Berlin Heidelberg 1999

rugged that it can be used for significant applications. PVS is a research prototype: it evolves and improves as we develop or apply new capabilities, and as the stress of real use exposes new requirements.

PVS is a large and complex system and it takes a long while to learn to use it effectively. You should be prepared to invest six months to become a moderately skilled user (less if you already know other verification systems, more if you need to learn logic or unlearn Z)

Math/pad and PVS have completely different design goals, stemming from the fact that Math/pad is intended to support the (formal) *construction* of computer programs, whereas PVS is designed to support the *verification* of existing programs. Thus Math/pad supports the language of mathematics, in its full generality, whereas PVS constrains its user to its own ASCII-based teletype language. But Math/pad does not purport to validate or verify the user's calculations in any way, that being the responsibility of the user, whereas PVS does.

The design of Math/pad reflects what we believe to be the highest priorities in developing tools to support the use of formal methods for software design. Above all, we concur wholeheartedly with Knuth's view [12] that programming is best viewed as a document preparation activity, the documentation serving to integrate the many different aspects (requirements, specification, implementation, testing etc.) of a highly complex process. Furthermore the language of programming specification is the language of mathematics — in other words, precise and concise, but unconstrained and subject to continual evolution and adaptation. Finally, the goal of formal methods is to ensure that programs are *correct by construction*, i.e. that the discipline of programming guarantees (when applied conscientiously and correctly) that the constructed program satisfies its specification.

This is not to say that program verification is not important. Independent checks on the validity of computer programs are vital to reliability guarantees and quality control. Formal verification, model checking, extensive (manual) testing and (independent) code walk-throughs all contribute in their own way, and none should be neglected in the real world of software design, particularly where safety is significant. But program verification can only be truly helpful if it doesn't require "unlearning" a mathematical specification language like Z in favour of spending six months becoming a moderately skilled user of an awkward teletype language.

This description of PVS might seem to be negative, but many interactive theorem provers fit this description. For many theorem provers, the user interface is not as important as the logical engine that does the reasoning. As a result, users of theorem provers are often confronted with a system-specific specification language, usually one-dimensional and based on ASCII. Since mathematics uses special symbols and operators, a translation is needed from the mathematically oriented language to the specification language, which reduces the readability and can introduce errors. If the specification becomes unreadable, the user might prefer the blackboard to do the calculations and consider using the theorem prover to check it afterwards.

Some constructors of theorem provers have recognized that the interface should be improved, as discussed during the User Interfaces for Theorem Provers (UITP) workshops [7, 4]. To improve the readability, the interface should use mathematical notations, as used, for example, during lectures on the blackboard. A good example of such an improved interface is the Jape system [20], where the user works with a familiar notation, albeit one-dimensional except for some specific in-built notations. The next step is to integrate the theorems, proofs and documentation into one single document, as in Mathematica [22] and Maple[16].

Now that we have successfully achieved our own initial goals, in the form of a stable, well-tested (mathematical-)document preparation system, the time is ripe to couple it to other tools, such as program verifiers. This document describes how we have combined Math∫pad with PVS. We discuss the potential benefits of the combination seen from the viewpoint of someone wanting to use formal methods for the construction of computer programs, and we discuss the architecture of the combined system for the benefit of anyone wanting to investigate combining the Math∫pad system with other programming tools. The system we have implemented runs under Unix and may be downloaded from http://www.win.tue.nl/cs/wp/mathspad.

2   User Model

The recent Ph.D. thesis by Matteo Vaccari [21] is illustrative of what we ultimately want to achieve. In his thesis, Vaccari discusses the calculational construction of hardware circuits, where the first 6 chapters contain theoretical discussions of relation algebra, circuits and regular language recognizers, while the later chapters contain simulations of the circuits using Tangram [18] and a machine verification of the theory using PVS [14]. Vaccari used Math∫pad in the process of developing and documenting the "theoretical" designs in the initial chapters, and then hand-coded these into the forms acceptable to Tangram and PVS. (See Fig. 1.)

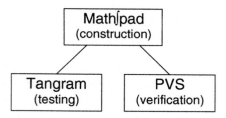

Fig. 1. The user model

The use of *two* additional and entirely independent systems to check the "theoretical" designs gives a remarkable level of confidence in the reliability of

Vaccari's designs that could not have been achieved by using any one of the systems on its own. Tangram is a system comprising a language, a simulator and a compiler developed at Philips Research Laboratories, Eindhoven, for the design of asynchronous hardware circuits. Using it, Vaccari was able to *test* that his designs functioned according to specification. In addition, Tangram has features to analyse the efficiency of a circuit design (including area, speed and energy consumption), and warns against unimplementable features. The PVS system comprises its own, quite different, specification language based on higher-order logic. Using it, Vaccari was able to formally *verify* all the lemmas and theorems leading up to and including the final circuit design. Vaccari comments in his thesis that neither systems showed up any errors in the calculated designs; however, the use of Tangram gave practical feedback, whereas the use of PVS obliged him to clarify certain elements in his calculations.

Independent checks are crucial to improving confidence, but there is one major weakness in the procedure adopted by Vaccari: namely, the lack of any formal link between the mathematical language in which his designs were constructed, the language of Tangram in which his designs were tested, and the language of PVS in which his designs were verified. This, however, is a weakness shared by all validation systems (theorem provers, model checkers, etc.) that we know of since such systems are invariably based on a language that is different to the actual implementation language used by "real" programmers. Practical reality compounds the problems drastically: since systems are subject to continual modification and evolution, it is almost inevitably the case that what is verified (or even tested) is not what is executed.

We believe that the use of a system like Math∫pad can make a substantial contribution to overcoming this weakness. Math∫pad is a structure editor — the user of Math∫pad manipulates, in fact, an abstract structure which is viewed on-screen as a mathematical expression but which can also be viewed as a Tangram program or as a collection of theorems and proofs in the PVS system.

Of course, matters are not quite as simple as we have just sketched. The process of viewing an abstract structure on screen involves, by design, a very simple transformation of the structure into display events, whereas the process of transforming the structure into a Tangram program is much less simple, and the process of converting it into a collection of PVS theorems and proofs – the topic of this paper – is far from trivial. But this is essentially what Vaccari did in his thesis, mostly by hand but also with the aid of a number of automated tools. Our goal in developing the interface with the PVS system was to automate this process as much as possible.

A tool like Math∫pad has the potential to be useful as an interface for several backend engines, such as symbolic computation systems and theorem provers. Many of those systems have a teletype interface and the mathematical content is often difficult to read and written in an unfamiliar syntax. Furthermore, each system uses its own syntax, which makes it virtually impossible to switch from one system to another. In Math∫pad, the user works with the familiar syntax, while the generated output is less important. As it is possible to generate output in another markup language, it is not too difficult to generate the input that is needed for a particular backend engine. For a normal user, Math∫pad should hide all the knowledge that is needed to use the backend engine and translate the input and output of the backend engine to the syntax familiar to the user. For an expert user, the connection with the backend engine should be easy to construct and maintain.

Since there are many possible backend engines with their own markup languages, the connection between Math∫pad and a backend engine should be as generic as possible. A connection with one particular backend engine would not be too difficult to construct and Math∫pad could be tuned for that backend engine. However, if a connection with a different backend engine is needed, the same work has to be done all over again. Therefore, the core Math∫pad system does not contain specific knowledge about one particular backend, but it provides the functionality to add that knowledge.

In the following sections, the connection we have made between Math∫pad and the PVS system is described. The PVS system was chosen because the Math∫pad documents with human readable proofs created by Vaccari and their PVS versions were available to us, thus providing a substantial test-base for our ideas. Furthermore, the PVS system is a non-trivial system and was likely to expose problems of a general nature when connecting Math∫pad to other systems.

3   An Example

A simple example will serve to illustrate the difference between mathematical calculation and PVS-style verification.

3.1   Mathematical Calculation

The example, in the popular Feijen style of proof presentation [11], in Fig. 2 is taken from Vaccari's thesis [21]. Figure 3 shows the example as the user sees it in the Math∫pad editor.

In the example, a law is given about *map* and *fold*, together with a proof that the law is correct. The proof, although very simple, illustrates well the advantages of good, clear mathematical notation.

Consider the calculation introduced by the words "For $n + 1$ we have". Note, first, the invisible use of the associativity of composition in the first two steps[1]. In the first step $fold_{n+1}.R$ is replaced by $R \circ \iota \times fold_n.R$, and $map_{n+1}.S$ is replaced by $S \times map_n.S$. The combined effect is to replace the top line in the calculation by

$$(R \circ \iota \times fold_n.R) \circ S \times map_n.S$$

where the parentheses indicate the grouping resulting from the two replacements. Note now that the second step groups the subterms differently. In the second

---

[1] Here multiplication has precedence over composition, denoted by a small circle. The meaning of the operators is not relevant to the current discussion.

A law about *map* and *fold* is the following: given R and S such that

$$R \circ S{\times}S \;=\; S \circ R$$

then

$$fold_n.R \circ map_n.S \;=\; S \circ fold_n.R$$

The proof is by induction on n; for $n = 1$ it is trivially true. For $n + 1$ we have

$$fold_{n+1}.R \circ map_{n+1}.S$$

$=$ { definitions }

$$R \;\circ\; \iota{\times}fold_n.R \;\circ\; S{\times}map_n.S$$

$=$ { fusion }

$$R \;\circ\; S{\times}(fold_n.R \circ map_n.S)$$

$=$ { induction hypothesis }

$$R \circ S{\times}(S \circ fold_n.R)$$

$=$ { proviso: $R \circ S{\times}S \;=\; S \circ R$; fusion }

$$S \;\circ\; R \;\circ\; \iota{\times}fold_n.R$$

$=$ { definition }

$$S \circ fold_{n+1}.R$$

Fig. 2. The formatted example

step the subterms $\iota \times fold_n.R$ and $S \times map_n.S$ are "fused" together to form the subterm $S{\times}(S \circ fold_n.R \circ map_n.S)$. That is, the associativity of composition has been applied implicitly between the first and second steps transforming the expression displayed above to

$$R \circ (\iota{\times}fold_n.R \;\circ\; S{\times}map_n.S)$$

Such uses of associativity occur very frequently in calculations and, as here, a practised scientist would not make its use explicit. (In fact, another invisible step in the proof involves exploiting the fact that the symbol ι denotes the identity of composition.)

A second point to note about this proof is that "fusion" appears twice in the hints (the remarks between curly bracktes). Both hints refer to the same law, but the law is used in different directions in the two instances (once from left to right and once from right to left).

A final point about this little calculation is the non-explicit use of the transitivity of equality. What is proved is that the top line

$$fold_{n+1}.R \circ map_{n+1}.S$$

A law about *map* and *fold* is the following: given R and S such that

$$R \circ S{\times}S = S \circ R$$

then

$$fold_n.R \circ map_n.S = S \circ fold_n.R$$

The proof is by induction on n; for $n{=}1$ it is trivially true.
For $n{+}1$ we have

$$fold_{n+1}.R \circ map_{n+1}.S$$
$$= \quad \{ \quad \text{definitions} \}$$
$$R \circ \imath{\times}fold_n.R \circ S{\times}map_n.S$$
$$= \quad \{ \quad \text{fusion} \}$$
$$R \circ S \times (fold_n.R \circ map_n.S)$$
$$= \quad \{ \quad \text{induction hypothesis} \}$$
$$R \circ S{\times}(S \circ fold_n.R)$$
$$= \quad \{ \quad \text{proviso:} R \circ S{\times}S = S \circ R; \text{fusion} \}$$
$$S \circ R \circ \imath{\times}fold_n.R$$
$$= \quad \{ \quad \text{definition} \}$$
$$S \circ fold_{n+1}.R$$

Fig. 3. The example as it appears in Math∫pad (as screendump)

is equal to the bottom line

$$S \circ fold_{n+1}.R$$

but this is not stated explicitly since it is immediately clear from the structure
and layout of the proof.

3.2   PVS Verification

Although the law and the proof are given in an informal manner, the manual
translation to PVS is straightforward, as is shown in Fig. 4.

The translation may indeed be easy to carry out by hand, but the result is
complex, is far from being readable and does not come anywhere near to the way
that human beings wish to see proofs presented. The statement of the theorem
is readable but this is misleading: the o and ∗ operators are overloaded. Since
you can not define new binary operators in PVS and the number of operators
that can be overloaded is small, it is very likely that the PVS specification will
become unreadable, as binary operators have to be replaced by functions with
two arguments. Furthermore, the precedence of the overloaded operators can not
be changed, which leads to confusion if another precedence is assumed. In the
example, the precedence of the o and ∗ operators is different in the PVS version,
which decreases the readability.

Another factor that contributes to the unreadability is the requirement to be
explicit about the use of the identity of composition. The line with the comment

The PVS definition:

```
fold_map:   THEOREM  R o (S*S) = S o R
                   IMPLIES fold(n,R) o map(n,S) = S o fold(n,R)
```

The PVS proof script:

```
(induct "n" 1)                              %induction
1  (grind)                                  %basis: trivial
   (rewrite "id0")
   (rewrite "id1")
2  (skolem!) (ground)                       %step
   (skolem!) (ground)
   (expand "fold" :if-simplifies t)         %definition
   (expand "map" :if-simplifies t)          %definition
   (assoc-rewrite "fusion" :dir RL)         %fusion lemma
   (inst?) (ground)                         %induction hypothesis
   (replace*)
   (rewrite "id1")                          %remove unit of composition
   (rewrite "id0" 1 ("R" "S!1") 1 RL)       %add unit of composition
   (assoc-rewrite "fusion")                 %fusion lemma
   (rewrite "id0")                          %remove unit of composition
   (replace*)                               %proviso
   (rewrite "comp_assoc")                   %associativity of composition
```

Fig. 4. The PVS example

"add unit of composition", for example, involves a complex "path expression" indicating to which subterm the rule is applied, in a manner akin to the way that paths through a directory structure had to be typed in before the existence of pointing devices.

But most importantly, the proof script as shown in the example is but a very small part of what the user sees while the proof is being built. After each step in the proof script, PVS will display the intermediate results and the current goal, which leads to several pages of formulae in the highly unreadable PVS-speak! A straightforward proof has thus been turned into an intellectual feat!

4   Building the Interface

4.1   Communication with PVS

From a user interface point of view, PVS is an extension of Emacs, which connects the proof engine to the Emacs interface and the Tcl toolkit. The user can edit files containing theorems and use the proof engine to construct the proof interactively. Since the proof engine is basically a lisp interpreter with state information, the user interface of the engine is hidden from the user by a collection of pull-down menus in Emacs. With these menus, the user can perform all the actions that might be needed to manipulate files, theorems, lemmas and proofs. However, to construct a PVS proof, the user has to enter plain lisp commands to apply tactics to a goal. To allow some proof planning, an interface with a Tcl program is available to keep track of the subgoals.

Since PVS is a closed system and cannot be modified, the available PVS interface had to be used. The first problem was the existing Emacs interface, which complicates the communication with PVS. Luckily, the PVS system consists of a core system connected to Emacs with a collection of Emacs lisp files, as shown in Fig. 5. Emacs contains a lisp interpreter which is used to load the lisp files for the PVS communication. These configuration files extend Emacs with new functions and menus to provide a PVS specific interface. With these additional functions, Emacs is able to communicate with the PVS core system, using its standard input and output.

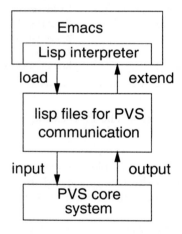

Fig. 5. The PVS structure

By using the PVS core system directly, the communication is simplified and easier to maintain. However, the protocol used between Emacs and the core system is not documented, probably because the constructors of PVS didn't envisage a different interface to that core system. Therefore, the protocol had to be extracted from the lisp configuration files used by Emacs and the messages that are sent between Emacs and the core system. With some detective work in the form of a wrapper script that monitors these messages, we were able to reconstruct the most important parts of the protocol, which was sufficient to use the core system without the Emacs interface.

The PVS core system is a lisp interpreter and receives lisp commands as input, which can be used to update or inspect the state of the system or to prove a theorem. The output of the core system consists of a combination of commands to update the state of Emacs and the results of proving a theorem. The core system might also construct temporary files and instruct Emacs to open them, which is mainly used for help files and the Tcl interface. The Emacs interface cleverly hides the lisp input with a collection of pull-down menus, while the mixed output is parsed and separated into several buffers. For the average user, only the buffer with the results of a proof are of interest.

The PVS core system operates in three modes: a mode for managing the state, a mode for making the proofs and a debug mode. Since the active mode affects the commands that Emacs has to send, the system uses synchronization points when it switches to a different mode and notifies Emacs. The debug mode is only used if the system receives incorrect input, and this mode is ended by resetting PVS.

To construct a different user interface for the PVS core system, the user interface had to simulate the actions performed by Emacs, such that the core system could not notice the difference. As our plan was to hide PVS as much as possible from the user, only a subset of the actions available in Emacs were made available in the new interface.

4.2   The Math∫pad Infrastructure

The PVS interface has been constructed as a loadable module. For this purpose, Math∫pad provides an interpreted language which can be used to extend the interface and to load modules. It is also possible for a loadable module to extend the language with new functions, variables and types. The infrastructure of the entire system is shown in Fig. 6.

The interpreter can be used to customise Math∫pad to a particular need. With the interpreted language, the user can define new functions to combine common sequences into a single function. These functions can be used in pop-up menus and keyboard definitions to customise the interface and the keyboard usage.

For each extension, Math∫pad will load an interface definition file to adjust the menus and keyboard definitions. Depending on the complexity of the extension, the interface definition file can include a dynamic library, which can extend the interpreted language with new functions, types and variables. With these new language items, the user can extend the menus and keyboard definitions and further customise the extension.

The combination of the interface definition file and the dynamic library can communicate with the external program through the standard input and output of the program. In order to do that, input has to be generated in the correct syntax for the particular program and the output of the program has to be parsed. As the interpreted language is not yet suited to the complex task of parsing the output, a dynamic library is usually needed if the output has to be parsed. When the output does not need to be parsed, some preprocessing of the output can be performed by adding a filter to the external program.

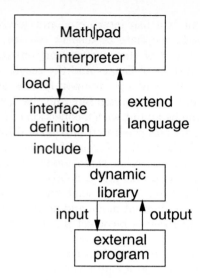

Fig. 6. The Math∫pad infrastructure

The interpreted language (see Fig. 7 for an example) is an imperative language, based on the guarded command language. It supports sequential composition, selection and repetition, but not recursion. Procedures are defined with a prototype, which is used to pass the arguments correctly, that is, to dereference variables where needed. Procedures can have local variables with the normal scope rules. To support callback functions, one additional operator is added to support lazy evaluation, that is, to pass an argument to a function such that it will be evaluated by that function at the correct time, for example after a filename is selected instead of before the file selector is opened.

The language supports a standard set of operators which can be overloaded by defining functions for each combination of arguments. This enables an extension to define new types with sensible operators, without the need to reconstruct the parser for the interpreted language.

Since some extension might have special needs for the content of menus, the strings in the interpreted language are in the Unicode encoding. This ensures that almost any symbol that an extension might need will be available for the pop-up menus and messages. For mathematical or foreign extensions, this will increase the readability.

4.3   The PVS Interface Library

The PVS module consists of a dynamic library for communicating with the PVS core system and an interpreted file to adjust the interface with Math∫pad. The purpose of the dynamic library is threefold. First, it interprets the Math∫pad document to extract theorems and proofs. Second, it generates the input that is sent to the PVS core system. Third, it parses the output that is generated by the core system.

As a Math/pad document is structured, the generation of theorems from a proof given in the Feijen style is not so difficult. For the example in Fig. 2, each of the five steps has to be correct, so we can generate a theorem for each step. Since the syntactical differences between the PVS input and the Math/pad version are not very different, generating these theorems is straightforward, once the definitions of the templates are correct. Extracting the proof for these theorems is also possible, as the hint contains keywords that indicate which strategies are applicable. In the example, the keyword "fusion" indicates that the fusion lemma is used as a rewrite rule. The keyword "definition" indicates that some definition has to be expanded and the keyword "induction" indicates that a premise is used as a rewrite rule, where the premise can be constructed from the proof itself by using the first and last expressions. However, the hints are not always precise enough, as is indicated by the PVS version of the proof. The additional details are automatically applied by a human reader of the formatted proof, without complaining. The reader will apply the trivial laws, such as the "identity of composition" and "associativity of composition", when needed and the direction in which an equality law is used is determined by trial and error. A complex dialogue with the author could be used to get these additional details, but we decided to define additional PVS strategies which simulate the behaviour of a human reader:

- a strategy to apply a rewrite rule in both directions,
- a strategy to retry a given strategy after applying the trivial laws, if that strategy fails the first time,
- a strategy to apply a rewrite rule modulo composition.

These strategies have their limitations, as it is likely that rewrite rules are applied incorrectly. However, the theorems are usually small and their proofs are short, so it is less likely that something will go wrong. In the event that a theorem can not be proven, an indication that the given hint is not sufficient to prove that step should be a reasonable reply from the system, as a reader might have the same problems with it as PVS.

For the other part of the example, the extraction of the theorems would require a combination of natural language processing and logical reasoning, for which a general solution is difficult. Therefore, this part is still missing from the current interface.

Once the theorems and proofs are known, they have to be converted to the specification language used by PVS. Since the output generated by Math/pad depends on the templates that are used, it is possible to generate valid PVS input from Math/pad expressions without much additional programming. However, the expressions appear in a certain context and the identifiers should have a certain type, otherwise PVS will generate parse or type errors. Although the context and type information can be stored in the document as hidden information, we chose to use a default context, where certain definitions and identifiers are predefined. This approach is quite common in documents with many identifiers, as it releases the author from the burden of mentioning the type of an identifier over and over again.

In order to give feedback to the user, the PVS output should be parsed and converted to familiar syntax. If a theorem is correct, all is well and a simple message should be sufficient. Otherwise, a warning or error message should be generated, indicating the problem and possibly a solution. If PVS does not need the generated proof completely, it might be that the given hint is incorrect or over-complete and Math∫pad will suggest to adjust the hint in order to avoid confusing the reader. If PVS is unable to prove the theorem, the hint might be incomplete or an error might have occurred. By inspecting the output and comparing the expressions Math∫pad could suggest that an identifier is incorrect or that a particular law might be applied. Since the user is not familiar with the PVS language, the output of PVS should be parsed and shown in the language as used in the document with a familiar syntax. However, the expressions in Math∫pad are constructed with templates, which are used to generate the PVS expression. Therefore, these templates should also be used to parse the PVS output, which is complicated by the possible ambiguities in the definition of these templates. At the moment, this part is still missing from the experimental interface.

The PVS output also contains commands which are handled by Emacs. For each command, the PVS module will either ignore it or translate it to the new interface. For example, after the PVS core system has finished a proof, it will tell Emacs to open a buffer with the PVS file that contains the proven theorem. In Math∫pad, that PVS file is generated by a step in a proof and of no interest to the user, so Math∫pad will highlight the step that generated the PVS file.

The library adds the functions `pvs_check_hint` (to check the selected hint), `pvs_start` (to start PVS) and `pvs_add_keyword` (to define a keyword like "induction" mentioned above and the related PVS strategies). These functions, together with the already available functions, are used in the pop-up menus to extend the interface of Math∫pad, for example to start PVS and to check a selected hint. The library also adds the variables `pvs_initialized` and `pvs_in_checker`, which can be used to inspect the status of PVS, and `pvs_context_dir`, `pvs_hint_file` and `pvs_lemma_name`, which are used to customise the generation of PVS files.

Since Math∫pad uses Unicode internally, the strings that are part of the library, such as error messages, have to be converted to Unicode before they are used. This conversion uses a translation table to check whether the string has been customised by the user. This leaves a library with an additional method of customisation: by converting a string with the translation table, it can be adjusted by the user. In the PVS module, the string "PVS_HEADER" is used as the header of the PVS file, which defines the context of the generated theorem. By defining a translation for this string, the correct header is used.

In addition to the theory-specific keywords, there are four keywords with a special meaning. Each of these keywords is used in a special case:

- INITSTEP is used to initialise the PVS proof and to remove universal quantifiers.
- FINISHSTEP is used to finalise the PVS proof by applying all the trivial steps,
- EXPRESSIONSTEP is used when an expression occurs within a hint. Expressions in hints are regarded as assumptions and will result in a premise.
- STOPPVSPROOF is used when the proof fails and PVS has to leave the proof mode.

Without these four keywords, a correct proof script can not be constructed. Therefore, the interface definition file has to define these keywords with the pvs_add_keyword function.

The dynamic library that is used to communicate with PVS is written in C and consists of about 1000 lines of code. 35 percent is used to separate the PVS output and to handle the lisp requests from PVS, 15 percent is used to parse the PVS proof output and 20 percent is used to extract theorem and proof from the selected hint.

4.4   The Definition File

The PVS dynamic library handles the communication with the PVS core system and provides the interpreted language with a collection of high-level functions. With these functions, the pop-up menus of Math∕pad have been extended with PVS specific commands or submenus. The interpreted language is also used to initialize and customize the PVS library, for example by filling the keyword list and setting up the context. Some parts of the definition file for PVS are shown in Fig. 7.

First, the dynamic library is included, meaning that the functions and variables from that library become available to the interpreter. It is also possible to include other definition files, which can be used to divide the different aspects of the interface over separate files.

After the dynamic library has been included, the function pvs_reset is defined, which is used to reset PVS if something goes wrong. This function could also be part of the dynamic library, but defining it in the interface definition file is more flexible, as it can be adjusted more easily.

Once all the functions are available, they can be linked to a pop-up menu and the keyboard. The interface definition language has special constructions to make this as easy as possible. A pop-up menu is defined by making a list of menu items, each containing a description and either the function to be called or the submenu to be opened. In the example, the menu called PVSMathSpad gives the user access to four PVS-specific functions. The menu itself is added as a submenu to the menu called Misc, which lists miscellaneous features.

Three functions are made available through keyboard shortcuts. After the Meta-p prefix, the key s will start PVS, the key c will check the selected hint and the key r will reset PVS.

```
Include "libpvs.so"

Function pvs_reset()
{
    if (pvs_initialized) {
        send_signal(2, "PVS Session");
        send_string(":reset\n", "PVS Session");
        pvs_in_checker := 0;
    }
}
Menu PVSMathSpad {
    Options Pin;
    Title "PVS Link";
    "Start"        : pvs_start("PVS Session");
    "Check Hint"   : pvs_check_hint(1);
    "Reset"        : pvs_reset();
    "Exit"         : send_string("(pvs::lisp (ILISP:ilisp-restore))
                         (pvs-errors (exit-pvs))\n", "PVS Session");
}
Menu  Misc {
    "PVS"    : PVSMathSpad;
}
Keyboard Global {
    'M-p' 's' : pvs_start("PVS Session");
    'M-p' 'c' : pvs_check_hint(1);
    'M-p' 'r' : pvs_reset();
}
Translation English {
  "PVS-shell"          : "PVS Session";
  "PVS_HEADER"         : " [t: TYPE+] : THEORY
 BEGIN
 IMPORTING tuples[t]
  n,m: VAR upfrom(1)
  R,S,T,U: VAR rel
";
}

pvs_context_dir := "/home/river/pvs-test";
pvs_hint_file := "hint";
pvs_lemma_name := "hintlemma";
pvs_add_keyword("STOPPVSPROOF", "(quit)\nY\n\"nil\"\nno\n",0);
...
pvs_add_keyword("induction",
                "(then* (inst?)(ground)
                 (try-triv-step (bidi-replace*)))\n", 1);
```

Fig. 7. The interface definition file

To customise the PVS library, two translation strings are defined. As explained earlier, a translation for the string "PVS_HEADER" is given to set the context for the generated theorems. In general, this translation mechanism is used to customise the messages from Math∕pad, as these are all in English and perhaps not clear enough (as in 'folder' versus 'directory').

At the end, the variables are initialised and the database of keywords is filled. At this point, the definition file is used as a script file to execute the functions while the definition file is loaded, which is used to futher customise the library.

5   Related Work

There are already some projects to improve the interface of PVS. TAME [2] is a layer on top of PVS for reasoning about timed automata and consists of a number of strategies to reduce the number of steps made in a typical PVS proof to the number of steps made in a hand-made proof. With these additional strategies, the user of TAME will not be exposed to the low-level steps and commands needed in PVS, thereby making the commands field specific. However, since the PVS interface is used, there is still a gap between the notational conventions used by PVS and those used in the documentation.

The system PAMELA [9] is designed to check partial correctness of VDM-like specifications in the area of code generators. By providing a connection with PVS, the system supports a larger class of specifications, using PVS to discharge proof obligations. The connection between PAMELA and PVS is made by extending PVS with additional commands and adding a Tcl/Tk interface which communicates with the Emacs system. Although this approach works, the modifications to PVS indicate that using a different theorem or a different interface would also require such changes. Furthermore, as the existing Emacs interfaces is still used, it does not remove the burden of using multiple interfaces and multiple specification languages.

Merriam constructed the PVS proof command prompter [13], which extends PVS with an additional input method for the proof commands to improve the PVS interface and to decrease the cognitive overhead for the user. The prompter uses a fill-in form to ask the user for the arguments that might be used for a given command.

GrammaTech and Formal Systems Design & Development are working on an environment for integrating formal methods tools to improve industrial acceptance of formal methods[1]. The environment will use active documents with embedded objects, with CORBA to handle the object distribution. The use of embedded object might cause some problems with the writability of the documents. That approach is also used by FrameMaker and Word, which are not the best word processors for mathematically oriented documents, as they have problems with context switches and treat mathematical expressions as images.

Simons has been working on a system to combine proofs in Isabelle [15] with documentation [19]. The system uses the structured documentation technique introduced by Knuth [12] to allow one file to contain both the proofs and the documentation and uses programs to separate those. This solves the problem of combining several files into one document, at the expense of using different languages in a single file, namely, LATEX for formatting the document, Isabelle for specifying the proof and the meta language to instruct the programs. For a user, this mix of languages might be confusing.

The ILF system [10] offers a uniform interface for several automated theorem provers and it removes the burden of translating the specification files to the languages used by these theorem provers. The ILF system does not require any changes to the existing theorem provers and works like a server, which sends proof obligations to the available theorem provers and handles the results. Although ILF hides the specific languages and options of the theorem provers, it does add its own specification language, based on PROLOG.

6   Conclusions

The goal we set ourselves in this project was to automatically translate mathematical calculations to PVS proofs. An automatic translation is of course much more difficult than one done by hand. Nevertheless the goal was feasible, given that Vaccari had written his thesis with the Math∫pad system so that all the documents needed to test the connection between PVS and Math∫pad were already available to us. The goal has been achieved except for the interpretation of natural language linking together different calculations. There are also still some problems hiding the PVS language from the user.

Math∫pad does not help the user to construct the PVS files which are needed to get started. Therefore, the connection only works if there are already some PVS files with the required definitions. These files must be constructed by someone who is conversant with both Math∫pad and PVS. However, only a limited number of such experts are needed; (ultimately) other users can exploit the benefits of formal verification with the PVS system without a six-month training period.

The connection has been made without adjusting PVS in any way. That is, the same version of PVS can be used with the Emacs interface and the Math∫pad interface. Although the Emacs interface had to be separated from the PVS core system, this process is not very difficult and can easily be repeated for the next version of PVS, assuming that the internal interface does not change drastically. The conversion from version 2.1 to version 2.2 of PVS was a matter of updating the initialization file for the PVS core system, which can be constructed by monitoring the communication between Emacs and the PVS core system.

In order to build a different user interface for an existing theorem prover, the theorem prover should have a clearly separated user interface and core system. For PVS, this structure is not directly visible, but after a closer look, the separation is not very difficult, although the documentation is missing.

The use of loadable modules in the form of dynamic libraries is a powerful technique and allows easy extension of a system, as is shown by applications like Netscape, the Linux kernel, the GIMP and Photoshop. It allows modules from different sources to combine their strength in order to improve the total system. If theorem provers were available as modules, the main system could choose the best module for a given job. With some effort, it is possible to use an existing theorem prover as a module. However, every theorem prover uses its own input format, output format and user interface, which makes it very difficult to combine the power of multiple theorem provers for a single project. Perhaps the MathML or OpenMath languages will be useful in this respect.

PVS seems to be at the correct level of automation for our purpose. An automatic theorem prover could not verify whether the hints are meaningful and would require additional testing. A low-level theorem prover would need additional information to finish the proof or high-level tactics have to be introduced.

References

[1] P. Anderson, M. Goldsmith, B. Scattergood, and T. Teitelbaum. An environment for intergrating formal methods tools. In Bertot [7]. See also: http://www.grammatech.com/papers/uitp.html.

[2] Myla Archer, Constance Heitmeyer, and Steve Sims. TAME: A PVS interface to simplify proofs for automata models. In Backhouse [4], pages 147–156. See also: http://www.win.tue.nl/cs/ipa/uitp/papers/Archer.ps.gz.

[3] R.C. Backhouse. Archive of the mathematics of program construction group. Available online at http://www.win.tue.nl/cs/wp/papers/, July 1998.

[4] R.C. Backhouse, editor. *Workshop on User Interfaces for Theorem Provers*, Computing Science Reports, July 1998. International Workshop, see also http://www.win.tue.nl/cs/ipa/uitp/proceedings.html.

[5] R.C. Backhouse, R. Verhoeven, and O. Weber. Math∫pad: A system for on-line preparation of mathematical documents. *Software – Concepts and Tools*, 18:80–89, 1997. See also: http://www.win.tue.nl/cs/wp/mathspad/.

[6] Roland Backhouse and Richard Verhoeven. Math∫pad *Ergonomic Document Preparation*, version 0.60 edition, February 1996. Manual of the Math∫pad system. See also: http://www.win.tue.nl/cs/wp/mathspad/.

[7] Yves Bertot, editor. *Workshop on User Interfaces for Theorem Provers*, September 1997. International Workshop, see also http://www-sop.inria.fr/croap/events/uitp97-papers.html.

[8] Eerke Boiten, John Derrick, Howard Bowman, and Maarten Steen. Consistency and refinement for partial specification in z. In Marie-Claude Gaudel and James Woodcock, editors, *FME '96: Industrial Benefit and Advances in Formal Methods*, volume 1051 of *LNCS*, pages 287–306. Springer, 1996.

[9] Bettina Buth. *Operation Refinement Proofs for VDM-like Specifications*. PhD thesis, Institute of Computer Science and Practical Mathematics of the Christian-Albrechts-University Kiel, February 1995. See also: http://www.informatik.uni-bremen.de/~bb.

[10] Ingo Dahn. Using ILF as an interface to many theorem provers. In Backhouse [4], pages 75–86. See also: http://www.win.tue.nl/cs/ipa/uitp/papers/Dahn.ps.gz.

[11] E.W. Dijkstra and C.S. Scholten. *Predicate Calculus and Program Semantics*. Springer-Verlag, Berlin, 1990.

[12] D.E. Knuth. Literate programming. *Computer Journal*, 27(2):97–111, 1984.

[13] N.A. Merriam and M.D. Harrison. What is wrong with GUIs for theorem provers. In Bertot [7]. See also: http://www.cs.york.ac.uk/~nam/uitp97.ps.gz.

[14] S. Owre, N. Shankar, and J. M. Rushby. *The PVS Specification Language*. Computer Science Laboratory, SRI International, Menlo Park, CA, February 1993. See also: http://pvs.csl.sri.com/.

[15] Lawrence C. Paulson. *Isabelle: a Generic Theorem Prover*. Number 828 in Lecture Notes in Computer Science. Springer – Berlin, 1994.

[16] Darren Redfern. *The Maple Handbook*. Springer, 1996.

[17] John Rushby. What is pvs? Available online at http://pvs.csl.sri.com/whatispvs.html, November 1998. Contains a description of PVS.

[18] Frits D. Schalij. Tangram manual. Technical Report UR 008/93, Philips Electronics N.V., 1996.

[19] Martin Simons. Proof presentation for Isabelle. In Elsa Gunter and Amy Felty, editors, *Theorem Proving in Higher Order Logics: 10th International Conference, TPHOLs '97*, volume 1275 of *Lecture Notes in Computer Science*, pages 259–274, Murray Hill, NJ, August 1997. Springer-Verlag.

[20] Bernard Sufrin and Richard Bornat. User interfaces for generic proof assistants part II: Displaying proofs. In Backhouse [4], pages 147–156. See also: http://www.win.tue.nl/cs/ipa/uitp/papers/Sufrin.ps.gz.

[21] Matteo Vaccari. *Calculational Derivation of Circuits*. PhD thesis, Dipartimento di Informatica, Università degli Studi di Milano, May 1998. See also: http://dotto.usr.dsi.unimi.it/~matteo/tesi.ps.gz.

[22] Stephen Wolfram. *The Mathematica Book*. Cambridge University Press, third edition edition, 1996.

Software Verification Based on Linear Programming⋆

S. Dellacherie⋆⋆, S. Devulder⋆ ⋆ ⋆, and J-L. Lambert†

GREYC, CNRS UPRESA 6072, Université de Caen,
BP 5186, 14032 Caen cedex, France
dellache@info.unicaen.fr, devulder@info.unicaen.fr, jll@info.unicaen.fr

Abstract. We introduce a new software verification method based on plain linear programming. The problematic is being given a software S and a property $\mathcal{P}$, to find whether there exists a path (i.e. a test sequence) of S satisfying $\mathcal{P}$, or a proof that $\mathcal{P}$ is impossible to satisfy.

The software S is modelized as a set of communicating automata which in turn is translated into a system of linear equations in positive numbers. Property $\mathcal{P}$ is then translated as extra linear equations added to this system.

We define the extended notion of flow-path (which includes the notion of path) permitting the automata to carry flows of data rather than undividable tokens. By applying linear programming in a sophisticated way to the linear system, it is possible, in time polynomial in the size of $(S, \mathcal{P})$, either to display a flow-path of S satisfying $\mathcal{P}$ or to prove that $\mathcal{P}$ is impossible to satisfy.

The existence of a flow-path does not always imply the existence of a path, as it can be non-integer valued. Yet, on all our modelized examples, the study of the flow-path solution always permitted either to display a path satisfying $\mathcal{P}$ or to underscore a reason proving $\mathcal{P}$ to be impossible to satisfy.

The first part of this document introduces the theoretical background of our method. The second part sums up results of the use of our method on some systems of industrial size.

Keywords: software, concurrent program, distributed system, formal verification, validation, simulation, test case generation, proof, linear programming, integer programming.

URL: http://www.info.unicaen.fr/lpv

⋆ This work was partly supported by CNET under grant n#95 5B 046, by Rgion Basse-Normandie and CNRS under contract CON950207DR19
⋆⋆ PhD Student, CNET and University of Caen
⋆ ⋆ ⋆ PhD Student, CNRS and University of Caen
† Professor, University of Caen

J. Wing, J. Woodcock, J. Davies (Eds.): FM'99, Vol. II, LNCS 1709, pp. 1147–1165, 1999.
© Springer-Verlag Berlin Heidelberg 1999

1   Introduction

Linear programming gathers means for optimizing a linear function subject to a set of linear constraints in real positive numbers [faq]. Due to its efficiency and the range of its applications areas (production management, networks organization, resources planification, ...), it is the cornerstone of combinatorial optimization techniques. Still at present, due to the arising of interior-point algorithms, linear programming attracts an important research power, both in theoretical and practical fields. Linear programming algorithms now routinely solve on a desktop computer problems involving hundreds of thousand rows per hundreds of thousand columns.

Linear programming is also a classical mean for tackling the much more difficult integer programming problem where all (or part of) variables need to have an integer value. A wide range of techniques are available for this particular problem.

Attempts to use linear programming in the verification domain is not new. The Petri-nets community has been using linear programming for almost fifteen years. Yet, it seems to be only used on very constrained models, not well suited for the modelization of real-world systems [ES92] or for the generation of the set of the model invariants, which is constructed blindly and whose size increases very quickly [LM89] [CHP92]. More recently, Corbett and Avrunin [CA95] studied the use of a general purpose integer programming algorithm directly on a communicating automata model. Unfortunately, the use of a general purpose integer programming algorithm destroys the efficiency of mere linear programming, and prevents the possibility of constructing proofs on the model.

Thus, to our knowledge, none of these attempts make a complete use of the powerful theoretical background bind to linear programming: the duality theory. We will overview in this document how the use of linear programming duality permits to obtain a non-trivial and efficient (polynomial time) completeness theorem on the proof of existence of a flow-path or the proof of non-existence of any flow-path.

Furthermore, as we will see in this document, our method shares very few features with other existing methods. Unlike *model-checking* techniques (see for example [McM93][Kur92] [Hol97]) our method works directly on the automata model without constructing a representation of the reachability graph, thus enabling the handling of huge models. Unlike *theorem-proving* techniques (see for example [Abr95][ORR+96] [GH93]), the proofs given by our method are automatic and fastly computed directly on the automata model.

Now considering its negative points, the main drawback of the method is the fact that if a flow-path is proved to exist, it does not always induce the existence of a path (i.e. a test sequence on the automata): linear programming works with real numbers, and the proposed flow-path is not always integer-valued. When such a fractional solution occurs, one has to make the property more precise and/or slightly transform the model in order to conclude.

Yet, as we will see in this document, a flow-path is not "very far" from a path. In practice on the automata models we have studied, the careful reading of the flow-path solution has always led us to find a path satisfying the property or a proof that the property is impossible to satisfy.

The first part of this document presents the theoretical background of the method. The first section formally defines the automata model, the set of properties handled, the synchronization and flow-synchronization rules. The second section explains how the automata model and a property are translated into a system of linear equations, and introduces the main theoretical result obtained using linear programming theory.

The second part of this document summarizes the results of the use of the method on three different systems:

1. A generic telephony system. We used our method on instances using from 5 to 7 telephones communicating through fifo-channels of size 3 to 7. Such a model uses more than 800 automata and 2500 different synchronization messages. The corresponding state space is more than 10^{40} wide. Resolutions took a few tens of minutes.
2. A generic access control system. We used our method on instances using up to 20 cards, 8 doors and 4 buildings, communications being done using buffers. Such a model uses 230 automata and 2800 different synchronization messages. The corresponding state space is more than 10^{52} wide. Resolutions took a few hours.
3. A generic bus arbiter. The method was used on instances going up to 1200 cells. The state space is then about 10^{500} wide. Resolutions took a few tens of minutes.

On all three systems we have always been able for all properties checked, either to find a test-suite or a proof of impossibility.

Note that the method described herein is subject to a patent[1] and is about to be industrialized.

2   Theoretical Principles

2.1   The Model

Our linear programming verification method works with a communicating automata formalism. Using communicating automata is quite common in the verification domain (StateCharts, part of the SDL and UML formalisms, ...). They are easy to understand and to use while being powerful enough to modelize a

---

[1]   patent #97 15217 registered on Dec. 3rd of 1997 and owned in common by France Telecom, the CNRS, and the University of Caen

large variety of software components. They also consitute a dynamic model of a software and are thus easily implementable and executable.

The use of communicating automata means that our verification method is mainly suited to verify the control part of a software, interactions between components of a software, and interactions between the control and the data of a software. A great part of verification needs in industrial software developments are of this kind.

Synchronized Automata   The automata we use communicate via rendez-vous, synchronizing themselves on messages carried by the transitions. We will call them in the remaining *synchronized automata*.

We modelize every possible component of the software with synchronized automata: the data, the control-flow, the communication channels (fifo-channels, stacks, ...). Of course, all these components need to have a finite domain, furthermore not too large. Yet we will see in the second part of this document that rather huge models can be handled by our verification method. Moreover, abstraction principles such as described in [CC77] can also be used in our approach to handle larger validity domains.

Figure 1 presents a small example that we are going to use to illustrate the method all along this document.

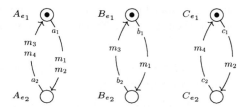

Fig. 1. A small example of synchronized automata.

Each automaton has states (the nodes, labeled A_{e_i}, B_{e_i} or C_{e_i}) and transitions (the arcs, labeled a_i, b_i or c_i). Each automaton has a single token that can move from state to state using the transitions. Transitions carry synchronization messages (m_1, m_2, m_3 and m_4). A transition may have multiple messages. For instance, arc a_1 bears two messages m_1 and m_2.

An automaton can go (i.e. move its token) from a state to another if and only if there exists a transition between those two states and all the synchronization messages present on that transition can be emitted. A message can be emitted if and only if all automata that know the message (ie. that have at least one transition carrying this message) can use simultaneously a transition carrying this message.

For example, automaton A can go from state A_{e_1} to state A_{e_2} if and only if both synchronization messages m_1 and m_2 can be emitted. This is possible if, for example, automata B and C are (ie. have their token) respectively in states B_{e_1} and C_{e_1}. In this situation, the three automata will arrive in state A_{e_2}, B_{e_2} and C_{e_2} respectively.

On the other hand, if A is in state A_{e_1} while automaton B is in state B_{e_2}, we are in a deadlock situation. Using transition a_1 requires the ability of emitting message m_1 which is impossible. Indeed B knows m_1 —carried by b_1— but is not in a state where it can emit it. So transition a_1 cannot be used and both m_1 and m_2 cannot be emitted which means that transition c_1 cannot be used and that all the automata will have to stay on the same state, thus the deadlock situation.

Let us state the formal definition of a system of automata, the definition of the synchronization rule, and then the definition of a system of synchronized automata.

Definition (automata). A *system of automata* S is composed of N sub-systems S_n, $1 \leq n \leq N$ called *automata*, and of a set $M = \{m^k, 1 \leq k \leq |M|\}$ containing the *messages* m^k of S. Every automaton S_n is described by

1. the set $E_n = \{e_n^i, 1 \leq i \leq |E_n|\}$ of its states;
2. the set $A_n = \{a_n^j, 1 \leq j \leq |A_n|\}$ of its transitions;
3. the set of messages $M_n \subset M$ carried by A_n.

To every transition a_n^j of S_n is associated a unique starting state $e_n^{j_1} \in E_n$ and a unique arriving state $e_n^{j_2} \in E_n$. Every transition a_n^j of S_n carries a set of messages $M_n^j \subset M_n$. $\diamond$

Definition (synchronization rule). Let us call *configuration* a mapping C which associates to every automaton S_n a unique state $e_n \in S_n$ called the *activated state* of S_n, and let us call *synchronization* a subset s of M. We then define the *synchronization rule* as follows: the synchronization s has S changed from configuration C to configuration C' if and only if $\forall S_n \in S$,

1. if $s \cap M_n = \emptyset$ then $C'(S_n) = C(S_n)$
2. if $s \cap M_n \neq \emptyset$ then $\exists a_n^j = (e_n^{j_1}, e_n^{j_2}) \in A_n$ such that
   (a) $M_n^j = s \cap M_n$
   (b) $e_n^{j_1} = C(S_n)$, $e_n^{j_2} = C'(S_n)$

We then say that transition a_n^j is *fired* and that messages $m \in M_n^j$ are *activated* during the change from C to C'. $\diamond$

Definition (synchronized automata). A *system of synchronized automata* is a system of automata endowed with the synchronization rule.
Furthermore, let C and C' be two configurations of S. The change from C to C' by synchronization s defines a *step* (C, s, C') for S. A succession of steps $(C_0, s_0, C_0'), \dots, (C_{n-1}, s_{n-1}, C_n')$ such that $C_{i+1} = C_i'$ defines a *path* for S. $\diamond$

The synchronization rule can be interpreted in two ways: an automaton which aims at firing a transition can be considered forcing the other automata to follow him, or having to ask the other automata the permission to do so. The appropriate interpretation has to be given at higher level by the semantic of the system.

To our knowledge this kind of synchronization rule we defined is not classical, as all automata have to get simultaneously in accordance to fire their transitions. Note however that more classical formalisms as Statecharts or the BLIF format were easily translated in our own formalism.

We now introduce a set of properties which can be verified with our method.

Accessibility Properties   The kind of requests we will check on a system of synchronized automata corresponds to the classical set of accessibility (or reachability) properties. For every automaton, we give a set of states within which is the activated state at start, and a set of states within which we want the activated state to arrive. The question is then whether there exists or not a path connecting these two sets.

On our small example, such a request could be: having each automaton in its state A_{e_1}, B_{e_1} or C_{e_1} respectively, can automata A and B reach its state A_{e_2} and B_{e_2} respectively, C being in state C_{e_1} or C_{e_2}?

Such a set of requests can be formally stated as follow:

Definition (accessibility property). Let S be a system of synchronized automata. An *accessibility property* on S is a couple $\mathcal{P} = (\mathcal{C}, \mathcal{C}')$ of sets of states of S.   ◇

Definition (path-satisfiability). An accessibility property $\mathcal{P} = (\mathcal{C}, \mathcal{C}')$ on S *has a path satisfying* $\mathcal{P}$ if and only if there exists a path in $k \in \mathbb{N}$ steps going from a configuration C_0 to a configuration C'_n such that $\forall S_n \in S$,

- if $E_n \cap \mathcal{C} \neq \emptyset$ then $C_0(S_n) \in \mathcal{C}$
- if $E_n \cap \mathcal{C}' \neq \emptyset$ then $C'_n(S_n) \in \mathcal{C}'$ ◇

The expressiveness of this set of properties is quite large if we consider the appending of "observing automata" to the system S. These observers permit to express the necessity of using a particular message before another, the necessity to avoid a particular message, to avoid a particular transition, etc. On such automata one can then state an accessibility request, and thus extend the amount of properties which can be expressed directly on S. It has been shown to have at least the ability of expressing *temporal logic safety formulae* [JPO95].

Sub-section 2.1 now introduces a different automata model based on a generalization of the synchronization rule. This new model will be useful to state the main theoretical result given later in this document.

Flow-Synchronized Automata Our method is based on mere linear programming, which means that results given by the linear programming solver won't always be integer results. This motivates the introduction (which will be fully relevant in section 2.2) of a non-integer variation of the synchronization rule and the definition of flow-synchronized automata. We begin with the introduction of various kinds of flows:

Definition (message-flow). A *message-flow* is a function f_m which associates to every message m of S a real quantity $f_m(m) \in [0,1]$. $\diamondsuit$

Definition (transition-flow). A *transition-flow* is a function f_a which associates to every transition a_n^j of S a real quantity $f_a(a_n^j) \in [0,1]$. $\diamondsuit$

Definition (state-flow). A *state-flow* is a function f_e which associates to every state e_n^i of S a real quantity $f_e(e_n^i) \in [0,1]$. $\diamondsuit$

We are now ready to state the definition of the non-integer variation of the synchronization rule:

Definition (flow-synchronization rule). Let

- A_n^m be the set of transitions of S_n carrying message m: $A_n^m = \{a_n^j \in A_n / m \in M_n^j\}$,
- E_n^{i+} be the set of transitions of S_n having e_n^i as starting state: $E_n^{i+} = \{a_n^j \in A_n / \exists e, \ a_n^j = (e_n^i, e)\}$,
- E_n^{i-} be the set of transitions of S_n having e_n^i as arriving state: $E_n^{i-} = \{a_n^j \in A_n / \exists e, \ a_n^j = (e, e_n^i)\}$.

Let us call

- *flow-configuration* a state-flow f_C such that $\forall S_n$, $\sum_{e_n^i \in S_n} f_C(e_n^i) = 1$ (i.e. the quantity of token on each automaton is equal to 1),
- *flow-synchronization* a pair $f_s = (f_m, f_a)$ such that $\forall m \in M$, $\forall S_n$, $A_n^m \neq \emptyset \Rightarrow f_s(m) = \sum_{a_n^j \in A_n^m} f_a(a_n^j)$ (i.e. for all automata that know m, the quantity of m emitted is equal to the flow going through the transitions carrying m).

We define the *flow-synchronization rule* as follows: the flow-synchronization $f_s = (f_m, f_a)$ has S changed from f_C to $f_{C'}$ if and only if $\forall e_n^i$, the following equations hold:

1. $\sum_{a_n^j \in E_n^{i+}} f_a(a_n^j) \leq f_C(e_n^i)$ (i.e. the flow leaving e_n^i is not greater than the quantity of token which is on e_n^i),
2. $\sum_{a_n^j \in E_n^{i-}} f_a(a_n^j) \leq f_{C'}(e_n^i)$ (i.e. the flow arriving on e_n^i is not greater than the total amount of token which is on e_n^i),
3. $f_C(e_n^i) - \sum_{a_n^j \in E_n^{i+}} f_a(a_n^j) = f_{C'}(e_n^i) - \sum_{a_n^j \in E_n^{i-}} f_a(a_n^j)$ (i.e. the new quantity of token on e_n^i is the previous quantity plus the flow arriving on e_n^i and less the flow leaving e_n^i).

If $f(a_n^j) > 0$ then we say that transition a_n^j is *flow-fired* and that messages $m \in M_n^j$ are *flow-activated* during the change from f_C to $f_{C'}$. $\diamond$

This flow-synchronization-rule then defines a new kind of automata:

Definition (flow-synchronized automata). A *system of flow-synchronized automata* is a system of automata endowed with the flow-synchronization rule. Furthermore, let f_C and $f_{C'}$ be two flow-configurations of S. The change from f_C to $f_{C'}$ by flow-synchronization f_s defines a *flow-step* $(f_C, f_s, f_{C'})$ for S. A succession of flow-steps $(f_{C_0}, f_{s_0}, f_{C_0'})$, ..., $(f_{C_{n-1}}, f_{s_{n-1}}, f_{C_n'})$ such that $f_{C_i'} = f_{C_{i+1}}$ defines a *flow-path* for S. $\diamond$

We also have by extension of path-satisfiability:

Definition (flow-path-satisfiability). A property $\mathcal{P} = (\mathcal{C}, \mathcal{C}')$ is *flow-path-satisfiable* if and only if there exists a flow-path going from $\mathcal{C}$ to $\mathcal{C}'$ in a finite number of flow-steps. $\diamond$

A system of flow-synchronized automata is a "continuous" version of the corresponding system of synchronized automata. On synchronized automata the quantity of information can be modelized for every automaton with a token that moves from state to state following the synchronization rule. On flow-synchronized automata, the information which is in quantity still equal to one token per automaton, can this time flow through states as would do a liquid, following the flow-synchronization rule.

The synchronization rule is obviously a special occurence of a flow-synchronization rule (it is an integer-valued flow-synchronization), which implies that all notions binded to this former rule are also special occurences of the equivalent notions binded to the latter rule (step, path, satisfiability, ...).

The flow-automata model will be used to state the theoretical result of section 2.2. We yet need one more automata model to fulfill this first section. This last model, derived from the two former ones, will be the one used in practice by our method.

The Storied Extension of Automata   The idea is to "unfold" through time the automata model in order to have each synchronization step (or flow-synchronization step) mapped to a given time step. Thus, during a time step, every automaton will have to use one of its transitions in accordance with the (flow-)synchronization rule, or to use a special transition, named an ε-transition, which will leave the automaton in the same state.

Figure 2 shows the storied version of the previous small example, unfolded through 3 time steps. All automata are respectively in their state $A_{e_1}(0)$, $B_{e_1}(0)$ and $C_{e_1}(0)$ before the first synchronization occurs. Suppose the first synchronization is the empty-set: all automata will use an ε-transition to stay in the same state, but ready for the second synchronization: respectively state $A_{e_1}(1)$, $B_{e_1}(1)$ and $C_{e_1}(1)$. Now if the second synchronization includes the emission of

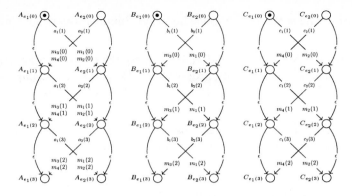

Fig. 2. storied automata of figure 1 on 3 time steps.

m_1 and m_2, this will make the automata to use respectively transitions $a_1(2)$, $b_1(2)$ and $c_1(2)$ to reach respectively $A_{e_2}(2)$, $B_{e_2}(2)$ and $C_{e_2}(2)$. And so on.

We see that there is a one to one correspondence between synchronization (or flow-synchronization) steps on the automata model and time steps on the storied extension. A solution on the latter will thus give directly a solution path (or flow-path) for the studied automata model. Section 2.2 explains how to use linear programming on this storied extension of the automata model.

Here is the formal definition of the storied extension of an automata model:

Definition (storied automata). Let S be a system of automata. We consider S on $T + 1$ time steps as follow: for each automaton $S_n \in S$ we associate

1. to every value $t \in \{0, \dots, T\}$ and every state e_n^i, a state $e_n^i(t)$;
2. to every value $t \in \{1, \dots, T\}$ and every transition $a_n^j = (e_n^{j_1}, e_n^{j_2})$, a transition $a_n^j(t) = (e_n^{j_1}(t-1), e_n^{j_2}(t))$;
3. to every value $t \in \{1, \dots, T\}$ and every message $m^k \in M_{a_n^j}$, a message $m^k(t) \in M_{a_n^j(t)}$;
4. to every value $t \in \{1, \dots, T\}$ and every state e_n^i, an ϵ-transition $\epsilon_n^i(t) = (e_n^i(t-1), e_n^i(t))$.

The system thus constructed from S is called the *storied system of automata S_T* of S on T time steps. $\diamond$

A storied system of automata S_T is clearly a special occurence of a system of automata, and both the definitions of synchronisation and flow-synchronisation rules are valid on S_T. The translation of an accessibility property from S to S_T is obvious: the starting set of configurations $\mathcal{C}$ is specified on the first time step $t = 0$, and the ending set of configurations $\mathcal{C}'$ is specified on the last time step $t = T$. Formally, it gives:

Definition. Let S be a system of automata and S_T the corresponding storied system. Let $(\mathcal{C}, \mathcal{C}')$ be an accessibility property on S. The corresponding accessibility property on S_T is given by $\mathcal{C} = \mathcal{C}(0)$ and $\mathcal{C}' = \mathcal{C}'(T)$. $\diamond$

Furthermore we have the trivial following result binding a path in S and a path in S_T:

Proposition. Let S be a system of automata, S_T the corresponding storied system of automata. An accessibility property $(\mathcal{C}, \mathcal{C}')$ on S is (flow-)path satisfiable in n steps if and only if $(\mathcal{C}(0), \mathcal{C}'(T))$ is (flow-)path satisfiable on S_T with $T = n$. $\diamond$

We are now ready to see how the storied system of automata is used in accordance with linear programming to verify accessibility properties.

2.2   The Use of Linear Programming

As stated in the introduction, linear programming is a very efficient mean for solving systems of linear equations in positive numbers when a real (i.e. not always integer) solution is searched for.

Here is a classical way of formally expressing the kind of problems treated by linear programming: the problem is to find an x^*, a vector of size n, optimal solution of

$$\begin{cases} \max c^t x \\ Ax = b \\ x \geq 0 \end{cases}$$

where A is an m rows, n columns matrix, c a vector of size n, b a vector of size m.

The optimization criteria $c^t x$ is optional, and the problem of only finding an x subject to $\{Ax = b, x \geq 0\}$ is of the same difficulty (it constitutes for example the first phase of the two-phases simplex algorithm). Our method relies mainly on finding such an x subject to a system of constraints that translates the properties of the automata system.

This implies first the necessity of constructing a system of linear constraints that catches the structural properties of the system of automata. This is the subject of the following sub-section.

Linear Constraints Drawn out of Automata   The system of linear equations in positive numbers is drawn out of the storied extension S_T of the automata system S as follows:

Two kinds of equations are constructed: flow equations which translate the preservation of information on every state of every automaton of S_T, and synchronization equations which translate the synchronization (or flow-synchronization) rule for every message of S_T.

To this set of equations are added equations which translate the accessibility property, by forcing the value of some states at step $t = 0$ and at step $t = T$ to be equal to 1.

Here are the equations drawn out of the storied extension ($T = 3$) of our small example, the accessibility property being given by $\mathcal{C}(0) = \{A_{e_1}(0), B_{e_1}(0), C_{e_1}(0)\}$ and $\mathcal{C}'(3) = \{A_{e_2}(3), B_{e_3}(3), C_{e_3}(3)\}$.

The flow equations are for $i \in \{0, \dots, 3\}$:

$$A_{e_1}(i) = a_1(i+1) + \epsilon_{A_{e_1}}(i+1)$$
$$A_{e_2}(i) = a_2(i+1) + \epsilon_{A_{e_2}}(i+1)$$
$$A_{e_1}(i+1) = a_2(i+1) + \epsilon_{A_{e_1}}(i+1)$$
$$A_{e_2}(i+1) = a_1(i+1) + \epsilon_{A_{e_2}}(i+1)$$

$$B_{e_1}(i) = b_1(i+1) + \epsilon_{B_{e_1}}(i+1)$$
$$B_{e_2}(i) = b_2(i+1) + \epsilon_{B_{e_2}}(i+1)$$
$$B_{e_1}(i+1) = b_2(i+1) + \epsilon_{B_{e_1}}(i+1)$$
$$B_{e_2}(i+1) = b_1(i+1) + \epsilon_{B_{e_2}}(i+1)$$

$$C_{e_1}(i) = c_1(i+1) + \epsilon_{C_{e_1}}(i+1)$$
$$C_{e_2}(i) = c_2(i+1) + \epsilon_{C_{e_2}}(i+1)$$
$$C_{e_1}(i+1) = c_2(i+1) + \epsilon_{C_{e_1}}(i+1)$$
$$C_{e_2}(i+1) = c_1(i+1) + \epsilon_{C_{e_2}}(i+1)$$

The synchronization equations are for $i \in \{1, \dots, 3\}$:

$$m_1(i) = a_1(i) \quad m_2(i) = a_1(i)$$
$$m_1(i) = b_1(i) \quad m_2(i) = c_1(i)$$

$$m_3(i) = a_2(i) \quad m_4(i) = a_2(i)$$
$$m_3(i) = b_2(i) \quad m_4(i) = c_2(i)$$

The property equations are:

$$A_{e_1}(0) = 1 \; B_{e_1}(0) = 1 \; C_{e_1}(0) = 1$$
$$A_{e_2}(3) = 1 \; B_{e_2}(3) = 1 \; C_{e_2}(3) = 1$$

Let us see the formal definition of these three sets of equations:

Definition (system of equations). Let S be a system of automata, S_T the storied extension of S on T time steps, and $\mathcal{P} = (\mathcal{C}, \mathcal{C}')$ an accessibility property on S. We recall that for every automaton $S_n \in S$, E_n^{i+} is the set of transitions having e_n^i as starting state, E_n^{i-} is the set of transitions having e_n^i as arriving state, and A_n^m is the set of transitions carrying message m.

The system of linear equations $L(S_T, \mathcal{P})$ drawn out of S_T and $\mathcal{P}$ is given by the three following sets of equations:

– *flow equations:* $\forall S_n \in S$, $\forall t \in \{1, \dots, T\}$, $\forall e_n^i \in S_n$, we have

$$e_n^i(t-1) = \sum_{j_1 \in E_n^{i+}} a_n^{j_1}(t) + \epsilon_n^i(t)$$

$$e_n^i(t) = \sum_{j_2 \in E_n^{i-}} a_n^{j_2}(t) + \epsilon_n^i(t)$$

– *synchronization equations:* $\forall S_n \in S$, $\forall t \in \{1, \dots, T\}$, $\forall m \in M_n$, we have

$$m(t) = \sum_{j_3 \in A_n^m} a_n^{j_3}(t)$$

– *property equations:* $\forall S_n \in S$, we have $\sum_{e_n^i \in E_n} e_n^i(0) = 1$

$$\text{if } C \cap E_n \neq \emptyset \text{ then } \sum_{e_n^i \in C \cap E_n} e_n^i(0) = 1$$

$$\text{if } C' \cap E_n \neq \emptyset \text{ then } \sum_{e_n^i \in C' \cap E_n} e_n^i(T) = 1$$

$\diamondsuit$

We clearly have a one to one correspondence between the use of a transition, a state or a message of the storied system of automata at a given time step and the value of the corresponding variable of the system of equations, whether the synchronization rule or the flow-synchronization rule is used.

If we use the synchronisation rule on S, we need to add to $L(S_T, \mathcal{P})$ positivity and integrality constraints on all its variables. If we use the flow-synchronisation rule on S, we need to add to $L(S_T, \mathcal{P})$ only the positivity constraints.

Proposition. Let S_T be a storied system of automata on T time steps, and $(\mathcal{C}(0), \mathcal{C}'(T))$ an accessibility property on S_T.
If the synchronization rule is used on S_T, then $(\mathcal{C}(0), \mathcal{C}'(T))$ is satisfiable on S_T if and only if $L(S_T, \mathcal{P})$ has a solution with all variables being positive and integer valued.
If the flow-synchronization rule is used on S_T, then $(\mathcal{C}(0), \mathcal{C}'(T))$ is satisfiable on S_T if and only if $L(S_T, \mathcal{P})$ has a solution with all variables being positive. $\diamondsuit$

Linear programming can handle systems of positive variables without integrality constraints. Thus we are only able to use linear programming on a system of automata using the flow-synchronization rule.

The solving of $L(S_T, \mathcal{P})$ gives either a flow-path or a proof (via the classical duality theory of linear programming) of the inexistence of any flow-path on a model of T stories. Subsection 2.2 will show that this completeness result on the existence or inexistence of flow-paths is independent of the number of steps T.

The Completeness Theorem Being given $L(S_T, \mathcal{P})$, the idea is to eliminate in an iterative way transitions, messages and states that, whatever the value of T is, can never be used if one wants to satisfy property $\mathcal{P}$. The fundamental point is that this iterative mechanism, called the *proof system*, works independently of the number of time steps T. This proof system permits to establish the following completeness theorem:

Theorem (completeness). Let S be a system of automata and $\mathcal{P}$ an accessibility property on S. The proof system establishes, in time polynomial in the size of $(S, \mathcal{P})$, the following alternative:

– it proves the existence of a *flow-path* on S satisfying $\mathcal{P}$ and gives an upper bound on the number of flow-steps;
– it proves the non-existence of any *flow-path* of S satisfying $\mathcal{P}$, and thus of any *path* of S satisfying $\mathcal{P}$.   ◇

The details of the proof of this theorem are technically difficult and too long to be given in this document (the proof system is fully developed in [Dev99]). We yet can give an idea of how the proof system works.

Let us suppose $\mathcal{P} = (C_0, C_f)$ (we ask the system to go from a configuration C_0 to a configuration C_f). The proof system is made of three kind of inferences. Each inference can deduce from the conclusions of the previous one that some data (transitions, states or messages) of the system are useless and can be eliminated safely, or that the accessibility property is impossible to satisfy.

First kind of inference:

   If one can find a set of states Q_1 such that any entering transition (say a) must flow-synchronize with another one (say b_1) that goes out of this set,

   then we infer: if $C_0 \cap Q_1 = \emptyset$ then $C_f \cap Q_1 = \emptyset$, which implies that all the in-going and out-going transitions of Q_1 (here a, b_1, b_2, b_3) cannot be used. These transitions are proved impossible to use and are thus eliminated.

Second kind of inference:

   Similarly, if one can find a set of states Q_2 such that any transition that goes out of it must flow-synchronize with another one that goes inside this set,

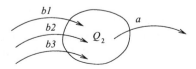

then we infer: if $C_f \cap Q_2 = \emptyset$ then $C_0 \cap Q_2 = \emptyset$, which implies that all the in-going and out-going transitions of Q_2 (here a, b_1, b_2, b_3) cannot be used. These transitions are proved impossible to use and are eliminated.

Third kind of inference:

If one can find a vector Y such that for any configuration C_n, we have $Y^t C_0 \leq Y^t C_n$, then we infer: if C_f satisfies $Y^t C_0 > Y^t C_f$, C_f cannot be accessed and the request is proved infeasible, or else we must have $Y^t C_0 = Y^t C_f$ and any transition that strictly increases $Y^t C_n$ is forbidden and eliminated.

All inferences are computed using linear programming, which is a numerical algorithm. All data eliminated by an inference are yet proved impossible to use. The key idea of the proof is given by the well known following linear programming result:

Lemma (Farkas). Let A be a m rows, n columns matrix, and b a vector of size m. Then one and only one of the following statements is true:

1. there exists a vector $x \geq 0$ such that $Ax = b$;
2. there exists a vector y such that $y^t A \geq 0$, $y^t b < 0$.   ◇

Based on this lemma, for all inferences linear programming gives a certificate (the y vector) justifying the elimination of the selected set of data.

The remaining question is whenever the existence of a flow-path is proved, how the existence of a true path can be proved and constructed.

The Effective Search of a Solution Path The proof of non-existence of any flow-path implies the non-existence of any path, which implies the accessibility property to be impossible to satisfy. In this case, the proof system is sufficient to conclude. On the contrary, whenever the proof of existence of a flow-path is given, it does not imply the existence of a path (as it is not always integer-valued), and it is thus not directly possible to know whether the accessibility property can be satisfied or not.

This constitutes the non-polynomial part of our method, and illustrates the intrinsic difficulty of software verification as the gap between linear programming and integer programming. Yet several remarks make this gap not so overwhelmingly difficult in our case. The remainder of this sub-section will give only pragmatic and rather subjective arguments to understand why it seems to work in practice.

The first thing to note is that the obtaining of a flow-path is very easy. It suffices to use a linear programming solver on the storied extension with enough time steps: the resulting solution is directly interpretable on the flow-synchronized automata model.

Having the flow-path solution, a general way of finding a path is to force some of the data to have integer values and to relaunch the linear programming solver. Iterating this technique permits eventually to find an all integer-valued solution, which is a path. A general strategy of this kind is yet heavily combinatorial, with a branching on every forced variable (0 or 1 value), and also combinatorial on the number of time steps.

However one has to notice that both the automata model and the flow-path have a semantic meaning. Taking into account this meaning in order to choose which data (transition, message or state) to force to a particular value, it reduces drastically the number of branching necessary to conclude. This guided branching strategy seems very efficient in practice when a path does exist: on all our examples, a few forcing steps were sufficient to find a true path.

When no paths exist, it gets more intricated and a guided branching strategy is not always sufficient. Indeed, the property has to be proved impossible whatever the number of time steps is. Yet, again guided by the semantic of the model and of the flow-path solution, the idea is then to find on the automata model the main reason permitting a non integer-valued solution to exist, and to slightly modify the automata model in order to eliminate this non integer solution (the theoretical meaning relying behind these slight modifications is given in [Del99b]).

Using this final technique together with some guided branching, we have always been able to conclude on all the examples we considered.

3   Some Case Studies

We summarize now some experiments we have done with our verification method on three different systems modelized with our automata-like formalism: a telephony system, an access control system and a bus arbiter.

All computations were done on a 168MHz UltraSparc2 with 256Mb of memory. The linear programming software used was CPLEX V4.0.

3.1   A Telephony System

This system modelizes mainly a connection/deconnection protocol between entities — telephones — which communicate between them using fifo channels. The system is not centralized, which means that any telephone can communicate directly with any other telephone by sending messages to its fifo channel. Some more details on this system are given at the end of article [DDL99].

The complexity of this telephony system is due to the increasing amount of different messages which can travel through the fifo channels. The connection/deconnection protocol uses 12 different messages (6 in emission and 6 in reception) for every possible pair of telephones, these messages being possibly stored on any place of the corresponding fifo channel.

A telephone is made of two automata (one of 16 states, and one of 3 states). A fifo channel of size k is made of a write automaton ($k + 1$ states), a read automaton (one state) and k memory-cell automata ($6 * n(n - 1) + 1$ states, n being the number of telephones).

The experiments were done with $n = 7$ telephones using fifo channels of size $k = 3$, or $n = 5$ telephones using fifo channels of size $k = 7$. The resulting systems is made of more than 800 automata and uses more than 2500 different synchronization messages. The state space is more than 10^{40} wide.

Here are some samples of properties for which a test-suite was found:

can phone#5 send a ABANDON to phone#6 ?
can phone#6 read a BUSY_LINE from phone#3 ?
can phone#3 send a STOPPING to phone#2 ?
can phone#4 be in its state S13_3.4 ?
can phone#1 and phone#4 be in conversation ?

Here are some samples of properties for which a proof of impossibility was found:

can phone#3 ring while offhooked ?
can phone#5 send BUSY_LINE to phone#1 while onhook ?
can phone#2 ring while nobody ever called it ?
can phone#7 be alone in communication ?
can phones #1, #4 and #6 be in circular communication ?

We also proved that with 5 telephones, fifo channels of size 6 were sufficient, by finding a test suite that fills a fifo of size 6 and by finding a proof that a fifo of size 7 can never be entirely filled.

In all cases, the computations took always less than an hour and used less than 200Mb of memory.

3.2   An Access Control System

The purpose of the system is to check in and out-goings of people through doors of some buildings. All doors have a reading-card device and communicate through buffers with a centralized controlling device. This centralized device controls the validity of the request (activated and authorized card for the given building), manages the opening-closing protocol of the door and records the entrance or exit of the card-bearer. An emergency circuit is also specified in order to open all doors of a given building in first priority, as well as a reset protocol to end the emergency and put the doors of the building in a ready-to-work state. The full technical details on this case study are in [Del99a].

The size of the system grows cubiquely with the number of cards i, the number of doors j and the number of buildings k. The complexity of this system relies in the amount of data which has to be maintained while processing the opening-closing and the emergency-reset protocols (for example the centralized controller knows for every card in which building it is).

A door is made of 6 automata (of respectively 7, 3, 2, 2, 2, and 2 states). The centralized controller is made of many automata which represent mainly data. A door's buffer has 6 states, and the centralized controller's buffer has $2ij + 3j + 1$ states.

The experiments were done on a small instance made of 5 cards, 4 doors and 2 buildings, and then checked again on a huge instance made of 20 cards, 8 doors and 4 buildings. On this last instance the resulting system is made of 230 automata and uses more than 2800 different synchronization messages. The state space is more than 10^{52} wide.

Here are some samples of properties for which a test-suite was found:

can card#1 go in and out of building#2 with all doors locked behind him?
can card#1 go in-out of building#1 and then get in-out of building#2?
can door#3 be open with all its data in its expected state?
can card#4, being deactivated, get in building#2 after being reactivated?
can all doors of a building on emergency be opened without using a card?

Here are some samples of properties for which a proof of impossibility was found:

can card#1 be in building#2 but registered out of it?
can card#1, who entered building#1, enter building#2 without getting first out of building#1?
can door#3 be open with one of its data in an unexpected state?
can card#4, which is deactivated, get in building#2 without being reactivated?
can a door of a building under emergency stay locked?
can a door being on a building not on emergency get an emergency message?

The computations on the small instance took always a few minutes and used a few tens of Mb of memory; on the huge instance it took from 4 to 15 hours and used less than 200Mb of memory.

3.3   A Bus Arbiter

The bus arbiter is a hardware circuit whose purpose is to give to a single client an access to a resource shared by several different clients. This is a well known example which has been treated with several techniques. The complete details on this case study are given in [Dev98].

The bus arbiter used for our experiments was a direct translation from the one given in the Xeve/Estrel package. It is made of several local cells which decide whether or not to allow the access to the resource for a client. The client claims the access by activating a cell which in turn activates a signal if it can access the resource. Cells are connected one to another to form a ring, allowing information to propagate. A token goes from one cell to the next on the ring. The cell who owns the token can access the bus if it wants to. If not, it tells the next cell that it can access the bus it it wants to. If this next cell doesn't want to use the bus, it tells the next cell and so on.

An arbiter with n cells has at least 2^n input configurations. We made experiments for systems with up to 1200 cells. The state space is then at least 10^{500} wide, and the computation took around one hour. The property checked was to know whether a client could access the bus at the same time as client#1. A proof of impossibility was found for all instances checked.

4   Conclusion

We have presented a new method for software verification which can be used either to exhibit test suites satisfying a property or proofs that a property is unsatisfiable.

In comparison with existing verification techniques, the main advantage of our method is its ability to handle huge models of automata without doing any abstraction, and to give at worse an answer which has always a semantic meaning helpful for further study. On the examples we modelized, the study of these answers has always permitted to conclude.

The modelization used (communicating automata) is dynamic and thus not far from an implementation. This means that the method is fitted for test suite generation. However, the relative poor computation time compared to probabilistic techniques indicates mostly an interest in finding probalistically hard test suites. The resolution time, though, is fast enough (both for path finding and proof finding) to allow interactivity to the model designer.

The resolution times given here can be improved easily. Our linear programming solver is not state-of-the-art and current solvers are now about 10 to 30 times faster while using less memory. The computer we use has a Specfp95 equal to 10, which is quite poor. Furthermore, we didn't work on optimizing the problem formulation given to the solver. The work involved is surely important but could decrease greatly the resolution time.

To finish, both test suites and (under some conditions) proofs can be found on a small instance of a generic specification and directly checked on a bigger instance. This is of great importance if the goal is to validate the specification and not only an instance of it.

References

[Abr95]   J-R. Abrial. *The B-book.* Cambridge University Press, 1995.

[CA95]   James C. Corbett and Georges S. Avrunin. Using integer programming to verify general safety and liveness properties. Technical report, University of Hawaii at Manoa, 1995.

[CC77]   P. Cousot and R. Cousot. Abstract interpretation: A unified lattice model for static analysis of programs by construction of approximation of fixed points. In *Proceedings of the 4th ACM Symposium on Principles of Programming Languages, Los Angeles*, pages 238–252, New York, NY, 1977. ACM.

[CHP92]   J.M. Couvreur, S. Haddad, and J.F. Peyre. parametrized resolution of families of linear systems. *RAIRO Recherche Operationnelle*, 26:183–206, 1992.

[DDL99]   S. Dellacherie, S. Devulder, and J-L. Lambert. (technical version) software verification based on linear programming. Technical report, GREYC, universit de Caen, 1999.

[Del99a]   S. Dellacherie. A case study: specification and verification of an access control system using the lpv technology. Technical report, GREYC, Universit de Caen, 1999.

[Del99b]   S. Dellacherie. *Vrification logicielle base sur la programmation linaire.* PhD thesis, Universit de Caen, 1999. To appear.

[Dev98]   S. Devulder. A comparison of lpv with other validation methods. Technical report, GREYC, Universit de Caen, 1998.

[Dev99]   S. Devulder. *Un modle de preuve de logiciels fond sur la programmation linaire.* PhD thesis, Universit de Caen, 1999. To appear.

[ES92]   J. Esparza and M. Silva. A polynomial-time algorithm to decide liveness of bounded free choice nets. *Theoretical Computer Science*, 102:185–205, 1992.

[faq]   www-unix.mcs.anl.gov/otc/Guide/faq/linear-programming-faq.html.

[GH93]   J.V. Guttag and J.J. Horning. *Larch: languages and tools for formal specification.* Springer-Verlag, 1993.

[Hol97]   G.J. Holtzmann. The model checker spin. *IEEE Transactions on Software Engineering*, 23(5), May 1997.

[JPO95]   Laeta Jategaonkar Jagadeesan, Carlos Puchol, and James E. Von Olnhausen. Safety porperty verification of esterel programs and applications to telecommunications software. In *Seventh Conference on Computer-aided verification*, 1995.

[Kur92]   R. P. Kurshan. Automata-theoretic verification of coordinating processes. Technical report, ATT Bell Laboratories, 1992.

[LM89]   J.B. Lasserre and F. Mahey. Using linear programming in petri net analysis. *RAIRO Recherche Operationnelle*, 23:43–50, 1989.

[McM93]   K.L. McMillan. *Symbolic Model Checking.* Kluwer Academic Publishers, 1993.

[ORR+96]   S. Owre, S. Rajan, J.M. Rushby, N. Shankar, and M. Srivas. Pvs: Combining specification, proof checking, and model checking. In *LNCS*, volume 1102, pages 411–414. Springer Verlag, 1996.

Sensors and Actuators in TCOZ

Brendan Mahony[1] Jin Song Dong[2]

[1] Information Technology Division
Defence Science and Technology Organisation (DSTO)
Brendan.Mahony@dsto.defence.gov.au
[2] School of Computing,
National University of Singapore,
dongjs@comp.nus.edu.sg

Abstract. Timed Communicating Object Z (TCOZ) combines Object-Z's strengths in modeling complex data and algorithms with Timed CSP's strengths in modeling real-time concurrency. TCOZ inherits CSP's channel-based communication mechanism, in which messages represent discrete synchronisations between processes. The purpose of most control systems is to observe and control analog components. In such cases, the interface between the control system and the controlled systems cannot be satisfactorily described using the channel mechanism. In order to address this problem, TCOZ is extended with continuous-function interface mechanisms inspired by process control theory, the **sensor** and the **actuator**. The utility of these new mechanisms is demonstrated through their application to the design of an automobile cruise control system.

1 Introduction

The design of complex systems requires powerful mechanisms for modeling data, algorithms, concurrency, and real-time behaviour; as well as for structuring and decomposing systems in order to control local complexity. In recognition of this, much recent work in the development of specification and design notations has concentrated on the blending of existing notations with strong mechanisms in one or the other of these areas. An early examples of this trend are the LOTOS language, which blends process algebras with algebraic modeling languages, and RAISE, which blends VDM, CSP, ML with algebraic modeling languages. More recently there has been active investigation of the integration of object-oriented data-structuring techniques with process description languages. The blending of Z/Object-Z with either CSP [19,6,18,21] or CCS [7,22] has been a popular approach. TCOZ lies in this last category. It is a blending of Object-Z and Timed CSP that is aimed at providing a powerful design notation for real-time and concurrent systems with digital components.

Many classes of complex digital systems are identified in the literature: concurrent, real-time, hybrid, embedded to name a few. In fact, many of these systems are better characterised as *control* systems [15]. Following Shaw [17], we contend that the architecture of control systems is an important structuring mechanism for the efficient design of complex digital systems. The (closed-loop) control architecture is depicted in Figure 1 (which is borrowed with minor modifications from Raven [15, Fig. 1.3]).

J. Wing, J. Woodcock, J. Davies (Eds.): FM'99, Vol. II, LNCS 1709, pp. 1166-1185, 1999.
© Springer-Verlag Berlin Heidelberg 1999

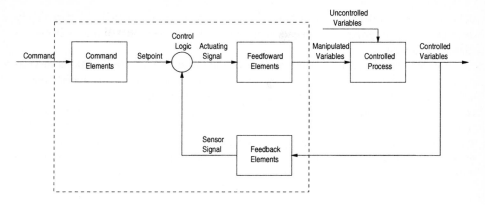

Fig. 1. Abstract control system architecture

Generally the controlled process is described by a differential or integral equation involving the controlled, uncontrolled, and manipulated variables, which are best modeled as continuous real-valued functions of real-valued time. The development of precise models for analog components is essentially beyond the scope of TCOZ, which is restricted by its nature to the description of discrete models. (Even though TCOZ adopts real-valued time, all of the events and quantities described in a TCOZ class remain essentially discrete in nature.) Higher level design languages such as the Timed Refinement Calculus [14] or Duration Calculus [24] should instead be employed to describe the behaviour of the analog components.

However, in a modern digital control system, the subsystem of Figure 1 enclosed within the dashed rectangle is composed solely of digital components. The feedforward, feedback, and command elements are generally digital-to-analog and analog-to-digital converters as appropriate. The actuating signal is used to generate an analog quantity and the sensor and setpoint signals are sampled from analog quantities. The control logic is a non-terminating reactive process executing on a digital processing unit. All of these elements should in theory be amenable to description within a discrete modeling language such as TCOZ.

In drawing the digital subsystem boundary to encompass the conversion elements of the control system, we present some challenges to the CSP channel-based communications mechanism used in TCOZ. The primary challenge lies in the analog nature of the quantities which make up the interfaces. The discrete modeling mechanisms of CSP and Object-Z cannot describe a continuously varying quantity. Another point is that the digital system thus described becomes an open system. CSP channels are better suited to describing closed systems because of CSP's view of communications as representing synchronisations between systems. A closed system is one in which all aspects of system behaviour are fully described, with no need to refer to, nor interface to, other systems. An open system is one which operates in the context of an environment which is determined solely by the interface it presents. Since CSP communications require synchronisation between processes, any system specified in CSP is subject to arbitrary delay by an uncooperative environment. Such a system cannot usually be completely decoupled from its environment because it relies on the co-operation of the environment to make progress.

In order to address these shortcomings of the basic CSP communications mechanism, we propose the introduction to TCOZ of two continuous-function interface mechanisms inspired by the control system architecture. The **sensor** provides a sampling channel linked to a global continuous variable. The **actuator** provides a local-variable linked to a global continuous variable. Sensors and actuators may appear either at the system boundary (describing how global analog quantities are sampled from or generated by the digital subsystem) or else within the system (providing a convenient mechanism for describing local communications which do not require synchronisations).

Outline of paper

It is assumed that the reader has some familiarity with both Object-Z [4] and CSP, since the mechanics of blending the two notations is considered only briefly in Section 2. The continuous-function interface mechanisms, **sensor** and **actuator**, are introduced in Section 3. Section 4 informally describes the high-level functionality of a standard case study in automatic control, the automobile cruise control. The TCOZ specification of the cruise control is presented and evaluated in Section 5.

2   Aspects of TCOZ

TCOZ is a blending of Object-Z [4] and Timed CSP [16], for the most part preserving them as proper sub-languages of the blended notation. The essential elements of this blending are the unification of the concepts of type, class, and process and the unification of Object-Z operation specification schemas with terminating CSP processes. Thus instances of process may be declared normally and occupy the same syntactic class as objects. Operation schemas and CSP processes also occupy the same syntactic category, operation schema expressions may appear wherever processes may appear in CSP and CSP process definitions may appear wherever operation definitions may appear in Object-Z. In this section we briefly consider the aspects of TCOZ which help to bring the two notations together. A detailed introduction to TCOZ and its Timed CSP and Object-Z features may be found elsewhere [12]. The semantics of TCOZ can be found in [10].

2.1   Declaring channels

CSP channels are given an independent, first class role in TCOZ. This allows the communications and control topology of a network of objects to be designed orthogonally to their class structure.

In order to support the role of CSP channels, the state schema convention is extended to allow the declaration of communication channels. If c is to be used as a communication channel by any of the operations of a class, then it must be declared in the state schema to be of type **chan**. Channels are type polymorphic and may carry communications of any type. Being based on ZF set theory, Z is not technically speaking a typed logic [20], so this presents no semantic challenge and prevents unnecessary proliferation of channel names. Channel variables act in the role of 'event constructors'. A channel c may either appear alone in the role of an event (applied to the null-value) or else be applied to a Z-value v like so $c.v$. The conventional usages $c?v$ and $c!v$ serve solely as visual feedback to document the intention that an event act in the role of an input or output respectively. They have no semantic implications.

Contrary to the conventions adopted for internal state variables, channels are viewed as shared rather than as encapsulated entities. This is a consequence of their role as communications interfaces *between* objects. The introduction of channels to TCOZ reduces the need to reference other classes in class definitions, thereby enhancing the modularity of system specifications.

2.2   A model of time and quantity

In TCOZ, all timing information is represented as real valued measurements in *seconds*. Describing time and other physical quantities in terms of standard units of measurement is an important aspect of ensuring the completeness and soundness of specifications of real-time, reactive, and hybrid systems. In order to support the use of standard units of measurement, extensions to the Z typing system suggested by Hayes and Mahony [8] are adopted. Under this convention, time quantities are represented by the type $\mathbb{R}$ s, where $\mathbb{R}$ represents the real numbers and s is the SI symbol for the standard unit of time. Time literals consist of a real number literal annotated with a symbol representing a unit of time. For example, $3 \mu s$ is a literal representing a period of three microseconds, that is three millionths of the standard time unit, the second. All the SI standard units symbols are supported and all the arithmetic operators are extended in the obvious way to allow calculations involving units of measurement.

2.3   Deadlines and delays

In order to describe the timing requirements of operations and sequences of operations, a deadline command along the lines described by Hayes and Utting [9] is introduced. If *OP* is an operation specification (defined through any combination of CSP process primitives and Object-Z operation schemas) then $OP \bullet$ DEADLINE t describes the process which has the same effect as *OP*, but is constrained to terminate no later than t.

The WAITUNTIL operator is a dual to the deadline operator. The process

$OP \bullet$ WAITUNTIL t

performs *OP*, but will not terminate until at least time t.

2.4   Guards and preconditions

A novel CSP operator, the state-guard, is used to *block* or *enable* execution of an operation on the basis of an object's local state. For example, the operation $[a \geq 0] \bullet [\Delta(a) \mid a \geq 0 \wedge a' = \sqrt{a}]$ will replace the state variable a with its square root if a is positive otherwise it will *deadlock*, that is be blocked from executing. The blocking or enabling of this operation is achieved by the state guard $[a \geq 0] \bullet \_$ and not by the precondition $a \geq 0$ within the operation schema. If the operation schema alone is invoked with a negative, it will *diverge* rather than block. The difference between deadlock and divergence is that a divergence may be refined away by making an operation more robust, while a deadlock can never be refined away.

An additional function of state guards is as a substitute for CSP's indexed external choice operator. The process $[n : \mathbb{N} \mid 0 \leq n \leq 5] \bullet c?n \to P(n)$ may input any value of n between 0 and 5 (from channel c) as chosen by its environment. CSP's indexed internal choice is replaced by the operation schema and sequential composition. The process $[n! : \mathbb{N} \mid 0 \leq n! \leq 5]; c!n \to P(n)$ may output any value of n between 0 and 5 according to its own designs.

2.5   Active and passive objects

Active objects have their own thread of control, while passive objects are controlled by other objects in a system. In TCOZ, an identifier MAIN (non-terminating process) is used to determine the behaviour of active objects of a given class [3]. The MAIN process is required to have neither input nor output parameters. If ob_1 and ob_2 are active objects of the class C, then the independent parallel composition behaviour of the two objects can be represented as $ob_1 \mid\mid\mid ob_2$, which means $ob_1.\text{MAIN} \mid\mid\mid ob_2.\text{MAIN}$

2.6   Complex network topologies

In TCOZ, a graph-based approach is adopted to describing network topologies [13]. For example, consider that processes A and B communicate privately through the channel ab, processes A and C communicate privately through the channel ca, and processes B and C communicate privately through the channel bc. This network topology may be described in TCOZ by the *network topology* expression

$$\big|\big|(A \xleftrightarrow{ab} B; \; B \xleftrightarrow{bc} C; \; C \xleftrightarrow{ca} A).$$

Network topology expressions are a notation intended to mimic the graphical communicating structure. They consist of interface specifications of the form

$$P_1, \ldots, P_n \xleftrightarrow{c_1, \ldots, c_n} Q_1, \ldots, Q_n,$$

indicating that the channels $c_1, \ldots, c_n$ are used to communicate from the processes $P_1, \ldots, P_n$ to the processes $Q_1, \ldots, Q_n$.

3   Adding continuous-function interfaces to TCOZ

Integrating TCOZ specifications with traditional control theory system models presents something of a challenge. The standard CSP communications interface is the channel, which represents a sequence of discrete synchronisations between system and environment. The standard model for system interfaces in control theory is the continuous,

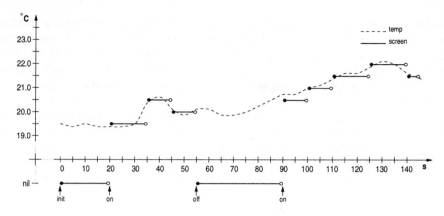

Fig. 2. The office communication scenario.

differentiable function. One approach to this problem is to require the system designer to resolve the mismatch at a higher-level of abstraction, handcrafting a translation from the continuous-function world to TCOZ's discrete world. We reject this approach on the grounds that, though it is very flexible, it constitutes a barrier to the ready acceptance of TCOZ as design tool for digital components of control systems. Instead we adopt an approach by which TCOZ takes it upon itself to become a `good corporate citizen' in the world of control engineering by providing standardised mechanisms for converting from the discrete to the continuous and vice versa, thus allowing TCOZ process classes to present a continuous-function interface to their environments. This allows subsystems specified in TCOZ to fit seamlessly into the overall design of a complex control system.

3.1   The digital temperature display

As a simple demonstration in the use of continuous-function interfaces in TCOZ and their interaction with CSP channels and Object-Z local variables, we consider the communication scenario between a digital temperature display (DTD) and the occupant of an office. The office occupant can turn on/off the DTD by pressing the `on'/`off' buttons on the unit. If the DTD is turned on, then it will monitor the rooms current temperature using its built-in thermometer and update the temperature display every 5 s to display the current temperature to the nearest half a degree Celsius. If the DTD is turned off, the temperature display goes blank. An example behaviour of the DTD is illustrated by Figure 2.

The communications interfaces to the DTD fall into three distinct classes. The on/off buttons of the unit are best represented using the channel mechanism, because they require explicit co-operation between the user and the DTD unit (that is a synchronisation) and because they are discrete events. A continuous interface could be used, but considerable effort would be required to ensure proper synchronisation. The temperature on the other hand is best modeled as a continuous function of time and is not well suited to being described as a CSP channel. Not only is the continuous function the standard scientific and engineering model for analog quantities, it is also common engineering practice to view digital signals as piece-wise continuous step-functions [14]. The temperature display falls into an area between the truly continuous and the truly discrete, either model may be preferred depending on the application. In this case, because the display falls at the system boundary, the difficulties of using CSP channels to describe open system interfaces mean that modeling the display as a CSP channel is not ideal. For example, the requirement that the display be updated every 5 s cannot easily be expressed if the display is a CSP channel which may be blocked by an uncooperative environment.

The on/off buttons can be modeled by using CSP channels, one for on-events and one for off-events. In order to describe the thermometer and the display we introduce two new continuous-function interface mechanisms.

The thermometer is introduced by a declaration of the form

$temp : \mathbb{R} \, ^\circ\mathrm{C}$ **sensor**,

which declares *temp* to be a continuous-function interface with public type $\mathbb{R} \, \mathsf{s} \to \mathbb{R} \, ^\circ\mathrm{C}$. Internally, *temp* takes the syntactic role of a CSP channel. The relationship between the public continuous-function variable and the internal channel is that whenever a value v is communicated on the internal channel at a time t, that value must be equal to the value of the continuous function at that time, that is $temp(t) = v$.

The temperature display is introduced by a declaration of the form

$screen : Display$ **actuator**,   where $Display ::= Temp\langle\!\langle \mathbb{N} * 0.5^\circ\mathrm{C} \rangle\!\rangle \mid nil$.

This declaration also introduces *screen* as a public continuous-function variable, but in this case the internal role is that of the local state variable. Thus *screen* may appear in the delta list of operations and any other place where a local variable may appear.

The TCOZ process class describing the DTD is below.

DTD

| $temp : \mathbb{R} \, ^\circ\mathrm{C}$ **sensor** |
| $screen : Display$ **actuator** |
| $on, off :$ **chan** |

INIT
$screen = nil$

SetScreen
$\Delta(screen)$
$t? : \mathbb{R} \, ^\circ\mathrm{C}$

$\exists dt : \mathbb{N} * 0.5^\circ\mathrm{C} \bullet$
$\quad dt = t \pm 0.5^\circ\mathrm{C} \land$
$\quad screen' = Temp(dt)$

$Show \mathrel{\widehat{=}} ([t : \mathbb{R} \, ^\circ\mathrm{C}] \bullet temp?t \to$
$\qquad SetScreen \bullet \textsc{Deadline}\,5\,\textsc{s} \bullet \textsc{WaitUntil}\,5\,\textsc{s};\ Show)$
$\qquad \nabla\ off \to NoShow$

$NoShow \mathrel{\widehat{=}} screen := nil;\ on \to Show$

$\textsc{Main} \mathrel{\widehat{=}} on \to Show$

A DTD object begins with the screen blanked (INIT), then when the on-button is pressed it passes into *Show* mode.

In *Show* mode it polls the temperature sensor and displays the result to the nearest one half degree Celsius. This behaviour is repeated with periodicity 5 s. A repeated activity with period T can be described by the CSP definition of the form

$$PA_0 \triangleq A; \ \text{WaitUntil} \ T; \ PA_0,$$

provided the activity A is guaranteed to terminate before T. In order ensure this a deadline is placed on the activity giving a definition of the form

$$PA \triangleq A \bullet \text{Deadline} \ T \bullet \text{WaitUntil} \ T; \ PA.$$

The definition of *Show* is of precisely this form, ensuring that the screen update occurs once every 5 s. The fact that the *temp* channel is a sensor is important in ensuring that the *Show* acts as expected. Since *temp* events do not represent synchronisations with the environment they happen immediately they are offered. A simple CSP channel could be blocked for an arbitrary time, making such a periodic behaviour impossible to guarantee.

If the off-button is pressed with the DTD in *Show* mode, it immediately passes to the *NoShow* mode by blanking the screen. This is expressed using the Timed CSP interrupt operator ($\_ \ \triangledown \ \_$), which shifts control to the interrupt routine as soon as an interrupt event (in this case *off*) is enabled. The DTD remains in *NoShow* mode until the on-button is once again pressed. Note that the expression *screen* $:=$ *nil* is a short form of the schema $[\Delta(screen) \mid screen' = nil]$

3.2   The local virtues

The experienced CSP practitioner is probably not entirely convinced by the preceding argument. After all the so-called `continuous-function interface' is really just an asynchronous communications medium and it is well known how to model such things in CSP. To a degree this criticism is valid, at least in a closed system. A local continuous-function interface a of type A may be modeled by the following TCOZ process, provided that it appears in a context in which the channels la and ra are hidden from the environment and therefore cannot be blocked.

```
┌─ loc_a ──────────────────────────────────────────────────────
│  la, ra : chan
│  a : A
├──────────────────────────────────────────────────────────────
│  Main ≙ μ LA • ([i : A] • la?i → a := i; LA) □ (ra!a → LA)
└──────────────────────────────────────────────────────────────
```

If B is a process which uses a as an actuator and C is a process that uses a as a sensor, then

$$P \triangleq \ \| \ B \xleftarrow{a} C$$

has the same behaviour as

$$P^* \triangleq \ \| \ B^* \xleftarrow{la} A; \ A \xleftarrow{ra} C^*,$$

where B^* is B with a replaced by la and updates to a replaced by outputs to la; and C^* is C with a replaced by ra. This interfacing model is inferior in two ways.

Firstly it is only effective when used in closed systems. This means that processes designed to interface with such a channel cannot be understood in isolation, leading to a highly coupled system design. In the above examples, the processes B^* and C^* have the correct timing behaviour only when placed in conjunction with A as in P^*. Unless la and ra are hidden, a hostile environment may interfere with their behaviour. In contrast the **sensor** and **actuator** mechanism provide a truly localised model of an asynchronous interface. Systems designed using these mechanisms are decomposed more easily because the individual components are more easily understood in isolation. In the DTD specification there is no need to describe the behaviour of system environment at all, only the interface it presents.

Secondly in the **sensor/actuator** mechanism the associated continuous function becomes a public interface to the TCOZ process. This means that TCOZ processes may be treated transparently as normal components in a formal approach to analog systems design. One such approach is being developed by Fidge and Hayes *et al* [5, 9], based on Mahony's timed refinement calculus [11, 14]. In any case, describing digital components as truly open subsystems seems preferable to requiring the designer to artificially close a system design by providing unsatisfactory digital approximations to analog system components.

3.3   Generating a real-time clock timer

As another example of the utility of continuous-function interfaces, consider the specification of a real-time system clock for a digital system. A real-time clock provides a synchronisation signal for the various components in a system, in the form of a simple square-wave which oscillates with a set frequency. Such clocks are generally rated in terms of the number of cycles per second (hz) which they generate.

In TCOZ the signal from the real-time clock can be modeled by using a boolean actuator and the square-wave generated by a periodic process.

$$
\begin{array}{|l}
\hline
\_RT\_Clock_____ \\
\quad \begin{array}{|l} \hline
\textit{freq} : \mathbb{R} \, \mathsf{hz} \\
\textit{per}, \textit{gain} : \mathbb{R} \, \mathsf{s} \\
\hline
\textit{per} * \textit{freq} = 1 \wedge \textit{gain} < \textit{per}/10 \\
\end{array} \\[6pt]
\hline
\quad \textit{rtc} : \mathbb{B} \, \textbf{actuator} \\
\hline
\quad \textsc{Main} \; \widehat{=} \; \mu \, C \bullet \textit{rtc} := \neg \, \textit{rtc} \bullet \textsc{Deadline} \, \textit{gain} \bullet \textsc{WaitUntil} \, \textit{per}/10; \; C \\
\hline
\end{array}
$$

The parameters of the *RT_Clock* represent the frequency *freq* and period *per* of the clock; and the time taken to change state *gain*, which is much smaller than the period.

3.4   Monitoring input signals

A number of the continuous-function interfaces in the cruise control specification in Section 4 represent digital signals, that is signals of type boolean. In such cases it is often of great interest to detect transitions in the signal, either from high to low or vice versa. The following TCOZ class describes a process which monitors a digital signal and raises events whenever it encounters a leading or a trailing edge.

Edges

$signal : \mathbb{B}\,\textbf{sensor}$
$up, dn : \textbf{chan}$

$High \mathrel{\widehat{=}} signal.\mathsf{false} \rightarrow dn \rightarrow Low$
$Low \mathrel{\widehat{=}} signal.\mathsf{true} \rightarrow up \rightarrow High$
$\textsc{Main} \mathrel{\widehat{=}} signal.\mathsf{false} \rightarrow Low \mathbin{\square} signal.\mathsf{true} \rightarrow High$

It may seem strange to introduce a signal interface and then re-interpret it as events, but this mechanism gives a more accurate local model of the situation than if the events themselves were the interface. With a channel based interface, a failure of the system to process the signal rapidly enough may simply result in the environment waiting till it is finished. With the continuous-function interface the missing of a processing deadline definitely results in the missing of an edge.

Sometimes we will be interested only in leading edges or else only in trailing edges.

$Lead \mathrel{\widehat{=}} (Edges \setminus dn)$
$Trail \mathrel{\widehat{=}} (Edges \setminus up)$

Both the *RT_Clock* and the *Edges* classes will be reused extensively in the cruise control specification.

4   Cruise control overview

The aim of a cruise control system for a car is to maintain the speed of the car even over varying terrain. The high-level system structure of a cruise control system of a car is illustrated in Figure 3. The *Car* is an analog system capable of moving forward, changing direction, producing heat, and many other observable behaviours which we represent as an abstract variable *perf*. The variable *perf* is a function of three inputs. The driver provides control inputs by by turning the steering-wheel, applying the brake, etc the aggregate of which we represent by the abstract variable *driver_inp*. The throttle setting, represented by *throttle*, controls the forward speed of the car. Finally, various environmental factors including wind drag, road incline, etc (represented by *env*) can affect the response of the system to the controlling variables.

The purpose of the *Cruise* class is to monitor the linear speed of the car and to modulate the throttle setting so as to maintain the speed of the car at a point determined by the driver inputs.

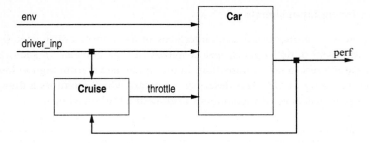

Fig. 3. Block diagram of cruise system and car.

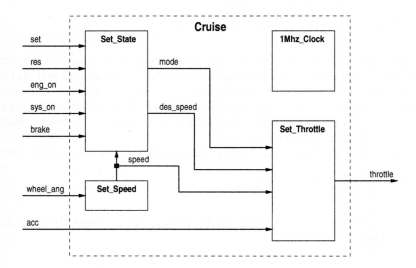

Fig. 4. Block diagram of throttle control.

Notice that the structure of the cruise control system is precisely that of the abstract control system presented in Figure 1. The controlled variable is *perf*, the uncontrolled variables are *env* and some components of *driver_inp*, the manipulated variable is *throttle*, and the command variables are the components of *driver_inp* which determine the mode of behaviour of the *Cruise* class. This gives *Cruise* class itself the same external interface as the subsystem enclosed by the dashed rectangle in Figure 1, suggesting the structure of that subsystem as a suitable architecture for the *Cruise* class. Section 5 is devoted to a formal TCOZ specification of the *Cruise* subsystem following this control system architecture.

5   TCOZ model of the cruise control system

The top-level design of the cruise control system, illustrated in Figure 4, follows the basic structure of the digital subsystem from Figure 1. The command variables are the components of *driver_inp* (driver input) that are devoted to operating the cruise control. These consist of the cruise-on/off button *sys_on*, the set-cruise button *set*, the resume-cruise button *res*, the accelerator pedal *acc*, and the brake pedal *brake*. The exact function of these command variables is described in Section 5.3, but for the moment it is sufficient to note that they are interpreted by the *Cruise* class command element *Set_State*. The setpoint signals are *des_speed*, *mode*, and *acc* which is passed through directly. The monitored components of the car are *eng_on* which indicates when the engine is running and *wheel_ang* which measures the angular position of a reference point on one of the wheels. The feedback element of the *Cruise* class is the *Set_Speed* class, which uses *wheel_ang* to calculate the current speed. The control function is performed by the *Set_Throttle* class which determines the correct *throttle* setting according to the current *speed*, *mode*, *des_speed*, and accelerator heel *pulses* and (acceleration) *acc*. The output from the cruise control is the *throttle*, which constitutes both the actuating signal and the manipulated variable. The feedforward element is the trivial process which propagates *throttle* through to the *Car* system. The final class is the real-time clock which is used to drive the activities of the other classes.

5.1   The clock

In order to drive the cruise control circuitry we introduce a 1 Mhz clock, that is $1 \text{ cu} = 1 \mu s$.

_ 1 Mhz *Clock* _____

   RT_Clock

   | $per = 1 \text{ cu} \land gain < 0.1 \text{ cu}$

5.2   Car speed

The speed of the car is determined by counting clock signals between pulses from a wheel sensor. This process consists of four components as shown in Figure 5: one to generate the wheel pulses, one to detect wheel pulses, one to detect clock signals, and one to actually count the clock signals in each period of revolution and calculate the speed. The speed is calculated with a precision of 0.1 km hr^{-1}, that is in units of $\text{su} == 0.1 \text{ km hr}^{-1}$, and also to an accuracy of 0.1 km hr^{-1}, under the assumptions that the maximum speed of the car is $max_s == 300 \text{ km hr}^{-1}$ and the wheel circumference is $C_w == 3 \text{ m}$. The period of revolution is calculated with a precision is ± 1 clock cycle, the wheel pulse timings may be so as to allow a whole extra clock signal when the time elapsed is a small fraction of a clock cycle or vice versa. To ensure that the overall accuracy of the speed calculation is better than $\pm 1 \text{ su}$, the clock unit cu must satisfy the condition

$$1 \text{ cu} \leq \frac{C_w}{max_s} * \frac{0.5 \text{ su}}{max_s - 0.5 \text{ su}}.$$

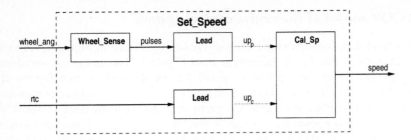

Fig. 5. Block diagram of speed calculation.

The suggested clock rate of 1 Mhz is adequate to ensure this condition.

The *Wheel_Sense* process monitors the *wheel_ang* variable and raises the pulse signal while the angle is between 0 rad and $\epsilon_a : \mathbb{R}$ rad. In order to ensure the precision of ± 1 cu, we require that raising and dropping the signal take no longer than $\delta_a == 0.1$ cu.

__*Wheel_Sense*_____

$wheel\_ang : \mathbb{R}$ rad **sensor** | INIT _____
$pulse : \mathbb{B}$ **actuator** | $pulse =$ false

MAIN $\widehat{=} \; \mu \; WS \; \bullet$
    $[a : \mathbb{R}$ rad $| \; 0$ rad $\leq a \leq \epsilon_a] \bullet wheel\_ang?a \rightarrow$
        $pulse :=$ true $\bullet$ DEADLINE δ_a;
    $[a : \mathbb{R}$ rad $| \; \epsilon_a \leq a] \bullet wheel\_ang?a \rightarrow$
        $pulse :=$ false $\bullet$ DEADLINE δ_a; WS

Between each wheel pulse the number of clock pulses is counted to determine the period of rotation to the nearest clock unit. The speed is then calculated in speed units by dividing the circumference (C_w) of the wheel by the period between pulses.

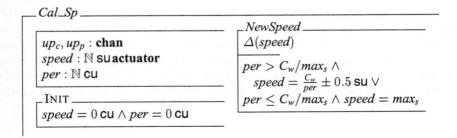

$Count \mathrel{\widehat{=}}$
$\qquad [per < C_w/1\,\mathsf{su}] \bullet ($
$\qquad\qquad (up_c \to per := per + 1\,\mathsf{cu} \bullet \text{DEADLINE}\,0.1\,\mathsf{cu};\ Count)\ \square$
$\qquad\qquad (up_p \to (NewSpeed;\ per := 0\,\mathsf{cu}) \bullet \text{DEADLINE}\,0.1\,\mathsf{cu};\ Count))$
$\qquad \square$
$\qquad [per \geq C_w/1\,\mathsf{su}] \bullet$
$\qquad\qquad (speed := 0\,\mathsf{su};\ per := 0\,\mathsf{cu}) \bullet \text{DEADLINE}\,0.1\,\mathsf{cu};$
$\qquad\qquad\qquad up_p \to Count$
$\text{MAIN} \mathrel{\widehat{=}} up_p \to Count$

Two exceptional behaviours are considered. If the wheel is rotating very slowly, the period calculation times out when the count exceeds C_w/max_s, the speed is set to $0\,\mathsf{su}$ and the count is not restarted until the next wheel pulse is encountered. If the wheel is rotating very fast then the speed is set to max_s.

─── Set_Speed ─────────────────────────────

$pe : Lead[\frac{pulses}{signal}, \frac{up_p}{up}]$
$ce : Lead[\frac{rtc}{signal}, \frac{up_c}{up}]$
$cs : Cal\_Sp$
$ws : Wheel\_Sense$

$\text{MAIN} \mathrel{\widehat{=}} \Big\| (ws \xleftarrow{\ pulses\ } pe;\ pe \xleftarrow{\ up_p\ } cs;\ ce \xleftarrow{\ up_c\ } cs)$

5.3   Cruise modes

When operating, the cruise control can be in any of four modes of operation.

$\qquad CM \mathrel{\widehat{=}} setpoint \mid accel \mid decel \mid rest$

setpoint The speed of the car is maintained at the desired speed by manipulating the throttle setting.
accel The speed of the car is increased by opening the throttle.
decel The speed of the car is decreased by closing the throttle.
rest No throttle manipulation is performed, but the desired speed is remembered.

The mode of operation of the cruise control is determined by the following input signals.

eng_on The cruise control cannot operate if the engine is off.
sys_on The cruise control is switched on and off by this signal.
set While the cruise control is in any operating mode, briefly raising the *set*-signal sets the desired speed to the current speed and initiates *setpoint*-mode. Holding the *set*-signal high for longer than

$\qquad t_h == 1\,\mathsf{s}$

causes the car to enter the *decel*-mode. When the *set*-signal falls the desired speed is set to the current speed, then control returns to *setpoint*-mode.

res While the cruise control is in any operating mode, briefly raising the *res*-signal initiates *setpoint*-mode, but does not alter the desired speed. Holding the *res*-signal high for longer than t_h causes the car to enter the *accel*-mode. When the *res*-signal falls the desired speed is set to the current speed, then control enters the *setpoint*-mode.

brake While the cruise control is in any operating mode, touching the brake causes the control to enter *rest*-mode, but does not alter the desired speed.

speed If operating, the cruise control cannot be in *setpoint*-mode if the desired speed is less than $min_d == 50.0 \, \text{km hr}^{-1}$.

The purpose of the *Set_State* process is to determine the correct operating mode and to maintain the value of the desired speed.

In order to correctly interpret the control signals from the driver, especially in light of the dual purpose nature of the *set* and *res* signals, monitors are placed on these signals to convert them to a sequence of driver events as depicted in Figure 6. The possible events on the *set* signal are *sp* for enaging cruise control and *dc* for decelerating. The possible events on the *res* signal are *rs* for resuming cruise control and *ac* for accelerating.

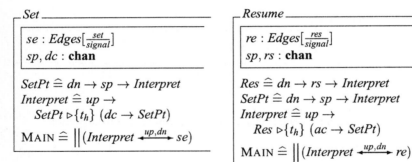

A simple edge monitor is used on the brake signal.

The normal behaviour of the cruise state is to set the *mode* and *des_speed* signals in accordance with driver cruise events and any brake events. However, this behaviour is suppressed if the *eng_on* or *sys_on* signals go low. When both signal go high again the *mode* is set to *rest* and the *des_speed* to 0 su.

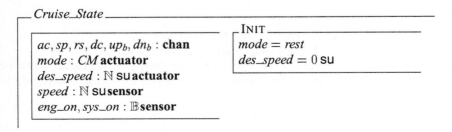

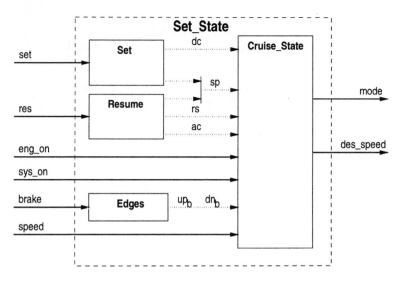

Fig. 6. Block diagram of cruise state determination.

$SP \cong sp \to [s : \mathbb{N} \, \textsf{su}] \bullet speed?s \to ($
$\qquad [s \geq min_d] \bullet des\_speed := s; \ mode := setpoint \ \Box$
$\qquad [s < min_d] \bullet \textsc{Skip})$

$RS \cong rs \to ($
$\qquad [des\_speed \geq min_d] \bullet mode := setpoint \ \Box$
$\qquad [des\_speed < min_d] \bullet \textsc{Skip})$

$AC \cong ac \to mode := accel$

$DC \cong dc \to mode := decel$

$Normal \cong (SP \ \Box \ RS \ \Box \ AC \ \Box \ DC); \ Normal$

$Active \cong Normal \ \triangledown \ up_b \to mode := rest; \ dn_b \to Active$

$Sys\_Off \cong sys\_on?\textsf{true} \to Active$
$\qquad \triangledown \ sys\_on?\textsf{false} \to mode := rest; \ des\_speed := 0 \, \textsf{su}; \ Sys\_Off$

$Eng\_Off \cong eng\_on?\textsf{true} \to Sys\_Off$
$\qquad \triangledown \ eng\_on?\textsf{false} \to mode := rest; \ des\_speed := 0 \, \textsf{su}; \ Eng\_Off$

$\textsc{Main} \cong Eng\_Off$

A *Set_State* class then consists of monitors on the *set*, *res*, and *brake* signals; and a *Cruise_State* class communicating with each other as described in Figure 6.

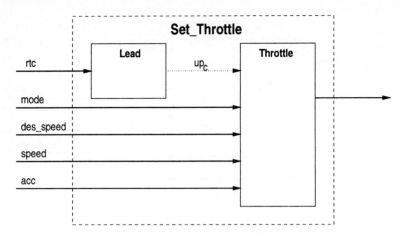

Fig. 7. Block diagram of throttle determination.

_Set_State_

> $sm : Set$
> $rm : Resume$
> $br : Edges[\frac{brake}{signal}, \frac{up_b}{up}, \frac{dn_b}{dn}]$
> $cs : Cruise\_State$

$\text{MAIN} \mathrel{\widehat{=}} \|\,(sm \xleftrightarrow{sp,dc} cs;\ rm \xleftrightarrow{sp,rs,ac} cs;\ br \xleftrightarrow{up_b,dn_b} cs)$

5.4   Throttle

The final component of the cruise control determines the appropriate throttle setting for all cruise modes. A block diagram of the _Set_Throttle_ component is depicted in Figure 7. It is a clocked component which calculates a new throttle setting each clock cycle, based on the current speed, the cruise mode, the accelerator pedal, and the desired speed (in _setpoint_-mode). The throttle and accelerator pedal quantities are represented abstractly by a unit symbol au.

Throttle

> $\delta_{th} : \mathbb{N}\,\text{au}$
> $max_{th}, min_{th} : \mathbb{N}\,\text{au}$
> $\ldots$
>
> $s_p : \mathbb{N}\,\text{su}$
> $speed, des\_speed : \mathbb{N}\,\text{su}\,\textbf{sensor}$
> $mode : CM\,\textbf{sensor}$
> $acc : \mathbb{N}\,\text{au}\,\textbf{sensor}$
> $throttle : \mathbb{N}\,\text{au}\,\textbf{actuator}$
>
> $\ldots$ [details omitted]

The details of the above class are omitted due to the space limitation.

The *Set_Throttle* class consists of a monitor on the clock signal and a *Throttle* class for updating the throttle every clock cycle.

$$
\begin{array}{|l}
\hline
\quad Set\_Throttle _____ \\
\hline
\quad ce : Lead[\frac{rtc}{signal}, \frac{up_c}{up}] \\
\quad th : Throttle \\
\hline
\quad \textsc{Main} \mathrel{\widehat{=}} \| (ce \xleftarrow{up_c} th) \\
\hline
\end{array}
$$

5.5 Cruise system

As stated in the introduction to this section, the *Cruise* class consists of a 1 Mhz clock, a speed monitor, a user input monitor, and a throttle actuator interacting as described in Figure 4.

$$
\begin{array}{|l}
\hline
\quad Cruise _____ \\
\hline
\quad c : 1\ \text{Mhz}\ Clock \\
\quad ss : Set\_State \\
\quad sd : Set\_Speed \\
\quad st : Set\_Throttle \\
\hline
\quad \textsc{Main} \mathrel{\widehat{=}} \| (c \xleftarrow{rtc} sd, st;\ ss \xleftarrow{mode, des\_speed} st;\ sd \xleftarrow{speed} ss, st) \\
\hline
\end{array}
$$

6 Conclusion

In this paper, Timed Communicating Object Z (TCOZ) has been extended with new communications mechanism, the *continuous-function interface*. The basic idea is to use a (usually real-valued) function of real-valued time as communications medium between objects. The **actuator** and **sensor** mechanism differ only in the manner in which the continuous-function interface is utilised by a class. A **actuator** takes on the role of a local variable through which an object `controls' the value of the continuous-function interface. A **sensor** takes on the role of a CSP channel through which the object `monitors' the value of the continuous-function interface.

The standard method of communication between components in an object-oriented architecture is the method invocation by which an object may request a service from another object if it knows the appropriate method name and object identifier. This form of communication leads to a high degree of coupling between object classes because so much information is needed to set up communications. In CSP the standard communications mechanism is the channel which provides a more abstract interface between processes. Each component interacts only with its channels and need have little detailed knowledge about the structure of other components. However, because communications on CSP channels represent explicit synchronisations between processes, each process must obey the correct 'protocol' for the channel in order to avoid deadlock situations. Thus there remains a residual amount of coupling between processes linked by CSP channels. This coupling is removed by the continuous-function interface mechanism which does not require a synchronisation between processes for communication to occur. Through judicious use of channels where synchronisation is truly required (as for service requests) and continuous-function interfaces where synchronisation is not required, it is possible to adopt a 'open' approach to systems design with a minimum of inter-module coupling. We believe the open systems approach to be essential to the treatment of large-scale formal systems design.

The coupling problem with CSP channels has also been recognised by Davies [2], who suggested the use of *signal* events as a means of addressing the problem. A signal event is simply an event which cannot be blocked by its environment. However, if no process is ready to accept the signal immediately, the information is lost forever. The continuous-function interface is superior to the signal mechanism, because the information transmitted on an **actuator** signal remains available to any other process until overwritten by the controlling process.

The **actuator** and **sensor** metaphors are drawn from the theory of automatic control systems. Following Shaw [17], we advocate the control system as an important architectural framework for the design of real-time, hybrid systems. In this paper we have demonstrated the power of the control systems architecture by applying it to the classic hybrid-system case-study, the automobile cruise control. Applying the control system template of Figure 1 to the cruise control allowed us to identify and describe the high-level components of the cruise control with a minimum of effort. By adopting the 'natural' architecture for the problem domain, we were able to produce a design with a low degree of coupling between components; a factor that is likely to make later development phases both cheaper and faster. The case study has also served as a vehicle for demonstrating the power of the continuous-function interface as a means of supporting the description of 'open' system components. The formal incarnation of the cruise control design was able to reflect the elegance of the informal architecture because the continuous-function interface does not bias the design toward higher coupling as would the method invocation and channel communications mechanisms.

The shift from closed to open systems necessitates close attention to issues of control, an area where both Z and CSP are weak [23]. We believe that TCOZ with the **actuator** and **sensor** can be a good candidate for specifying open control systems.

Acknowledgements

We would like to thank Neale Fulton, Ian Hayes and anonymous referees for many useful comments. This work is supported in part by the DSTO/CSIRO Fellowship programme.

References

1. K. Araki, A. Galloway, and K. Taguchi, editors. *IFM'99: Integrated Formal Methods, York, UK*. Springer-Verlag, June 1999.

2. J. Davies. *Specification and Proof in Real-Time Systems*. PhD thesis, Oxford University Computing Laboratory, Programming Research Group, 1991.

3. J.S. Dong and B. Mahony. Active Objects in TCOZ. In J. Staples, M. Hinchey, and S. Liu, editors, *the 2nd IEEE International Conference on Formal Engineering Methods (ICFEM'98)*, pages 16–25. IEEE Press, December 1998.

4. R. Duke, G. Rose, and G. Smith. Object-Z: a Specification Language Advocated for the Description of Standards. *Computer Standards and Interfaces*, 17:511–533, 1995.

5. C. J. Fidge, I. J. Hayes, A. P. Martin, and A. K. Wabenhorst. A set-theoretic model for real-time specification and reasoning. In *Mathematics of Program Construction*, 1998.

6. C. Fischer. CSP-OZ: A combination of Object-Z and CSP. In H. Bowmann and J. Derrick, editors, *Formal Methods for Open Object-Based Distributed Systems (FMOODS '97)*, volume 2, pages 423–438. Chapman & Hall, 1997.

7. A. J. Galloway and W. J. Stoddart. An operational semantics for ZCCS. In M. Hinchey and S. Liu, editors, *the IEEE International Conference on Formal Engineering Methods (ICFEM'97)*, pages 272–282, Hiroshima, Japan, November 1997. IEEE Press.

8. I. J. Hayes and B. P. Mahony. Using units of measurement in formal specifications. *Formal Aspects of Computing*, 7(3), 1995.

9. I. J. Hayes and M. Utting. Coercing real-time refinement: A transmitter. In D. J. Duke and A. S. Evans, editors, *BCS-FACS Northern Formal Methods Workshop*, Electronic Workshops in Computing. Springer Verlag, 1997.

10. B. Mahony and J.S. Dong. Overview of the semantics of TCOZ. In Araki et al. [1].

11. B. P. Mahony. *The Specification and Refinement of Timed Processes*. PhD thesis, University of Queensland, 1991.

12. B. P. Mahony and J.S. Dong. Blending Object-Z and Timed CSP: An introduction to TCOZ. In K. Futatsugi, R. Kemmerer, and K. Torii, editors, *The 20th International Conference on Software Engineering (ICSE'98)*, pages 95–104, Kyoto, Japan, April 1998. IEEE Press.

13. B. P. Mahony and J.S. Dong. Network topology and a case-study in TCOZ. In *ZUM'98 The 11th International Conference of Z Users*. Springer-Verlag, September 1998.

14. B. P. Mahony and I. J. Hayes. A case-study in timed refinement: A mine pump. *IEEE Transactions on Software Engineering*, 18(9):817–826, 1992.

15. F. H. Raven. *Automatic Control Engineering*. McGraw-Hill, second edition, 1968.

16. S. Schneider and J. Davies. A brief history of Timed CSP. *Theoretical Computer Science*, 138, 1995.

17. M. Shaw. Beyond objects. *ACM Software Engineering Notes*, 20(1), January 1995.

18. A. Simpson, J. Davies, and J. Woodcock. Security management via Z and CSP. In J. Grundy, M. Schwenke, and T. Vickers, editors, *IRW/FMP'98*. Springer-Verlag, 1998.

19. G. Smith. A semantic integration of Object-Z and CSP for the specification of concurrent systems. In J. Fitzgerald, C. Jones, and P. Lucas, editors, *Proceedings of FME'97: Industrial Benefit of Formal Methods*, Graz, Austria, September 1997. Springer-Verlag.

20. J. M. Spivey. *Understanding Z: A Specification Language and its Formal Semantics*, Cambridge University Press, 1988.

21. C. Suhl. RT-Z: An integration of Z and timed CSP. In Araki et al. [1].

22. K. Taguchi and K. Araki. The State-Based CCS Semantics for Concurrent Z Specification. In M. Hinchey and S. Liu, editors, *the IEEE International Conference on Formal Engineering Methods (ICFEM'97)*, pages 283–292, Hiroshima, Japan, November 1997. IEEE Press.

23. P. Zave and M. Jackson. Four dark corners of requirements engineering. *ACM Trans. Software Engineering and Methodology*, 6(1):1–30, January 1997.

24. C. Zhou, C. A. R. Hoare, and A. P. Ravn. A calculus of durations. *Information Processing Letters*, 40:269–276, 1991.

The UniForM Workbench,
a Universal Development Environment
for Formal Methods

Bernd Krieg-Brückner[1], Jan Peleska[1], Ernst-Rüdiger Olderog[2], Alexander Baer[3]

[1] Bremen Institute of Safe Systems, University of Bremen, PBox 330440, D-28334 Bremen
bkb@Informatik.Uni-Bremen.DE, jp@Informatik.Uni-Bremen.DE
[2] University of Oldenburg, PBox 2593, D-26111 Oldenburg
Olderog@Informatik.Uni-Oldenburg.DE
[3] INSY, Marzahnerstr. 34, D-13053 Berlin
insy_abaer@compuserve.com

Abstract. The UniForM Workbench supports combination of Formal Methods (on a solid logical foundation), provides tools for the development of hybrid, real-time or reactive systems, transformation, verification, validation and testing. Moreover, it comprises a universal framework for the integration of methods and tools in a common development environment. Several industrial case studies are described.

1 Introduction

The UniForM Workbench (Universal Formal Methods Workbench, cf. [K+96, K+99, Kri99]) has been developed by the Universities of Bremen and Oldenburg, and *Elpro*, Berlin, funded by the German Ministry for Education and Research, BMBF.

Formal Methods are used in modelling, using a mathematically well-founded specification language, proving properties about a specification and supporting correct development. The need arises in many aspects and properties of software, or more generally systems: for the physical environment of a hybrid hardware / software system, for the timing behaviour and real-time constraints of an embedded system, for the hazards and safety requirements of a safety-critical system, for the concurrent interactions of a reactive system, for deadlock and livelock prevention, for performance and dependability analysis, for architectural and resource requirements, and, finally, at many stages of the software development process for requirements and design specifications, etc., to the implementation of a single module.

It is unrealistic to expect a unique standard formalism to cover all the needs listed above. Instead, the solution is a variety of formalisms that complement each other, each adapted to the task at hand: specification languages and development methodologies, specific development methods or proof techniques, with a whole spectrum of tool support. Thus the challenge is to cater for correct combination of formalisms to

J. Wing, J. Woodcock, J. Davies (Eds.): FM'99, Vol. II, LNCS 1709, pp. 1186-1205, 1999.
© Springer-Verlag Berlin Heidelberg 1999

(1) ensure correct transition from abstract to concrete specifications when switching between formalisms during the development process ("vertical composition"),

(2) ensure correct combination of formalisms in a heterogeneous situation, e.g. combining concurrent and sequential fragments ("horizontal composition"),

(3) enable verification of particular properties, e.g. adherence to a security model, absence of deadlocks or satisfaction of performance requirements.

Another issue is the correct combination and integration of tools to support Formal Methods. Tools invariably differ in the exact language or semantics they support; the tool combination has to realize a correct combination of the resp. methods.

2 Combination of Methods

2.1 Integration into the Software Life Cycle

Integration of Formal Methods into Existing Process Models is important for success in industry. The Software Life Cycle Process Model V-Model [VMOD] originally a German development standard, has become internationally recognised. As many such standards, it loads a heavy burden on the developer by prescribing a multitude of documents to be produced. Thus tool support is essential to

(1) tailor the V-model first to the needs of a particular enterprise, then

(2) tailor the V-model to the special project at hand, fixing methods and tools,

(3) support its enactment guiding and controlling the use of methods and tools, and

(4) provide automatically generated development documents.

Up to now, tool support for working with the V-Model has mostly been provided by stand-alone project management components, facilitating the document production process for the project manager. In the UniForM project, we have adopted a different approach to V-Model utilisation: Formally speaking, the V-Model is a generic specification for the system development process. Tailoring the V-Model for a particular enterprise means instantiating this development process specification by determining

• the products (specifications, code, hardware, tests, proofs etc.) to be created,

• the activities and people responsible for each product,

• the methods to be used for each development step, and

• the tools to be used for application of these methods.

We are convinced that this instantiation process is best performed in the development environment itself, so that the tailoring process will not only have project management documents as output but simultaneously configure the Workbench for the specific configuration to be used in the development project.

This approach is presently implemented by Purper [BW98, Pur99a, b] in the Graphical Development Process Assistant, adapting the V-model to formal methods, where development and quality assurance are intimately related. The V-model is presented as a heavily interwoven hypertext document, generated from a common database, and tool support items 1 to 4 above; cf. also fig.1. Integration into a development environment such as the UniForM Workbench allows the coordination with its methods and tools (item 3). Tools themselves can generate development documents in conformance with the V-model (cf. item 4), such as the development history of fig. 6.

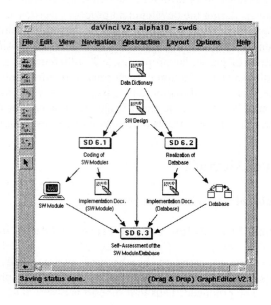

Fig. 1. *Example of a V-Model Process Graph as supported by the* UniForM Workbench

Combination of Conventional, Semi-Formal and Formal Techniques arises naturally when interfacing with other methods in the context of the V-model. Safety considerations, and thus the employment of formal methods, will often be restricted to parts of a system. Ideally, graphical interfaces will give the illusion of working with an informal method while an underlying formal semantics provides hooks to the use of formal methods (cf. PLC-Automata in section 2.2 and 3.1).

At the same time, it is sometimes advisable to flip back and forth between informal techniques at a high level of abstraction, e.g. requirements analysis, and formal methods, once more detail is required; complete formalisation might be premature and rather a burden, but formal methods are already useful at an early stage to support the analysis. An example is the specialisation of fault trees for hazard analysis to develop safety requirements and safety mechanisms [LMK98].

2.2 Combination of Formal Methods

Combinations of Formal Methods are by no means easy to achieve. The need for research has been recognised and requires demanding mathematical foundations, such as advanced methods in category theory. This has lead to languages for "institution independent" heterogeneous composition of modules ("in the large", see e.g. [AC94, Tar96, Dia98]); approaches for reasoning about correct composition of the logics capturing the semantics "in the small" (see e.g. [Mos96, Mos99b, MTP97, MTP98, SSC98, S+98]) introduce notions such as *embedding, translating* one formalism to another, *combination* of two formalisms, or *projecting* to either from the combination.

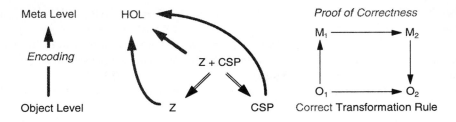

Fig. 2. *Semantic Representation in UniForM*

Semantic Representation. The approach of UniForM is to represent the semantics underlying a particular formalism or language in higher-order logic (HOL) as it is realized in the logical framework Isabelle [Pau95]. Fig. 2 shows a tiny Logic Graph for Z, CSP and their projections from the combination Z+CSP, plus the logic encoding into HOL at the meta level. Specifications in these languages are represented as theories in Isabelle and used for theorem proving with the verification system IsaWin on top of Isabelle (cf. section 3.3), and, as a basis for transformational development (cf. section 3.4), for proving the correctness of transformation rules.

HOL-Z, HOL-CSP and HOL-CASL. In HOL-Z, the logic of Z has been represented (cf. [KSW96a, KSW96b, K+97, Kol97, L+98]) and the mathematical tool kit has been proved correct (in co-operation with the ESPRESS project); this resulted in ca. 1k theorems, a 4k line proof script, and ca. 3 person-years of effort.

HOL-CSP represents the logic of CSP; a small but pervasive error in the 20 year old theory of CSP has been found and corrected [TW97, Tej99]. The process algebra has been proved correct; this resulted in ca. 3k theorems, a 17k line proof script, and ca. 3 person-years of effort. The example shows that such an endeavour is by no means trivial but pays off in the end. The proof of correctness of transformation rules, in particular, is now much easier. The above statistics includes the effort of becoming familiar with the intricacies of Isabelle, and most of the effort went into the proof of the process algebra of CSP. A subsequent representation of the logics and static semantics of CASL basic specifications (including an intricate overloading resolution) only required about 1 person-year of effort [MKK98].

Reactive Real-Time Systems. The first instantiation of UniForM has been for Z and CSP since these are considered to be rather mature and have been successfully applied to industrial cases. At the moment, we are working on methods ("structural transformations") to project not only from Z+CSP (actually Object-Z, cf. [Fis97, FS97]), but also from CSP+t, i.e. CSP with real-time constraints, to CSP without such constraints on the one hand, and simple timer processes on the other, cf. fig. 3. Thus specialised methods can be used in the projected domains. This breakdown is also successfully used for testing of real-time and hybrid systems (cf. section 3.4).

Combination of CSP and Object-Z. Whereas CSP is well suited for the description of communicating processes, Object-Z is an object based specification method for data, states and state transformations. Motivated by previous work at Oldenburg in the ESPRIT Basic Research Action ProCoS (Provably Correct Systems) [ProCoS], a combination of both methods into the specification language CSP-OZ has been proposed in [Fis97, FS97]. In CSP-OZ the process aspects are described using CSP and the data aspects using Object-Z. A specific achievement is the simple semantics of the combination which is based on two ideas:

- the embedding of Object-Z into the standard semantic model of CSP, the so-called failures/divergences model [Ros97]
- the semantic definition of the combination by the synchronous, parallel composition of the CSP part and the Object-Z part of a CSP-OZ specification.

Thus to each CSP-OZ specification a semantics in the failures/divergences model is assigned. As a consequence the concept of refinement of this model is also applicable to CSP-OZ. It has been shown that both process refinement of the CSP part and data refinement of the Object-Z part yield refinement of the whole CSP-OZ specification [Hal97]. Thus FDR (failures/divergences refinement), a commercially available model checker for CSP [FDR96], can also be applied to CSP-OZ specifications.

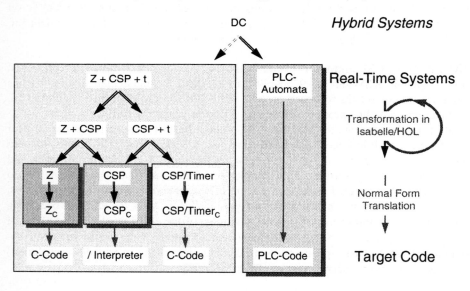

Fig. 3. *Method Combination in UniForM*

Combination of PLCs and Duration Calculus. For the specification of time critical aspects of computer systems, the Duration Calculus (DC for short, cf. [ZHR92]) was chosen from the start of the UniForM project. DC is intended for a formalization of high-level requirements.

On the lowest level, Programmable Logic Controllers (PLCs for short) were considered because they are simple devices that are widespread in control and automation technology. A PLC interacts with sensors and actuators in a cyclic manner. Each cycle consists of three phases: an input phase where sensor values are read and stored in local variables, a state transformation phase where all local variables are updated according to the stored program, and an output phase where the values of some of the local variables are output to the actuators. Real-time constraints can be implemented on PLCs with the help of timers that can be set and reset during the state transformation phase. The reaction time of a PLC depends on the cycle time.

One of the challenges of the UniForM project was to bridge the gap between Duration Calculus and PLCs in such a way that the correctness of the PLC software can be proven against the requirements formalised in DC. One of the discoveries in the UniForM project was that the behaviour of PLCs can very well be modelled using a novel type of automaton called *PLC-Automaton* [Die97], cf. fig. 4. The semantics of PLC-Automata describes the cyclic behaviour of a PLC; it is defined in terms of the Duration Calculus. Thus PLC-Automata represent a combination of the concept of PLC with DC. This enables us to integrate PLC-Automata into a general methodology for the design of real-time systems based on DC [Old98].

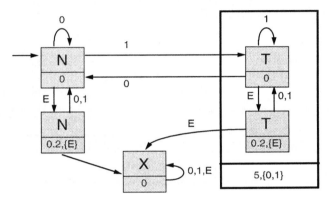

Fig. 4: PLC-Automaton

The CoFI Standard Family of Specification Languages. A standard formalism for all aspects of formal methods seems pragmatically undesirable (if not impossible) since a projection to a restricted and supposedly simpler formalism allows easier reasoning and specialised tools. However, standardisation should be aimed for in well-defined areas. IFIP WG 1.3 (Foundations of System Specification), based on more than 7 years of experience of the ESPRIT WG COMPASS, (cf. [Kri96]), started the Common Framework Initiative for Algebraic Specification and Development, CoFI.

CoFI, an international effort by primarily European groups, is developing a family of specification languages, a methodology guide and associated tools. The major language in this family, the Common Algebraic Specification Language CASL, has just been completed; it is the basis for sublanguages and extensions in the family. It has a complete formal semantics. CASL is a rather powerful and general specification language for first-order logic specifications with partial and total functions, predicates, subsorting, and generalized overloading [CoFI, C+97, Mos97]. Sublanguages of CASL, in connection with the planned extensions towards higher-order, object-oriented and concurrent aspects, allow interfacing to specialised tools and mapping from/to other specification languages [Mos99a]; this aspect is crucial for its intended impact. Various parsers exist; the first prototype implementation in the UniForM

Workbench [MKK98] comprises static semantic analysis for basic specifications and theorem proving in Isabelle; it will be the basis for transformational development.

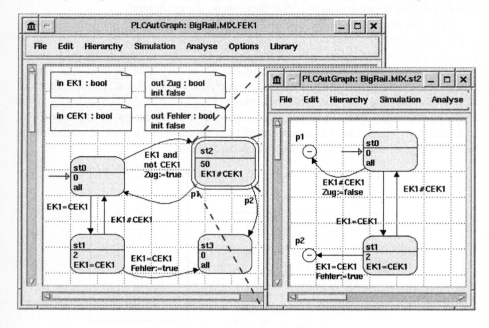

Fig. 5: *The Moby/PLC tool for the development of PLC-Automata*

3 Tools for Development

3.1 Development of PLC Software

At the University of Oldenburg a tool called Moby/PLC was designed and implemented that supports the work with PLC-Automata [DT98], see fig. 5. The tool comprises the following components:

- a graphical editor for drawing PLC-Automata
- a simulator for networks of PLC-Automata
- a compiler for generating PLC code in ST (Structured Text), a dedicated programming language for PLCs
- an algorithm for the static analysis of real-time constraints
- compilers for generating input for the real-time model checkers UPPAAL [B+95] and KRONOS [D+96]
- a synthesis algorithm for generating PLC-Automata from specifications written in a subset of Duration Calculus, so-called DC Implementables.

3.2   Tools for CSP-OZ

For the combined specification language CSP-OZ a graphical editor called Moby/OZ was developed. It is based on the same class library as the Moby/PLC tool. The editor enables the user to perform type checking using the Object-Z type checker "wizard".

3.3   Verification

Formal Methods are meant for the development of dependable systems: apart from safety and security, aspects of availability, reliability, fault-tolerance, and a general adherence to functionality requirements are important. Thus correctness is only one aspect, but obviously at the heart of the matter. In particular in safety-critical domains, application developers become increasingly aware of the importance of methods *guaranteeing* correctness w.r.t. a formal specification requirements, be it by the invent-and-verify paradigm, synthesis or transformation.

Abstraction to Verify Special Properties. In [B+97, BPS98, UKP98], a technique for abstracting from an existing program to verify the absence of deadlocks and livelocks was developed. It was applied successfully to more than 25k lines of Occam implementing a safety layer of a fault tolerant computer to be used in the International Space Station Alpha developed by DASA RI, Bremen; thus it is scalable and applicable to realistic applications.

The concrete program is abstracted to a formal specification in CSP containing only the *essential communication behaviour*; the approach guarantees that the proof for the abstract program implies the proved property for the concrete one. If the proof fails, the property does not hold, or the abstraction is not yet fine enough. The task is split into manageable subtasks by modularisation according to the process structure, and a set of generic composition theories developed for the application. The modules are then model-checked using the tool FDR [FDR96].

The abstraction was done by hand; future research will focus on implementing formal abstraction transformations in the UniForM Workbench to support the process.

Model-Checking is a very important technique in practice. The FDR tool [FDR96] is very useful for CSP, mostly for validating specifications, proving properties such as deadlock-freeness, and for development, proving the correctness of a refinement in the invent-and-verify paradigm. But it can do more: the transition graph it generates can be interpreted at run-time; this technique has been used for the safety layer of a computer on-board a train (see section 5.3). The abstraction and modularisation method applied to the International Space Station, described in the preceding paragraphs, shows two things:

- Model-checking is extremely useful when the resp. data-types are essentially enumeration types and the systems small enough.
- For large systems, these properties are likely to be violated; reasoning about modularisation and composition properties is necessary; proof tools are desirable.

Thus both model-checking and (interactive) proofs should go hand in hand. In the UniForM Workbench, the FDR tool can be used within the interactive proof tool.

Moreover, the experience of [HP98] when solving the train control problem in general (cf. also section 5.3) has been that reasoning about algebraic properties at a high level of abstraction is necessary, with subsequent refinements; model-oriented specifications and model-checking are not enough for this very practical problem that had defied a general solution thus far.

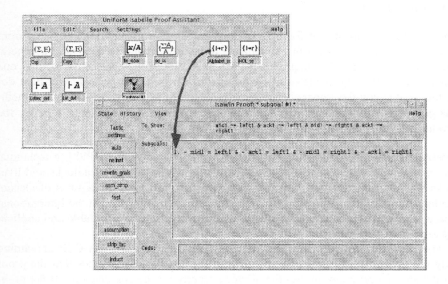

Fig. 6. *The* **Isabelle** *Proof Assistant* **IsaWin** *in* **UniForM**

A Window to Isabelle. The UniForM Workbench makes extensive use of the generic theorem prover Isabelle [Pau95], and heavily relies on the possibilities for interaction and tactic definition. A graphical user interface, a "window to Isabelle", IsaWin, has been constructed that hides unnecessary details from the uninitiated user [K+97, LW98]. Objects such as theories, substitutions, proof rules, simplification sets, theorems and proofs are typed (cf. fig. 6); icons can be dragged onto each other or onto the manipulation window to achieve various effects. This graphical and gesture-oriented approach is as a major advance over the rather cryptic textual interface. In the example, a set of rewrite rules for simplification is dragged onto the ongoing proof goal in the manipulation.

3.4   Development by Transformation

Architecture of the UniForM Transformation and Verification System. In fact, theorem proving and transformation, both a form of deduction, are so analogous, that the UniForM Verification System IsaWin shares a substantial part of its implementation with the Transformation System TAS (cf. fig. 7, see [LW98, L+98, L+99]). Like Isabelle, it is implemented in Standard ML; sml_tk [LWW96] is a typed interface in

SML to Tcl/Tk; on top, the generic user interface GUI provides the appearance of fig. 6 and fig. 8. This basic system is then parametrized (as a functor in SML terminology) either by the facilities for theorem proving of IsaWin or those for transformation of TAS. In addition, both share focussing and manipulation of scripts, i.e. proofs or development histories.

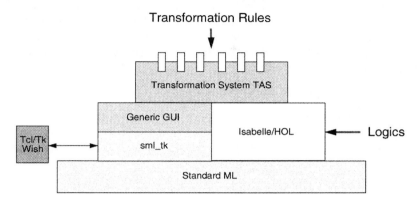

Fig. 7. Architecture of TAS, the UniForM Transformation System

Synthesis by Transformation. While the invent-and-verify paradigm is already supported by IsaWin, we definitely prefer synthesis-by-transformation over invent-and-verify as the pragmatically more powerful paradigm. First of all, the latter can be implemented by the former as a transformation rule that generates the necessary verification condition from the applicability condition. Secondly, this *automatic* generation of the required verification conditions is precisely one of the advantages of the transformational approach. The developer can concentrate on the development steps (viz. applications of transformation rules) first while the verification conditions are generated on the side and tabled for later treatment. Above all perhaps, single transformation rules and automated transformation methods embody development knowledge in a compact and accessible form like design patterns. Transformation rules preserve correctness; they can themselves be proved correct in UniForM against the semantics of the object language, e.g. at the level of the logic representation in HOL, cf. fig. 2.

TAS, the UniForM Transformation System. TAS may be parametrized by a logic (e.g. semantic representation of Z, CSP or CASL) at the Isabelle level, and by transformation rules at the level of TAS itself, cf. fig. 7 [Lüt97, L+99]. On top of the basic architecture that it shares with IsaWin, TAS provides icons for (program or specification) texts, transformation rules (possibly parametrized) and transformational developments in progress, in analogy to proofs (cf. shaded icon and manipulation window in fig. 8). In the example, a parametrized transformation rule is applied to the highlighted fragment denoted by focussing, and a window for the editing of parameters is opened. Once input of parameters is completed, the rule is applied, and a further proof obligation is possibly generated. A proof obligation may be discharged during or after the development by transferring it to IsaWin or another verification system such as a model checker (presently FDR). The example shows the development of a communication protocol with send / receive buffers by a sequence of transformations in CSP.

The functionality of TAS subsumes that of a forerunner, the PROSPECTRA system [HK93]. However, the basis of Isabelle allows a more compact, more flexible and more powerful realisation: parametrization by additional transformation rules is a matter of minutes (instantiation of a functor rather than recompilation of the whole system!); static semantic analysis can often be mapped to type checking of Isabelle; proof tactics can be defined as SML programs and often allow the automation of applicability conditions, such that much fewer residual verification conditions need to be interactively proved by the user.

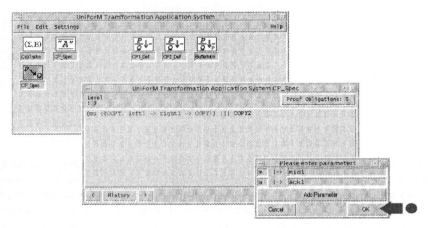

Fig. 8. Application of a Parametrized Transformation Rule

Development History. Note also the History button that allows navigation in the development history, in particular partial undo for continuation in a different way. The whole development is documented automatically and can be inspected in a WWW browser: initial and current specification, proof obligations, and development history.

Reusability of Developments. The development history is a formal object as well, (partial) replay is possible. A development can be turned into a new transformation rule by command; the generated verification conditions are then combined to a new applicability condition. Combined with abstraction, *developments themselves* become reusable in new situations, not just their products.

3.5 Validation, Verification, and Test Environment for Reactive Real-Time Systems

For real-world large-scale systems, complete formal development is still unrealistic: The amount of code implementing the application, operating system, drivers and firmware is simply too large to admit complete formal treatment. Furthermore, many correctness aspects of reactive systems depend on the interaction of software and hardware, and the number of different hardware components is too high to allow for the creation of formal behavioural models of these components. As a consequence, our recommendation to the Formal Methods practitioner is as follows:

* Try to develop the logical concepts (communication flow, control algorithms, data transformation algorithms etc.) in a formal way, in order to avoid logical flaws creeping into system design and implementation.
* Perform formal code development as far as possible, with emphasis on the critical modules of the system, otherwise use testing and inspection techniques.
* Use automated testing to check the proper integration of software and hardware. To support such an approach, the VVT-RT (Verification, Validation and Test for Real-Time Systems) tool kit is currently integrated into the UniForM Workbench:

Verification, Validation, and Testing. The methodology and tool kit VVT-RT [Pel96, PS96, PS97] allows *automatic* testing and verification and validation of (test) specifications. Test cases are generated from a real-time specification; they drive the completed hardware/software system as a "black box" in a hardware-in-the-loop configuration from a separate computer containing the test drivers, simulating a normal or faulty environment. The testing theory ensures, that each test will make an actual contribution, approximating and converging to a complete verification.

Even more important is the automatic test evaluation component of the tool kit: In practice, the execution of real-time tests will lead to thousands of lines of timed traces recording the occurrence of interleaved inputs and outputs over time. Manual inspection of these traces would be quite impossible. Instead, VVT-RT performs automatic evaluation of timed traces against a binary graph representation of the formal specification. This approach is very cost-effective. It has been applied successfully to one of the case studies of UniForM, a control computer on board of a train for railway control (see section 5.3), and to an electric power control component of a satellite developed by OHB, Bremen [Mey98, SMH99].

4 Universal Development Environment

The UniForM Workbench is an open ended tool integration framework for developing (formal) software development environments from the basis of pre-fabricated off-the-shelf development tools. The Workbench uses Concurrent Haskell as its central integration language, extended with a higher order approach to event handling akin to the one found in process algebras. Integration can therefore be done at a high level of abstraction, which combines the merits of functional programming with state-of-the-art concurrent programming languages.

The Workbench provides support for data, control and presentation integration as well as utilities for wrapping Haskell interfaces around existing development tools. It views the integrated Workbench as a reactive (event driven) system, with events amounting to database change notifications, operating system events, user interactions and individual tool events. The unique feature of the Workbench is that it provides a uniform and higher order approach to event handling, which improves on traditional approaches such as callbacks, by treating events as composable, first class values.

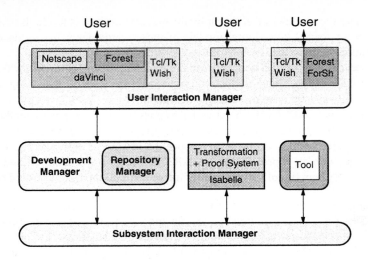

Fig. 9: *System Architecture of the* UniForM Workbench

Integration of Tools in the UniForM Workbench is described in detail in [Kar99] (see also [Kar98]), cf. fig. 9. *Control integration* is provided by the Subsystem Interaction Manager; based on the UniForM Concurrency Toolkit, tools interact in a fine grained network of communicating concurrent agents and are, in general, loosely coupled by intermittent adaptors (cf. [Kar97a, Kar97b]). The Repository Manager [KW97] takes care of *data integration* with an interface to a public domain version of the industry standard Portable Common Tool Environment [PCTE94, HPCTE] and provides version and configuration control, etc. with a graphical interface (using daVinci; cf. also fig. 10).

The User Interaction Manager provides *presentation integration*, incorporating interfaces to daVinci (see [FW94, Frö97], and cf. fig. 7 and fig. 10) and its extension Forest, a WWW-browser, and Tcl/Tk for window management. In particular the latter two become much more manageable and homogeneous by encapsulation into a typed, high-level interface in Haskell.

Haskell is the internal integration language; thus even higher-order objects and processes can be transmitted as objects. External tools are wrapped into a Haskell interface; we are working on an adaptation of the Interface Definition Language of the industry standard CORBA to Haskell that will shortly open more possibilities to integrate tools in, say, C, C++, or Java.

Architectures for development tools should avoid self-containment and allow integration with others. The possibility for control and data integration of a tool as an "abstract data type" is the most important (and not obvious since the tool may e.g. not allow remote control and insist on call-backs); integration of persistent data storage in a common repository is next (this may require export and import w.r.t. local storage); presentation integration with the same user interface is last - in fact it is most likely that the tool has its own graphical user interface. However, interactive Posix tools usually have a line-oriented interface that can easily be adapted [Kar97b].

This way, a graphical interface to HUGS was developed in a matter of weeks. Isabelle, IsaWin and TAS have been integrated, and a Z-Workbench with various tools has been instantiated from the UniForM Workbench (L+98), cf. fig. 10.

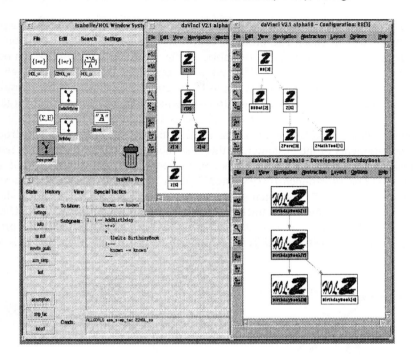

Fig. 10: Z-Workbench

Increase of Productivity by Functional Languages. It is quite obvious that we should use formal methods eventually to produce our own tools; but is this realistic at the moment for really large systems? Our experience has been best with functional programming languages so far; we estimate the increase of productivity over, say, C, to a factor of 3 (in number of lines, backed by empirical evidence). Without them, the development of large, non-trivial tools over a period of several years would have been impossible in an academic environment. TAS and IsaWin are extensions of Isabelle and comprise about 25k lines of SML; the graph visualisation system daVinci with was developed by Fröhlich and Werner [FW94, Frö97] over a period of 5 years comprising about 35k lines of a functional language developed at Bremen, plus about 10k lines of C for interfacing; the tool integration framework of the UniForM Workbench was developed almost entirely by Karlsen [Kar99] in about 50k lines of Haskell.

5 Case Studies

5.1 Control of a Single Track Segment

In close cooperation with the industrial partner Elpro, a case study "control of a single track segment" was defined. The problem concerns the safety of tram traffic on a segment where only a single track is available, see fig. 11. Such a bottle-neck can occur for example during repair work. The task is to control the traffic lights in such a way that collisions of trams driving in opposite direction is avoided and that certain general traffic rules for trams are obeyed. Real-time requirements occur locally at the sensor components ES1, CS1, LS1, ES2, CS2, LS2 near the track.

The methodology of PLC-Automata was applied to this case study. Starting from informal requirements of the customer, in this case the Berlin traffic company, a network consisting of 14 PLC-Automata was constructed using the Moby/PLC tool as part of the UniForM Workbench [DT98, Die97]. With Moby/PLC the whole network could be simulated [Tap97]. Essential safety properties were proven, for example that at most one direction of the single track segment will have a green traffic light. Then the network of PLC-Automata was compiled into 700 lines of PLC code in the programming language ST (Structured Text), which can be distributed over the PLCs as indicated in fig. 11.

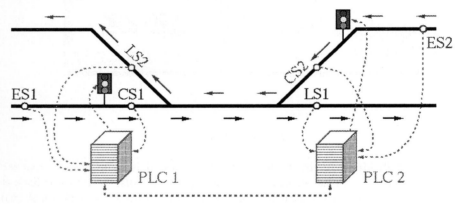

Fig. 11: Tram Control

5.2 Control of Jena Steinweg

After this first successful experiment with Moby/PLC, the Oldenburg group was challenged by Elpro to attack a more demanding case study where trams are allowed to drive into and out of the single track segment in many different ways. This control was actually implemented by Elpro in the city of Jena, hence the name. The complexity of this case study is due to the fact that the signalling of the traffic lights critically depends on the history of the last tram movements.

This case study could also be modelled with Moby/PLC as a network consisting of 110 PLC-Automata. While simulation still worked well, attempts to perform automatic verification of properties by translating the PLC-Automata into input for the real-time model checkers UPPAAL [B+95] and KRONOS [D+96] failed so far due to the complexity of the resulting timed automata. This complexity is caused by the fact that PLC automata take the cycle times of PLCs explicitly into account, in order to detect problems between communicating PLCs with different cycle times.

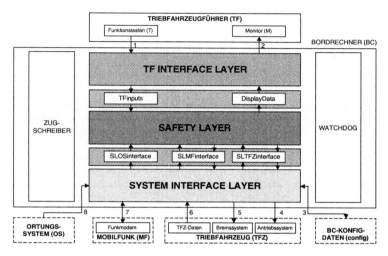

Fig. 12: *Architecture of the On-Board Computer*

5.3   On-Board Computer for Railway Control

Another case study was the development of a control computer on board of a train for railway control [AD97]. It is part of a distributed train and switching control system developed by *Elpro*, Berlin, where decentralised track-side safety-units control local points and communicate with trains via mobile phones. The whole system (with single tracks and deviations) has been modelled and specified with CSP in a student project at Bremen (cf. also [HP98] for a solution of the general train control problem).

The on-board computer has a layered architecture (see fig. 12). The TF INTERFACE LAYER communicates with the driver, the SYSTEM INTERFACE LAYER with a localization subsystem (e.g. GPS), a mobile phone subsystem and the train. The SAFETY LAYER contains all safety-relevant modules, determining the local state of the train, the requirements on the decentralized units on the track and their answers, finally leading to a decision about the permission to continue for the driver, or, alternatively, a forced-braking command to the train.

The design of the abstracts away from physical data formats in the concrete interfaces. The formal specification in CSP as an abstract transition system could be directly transliterated into an executable program that calls C++ functions of the interfaces [AD97, Pel96b].

The mobile phone based communication of the on-board computer with the track-side units in the SYSTEM INTERFACE LAYER is an example of the combination of CSP and OZ [Fis97, FS97], cf. sections 2.2 and 3.2.

The above case studies were done within the UniForM project; for other industrial applications of the UniForM Workbench cf. the verification of absence of deadlocks and livelocks for the International Space Station ([B+97, BPS98, UKP98], see section 3.3) or the automatic testing of an electric power control component of a satellite ([Mey98, SMH99], see section 3.5).

6 References

[AD 97]   Amthor, P., Dick, S.: Test eines Bordcomputers für ein dezentrales Zugsteuerungssystem unter Verwendung des Werkzeuges VVT-RT. 7. *Kolloquium Software-Entwicklung Methoden, Werkzeuge, Erfahrungen: Mächtigkeit der Software und ihre Beherrschung*, Technische Akademie Esslingen (1997).

[AC94]   Astesiano, E., Cerioli, M.: Multiparadigm Specification Languages: a First Attempt at Foundations, In: C.M.D.J. Andrews and J.F. Groote (eds.), *Semantics of Specification Languages (SoSl '93)*, Workshops in Computing, Springer (1994) 168-185.

[BW98]   Blank Purper, C., Westmeier, S.: A Graphical Development Process Assistant for Formal Methods. In: *Proc. VISUAL'98 (short papers)*, at ETAPS'98, Lisbon (1998). http://www.tzi.de/~uniform/gdpa

[B+95]   Bengtsson, J., Larsen, K.G., Larsson, F., Pettersson, P., Yi, W.: UPPAAL -- a tool suite for automatic verification of real-time systems. Proc. 4th DIMACS Workshop: *Verification and Control of Hybrid Systems*. New Brunswick, New Jersey, 1995.

[B+97]   Buth, B., Kouvaras, M., Peleska, J., Shi, H.: Deadlock Analysis for a Fault-Tolerant System. In Johnson, M. (ed.): *Algebraic Methodology and Software Technology, AMAST'97*. LNCS 1349. Springer (1997) 60-75.

[BPS98]   Buth, B., Peleska, J., Shi, H.: Combining Methods for the Livelock Analysis of a Fault-Tolerant System. In Haeberer, A.M. (ed.): *Algebraic Methodology and Software Technology, AMAST'98*. LNCS 1548. Springer (1999) 124-139.

[C+97]   Cerioli, M., Haxthausen, A., Krieg-Brückner, B., Mossakowski, T.: Permissive Subsorted Partial Logic in CASL. In Johnson, M. (ed.): *Algebraic Methodology and Software Technology, AMAST 97*, LNCS 1349, Springer (1997) 91-107.

[CoFI]   *CoFI: The Common Framework Initiative for Algebraic Specification and Development.* http://www.brics.dk/Projects/CoFI

[Dia98]   Diaconescu, R.: Extra Theory Morphisms for Institutions: logical semantics for multi-paradigm languages. *J. Applied Categorical Structures 6* (1998) 427-453.

[Die97]   Dierks, H.: PLC-Automata: A New Class of Implementable Real-Time Automata. Proc. *ARTS'97*, LNCS 1231, Springer (1997) 111-125.

[DT98]   Dierks, H., Tapken, J.: Tool-Supported Hierarchical Design of Distributed Real-Time Systems. *Euromicro Workshop on Real Time Systems*, IEEE (1998) 222-229.

[D+96]   Dawsa, C., Olivero, A., Tripakis, S., Yovine, S.: The tool KRONOS. In: R. Alur, T.A. Henzinger, E.D. Sontag (Eds.): *Hybrids Systems III – Verfication and Control.* LNCS 1066, Springer, (1996).

[FDR96]   Formal Systems Ltd.: *Failures Divergence Refinement.* User Manual and Tutorial Version 2.0. Formal Systems (Europe) Ltd. (1996).

[Fis97]   Fischer, C.: CSP-OZ: A Combination of Object-Z and CSP. In H. Bowmann, J. Derrick (eds.): *Formal Methods for Open Object-Based Distributed Systems, FMOODS `97*, volume 2, Chapmann & Hall (1997) 423-438.

[FS97]   Fischer, C., Smith, G.: Combining CSP and Object-Z: Finite or infinite trace-Semantics? *Proc. FORTE/PSTV 97*, Chapmann & Hall(1997) 503-518.
[Frö97]   Fröhlich, M.: Inkrementelles Graphlayout im Visualisierungssystem daVinci. Dissertation. 1997. *Monographs of the Bremen Institute of Safe Systems 6*, ISBN 3-8265-4069-7, Shaker , 1998.
[FW94]   Fröhlich, M., Werner, M.: The interactive Graph-Visualization System daVinci – A User Interface for Applications. Informatik Bericht Nr. 5/94, Universität Bremen, 1994. updated doc.: http://www.tzi.de/~daVinci
[Hal97]   Hallerstede, S.: Die semantische Fundierung von CSP-Z. Diplomarbeit, Universität Oldenburg, 1997.
[HPCTE]   The H-PCTE Crew: H-PCTE vs. PCTE, Version 2.8, Universität Siegen, 1996.
[HP98]   Haxthausen, A. E., Peleska, J.: Formal Development and Verification of a Distributed Railway Control System. In *Proc. 1st FMERail Workshop*, Utrecht (1998).
[HK93]   Hoffmann, B., Krieg-Brückner, B. (eds.): *PROgram Development by Specification and Transformation, The PROSPECTRA Methodology, Language Family, and System*. LNCS 680. Springer, 1993. http://www.tzi.de/~prospectra
[Kar97a]   Karlsen, E.W.: The UniForM Concurrency ToolKit and its Extensions to Concurrent Haskell. In: O'Donnald, J. (ed.): *GFPW'97, Glasgow Workshop on Functional Programming '97*, Ullapool.
[Kar97b]   Karlsen, E.W.: Integrating Interactive Tools using Concurrent Haskell and Synchronous Events. In *ClaPF'97, 2nd Latin-American Conference on Functional Programming*, La Plata, Argentina (1997).
[Kar98]   Karlsen, E.W.: The UniForM Workbench - a Higher Order Tool Integration Framework. In: *Int'l Workshop on Current Trends in Applied Formal Methods*. LNCS. Springer (*to appear*).
[Kar99]   Karlsen, E.W.: *Tool Integration in a Functional Setting*. Dissertation. Universität Bremen (1998) 364pp (to appear)
[KW97]   Karlsen, E.W., Westmeier, S.: Using Concurrent Haskell to Develop User Interfaces over an Active Repository. In *IFL'97, Implementation of Functional Languages 97*, St. Andrew, Scotland. LNCS 1467. Springer (1997).
[Kol98]   Kolyang: HOL-Z, An Integrated Formal Support Environment for Z in Isabelle/HOL. Dissertation, 1997. *Monographs of the Bremen Institute of Safe Systems 5*, ISBN 3-8265-4068-9, Shaker, 1998.
[KSW96a]   Kolyang, Santen, T., Wolff, B.: A Structure Preserving Encoding of Z in Isabelle/HOL. In *Proc. Int'l Conf. on Theorem Proving in Higher Order Logic*. LNCS 1125. Springer (1996). http://www.tzi.de/~kol/HOL-Z
[KSW96b]   Kolyang, Santen, T., Wolff, B.: Correct and User-Friendly Implementations of Transformation Systems. In: Gaudel, M.-C., Woodcock, J. (eds.): *FME'96: Industrial Benefit and Advances in Formal Methods*. LNCS 1051 (1996) 629-648.
[Kri96]   Krieg-Brückner, B.: Seven Years of COMPASS. In: Haveraaen, M., Owe, O., Dahl, O.-J. (eds.): *Recent Trends in Data Type Specification, LNCS 1130* (1996) 1-13.
[Kri99]   Krieg-Brückner, B.: UniForM Perspectives for Formal Methods. In: *Int'l Workshop on Current Trends in Applied Formal Methods*. LNCS. Springer (*to appear*).
[K+96]   Krieg-Brückner, B., Peleska, J., Olderog, E.-R., Balzer, D., Baer, A. (1996): UniForM, Universal Formal Methods Workbench. in: Grote, U., Wolf, G. (eds.): *Statusseminar des BMBF: Softwaretechnologie*. Deutsche Forschungsanstalt für Luft- und Raumfahrt, Berlin 337-356. http://www.tzi.de/~uniform
[K+97]   Kolyang, Lüth, C., Meyer, T., Wolff, B.: TAS and IsaWin: Generic Interfaces for Transformational Program Development and Theorem Proving. In Bidoit, M., Dauchet, M. (eds.): *Theory and Practice of Software Development '97*. LNCS 1214. Springer (1997) 855-859.
[K+99]   Krieg-Brückner, B., Peleska, J., Olderog, E.-R., Balzer, D., Baer, A: UniForM Workbench, Universelle Entwicklungsumgebung für Formale Methoden; Schlußbericht. 1998. *Monographs of the Bremen Institute of Safe Systems 9*. ISBN 3-8265-3656-8. Shaker, 1999.

[LMK98]   Lankenau, A., Meyer, O., Krieg-Brückner, B.: Safety in Robotics: The Bremen Autonomous Wheelchair. In: *Proc. AMC'98, 5th Int. Workshop on Advanced Motion Control*, Coimbra, Portugal 1998. ISBN 0-7803-4484-7, pp. 524-529.

[Lüt97]   Lüth, C.: Transformational Program Development in the UniForM Workbench. Selected Papers from the 8th Nordic Workshop on Programming Theory, Oslo, Dec. 1996. Oslo University Technical Report 248, May 1997.

[LW98]   Lüth, C. and Wolff, B.: Functional Design and Implementation of Graphical User Interfaces for Theorem Provers. *J. of Functional Programming* (to appear).

[L+98]   Lüth, C., Karlsen, E. W., Kolyang, Westmeier, S., Wolff, B.: HOL-Z in the UniForM Workbench - a Case Study in Tool Integration for Z. In J. Bowen, A. Fett,, M. Hinchey (eds.): *Proc. ZUM'98, 11th International Conference of Z Users*, LNCS 1493, Springer (1998) 116-134.

[L+99]   Lüth, C., Tej, H., Kolyang, Krieg-Brückner, B.: TAS and IsaWin: Tools for Transformational Program Development and Theorem Proving. In J.-P. Finance (ed.): *Fundamental Approaches to Software Engineering (FASE'99, at ETAPS'99).* LNCS 1577. Springer (1999) 239-243. http://www.tzi.de/~agbkb

[LWW96]   Lüth, C., Westmeier, S., Wolff, B.: sml_tk: Functional Programming for Graphical User Interfaces. Informatik Bericht Nr. 8/96, Universität Bremen. http://www.tzi.de/~cxl/sml_tk

[Mey98]   Meyer, O.: Automated Test of a Power and Thermal Controller of a Satellite. In: Test Automation for Reactive Systems - Theory and Practice. Dagstuhl Seminar 98361, Schloss Dagstuhl, (1998).

[Mos96]   Mossakowski, T.: Using limits of parchments to systematically construct institutions of partial algebras. In M. Haveraaen, O. Owe, O.-J. Dahl, eds.: *Recent Trends in Data Type Specification, LNCS 1130*, Springer (1996) 379-393.

[Mos97]   Mosses, P.: CoFI: The Common Framework Initiative for Algebraic Specification and Development. In Bidoit, M., Dauchet, M. (eds.): *Theory and Practice of Software Development '97.* LNCS 1214, Springer (1997) 115-137.

[Mos99a] Mossakowski, T.: Translating OBJ3 to CASL: the Institution Level. In J. L. Fiadeiro (ed.): *Recent Trends in Algebraic Development Techniques.* 13th Int'l Workshop, WADT'98, Lisbon, Selected Papers. *LNCS 1589* (1999) 198-214.

[Mos99b] Mossakowski, T.: Representation, Hierarchies and Graphs of Institutions. Dissertation, Universität Bremen, 1996. Revised version. *Monographs of the Bremen Institute of Safe Systems 2*, ISBN 3-8265-3653-3, Shaker, 1999.

[MKK98]   Mossakowski, T., Kolyang, Krieg-Brückner, B.: Static Semantic Analysis and Theorem Proving for CASL. In Parisi-Pressice, F. (ed.): *Recent Trends in Algebraic Development Techniques.* WADT'97, LNCS 1376, Springer (1998) 333-348.

[MTP97]   Mossakowski, T., Tarlecki, A., Pawlowski, W.: Combining and Representing Logical Systems, In Moggi, E. and Rosolini, G. (eds.): *Category Theory and Computer Science,* 7th Int. Conf. LNCS 1290, Springer (1997) 177-196.

[MTP98]   Mossakowski, T., Tarlecki, A., Pawlowski, W.: Combining and Representing Logical Systems Using Model-Theoretic Parchments. In Parisi-Pressice, F. (ed.): *Recent Trends in Algebraic Development Techniques.* WADT'97, LNCS 1376, Springer (1998) 349-364.

[Old98]   Olderog, E.-R.: Formal Methods in Real-Time Systems. In *Proc. 10th EuroMicro Workshop on Real Time Systems.* IEEE Computer Society (1998) 254-263.

[Pau95]   Paulson, L. C.: *Isabelle: A Generic Theorem Prover.* LNCS 828, 1995.

[PCTE94] European Computer Manufacturers Association: *Portable Common Tool Environment (PCTE), Abstract Specification,* 3rd ed., ECMA-149. Geneva, 1994.

[Pel96a] Peleska, J.: Formal Methods and the Development of Dependable Systems. Bericht 1/96, Universität Bremen, Fachbereich Mathematik und Informatik (1996) 72p. http://www.tzi.de/~jp/papers/depend.ps.gz

[Pel96b] Peleska, J.: Test Automation for Safety-Critical Systems: Industrial Application and Future Developments. In: M.-C. Gaudel, J. Woodcock (eds.): *FME'96: Industrial Benefit and Advances in Formal Methods.* LNCS 1051 (1996) 39-59.

[ProCoS]   He, J., Hoare, C.A.R., Fränzle, M., Müller-Olm, M., Olderog, E.-R., Schenke, M., Hansen, M.R., Ravn, A.P., Rischel, H.: Provably Correct Systems. In H. Langmaack, W.-P., de Roever, J., Vytopil (Eds.): *Formal Techniques in Real-Time and Fault-Tolerant Systems.* LNCS 863, Springer (1994).288–335.

[PS96]   Peleska, J., Siegel, M.: From Testing Theory to Test Driver Implementation. in: M.-C. Gaudel, J. Woodcock (eds.): *FME'96: Industrial Benefit and Advances in Formal Methods.* LNCS 1051 (1996) 538-556.

[PS97]   Peleska, J., Siegel, M.: Test Automation of Safety-Critical Reactive Systems. *South African Computer Jounal 19* (1997) 53-77. http://www.tzi.de/~jp/papers/sacj97.ps.gz

[Pur99a]   Purper, C.: GDPA: A Process Web-Center. *Proc. 2nd Workshop on Software Engineering over the Internet,* with ICSE'99, Los Angeles, 1999. http://sern.cpsc.ucalgary.ca/ ~maurer/ICSE99WS/Program.htm

[Pur99b]   Purper, C.: An Environment to support flexibility in process standards. *Proc. 1st IEEE Conf. on Standardization and Innovation in Information Technology.* Aachen, 1999 (to appear).

[Ros97]   Roscoe, A.W.: *The Theory and Practice of Concurrency.* Prentice Hall, 1997.

[SMH99]   Schlingloff, H., Meyer, O., Hülsing, Th.: Correctness Analysis of an Embedded Controller. In *Data Systems in Aerospace, DASIA '99,* Lissabon (May 1999).

[SSC98]   Sernadas, A., Sernadas, C., Caleiro, C.: Fibring of logics as a categorial construction. *Journal of Logic and Computation 8:10* (1998) 1-31.

[S+98]   Sernadas, A., Sernadas, C., Caleiro, C., Mossakowski, T.: Categorical Fibring of Logics with Terms and Binding Operators. In Gabbay, D., van Rijke, M. (eds.): *Frontiers of Combining Systems.* Research Studies Press (to appear).

[Tap97]   Tapken, J.: Interactive and Compilative Simulation of PLC-Automata. In Hahn, W., Lehmann, A. (eds.): *Simulation in Industry, ESS`97.* Society for Computer Simulation (1997) 552-556.

[Tap98]   Tapken, J.: MOBY/PLC – A Design Tool for Hierarchical Real-Time Automata. In: Astesiano, E. (ed.): *Fundamental Approaches to Software Engineering, FASE'98,* at ETAPS'98, Lisbon. LNCS 1382, Springer (1998) 326-329.

[TD98]   Tapken, J., Dierks, H.: Moby/PLC – Graphical Development of PLC-Automata. In Ravn, A.P., Rischel, H. (eds.): *FTRTFT`98,* LNCS 1486, Springer (1998) 311-314.

[Tar96]   Tarlecki, A: Moving between logical systems. In M. Haveraaen, O. Owe, O.-J. Dahl, eds.: *Recent Trends in Data Type Specifications, LNCS 1130,* 478-502. Springer, 1996.

[Tej99]   Tej, H. (1999): HOL-CSP: Mechanised Formal Development of Concurrent Processes. Dissertation. (forthcoming)

[TW97]   Tej, H., Wolff, B.: A Corrected Failure-Divergence Model for CSP in Isabelle / HOL. *Formal Methods Europe, FME'97.* LNCS 1313, Springer (1997) 318-337.

[UKP98]   Urban, G., Kolinowitz, H.-J., Peleska, J.: A Survivable Avionics System for Space Applications. in *Proc. FTCS-28, 28th Annual Symposium on Fault-Tolerant Computing,* Munich, Germany, 1998.

[VMOD]   V-Model: *Development Standard for IT Systems of the Federal Republic of Germany.* General Directives: 250: Process Lifecycle; 251: Methods Allocation; 252: Functional Tool Requirements. (1997).

[ZHR92]   Zhou, C., Hoare, C.A.R., Ravn, A.P.: A Calculus of Durations. *Information Processing Letters 40(5)* (1992) 269-276.

Integrating Formal Description Techniques

Bernhard Schätz and Franz Huber[*]

Fakultät für Informatik, Technische Universität München,
Arcisstraße 21, 80333 München
Email: {schaetz|huberf}@in.tum.de

Abstract. Using graphical description techniques for formal system development has become a common approach in many tools. Often multiple description techniques are used to represent different views of the same system, only together forming a complete specification. Here, the question of the integration of those description techniques and views becomes a major issue, raising questions of consistency and completeness. In this paper, we present an approach to ensuring conceptual and semantic consistency, influenced by experience gained from a first implementation of the AUTOFOCUS tool prototype. Finally, we show how this approach forms the basis for the definition of specification modules.

1 Introduction

Using multiple description techniques has become a common approach for the tool-based system development. Prominent examples are SDL-based tools (e.g., ObjectGeode [19], SDT [18]) and automata-based approaches (e.g., ObjecTime [17]). Here, the specification of a system is spread out over several documents, each one describing a certain view of the system, like its structure, its behavior, its data types, or some of its sample runs. Only by combining those views we obtain the complete system specification. However, while this structuring mechanism makes specifications more readable and manageable, it also poses a major problem: inconsistencies may arise, for example by

- conflicts between the external and internal interface of a system or component,
- conflicts between the behavior of a system and of its combined subsystems, or
- conflicts between the specified behavior and given sample runs of a system.

To form a reasonable specification, inconsistencies between those views must be avoided. Thus a tool should support detecting and fixing those inconsistencies. In other words, for the usability of a tool supporting a view-based specification method, the integration of those views is a prime requisite. This article describes an approach towards this integration within the tool prototype AUTOFOCUS.

---

[*] This work was carried out within the sub-project A6 of "Sonderforschungsbereich 342 (Werkzeuge und Methoden für die Nutzung paralleler Rechnerarchitekturen)" and the project SysLab, sponsored by the German Research Community (DFG) under the Leibniz program and by Siemens-Nixdorf.

J. Wing, J. Woodcock, J. Davies (Eds.): FM'99, Vol. II, LNCS 1709, pp. 1206-1225, 1999.
© Springer-Verlag Berlin Heidelberg 1999

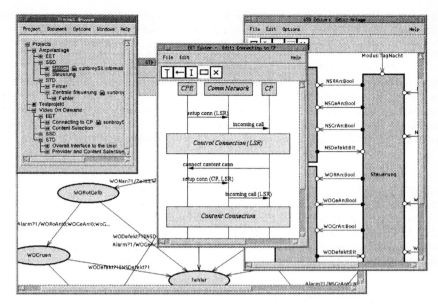

Fig. 1. The AUTOFOCUS Client Application – Project Browser and Editors

The remainder gives a short introduction of the AUTOFOCUS description techniques. Section 2 explains our notion of integrated formalisms, sections 3 and 4 sketch the idea of a conceptual model to base those formalisms on. Section 5 illustrates the capabilities of a conceptual model for the reuse of. Finally, section 6 concludes the approach with a short summary and outlook. As mentioned throughout the article, part of this introduced approach is already implemented in the current version of AUTOFOCUS, the remainder describes work in progress.

1.1 View-Based Systems Development

To support the development of distributed systems, AUTOFOCUS [11] does not aim at capturing a complete system within a single formalism. Instead, different views of a system are each specified using an appropriate notation. In the AUTOFOCUS approach, a distributed system is characterized from several points of view, as

- the structure of a system including its components and channels,
- the behavioral description of the system as a whole or of one of its components,
- the data processed by the system and transmitted across the channels, and
- the interaction of the components and the environment via message exchange.

In general, only a description including all views forms a complete picture of the system. Thus, AUTOFOCUS offers multiple description techniques: system structure diagrams (SSDs), state transition diagrams (STDs), data type definitions (DTDs), component data declarations (CDDs), and extended event traces (EETs), covering all those aspects. Like the hierarchical concepts of the underlying theory FOCUS [4], each description technique allows to model on different levels of detail, where, for example, components can be either atomic or consist of sub-components themselves.

1.1.1   Document Oriented Description

In AUTOFOCUS, a project, representing a system under development, consists of a number of documents that are representations of views using the description techniques introduced above. Thus each description technique is mapped to a corresponding class of documents ("diagrams"). Combined, these documents provide a complete characterization of a system in its current development status.

1.1.2   Hierarchical Documents

All graphical AUTOFOCUS description techniques share the concept of hierarchy. SSDs, STDs and EETs allow hierarchical decomposition. In an SSD, a system component may be viewed as a conceptual unit of sub-components specified in another SSD. In the same way, a state in an STD can be characterized by another STD document describing this state on a more detailed level. In EETs, so-called "boxes" are introduced as an abbreviating notation for partial runs specified in different EETs.

1.1.3   Integrated Documents

From the user's point of view, the documents of a development project are integrated, both vertically along the refinement hierarchies and horizontally along the relationships between documents of different kinds. For instance, an STD can be associated with a component in an SSD denoting that this STD specifies the behavior of the component. Along relationships like these, quick and intuitive navigation mechanisms between the documents are available.

1.1.4   System Structure Diagrams (SSDs)

System structure diagrams describe a distributed system as a network of components exchanging messages over directed channels. Each component has a set of input and output ports to which the channels are attached. Channels have associated data types describing the sets of messages sent across them. Components can be hierarchically refined by networks of sub-components. Then, the complete sub-network has the same set of communication ports as the higher-level component this refined view belongs to. Graphically, as in Fig. 1, SSDs are represented with boxes as components and arrows for channels. Both are annotated with identifiers and, in the case of channels, also with their data types. Input and output ports are visualized as small hollow and filled circles, respectively.

1.1.5   State Transition Diagrams (STDs)

State transition diagrams are extended finite automata similar to the concepts introduced in [8]. They are used to describe the behavior of a system or component. Each component can be linked to an STD consisting of states and transitions between them. Each transition has a set of annotations: a pre- and post-condition, encoded as predicates over the data state of the component satisfied before and after the transition, and a set of input and output patterns describing the messages read from or written to the input and output ports. For hierarchical refinement of states in STDs, we use a concept similar to the SSD case. Graphically, automata are represented as graphs with labeled ovals as states and arrows as transitions. Fig. 1 shows an example of an AUTOFOCUS state transition diagram.

1.1.6   Datatype Definitions (DTDs)
The types of the data processed by a distributed system are defined in a textual notation. We use basic types and data type constructors similar to those found in the functional programming language Gofer [14]. The data types defined here may be referenced from within other development documents, for example, as channel data types in SSDs.

1.1.7   Component Data Declaration (CDDs)
Additionally to receiving and sending messages, components generally store information locally to process those messages. For this purpose, local variables may be defined for each component by associating a component data declaration to it. A CDD simply consists of a set of variable identifiers and their associated types as defined in the DTD of the system, plus a possible initial value. Those variables locally defined for a component may be addressed in the definition of the STD of this component in the input and output patterns as well as in the pre- and post-conditions.

1.1.8   Extended Event Traces (EETs)
Extended event traces (cf. [16]) describe sample system runs from a component-based view. As shown in Fig. 1, we use a notation similar to the ITU-standardized message sequence charts MSC'96 (ITU Z.120, [13]). Using "boxes" EETs, support hierarchy and specify variants of behavior. Indicators can be used to define optional or repeatable parts of an EET. From a methodological point of view they are used in the early stages of systems development to specify the functionality of a system on a sample basis as well as system behavior in error situations. Later in the development process, the system specifications given by SSDs, STDs, and DTDs can be checked against the EETs, whether they fulfill the properties specified in them.

2   Integration of Formalisms

We use the term *integration of description formalisms* to express the influence of the description formalisms on each other. To judge the integration we must answer the question "How well do the formalisms play together to form a reasonable description of the system to be developed?" In other words, "What are the necessary side conditions on the formalisms to form a consistent system specification?" Here, we use "consistency" in a rather general interpretation (cf. [10]) to express several forms of conditions like:

- **Document Interface Correctness:** If a document is hierarchically embedded into another one, these documents must have compatible interfaces (components in SSDs, states in STDs, or boxes in EETs).

- **Definedness:** If a document makes use of objects not defined in the document itself, those objects must be defined in a corresponding document (like channel types in SSDs or STDs).
- **Inter-View Consistency:** If two or more formalisms describe the same aspect of a system, the descriptions must be consistent (like SSDs and STDs with EETs).
- **Completeness:** All necessary documents of a project have to be present.

From a methodological point of view we distinguish two kinds of conditions:

- **Conceptual Consistency Conditions** can be defined solely in terms of the description technique concepts. Examples are the interface consistency, the definedness conditions or the well-typedness of specifications.
- **Semantical Consistency Conditions** can only be defined using semantical notions. Examples are the refinement of a system including its behavioral description by an implementation through a set of sub-components including their behavioral description; or the compatibility of a sample EET of a system with the behavioral description of is sub-components.

Most developers expect the first class of conditions to generally hold during the development process. Luckily, there are simple mechanisms to check their validity (cf. Subsection 2.1). The second class is quite the opposite: very complex mechanisms are needed to validate those semantical consistency conditions (cf. Subsections 2.2.1 and 2.2.2), if possible at all. Since those conditions are quite complex, however, developers generally do not expect them to hold throughout the development process.

The distinction between conceptual and semantical consistency conditions plays an important role with the introduction of the conceptual model as described in section 3. There we introduce a notion of a specification based on a general conceptual model for AUTOFOCUS instead of a collection of AUTOFOCUS description techniques.

2.1 Conceptual Consistencies

Conceptual consistency conditions generally are considered to hold invariantly during the development process. However, mainly due to its originally document-oriented approach, AUTOFOCUS so far does not strictly enforce conceptual consistency throughout the development process. It rather offers developers the possibility to check the violation of conceptual consistency conditions and locate those elements of the specification causing these violations. With AUTOFOCUS, conditions can be formalized using a consistency condition description language based on a typed first-order logic. The language and the user interface are described in [10] and [6]. Experiences with AUTOFOCUS and this form of conceptual consistency conditions, however, suggest using a more rigorous approach, as discussed in section 2.3

2.2 Semantic Consistencies

Integration of views on the semantical level is more complicated. Those consistency conditions can only be expressed by proof obligations defined using the semantical basis. Thus a formal semantics of the description techniques and a sufficiently powerful proof-mechanism are needed. Providing a semantical basis for intuitive graphical description techniques is becoming more and more state of the art (cf. StateChart,

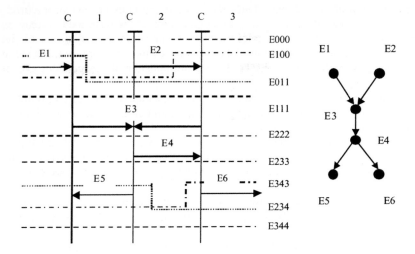

Fig. 2. Reachable Cuts of an EET and its Partial Order Trace

Rhapsody [12], ObjectGeode, SDT [18]). However, strong verification support, especially automatic support, is commonly found only in more mathematically oriented description techniques (e.g., Atelier B [1], FDR [7]). For a strictly integrated use of those user-friendly description techniques it is not sufficient to support a translation into a format suitable for a prover. For an integrated approach we furthermore require a tool to support the user on the level of those description techniques.

2.2.1   Hierarchical Consistencies

In the AUTOFOCUS approach only one form of hierarchical consistency on the semantic level is required: behavioral refinement of systems. Consistency violation may occur if a component is assigned behavior using a corresponding STD; furthermore a substructure is defined for this component via an SSD with STDs for all the components of this SSD. The AUTOFOCUS approach requires the behavior of the refined component (substructure components and their behaviors) to be a refinement of the behavior originally associated with the component. To check the validity of the refinement and thus the semantical consistency AUTOFOCUS offers an automatic check based on the relational μ calculus model checker μcke [3]. The formal basis for this check can be found in [10].

2.2.2   Inter-View Consistencies

To ensure semantic inter-view consistency in AUTOFOCUS, again, only one form of check is required. Since the combination of SSDs and STDs on the one hand and EETs on the other hand characterize system behavior, we require sample runs of the EETs to be a legal behavior as described by the SSD/STD combination. Again, we use μcke to check the consistency of the SSD/STD and the EET view.

As mentioned in Section 1.1.8, EETs are interpreted as positive or negative requirements in the form of sample runs. Formally, an EET is interpreted as a relation between two system states, relating a state before the execution of the EET to a state after the execution of all EET events. Thus, its μ formalization makes use of the product state and product transition relation of all components of the described system as described in [10]. Thus, an EET is interpreted as a state transition diagram of the complete system. *Reachable cuts* are used as the states of this diagram, defined using the independence expressed by the EETs. Events are considered independent except in two cases:

- All send and receive events of one component (represented as start or end point of arrows on a single component axis) are causally dependent in the downward direction to represent the passing of time.

Send and receive events of a single message event are causally dependent.[1] Fig. 2 shows the different reachable cuts of an EET consisting of components C1, C2 and C3.[2] Since a reachable cut marks a possible intermediate state of an EET, we define a *reachable cut* by the following rules:

- The start state of an EET (before any event) is a reachable cut.
- If a reachable cut is followed by a set of independent actions, all states reached by the execution of any subset of this set are reachable cuts.

As shown in Fig. 2, an EET can be equivalently expressed using a partial order trace (cf. [5]). Here, with independent E1 and E2, we obtain the reachable cuts:

- E000 is reachable by the first rule.
- E100 reachable from E000 through E1 by the second rule,
- E011 reachable from E000 through E2 by the second rule,
- E111 reachable from E100 through E2, from E011 through E1, or from E000 through simultaneously applying E1 and E2 by the second rule.

With E3 being dependent on E1 and E2, the next reachable cut is E222, and – similarly – E233. Analogously E5 and E6 lead to the cuts E343, E234, and E344.

For the μ formalization, we introduce a relation for each reachable state. A relation corresponds to executing pending events and reaching the associated cuts. For each execution of a set of events a clause is introduced reflecting the transfer of messages v_i on channels c_i and the reached cut EET_i. Furthermore, a clause is introduced with empty messages $c_i = nil$ representing a "nil round" of the system with no messages sent. Finally, all clauses are combined using disjunction:

$$\mu EET(s,s') \equiv (s.c_1 = nil \wedge \ldots \wedge s.c_n = nil \wedge \exists t.(T(s,t) \wedge EET(t,s'))) \vee$$

$$(s.c_1 = v_{1,1} \wedge \ldots \wedge s.c_n = v_{1,n} \wedge \exists t.(T(s,t) \wedge EET_1(t,s'))) \vee$$

$$\vdots$$

$$(s.c_1 = v_{1,k} \wedge \ldots \wedge s.c_n = v_{n,k} \wedge \exists t.(T(s,t) \wedge EET_k(t,s')))$$

Here, the μ operator is used to define the relation as the least fixed point of this recursive definition. T corresponds to the transition relation of the system composed of C1, C2 and C3, formalized as product transition relation as in [10].

To formalize hierarchic elements of an EET, a single relation is introduced for those elements. To formalize those sub-parts the above strategy is applied to them. Depending on the kind of hierarchical structuring mechanism (indicators/boxes) those

---

[1] Here send/receive events of a message are considered to happen simultaneously and are therefore interpreted as a single event.

[2] For the sake of brevity, we use labels E1, E2, ... instead of regular annotations.

sub-EETs are inserted in the relation of the embedding EET analogously to the execution of a single event:

$$EET(s,s') \equiv \exists t.(EET_b(s,t) \wedge EET'(t,s'))$$

with $EET_b(s,t)$ denoting the relation for the embedded EET constructed as described below, and $EET'(t,s')$ denoting the relation for the remainder of the embedding EET. The relation for an EET embedded using an indicator is constructed depending on the kind of the indicator (optional/repetitive/optional repetitive):

- **Optional**: $\mu EET_b(s,s') \equiv EET_i(s,s') \vee s = s'$
- **Repetitive**: $\mu EET(s,s') \equiv \exists t.EET_i(s,t) \wedge (s' = t \vee EET(t,s'))$
- **Optional repetitive**: $\mu EET(s,s') \equiv (s = s' \vee \exists t.EET_i(s,t) \wedge EET(t,s'))$

Here, $EET_i(s,s')$ denotes the relation for the indicated sub-EET. Similarly, boxes are formalized by a relation comprising the "boxed" EETs by simply forming a disjunction over them, thus allowing any of those EETs to substitute the box:

$$\mu EET_o(s,s') \equiv EET_1(s,s') \vee ... \vee EET_n(s,s'),$$

where $EET_1(s,s'),...,EET_n(s,s')$ denote the relations for the boxed EETs.

Since the formalisation of an EET represents a property about the transition relation of the whole system, it can be used to express different positive and negative requirements about the system using an embedded clause as described in [2]. In case such a requirement does not hold for the system, the counter example generated of the model checker can be used to generate a counter example as discussed in [10].

2.3 Lessons Learned

AUTOFOCUS was originally implemented with a user controlled consistency mechanism (cf. [10]). Only syntactic consistency criteria of the description techniques where controlled automatically during the development process, all other conceptual consistency condition had to be initiated by the user. Experiences have shown that developers using AUTOFOCUS were willing to trade in a maximally flexible development process for an enforcement of conceptual consistency if offered a comfortable interface for the development of consistent specifications (see Section 5.5). Thus, the weak integration of description techniques in AUTOFOCUS is currently strengthened using a single conceptual model. This conceptual model and the resulting approach currently under implementation are described in Sections 3 and 5.

3   Conceptual Models

This section introduces a simplified version of a conceptual model for AUTOFOCUS. Here, specifications are *instances* of this conceptual model and describe systems in an integrated fashion. Developers create and manipulate them using concrete notations representing views upon them. Even different graphical or textual views on the same parts of the model may be offered. The notations representing these views are the same used in the document-based initial version of AUTOFOCUS and were introduced in sections 1.1.4 through 1.1.8.

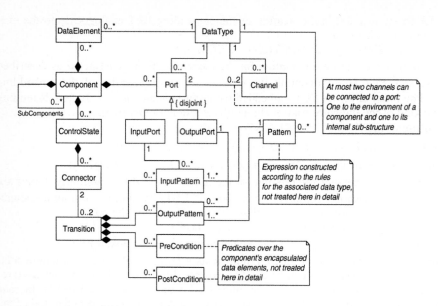

Fig. 3. Simplified Conceptual Model of AUTOFOCUS

The elements in the conceptual model make up the essence of the notations used, like abstract syntax trees generated by parsers for programming languages. In programming languages, however, source code "documents" are the important modeling concept, the syntax tree is generated by the parser unnoticed by the user. Many software engineering tools offer a similar approach, treating system descriptions as—at most loosely related—documents of different kinds. In the model-based approach, the abstract model is the central concept, both from the tool developer's and from the methodologist's point of view. Developers deal directly with the elements of the abstract model without encapsulation in artificial constructs such as documents. The modeling elements of AUTOFOCUS are shown in Fig. 3 using a UML-style notation. For a more detailed description of the modeling concepts we refer to [11].

Subsequently, we describe the elements in the conceptual model, which are, of course, the concepts described by the notations introduced in Section 1.

- **Components** encapsulate *data*, *structure*, and *behavior*, communicating with their environment.
- **Data types** define data structures used by components.
- **Data** are encapsulated by a component and provide a means to store persistent state information inside a component, realized by typed state variables.
- **Ports** are a component's means of communicating with its environment. Components read data on input ports and send data on output ports.
- **Channels** are directed, named, and typed. They connect component ports. They define the communication structure (topology) of a distributed system.
- **Control States** and **Transitions** between their entry and exit points—called **Connectors**—define the control flow of a component. Transitions carry four kinds of annotations determining their firing conditions,

- pre-conditions and post-conditions, which are predicates over the data elements of the component to be fulfilled before and after the transition, respectively, and
- input and output patterns, determining which values must be available on the component's input ports to fire the transition and which values are then written to the output ports.

The elements of the conceptual model can be regarded as abstractions of both the underlying formal model and their concrete notations. Thus, the conceptual model represents the common denominator of both the description techniques and a formal model.

Viewing specifications as graphs of specification elements, it is possible to construct a multitude of graphs using only instances of the elements and relationships in the conceptual model, leaving aside the arities given for the relationships. Then, of course, most of the possible graphs will not conform to the conceptual model.[3] In this respect, the conceptual model acts as a requirement specification for well-formedness (see Subsection 5.1.1), discriminating well-formed from ill-formed specifications.

4   Views and Description Techniques

How do developers develop system specifications using a conceptual model? In the model-based approach, a system specification is an *instance* of the conceptual model, i.e., a graph consisting of individual nodes, which are atomic modeling entities, and of arcs capturing their relationships. Such a model instance must obey the well-formedness conditions defined by the conceptual model; arbitrary graphs are not allowed since they do not represent well-formed specifications. As stated in Section 3, developers do not manipulate these "specification graphs" as a whole, but by picking only specific parts of it, which are of interest during particular development activities. These parts, usually closely related with each other, make up *views* of the system. For instance, the structural view in AUTOFOCUS considers only elements from the conceptual model describing the interface of components and their interconnection. The view on the control flow focuses on the state space of components and the transitions possible within the state space.

To manipulate elements of these views we represent them visually. In AUTOFOCUS we use the notations introduced in Sections 1.1.4 through 1.1.8. Although the notations used to represent modeling entities are the same as in the document-based approach, their purpose in the model-based approach differs substantially from a methodological point of view. In document-based development documents are *closed* modeling artifacts with no explicit references to modeling elements defined in a different context, outside a specific document. Only implicit references are defined, like references by equality of names of port elements or of names of variables. Only the assembly of all the individual documents and the resolution of these implicit references gives the complete view of the specification. In the model-based approach the specification of the system as a whole is incrementally constructed by adding new modeling elements to the specification. This complete specification thus really repre-

---

[3] Although well-formedness is considered an invariant in the development process (see Subsection 5.1.1), allowing ill-formed specifications can be reasonable for some, mostly internal, operations on specifications invisible to the user (see Subsection 5.4.2).

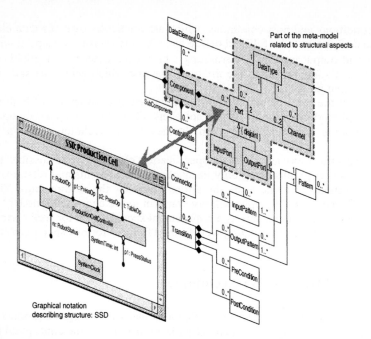

Fig. 4. Structural View of Conceptual Model and Notation Representing its Elements

sents a *model* of the system, an abstraction of the complete system, which is the goal of the development process. The notations do not represent self-contained documents but a visualization of a clipping from the complete specification graph. This clipping *does* contain explicit references to other parts of the specification, as in Fig. 4, where the gray area in the conceptual model encompasses all elements carrying information about the structure of a system. Within this structural description, other information, such as the interface view of components (collection of ports of a component) and the data type view (necessary to describe both the component ports and the channels) is contained as well. Thus, ports and data types are *explicitly referenced* in the structural view. One possible graphical representation of the structural view of a system is given by SSDs as symbolized in Fig. 4. This sample SSD represents a part of a fault-tolerant production cell controller, which will also be used as an example in Section 5.2.2. We call this collection of a view and a notation together with their interrelationships a *description technique*. More formally, a description technique consists of

- a subset of modeling elements from the conceptual model and the relationships between them, which, together, define a specific view on the system,
- a concrete syntax (graphical or textual notation) representing these elements, and
- rules to map the concrete syntax to the modeling elements and vice-versa.

A description technique thus serves as a kind of peephole through which developers can see (and change) parts of a specification.

5 Specification Modules

The conceptual model introduces the terms and relations needed to describe the system specified by the developer. We show how those terms and relations are combined to form specifications. In Subsection 5.1 we define when a description of a system is considered a system specification. In Subsection 5.2 we show how specifications and specification modules are related and what it means to define an incomplete specification module. Finally, in Subsection 5.4 we demonstrate how specification modules are applied to support reuse of specifications.

5.1 Module Criteria

To support reuse of specifications or specification parts, a clear meaning of a specification has to be defined. Based on the conceptual model discussed above we introduce the notion of a *specification* of a system. A *specification*

- is a *well-formed* description of one or more aspects of a system,
- may fulfill additional conceptual consistency conditions,
- does not necessarily need to be *complete*.

Like the conceptual model, a specification is an abstract concept and can have several concrete syntactical representations. The choice of the conceptual model determines the notion of a specification by defining the *well-formedness* and additional *conceptual consistency conditions* of a specification. The first describes invariant conceptual consistency conditions of a specification, the latter conditions required only at certain development steps. Since the distinction between a well-formedness condition and a consistency condition depends on the definition of the conceptual model, this definition—as a methodological decision—influences the strictness of the design process. For example, the assignment of a data type to a port or channel may be considered a well-formedness condition as well as a consistency condition. In the first case a port or a channel cannot be created without assigning an appropriate type. In the latter case, a type may be assigned at a later step in the design process.

5.1.1 Well-Formedness

Well-formedness conditions are invariant conditions that hold for specifications invariantly throughout the design process. Those invariances are defined by the conceptual model and typically include syntactic properties. Examples are:

- Each channel has two adjacent ports, an output port at its beginning, and an input port at its end, and an associated data type.
- Each transition has two adjacent connectors.

5.1.2 Consistency

Consistency conditions are defined as additional properties of the conceptual model that must hold for reasonable specifications but may be violated throughout the design process. At certain steps in the design process, consistency of the specification is required. Typical steps are code generation, verification, and specification module definition. Different consistency conditions may be required for different steps. While code generation or simulation require completely defined data types, this is not necessary for verification or specification module definition. Example conditions are:

- Each port, channel, etc. has a defined (i.e., non-empty) type.
- Port names are unique for each system component.

While the first condition is a necessary consistency condition for simulation or code generation, the second consistency condition is not formally; it may, however, be formulated and checked to support better readability or clarity of documents generated from the conceptual model.

5.1.3   Completeness

A third condition to be raised throughout the development process but not mentioned so far is the *completeness* of a specification. A specification is called complete if all relevant objects of the specification are contained in the specification itself. Similar to the consistency of a specification, completeness is only required at certain steps of the development process like simulation, code generation or verification. Actually, completeness can be defined as a consistency condition and checked the same way (see [10]). However, the incompleteness of a specification module can be used to define parameterized modules, and is thus treated as a separate property for methodological reasons: since an instantiation mechanism is needed for incomplete or parameterized specification modules, incomplete modules are distinguished form other forms of inconsistency. Subsection 5.2.2 treats this question in more detail.

5.2   Module Definition

Given the modeling concepts introduced above, the notion of a specification module can be introduced. Typical examples of specification modules are:

- System structure module: A specification module of a system as defined by a corresponding component possibly including its sub components.
- Behavioral module: The behavior assigned to a component or a subpart of it.

In our approach a specification module is *not* distinguished from a specification. Thus, every well-formed part of a specification is considered a specification module. A well-formed part of a specification need not be complete. However, for a reasonable reuse of a specification module, it has to obey several consistency conditions. This leads to a simple distinction of two different specification module concepts:

- *Complete specification module:* A specification module is *complete* if all referenced elements (e.g., type definitions of used port types or local data, subcomponents of a component) are contained in the module.
- *Parameterized specification module:* A specification module is *parameterized* if some referenced elements are not included in the specification (e.g., incomplete type definitions of a component, undefined behavior of a component).

Specification modules are well-formed specification parts possibly obeying additional consistency conditions. Therefore, specification modules can either be developed as in the case of a usual specification or reused form a larger specification by a selection process based on the conceptual model.

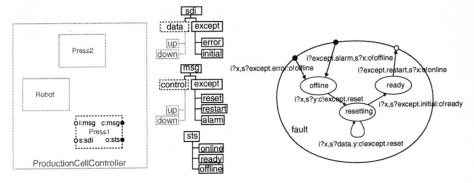

Fig. 5. Parameterized Error Treatment Module

5.2.1   Complete Modules

The simplest form of a specification module is the one containing all relevant information. Since—unlike in the parameterized case—no instantiating of the module is needed, all information of the module can simple be added to the target specification. A simple example of a complete specification module is the press controller module of the production cell consisting of

- the data types describing the actuatory and sensory data,
- the interface description of the controller (typed input and output ports),
- the (empty) list of variables of the controller unit, and
- the behavioral description of the controller unit given by an STD using the typed port, component, and transition variables of the controller.

This module is complete since all entities referenced in this module (data types, ports, variables, etc) are also defined in this module.

5.2.2   Parameterized Modules

As a simple example we define a behavioral specification module as shown in Fig. 5. The module is used to handle fault situations of the production cell units. Upon entering the module, an offline status message is issued. The unit is then brought to a defined state and stability of the unit is reported. Upon receipt of a restart message, the unit is restarted. Since all of the units of the production cell must support this kind of error treatment, it is useful to define a general fault module to be instantiated for all components. The defined specification module consists of three parts:

- The minimal interface to be supplied by a component intended to offer this fault recovery strategy. The interface is defined by the corresponding ports (i, o, c, s).
- The type of messages used to indicate the status of the unit or to influence its behavior. As the behavior is independent of the kind of unit (press, robot arm, etc.), the unit-dependent part of the message types (data, control) is not specified by the module but defined as a parameter to be instantiated upon use of the module.
- The behavior relevant for fault recovery. Only a part of a complete behavioral description of a unit is described by giving the necessary states (offline, resetting, ready), and the corresponding transitions and entry- and exit-points. Applying the module adds the fault-recovery routine to the target specification to be extended to a complete specification for the corresponding unit.

To apply a parameterized module to a target specification the parameters are instantiated and the resulting module is added to the specification. In Section 5.3 we give a more precise definition of the concepts of specification modules and their elements; in Section 5.4 we show how to apply complete or parameterized modules to a target specification.

5.3   Mathematical Model

In the previous sections we gave an intuitive interpretation of the terms *specification* and *complete* and *parameterized specification module*. However, to introduce the application or reuse of specification modules we need a more precise definition of those terms. Therefore, we define a mathematical model for the above-introduced concepts. In Subsection 5.3.1 we define the mathematical concept of modules and their combination using the notion of colored graphs and typed binary relations.[4] Based on this model we will introduce the necessary formal operations *union construction* and *renaming*, which will be used to define the module application in Section 5.4.

5.3.1   Model of Specification Modules

A specification is considered a graph with the specification elements of the conceptual model as nodes and the relations between these elements as the edges of the graph.[5] Since the conceptual model is typed (the elements of the conceptual model are elements of distinct classes like components, ports, channels, etc.), the node set is partitioned. Thus a specification can be described by a pair *(E,R)* with

- a collection of sets of elements $E = (E_1, E_2, \ldots, E_{m-1}, E_m)$
- a collection of binary relations $R = (R_1, R_2, \ldots, R_{n-1}, R_n)$

with $E_i \subseteq \mathcal{E}_i$ and $R_j \subseteq \mathcal{R}_j$, where $\mathcal{R}_j = \mathcal{E}_k \times \mathcal{E}_l$, as well as corresponding definitions for $\mathcal{E}$ and $\mathcal{R}$. The definitions of $\mathcal{E}_i$ and $\mathcal{R}_j$ depend on the definition of the conceptual model as described in Section 3. In the AUTOFOCUS conceptual model, for example,

- the collection $\mathcal{E}$ contains the set of input ports $\mathcal{I}$, the set of system components $\mathcal{S}$, the set of channels $\mathcal{C}$, or the set of types $\mathcal{T}$, and
- the collection $\mathcal{R}$ contains the relation $\mathcal{SS}$ between a system component and its sub components, the relation $\mathcal{IC}$ between an input port and connected channel, $\mathcal{IT}$ between an input port and its type as well as $\mathcal{CT}$ between an channel and its type.

Generally R_i will not cover the complete range of sub relations of $\mathcal{R}_i$. As, for example,

- a system component cannot be its own sub component, the sub component relation is not reflexive

$$\forall x{:}\,S, y{:}\,S.\,(x,y) \in SS \Rightarrow x \neq y$$

- it is not possible to connect one port to two input channels, the channel-input port relation will not contain two different channels for one port:

$$\forall i{:}\,I, c_1{:}\,C, c_2{:}\,C.\,(i,c_1) \in IC \wedge (i,c_2) \in IC \Rightarrow c_1 = c_2$$

---

[4] See [15] for an elaborate treatment of using algebraic approaches to model specifications.

[5] For reasons of simplicity we will only consider binary relations; the extension to relations of higher cardinality is straight-forward.

Furthermore, the collection of relations will not cover the complete range of possible sets of relations fulfilling those above conditions. For example, if a pattern is defined for an input port in a state transition diagram, both pattern and input port are of the same type

$$\forall i: I, p: P, t1: T, t2: T. ((i, t1) \in IT \wedge (p, t2) \in PT \wedge (i, p) \in IP) \Rightarrow t1 = t2$$

Those additional conditions fulfilled by the pair *(E,R)* of a specification module represent the well-formedness conditions described in Subsection 5.1. Some of those conditions above are typically described using arity-annotations of class diagrams. Those conditions can be expressed in typed first-order predicate logic with equality and can thus be automatically checked by a consistency checker as described in [10].

5.3.2   Operations on Specification Modules

To combine two modules (E, R) and (E', R'), the union $(E \cup E', R \cup R')$ is constructed with $E \cup E' = (E_1 \cup E_1', ..., E_m \cup E_m')$ and $R \cup R' = (R_1 \cup R_1', ..., R_n \cup R_n')$. E and E' are neither required to be disjoint nor to be identical. Thus, the union of two specification modules can introduce

- new specification elements like components, ports, types, states, etc.
- new relations between both old and new specification elements like adding a new port to an already existing system component.

It is important to note, however, that the union construction of two well-formed or consistent non-disjoint specification modules in general will not lead to a well-formed or consistent specification. Subsection 5.4.2 considers this aspect.

Finally, specification modules can be renamed prior to the union application to allow the identification of specification elements. Thus, parameterized specification modules can be applied to specifications. To rename specification modules, isomorphic mappings $M: \mathcal{E} \times \mathcal{R} \rightarrow \mathcal{E} \times \mathcal{R}$, $M_{\mathcal{E}_i}: \mathcal{E}_i \rightarrow \mathcal{E}_i$, and $M_{\mathcal{R}_j}: \mathcal{R}_j \rightarrow \mathcal{R}_j$ are defined with $M = (M_{\mathcal{E}_1} \times ... \times M_{\mathcal{E}_m}, M_{\mathcal{R}_1} \times ... \times M_{\mathcal{R}_n})$, as well as

$$M_{\mathcal{R}}(R_i) = \{(M_{\mathcal{E}_j}(e1), M_{\mathcal{E}_k}(e2)) | (e1, e2) \in R_i \wedge R_i \subseteq \mathcal{E}_j \times \mathcal{E}_k\}$$

Based on the techniques of renaming and union construction we will describe how a specification module can be applied as a complete or parameterized module in the following section.

5.4   Module Application

Basically, the application of a specification module can be defined as an embedding operation on the conceptual model with additional mappings of common elements of the module and the specification. In Subsection 5.4.1 we outline renaming as the basic difference between the application of a complete and a parameterized specification module. Subsection 5.4.2 sketches how such a renaming mapping is used to define parameterized modules using the example of Subsection 5.2.2.

5.4.1   Complete and Parameterized Specification Modules

As mentioned in Subsection 5.2 we distinguish between parameterized and complete specification modules. Having introduced a mathematical model for specification modules, it is obvious that this distinction is not a technical but a methodical one. To add a *complete* specification module we simply construct the union as defined above. Assuming disjoint sets of specification elements no further renaming is necessary.[6] For example, we can simply add the press controller module defined in Subsection 5.2.1 to the specification to add another press to the system. To make use of the controller module we then connect the ports of the module to the ports of the system.

To make use of a *parameterized* specification module it is necessary to instantiate its parameters before adding it to the specification. Therefore, the parameter elements must be renamed to elements of the target specification prior to the union construction. Like specification parameters in algebraic specification languages like SPEC-TRUM [9], the parameter elements are considered the interface of a module used to apply it to the target specification. Again, consider the example of the press controller module defined in Subsection 5.2.2. The specification can be used as a behavioral specification module with type parameters (control and data), a system component parameter (Press1) and a state parameter (fault). To avoid the introduction of new types for the actuatory and sensory data we identify the types used in the press controller module with the types already defined in the system specification.

5.4.2   Module Instantation

As mentioned in Subsection 5.4.1, specification modules can be compared to algebraic specifications. The combination of specification modules is similar to the combination of algebraic specifications: elements of the interface of the applied specification module are identified with elements of the specification (or module) it is applied to. Thus, to apply a specification module, a mapping must be constructed to map the interface elements to elements of the same type in the target application. Furthermore, the resulting specification must again be well-formed. To illustrate module application we consider the module introduced in Fig. 5. Here, the mapping

- introduces new port elements (i,o,s,c), new type elements (msg, except, alarm, etc.), new state elements (offline, resetting, online), as well as the new transition elements and pattern elements found in Fig. 5,
- identifies old and new elements like the system component Press1, the type elements data or control and the state fault, and therefore
- introduces new relations, like the component-port relation between Press1 and i, or the state-sub state relation between fault and offline.

Fig. 5 shows the resulting specification after the mapping and the union construction including the newly introduced elements, the already defined elements (grayed out) and the identified elements (dashed).

5.5   User Interface

Developers manipulate a specification as instance of the conceptual model using concrete notations, e.g., as in Sections 1.1.4 through 1.1.8, representing its elements and their structure. Users interacting with such notations need appropriate operations on the presented specification part. These operations must fulfill two criteria. First, they

---

[6] The disjointness condition might be relaxed to support the common use of predefined data types like *bool* or *int* as well as identifiers of specification elements.

must not allow to create ill-formed specifications in terms of the conceptual model: Each operation must preserve conceptual consistency (cf. Sections 2 and 5.1). Second, they must be flexible and comfortable enough, so users do not regard them as too restrictive. Since notations are *visual* elements, interaction mechanisms developed in the GUI domain that have proven their user-friendliness are candidates to be considered here. For the AUTOFOCUS approach, the following two concepts are envisaged.

5.5.1   Drag and Drop

One paradigm to exchange information is "drag-and-drop", a mouse-based interaction scheme, which aims at several different purposes of information interchange. First, relocation of information can be accomplished by drag-and-drop: Grabbing an information element, a piece of text or a graphics element, for instance, and dragging it somewhere else results in removing (or copying) it from its source location and placing it in the target location.

Thus, drag-and-drop can be used to move representations of specification elements around within their graphical context. These are, however, usually operations that change only layout information and are thus not semantically relevant.[7] With respect to the specification, drag-and-drop can create new associations between elements of specifications. Thus, by grabbing a specification element, for example a type defined in an DTD, in a given context and dragging it into a different context, like a port, a relationship between the two contexts, the definition of a port of this type, is created. The target context uses the specification element defined in the source context.

5.5.2   Contextual Menus

Contextual menus provide users with a range of possible operations that are applicable in a certain context. In graphical file managers selecting file or directory icons and activating the contextual menu presents a set of possible operations that can be carried out upon the selected files/directories such as deleting or changing properties. We use contextual menus again to help users establish relationships between specification elements, for example type constructors to build messages for EET events, and, to preserve the well-formedness of the specification, to make only *suitable* specification constructs available to users.

5.5.3   Example

Consider the use of ports as example. When defining an input pattern for an STD-transition, an input port has to be specified along with the value or pattern to be present at the port for the transition to fire. Assigning the port can be done by dragging one of the component's input ports (and only input ports) from the SSD of the component into the property sheet of the transition. Alternatively, in the property sheet a contextual menu can be used to specify the port. In this menu, only the input ports of the component are available. The data required at the input port can be specified again by drag and drop of a data type constructor element from the data type definition used by the port. Alternatively, all possible constructors of component variables (or available local transition variables) could be given in a contextual menu.

---

[7] In EETs the vertical layout of the messages is relevant and relocating them has a meaning.

6   Conclusion

We discussed the need for an integration of description formalisms in tool-supported formal system development. We showed that the introduction of a conceptual model and the interpretation of description techniques as views on the model on the one hand and the integration of powerful proof tools on the other hand support a manageable conceptually and semantically consistent development process. The introduction of a conceptual model additionally allows the introduction of specification modules and eases the reuse of specifications. However, as discussed in Section 5.5, sufficient usability is a prime requisite for the success of such an approach.

Thus, while the introduced approach is consequently carrying further approaches found in state-of-the-art system development tools, finally its acceptance can only be affirmed after the introduced concepts are implemented in the current prototype.

7   References

1. Abrial, J.-R.: The B-Book: Assigning Programs to Meanings. Cambridge University Press (1996)
2. Bechtel, R.: Einbettung des µ-Kalkül Model-Checkers µ-cke in AutoFocus (in English). Master's Thesis. Institut für Informatik, TU München (1999)
3. Biere, A.: Effiziente Modellprüfung des µ-Kalküls mit binären Entscheidungsdiagrammen. Ph.D.Thesis. Universität Karlsruhe (1997)
4. Broy, M., Dendorfer, C., Dederichs, F., Fuchs, M., Gritzner, T., Weber, R.: The Design of Distributed Systems – An Introduction to Focus. Technical Report TUM-I9225, Technische Universität München (1992)
5. Diekert, V., Rozenberg, G.: The Book of Traces. Singapore World Scientific (1995)
6. Einert, G.: Ein Framework zur Konsistenzprüfung von Spezifikationen im AutoFocus-Werkzeug. Master's Thesis. Institut für Informatik, TU München (1998)
7. Formal Systems (Europe) Ltd.: Failures-Divergence Refinement: FDR2 User Manual. Oxford (1997)
8. Grosu, R., Klein, C., Rumpe, B., Broy, M.: State Transition Diagrams. Technical Report TUM-I9630. Technische Universität München (1996)
9. Grosu, R., Nazareth, D.: The Specification Language SPECTRUM – Core Language Report V1.0. Technical Report TUM-I9429. Technische Universität München (1994)
10. Huber, F., Schätz, B., Einert, G.: Consistent Graphical Specification of Distributed Systems. In: Fitzgerald, J., Jones, C. B., Lucas, P. (eds.): Proceedings of FME '97, 4th International Symposium of Formal Methods Europe, Lecture Notes in Computer Science, Vol. 1313. Springer (1997)
11. Huber, F., Schätz, B., Spies, K.: AUTOFOCUS – Ein Werkzeugkonzept zur Beschreibung verteilter Systeme. In Herzog, U., Hermanns, H. (eds.): Formale Beschreibungstechniken für verteilte Systeme. Universität Erlangen - Nürnberg (1996) 165–174
12. i-Logix Inc.: Rhapsody Reference (1997)
13. International Telecommunication Union: ITU-TS Recommendation Z.120: Message Sequence Chart (MSC). ITU, Geneva (1996)
14. Jones, M. P.: An Introduction to Gofer. User's Manual (1993)
15. Paech, B.: Algebraic View Specification. In Wirsing, M., Nivat, M. (eds.): Proceedings of AMAST '96: Algebraic Methodology and Software Technology. Lecture Notes in Computer Science, Vol. 1101. Springer (1996) 444–457

16. Schätz, B., Hußmann, H., Broy, M.: Graphical Development of Consistent System Specifications. In Gaudel, M.-C., Woodcock, J. (eds.): FME '96: Industrial Benefit and Advances
in Formal Methods. Lecture Notes in Computer Science, Vol. 1051. Springer (1996) 248–
267
17. Selic, B., Gullekson, G., Ward, P.T.: Real-Time Object-Oriented Modeling. Wiley Professional Computing (1994)
18. Telelogic AB: SDT 3.1 Reference Manual. Telelogic AB (1996)
19. Verilog: ObjectGEODE Method Guidelines. Verilog (1997)

A More Complete TLA

Stephan Merz

Institut für Informatik, Universität München
merz@informatik.uni-muenchen.de

Abstract. This paper defines a generalization of Lamport's Temporal Logic of Actions. We prove that our logic is stuttering-invariant and give an axiomatization of its propositional fragment. We also show that standard TLA is as expressive as our extension once quantification over flexible propositions is added.

1 Background

Temporal logics are routinely used for the specification and analysis of reactive systems. However, Lamport [10] has identified a shortcoming of standard linear-time temporal logic (LTL): because it is based on a global notion of "next state", it does not allow to relate specifications written at different levels of abstraction. He has therefore maintained that specifications should be invariant under "stuttering", that is, finite repetitions of identical states, and has proposed the Temporal Logic of Actions (TLA) [12, 13, 6]. Characteristically, TLA formulas contain the "next-time" operator only in a restricted form and can therefore not distinguish between stuttering-equivalent behaviors. Several case studies have established TLA as a useful formalism for describing systems; on the theoretical side, researchers have studied questions such as the description of real-time and hybrid systems [3, 11], the representation of assumption-commitment reasoning [4, 5], and the expressiveness of propositional TLA [18]. Moreover, Lamport has developed a formal specification language TLA+ based on TLA.

Although TLA has been found to be expressively complete for stuttering-invariant ω-regular languages [18], this does not necessarily imply that specifications can be expressed in a natural way. In fact, the syntactic restrictions imposed by Lamport that ensure invariance under stuttering occasionally make it hard to express seemingly simple properties. For example, whereas the requirement "eventually P will be true, and Q will hold at some later state" is expressed by the formula $\Diamond(P \wedge \Diamond Q)$, as in standard LTL, the analogous requirement "eventually action A will be performed, some time later followed by action B" is not expressed as easily. Eventual occurrence of action A is expressed by the formula $\Diamond \langle A \rangle_v$, where A describes the action as a relation on pairs of states, and v is (roughly speaking) the tuple of all state components of interest. One might therefore expect to express the informal requirement above by a formula such as $\Diamond \langle A \wedge \Diamond \langle B \rangle_v \rangle_v$, but TLA does not allow temporal formulas to occur inside an action formula (i.e., inside angle brackets). In some cases one can identify a state formula pA that is true iff action A has happened sometime in the past: for example, A might represent a request for a resource, and pA could be defined from the system's log-file. In those cases, we can express our requirement by the formula $\Diamond \langle pA \wedge B \rangle_v$. This

J. Wing, J. Woodcock, J. Davies (Eds.): FM'99, Vol. II, LNCS 1709, pp. 1226–1244, 1999.
© Springer-Verlag Berlin Heidelberg 1999

formula requires that eventually action B occurs with pA being true—hence A must have occurred before. Observe, however, that the "point of reference" has changed with respect to the informal statement of the requirement, and that action A is no longer mentioned directly. If no suitable formula pA exists, we can "create" one using TLA's quantification over state variables, and write[1]

$$\exists\, pA : \neg pA \wedge \Box[pA' \equiv (pA \vee A)]_v \wedge \Diamond\langle pA \wedge B\rangle_v$$

This formula defines pA to become true at the first occurrence of action A and then remain true forever; it is an example for a so-called *history variable* [2]. Although the formula can be shown to capture the informal requirement, it is certainly not natural.

Another concern that has not been resolved in a satisfactory way is the question of proof systems, even for propositional TLA. Lamport [12] states a relative completeness result for first-order TLA, subject to expressiveness assumptions similar to those for Hoare logics, for specifications in so-called "normal form". Formulas that deviate from "normal form" specifications arise naturally when specifications are composed [4]. Abadi [1] has proposed an axiomatization of an earlier version of TLA, but it is not clear whether his proof system can be adapted to the present-day TLA. This is in contrast to standard propositional temporal logic (PTL) whose axiomatization has been well understood since a landmark paper by Gabbay et al [8]. Complete axiomatizations are perhaps of rather academic interest; nevertheless they supply important information about the principles that underly a given logic, and they can form the basis of practical verification systems. For example, an accepted axiomatization would have helped us with the mechanization of TLA in the generic interactive theorem prover Isabelle [15].

In this paper we argue that the two shortcomings of TLA identified above are in fact related: we define the logic GTLA, which is a variant of TLA, but has a more liberal syntax. For example, $\Diamond\langle A \wedge \Diamond\langle B\rangle_v\rangle_v$ is a GTLA formula. We prove that GTLA, like TLA, is invariant under stuttering and provide a sound and complete axiomatization, via two different presentations. Finally, we show that TLA and GTLA are equally expressive once we add quantification over flexible propositions, preserving stuttering invariance. More precisely, while TLA is a sublogic of GTLA, every GTLA formula (possibly containing quantifiers) can be effectively translated to a quantified TLA formula. We argue that GTLA is better suited for verification than TLA. The added flexibility in expressiveness, which comes at no extra cost, may prove useful for writing specifications.

The plan of the paper is as follows: section 2 defines GTLA and contains the proof of stuttering invariance. Sections 3 and 4 introduce the first, heterogeneous version of an axiomatization for GTLA; an alternative, homogeneous presentation is derived in section 5. Section 6 compares the expressiveness of TLA and GTLA. Section 7 concludes the paper. Throughout, we restrict ourselves to propositional (or quantified propositional) logics, although the logic is easily extended to a first-order language.

---

[1] The formula becomes even more complex if A and B are allowed to occur simultaneously.

2   A Generalized TLA

We define the syntax and semantics of propositional GTLA and prove that all formulas
are invariant under stuttering.

2.1   Syntax and Semantics

Assume given a denumerable set $\mathcal{V}$ of atomic propositions.

Definition 1. *Formulas and pre-formulas of GTLA are inductively defined as follows.*

1. *Every atomic proposition $v \in \mathcal{V}$ is a formula.*
2. *If F, G are formulas then $\neg F$, $F \Rightarrow G$, and $\square F$ are formulas.*
3. *If P is a pre-formula and $v \in \mathcal{V}$ then $\square[P]_v$ is a formula.*
4. *If F is a formula then F and $\bigcirc F$ are pre-formulas.*
5. *If P, Q are pre-formulas then $\neg P$ and $P \Rightarrow Q$ are pre-formulas.*

   The pre-formulas of GTLA generalize the transition formulas (actions) of TLA. In
fact, propositional TLA can be defined similarly, except that clause (4) above should
then be changed to

   4'. If $v \in \mathcal{V}$ is an atomic proposition then v and $\bigcirc v$ are pre-formulas.

We will use symbols such as F, G for formulas, P, Q for pre-formulas, and A, B for
either formulas or pre-formulas. Note that, as in TLA, we consider $\square$ and $\square[\_]_v$ to be
different operators, for each $v \in \mathcal{V}$.

   In the following we assume standard abbreviations such as **true**, $\wedge$, $\vee$, $\equiv$, and $\not\equiv$
(equivalence, non-equivalence) for both formulas and pre-formulas. For compatibility
with standard TLA syntax, we sometimes write v' instead of $\bigcirc v$ when v is an atomic
proposition. For a finite set $V = \{v_1, \ldots, v_n\} \subseteq \mathcal{V}$ of atomic propositions we let
$\square[P]_V$ denote the formula $\square[P]_{v_1} \wedge \ldots \wedge \square[P]_{v_n}$; in particular, $\square[P]_\emptyset$ equals **true**.
Stretching the notation even further, we write $\square[P]_F$ (where F is any formula) for[2]
$\square[P \vee (\bigcirc F \equiv F)]_{At(F)}$ where $At(F) \subseteq \mathcal{V}$ denotes the set of atomic propositions
that occur in F. We write $\Diamond F$ for the formula $\neg\square\neg F$ and $\Diamond\langle P\rangle_v$ for $\neg\square[\neg P]_v$. Con-
sequently, $\Diamond\langle P\rangle_{\{v_1,\ldots,v_n\}}$ denotes $\Diamond\langle P\rangle_{v_1} \vee \ldots \vee \Diamond\langle P\rangle_{v_n}$, and $\Diamond\langle P\rangle_F$ abbreviates
$\Diamond\langle P \wedge (\bigcirc F \not\equiv F)\rangle_{At(F)}$. Finally, we let $[P]_F$ and $\langle P\rangle_F$ abbreviate the pre-formulas
$P \vee (\bigcirc F \equiv F)$ and $P \wedge (\bigcirc F \not\equiv F)$, respectively.

   A *state* is a boolean valuation $s : \mathcal{V} \to \{\text{tt}, \text{ff}\}$ of the atomic propositions. A *behav-
ior* $\sigma = s_0 s_1 \ldots$ is an infinite sequence of states. For any $i \geq 0$, we denote by $\sigma|_i$ the
suffix of σ starting at state s_i, that is, the sequence $s_i s_{i+1} \ldots$. We now define what it
means for a (pre-)formula to hold of a behavior σ, written $\sigma \models F$ or $\sigma \approx\!\!\!| P$.

Definition 2. *The semantics of (pre-)formulas is given by the relation $\approx\!\!\!|$, which is in-
ductively defined as follows:*

---

[2] This notation introduces an ambiguity when $F \equiv v$ is an atomic proposition. However, both
possible interpretations are equivalent under the semantics of definition 2 below.

$$\sigma \models v \qquad \textit{iff} \qquad s_0(v) = \text{tt} \qquad \textit{(for } v \in \mathcal{V}\textit{)}.$$
$$\sigma \models \neg A \qquad \textit{iff} \qquad \sigma \models A \textit{ does not hold}.$$
$$\sigma \models A \Rightarrow B \quad \textit{iff} \qquad \sigma \models A \textit{ implies } \sigma \models B.$$
$$\sigma \models \Box F \qquad \textit{iff} \qquad \sigma|_i \models F \textit{ holds for all } i \geq 0.$$
$$\sigma \models \Box[P]_v \qquad \textit{iff} \qquad \textit{for all } i \geq 0, \ s_i(v) = s_{i+1}(v) \textit{ or } \sigma|_i \models P.$$
$$\sigma \models \bigcirc F \qquad \textit{iff} \qquad \sigma|_1 \models F.$$

For a formula F, we usually write $\sigma \models F$ instead of $\sigma \models F$.

We say that a formula F is *valid over a behavior* σ iff $\sigma|_n \models F$ holds for all $n \geq 0$. Formula F *follows from* a set $\mathcal{F}$ of formulas (written $\mathcal{F} \models F$) iff F is valid over all behaviors over which all formulas $G \in \mathcal{F}$ are valid. Finally, F is *valid* (written $\models F$) iff it is valid over all behaviors, which is equivalent to saying that it follows from $\emptyset$.

Note that we have chosen the definition of *floating validity*, which is the traditional definition for modal logics, rather than the alternative *anchored validity*, which Lamport [12] uses. It is well known that either choice leads to the same set of valid formulas, although the consequence relation is different. We prefer floating validity because it is usually easier to axiomatize.

We say that a (pre-)formula is tautological if it results from a propositional tautology A of classical logic by consistently replacing atomic subformulas of A by formulas or pre-formulas. It is easy to see that every tautological formula is valid.

2.2 Stuttering Invariance

Definition 1 allows the $\Box$ operator to be applied only to formulas. For example, $\Box \bigcirc v$ is not a pre-formula, although $\bigcirc \Box v$ is. Had we allowed pre-formulas to freely contain outermost boxes, we would not obtain invariance under stuttering: consider, for example, $\Box[\Box(p \Rightarrow \bigcirc q)]_p$, which is not a GTLA formula, and the behaviors σ and τ, where τ differs from σ only in the repetition of a single state, as illustrated by the following diagram (where $\sim$ means "don't care"):

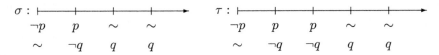

Assuming the last state to repeat indefinitely, $\Box[\Box(p \Rightarrow \bigcirc q)]_p$ clearly holds of σ, but not of τ.

We now formally define stuttering equivalence and prove that GTLA formulas do not distinguish between stuttering equivalent behaviors.

Definition 3 (stuttering equivalence). *Let $V \subseteq \mathcal{V}$ be a set of atomic propositions.*

1. *Two states s, t are called V-similar, written $s \simeq_V t$ iff $s(v) = t(v)$ for all $v \in V$.*
2. *V-stuttering equivalence, again written $\simeq_V$, is the smallest equivalence relation on behaviors that identifies $\rho \circ \langle s \rangle \circ \sigma$ and $\rho \circ \langle tu \rangle \circ \sigma$, for any finite sequence of states ρ, infinite sequence of states σ, and pairwise V-similar states s, t, u.*
3. *Stuttering equivalence (written $\simeq$) is $\mathcal{V}$-stuttering equivalence.*

It follows that $\sigma \simeq_V \tau$ implies $\sigma \simeq_W \tau$ whenever $W \subseteq V$ holds. In particular, stuttering equivalence is the finest relation among all $\simeq_V$. Let us list some elementary facts about stuttering equivalent behaviors.

Proposition 4. *Assume that $\sigma \simeq_V \tau$ holds for behaviors $\sigma = s_0 s_1 \ldots$ and $\tau = t_0 t_1 \ldots$.*

1. $t_0 \simeq_V s_0$.
2. For every $n \geq 0$ there is some $m \geq 0$ such that $\sigma|_n \simeq_V \tau|_m$ and $\sigma|_{n+1} \simeq_V \tau|_{m+1}$.

Theorem 5 (stuttering invariance). *For any GTLA formula F and any behaviors σ, τ such that $\sigma \simeq_{At(F)} \tau$, we have $\sigma \models F$ iff $\tau \models F$.*

Proof. We simultaneously prove the following assertions by induction on the structure of (pre-)formulas, for all behaviors $\sigma = s_0 s_1 \ldots$ and $\tau = t_0 t_1 \ldots$.

1. If $\sigma \simeq_{At(F)} \tau$ then $\sigma \models F$ iff $\tau \models F$.
2. If $\sigma \simeq_{At(P)} \tau$ and $\sigma|_1 \simeq_{At(P)} \tau|_1$ then $\sigma \approx P$ iff $\tau \approx P$.

We first consider the different cases in the definition of formulas F.

$F \in \mathcal{V}$: The assertion follows from proposition 4.1, since $s_0(F) = t_0(F)$.
$\neg F$: immediate from the induction hypothesis.
$F \Rightarrow G$: Since $At(F) \subseteq At(F \Rightarrow G)$ and $At(G) \subseteq At(F \Rightarrow G)$, the assumption $\sigma \simeq_{At(F \Rightarrow G)} \tau$ implies both $\sigma \simeq_{At(F)} \tau$ and $\sigma \simeq_{At(G)} \tau$. This observation, together with the induction hypothesis, implies the assertion.
$\Box F$: By symmetry of $\simeq_{At(\Box F)}$, it is enough to prove "if". So assume that $\tau \models \Box F$, and let $n \geq 0$ be arbitrary. Proposition 4.2 implies that there exists some $m \geq 0$ such that $\sigma|_n \simeq_{At(\Box F)} \tau|_m$. From $\tau \models \Box F$ we conclude $\tau|_m \models F$, and therefore $\sigma|_n \models F$ by induction hypothesis, since $At(\Box F) = At(F)$.
$\Box[P]_v$: Again, we need only prove the "if" part. Assume that $\tau \models \Box[P]_v$, and let $n \geq 0$ be arbitrary. Choose $m \geq 0$ such that $\sigma|_n \simeq_{At(\Box[P]_v)} \tau|_m$ and also $\sigma|_{n+1} \simeq_{At(\Box[P]_v)} \tau|_{m+1}$; proposition 4.2 ensures that m exists. Proposition 4.1 implies that $s_n(v) = t_m(v)$ and $s_{n+1}(v) = t_{m+1}(v)$. If $t_m(v) = t_{m+1}(v)$, it follows that $s_n(v) = s_{n+1}(v)$, and we are done. Otherwise, by the assumption $\tau \models \Box[P]_v$ it follows that $\tau|_m \approx P$, and the induction hypothesis (for assertion 2) gives $\sigma|_n \approx P$ because $\simeq_{At(\Box[P]_v)} \subseteq \simeq_{At(P)}$.

Turning to assertion 2, we consider the cases in the definition of pre-formulas:

P a formula : immediate from the induction hypothesis for assertion 1.
$\bigcirc F$: The assumption that $\sigma|_1 \simeq_{At(\bigcirc F)} \tau|_1$ and the induction hypothesis for assertion 1 imply $\sigma|_1 \models F$ iff $\tau|_1 \models F$, and therefore $\sigma \approx \bigcirc F$ iff $\tau \approx \bigcirc F$.
$\neg P, P \Rightarrow Q$: analogous to the corresponding cases for formulas. $\therefore$

(ax0)	$\vdash F$ whenever F is tautological	(pax0)	$\hspace{-0.3em}\sim P$ whenever P is tautological
(ax1)	$\vdash \Box F \Rightarrow F$	(pax1)	$\hspace{-0.3em}\sim \bigcirc \neg F \equiv \neg \bigcirc F$
(ax2)	$\vdash \Box F \Rightarrow \Box[\Box F]_v$	(pax2)	$\hspace{-0.3em}\sim \bigcirc(F \Rightarrow G) \Rightarrow (\bigcirc F \Rightarrow \bigcirc G)$
(ax3)	$\vdash \Box[F \Rightarrow \bigcirc F]_F \Rightarrow (F \Rightarrow \Box F)$	(pax3)	$\hspace{-0.3em}\sim \Box F \Rightarrow \bigcirc \Box F$
(ax4)	$\vdash \Box[P \Rightarrow Q]_v \Rightarrow (\Box[P]_v \Rightarrow \Box[Q]_v)$	(pax4)	$\hspace{-0.3em}\sim \Box[P]_v \equiv [P]_v \wedge \bigcirc\Box[P]_v$
(ax5)	$\vdash \Box[v' \not\equiv v]_v$	(pax5)	$\hspace{-0.3em}\sim \bigcirc\Box F \Rightarrow \Box[\bigcirc F]_v$

$$(\text{mp}) \quad \frac{\vdash F \qquad \vdash F \Rightarrow G}{\vdash G} \qquad\qquad (\text{pmp}) \quad \frac{\hspace{-0.3em}\sim P \qquad \hspace{-0.3em}\sim P \Rightarrow Q}{\hspace{-0.3em}\sim Q}$$

$$(\text{sq}) \quad \frac{\hspace{-0.3em}\sim P}{\vdash \Box[P]_v} \qquad\qquad (\text{pre}) \quad \frac{\vdash F}{\hspace{-0.3em}\sim F} \qquad (\text{nex}) \quad \frac{\vdash F}{\hspace{-0.3em}\sim \bigcirc F}$$

Fig. 1. The proof system Σ_{GTLA}.

3 An Axiomatization of GTLA

We now present a proof system Σ_{GTLA} for GTLA and prove its adequacy. Σ_{GTLA} is based on two provability relations $\vdash$ and $\hspace{-0.3em}\sim$ for formulas and pre-formulas; we therefore call Σ_{GTLA} a heterogeneous proof system. An alternative "homogeneous" proof system will be given in section 5. Figure 1 contains the axioms and rules that define $\vdash$ and $\hspace{-0.3em}\sim$. We extend $\vdash$ to a relation between sets of formulas and formulas by defining $\mathcal{F} \vdash F$ iff $\vdash F$ can be established from the axioms and rules of Σ_{GTLA} if additionally $\vdash G$ is assumed for all formulas $G \in \mathcal{F}$, and similarly define $\mathcal{F} \hspace{-0.3em}\sim P$. Because we are ultimately only interested in the relation $\vdash$ for formulas, we do not allow pre-formulas to occur in the set $\mathcal{F}$ of hypotheses.

Many of the axioms and rules of Σ_{GTLA} are familiar from propositional linear-time temporal logic [8, 9]. First observe that both $\vdash$ and $\hspace{-0.3em}\sim$ contain full propositional calculus. Axiom (ax3) is a "stuttering-invariant" version of the induction axiom. Its formulation relies essentially on the GTLA syntax that allows temporal formulas in the scope of the $\Box[\_]_v$ operator. Axiom (ax5) effectively asserts that the pre-formula P in $\Box[P]_v$ is evaluated only when v changes value. Axiom (pax1) expresses that time is linear. We cannot state an induction principle for formulas of the form $\Box[P]_v$ because $\bigcirc P$ or $\bigcirc[P]_v$ are not even pre-formulas. For this reason, (pax4) is stronger than its counterparts (ax1) and (pax3). Axiom (pax5) asserts a form of commutativity for the $\bigcirc$ and $\Box$ operators. The rules (sq) and (nex) reflect the floating definition of validity. The necessitation rule

$$(\text{alw}) \quad \frac{\vdash F}{\vdash \Box F}$$

is easily derived in Σ_{GTLA}. Note also that the axioms (ax2), (ax4), (pax4), (pax5) and the rule (sq) are easily generalized to versions where the "index" v is replaced by a finite set V of atomic propositions, or by a GTLA formula.

Theorem 6 (Soundness). *For any set $\mathcal{F}$ of formulas, $\mathcal{F} \vdash F$ implies $\mathcal{F} \models F$.*

Proof. The proof is by induction on the assumed derivation of F from $\mathcal{F}$, also proving that $\mathcal{F} \mathrel{\vdash\!\!\!\sim} P$ implies that $\sigma|_n \mathrel{\approx\!\!\!\mid} P$ holds for every $n \geq 0$ and every behavior σ such that all formulas in $\mathcal{F}$ are valid over σ. We only consider a few cases.

(ax3) It suffices to prove $\sigma \models \Box[F \Rightarrow \bigcirc F]_F \Rightarrow (F \Rightarrow \Box F)$, for any formula F and any behavior $\sigma = s_0 s_1 \dots$. So suppose $\sigma \models \Box[F \Rightarrow \bigcirc F]_F$ and $\sigma \models F$. We prove $\sigma|_n \models F$ for every $n \geq 0$, by induction on n. The base case being trivial, assume that $\sigma|_n \models F$. If $s_n \simeq_{At(F)} s_{n+1}$, we have $\sigma|_n \simeq_{At(F)} \sigma|_{n+1}$, and theorem 5 ensures that $\sigma|_{n+1} \models F$. Otherwise, there is some $v \in At(F)$ such that $s_n(v) \neq s_{n+1}(v)$, and the assumption $\sigma \models \Box[F \Rightarrow \bigcirc F]_F$ implies that $\sigma|_n \mathrel{\approx\!\!\!\mid} (F \Rightarrow \bigcirc F) \vee (\bigcirc F \equiv F)$, hence again $\sigma|_{n+1} \models F$.

(pax5) Suppose $\sigma \mathrel{\approx\!\!\!\mid} \bigcirc\Box F$, that is, $\sigma|_{n+1} \models F$, for every $n \geq 0$. We prove that $\sigma \models \Box[\bigcirc F]_v$. Let $m \geq 0$ be arbitrary. The assumption ensures that $\sigma|_{m+1} \models F$, and therefore $\sigma|_m \mathrel{\approx\!\!\!\mid} \bigcirc F$. This suffices.

(sq) Assume that $\mathcal{F} \mathrel{\vdash\!\!\!\sim} P$, that σ is some behavior such that all formulas in $\mathcal{F}$ are valid over σ, and that $n \geq 0$. We need to prove that $\sigma|_n \models \Box[P]_v$. So let $m \geq 0$ be arbitrary. By induction hypothesis, we know that $\sigma|_{n+m} \mathrel{\approx\!\!\!\mid} P$, and therefore $(\sigma|_n)|_m \mathrel{\approx\!\!\!\mid} P$. This suffices. $\because$

We also have a version of the deduction theorem for Σ_{GTLA}, as stated in the following theorem.

Theorem 7. *For any set $\mathcal{F}$ of formulas, any formulas F, G, and any pre-formula P we have $\mathcal{F} \cup \{F\} \vdash G$ iff $\mathcal{F} \vdash \Box F \Rightarrow G$ and $\mathcal{F} \cup \{F\} \mathrel{\vdash\!\!\!\sim} P$ iff $\mathcal{F} \mathrel{\vdash\!\!\!\sim} \Box F \Rightarrow P$.*

Proof. "if": Assume $\mathcal{F} \vdash \Box F \Rightarrow G$. A fortiori, we have $\mathcal{F} \cup \{F\} \vdash \Box F \Rightarrow G$. The derived rule (alw) implies that $\mathcal{F} \cup \{F\} \vdash \Box F$, and therefore we have $\mathcal{F} \cup \{F\} \vdash G$ by (mp). The second assertion is proven similarly.

"only if": The proof is by induction on the assumed derivations of $\mathcal{F} \cup \{F\} \vdash G$ and $\mathcal{F} \cup \{F\} \mathrel{\vdash\!\!\!\sim} P$ (simultaneously for all F and P).

- If G is an axiom or $G \in \mathcal{F}$, we have $\mathcal{F} \vdash G$, and $\mathcal{F} \vdash \Box F \Rightarrow G$ follows by propositional reasoning. The same argument applies for the second assertion when P is an axiom.
- If G is F, then $\mathcal{F} \vdash \Box F \Rightarrow F$ is an instance of (ax1).
- If G results from an application of (mp) to previously derived formulas $H \Rightarrow G$ and H, then the induction hypothesis implies $\mathcal{F} \vdash \Box F \Rightarrow (H \Rightarrow G)$ as well as $\mathcal{F} \vdash \Box F \Rightarrow H$, from which we conclude $\mathcal{F} \vdash \Box F \Rightarrow G$ by propositional reasoning. The same argument holds for (pmp).
- Assume that G results from an application of (sq), say, $G \equiv \Box[Q]_v$. By induction hypothesis, we have $\mathcal{F} \mathrel{\vdash\!\!\!\sim} \Box F \Rightarrow Q$, and we continue as follows:

(1) $\mathrel{\vdash\!\!\!\sim} \Box F \Rightarrow Q$ (ind.hyp.)

(2) $\vdash \Box[\Box F \Rightarrow Q]_v$ (sq)(1)

(3) $\vdash \Box[\Box F \Rightarrow Q]_v \Rightarrow (\Box[\Box F]_v \Rightarrow \Box[Q]_v)$ (ax4)

(4) $\vdash \Box F \Rightarrow \Box[\Box F]_v$ (ax2)

(5) $\vdash \Box F \Rightarrow \Box[Q]_v$ (prop)(2)(3)(4)

- If G results from an application of (pre), then by induction hypothesis we have $\mathcal{F} \vdash \Box F \Rightarrow G$, and therefore also $\mathcal{F} \mathbin{\vdash\!\!\!\sim} \Box F \Rightarrow G$, by (pre).
- If $G \equiv \bigcirc H$ results from an application of (nex), then the induction hypothesis yields $\mathcal{F} \vdash \Box F \Rightarrow H$. Rule (nex) shows $\mathcal{F} \mathbin{\vdash\!\!\!\sim} \bigcirc(\Box F \Rightarrow H)$, and we obtain $\mathcal{F} \mathbin{\vdash\!\!\!\sim} \bigcirc\Box F \Rightarrow \bigcirc H$ by (pax2) and (pmp). The conclusion $\mathcal{F} \mathbin{\vdash\!\!\!\sim} \Box F \Rightarrow \bigcirc H$ follows with the help of (pax3).   ∴

The following are some derived theorems of Σ_{GTLA}, which will be used later. Derivations of these theorems can be found in the full version of this paper [14].

(T1) $\vdash \Box F \equiv \Box\Box F$ (T2) $\vdash \Box[P]_v \equiv \Box\Box[P]_v$

(T3) $\vdash \Box[[P]_v]_v \equiv \Box[P]_v$ (T4) $\vdash \Box[P]_v \Rightarrow \Box[[P]_v]_w$

(T5) $\vdash \Box[[P]_w]_v \Rightarrow \Box[[P]_v]_w$ (T6) $\vdash \Box F \Rightarrow \Box[\bigcirc F]_v$

(T7) $\mathbin{\vdash\!\!\!\sim} \Box F \equiv F \wedge \bigcirc\Box F$ (T8) $\mathbin{\vdash\!\!\!\sim} \bigcirc(F \wedge G) \equiv \bigcirc F \wedge \bigcirc G$

By rule (pre), every provable formula is also provable as a pre-formula. An important result for Σ_{GTLA} shows that the converse is also true. This can be shown by a careful analysis of the derivations in Σ_{GTLA}; the full proof is given in [14].

Theorem 8. *For any set $\mathcal{F}$ of formulas and any formula F:*

$$\mathcal{F} \vdash F \quad \textit{iff} \quad \mathcal{F} \mathbin{\vdash\!\!\!\sim} F \quad \textit{iff} \quad \mathcal{F} \mathbin{\vdash\!\!\!\sim} \bigcirc F$$

4   Completeness of Σ_{GTLA}

We will now prove the completeness of Σ_{GTLA}. Let us first note that GTLA, just as PTL, is not compact:

Example 9. Let $\mathcal{F} = \{\Box[v_i \Rightarrow v'_{i+1}]_{v_i}, \Box(v_i \Rightarrow w) : i \geq 0\}$. It is easy to see that $\mathcal{F} \models v_0 \Rightarrow \Box w$, but we can clearly not derive $\mathcal{F} \vdash v_0 \Rightarrow \Box w$, because this would require the infinitary invariant $\Box \bigvee_{i \geq 0} v_i$.

We can therefore only hope for completeness when $\mathcal{F}$ is a finite set, and by theorem 7 it is enough to show that $\models F$ implies $\vdash F$.

Our completeness proof follows the standard approach [9] of constructing a model for a finite and consistent set of formulas. To do so, we have to assemble information about pre-formulas as well as formulas. Nevertheless, the critical step in the proof is to show that all the essential information is contained in the formulas used for the construction; this is due to the fact that the assumptions in a derivation $\mathcal{F} \vdash F$ do not contain pre-formulas. For a set $\mathcal{G}$ of formulas and pre-formulas, we denote by $\mathcal{G}^F$ the set of all formulas contained in $\mathcal{G}$. We also use $\mathcal{G}$ to denote the conjunction of all (pre-) formulas in $\mathcal{G}$; it will always be clear from the context whether we refer to the set or the (pre-)formula.

A set $\mathcal{G}$ is called *inconsistent* if $\mathbin{\vdash\!\!\!\sim} \neg\mathcal{G}$, otherwise it is called *consistent*. Note that if $\mathcal{G}$ is consistent and A is any formula or pre-formula, one of the sets $\mathcal{G} \cup \{A\}$ or $\mathcal{G} \cup \{\neg A\}$ is again consistent.

We inductively define a set $\tau(A)$ for any formula or pre-formula A, as follows:

$$\tau(v) = \{v\} \qquad\qquad \tau(\neg A) = \{\neg A\} \cup \tau(A)$$
$$\tau(A \Rightarrow B) = \{A \Rightarrow B\} \cup \tau(A) \cup \tau(B) \qquad \tau(\Box F) = \{\Box F\} \cup \tau(F)$$
$$\tau(\Box[P]_v) = \{\Box[P]_v, v, \bigcirc v\} \cup \tau(P) \qquad \tau(\bigcirc F) = \{\bigcirc F\}$$

For a set $\mathcal{G}$, we define $\tau(\mathcal{G})$ as the union of all $\tau(A)$, for all (pre-)formulas A contained in $\mathcal{G}$. Note that our definitions ensure that $\tau(\mathcal{G})$ is finite whenever $\mathcal{G}$ is finite.

We say that $\mathcal{G}$ is *complete* if it contains either A or $\neg A$, for every (pre-)formula A from $\tau(\mathcal{G})$. Observe that for every finite and consistent $\mathcal{G}$ there exist only finitely many finite, consistent, and complete $\mathcal{G}^* \supseteq \mathcal{G}$, since $\tau(\mathcal{G})$ is itself finite; we call any such $\mathcal{G}^*$ a *completion* of $\mathcal{G}$. We note the following elementary facts about complete sets. The proofs of assertions 1 and 3 are standard, whereas the second assertion follows from the first and theorem 8 by propositional reasoning, since $\mathcal{G} \Rightarrow \mathcal{G}^F$ holds for any set $\mathcal{G}$ by (ax0).

Proposition 10.

1. *Assume that $\mathcal{G}$ is finite and consistent, and that $\mathcal{G}_1^*, \ldots, \mathcal{G}_n^*$ are all the different completions of $\mathcal{G}$. Then $\hspace{0.1cm}\vdash\hspace{-0.35cm}\sim\hspace{0.1cm} \mathcal{G} \Rightarrow \mathcal{G}_1^* \vee \ldots \vee \mathcal{G}_n^*$.*
2. *Assume that $\mathcal{F}$ is a finite and consistent set of formulas, and that $\mathcal{G}_1, \ldots, \mathcal{G}_n$ are all the different completions of $\mathcal{F}$. Then $\vdash \mathcal{F} \Rightarrow \mathcal{G}_1^F \vee \ldots \vee \mathcal{G}_n^F$.*
3. *Assume that $\mathcal{G}$ is consistent and complete and that A, B are (pre-)formulas.*
   (a) *If $A \in \mathcal{G}$, $B \in \tau(\mathcal{G})$ and $\vdash A \Rightarrow B$ or $\hspace{0.1cm}\vdash\hspace{-0.35cm}\sim\hspace{0.1cm} A \Rightarrow B$ then $B \in \mathcal{G}$.*
   (b) *If $A \Rightarrow B \in \tau(\mathcal{G})$ then $A \Rightarrow B \in \mathcal{G}$ iff $A \notin \mathcal{G}$ or $B \in \mathcal{G}$.*

We now define a set $\sigma(\mathcal{G})$ of formulas that, intuitively, transfer information from one state of the model under construction to the next one.

$$\sigma_1(\mathcal{G}) = \{F : \bigcirc F \in \mathcal{G}\} \qquad\qquad \sigma_2(\mathcal{G}) = \{\neg F : \neg \bigcirc F \in \mathcal{G}\}$$
$$\sigma_3(\mathcal{G}) = \{\Box F : \Box F \in \mathcal{G}\} \qquad\qquad \sigma_4(\mathcal{G}) = \{\neg \Box F : \neg \Box F \in \mathcal{G}, F \in \mathcal{G}\}$$
$$\sigma_5(\mathcal{G}) = \{\Box[P]_v : \Box[P]_v \in \mathcal{G}\}$$
$$\sigma_6(\mathcal{G}) = \{\neg\Box[P]_v : \neg\Box[P]_v \in \mathcal{G} \text{ and }$$
$$P \in \mathcal{G} \text{ or } \{v, \bigcirc v\} \subseteq \mathcal{G} \text{ or } \{\neg v, \neg \bigcirc v\} \subseteq \mathcal{G}\}$$
$$\sigma(\mathcal{G}) = \sigma_1(\mathcal{G}) \cup \sigma_2(\mathcal{G}) \cup \sigma_3(\mathcal{G}) \cup \sigma_4(\mathcal{G}) \cup \sigma_5(\mathcal{G}) \cup \sigma_6(\mathcal{G})$$

Lemma 11. *Assume that $\mathcal{G}$ is finite.*

1. $\hspace{0.1cm}\vdash\hspace{-0.35cm}\sim\hspace{0.1cm} \mathcal{G} \Rightarrow \bigcirc\sigma(\mathcal{G})$.
2. *If $\mathcal{G}$ is consistent, then so is $\sigma(\mathcal{G})$.*

Proof. 1. By (T8), it is enough to show $\hspace{0.1cm}\vdash\hspace{-0.35cm}\sim\hspace{0.1cm} \mathcal{G} \Rightarrow \bigcirc F$, for every formula $F \in \sigma(G)$. We distinguish the different cases in the definition of $\sigma(\mathcal{G})$.
   - For $F \in \sigma_1(\mathcal{G})$, we have $\bigcirc F \in \mathcal{G}$, so the assertion follows by (pax0).
   - If $F \equiv \neg G \in \sigma_2(\mathcal{G})$, then $\neg \bigcirc F \in \mathcal{G}$, and the assertion follows using (pax1).
   - If $F \equiv \Box G \in \sigma_3(\mathcal{G})$, we have $\Box G \in \mathcal{G}$; use (pax3) to prove the assertion.
   - If $F \equiv \neg \Box G \in \sigma_4(\mathcal{G})$, the definition ensures $\hspace{0.1cm}\vdash\hspace{-0.35cm}\sim\hspace{0.1cm} \mathcal{G} \Rightarrow G \wedge \neg\Box G$, and the assertion follows by (T7), (pax1), and propositional logic.

- For $F \equiv \Box[P]_v \in \sigma_5(\mathcal{G})$, use (pax4) to prove the assertion.
- If $F \equiv \neg\Box[P]_v \in \sigma_6(\mathcal{G})$, the definition and (pax0) yield $\mathcal{G} \Rightarrow [P]_v \wedge \neg\Box[P]_v$, and the assertion follows by (pax4) and (pax1).

2. If $\sigma(\mathcal{G})$ is inconsistent, we have $\mathrel{\vdash\mkern-9mu\sim} \neg\sigma(\mathcal{G})$. By rule (nex), we obtain $\mathrel{\vdash\mkern-9mu\sim} \bigcirc\neg\sigma(\mathcal{G})$. Using axiom (pax1) and propositional logic, assertion (1) implies $\mathrel{\vdash\mkern-9mu\sim} \neg\mathcal{G}$, that is, $\mathcal{G}$ is inconsistent. $\therefore$

Given a finite and consistent set $\mathcal{F}$ of formulas, we inductively define a graph $\mathcal{T}(\mathcal{F})$ of sets of pre-formulas as follows:

- All different completions of $\mathcal{F}$ are nodes of $\mathcal{T}(\mathcal{F})$, called the *roots* of $\mathcal{T}(\mathcal{F})$.
- If $\mathcal{G}$ is a node in $\mathcal{T}(\mathcal{F})$ then its successors are all different completions of $\sigma(\mathcal{G})$.

It follows that every node $\mathcal{G}$ is finite, consistent, and complete. Also, the sub-graph of $\mathcal{T}(\mathcal{F})$ that consists of all nodes reachable from the successors of $\mathcal{G}$ is just $\mathcal{T}(\sigma(\mathcal{G}))$.

Lemma 12. *Assume that $\mathcal{F}$ is a finite and consistent set of formulas.*

1. *$\mathcal{T}(\mathcal{F})$ contains only finitely many different nodes $\mathcal{G}_1, \ldots, \mathcal{G}_n$.*
2. *Assume that $\mathcal{G}_1, \ldots, \mathcal{G}_n$ are all the different nodes in $\mathcal{T}(\mathcal{F})$.*
   (i) $\mathrel{\vdash\mkern-9mu\sim} \mathcal{G}_i^F \Rightarrow \mathcal{G}_1 \vee \ldots \vee \mathcal{G}_n$ *(for $i = 1, \ldots, n$).*
   (ii) $\mathrel{\vdash\mkern-9mu\sim} \mathcal{G}_1^F \vee \ldots \vee \mathcal{G}_n^F \Rightarrow \bigcirc(\mathcal{G}_1^F \vee \ldots \vee \mathcal{G}_n^F)$.
   (iii) $\vdash \mathcal{F} \Rightarrow \Box(\mathcal{G}_1^F \vee \ldots \vee \mathcal{G}_n^F)$.

Proof. 1. The completions of a finite set $\mathcal{G}$ only contain – possibly negated – pre-formulas from the set $\tau(\mathcal{G})$, which is also finite. On the other hand, the only pre-formulas in $\sigma(\mathcal{G})$ that are possibly not in $\tau(\mathcal{G})$ are of the form F or $\neg F$ such that $\mathcal{G}$ contains $\bigcirc F$ or $\neg\bigcirc F$, hence the number of $\bigcirc$ operators decreases, which is possible only finitely often. Therefore, only finitely many different (pre-)formulas occur in $\mathcal{T}(\mathcal{F})$, hence $\mathcal{T}(\mathcal{F})$ can contain only finitely many different nodes.

2. (i) Let $i \in \{1, \ldots, n\}$ be arbitrary, and consider the set $\mathcal{F}'$ of formulas from which the node $\mathcal{G}_i$ was constructed—either the initial set $\mathcal{F}$ or the set $\sigma(\mathcal{G}')$ where $\mathcal{G}'$ is a predecessor of $\mathcal{G}$ in $\mathcal{T}(\mathcal{F})$. Proposition 10.1 implies $\mathrel{\vdash\mkern-9mu\sim} \mathcal{F}' \Rightarrow \mathcal{G}_1 \vee \ldots \vee \mathcal{G}_n$ because all consistent completions of $\mathcal{F}'$ are contained in $\mathcal{T}(\mathcal{F})$. Since $\mathcal{G}_i$ is a completion of $\mathcal{F}'$, it follows that $\mathcal{F}' \subseteq \mathcal{G}_i^F$, hence we have $\vdash \mathcal{G}_i^F \Rightarrow \mathcal{F}'$ by (ax0), and therefore the assertion.
   (ii) We first note $\mathrel{\vdash\mkern-9mu\sim} \mathcal{G}_j \Rightarrow \bigcirc\sigma(\mathcal{G}_j)$, for every node $\mathcal{G}_j$ of $\mathcal{T}(\mathcal{F})$, by lemma 11. Proposition 10.2 ensures $\vdash \sigma(\mathcal{G}_j) \Rightarrow \mathcal{G}_1^F \vee \ldots \vee \mathcal{G}_n^F$. Applying rule (nex) and (pax2), we obtain $\mathrel{\vdash\mkern-9mu\sim} \mathcal{G}_j \Rightarrow \bigcirc(\mathcal{G}_1^F \vee \ldots \vee \mathcal{G}_n^F)$, for every j, hence also $\mathrel{\vdash\mkern-9mu\sim} \mathcal{G}_1 \vee \ldots \vee \mathcal{G}_n \Rightarrow \bigcirc(\mathcal{G}_1^F \vee \ldots \vee \mathcal{G}_n^F)$. The assertion follows with the help of (i) and propositional logic.
   (iii) Let $\mathcal{I}$ denote the formula $\mathcal{G}_1^F \vee \ldots \vee \mathcal{G}_n^F$. Assertion (ii) and rule (sq) imply $\vdash \Box[\mathcal{I} \Rightarrow \bigcirc\mathcal{I}]_\mathcal{I}$, hence $\vdash \mathcal{I} \Rightarrow \Box\mathcal{I}$ by axiom (ax3). On the other hand, proposition 10.2 implies $\vdash \mathcal{F} \Rightarrow \mathcal{I}$, and the assertion follows. $\therefore$

We will construct a model for $\mathcal{F}$ from the paths in $\mathcal{T}(\mathcal{F})$. Let us call a path $\mathcal{G}_0, \mathcal{G}_1, \ldots$ *complete* iff it satisfies the two following conditions, for every $i \geq 0$:

- If $\neg\Box F \in \mathcal{G}_i$ then $\neg F \in \mathcal{G}_j$ for some $j \geq i$.
- If $\neg\Box[P]_v \in \mathcal{G}_i$ then for some $j \geq i$, $\neg P \in \mathcal{G}_j$ and either $\{v, \neg \circ v\} \subseteq \mathcal{G}_j$ or $\{\neg v, \circ v\} \subseteq \mathcal{G}_j$.

Lemma 13. *Assume that $\mathcal{F}$ is a finite and consistent set of formulas. Then $\mathcal{T}(\mathcal{F})$ contains a complete path starting at some root.*

Proof. We first prove that for every node $\mathcal{G}$ of $\mathcal{T}(\mathcal{F})$ and any formula F such that $\{\neg\Box F, F\} \subseteq \mathcal{G}$ there is some node $\mathcal{H}$ in $\mathcal{T}(\sigma(\mathcal{G}))$ that contains $\neg F$. Suppose not. Then, in particular, every root $\mathcal{W}$ of $\mathcal{T}(\sigma(\mathcal{G}))$ contains $\neg\Box F$ and F (because $F \in \tau(\sigma(\mathcal{G}))$ and $\mathcal{W}$ is a completion of $\sigma(\mathcal{G})$), hence $\neg\Box F \in \sigma(\mathcal{W})$. Inductively, it follows that $\{\neg\Box F, F\} \subseteq \mathcal{H}$ holds for every node $\mathcal{H}$ of $\mathcal{T}(\sigma(\mathcal{G}))$. Let $\mathcal{G}_1, \ldots, \mathcal{G}_n$ be all nodes of $\mathcal{T}(\sigma(\mathcal{G}))$, and let $\mathcal{I}$ denote the formula $\mathcal{G}_1^F \vee \ldots \vee \mathcal{G}_n^F$. Then (ax0) gives $\mathcal{I} \Rightarrow F$, which proves $\mathcal{I} \vdash \Box F$, using rule (alw). By theorem 7, we conclude $\vdash \Box\mathcal{I} \Rightarrow \Box F$. Lemma 12.2(iii) yields $\vdash \sigma(\mathcal{G}) \Rightarrow \Box F$, but on the other hand we have $\vdash \sigma(\mathcal{G}) \Rightarrow \neg\Box F$ because $\neg\Box F \in \sigma(\mathcal{G})$. Therefore, $\sigma(\mathcal{G})$ and (by lemma 11.2) also $\mathcal{G}$ is inconsistent, and a contradiction is reached.

Similarly, we show that there is some node $\mathcal{H}$ in $\mathcal{T}(\sigma(\mathcal{G}))$ that contains $\neg P$ and either $\{v, \neg\circ v\}$ or $\{\neg v, \circ v\}$ whenever $\neg\Box[P]_v \in \mathcal{G}$ and either $P \in \mathcal{G}$ or $\{v, \circ v\} \subseteq \mathcal{G}$ or $\{\neg v, \neg\circ v\} \subseteq \mathcal{G}$. Suppose not. Then an argument analogous to the one above establishes that every node $\mathcal{H}$ contains P or $\{v, \circ v\}$ or $\{\neg v, \neg\circ v\}$. By axiom (pax0), this shows $\vdash \mathcal{H} \Rightarrow [P]_v$. Lemma 12.2(i) implies $\vdash \mathcal{I} \Rightarrow [P]_v$, and by (ax1) and (pre), a fortiori $\vdash \Box\mathcal{I} \Rightarrow [P]_v$. Using rule (sq) and (ax4), this shows $\vdash \Box[\Box\mathcal{I}]_v \Rightarrow \Box[[P]_v]_v$, and (T3) implies that $\vdash \Box[\Box\mathcal{I}]_v \Rightarrow \Box[P]_v$. But as above we have $\vdash \sigma(\mathcal{G}) \Rightarrow \Box\mathcal{I}$, and thus also $\vdash \sigma(\mathcal{G}) \Rightarrow \Box[\Box\mathcal{I}]_v$ by (ax2), which proves $\vdash \sigma(\mathcal{G}) \Rightarrow \Box[P]_v$. On the other hand, we know $\vdash \sigma(\mathcal{G}) \Rightarrow \neg\Box[P]_v$ by assumption and reach a contradiction.

These two claims ensure that for every node $\mathcal{G}$ in $\mathcal{T}(\mathcal{F})$ that contains either $\neg\Box F$ or $\neg\Box[P]_v$ there exists some node $\mathcal{G}'$ reachable from $\mathcal{G}$ that satisfies the condition from the definition of a complete path. For if $\mathcal{G}$ itself does not satisfy the condition, the formula is contained in $\sigma(\mathcal{G})$, hence $\mathcal{T}(\sigma(\mathcal{G}))$, which is just the subgraph of $\mathcal{T}(\mathcal{F})$ whose roots are the sons of $\mathcal{G}$, contains a node as required.

The assertion is now proved by fixing some order on the finite set of formulas $\neg\Box F$ and $\neg\Box[P]_v$ that occur in $\mathcal{T}(\mathcal{F})$ and an iterative construction that constructs a complete path piecewise by repeatedly considering the eventuality formulas in the chosen order. The details of this construction are standard [8, 9].   ∴

Lemma 14. *Assume that $\mathcal{F}$ is a finite and consistent set of formulas and that $\mathcal{G}_0, \mathcal{G}_1, \ldots$ is a complete path in $\mathcal{T}(\mathcal{F})$. For every $i \geq 0$, the following assertions hold:*

1. *If $\circ F \in \tau(\mathcal{G}_i)$ then $\circ F \in \mathcal{G}_i$ iff $F \in \mathcal{G}_{i+1}$.*
2. *If $\Box F \in \tau(\mathcal{G}_i)$ then $\Box F \in \mathcal{G}_i$ iff $F \in \mathcal{G}_j$ for all $j \geq i$.*
3. *If $\Box[P]_v \in \tau(\mathcal{G}_i)$ then $\Box[P]_v \in \mathcal{G}_i$ iff for all $j \geq i$, $P \in \mathcal{G}_j$ or $\{v, \circ v\} \subseteq \mathcal{G}_j$ or $\{\neg v, \neg\circ v\} \subseteq \mathcal{G}_j$.*

Proof. 1. If $\circ F \in \mathcal{G}_i$ then $F \in \sigma(\mathcal{G}_i)$ and therefore $F \in \mathcal{G}_{i+1}$, which is a completion of $\sigma(\mathcal{G}_i)$.

If $\circ F \notin \mathcal{G}_i$ then $\neg\circ F \in \mathcal{G}_i$ (because $\mathcal{G}_i$ is complete), so $\neg F \in \sigma(\mathcal{G}_i)$, and again $\neg F \in \mathcal{G}_{i+1}$. The consistency of $\mathcal{G}_{i+1}$ implies $F \notin \mathcal{G}_{i+1}$.

2. Assume $\Box F \in \mathcal{G}_i$. Then we have $F \in \tau(\mathcal{G}_i)$, and because of $\vdash \Box F \Rightarrow F$ (ax1) and proposition 10.3, it follows that $F \in \mathcal{G}_i$. Moreover, $\Box F \in \sigma(\mathcal{G}_i)$ and therefore $\Box F \in \mathcal{G}_{i+1}$. Inductively, we conclude that $F \in \mathcal{G}_j$ holds for all $j \geq i$.

   Conversely, if $F \in \mathcal{G}_j$ for all $j \geq i$ then the definition of a complete path and the consistency of the $\mathcal{G}_j$ ensure that $\neg \Box F \in \mathcal{G}_i$ cannot hold. The assumption $\Box F \in \tau(\mathcal{G}_i)$ and the fact that $\mathcal{G}_i$ is complete imply $\Box F \in \mathcal{G}_i$.

3. Assume $\Box[P]_v \in \mathcal{G}_i$. Then $\{P, v, \bigcirc v\} \subseteq \tau(\mathcal{G}_i)$, and by $\vdash \Box[P]_v \Rightarrow [P]_v$ (pax4) and proposition 10.3, the assertion follows for $j = i$ using the completeness and consistency of $\mathcal{G}_i$ and propositional logic. Moreover, $\Box[P]_v \in \sigma(\mathcal{G}_i)$ and therefore $\Box[P]_v \in \mathcal{G}_{i+1}$. Inductively, the assertion follows for all $j \geq i$.

   Conversely, if $P \in \mathcal{G}_j$ or $\{v, \bigcirc v\} \subseteq \mathcal{G}_j$ or $\{\neg v, \neg \bigcirc v\} \subseteq \mathcal{G}_j$ holds for all $j \geq i$, the consistency of the $\mathcal{G}_j$ implies that there can be no $j \geq i$ such that $\neg P \in \mathcal{G}_j$ and either $\{v, \neg \bigcirc v\} \subseteq \mathcal{G}_j$ or $\{\neg v, \bigcirc v\} \subseteq \mathcal{G}_j$. Therefore, using the definition of a complete path, it follows that $\neg \Box[P]_v \in \mathcal{G}_i$ cannot hold, hence $\Box[P]_v \in \mathcal{G}_i$.   ∵

We now have all the bits and pieces to construct a model for a finite and consistent set $\mathcal{F}$ from $\mathcal{T}(\mathcal{F})$.

Lemma 15. *For every finite and consistent set $\mathcal{F}$ of formulas there is a behavior σ such that $\sigma \models F$ holds for all $F \in \mathcal{F}$.*

Proof. Assume that $\mathcal{F}$ is a finite and consistent set of formulas. Construct $\mathcal{T}(\mathcal{F})$ and choose some complete path $\mathcal{G}_0, \mathcal{G}_1, \ldots$ that starts at some root of $\mathcal{T}(\mathcal{F})$; such a path exists by lemma 13. Now define the behavior $\sigma = s_0 s_1 \ldots$ by $s_i(v) = \text{tt}$ iff $v \in \mathcal{G}_i$, for every $v \in \mathcal{V}$.

By induction on the structure of (pre-)formulas, we prove that for all (pre-)formulas A and all $i \geq 0$, if $A \in \tau(\mathcal{G}_i)$ then $\sigma|_i \approx A$ iff $A \in \mathcal{G}_i$.

Because of $\mathcal{F} \subseteq \mathcal{G}_0$ and $F \in \tau(\mathcal{F}) = \tau(\mathcal{G}_0)$ for every $F \in \mathcal{F}$, this in particular implies $\sigma \models F$ for all formulas $F \in \mathcal{F}$.

The inductive proof of the assertion is again standard; we only give a few cases:

$\Box[P]_v$: Assume $\Box[P]_v \in \tau(\mathcal{G}_i)$. Therefore, either $\Box[P]_v \in \mathcal{G}_i$ or $\neg \Box[P]_v \in \mathcal{G}_i$. In the former case, lemma 14.3 implies that, for all $j \geq i$, $P \in \mathcal{G}_j$ or $\{v, \bigcirc v\} \subseteq \mathcal{G}_j$ or $\{\neg v, \neg \bigcirc v\} \subseteq \mathcal{G}_j$. By induction hypothesis and lemma 14.1, this implies that, for all $j \geq i$, $\sigma|_j \approx P$ or $s_j(v) = s_{j+1}(v)$, and therefore $\sigma|_i \approx \Box[P]_v$.

   If $\neg \Box[P]_v \in \mathcal{G}_i$, then the definition of a complete path ensures that for some $j \geq i$, we have $\neg P \in \mathcal{G}_j$ and either $\{v, \neg \bigcirc v\} \subseteq \mathcal{G}_j$ or $\{\neg v, \bigcirc v\} \subseteq \mathcal{G}_j$, and the induction hypothesis and lemma 14.1 ensure $\sigma|_i \approx \neg \Box[P]_v$.

$\bigcirc F$: Assume $\bigcirc F \in \tau(\mathcal{G}_i)$. By lemma 14.1, $\bigcirc F \in \mathcal{G}_i$ iff $F \in \mathcal{G}_{i+1}$ iff (by induction hypothesis) $\sigma|_{i+1} \approx F$ iff $\sigma|_i \approx \bigcirc F$.   ∵

Theorem 16 (Completeness). *For every formula F, if $\models F$ then $\vdash F$.*

Proof. Assume $\models F$. Then $\sigma \models \neg F$ holds for no behavior σ, and lemma 15 implies that $\{\neg F\}$ is inconsistent, that is $\vdash \neg\neg F$, from which $\vdash F$ follows by theorem 8.1 and propositional logic.   ∵

(hx0)	F whenever F is tautological
(hx1)	$\Box F \Rightarrow F$
(hx2)	$\Box F \Rightarrow \Box[F]_v$
(hx3)	$\Box F \Rightarrow \Box[\Box\Box F]_v$
(hx4)	$\Box[F \Rightarrow \bigcirc F]_F \Rightarrow (F \Rightarrow \Box F)$
(hx5)	$\Box[P \Rightarrow Q]_v \Rightarrow (\Box[P]_v \Rightarrow \Box[Q]_v)$
(hx6)	$\Box[v' \not\equiv v]_v$
(hmp)	$F, F \Rightarrow G \vdash^h G$

(hx7)	$\Box[P]_v$ whenever P is tautological
(hx8)	$\Box[\bigcirc\neg F \equiv \neg\bigcirc F]_v$
(hx9)	$\Box[\bigcirc(F \Rightarrow G) \Rightarrow (\bigcirc F \Rightarrow \bigcirc G)]_v$
(hx10)	$\Box[\Box[P]_v \Rightarrow [P]_v]_w$
(hx11)	$\Box[P]_v \Rightarrow \Box[\bigcirc\Box[P]_v]_w$
(hx12)	$\Box[[P]_v \wedge \bigcirc\Box[P]_v \Rightarrow [P]_v]_w$
(hx13)	$\Box[\bigcirc\Box F \Rightarrow \Box[\bigcirc F]_v]_w$
(alw)	$F \vdash^h \Box F$

Fig. 2. The proof system Σ^h_{GTLA}.

5   A Homogeneous Axiomatization

The system Σ_{GTLA} is based on the auxiliary relation $\vdash\hspace{-0.5em}\sim$ besides the relation $\vdash$ that we are really interested in. One may argue that one could instead simply translate propositional (G)TLA to PTL and use any standard PTL proof system. Still, proofs may then contain PTL formulas such as $\Box\bigcirc F$ that are not even pre-formulas of GTLA. We now show that it is possible to eliminate the auxiliary relation $\vdash\hspace{-0.5em}\sim$ and define a "homogeneous" axiomatization of GTLA based on a single provability relation $\vdash^h$. The key observation is that in Σ_{GTLA}, a derived pre-formula can only be used via rule (sq) in the derivation of a formula. It therefore suffices to "box" the axioms (pax0)–(pax5) and rephrase (pre), (nex), and (pmp) accordingly. The proof system Σ^h_{GTLA} shown in figure 2 is based on this idea and some further simplifications. The following theorems and rules can be derived in Σ^h_{GTLA}; again, we refer to the full version [14] of this paper.

(H1)	$\Box[P]_v, \Box[P \Rightarrow Q]_v \vdash^h \Box[Q]_v$
(H3)	$\Box[P \Rightarrow Q]_v, \Box[Q \Rightarrow R]_v \vdash^h \Box[P \Rightarrow R]_v$
(H4)	$\Box[[P]_v \Rightarrow P]_v$

(H2)	$F \vdash^h \Box[F]_v$
(H5)	$\Box[\Box F \Rightarrow \bigcirc\Box F]_v$

Again, it is easy to derive analogues of these rules where the "index" v is replaced by a finite set of atomic propositions, or by a GTLA formula.

We now prove that the two provability relations agree (where $\mathcal{F} \vdash^h F$ is defined in the obvious way). In particular, Σ^h_{GTLA} is also sound and complete. It is therefore a matter of taste and convenience which axiomatization to use. The homogeneous proof system is aesthetically more satisfactory, but the heterogeneous system may be easier to use. (This is why the completeness proof was given for Σ_{GTLA}.)

Theorem 17. *For any set $\mathcal{F}$ of formulas and any formula F, $\mathcal{F} \vdash F$ iff $\mathcal{F} \vdash^h F$.*

Proof. "only if": By induction on the length of the assumed derivation in Σ_{GTLA}, we prove that $\mathcal{F} \vdash^h F$ whenever $\mathcal{F} \vdash F$ and that $\mathcal{F} \vdash^h \Box[P]_v$, for all atomic propositions v, whenever $\mathcal{F} \vdash\hspace{-0.5em}\sim P$, for any pre-formula P.

If F is from $\mathcal{F}$ or if it is an instance of (ax0), (ax1), (ax3), (ax4) or (ax5) then the assertion holds trivially because these axioms are also contained in Σ^h_{GTLA}. Axiom (ax2) is derived in Σ^h_{GTLA} as follows:

(1) $\Box[\Box F \Rightarrow \bigcirc\Box F]_F$ (H5)

(2) $\Box F \Rightarrow \Box\Box F$ (1)(hx4)(mp)

(3) $\Box\Box F \Rightarrow \Box[\Box F]_v$ (hx2)

(4) $\Box F \Rightarrow \Box[\Box F]_v$ (prop)(2)(3)

If the last step in the derivation of $\mathcal{F} \vdash F$ is an application of (mp) to previously derived formulas G and $G \Rightarrow F$ then by induction hypothesis we have $\mathcal{F} \overset{h}{\vdash} G$ and $\mathcal{F} \overset{h}{\vdash} G \Rightarrow F$, so $\mathcal{F} \overset{h}{\vdash} F$ follows by rule (hmp).

If the last step in the derivation of $\mathcal{F} \vdash F$ is an application of (sq) to some previously derived pre-formula P (so F is $\Box[P]_v$) then by the induction hypothesis for the second assertion we already have $\mathcal{F} \overset{h}{\vdash} \Box[P]_v$.

The second assertion is trivial if the last step in the derivation of $\mathcal{F} \mathrel{\vdash\!\!\!\sim} P$ is an instance of (pax0), (pax1), (pax2) or (pax5) because Σ_{GTLA} contains corresponding axioms. The case of (pax3) is taken care of by (H5). As for (pax4), it could obviously be replaced by

(pax4a) $\mathrel{\vdash\!\!\!\sim} \Box[P]_v \Rightarrow [P]_v$

(pax4b) $\mathrel{\vdash\!\!\!\sim} \Box[P]_v \Rightarrow \bigcirc\Box[P]_v$

(pax4c) $\mathrel{\vdash\!\!\!\sim} [P]_v \wedge \bigcirc\Box[P]_v \Rightarrow \Box[P]_v$

without changing the set of pre-formulas derivable in Σ_{GTLA}. The axioms (hx10) and (hx12) directly correspond to (pax4a) and (pax4c), so it remains to consider the case of (pax4b):

(1) $\Box[P]_v \Rightarrow \Box[\bigcirc\Box[P]_v]_w$ (hx11)

(2) $\Box[\Box[P]_v \Rightarrow \Box[\bigcirc\Box[P]_v]_w]_w$ (H2)(1)

(3) $\Box[\Box[\bigcirc\Box[P]_v]_w \Rightarrow [\bigcirc\Box[P]_v]_w]_w$ (hx10)

(4) $\Box[\Box[P]_v \Rightarrow [\bigcirc\Box[P]_v]_w]_w$ (H3)(2)(3)

(5) $\Box[[\bigcirc\Box[P]_v]_w \Rightarrow \bigcirc\Box[P]_v]_w$ (H4)

(6) $\Box[\Box[P]_v \Rightarrow \bigcirc\Box[P]_v]_w$ (H3)(4)(5)

Considering the rules, the case of (pmp) is handled by the induction hypothesis and (H1). If the last step in the derivation of $\mathcal{F} \mathrel{\vdash\!\!\!\sim} P$ is an application of (pre), then P is actually a formula and has already been derived, so we may assume $\mathcal{F} \overset{h}{\vdash} P$ by induction hypothesis. We obtain $\mathcal{F} \overset{h}{\vdash} \Box[P]_v$ by (H2).

If the last step is an application of (nex), then P is $\bigcirc F$, for some previously derived formula F, and by induction hypothesis we may assume $\mathcal{F} \overset{h}{\vdash} F$. We continue as follows:

(1) F (ind.hyp.)

(2) $\Box F$ (alw)(1)

(3) $\Box[\circ\Box F]_v$ (2)(hx3)(hmp)

(4) $\Box[\circ\Box F \Rightarrow \Box[\circ F]_v]_v$ (hx13)

(5) $\Box[\Box[\circ F]_v]_v$ (H1)(3)(4)

(6) $\Box[\Box[\circ F]_v \Rightarrow [\circ F]_v]_v$ (hx10)

(7) $\Box[[\circ F]_v]_v$ (H1)(5)(6)

(8) $\Box[\circ F]_v$ (7)(H4)(H1)

"if": The proof is again by induction on the assumed derivation of $\mathcal{F} \vdash^h F$. The cases of (hx0), (hx1), (hx4), (hx5), and (hx6) are trivial because Σ_{GTLA} contains the same axioms. For (hx7), (hx8), (hx9), (hx10), (hx12), and (hx13), the proof uses the corresponding axioms of Σ_{GTLA} and rule (sq). For (hmp) and (alw), the assertion follows from the induction hypothesis and rules (mp) and (alw), which is a derived rule in Σ_{GTLA}.

The axiom (hx2) is derived in Σ_{GTLA} as follows:

(1) $\vdash \Box F \Rightarrow F$ (ax1)(pre)

(2) $\vdash \Box[\Box F \Rightarrow F]_v$ (sq)(1)

(3) $\vdash \Box[\Box F]_v \Rightarrow \Box[F]_v$ (2)(ax4)(mp)

(4) $\vdash \Box F \Rightarrow \Box[\Box F]_v$ (ax2)

(5) $\vdash \Box F \Rightarrow \Box[F]_v$ (prop)(3)(4)

The derivation of (hx3) is similar, using (pax3) instead of (ax1). The derivation of (hx11) is very similar to that of (T4) and is omitted.   ∴

6 Quantification and Expressiveness

We have remarked in section 2 that propositional TLA is a sublanguage of GTLA whose pre-formulas are restricted to boolean combinations of primed and unprimed proposition symbols. On the other hand, GTLA can be considered as a sublanguage of PTL by removing the distinction between formulas and pre-formulas and considering $\Box[P]_v$ as a short-hand notation for the PTL formula $\Box(P \vee (\circ v \equiv v))$. Lamport's intention in introducing TLA was to allow the implementation relation between two descriptions of systems, even at different levels of abstraction, to be represented by model inclusion on the semantic side, and by validity of implication inside the logic [13]. Theorem 5 gives a formal expression to this intention, so GTLA satisfies Lamport's requirement.

Does GTLA add any undesired expressiveness to TLA? We will now show that this is not the case by proving that TLA and GTLA become equi-expressive once we add quantification over atomic propositions.

We introduce two auxiliary relations on behaviors that are used in a stuttering-invariant semantics of quantification over atomic propositions.

Definition 18. *For $v \in \mathcal{V}$ we define the relations $=_v$ and $\approx_v$ on behaviors as follows:*

1. *Two behaviors $\sigma = s_0 s_1 \ldots$ and $\tau = t_0 t_1 \ldots$ are equal up to v, written $\sigma =_v \tau$ if $s_i(w) = t_i(w)$ for all $i \geq 0$ and $w \in \mathcal{V}$, except possibly v.*
2. *The relation $\approx_v$, called similarity up to v, is defined as $\approx_v = (\simeq \circ =_v \circ \simeq)$, where $\simeq$ is stuttering equivalence and $\circ$ denotes relational composition.*

Proposition 19.

1. *For any $v \in \mathcal{V}$, the relations $=_v$ and $\approx_v$ are equivalence relations.*
2. *$(\simeq_V \circ \approx_v) = (\approx_v \circ \simeq_{V \cup \{v\}})$, for any $v \in \mathcal{V}$ and $V \subseteq \mathcal{V}$.*

We now extend GTLA by quantification over atomic propositions. Conceptually, existential quantification corresponds to the hiding of state components in specifications. Following Lamport, we use a bold quantifier symbol $\boldsymbol{\exists}$ to emphasize that its semantics is non-standard, which helps to preserve stuttering invariance.

Definition 20 ($\boldsymbol{\exists}$-GTLA).

1. *Formulas and pre-formulas of $\boldsymbol{\exists}$-GTLA are given inductively as in definition 1, except by adding the following clause:*
   6. *If F is a formula and $v \in \mathcal{V}$ then $\boldsymbol{\exists} v : F$ is a formula.*
2. *The semantics of $\boldsymbol{\exists}$-GTLA is obtained by adding the following clause to definition 2.*
   $$\sigma \models \boldsymbol{\exists} v : F \quad \text{iff} \quad \tau \models F \text{ holds for some } \tau \approx_v \sigma.$$

For a formula $F \equiv \boldsymbol{\exists} v : G$, we define the set $At(F)$ as $At(G) \setminus \{v\}$, since v becomes bound by the quantifier. Our definition of the semantics of quantification agrees with that of Lamport [12] who motivates it by showing that a naive definition would not preserve stuttering invariance. In fact, $\boldsymbol{\exists}$-GTLA is again insensitive to stuttering:

Theorem 21. *For any $\boldsymbol{\exists}$-GTLA formula F and behaviors σ, τ such that $\sigma \simeq_{At(F)} \tau$, we have $\sigma \models F$ iff $\tau \models F$.*

Proof. Extending the proof of theorem 5, we need only consider the case of a quantified formula $F \equiv \boldsymbol{\exists} v : G$. So assume that $\sigma \models F$ and that $\tau \simeq_{At(F)} \sigma$. Choose some behavior $\rho \approx_v \sigma$ such that $\rho \models G$, by the definition of $\sigma \models \boldsymbol{\exists} v : G$. Then $\tau (\simeq_{At(F)} \circ \approx_v) \rho$, and by proposition 19 it follows that $\tau (\approx_v \circ \simeq_{At(F) \cup \{v\}}) \rho$, which in turn implies $\tau (\approx_v \circ \simeq_{At(G)}) \rho$, because $\simeq_{At(F) \cup \{v\}} \subseteq \simeq_{At(G)}$. Hence, there exists some behavior π such that $\tau \approx_v \pi$ and $\pi \simeq_{At(G)} \rho$. By induction hypothesis it follows that $\pi \models G$, and thus $\tau \models F$ as required. $\therefore$

The semantics of quantified formulas is defined for $\boldsymbol{\exists}$-GTLA in the same way as for TLA. It is therefore immediate that quantified propositional TLA is again a sublogic of $\boldsymbol{\exists}$-GTLA. We now show that the two logics are equally expressive by effectively constructing an equivalent (quantified) TLA formula for every $\boldsymbol{\exists}$-GTLA formula.

Theorem 22. *For every $\boldsymbol{\exists}$-GTLA formula F there is a TLA formula F^{TLA} such that for every behavior σ, $\sigma \models F$ iff $\sigma \models F^{\mathrm{TLA}}$.*

Proof. In a first step, eliminate all quantified subformulas of F by successively choosing a fresh atomic proposition u for every (innermost) subformula $\exists\, v : G$ of F, and replacing F by $\exists\, u : \Box(u \equiv \exists\, v : G) \wedge F^*$, where F^* is obtained from F by replacing the subformula $\exists\, v : G$ by u. It is easy to see that the resulting formula is equivalent to the original formula F.

If F does not contain any quantified subformulas except those introduced above, the final formula F^* and every formula G in $\exists\, v : G$ is translated as follows: choose a new atomic proposition v_H for every (topmost) non-atomic formula H such that H or $\bigcirc H$ occurs inside a subformula $\Box[P]_v$. If $v_{H_1}, \ldots v_{H_n}$ are all the atomic propositions added in this way, replace the formula G under consideration by the TLA formula

$$\exists\, v_{H_1}, \ldots v_{H_n} : \Box(v_{H_1} \equiv H_1) \wedge \ldots \wedge \Box(v_{H_n} \equiv H_n) \wedge G^\dagger$$

where $G^\dagger$ results from G by replacing H_i by v_{H_i}, $\bigcirc H_i$ by v'_{H_i}, and all remaining preformulas $\bigcirc u$ by u'.

For example, if F is the formula

$$\Box[\Box v \Rightarrow \bigcirc\exists\, w : \Box[u \Rightarrow \bigcirc\Box w]_u]_v$$

the first step produces

$$\exists\, x : \Box(x \equiv \exists\, w : \Box[u \Rightarrow \bigcirc\Box w]_u) \wedge \Box[\Box v \Rightarrow \bigcirc x]_v$$

and F^{TLA} is the TLA formula

$$\exists\, x : \Box(x \equiv \exists\, w, y : \Box(y \equiv \Box w) \wedge \Box[u \Rightarrow y']_u) \wedge \exists\, z : \Box(z \equiv \Box v) \wedge \Box[z \Rightarrow x']_v$$

Given a behavior $\sigma = s_0 s_1 \ldots$, define the behavior $\tau = t_0 t_1 \ldots$ such that, for all $i \geq 0$, s_i and t_i agree on all propositions, except possibly on $v_{H_1}, \ldots v_{H_n}$, and where $t_i(v_{H_j}) = \text{tt}$ iff $\sigma|_i \models H_j$. The assertion now follows from the following fact, which is proved by structural induction: For any subformula H of G, $\sigma|_i \models H$ iff $\tau|_i \models H^\dagger$ where $H^\dagger$ is obtained from H in the same way as $G^\dagger$ is obtained from G.   ∵

For the GTLA formula $\Diamond\langle A \wedge \langle B \rangle_v \rangle_v$ considered in section 1, the procedure outlined in the proof of theorem 22 produces the TLA formula

$$\exists\, x : \Box(x \equiv \langle B \rangle_v) \wedge \Diamond\langle A \wedge x \rangle_v$$

7   Conclusion

The logic GTLA defined in this paper is a variant of Lamport's Temporal Logic of Actions. Like TLA, its formulas do not distinguish between behaviors that are stuttering equivalent. However, GTLA removes some apparently unnecessary restrictions on the syntax of formulas. We have also shown that the propositional fragment of GTLA admits a complete and reasonably simple axiomatization. In fact, our proof systems Σ_{GTLA} and Σ^h_{GTLA} are much simpler than Abadi's axiomatization [1] of a previous version of TLA. We have been careful to adhere to TLA as closely as possible. In particular, every TLA formula is a GTLA formula, and the two logics are equally expressive once we add (stuttering-invariant) quantification over flexible proposition symbols, as proposed by Lamport. By Rabinovich's result of expressive completeness for TLA [18], it follows that $\exists$-GTLA is expressively complete for all stuttering-invariant ω-languages definable in the monadic second-order theory of linear orders. We believe that GTLA is a more natural explanation of TLA's concepts. The difference between TLA and GTLA lies in the fact that in GTLA, formulas and pre-formulas are defined by mutual induction, whereas the syntax of TLA is defined in succeeding layers. In particular, GTLA allows temporal formulas to occur inside the $\square[\_]_v$ operator. The fact that such formulas can already expressed in TLA via quantification over flexible variables (cf. the proof of theorem 22) is easily overlooked in the original definition of TLA. It will remain to be seen whether the added flexibility of GTLA is useful for writing system specifications.

There are alternative definitions of stuttering-invariant temporal logics. The easiest way to obtain invariance under stuttering is to interpret the $\bigcirc$ operator of PTL not as referring to the immediate successor state, but to the first state in the future that differs in the valuation of some proposition (and to let $\bigcirc F$ be true if no such state exists). The resulting logic is axiomatized by a minor variant of the standard PTL proof system, and it is "globally" stuttering-invariant with respect to $\simeq$, but not "locally" with respect to $\simeq_{At(F)}$, as determined by the formula under consideration. Unfortunately, "global" stuttering invariance is not enough to represent implementation by model inclusion. Another example for a globally stuttering-invariant logic is Pnueli's TLR [17]. The logic MTL defined by Mokkedem and Méry [16] is "locally" stuttering-invariant, but the authors did not prove a completeness result. On the other hand, one could obtain an axiomatization of TLA or GTLA by interpreting their formulas in PTL. However, this approach breaks when it comes to quantified formulas, due the stuttering-invariant definition of the semantics for $\exists$ (see also [18]).

GTLA is easily extended to a first-order logic where atomic propositions are replaced by atomic predicate-logic formulas, except for the "subscripts" v in formulas $\square[P]_v$, which should then be state variables. (The generalization to arbitrary terms can be introduced as a short-hand notation as we have done in this paper.) Of course, one cannot hope for full completeness of first-order GTLA. Nevertheless, the ability to reason about the propositional fragment, together with some simple rules about (rigid) quantification has turned out to be extremely useful in the application of standard linear-time temporal logic, and we believe the same to be true for TLA.

References

[1] Martín Abadi. An axiomatization of Lamport's Temporal Logic of Actions. In Jos C. M. Baeten and Jan W. Klop, editors, *CONCUR '90, Theories of Concurrency: Unification and Extension*, volume 458 of *Lecture Notes in Computer Science*, pages 57–69, Berlin, 1990. Springer-Verlag. A revised version is available on the Web at http://www.research.digital. com/SRC/personal/Martin_Abadi/allpapers.html.

[2] Martín Abadi and Leslie Lamport. The existence of refinement mappings. *Theoretical Computer Science*, 81(2):253–284, May 1991.

[3] Martín Abadi and Leslie Lamport. An old-fashioned recipe for real time. Research Report 91, Digital Equipment Corporation, Systems Research Center, 1992. An earlier version, without proofs, appeared in [7, pages 1–27].

[4] Martín Abadi and Leslie Lamport. Conjoining specifications. *ACM Transactions on Programming Languages and Systems*, 17(3):507–534, May 1995.

[5] Martín Abadi and Stephan Merz. An abstract account of composition. In Jiří Wiedermann and Petr Hajek, editors, *Mathematical Foundations of Computer Science*, volume 969 of *Lecture Notes in Computer Science*, pages 499–508, Berlin, 1995. Springer-Verlag.

[6] Martín Abadi and Stephan Merz. On TLA as a logic. In Manfred Broy, editor, *Deductive Program Design*, NATO ASI series F, pages 235–272. Springer-Verlag, Berlin, 1996.

[7] J. W. de Bakker, C. Huizing, W. P. de Roever, and G. Rozenberg, editors. *Real-Time: Theory in Practice*, volume 600 of *Lecture Notes in Computer Science*. Springer-Verlag, Berlin, 1992. Proceedings of a REX Real-Time Workshop, held in The Netherlands in June, 1991.

[8] Dov Gabbay, Amir Pnueli, S. Shelah, and Jonathan Stavi. On the temporal analysis of fairness. In *Proceedings of the 7th Annual ACM Symposium on Principles of Programming Languages*, pages 163–173. ACM, 1980.

[9] Fred Kröger. *Temporal Logic of Programs*, volume 8 of *EATCS Monographs on Theoretical Computer Science*. Springer-Verlag, Berlin, 1987.

[10] Leslie Lamport. What good is temporal logic? In R. E. A. Mason, editor, *Information Processing 83: Proceedings of the IFIP 9th World Congress*, pages 657–668, Paris, September 1983. IFIP, North-Holland.

[11] Leslie Lamport. Hybrid systems in TLA$^+$. In Robert L. Grossman, Anil Nerode, Anders P. Ravn, and Hans Rischel, editors, *Hybrid Systems*, volume 736 of *Lecture Notes in Computer Science*, pages 77–102. Springer-Verlag, 1993.

[12] Leslie Lamport. The Temporal Logic of Actions. *ACM Transactions on Programming Languages and Systems*, 16(3):872–923, May 1994.

[13] Leslie Lamport. Refinement in state-based formalisms. Technical Note 1996–001, Digital Equipment Corporation, Systems Research Center, Palo Alto, California, December 1996.

[14] Stephan Merz. A more complete TLA. Technical Report, Institut für Informatik, Universität München. Available on the WWW at URL http://www.pst.informatik.uni-muenchen. de/~merz/papers/gtla.html, 1999.

[15] Stephan Merz. Isabelle/TLA. Available on the WWW at URL http://www.pst.informatik. uni-muenchen.de/~merz/isabelle/, 1997. Revised 1999.

[16] Abdelillah Mokkedem and Dominique Méry. A stuttering closed temporal logic for modular reasoning about concurrent programs. In *Temporal Logic (ICTL '94)*, volume 827 of *Lecture Notes in Computer Science*, pages 382–397, Bonn, 1994. Springer-Verlag.

[17] Amir Pnueli. System specification and refinement in temporal logic. In R.K. Shyamasundar, editor, *Foundations of Software Technology and Theoretical Computer Science*, volume 652 of *Lecture Notes in Computer Science*, pages 1–38. Springer-Verlag, 1992.

[18] Alexander Rabinovich. Expressive completeness of temporal logic of action. In L. Brim, J. Gruska, and J. Zlatuska, editors, *Mathematical Foundations of Computer Science*, volume 1450 of *Lecture Notes in Computer Science*, Brno, Czech Republic, August 1998. Springer-Verlag.

Formal Justification of the Rely-Guarantee Paradigm for Shared-Variable Concurrency: A Semantic Approach

F.S. de Boer[1], U. Hannemann[2], and W.-P. de Roever[3]

[1] Utrecht University, Department of Computer Science, Utrecht, The Netherlands,
frankb@cs.uu.nl
[2] Christian-Albrechts-Universität zu Kiel, Institut für Informatik und Praktische
Mathematik II, Kiel, Germany,
{uha,wpr}@informatik.uni-kiel.de

Abstract. This paper introduces a semantic analysis of the Rely-Guarantee
(R-G) approach to the compositional verification of shared-variable concurrency. The main contribution is a new completeness proof.

1 Introduction

In the Rely-Guarantee (R-G) approach to the compositional verification of shared-
variable concurrency [9, 10, 13] a property of a component process is, in essence,
stated as a pair (R, G) consisting of a guarantee property G that the component will satisfy provided the environment of the component satisfies the rely
property R. The interpretation of (R, G) has to be carefully defined so as to be
non-circular. Informally, a component P satisfies (R, G) if the environment of
P violates R *before* component P fails to satisfy G. In this paper we develop
a semantic approach to the formal justification of the Rely-Guarantee proof
method.

There are two basically different compositional semantic models for shared
variable concurrency: *reactive-sequence* semantics [4], and *Aczel-trace* semantics
[5]. A reactive sequence of a process P is a sequence of computation steps $\langle \sigma, \sigma' \rangle$
which represent the execution of an atomic action of P in state σ with resulting
state σ'. The resulting state of a computation step does not necessarily coincide
with the initial state of the subsequent computation step in the sequence. These
'gaps' represent the state-changes induced by the (parallel) environment. Note
that thus a reactive sequence abstracts from the *the number and granularity* of
the environmental actions. In contrast, an Aczel-trace of a process records all
the state-changes (both of the process and its environment) at the level of the
atomic actions.

Which of these two semantics of shared-variable concurrency provides a suitable basis for a formal justification of the R-G proof method? A seemingly natural interpretation of R-G specifications in terms of reactive sequences consists
of the following.

J. Wing, J. Woodcock, J. Davies (Eds.): FM'99, Vol. II, LNCS 1709, pp. 1245–1265, 1999.
© Springer-Verlag Berlin Heidelberg 1999

> If the gaps of a reactive sequence satisfy the rely condition then the computation steps of the sequence itself should satisfy the guarantee condition.

However under this interpretation the R-G proof rule for parallel composition will allow the derivation of incorrect R-G specifications. A proper semantic analysis based on reactive sequences can be obtained by the introduction of *stutter steps* as studied in [4]. In fact the addition of arbitrary stutter steps allows one to interpret the gaps of a reactive sequence as stemming from the execution of a single atomic action by the environment. In that case the reactive sequences semantics actually coincides with the Aczel semantics. In the Aczel semantics then we have the following interpretation of R-G specifications.

> If all the atomic environmental actions satisfy the rely condition then the computation steps of the sequence itself should satisfy the guarantee condition.

The main contribution of this paper consists of a new semantic completeness proof of the R-G proof method. An essential aspect of the R-G paradigm is that of finding a characterization of validity of a R-G specification which is non-circular. Indeed, the explicit breaking of cycles in chains of implications between R and G properties associated with the different processes which constitute an (open) network occurs already in Misra and Chandy's formulation of the *Assumption-Commitment* method [12] . As our completeness proof for the R-G paradigm demonstrates, preventing such circularities is straightforward once the appropriate concepts have been defined, and certainly simpler than any method proposed before. As worked out in [1], at an abstract level the breaking of such cycles of dependencies is connected to the use of constructive logics for reasoning about such dependencies, and is related to the use of such logics by Gerard Berry in his work on the semantics of the synchronous language Esterel [2]. The completeness proof for our proposed formalization of the Rely-Guarantee paradigm shows that there is a simple alternative to introducing such logics. The practical relevance of the new formal justification of the R-G paradigm presented in this paper lies in the fact that it determines the exact nature of the rely and guarantee predicates and, consequently, it provides a clear view on the way the R-G proof method is to be applied.

The approach which is followed in this paper is based on the inductive-assertion method [7] which is a methodology for proving state-based transition diagrams correct. It consists of the construction of an *assertion network* by associating with each location of a transition diagram a (state) predicate and with each transition a *verification condition* on the predicates associated with the locations involved; semantically, these predicates are viewed as sets of states. Thus it reduces a statement of correctness of a transition diagram, which consists of a finite number of locations, to a correspondingly finite number of verification conditions on predicates.

The inductive assertion method can be trivially generalized to concurrency by viewing a concurrent transition diagram as the product of its components and thus reducing it to a sequential system. However this global proof method leads to a number of verification conditions which is exponential in the number of components.

Compositional proof methods in general provide a reduction in the complexity of the number of verification conditions. In this paper we investigate the semantic foundations of the Rely-Guarantee proof method for concurrent systems obtained by sequential and parallel composition from basic transition diagrams. The components of such a concurrent system communicate via shared variables.

Technically, we introduce the new concept of R-G-inductive assertion networks for reasoning about the sequential components, i.e., the transition diagrams, of a concurrent system. By means of compositional proof rules such assertion networks can be used for deducing properties of the whole system.

The paper is organized as follows: we first introduce transition diagrams as our basic control structure and define in section 3 the reactive-sequence semantics. R-G correctness formulae are introduced in section 4 together with our proof system for them. In section 5 we formally define validity of R-G specifications w.r.t. the reactive sequence semantics and give an example why this choice of semantics is not appropriate. On top of the reactive sequence semantics we introduce the Aczel semantics, for which we prove in section 8 completeness of the proof system given in section 4. In section 7 we continue the comparison between Aczel semantics and reactive sequence semantics by extending the latter with stutter steps and proving that this change suffices to get a notion of validity of R-G formulae which is equivalent to the one based on Aczel semantics.

2 Syntax

The basic control construct of our semantical analysis of the Rely-Guarantee (R-G) proof system is that of a transition diagram, i.e., a labeled directed graph where each label denotes an instruction. Given a set of states Σ, an instruction has the following form: a boolean condition $b \in \mathcal{P}(\Sigma)$ followed by a state transformation $f \in \Sigma \to \Sigma$, notation: $b \to f$. The set of states Σ, with typical element σ, is given by $VAR \to VAL$, where VAR, with typical elements $x, y, z, \ldots$, is an infinite set of variables and VAL denotes the underlying domain of values. In the sequel sets of states often will be called *predicates* and (sets of) pairs of states will be called *action predicates*, with typical element *act*, as they reflect the effect of a state transformation (or action) upon the state. We have the following semantic characterization of the variables *involved* in a (action) predicate and a state transformation. This characterization is an approximation of the corresponding syntactic notion of *occurrence* of a variable.

Definition 1. *Let $\bar{x}$ denote a sequence $x_1, \ldots, x_n$ of distinct variables. By $\sigma(\bar{x}) = \sigma'(\bar{x})$ we then abbreviate $\bigwedge_{i=1}^{n} \sigma(x_i) = \sigma'(x_i)$. A predicate $\phi \in \mathcal{P}(\Sigma)$ involves the variables $x_1, \ldots, x_n$ if*

- $\forall \sigma, \sigma' \in \Sigma.\ \sigma(\bar{x}) = \sigma'(\bar{x}) \Rightarrow (\sigma \in \phi \Leftrightarrow \sigma' \in \phi).$

This condition expresses that the outcome of ϕ only depends on the variables $x_1, \ldots, x_n$.

Similarly, an action predicate $act \in \mathcal{P}(\Sigma \times \Sigma)$ involves the variables $x_1, \ldots, x_n$ if

- $\forall \langle \sigma_1, \sigma_1' \rangle, \langle \sigma_2, \sigma_2' \rangle \in \mathcal{P}(\Sigma \times \Sigma).$
  $(\sigma_1(\bar{x}) = \sigma_2(\bar{x}) \wedge \sigma_1'(\bar{x}) = \sigma_2'(\bar{x})) \Rightarrow (\langle \sigma_1, \sigma_1' \rangle \in act \Leftrightarrow \langle \sigma_2, \sigma_2' \rangle \in act).$

Finally, a function $f \in \Sigma \to \Sigma$ involves the variables $\bar{x}$ if

- $\forall \sigma, \sigma' \in \Sigma.\ \sigma(\bar{x}) = \sigma'(\bar{x}) \Rightarrow f(\sigma)(\bar{x}) = f(\sigma')(\bar{x})$
- $\forall \sigma \in \Sigma, y \notin \bar{x}.\ f(\sigma)(y) = \sigma(y)$

The first condition expresses that if two states σ and σ' agree with respect to the variables $\bar{x}$, then so do their images under f. The second condition expresses that any other variable is not changed by f.

We restrict ourselves to state-transformations and (action) predicates for which there exists a *finite* set of variables which are involved. The set of variables involved in the state-transformation f, (action) predicates ϕ and act, we denote by $var(f)$, $var(\phi)$ and $var(act)$, respectively. For predicate ϕ and action predicate act let $\sigma \models \phi$ denote $\sigma \in \phi$, and $\langle \sigma, \sigma' \rangle \models act$ denote $\langle \sigma, \sigma' \rangle \in act$. By $\models \phi$ (and $\models act$) we denote the validity of ϕ (and act), i.e., for all σ, $\sigma \models \phi$ (and for all $\langle \sigma, \sigma' \rangle$, $\langle \sigma, \sigma' \rangle \models act$).

Given a sequence of distinct variables $\bar{x} = x_1, \ldots, x_n$ and a sequence of values $\bar{v} = v_1, \ldots, v_n$, the state-transformation $(\sigma : \bar{x} \mapsto \bar{v})$ is defined by

$$(\sigma : \bar{x} \mapsto \bar{v})(y) \stackrel{\text{def}}{=} \begin{cases} \sigma(y) \text{ if } y \notin \{x_1, \ldots, x_n\} \\ v_i \quad \text{ if } y = x_i \end{cases}$$

For a sequence of distinct variables $\bar{x} = x_1, \ldots, x_n$, $\exists \bar{x}.\phi$ denotes the set of states σ such that $(\sigma : \bar{x} \mapsto \bar{v}) \in \phi$, for some sequence of values $\bar{v} = v_1, \ldots, v_n$. Similarly, $\exists \bar{x}.act$, act an action predicate, denotes the set of pairs of states $\langle \sigma, \sigma' \rangle$ such that $\langle (\sigma : \bar{x} \mapsto \bar{v}), (\sigma' : \bar{x} \mapsto \bar{v'}) \rangle \in act$, for some sequences of values $\bar{v} = v_1, \ldots, v_n$ and $\bar{v'} = v_1', \ldots, v_n'$. Finally, given a state-transformation f, the state-transformation $\exists \bar{x}.f$ is defined by $\exists \bar{x}.f(\sigma) \stackrel{\text{def}}{=} (f(\sigma) : \bar{x} \mapsto \sigma(\bar{x}))$, where $\sigma(\bar{x})$ denotes the sequence of values $\sigma(x_1), \ldots, \sigma(x_n)$.

We have the following formal definition of a transition diagram.

Definition 2. *A basic transition diagram is a quadruple (L, T, s, t), where L is a finite set of locations l, T is a finite set of transitions $(l, b \to f, l')$, and s and t are the entry and exit locations, respectively, which are different ($s \neq t$). There are no outgoing transitions starting in t.*

A program P is either a basic transition diagram or defined inductively as a sequential composition $P_1; P_2$ or parallel composition $P_1 \parallel P_2$ of two programs P_1 and P_2.

3   Reactive Sequence Semantics

The Rely-Guarantee paradigm aims at specifying both terminating *and nonterminating* computations in a compositional style. We denote termination by the symbol $\sqrt{}$.

For the formal definition of reactive sequence semantics as introduced in, e.g., [4], we use the following transition relation.

Definition 3. *For a given basic transition diagram* $P = \langle L, T, s, t \rangle$,

$$l \xrightarrow{\langle \sigma, \sigma' \rangle} l'$$

denotes a transition of P *when for some* $(l, b \to f, l') \in T$ *one has that* $\sigma \models b$ *and* $\sigma' = f(\sigma)$.

The following axiom and rule allow to compute the reflexive transitive closure of this transition relation:

$$l \xrightarrow{\epsilon} l \quad and \quad \frac{l \xrightarrow{w} l', l' \xrightarrow{w'} l''}{l \xrightarrow{w \cdot w'} l''},$$

where ϵ *denotes the empty sequence, and* "$\cdot$" *the operation of concatenation.*

Given a basic transition diagram P, $l \xrightarrow{w} l'$ thus indicates that starting at l execution of P can generate the sequence of computation steps w arriving at l'. Such a sequence w is called a *reactive sequence*. For a non-empty reactive sequence $w = w' \cdot \langle \sigma, \sigma' \rangle$ we define $laststep(w) \overset{\text{def}}{=} \langle \sigma, \sigma' \rangle$. A reactive sequence $w = \langle \sigma_1, \sigma_1' \rangle \langle \sigma_2, \sigma_2' \rangle \cdots \langle \sigma_n, \sigma_n' \rangle$ is called a *connected* sequence if for all $i = 1, \ldots, n-1$ we have that $\sigma_i' = \sigma_{i+1}$. A 'gap' $\langle \sigma_i', \sigma_{i+1} \rangle$ between two consecutive computation steps $\langle \sigma_i, \sigma_i' \rangle$ and $\langle \sigma_{i+1}, \sigma_{i+1}' \rangle$ represents the state-transformation induced by the (parallel) environment. Note that such a gap, therefore, abstracts from the *granularity* of the environment, i.e., the actual number of atomic computation steps performed by the environment.

Definition 4. *For a basic transition diagram* $P = \langle L, T, s, t \rangle$, $l \in L$ *we define* $\mathcal{R}_l \llbracket P \rrbracket \overset{\text{def}}{=} \{w \mid s \xrightarrow{w} l\}$.

We distinguish sequences which are *terminated* w.r.t. the executing process by ending them with the $\sqrt{}$ symbol. *Computations* are either reactive sequences or reactive sequences followed by a $\sqrt{}$ symbol. Therefore, if a computation w contains a $\sqrt{}$, it is of the form $w'\sqrt{}$ with w' a reactive sequence containing no $\sqrt{}$ symbol.

Definition 5. *The reactive-sequence semantics* $\mathcal{R} \llbracket P \rrbracket$ *of a program* P *is defined as follows: For* $P = \langle L, T, s, t \rangle$ *we define*

$$\mathcal{R} \llbracket P \rrbracket \overset{\text{def}}{=} \bigcup_{l \in L} \mathcal{R}_l \llbracket P \rrbracket \cup \{w\sqrt{} \mid w \in \mathcal{R}_t \llbracket P \rrbracket \}.$$

For $P = P_1; P_2$ we define

$$\mathcal{R}\,[\![P]\!] \stackrel{\text{def}}{=} \{w \,|\, w \in \mathcal{R}'\,[\![P_1]\!]\,\} \cup \{w \cdot w' \,|\, w\sqrt{} \in \mathcal{R}\,[\![P_1]\!] \wedge w' \in \mathcal{R}\,[\![P_2]\!]\,\},$$

where $\mathcal{R}'\,[\![P_1]\!]$ denotes the set of non-terminated sequences of P_1, that is, those sequences not ending with $\sqrt{}$. Finally, for $P = P_1 \parallel P_2$ we define

$$\mathcal{R}\,[\![P]\!] \stackrel{\text{def}}{=} \{w \,|\, w \in w_1 \tilde{\parallel} w_2, w_1 \in \mathcal{R}\,[\![P_1]\!]\,, w_2 \in \mathcal{R}\,[\![P_2]\!]\,\},$$

where $w_1 \tilde{\parallel} w_2$ denotes the set of all interleavings of w_1 and w_2, ending in $\sqrt{}$ if and only if both w_1 and w_2 end in $\sqrt{}$.

The semantics $\mathcal{R}\,[\![P]\!]$ contains all the finite prefixes of all the computations of P, including the *non-terminating* computations. Recall from the introduction that a process P satisfies (R, G) provided P's environment violates R *before* P violates G, i.e., *at any stage of an on-going computation P's actions should satisfy G as long as R remains satisfied by P's environment.* This is mathematically expressed by requiring (R, G) to be satisfied by all prefixes of a computation of P.

So how does one characterize the semantics of programs in which the this process of parallel composition with new environments has come to an end, i.e., the semantics of a closed system? This is done by considering only reactive sequences in which the gaps are "closed", i.e., by considering the subset of connected sequences.

4   The Rely-Guarantee Proof Method

In this section we first give an intuitive definition of Rely-Guarantee correctness formulae and their interpretation and then present a proof system for this type of correctness formula that is fairly standard as far as the composition rules are concerned [15]. For correctness formulae that reason about basic transition diagrams we adapt Floyd's inductive assertion network method [7] to the additional requirements of the R-G method.

Definition 6. *Let pre and post be predicates denoting sets of states, rely and guar be action predicates, and P be a program, then $\langle rely, guar \rangle : \{pre\}\ P\ \{post\}$ is called an R-G correctness formula.*

Traditionally, *pre* and *post* impose conditions upon the initial, respectively, final state of a computation, whereas *rely* and *guar* impose conditions upon environmental transitions, respectively, transitions of the process itself. This is captured by the following intuitive characterization of validity of an R-G formula:
    Whenever

1) P is invoked in an initial state which satisfies *pre*, and
2) the environment satisfies *rely*,

then

3) any transition of P satisfies $guar$, and
4) if a computation terminates, its final state satisfies $post$.

We generalize Floyd's method to the additional requirements of R-G formulae and define for $P = \langle L, T, s, t \rangle$ an R-G-inductive assertion network $\mathcal{Q}(rely, guar)$: $L \to \mathcal{P}(\Sigma)$, i.e., we associate with each location l a predicate $\mathcal{Q}_l$ as follows:

Definition 7 (R-G-inductive assertion networks). *An assertion network $\mathcal{Q}$ is R-G-inductive w.r.t. rely and guar for $P = \langle L, T, s, t \rangle$ if:*

- *For every $(l, b \to f, l') \in T$ and state σ: if $\sigma \models \mathcal{Q}_l \wedge b$ then $\langle \sigma, f(\sigma) \rangle \models guar$ and $f(\sigma) \models \mathcal{Q}_{l'}$.*
- *For every $l \in L$ and states σ and σ': if $\sigma \models \mathcal{Q}_l$ and $\langle \sigma, \sigma' \rangle \models rely$ then $\sigma' \models \mathcal{Q}_l$.*

We abbreviate that $\mathcal{Q}$ is an R-G-inductive assertion network w.r.t. $rely$ and $guar$ for P by $\mathcal{Q}(rely, guar) \vdash P$. We have the following rule for deriving R-G specifications about basic transition diagrams.

Rule 8 (Basic diagram rule)   *For $P = \langle L, T, s, t \rangle$:*

$$\frac{\mathcal{Q}(rely, guar) \vdash P}{\langle rely, guar \rangle : \{\mathcal{Q}_s\} \; P \; \{\mathcal{Q}_t\}}$$

The following rules are standard.

Rule 9 (Sequential composition rule)

$$\frac{\langle rely, guar \rangle : \{\phi\} \; P_1 \; \{\chi\}, \; \langle rely, guar \rangle : \{\chi\} \; P_2 \; \{\psi\}}{\langle rely, guar \rangle : \{\phi\} \; P_1; P_2 \; \{\psi\}}$$

Rule 10 (Parallel composition rule)

$$\frac{\begin{array}{c} \models rely \vee guar_1 \to rely_2 \\ \models rely \vee guar_2 \to rely_1 \\ \models guar_1 \vee guar_2 \to guar \\ \langle rely_i, guar_i \rangle : \{pre\} \; P_i \; \{post_i\}, \; i = 1, 2 \end{array}}{\langle rely, guar \rangle : \{pre\} \; P_1 \| P_2 \; \{post_1 \wedge post_2\}}$$

Rule 11 (Consequence rule)

$$\frac{\begin{array}{c} \langle rely, guar \rangle : \{\phi\} \; P \; \{\psi\} \\ \models \phi_1 \to \phi, \; \models \psi \to \psi_1, \\ \models rely_1 \to rely, \models guar \to guar_1 \end{array}}{\langle rely_1, guar_1 \rangle : \{\phi_1\} \; P \; \{\psi_1\}}$$

Definition 12. *A set of program variables* $\bar{z} = z_1, \ldots, z_n$ *is called a set of auxiliary variables of a program P if:*

- *For any boolean condition b of P we have $\bar{z} \cap var(b) = \emptyset$, and*
- *any state transformation of P can be written as $f \circ g$, i.e., a composition of state-transformations f and g, such that $\bar{z} \cap var(f) = \emptyset$, and the write variables of g, i.e, those variables x such that $g(\sigma)(x) \neq \sigma(x)$, for some state σ, are among $\bar{z}$.*

We have the following rule for deleting auxiliary variables:

Rule 13 (Auxiliary variables rule)

$$\frac{\langle rely, guar \rangle : \{\phi\}\ P'\ \{\psi\}}{\langle \exists \bar{z}.rely, guar \rangle : \{\exists \bar{z}.\phi\}\ P\ \{\psi\}},$$

where $\bar{z}$ is a set of auxiliary variables of P', guar and ψ do not involve $\bar{z}$, and P is obtained from P' by replacing every state transformation f in P' by $\exists \bar{z}.f$.

Finally, how does one reason about closed programs? This is done by requiring $rely$ to be id, the identity on states.

Derivability of an R-G formula $\langle rely, guar \rangle : \{\phi\}\ P\ \{\psi\}$ in this proof system is expressed by

$$\vdash \langle rely, guar \rangle : \{\phi\}\ P\ \{\psi\}.$$

5   R-G Validity w.r.t. Reactive Sequences Semantics

In order to define the validity of a R-G specification $\langle rely, guar \rangle : \{\phi\}P\{\psi\}$ we have first to determine the exact meaning of the precondition ϕ and the postcondition ψ: Are these predicates referring to the initial and final state of P itself or of the complete system (which includes the environment of P)? Following the literature we choose the latter option. Therefore we define the validity of a R-G specification for P in terms of a triple consisting of an initial (i.e., w.r.t. the complete system) state σ, a reactive sequence w of P, which records the sequence of computation steps of P, and a final state σ', which is final under the assumption that the environment has terminated as well. Whereas for terminated computations σ' is the final state of the complete system, we can interpret it as the "current" state for non-terminating computations, i.e., the last observation point at hand.

We define for a reactive sequence w and states σ, σ' the *complement* of w with respect to initial state σ and final state σ', denoted by $\overline{\langle \sigma, w, \sigma' \rangle}$, as follows:

Definition 14.   *We define*

$$\overline{\langle \sigma, \epsilon, \sigma' \rangle} \stackrel{\text{def}}{=} \langle \sigma, \sigma' \rangle,$$
$$\overline{\langle \sigma, \langle \sigma_1, \sigma_2 \rangle \cdot w, \sigma' \rangle} \stackrel{\text{def}}{=} \langle \sigma, \sigma_1 \rangle \cdot \overline{\langle \sigma_2, w, \sigma' \rangle}.$$

The complement of a reactive sequence w with respect to a given initial state σ and final state σ' thus specifies the behavior of the environment.

Definition 15. *For a reactive sequence* $w = \langle\sigma_1,\sigma_1'\rangle\cdots\langle\sigma_n,\sigma_n'\rangle$, $w \models act$ *indicates that* $\langle\sigma_i,\sigma_i'\rangle \models act$, $i = 1,\ldots,n$, *(and* $w\sqrt{} \models act$ *indicates that* $w \models act$).

Now we are sufficiently equipped to introduce the following notion of validity of R-G specifications.

Definition 16 (R-Validity of R-G specifications). *We define*

$$\models_R \langle rely,\ guar\rangle : \{\phi\}\ P\ \{\psi\}$$

by

for all $w \in \mathcal{R}\,[\![P]\!]$, *states* σ *and* σ', *if* $\sigma \models \phi$ *and* $\overline{\langle\sigma,w,\sigma'\rangle} \models rely$ *then* $w \models guar$ *and* $w = w'\sqrt{}$, *for some* w', *implies* $\sigma' \models \psi$.

Intuitively, a R-G specification $\langle rely,\ guar\rangle : \{\phi\}\ P\ \{\psi\}$ is R-valid if for every reactive sequence w of P, initial state σ and final state σ' (of the parallel composition of P with its environment) the following holds: if the initial state σ satisfies ϕ and all the steps of the environment as specified by $\overline{\langle\sigma,w,\sigma'\rangle}$ satisfy $rely$ then all the steps of w satisfy $guar$ and upon termination the final state σ' satisfies ψ.

Example 1. We have the following *counter-example* to the soundness of the parallel composition rule with respect to the notion of R-validity above: It is not difficult to check that

$$\models_R \langle x' = x + 1, x' = x + 1\rangle : \{x = 0\}x := x + 1\{x = 3\}.$$

By an application of the parallel composition rule to $x := x + 1 \,\|\, x := x + 1$, where both assignments $x := x + 1$ are specified as above, we then would derive

$$\langle true, x' = x + 1\rangle : \{x = 0\}x := x + 1 \,\|\, x := x + 1\{x = 3\}$$

which is clearly not R-valid.

(Here $x := x + 1$ abbreviates the transition diagram $\langle\{s,t\}, \{(s, true \to f, t)\}, s, t\rangle$, where f increments x by 1.)

In the full paper we show that soundness of the parallel composition rule with respect to this notion of validity requires all *rely*-predicate to be *transitive*, i.e., that $\langle\sigma,\sigma'\rangle \models rely$ and $\langle\sigma',\sigma''\rangle \models rely$ imply $\langle\sigma,\sigma''\rangle \models rely$.

This observation motivates our next section where we give a different interpretation of R-G specifications in terms of Aczel-traces. These Aczel-traces will provide more detailed information about environmental steps.

6   Aczel Semantics

An Aczel-trace is a connected sequence of process-indexed state pairs. It can thus be seen as the extension of connected reactive sequence in which every atomic action contains as additional information an identifier which represents the executing process.

We assume to have a set Id of *process identifiers* with typical element $I_1, I_2, \ldots$. The complement of a set of identifiers $V \subseteq Id$ is denoted by $\overline{V} \stackrel{\text{def}}{=} Id \setminus V$.

Definition 17. *A process-indexed state pair is a triple $\langle \sigma, I, \sigma' \rangle \in \Sigma \times Id \times \Sigma$. An Aczel-trace π is a non-empty connected sequence of process-indexed state pairs, that might end with a $\sqrt{}$-symbol.*
For an Aczel-trace π we define $first(\pi)$ and $last(\pi)$ by the first and last state of the sequence, respectively: $first(\langle \sigma, I, \sigma' \rangle \cdot \pi') = \sigma$ and $last(\pi' \cdot \langle \sigma, I, \sigma' \rangle) = \sigma'$. ($last(\pi \sqrt{}) = last(\pi)$).

In order to define the set of Aczel-traces of a program in terms of its reactive-sequence semantics we introduce the following projection operation on Aczel-traces.

Definition 18. *Let $V \subseteq Id$ be a set of identifiers.*

$$\epsilon[V] \stackrel{\text{def}}{=} \epsilon,$$
$$(\langle \sigma, I, \sigma' \rangle \cdot \pi)[V] \stackrel{\text{def}}{=} \pi[V], \;\; if \; I \notin V,$$
$$(\langle \sigma, I, \sigma' \rangle \cdot \pi)[V] \stackrel{\text{def}}{=} \langle \sigma, \sigma' \rangle \cdot \pi[V], \;\; if \; I \in V,$$
$$\pi \sqrt{}[V] \stackrel{\text{def}}{=} \pi[V] \sqrt{}.$$

We define the Aczel semantics of a program P parametric with respect to a set of identifiers V. The elements of V are used to identify the transitions of P. Thus we can extract a reactive sequence of P out of an Aczel-trace by projecting onto this set of identifiers. Within Aczel-traces, the purpose of these identifiers is to distinguish between steps of the process and steps of the environment.

Definition 19. *For $P = \langle L, T, s, t \rangle$ a basic transition diagram, $l \in L$, and $V \subseteq Id$, we define*

$$Acz_V^l \llbracket P \rrbracket \stackrel{\text{def}}{=} \{\pi \mid \pi[V] \in \mathcal{R}_l \llbracket P \rrbracket \}.$$

By $Acz_V \llbracket P \rrbracket$ then we denote $Acz_V^t \llbracket P \rrbracket$. For composed systems P we define

$$Acz_V \llbracket P \rrbracket \stackrel{\text{def}}{=} \{\pi \mid \pi[V] \in \mathcal{R} \llbracket P \rrbracket \}.$$

The proof of the following proposition is straightforward and therefore omitted.

Proposition 20. *Let V_1 and V_2 be disjoint sets of identifiers. We have for every $P = P_1 \parallel P_2$*

$$Acz_{V_1} \llbracket P_1 \rrbracket \cap Acz_{V_2} \llbracket P_2 \rrbracket \subseteq Acz_V \llbracket P \rrbracket,$$

with $V = V_1 \cup V_2$. Note that in general the converse does not hold.

We have the following interpretation of R-G specifications.

Definition 21 (Aczel-Validity of R-G specifications). *We define*

$$\models_A \langle rely, \, guar \rangle : \{\phi\} \; P \; \{\psi\}$$

by

> *For all sets of identifiers V and $\pi \in \mathcal{A}cz_V \llbracket P \rrbracket$ if $first(\pi) \models \phi$ and $\pi[\overline{V}] \models rely$ then $\pi[V] \models guar$ and $\pi = \pi' \sqrt{}$ implies $last(\pi) \models \psi$.*

The R-G method as presented above is sound with respect to the Aczel-trace semantics, for the soundness proof of the basic diagram rule we refer to the full paper. For the other rules detailed proofs in the Aczel-trace set-up are given in [15].

The main difference between this notion of validity and the one based on reactive sequences is that now *every atomic* computation step of the environment has to satisfy the rely condition. Consequently, for Example 1 we have

$$\not\models_A \langle x' = x + 1, x' = x + 1 \rangle : \{x = 0\} x := x + 1 \{x = 3\},$$

since there is an arbitrary number of environmental steps possible.

7   Reactive Sequences Reconsidered

As observed above the reactive sequences semantics $\mathcal{R}$ does not provide a correct interpretation of R-G specifications. More precisely, it requires the predicates $rely_1$ and $rely_2$ in the parallel composition rule to be transitive. However, we can obtain such a correct interpretation of R-G specifications by the introduction of arbitrary *stutter steps* of the form $\langle \sigma, \sigma \rangle$.

Definition 22. *Let $\mathcal{R}_\tau \llbracket P \rrbracket$ be the smallest set containing $\mathcal{R} \llbracket P \rrbracket$ which satisfies the following:*

$$w_1 \cdot w_2 \in \mathcal{R}_\tau \llbracket P \rrbracket \text{ implies } w_1 \cdot \langle \sigma, \sigma \rangle \cdot w_2 \in \mathcal{R}_\tau \llbracket P \rrbracket.$$

This abstraction operation is required in order to obtain a *fully abstract* semantics (see [4, 3, 11]). We observe that the corresponding notion of validity, which we denote by $\models_{R_\tau}$, requires the *guar* predicate to be *reflexive*, i.e. $\langle \sigma, \sigma \rangle \models guar$, for every state σ. However, given this restriction we do have that the two different notions of validity $\models_A$ and $\models_{R_\tau}$ coincide.

Theorem 23. *Let $\langle rely, guar \rangle : \{\phi\} P \{\psi\}$ be such that guar is reflexive. Then*

$$\models_A \langle rely, guar \rangle : \{\phi\} P \{\psi\} \text{ if and only if } \models_{R_\tau} \langle rely, guar \rangle : \{\phi\} P \{\psi\}.$$

Proof. Let $\models_A \langle rely, guar \rangle : \{\phi\} P \{\psi\}$ and $w \in \mathcal{R}_\tau [\![P]\!]$. Furthermore let σ and σ' be such that $\sigma \models \phi$, $\langle \sigma, w, \sigma' \rangle \models rely$. Then the requirements of $\models_{R_\tau}$ are satisfied because of the existence of a corresponding $\pi \in \mathcal{A}cz_V [\![P]\!]$, for any (non-empty) V. Formally, we obtain such a corresponding π by defining the Aczel-trace $A(\sigma, w, \sigma')$ by induction on the length of w. Let $E \notin V$ and $I \in V$. Then

$$A(\sigma, \epsilon, \sigma') \stackrel{\text{def}}{=} \langle \sigma, E, \sigma' \rangle,$$
$$A(\sigma, \langle \sigma_1, \sigma_2 \rangle \cdot w, \sigma') \stackrel{\text{def}}{=} \langle \sigma, E, \sigma_1 \rangle \cdot \langle \sigma_1, I, \sigma_2 \rangle \cdot A(\sigma_2, w, \sigma').$$

Conversely, let $\models_{R_\tau} \langle rely, guar \rangle : \{\phi\} P \{\psi\}$ and $\pi = \langle \sigma_1, I_1, \sigma_2 \rangle \cdots \langle \sigma_n, I_n, \sigma_{n+1} \rangle \in \mathcal{A}cz_V [\![P]\!]$ such that $\sigma_1 \models \phi$ and $\langle \sigma_k, \sigma_{k+1} \rangle \models rely$, for $I_k \notin V$. Then the requirements of $\models_A$ are satisfied because of the existence of a corresponding $w \in \mathcal{R}_\tau [\![P]\!]$. Formally, we define $R(\pi)$ by induction on the length of π:

$$R(\epsilon) \stackrel{\text{def}}{=} \epsilon,$$
$$R(\langle \sigma_1, I_1, \sigma_2 \rangle \cdot \pi) \stackrel{\text{def}}{=} \begin{cases} \langle \sigma_1, \sigma_2 \rangle \cdot R(\pi) & I_1 \in V \\ \langle \sigma_2, \sigma_2 \rangle \cdot R(\pi) & I_1 \notin V, \end{cases}$$

and use $R(\pi) \in \mathcal{R}_\tau [\![P]\!]$ as reactive sequence corresponding to π to prove that *guar* and ψ hold in their respective (pairs of) states. Note that thus the insertion of stutter steps is used to obtain the 'gaps' corresponding to the environmental steps in π, providing extra observation points.

8   Completeness

This section presents the completeness proof for our proof system and constitutes the very justification of the paper. We have the following main theorem (the remainder of this section is devoted to its proof).

Theorem 24. *The proof system presented in section 4 is (relative) complete w.r.t. the Aczel-trace semantics, i.e.,*

$$\models_A \langle rely, guar \rangle : \{\phi\} \ P \ \{\psi\} \ implies \vdash \langle rely, guar \rangle : \{\phi\} \ P \ \{\psi\}.$$

We prove the derivability of an Aczel-valid R-G specification by induction on the structure of the program P.

Basic case

Given a valid R-G specification $\models_A \langle rely, guar \rangle : \{\phi\} P \{\psi\}$, with $P = \langle L, T, s, t \rangle$ a basic transition diagram, we associate with every location l of P the *strongest postcondition* $SP_l(\phi, rely, P)$. The resulting network we denote by $\mathcal{SP}$. Intuitively, a state σ belongs to $SP_l(\phi, rely, P)$ if there is a computation of P *together with its environment* that reaches location l of P, starting in a state satisfying ϕ, such that all environment steps satisfy *rely*.

Definition 25. *For $P = \langle L, T, s, t \rangle$ we define*

$$\sigma \models SP_l(\phi, rely, P)$$

by

> $\sigma \models \phi$ *(in case l equals s) or* $first(\pi) \models \phi$ *and* $\pi[\overline{V}] \models rely$, *for some set V of process identifiers and some* $\pi \in Acz_V^l \llbracket P \rrbracket$, *with* $last(\pi) = \sigma$.

Note that any state σ' which can be reached from a state σ which satisfies $SP_l(\phi, rely, P)$ by a sequence of *rely*-steps also satisfies $SP_l(\phi, rely, P)$, because any computation sequence of P together with its environment that reaches location l of P in state σ can be extended to a similar sequence reaching σ'. Hence $SP_l(\phi, rely, P)$ is invariant under *rely*.

We also need a characterization of the computation steps of a program P. This is given by the *strongest guarantee* $SG(\phi, rely, P)$, an action predicate describing those transitions of P which are actually executed by P in some computation, provided ϕ is satisfied initially, and every environment transition satisfies *rely*.

Definition 26. *Let P be an arbitrary program. We define*

$$\langle \sigma, \sigma' \rangle \models SG(\phi, rely, P)$$

by

> $first(\pi) \models \phi$ *and* $\pi[\overline{V}] \models rely$, *for some set V of process identifiers and* $\pi \in Acz_V \llbracket P \rrbracket$, *with* $\langle \sigma, \sigma' \rangle = laststep(\pi[V])$.

The following basic properties of SP_l and SG follow immediately from their definitions.

Lemma 27. *For P a basic transition diagram we have*

i) $\models_A \langle rely, SG(\phi, rely, P) \rangle : \{\phi\} \ P \ \{SP_t(\phi, rely, P)\}$.
ii) $\models_A \langle rely, guar \rangle : \{\phi\} \ P \ \{\psi\}$ *implies*
    a) $\models SP_t(\phi, rely, P) \rightarrow \psi$.
    b) $\models SG(\phi, rely, P) \rightarrow guar$.
iii) $\models \phi \rightarrow SP_s(\phi, rely, P)$.

Moreover, we have the following lemma.

Lemma 28. *Given a basic transition diagram P, $\mathcal{SP}$ is an R-G-inductive assertion network w.r.t. rely and $SG(\phi, rely, P)$.*

Proof. Let $l \in L$ and $\sigma \models SP_l(\phi, rely, P)$. So, for some set V of process identifiers, there exists π such that $\pi \in Acz_V^l \llbracket P \rrbracket$, $first(\pi) \models \phi$, $\pi[\overline{V}] \models rely$ and $last(\pi) = \sigma$.

- Let $\sigma \models b$ and $(l, b \rightarrow f, l') \in T$. By executing $(l, b \rightarrow f, l')$ we reach l' with $\sigma' = f(\sigma)$. We first prove that $\sigma' \models SP_{l'}(\phi, rely, P)$. Without loss of generality we may assume that V is non-empty. Let $I \in V$. Since $\pi \in Acz_V^l \llbracket P \rrbracket$ we get that $\pi' = \pi \cdot \langle \sigma, I, \sigma' \rangle \in Acz_V^{l'} \llbracket P \rrbracket$. We have that $first(\pi) = first(\pi') \models \phi$ (note that π is non-empty). Moreover, $\pi[\overline{V}] \models rely$ and $\pi[\overline{V}] = \pi'[\overline{V}]$. Thus, $\pi'[\overline{V}] \models rely$. Obviously we have $last(\pi') = \sigma'$ and therefore $\sigma' \models SP_{l'}(\phi, rely, P)$. Additionally, since $\langle \sigma, \sigma' \rangle = laststep(\pi'[V])$ we derive that $\langle \sigma, \sigma' \rangle \models SG(\phi, rely, P)$.

– Next let $\langle \sigma, \sigma' \rangle \models rely$. We have for $I \notin V$ that $\pi' = \pi \cdot \langle \sigma, I, \sigma' \rangle \in Acz_V^l \llbracket P \rrbracket$. Again we have that $first(\pi) = first(\pi') \models \phi$. Since $\pi[\overline{V}] \models rely$, $\langle \sigma, \sigma' \rangle \models rely$ and $\pi'[\overline{V}] = \pi[\overline{V}] \cdot \langle \sigma, \sigma' \rangle$ we conclude that $\pi'[\overline{V}] \models rely$. Finally, $last(\pi') = \sigma'$. Thus, $\sigma' \models SP_l(\phi, rely, P)$.

By our basic rule 8 we thus derive that

$$\vdash \langle rely, SG(\phi, rely, P) \rangle : \{SP_s(\phi, rely, P)\} \ P \ \{SP_t(\phi, rely, P)\}.$$

Since by Lemma 27

– $\models \phi \to SP_s(\phi, rely, P)$,
– $\models SP_t(\phi, rely, P) \to \psi$, and
– $\models SG(\phi, rely, P') \to guar$

hold, we derive by the consequence rule

$$\vdash \langle rely, guar \rangle : \{\phi\} \ P \ \{\psi\}.$$

Composed programs

Next we consider the remaining cases $P = P_1; P_2$ and $P = P_1 \parallel P_2$. First we generalize definition 25.

Definition 29. *We define for every system P,*

$$\sigma \models SP(\phi, rely, P)$$

if

$first(\pi) \models \phi$ and $\pi[\overline{V}] \models rely$, for some set V of process identifiers and some $\pi\surd \in Acz_V \llbracket P \rrbracket$, with $last(\pi) = \sigma$.

Note that for $P = (L, T, s, t)$ a basic transition diagram $SP(\phi, rely, P) = SP_t(\phi, rely, P)$. The basic properties of Lemma 27 carry over to the general case.

Lemma 30. *For every system P we have*

i) $\models_A \langle rely, SG(\phi, rely, P) \rangle : \{\phi\} \ P \ \{SP(\phi, rely, P)\}$.
ii) $\models_A \langle rely, guar \rangle : \{\phi\} \ P \ \{\psi\}$ *implies*
     a) $\models SP(\phi, rely, P) \to \psi$.
     b) $\models SG(\phi, rely, P) \to guar$.

Sequential composition

Now consider the case of sequential composition. Let

$$\models_A \langle rely, guar \rangle : \{\phi\} P_1; P_2 \{\psi\}.$$

By the induction hypothesis we thus obtain

$$\vdash \langle rely, SG(\phi, rely, P_1) \rangle : \{\phi\} P_1 \{SP(\phi, rely, P_1)\}$$

and

$$\vdash \langle rely, SG(\phi', rely, P_2)\rangle : \{\phi'\}P_2\{SP(\phi', rely, P_2)\},$$

where $\phi' = SP(\phi, rely, P_1)$. Furthermore,

$$\models_A \langle rely, guar\rangle : \{\phi\}P_1; P_2\{\psi\}$$

implies

$$\models_A \langle rely, guar\rangle : \{\phi\}P_1\{SP(\phi, rely, P_1)\}$$

and

$$\models_A \langle rely, guar\rangle : \{SP(\phi, rely, P_1)\}P_2\{\psi\}.$$

Using the above lemma we thus obtain by the consequence rule

$$\vdash \langle rely, guar\rangle : \{\phi\}P_1\{SP(\phi, rely, P_1)\}$$

and

$$\vdash \langle rely, guar\rangle : \{SP(\phi, rely, P_1)\}P_2\{\psi\}.$$

An application of the rule for sequential composition concludes the proof.

Parallel composition

We have now arrived at the most interesting case $P = P_1 \| P_2$. Let

$$\models_A \langle rely, guar\rangle : \{\phi\}P_1 \| P_2\{\psi\}.$$

Our task is to construct predicates that fit the parallel composition rule 10. In particular we have to define predicates $rely_i, guar_i, pre, post_i$, $i = 1, 2$, such that for some augmentation P_i' of P_i with auxiliary variables the R-G specifications

$$\models_A \langle rely_i, guar_i\rangle : \{pre\}\, P_i'\, \{post_i\}, i = 1, 2,$$

and the corresponding side conditions hold.

In order to define such predicates we introduce *histories*.

Definition 31. *A history θ is a sequence of indexed states (I, σ), with $I \in Id$.*

An indexed state (I, σ) indicates that the process I is active in state σ.

We assume given a set of history variables $HVAR \subseteq VAR$ with typical element h. For h a history variable, $\sigma(h)$ is a history.

Our next step is to augment every transition of $P_1 \| P_2$ with a corresponding update to the fresh history variable h (i.e., h does not occur in P nor in the given predicates $rely, guar, \phi$, and ψ). This history variable h records the history of P, i.e., the sequence of state changes of process P *together with its environment*, plus the active components responsible for these changes. Without loss of generality we may assume that P_1 and P_2 are two distinct process identifiers. We then transform each transition $(l, b \to f, l')$ of a constituent of P_i to $(l, b \to f \circ g, l')$, where $g \stackrel{\text{def}}{=} (\sigma : h \mapsto h \cdot (P_i, \sigma))$, i.e., $g(\sigma)$ is like σ, except for the value of h which is extended by (P_i, σ). This augmented version of P_i will be denoted by P_i'.

Note that in the augmented process $P' = P_1'\|P_2'$ boolean conditions do not involve the history variable h, and that h does not occur in assignments to non-history variables. I.e., the history variable h is an *auxiliary variable* which does not influence the flow-of-control of a process.

We have to ensure, *in order to have the complete computation history recorded in h*, that every possible environmental action should update the history variable correctly. I.e., we should prevent that some process is setting, e.g., $h := \epsilon$, by formulating additional requirements upon *rely*; also we change the given precondition ϕ to ensure that initially h denotes the empty sequence.

Definition 32. *We define*

- $\langle \sigma, \sigma' \rangle \models rely'$ *if and only if* $\langle \sigma, \sigma' \rangle \models rely$ *and* $\sigma'(h) = \sigma(h) \cdot (E, \sigma)$
- $\sigma \models \phi'$ *if and only if* $\sigma \models \phi$ *and* $\sigma(h) = \epsilon$,

where $E \in Id$ is a process identifier distinct from P_1 and P_2, representing "the environment".

It is straightforward to prove that

$$\models_A \langle rely, guar \rangle : \{\phi\}P_1\|P_2\{\psi\}$$

implies

$$\models_A \langle rely', guar \rangle : \{\phi'\}P_1'\|P_2'\{\psi\}.$$

Moreover, we introduce the following rely condition e_i which ensures a correct update of the history variable h by the environment of P_i' when executed in the context $P_1' \| P_2'$. Note that the environment of P_i' in the context of $P_1' \| P_2'$ consists of the common environment of P_1' and P_2' and the other component P_j', $i \neq j$.

Definition 33. *Let for $i = 1, 2$,*

$$\langle \sigma, \sigma' \rangle \models e_i$$

be defined by

$$\sigma'(h) = \sigma(h) \cdot (E, \sigma) \text{ or } \sigma'(h) = \sigma(h) \cdot (P_j, \sigma),$$

where $i \neq j (\in \{1, 2\})$.

We are now in a position to define the predicates that will satisfy the requirements of the parallel composition rule.

Definition 34. *We define for $i = 1, 2$ the following predicates*

- $rely_i \stackrel{\text{def}}{=} rely' \vee SG(\phi', e_j, P_j')$ $(i \neq j)$;
- $post_i \stackrel{\text{def}}{=} SP(\phi', rely_i, P_i')$;
- $guar_i \stackrel{\text{def}}{=} SG(\phi', rely_i, P_i')$.

The predicate $rely_i$ is intended to specify the steps of the environment of P_i' in the context of $P_1' \parallel P_2'$. The computation steps of the common environment of P_1' and P_2' are specified by the action predicate $rely'$ whereas the computation steps of the other component are specified by the action predicate $SG(\phi', e_j, P_j')$ which states the existence of a corresponding computation of P_j' in which the environment correctly updates the history variable h.

By Lemma 30 we have for $i = 1, 2$

$$\models_A \langle rely_i, guar_i \rangle : \{\phi'\} \ P_i' \ \{post_i\}.$$

By the induction hypothesis we thus have

$$\vdash \langle rely_i, guar_i \rangle : \{\phi'\} P_i' \{post_i\}.$$

We therefore now prove the corresponding requirements of the parallel composition rule.

Lemma 35. *We have for $i, j = 1, 2$ and $i \neq j$*

$$\models rely' \lor guar_i \rightarrow rely_j,$$

and

$$\models guar_1 \lor guar_2 \rightarrow guar.$$

Proof. The validity of the implication

$$rely' \lor guar_i \rightarrow rely_j$$

follows from the validity of the implication

$$SG(\phi', rely_i, P_i') \rightarrow SG(\phi', e_i, P_i').$$

Validity of this latter implication in turn follows from the validity of the implication $rely_i \rightarrow e_i$. Let $\langle \sigma, \sigma' \rangle \models rely_i$. In case $\langle \sigma, \sigma' \rangle \models rely'$, by definition of $rely'$, we have that $\sigma'(h) = \sigma(h) \cdot (E, \sigma)$, otherwise $\langle \sigma, \sigma' \rangle \models SG(\phi', e_j, P_j')$, and so we have by definition of SG and the construction of P_j', that $\sigma'(h) = \sigma(h) \cdot (P_j, \sigma)$.

In order to prove the validity of the implication

$$guar_1 \lor guar_2 \rightarrow guar$$

let $\langle \sigma, \sigma' \rangle \in guar_i$. By definition of $guar_i$ there exists

$$\pi = \langle \sigma_1, I_1, \sigma_2 \rangle \cdots \langle \sigma_n, I_n, \sigma_{n+1} \rangle \in \mathcal{A}cz_V \left[\!\left[P_i' \right]\!\right],$$

for some set of process identifiers V such that $\sigma_1 \models \phi'$, $\sigma_n = \sigma$, $\sigma_{n+1} = \sigma'$, and $\langle \sigma_k, \sigma_{k+1} \rangle \models rely_i$, whenever $I_k \notin V$. Note that by definition of $rely_i$ and construction of P_j', $(i \neq j)$, $I_k \notin V$ implies either $\sigma_{k+1}(h) = \sigma_k(h) \cdot (E, \sigma_k)$ or $\sigma_{k+1}(h) = \sigma_k(h) \cdot (P_j, \sigma_k)$. Moreover, for $I_k \in V$ we have by construction of P_i' that $\sigma_{k+1}(h) = \sigma_k(h) \cdot (P_i, \sigma_k)$. Thus we may assume without loss of generality that $\sigma_{k+1}(h) = \sigma_k(h) \cdot (I_k, \sigma_k)$, $k = 1, \ldots, n$ (simply rename the identifiers I_k accordingly). Since, $\sigma_1(h) = \epsilon$, we derive by a straightforward induction that $\sigma_{k+1}(h) = (I_1, \sigma_1) \cdots (I_k, \sigma_k)$, $k = 1, \ldots, n$.

Either there is a last P_j step in the Aczel trace π or there isn't one. If there is no such step in π then also $\pi \in \mathcal{A}cz_{V \cup W} \llbracket P_1' \| P_2' \rrbracket$, for any set W of identifiers, because there are no P_j steps in π. Otherwise, let $\langle \sigma_l, P_j, \sigma_{l+1} \rangle$ be the last P_j $(i \neq j)$ step of the Aczel-trace π. We have that $\langle \sigma_l, \sigma_{l+1} \rangle \models SG(\phi', e_j, P_j')$. By definition of $SG(\phi', e_j, P_j')$ there exists

$$\pi' = \langle \sigma_1', I_1', \sigma_2' \rangle \cdots \langle \sigma_m', I_m, \sigma_{m+1}' \rangle \in \mathcal{A}cz_W \llbracket P_j' \rrbracket,$$

for some set of process identifiers W such that $\sigma_1' \models \phi'$, $\sigma_m' = \sigma_l$, $\sigma_{m+1}' = \sigma_{l+1}$, and $\langle \sigma_k', \sigma_{k+1}' \rangle \models e_j$, whenever $I_k' \notin W$. By definition of e_j and the construction of P_j', in a similar manner as argued above, we may assume without loss of generality that $\sigma_{k+1}'(h) = \sigma_k'(h) \cdot (I_k', \sigma_k')$, $k = 1, \ldots, m$. Since, $\sigma_1'(h) = \epsilon$, we thus derive by a straightforward induction that $\sigma_{k+1}'(h) = (I_1', \sigma_1') \cdots (I_k', \sigma_k')$, $k = 1, \ldots, m$. But $\sigma_{m+1}'(h) = \sigma_{l+1}(h)$, and consequently we derive that π' is a prefix of π. Since π is an extension of π' consisting of non-P_j steps only, by definition of $\mathcal{A}cz_W \llbracket P_j' \rrbracket$ we subsequently derive that $\pi \in \mathcal{A}cz_W \llbracket P_j' \rrbracket$. By proposition 20, $\mathcal{A}cz_V \llbracket P_1' \rrbracket \cap \mathcal{A}cz_W \llbracket P_2' \rrbracket \subseteq \mathcal{A}cz_{V \cup W} \llbracket P_1' \| P_2' \rrbracket$. From this we derive that $\pi \in \mathcal{A}cz_{V \cup W} \llbracket P_1' \| P_2' \rrbracket$. Since $\pi[\overline{V \cup W}] \models rely'$ and $\sigma_1 \models \phi'$ we thus infer from the validity of

$$\models_A \langle rely', guar \rangle : \{\phi'\} P_1' \| P_2' \{\psi\}$$

that $\langle \sigma, \sigma' \rangle \models guar$.

By an application of the parallel composition rule we thus obtain

$$\vdash \langle rely', guar \rangle : \{\phi'\} P_1' \| P_2' \{post_1 \wedge post_2\}.$$

In order to proceed we first show that $\models post_1 \wedge post_2 \rightarrow \psi$. Let $\sigma \models post_1 \wedge post_2$. By definition of $post_1$ and $post_2$ there exist computations

$$\pi = \langle \sigma_1, I_1, \sigma_2 \rangle \cdots \langle \sigma_n, I_n, \sigma_{n+1} \rangle \sqrt{} \in \mathcal{A}cz_{V_1} \llbracket P_i' \rrbracket$$

and

$$\pi' = \langle \sigma_1', I_1', \sigma_2' \rangle \cdots \langle \sigma_m', I_m', \sigma_{m+1}' \rangle \sqrt{} \in \mathcal{A}cz_{V_2} \llbracket P_j' \rrbracket$$

such that $\sigma = \sigma_{n+1} = \sigma_{m+1}'$, $\sigma_1 \models \phi'$, $\sigma_1' \models \phi'$, $\langle \sigma_k, \sigma_{k+1} \rangle \models rely_1$, $I_k \notin V_1$, and $\langle \sigma_k', \sigma_{k+1}' \rangle \models rely_2$, $I_k' \notin V_2$. By definition of $rely_i$ and construction of P_i' $(i = 1, 2)$, we may assume without loss of generality that $V_1 = \{P_1\}$, $V_2 = \{P_2\}$, $\sigma_{k+1}(h) = \sigma_k(h) \cdot (I_k, \sigma_k)$, $k = 1, \ldots, n$, and $\sigma_{k+1}'(h) = \sigma_k'(h) \cdot (I_k', \sigma_k')$, $k = 1, \ldots, m$ (simply rename the identifiers I_k, $k = 1, \ldots, n$, and I_l', $l = 1, \ldots, m$, accordingly). Since $\sigma_1(h) = \sigma_1'(h) = \epsilon$, we derive by a straightforward induction that $\sigma_{n+1}(h) = (I_1, \sigma_1) \cdots (I_n, \sigma_n)$ and $\sigma_{m+1}'(h) = (I_1', \sigma_1') \cdots (I_m', \sigma_m')$. Thus we derive from $\sigma_{n+1}(h) = \sigma_{m+1}'(h)$ that $\pi = \pi'$. Since $\mathcal{A}cz_{V_1} \llbracket P_1' \rrbracket \cap \mathcal{A}cz_{V_2} \llbracket P_2' \rrbracket \subseteq$

$\mathcal{A}cz_V \, [\![P_1'\|P_2']\!]$, we derive that $\pi \in \mathcal{A}cz_V \, [\![P_1'\|P_2']\!]$. By the given validity of the R-G-specification

$$\models_A \langle rely, guar \rangle : \{\phi\} P_1 \| P_2 \{\psi\}$$

(note that ϕ' implies ϕ and $rely'$ implies $rely$) we thus derive that $\sigma \models \psi$.

By an application of the consequence rule we thus obtain

$$\vdash \langle rely', guar \rangle : \{\phi'\} P_1' \| P_2' \{\psi\}.$$

Next we apply the auxiliary variables rule:

$$\vdash \langle \exists h.rely', guar \rangle : \{\exists h.\phi'\} P_1 \| P_2 \{\psi\}.$$

Finally, by an application of the consequence rule (using $\models rely \rightarrow \exists h.rely'$ and $\models \phi \rightarrow \exists h.\phi'$), we conclude

$$\vdash \langle rely, guar \rangle : \{\phi\} P_1 \| P_2 \{\psi\}.$$

9   Conclusion, Future, and Related Work

This paper advocates the usefulness of a semantic analysis of proof methods for concurrency. Such an analysis abstracts away from any expressibility issues and is especially effective in case of giving soundness and completeness proofs. By focussing on the semantic issues we discovered facts which were not known before about the R-G paradigm: that reactive-sequence semantics are inappropriate for modeling this paradigm, that Aczel-trace semantics does provide a correct interpretation for R-G validity, and that by adding finite stutter steps to reactive sequences a model is obtained which does model R-G validity adequately.

Furthermore, in such a semantic analysis one separates reasoning about sequential components from reasoning about parallel composition, by defining for the former an appropriate concept of inductive assertion networks (here: R-G-inductive assertion networks), and reasoning about the latter by Hoare-like proof rules. This considerably simplifies the reasoning process (just compare [15]), and focusses attention on the one central issue, namely, how to formulate a minimal number of rules for reasoning compositionally about shared-variable concurrency for open systems in a sound and semantically complete way. Such rules provide the basis for machine-supported compositional reasoning about concurrency in PVS, as used in, e.g., Hooman's work [8].

Finally, by focussing on the essential elements underlying completeness of the proposed proof method we discovered a proof which is much simpler than any previous "proof" appearing in the literature (of the correctness of none of which we are convinced anymore), and which extends the usual patterns of completeness proofs for Hoare-like reasoning about concurrency in a straightforward way.

This work arose out of a careful analysis of of the completeness proof presented in [14, 15], which is based on reduction to the completeness proof of the method of Owicki & Gries. We believe that our direct completeness proof provides more insight in the R-G proof method. Also it is much simpler and therefore easier to check its correctness.

An interesting avenue of research opens up by applying the various methods which Gérard Berry employed, in his characterizations of the semantics of Esterel, to the Assume-Guarantee paradigm (the name of which was invented by Natarajan Shankar).

The present paper is the third one in a series of papers on the semantical analysis of compositional proof methods for concurrency, and will eventually appear as part of a chapter on compositional proof methods for concurrency in [6].

References

[1] M. Abadi and G. D. Plotkin. A logical view of composition. *Theoretical Computer Science*, 114(1):3–30, 1993.

[2] G. Berry. The Constructive Semantics of Esterel. Book in preparation, http://www-sop.inria.fr/meije/esterel/doc/main-papers.html, 1999.

[3] S. Brookes. *A fully abstract semantics of a shared variable parallel language.* In Proceedings 8th Annual IEEE Symposium on Logic in Computer Science, IEEE Computer Society Press, pages 98–109, 1993.

[4] F.S. de Boer, J.N. Kok, C. Palamedessi, and J.J.M.M. Rutten. The failure of failures: towards a paradigm for asynchronous communication. In Baeten and Groote, editors, *CONCUR'91*, LNCS 527. Springer-Verlag, 1991.

[5] W.-P. de Roever. The quest for compositionality - a survey of assertion-based proof systems for concurrent programs, part 1: Concurrency based on shared variables. In *Proc. of IFIP Working Conf, The Role of Abstract Models in Computer Science, North-Holland*, 1985.

[6] W.-P. de Roever, F.S. de Boer, U. Hannemann, J. Hooman, Y. Lakhnech, M. Poel, and J. Zwiers. Concurrency Verification: An Introduction to State-based Methods. To appear.

[7] R.W. Floyd. Assigning meanings to programs. In *Proceedings AMS Symp. Applied Mathematics*, volume 19, pages 19–31, Providence, R.I., 1967. American Mathematical Society.

[8] J.Hooman. Compositional Verification of Real-Time Applications. In W.-P. de Roever, H. Langmaack, and A. Pnueli (eds.) *Compositionality: The Significant Difference. International Symposium, COMPOS'97, Bad Malente, Germany, September 8 –12, 1997*. pp. 130–149, Springer-Verlag, LNCS 1536, 1998.

[9] C.B. Jones. *Development methods for computer programs including a notion of interference*. PhD thesis, Oxford University Computing Laboratory, 1981.

[10] C.B. Jones. Tentative steps towards a development method for interfering programs. *ACM Transactions on Programming Languages and Systems*, 5(4):596–619, 1983.

[11] L. Lamport. The Temporal Logic of Actions. *ACM Transactions on Programming Languages and Systems*, 16(3), pp. 872–923, 1994.

[12] J. Misra and K.M. Chandy. Proofs of networks of processes. *IEEE Transactions on Software Engeneering*, 7(7):417–426, 1981.

[13] E. Stark. A proof technique for rely/guarantee properties. In *Proceedings of 5th Conference on Foundations of Software Technology and Theoretical Computer Science*, LNCS 206, pages 369–391. Springer-Verlag, 1985.

[14] Q. Xu. *A theory of state-based parallel programming.* DPhil. Thesis, Oxford University computing Laboratory, 1992.

[15] Q. Xu, W.-P. de Roever, and J. He. The rely-guarantee method for verifying shared-variable concurrent programs. *Formal Aspects of Computing*, 9(2):149–174, 1997.

Relating Z and First-Order Logic

Andrew Martin*

Oxford University Software Engineering Centre
Computing Laboratory, Wolfson Building
Parks Road, Oxford OX1 3QD, UK.
apm@comlab.ox.ac.uk

Abstract Despite being widely regarded as a gloss on first-order logic and set theory, Z has not been found to be very supportive of proof. This paper attempts to distinguish between the different philosophies of proof in Z. It discusses some of the issues which must be addressed in creating a proof technology for Z, namely schemas, undefinedness, and what kind of logic to use.

1 Introduction

The Z notation [26] is gaining widespread acceptance as a useful means of specifying software systems. Tool support for Z, though given impetus by the Z standardization activity [20], is quite varied, especially in the area of proof. There appears to be little consensus about what proving properties of Z specifications actually means. Different people seem to understand Z and proof differently.

Z has been widely regarded as a sylized form of classical first-order logic and set theory, with a simple type system (but this is not a universal view; see below). The schema language complicates this relationship considerably. As the semantics of schemas has become more complex, it has been increasingly unclear whether Z needs its own logic, or whether it can be manipulated using a familiar system. In creating proof tools, some authors do not appear to have even asked this question, but have assumed a Z semantics which corresponds exactly with the computational logic of some host system.

Therefore, the language of discourse has become surprisingly clouded. The aim of this paper is to relate the different understandings of the nature of proof in Z, and to explain the issues involved. Automatic translations from one notational system to another—or one logic to another—are of course part of any total logical system for Z. Since Z is a large and rich notation, the verification of those translations becomes an issue itself.

Outline of the paper The following section sets the scene, discussing the notion and purpose of proof in Z. Section 3 defines many terms, according to long-standing logical terminology. Somehow these have not always been followed in the Z community, or have come to mean different things to different people. The

---

* Paper written at the University of Southampton.

J. Wing, J. Woodcock, J. Davies (Eds.): FM'99, Vol. II, LNCS 1709, pp. 1266–1280, 1999.

next section surveys some of the leading approaches to this topic—and points to a more detailed survey elsewhere. Sections 5 and 6 detail the two most basic issues which affect reasoning in Z: schemas, and the issue of undefinedness. Section 7 considers related and future work. Alternative approaches are not based on first-order logic at all. For the future, the key challenge seems to be in finding ways to manage the complexity of Z proofs. The paper finishes with some conclusions.

2   Z, Logical Calculi, and Semantics

Z is quite clearly a logical notation. The central task of writing a Z specification is writing schemas. The main content of a schema is found in its predicate part. This is a collection of sentences of first-order logic. The syntax which Z has settled upon is slightly different from that found in most logical texts, but this is not significant.

Whilst in some philosophical disciplines logical notation may be introduced largely as a means to add precision to statements, in mathematical work, and in particular, in software engineering, it is more usual to add a calculus to the presentation of a logical notation. Logic is not used as a language in its own right, but as a means to facilitate proof activity.

In this regard, Z is unusual, since whilst it is not 'semantics free' it has arisen with a rich language, but little in the way of logic. Spivey [25] presents a denotational semantics, and also elements of a logical calculus for the schema notation. More mundane logical proof rules are assumed and not stated.

This reminds us that there are at least two possible approaches to giving meaning to a piece of formal text: we can give a denotational semantics; a model in some system which is already understood—this is Spivey's main approach (despite the use of Z as the metalanguage). Alternatively, we can give a logical calculus, a system of reasoning which relates terms of the language without interpreting them. Such a logic is a higher-level description, and is, in general more practical.

Of course, many writers of specifications will be concerned neither with the model nor with the logic. They are interested in writing specifications and communicating ideas unambiguously, but not in proving that their specifications are complete, say. Nevertheless, a logical system—however expressed—is an important mental tool in writing specifications. The specifier needs to know whether, for example, writing

$$x \notin \operatorname{dom} f \wedge f' = f \cup \{x \mapsto y\}$$

is equivalent to writing

$$f' = f \oplus \{x \mapsto y\} \quad .$$

The application of the definitions of the various operators is a logical process. Some such questions are easily answered, others will require careful detailed reasoning. The answer depends upon the choice of logical system, and will not usually be answered with reference to the model. Most logics will agree on most answers, but in some cases—particularly where application of partial functions is involved—the answers will vary.

If the Z user *does* wish to undertake more formal reasoning (in calculation of preconditions, for example) then the detailed choice of logical system (whether to support a proof by hand, or by machine) will have a significant effect, potentially on both the ease or difficulty of the proof, and perhaps the outcome.

A number of approaches to proof in Z have been taken as a result of the lack of a 'standard' answer. Some of these are explored below; a comprehensive survey is presented in [18], covering both traditional logical presentations, and computational logics/proof tools for Z.

3   Languages and Logic

For some reason, the language used to discuss Z semantics and logic is frequently at odds with the usual terminology of mathematical logic [19, 8]. This section seeks to establish some definitions.

3.1   Terminology

In this paper, we see the Z notation as a *language* in the logical sense. The study of how Z is to be expressed is a matter of *syntax*. The study of meaning, and the relationship of one Z specification (or predicate) with another—whether via models or logics—is the concern of *semantics*.

We may construct a semantics for Z by associating with each term in the language some object in an underlying structure (typically, a set). A particular semantic construction is a *model* of a particular Z specification (or predicate) if the relationships between terms in the specification also hold in the model (if it makes the predicate *true*). A predicate is *logically valid* if it holds in all models. It is logically valid relative to a specification if it holds in all the models of that specification.

A *logic for Z* is a collection of axioms and rules of inference written using the Z notation. These rules and axioms may be used inductively to define which predicates are *logical consequences* of others. Those which are the logical consequence of the empty set of predicates (or, equivalently, the logical consequence of only the axioms of the logic) are known as *theorems*. Usually, such a logic will allow the use of the definitions in a specification (schemas, generic definitions, etc.), so that a predicate may be a theorem *of a specification*, if it is a logical consequence of the definitions in that specification.

A logic for Z may be proven *sound* in some model by showing that each of its theorems is logically valid. It is traditional to ask whether a logic is also *complete* — i.e. whether every logically valid predicate is also a theorem. A consequence of Gödel's incompleteness theorem is that it is not possible to find a complete logic for Z with respect to any conventional underlying theory of sets.

A different question is to ask whether a logic for Z is complete with respect to the mapping into the underlying set theory: this relies on treating the underlying theory as itself a formal system, rather than a model as above. Such an alternative understanding will be discussed below.

Alternative Views Z has often been seen not as a language, but as a sugared syntax for ZF set theory. In this view, most of the foregoing terminology is not used. Instead, one seeks to exhibit a mapping from Z to an underlying language of sets, and to conduct all one's reasoning in the corresponding theory of sets. Since the core parts of Z are simple set theory, the mapping is sometimes invisible, and one is able to use the normal rules of set theory on Z terms. If a partial inverse for the mapping can be found (it will not be bijective, since the richness of Z syntax is not typically present in the underlying system) then the underlying theory might be said to induce a logic for Z, though this construction has not been explored.

Noteworthy is that this process of translation is *largely indistinguishable* from the process of providing a model for Z, as described above. This may help to explain why the process of Z standardization which began by seeking to provide a logic for Z has lately focussed most of its semantic efforts on the model theory of Z.

In many of the proof tools described in the literature, there is no attempt to describe a logic for Z. Instead, the tool is constructed by 'embedding' Z in some computational logic system. The most successful embeddings use higher-order logic (as described in the HOL tool, or in Isabelle's HOL theory) as the 'host'. The embeddings are on a spectrum from 'shallow' to 'deep', depending on how much of Z's semantic structure is retained in the translation. To produce a deep embedding (i.e. one which retains much of Z's structure) is a non-trivial task. As a result, the question arises of how to validate this translation.

A proof in the underlying theory may be demonstrably sound for models of that theory, but the embedding approach is unable to ask whether this represents a sound proof for Z, since there is nothing against which to judge the translation. The difference between truth and provability clearly borders at some point on the philosophical, and is outside the scope of this paper.

3.2   Theorems

It has long been customary to write conjectures (or theorems) in Z specifications as

$$\vdash pred$$

the intention being to speculate (or indicate) that *pred* is a logical consequence of the foregoing specification. Various Z paragraphs have been written to the left of the turnstile ($\vdash$)—schemas, declarations and predicates, etc.—the intended meaning being that the foregoing specification, augmented with those paragraphs, has *pred* as a logical consequence,

Thus, for example, in Spivey's [26] *BirthdayBook* specification, he demonstrates (without writing $\vdash$) that

$$AddBirthday \vdash known' = known \cup \{name?\}$$

meaning that in the context of this specification, and further, within the scope of *AddBirthday* as a definition, *known* has the property shown.

Spivey avoids use of $\vdash$ in this way, but other authors do not. Since the system of logic to be used in such a proof is usually ill-defined, this is a most remarkable abuse of notation, or else a philosophical oddity even for the most ardent Platonist. In the mentioned texts on logic, and others, the turnstile is used as a metalogical symbol to indicate (conjectured) theoremhood with respect to some particular logical calculus. The calculus is either understood from the context, or its name is supplied as an explicit decoration. For a Z specification, where there is no calculus to be understood from the context, it is far from clear what such a conjecture (or theorem) is to mean.

On the 'alternative view' given above, the calculus is presumably understood to be classical first-order logic and set theory. The variety of available presentations (and as a result, of sets of theorems), especially for the latter, would seem to leave the statement of a theorem in this way dangerously close to meaningless.

The Draft Z Standard [20] has given a meaning for statements of Z conjectural theorems which is entirely independent of any logical calculus. This is of course quite a feat. In fact, the Standard's definition does not touch theoremhood at all, but instead deals with model-theoretic truth. That is, the Standard says that

$$\vdash pred$$

holds in a specification *Spec* exactly when all the models of the specification satisfy the predicate. That is, in the notation of the Standard,

$$\{\!| \; Spec \; |\!\}^{\mathcal{M}} \subseteq \{\!| \; pred \; |\!\}^{\mathcal{M}} \quad .$$

This form of proposition is more traditionally written

$$Spec \models pred \quad .$$

As we have observed, one might expect a logic for Z to be sound—that is, that every theorem of a specification is true in every model of that specification (or, '$\vdash$' $\Rightarrow$ '$\models$'). In pure first-order logic, the converse property (completeness) also holds, so every logically valid predicate is a theorem. This property does not extend to axiomatic set theory (if it is consistent), so it is not the case that the notions of theoremhood and logical validity can be used interchangeably in Z.

As a result, we must conclude that the unqualified use of statements such as the one which began this subsection is unfortunate, if not misleading.

4   Approaches to Logic and Semantics

A logical presentation is able to give meaning to a metalogical statement like $\vdash pred$. A denotational semantics—giving models for the language—is able to give meaning to statements like $\models$ *pred*. The most tractable way to demonstrate inductively that a logical calculus is consistent is to exhibit a semantic structure and demonstrate that the logic is sound with respect to the semantics. This has been the intention of the Z Standards activity [20], though lately most effort has been spent on the model.

Many texts have given elements of a logical calculus for Z, [25] and [30] being the among the first. Later, Spivey [26] remarks that his Z Reference Manual has not included a full set of inference rules, not least because there is insufficient experience of how to present such rules so that they interact helpfully. Potter et al. [22] devote a chapter to formal reasoning in Z, but for pedagogical reasons, rather than to present a systematic reasoning system for Z. Perhaps Woodcock and Davies [29] give the fullest textbook treatment of reasoning in Z, but again, this is presented as a good means of understanding the complexities and nuances of the notation.

Separate accounts have described logics for Z in a more systematic manner. $\mathcal{W}$ [28] was perhaps the first; it has been followed by $\mathcal{V}$ [7], which corrects a number of shortcomings in the account of $\mathcal{W}$. These logics have been developed to be part of the Z Standardization activity. Henson and Reeves [11] have also produced a logic for Z, which they have named Z_C. Their logic and conclusions mirror the $\mathcal{W}$ family in some respects, but achieve a higher level of rigour and a greater separation of concerns. They argue that some of the innovations of $\mathcal{W}$, such as a novel treatment of substitution, are unnecessary—see below.

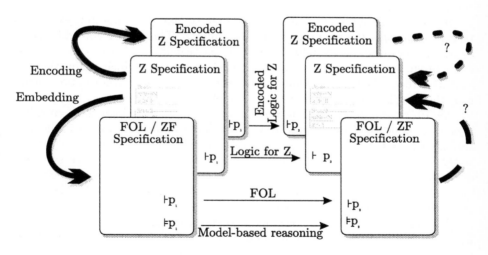

Fig.1. Some approaches to reasoning

Figure 1 illustrates some of the approaches to giving meaning to, and/or reasoning about, Z specifications. Logics for Z transform one conjecture into another—or discharge the proof obligation to show that the conjecture is a theorem—without leaving the Z notation. In each case, the turnstile symbol $\vdash$ is understood relative to the logic in use, be it $\mathcal{W}$, $\mathcal{V}$, Z_C, etc.

The figure also illustrates the possibility of transforming a Z specification into a model, in, say the language of first-order logic and set theory. It is then possible to re-cast the conjecture in two different ways—as a possible theorem of the formal system of first-order logic and set theory, or as a property of the model. These two activities appear very similar indeed, but are in fact quite different endeavours. Working in the former system will be a formal logical activity; work in the latter is more akin to mainstream mathematics. One is in the domain of proof theory, the other, model theory.

Most proof tools take the first of these approaches. Z/EVES [23] does precisely this; ProofPower [13] and Z-in-Isabelle/HOL [14] use higher-order, rather than first-order, logic. Bowen and Gorden [5] explain that these embeddings of one logic in another may take place at a number of different *depths*, depending upon the extent to which the artefacts of the high-level language (Z) are modelled directly in the host logic. In Z, the principal interest is with the modelling of schemas—see below. A comparison of tools on this basis is included in [18].

It is worthwhile noting that the soundness of these formal logical manipulations is itself guaranteed by an embedding in some model. The soundness (where proven) of each logical approach means that the sets of transformations *increase* when passing down the page—that is, the available logical steps in a logic for Z is a subset of those available by reasoning about a representation of Z in FOL/ZF, etc. As we have observed, properties true in the model may not be provable in the logic, so the inclusion is typically as a *proper* subset.

Having performed logical reasoning in FOL or HOL, it is not always an easy task to transform the resulting terms back into Z. The deeper embeddings accomplish this quite successfully. Z/EVES, in particular, is able to recast virtually every predicate back into a Z form. Z/EVES is one system which might, then, be said to induce a logic for Z, though the complexity of the transformation means that the details of this logic have not been elucidated.

An alternative to embedding the Z notation in another logic is to encode a logical calculus for Z in a logical framework [17, 15], or in a custom implementation such as CADiZ [27]. The soundness of these encodings is usually called *faithfulness*. An encoding is called *adequate* if it allows precisely the same set of manipulations as the logic it encodes. In practice this is rarely the case, so encodings are shown in the diagram with a transformation arrow the highest on the page; it may be imagined to admit the smallest set of transformations.

The diagram is of course only indicative. Particular logics, encodings, embeddings, and models will not necessarily form a neat hierarchy, because there is no general agreement on the class of Z theorems and derivations.

5   Schemas

Schemas are without doubt the most important and distinctive feature of the Z notation. Semantically, they represent a challenge, and framing suitable inference rules for dealing with them has been a significant research activity, which is reported elsewhere [9, 6]. The difficulty with schemas has been in finding a uniform representation which can represent a schema abstractly, and used to give its properties in each situation in which it may appear.

Consider the following schema, which describes a size-limited phone directory, assuming that MAX has been given some natural number value.

$$S == [n : NAME \nrightarrow PHONE \mid \#n < MAX]$$

S might be used as a declaration, as in the following predicate which says that only international numbers are stored:

$$\forall S \bullet (\forall p : \mathrm{dom}\, n \bullet p \in INTERNATIONAL)$$

S might be used as an expression, as in the following predicate which says the same thing:

$$\forall s : S \bullet (\forall p : \mathrm{dom}\, s.n \bullet p \in INTERNATIONAL)$$

S might be used as a predicate, as in

$$\forall n : NAME \nrightarrow PHONE \bullet S$$

which we might interpret as saying that *all* phone directories are limited in size.

The difficulty arises because when S is used as a predicate, the component labelled n behaves like a free variable—it can be captured by a quantifier. Incidentally, MAX cannot be captured by a quantifier; in all instances of S it takes the value it did at the point where S is defined. When S is used as an expression, n is more like a bound variable—though not entirely, as alpha-conversion would affect the type of the expression. Moreover, in Draft Standard Z, a schema-type object can be created at any level of scope, not just at the top level, so the boundness/freeness of variables depends critically on the *context* of the term.

Dealing with these issues led the designers of $\mathcal{W}/\mathcal{V}$ etc. to create an elaborate calculus of bound and free variables, and eventually an object-level notion of substitution. When a schema is used as an expression, it denotes a set of *bindings*, which are associations of labels with values. For example, the schema

$$
\begin{array}{|l}
\hline
T \\\hline
x, y : \mathbb{N} \\\hline
x < y \\\hline
\end{array}
$$

has as members bindings such as

$$\langle\!\mid x == 3, y == 4 \mid\!\rangle, \langle\!\mid x == 2, y == 6 \mid\!\rangle$$

etc. A binding such as $\langle\!\mid x == e \mid\!\rangle$ carries the same semantic content as a traditional substitution $[x/e]$. Instead of writing $P[x/e]$, we might write

$$P \odot \langle\!\mid x == e \mid\!\rangle$$

the latter being a wholly Z predicate.

Henson and Reeves [11] have since suggested that this innovation was unnecessary and over-complicates the logic. Their logic avoids needing schema components to be sometimes bound and sometimes free, and consequentially is able to use a more usual notion of substitution.

The $\mathcal{V}$ logic presents a complete calculus for schemas based on this approach to bindings and substitution. Henson and Reeves [9] present a similar calculus, based upon their logic Z_C, retaining a more traditional notion of substitution, and basing their rules on a notion of schema membership which is more liberal. Both pieces of work demonstrate sufficient inference rules to allow schema objects to be eliminated entirely—demonstrating that a logic for the whole of Z can be constructed using ordinary ZF and adding one new construction (the labelled product/schema type/binding).

These calculi also make formal many of the results that have been used by Z practitioners (and schema expansion tools) over many years for the analysis of operators in the schema calculus. For example, if D_1 and D_2 represent schema declaration parts in 'normalized' form (itself typically described informally) then

$$[D_1 \mid P_1] \wedge [D_2 \mid P_2] = [D_1 \sqcup D_2 \mid P_1 \wedge P_2]$$

where $\sqcup$ is some signature-compatible union. A proof of this property is presented by Henson and Reeves [9], though it was also possible using $\mathcal{W}$ [28].

6   Undefinedness

Whilst most well-formed expressions in Z can be given a meaning quite readily, there are two places where a problem arises with potentially undefined terms. One is in the area of function application; the other with improper μ-terms. The latter may be seen as a special case of the former (and vice versa), and so we restrict our attention to function application. (The μ operator is used to select from a set the unique member having a given property. Where no such unique member exists—either through there being no member with the property, or several members with the property—the μ-term is called improper. It is a simple matter to reconstruct this as a discussion of functions and relations.)

Z allows functions to be total or partial. In Z, both functions and relations are sets of pairs. There is no uniform procedure to check whether a given relation is in fact a function, so the language allows relations to be applied to arguments as if they were functions. Problems may arise if a partial function is applied to an argument not in its domain, or if a relation is applied at a point where it is not functional (i.e. it maps its argument to more than one value): what is the function application to denote, and how does this value affect the surrounding terms, or the predicate in which it occurs?

This is not merely an academic enquiry, since it may materially alter the meaning of a specification. Moreover the use of partial functions is very common Z style, so the question potentially affects very many Z specifications. Z has been criticised on these grounds, particularly by the creators of PVS [21]. In PVS all functions are total—the burden is thereby shifted into the type system, which unlike Z's is therefore undecidable.

The tool Z/EVES [23] incorporates a similar check that each function application is well-formed. Its authors report that the majority of 'real' Z specifications examined have failed this test. Many have argued (notably, the late Peter Lupton [16]) that a specification which exploits any interpretation of undefinedness is a bad specification.

6.1 Approaches to Undefinedness

A comprehensive treatment of the possible approaches to undefined terms is given by Arthan [1]. These include the possibility of allowing undefined terms to be reflected in making the predicates in which they arise also undefined. That approach gives rise to a three-valued logic, as used in VDM [12], but it is not generally embraced by Z users (the Cogito project [3] is an exception).

The two most popular approaches are characterised by Arthan as 'UPF' (undefined propositions are false) and 'UED' (undefined expressions denote). In the latter case, all expressions are assumed to denote a value, but it may not be possible to determine which one.

The Draft Z Standard has accommodated the variety of approaches by loosely defining the semantics of function application. Whereas most expressions are defined by an *equation*, so that the meaning of a particular expression is a particular set or relation in the underlying set theory, function application is defined by a *set inclusion*. Thus, the value of an expression involving a relation applied outside is domain, or where it is not functional, is not prescribed.

Different logical systems may resolve this in different ways, and nevertheless be considered compliant (arguably, sound). For example, each type could be given a non-Z error value, and this could be taken as the value of the undefined term. Or, possibly, there could be a different error value for each term, to ensure that undefined terms are not inadvertently made equal. The resolution chosen by the $\mathcal{W}/\mathcal{V}$ family of logics is to determine that undefined expressions denote a Z value of the appropriate type, but not to allow sufficient apparatus to determine which value that is.

6.2 Baumann's Question

The $\mathcal{W}/\mathcal{V}$ resolution described above gives rise to a question posed by Baumann [2].

If every expression denotes a Z value of the appropriate type, then surely

$$\vdash \forall f : X \nrightarrow Y \bullet \left(\forall x : X \bullet (\exists y : Y \bullet f\ x = y) \right)$$

therefore

$$\vdash \forall f : X \nrightarrow Y \bullet (\forall x : X \bullet (\exists y : Y \bullet x \mapsto y \in f))$$

therefore

$$\vdash \forall f : X \nrightarrow Y \bullet (\forall x : X \bullet x \in \operatorname{dom} f)$$

therefore

$$\vdash \forall f : X \nrightarrow Y \bullet f \in X \rightarrow Y$$

That is to say, all partial functions in Z are also total functions. This is clearly undesirable; indeed, it is at odds with most users' understanding of Z.

The resolution of this apparent paradox lies in the difference between *truth* (in the model) and *provability* (in the logic). Writing $\models_D$ *pred* to mean that *pred* holds in the model extended so that it has the property 'every term denotes', the following may be true

$$\models_D \forall f : X \nrightarrow Y \bullet \big(\forall x : X \bullet (\exists y : Y \bullet f\ x = y) \big) \quad ,$$

but it does not follow (indeed, it is not the case) that this predicate is a theorem of $\mathcal{W}$ etc. (Its truth is not certain, because the extension of the model may be made in a number of different ways: the model might determine that any application of a function outside its domain results in a 'bottom' value which is outside the type system, or a distinguished value of the appropriate type, or an entirely unspecified member of the type. The predicate above would be true in the latter two cases—provided Y is a basic type, and not some subset—but not in the first.)

6.3   Issues of Methodology

We have already argued that matters of logic are important not only to those who wish to prove properties of their specifications, but to all who try to *understand* Z specifications. In particular, a working knowledge of logic will enable the reader to ask questions about what would have happened if something had been written differently.

The treatment of undefinedness has an impact on how one writes specifications as well as how one reasons about them. An oft-cited example is the specification which declares a (possibly infinite) set and then asserts that its cardinality is fixed.

$$\begin{array}{|l}
s : \mathbb{P}\,\mathbb{N} \\
\hline
\#s = 4
\end{array}$$

The cardinality function $\#$ is partial; its value is defined only on finite sets. The question of whether or not the definition of s is a useful one depends upon one's treatment of undefined terms. If every expression denotes ('UED'), then $\#s$ and 4 can be used interchangeably in the sequel, which is probably almost what the specifier intended—but not quite. On the other hand one interpretation of the position 'UPF' would mean that the very possibility that $\#s$ may be undefined would be enough to make the predicate false, and therefore the whole specification inconsistent (and useless). Another interpretation of 'UPF' would be to rule out those models in which $\#s = 4$ is false (for whatever reason, including undefinedness), leaving a specification which performs as 'intended'. The apparatus for achieving the latter is non-trivial.

Conversely, we can easily exhibit specifications—such as set comprehensions or schemas—where we would like undefined terms to give rise to false predicates, so that the rogue terms are excluded from the set/schema. For example, writing

$$S_4 == \{\ s : \mathbb{P}\,\mathbb{N} \mid \#s = 4\ \}$$

we would hope that S_4 would be the set of all sets of natural numbers having cardinality 4—and no others. On the 'UED' interpretation, we can be sure that the sets of four natural numbers are members of S_4, but we cannot prove that, say, $\mathbb{N}$ is not. In 'UPF', however, S_4 would contain exactly the sets of natural numbers having four elements, and nothing else.

The study of undefinedness has a long history in classical mathematics, with no universal answer, and often no need for one because the 'intuitive' answer is usually the right one (normal mathematical practice not being overly formal). That there should be no ready answer in Z is therefore not surprising.

7   Future and Related Work

7.1   Managing Complexity

Just as undefinedness is a widespread problem, so too is the issue of managing complexity. Z's schema notation provides the specifier with the opportunity to write very deeply-nested specifications in a very compact way. Anyone who has used a schema expansion tool will know how readily an innocuous-looking five-line schema can when fully expanded occupy several printed pages.

A challenge in supporting proof is to find ways to manage this complexity. This issue is almost orthogonal to the logical concerns already raised, but has a profound impact on the tractability of formal proof for anything but the smallest specification.

Moreover, the language is quite rich, and uses a variety of specialised symbols. Again, these are a means to the management of complexity, since they allow complex ideas to be expressed succinctly. They are, however, outside the general abilities of most proof tools today, though they need not be, since on-screen display of symbol fonts is now quite commonplace.

Support for practical reasoning will require solving these two difficulties in tool implementations. The first is ideally a methodological issue as well as an interface one. Despite discovering logics for schemas, no practical method for using schemas to structure proofs as well as specifications has been discovered.

7.2   Other Logics

Whilst this paper has largely described Z in relation to first-order logic, higher-order logic has been found to be a good basis for Z semantics. In particular, it offers a very appropriate type model (provided schema types/bindings are incorporated). [24] has described an isomorphism between Z and HOL (disregarding names in schema types). This provides the theory underlying the Z in Isabelle/HOL work described above.

Others have considered using constructive logics [10]. In this approach, proof becomes a means of program development. In other contexts, second-order logic has been found to be a useful tool; perhaps it could also add expressiveness to Z.

8   Conclusions

Z now has quite a lengthy history, and sometimes the original motivations and assumed theory have become obscured. This paper's purpose is to make some observations about the purpose and role of proof in Z, and its relationship to first-order logic. General understanding of these topics has been divergent, and the hope is to promote some common acceptance and understanding; in essence to provide a framework for a philosophy of proof in Z. Much of the paper has been devoted to documenting issues that are 'part of the folklore' of Z proof but do not seem to have been recorded anywhere—to the annoyance of newcomers to the field.

The original connection between Z and first-order logic was very close. Various developments have served to obscure this relationship. Two pieces of recent work [11, 6] show that the relationship persists, and indeed a first-order logic can be described which, with the single addition of schema *types* can be used to reason about the whole language. Insofar as demonstrating this relationship is non-trivial it also suggests that Z adds some significant structure to the language of first-order logic and set theory. Experience suggests that this structure is useful for specification. It appears that it may also be useful for proof.

References

[1] R. D. Arthan. Undefinedness in Z: Issues for specification and proof, 1996. Presented at CADE-13 Workshop on Mechanization of Partial Functions.

[2] Peter Baumann. Private Communication, April 1994.

[3] Anthony Bloesch, Ed Kazmierczak, Peter Kearney, and Owen Traynor. The Cogito methodology and system. In *Asia–Pacific Software Engineering Conference '94*, pages 345–355, 1994.

[4] J. P. Bowen, A. Fett, and M. G. Hinchey, editors. *ZUM'98: The Z Formal Specification Notation, 11th International Conference of Z Users, Berlin, Germany, 24–26 September 1998*, volume 1493 of *Lecture Notes in Computer Science*. Springer-Verlag, 1998.

[5] J. P. Bowen and M. J. C. Gordon. A shallow embedding of Z in HOL. *Information and Software Technology*, 37(5–6):269–276, 1995.

[6] Stephen Brien and Andrew Martin. A calculus for schemas in Z. *J. Symbolic Computation*, 2000. To appear.

[7] Stephen M. Brien. *A Logic and Model for the Z Standard*. D.Phil. thesis, University of Oxford, 1998.

[8] Herbert B. Enderton. *A Mathematical Introduction to Logic*. Academic Press, 1972.

[9] M. C. Henson and S. Reeves. A logic for the schema calculus. In Bowen et al. [4], pages 172–191.

[10] Martin Henson and Steve Reeves. New foundations for Z. In Jim Grundy, Martin Schwenke, and Trevor Vickers, editors, *IRW/FMP'98*. Springer-Verlag, 1998.

[11] Martin C. Henson and Steve Reeves. Investigating Z. Technical Report CSM-317, Department of Computer Science, University of Essex, 1998. *Journal of Logic and Computation*, to appear.

[12] Cliff B. Jones. *Systematic Software Development Using VDM*. Prentice-Hall Intenational, second edition, 1990.

[13] R. B. Jones. ICL ProofPower. *BCS FACS FACTS*, Series III, 1(1):10–13, Winter 1992.

[14] Kolyang, T. Santen, and B. Wolff. A structure preserving encoding of Z in Isabelle/HOL. In *1996 International Conference on Theorem Proving in Higher Order Logic*. Springer-Verlag, 1996.

[15] Ina Kraan and Peter Baumann. Implementing Z in Isabelle. In Jonathan P. Bowen and Michael G. Hinchey, editors, *ZUM'95: The Z Formal Specification Notation*, volume 967 of *LNCS*, pages 355–373. Springer-Verlag, 1995.

[16] Peter J. L. Lupton. Z and undefinedness. Technical Report PRG/91/68, Z Standards Panel / Programming Research Group, 1991.

[17] A. Martin. Encoding W: A logic for Z in 2OBJ. In J. C. P. Woodcock and P. G. Larsen, editors, *FME'93: Industrial-Strength Formal Methods*, volume 670 of *Lecture Notes in Computer Science*, pages 462–481. Formal Methods Europe, Springer-Verlag, 1993.

[18] Andrew Martin. Why effective proof tool support for Z is hard. Technical report 97-34, Software Verification Research Centre, School of Information Technology, The University of Queensland, Brisbane 4072. Australia, November 1997.

[19] Elliott Mendelson. *Introduction to Mathematical Logic*. Mathematics Series. Wadsworth and Brooks/Cole, 1987.

[20] John Nicholls, editor. *Z Notation*. Z Standards Panel, ISO Panel JTC1/SC22/WG19 (Rapporteur Group for Z), 1995. Version 1.2, ISO Committee Draft; CD 13568.

[21] S. Owre, S. Rajan, J.M. Rushby, N. Shankar, and M.K. Srivas. PVS: Combining specification, proof checking, and model checking. In Rajeev Alur and Thomas A. Henzinger, editors, *Computer-Aided Verification, CAV '96*, number 1102 in Lecture Notes in Computer Science, pages 411–414, New Brunswick, NJ, July/August 1996. Springer-Verlag.

[22] B. F. Potter, J. E. Sinclair, and D. Till. *An Introduction to Formal Specification and Z*. Prentice Hall International Series in Computer Science, 2nd edition, 1996.

[23] M. Saaltink. The Z/EVES system. In J. P. Bowen, M. G. Hinchey, and D. Till, editors, *ZUM'97: The Z Formal Specification Notation*, volume 1212 of *Lecture Notes in Computer Science*, pages 72–85. Springer-Verlag, 1997.

[24] T. Santen. On the semantic relation of Z and HOL. In Bowen et al. [4], pages 96–115.

[25] J. M. Spivey. *Understanding Z: A Specification Language and its Formal Semantics*, volume 3 of *Cambridge Tracts in Theoretical Computer Science*. Cambridge University Press, January 1988.

[26] J. M. Spivey. *The Z Notation: A Reference Manual*. Prentice-Hall, second edition, 1992.

[27] I. Toyn. Formal reasoning in the Z notation using CADiZ. In *Proc. 2nd Workshop on User Interfaces to Theorem Provers, York*, July 1996.

[28] J. C. P. Woodcock and S. M. Brien. *W*: A Logic for Z. In *Proceedings 6th Z User Meeting*. Springer-Verlag, 1992.

[29] J. C. P. Woodcock and J. Davies. *Using Z: Specification, Proof and Refinement*. Prentice Hall International Series in Computer Science, 1996.

[30] J. C. P. Woodcock and M. Loomes. *Software Engineering Mathematics: Formal Methods Demystified*. Pitman, 1988.

Acknowledgements

If I have any insight in this area, it has been gained in discussions with members of the Z Standards panel. Anthony Hall helped to make stark the choices faced in dealing with undefinedness, and discussions with Martin Henson have greatly helped my understanding and exposition.

Formal Modeling of the Enterprise JavaBeans™ Component Integration Framework

João Pedro Sousa and David Garlan

School of Computer Science
Carnegie Mellon University
Pittsburgh, PA 15213 USA
{jpsousa|garlan}@cs.cmu.edu
http://www.cs.cmu.edu/~able/

Abstract. An emerging trend in the engineering of complex systems is the use of component integration frameworks. Such a framework prescribes an architectural design that permits flexible composition of third-party components into applications. A good example is Sun Microsystems' *Enterprise JavaBeans*™ (*EJB*) framework, which supports object-oriented, distributed, enterprise-level applications, such as account management systems. One problem with frameworks like EJB is that they are documented informally, making it difficult to understand precisely what is provided by the framework, and what is required to use it. We believe formal specification can help, and in this paper show how a formal architectural description language can be used to describe and provide insight into such frameworks.

Keywords: Software architecture, software frameworks, component integration standards, component-based software, Enterprise JavaBeans.

1 Introduction

Component integration frameworks[1] are becoming increasingly important for commercial software systems. The purpose of a component integration framework is to prescribe a standard architectural design that permits flexible composition of third-party components. Usually a framework defines three things: (a) the overall structure of an application in terms of its major types of constituent components; (b) a set of interface standards that describe what capabilities are required of those components; and (c) reusable infrastructure that supports the integration of those components through shared services and communication channels.

A successful framework greatly simplifies the development of complex systems. By providing rules for component integration, many of the general problems of component mismatch do not arise [8]. By providing a component integration platform for third-party software, application developers can build new

---

[1] Component integration frameworks are sometimes referred to as *component architectures*

J. Wing, J. Woodcock, J. Davies (Eds.): FM'99, Vol. II, LNCS 1709, pp. 1281–1300, 1999.
© Springer-Verlag Berlin Heidelberg 1999

applications using a rich supply of existing parts. By providing a reusable infrastructure, the framework substantially reduces the amount of custom code that must be written to support communication between those parts.

A good example of a framework is Microsoft's Visual Basic^{TM} system, which defines an architecture for component integration (Visual Basic Controls), rules for adding application-specific components (such as customized widgets, forms, graphics, etc.), and code that implements many shared services for graphical user interfaces (for example, to support coordination and communication among the parts via events.)

Another, more recent example is Sun's Enterprise JavaBeans^{TM} (EJB) architecture. EJB is intended to support distributed, Java-based, enterprise-level applications, such as business information management systems. Among other things, it prescribes an architecture that defines a standard, vendor-neutral interface to information services including transactions, persistence, and security. It thereby permits application writers to develop component-based implementations of business processing software that are portable across different implementations of those underlying services.

One critical issue for users and implementors of a framework is the documentation that explains what the framework provides and what is required to instantiate it correctly for some application. Typically a framework is specified using a combination of informal and semi-formal documentation. On the informal side are guidelines and high-level descriptions of usage scenarios, tips, and examples. On the semi-formal side one usually finds a description of an application programmer's interface (API) that explains what kinds of services are provided by the framework. APIs are formal to the extent that they provide precise descriptions of those services – usually as a set of signatures, possibly annotated with informal pre- and post-conditions.

Such documentation is clearly necessary. However, by itself it leaves many important questions unanswered – for component developers, system integrators, framework implementers, and proposers of new frameworks. For example, the framework's API may specify the names and parameters of services provided by the infrastructure. However, it may not be clear what are the restrictions (if any) on the ordering of invocations of those services. Usage scenarios may help, but they only provide examples of selected interactions, requiring the reader to infer the general rule. Moreover, it may not be clear what facilities *must* be provided by the parts added to the framework, and which are optional.

As with most forms of informal system documentation and specification, the situation could be greatly improved if one had a precise description as a formal specification of the framework. However, a number of critical issues arise immediately. What aspects of the framework should be modeled? How should that model be structured to best expose the architectural design? How should one model the parts of the framework to maintain traceability to the original documentation, and yet still improve clarity? How should one distinguish optional from required behavior? For object-oriented frameworks what aspects of the object-oriented design should be exposed in the formal model?

In this paper we show how one can use formal architectural modeling to provide one set of answers to these questions. The key idea is to provide an abstract structural description of the framework that makes clear what are the high-level interfaces and interactions, and to characterize their semantics in terms of protocols. By making explicit the protocols inherent in the integration framework, we make precise the requirements on both the components and on the supporting infrastructure itself. This in turn yields a deeper understanding of the framework, and ultimately supports analysis of its properties. Furthermore, we can validate that the model is a useful abstraction of "reality" by checking that the model exhibits the properties that are required informally in the specification of the software framework.

In the remainder of this paper we describe our experience in developing a specification of Sun's Enterprise JavaBeans integration framework. The primary contributions of this paper are twofold. First, we show how formal architectural models based on protocols can clarify the intent of an integration framework, as well as expose critical properties of it. Second, we describe techniques to create the model, and structure it to support traceability, tractability, and automated analysis for checking of desirable properties. These techniques, while illustrated in terms of EJB, shed light more generally on ways to provide formal architectural models of object-oriented frameworks.

2   Related Research

This work is closely related to three areas of prior research. The first area is the field of *architectural description and analysis*. Currently there are many architecture description languages (ADLs) and tools to support their use (such as [11], [17], [14], [13]). While these ADLs are far from being in widespread use, there have been numerous examples of their application to realistic case studies. This paper contributes to this body of case studies, but pushes on a different dimension – namely, the application of architectural modeling to component integration frameworks.

Among existing ADLs the one used here, Wright, is most closely related to Rapide [11], since both use event patterns to describe abstract behavior of architectures. Wright differs from Rapide insofar as it supports definition of connectors as explicit semantic entities and permits static analysis using model checking tools. As we will see, this capability is at the heart of our approach for modeling integration frameworks.

The second related area is research on the *analysis of architectural standards*. An example close in spirit to our work is that of Sullivan and colleagues, who used Z to model and analyze the Microsoft COM standard [18]. In our own previous work we looked at the High Level Architecture (HLA) for Distributed Simulation [2]. HLA defines an integration standard for multi-vendor distributed simulations. We demonstrated that Wright could be used to model this framework and identify potential flaws in the HLA design. EJB differs from HLA in that it provides a different set of challenges. In particular, unlike HLA, EJB is an object-oriented framework; it has a diverse set of interface specifications; and its has weaker (but more typical) documentation.

The third related area is *protocol specification and analysis*. There has been considerable research on ways to specify protocols using a variety of formalisms, including I/O Automata [12], SMV [4, 5], SDL [10], and Petri Nets [15]. While our research shares many of the same goals, there is one important difference. Most protocol analysis assumes one is starting with a complete description of the protocol. The problem is then to analyze that protocol for various properties. In contrast, in architectural modeling of systems like EJB, protocols are typically *implicit* in the APIs described in the framework documentation. Discovering what the protocols are, and how they determine the behavior of the system is itself a major challenge.

3   Enterprise JavaBeans™

3.1   Background

One of the most important and prevalent classes of software systems are those that support business information applications, such as accounting systems and inventory tracking systems. Today these systems are usually structured as multi-tiered client-server systems, in which business-processing software provides services to client programs, and in turn relies on lower level information management services, such as for transactions, persistence, and security (see Fig. 1.)

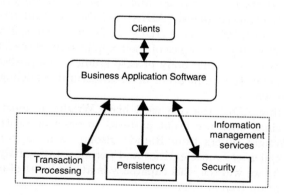

Fig. 1. A three-tiered business application

Currently one of the problems with writing such software is portability: application software must be partially rewritten for each vendor's support facilities because information management services provided by different venders often have radically different interfaces.

Additionally, clients of application software are faced with a huge variety
of interfaces to those applications. While some differences are inevitable, given
that different applications must provide different capabilities, one would wish
for certain levels of standardization for generic operations such as creating or
deleting business process entities (such as accounts).

To address this problem several vendors have proposed component integration frameworks for this class of system. One of these is Sun Microsystems'
Enterprise JavaBeans^{TM} framework, a component architecture for building distributed, object-oriented, multi-vendor, business applications in the Java programming language. The basic idea of the framework is to standardize on three
things. First, the framework defines a standard interface to information management services, insulating application software from gratuitous differences in
vendors' native interfaces. Second, the framework defines certain standard operations that can be used by client software to create, delete, and access business
objects, thereby providing some uniformity across different business applications
software. Third, the framework defines rules for composing object-oriented business applications using reusable components called *beans*.

By standardizing on these aspects of an information management application,
EJB intends to promote application portability, multi-vendor interoperability,
and rapid composition of applications from independently developed parts.

The remainder of this section elaborates on the elements of EJB that are
necessary to follow the formalization in Sect. 6.

3.2   Overview of Enterprise JavaBeans^{TM}

Sun's "Specification of the Enterprise JavaBeansTM Architecture" [6], (henceforth, *EJB spec*) defines a standard for third parties to develop Enterprise
JavaBeans^{TM} deployment environments (henceforth, *EJB servers*). An application running in one of these environments would access information management services by requesting them of the EJB server, via the EJB API, in the
way prescribed by the EJB spec.

Figure 2 illustrates a system with a remote client calling an application that
implements some business logic, for which Orders and Accounts are relevant
operational entities. In the object-oriented paradigm, such entities are termed
objects. An object can be viewed as a unit that holds a cohesive piece of information and that defines a collection of operations (implemented by methods) to
manipulate it.

The EJB framework defines particular kinds of objects, termed Enterprise
JavaBeans^{TM} (*beans*, for short). Beans must conform to specific rules concerning
the methods to create or remove a bean, or to query a population of beans for the
satisfaction of some property. Hence, whenever client software needs to access a
bean, it can take some features for granted.

It is the job of EJB server *providers* to map the functionality that the EJB
spec describes into available products and technologies. In version 1.0, released
in March 1998, the EJB spec covers transaction management, persistence, and

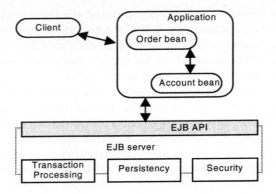

Fig. 2. The EJB server offering access to information management services.

security services.[2] The EJB spec does not regulate how these services are to be implemented, however: they may be implemented by the EJB server provider, as part of the server; or they may rely on external products, eventually supplied by other vendors. Such products, however, are invisible to the beans.

A typical example of the symbiosis between an EJB server and an external product would be for an EJB server provider to offer access to one or more industry standard databases. The customer organization could then develop new applications that access existing corporate databases, using the persistency services provided by the EJB server. All that the developers of the new application would need to be aware of is the logical schema of the existing databases.

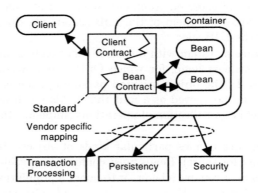

Fig. 3. The EJB container.

---

[2] Actually, version 1.0 views persistency services to be optional.

The EJB spec refers to the collection of services that both the beans and the client software use as a *container* (see Fig. 3). A container provides a deployment environment that wraps the beans during their lifecycle. Each bean lives within a container. The container supports (directly or indirectly) all aspects that the bean assumes about the outside world, as defined in the EJB spec.[3] The protocols that regulate the dialog between a bean and its container are termed the *bean contract*.

The container also supports a set of protocols, termed the *client contract*, that regulate the dialog between client software and a bean. The client contract defines two interfaces that a client uses to communicate with a specific bean: the *Home Interface* and the *Remote Interface*. Both interfaces are implemented at deployment-time by special-purpose tools supplied by the EJB server provider.[4] The Remote Interface reflects the functionality of the bean it represents, as it publishes the so-called business methods of the bean. Each bean has one such interface. The Home Interface contains the methods for creation and removal of beans, as well as optional methods for querying the population of beans (*finder* methods). There is one such interface per bean class.

To use the services of a bean a client first obtains a reference to the bean's class Home Interface using the Java Naming and Directory Interface^{TM} (JNDI). Using this reference, the client software can call a `create` method in the class's Home Interface, thus obtaining a reference to the bean's Remote Interface implemented by the container. The Remote Interface then delegates subsequent method calls to the corresponding bean. The fact that the client uses JNDI to obtain a reference to the Home Interface of the class is a necessary condition for distribution transparency. Any piece of software, including a bean, may use the client contract to communicate with some bean if the software does not know (or care) where the target bean is actually being deployed. Such software calls the interfaces in the container holding the target bean using Java's Remote Method Invocation.

An EJB server manages the population of beans that reside in main memory in a way that is transparent to the client software. As the population of beans inside a container grows beyond a certain limit, determined by the EJB server, the container sends some number of the least recently used beans to secondary memory. The EJB spec refers to the beans that are subject to this operation as *passivated*. Since every call to a bean flows through the interfaces in the

---

[3] This does not mean the container restrains beans from accessing the world outside EJB. For instance, a bean may include Java Database Connectivity (JDBC) code to access a database directly. However, in doing so, the bean sacrifices implementation independence and distribution transparency.

[4] In Java, the Home and Remote Interface are termed `EJBHome` and `EJBObject`, respectively. These two interfaces in the EJB spec are *extended* by user-written, domain-specific, Java interfaces. Such domain-specific Java interfaces are read by the deployment tools to produce the container-specific classes that implement the two interfaces. The latter classes are, however, invisible to the user. For the sake of clarity we will continue to refer to the user-specified interfaces as Home and Remote Interface.

container, it is the container that relays the call to the bean, as appropriate. So, whenever a method call is addressed to a passivated bean, the bean is brought back to primary memory by the container. The EJB spec refers to beans that are subject to this latter operation as *activated*.

Although passivation and activation are transparent to the client calling the bean, it is not so to the bean itself. Before being passivated, the bean is required to release the shared resources it acquired previously, so as not to lock them during passivation time. Likewise, upon activation, the bean may have to reacquire the resources to serve the client's request. Therefore, in order to allow the bean to perform these actions, the container issues synchronization messages to the bean just before passivation and immediately after activation, before the client's call is relayed (`ejbPassivate` and `ejbActivate`, in Fig. 4.)

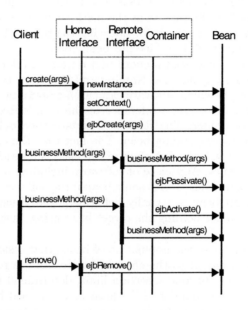

Fig. 4. Sample event trace for the lifecycle of a bean.

3.3   The Enterprise JavaBeans™ Specification

The EJB spec [6] released by Sun is a 180-page document, in which the concepts and their interplay are described in English, much in the same way as Sect. 3.2. A few informal state diagrams complement the explanation. There are also some chapters dedicated to the presentation of illustrative scenarios of interactions described using event trace diagrams. For instance, the event trace in Fig. 4 is an adaptation of the ones in pages 32 to 36 of the EJB spec. The document has an appendix enumerating the Java API that the elements of the architecture should follow. The signature and purpose of each method is briefly described, in English, along with an enumeration of the exceptions that may be raised. No pre- and post-conditions are provided.

Although voluminous, documentation such as this has two intrinsic problems. First, related information is spread throughout the document. For example, to determine what sequence of method calls a bean must follow to request a typical service from the container, the reader must locate the explanation in the text (hopefully covering all relevant operations), refer to the API method descriptions, examine any examples of sample executions, and consult the list of possible raised exceptions.

Second, the lack of a precise definition makes it difficult for a reader to resolve inconsistencies and ambiguities, and to determine the intended semantics of the framework. As an example of unresolvable inconsistencies, in one place the documentation says the Home Interface should "define *zero* or more `create` methods" (page 14), while in another it says "*one* or more `create` methods" (page 20). Without a single place in the document that has the precise definition, it is impossible to determine which of the two (if either) is correct (even assuming we can determine what a `create` method should do).

As another example, consider the issue of the interaction between bean deletion and bean passivation. Suppose a client decides to remove a bean that the client has not accessed in some time. If the container has passivated that bean, it is not clear what happens. The normal rules of method invocation would imply that the bean would first have to be activated (reacquiring all resources needed for its normal operation), only to be immediately removed. This seems like a strange kind of behavior, and it is not clear if it is intended by the standard.

Finally, as with any documentation that only provides *examples* of method sequences, rather than formal *rules*, it is impossible for a reader to be sure what generalization is intended.

It seems clear that much could be gained by a formal unambiguous specification of EJB as a supplementary (or even central) resource for framework implementers, bean providers, and developers of client software. In the remainder of this paper we examine one such specification.

4 Wright

Wright is a formal language for describing software architecture. As with most architecture description languages, Wright describes the architecture of a system as a graph of components and connectors. Components represent the main centers of computation, while connectors represent the interactions between components. While all architecture description languages permit the specification of new component types, unlike many languages, Wright also supports the explicit specification of new architectural connector types [1].[5]

---

[5] Wright also supports the ability to define architectural styles, check for consistency and completeness of architectural configurations, and check for consistent specifica-

A simple Client-Server system description is shown below:

```
Configuration SimpleExample
   Component Server
       Port Provide = <provide protocol>
       Computation  = <Server specification>
   Component Client
       Port Request = <request protocol>
       Computation  = <Client specification>
   Connector C-S-connector
       Role Client = <client protocol>
       Role Server = <server protocol>
       Glue = <glue protocol>
   Instances
       s: Server
       c: Client
       cs: C-S-connector
   Attachments
       s.Provide as cs.Server;
       c.Request as cs.Client
   end SimpleExample.
```

This example shows three basic elements of a Wright system description: component and connector type declarations, instance declarations, and attachments. The instance declarations and attachments together define a particular system configuration.

In Wright, the description of a component has two important parts, the *interface* and the *computation*. A component interface consists of a number of *ports*. Each port defines a point of interaction through which the component may interact with its environment.

A connector represents an interaction among a collection of components. For example, a pipe represents a sequential flow of data between two filters. A Wright description of a connector consists of a set of *roles* and the *glue*. Each role defines the allowable behavior of one participant in the interaction. A pipe has two roles, the source of data and the recipient. The glue defines how the roles will interact with each other.

The specification of both components and connectors can be parameterized, either with a numeric range – allowing a variable number of ports or roles with identical behaviors – or with a process description – instantiating the generic structure of a component (or connector) to a specific behavior. A typical case of parameterization is a Client-Server connector that allows the attachment of a variable number of Clients, multiplexing their requests according to rules defined in the glue protocol:

---

tions of components and connectors. In this paper we restrict our presentation to just those parts of Wright that concern the specification of EJB. See [3] for further details.

```
Connector C-S-connector(nClients:1..)
    Role Client₁..nClients = <client protocol>
    Role Server = <server protocol>
    Glue = <client multiplexing glue protocol>
```

Each part of a Wright description – port, role, computation, and glue – is defined using a variant of CSP [9]. Each such specification defines a pattern of events (called a process) using operators for sequencing (" → " and " ; "), choice (" ⊓ " and " [] "), parallel composition (" ‖ ") and interruption (" △ ").[6]

Wright extends CSP in three minor syntactic ways. First, it distinguishes between *initiating* an event and *observing* an event. An event that is initiated by a process is written with an overbar. Second, it uses the symbol § to denote the successfully-terminating process.[7] (In CSP this is usually written "SKIP".) Third, Wright uses a quantification operator: `<op> x : S • P(x)`. This operator constructs a new process based on the process expression `P(s)`, and the set `S`, combining its parts by the operator `<op>`.

For example, `[] i:1,2,3 • Pᵢ = P₁ [] P₂ [] P₃` .

5   Component or Connector?

When defining the architectural structure of a framework, a key question is what are the connectors. This question is important because many frameworks are essentially concerned with providing mediating infrastructure between components that are provided by the user of the framework. Making a clear distinction between the replaceable componentry, and the mechanisms that coordinate their interaction greatly improves the comprehensibility of the framework.

From our perspective, the entities that are a locus of application-specific computation are best represented as components. The infrastructure that is prescribed by the framework to assure the interconnection between application components is a likely candidate to be represented as a (set of) connector(s).

In general, however, it may not always be obvious what should be represented as a component and what should be represented as a connector. Consider the system illustrated in Fig. 5a, consisting of three components: A, B, and C. In some cases the purpose of C is to enable the communication between A and B, using an A-C protocol over connector X, and a C-B protocol over connector Y. If those two protocols are completely independent, it makes sense to represent C as a distinct component, and keep X and Y as separate connectors.

On the other hand, if events on X are tightly coupled with those on Y (or vice versa), then it may make more sense to represent the protocol between X

---

[6] We assume familiarity with CSP. For details on the semantics of the mentioned operators see the extended version of this paper in electronic format, available from Springer Verlag.

[7] Wright uses a non-standard interpretation of external choice in the case in which one of the branches is § : specifically, the choice remains external, unlike, for example, the treatment in [16]. See [3] for technical details.

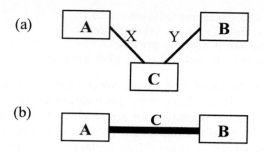

Fig. 5. Component or connector?

and Y directly using a single connector, as indicated in Fig. 5b. In this case, the connector itself encapsulates the mediating behavior of C as *glue*.

Representing a complex piece of software as a connector is a judgement call that is enabled by describing connectors as first class architectural entities. This perspective departs from a notion of connection that is restricted to relatively simple mechanisms like method calling, event announcing, or data pipelining. It requires the ability to describe the protocols that go on at each end of the connector (the *roles* in Wright) as well as the rules that tie those protocols together (the *glue*). In addition, it requires the ability describe complex topologies of connection, beyond simple point-to-point, like having multiple clients communicating with a server over the same set of protocols (a parametric multi-role connector in Wright – see Sect. 4.)

6   Formalizing Enterprise JavaBeans™

Turning now to EJB (as illustrated in Fig. 3), it seems clear that clients and beans should be represented as components. Each performs significant application-specific computation, and is best viewed as a first class type of computational entity in the architectural framework. However, as the actual computations of the clients and beans cannot be defined at the framework level (since they will be determined when the framework is used to develop a particular application), we will represent those components parametrically. That is, the actual application code will be used to instantiate them at a later time.

What about the EJB container? While it would be possible to represent it as a component, as in Fig. 5a, it seems far better to consider it a rich connector, as in Fig. 5b. Not only is the container primarily responsible for bridging the gap between clients and beans, but also the container-client and container-bean sub-protocols are so tightly interwoven that it is makes sense to describe them as a single semantic entity (i.e., the connector glue). For example, the effect of a remote method call from a client to a bean is mediated by the container so that if the target bean is passivated it can be activated using the container-bean activation protocol. The resulting general structure is illustrated in Fig. 6.

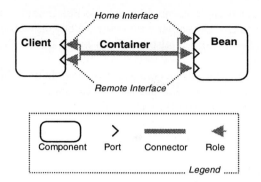

Fig. 6. One Client connected to one Bean.

In this case the Remote and Home interfaces become roles in the Container connector that both a Client and a Bean interact with. In Wright this structure is described (schematically) as:

```
Configuration one-Client-one-Bean
   Component Client (BusinessLogic: Process)
        Port UseHomeInterface = <...>
        Port UseRemoteInterface = BusinessLogic
        Computation = <...>
   Component EJBean (BusinessLogic: Process)
        Port BeanHome = <...>
        Port JxBean = <...>
        Port RemoteInterface = BusinessLogic
        Computation = <...>
   Connector Container (BusinessLogic: Process)
        Role HomeInterface = <...>
        Role RemoteInterface = BusinessLogic
        Role UseBeanHome = <...>
        Role UseJxBean = <...>
        Role UseRemoteInterface = BusinessLogic
        Glue = <...>
   Process SomeBusinessLogic = <...>
   Instances
        A: Client(SomeBusinessLogic)
        B: EJBean(SomeBusinessLogic)
        C: Container(SomeBusinessLogic)
   Attachments
        A.UseHomeInterface as C.HomeInterface
        A.UseRemoteInterface as C.RemoteInterface
        C.UseBeanHome as B.BeanHome
        C.UseRemoteInterface as B.RemoteInterface
        C.UseJxBean as B.JxBean
   end one-Client-one-Bean.
```

As indicated earlier, we use a placeholder process `BusinessLogic` as a parameter to clients, beans, and the Container connector. (The connector is parameterized by the business logic because it also needs to know about the `BusinessLogic` protocol.)

The Wright specification of the configuration also defines the attachments between the ports of each component and the corresponding roles in the Container. The next sections examine each part in turn.

6.1   The Client

The specification of a Client component is:

```
Component Client (BusinessLogic: Process)
    Port UseRemoteInterface = BusinessLogic
    Port UseHomeInterface
        = create→ ( GoHomeInterface
                    △ noSuchObjectException
                            → UseHomeInterface )
                △ remove → ( § ▯ removeException → § ))
    Where GoHomeInterface
        = getEJBMetaData → GoHomeInterface
    Computation = create → CallBean
    Where CallBean
        = ( (UseRemoteInterface ‖ GoHomeInterface)
            △ noSuchObjectException → create → CallBean )
        △ remove → ( § ▯ removeException → § )
```

It has two ports for accessing the Bean: `UseHomeInterface` and `UseRemote-Interface`. As noted above, the latter is defined by a process that describes the application logic implemented by the Bean and is passed to the Client as a parameter (`BusinessLogic`).

The process describing the client's view of the Home Interface consists of three events: `create` and `remove`, with the obvious meaning, and `getEJBMeta-Data`, which is a service provided by the container that returns meta-information about the methods supported by the bean. Note that the port is initialized by a `create` event and terminated by a `remove` event. The auxiliary process definition `GoHomeInterface`, describes the Home Interface perspective of what may go on between the creation of a bean and its removal: getting the bean's meta-data.

An event that may occur at any time after the creation, `noSuchObject-Exception`, corresponds to an exception being raised by the container. In fact, the EJB spec says that "*a Client must always be prepared to recreate a new instance* (of a bean) *if it looses the one it is using*" (pp. 24).[8] Hence, if the Client gets a `noSuchObjectException`, it should go back to create another bean. The

---

[8] In a distributed computing environment, it is possible to loose communication with a remote server. The distribution transparency provided by EJB, however, has the potential to hide from the client whether the reinitialized home interface is directed to the same, recovered, server or to another that supports the same bean class.

Wright specification exhibits this property in both the specification of the process
`GoHomeInterface` and in the process CallBean in the Client's computation: the
occurrence of a `noSuchObjectException` event causes the Client to reinitialize
the Home Interface by issuing a `create` event. In Sect. 7 we see how less trivial
properties can be checked by the use of automated tools.

The main body of computation, once it is initialized by a `create`, is the parallel composition of the processes `UseRemoteInterface` and `GoHomeInterface`.
What goes on in this composition is dictated by the application logic, passed
as a parameter to the client, in parallel with the initialized Home Interface. Finally, at any time (after initialization) the client may decide to remove the bean.
This is signaled by the client-initiated `remove` event interrupting the process
described above (using the △ operator). However, the Client must be prepared
to handle a `removeException`, thrown by the Container. After a `remove`, either
the computation successfully terminates, or it accepts a `removeException`, after
which it also terminates. The EJB spec does not define how components should
handle exceptions. So we only note the fact that an exception may be received.
It should be clear now that the specification of the `UseHomeInterface` port is
actually a view of the Client's computation, restricted to the events recognized
by the Home Interface.

The `HomeInterface` role in the container expresses the possible behaviors of
the client that attaches to this role:

```
Connector Container (BusinessLogic: Process)
    Role HomeInterface = create → GoHomeInterface
    Where GoHomeInterface
        = ( getEJBMetaData → GoHomeInterface
            [] noSuchObjectException → HomeInterface )
        ⊓ remove → ( § [] removeException → § )
```

The process specification for this role is equivalent to the process in the `Use-`
`HomeInterface` of the Client component, in the sense that it will generate the
same set of traces. After being initialized by `create`, the attached component will
choose (internally) whether or not to `remove` the bean. If the component chooses
not to remove the bean, it may initiate a request for meta-data. It also admits
a `noSuchObjectException`, which resets the role. If the component chooses to
remove the bean, it admits a `removeException`, but terminates afterwards, in
either case.[9]

6.2   The Container and the Bean

In the container, there are three Wright roles that are involved in the creation of
a bean. The first is the `HomeInterface` role, as discussed in Sect. 6.1, to which

---

[9] Again, for simplicity, we focus on a single run of the protocols between the client
and the container, in order to distinguish between a situation where the protocol
demands a reset, from a situation where it runs through successfully and could go
back to create another bean.

the client attaches. The other two are the `UseBeanHome` and `UseJxBean` roles, to which the bean attaches:

```
Connector Container (BusinessLogic: Process)
    alpha Created = αUseJxBean \ {setContext, ejbRemove}
    . . .
    Role UseBeanHome = newInstance → ejbCreate → §
    Role UseJxBean   = setContext → GoJxBean
    Where GoJxBean
        =  ejbPassivate → ejbActivate → GoJxBean
        [] ejbRemove → UseJxBean
    Glue = ...
    Where BeanLive
        = create →  newInstance  →  setContext  →  ejbCreate
        → ( RUN_Created
            △ remove →  ejbRemove  → § )
    . . .
Component EJBean (EJBObject: Process)
    Port BeanHome = newInstance → ejbCreate → §
    Port JxBean = setContext → GoJxBean
    Where GoJxBean
        =  ejbPassivate → ejbActivate → GoJxBean
        [] ejbRemove → §
```

Since it is often the case that a protocol refers to events in more than one role, the perspective that a specific role has of a protocol is limited by the alphabet of the role. It is the *glue* that links what goes on in each role, thus completing the protocol followed by the connector.

In order to single out each piece of the glue that corresponds to a particular protocol in the software framework, we introduce auxiliary process definitions. BeanLive is one of them. Since this is a glue process, it takes the viewpoint of the container: hence, the `create` event is initiated by the environment (in the `HomeInterface` role). After receiving a `create`, the container initiates the `newInstance` event in the `UseBeanHome` role, sets the newly created bean's run-time context (`setContext` in the `UseJxBean` role,) and signals the new bean to run the appropriate initialization method (`ejbCreate` in `UseBeanHome`).

The `BeanLive` process then accepts any event in the alphabet of the `UseJx-Bean` role, except for `setContext` (part of the initialization) and `ejbRemove` (part of the termination). When interrupted by a `remove` event in the `HomeInterface` role, the `BeanLive` process signals the bean to run the appropriate termination method (`ejbRemove` in the `UseJxBean` role) and then terminates.[10]

The Container relays the business logic events in the role `RemoteInterface` (to which the Client attaches) to the role `UseRemoteInterface` (to which the

---

[10] The roles take the viewpoint of the environment (of the components that attach to the roles,) as opposed to the viewpoint of the container. So, the parity of initiation is reversed in the glue and in the roles. Note also that the processes in the roles UseBeanHome and UseJxBean match the processes in the corresponding ports in the Bean component, BeanHome and JxBean.

Bean attaches). The glue process `Delegate` assures this by simply stating that any event e in the `RemoteInterface` role is followed by the (container-initiated) same event $\bar{e}$ in the `UseRemoteInterface` role.

Recall now that the container may decide to passivate a bean according to a least recently used policy. The glue process `SwapBean` (see below) accepts any event in the alphabet of the Container,[11] except for the events `ejbPassivate` and `ejbActivate`. Whenever the container decides to initiate an `ejbPassivate` event, the `SwapBean` process waits for the next event in the `RemoteInterface` role. After that, and before the event is relayed to the `UseRemoteInterface` role, an `ejbActivate` event is interleaved. The parallel combination of the processes `SwapBean` and `Delegate` in the glue produces the desired effect: the business logic events are normally relayed, but whenever the bean was passivated, it receives an activation event just before the business logic event is sent.

```
Connector Container (BusinessLogic: Process)
    alpha Activated = αContainer \ {ejbPassivate, ejbActivate}
    Role UseJxBean = setContext → GoJxBean
    Where GoJxBean
        =   ejbPassivate → ejbActivate → GoJxBean
        [] ejbRemove → UseJxBean
    ...
    Role RemoteInterface = BusinessLogic
    Role UseRemoteInterface = BusinessLogic
    Glue =   BeanLive
           || Delegate
           || SwapBean
    Where Delegate = [] e: αRemoteInterface •
        RemoteInterface.e → UseRemoteInterface.ē → Delegate
    Where SwapBean
        = RUN_Activated △ ejbPassivate
        → ( [] e: αRemoteInterface • RemoteInterface.e
            → ejbActivate → UseRemoteInterface.ē → SwapBean )
```

7 Using the Model

By precisely specifying the implied protocols of interaction for EJB, one achieves a number of immediate benefits. First, the formal specification is explicit about permitted orderings of method calls, and about where the locus of choice lies. Second, the specification makes explicit where different parts of the framework share assumptions. In particular, the role of `BusinessLogic` as a parameter helps clarify the way in which assumptions about the application-specific behavior are shared among the parts of the framework. Third, the model helps clarify some of the more complex aspects of the model by localizing behavior. For example, the murky role of passivation becomes clear in the `Container` glue.

Furthermore, it is also possible to submit the model to formal analysis via model checking tools. To do this we used the FDR™ model checker for CSP [7]

---

[11] Taken here as the union of the alphabets in all roles.

to check for deadlocks in the container.[12] In addition to checking for deadlocks, FDR can also be used to make sure that specific required behaviors[13] still hold in the overall result of the composition of all local specifications. For that we use the CSP notion of process refinement. Specifically, we can check if a process describing the desired behavior is *refined* by the overall specification; for instance, if a process describing the client's recovery after a container failure is refined by the one-Client-one-Server specification. If that is the case, that means that the intended behavior was not lost due to a mistake during the process of specifying all the interacting behaviors.

For the current model, analysis revealed one significant problem. The problem concerns a possible race condition between the delegation and passivation processes inside the Container. Suppose that the Client initiates an event in the RemoteInterface role. Then, before the Delegate process relays the event to the bean through the UseRemoteInterface role, the SwapBean process, operating concurrently, decides to passivate the bean. Now, the Delegate process must relay the received business logic event to the UseRemoteInterface role, before it can accept the next event in the RemoteInterface role. However, the SwapBean process just issued an ejbPassivate notification to the bean, and hence it waits for the next event in the RemoteInterface role to reactivate the bean. Therefore, the processes that go on inside the Container cannot agree on what to do next, and the connector deadlocks.

A simple correction for the deadlock is:

```
Connector Container (EJBObject: Process)
    ...
    Where Delegate
        = ( [] e: αRemoteInterface •
            RemoteInterface.e → UseRemoteInterface.ē → Delegate )
        [] ejbPassivate → Delegate
    ...
```

That is, the Delegate process must prevent passivation between receiving an event in the RemoteInterface role and relaying it to the UseRemoteInterface role. One way to model it in CSP is to explicitly allow the ejbPassivate event outside the mentioned "critical section".

While arguably one might attribute the detected problem to *our* specification, and not to Sun's EJB spec, it does point out a place where the complexity of the specification can lead to errors that might be hard to detect otherwise. Without a precise model and effective automated analysis tools to identify problem areas, such errors could easily be introduced, undetected, into an implementation.

---

[12] Translation from Wright to FDR is accomplished semi-automatically using the Wright tool set. See [1].
[13] For instance, Sun's document (pp. 24) states that any implementation of the EJB protocol between a client and an EJB server must allow the client to recover from EJB server crashes.

8   Conclusions and Future Work

In this paper we have outlined a formal architectural model of part of Sun's EJB component integration framework. In doing this we have attempted to shed light both on EJB itself, and on the way in which one can go about modeling object-oriented architectural frameworks. The key idea in our approach is to take an architectural view of the problem that makes explicit the protocols of interaction between the principle parts of the framework. In particular, we have shown how representing the framework's mediating infrastructure as a connector with a well-defined protocol helps to clarify the overall structure of the framework and to localize the relationships between the various method calls that connect the parts.

The use of formal architectural modeling languages to represent frameworks such as EJB opens up a number of important questions to investigate. First, while our specification focused on certain properties of the framework, there are many others that one might want to model. For example, although potential deadlocks are highlighted by our model, we do not handle important issues such as performance, reliability, and security. For many frameworks finding notations that expose such properties will be crucial.

Second, given a formal specification, such as the one we have presented, it should be possible to influence conformance testing. Currently, conformance to a framework can only be loosely checked – for example, by making sure that an implementation provides the full API. However, given a richer semantic model, it should be possible to do much better.

Third, the EJB spec uses inheritance to organize the presentation of many of its concepts. For example, the `SessionBean` class inherits behavior from the `EnterpriseBean` class, which in turn inherits from the `java.io.Serializable` class. In contrast, the formal model that we have presented is essentially flat. To come up with our model we had to fold together the implicit semantic behavior defined in several classes. It would have been much nicer to have been able to mirror the inheritance structure in the architectural specification. While such extension is relatively well-understood with respect to signatures, it is not so clear what is needed to handle interactive behaviors – such as protocols of inter-action. Finding a suitable calculus of protocol extension is an open and relevant topic for future research.

Acknowledgments

This research was supported by the US Defense Advanced Research Projects Agency and Rome Laboratory, USAF, under Cooperative Agreement F30602-97-2-0031, and by the US National Science Foundation under Grant CCR-9357792. Views and conclusions contained in this document are those of the authors and should not be interpreted as representing the official policies, either expressed or implied, of Rome Laboratory, the US Department of Defense, or the US National Science Foundation. The US Government is authorized to reproduce and distribute reprints for Government purposes, notwithstanding any copyright notation thereon.

References

[1] Robert Allen and David Garlan. A formal basis for architectural connection. In *ACM Trans. on Software Engineering and Methodology*, July 1997.

[2] Robert Allen, David Garlan, and James Ivers. Formal modeling and analysis of the HLA component integration standard. In *Sixth Intl. Symposium on the Foundations of Software Engineering* (FSE-6), Nov. 1998.

[3] Robert Allen. A Formal Approach to Software Architecture. PhD thesis, CMU, School of Computer Science, January 1997. CMU/SCS Report CMU-CS-97-144.

[4] Edmund Clarke et al. Automatic verification of finite state concurrent systems using temporal logic specifications. In *ACM Trans. on Programming Languages and Systems*, April 1986.

[5] Edmund Clarke et al. Verification Tools for Finite-State Concurrent Systems. A Decade of concurrency - Reflections and Perspectives. *Springer Verlag LNCS 803*, 1994.

[6] Vlada Matena, Mark Hapner, Enterprise JavaBeans™, Sun Microsystems Inc., Palo Alto, California, 1998.

[7] Failures Divergence Refinement: User Manual and Tutorial, 1.2β. Formal Systems (Europe) Ltd., Oxford, England, 1992.

[8] David Garlan, Robert Allen, and John Ockerbloom. Architectural mismatch: Why reuse is so hard. *IEEE Software*, November 1995.

[9] C. A. R. Hoare. *Communicating Sequential Processes*. Prentice Hall, 1985.

[10] Gerald J. Holzmann. *Design and Validation of Computer Protocols*. Prentice Hall, 1991.

[11] David C Luckham, et al. Specification and analysis of system architecture using Rapide. In *IEEE Trans. on Software Engineering*, April 1995.

[12] Nancy A. Lynch and Mark R. Tuttle. An introduction to input/output automata. Technical Report MIT/LCS/TM-373, MIT LCS, 1988.

[13] J. Magee, N. Dulay, S. Eisenbach, and J. Kramer. Specifying distributed software architectures. In *Proceedings ESEC'95*, Sept. 1995.

[14] M. Moriconi, X. Qian, and R. Riemenschneider. Correct architecture refinement. In *IEEE Trans. on Software Engineering*, April 1995.

[15] J.L. Peterson. *Petri nets*. ACM Computing Surveys, September 1977.

[16] A. W. Roscoe. *The Theory and Practice of Concurrency*. Prentice Hall, 1998.

[17] Mary Shaw, et al. Abstractions for software architecture and tools to support them. In *IEEE Trans. on Software Engineering*, April 1995.

[18] K.J. Sullivan, J. Socha, and M. Marchukov. Using formal methods to reason about architectural standards. In *1997 Intl. Conf. on Software Engineering*, May 1997.

Developing Components in the Presence of Re-entrance

Leonid Mikhajlov[1], Emil Sekerinski[2], and Linas Laibinis[1]

[1] Turku Centre for Computer Science,
Lemminkäisenkatu 14A, Turku 20520, Finland
`Leonid.Mikhajlov,Linas.Laibinis@abo.fi`
[2] McMaster University,
1280 Main Street West, Hamilton, Ontario, Canada, L8S4K1
`Emil.Sekerinski@mcmaster.ca`

Abstract. Independent development of components according to their specifications is complicated by the fact that a thread of control can exit and re-enter the same component. This kind of re-entrance may cause problems as the internal representation of a component can be observed in an inconsistent state. We argue that the ad-hoc reasoning used in establishing conformance of components to their specifications that intuitively appears to be correct does not account for the presence of re-entrance. Such reasoning leads to a conflict between assumptions that component developers make about the behavior of components in a system, resulting in the component re-entrance problem. We formulate the modular reasoning property that captures the process of independent component development and introduce two requirements that must be imposed to avoid the re-entrance problem. Then we define a customized theory of components, component systems, and component refinement which models the process of component development from specifications. Using this theory, we prove that the formulated requirements are sufficient to establish the modular reasoning property.

1 Introduction

In this paper we study a problem which hinders the development of a component market. One of the characteristic features of component-based systems and standards is the fact that components are developed by independent developers and an integration phase is either completely absent or minimized. When the integration phase is missing as, e.g., in CI Labs OpenDoc [8], components are composed by end users; when the integration phase is postponed, as in the case of Sun Java Beans [16] and Microsoft COM [15], components are composed by application developers. With both composition scenarios, components communicate by invoking each other's methods through the interfaces they implement. Interfaces are syntactic and only syntactic compatibility of components implementing them can be verified in the integration phase. It has been recognized [10, 17] that the verification of syntactic compatibility is insufficient to guarantee seamless interoperation of components in the resulting system. Interfaces

J. Wing, J. Woodcock, J. Davies (Eds.): FM'99, Vol. II, LNCS 1709, pp. 1301–1320, 1999.
© Springer-Verlag Berlin Heidelberg 1999

component *Model*
    $s : seq\ of\ char := \langle\rangle,$
    $get\_s() \ \widehat{=} \ \mathbf{return}\ s,$
    $get\_num() \ \widehat{=} \ \mathbf{return}\ \#s,$
    $append(\mathbf{val}\ t : seq\ of\ char) \ \widehat{=}$
        $s := s\ \widehat{}\ t;\ View \rightarrow update()$
end

component *View*
    $update() \ \widehat{=}$
        $print(\#\ Model \rightarrow get\_s())$
end

Fig. 1. Specification of the Model-View component system. The operator $\#$ returns the length of a sequence and the operator $\widehat{}$ concatenates two sequences.

should be augmented with behavioral specifications of the expected functionality to stipulate the contractual obligations that the components implementing such interfaces are required to meet. Due to the missing integration phase, it becomes impossible to analyze semantic integrity of the composed system. Therefore, a specification and verification method should provide for modular reasoning: verifying that participating components meet their contractual obligations should be sufficient to guarantee that the composed system operates correctly.

The independent development of components according to their specifications is complicated by the fact that, in general, a thread of control can exit and re-enter the same component. Suppose that we have two communicating components $\mathcal{A}$ and $\mathcal{B}$, each with its own attributes. A method of component $\mathcal{A}$ invokes a method of component $\mathcal{B}$. At the moment when the method of $\mathcal{B}$ is invoked, instance variables of $\mathcal{A}$ might be in transition between consistent states. The component $\mathcal{B}$ can observe and modify the state of $\mathcal{A}$ by calling back its methods. Such a re-entering method invocation pattern is problematic because $\mathcal{B}$ can observe $\mathcal{A}$ in an unexpected inconsistent state and become invalidated. Further on we refer to this problem as the *component re-entrance problem*. In order to show the implications of the component re-entrance problem on the independent development of components, we analyze the example in Fig. 1.

Let us first remark on the specification notation that we use in our examples. It was pointed out [13, 2, 10, 5, 6] that a specification can be viewed as an abstract program. In fact, specifications differ from executable programs only by the degree of nondeterminism and data structures that are used. Typically, an executable program is just a deterministic specification operating on implementable data structures. Such an approach to formal specification is advantageous, because it permits to include method calls in a component specification to fix a certain communication protocol. This approach is state-based, and in order to specify the behavior of component methods we need to model data attributes of this component. Even though component attributes are present in its specification, they cannot be accessed by clients of this component and, therefore, can be changed in a development step. When such a change is made, component methods must be modified to work with the new attributes.

As the problem that we consider does not depend on a programming language, in the example in Fig. 1 we use a simple specification notation which should appeal to the reader's intuition. Weakest precondition and operational semantics for statements in this notation can be found in [2]. Note that each statement explicitly indicates which variables it modifies; the other variables remain unchanged.

The example follows the Observer pattern [9], which allows separating the presentational aspects of the user interface from the underlying application data, by defining two components *Model* and *View*. The components *Model* and *View* refer to each other. Note that we deliberately abstract away from the mechanism by which such mutual reference can be achieved, because we want to keep our component model as general as possible. Components can be static entities, such as modules, or dynamic entities, such as objects. In the case of static entities mutual reference can be established by mutual inclusion of syntactic interfaces, whereas with dynamic entities it can be achieved, for example, by passing pointers to components as method parameters.

The specification *Model* maintains a string *s*, represented by a sequence of characters and initialized with an empty sequence. Every time a new string is appended to the string in *Model*, the method *update* of *View* is called. In turn, *update* calls back *Model*'s *get_s*() method and prints out the number of elements in the received string. In a component market, these specifications are published and independent developers are offered to implement these components.

Suppose that one software company decides to implement the specification of *Model*. To avoid counting characters in the method *get_num*, the developers introduce an integer attribute *n* to represent the number of characters in the sequence. Accordingly, they implement a component *Model'* as follows:

```
component Model'
    s :  seq of char := ⟨⟩,
    n : int := 0,
    get_s()  ≙ return s,
    get_num()  ≙ return n,
    append(val t :  seq of char)  ≙
        s := s ^ t; View ⊳ update(); n := n + #t
end
```

Note that taking into account the specification of the method *update* in *View*, the implementation of the method *append* appears to be perfectly valid. In fact, updating the screen as early as possible is a reasonable policy.

Now suppose that another software company decides to implement a component *View'* according to the specification. Note that the developers of *View'* do not have access to the code of *Model'*, so the only thing they can rely on is its specification. To avoid passing a sequence of characters as a parameter, the method *update* can be implemented to invoke the method *get_num* of *Model*:

component $View'$
$\quad update() \ \widehat{=} \ print(Model \rightarrow get\_num())$
end

Here we face the component re-entrance problem. Even though components $Model'$ and $View'$ appear to implement the specification correctly, their composition behaves incorrectly: the number of elements in the string s that $update$ prints out is wrong.

In a component market, where developments have to be independent, this constitutes a major obstacle. However, if we view $Model$ and $View$ as implementations and $Model'$ and $View'$ as more efficient implementations, we see that this problem occurs not only during development, but also during maintenance of component systems. The formalism in which we study the problem encompasses both situations in a uniform way.

A recommendation known from practice suggests always to establish a component invariant before the thread of control leaves the component. In fact, this is the recommendation for implementing the Observer pattern as it can be found in [9]. In the example above, the developers of $Model'$ should have established the component invariant $n = \#s$ before invoking the method $update$.

In this paper we present a formal analysis of the problem that supports this requirement, but reveals that it is not sufficient in the general case. Two further restrictions should be imposed according to "no call-back assumptions" and "no accidental mutual recursion" requirements.

The rest of the paper is organized as follows. We begin with a detailed analysis of the component re-entrance problem and explain why we view it as the conflict of assumptions that developers of components make about the behavior of other components in the system. We formulate the modular reasoning property that captures the process of independent component development. Using simple examples, we then justify the introduction of two requirements that must be imposed to avoid the re-entrance problem. Next we develop a customized theory of components, component composition, and refinement and prove a modular reasoning theorem which states that the modular reasoning property reinforced with our requirements holds in the presence of re-entrance. Finally, we offer a discussion of implications of the modular reasoning theorem, discuss related work, and provide some insights on our future work.

2   The Essence of the Component Re-entrance Problem

A component operates by communicating with an environment. Unlike in the case of procedure libraries, the environment calls back the component's methods. The component and its environment play symmetrical roles: the component is a client of the environment, while the environment is a client of the component. Therefore, we can view the entire system as consisting of only two components, the component under consideration and the component "environment".

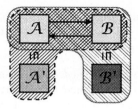

Fig. 2. Independence of component development. Developers can access only the components in the corresponding hatched areas.

Let us now define the notion of behavioral conformance more precisely. We say that a system (or a component) **S** *is refined by* a system (or a component) **S′** if the externally observable behavior of **S′** is the externally observable behavior of **S** or an improvement of it. In other words, if **S′** is a refinement of **S** then it is substitutable for **S** in any context.[1] Note that **S** and **S′** can be, respectively, a specification and a more concrete specification, a specification and an implementation, or an implementation and a more efficient implementation.

Now suppose that we have a specification of a system composed of two components $\mathcal{A}$ and $\mathcal{B}$ invoking each other's methods. Ultimately, independent developers of refining components $\mathcal{A}'$ and $\mathcal{B}'$ would like to achieve that the system resulting from the composition of these components be a refinement of the composition of the original components $\mathcal{A}$ and $\mathcal{B}$, namely,

$$\mathcal{A}\,\mathbf{comp}\,\mathcal{B} \ is \ refined \ by \ \mathcal{A}'\,\mathbf{comp}\,\mathcal{B}' \tag{1}$$

where **comp** composes two components into a component system. A composition of two components has all the methods of both components with all mutual method calls resolved. Due to the late integration phase, which is characteristic of component systems, developers of a component cannot analyze the source code of the new environment this component will be used in, and can rely only on the original specification of the system. This setting is illustrated in Fig. 2.

The behavior of a component invoking methods of another component depends on the behavior of these methods. Therefore, when reasoning about the conformance of the component $\mathcal{A}'$ to the component $\mathcal{A}$, the developers need to make assumptions about the behavior of the component $\mathcal{B}$. The ad-hoc method for taking such assumptions into account is to reason about the refinement between the results of composition of $\mathcal{A}'$ and $\mathcal{A}$ with $\mathcal{B}$:

$$\mathcal{A}\,\mathbf{comp}\,\mathcal{B} \ is \ refined \ by \ \mathcal{A}'\,\mathbf{comp}\,\mathcal{B}, \tag{2}$$

and dually for the components $\mathcal{B}'$ and $\mathcal{B}$:

$$\mathcal{A}\,\mathbf{comp}\,\mathcal{B} \ is \ refined \ by \ \mathcal{A}\,\mathbf{comp}\,\mathcal{B}' \tag{3}$$

---

[1] The formal definition of refinement is given in Sec.4.3.

Unfortunately, in the general case, the two requirements (2) and (3) are insufficient to establish the goal (1), as demonstrated by the previous example. In other words, the desired property

$$\begin{aligned}
&\textit{if } \mathcal{A} \, \textsf{comp} \, \mathcal{B} \textit{ is refined by } \mathcal{A}' \, \textsf{comp} \, \mathcal{B} \textit{ and} \\
&\quad \mathcal{A} \, \textsf{comp} \, \mathcal{B} \textit{ is refined by } \mathcal{A} \, \textsf{comp} \, \mathcal{B}' \\
&\textit{then } \mathcal{A} \, \textsf{comp} \, \mathcal{B} \textit{ is refined by } \mathcal{A}' \, \textsf{comp} \, \mathcal{B}'
\end{aligned} \tag{4}$$

does not hold. We believe that this fact constitutes the essence of the component re-entrance problem. The problem occurs due to the conflict of assumptions the developers of components make about the behavior of other components in the system. In the previous example the developers of the component *View'* assumed that at the moment when the method *update* is called the invariant of the implementation of *Model* would hold. Similarly, the developers of *Model'* assumed that they did not need to establish the invariant before invoking *update*, because its specification did not rely on it. These conflicting assumptions led to the problem during composition.

This consideration brings us to the questions how we can guide the process of component development, so that the system composed of the refining components would always be safely substitutable for the original one, and how while developing a component one can make assumptions about the behavior of the other components in the system, in a consistent manner.

3   Modular Reasoning Required

Apparently, it would be desirable if for establishing refinement between composed systems it would be sufficient to verify refinement between the corresponding components. In other words, we would like the following property to hold:

$$\begin{aligned}
&\textit{if } \mathcal{A} \textit{ is refined by } \mathcal{A}' \textit{ and} \\
&\quad \mathcal{B} \textit{ is refined by } \mathcal{B}' \\
&\textit{then } \mathcal{A} \, \textsf{comp} \, \mathcal{B} \textit{ is refined by } \mathcal{A}' \, \textsf{comp} \, \mathcal{B}'
\end{aligned}$$

However, establishing refinement between the participating components is complicated due to their mutual dependence. In principle, we can say that a component is refined by another component if the systems resulting from the composition of these components with an arbitrarily chosen component are in refinement:

$$\mathcal{A} \textit{ is refined by } \mathcal{A}' \; \widehat{=} \; \mathcal{A} \, \textsf{comp} \, \mathcal{B} \textit{ is refined by } \mathcal{A}' \, \textsf{comp} \, \mathcal{B}, \textit{ for any } \mathcal{B}$$

In fact, it is possible to prove that this definition of refinement indeed establishes the property (4) for the case of mutually dependent components. Unfortunately, this definition of refinement is too restrictive to be used in practice. According to this definition, one can only refine bodies of methods around method invocations, without being able to assume anything about the called methods.

For the definition of component refinement to be useful in practice it should permit to make assumptions about the context in which the component under consideration operates. As the context (environment) of a component can be seen as the other component, we would like the following *modular reasoning property* to hold:

> *if A is refined by A' in context of B and*
> *B is refined by B' in context of A*
> *then A comp B is refined by A' comp B'*

In the case when the complete context is assumed in a refinement step, the modular reasoning property is equivalent to the property (4). However, as was demonstrated by the previous example, the conclusion of the modular reasoning property does not hold in this case. In order to establish refinement between the composed systems, it is necessary to restrict the assumptions that component developers can make about the context in which the component is going to operate. To identify the restrictions that should be imposed on the assumptions about the component context, let us consider two counter examples invalidating the property (4).

In the following example we use an assertion statement $\{p\}$, where p is a state predicate. If p is true in the current state, the assertion skips, otherwise it aborts. Therefore, the assertion statement can be seen as an abbreviation for the conditional **if** p **then skip else abort**.

component A
$\quad m_1(\textbf{valres } x : int) \;\widehat{=}\; \{x > 5\}; x := 5,$
$\quad m_2(\textbf{valres } x : int) \;\widehat{=}\; \{x > 0\}; x := 5$
end
component A'
$\quad m_1(\textbf{valres } x : int) \;\widehat{=}\; \{x > 0\}; x := 5,$
$\quad m_2(\textbf{valres } x : int) \;\widehat{=}\; B{\to}n(x)$
end

component B
$\quad n(\textbf{valres } x : int) \;\widehat{=}$
$\qquad A{\to}m_1(x)$
end
component B'
$\quad n(\textbf{valres } x : int) \;\widehat{=}$
$\qquad \{x > 5\}; x := 5$
end

If we expand the bodies of the method m_2 in the composed systems then we have:

$(A \textbf{ comp } B) :: m_2 = \{x > 0\}; x := 5 \quad (A' \textbf{ comp } B) :: m_2 = \{x > 0\}; x := 5$
$(A \textbf{ comp } B') :: m_2 = \{x > 0\}; x := 5 \quad (A' \textbf{ comp } B') :: m_2 = \{x > 5\}; x := 5$

Therefore,

$(A \textbf{ comp } B) :: m_2$ *is refined by* $(A' \textbf{ comp } B) :: m_2$ and
$(A \textbf{ comp } B) :: m_2$ *is refined by* $(A \textbf{ comp } B') :: m_2$

However, it is not the case that

$(A \textbf{ comp } B) :: m_2$ *is refined by* $(A' \textbf{ comp } B') :: m_2$

Due to the presence of assertions, the precondition $x > 5$ of $(\mathcal{A}' \operatorname{\mathbf{comp}} \mathcal{B}') :: m_2$ is stronger than the precondition $x > 0$ of $(\mathcal{A} \operatorname{\mathbf{comp}} \mathcal{B}) :: m_2$, while to preserve refinement, preconditions can only be weakened.

This example motivates us to formulate the following "no call-back assumptions" requirement:

> *While developing an implementation of a method, implementations of other methods of the same component cannot be assumed; their specifications should be considered instead.*

As the behavior of the environment serving as a context depends on the behavior of the component under consideration, assuming that the environment is going to call back on the refined component would implicitly modify the specification.

However, there exists another aspect of the component re-entrance problem which cannot be handled by simply restricting the context for refinement. The following rather trivial example illustrates this aspect of the problem.

component $\mathcal{A}$	**component** $\mathcal{B}$
$\quad m(\mathbf{res}\ r : int) \;\widehat{=}\; r := 5$	$\quad n(\mathbf{res}\ r : int) \;\widehat{=}\; r := 5$
end	**end**
component $\mathcal{A}'$	**component** $\mathcal{B}'$
$\quad m(\mathbf{res}\ r : int) \;\widehat{=}\; \mathcal{B} \text{-}\!\triangleright n(r)$	$\quad n(\mathbf{res}\ r : int) \;\widehat{=}\; \mathcal{A} \text{-}\!\triangleright m(r)$
end	**end**

It is easy to see that a call to any method in the composition $\mathcal{A}' \operatorname{\mathbf{comp}} \mathcal{B}'$ of the refined components leads to a never terminating recursion of method invocations. Obviously, such a behavior does refine the behavior of the original system. In fact, a similar problem was described by Carroll Morgan in [13]. He mentions that in case of mutually dependent modules their independent refinements can accidentally introduce mutual recursion. Based on this example, we formulate the following "no accidental mutual recursion" requirement:

> *Independent development of components should not introduce unexpected mutual recursion.*

We claim that if the "no call-back assumptions" and "no accidental mutual recursion" requirements are satisfied, then the modular reasoning property holds. For proving this claim formally we develop a customized theory of components, component systems, and their refinement.

4 Formalization of Components, Composition, and Refinement

We formalize components, component systems, and refinement between them within the refinement calculus [2, 13]. For simplicity, we assume that components do not have self-calls and component implementations do not introduce new methods. Here we only consider components which do not have recursive and mutually recursive methods. Our model is tailored specifically to allow for reasoning about the properties under consideration.

4.1   Statements and Statement Refinement

This subsection is based on the work by Ralph Back and Joakim von Wright as presented in [2, 3, 4]. The refinement calculus is a logical framework for reasoning about correctness and refinement of imperative programs. The language used to express programs and specifications is essentially Dijkstra's language of guarded commands, with some extensions. Each command of this language is identified with its weakest precondition predicate transformer. Therefore, program statements are modeled as functions that map postconditions to preconditions.

The predicates over a state space (type) Σ are functions from Σ to *Bool*, denoted by $\mathcal{P}\Sigma$. The relations from Σ to Γ are functions from Σ to a predicate (set of values) over Γ, denoted by $\Sigma \leftrightarrow \Gamma$. The predicate transformers from Σ to Γ are functions mapping predicates over Γ to predicates over Σ, denoted by $\Sigma \mapsto \Gamma$ (note the reversion of the direction), or by $Ptran(\Sigma)$ in the case of $\Sigma \mapsto \Sigma$.

The entailment ordering $p \subseteq q$ on predicates $p, q : \mathcal{P}\Sigma$ is defined as universal implication on booleans, i.e.

$$p \subseteq q \;\; \widehat{=} \;\; (\forall \sigma : \Sigma \bullet p.\sigma \;\Rightarrow\; q.\sigma)$$

The conjunction and disjunction on predicates $\cup$ and $\cap$ are defined pointwise. The predicates *true* and *false* over Σ map every $\sigma : \Sigma$ to the boolean values **T** and **F**, respectively. The refinement ordering $S \sqsubseteq T$, read S *is refined by* T, on statements $S, T : \Sigma \mapsto \Gamma$ is defined by universal entailment:

$$S \sqsubseteq T \;\; \widehat{=} \;\; (\forall q : \mathcal{P}\Gamma \bullet S.q \subseteq T.q)$$

A predicate transformer $S : \Sigma \mapsto \Gamma$ is said to be *monotonic* if for all predicates p and q, $p \subseteq q$ implies $S.p \subseteq S.q$. Statements from Σ to Γ are identified with monotonic predicate transformers from Σ to Γ. Statements of this kind may be concrete, i.e. executable, or abstract, i.e. specifications. The refinement calculus includes all standard program statements, such as assignments, conditionals, and loops. Here we only present the definitions of the constructs that are used later in the paper.

The sequential composition of statements $S : \Sigma \mapsto \Gamma$ and $T : \Gamma \mapsto \Delta$ is modeled by their functional composition, for $q : \mathcal{P}\Delta$,

$$(S;T).q \;\; \widehat{=} \;\; S.(T.q)$$

The statement **abort** does not guarantee any outcome or termination, therefore, it maps every postcondition to *false*. The statement **magic** is *miraculous*, since it is always guaranteed to establish any postcondition. The statement **skip** leaves the state unchanged. Thus, we have:

$$\textbf{abort}.q \;\widehat{=}\; false \qquad\qquad \textbf{magic}.q \;\widehat{=}\; true \qquad\qquad \textbf{skip}.q \;\widehat{=}\; q$$

The *assertion* statement $\{p\}$ indicates that the predicate p is known to hold at a certain point in the program. The assertion $\{p\}$ behaves as **abort** if p does not hold, and as **skip** otherwise. Formally, it is defined as follows:

$$\{p\}.q \;\widehat{=}\; p \cap q$$

The language supports two kinds of non-deterministic updates which, in fact, represent specification statements. Given a relation $P : \Sigma \leftrightarrow \Gamma$, the *angelic update* $\{P\} : \Sigma \mapsto \Gamma$, and the *demonic update* $[P] : \Sigma \mapsto \Gamma$ are defined by

$$\{P\}.q.\sigma \; \widehat{=} \; (\exists \gamma : \Gamma \bullet P.\sigma.\gamma \,\wedge\, q.\gamma) \qquad [P].q.\sigma \; \widehat{=} \; (\forall \gamma : \Gamma \bullet P.\sigma.\gamma \,\Rightarrow\, q.\gamma)$$

When started in a state σ, $\{P\}$ angelically chooses a new state γ such that $P.\sigma.\gamma$ holds, while $[P]$ demonically chooses a new state γ such that $P.\sigma.\gamma$ holds. If no such state exists, then $\{P\}$ aborts, whereas $[P]$ behaves as **magic**. Traditional pre-postcondition specifications can be easily expressed in the refinement calculus. For example, a specification with the precondition $x > 0$ and postcondition $x' > x$, where x' stands for the new value of the program variable x, can be expressed by the statement $\{p\}; [P]$, where $p.x = x > 0$ and $P.x.x' = x' > x$.

The cartesian product of state spaces Σ and Γ is written $\Sigma \times \Gamma$. For predicates $p : \mathcal{P}\Sigma$ and $q : \mathcal{P}\Gamma$, their product $p \times q$ is a predicate of type $\mathcal{P}(\Sigma \times \Gamma)$ defined by

$$(p \times q).(\sigma, \gamma) \; \widehat{=} \; p.\sigma \,\wedge\, q.\gamma$$

For relations $P_1 : \Sigma_1 \leftrightarrow \Gamma_1$ and $P_2 : \Sigma_2 \leftrightarrow \Gamma_2$, their product $P_1 \times P_2$, is a relation of type $(\Sigma_1 \times \Sigma_2) \leftrightarrow (\Gamma_1 \times \Gamma_2)$, where for $\sigma_1 : \Sigma_1$, $\sigma_2 : \Sigma_2$, $\gamma_1 : \Gamma_1$, and $\gamma_2 : \Gamma_2$, we have:

$$(P_1 \times P_2).(\sigma_1, \sigma_2).(\gamma_1, \gamma_2) \; \widehat{=} \; (P_1.\sigma_1.\gamma_1) \,\wedge\, (P_2.\sigma_2.\gamma_2)$$

For predicate transformers $S_1 : \Sigma_1 \mapsto \Gamma_1$ and $S_2 : \Sigma_2 \mapsto \Gamma_2$, their product $S_1 \times S_2$ is a predicate transformer of type $\Sigma_1 \times \Sigma_2 \mapsto \Gamma_1 \times \Gamma_2$ whose execution has the same effect as the simultaneous execution of S_1 and S_2:

$$(S_1 \times S_2).q \; \widehat{=} \; (\cup q_1, q_2 \mid q_1 \times q_2 \subseteq q \bullet S_1.q_1 \times S_2.q_2)$$

The cross products operators are not associative in the sense that, e.g., $S_1 \times (S_2 \times S_3) \neq (S_1 \times S_2) \times S_3$. As different associations of the cross product operators are isomorphic to each other, for simplicity we disregard the non-associativity.

A statement S operating on the state space Σ can be coerced to operate on the state space Σ' using an *encoding* operator $\downarrow$ with a relation $R : \Sigma' \leftrightarrow \Sigma$ [3]. By lifting the relation R to the level of predicate transformers, we get the update statements $\{R\} : \Sigma' \mapsto \Sigma$ and $[R^{-1}] : \Sigma \mapsto \Sigma'$ that can be used to define the encoding operator $\downarrow$ as follows:

$$S{\downarrow}R \; \widehat{=} \; \{R\}; S; [R^{-1}]$$

Note that the statement $S \downarrow R$ operates on the state space Σ'. For tuples of statements, the encoding operator is defined elementwise. The encoding operator is left-associative and has a higher precedence than function application.

The encoding operator can be used to define *data refinement* in terms of ordinary refinement [19]. A statement $S : Ptran(\Sigma)$ is data refined by a statement $S' : Ptran(\Sigma')$ via a relation $R : \Sigma' \leftrightarrow \Sigma$, connecting concrete and abstract states, if S concretely coerced with R is refined by S', i.e.

$$S \sqsubseteq_R S' \; \widehat{=} \; S{\downarrow}R \sqsubseteq S'$$

A statement is said to be *indifferent* with respect to an encoding relation if it does not operate on the state component coerced with the relation. An indifferent statement **skip** $\times S$ is characterized by the following property:

$$(\textbf{skip} \times S)\!\downarrow\!(R \times Id) \sqsubseteq (\textbf{skip} \times S)$$

Relations of the form $R \times Id$ and $Id \times P$ are said to be *orthogonal* to each other. Further on, we use the following property of the encoding operator for the orthogonal relations $R \times Id$ and $Id \times P$:

$$S\!\downarrow\!(R \times Id)\!\downarrow\!(Id \times P) = S\!\downarrow\!(Id \times P)\!\downarrow\!(R \times Id) = S\!\downarrow\!(P \times R)$$

Forward functional composition is denoted by $\circ$ and defined in the usual way:

$$(f \circ g).x \;\; \widehat{=} \;\; f.(g.x)$$

Repeated function application f^n is defined inductively by

$$\begin{aligned} f^0.x &= x \\ f^{n+1}.x &= f^n.(f.x) \end{aligned}$$

4.2   Components and Composition

As we have mentioned, any component system can be seen as consisting of two components $\mathcal{A}$ and $\mathcal{B}$. Suppose that $\mathcal{A}$ has m and $\mathcal{B}$ has n methods. The components communicate by invoking each other's methods and passing parameters. For simplicity, we model method parameters by global variables that methods of both components can access in turns. For every formal parameter of a method we introduce a separate global variable which is used for passing values in and out of components. It is easy to see that parameter passing by value and by reference can be modeled in this way. As due to encapsulation the type of the internal state of the other component is not known, we say that the body of a method of the component $\mathcal{A}$ has the type $Ptran(\Sigma \times \Delta \times \beta)$, where Σ is the type of $\mathcal{A}$'s internal state, Δ is the type of global variables modeling method parameters, and β is the type variable to be instantiated with the type of the internal state of the other component during composition. As the internal state of the other component is not accessible, we assume that methods of $\mathcal{A}$ operate only on their internal state and the state representing method parameters and are, therefore, of the form $S \times \textbf{skip}$. Similarly, methods of $\mathcal{B}$ have bodies that are of the form $\textbf{skip} \times S$ and of the type $Ptran(\alpha \times \Delta \times \Gamma)$, where α is the type variable.

The behavior of a component method depends on the behavior of the methods it invokes. We can model a method of the component $\mathcal{A}$ as a function of a tuple of method bodies returning a method body[2]:

$$a_i \;\widehat{=}\; \lambda Bb \bullet ab_i$$

---

[2] We accept the following scheme for naming variables: a variable starting with a capital letter represents a tuple of variables; the second letter b in the name of a variable means that it represents a method body (statement) or a tuple of method bodies.

If we introduce an abbreviation Ψ^n to stand for $\Psi \times ... \times \Psi$ with n occurrences of Ψ, we can write out the type of a_i as $Ptran^n(\Sigma \times \Delta \times \beta) \to Ptran(\Sigma \times \Delta \times \beta)$, where n is the number of methods of $\mathcal{B}$. Methods of $\mathcal{B}$ are defined in the same manner, but have the type $Ptran^m(\alpha \times \Delta \times \Gamma) \to Ptran(\alpha \times \Delta \times \Gamma)$, where m is the number of methods in $\mathcal{B}$. We assume that every method is monotonic in its argument. Accordingly, we can collectively describe all methods of $\mathcal{A}$ as a function A given as follows:

$$A \mathrel{\widehat{=}} (\lambda Bb \bullet (ab_1, ..., ab_m)) : Ptran^n(\Sigma \times \Delta \times \beta) \to Ptran^m(\Sigma \times \Delta \times \beta)$$

Therefore, the component $\mathcal{A}$ is a tuple (a_0, A), where $a_0 : \Sigma$ is an initial value of the internal state and A is the function as defined above. The definition of the component $\mathcal{B}$ is similar but with the corresponding differences in typing.

Composing components $\mathcal{A}$ and $\mathcal{B}$ results in a component system that has methods of both components with all mutual calls resolved. The methods of the component $\mathcal{A}$ in the composed system can be approximated by $A.B.\textbf{Abort}$, where $\textbf{Abort}$ is a tuple of $\textbf{abort}$ statements. Using functional composition, this can be rewritten as $(A \circ B).\textbf{Abort}$. Methods in such an approximation behave as the methods of $\mathcal{A}$ with all external calls redirected to $\mathcal{B}$, but with external calls of $\mathcal{B}$ aborting rather then going back to $\mathcal{A}$. Hence a better approximation of the methods of $\mathcal{A}$ in the composed system would be $(A \circ B \circ A \circ B).\textbf{Abort}$, and yet a better one $(A \circ B \circ A \circ B \circ A \circ B).\textbf{Abort}$, etc. The desired result is then the limit of this sequence. This limit can be expressed as the least fixed point $(\mu\ A \circ B)$, which is the least Xb with respect to the refinement ordering on tuples of statements such that $Xb = (A \circ B).Xb$. Choosing the least fixed point means that a non-terminating sequence of calls from $\mathcal{A}$ to $\mathcal{B}$ and back is equivalent to $\textbf{abort}$, which is the meaning of a non-terminating loop. According to the theorem of Knaster-Tarski [18], a monotonic function has a unique least fixed point in a complete lattice. Statements form a complete lattice with the refinement ordering $\sqsubseteq$ and the function $(A \circ B)$ is monotonic in its argument, therefore, $(\mu\ A \circ B)$ exists and is unique. Similarly, the methods of the component $\mathcal{B}$ in the composed system are defined by $(\mu\ B \circ A)$.

The component system resulting from the composition of the components $\mathcal{A}$ and $\mathcal{B}$ can now be defined as follows:

$$(\mathcal{A}\,\textbf{comp}\,\mathcal{B}) \mathrel{\widehat{=}} ((a_0, b_0), (\mu\ A \circ B, \mu\ B \circ A))$$

Note that during composition, the type variables α and β, representing unknown state spaces of the components $\mathcal{B}$ and $\mathcal{A}$, get instantiated with Σ and Γ respectively, so that the composed system has methods operating on the state space $\Sigma \times \Delta \times \Gamma$.

4.3   Refining Components and Component Systems

Let $A : Ptran^n(\Sigma \times \Delta \times \beta) \to Ptran^m(\Sigma \times \Delta \times \beta)$ and $A' : Ptran^n(\Sigma' \times \Delta \times \beta) \to Ptran^m(\Sigma' \times \Delta \times \beta)$ be methods of components $\mathcal{A}$ and $\mathcal{A}'$, respectively. We say that A is data refined by A' in the context of component $\mathcal{B}$ via a relation $R \times Id \times Id$ if

$$A \overset{\mathcal{B}}{\sqsubseteq}_R A' \mathrel{\widehat{=}} (\mu\ A \circ B) \downarrow (R \times Id \times Id) \sqsubseteq A' . (\mu\ B \circ A) \downarrow (R \times Id \times Id))$$

For methods of components $\mathcal{B}$ and $\mathcal{B}'$ we have a similar definition but via a relation $Id \times Id \times P$.

As method bodies of the components $\mathcal{A}'$ and $\mathcal{B}'$ are indifferent to the relations $Id \times Id \times P$ and $R \times Id \times Id$ respectively, we use the following *encoding propagation lemma* :

$$(A'.\ Xb) \downarrow (Id \times Id \times P) \sqsubseteq A'.\ Xb \downarrow (Id \times Id \times P)$$
$$(B'.\ Yb) \downarrow (R \times Id \times Id) \sqsubseteq B'.\ Yb \downarrow (R \times Id \times Id)$$

The proof of this lemma can be found in [12].

We say that $\mathcal{A} = (a_0 : \Sigma, A : Ptran^n(\Sigma \times \Delta \times \beta) \to Ptran^m(\Sigma \times \Delta \times \beta))$ is refined by $\mathcal{A}' = (a'_0 : \Sigma', A' : Ptran^n(\Sigma' \times \Delta \times \beta) \to Ptran^m(\Sigma' \times \Delta \times \beta))$ in the context of $\mathcal{B}$, if there exists a relation $R : \Sigma' \leftrightarrow \Sigma$ such that this relation holds between the initial values, and methods of $\mathcal{A}$ are data refined by methods of $\mathcal{A}'$ in the context of $\mathcal{B}$ via the relation $R \times Id \times Id$. Formally,

$$\mathcal{A} \overset{\mathcal{B}}{\sqsubseteq} \mathcal{A}' \mathrel{\widehat{=}} (\exists R \bullet (R.\ a'_0.\ a_0) \ \wedge \ A \overset{\mathcal{B}}{\sqsubseteq}_R A')$$

For the components $\mathcal{B} = (b_0 : \Gamma, B)$ and $\mathcal{B}' = (b'_0 : \Gamma', B')$ the definition of refinement is similar, only that the initial values are connected via a relation $P : \Gamma' \leftrightarrow \Gamma$ and methods of $\mathcal{B}$ are data refined by methods of $\mathcal{B}'$ in the context of $\mathcal{A}$ via the relation $Id \times Id \times P$.

We say that the component system $\mathcal{A}\,\mathbf{comp}\,\mathcal{B}$ is refined by the component system $\mathcal{A}'\,\mathbf{comp}\,\mathcal{B}'$, if there exist such relations R and P that initial values of these component systems are related via the relation $R \times P$ and tuples of method bodies are related via the relation $R \times Id \times P$. Formally, we have:

$$\mathcal{A}\,\mathbf{comp}\,\mathcal{B} \sqsubseteq \mathcal{A}'\,\mathbf{comp}\,\mathcal{B}' \mathrel{\widehat{=}}$$
$$(\exists R, P \bullet (R \times P).\ (a'_0, b'_0).\ (a_0, b_0) \ \wedge$$
$$(\mu\ A \circ B) \downarrow (R \times Id \times P) \sqsubseteq (\mu\ A' \circ B') \ \wedge$$
$$(\mu\ B \circ A) \downarrow (R \times Id \times P) \sqsubseteq (\mu\ B' \circ A'))$$

5   Modular Reasoning Theorem

Our objective is to prove that the modular reasoning property holds for mutually dependent components if the "no call-back assumptions" and "no accidental mutual recursion" requirements are satisfied. First we formulate and prove the modular reasoning theorem which captures the mathematical meaning of the modular reasoning property reinforced with the requirements. Then we explain how the requirements are reflected in the assumptions of the theorem. As the "no accidental mutual recursion" requirement is non-modular, in the sense that it requires checking for the absence of mutual recursion in the system composed from refining components, we then discuss techniques which permit to satisfy this requirement in a modular fashion.

5.1   Formulating and Proving the Theorem

Modular Reasoning Theorem. *Let components* $\mathcal{A}$, $\mathcal{B}$, $\mathcal{A}'$, *and* $\mathcal{B}'$ *be given as follows*:

$$\mathcal{A} = (a_0 : \Sigma, A : Ptran^n(\Sigma \times \Delta \times \beta) \to Ptran^m(\Sigma \times \Delta \times \beta)),$$
$$\mathcal{B} = (b_0 : \Gamma, B : Ptran^m(\alpha \times \Delta \times \Gamma) \to Ptran^n(\alpha \times \Delta \times \Gamma)),$$
$$\mathcal{A}' = (a_0' : \Sigma', A' : Ptran^n(\Sigma' \times \Delta \times \beta) \to Ptran^m(\Sigma' \times \Delta \times \beta)),$$
$$\mathcal{B}' = (b_0' : \Gamma', B' : Ptran^m(\alpha \times \Delta \times \Gamma') \to Ptran^n(\alpha \times \Delta \times \Gamma'))$$

Then we have:

$$\mathcal{A} \overset{\mathcal{B}}{\sqsubseteq} \mathcal{A}' \;\wedge \tag{a}$$
$$\mathcal{B} \overset{\mathcal{A}}{\sqsubseteq} \mathcal{B}' \;\wedge \tag{b}$$
$$(\exists k \bullet \forall Xb \bullet (\mu\ A' \circ B') = (A' \circ B')^k . Xb)\ \wedge \tag{c}$$
$$(\exists l \bullet \forall Yb \bullet (\mu\ B' \circ A') = (B' \circ A')^l . Yb) \Rightarrow \tag{d}$$
$$\mathcal{A}\,\mathbf{comp}\,\mathcal{B} \sqsubseteq \mathcal{A}'\,\mathbf{comp}\,\mathcal{B}'$$

Proof Expanding the definitions and making simple logical transformations, we get three subgoals

1. $(R.\,a_0'.\,a_0)\ \wedge\ (P.\,b_0'.\,b_0)\ \Rightarrow\ (R \times P).\,(a_0', b_0').\,(a_0, b_0)$
2. $A \overset{\mathcal{B}}{\sqsubseteq}_R A'\ \wedge\ B \overset{\mathcal{A}}{\sqsubseteq}_P B'\ \wedge\ (c)\ \wedge\ (d)\ \Rightarrow\ (\mu\ A \circ B){\downarrow}(R \times Id \times P) \sqsubseteq (\mu\ A' \circ B')$
3. $A \overset{\mathcal{B}}{\sqsubseteq}_R A'\ \wedge\ B \overset{\mathcal{A}}{\sqsubseteq}_P B'\ \wedge\ (c)\ \wedge\ (d)\ \Rightarrow\ (\mu\ B \circ A){\downarrow}(R \times Id \times P) \sqsubseteq (\mu\ B' \circ A')$

where R and P are fixed but arbitrary relations. The first subgoal is obviously true. To prove the second and the third subgoals, we first prove the following lemma.

Lemma. *For functions* A, B, A' *and* B' *defined as above, relations* $R : \Sigma' \leftrightarrow \Sigma$ *and* $P : \Gamma' \leftrightarrow \Gamma$, *and any natural number* k, *we have*:

$$A \overset{\mathcal{B}}{\sqsubseteq}_R A' \wedge B \overset{\mathcal{A}}{\sqsubseteq}_P B' \Rightarrow (\mu\ A \circ B){\downarrow}(R \times Id \times P) \sqsubseteq (A' \circ B')^k.\,(\mu\ A \circ B){\downarrow}(R \times Id \times P)$$

Proof We prove this lemma by induction over k.
Base case:

$$(A' \circ B')^0.\,(\mu\ A \circ B){\downarrow}(R \times Id \times P)$$
$$= \{\textit{definition of } f^0\}$$
$$(\mu\ A \circ B){\downarrow}(R \times Id \times P)$$

Inductive case:
Assuming $(\mu\ A \circ B){\downarrow}(R \times Id \times P)\ \sqsubseteq\ (A' \circ B')^k.\,(\mu\ A \circ B){\downarrow}(R \times Id \times P)$, we calculate:

$$(\mu\ A \circ B){\downarrow}(R \times Id \times P)$$

$\sqsubseteq$ {*induction assumption*}
$\quad (A' \circ B')^k . (\mu\ A \circ B) \!\downarrow\! (R \times Id \times P)$

$=$ {*the property of encoding operator for the orthogonal relations*}
$\quad (A' \circ B')^k . (\mu\ A \circ B) \!\downarrow\! (R \times Id \times Id) \!\downarrow\! (Id \times Id \times P)$

$\sqsubseteq$ {*assumption* $A \sqsubseteq_R^{\mathcal{B}} A'$}
$\quad (A' \circ B')^k . (A'. (\mu\ B \circ A) \!\downarrow\! (R \times Id \times Id)) \!\downarrow\! (Id \times Id \times P)$

$\sqsubseteq$ {*encoding propagation lemma* }
$\quad (A' \circ B')^k . A'. (\mu\ B \circ A) \!\downarrow\! (R \times Id \times Id) \!\downarrow\! (Id \times Id \times P)$

$=$ {*the rule for encoding with orthogonal relations*}
$\quad (A' \circ B')^k . A'. (\mu\ B \circ A) \!\downarrow\! (Id \times Id \times P) \!\downarrow\! (R \times Id \times Id)$

$\sqsubseteq$ {*assumption* $B \sqsubseteq_P^{\mathcal{A}} B'$}
$\quad (A' \circ B')^k . A'. (B'. (\mu\ A \circ B) \!\downarrow\! (Id \times Id \times P)) \!\downarrow\! (R \times Id \times Id)$

$\sqsubseteq$ {*encoding propagation lemma* }
$\quad (A' \circ B')^k . A'. B'. (\mu\ A \circ B) \!\downarrow\! (Id \times Id \times P) \!\downarrow\! (R \times Id \times Id)$

$=$ {*the property of encoding operator for the orthogonal relations*}
$\quad (A' \circ B')^k . A'. B'. (\mu\ A \circ B) \!\downarrow\! (R \times Id \times P)$

$=$ {$f^{k+1}. x = f^k . (f. x)$, *definition of composition*}
$\quad (A' \circ B')^{k+1} . (\mu\ A \circ B) \!\downarrow\! (R \times Id \times P)$ $\square$

Now using this lemma we can prove the second subgoal of the Modular Reasoning Theorem. Assume $A \sqsubseteq_R^{\mathcal{B}} A'$, $B \sqsubseteq_P^{\mathcal{A}} B'$, and $\forall X b \bullet (\mu\ A' \circ B') = (A' \circ B')^k . X b$, for fixed but arbitrary k. The conclusion is then proved as follows:

$\quad (\mu\ A \circ B) \!\downarrow\! (R \times Id \times P)$

$\sqsubseteq$ {*Lemma*}
$\quad (A' \circ B')^k . (\mu\ A \circ B) \!\downarrow\! (R \times Id \times P)$

$=$ {*assumption* (c), *instantiating Xb with* $(\mu\ A \circ B) \!\downarrow\! (R \times Id \times P)$}
$\quad (\mu\ A' \circ B')$

The proof of the third subgoal is similar. $\square$

5.2   Interpretation and Implications of the Theorem

Let us consider how the requirement "no call-back assumptions" is reflected in the formulation of the theorem. In fact, this requirement is not captured by a separate assumption in the theorem, rather the definition of component refinement in context accommodates for it. As stipulated by this requirement, when refining the component $\mathcal{A}$ to $\mathcal{A}'$ we should not assume that the component $\mathcal{B}$ calls back methods of $\mathcal{A}'$, because in doing so we would implicitly modify the specification of the component system. The specification of method bodies of $\mathcal{A}$ is mathematically defined by $(\mu \; A \circ B)$, whereas the specification of method bodies of $\mathcal{B}$ is defined by $(\mu \; B \circ A)$. Accordingly, refinement between the specification of method bodies of $\mathcal{A}$ and the implementation of methods of $\mathcal{A}'$ in the context of the specification of method bodies of $\mathcal{B}$ is expressed as follows:

$$(\mu \; A \circ B) \!\downarrow\! (R \times Id \times Id) \sqsubseteq A'. \, (\mu \; B \circ A) \!\downarrow\! (R \times Id \times Id)$$

Here the encodings are necessary for adjusting the state spaces of the participating components. The same requirement for the refinement between B and B' in context of A is treated similarly.

Unlike in the case of "no call-back assumptions", the "no accidental mutual recursion" requirement is captured in the assumptions (c) and (d) of the theorem explicitly. Let us consider the assumption (c) (the assumption (d) is treated similarly):

$$(\exists n \bullet \forall Xb \bullet (\mu \; A' \circ B') = (A' \circ B')^k.Xb)$$

In this formula $(A' \circ B')^k$ is the function resulting from composing the function $(A' \circ B')$ with itself $n-1$ times. The intuition here is as follows. If the result of applying the function $(A' \circ B')$ to an arbitrary tuple of method bodies a finite number of times is equal to the complete unfolding of method invocations between $\mathcal{A}'$ and $\mathcal{B}'$, then the bodies of methods of $\mathcal{A}'$ are completely defined. This, of course, can only be achieved if the unfolding terminates, i.e. there is no infinite mutual recursion.

The "no accidental mutual recursion" requirement is non-modular in the sense that it requires checking for the absence of mutual recursion in the system composed from refined components. We envision several approaches to satisfying this requirement in a modular manner. For example, component methods in the original specification can be marked as atomic if they do not call other methods. While refining a component, atomic methods must remain atomic and non-atomic ones can introduce new calls only to atomic methods. Although being apparently restrictive, this approach guarantees the absence of accidental mutual recursion in the refined composed system. With another approach, we can assign to every method an index which indicates the maximal depth of method calls that this method is allowed to make. This approach apparently only works if the original specification does not have mutually recursive method calls. For example, a method m which does not invoke any other method will have index 0, whereas a method n invoking m will have index 1. If a method invokes several methods with different indices, it is assigned the maximal of these indices plus one. With the original specification annotated in this manner we can require that, while refining a method, calls to methods with indices higher than the indices of the methods that were called before cannot be introduced. However, the detailed analysis of the different methods for establishing the "no accidental mutual recursion" requirement in a modular manner is outside the scope of this paper.

6 Discussion, Conclusions, and Related Work

We study a problem which hinders independent development of components in the presence of re-entrance. A formal analysis of this problem allowed us to recognize the essence of the problem in the conflict of assumptions that developers of components make about the behavior of other components in the system.

Problems related to compositionality of systems have been and remain a subject of intensive studies in the formal methods community, e.g. [7]. In particular, compositionality of concurrently executing processes communicating through global variables has been the focus of formal analysis by Abadi and Lamport in [1]. However, the setting that they consider is rather different from our, as we consider sequential communication of components.

Problems with re-entrance are also often discussed in the context of concurrent programming. In a multithreaded environment several instances of the same procedure modifying global variables can be executed simultaneously. One thread of control can enter the procedure and, before the end of the procedure is reached, a second thread of control can re-enter the same procedure. Apparently, such a situation is problematic because the second instance of the procedure might observe the global variables in an inconsistent state, or it can modify these global variables and then the first instance will observe them in an inconsistent state.

The problem that we consider is sufficiently different from the re-entrance problem as known in concurrent programming to deserve a separate name, the "component re-entrance problem". There are two scenarios in which this problem can occur; firstly, when components are independently developed from specifications and, secondly, during independent maintenance of components.

One of the recommendations in concurrent programming is to circumvent the re-entrance problem by avoiding the re-entrance setting, which can be achieved using various locking mechanisms. In object-oriented and component-based programming the re-entrance setting can be avoided by following what is known as the "push" communication style. Adhering to this style requires passing to a client component all the data it might possibly need as method parameters. Apparently, such an approach to component communication is rather inefficient, and it is often preferable to pass to the client component just a reference to itself and permit it to obtain all the data it might need. However, the latter approach, which is often referred to as the "pull" approach, matches the re-entrance setting.

Several researchers have pointed out that components should specify relevant information about their environments, such as required interfaces [14]. It was also recognized that accidental reuse does not lead to the development of robust maintainable systems [9]. To be really useful, reuse must be pre-planned by system developers. Agreeing with these ideas, we advocate a specification method where component environments are described by abstract specifications of their behavior. We believe that the specification of the environment should be split into components specifying certain interfaces to indicate the communication protocol between the components. As the specifications of the environment components can be given in terms of abstract mathematical data structures and non-deterministic specification statements, this would permit a multitude of different implementations.

Similar problems occurring during maintenance of mutually dependent components have been mentioned by several researchers, e.g., Bertrand Meyer in [11] and Clemens Szyperski in [17]. Meyer considers the setting with two mutually dependent classes whose invariants include each other's attributes. His method for verification of conformance between two implementations of one class requires that the new implementation respect the invariant of the original implementation. He notices that this requirement alone is not sufficient for establishing correctness of the composed system and refers to this problem as "indirect invariant effect". He then makes the conjecture that mirroring such interclass invariants in the participating classes would be sufficient to avoid the problem. Although we disagree with the practice of stating interclass invariants, it appears that the problem considered by Meyer is just a special case of the component re-entrance problem as formulated in this paper. As our examples demonstrate, preserving invariants, taken alone, does not eliminate the problem.

Szyperski describes a similar problem but sees it rather as an instance of the re-entrance problem as occurring in concurrent systems. He reiterates the common recommendation for avoiding the problem, which suggests to establish a component invariant before invoking any external method. Interestingly enough, the recommendation to re-establish the invariant before all external method calls does not follow from the specification and is rather motivated by empirical expertise. As demonstrated by our examples, this recommendation, although being necessary, is insufficient.

In fact, our "no call-back assumptions" requirement subsumes this recommendation. Let us reconsider our first example. According to the Modular Reasoning Theorem, to demonstrate that $Model'$ is a valid implementation of $Model$ in the context of $View$, we would need to show that every method of $Model'$ calling methods of $View$ composed with methods of $Model$ refines the corresponding methods of $Model$ composed with methods of $View$. Since $Model$ and $Model'$ operate on different attributes, to express, for example, in the method $append$ of $Model'$ the behavior of a call to $View.update$, which calls get_s of $Model$, we need to coerce this call using an abstraction relation. Such an abstraction relation usually includes component invariants, and in this case includes the component invariant $n = \#s$ of $Model'$, i.e. $R.(s',n').s \mathrel{\widehat{=}} s' = s \land n' = \#s'$. Note that in the definition of R the attributes of $Model'$ are primed in order to distinguish them from the attributes of $Model$. According to the definition of refinement in context, the proof obligation for the method $append$ after expansion and simplification is

$$(s := s \hat{\ } t; print(\#s)) \!\downarrow\! R \sqsubseteq s := s \hat{\ } t; (print(\#s)) \!\downarrow\! R; n := n + \#t$$

The right hand side can be expanded to $s := s \hat{\ } t; \{R\}; print(\#s); [R^{-1}]; n := n + \#t$. The abstraction statement preceding the invocation of $print$ aborts, because it tries to find an abstract value of a sequence s satisfying the invariant $\#s = n$ which obviously does not hold at this point. Certainly, an aborting method is not a refinement of a non-aborting one and, therefore, *Model'* fails to correctly implement *Model* in the context of *View*, breaching our requirement.

The requirement to re-establish a component invariant before all external calls is rather restrictive, because re-establishing the invariant might require a sequence of method calls to this and other components. Besides, it is not always necessary to establish the entire component invariant before external calls, because clients of the component can depend on some parts of the component invariant while being indifferent to the other parts. Szyperski in [17] proposes to "weaken invariants conditionally and make the conditions available to clients through test functions". In a way, he proposes to make assumptions that component developers make about other components more explicit. This idea can be elaborated through augmenting the specification of components with require/ensure statements stipulating assumptions and guarantees that the components make. To avoid a conflict of assumptions, the component specification can make explicit the information the component relies on and provides to other components. For instance, every method can begin with a require condition and end with an ensure condition. Also every method invocation can be surrounded by an ensure/require couple. Then, while implementing a method, the developer can assume the information as stipulated in the require condition and ought to establish the ensure condition. Such an explicit statement of mutual assumptions and guarantees between components would reduce the need to unfold method invocations when verifying refinement in context. Note that the theoretical underpinning of such an approach to specification of component systems is an interpretation of the results presented in this paper, as the refinement calculus includes constructs for expressing the require/ensure statements.

A specification and verification method for component systems based on such an approach should additionally provide for satisfying the "no accidental mutual recursion" requirement in a modular manner. The detailed elaboration of such a method represents the subject of current research.

As was already mentioned, we have made a number of simplifications in the component model. In particular, we have assumed that components do not have self-calls and component implementations do not introduce new methods. Relaxing these confinements on the component model is the subject of future work.

Acknowledgments

We would like to express our gratitude to Anna Mikhajlova for useful comments. Ralph Back and Joakim von Wright have provided valuable feedback on an earlier version of this paper. Discussions with Eric Hehner and his colleagues while presenting this work at the University of Toronto helped us to improve the presentation of the material.

References

[1] M. Abadi and L. Lamport. Composing specifications. *ACM Transactions on Programming Languages and Systems*, 15(1):73–132, Jan. 1993.

[2] R. J. R. Back and J. von Wright. *Refinement Calculus: A Systematic Introduction.* Springer-Verlag, April 1998.

[3] R. J. R. Back and J. von Wright. Encoding, decoding and data refinement. Technical Report TUCS-TR-236, Turku Centre for Computer Science, Finland, Mar. 1, 1999.

[4] R. J. R. Back and J. von Wright. Products in the refinement calculus. Technical Report TUCS-TR-235, Turku Centre for Computer Science, Finland, Feb. 11, 1999.

[5] M. Büchi and E. Sekerinski. Formal methods for component software: The refinement calculus perspective. In W. Weck, J. Bosch, and C. Szyperski, editors, *Proceedings of WCOP'97*, volume 5 of *TUCS General Publication*, pages 23–32, June 1997.

[6] M. Büchi and W. Weck. A plea for grey-box components. Technical Report TUCS-TR-122, Turku Centre for Computer Science, Finland, Sept. 5, 1997.

[7] W.-P. de Roever, H. Langmaack, and A. Pnueli. *Compositionality: The Significant Difference. Proceedings of COMPOS'97*, volume 1536 of *LNCS*. Springer-Verlag, 1997.

[8] J. Feiler and A. Meadow. *Essential OpenDoc.* Addison-Wesley, 1996.

[9] E. Gamma, R. Helm, R. Johnson, and J. Vlissides. *Design Patterns: Elements of Reusable Object-Oriented Software.* Addison-Wesley, 1995.

[10] R. Helm, I. M. Holland, and D. Gangopadhyay. Contracts: Specifying behavioural compositions in object-oriented systems. In *Proceedings OOPSLA/ECOOP'90, ACM SIGPLAN Notices*, pages 169–180, Oct. 1990.

[11] B. Meyer. *Object-Oriented Software Construction.* Prentice Hall, New York, N.Y., second edition, 1997.

[12] L. Mikhajlov, E. Sekerinski, and L. Laibinis. Developing components in the presence of re-entrance. Technical Report TUCS-TR-239, TUCS - Turku Centre for Computer Science, Feb. 9 1999. Tue, 9 Jan 1999 8:17:45 GMT.

[13] C. C. Morgan. *Programming from Specifications.* Prentice–Hall, 1990.

[14] A. Olafsson and D. Bryan. On the need for "required interfaces" of components. In M. Muehlhaeuser, editor, *Special Issues in Object Oriented Programming*, pages 159–165. dpunkt Verlag Heidelberg, 1997. ISBN 3-920993-67-5.

[15] D. Rogerson. *Inside COM: Microsoft's Component Object Model.* Microsoft Press, 1997.

[16] Sun Microsystems. *Java Beans(TM)*, July 1997. Graham Hamilton (ed.). Version 1.0.1.

[17] C. Szyperski. *Component Software – Beyond Object-Oriented Software.* Addison-Wesley, 1997.

[18] A. Tarski. A lattice theoretical fixed point theorem and its applications. *Pacific J. Mathematics*, 5:285–309, 1955.

[19] J. Wright. Program refinement by theorem prover. In *6th Refinement Workshop*, London, 1994. Springer–Verlag.

Communication and Synchronisation Using Interaction Objects

H.B.M. Jonkers

Philips Research Laboratories Eindhoven,
Prof. Holstlaan 4, 5656 AA Eindhoven, The Netherlands
`jonkers@natlab.research.philips.com`

Abstract. In this paper we introduce a model of process communication and synchronisation, based on the concept of interaction objects. Interaction objects define an abstraction mechanism for concurrent access to data, based on a strict separation of process interaction and data access. Process interaction can be controlled by means of three basic interaction operators that operate on interaction objects. The interaction operators can be used to define various forms of communication and synchronisation including a general form of condition synchronisation. We define the concept of an interaction object and the interaction operators, and give examples of a number of interaction objects. Various aspects of interaction objects are discussed, such as the formal specification and implementation of interaction objects, and the verification of programs that use interaction objects.

1 Introduction

Most operating systems and concurrent programming languages in wide use today are based on the same basic model of process communication and synchronisation. Processes communicate and synchronise by means of intermediate objects such as shared variables, semaphores, monitors, message queues, channels, etc. The operations associated with these intermediate objects can be used concurrently by processes to pass information to each other, or to wait until certain synchronisation conditions are met. The communication and synchronisation mechanisms associated with these objects have been subject of extensive study, leading to a rich theory; see e.g. [1, 22] for comprehensive surveys.

In this paper we introduce a model of process communication and synchronisation, based on a specific type of intermediate object called an *interaction object*. Interaction objects define an abstraction mechanism for concurrent access to data, based on a strict separation of process interaction and data access. Interaction objects have non-blocking and atomic operations only, implying that they can be specified using standard sequential techniques. Interaction between processes, including blocking, is controlled by means of three basic *interaction operators* that operate on interaction objects. In combination with various types of interaction objects, these operators can be used to define several forms of

J. Wing, J. Woodcock, J. Davies (Eds.): FM'99, Vol. II, LNCS 1709, pp. 1321–1342, 1999.

communication and synchronisation, including a general form of condition synchronisation.

As we will argue in the paper, programming with interaction objects and interaction operators helps in minimising and making explicit the interference in concurrent programs, and thereby in reducing their complexity. This argument is supported by practical experience with the CoCoNut software component [16] that has been used in several applications in Philips. CoCoNut provides a full implementation of the programming model discussed in this paper and includes a collection of ready-made interaction objects.

This paper consists of two main parts. In the first part, Section 2, we define the basic concepts such as the interaction point, interaction object and interaction operator, and give an example of an interaction object. In the second part, Section 3, we deal with various aspects of the use of interaction objects, such as how to specify and implement them, and how to verify programs that use interaction objects. In Section 4 we compare interaction objects with related approaches.

The concept of an interaction object, as defined in this paper, originated from work on the SPRINT method [15, 8]. It should not be confused with the concept of an interaction object as used in the context of user interfaces, where it refers to a user-interface widget. In order to distinguish the two, the first type of objects can be characterised as *process* interaction objects and the second type as *computer-human* interaction objects.

2   Basic Concepts

2.1   Objects and Processes

We consider systems consisting of two types of entities: passive *objects* and active *processes*. An object consists of a collection of *variables* and a set of *operations*. The sets of variables of objects are disjoint. In any given state of the system a variable has a certain *value*. The values of all variables of an object define the *state* of the object. The state of an object can only be inspected or changed by means of the operations associated with the object. An operation of an object accesses the variables of that object only. An operation is said to be *enabled* if its precondition is true and *disabled* if its precondition is false.

A process is an autonomous sequential activity that operates on objects, i.e., it may inspect and change the values of variables using the operations associated with the objects. Each process has a *domain* defining the *local variables* of the process. The domains of processes are *disjoint*. Variables not in the domain of any process are referred to as *global variables*.

The operations of objects are divided into two classes: *access operations* and *interaction operations*. An access operation of an object X is an operation that, when called by a process P, will access variables of X in the domain of P only. Since process domains are disjoint, processes can never interfere by calling access operations. An interaction operation of an object X is an operation that, when called by a process P, may access variables of X outside the domain of P, i.e., global variables or variables in the domains of other processes.

Objects and processes partition the set of variables orthogonally, as illustrated in Figure 1. In this and other figures, objects are represented by rectangles, processes by ellipses, variables by small rounded rectangles and operations by arrows. The variables associated with an object may be contained in different processes. For example, the variables v_1 and v_3 of object X are contained in the domains of processes P and Q, respectively. Likewise, the variables associated with a process may be part of different objects. For example, the variables v_3 and v_5 from the domain of Q are contained in the objects X and Y, respectively. There may also be variables that are not contained in any process, such as the global variable v_2 of X, or in any object, such as the internal variable v_4 of Q.

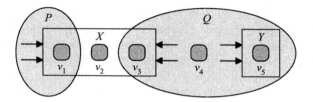

Fig. 1. Objects and Processes

2.2   Interaction Points

In the model defined above, all interaction between processes occurs by means of interaction operations of objects. Most existing communication and synchronisation mechanisms such as monitors, channels, pipes, etc., can be viewed as objects with interaction operations. For example, a message queue, as supported by most operating systems, can be seen as an object containing one global variable (a message buffer) and two interaction operations: *send* and *receive* (see Figure 2).

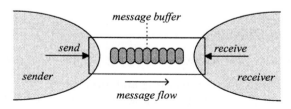

Fig. 2. Message Queue

We define an *interaction point* as a point in the code or execution of a process where the process interacts with other processes, i.e., where it potentially *influences* the behaviour of other processes (*outgoing* interaction point) or *is* potentially *influenced by* other processes (*incoming* interaction point). We use the word "potentially" because the influence of an action of one process on another may be indirect or may depend on dynamic conditions. For example, calling a *send* operation of a message queue introduces an outgoing interaction point in the sender process. The receiver process will only be influenced by this when it calls the *receive* operation of the message queue, introducing an incoming interaction point in the receiver process. There may even be no influence at all if the receiver process chooses to ignore the message queue.

A *synchronisation point* is a special type of incoming interaction point where the *progress* of a process is influenced by other processes, i.e., where the process may *block*. Calling the *receive* operation of a message queue will typically introduce a synchronisation point: if the message queue is empty, the receiver will block until a message is put into the queue by the sender. If the message queue is bounded, a *send* operation could also introduce a synchronisation point in addition to an outgoing interaction point: if the message queue is full, the sender will block until the receiver removes a message from the queue.

The complexity of concurrent programs is closely related to the number of interaction points contained in them. Even a relatively small number of interaction points can give rise to a very large number of interleavings of process actions, making it hard to establish the correctness of such programs. It is therefore important to keep the number of interaction points as small as possible, i.e., to achieve as much decoupling of processes as possible. The mechanisms referred to above only support this to a certain extent, since most operations of monitors, channels, etc., contain interaction points. This is even true for those operations that read information only. For example, an operation of a message queue that allows the receiver to determine the number of messages in the queue introduces an incoming interaction point in the receiver, since the number of messages in the queue may be influenced by the sender.

The model introduced in this paper takes a rather drastic approach in curtailing the number of interaction points. It limits process interaction to three general *interaction operators* which can be used to insert explicit interaction points in the process code. Process code not containing any of these interaction operators will not contain interaction points. The key to this approach is the concept of an interaction object, as defined in the next section.

2.3   Interaction Objects

An interaction object X is an object satisfying the following requirements:

1. All operations of X are non-blocking and atomic.
2. The variables of X consist of the following disjoint subsets per process P:
   (a) $in_{X,P}$: the *input variables* of X for P, which are local variables of P.
   (b) $iav_{X,P}$: the *interaction variables* of X for P, which are global variables.
   (c) $out_{X,P}$: the *output variables* of X for P, which are local variables of P.
3. X has exactly two interaction operations:
   (a) $commit_X$, which has no parameters. The call of $commit_X$ from a process P will be denoted as $commit_{X,P}$. It accesses variables in $in_{X,P} \cup iav_{X,P}$ only, modifies variables in $iav_{X,P}$ only, and disables itself.

(b) $sync_X$, which has a process as its parameter. The call of $sync_X$ from a process P with parameter Q will be denoted as $sync_{X,P,Q}$. It accesses variables in $iav_{X,Q} \cup out_{X,P}$ only, modifies variables in $out_{X,P}$ only, and disables itself.

The *commit* and *sync* operations of interaction objects will be represented in diagrams by curved arrows as indicated in Figure 3.

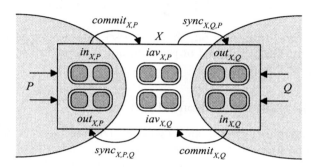

Fig. 3. Commit and Sync Operations

The following remarks can be made about the requirements listed above:

Item 1: This requirement implies that operations of interaction objects do not contain synchronisation points. It also implies that interaction objects can be fully specified using classical pre- and post-condition techniques.

Item 2: Input and output is seen from the point of view of interaction objects rather than processes. That is, the input and output variables provide input to and output from an interaction object. The interaction variables are the intermediaries between input and output variables.

Item 3a: $commit_{X,P}$ can be seen as an action that "commits" a local state change of P by making its effect visible in the interaction variables $iav_{X,P}$, thus introducing an *outgoing* interaction point in P. The self-disabling requirement reflects the fact that there is no sense in committing a local state change twice if the local state has not changed. The only way $commit_{X,P}$ can be enabled after being disabled is by calls of access operations of X by P, modifying the variables in $in_{X,P}$.

Item 3b: $sync_{X,P,Q}$ can be seen as an action that "synchronises" the local state of P with the state of the interaction variables $iav_{X,Q}$, thus introducing an *incoming* interaction point in P. The self-disabling requirement reflects the fact that there is no sense in synchronising twice to a global state change if the global state has not changed. The only way $sync_{X,P,Q}$ can be enabled after being disabled is by calls of $commit_{X,Q}$ modifying the variables in $iav_{X,Q}$.

In the remainder of this paper we will use the definition of an interaction object in a somewhat more liberal way. An object is an interaction object if its representation in terms of variables can be turned into a behaviourally equivalent representation satisfying the above requirements. This approach is justified because objects are fully encapsulated: they can be accessed by means of operations only. It does not matter which variables are used to represent the object, as long as the external behaviour of the object remains the same. This freedom can often be used to write more natural specifications of interaction objects. The disadvantage is that we may have to prove behavioural equivalence of specifications; we will use standard data transformation techniques to do this (see Section 3.2).

We will assume, from now on, that processes interact by means of interaction objects only. Other types of objects are not relevant in the context of this discussion and will be ignored.

2.4   Example of an Interaction Object

As a simple example of interaction objects we consider *observers*. An observer is an interaction object that allows one process, the *reader*, to observe the value of a variable that is changed concurrently by another process, the *writer*. An observer is similar to a shared variable except that write and read operations are "cached", with the cache being controlled by *commit*s and *sync*s. Both the writer and the reader have a cached copy of the shared variable. The writer writes to its own cached copy of the variable. These changes will not become externally visible until the writer performs a *commit* on the observer. The reader reads from its cached copy and will not see any changes until it performs a *sync* on the observer.

Conceptually, an observer X contains three variables: an input variable wv, an interaction variable iv, and an output variable rv. More precisely:

$$
\begin{aligned}
in_{X,P} &= \textbf{if } P = writer \textbf{ then } \{wv\} \textbf{ else } \emptyset \\
iav_{X,P} &= \textbf{if } P = writer \textbf{ then } \{iv\} \textbf{ else } \emptyset \\
out_{X,P} &= \textbf{if } P = reader \textbf{ then } \{rv\} \textbf{ else } \emptyset
\end{aligned}
$$

These variables are depicted in Figure 4. In diagrams of interaction objects such as Figure 4, we label the arrows representing $commit_{X,P}$ and $sync_{X,P,Q}$ actions without indicating the X, P and Q, since that information follows from the position of the arrows. Furthermore, we omit arrows representing *commit*s and *sync*s that are always disabled, such as $commit_{X,R}$ and $sync_{X,W,R}$ where $W = writer$ and $R = reader$.

We will specify interaction objects in a small subset of Z [24]. The model of an interaction object is defined by a Z schema containing the processes and variables associated with the interaction object (see the *Observer* schema below). The initial state is defined by the *init* schema and the operations by schemas with the same name as the operation (see the *write*, *read*, *commit* and *sync* schemas below). In the specifications we treat the process P calling an operation as a parameter of that operation (indicated by "P" rather than "P?"), though in actual code this parameter will normally be implicit. The first line in the axiom

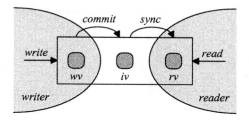

Fig. 4. Model of an Observer

part of an operation schema can be read as its pre-condition and the rest as its post-condition.

The full specification of observers is given below, where *Process* and *Value* (the values of observers) are given sets.

Observer

writer, reader : Process
wv, iv, rv : Value

---
init

Observer
v? : Value
_____
wv = iv = rv = v?

ΔObserver

Observer
Observer'
_____
writer' = writer ∧ reader' = reader

---
write

ΔObserver
P : Process
v? : Value
_____
P = writer
wv' = v? ∧ iv' = iv ∧ rv' = rv

---
read

ΞObserver
P : Process
v! : Value
_____
P = reader
v! = rv

$$\boxed{\begin{array}{l} \underline{\quad commit \quad\rule{18em}{0pt}} \\ \Delta Observer \\ P : Process \\ \hline P = writer \land wv \neq iv \\ wv' = wv \land iv' = wv \land rv' = rv \end{array}}$$

$$\boxed{\begin{array}{l} \underline{\quad sync \quad\rule{18em}{0pt}} \\ \Delta Observer \\ P, Q : Process \\ \hline P = reader \land Q = writer \land rv \neq iv \\ wv' = wv \land iv' = iv \land rv' = iv \end{array}}$$

We can easily verify that observers, as specified above, meet all requirements of interaction objects. It is also quite simple to generalise this specification for observers with multiple readers.

2.5 Basic Interaction Operators

When dealing with configurations of processes and interaction objects the pictorial representations used so far are somewhat clumsy. To represent such configurations, we introduce an additional graphical notation which is similar to the one used in [9]. As illustrated in Figure 5, processes are represented by parallelograms and interaction objects by rectangles. A line connecting a process P to

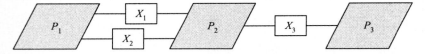

Fig. 5. Configuration of Processes and Interaction Objects

an interaction object X indicates that P is *attached to* X, i.e., that there is some form of interaction between P and X, by means of *commits*, *syncs*, or both. If P is not attached to X, $commit_{X,P}$ and $sync_{X,P,Q}$ are always disabled and can therefore be ignored. The rectangles represent general interaction objects; we will introduce special symbols for particular types of interaction objects. The symbol for an observer, with multiple readers, is shown in Figure 6.

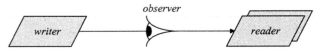

Fig. 6. Observer Symbol

Programming with interaction objects would be a nuisance if each interaction had to be programmed in terms of calls of individual *commit* and *sync* operations. For example, all interactions in process P_2, in Figure 5, would have to be programmed in terms of the *commits* and *syncs* of interaction objects X_1, X_2 and X_3. Instead of this, we will define three basic *interaction operators* that provide a general way to control interaction. In practice, one can even make it impossible to access the individual *commit* and *sync* operations other than by means of these interaction operators (as done in CoCoNut, see Section 3.4).

The first two interaction operators, called **commit** and **sync**, are more or less obvious. When used in a process P, **commit** performs all enabled *commits* and **sync** performs all enabled *syncs* on the interaction objects that P is attached to. Use of **commit** and **sync** in a process P will be denoted as **commit**$_P$ and **sync**$_P$, respectively. So, when programming process P_2 in Figure 5, the programmer could perform a number of access operations on the interaction objects X_1, X_2 and X_3, and then use **commit** to make their effect visible to P_1 and P_3, or use **sync** to synchronise with any changes made by P_1 and P_3 to the global variables in X_1, X_2 and X_3.

Statically, i.e., in the process code, **commit**$_P$ introduces a single outgoing interaction point and **sync**$_P$ introduces a single incoming interaction point in P. Dynamically, both **commit**$_P$ and **sync**$_P$ may amount to the execution of a sequence of individual atomic actions, and they may thereby introduce multiple interaction points in P. For **sync**$_P$, this is more or less natural since the individual *syncs* executed by **sync**$_P$ are enabled asynchronously by the *commits* of other processes. Even while executing **sync**$_P$, new *syncs* may be enabled. In order to avoid potential unboundedness in the execution of **sync**$_P$, we will assume that *syncs* that are enabled during the execution of **sync**$_P$ are ignored; they will be executed in the next call of **sync**$_P$.

For **commit**$_P$, the situation is different. The set of *commits* that are executed by **commit**$_P$ is fully predictable since these *commits* have been enabled by P itself. Moreover, the order of execution of these *commits* is irrelevant since each $commit_{X,P}$ operates on a disjoint set of variables: it reads from $in_{X,P} \cup iav_{X,P}$ and writes to $iav_{X,P}$. We will therefore assume that the *commits* executed by **commit**$_P$ are executed in a single atomic action. This can be implemented in an efficient way, as discussed in Section 3.4.

Both **commit** and **sync** are non-blocking operators. In order to provide a general interaction mechanism, we also need some way to block a process, i.e., some way to introduce a synchronisation point in the code of a process. The third interaction operator, called **wait**, does just that. When used in a process P it will block P until at least one $sync_{X,P,Q}$ is enabled for some X and Q. Use of **wait** in a process P will be denoted as **wait**$_P$.

We will say that a process P is *in sync* with an interaction object X if $sync_{X,P,Q}$ is disabled for all Q. Otherwise we will say that P is *out of sync* with X. We will say that a process is *in sync* if it is in sync with all interaction objects it is attached to. Otherwise we will say that it is *out of sync*. So, the effect of **wait**$_P$ can also be described as "block P until it is out of sync".

The definitions of the three interaction operators are summarised below:

commit$_P$: Perform all enabled *commit*s of the interaction objects to which P is attached in *one* atomic action.

sync$_P$: Perform all enabled *sync*s of the interaction objects to which P is attached, where each *sync* is an individual atomic action.

wait$_P$: Block until at least one *sync* of an interaction object attached to P is enabled.

2.6   Composite Interaction Operators

The three interaction operators defined above constitute a complete set in the sense that, in combination with the proper interaction objects, they can be used to define most of the standard communication and synchronisation mechanisms. Rather than defining these mechanisms directly in terms of the basic interaction operators, it is useful to use a few composite interaction operators. In defining these operators, and also in the example process code, we will use C(++)-like macro definitions, control structures and parameter passing conventions. We will use ":=" rather than "=" as the assignment operator, and "=" rather than "==" as the equality operator.

The first composite interaction operator is the **next** operator defined by:

   #define next   { commit; sync; }

It is typically used after a sequence of access operations $S_1; \ldots; S_n$ in a process to make the effect of the operations globally visible and, at the same time, to synchronise with global state changes of other processes. Note that the sequence of actions:

   $S_1; \ldots; S_n;$ **commit**;

constitutes a single atomic state transition. The name of the **next** operator is inspired by the similar **nextstate** operator of SDL [6]. That is, we can read it as "finish the current atomic state transition, synchronise, and start with the next".

The second composite interaction operator is the parameterised **await** operator defined by:

   #define await(C) **{ next; while($\neg$ C){ wait; sync; } }**

await(C) will make a process wait until condition C becomes true. Any condition C is allowed, provided that only local variables of the process and side-effect free access operations of objects are used in C. (We will weaken this restriction later on.) The **await** operator provides what is known as *condition synchronisation* and can be seen as a restricted, though still fairly general form of the *await statement* [1]. Unlike the general await statement, it can be implemented very efficiently. All that is required is efficient implementations of the **commit**, **sync** and **wait** operators (see Section 3.4).

When executing **await**(C), a process P will perform a **commit** and then repeatedly perform a **sync**, evaluate C, and call **wait** as long as C returns *false*. Calling **wait** when C returns *false* is safe because C depends only on the values of local variables in P. C can only become true due to the execution of *syncs* that modify the local variables of P. If no *sync* is enabled, P can safely block in **wait** until a *sync* is enabled. Note that C may be true temporarily during the execution of a **sync**, while still being false immediately after the execution of **sync**. However, if C finally becomes true it will still be true at the beginning of the statement immediately following **await**(C). So, irrespective of the condition C, the following **assert** statement will never fail:

await(C); **assert**(C);

In the examples discussed in the remainder of this paper, we will only use **next** and **await** rather than **commit**, **sync** and **wait**. Strictly speaking, we could even restrict ourselves to using **await** since **next** is equivalent to **await**(*true*).

3   Using Interaction Objects

3.1   Using the Interaction Operators

In order to demonstrate the use of the interaction operators we consider a simple alarm control system (inspired by an example from [5]). The system should measure the temperature and humidity in a room every 50 and 100 ms, respectively, and ring a bell while the temperature and humidity are in the unsafe range. The predicate *safe*(t, h) indicates whether the combination of temperature t and humidity h is in the safe range. We use three processes: *measure_temperature* and *measure_humidity* to measure temperature and humidity, respectively, and *alarm_control* to control the alarm bell. The *alarm_control* process can read the temperature and humidity by means of two observers *temp* and *humi*, that are written to by the two measurement processes (see Figure 7).

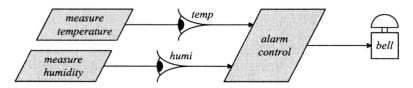

Fig. 7. Temperature Humidity Alarm System

The code of the three processes is given below, where *sleep*(n) delays a process for n milliseconds, and *measure_temp*(&t) and *measure_humi*(&h) perform measurements of temperature and humidity and assign the measured values to the variables t and h, respectively. The bell is represented by the variable *bell* with two possible values: *on* and *off*. Initially the temperature and humidity are in the safe range and the bell is off.

```
#define T    temp.read()
#define H    humi.read()
```

```
measure_temperature:        measure_humidity:        alarm_control:
  Temperature t;              Humidity h;              while(true)
  while(true)                 while(true)              { await(¬ safe(T, H));
  { sleep(50);                { sleep(100);              bell := on;
    measure_temp(&t);           measure_humi(&h);        await(safe(T, H));
    temp.write(t);              humi.write(h);           bell := off;
    next;                       next;                  }
  }                           }
```

Informally we can argue the correctness of this program as follows. At the two synchronisation points in the *alarm_control* process, i.e., at the two occurrences of **wait** in the **await** statements, the following invariant holds:

$$(\neg \ safe(T, H) \wedge bell = on) \vee (safe(T, H) \wedge bell = off)$$

When blocked at one of its synchronisation points, the *alarm_control* process is in sync with the *temp* and *humi* observers and hence T and H are equal to the measured temperature and humidity, respectively. So, as long as the *alarm_control* process is blocked, the system has the desired properties. As soon as it gets out of sync because of changes of the measured temperature or humidity, the process will de-block, re-synchronise and block again at either the same or the next synchronisation point, thereby restoring the invariant. The blocking will occur because *syncs* disable themselves and the two conditions in the **await** operators are mutually exclusive. The assumption in all of this is, of course, that the execution of the code in the body of the while loop of the *alarm_control* process takes substantially less time than the average time between two successive "out of sync" events in the observers *temp* and *humi* (which is always ≥ 33 ms). Note that the **next** operator in the measurement processes could be replaced by **commit**.

3.2   Specifying Interaction Objects

In Section 2.4 we have already seen a specification of a simple interaction object. Some of the more subtle details of specifying interaction objects will be illustrated here using the example of a *mailbox*. A mailbox is similar to a message queue as discussed earlier (see Figure 2) in that it provides a way to pass messages from a sender process to a receiver process asynchronously. The difference is that mailboxes satisfy the requirements of interaction objects, as reflected by the model of a mailbox in Figure 8. The *send* and *receive* operations operate on the local message queues *sm* and *rm* in the domains of the sender and receiver processes, respectively. Interaction between sender and receiver occurs through the global message queue *im* using *commits* and *syncs*.

We will allow mailboxes to be used simultaneously by multiple senders, leading to the generalised mailbox model indicated in Figure 9. In this model, each

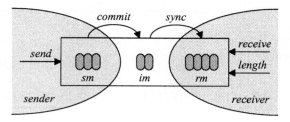

Fig. 8. Model of a Mailbox with a Single Sender

sender process P has its own local and global message queues. This is represented in the formal specification of a mailbox below, by means of the functions sm and im that map a sender process P to its associated message queues $sm(P)$ and $im(P)$. In the specification we use the types *Process* and *Message* as given sets.

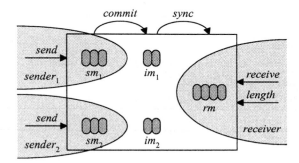

Fig. 9. Model of a Mailbox with Multiple Senders

Mailbox _____

$senders : \mathbb{F}\ Process$
$receiver : Process$
$sm, im : Process \nrightarrow \text{seq}\ Message$
$rm : \text{seq}\ Message$

_____

$\text{dom}\ sm = \text{dom}\ im = senders$

---

init _____

Mailbox

_____

$(\forall P : senders \bullet sm(P) = im(P) = \langle\rangle) \wedge rm = \langle\rangle$

$\Delta Mailbox$ _____

Mailbox
Mailbox$'$

_____

$senders' = senders \wedge receiver' = receiver$

---

send
$\Delta Mailbox$
$P : Process$
$m? : Message$

$P \in senders$
$sm' = sm \oplus \{P \mapsto \langle m? \rangle \frown sm(P)\} \wedge im' = im \wedge rm' = rm$

---

receive
$\Delta Mailbox$
$P : Process$
$m! : Message$

$P = receiver \wedge rm \neq \langle \rangle$
$sm' = sm \wedge im' = im \wedge rm' \frown \langle m! \rangle = rm$

---

length
$\Xi Mailbox$
$P : Process$
$n! : \mathbb{N}$

$P = receiver$
$n! = \#rm$

---

commit
$\Delta Mailbox$
$P : Process$

$P \in senders \wedge sm(P) \neq \langle \rangle$
$sm' = sm \oplus \{P \mapsto \langle \rangle\} \wedge im' = im \oplus \{P \mapsto sm(P) \frown im(P)\} \wedge rm' = rm$

---

sync
$\Delta Mailbox$
$P, Q : Process$

$P = receiver \wedge Q \in senders \wedge im(Q) \neq \langle \rangle$
$sm' = sm \wedge im' = im \oplus \{Q \mapsto \langle \rangle\} \wedge rm' = im(Q) \frown rm$

In contrast with observers, it is not immediately clear that mailboxes satisfy all requirements of interaction objects. The obvious way to define the sets of input, interaction and output variables of a mailbox X is as follows:

$$in_{X,P} = \textbf{if } P \in senders \textbf{ then } \{sm(P)\} \textbf{ else } \emptyset$$
$$iav_{X,P} = \textbf{if } P \in senders \textbf{ then } \{im(P)\} \textbf{ else } \emptyset$$
$$out_{X,P} = \textbf{if } P = receiver \textbf{ then } \{rm\} \qquad \textbf{else } \emptyset$$

In this definition we took the liberty of interpreting $sm(P)$ and $im(P)$ as individual variables rather than as references to parts of the variables sm and im.

The reason why the above definition does not work is that $commit_{X,P}$ modifies the variables in $in_{X,P}$, and $sync_{X,P,Q}$ modifies the variables in $iav_{X,Q}$. This is not allowed according to the definition of interaction objects. It can be remedied by transforming the above specification into another behaviourally equivalent specification using a different set of variables, as sketched briefly below. We use the method of "adding and removing variables" as described in [14, 20]. Step 1 is to augment the model of a mailbox with three new variables: the input variable st, the interaction variable it and the output variable rt.

$$\begin{array}{|l}
\hline
\;\underline{Mailbox2} \\
\;\;Mailbox \\
\;\;st, it, rt : Process \nrightarrow \text{seq } Message \\
\;\underline{} \\
\;\;\text{dom } st = \text{dom } it = \text{dom } rt = senders \\
\hline
\end{array}$$

The idea is to make $st(P)$ equal to the trace of *all* messages sent to the mailbox by process P, with $commit$ making copies of $st(P)$ in $it(P)$ and $sync$ making copies of $it(P)$ in $rt(P)$. Step 2 is to augment the operation specifications accordingly, and prove the following mailbox invariant:

$$\forall P : senders \bullet st(P) = sm(P) \frown it(P) \wedge it(P) = im(P) \frown rt(P)$$

This invariant allows sm and im to be expressed entirely in terms of st, it and rt. Step 3 is to eliminate all applied occurrences of sm and im by means of replacements. Step 4 is to remove the now redundant defining occurrences of sm and im from the model as well. The new definition of a mailbox, thus obtained, satisfies all interaction object requirements, where:

$$\begin{aligned}
in_{X,P} &= \textbf{if } P \in senders \textbf{ then } \{st(P)\} \quad \textbf{else } \emptyset \\
iav_{X,P} &= \textbf{if } P \in senders \textbf{ then } \{it(P)\} \quad \textbf{else } \emptyset \\
out_{X,P} &= \textbf{if } P = receiver \textbf{ then } \{rt(P), rm\} \textbf{ else } \emptyset
\end{aligned}$$

3.3   Communicating Using Interaction Objects

We will use mailboxes to illustrate how interaction objects can be used to communicate between processes. The symbol for a mailbox is shown in Figure 10. A

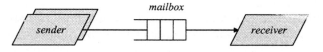

Fig. 10. Mailbox Symbol

sender process can send a message x to a mailbox mbx like this:

$mbx.send(x);$ **next**;

The receiver process can receive the message in a variable m like this:

await$(mbx.length > 0)$; $mbx.receive(\&m)$;

Here we have assumed that the output parameter $m!$, in the specification of the *receive* operation, has been implemented as a reference parameter. Compared with the normal way of receiving a message from a message queue using a single blocking call, the above may seem somewhat clumsy. This can be remedied by implementing the precondition of *receive* as a boolean return value. If the precondition is not valid, the operation returns *false* and has no side effect, allowing a message to be received like this:

await$(mbx.receive(\&m))$;

This approach requires the use of assertions with side effects. A safe rule to contain the negative effects of this is to require that the condition C in **await**(C) has no effect when it returns *false*. This implies that, in the execution of the await statement, the side effect will occur only once, i.e., when the assertion C returns *true*.

Using **or** and **and** as conditional versions of the logical operators $\lor$ and $\land$ (similar to the $||$ and $\&\&$ operators in C), several standard communication constructs can be defined directly in terms of the **await** construct. A process that has to receive data from one of two mailboxes $mbx1$ and $mbx2$ can do so by means of the following construct:

await$(mbx1.receive(\&m)$ **or** $mbx2.receive(\&m))$;

By adding guards and actions, this can be extended to a general guarded input statement:

await((*GUARD1* **and** $mbx1.receive(\&m)$ **and** *ACTION1*)
    or (*GUARD2* **and** $mbx2.receive(\&m)$ **and** *ACTION2*)
    );

The only assumption we make here is that the guards have no side effect and that the actions return *true*. By replacing mailboxes by interaction objects supporting synchronous communication (such as CoCoNut channels, see Section 3.4), we can even implement a rendezvous mechanism without introducing any additional language constructs. The above guarded input statement then corresponds to an Ada select statement.

In order to demonstrate what happens if multiple processes are concurrently sending data to the same mailbox, consider a simple configuration of two producers and one consumer, as depicted in Figure 11. Each producer repeatedly sends a pair of consecutive numbers to the mailbox in a single atomic action. The consumer also receives the natural numbers in pairs, as described by the code of producers and consumer below.

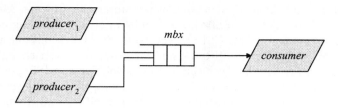

Fig. 11. Producers and Consumer

$producer_i$ $(i = 1, 2)$:
  $int\ n := 0$;
  while($true$)
  { $mbx.send(n)$;
   $mbx.send(n + 1)$;
   next;
   $n := n + 1$;
  }

$consumer$:
  $int\ n1, n2$;
  while($true$)
  { **await**($mbx.length \geq 2$);
   $mbx.receive(\&n1)$;
   $mbx.receive(\&n2)$;
   assert($n2 = n1 + 1$);
  }

It is easy to infer from the specification of mailboxes that, despite the fact that the individual *send* operations of the producers are interleaved, the consumer will always receive pairs of two consecutive numbers. Hence, the **assert** statement in the consumer code will never fail. Though not advisable from the point of view of defensive programming, we could even replace the **await** statement in the consumer code by:

await($mbx.length > 0$);

3.4   Implementing Interaction Objects

In discussing the implementation of interaction objects, we will restrict ourselves to the situation that all processes execute in the same address space, i.e., that processes are *threads*. This situation is typical for embedded systems in the context of which the concept of an interaction object originated. Embedded systems often use real-time kernels to provide basic thread management, synchronisation and communication. Implementing interaction objects in distributed systems is a separate story that will not be discussed here.

The implementation problem of interaction objects is essentially the problem of implementing the three interaction operators **commit**, **sync**, and **wait**. First consider the problem of guaranteeing the atomicity of **commit** and the individual *syncs* executed by **sync**. This problem can be solved by associating a mutual exclusion mechanism with each process P. When executing **commit**, P uses this mechanism to disable access to all of its associated interaction variables, i.e., the variables in the sets $iav_{X,P}$ for all X attached to P (see Figure 3). Another process Q executing $sync_{X,Q,P}$ uses the same mechanism to disable access to the variables $iav_{X,P}$.

The mutual exclusion mechanism can be chosen per process. Mutexes and pre-emption disabling are typical choices, while interrupt disabling can be used for interrupt service routines (ISRs). Note that, insofar as interaction objects are concerned, we can treat ISRs as normal processes, even though they are dealt with differently at the operating system level. For non-ISR processes, pre-emption disabling is often a good choice because *commits* and *syncs* are normally very short actions. For example, in a typical mailbox implementation, they amount to append operations on linked lists.

The problem of how to determine which *commits* and *syncs* should be executed by **commit** or **sync** can be solved by introducing flags $c_{X,P}$ and $s_{X,P,Q}$ for each $commit_{X,P}$ and $sync_{X,P,Q}$, respectively, while maintaining the following invariant:

$$commit_{X,P} \text{ is enabled} \Rightarrow c_{X,P} \text{ is set}$$
$$sync_{X,P,Q} \text{ is enabled} \Rightarrow s_{X,P,Q} \text{ is set}$$

According to the definition of an interaction object, only the access operations of X can enable $commit_{X,P}$, so access operations of X should set $c_{X,P}$ when called by P. Likewise, only $commit_{X,Q}$ can enable $sync_{X,P,Q}$, so $commit_{X,Q}$ should set $s_{X,P,Q}$ when called by Q. **commit** and **sync** can use the flags to determine which *commits* or *syncs* to execute. They should clear a flag immediately before the execution of the corresponding *commit* or *sync*. This cannot violate the invariant because of the self-disabling property of *commits* and *syncs*. **wait** can use the $s_{X,P,Q}$ flags to determine whether a process should be blocked or de-blocked, without affecting the flags themselves. Note that there could be situations where a flag is set while the corresponding *commit* or *sync* is disabled. This can do no harm provided that disabled *commits* and *syncs* have no effect when executed. Note also that in a real implementation, it is more efficient to use lists of function pointers rather than flags (similar to *active messages* [10]).

The CoCoNut component [16], developed by Philips Research, provides a full implementation of interaction objects along the lines sketched above. CoCoNut ("Control Component in a Nutshell") is a scalable, platform-independent software component defining an operating system abstraction on top of which applications using interaction objects can be developed. It provides implementations of the interaction operators and a number of interaction objects such as *observers* (see Section 2.4), *mailboxes* (see Section 3.2), *events* (asynchronous push buttons), *channels* (one-slot buffers supporting synchronous communication), *buffers* (multi-slot bounded communication buffers), *locks* (mutexes according to the interaction object model), and *timers* (programmable objects supporting timed actions). In addition to this, CoCoNut supports dynamic creation of interaction objects, dynamic attachment of processes to interaction objects, and facilities for the construction of custom-made interaction objects.

Another feature of CoCoNut is the support for organising applications as collections of *communicating state machines*, with the ability to allocate state machines to processes at compile time. This allows systematic *task inversion* [9] which is important in resource-constrained embedded systems that can only afford a small number of processes. In the extreme case that all state machines are allocated to the same process, a single-process version of CoCoNut can be used requiring no real-time kernel. Kernel-based applications of CoCoNut should nevertheless be preferred since they can take full, real-time advantage of the loose process coupling provided by interaction objects, using the pre-emptive priority-based scheduling support of the kernel. In practice, CoCoNut has been used both with and without real-time kernels.

3.5   Verifying Programs That Use Interaction Objects

Programs that use interaction objects can be verified using standard verification techniques for concurrent programs such as [7, 18, 17]. The verification task is simplified because these programs, if properly designed, can be dissected into relatively large pieces of atomic code. We exemplify this by sketching how a program that uses interaction objects can be mapped to a *transition system*, thus enabling the use of standard techniques for proving properties of transition systems (see [23], for example).

We will assume that programs use **await** and **next** as interaction operators only, and that all conditions in **await** statements are free of side effects. With the **await** and **next** macros expanded, the code of each process consists of atomic sequences of statements ending in **commit**, where each **commit** is followed by one or more executions of **sync**. For example, the code of the *alarm_control* process from the temperature/humidity alarm system in Section 3.1 expands, with some rewriting, to:

```
commit;
while(true)
{ sync; while(safe(T, H)){ wait; sync; }; bell := on; commit;
  sync; while(¬ safe(T, H)){ wait; sync; }; bell := off; commit;
}
```

Using an auxiliary control variable to model the program counter, code like this can be mapped in a standard way to a transition system. In this case we do not even need the auxiliary variable because the *bell* variable, whose initial value is *false*, can be used as the control variable. In programs that use interaction objects, the transitions will be of two types: *outgoing* transitions (the ones ending in **commit**) and *incoming* transitions (the individual *syncs* contained in **sync**). We can ignore the occurrences of **wait** because they are only there to keep the program from useless busy waiting. Since the **sync** operator is used between *all* outgoing transitions, we decouple the incoming transitions from the control flow and treat the *syncs* as autonomous transitions in the transition system. For example, the *alarm_control* process breaks down into the following transitions:

$$bell = off \land \neg \, safe(T, H) \rightarrow bell := on; \textbf{commit}_{P_A};$$
$$bell = on \land safe(T, H) \rightarrow bell := off; \textbf{commit}_{P_A};$$
$$enabled(sync_{temp, P_A, P_T}) \rightarrow sync_{temp, P_A, P_T};$$
$$enabled(sync_{humi, P_A, P_H}) \rightarrow sync_{humi, P_A, P_H};$$

Here P_A, P_T and P_H represent the *alarm_control*, *measure_temperature* and *measure_humidity* processes, respectively. The part on the left-hand side of an arrow is the *enabling condition* of the transition, and the part on the right-hand side is the atomic *action* of the transition. Using the formal specifications of the interaction objects, the transition rules can be expressed in terms of operations on variables and can be further simplified. For example, the input variables of interaction objects can generally be completely eliminated. In the above case, the occurrences of **commit**$_{P_A}$ can even be omitted because they have no effect.

The decoupling of synchronisation actions from the control flow in the above mapping of programs to transition systems implies that we are actually using a more nondeterministic of version of the **sync** operator than the one defined in Section 2.5. Rather than assuming that **sync** executes *all* enabled *syncs* in a process, we assume that it executes *some* enabled *syncs*, where "some" could be anything between none and all. Fairness is assumed in the sense that an enabled *sync* will eventually be executed. This is the natural interpretation of the **sync** operator in a distributed setting. We prefer this interpretation in proving properties of programs, since it leads to simpler transition systems and wider applicability of programs. As a consequence, we should design our programs in such a way that their desired properties can be proven irrespective of the order of execution of the synchronisation actions. Note that if timing is important, as in the temperature/humidity alarm system, time steps can be added as transitions to the transition systems leading to a *timed transition systems* approach [11].

4   Related Work

In this section, we compare our concurrent system model (processes communicating by means of interaction objects) to related approaches. A common aim of our model and more fundamental models, such as transition systems [18, 7] and action systems [2], including language outgrowths such as Seuss [19] and DisCo [13], is to support the use of sequential techniques in dealing with concurrent systems, based on an interleaving model of concurrency. The link with transition systems was already discussed in Section 3.5. In terms of action systems, access operations of objects would be *private actions* and interaction operations would be *joint actions* of processes. The difference is that we restrict ourselves to very special types of joint actions (*commits* and *syncs*) allowing the definition of general interaction operators that can be inserted in the control flow of a process. Neither transition systems nor action systems consider processes at the level of control flow.

Interaction operators similar to the ones defined in this paper can be found, for example, in the Mianjin language [21] and in SDL [6]. Mianjin is a parallel programming language supporting the concept of global objects and the ability to call methods of global objects asynchronously from different processes. The process owning the global object will not be interfered with until it calls the **poll** operator, which has a similar effect as a **sync** operator in that it executes all pending global method calls and thereby introduces an incoming interaction point in the process. The main differences are that **sync** is more restricted than

poll since it executes synchronisation actions only, and that there is no equivalent of the **commit** operator in Mianjin.

As already noticed in Section 2.6, the **nextstate** operator of SDL is similar to the **next** interaction operator. SDL is a concurrent programming language supporting state machines that communicate asynchronously using "signals". At the beginning of a transition, a state machine can receive signals and during the transition it can send signals. The **nextstate** operator is used to terminate a transition. This can conceptually be seen as "committing" any pending output and "synchronising" to new input, before going to the next transition. The model defined in this paper is more general than the SDL programming model in that it allows state machines to communicate using any type of communication mechanism (interaction object). During a transition, a state machine can perform arbitrary input and output actions (access operations on interaction objects) without the danger of affecting the atomicity of the transition.

Monitors [3, 12, 4] and interaction objects are similar in the sense that both define an abstraction mechanism for concurrent access to data. There is one essential difference: in monitors all interaction between processes accessing the data is controlled from within the monitor. Synchronisation is controlled internally e.g. using condition variables, implying that monitor operations are generally *blocking* operations. In contrast, the operations of an interaction object do not contain interaction points at all *except* for the two interaction operations *commit* and *sync* which are non-blocking. All interaction between processes is controlled *outside* an interaction object by means of three basic interaction operators. This has a number of consequences. First of all, processes can use a general form of condition synchronisation, using the **await** operator, instead of the dedicated condition synchronisation implemented by a monitor. Secondly, processes can define synchronisation conditions that involve multiple interaction objects. With monitors this is not possible because monitor operations may block. Finally, interaction objects are simpler to specify and verify than monitors: they can e.g. be specified completely using pre- and post-condition techniques.

5   Conclusion

We conclude by recapitulating some of the salient features of the model of communication and synchronisation introduced in this paper. The key characteristic of this model is the strict separation of process interaction and data access as reflected in the definition of an interaction object. All process interaction is established by means of three interaction operators and all data access is non-interfering. As a consequence of this separation of concerns, programmers get full control over the interaction points in their programs and can deal with data access using standard sequential techniques. Furthermore, various standard ways of communication and synchronisation can be be modelled directly in terms of combinations of interaction operators and interaction objects. The model can be implemented in an efficient and platform-independent way, as demonstrated by the CoCoNut component [16]. Distributed implementations of interaction objects have not been discussed in this paper and are subject of future work.

References

[1] Andrews, G.R., *Concurrent Programming*, Benjamin/Cummings (1991).
[2] Back, R.J.R., Kurki-Suonio, R., *Distributed Cooperation with Action Systems*, ACM Transactions on Programming Languages and Systems, Vol. 10, 4 (1988), 513–554.
[3] Brinch Hansen, P., *Operating System Principles*, Prentice-Hall (1973).
[4] Buhr, P.A., Fortier, M., Coffin, M.H., *Monitor Classification*, ACM Computing Surveys 27, 1 (1995), 63–107.
[5] Bustard, D., Elder, J., Welsh, J., *Concurrent Program Structures*, Prentice Hall (1988).
[6] CCITT Recommendation Z.100: *Specification and Description Language SDL*, Blue Book, Volume X.1–X.5, ITU (1988).
[7] Chandy, K.M., Misra, J., *Parallel Program Design*, Addison Wesley (1988).
[8] Feijs, L.M.G., Jonkers, H.B.M., *History, Principles and Application of the SPRINT Method*, Journal of Systems and Software 41 (1998), 199-219.
[9] Gomaa, H., *Software Design Methods for Concurrent and Real-Time Systems*, Addison-Wesley (1993).
[10] von Eicken, T., Culler, D., Goldstein, S.C., Schauser, K.E., *Active Messages: a Mechanism for Integrated Communication and Computation*, in: Proceedings of the 19th International Symposium on Computer Architecture (1992).
[11] Henzinger, T.A., Manna, Z., Pnueli, A., *Timed Transition Systems.* In: Real-Time: Theory in Practice, Lecture Notes in Computer Science, Vol. 600, Springer-Verlag (1992), 226–251.
[12] Hoare, C.A.R., *Monitors: An Operating System Structuring Concept*, Communications of the ACM, Vol. 17, 10 (1974), 549–557.
[13] Järvinen, H.-M., Kurki-Suonio, R., *DisCo specification language: marriage of actions and objects.* In: Proceedings of the 11th International Conference on Distributed Computing Systems, IEEE Computer Society Press (1991), 142–151.
[14] Jonkers, H.B.M., *Abstraction, Specification and Implementation Techniques*, Mathematical Centre Tracts, Vol. 166, Mathematisch Centrum (1983).
[15] Jonkers, H.B.M., *An Overview of the SPRINT Method.* In: Woodcock, J.C.P., Larsen, P.G. (Eds.), Industrial Strength Formal Methods, Lecture Notes in Computer Science, Vol. 670, Springer-Verlag (1993), 403-427.
[16] Jonkers, H.B.M., *Survey of CoCoNut 1.0*, Technical Report RWB-506-ir-96022, Philips Research, Information and Software Technology (1996).
[17] Lamport, L., *The Temporal Logic of Actions*, ACM Transactions on Programming Languages and Systems, Vol. 16, 3 (1994), 872–923.
[18] Manna, Z., Pnueli, A., *The Temporal Logic of Reactive and Concurrent Systems: Specification*, Springer-Verlag (1992).
[19] Misra, J., *An Object Model for Multiprogramming*, Proc. 10th IPPS/SPDP 98 Workshops, Jose Rolim (ed.), Lecture Notes in Computer Science, Vol. 1388, Springer-Verlag (1998), 881–889.
[20] Morgan, C., *Programming from Specifications*, Prentice Hall (1990).
[21] Roe, P., Szyperski, C., *Mianjin is Gardens Point: A Parallel Language Taming Asynchronous Communication.* In: Fourth Australasian Conference on Parallel and Real-Time Systems (PART'97), Springer-Verlag (1997).
[22] Schneider, F.B., *On Concurrent Programming*, Springer-Verlag (1997).
[23] Shankar, A.U., *An Introduction to Assertional Reasoning for Concurrent Systems*, ACM Computing Surveys, Vol. 25, 3 (1993), 225–262.
[24] Spivey, J.M., *The Z Notation: A Reference Manual*, Second Edition, Prentice Hall (1992)

Modelling Microsoft COM Using π-Calculus

Loe M.G. Feijs

Philips Research Laboratories and EESI TUE
feijs@natlab.research.philips.com and feijs@win.tue.nl

Abstract. We use the π-calculus to model aspects of Microsoft's COM architecture. The paper introduces certain aspects of COM, first using IDL and C++, and then using a sugared version of the π-calculus (with numbers and lists added). Most of the complexities arise in dynamic interface management. We explore using the reduction rules of the calculus to show that two components (a stack and stack-observer) do indeed connect to each other in the required manner.

1 Introduction

There is considerable experience with using formal techniques for modelling and analysis of classical communication protocols, by which we mean those protocols which deal with such issues as splitting and assembling protocol data units, error control and flow control. Languages like CCS [1], ACP [2], LOTOS [3], PSF [4], SDL [5], MSC [6] etc. have proven to be useful for this. The component technology [7, 8] which is emerging presently, brings with it protocols of a slightly different type: they are concerned with dynamic binding and with negotiating about a component's capabilities. Configurations change dynamically and processes not only exchange data, but they also exchange link-names.

Therefore we consider it worthwhile to experiment with the π-calculus [9], which provides precisely this extra expressive power. We apply the π-calculus to key aspects of one of the most successful component technologies presently available: Microsoft's Component Object Model (COM) [10]. This is the basic technology which makes it possible, among other things, to perform run-time negotiations and establish run-time bindings. COM is the basis of what Microsoft calls Active-X, whose forerunner was called OLE (Object Linking and Embedding) [11]. It is Active-X or OLE which allows to copy-paste a bitmap made by MS-Paint into a MS-Word document, and then find that when the bitmap is embedded in the Word document, it still can be edited in a wysiwyg style.

Survey of the paper: in Sect. 2 we present a brief discussion of the relevance of component technology and introductory remarks on Microsoft COM. In Sect. 3 we present a summary of the π-calculus. In Sect. 4 we present the principles of our approach to modelling COM using π-calculus. Sects. 5 and 6 together form the first part of our case study: the former explaining concrete aspects of COM for a component MyStack by using only IDL and C++ as notations, the latter section describing precisely the same aspects but using π-calculus instead of IDL and C++. Then in Sect. 7 we discuss the key aspect of COM (manipulating

J. Wing, J. Woodcock, J. Davies (Eds.): FM'99, Vol. II, LNCS 1709, pp. 1343–1363, 1999.
© Springer-Verlag Berlin Heidelberg 1999

interface pointers) and in Sect. 8 we extend the formal π-calculus model in order to properly deal with these key aspects of COM as well. A sample calculation using the rules of π-calculus is given in Sect. 9. Finally Sect. 10 contains some concluding remarks. The paper demands no a-priori knowledge of COM or π-calculus: Sects. 5 and 7 introduce COM and Sect. 3 summarises the π-calculus.

Acknowledgements: the author would like to thank Hans Jonkers for the help and cooperation on the subject of this paper; the author also wants to thank the anonymous referees for their helpful comments.

2   Component Technology

The idea of component technology is that custom programs are composed from reusable parts that serve to perform certain sub-tasks. In the model proposed by Microsoft, components are reused in binary executable form. It includes a binary interfacing mechanism which lets components communicate with each other in an open system. There is a need to add components to an open system and to add new interfaces to a system. The connection and communication mechanisms are standardised and do not depend on the specific interfaces themselves. The set of components in a system can change over time. So there are situations where a newer component that is capable of exploiting a certain new interface encounters an old component that does not know about this new interface. For this purpose there is a negotiation mechanism in COM by which one component or application can find out if a desired interface is supported by another component. It makes sense to think of interfaces as formal legal contracts. Implementers must make sure their implementations meet the contracts. In COM, contracts are identified by interface identifiers (IIDs). When components are enhanced, they get new interfaces, while preserving possibly some of the older interfaces. It is also possible to remove some of the older interfaces. The interfaces themselves are not changed. Each IID identifies a contract which may or may not be supported by a given component (or better, by a given object; in this paper we do not go into the distinction between components and objects). Once the IID is fixed and released, no one is supposed to make even the smallest modification to the signature or the semantics of the interface. The signature is fixed by means of the language IDL. Although most of the COM literature insists that the semantics of the interfaces for a given IID be fixed, there is no dedicated specification language for COM and often the semantic aspects of the contracts are not formally specified. Williams in [12] provides an exposé of the ideas of system evolution underlying COM (this paragraph is based on Williams' text).

The internal operation of a COM component is hidden because COM is a binary standard. A COM component is obtained by compilation of for example, a C++ program, or a Java program. The source code is not released for distribution. Usually only the compiled version, i.e. the machine code is released. It is not possible to read to or write from a component's data structures directly. All access must be done via procedure calls. This approach preserves the freedom for choosing another data structure in a next version of the component. Secondly, it is relatively easy to replace a local function call by a call to a stub, which at its turn executes an RPC (remote procedure call). This kind of replacement, which is easy for procedure calls, would not be so easy to realise for direct access to data structures.

All functions (procedures) are grouped into so-called interfaces. An interface is a set of functions whose semantics is somehow related. This resembles the well-known concept of 'signature' from the theory of algebraic datatypes. An interface however only contains functions, no abstract types. There are auxiliary types such as void, long, etc, and also "struct"s or other interface types; but the main type, the component's type itself remains implicit. Usually a component has several interfaces (which is an important difference with algebraic data types).

3   The π-Calculus

The π-calculus was proposed by Milner, Parrow and Walker in 1992. It is also called 'a calculus of mobile processes', but actually no processes are moved around, only the identities of the ports of the processes can be communicated from one process to another. The π-calculus has a certain simplicity which comes from the fact that all distinction between variables and constants has been removed. The main idea is that the calculus is like CCS, except for the fact that not only values are communicated, but also port identifiers.

A very brief summary of the calculus is given here. If p is a port, then $\bar{p}v . P$ is the process which sends value v along port p and then proceeds as P. Conversely, $p(x) . Q$ is the process which receives a value over port p, binds the value thus received to x, and proceeds as Q. In the body Q, this x may be used. The special thing about π-calculus is that port identifiers may be sent and received as well. For example $q(p) . \bar{p}v . R$ is the process which receives port identifier p via port q, and then uses this p for sending something else, viz. v (and proceeds as R).

Further operators of the π-calculus include $+$ for alternative composition, $|$ for parallel composition, recursive definition, inaction $\mathbf{0}$, silent step τ, matching prefix $[x = y]$ and binding prefix (x). The main rule of computation is that $(... + \bar{y}x.P + ...) \,|\, (... + y(z).Q + ...) \xrightarrow{\ \tau\ } P|Q\{x/z\}$.

4   Modelling Approach

The main modelling techniques that we propose and that we shall put into action in Sects. 6 and 8 are the following:

- invocation of a procedure with n input and m output parameters is modelled by $n + 1$ send actions followed by m receive actions. HRESULT (handle to a result) and call-by-reference parameters are treated in the same way.
- interface pointers are modelled as π-calculus ports, for example if the one-argument procedure p belongs to interface i, then invoking p is modeled as $\bar{i}p . \bar{i}a . i(h) . \cdots$. So p is the procedure's name, a is its input argument and h is the result (of type HRESULT).

– the state-based behaviour of the component is modelled by recursive equations where the various parts of the state are parameters.

5 The 'Interface' Concept of COM

Our example is about a stack. We begin with its main interface (the push and pop behaviour). Each interface has a name. In COM this name always starts with a capital I. So we assume that the usual push and pop functions are inside IManipulate. There is a language for describing interfaces called IDL (Interface Definition Language). For the first interface, we assume a few auxiliary types:

– HRESULT, whose value set has 2^{32} elements, among which are S_OK, S_FALSE, E_NOINTERFACE, E_NOTIMPL and E_FAIL.
– The set ITEM (the values that will be pushed onto the stack), with a value set which is considered not being interesting now (32 bits integers).

For the purpose of classifying the obtained HRESULT values there are two auxiliary functions, FAILED(...) and SUCCEEDED(...), which we fix for the time being by means of equations: FAILED(S_OK) = FALSE, FAILED(S_FALSE) = FALSE, FAILED(E_NOINTERFACE) = TRUE, etcetera. Generally FAILED(S_...) = FALSE and SUCCEEDED(S_...) = TRUE. Conversely FAILED(E_...) = TRUE and SUCCEEDED(E_ ...) = FALSE.

Now we are ready to present our first interface definition in IDL (we have left out a few things, viz. [in], [out] which serve for classifying parameters, and : IUnknown, which indicates inheritance on interfaces).

```
interface IManipulate
{
    HRESULT clear();
    HRESULT is_empty();
    HRESULT push(ITEM i);
    HRESULT pop(ITEM *retval);
}
```

First we discuss the syntax of this specification. The first word, "interface" is a key-word. The second word, "IManipulate" is the name that is given to the newly defined interface. Thereafter, between "{" and "}" there is a set of four function headers. These function headers are denoted with a syntax which resembles C or C++. Recall that in C and C++ declarations always mention the type first, followed by the name of the variable or parameter of that type. So for example HRESULT push(ITEM i); means that push is a function that takes an ITEM value and that yields a HRESULT value. Please note that push is a function in the sense of the programming languages C and C++, that is, a procedure with side-effect. The IDL description only contains signature information; in particular, it does not say which variables are assigned to. For is_empty we can use the distinction between S_OK and S_FALSE to indicate whether the stack is empty (S_OK) or not empty (S_FALSE). Usually this is not recommended, but it is possible. Also note the asterisk in (ITEM *retval): the C or C++ conventions apply. So this function has to be called having as its argument a pointer to a variable in which an ITEM will fit. This variable could be called retval. In that case &retval is a pointer to this variable. Therefore the call pop(&retval) has the effect that upon return we find that retval contains the ITEM value which was first on top of the stack (assuming that HRESULT delivered the value S_OK).

If we have a stack object, we can perform push and pop operations, etc. But we shall never have objects as such; we will only have direct access to pointers which refer to interfaces. These interface pointers can be dereferenced (which gives us interfaces), and by using an interface we can call clear, is_empty, push and pop. Suppose for example that ps is a pointer to an IManipulate interface of a component with stack behaviour, then we can run the following fragment of C++ (if we prefer Java we have to write "." instead of "->"). So this is code of some component or application which has to use a stack.

```
HRESULT hr;
ITEM i,retval;
BOOL test = FALSE;

hr = ps->clear();
if (SUCCEEDED(hr))
{
    hr = ps->push(i);
    if (SUCCEEDED(hr))
    {
        hr = ps->pop(&retval);
        if (SUCCEEDED(hr))
        {
            test = (retval == i);
        } else // failed to pop
    } else // failed to push
} else // failed to clear
```

6   Modelling Interface Behaviour in π-Calculus

We show a recursive definition of a process MyStack which models the interface behaviour of the IManipulate interface. It is based on the principles of Sect. 4.

The state-based behaviour of the various components is modelled again by recursive process equations where the various parts of the state are carried along as parameters of the processes. Although the pure π-calculus does not provide for built-in data types and process parameters, we assume that these can be simulated thanks to the power of the π-calculus (which is known to simulate full λ-calculus). We assume additional operators <>, <.> and ++ for lists of items. Here <> denotes the empty stack, <.> is the operator which makes a one-element list, and ++ denotes concatenation.

The process MyStack has two parameters. The first of these, pIman, models the interface pointer along which all communication takes place. The second parameter is the contents of the stack.

```
MyStack(pIman,<>) =
( pIman (f) .
    ( [f = clear] .
      pIman S_OK .
      MyStack(pIman,<>)
    + [f = is_empty] .
      pIman S_OK .
      MyStack(pIman,<>)
    + [f = push] .
      pIman (j) .
      pIman S_OK .
      MyStack(pIman,<j>)
    + [f = pop] .
      pIman E_FAIL .
      MyStack(pIman,<>)
)   )

MyStack(pIman,<i>++s) =
( pIman (f) .
  ( [f = clear] .
    pIman S_OK .
    MyStack(pIman,<>)
  + [f = is_empty] .
    pIman S_FALSE .
    MyStack(pIman,<i>++s)
  + [f = push] .
    pIman (j) .
    pIman S_OK .
    MyStack(pIman,<j>++<i>++s)
  + [f = pop] .
    pIman S_OK .
    pIman i .
    MyStack(pIman,s)
) )
```

There is nothing special about this model yet. It could be written in CCS or any process algebraic formalism. But in the next section we present other aspects and other examples in COM, the modelling of which becomes more interesting.

7   Manipulating COM Interface Pointers

An important question to be addressed now is: "how do we get an interface pointer of a stack"? There are two answers: (1) get it from somebody else, (2) create it yourself.

For the first case (got it from somebody else) it is best to first perform some querying in order to make sure that we have a valid interface pointer of the desired interface identifier (IID); there is a general mechanism for that. For a given interface pointer it is possible to ask in a dynamic way whether its component has an interface with IManipulate behaviour (that is, whether the component implements stack behaviour). This asking in a dynamic way is important because objects are created in a dynamic way, on different machines, possibly from different or even incompatible component versions. So it is very essential first to find out more about the component behind a given pointer. This asking/testing mechanism makes it possible to obtain other interface pointers once we have the first one that belongs to a certain component. The mechanism is implemented as a procedure which is called QueryInterface.

For the second case it is possible to get hold of an interface pointer via a so-called "factory". Once we have the first, we can use QueryIterface to get the others. First we discuss the QueryInterface mechanism. Each component supports one interface that is obligatory: IUnknown. Later we shall show more of our component MyStack which happens to have three interfaces. These will be called IUnknown, IManipulate and IOverflow (see figure). The interface IUnknown has to be supported by every component. There is no language construct to express that MyStack has these three interfaces.

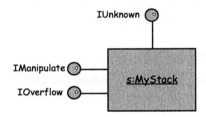

Fig. 1. MyStack object having three interfaces.

MyStack is a concrete component which contains a 'class', of which instances can be created. In Figure 1 we show an instance (which is why we underlined s:MyStack). The asking/testing mechanism is provided by IUnknown, which has the following IDL:

```
interface IUnknown
{
    HRESULT QueryInterface(REFIID iid, void** ppv);
    HRESULT AddRef();
    HRESULT Release();
}
```

REFIID is the type of pointers to IID, where IID is the type of interface identifiers. Interface identifiers are statically determined identifications. Note: this iid must be viewed as an input parameter; the fact that REFIID is a pointer itself is only an efficiency trick which amounts to a call-by-reference mechanism. The second parameter yields an untyped pointer (an interface pointer). This QueryInterface function embodies the mentioned asking/testing mechanism.

What comes next is an intermezzo about interface identifiers and interface pointers. Interface pointers indicate specific instances of interfaces, associated with corresponding object instances, whereas interface identifiers effectively give the "type" of the interface. An interface identifier is obtained statically using a special number generator (uuidgen, to be run by the interface designer, no central registering). This could yield 6A92D9A0-C04D-11D3-A11B-00A024674DFA for IManipulate. In the same way IUnknown has its own interface identifier, but this is always the same, on all machines, viz. 00000000-0000-0000-C000000000000046. This takes care of all numbers being unique. Using the number generator at another point in time or at another machine yields a different number. This number 00000077-0000-0000-C000-000000000048 could be the IID that belongs to all IManipulate interfaces. If we have ten stacks then we have 30 interfaces: ten of the first IID (00000000-0000-0000-C000-000000000046), and ten of the IID of IManipulate, and yet another 10 of that of IOverflow. But all 30 of them have another interface, and hence another interface pointer.

Next we put the asking/testing mechanism into operation. Let us presuppose constants for the interface identifiers, typically fixed by a #define IID_IUNKNOWN 00000000-0000- 0000-C000-000000000046, etc. Now assume that the factory has given us a pointer, pStack say, as in the following program fragment:

```
void* pStack;
pStack = ... // from the factory
```

Then we can test pStack by asking if indeed the IID of IUnknown is known.

```
void* pStack_;
HRESULT hr;
hr = pStack->QueryInterface(IID_IUNKNOWN, &pStack_);
```

If hr equals S_OK, or if it is one of the other S_ values, then we know that we have got an IUnknown interface pointer. Besides that, QueryInterface also provides a result, in this case in pStack_, and if all is right, this is again a pointer to the same interface as pStack. Although this was a nice test, it does not seem to advance us much. So next we shall use QueryInterface to obtain a pointer to another interface, IManipulate. This works the same as just before: call QueryInterface, but now giving it the IID (obtained once from the special number generator) of IManipulate

```
void* pIman;
HRESULT hr;
hr = pStack->QueryInterface(IID_IMANIPULATE, &pIman);
```

If hr equals S_OK, or one of the other S_ values, then we know that in pIman we have got an IManipulate interface pointer. We may assume that a stack has been created (or at least something else that implements IManipulate behaviour). Now we are ready to use this object.

```
hr = pIman->clear();
hr = pIman->push(i);
hr = pIman->pop(&retval);
```

This was quite involved, but the advantage is that, starting from a suspect pointer, which may or may not come from the appropriate "factory", we have verified that it belongs to an object with stack behaviour. And in this way we arrived at functions for which there is no more reason to doubt that they will meet our expectations.

Now let us have a look at the third interface of MyStack, the IOverflow. The idea is that it is employed for connecting "callbacks". We imagine that heavy usage of the push operation (much more push'es than pop's) could lead to an overflow of the stack. In fact, each stack has only a limited memory capacity (1000 items say) and if this is exceeded, the normal stack behaviour can no longer be guaranteed. It should be tried to prevent this, which is better than trying to restore a stack where the damage has already occurred. Therefore we assume that there is another component, for example called MyStackObserver, which has to be warned whenever the threat for overflow occurs (MyStackObserver is only a concrete example, in fact we are concerned with the general idea of a component which observes a stack). Of course it would be possible to have the calls of the observer's procedures "hard-coded" in MyStack. But assume that we refrain from doing so, and instead of that let us demand that objects with stack behaviour work for arbitrary observers, not just this specific MyStackObserver. So an arbitrary component must be able to subscribe to warnings concerning stack overflow. Therefore such an object (e.g. MyStackObserver) must tell the object with stack behaviour which procedure must be called if an overflow threat occurs and which procedure must be called if an overflow happened nevertheless. In this context we call these procedures of the observer "callback procedures". In general there may be several callbacks procedures; it is COM-style to group them into an interface. In our running example we choose for naming this interface IStackObserver; it has to be implemented by MyStackObserver.

In this example we want two call back procedures, onStackHalfFull() for when the stack is about half full and onStackOverflow() for handling a real overflow. We give the IDL description of this interface:

```
interface IObserver
{
    HRESULT onStackHalfFull();
    HRESULT onStackOverflow();
}
```

MyStackObserver has to "inform" the stack object of these two procedures, but it will not do so for each procedure separately. It does so in a single step, namely by sending its IStackObserver interface pointer to the object with stack behaviour. Now the problem of "informing" has been reduced to transferring an interface pointer. That is easy if we choose the IOverflow interface as follows:

```
interface IOverflow
{
    HRESULT subscribe(int p, IStackObserver* obs);
    HRESULT unsubscribe(IStackObserver* obs);
}
```

The parameter p of subscribe indicates at which percentage of the stack space the warning is generated. For example if p equals 50 then the warning will come when precisely half of the available stack space has been used up. Now the intention of all this is that two component instances will get connected as shown in Figure 2 below.

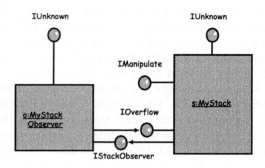

Fig. 2. MyStackObserver and MyStack coupled.

The arrow from MyStack to the lollipop of IStackObserver indicates that object s, being an instantiation of component MyStack can perform calls to procedures of the object IStackObserver. Whereas IOverflow is an *incoming interface* of the object with stack behaviour, we say that IStackObserver is an *outgoing interface* of it. Somewhere in the initialisation of MyStackObserver there is a call of subscribe(...) as we shall show in the corresponding program fragment given below. Let us assume that pStack is pointing to the IUnknown interface of an object with stack behaviour. Also assume that IID_IOVERFLOW is defined by means of a #define.

```
IUnknown * pStack;      // IUnknown pointer of e.g. MyStack      (given)
IStackObserver* pIobs;  // interface pointer of observator self  (given)
IOverflow* pIovr;       // interface pointer              (to be filled in)
HRESULT hr;

hr = pStack->QueryInterface(IID_IOVERFLOW, &pIovr);
if SUCCEEDED(hr) {
   hr = pIovr->subscribe(50, pIobs);
   if SUCCEEDED(hr) {
      // coupling made
   } else ...
} else ...
```

We assume that somewhere inside the object with stack behaviour this value 50 is stored, for example in a variable called warninglevel. We also assume that this object with stack behaviour can only deal with one subscriber, whose IStackObserver interface pointer is kept in the variable pIobs (internally in the object with stack behaviour). So the implementation of `subscribe`, possibly being a part of the implementation of `MyStack`, could look as follows:

```
int warninglevel;            //            (to be filled in)
IStackObserver* pIobs;       // subscriber (to be filled in)

HRESULT subscribe(int p, IStackObserver* obs)
{   warninglevel = p
    pIobs = obs;
    return S_OK;
}
```

Figure 3 below illustrates the entire structure of pointers built-up in this way. In this state we find that the system consisting of `MyStackObserver` and `MyStack` is sufficiently coupled in order that the operational behaviour of the component with stack behaviour can begin.

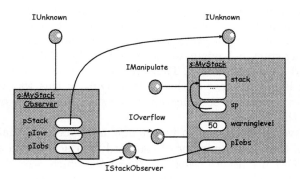

Fig. 3. Implementation of MyStackObserver and MyStack coupling.

It can be seen how the outgoing arrows of Figure 2 are nothing but abstractions of the implementation-level arrows (that is, pointers). Of course Figure 3 is not suited for specification purposes because it reveals too much implementation detail. It is an illustration of one of the possible ways the implementation could work; but variables such as `pStack`, `pIovr`, `pIobs`, `stack`, `sp`, `warninglevel` and (the other) `pIobs` are not visible from the ouside of the component.

Once the coupling has been established, the object with stack behaviour can perform calls of `onStackHalfFull()` and `onStackOverflow()`. Let us have a look at a possible implementation of `push(...)` inside `MyStack`. We repeat the declarations of `warninglevel` and `pIobs`.

```
#define MAX 1000

int warninglevel;      //                  (given)
IStackObserver* pIobs; // subscriber  (given)
```

```
int sp;                 // stack pointer
ITEM stack[MAX];        // contents of the stack
HRESULT hr;

HRESULT push(Item i)
{   if (sp >= MAX) {
        hr = pIobs->onStackOverflow();
        return E_FAIL;
    }
    else {
        if (sp >= warninglevel*(MAX / 100)) {
            hr = pIobs->onStackHalfFull();
        }
        stack[sp++] = i;
        return S_OK;
}   }
```

By now it should be clear that Figure 1 (stack behaviour with three interfaces) is somehow incomplete: the view of an object with stack behaviour is only complete if we include its outgoing interface as well. Whenever we want to fix a contract concerning stack behaviour we have to describe IUnknown, IManipulate, IOverflow and IStackObserver. Then we have an interface suite of stack behaviour which is independent of the context. Only in this way it may become possible to have a complete specification of the suite (and hence of a component that supports that suite).

Although everybody is free to invent new interfaces and make agreements on their usage, there are a number of standard interfaces which are themselves part of the COM framework. Next to IUnknown which was discussed above, the following four interfaces are frequently used; these belong together, providing a general mechanism for binding all kinds of subscribers to components that will perform callbacks: IConnectionPoint, IConnectionPointContainer, IEnumConnectionPoints and IEnumConnections. They resemble IOverflow, but are much more general. The basic idea is that for each outgoing interface (such as IStackObserver) there is an extra incoming interface that offers the possibility of subscribing to certain events (coupling them to callback functions). This extra incoming interface is called IConnectionPoint. It makes it possible to have more than one subscriber. Moreover, IConnectionPoint is standardised: there is no need to invent from scratch what the interface will look like. The interface can always be the same, quite independently of the precise nature of the outgoing interface itself.

8   Modelling COM Interface Manipulation in π-Calculus

In this section we present a formal model of MyStack which support the interfaces IUnknown, IManipulate and IOverflow. We also show parts of MyStackObserver which supports the interfaces IUnknown and IStackObserver. Finally we show a part of StackUser, which supports no interfaces but which does have a certain active behaviour. As before, we assume operators <>, <.> and ++ for lists of items. Moreover, if s is a list of items, we let $|s|$ be the length of the list. We assume 0,1,... and $+$ for natural numbers. We assume IID_IUNKNOWN, IID_IMANIPULATE, IID_IOVERFLOW and IID_ISTACKOBSERVER for interface identifiers. And we assume i_0 to be some value of type ITEM. We adopted a simplification, viz. to have only one reference counter keeping the total number of references to any of the interfaces of the object (this is done often although conceptually there is one counter per interface). The present model does not build further on the model of Sect. 6, we just start from scratch again. There is one COM feature which we have left out in order to simplify the presentation; this is the fact that all interfaces 'inherit' from IUnknown.

```
MyStack(pIunk,pIman,pIovr,pIobs,refs,stack,wl) =
  ( IUnknown(pIunk,pIman,pIovr,pIobs,refs,stack,wl)
  + IManipulate(pIunk,pIman,pIovr,pIobs,refs,stack,wl)
  + IOverflow(pIunk,pIman,pIovr,pIobs,refs,stack,wl)
  )
```

The state-based behaviour of the various components is modelled again by recursive process equations where the various parts of the state are parameters of the processes. The remarks of Sect. 6 apply here too.

```
IUnknown(pIunk,pIman,pIovr,pIobs,refs,stack,wl) =
( pIunk (f) .
  ( [f = QueryInterface] .
    pIunk (iid) .
    ( [iid = IID_IUNKNOWN]
      p̄Iunk S_OK .
      p̄Iunk pIunk .
      MyStack(pIunk,pIman,pIovr,pIobs,refs + 1,stack,wl)
    + [iid = IID_IMANIPULATE]
      p̄Iunk S_OK .
      p̄Iunk pIman .
      MyStack(pIunk,pIman,pIovr,pIobs,refs + 1,stack,wl)
    + [iid = IID_IOVERFLOW]
      p̄Iunk S_OK .
      p̄Iunk pIovr .
      MyStack(pIunk,pIman,pIovr,pIobs,refs + 1,stack,wl)
    + ["otherwise"]
      p̄Iunk E_NOINTERFACE .
      p̄Iunk NULL .
      MyStack(pIunk,pIman,pIovr,pIobs,refs,stack,wl)
    )
  + [f = AddRef] .
    p̄Iunk S_OK .
    MyStack(pIunk,pIman,pIovr,pIobs,refs + 1,stack,wl)
  + [f = Release] .
    ( [refs = 1]
      p̄Iunk S_OK .
      0
```

```
      + [refs > 1]
        pIunk S_OK .
        MyStack(pIunk,pIman,pIovr,pIobs,refs - 1,stack,wl)
) ) )


IManipulate(pIunk,pIman,pIovr,pIobs,refs,<>,wl) =
( pIman (f) .
    ( [f = clear] .
      pIman S_OK .
      MyStack(pIunk,pIman,pIovr,pIobs,refs,<>,wl)
    + [f = is_empty] .
      pIman S_OK .
      MyStack(pIunk,pIman,pIovr,pIobs,refs,<>,wl)
    + [f = push] .
      pIman (j) .
      pIman S_OK .
      MyStack(pIunk,pIman,pIovr,pIobs,refs,<j>,wl)
    + [f = pop] .
      pIman E_FAIL .
      MyStack(pIunk,pIman,pIovr,pIobs,refs,<>,wl)
) )


IManipulate(pIunk,pIman,pIovr,pIobs,refs,<i>++s,wl) =
( pIman (f) .
  ( [f = clear] .
    pIman S_OK .
    MyStack(pIunk,pIman,pIovr,pIobs,refs,<>,wl)
  + [f = is_empty] .
    pIman S_FALSE .
    MyStack(pIunk,pIman,pIovr,pIobs,refs,<i>++s,wl)
  + [f = push] .
    pIman (j) .
    ( [|<i>++s| ≥ MAX]
      pIobs onStackOverflow .
      pIobs (h) .
      pIman E_FAIL .
      MyStack(pIunk,pIman,pIovr,pIobs,refs,<i>++s,wl)
    + [|<i>++s| < MAX]
      ( [|<i>++s| ≥ wl*(MAX/100)]
        pIobs onStackHalfFull .
        pIobs (h) .
        pIman S_OK .
        MyStack(pIunk,pIman,pIovr,pIobs,refs,<j>++<i>++s,wl)
      + [|<i>++s| < wl*(MAX/100)]
        pIman S_OK .
        MyStack(pIunk,pIman,pIovr,pIobs,refs,<j>++<i>++s,wl)
      )
    )
  + [f = pop] .
    pIman S_OK .
```

```
     pIman i .
     MyStack(pIunk,pIman,pIovr,pIobs,refs,s,wl)
) )
```

For IOverflow we only show the subscribe procedure; because of space limitations we leave out our earlier unsubscribe (which poses no special problems).

```
IOverflow(pStack,pIman,pIovr,pIobs,refs,stack,wl) =
( pIovr (f) .
  [f = subscribe] .
  pIovr (w) .
  pIovr (b) .
  pIovr S_OK .
  MyStack(pStack,pIman,pIovr,b,refs,stack,w)
)
```

Next we present MyStackObserver, which is described by a few initialisation steps where the subscription takes place, followed by MyStackObserverCont (for continuation) which is described by recursion. Note that MyStackObserver supports two interfaces.

```
MyStackObserver(pIunk,pIobs,pStack,refs) =
  pStack QueryInterface .
  pStack IID_IOVERFLOW .
  pStack (h) .
  pStack (pIovr) .
  pIovr subscribe .
  pIovr 50 .
  pIovr pIobs .
  pIovr (h) .
  MyStackObserverCont(pIunk,pIobs,pStack,pIovr,refs,0,0)

MyStackObserverCont(pIunk,pIobs,pStack,pIovr,refs,x,y) =
  ( IUnknown'(pIunk,pIobs,pStack,pIovr,refs,x,y)
  + IStackObserver(pIunk,pIobs,pStack,pIovr,refs,x,y)
  )
```

Next we present IUnknown', which is the implementation of COM's IUnknown interface for the stack observer. Note that although it is said that each component has to implement COM's IUnknown, we see that the implementation of this IUnknown' is slightly different from the IUnknown given before, just because MyStackObserver has different interfaces than MyStack.

```
IUnknown'(pIunk,pIobs,pStack,pIovr,refs,x,y) =
( pIunk (f) .
  ( [f = QueryInterface] .
    pIunk (iid) .
    ( [iid = IID_IUNKNOWN]
      pIunk S_OK .
      pIunk pIunk .
      MyStackObserverCont(pIunk,pIobs,pStack,pIovr,refs + 1,x,y) =
```

```
    + [iid = IID_ISTACKOBSERVER]
      pIunk S_OK .
      pIunk pIobs .
      MyStackObserverCont(pIunk,pIobs,pStack,pIovr,refs + 1,x,y) =
    + ["otherwise"]
      pIunk E_FAIL .
      MyStackObserverCont(pIunk,pIobs,pStack,pIovr,refs,x,y) =
    )
  + [f = AddRef] .
    pIunk S_OK .
    MyStackObserverCont(pIunk,pIobs,pStack,pIovr,refs + 1,x,y) =
  + [f = Release] .
    ( [refs = 1]
      pIunk S_OK .
      0
    + [refs > 1]
      pIunk S_OK .
      MyStackObserverCont(pIunk,pIobs,pStack,pIovr,refs - 1,x,y) =
) ) )

IStackObserver(pIunk,pIobs,pStack,pIovr,refs,x,y) =
( pIobs (f) .
  ( [f = onStackHalfFull] .
    pIobs S_OK .
    IStackObserver(pIunk,pIobs,pStack,pIovr,refs,x + 1,y)
  + [f = onStackOverflow] .
    pIobs S_OK .
    IStackObserver(pIunk,pIobs,pStack,pIovr,refs,x,y + 1)
) )
```

Now we may compose a system out of various instances of these components. We show the obvious combination having one instance of each. So we assume three initial interface pointers to the three interfaces of MyStack. We also assume two interface pointers to the two interfaces of MyStackObserver. Finally we assume one interface pointer to the IUnknown interface of StackUser. Of course all these six interface pointers are different. Let these initial interface pointers be called PSTACK, PIMAN, PIOVR, PIUNK, PIOBS and PUSER, respectively. Upon initialisation, the MyStack instance only knows its own interfaces, whereas MyStackObserver and StackUser know, next to their own interfaces, also the IUnknown interface pointer of the instance of MyStack.

```
System = (  MyStack(PSTACK,PIMAN,PIOVR,NULL,1,<>,100)
         |  MyStackObserver(PIUNK,PIOBS,PSTACK,1)
         |  StackUser(PUSER,PSTACK)
         )
```

9   Calculations

In this section we show an example of a calculation. This shows one way of using the formal model. Let us consider only the first two parallel components of System, leaving out the stack user. Now we are ready to do some calculation work.

```
(  MyStack(PSTACK,PIMAN,PIOVR,NULL,1,<>,100)
|  MyStackObserver(PIUNK,PIOBS,PSTACK,1)
)
```

=

```
( ( PSTACK (f) .
    ( [f = QueryInterface]
      PSTACK (iid) .
      ( [iid = IID_IOVERFLOW]
        PSTACK S_OK .
        PSTACK PIOVR .
        MyStack(PSTACK,PIMAN,PIOVR,NULL,2,<>,100)
      + [''other iid values''] ...
      )
    + [''other f values''] . ...
    )
  + PIMAN (f) . ...
  + PIOVR (f) . ...
  )
| ( PSTACK QueryInterface .
    PSTACK IID_IOVERFLOW .
    PSTACK (h) .
    PSTACK (pIovr) .
    pIovr subscribe .
    pIovr 50 .
    pIovr PIOBS .
    pIovr (h) .
    MyStackObserverCont(PIUNK,PIOBS,PSTACK,pIovr,1,0,0)
) )
```

$\xrightarrow{\tau}$

```
( PSTACK (iid) .
  ( [iid = IID_IOVERFLOW]
    PSTACK S_OK .
    PSTACK PIOVR .
    MyStack(PSTACK,PIMAN,PIOVR,NULL,2,<>,100)
  + [''other iid values''] ...
  )
| ( PSTACK IID_IOVERFLOW .
    PSTACK (h) .
    PSTACK (pIovr) .
    pIovr subscribe .
    pIovr 50 .
    pIovr PIOBS .
    pIovr (h) .
    MyStackObserverCont(PIUNK,PIOBS,PSTACK,pIovr,1,0,0)
) )
```

$$\xrightarrow{\tau}$$
$$\xrightarrow{\tau}$$

```
( ( PSTACK PIOVR .
    MyStack(PSTACK,PIMAN,PIOVR,NULL,2,<>,100)
  )
| ( PSTACK (pIovr) .
    pIovr subscribe .
    pIovr 50 .
    pIovr PIOBS .
    pIovr (h) .
    MyStackObserverCont(PIUNK,PIOBS,PSTACK,pIovr,1,0,0)
) )
```

$$\xrightarrow{\tau}$$

```
( MyStack(PSTACK,PIMAN,PIOVR,NULL,2,<>,100)
| ( PIOVR subscribe .
    PIOVR 50 .
    PIOVR PIOBS .
    pIovr (h) .
    MyStackObserverCont(PIUNK,PIOBS,PSTACK,PIOVR,1,0,0)
) )
```

This can be interpreted as: the composition of `MyStack(PSTACK,PIMAN, PIOVR, NULL, 1,<>,100)` and `MyStackObserver(PIUNK,PIOBS,PSTACK,1)` can evolve to the situation of Fig. 4. The calculation result represents the state where the link indicated by the arrow from the `pIovr` variable of `o:MyStackObserver` to the `IOverflow` lollipop of `s:MyStack` has been established. This means that we have the situation of Figure 4.

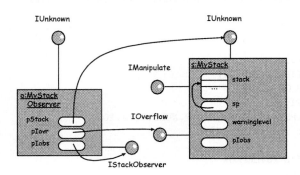

Fig. 4. MyStackObserver and MyStack partially coupled.

The link from the `pIobs` variable in `s:MyStack` to the lollipop of `IStackObserver` has not been established yet (that is why the `MyStack` term still has one `NULL` argument), but of course this is what will happen next if we would continue our calculation. The arrow from pStack, and pIobs of o:MyStackObserver were assumed to be available from the very beginning; these are PSTACK and PIOBS. continuing the calculation, the situation of Figure 3 will be reached in a finite number of steps. It will be reached necessarily because there are no alternative receive constructs that match the names sent.

So the above calculation shows one way of exploiting the model. In general, the exploitation can be done in various ways analogous to the exploitation of classical communication protocol models in CCS and other process algebraic formalism such as ACP, μCRL, PSF, LOTOS:

- equational reasoning to show behavioural congruence of specifications and implementations (there is a theory of bisimulation for the π-calculus),
- simulation to demonstrate, visualise or test the operational behaviour of a given model in a given context (as demonstrated above).

10   Concluding Remarks

The modelling of COM mechanisms turned out easy and natural (interface pointer manipulations and π-calculcus have good semantic match). The case study was about modelling a component with stack-manipulation behaviour, the obligatory QueryInterface behaviour, and an 'observer' which is more or less similar to the well-known observer pattern [13].

Related work: Kramer and Magee defined the ADL called Darwin [14]. It is a combination of a Module Interconnection Language (MIL) and a behavioural specification language. A key ingredients of the MIL part of Darwin is the 'bind' construct: $r -- p$ means that a required service r is bound to a provided service p. It gets its semantics via π-calculus as follows: to the semantic models of r and p a special agent is added (as a component in a parallel composition); the task of the agent is to send the name of p to r. See [15]. A special elaboration algorithm guarantees that all the bindings specified in Darwin lead to the desired exchange of names. A difference with our work is that we use no intermediate ADL with built-in solutions for the exchange of names.

Sullivan et al. [16] model aspects of COM using Z. Components are modelled as consisting of a finite set of interfaces, a corresponding set of IIDs, and an iunknown interface (which is an element of this former finite set). Every interface supports the QueryInterface operation, which is modelled as a partial function QI that maps the interface and a given IID to another type. They show how formal specification techniques help in explaining and analysing the complexities of COM. Neither COM interfaces nor COM function calls are mapped directly to Z schemas (indirections are modelled as functions, e.g. QI).

Other interesting references include [17] (OO notation $\pi o \beta \lambda$ based on π-calculus), [18] (a research program for component frameworks, including a discussion on use of π-calculus for open systems components) and [19] (components are interactive systems communicating asynchronously through channels).

There are several issues not addressed but worth further investigation: adding features to π-calculus, concurrency aspects (see the notes on molecular actions and private names in [9]), and re-entrant procedures. The present paper is an exercise in trying to understand component-technology. We do not yet advocate the direct usage of π-calculus. Most of the semantic aspects of interfaces can be described well by languages in the tradition of VDM [20], Z [21] and COLD [22], but there may be a need for special syntactic sugar and special methodogical and tool-based support.

References

[1] Milner, R.: Communication and concurrency, Prentice Hall (1989)
[2] Bergstra, J.A., Klop, J.W.: Process algebra for synchronous communication. Information and Computation, **60**(1/3):109-137 (1984)
[3] Bolognesi, T., Brinksma, E.: Introduction to the ISO specification language LOTOS, Computer Networks and ISDN Systems, **14**, (1987) 25–59
[4] Mauw, S., Veltink, G.J. (Eds.): Algebraic specification of communication protocols, Cambridge Tracts in Theoretical Comp. Sc. **36**, CUP (1993)
[5] CCITT. Specification and Description Language (SDL), Rec. Z.100
[6] CCITT. Message Sequence Chart (MSC), Rec. Z.120, Study Group X (1996)
[7] Szyperski, C.: Component Software, Beyond Object-oriented Programming, Addisson Wesley, ISBN 0-201-17888-5
[8] Orfali, R., Harkey, D., Edwards, J.: The essential distributed objects survival guide, John Wiley & Sons, Inc. (1996)
[9] Milner, R., Parrow, J., Walker, D.: A Calculus of Mobile Processes Pt.1 Information and Computation **100**(1) (1992) 1–40
[10] Microsoft Corporation. The Component Object Model Specification, Version 0.9, Microsoft (1995)
[11] Brockschmidt, K.: How OLE and COM solve the problems of component software design, Microsoft Systems Journal, (1996) 63–80
[12] Williams, T.: Reusable Components for Evolving Systems, IEEE 1998 Software Reuse Conference (pp. 12–16)
[13] Gamma, E.,, Helm, R., Johnson, R., Vlissides, J.: Design patterns: elements of reusable object-oriented software, Addison-Wesley (1994)
[14] Magee, J., Kramer, J.: Dynamic Structure in Software Architectures, in: Proc. 4th ACM SIGSOFT Symp. on the Foundations of Software Engineering
[15] Eisenbach, S., Paterson, R.: pi-Calculus semantics for the concurrent configuration language Darwin, Hawaii Int. Conf. on System Sciences (1993)
[16] Sullivan, K.J., Socha, J., Marchukov, M.: Using formal methods to reason about architectural standards, International conference on software engineering ICSE '97, (1997) 503–512
[17] Jones, C.B.: A π-calculus semantics for an object-based design notation, in: E. Best (Ed.), Proceedings of CONCUR'93, Springer-Verlag LNCS 715, (1993) 158–172
[18] Nierstrasz, O.: Infrastructure forsoftware component frameworks, Internet http://www.iam.unibe.ch/~scg/Archive/NFS/iscf.html (1996)
[19] Broy, M.: Towards a mathematical concept of a component and its use, Software – concepts and tools **18**, (1997) 137–148
[20] Jones, C.B.: Systematic software development using VDM, Prentice Hall (1986)

[21] Spivey, J.M.: Understanding Z: a specification language and its formal semantics, Volume 3 of Cambridge Tracts in Theoretical Computer Science. Cambridge University Press (1988)

[22] Feijs, L.M.G., Jonkers, H.B.M., Middelburg, C.A.: Notations for Software Design, FACIT Series, Springer-Verlag (1994)

Validation of Mixed SIGNAL-ALPHA Real-Time Systems through Affine Calculus on Clock Synchronisation Constraints

Irina M. Smarandache[1], Thierry Gautier[2], and Paul Le Guernic[2]

[1] The University of Reading, Department of Computer Science
Whiteknights, PO Box 225, Reading RG6 6AY, United Kingdom
Tel.: (44) 118 931 8611 (7626), Fax: (44) 118 975 1994
I.M.Smarandache@reading.ac.uk
[2] IRISA-INRIA, Campus de Beaulieu, 35042 Rennes Cedex, France
Thierry.Gautier@irisa.fr, Paul.LeGuernic@irisa.fr

Abstract. In this paper we present the affine clock calculus as an extension of the formal verification techniques provided by the SIGNAL language. A SIGNAL program describes a system of clock synchronisation constraints the consistency of which is verified by compilation (clock calculus). Well-adapted in control-based system design, the clock calculus has to be extended in order to enable the validation of SIGNAL-ALPHA applications which usually contain important numerical calculations. The new affine clock calculus is based on the properties of affine relations induced between clocks by the refinement of SIGNAL-ALPHA specifications in a codesign context. Affine relations enable the derivation of a new set of synchronisability rules which represent conditions against which synchronisation constraints on clocks can be assessed. Properties of affine relations and synchronisability rules are derived in the semantical model of traces of SIGNAL. A prototype implementing a subset of the synchronisability rules has been integrated in the SIGNAL compiler and used for the validation of a video image coding application specified using SIGNAL and ALPHA.

1 Introduction

Real-time systems, and more generally reactive systems [4], are in continuous interaction with their environment. Therefore, they must respond *in time* to external stimuli. Moreover, real-time systems must be safe, thus one would wish to prove their correctness. Time constraints and safety are two important aspects to be considered in the design of a real-time application.

Real-time systems may be constrained by very tight real-time deadlines. Moreover, a hardware implementation of parts of these systems is sometimes required, to meet specific constraints for instance. An example is an application consisting of numerical calculations performed iteratively on large structures of regular multidimensional data. In this case, a hardware/software implementation may be envisaged, in which the numerical calculations are conveyed to hardware

J. Wing, J. Woodcock, J. Davies (Eds.): FM'99, Vol. II, LNCS 1709, pp. 1364–1383, 1999.

for efficiency reasons, while the control relating these parts is implemented in software.

In general, designing a mixed hardware/software real-time system requires a rigorous methodology that comprises methods and tools addressing, among others, system specification and validation, optimal code generation and hardware synthesis. These aspects are dealt with in *codesign* [7] [9] which denotes the specification, validation and implementation of an application which consists both of a hardware part, in the form of a set of specialised integrated circuits, and a software part implemented on general programmable processors. The idea is to explore various possible implementations of hardware/software systems in order to improve their performance and to ensure the respect of cost constraints.

1.1   Real-Time System Codesign

System codesign is a complex process which can be decomposed into three main activities [7]: 1. The *cospecification* of an application at various levels of abstraction; 2. The validation of a specification by formal verification or simulation, also known as *cosimulation*; 3. The hardware/software partitioning of an application, the evaluation of a partitioning from the point of view of the time constraints and cost, the generation of executable code, the synthesis of hardware, and the production of the interface between hardware and software, i.e *cosynthesis*. A lot of work has been done, the purpose of which was to define a well-structured methodology for codesign [7] [11] [19]. An important point was generally the description of both hardware and software using the same language, like for instance VHDL enhanced with mechanisms for calling C functions [14], or high-level languages like C, C++ or FORTRAN extended with facilities for the description of hardware systems [10]. These approaches enable the programming of both the hardware and software parts of a system in a unique framework and their validation by simulation. However, they cannot guarantee system correctness. This aspect can be much improved by using formal languages for system specification, refinement of specifications towards lower levels of abstraction (implementation) and validation of the various specifications by formal verification.

Defining a complete methodology of codesign requires addressing other relevant problems, most of them concerning cosynthesis. Among these problems there are the automatic partitioning into hardware and software, the synthesis of hardware and the generation of optimal code for software implementation.

The work presented in this paper is part of a more general effort for building a hybrid framework in which the SIGNAL [12] [13] and ALPHA [20] languages can be used for real-time system codesign.

1.2   Cospecification and Cosimulation of SIGNAL-ALPHA Systems

SIGNAL is a *synchronous* [4] language developed for the specification, validation and implementation of real-time systems. SIGNAL variables represent finite or infinite sequences of values (data) which can be filtered or merged before being submitted to classical boolean or mathematical operations. A *clock* is implicitly associated with each SIGNAL variable: it represents a set of temporal indices which denote the logical instants where the variable is present and has a value. The semantics of a SIGNAL program can be described by a system of constraints (relations) on clocks and values, which is constructed and verified for consistency during compilation. The verification of the clock constraints is called *clock calculus*. The SIGNAL environment is enhanced with tools for C [5] and VHDL [3] code generation and formal verification of dynamic properties [2].

In its present form, SIGNAL is well-adapted for the design of control-based real-time systems. Firstly, this is due to its limitations concerning the treatment of computations on multidimensional data such as matrices. Only simple algorithms can be expressed in SIGNAL and no significant optimisation is performed at the level of the generation of executable C or VHDL code concerning vectors. In contrast with SIGNAL, the ALPHA language has been developed primarily for the specification and implementation of algorithms on multidimensional data. Such algorithms can be described in ALPHA using affine recurrence equations over convex polyhedral domains [20] and be further transformed for optimal hardware or software implementation on parallel or sequential architectures [21].

Given their complementary properties, the SIGNAL and ALPHA languages can be used jointly for the design of real-time systems containing important numerical calculations on multidimensional data and control: numerical computations are expressed in ALPHA and the control is conveyed to SIGNAL. When the real-time requirements of the system are very tight, a mixed hardware/software implementation may be envisaged. In [9] we propose a hybrid framework for the combined use of SIGNAL and ALPHA in real-time system codesign. In order for this framework to be operational, it is necessary to interface SIGNAL and ALPHA programs both at the functional and architectural level. The former corresponds to a high-level mathematical representation of an algorithm in ALPHA, while the latter contains a set of new temporal indices corresponding to the execution of the algorithm on a parallel or sequential architecture.

In SIGNAL-ALPHA systems, the refinement of an ALPHA program from a functional level to an architectural level oriented toward a particular implementation also induces a refinement of the temporal indices in SIGNAL. The new time indices are obtained through *affine transformations* on the instants of time of the initial SIGNAL specification. Consider clocks c and c_1 in SIGNAL which are identical at the functional level (they are also denoted as *synchronous*). After refinement, their relative position is such that clock c_1 can be obtained by an *affine transformation* applied to clock c: the instants of time of c and c_1, denoted respectively T and T_1, can be described by a pair of *affine functions* $T = \{nt + \varphi_1 \mid t \in \mathcal{T}\}$, $T_1 = \{dt + \varphi_2 \mid t \in \mathcal{T}\}$, on the same set of instants $\mathcal{T}$. With $\varphi = \varphi_2 - \varphi_1$, we will say that clock c_1 is obtained by an (n, φ, d)-affine transformation applied to clock c, where $n, d \in \mathbb{N}^*$ the set of strictly positive integers and $\varphi \in \mathbb{Z}$ the set of integers. Clocks c and c_1 are also said to be in an (n, φ, d)-*affine relation*.

Clocks obtained by affine transformation may be re-synchronised at the architectural level. As an example, consider clocks c, c_1 and c_2 which are identical in the SIGNAL functional specification. At the architectural level, clocks c_1 and c_2 have been transformed such that c, c_1 and c, c_2 are respectively in affine relations of parameters (n_1, φ_1, d_1) and (n_2, φ_2, d_2). Whether clocks c_1 and c_2 can be re-synchronised depends on the properties of the affine relations which are induced from the values of (n_1, φ_1, d_1) and (n_2, φ_2, d_2). Moreover, the relations between c, c_1 and respectively, c, c_2 may be expressions on (n, φ, d)-affine relations constructed using operations like composition, union, etc. In this case, the re-synchronisation of clocks c_1 and c_2 depends on the properties of these operations.

The SIGNAL clock calculus performs the verification of clock synchronisation constraints using a set of *synchronisability rules*, i.e. conditions against which these constraints can be assessed. The current clock calculus depends on boolean equation resolution methods [5] [1] which have been successfully used for the validation of numerous control-based real-time applications. However, in order to validate mixed SIGNAL-ALPHA systems as presented above, it is necessary to extend the current clock calculus with a set of synchronisability rules deduced from the properties of (n, φ, d)-affine relations. The new set of rules defines the *affine clock calculus*, which constitutes the main topic of this paper. We explore the space of (n, φ, d)-affine relations and study to which extent it is closed under the main operations that can be performed on affine relations. Following this study, we define a set of synchronisability rules which, although incomplete, enables the validation of the principles underlying the cospecification and cosimulation using SIGNAL and ALPHA. The semantical model of traces of SIGNAL [12] [16] constitutes the support for the study of the properties of affine relations and for the definition of the new synchronisability rules.

1.3 Organisation of the Paper

In Section 2 we present the integration of SIGNAL and ALPHA for system codesign. Section 3 is the central core of this paper and is dedicated to the definition and implementation of the affine clock calculus. The main concepts useful for this purpose are progressively introduced: these are the model of traces of the SIGNAL language, the properties of affine relations on clocks, the set of synchronisability rules induced by the latter, and finally the necessary elements for the integration of the affine clock calculus in the compiler. The affine clock calculus has been applied to the cospecification and cosimulation of a video image coding application; this is briefly illustrated in Section 4. In the same section we discuss in which way the SIGNAL and ALPHA environments may further contribute to the development of a complete codesign methodology based on both languages. Finally, in Section 5 we present conclusions and perspectives of our work.

2   SIGNAL and ALPHA in Real-Time System Codesign

Figure 1 summarizes the main elements of the environments around SIGNAL and ALPHA that make both languages well-adapted for real-time system codesign.

SIGNAL and ALPHA programs represent mathematical notations for the properties of the processes they define. The system of constraints on clocks and values associated with a SIGNAL program is transformed by compilation into a *synchronised data flow graph* (SDFG). This data structure constitutes the support for executable code generation (C or VHDL) or verification of dynamic properties using the formal tool SIGALI [2].

The ALPHA compiler includes a powerful type checking mechanism based on the structure of an ALPHA variable as a function over convex polyhedra. The syntax tree obtained after compilation can be directly translated into C code for functional simulation, or it can be transformed into a subset of ALPHA called AL-PHA0 which exhibits the details of a parallel or sequential implementation. The syntax tree in ALPHA0 form can be further translated in C or VHDL executable code or directly mapped on a netlist [21].

The interface between SIGNAL and ALPHA is based on the fact that both languages can be translated in C and executed for functional simulation. Furthermore, SIGNAL offers the possibility to call *external processes*: such a process can be the specification of an algorithm in a language other than SIGNAL. A particular type of an external process is a *function*, the execution of which is considered instantaneous from the point of view of SIGNAL. A SIGNAL function can be a predefined or a user-defined C function.

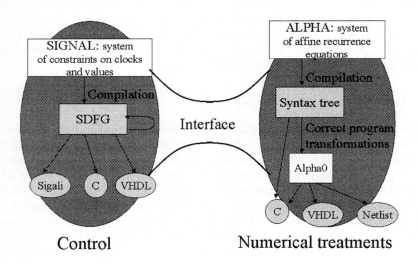

Fig. 1. SIGNAL and ALPHA in system codesign.

2.1 Functional Cospecification and Cosimulation

Being a synchronous language, SIGNAL is based on the following hypotheses [4]:
1. All actions (communications and calculations) in a system have zero *logical*

duration (the elapsed time is represented by the precedence of successive values on a same data flow); 2. Two or more actions can take place at the same logical instant, such actions being termed "simultaneous". From the point of view of the logical temporal properties of a system, only succession and simultaneity of instants are of interest. Although their exact time values are not considered, note however that they will be considered for a given implementation. The process associated with a SIGNAL program represents thus a succession of logical instants, with each instant being associated one or more actions considered of zero logical duration and involving process variables present at that instant.

Consider for example a coding system for sequences of video images at 34 Mbits/s [8]. A system of this type consists of a set of numerical treatments applied iteratively on images of the same dimension. Images are divided into luminance and chrominance blocks and treatments are applied to each block. Numerical treatments consist mainly of algorithms for inter and intra image coding which require operations like a discrete cosine transformation (DCT). In order to illustrate the interfacing between SIGNAL and ALPHA, we have isolated from the coding application a simple SIGNAL program and have illustrated the associated process in Fig. 2. It consists of a DCT operation applied in sequence to different values A_i of the matrix of pixels A present at each logical instant of time t_i. The matrix A corresponds to a block of luminance or chrominance of an image. The DCT can be expressed in SIGNAL as $B := Dct(A)$, where DCT is actually an external process. The DCT is a time consuming algorithm, particularly for large matrices or when applied to images containing a large number of blocks. In order to improve the overall performance of the coding application, one would wish to execute each instance $B_i := Dct(A_i)$ on a parallel integrated architecture as derived by the ALPHA environment.

The DCT can be easily described in ALPHA. The SIGNAL-ALPHA cospecification and cosimulation of the new system is made possible at the *functional* level as follows (see Fig. 2): 1. The ALPHA *system* is translated in executable C code; 2. The C function $ALPHA\_C$ obtained at step 1 represents the external process implementing the DCT in SIGNAL. The function $ALPHA\_C$ is considered instantaneous in SIGNAL; the clocks of the matrices A and B, denoted respectively by c and c_1, are therefore synchronous. The overall system is thus represented as a SIGNAL specification executing instantaneously the functional description of the ALPHA specification. The system can be validated in the SIGNAL environment by formal verification (compilation, model checking with SIGALI) and/or simulation.

2.2 Implementation-Oriented Cospecification and Cosimulation

A mixed SIGNAL-ALPHA specification at the functional level may be refined in order to take into consideration the details of a particular implementation. The ALPHA program of Section 2.1 describing a DCT may be submitted to a sequence of transformations for a parallel or sequential implementation. These transformations guarantee the equivalence of the final specification, noted $ALPHA'$ in Fig. 3, with the initial $ALPHA$ system of Fig. 2. The system $ALPHA'$ contains

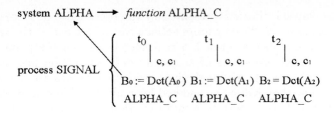

Fig. 2. SIGNAL-ALPHA interface at functional level.

the time indices corresponding to a particular scheduling of the DCT operation. In Fig. 3 these time indices are represented as the diagonal sets of *micro*-instants μt_i^j associated with each *macro*-instant t_i.

The SIGNAL specification has to be refined accordingly in order to enable the validation of the overall system. Therefore, the micro-instants of time of *ALPHA'* are taken into consideration in the new process *SIGNAL'* and described as the sets of instants μSt_0^i, μSt_1^i, etc. (see Fig. 3). The C function *ALPHA'_C* has been derived from *ALPHA'* and transformed in order to describe the sequence of operations performed at each micro-instant of time.

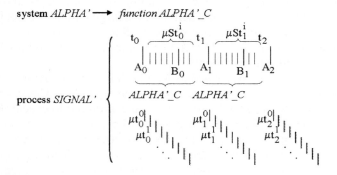

Fig. 3. SIGNAL-ALPHA interface at architectural level.

The regularity of ALPHA values manifests itself in SIGNAL in several ways. First, the sets of micro-instants μSt_0^i, μSt_1^i, etc. have the same cardinality. Also, successive values for B are provided at specific micro-instants between any two successive macro-instants t_i and t_{i+1} in a regular manner. This situation is illustrated in Fig. 4 where the clocks of matrices A and B, denoted respectively by c and c_1, are defined by the following instants of time: $c = \{0, 9, 18, ...\}$ and $c_1 = \{6, 15, ...\}$ (after providing the values B_i at the instants of time defined by c_1, the architecture implementing the operation $B_i := Dct(A_i)$ may execute further computations like initialisations for the next operation $B_{i+1} := Dct(A_{i+1})$).

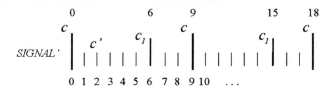

Fig. 4. Illustration of an affine relation.

In Fig. 4, clock c' is defined by the set of instants $\{0, 1, 2, 3, 4, 5, ...\}$. It can be noticed that clocks c and c_1 are placed in a regular manner on the support clock c': their relative position is such that c_1 has been obtained through an $(9, 6, 9)$-affine transformation applied to c. By definition, clock c_1 is the result of an (n, φ, d)-affine transformation applied to clock c if it can be obtained from c through steps 1 and 2 as follows: 1. Constructing a new clock c' as the union of c with the set of instants obtained by introducing $n - 1$ *fictive* instants between any two successive instants of c (and $-\varphi$ fictive instants before the first instant of c when φ is negative). 2. Defining the clock c_1 as the set of instants $\{dt + \varphi \mid t \in c'\}$, with $c' = \{t \mid t \in \mathbb{N}\}$ (in other words, counting every d instant, starting with the φth instant of c', or with the first instant of c' when φ is negative). Clocks c and c_1 are then said to be in an (n, φ, d)-affine relation. The above definition can be expressed in an equivalent form as follows: clocks c and c_1 are in (n, φ, d)-affine relation if there exists a clock c' such that c and c_1 can be respectively expressed using the *affine functions* $\lambda t.(nt + \varphi_1)$ and $\lambda t.(dt + \varphi_2)$, with $\varphi_2 - \varphi_1 = \varphi$, with respect to the time indices of c': $c' = \{t \mid t \in \mathbb{N}\}$, $c = \{nt + \varphi_1 \mid t \in c'\}$, $c_1 = \{dt + \varphi_2 \mid t \in c'\}$.

Properties on affine relations can be exploited in order to verify that clocks are *synchronisable*, that is, their sets of instants can be identified (re-synchronised). Consider (Fig. 2) a SIGNAL program which executes two successive DCT operations at each macro-instant t_i, one on a luminance block of an image, noted $B := Dct(A)$, and the second one on the next block of red chrominance of the same image, described by $D := Dct(C)$.

Each DCT function is expressed in ALPHA at the functional level and further refined according to a particular implementation. The SIGNAL specification is refined accordingly and we obtain the timing diagrams of Fig. 5: the clocks of A and C are synchronous and equal to c, the clocks of B and D are respectively c_1 and c_2, and the clocks c' and c'' describe the instants of the excution of the DCT functions on a potential architecture derived in the ALPHA environment.

In the functional SIGNAL-ALPHA specification, clocks c, c_1 and c_2 were synchronous (see Section 2.1 for details). After refinement of the time indices in the SIGNAL-ALPHA specification, the clocks c_1 and c_2 should be re-synchronised in order to preserve the temporal properties of the whole application. Whether the re-synchronisation of c_1 and c_2 is possible given their relative position as illustrated in Fig. 5, or after further adjustments of their time indices, can be decided based on the properties of the affine relations existing between c, c_1

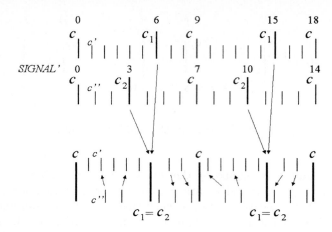

Fig. 5. Synchronisable clocks in the context of codesign with SIGNAL and AL-PHA.

and c, c_2 respectively. Clocks c, c_1 and c, c_2 are respectively in $(9, 6, 9)$ and $(7, 3, 7)$-affine relation in the process *SIGNAL'*. The relation existing between the triplets $(9, 6, 9)$ and $(7, 3, 7)$ guarantees the equivalence of the corresponding affine relations. This will be detailed in Section 3. Informally, the equivalence of the above affine relations expresses the fact that the *relative positions* of clocks c and c_1, respectively c and c_2, are identical. Based on this observation, clocks c_1 and c_2 can be identified without contradicting the temporal behaviour of the other clocks in the SIGNAL program. The instants of time of clocks c' and c'' situated between two successive instants of c and c_1 (or c_2) are independent and can be positioned with respect to each other in various manners; in Fig. 5 we have illustrated one possibility. Therefore, c_1 and c_2 can be re-synchronised; we say that c_1 and c_2 are *synchronisable*.

The aim of the affine clock calculus discussed in Section 3 is to define necessary and sufficient conditions for clock synchronisability based on the properties of affine relations on clocks. These conditions are expressed as a set of *synchronisability rules* and are derived in the *semantical model of traces* of SIGNAL. Section 3 begins with an introdution to these concepts.

3   Affine Calculus on Clocks in SIGNAL

Figure 6 introduces the reader to the semantics of traces [12] [16] of SIGNAL. The most important concepts in SIGNAL are: 1. the *signal*, which denotes a variable of the language and represents a finite or infinite sequence of values; 2. the *clock*, a variable associated with each signal which represents the set of logical instants where the values of the signal are present. SIGNAL operators manipulate signals by imposing implicit or explicit constraints on their values and clocks. Constraints on clocks are usually expressed as identities between clock expressions constructed using the operators of intersection ($\wedge$), union ($\vee$) or difference ($\backslash$). Clocks can be also subsets of other clocks defined as samplings by boolean conditions. When no condition is explicitly or implicitly stated on a pair of clocks, they are independent.

process SIGNAL

P

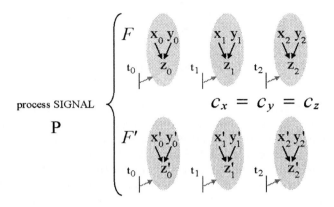

Fig. 6. Illustration of SIGNAL semantics of traces.

A SIGNAL program describes a real-time system, which is in continuous inter-action with its environment. Input values are transformed corresponding to the actions of a given specification and the results are provided to the environment. This situation is illustrated in Fig. 6 in the case of a program manipulating in-puts x and y and providing output z depending on the values of x and y. In case z is the addition of x and y, signals x, y and z are implicitly constrained by the $+$ operator in SIGNAL to have the same clocks $c_x = c_y = c_z$.

The configurations F and F' illustrated in Fig. 6 correspond to two different executions of the SIGNAL program, involving sequences x_i, y_i and z_i and respec-tively x'_i, y'_i and z'_i. The set of all possible configurations, called *traces*, which can be exhibited during the execution of a SIGNAL program, defines completely the *process* P associated with the program. Consider A a subset of the set B of signals manipulated by a program. A trace may contain instants with no action involving signals from A. However, each instant of this type contains actions which involve other signals from the set $B\backslash A$. Given a subset A of signals, a *flow* on A is a trace with at least one action involving signals from A for each logical instant. In the particular case of Fig. 6, if we consider the subset of signals to be $\{x, y, z\}$, the traces illustrated are actually flows.

More generally, the process P associated with a SIGNAL program is a set of flows on the variables of the program. Each flow F in P is constrained by a system of equations on the clocks and values of signals manipulated by P. Equations on values can be further expressed in the abstract form of a data dependency graph (an example of a data dependency graph is illustrated in Fig. 6 for the $+$ operator). Besides the clock calculus, the compiler verifies data consistency by checking the absence of cycles in the data dependency graph. In the next section however, we will concentrate mainly on the clock calculus.

3.1   Clock Calculus & Synchronisability

The clock calculus is equivalent to the resolution of a system of clock equations. For example:

$$
\begin{aligned}
c &= c_1 \\
c' &= (c_1 \wedge c_2) \vee c_1 \\
c &= c'
\end{aligned}
\tag{1}
$$

can be a system derived from a SIGNAL program which manipulates clocks c, c', c_1 and c_2. In this simple system, c_1 and $(c_1 \wedge c_2) \vee c_1$ have clearly to be proved equivalent, which is an immediate consequence of the axioms of the *boolean lattice*. The space of clocks associated with a SIGNAL program is a boolean lattice [6] the properties of which are extensively used for the proof of equivalences. The resolution of the system is performed by *triangularisation* of the system [5] [1].

Given a boolean signal Cd, its clock, denoted $\hat{C}d$, can be partitioned into the clock $[Cd]$ where the signal Cd is present and true and the clock $[\neg Cd]$ where Cd is present and false (the clocks $[Cd]$ and $[\neg Cd]$ represent *samplings by boolean conditions*). The relations between clocks $\hat{C}d$, $[Cd]$ and $[\neg Cd]$ are expressed by the *partition equations* below:

$$
\begin{aligned}
{}[Cd] \vee [\neg Cd] &= \hat{C}d \\
[Cd] \wedge [\neg Cd] &= \emptyset
\end{aligned}
\tag{2}
$$

The axioms of the boolean lattice together with the partition equations induce on the space of clocks a lattice of an order $\preceq$ "coarser" than the order $\leq$ of the boolean lattice [5]. Clocks can be boolean formulas constructed either with samplings by boolean conditions $[Cd]$, $[\neg Cd]$ or with free variables of the boolean lattice. The properties of the lattice of order $\preceq$ are actually used during the triangularisation of any system of clock equations.

The axioms of the lattice $\preceq$ represent a system of *synchronisability rules* in the sense described below. Clocks c and c' are *synchronisable* in the process P, which is denoted by $c \overset{P}{\odot} c'$, if there *exists* a flow F in P in which c and c' are *synchronous*:

$$
c \overset{P}{\odot} c' \Leftrightarrow \exists F \in P, c \overset{F}{=} c'
\tag{3}
$$

(we note $c \overset{F}{=} c'$ the fact that c and c' are synchronous in F).

Whenever the property expressed by equation 3 is valid *for each flow F in P*, the clocks c and c' are said to be *synchronous* in P, which is denoted by $c \overset{P}{=} c'$. This definition can be expressed as follows:

$$
c \overset{P}{=} c' \Leftrightarrow \forall F \in P, c \overset{F}{=} c'
\tag{4}
$$

Unless explicitly constrained through the SIGNAL program, clocks c and c' are completely independent in the associated P process. Therefore, their relative position can be such that in some flows F in P they are identical, while in some other flows F' in P their instants interleave in an arbitrary manner: obviously, if c and c' are independent in P, they are synchronisable. When the relative position of clocks c and c' is implicitly or explicitly constrained by the SIGNAL operators, flows F in P are subsequently constrained and the synchronisability of c and c' depends on these constraints.

In order to better understand the use of the synchronisability rules, consider for example a process P derived from a SIGNAL program Prg in which clocks c and c' are defined by the first two equations of the system (1):

$$c = c_1$$
$$c' = (c_1 \wedge c_2) \vee c_1 \tag{5}$$

Program Prg may be transformed into Prg' in which an additional constraint has been expressed on clocks c and c': $c = c'$ (in the SIGNAL-ALPHA context, Prg could be part of a transformed SIGNAL-ALPHA specification, as seen above, and Prg' the same specification, in which clocks are resynchronised). Consider the process P' corresponding to the program Prg'. The system of clock equations associated with Prg' is (1). Given the set of flows $\mathcal{F}' \subseteq P$ such that $c \overset{F}{=} c'$, $\forall F \in \mathcal{F}'$, it results $P' = \mathcal{F}'$. Therefore, verifying the consistency of (1), which is equivalent to testing that clocks c and c' are equivalent in P', is further equivalent to testing the synchronisability of c and c' in P. The rule $(c_1 \wedge c_2) \vee c_1 = c_1$ from the boolean lattice is indeed a *synchronism rule*: $(c_1 \wedge c_2) \vee c_1 \overset{P}{=} c_1$ for every process P. The same axiom holds for the process P associated with Prg. And thus $(c_1 \wedge c_2) \vee c_1 \overset{P}{\odot} c_1$, since synchronism implies synchronisability. Therefore in the example, $\mathcal{F}'$ is not empty and it can be concluded that P' is consistent from the point of view of the constraints expressed on its clocks.

The rules of the lattice $\preceq$ represent synchronisability rules: each identity $f_1 = f_2$, with f_1, f_2 boolean formulas on clocks, is equivalent to $f_1 \overset{P}{=} f_2$ which implies $f_1 \overset{P}{\odot} f_2$ for every process P. These rules can be further extended using the properties of the affine relations between clocks. Figure 5 illustrates this idea: if P is the process associated with the program *SIGNAL'*, the configuration in which clocks c_1 and c_2 coincide represent a flow $F \in P$ such that $c_1 \overset{F}{=} c_2$. Thus, c_1 and c_2 are synchronisable in P. The reason here is that the $(9, 6, 9)$ and $(7, 3, 7)$-affine relations existing respectively between c, c_1 and c, c_2 are equivalent. In the next section, we define the affine relation associated with a flow and a process and further explicitate the concept of equivalence of affine relations.

3.2   Affine Relations in SIGNAL

Given $n, d \in \mathbb{N}^*$ and $\varphi \in \mathbb{Z}$ fixed, clocks c and c_1 are in (n, φ, d)-affine relation in the flow F—which is denoted $c \, \mathcal{R}^F_{(n,\varphi,d)} \, c_1$ or $(c, c_1) \in \mathcal{R}^F_{(n,\varphi,d)}$—if the relative position of c and c_1 in F can be induced by an (n, φ, d)-affine transformation as defined in Section 2.2.

Clocks c and c_1 are in (n, φ, d)-affine relation in process P, denoted $c \, \mathcal{R}^P_{(n,\varphi,d)} \, c_1$ or $(c, c_1) \in \mathcal{R}^P_{(n,\varphi,d)}$, if they are in (n, φ, d)-affine relation in each flow F of P, i.e. $c \, \mathcal{R}^F_{(n,\varphi,d)} \, c_1, \forall F \in P$. Flows and processes are defined over the set of variables they manipulate. For a given set A, a flow F on A is a member of the set of flows $\mathcal{F}_A$ that can be constructed with the variables of A. In a similar manner, a process P on A belongs to the set of processes on A, i.e. $P \in \mathcal{P}_A$. Because of the finite nature of the sets of variables associated with flows and processes, affine relations can be defined as finite sets as follows:

$$\forall F \in \mathcal{F}_A, \mathcal{R}^F_{(n,\varphi,d)} = \{(c, c_1) \in A \times A \mid c \, \mathcal{R}^F_{(n,\varphi,d)} \, c_1\} \tag{6}$$

$$\forall P \in \mathcal{F}_A, \mathcal{R}^P_{(n,\varphi,d)} = \{(c, c_1) \in A \times A \mid c \, \mathcal{R}^P_{(n,\varphi,d)} \, c_1\} \tag{7}$$

Consider the process $P \in \mathcal{P}_{\{c,c_1,c_2\}}$ defined as follows:

$$P = \{F \in \mathcal{F}_{\{c,c_1,c_2\}} \mid c \, \mathcal{R}^F_{(n_1,\varphi_1,d_1)} \, c_1, c \, \mathcal{R}^F_{(n_2,\varphi_2,d_2)} \, c_2\} \tag{8}$$

(induced by a SIGNAL program that manipulates only the clocks c, c_1 and c_2).

From the definition of an affine relation associated with a process it results $c \, \mathcal{R}^P_{(n_1,\varphi_1,d_1)} \, c_1$ and $c \, \mathcal{R}^P_{(n_2,\varphi_2,d_2)} \, c_2$. Clocks c_1 and c_2 are synchronisable in P if there exists $F \in P$ satisfying $c_1 \overset{F}{=} c_2$. Consider $F_s \in P$ satisfying $c_1 \overset{F_s}{=} c_2$. Obviously $c \, \mathcal{R}^{F_s}_{(n_1,\varphi_1,d_1)} \, c_1$ and $c \, \mathcal{R}^{F_s}_{(n_2,\varphi_2,d_2)} \, c_2$. Being identical in F_s, clocks c_1 and c_2 can be replaced with each other and therefore $c \, \mathcal{R}^{F_s}_{(n_1,\varphi_1,d_1)} \, c_1$ implies $c \, \mathcal{R}^{F_s}_{(n_1,\varphi_1,d_1)} \, c_2$ and $c \, \mathcal{R}^{F_s}_{(n_2,\varphi_2,d_2)} \, c_2$ implies $c \, \mathcal{R}^{F_s}_{(n_2,\varphi_2,d_2)} \, c_1$. It results therefore that $\mathcal{R}^{F_s}_{(n_1,\varphi_1,d_1)} = \mathcal{R}^{F_s}_{(n_2,\varphi_2,d_2)} = \{(c, c_1), (c, c_2)\}$. In conclusion, a necessary condition for clocks c_1 and c_2 to be synchronisable in P is that $\mathcal{R}^{F_s}_{(n_1,\varphi_1,d_1)}$ and $\mathcal{R}^{F_s}_{(n_2,\varphi_2,d_2)}$ be *equivalent*. In the case of the process P defined by (8), it can be proved that this condition is also sufficient.

The equivalence of affine relations depends on the closure properties of the space of affine relations with respect to the main operations that can be applied to it. These are either union, intersection or difference induced by the homonym operations on clocks, or general operations on relations like inverse and composition [15]. In the next section we propose a study of these properties in the semantical model of traces of SIGNAL.

3.3   Properties on Affine Relations & Synchronisability Rules

The Semantics of Traces. Consider a finite set of signals A. The set of all possible flows defined on A is denoted $\mathcal{F}_A$. Subsets of flows from $\mathcal{F}_A$ can be grouped in processes which are members of the set $\mathcal{P}_A$ of all processes that can be defined on A. A SIGNAL program on A defines a process $P \in \mathcal{P}_A$; each flow

$F \in P$ satisfies some constraints imposed by the SIGNAL operators on the clocks and values of the signals from A.

SIGNAL disposes of four basic operators (kernel) which are sufficient for the construction of any program regardless of its complexity. Kernel operators are combined through composition and restriction in order to build programs. The composition and restriction of programs induce naturally the corresponding operations on processes and flows. Intuitively, the restriction of a flow F to a set of variables $A' \subseteq A$ is the flow $\Pi_{A'}(F)$ which contains only those instants of F with actions involving signals from A'.

Concerning processes, the main operations are defined as follows. Given a set of variables $A' \subseteq A$, the restriction of $P \in \mathcal{P}_A$ to A' (the projection of P on A') contains the flows $F \in P$ manipulating exclusively variables of A':

$$\Pi_{A'}(P) = \{F' \in \mathcal{F}_{A'} \mid F' = \Pi_{A'}(F), \forall F \in P\} \qquad (9)$$

The composition of processes $P_1 \in \mathcal{P}_{A_1}$ and $P_2 \in \mathcal{P}_{A_2}$, with A_1, A_2 arbitrary sets of variables, is defined by:

$$P_1 \mid P_2 = \{F \in \mathcal{F}_{A_1 \cup A_2} \mid \Pi_{A_1}(F) \in P_1, \Pi_{A_2}(F) \in P_2\} \qquad (10)$$

The following lemma describes the necessary and sufficient conditions— stated as $\Pi_{A_2}(P) \subseteq Q$—for a property valid in the process Q to be also also in P:

Lemma 1. $\forall P \in \mathcal{P}_{A_1}$, $\forall Q \in \mathcal{P}_{A_2}$, $A_2 \subseteq A_1$,

$$\Pi_{A_2}(P) \subseteq Q \Leftrightarrow P \mid Q = P \qquad (11)$$

In other words, given the hypothesis described by the left hand side of (11), Q expresses a property valid also in P.

Properties on Affine Relations. Operations specific to relations in general, like inverse $()^{-1}$ and composition $*$, can be applied to affine relations [15]. As an example, consider a process $P \in \mathcal{P}_{\{c,c_1,c_2,c_3\}}$ with clocks c, c_1, c_2 and c_3 satisfying $c \, \mathcal{R}^P_{(n_1,\varphi_1,d_1)} \, c_1$, $c_1 \, \mathcal{R}^P_{(n_2,\varphi_2,d_2)} \, c_2$ and $c \, \mathcal{R}^P_{(n_3,\varphi_3,d_3)} \, c_3$. Obviously, it results that $c \, \mathcal{R}^P_{(n_1,\varphi_1,d_1)} \, * \, \mathcal{R}^P_{(n_2,\varphi_2,d_2)} \, c_2$ and the synchronisability of c_2 and c_3 depends on properties of the composition. When the space of affine relations is closed under composition, the test of the synchronisability of c_2 and c_3 reduces itself to the verification of the equivalence of affine relations.

Affine relations can be further combined through union $\cup_r$, intersection $\cap_r$ and difference $\backslash_r$ induced by the homonym operations on clocks $(\vee, \wedge, \backslash)$. A similar argument as before conducts to the necessity of studying closure properties of these operators with respect to the space of affine relations.

Here is a brief presentation of the main steps and results obtained in the study of affine relations.

Equivalence of Affine Relations. An equivalence relation, noted $\sim$, can be defined between triplets (n, φ, d) as follows: $(n, \varphi, d) \sim (n', \varphi', d')$ iff either $nd' = n'd$ and $n\varphi' = n'\varphi$, for $G \mid \varphi$ (i.e., G is a divisor of φ) and $G' \mid \varphi'$, or $nd' = n'd$ and $\left[\frac{dt+\varphi}{n}\right] = \left[\frac{d't+\varphi'}{n'}\right], \forall t \in \mathbb{N}, dt+\varphi \geq 0$, for $G \nmid \varphi$ and $G' \nmid \varphi'$, with $G = gcd(n, d)$ the greatest common divisor of n and d, $G' = gcd(n', d')$ and $[x]$ the integer part of $x \in \mathbb{N}$. The equivalence of affine relations depends exclusively on the values of the associated triplets (n, φ, d) [17]:

Proposition 1.

$$\mathcal{R}^F_{(n,\varphi,d)} = \mathcal{R}^F_{(n',\varphi',d')}, \ \forall \ F \in \mathcal{F}_A \Leftrightarrow (n, \varphi, d) \sim (n', \varphi', d') \qquad (12)$$

Canonical Form. In order to reduce the complexity of the test of the equivalence $\sim$, we have then defined a canonical form $(n_{CF}, \varphi_{CF}, d_{CF})$ for a triplet (n, φ, d) [18] as follows:

Proposition 2.

$$\begin{array}{ll} a) & G \mid \varphi \Rightarrow (n_{CF}, \varphi_{CF}, d_{CF}) = (\frac{n}{G}, \frac{\varphi}{G}, \frac{d}{G}) \\ b) & G \nmid \varphi \Rightarrow (n_{CF}, \varphi_{CF}, d_{CF}) = (2\frac{n}{G}, (2\left[\frac{\varphi}{G}\right] + 1), 2\frac{d}{G}) \end{array} \qquad (13)$$

Consequently, the canonical form of $\mathcal{R}^F_{(n,\varphi,d)}$ is $\mathcal{R}^F_{(n_{CF},\varphi_{CF},d_{CF})}$ and the verification of the identity of two affine relations is thus reduced to the verification that two triplets of integers are identical:

Proposition 3.

$$\mathcal{R}^F_{(n,\varphi,d)} = \mathcal{R}^F_{(n',\varphi',d')} \Leftrightarrow (n_{CF}, \varphi_{CF}, d_{CF}) = (n'_{CF}, \varphi'_{CF}, d'_{CF}) \qquad (14)$$

Operations on affine relations. If any expression on affine relations could be rewritten as an affine relation, the verification of clock synchronisability would consist only in a test of equivalence on affine relations as above. But it has been observed that this was not the case in general. The closure property is true for the inverse of an affine relation. Also, the affine relation $\mathcal{R}^F_{(1,0,1)}$ is neutral with respect to composition. However, the closure property is lost when dealing with composition. The composition of two general affine relations $\mathcal{R}^F_{(n,\varphi,d)}$ and $\mathcal{R}^F_{(n',\varphi',d')}$ does not generally produce an affine relation. Nevertheless, it has been possible to identify in the space of the affine relations $\mathcal{R}^F_{(n,\varphi,d)}$ a subspace consisting of relations of the form $\mathcal{R}^F_{(1,\varphi,d)}$, with $\varphi \geq 0$, in which the closure property is true. Following this observation, we have distinguished two cases, as detailed in the sequel.

Properties of affine relations $\mathcal{R}^F_{(1,\varphi,d)}$, with $\varphi \geq 0$. It has been demonstrated [16] that the space of affine relations $\mathcal{R}^F_{(1,\varphi,d)}$, although closed under composition $*$ and intersection $\cap_r$, is not closed under union $\cup_r$ and difference $\backslash_r$. It is therefore necessary to define necessary and sufficient conditions for the equivalence of arbitrary expressions constructed with affine relations of the form $\mathcal{R}_{(1,\varphi,d)}^F$ using composition, union, intersection and difference. Given the complexity of the space of expressions on affine relations $\mathcal{R}_{(1,\varphi,d)}^F$ and the necessity of efficient algorithms for testing their equivalence, the question of the existence of a canonical form appears. Our attempt to provide a canonical form using exclusively the $\cup_r$ operator—based on the observation that any expression in this space can be rewritten as a union of affine relations $\mathcal{R}_{(1,\varphi,d)}^F$—has failed because of the infinite number of possibilities in which a relation $\mathcal{R}_{(1,\varphi,d)}^F$ can be rewritten as a union of affine relations of the same type. However, in [16] we propose a *relative normal form* which reduces partially the complexity of the equivalence calculus.

Properties of general affine relations $\mathcal{R}_{(n,\varphi,d)}^F$. Deciding that two arbitrary expressions on general affine relations are equivalent is a difficult problem. An initial step may be to isolate subsets of triplets (n, φ, d) and (n', φ', d') which respect the condition that the result of the operation $\mathcal{R}_{(n,\varphi,d)}^F$ op_r $\mathcal{R}_{(n',\varphi',d')}^F$, with $op_r \in \{*, \cup_r, \cap_r, \backslash_r\}$, is an affine relation. In [16] we propose a subset of such triplets $\{(n, \varphi, d), (n', \varphi', d')\}$, for which the above property is true, for the composition. Computing this subset $\{(n, \varphi, d), (n', \varphi', d')\}$ is an NP-complete problem. Future work may consider the applicability of heuristic search methods for this computation. Another open problem is the study of the properties of the union $\cup_r$, intersection $\cap_r$ and difference $\backslash_r$ of general affine relations.

Synchronisability Rules. The main results concerning the particular affine relations $\mathcal{R}_{(1,\varphi,d)}^F$, with $\varphi \geq 0$, and the general ones $\mathcal{R}_{(n,\varphi,d)}^F$ have respectively permitted the induction of a set of synchronism rules and a set of synchronisability rules. These rules actually represent a set of conditions which are necessary and sufficient for the synchronism and respectively the synchronisability of two clocks.

An example of synchronism rule is given below. Consider the process $P \in \mathcal{P}_{\{c,c_1,c_2,c_3\}}$ defined by:

$$P = \{F \in \mathcal{F}_{\{c,c_1,c_2,c_3\}} \mid c\ \mathcal{R}_{(1,\varphi_1,d_1)}^F\ c_1, c_1\ \mathcal{R}_{(1,\varphi_2,d_2)}^F\ c_2, c\ \mathcal{R}_{(1,\varphi_3,d_3)}^F\ c_3\} \quad (15)$$

Obviously $c\ \mathcal{R}_{(1,\varphi_1,d_1)}^P\ c_1,\ c_1\ \mathcal{R}_{(1,\varphi_2,d_2)}^P\ c_2$ and $c\ \mathcal{R}_{(1,\varphi_3,d_3)}^P\ c_3$. The calculus on affine relations $\mathcal{R}_{(1,\varphi,d)}^F$ induces $\mathcal{R}_{(1,\varphi_1,d_1)}^F * \mathcal{R}_{(1,\varphi_2,d_2)}^F = \mathcal{R}_{(1,\varphi_1+d_1\varphi_2,d_1d_2)}^F$ which is valid also for processes: $\mathcal{R}_{(1,\varphi_1,d_1)}^P * \mathcal{R}_{(1,\varphi_2,d_2)}^P = \mathcal{R}_{(1,\varphi_1+d_1\varphi_2,d_1d_2)}^P$. Therefore $c\ \mathcal{R}_{(1,\varphi_1+d_1\varphi_2,d_1d_2)}^P\ c_2$, and c_2 and c_3 are synchronisable if and only if $\mathcal{R}_{(1,\varphi_1+d_1\varphi_2,d_1d_2)}^P = \mathcal{R}_{(1,\varphi_3,d_3)}^P$. With Propositions 2 and 3, $\mathcal{R}_{(1,\varphi_1+d_1\varphi_2,d_1d_2)}^P$ and $\mathcal{R}_{(1,\varphi_3,d_3)}^P$ are equivalent if and only if $(1, \varphi_1 + d_1\varphi_2, d_1d_2)$ and $(1, \varphi_3, d_3)$ are identical, that is, $\varphi_1 + d_1\varphi_2 = \varphi_3$ and $d_1d_2 = d_3$. This result is expressed in the following synchronism rule:

Proposition 4. $\forall P \in \mathcal{P}_{\{c,c_1,c_2,c_3\}}$ *with* $c,\ c_1,\ c_2$ *and* c_3 *satisfying* $c\ \mathcal{R}_{(1,\varphi_1,d_1)}^P\ c_1, c_1\ \mathcal{R}_{(1,\varphi_2,d_2)}^P\ c_2$ *and* $c\ \mathcal{R}_{(1,\varphi_3,d_3)}^P\ c_3$, *the following equivalences are verified:*

$$c_2 \overset{P}{\odot} c_3 \Leftrightarrow \left\{ \begin{array}{l} \varphi_1 + d_1\varphi_2 = \varphi_3 \\ d_1 d_2 = d_3 \end{array} \right\} \Leftrightarrow c_2 \overset{P}{=} c_3 \tag{16}$$

In Fig. 7 the particular case $\varphi_1 = 6$, $d_1 = 2$, $\varphi_2 = 1$, $d_2 = 2$, and $\varphi_3 = 8$, $d_3 = 4$ is illustrated. It can be observed that clock c_1 is an *affine sampling* of phase φ_1 and period d_1 on clock c. Clock c_2 is defined similarly by an affine sampling of parameters φ_2 and d_2 on c_1. The same clock c_2 can be obtained by an affine sampling of φ_3 and d_3 on c; the clock c_3 constructed in this manner is synchronous, and therefore synchronisable, with c_2.

Following a sequence of steps similar as for Proposition 4, we have derived a system of synchronism rules which is minimal; it enables the verification of the synchronisability of two arbitrary clocks related by an expression on affine relations $\mathcal{R}^F_{(1,\varphi,d)}$, with $\varphi \geq 0$. The results concerning the equivalence of general affine relations $\mathcal{R}^F_{(n,\varphi,d)}$, summarized by Propositions 1, 2 and 3, and the partial result on composition of general affine relations, have allowed the derivation of a set of synchronisability rules which are sufficient for the validation of SIGNAL programs for which the single operation performed on affine relations is composition. Further work should be dedicated to the study of the union $\cup_r$, intersection $\cap_r$ and difference $\backslash_r$ of general affine relations.

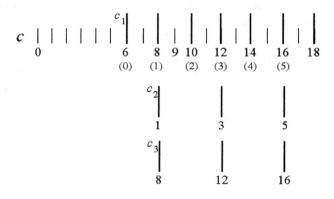

Fig. 7. Illustration of Proposition 4.

3.4   Implementation of the Affine Clock Calculus

A prototype implementing the synchronisability rules introduced in Section 3.3 has been integrated with the existing clock calculus and used for the validation of the SIGNAL-ALPHA interface on the video image coding application introduced in Section 2. In Section 3.1 we have explained that the existing (boolean) clock calculus relies on the properties of the lattice $\preceq$ existing on the space of clocks, and that it is equivalent to a system of synchronisability rules. The implementation of the affine clock calculus is briefly described now. By choosing an appropriate implementation of a general affine relation $\mathcal{R}^P_{(n,\varphi,d)}$ as detailed in [16], the considered clock expressions contain formulas constructed only with *affine clocks*, that is, affine samplings of specified phase and period on a given basis clock. Thus, the order $\preceq_{aff}$ defined by

$$\preceq_{aff} = \{(c_1, c_2) | \exists \varphi_i \geq 0, d_i > 1, \mathcal{R}^P_t = \mathcal{EXP}(\ldots, \mathcal{R}^P_{(1,\varphi_i,d_i)}, \ldots), c_1 \mathcal{R}^P_t c_2\} \quad (17)$$

with $\mathcal{EXP}$ a general expression on affine relations, induces on the space of *affine clocks* a lattice structure. The system of equations on affine clocks associated with a SIGNAL program is solved by triangularisation. When the equivalence of two clock expressions has to be demonstrated, synchronisability rules such that deduced in Section 3.3 are applied. Finally, for the integration of the affine and boolean clock calculus, each synchronisability rule which has been deduced in a process $Q \in \mathcal{P}_{A_2}$, is used in a larger context $P \in \mathcal{P}_{A_1}$, with $A_2 \subseteq A_1$, satisfying $\Pi_{A_2}(P) \subseteq Q$. Following Lemma 1, the synchronisability rule is also valid in P.

4   Application

The affine clock calculus has been used for the validation of the video image coding application described in Section 2. This application contains an important control part, which has been programmed in SIGNAL, and operations like the DCT, which have been expressed in ALPHA. The application has been specified and simulated at both functional and architectural levels as described in Section 2. In the coding system described in [8], each image is decomposed into a fixed number of macro-blocks, each macro-block consisting of one block of luminance and two blocks of chrominance (red and blue). At the architectural level, we have refined the ALPHA specifications of the DCTs corresponding to the blocks of luminance and red chrominance of a macro-block. These temporal refinements have been expressed in SIGNAL by means of two general affine relations between clocks c, c_1 and c, c_2 as illustrated in Fig. 5. The synchronisability of c_1 and c_2 has been verified by compilation and the entire SIGNAL-ALPHA system has been simulated in C.

Most of the operations involved in image coding applications are critical from the point of view of execution time or resources. Therefore, a codesign approach can be considered. The affine clock calculus represents an important element in defining a complete codesign methodology based on the SIGNAL and ALPHA languages. Besides the cospecification and cosimulation of an application, using SIGNAL and ALPHA in a codesign framework is interesting since it offers solutions to other codesign problems such as the automatic synthesis of specialised circuits for regular algorithms, or the generation of optimal code for the software implementation of both calculations and control. Concerning the latter, one might consider the hardware/software partitioning of an application corresponding to the partitioning into SIGNAL and ALPHA subsystems. Therefore, ALPHA processes would be implemented in hardware by automatic synthesis, while SIGNAL processes would be translated into C code for general purpose architectures. However, the proposed partitioning is not unique and automatic hardware/software partitioning remains an open problem, as it is the implementation of the hardware/software interface.

5   Conclusion

The joint use of the SIGNAL and ALPHA languages in hardware/software codesign has introduced the problem of the validation of mixed SIGNAL-ALPHA specifications both at the functional and architectural levels. The refinement of SIGNAL-ALPHA specifications towards the architectural level and their subsequent validation necessitates the extension of the formal clock calculus implemented in the SIGNAL compiler. This paper presents the new affine clock calculus based on the properties of affine relations induced between clocks by the refinement of SIGNAL-ALPHA specifications. The properties of affine relations are studied in the semantical model of traces of the SIGNAL language, but can be extended to any general model with similar characteristics. Based on this study, a new set of synchronisability rules is defined and integrated with the set already implemented by the existing formal clock calculus.

The affine clock calculus is relevant for the definition and implementation of a codesign methodology using the SIGNAL and ALPHA languages. Techniques for real-time system validation (formal verification, simulation) available in the SIGNAL and ALPHA environments can be used for cospecification and cosimulation. Both environments also have tools for automatic generation of optimal implementations which can be used in a complementary manner for hardware synthesis and/or implementation on general architectures. Further work should be devoted to the complete integration of the SIGNAL and ALPHA languages thus making possible the use of the most adapted formalism and environment for a given application.

References

[1] Amagbegnon T., Besnard L., Le Guernic P.: *Arborescent Canonical Form of Boolean Expressions.* INRIA Research Report 2290, IRISA/INRIA - Rennes, France, 1994
[2] Amagbegnon T., Le Guernic P., Marchand H., Rutten E.: *The SIGNAL dataflow methodology applied to a production cell.* IRISA Research Report 917, IRISA/INRIA - Rennes, France, 1995
[3] Belhadj M.: "Using VHDL for Link to Synthesis Tools". *Proceedings of the North Atlantic Test Workshop*, June 1994, Nmes, France
[4] Benveniste A., Berry G.: "Real-Time systems design and programming", *Proceedings of the IEEE*, September 1991, **79**, (9)
[5] Besnard L.: *Compilation de SIGNAL : horloges, dpendances, environnement*, PhD Thesis, University of Rennes 1, France, September 1992
[6] Birkhoff G.: *Lattice Theory*, AMS colloquium publications, 1973
[7] De Micheli G.: "Computer-Aided Hardware-Software Codesign", *IEEE Micro*, August 1994, **14**, (4)

[8] ETSI (European Telecommunication Standards Institute) *Specification of Component TV codecs 32-45 Mbit/s.* December 1990

[9] Gautier T., Le Guernic P., Quinton P., Rajopadhye S., Risset T., Smarandache I.: "Projet CAIRN: conception d'architectures partir de SIGNAL et ALPHA" *CODESIGN Conception conjointe logiciel-matriel*, Eyrolles, Collection Technique et Scientifique des Tlcommunications, 1998

[10] Gupta R.K., Coelho C.N., De Micheli G.: "Program Implementation Schemes for Hardware-Software Systems" *Computer*, January 1994, pp. 48-55

[11] Kalavade A., Lee E.A.: "A Hardware-Software Codesign Methodology for DSP Applications" *IEEE Design & Test of Computers*, September 1993, **10**, (3), pp. 16-28

[12] Le Guernic P., Gautier T.: "Data-Flow to von Neumann: the SIGNAL Approach", *Advanced Topics in Data-Flow Computing*, (Gaudiot J.-L. and Bic L., 1991), pp. 413-438

[13] Le Guernic P., Gautier T., Le Borgne M., Le Maire C.: "Programming Real-time Applications with SIGNAL", *Proceedings of the IEEE*, September 1991, **79**, (9), pp. 1321-1336

[14] Salinas M.H., Johnson B.W., Aylor J.H.: "Implementation-Independent Model of an Instruction Set Architecture in VHDL" *IEEE Design & Test of Computers*, September 1993, **10**, (3), pp. 42-54

[15] Sanderson J.G.: *A Relational Theory of Computing*, Springer Verlag 1980, **80**, Goss G. and Hartmanis J.

[16] Smarandache I.: *Transformations affines d'horloges : application au codesign de systèmes temps-réel en utilisant les langages SIGNAL et ALPHA*, PhD Thesis, University of Rennes 1, France, October 1998

[17] Smarandache I., Le Guernic P.: "Affine Transformations in SIGNAL and Their Applications in the Specification and Validation of Real-Time Systems" *Transformation-Based Reactive Systems Development*, Proceedings of the 4th International AMAST Workshop on Real-Time Systems and Concurrent and Distributed Software, Palma, Spain, LNCS **1231**, Springer Verlag, 1997

[18] Smarandache I., Le Guernic P.: *A Canonical Form for Affine Relations in SIGNAL.* INRIA Research Report 3097, IRISA/INRIA - Rennes, France, 1997

[19] Thomas D.E., Adams J.K., Schmit H.: "A Model and Methodology for Hardware-Software Codesign" *IEEE Design & Test of Computers*, September 1993, **10**, (3), pp. 6-15

[20] Wilde D.: *The ALPHA Language.* IRISA Research Report 827, IRISA/INRIA - Rennes, France, 1994

[21] Wilde D., Sié O.: *Regular array synthesis using ALPHA.* IRISA Research Report 829, IRISA/INRIA - Rennes, France, 1994

Combining Theorem Proving and Continuous Models in Synchronous Design

Simin Nadjm-Tehrani[1] and Ove Åkerlund[2]

[1] Dept. of Computer and Information Science, Linköping University
S-581 83 Linköping, Sweden
simin@ida.liu.se
[2] Saab AB, S-581 88 Linköping, Sweden
ove.akerlund@saab.se

Abstract. Support for system specification in terms of modelling and simulation environments has become a common practice in safety-critical applications. Also, a current trend is the automatic code-generation, and integration with formal methods tools in terms of translators from a high level design – often using common intermediate languages.

What is missing from current formal methods tools is a well-founded integration of models for different parts of a system, being software/hardware or control-intensive/data-intensive. By hardware we mean here the full range of domains in engineering systems including mechanics, hydraulics, electronics. Thus, there is a methodological gap for proving system properties from semantically well-defined descriptions of the parts.

We report on the progress achieved with the European SYRF project with regard to verification of integrated analog/discrete systems. The project pursues the development of new theories, application to case studies, and tool development in parallel. We use a ventilation control system, a case study provided by Saab Aerospace, to illustrate the work in progress on how hardware and software models used by engineers can be derived, composed and analysed for satisfaction of safety and timeliness properties.

Keywords: control system, synchronous languages, theorem proving, hybrid system, proof methodology

1 Introduction

Many applications of formal methods in system development are in the requirements specification phase – often formalising a subset of requirements corresponding to functional behaviour of the system [9, 6]. In embedded systems, these requirements commonly refer to the component which is under design – typically the controller for some physical devices (realised either as software or electronics). However, there is a class of properties arising as a result of interaction between the controller and the controlled environment, the verification of which requires an explicit model of the environment. This paper addresses

J. Wing, J. Woodcock, J. Davies (Eds.): FM'99, Vol. II, LNCS 1709, pp. 1384–1399, 1999.
© Springer-Verlag Berlin Heidelberg 1999

verification methodologies for such types of requirements in the context of synchronous languages.

A growingly popular approach to controller design or programming uses the family of synchronous languages (Lustre, Esterel, Signal and statecharts) [7, 8]. One reason for choosing such languages is the support provided in the development environments: the controller can be analysed to eliminate causal inconsistencies, and to detect nondeterminism in the reactive software. The clock calculii in Lustre and Signal, as well as constructive semantics in Esterel can be seen as verification support provided directly by the compiler (comparable to several properties verified by model checking in [5]). Most of the works reported within this community, however, apply verification techniques to check the controller *on its own.*

Modelling the controlled environment is common in control engineering. However, the analysis tools within this field primarily provide support for continuous system simulation, and are less adequate for proving properties of programs with discrete mode changes and (or) complex non-linear dynamics in the plant.

Within the Esprit project SYRF (on SYnchronous Reactive Formalisms), we present an approach whereby modelling tools used for analysis of analog systems can be used to substantiate the properties of the environment when formally verifying a closed loop system. We use the continuous model of the environment in two different settings. In the first approach, compositional verification is performed across different modelling platforms [14]. A required property is split into a number of conjuncts (proof obligations). Some of these are discharged by proofs in the discrete platform, using the controller properties. Others are verified in the environment model by simulation and extreme case analysis. Certain properties are refined in several steps before they are reduced to dischargable components.

In the second approach we model (aspects of) the continuous subsystem in the same (discrete) proof environment as the controller. Here, the restrictions in the physical model provide a sufficient condition: The proof of the property in the closed loop model holds provided that the restrictions leading to the discretised model holds.

A case study provided by Saab Aerospace is used to illustrate the alternative approaches, the properties for which they are appropriate, and some verification results obtained. However, some comparative studies are still in progress, and will be conclusively presented in the final report of the project.

2   The Air Control Case Study

The case study consists of a climatic chamber. A control system regulates and monitors the flow and the temperature of air which is circulating in the chamber. Originally, it was developed as a demo system which demonstrates the kind of problems appearing in developing realistic subsystems such as the ventilation system in the JAS 39 Gripen aircraft. It was presented to the project partners in terms of a 4 page textual specification and an implemented code for a controller in hierarchical block diagrams with state machines at the lowest level.

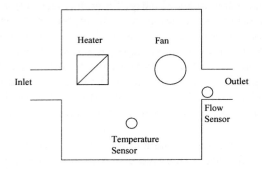

Fig. 1. The hardware components of the air control system.

The chamber is to be ventilated through the inlet and outlet and has a given volume. It has two sensors for measuring the internal air temperature and the air flow. Figure 1 presents the component model of the chamber, while Figure 2 shows the interface between the system and the operator. The external interface primarily consists of an on-off button, two analog knobs for setting the values for required temperature and flow (reference values), as well as warning signals in terms of a light and a sound. It also includes lights for showing some of its internal modes of operation.

User input		System output			
ON/OFF ☐		Mode	Wait	Work	Block
⊚	Reference Temperature		Actual Temperature		
⊚	Reference Flow		Actual Flow		
		Warnings	Light	Sound	

Fig. 2. The external interface to the system.

The controller has three modes while it is on. It has an initialising "wait" mode in which the heater and the fan are used to bring the chamber temperature and flow within a given scope. It also has two active modes in which more accurate regulation is achieved. One is the "solution" mode in which the actual temperature and flow values are brought to levels close to the reference values. The other, the "work" mode in which the actual values are maintained in the required region (within Δ of the reference values). The final mode, denoted as the "block" mode, is devoted to abnormal situations and it is intended as a shut-down mode. It is brought about when the earlier sound and light warnings have not led to changes in the reference values by the operator, or when the actual values fall outside the allowed scope despite manual intervention (for example due to unforeseen changes in unmodelled inputs, e.g. the incoming air temperature).

2.1   Requirements Specifications

The textual description mentioned above has a prescriptive nature. It describes how a controller should be implemented, giving some details about what should happen in each mode. To focus the formal verification work we had to deduce the overall goals of the control system: those requirements which are to be enforced by the suggested design.

The result of this study has been identification of the following global requirements.

- Keeping the reference values constant,
  - the work light will be lit within a time bound from the start of the system, and
  - the system will be stable in the work mode.
- Chamber temperature never exceeds a given (hazardous) limit.
- Whenever the reference values are (re)set, the system will (re)stablise within a time bound or warnings are issued.

Note that these are not properties of the controller on its own. Note also that our formulations are intended to fit in a framework where different proof techniques are applied where they suit best. Although "being stable in the work mode" can be seen as a safety property (the conditions for leaving the mode will not be true), it is most expedient to use control theory methods for proving this property. This is due to the fact that not *all* inputs to the system are kept constant (see the result of the physical modelling step). Hence, it is formulated as a stability property.

Another aspect to point out is on the second (safety) property. Here we look beyond the functional demand on the system to monitor and warn when the temperature falls outside given intervals. We rather attempt to see what is the goal of devising such intervals and mode changes and envisage as a (mode-independent) goal of the system that the air is never heated to a hazardous level (even in the block mode and *after* warnings are issued).

3   Model of the Controller

The controller has been modelled in several synchronous languages both in the data flow style (Lustre), and the control flow style (Esterel, statecharts). It represents the typical case where it is most naturally described in a combination of these paradigms. Thus, mode automata [12] and the synchronie workbench [1] use this as a demonstrator system. Also, a multi-formalism representation of the example used for distributed code generation can be found in [3].

Having models which reflect the nature of the computations naturally, surely avoids some development errors. Moreover, once the models are analysed with respect to the required properties they can be automatically translated to intermediate and lower layer programming languages. For example from mode-automata to Lustre, to DC, and to C (see work package 2 in the project [17]). Note that code generation is also available in tools which support analysis of continuous systems and analog (periodic) controllers (e.g. Matlab and MatrixX [10]). However, these are not targeted for cases with complex software with hierarchical structure and do not support formal verification.

It is also essential to obtain integration with analysis tools if the detailed design is to be formally verified prior to code generation. This is much more obvious where the controller has a hierarchical description, discrete mode changes, and complex control structures. Here, the work in the project is still in preliminary stages. Prototype translators from Lustre to PVS [16], and Lustre to the first order theorem prover NP-Tools by Prover technology have been developed (see work package 3.4 in [17]). However, the applications are still in progress.

Here we report on one such translator used in the case study: the prototype developed by Prover technology which translates a subset of the Statemate languages (with a synchronous interpretation) to NP-Tools with integer arithmetic [4]. The model of the controller in statecharts is too large for being presented here. However, the size of the translated NP-Tools model provides a feel for the size. The insect-like macro resulting from the translation to NP-Tools has 96 input variables and 88 output variables (seen as a circuit).

3.1   Lessons Learnt

Our experience with the modelling activities for climatic chamber controller can be summarised as follows. The NP-Tools [18] environment should obviously be seen as an analysis environment, not a primary modelling environment. The description of the controller at the circuit level loses much of the inherent structure and does not provide an overview when compared with the statechart model. On the other hand, using statecharts alone was not ideal for description of such a controller either. The model we developed prior to translation to NP-Tools used only a subset of the Statemate (statechart) notation. In particular, activity charts could not be used. Thus, all (continuous) control activities which are ideally described in a language like Lustre give rise to several self-loops within every active regulation mode, each loop having its own enabling condition.

The result of the translation from statecharts to NP-Tools was a macro with all the inner logic hidden. Each dynamic variable was modelled as an in-pin representing the value before each step, and an out-pin for the value after the step (additional pins for initial values are also provided). During the verification step counter-models presented by the theorem prover showed errors in the design model. However, after every modification to the design (in the statechart model), one needed to recompile to the NPTool format, which soon became impractical.

As a result of the childhood problems with the translators, we have so far attempted all our closed loop verifications on models directly developed in NP-Tools and a physical environment model. When modelling in NP-Tools we have used a similar style to modelling (variable naming conventions for values before and after a step, etc), as if the model was the result of translation from the statechart model.

The experience here shows, however, that much of the value in high level modelling is lost. To show, for example, that the control system is only in one mode at any time produced a number of counter examples and several modifications to the model. This is trivially achieved by competent compilers (e.g. the Esterel compiler based on constructive semantics [2]).

We are currently experimenting with the Lucifer tool which is a similar translator from Lustre to NP-Tools (see SYRF deliverable 2.2 [17]). Here, translation provides an improvement. The hierarchical structure of the Lustre program, not so visible in the textual language, becomes more visible in the NP-Tools version. This is due to preservation of the structure at the Lustre "node" level (one NP-Tools macro for each Lustre node).

4   Models of the Physical Environment

The physical model developed for the climatic chamber case study and the underlying assumptions were detailed in [14]. In the simplest form, the continuous model for the example, as derived from engineering models, has one differential equation describing changes in the chamber temperature as a function of three inputs: the incoming air temperature, the applied voltage, and the air flow in the chamber.

An initial hybrid model for this part (under the given assumptions) is seemingly simple: consisting of one discrete mode and one equation. The differential equation, in which u_i are inputs, x is the only state variable, and a, b and c are constants, has the following form:

$$\dot{x} = au_1x + bu_2 + cu_1u_3$$

Here, u_1 denotes the air flow $[m^2/s]$, u_2 is the square of the controller-applied voltage $[V]$, and u_3 is the temperature for the incoming air $[K]$. x denotes the chamber temperature which is prescribed to be within allowed ranges in different modes by the requirements/design document. Namely, the document refers to the chamber temperature being "within Δ of the reference temperature", or being " within 2Δ the reference temperature" as part of the transition condition between various modes.

4.1   Transformations on the Model

Ideally we would like to combine this model and the synchronous controllers described above, and perform analysis on the closed loop system. However, prototypical analysis environments in which hybrid models can be analysed are much more restrictive. Note that despite simplifying assumptions this model is still non-linear, and in particular the evolutions in state are not linear in time. We therefore propose a number of transformations on the model which makes some specific instances of it analysable. Two obvious "specialisations" are transformation to hybrid automata (HA) and transformation to a discrete time model.

Thus, we look at certain restrictions to the model which yield a "simpler" representation. Though simplicity might mean a larger number of discrete modes with simpler dynamics in each mode.

Another reason for looking at these restrictions is that the environment model above is an open system. One of the "simpler" models, hybrid automata, requires us to give invariances over every mode and differential equations describing each variable of the system. The distinction between state and input is thus removed, and the model is expected to incorporate full information both about control signals (here the voltage), and the disturbances (here the incoming air temperature).

On the other hand, we wish to keep a modular version of the environment (although simpler). We would like to plug and play with different control programs and verify each property in that context. Thus, there is a conflict between making the model simpler (e.g. turning it into HA) and keeping it modular.

We therefore propose a number of restrictions which can be applied with as little impact on modularity as possible. In particular, we distinguish between restricting:

- unmodelled inputs, and
- modelled inputs.

With unmodelled inputs we mean those which are completely outside our control. In the context of the case study the incoming air temperature is such an input. Since we do not have any information on how they can vary, restriction to a class, in any case proves something about the closed loop system when inputs are in that class. For these inputs we assume piecewise constant signals with a finite range of values.

For modelled inputs, either the input is described in detail as the state of another continuous state system, or the input is a control signal generated by a control program. In the former case, a parallel composition of the hybrid transition system eliminates those variables as inputs and makes them state variables. In the latter case – for control signals – we again restrict the signal to a class without making the controller behaviour fixed. In particular, control signals issued from a synchronous controller, depending on being periodic or not, lead to different abstractions of the physical model.

(a) piecewise constant control signal with changes allowed at equidistant points in time, lead to the discrete-time abstraction of the model as difference equations.

(b) piecewise constant control signals which set the rate of change of a continuous variable (e.g. increase, decrease, steady), lead to piecewise constant slopes incorporated in a hybrid automaton model.

We attempt both approximations in the project case study (see section 5 below). As far as other continuous (non-control) inputs are concerned, as a first approximation it is reasonable to assume that they are constant. This is standard practice in control engineering, and again, gives valid results for those system trajectories brought about by the constant input.

In the climatic chamber, as a first approximation we assume that the flow (u_1) is constant at all times. We further assume that the incoming air temperature (u_3) is piecewise constant with a finite range of values.

Thus the model of the system can be transformed to a hybrid transition system (HTS) [15] with one mode for every possible value of u_3. This analysis gives us Figure 3 as the first approximation.

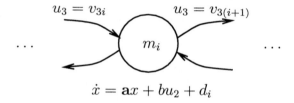

$$\dot{x} = \mathbf{a}x + bu_2 + d_i$$

Fig. 3. Assuming that domain of $u_3 = \{v_{31}, \ldots, v_{3n}\}, \mathbf{a} = au_1$, and $d_i = cu_1v_{3i}$

4.2   The Hybrid Automaton Model

One restriction to the incoming control signal assumes the controller to have three modes of operation with regard to the control signal: increasing, decreasing and keeping constant. In this section we take the model of Figure 3 and restrict u_2 to be of this type. This assumption leads to a model of the chamber whereby every mode in Figure 3 will be replaced by three modes as displayed in Figure 4. The figure shows the obtained hybrid automaton fragment, where the conditions for incoming and outgoing transitions from the fragment are left out.

It should be clear that by specifically stating the rate of change for u_2 this variable can no longer be considered as an input variable in the original transition system. In order to utilise the added knowledge for simplifying the equation for x, we need to relate rate of change of u_2 with the changes in x. Thus, we need to explicitly represent a clock which measures how long the system has resided in

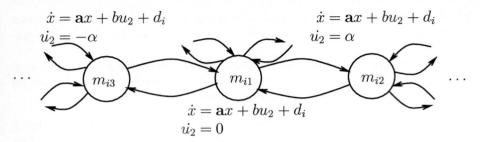

Fig. 4. An HTS model with u_2 as a state variable: assuming that it may stay constant, or increase/decrease at a constant rate.

each mode since the last time it was entered. We use the clock t for this purpose. This variable has to be reset to zero every time a mode is entered. Furthermore, we need to establish the condition for leaving a mode and entering a new one, which obviously arises due to actions of the controller. In HA, this is achieved by adding synchronisation labels corresponding to controller actions. The HA in Figure 5 allows arbitrary changes of slope within the range $\{-\alpha, 0, \alpha\}$ by the controller. Note that the value of x is now dependent on the (apriori unknown) value of u_2 on entry to the mode. This value on entry is captured by adding a piece-wise constant variable (g_i) and an assignment at each mode change.

It can be observed that the obtained hybrid automaton still is not analysable algorithmically. That is, it is not yet a *linear* hybrid automaton (x does not vary with constant slope). To make this model analysable using the existing (hybrid automata) verification tools, we need to add bounds on the evolution of x (otherwise the value of x will increase or decrease infinitely as time goes by in each mode). Adding these bounds is possible once the plant model is composed with a particular controller – a controller which has output signals of the type assumed in this plant model, i.e. an on-off controller with three values for u_2. Since the Saab program is not of this type this track will not be continued any further.

4.3   The Discrete Time Model

Considering constant flow and piecewise constant incoming air temperature as in previous case, but a different restriction for the control signal we obtain a different approximation in this subsection.

Here, we assume that the heater is controlled by a synchronous program. Moreover we assume the incoming control signal (voltage) and its square u_2 to change only at equidistant points in time. After this assumption, one can rewrite the differential equations into a discrete-time form by making the sampling interval T a parameter of the model. Thus, every differential equation in Figure 3 may be replaced by the difference equation:

$$\dot{x} = \mathbf{a}x - b\alpha t + g_i \qquad\qquad\qquad \dot{x} = \mathbf{a}x + b\alpha t + g_i$$
$$\dot{u}_2 = -\alpha \qquad\qquad\qquad\qquad\qquad \dot{u}_2 = \alpha$$
$$\dot{t} = 1 \qquad\qquad\qquad\qquad\qquad\qquad \dot{t} = 1$$
$$\dot{g}_i = 0 \qquad\qquad\qquad\qquad\qquad\qquad \dot{g}_i = 0$$

$$\dot{x} = \mathbf{a}x + g_i$$
$$\dot{u}_2 = 0$$
$$\dot{t} = 1$$
$$\dot{g}_i = 0$$

Fig. 5. Fragment of a hybrid automaton model with the same assumptions as in Figure 4 – the clock t and the piece-wise constant function $g_i = bu_2 + d_i$ have been added to relate the changes in x to u_2.

$$x((k+1)T) = x(kT)e^{\mathbf{a}T} + b/\mathbf{a}(e^{\mathbf{a}T} - 1)\, u_2(kT) + d_i/\mathbf{a}(e^{\mathbf{a}T} - 1)$$

That is, the $(k+1)$th value of x is defined in terms of the kth value of x and the kth value of u_2 (which is assumed constant during the interval $[kT, (k+1)T]$). This reduces the chamber model to a mode-automaton which is a hierachical model compilable to a Lustre program [12]. The syntax and semantics of mode-automata can also be found in the SYRF deliverable 2.1 [17].

4.4 Lessons Learnt

In the last two subsections we have seen how treatments of the control signal in two different ways results in two different "simplified" models, each useful in the context of some verification environment (see section 5).

Alhough it might seem that these guidelines are ad hoc, they rest on underlying general principles which justifies them in the context of verification. For example, to restrict the control signal in the above two ways is definitely superior to treatment of such a signal in a way similar to unmodelled inputs. Consider for example the case that the input u_2 (representing the square of the issued voltage) is piecewise constant with a finite range (with no further restrictions).

This leads to a new model, starting from the HTS in Figure 3 and repeating the same step earlier performed for u_3. That is, the voltage signalis assumed to have a finite range of values leading to the finite range $\{v_{21}, \ldots, v_{2p}\}$ for u_2. Replacing every mode of the HTS in Figure 3 with p modes, we get a totally connected HTS of the form shown in Figure 6.

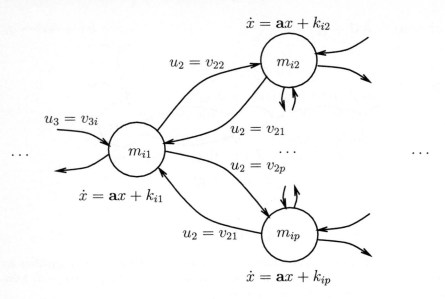

Fig. 6. The HTS obtained with piecewise constant restriction on the control variable u_2 – where $k_{ij} = bv_{2j} + d_i$.

Note that "simplifying" with the same treatment for two different types of input variables gives different results. In the case of a physical variable (the incoming temperature), it is reasonable to assume that values $v_{31}, \ldots, v_{3n}$ can be taken by u_3 in that order. In the case of the control signal u_2 we should assume that the variable may be set to any of the values $v_{21}, \ldots, v_{2p}$ in any order. We simply have no continuity assumptions on a discrete signal. Here, simplification of the continuous dynamics in a mode comes at a much higher price in terms of the increase in the number of (discrete) modes.

In those cases where the nature of the controller is intentionally left open (e.g. not restricted to be periodic) this might be a suitable abstraction. However, it is unnecessarily complex if we already intend to test a particular controller with specific characteristics (on/off controller in the HA case, and a sampled program in the case of the discrete time model).

5   Verification Techniques

In the project we have experimented with two different approaches to verifca- tion. The first one is compositional: a given requirement is decomposed into several conjuncts (prrof obligations). Different subsystem models (represented in different modelling environments) are used to verify that different proof obli- gations hold. The second approach, referred to as one-shot verification, models the physical system in the same proof environment and at the same abstraction level as the controller.

5.1 Compositional Verification

Our approach combines formal and informal reasoning as well as continuous analysis. In this approach we combine proofs in the NP-Tools theorem prover and simulations in the SystemBuild environment of the MatrixX tool [10].

First, we attempt to find sufficient conditions which facilitate proving a property using our knowledge of the system. These auxiliary properties may be of the following kinds:

- an assumption which we discharge informally
- a property of the controller or the environment which we formally prove locally
- another property arising as an interaction of the two, which we further refine by finding further sufficient conditions

Then the system satisfies the top requirement under the informally discharged assumptions.

Consider the second property which is a safety property. The only actuator in the system causing hazards is the heater which must be shown to heat the air to desired levels but *not* to hazardous levels. Let **R₂** express this property.

> **R₂**: The chamber temperature x never exceeds a limit T_H

The aim is to find (strong enough) properties **R₂ᵢ** such that $\bigwedge R_{2i}$ is sufficient for proving **R₂**. We start with the following conditions:

> **R₂₀**: The chamber temperature is equal to the incoming temperature u_3 at start time
> **R₂₁**: The reference temperature T_{Ref} can never exceed $T_{Ref_{max}}$, and $T_{Ref_{max}} + 2\Delta < T_H$
> **R₂₂**: Whenever the system is in wait-, solution-, or work-mode, we have $x < T_H$
> **R₂₃**: The system is never in block-mode while $x > T_H$

These properties can be discharged informally or proved within the NP-Tools model except for **R₂₃** which we continue to refine:

> **R₂₃₁**: $x = T_{Ref} + 2\Delta < T_H$ when entering the block-mode
> **R₂₃₂**: the applied voltage $u = 0$ throughout the stay in block-mode
> **R₂₃₃**: The system leaves the block-mode after *tblock* seconds, and enters the off-mode
> **R₂₃₄**: The temperature x does not increase while the system is in the block mode

This is sufficient for proving the safety property provided that
R₂₃₁ ∧ R₂₃₂ ∧ R₂₃₃ ∧ R₂₃₄ → R₂₃.
Properties **R₂₃₁** to **R₂₃₃** are easily proved using the NP-Tools model of the controller. For the proof of **R₂₃₄** we use continuous reasoning based on the simulation models.

5.2   One-Shot Verification

Here we describe the approach whereby some aspects of the environment model are directly stated in the same verification environment as the controller is.

Consider now the first requirement. The stability component of this requirement can best be verified using control theory and exact knowledge of the control algorithm in the work mode. Here, we concentrate on the first component, denoting it by $\mathbf{R_1}$.

$\mathbf{R_1}$: Keeping the reference values constant, the work light will be lit within t_1 from the start of the system

First, we provide sufficient conditions for $\mathbf{R_1}$ to hold in the design model:

$\mathbf{R_{11}}$: The system starts in the wait mode with the chamber temperature equal to u_3

$\mathbf{R_{12}}$: While T_{Ref} is constant, the only successor to the wait mode is the solution mode

Given input restrictions $\mathbf{R_{10}}$,

$\mathbf{R_{13}}$: The system leaves the wait mode within *wait_time* from the start of the system

$\mathbf{R_{14}}$: the system leaves the solution mode within *solution_time* from entering the mode

$\mathbf{R_{15}}$: While T_{Ref} is constant, the only successor to the solution mode is the work mode, and the work light is turned on whenever work mode is entered

$\mathbf{R_{16}}$: *wait_time* + *solution_time* $\leq t_1$

We initially claim that

$$\mathbf{R_{11}} \wedge \mathbf{R_{12}} \wedge \mathbf{R_{13}} \wedge \mathbf{R_{14}} \wedge \mathbf{R_{15}} \wedge \mathbf{R_{16}} \rightarrow \mathbf{R_1}$$

At a later stage we may drop $\mathbf{R_{11}}$ and replace it with the assumption that the initial chamber temperature is different from u_3. But to begin with, we make the restrictions in $\mathbf{R_{10}}$ more explicit, and show that

$$\mathbf{R_{10}} \rightarrow \mathbf{R_{13}} \wedge \mathbf{R_{14}}$$

Here, we have several paths to take, but the choice is guided by the verification techniques we intend to utilise. For example, the following restrictions justify the adoption of a discrete-time model of the environment in a mode-automaton [12] with n discrete modes. Each mode is then governed by a difference equation derived from the continuous model (see section 4.3) in the standard manner.

$\mathbf{R_{101}}$: u_1 stays constant at Q $[m^3/s]$

$\mathbf{R_{102}}$: u_2 may vary every t_{sample} seconds

$\mathbf{R_{103}}$: u_3 is piecewise constant taking the values $\{v_1, \ldots, v_n\}$

Note that using mode-automata [12], changes in state variables in each mode are defined in terms of a Lustre program. Each state variable is thus defined by an equation relating the state variables at the previous (clock) step and the current input.

Adopting the restrictions above, the verification method would be as follows: using a scheme for compilation from mode-automata to Lustre we obtain a model of the environment in Lustre which can be composed with a controller in Lustre, and further compiled to NP-Tools. In NP-Tools it is possible (but tedious) to show that the number of steps leading to the work light coming on is $\leq N$ for some N (this proves $\mathbf{R_1}$ for a given t_{sample} provided that $t_1 \geq Nt_{sample}$).

The tool Lucifer which translates Lustre programs to NP-Tools models makes these proofs easier. It facilitates inductive proofs with a base larger than 1. That is, it is possible to compose n copies of the transition relation for the system, and show the initial condition holding in the first n steps, followed by the inductive step. This is a track we are currently exploring in the project.

Note that this is one reason for not choosing a "too short" sampling interval [14]. As well as other disadvantages associated with oversampling, a large N makes the proof more difficult. Our approach is based on proving the bounded response property for as small N as feasible.

6   Related Works

The work we have reported is at a too early stage for making definitive remarks about feasibility of combining "push-botton" theorem provers and simulation environments. More work is also needed to compare the method with "heavy duty" theorem proving in the spirit of [6]. However, some preliminary points for discussion have already emerged. Some of the shortcomings are reminiscent of those reported in [5]: the limitation to interger arithmetic, for example, means that the counter proofs presented by the system are more informative than the safety proofs holding over a limited range. This is, however, compensated in our approach by departing from fully formal proofs and combining with a simulation analysis when (local) reasoning over reals is crucial to the property in question.

Our model of the heat process intentionally made several simplifications to fit an early experimental set up [14]. The interested reader may for example refer to a more complex model of heat exchangers in [13] where some of our restrictions are relaxed. The purpose of that paper is the illustration of a rich simulation language and only the plant part of the heat exchanger is subjected to validation by simulation.

It is also interesting to note that the size of the real ventilation subsystem, compared to the demo system, in the same format as the one discussed in section 3 (NP-Tools circuit), is 700 input variables and 500 output variables. Despite the seemingly large state space, the size of the reachable states set – as far as required for the types of properties mentioned – is small enough for practical purposes, even in the real system [11].

Further work in the other parts of the project, specially extensions to the Lucifer prototype are very interesting for enhancing our verification methodology and incorporation of our methods in the system development process.

Acknowledgements

This work was supported by the Esprit LTR project SYRF, the Swedish board for technical research (TFR), and the Swedish board for technical development (NUTEK).

References

[1] A. Poigné and M. Morley and O. Maffeïs and L. Holenderski. The Synchronous Approach to Designing Reactive Systems . *Formal Methods in System Design*, 12(2):163–187, March 1998.
[2] G. Berry. The Foundations of Esterel. In *Proofs, Languages and Interaction: Essays in Honour of Robin Milner*. MIT Press, 1998. To appear.
[3] L. Besnard, P. Bournai, T. Gautier, N. Halbwachs, S. Nadjm-Tehrani, and A. Ressouche. Design of a Multi-formalism Application and Distribution in a Data-flow Context: An Example. In *Proceedings of the 12th international Symposium on Languages for Intentional programming, Athens, June 1999*. World Scientific.
[4] B. Carlson, M. Carlsson, and G. Stålmarck. NP(FD): A Proof System for Finite Domain Formulas. Technical report, Logikkonsult NP AB, Sweden, April 1997. Available from http://www-verimag.imag.fr//SYNCHRONE/SYRF/HTML97/a321.html.
[5] W. Chan, R.J. Anderson, P. Beame, S. Burns, F. Modugno, D. Notkin, and J.D. Reese. Model Checking Large Software Specifications. *IEEE Transactions on Software Engineering*, 24:498–519, July 1998.
[6] B. Dutertre and V. Stavridou. Formal Requirements Analysis of an Avionics Control System. *IEEE Transactions on Software Engineering*, 25(5):267–278, May 1997.
[7] N. Halbwachs. *Synchronous Programming of Reactive Systems*. Kluwer Academic Publishers, 1993.
[8] D. Harel. STATECHARTS: A Visual Formalism for Complex Systems. *Science of Computer Programming*, 8:231–274, 1987.
[9] M. Heimdahl and N. Leveson. Completeness and Consistency in Heirarchical State-based Requirements. *IEEE transactions on Software Engineering*, 22(6):363–377, June 1996.
[10] Integrated Systems Inc. *SystemBuild v 5.0 User's Guide*. Santa Clara, CA, USA, 1997.
[11] O. Åkerlund. Application of Formal Methods for Analysis of the Demo System and parts of the Ventilation System of JAS 39 (in swedish). Technical report, Saab Aerospace AB, Linköping, Sweden, January 1997.
[12] F. Maraninchi and Y. Rémond. Mode-automata: About modes and states for reactive systems. In *Programming Languages and Systems, Proceedings of the 7th European Symposium On Programming, Held as part of ETAPS'98, Lisbon, Portugal, LNCS 1381*. Springer verlag, March 1998.

[13] S.E. Mattsson. On modelling of heat exchangers in modelica. In *Proc. 9th European Simulation Symposium*, Passau, Germany, October 1997. Currently available through `http://www.modelica.org/papers/papers.shtml`.

[14] S. Nadjm-Tehrani. Integration of Analog and Discrete Synchronous Design. In *Hybrid Systems: Computation and Control, Proceedings of the second international workshop, March 1999, LNCS 1569*, pages 193–208. Springer Verlag, March 1999.

[15] S. Nadjm-Tehrani. Time-Deterministic Hybrid Transition Systems. In *Hybrid Systems V, Proceedings of the fifth international workshop on hybrid systems, September 1997, LNCS 1567*, pages 238–250. Springer Verlag, 1999.

[16] N. Owre, J. Rushby, and N. Shankar. PVS: A Prototype Verification System. In *Proc. 11th International Conference on Automated Deduction, LNCS 607*. Springer Verlag, 1992.

[17] The SYRF Project. Deliverables for Work packages 1 to 7. Available from `http://www-verimag.imag.fr//SYNCHRONE/SYRF/deliv1.html`, 1997-99.

[18] Prover Technology. *NPTools v 2.3 User's Guide*. Stockholm, Sweden. Contact: `http://www.prover.com`.

ParTS
A Partitioning Transformation System

Juliano Iyoda, Augusto Sampaio, and Leila Silva

Departamento de Informática - UFPE
Caixa Postal 7851 - Cidade Universitária
CEP 50740-540 Recife - PE - Brazil
{jmi,acas,lmas}@di.ufpe.br

Abstract. This paper describes a system (ParTS) for automatic hardware/software partitioning of applications described in the concurrent programming language occam. Based on algebraic transformations of occam programs, the strategy guarantees, by construction, that the partitioning process preserves the semantics of the original description. ParTS has been developed as an extension of OTS — a tool implemented at Oxford University which allows one to apply basic algebraic laws to an occam program in an interactive way. ParTS extends OTS with elaborate transformation rules which are necessary for carrying out partitioning automatically. To illustrate the partitioning methodology and our system, a convolution program is used as a case study.

1   The Hardware/Software Partitioning Problem

The specification of a computer system is usually fully implemented as a software solution (executed in a general hardware like a microprocessor). On the other hand, some strong requirements (like performance or size) demand an implementation completely in hardware. Nevertheless, in between these two extremes, there are applications that favour a combined implementation with software and hardware components. This has become a recent trend in Computing called Hardware/Software Codesign, which has been widely adopted in the design of embedded systems.

The problem of how to divide a specification into hardware and software components, the hardware/software partitioning problem, raises at least two major and orthogonal problems: 1) How can the partitioning be done so that the result satisfies the efficiency requirements? 2) Does the final system execute its tasks according to the original specification?

The first question can be solved by heuristic algorithms and the second by formal verification that the partitioned system preserves the semantics of the original description.

Several approaches to hardware/software partitioning have been developed, as described, for example, in [2, 8, 12, 13]. All the approaches above emphasise the algorithmic aspects of hardware/software partitioning. More recently, some works have suggested the use of formal methods in the partitioning process, as

J. Wing, J. Woodcock, J. Davies (Eds.): FM'99, Vol. II, LNCS 1709, pp. 1400–1419, 1999.
© Springer-Verlag Berlin Heidelberg 1999

reported, for example, in [1, 6, 7]. Although these approaches use formal methods to hardware/software partitioning, neither of them includes a formal verification that the partitioning preserves the semantics of the original description.

In [3] Barros and Sampaio presented some initial ideas towards a partitioning approach whose emphasis is correctness. This work was the seed of the PISH project, a co-design environment which is being developed by four Brazilian universities [4]. The project comprises all the steps from the partitioning of (an initial description of) the system into hardware and software components to the layout generation of the hardware.

Silva *et al.* [18, 19] further develop the ideas presented in [3] by giving a precise characterisation of the partitioning process as a program transformation task. These works apply algebraic rules to guarantee that the partitioned system has the same functionality of the original description.

The main purpose of this paper is to present an environment which implements the strategy described in [3, 18, 19] to provide automatic hardware/software partitioning. This environment, the Partitioning Transformation System — ParTS, is an extension of the Oxford occam Transformation System (OTS) [10] — a tool developed at Oxford University constructed to perform transformations of occam programs [16]. While the basic algebraic laws implemented in OTS are useful for program transformation in general, they express only simple transformations, and are not suitable to capture the partitioning problem. ParTS extends OTS with new transformation rules specific for the partitioning strategy adopted. Also, ParTS deals with new language constructs not addressed by OTS (see Section 3) and provides a new graphical user interface. The transformation rules are coded as functions in the SML [15] functional language and the strategy is also a function that applies the rules in an appropriate order. Then the final system generated by ParTS is derived from the application of several semantic-preserving rules which guarantees the correctness of the solution by construction.

The next sections are organised as follows. Section 2 presents a brief description of the occam language and some of its laws. Section 3 explains the strategy adopted to carry out the partitioning. The implementation issues of ParTS are described in Section 4 and a case study of a hardware/software partitioning (of a convolution program) is shown in Section 5. Finally, Section 6 summarises the contribution of this paper and discusses topics for further research.

2   A Language of Communicating Processes

The goal of this section is to present the language which is used both to describe the applications and to reason about the partitioning process itself. This language is a representative subset of occam. For convenience, we sometimes linearise occam syntax in this paper. For example, we may write SEQ(P_1, P_2,..., P_n) instead of the standard vertical style. The subset of occam adopted here is defined by the following BNF-style syntax definition, where [**clause**] has the usual meaning that **clause** is an optional item.

```
P ::= SKIP | STOP | x := e
   | ch ? x | ch ! e
   | IF [ rep](c₁ P₁, c₂ P₂,..., cₙ Pₙ)
   | ALT [ rep] (c₁&g₁ P₁, c₂&g₂ P₂,..., cₙ&gₙ Pₙ)
   | SEQ [ rep] (P₁, P₂,..., Pₙ)
   | PAR [ rep] (P₁, P₂..., Pₙ)
   | WHILE c P
   | VAR x: P
   | CHAN ch: P
```

Informally, these processes behave as explained in what follows. The SKIP construct has no effect and always terminates successfully. STOP is the canonical deadlock process which can make no further progress. The commands x := e, ch ? x and ch ! e, are assignment, input and output commands, respectively; the communication in occam is synchronous. The commands IF and ALT select a process to execute, based on a condition (IF) or on a guard (ALT). While IF's conditions are always boolean expressions, ALT's guards involve input commands. IF's selection is deterministic; the lowest index boolean condition to be true activates the corresponding process. If none of the conditions is TRUE it behaves like STOP. On the other hand, ALT's selection is non-deterministic and randomly activates the process corresponding to the first guard to be satisfied. If more than one guard is satisfied at the same time, ALT activates non-deterministically one of the corresponding processes. If none of the guards is no satisfied ALT behaves like STOP. The commands SEQ and PAR denote the sequential and parallel composition of processes, respectively. Processes within a PAR constructor run concurrently, with the possibility of communication between them. Communication is the only way two parallel processes can affect one another, so (when combined in parallel) one process cannot access a variable that another one can modify. The command WHILE denotes a loop which executes a process until the WHILE's condition becomes false. The constructs VAR and CHAN declare local variables and channels, respectively. Here we avoid mentioning a particular type for the declared variables or channels. The optional argument **rep** which appears in the IF, ALT, SEQ and PAR constructors stands for a replicator of the form i = m FOR n where m and n are integer expressions. A more detailed description of these commands can be found in [16].

As shown in [17], there are many algebraic laws which hold of the occam constructs. Such laws change the syntax of a program but preserve its semantics. A set of algebraic laws which completely characterises the semantics of WHILE-free occam programs is given in [17]. In this section we present only a few of these laws for the purpose of illustration.

The SEQ operator runs a number of processes in sequence. If it has no arguments it simply terminates.

Law 2.1 (*SEQ-SKIP unit*) SEQ() = SKIP

Otherwise it runs the first argument until it terminates and then runs the rest in sequence. Therefore it obeys the following associative law.

Law 2.2 (*SEQ-assoc*) SEQ(P$_1$, P$_2$,..., P$_n$) = SEQ(P$_1$, SEQ(P$_2$, P$_3$,..., P$_n$))

It is possible to use the above laws to transform all occurrences of SEQ within a program to binary form.

PAR is an associative operator.

Law 2.3 (*PAR-assoc*) PAR(P$_1$, P$_2$,..., P$_n$) = PAR(P$_1$, PAR(P$_2$, P$_3$,..., P$_n$))

As with SEQ, we can reduce all occurrences of PAR to a binary form. The next law shows that the order in which the processes are combined in parallel is not important (PAR is symmetric).

Law 2.4 (*PAR-sym*) PAR(P$_1$, P$_2$) = PAR(P$_2$, P$_1$)

3   The Partitioning Approach

The hardware/software partitioning approach considered in this work performs the partitioning by applying a set of algebraic rules to the original system description. This is carried out in four major phases, as captured by Figure 1 and explained below.

Splitting The initial description of the system (written in occam) is transformed into the parallel composition of a number of *simple* processes. The formal definition of a simple process is given in [18], but it is enough to think of it as a process with granularity of a primitive command, possibly as a branch of a conditional (IF) or choice (ALT) statement.

Classification A set of implementation alternatives for each simple process is established by considering some features such as concurrent behaviour, data dependency, multiplicity, non-determinism and mutual exclusion.

Clustering Among the implementation alternatives of each process, one is chosen based on the minimisation of an area-delay cost function. The simple processes are grouped in clusters according to the similarity of functionality and the degree of parallelism. Each cluster groups simple processes that will be implemented in hardware or in software (this is determined by annotations). The fact that the simple processes generated by the splitting are in parallel gives full flexibility for this phase: as PAR is symmetric (Law 2.4) all possible permutations can be analysed.

Joining The processes in each cluster are effectively combined (either in sequence or in parallel), as determined by the result of the clustering process.

It is worthwhile mentioning that the phases that use algebraic transformations are splitting and joining. It has been proved that the use of algebraic rules in these phases preserves the semantics of the system while the program is being transformed [18, 19]. The classification and clustering phases implement heuristics to produce an efficient final system and the produced output is a mere permutation of the simple processes inside the PAR construction. Note that this

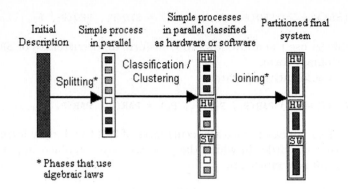

Fig. 1. The partitioning approach

procedure also does not affect the system behaviour once the PAR is associative and symmetric, as captured by laws 2.3 and 2.4.

ParTS is concerned only with splitting and joining since these are implemented by program transformation. In the rest of this section we describe these two phases in more detail. More information about the other two phases and about the tool which implements them can be found in [4]. In any case we will make clear how ParTS interacts with this tool to generate the partitioned system.

3.1   The Splitting Strategy

To improve flexibility concerning user interaction, the subset of occam presented in Section 2 was extended to consider new constructors: BOX, HBOX, SBOX and CON.

The syntax of these constructors is BOX P, HBOX P, and so on, where P is a process. The introduction of these constructors in occam has no semantic effect; they can be regarded just as annotations, useful not only for the splitting, but also for the other phases.

A process included into a constructor BOX is not split and its cost is analysed as a whole at the clustering phase. The HBOX and SBOX constructors denote a BOX which must be implemented in hardware and in software, respectively. They are used to raise the granularity level of the splitting phase when this happens to be convenient for a given application.

The constructor CON is an annotation for a *controlling process*; this is further explained in this section.

The goal of the splitting phase is to transform any initial description into a set of simple parallel processes by the application of a reduction strategy. This strategy applies algebraic rules and has two main steps. The first step transforms all IF's and ALT's commands into simple processes. As a simple process has at most one statement in its internal level, IF's and ALT's commands with multiple branches must be broken. Moreover, if a branch of a conditional command is a SEQ, PAR or WHILE process, it is necessary to distribute the conditional over these processes. Rule 1 and Rule 2 are examples of the rules employed in this step.

Rule 1:

$$\text{IF}(b_1\ P_1, ..., \ b_n\ P_n)$$
$$= \text{VAR } c_1, ..., \ c_n: \ \text{SEQ}(c_1, ..., \ c_n := \text{FALSE}, ..., \ \text{FALSE},$$
$$\text{IF}(b_1\ c_1 := \text{TRUE}, ..., \ b_n\ c_n := \text{TRUE}),$$
$$\text{IF}(c_1\ P_1, \text{TRUE SKIP}), ..., \ \text{IF}(c_n\ P_n, \text{TRUE SKIP}))$$

`provided each` c_k `is a fresh variable (occurring only where explicitly shown).`

This rule transforms any conditional process into a sequence of IF's to allow the analysis of each subprocess of the original conditional.

Note that the first IF of the right-hand side makes the choice (and saves the result in one of the fresh variables) allowing the subsequent conditionals to be carried out in sequence.

Rule 2:

$$\text{IF}(b\ \text{VAR } x: \ \text{SEQ}(P_1, ..., \ P_n), \ \text{TRUE SKIP})$$
$$= \text{VAR } c: \ \text{SEQ}(c := b,$$
$$\text{VAR } x: \text{SEQ}(\text{IF}(c\ P_1, \text{TRUE SKIP}), ..., \ \text{IF}(c\ P_n, \text{TRUE SKIP})))$$

`provided that` c `is a fresh variable.`

This rule distributes IF over SEQ. Note that after exhaustive application of this rule, no IF will include any SEQ in its internal process. Similar rules distribute IF over ALT and over WHILE.

The second step of the splitting strategy transforms the intermediary description generated by the first step in the *normal form* of the splitting phase, which is a set of parallel (simple) processes. Two crucial transformations of this step are: 1) To turn simple processes closed in the sense that all variable used and assigned in the process are local. 2) To introduce a *controlling process* between every two simple processes. The controlling process acts as the interface between the processes under its control and the environment.

To understand the usefulness of a controlling process, consider two processes P_1 and P_2 with data-dependency and originally in sequence. To put P_1 and P_2 in parallel, as required by the normal form, communication must be introduced between them, as occam does not allow parallel processes to share variables. The purpose of the controlling process is to manage this communication. Except for communication commands of the original description, each P_i interacts with the environment through the controlling process.

Rule 3 shows how sequential processes can be combined in parallel.

Rule 3:

> VAR z : SEQ(P_1, P_2)
>
> = CHAN ch_1, ch_2, ch_3, ch_4: PAR(VAR x_1: SEQ(ch_1 ? x_1, P_1, ch_2 ! x_1'),
>
>   VAR x_2: SEQ(ch_3 ? x_2, P_2, ch_4 ! x_2'),
>
>   VAR z : CON(SEQ(ch_1 ! x_1, ch_2 ? x_1', ch_3 ! x_2, ch_4 ? x_2')))

provided x_i = USED(P_i) ∪ ASS(P_i) **and** x_i' = ASS(P_i) **and** ch_1, ch_2, ch_3 **and** ch_4 **are not free in** P_1 **or** P_2.

It is denoted by ASS(P) the list of free[1] variables that are assigned in process P and by USED(P) the list of free variables used in expressions of P (either on the right-hand side of an assignment or in a boolean expression or in an output command).

Observe that although P_1 and P_2 are in parallel on the right-hand side of the rule above, in fact their behaviour are sequential. Process P_2 can executes only after the controlling process synchronises with P_1 through channel $ch2$.

3.2   The Joining Strategy

To indicate the result of the clustering phase, other new constructors are introduced: PARhw, PARsw, PARser and PARpar. These constructors have the same semantics of the standard PAR. The constructors PARhw and PARsw serve as annotations to denote the hardware and the software cluster, respectively. The constructors PARser and PARpar denote that the sub-processes included in each of them must be serialised and parallelised, respectively.

The goal of the joining strategy is to combine the processes that belong to the same cluster with the aim to implement the decisions taken by the clustering phase. Basically the joining phase applies algebraic rules to parallelise and serialise arbitrary simple processes. The parallelisation and serialisation must eliminate the communication introduced during the splitting phase, as well as the introduced variables on the case of IF's and ALT's recomposition.

As an example of the rules employed in this phase, consider Rule 4 below:

Rule 4:

```
CHAN ch,ch₁,ch₂,ch₃,ch₄,ch₅,ch₆:
PAR
  Q₁
  F(PARpar
      VAR x₁: SEQ(ch₁? x₁, P₁, ch₂! x₁')
      VAR x₂: SEQ(ch₃? x₂, P₂, ch₄! x₂')
      Q₂)
  VAR x:CON(SEQ(ch₅? x,VAR z:SEQ(ch₁!x₁,ch₂?x₁',ch₃!x₂,ch₄?x₂'),
             ch₆! x'))
```

---

[1] If P is some occam term and x is a variable, we say that an occurrence of x in P is *free* if it is not in the scope of any declaration of x in P, and *bound* otherwise.

$=$
CHAN ch,ch_5,ch_6 :
PAR
  Q_1
  F(PARpar VAR x:SEQ(ch_5?x, PAR(VAR z_1:P_1,VAR z_2:P_2), ch_6!x'))
    Q_2)
provided that $x_1' \cap x_2 = \emptyset$ and $x_2' \cap x_1 = \emptyset$
where $x = x_1 \cup x_2$, $x' = x_1' \cup x_2'$, $x_i = \text{USED}(P_i) \cup \text{ASS}(P_i)$,
$x_i' = \text{ASS}(P_i)$ and $z_i = z \cap x_i$, for $i = 1,2$.

To understand this rule, observe that the process P_1 and P_2 on the left-hand side of the rule are executed in sequence and their execution is controlled by the controlling process annotated with the construct CON. Note also that P_1 and P_2 are included in a PARpar constructor which means that they should be parallelised. The side conditions of the rule requires that P_1 and P_2 do not have data-dependency. The effect of the rule is to combine P_1 and P_2 in parallel, with the elimination of the controlling process, as can be noticed from the right-hand side of the rule.

4 ParTS Implementation

This section describes some implementation issues of ParTS such as its architecture, the programming languages used and the system it extends, OTS.

ParTS comprises two software layers: the transformation system in SML [15] and a graphical user interface in Java [5]. The core of ParTS is the SML module which implements the strategy to perform the hardware/software partitioning. This module extends the OTS environment including the specific rules of the splitting and the joining phases.

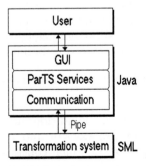

Fig. 2. The ParTS architecture

As shown in Figure 2 the Java module comprises three sub-modules which are concerned with communication with the SML module via a pipe (Communication module), concealment of the SML functions (ParTS Services module) and interface presentation (GUI module).

This architecture properly separates the system functionality from its graphical interface.

4.1   The Transformation Layer in SML

The OTS is implemented using the Edinburgh SML which is an interactive programming environment for a strongly-typed strict functional language. A functional program is defined as a set of values and functions. The SML also includes some imperative programming features which enables the construction of input/output commands and side-effect operations (assignment).

Collections of items are processed in SML using lists, a pre-defined type of the language. The lists are denoted by [] (the empty list) or by enumeration of its elements (such as [1,2,3]). The infix operator :: (pronounced 'cons') constructs a new list by adding an element in front of an existing list (if l is the list [x1,...,xn] and x is a value of the correct type then x::l is the list [x,x1,...,xn]).

New types are defined by the `datatype` declaration which allows the creation of heterogeneous classes (a class constructed from several distinct subclasses). A simple example of `datatype` declaration is shown below:

```
datatype process = SKIP
                 | STOP
                 | seq of process list;
```

This example defines a very small subset of the occam language. The new type **process** and the *constructors* SKIP, STOP and seq are created. Constructors are regarded as functions which create values of a datatype. The constructors SKIP and STOP receive no arguments and returns a **process** and the constructor seq receives a **process** list and returns a **process**.

A function is defined as a set of equations containing a pattern as parameter and an expression as result. The argument passed is compared with the patterns and if some pattern matches then the corresponding expression is evaluated.

```
fun binary_seq (seq (p1::p2::p)) = seq (p1::[seq (p2::p)])
  | binary_seq p = p;
```

The first equation uses on its left-hand side the pattern (seq (p1::p2::p)) — a sequence with at least two processes — and, on its right-hand side, the expression seq (p1::[seq (p2::p)]) which constructs a binary sequential process. The second equation performs no transformation on the argument. Whenever the argument does not match the pattern stated in the first equation, it will always match the second equation which uses a variable p to stand for a general pattern. For example, the evaluation of binary_seq(SKIP) reduces to SKIP.

The last version of OTS (released in 1988) was implemented by Goldsmith [10] in the SML functional language. An abstract syntax for occam was defined in SML as a set of recursive datatypes. The basic algebraic laws of occam are implemented as functions. A parse function is used to input a text file containing an occam process and translates it to the abstract syntax.

A sample of how an abstract syntax can be implemented using SML datatypes is shown below.

An identifier is represented as a string.

```
datatype identifier = ident of string;
```

Variables and channels are identifiers.

```
datatype variable = var of identifier;
datatype channel = chan of identifier;
```

Each operator of the language is a constructor of the type `process` with the relevant arguments. For example, an assignment statement is represented by the `assign` constructor and has as arguments a list of variables and a list of expressions.

```
datatype process = assign of (variable list) * expression list
                 | input_proc of channel * (variable list)
                 | output_proc of channel * (expression list)
                 | SKIP
                 | STOP
                 | dec of declaration * process
                 | seq_con of process list
                 | par_con of process list
                 | if_con of conditional list
                 | ...
and declaration = var_dec of variable list
                | chan_dec of channel list
and conditional = sim_cond of expression * process
                | if_cond of conditional list
and expression = TRUE
               | FALSE
               | num of int
               | varexp of variable
               | ...
```

As an example, the parser of OTS reads a file containing the following process

```
SEQ
  x := y
  ch ? y
```

and translates it to

```
seq_con [ assign( [var(ident ''x'')],[varexp(var(ident ''y''))] ),
          input_proc( chan(ident ''ch''),[var(ident ''y'')] ) ]
```

ParTS implements the transformation rules for the partitioning as functions. Nevertheless, these rules usually express much more complex transformations than the basic algebraics laws implemented in OTS.

As an example, we discuss the implementation of Rule 2 which will be called distIF(). The implementation of this rule has some auxiliary definitions. The function freshVar() receives a process P and returns a fresh variable (a variable that does not occur free in P). The function map() receives a function f and a list l and applies f to each element of l.

We also need to construct a function that builds each IF of the right-hand side of Rule 2. The oneIF() function receives as parameters a boolean expression and a process and returns a conditional process.

We also use the let expressions facility of SML. A let expression has the general form let D in E end. D is a declaration of values that is evaluated first. Then the expression E is evaluated inside the context of names declared in D.

Now we can define the distIF() function that implements Rule 2.

```
fun distIF (proc as
            if_con [
              sim_cond(b,
                dec(var_dec x,
                seq_con Pn)),
              sim_cond(TRUE,
                SKIP) ]) =
         let val c = freshVar(proc)
             val c_exp = varexp c
         in dec(var_dec [c],
              seq_con [
                assign([c],[b]),
                dec(var_dec x,
                seq_con (map (oneIF c_exp) Pn)) ])
         end;
```

The proc as clause before the pattern creates the name proc that is bound to the conditional process received as argument. Then, proc is used as the argument of freshVar() function to generate a fresh variable (c); c_exp is just the fresh variable transformed into an expression type. The expression (map (oneIF c_exp) Pn) applies the (oneIF c_exp) function to each element of the process list Pn.

Clearly, the abstract syntax of occam (and the auxiliary functions) makes the implementation less readable. Even so, each rule is implemented in an elegant and abstract way as an SML function.

In a similar way, ParTS implements all the rules of the splitting and the joining phases. These new functions form the main code of ParTS. The splitting and the joining strategies are also implemented as functions. Each one is defined as the composition of the transformation rules (coded as functions) for the relevant phase. These rules are applied in an appropriate order to produce the desired result. The application of a rule is achieved through a higher-order function that takes the rule as argument and applies it to the current process.

4.2   The Graphical User Interface

A great improvement with respect to OTS is that the interface of OTS was specific for the Sun View environment and requires the user to interact at the level of SML functions. We have also implemented some facilities not available in OTS; this is further discussed below.

The GUI of ParTS implemented in Java allows users to manipulate several occam processes in different windows. The portability of Java makes possible the implementation of different versions of ParTS, for Unix SunOS and Windows95. The Windows95 version uses the Moscow SML instead of Edinburgh SML without any loss of functionality.

Figure 3 shows the interface of ParTS. A brief description of some elements of the screen is given below.

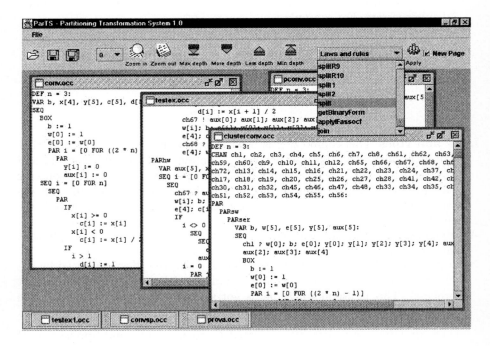

Fig. 3. The ParTS interface

File Menu The file menu provides commands to load occam files and save them (in general after performing transformations). It is possible to open various different files at the same time.

Zoom in Using this facility one can focus on any internal subprocess of the process, allowing the user to apply laws whose effect is restricted to internal parts of the process.

Zoom out This button has the opposite effect of the *Zoom in* button. For example:

```
SEQ                          SEQ
   SEQ                          P₁
      P₁    Zoom in            P₂
                 ⟹
      P₂    Zoom out
                 ⟸
   Q
```

$$
\begin{array}{ll}
\text{SEQ} & \quad \text{SEQ} \\
\quad \text{SEQ} & \quad\quad \text{P}_1 \\
\quad\quad \text{P}_1 & \quad\quad \text{P}_2 \\
\quad\quad \text{P}_2 & \\
\quad \text{Q} &
\end{array}
$$

Max depth / More depth ParTS allows the user to visualise a process partially. The *Max depth* button shows the process completely, without hiding any subprocess. The effect of the *More depth* button is to show the hidden subprocesses incrementally.

Less depth / Min depth The opposite effect of *More depth* is achieved with *Less depth* button. There is also the equivalent *Min depth* button that hides all subprocesses. For example,

$$
\begin{array}{ll}
\text{SEQ} & \quad\quad\quad \text{SEQ} \\
\quad \dots \text{ SEQ [2 clauses]} & \quad\quad\quad\quad \text{SEQ} \\
\quad\quad \text{P}_3 \quad\quad\quad \xrightarrow{More\ depth} & \quad\quad\quad\quad\quad \text{P}_1 \\
\quad\quad\quad\quad \xleftarrow{Less\ depth} & \quad\quad\quad\quad\quad \text{P}_2 \\
& \quad\quad\quad\quad \text{P}_3
\end{array}
$$

Laws and rules This combo box is used to select the name of law/rule that will be applied to the current process (it contains rules named as `split` and `join` which perform the transformations to carry out the hardware/software partitioning). Also there exist all the laws that construct the split and the join strategies, allowing the user to do the partitioning step by step, if desired.

Apply The apply button must be used after choosing a law. It will apply that law and transform the current process accordingly.

New page If it is set before the application of a law, the effect produced by applying the law is shown in a separate window (without changing the current process). This is useful when one is not sure whether the law will provide the desired transformation.

OTS already included facilities related to zoom, depth and application of laws. Nevertheless, the interaction with the user is at the level of SML syntax. In ParTS all the interaction is directly in the occam notation. Furthermore, all the facilities concerning file manipulation and multiple windows are entirely new.

5   A Small Case Study

This section illustrates the hardware/software partitioning process of a vector convolution program used as a case study. For conciseness reasons, the explanation will emphasise particular aspects of the partitioning process, instead of trying to address all the details of the transformations involved.

Figure 4a shows the original description of the convolution program, and Figure 4b the partial result of the splitting phase generated by ParTS. The system exhaustively applies the rules of the splitting phase coded as functions in SML, as explained in the previous section. Using an Intel Pentium II 300 MHz and 64 MB of RAM as the hardware platform, ParTS takes about 15 seconds to perform the splitting of this program, and transforms the original description into 37 simple processes, combined in parallel.

Observe from Figure 4b that each of these processes has at most one assignment in its most internal level. The only exception is Process 1, where all subprocesses included into a BOX constructor are considered as an atomic process and therefore it has not been split.

Another point to notice is that all simple processes have been turned *closed* (their variables are local). Moreover, each original process is encapsulated (preceded and followed by communication commands).

The application of Rule 1 to Process 2 of Figure 4a transforms it into four simple processes (see Process 2.1, 2.2, 2.3 and 2.4 of Figure 4b) and the application of Rule 3 introduces communication between each pair of these simple processes. Process 3 in Figure 4b is the controlling process of Process 2.3 and 2.4.

After the splitting phase, the classification and the clustering phases take place. As we have mentioned before, these phases are related to the efficiency issue of partitioning process. The classification and clustering phases are being implemented as a separate tool which is under development and communicates with ParTS via shared files.

The classification phase defines for each simple process a set of implementations alternatives such as parallel, sequential, independent, etc. (see Figure 5a). The clustering phase builds a clustering tree which defines the clusters and how their processes must be combined (Figure 5b). Observe that the processes 2.1 – 2.4 of Figure 4b are grouped in the same cluster and must be combined in sequence. The *cut line* shown in Figure 5b separates the hardware and software clusters based on the heuristics defined in [2]. The clustering phase is responsible only for determining which processes should be combined to form the clusters, but do not carry out the transformations to effectively combine them.

Figure 6a shows the program after the classification and the clustering phases. This program reflects the design decision of the clustering phase. Note that the only changes concerning the occam program of Figure 4b are the annotations to identify the software (PARsw) and the hardware (PARhw) clusters, and whether each group of processes must be combined in sequence (PARser) or in parallel (PARpar).

Regarding the preservation of semantics, the transformation of the program in Figure 4b into the one in Figure 6a is immediately justified by the associativity and symmetry of parallel composition (see laws 2.3 and 2.4 of Section 2). This emphasises the fact that classification and clustering are concerned with the efficiency of the partitioning process, and have very little to do with program transformation.

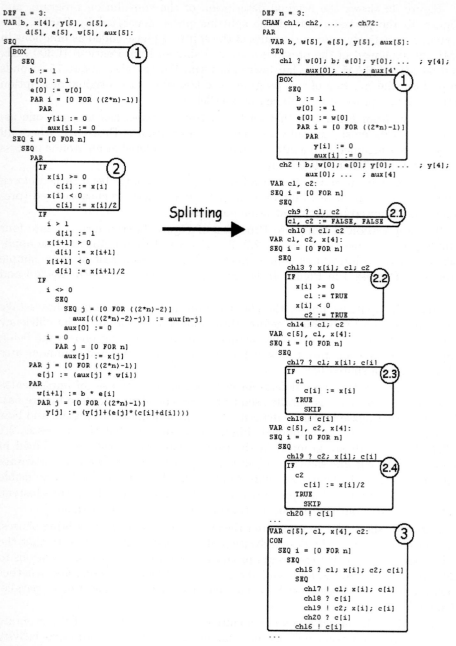

a) Original description

Splitting

b) After splitting

Fig. 4. The splitting phase

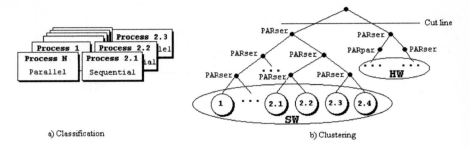

a) Classification   b) Clustering

Fig. 5. The classification and the clustering phases

The final partitioned system is shown in Figure 6b. Observe that the BOX annotation has been eliminated. Since all subprocesses 2.1 – 2.4 belongs to the same cluster, the IF process is re-arranged and Process 3 is eliminated. ParTS combines the processes in the joining phase by applying the `join` strategy to the file generated by the clustering phase. This process takes about 2 seconds to complete (using the same hardware previously mentioned).

In fact, all controlling processes are eliminated and the only remaining communication is the one necessary for the synchronisation between the hardware and the software components (Observe channels `ch67` and `ch68` in Figure 6b).

6   Conclusions

We have used an intentionally small case study to illustrate an innovative approach to the implementation of hardware/software partitioning. The Partitioning Transformation System (ParTS) realises the partitioning process as a program transformation task, based on algebraic rules which ensure that the resulting program is correct (with respect to the original input) by construction.

The approach to partitioning is structured into four major phases, as summarised by Figure 7.

The first task performed by ParTS (Figure 7a-b) is to split a process in several simple processes operating in parallel. The phases of classification and clustering are concerned with the efficiency of the partitioned program. From the result of the splitting, a graph is constructed to allow a cost analysis to be carried out. However, this tree is suitable only as an intermediate representation, and, as already said, the implementation of classification and clustering are separate from ParTS which is exclusively concerned with program transformation.

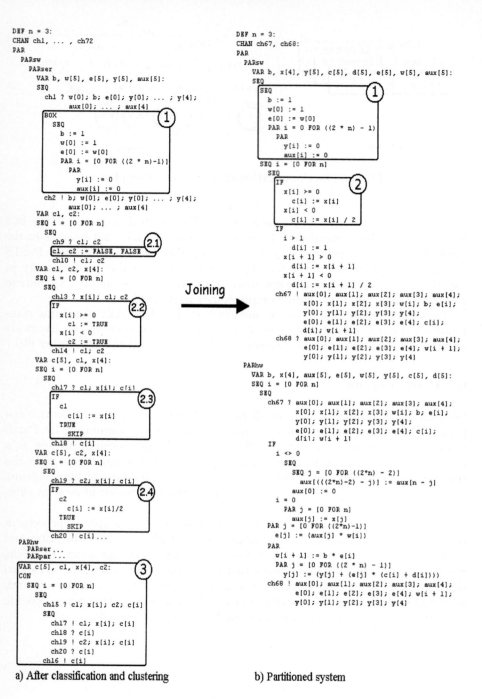

a) After classification and clustering

b) Partitioned system

Fig. 6. The joining phase

The following step is to represent the clustering tree as a program with the form shown in Figure 7c, where annotations are used to determine which clusters are to be implemented in hardware and in software. Also note that we use an annotation for each cluster. This contains useful information (generated during the clustering) to guide the combination of the processes in each cluster; basically, this indicates whether process must be combined in sequence (`PARser`) or in parallel (`PARpar`).

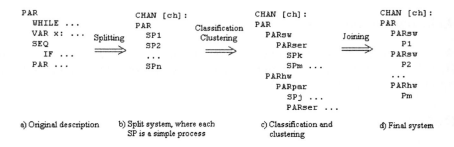

```
PAR                          CHAN [ch]:                    CHAN [ch]:                    CHAN [ch]:
   WHILE ...                 PAR           Classification   PAR                          PAR
   VAR x: ...   Splitting       SP1        Clustering          PARsw        Joining         PARsw
   SEQ          ======>         SP2        ======>             PARser       ======>         P1
      IF ...                    ...                            SPk                          PARsw
   PAR ...                      SPn                            SPm ...                      P2
                                                            PARhw                          ...
                                                               PARpar                      PARhw
                                                               SPj ...                     Pm
                                                            PARser ...
```

a) Original description   b) Split system, where each   c) Classification and   d) Final system
                              SP is a simple process   clustering

Fig. 7. The partitioning approach

Finally, the joining phases takes a program as in Figure 7c, carries out the necessary transformations to combine the processes in each cluster, and generates the final result, which is a precise abstract representation of our intended target architecture: with one software process and an arbitrary number of hardware processes (Figure 7d).

In terms of implementation, ParTS was built as an extension of the *Oxford occam Transformation System* (OTS), keeping all the original functionality of OTS, but adding specific notation and rules to allow a precise capture of the partitioning process, apart from a new user interface.

While the splitting has been completely formalised and implemented, the joining is still our major current focus of attention. A strategy for the joining phase is proposed in [19] based on transformation and reduction of configurations in a binary tree which represents the result of the clustering phase. While we have already implemented some general rules of the joining phase (which allows us to automatically partition some small examples like the one presented here) the full implementation of the joining strategy is still under development.

The integration between ParTS and the tool which implements the classification and clustering phases is also a topic for further research.

There are several systems which perform automatic hardware/software partitioning based on different approaches. The COSYMA system [8] assumes an all-software implementation as initial solution. A simulated annealing algorithm moves software code to hardware until the time constraints are met. The VULCAN system [11] starts by an all-hardware solution and uses an iterative approach to move operations from hardware to software. The SpecSyn [9] supports several partitioning algorithms and presents an approach combining clustering and greedy algorithms. The Lycos [14] achieves the partitioning by a dynamic-programming algorithm that uses the information of the profiling and the time and area estimation steps.

None of these systems is concerned with the formal correctness of the partitioning process. To our knowledge, ParTS is the only existing tool which implements hardware/software partitioning based on algebraic transformations which ensures the preservation of semantics.

Acknowledgements

We are grateful to Michael Goldsmith for making available the source code of OTS. We also thank the Brazilian Research Council (CNPq) for financial support through the grants 130264/98-9 and 521039/95-9.

References

[1] A. Balsoni, W. Fornaccari, D. Sciuto. Partitioning and Exploration Strategies in the TOSCA Co-Design Flow. In *Proceedings of Fourth International Workshop on HW/SW Codesign*, (1996) 62–69.

[2] E. Barros. *Hardware/Software Partitioning using UNITY*. PhD thesis, Universität Tübingen, Germany, 1993.

[3] E. Barros and A. Sampaio. Towards Probably Correct Hardware/Software Partitioning Using Occam. In *Proceedings of the Third International Workshop on HW/SW Codesign (CODES'94), Grenoble, France. IEEE Press*, (1994) 210-217.

[4] E. Barros *et al.* The PISH Methodology for Hardware/Software Codesign. In *Workshop of ProTem-CC, CNPq*, (1998) 65–98.

[5] M. Campione and K. Walrath. The Java Tutorial: Object-Oriented Programming for the Internet. Addison Wesley Pub Co., 1998.

[6] C. Carreras, J. C. López, M. L. López, C. Delgado-Kloos, N. Martinéz, L. Sánchez. A Co-Design Methodology Based on Formal Specification and High-level Estimation. In *Proceedings of Fourth International Workshop on HW/SW Codesign* (1996) 28–35.

[7] T. Cheung, G. Hellestrand and P. Kanthamanon. A Multi-level Transformation Approach to HW/SW Co-Design: A Case Study. In *Proceedings of Fourth International Workshop on HW/SW Codesign*, (1996) 10–17.

[8] R. Ernst and J. Henkel. Hardware-Software Codesign of Embedded Controllers Based on Hardware Extraction. In *Handouts of the International Workshop on Hardware-Software Co-Design*, October 1992.

[9] D. Gajski and F. Vahid. Specification and Design of Embedded Hardware-Software Systems. In *IEEE Design and Test of Computers*, Spring 1995, 53-67.

[10] M. Goldsmith. The Oxford occam Transformation System. *Technical report, Oxford University Computing Laboratory*, January 1988.

[11] R. Gupta, C. N. Coelho and G. De Micheli. Synthesis and Simulation of Digital Systems Containing Interacting Hardware and Software Components. In *Proceedings of 29th Design Automation Conference*,1992.

[12] R. Gupta and G. De Micheli. System-level Synthesis Using Re-programmable Components. In *Proceedings of EDAC*, (1992) 2–7, IEEE Press.

[13] P. V. Knudsen and J. Madsen. PACE: A Dynamic Programming Algorithm for Hardware/Software Partitioning.In *Proceedings of Fourth International Workshop on HW/SW Codesign*, (1996) 85–92.

[14] J. Madsen. J. Groge, P. V. Knudsen, M. E. Petersen and A. Haxthausen. Lycos: The Lyngby Co-synthesis System. In *Design Automation of Embedded Systems*, 1997,2(2):195-235.

[15] L. Paulson. ML for the working programmer. Cambridge University Press, 1991.

[16] D. Pountain and D. May. A tutorial introduction to occam programming. INMOS, BSP Professional Books, 1987.

[17] A. Roscoe and C. A. R. Hoare. The laws of **occam** programming. In *Theoretical Computer Science*, 60, (1988) 177–229.

[18] L. Silva, A. Sampaio and E. Barros. A Normal Form Reduction Strategy for Hardware/Software Partitioning. In *Formal Methods Europe (FME) 97. Lecture Notes in Computer Science 1313*, (1997) 624–643.

[19] L. Silva, A. Sampaio, E. Barros and J. Iyoda. An Algebraic Approach for Combining Processes in a Hardware/Software Partitioning Environment. In *Proceedings of the Seventh International Conference on Algebraic Methodology and Software Technology (AMAST)*, (1998) 308–324

A Behavioral Model for Co-design

He Jifeng*

International Institute For Software Technology
The United Nations University
P.O.Box 3058, Macau
jifeng@iist.unu.edu

1   Introduction

With chip size reaching one million transistors, the complexity of VLSI algorithms – i.e., algorithms implemented as a digital VLSI circuit – is approaching
that of software algorithms – i.e., algorithms implemented as code. However, the
design methods for circuits that are commonly found in textbooks resemble the
low-level machine language programming methods. Selecting individual logical
gates and registers in a circuit like selecting individual machine instruction in a
program. State transition diagrams are like flowcharts. These methods may have
been adequate for small circuit design when they were introduced, but they are
not adequate for circuits that perform complicated customer algorithms.

Oftenly we do not build circuits to perform complicated algorithms directly. We build general-purpose processor, and customise them for a particular
algorithm by writing a program. For many application, particularly where speed
of execution or security is important, a customer-built in circuit is better than
the traditional processor-and-software combination. The speed is improved by
the absence of the machine language layer and introducing parallelism, whereas
security is improved by the impossibility of reprogramming. Moreover, there are
space saving compared to a combination of software and processor.

In principle, there is no difference between hardware and software; what
can be done with one can be done with the other. For example, an assignment
statement $x := b$, where x is a Boolean variable, can be realised by a clocked circuit, wherein the output port of a combination device which generates the value
of expression b is connected to the input port of a register, which is allocated
to hold the value of x. An incoming clock signal triggers the execution of the
circuit which propagates the value of b to the output port of the register. On
the other hand, the instruction set of a general-purpose processor can often be
described by an interpreter [2, 6].

Out of the previous analysis has come an increasing awareness of the need
for behavioural models suited for specifying and reasoning about both programs
and digital devices. Contemporary hardware description languages (for example
[7, 10, 11]) are not sufficient because of the following limitations:

---

* On leave from East China Normal University, Shanghai. This work was partly supported by EPSRC research grant GR/K58708 "Linking theories for computer science"

J. Wing, J. Woodcock, J. Davies (Eds.): FM'99, Vol. II, LNCS 1709, pp. 1420–1438, 1999.
© Springer-Verlag Berlin Heidelberg 1999

1. Most such tools are intended much more for simulation than for mathematically sound reasoning.
2. Difficulties arise in developing circuit specifications that may refer to different levels of behavioral abstraction.
3. Existing formal frameworks for such languages are in general too restrictive to deal with the inherent parallelism of digital circuits.

An extended linear-time temporal logic based on intervals was developed in [4, 5, 9] for presenting the kinds of quantitative timing properties and signal transitions that occur in hardware devices. The behaviour of programs and circuits can often be decomposed into successively smaller intervals of activity. State transitions of programs can be characterised by properties relating the initial and final values of variables over interval of times. However in the treatment of hybrid systems where the physical world evolve continuously, this approach seems inappropriate.

We have used the notations of DC (Duration Calculus [12]) to describe hybrid systems. Case studies show that many quantitative timing properties can be handled effectively in DC. Nevertheless, it is not designed to model event-based languages, and lacks the mechanisms to synchronise systems with different time granularity. Section 2 presents a specification language, which is a variant of DC, enriched with a novel parallel operator to integrate systems evolved at various time rate. Its mixed interval structure enables us to model both discrete-time and continuous-time systems. This framework provides a unifying means for presenting the various features of event-based hardware description languages and state-based imperative programming languages.

The main purpose of the mathematical definition of temporal operators is to deduce their interesting properties. These are most elegantly expressed as algebraic laws – equations usually, but sometimes inequations, with implication between formulae rather than equivalence. Section 3 is devoted to the algebraic properties of our specification language. Algebra is well-suited for direct use by engineers in symbolic calculation of parameters and structure of an optimal design. Algebraic proofs by term rewriting are the most promising way in which computers can assist in the process of reliable design.

Section 4 gives a number of tests, known as *healthiness conditions*, which can be applied to specifications and intermediate designs to maintain their feasibility during the development process. It also explores the mathematical links between theories satisfying individual healthiness conditions, and shows that the set of formulae expressible in each theory is closed under relevant operators.

The VERILOG hardware description language (HDL) [11] is widely used to model the structure and behaviour of digital systems ranging from simple hardware building blocks to complete systems. It has a simulation oriented semantics based on *events*, i.e., changes to the values of wires and registers. This *event semantics* can actually model detailed asynchronous behaviour, but is very fine-grained and does not support formal verification. Section 5 shows the utility of our theory in dealing with hardware, and provides an observation-oriented semantics to the core of VERILOG.

TEMPURA [4, 9] is an imperative language based on interval temporal logic. It has been put forward as a useful tool for reasoning about concurrent programs and hardware. Every TEMPURA statement is a temporal logic formula. TEMPURA is formalised in Section 6 as a sub-theory which satisfies additional healthiness conditions.

2   Specification Language

Our specification language is based on continuous time represented by reals

$$Time =_{df} Real$$

It adopts two types of time intervals: *closed continuous interval* $[b, e]$ and *finite discrete intervals* $< t_0, \ldots, t_n >$. Let $\mathcal{E} \subseteq Time$, the set $I(\mathcal{E})$ of intervals with the end points of $\mathcal{E}$ is defined by

$$I(\mathcal{E}) =_{df} CI \cup DI$$

$$CI =_{df} \{[b, e] \mid b \leq e \ \wedge \ \{b, e\} \subset \mathcal{E}\}$$

$$DI =_{df} \{\{t_0, \ldots, t_n\} \mid \{t_0, \ldots, t_n\} \subseteq \mathcal{E} \wedge \ (t_0 < \ldots < t_n)\}$$

In the following, we will use σ to range over intervals, and $\sigma.b$ and $\sigma.e$ to represent its left and right end points. Adjacent intervals of the same type can be combined into a big one by the catenation operator $\frown$

$$\sigma_1 \frown \sigma_2 =_{df} \sigma_1 \cup \sigma_2 \quad \textbf{if} \ \sigma_1.e = \sigma_2.b \ \textbf{and} \ (\{\sigma_1, \sigma_2\} \subseteq CI \ \textbf{or} \ \{\sigma_1, \sigma_2\} \subseteq DI)$$

We adopt an inclusion-like partial order $\leq$ among intervals

$$\sigma_1 \leq \sigma_2 =_{df} (\sigma_1.b = \sigma_2.b) \ \wedge \ (\sigma_1.e = \sigma_2.e) \ \wedge \ (\sigma_1 \subseteq \sigma_2)$$

Clearly, this ordering is preserved by the catenation operator.

As a specification mechanism based on interval temporal logic, our language includes

- *global variables*, which represent *constant* (i.e., independent of time) and are denoted by lower letters $x, y, \ldots, z$.
- *state variables*, which stand for real functions over $Time$, and are denoted by capital letters $X, Y, \ldots, Z$.
- *temporal variables*, which are identified as real functions on intervals. and denoted by lower letters $u, v, \ldots, w$.

Two specific temporal variables l and $\sharp$ are present to characterise the type of intervals, where the first one stands for the length of interval

$$l(\sigma) =_{df} \sigma.e - \sigma.b$$

and the second is used to count the *isolated* time points of interval

$$\sharp([b, e]) =_{df} \textbf{if} \ b < e \ \textbf{then} \ 0 \ \textbf{else} \ 1$$

$$\sharp(< t_0, \ldots, t_n >) =_{df} n + 1$$

The terms of the language can conveniently be defined by induction

(1) global variables are terms.
(2) temporal variables (including l and $\sharp$) are terms.
(3) if X is a state variable, then $\overleftarrow{X}$ $\overrightarrow{X}$ and $\bigcirc X$ are terms.
(4) if $r_1, \ldots, r_n$ are terms and f is an n-ary function name, then $f(r_1, \ldots, r_n)$ is also a term.

The set of well-formed formulae is generated by the following rules:

(1) if $r_1, \ldots, r_n$ are terms, and p is an n-ary predicate name, then $p(r_1, \ldots, r_n)$ is a well-formed formula
(2) **true** and **false** are well-formed formulae.
(3) if F and G are well-formed formulae, so are $\neg F$ and $F \wedge G$ and $\exists h \bullet F$, where h is either a (global or state) variable.
(4) if both F and G are well-formed formulae, so are F^*, $F^\frown G$ and $F \backslash\backslash G$.

A model $\mathcal{M}$ assigns every variable a constant of the proper type

(1) Temporal variable v is associated with an interval function $\mathcal{M}(v)$.
(2) State variable X is interpreted as a time function $\mathcal{M}(X)$
(3) Global variable x is assigned a real $\mathcal{M}(x)$
(4) Function names f and predicate names p are interpreted as functions $\mathcal{M}(f)$ on *Real* and relations $\mathcal{M}(p)$ over *Real* respectively.

Let h be a variable. Two models $\mathcal{M}1$ and $\mathcal{M}2$ are called to be h-*equivalent*, denoted by $\mathcal{M}1 \equiv_h \mathcal{M}2$, if for all variables v different from x

$$\mathcal{M}1(v) = \mathcal{M}2(v)$$

Terms are interpreted over intervals. Given a model $\mathcal{M}$ and an interval $\sigma \in I(\mathcal{E})$ the value of a term r over σ is defined by

$$\mathcal{M}_\sigma(x) =_{df} \mathcal{M}(x)$$
$$\mathcal{M}_\sigma(l) =_{df} l(\sigma)$$
$$\mathcal{M}_\sigma(\sharp) =_{df} \sharp(\sigma)$$
$$\mathcal{M}_\sigma(v) =_{df} \mathcal{M}(v)(\sigma)$$
$$\mathcal{M}_\sigma(\overleftarrow{X}) =_{df} \mathcal{M}(X)(\sigma.b)$$
$$\mathcal{M}_\sigma(\overrightarrow{X}) =_{df} \mathcal{M}(X)(\sigma.e)$$
$$\mathcal{M}_\sigma(\bigcirc X) =_{df} \mathcal{M}(X)(\sigma.e) \qquad \text{if } \sigma \in CI$$
$$\qquad\qquad =_{df} \mathcal{M}(X)(t_1) \qquad \text{if } \sigma =< t_0, t_1, \ldots, t_n >$$
$$\mathcal{M}_\sigma(f(r_1, \ldots, r_n)) =_{df} \mathcal{M}(f)(\mathcal{M}_\sigma(r_1), \ldots, \mathcal{M}_\sigma(r_n))$$

Formulae are interpreted as functions from intervals to the Boolean values $\{tt, ff\}$.

$$\mathcal{M}_\sigma(\textbf{true}) =_{df} tt$$

$$\mathcal{M}_\sigma(\textbf{false}) =_{df} ff$$

$$\mathcal{M}_\sigma(p(r_1,\ldots,r_n)) =_{df} \mathcal{M}_\sigma(p)(\mathcal{M}_\sigma(r_1),\ldots,\mathcal{M}_\sigma(r_n))$$

$$\mathcal{M}_\sigma(\neg F) =_{df} \neg \, \mathcal{M}_\sigma(F)$$

$$\mathcal{M}_\sigma(F \wedge G) =_{df} \mathcal{M}_\sigma(F) \wedge \mathcal{M}_\sigma(G)$$

$$\mathcal{M}_\sigma(F^*) =_{df} l(\sigma) = 0 \ \vee$$

$$\exists \sigma_0, \ldots, \sigma_n \bullet \sigma = (\sigma_0 \hat{\ } \ldots \hat{\ } \sigma_n) \wedge \forall i \bullet \mathcal{M}_{\sigma_i}(F)$$

$$\mathcal{M}_\sigma(\exists h \bullet F) =_{df} \exists \mathcal{M}' \bullet \mathcal{M}'_\sigma(F) \wedge (\mathcal{M} \equiv_h \mathcal{M}')$$

$$\mathcal{M}_\sigma(F \hat{\ } G) =_{df} \exists \sigma_1, \sigma_2 \bullet \sigma = (\sigma_1 \hat{\ } \sigma_2) \wedge \mathcal{M}_{\sigma_1}(F) \wedge \mathcal{M}_{\sigma_2}(G)$$

$$\mathcal{M}_\sigma(F \backslash\backslash G) =_{df} \exists \rho, \sigma_0, \ldots, \sigma_n \bullet \sigma = (\sigma_0 \hat{\ } \ldots \hat{\ } \sigma_n) \wedge \forall i \bullet \mathcal{M}_{\sigma_i}(F) \wedge$$

$$\rho = \ <\sigma_0.b, \sigma_1.b, \ldots, \sigma_n.b, \sigma_n.e> \ \wedge \ \mathcal{M}_\rho(G)$$

All the usual logical connectives (disjunction, implication, etc.) and quantifiers can be defined in interval term. For example

$$F \vee G =_{df} \neg \, (\neg F \wedge \neg G)$$

$$\forall h \bullet F =_{df} \neg(\exists h \bullet \neg F)$$

The modal operators $\Diamond$ and $\Box$ can be defined in terms of the chop operator.

(1) The formula $\Diamond F$ holds on the interval σ if F does so on one of its subintervals.

$$\Diamond F =_{df} \textbf{true}\hat{\ }(F\hat{\ }\textbf{true})$$

$\Diamond_t F$ holds on σ if F holds in its suffix subinterval.

$$\Diamond_t F =_{df} \textbf{true}\hat{\ }F$$

(2) The formula $\Box F$ holds if F holds on all its subintervals.

$$\Box F =_{df} \neg\Diamond(\neg F)$$

$\Box_t F$ holds on σ if F holds on all its suffix subintervals.

$$\Box_t F =_{df} \neg\Diamond_t(\neg F)$$

(3) We use the notation **unit** to denote the interval of zero length

$$\textbf{unit} =_{df} (l = 0)$$

(4) Let b be a Boolean expression of state variables. Define

$$F \lhd b \rhd Q =_{df} (F \wedge b) \vee (G \wedge \neg b)$$

3   Algebraic Laws

The great merit of algebra is as a powerful tool for exploring family relationship over a wide range of different theories. For example, study of foundations of interval temporal logic has given denotations to a wide variety of Duration Calculus – Mean Value Calculus of Durations, Extended Duration Calculus, Super-dense

Duration Calculus, etc. Distinctions are revealed in the structure and content of each kind of time domain and state variable so defined. It is only their algebraic properties that emphasise the family likeness across the range of Duration systems.

3.1   Chop

The chop operator $^\frown$ is used to model sequential systems. Like its counterpart in ITL, its behaviour is subject to the following familiar laws.

(int-1) (associativity)
$$F^\frown(G^\frown H) \ = \ (F^\frown G)^\frown H$$

(int-2) (unit)
$$\textbf{unit}^\frown G \ = \ G \ = G^\frown \textbf{unit}$$

(int-3) (disjunctivity)
$$F^\frown(G1 \ \vee \ G2) = (F^\frown G1) \ \vee \ (F^\frown G2)$$
$$(F1 \ \vee \ F2)^\frown G = (F1^\frown G) \ \vee \ (F2^\frown G)$$

(int-4) (conjunctivity)   If $L = (l = x)$ or $L = (\sharp = n + 1)$ (for $n \geq 0$), then
$$L^\frown(G1 \ \wedge \ G2) = (L^\frown G1) \ \wedge \ (L^\frown G2)$$
$$(F1 \ \wedge \ F2)^\frown L = (F1^\frown L) \ \wedge \ (F2^\frown L)$$

(int-5) (scope extension)   If h is not free in G, then
$$(\exists h \bullet F)^\frown G \ = \ \exists h \bullet (F^\frown G)$$

(int-6) (dense time)
$$(l = r)^\frown(l = s) \ \Rightarrow \ (l = r + s)$$

(int-7) (interval independency)   If F does not contain temporal variables, nor temporal propositional letter, then
$$(F^\frown G) \Rightarrow F$$
$$(G^\frown F) \Rightarrow F$$

(int-8) (zero)
$$\textbf{false}^\frown G \ = \ \textbf{false} \ = F^\frown\textbf{false}$$

(int-9) (intermediate state)   If p is a predicate, then
$$(F \wedge p(\overrightarrow{X}))^\frown G) \ = \ F^\frown(p(\overleftarrow{X}) \wedge G)$$

(int-10) (initial and final states)   If p is a predicate, then
$$(p(\overleftarrow{X}) \wedge F)^\frown Q = p(\overleftarrow{X}) \wedge (F^\frown G)$$
$$F^\frown(G \wedge p(\overrightarrow{X})) = (F \wedge G) \wedge p(\overrightarrow{X})$$

Adjacent intervals of the same type can be combined into a single one.

(int-11) (closure of interval catenation)
$$(\sharp = 0)^\frown (\sharp = 0) = (\sharp = 0)$$
$$(\sharp = m + 1)^\frown (\sharp = n + 1) = (\sharp = m + n + 1)$$

(int-12) (validity of catenation)
$$(\sharp = 0)^\frown (\sharp \geq 2) = \mathbf{false} \; (\sharp \geq 2)^\frown (\sharp = 0)$$

The length and number of isolated time points of interval are governed by the following laws.

(int-13) (non-empty length)
$$(\sharp \geq 0) = \mathbf{true} = (l \geq 0)$$

(int-14) (singleton sets)
$$(l = 0) = (\sharp = 1)$$

3.2   Parallel

The definition of $\backslash\backslash$ is complicated; so it is comforting that it shows many of the algebraic properties of other familiar parallel operators.

($\backslash\backslash$-1) (associativity)
$$(F\backslash\backslash G)\backslash\backslash H = F\backslash\backslash (G\backslash\backslash H)$$

($\backslash\backslash$-2) (time synchronisation)
$$F\backslash\backslash (\mathbf{unit} \wedge G) = (F \wedge \mathbf{unit})\backslash\backslash G = (F \wedge \mathbf{unit} \wedge G)$$
$$F\backslash\backslash (l > 0 \wedge G) = (F \wedge l > 0)\backslash\backslash G$$

($\backslash\backslash$-3) (disjunctivity)
$$F\backslash\backslash (G1 \vee G2) = (F\backslash\backslash G1) \vee (F\backslash\backslash G2)$$

($\backslash\backslash$-4) (conjunctivity)
$$(F \wedge l = x)\backslash\backslash (G1 \wedge G2) = ((F \wedge l = x)\backslash\backslash G1) \wedge ((F \wedge l = x)^\frown G2)$$
$$(F1 \wedge (l = x) \wedge F2)\backslash\backslash G = ((F1 \wedge l = x)\backslash\backslash G) \wedge ((F2 \wedge l = x)\backslash\backslash G)$$

($\backslash\backslash$-5) ($\backslash\backslash - \frown$ distribution)
$$F\backslash\backslash (G^\frown H) =$$
$$(\mathbf{unit}\backslash\backslash G)^\frown (F\backslash\backslash H) \vee (F\backslash\backslash G)^\frown (F\backslash\backslash H) \vee (F\backslash\backslash G)^\frown (\mathbf{unit}\backslash\backslash H)$$

($\backslash\backslash$-6) (locality of state variable)   If h is not free in F, then
$$F\backslash\backslash (\exists h \bullet G) = \exists h \bullet (F\backslash\backslash G)$$

($\backslash\backslash$-7) (monotonicity)   If $H_1 \Rightarrow H_2$, then
$$(H_1\backslash\backslash G) \Rightarrow (H_2\backslash\backslash G)$$

($\backslash\backslash$-8) (exclusiveness)
$$\neg(\mathbf{true}\backslash\backslash (\sharp = 0))$$

(\\-9) (single transition)
$$F\backslash\backslash(G \wedge \sharp = 2) \;=\; F \wedge (\mathbf{true}\backslash\backslash(G \wedge \sharp = 2))$$

(\\-10) (void synchronisation)
$$(\mathbf{true}\backslash\backslash(\sharp = 2)) \;=\; l > 0$$

(\\-11) ($\widehat{} - \vee$ distribution)
$$(\mathbf{unit} \vee F)\backslash\backslash G \;=\; (\mathbf{unit}\backslash\backslash G) \vee (F\backslash\backslash G)$$

(\\-12) (interval decomposition independency)   If p is a predicate, then
$$F\backslash\backslash(G \wedge p(\overleftarrow{X}, \overrightarrow{X}, l)) \;=\; (F\backslash\backslash G) \wedge p(\overleftarrow{X}, \overrightarrow{X}, l)$$

(\\-13) (invariant)   If p is a predicate, then
$$(F \wedge p(\overleftarrow{X}, \overrightarrow{X}))\backslash\backslash(G \wedge (\sharp \geq 2)) \;=\; F\backslash\backslash(G \wedge \Box_t(l > 0 \Rightarrow p(\overleftarrow{X}, \bigcirc X)))$$

Theorem 3.1

(1) $\mathbf{true}\backslash\backslash\mathbf{true} \;=\; \mathbf{true}$

(2) $\mathbf{false}\backslash\backslash G \;=\; \mathbf{false} \;=\; F\backslash\backslash\mathbf{false}$

(3) $F\backslash\backslash(\sharp \leq 2) \;=\; F$

(4) $F\backslash\backslash(\sharp = n + 1) \;=\; (F \wedge l > 0))^n,$ for $n \geq 1$

where $F^0 =_{df} \mathbf{unit}$ and $F^{n+1} =_{df} F\widehat{}F^n$.

Proof of (1) $\mathbf{true}\backslash\backslash\mathbf{true}$ $\{(int - 1)$ and $(\backslash\backslash - 3)\}$

$\Leftarrow \mathbf{true}\backslash\backslash(\sharp = 1) \vee \mathbf{true}\backslash\backslash(\sharp = 2)$ $\{(\backslash\backslash - 2)$ and $(\widehat{} - 10)\}$

$= (l = 0) \vee (l > 0)$ $\{(int - 1)\}$

$= \mathbf{true}$

The conclusion (4) can be proved by induction.

$F\backslash\backslash(\sharp = 2)$ $\{(\backslash\backslash - 9)$ and $(\backslash\backslash - 10)\}$

$= F \wedge (l > 0)$

$F\backslash\backslash(\sharp = n + 2)$ $\{(int - 10)\}$

$= F\backslash\backslash((\sharp = 2)\widehat{}(\sharp = n + 1))$ $\{(\backslash\backslash - 5)\}$

$= (\mathbf{unit}\backslash\backslash(\sharp = 2))\widehat{}(F\backslash\backslash(\sharp = n)) \vee$

$(F\backslash\backslash\sharp = 2)\widehat{}(F\backslash\backslash\sharp = n) \vee$

$(F\backslash\backslash(\sharp = 2))\widehat{}(\mathbf{unit}\backslash\backslash(\sharp = n))$ $\{(\backslash\backslash - 2)$ and $(int - 12)\}$

$= (F\backslash\backslash\sharp = 2)\widehat{}(F\backslash\backslash\sharp = n)$ $\{$inductive hypothesis$\}$

$= (F \wedge l > 0)\widehat{}(F \wedge l > 0)^n$ $\{$Def of $F^{n+1}\}$

$= (F \wedge l > 0)^{n+1}$ $\square$

Corollary

If $\mathbf{unit} \Rightarrow F$ then $F\backslash\backslash\mathbf{true} \;=\; F^*$ $\square$

4   Healthiness Conditions

In this section, we work towards to a more precise characterisation of the class of formulae that are useful in software/hardware design. As usual, we follow the standard practice of mathematics, which is to classify the basic concepts by their important properties. For example, among the functions of real numbers, it is useful to single out those are integrable, or continuous, or rational, or differentiable. A similar classification of the basic concept of a interval formula is essential to our goal of unifying theories of co-design. This section gives a set of healthiness conditions, and shows that the set of healthy formulae is closed under relevant operators. In the later sections we will demonstrate that all actual software/hardware systems satisfy all the the stated healthiness conditions (and more).

4.1   Monotonicity

Definition 4.1 (Monotonic formulae)
As a predicate of intervals, a formula F is monotonic if it respects the ordering relation $\leq$ over I, i.e., for any model $\mathcal{M}$ and any intervals σ_1 and σ_2

$$(\sigma_1 \leq \sigma_2) \;\Rightarrow\; (\mathcal{M}_{\sigma_1}(F) \;\Rightarrow\; \mathcal{M}_{\sigma_2}(F)) \qquad\qquad \square$$

Examples 4.2
(1) **true** and **false** are monotonic.
(2) Let X be a state variable and p a predicate letter, then $p(l, \overleftarrow{X}, \overrightarrow{X})$ is monotonic.
(3) The formula $\sharp \leq 1$ is monotonic, but $\sharp \leq n$ is not monotonic for $n \geq 2$.
(4) Let X be a state variable, then

$$\mathbf{stb}(X) \;=_{df}\; \exists x \bullet \Box_t(\overleftarrow{X} = x)$$

is not monotonic. $\qquad\qquad \square$

Define

$$\Phi_1(F) \;=_{df}\; F \;\vee\; (\mathbf{true} \backslash\backslash F)$$

Theorem 4.3 (Fixed point representation)
F is monotonic iff $F \;=\; \Phi_1(F)$ $\qquad\qquad \square$

Corollary Monotonic formulae form a complete lattice.

Proof From the monotonicity of Φ_1 and Tarski's fixed point theorem. $\qquad\qquad \square$

Theorem 4.4
F is monotonic **iff** it lies in the image set of Φ_1.

Proof We are going to show that Φ_1 is idempotent.

$$\Phi_1^2(G) \qquad\qquad \{\text{Def of } \Phi_1\}$$
$$= \Phi_1(G) \ \vee \ (\mathbf{true}\backslash\backslash\Phi_1(G)) \qquad \{(\backslash\backslash - 3) \text{ and } (\backslash\backslash - 1)\}$$
$$= \Phi_1(G) \ \vee \ (\mathbf{true}\backslash\backslash G) \ \vee \ ((\mathbf{true}\backslash\backslash\mathbf{true})\backslash\backslash G) \qquad \{\text{Theorem 3.(1)}\}$$
$$= \Phi_1(G) \ \vee \ (\mathbf{true}\backslash\backslash G) \qquad\qquad \{\text{Def of } \Phi_1\}$$
$$= \Phi_1(G) \qquad\qquad \square$$

Theorem 4.5

(1) $\Phi_1(F \vee G) \ = \ \Phi_1(F) \ \vee \ \Phi_1(G)$

(2) $\Phi_1(F \wedge G) \ \Rightarrow \ \Phi_1(F) \wedge \Phi_1(G)$

(3) $\Phi_1(\exists h \bullet F) \ = \ \exists h \bullet \Phi_1(F)$

(4) $\Phi_1(F\,\hat{}\,G) \ \Rightarrow \ \Phi_1(F)\,\hat{}\,\Phi_1(G)$

(5) $\Phi_1(F^*) \ \Rightarrow \ (\Phi_1(F))^*$

(6) $\Phi_1(F\backslash\backslash G) \ \Rightarrow \ (\Phi_1(F)\backslash\backslash\Phi_1(G))$

(7) $\Phi_1(F \lhd b(\overleftarrow{X}) \rhd G) \ = \ \Phi_1(F) \ \lhd b(\overleftarrow{X}) \rhd \ \Phi_1(G)$

Proof of (3) $\Phi_1(F\,\hat{}\,Q) \qquad\qquad \{(\backslash\backslash - 5)\}$
$$= \quad (F\,\hat{}\,G) \ \vee \ ((\mathbf{unit}\backslash\backslash F)\,\hat{}\,(\mathbf{true}\backslash\backslash G)) \ \vee$$
$$((\mathbf{true}\backslash\backslash F)\,\hat{}\,(\mathbf{true}\backslash\backslash Q)) \ \vee \ (\mathbf{true}\backslash\backslash F)\,\hat{}\,(\mathbf{unit}\backslash\backslash G) \qquad \{(\backslash\backslash - 7)\}$$
$$= \quad (F\,\hat{}\,G) \ \vee \ (\mathbf{true}\backslash\backslash F)\,\hat{}\,(\mathbf{true}\backslash\backslash G) \qquad \{(int - 4)\}$$
$$\Rightarrow \quad (F \vee (\mathbf{true}\backslash\backslash F))\,\hat{}\,(G \vee (\mathbf{true}\backslash\backslash G)) \qquad \{\text{Def of } \Phi_1\}$$
$$= \quad \Phi_1(P)\,\hat{}\,\Phi_1(Q) \qquad\qquad \square$$

Theorem 4.6 (Closure of monotonic formulae)

If F and G are monotonic, so are $F \vee G$, $F \wedge G$, $F\,\hat{}\,G$, F^*, $F\backslash\backslash G$, $F \lhd b(\overleftarrow{X}) \rhd G$, and $\exists h \bullet F$.

Proof Assume that both F and G are monotonic.
$$F\,\hat{}\,G \qquad\qquad \{(X \Rightarrow \Phi_1(X))\}$$
$$\Rightarrow \Phi_1(F\,\hat{}\,G) \qquad\qquad \{\text{Theorem 4.5(3)}\}$$
$$\Rightarrow \Phi_1(F)\,\hat{}\,\Phi_1(G) \qquad \{F \ = \ \Phi_1(F) \text{ and } G \ = \ \Phi_1(G)\}$$
$$= F\,\hat{}\,G$$
which implies that $F\,\hat{}\,G \ = \ \Phi_1(F\,\hat{}\,G)$ as required. $\qquad\qquad \square$

4.2   *DI* Approachable

Definition 4.7 (*DI* approachable formulae)

If the behaviour of F over continuous intervals is determined by its behaviour over discrete intervals, then it is said to be *DI* approachable, i.e.,

$$\forall \mathcal{M}, \forall \sigma \bullet (\sigma \in CI \Rightarrow (\mathcal{M}_\sigma(F) \ = \ \bigvee_{\rho \in DI \ \wedge \ \rho \leq \sigma} \mathcal{M}_\rho(F))) \qquad \square$$

Examples 4.8

(1) **true, false, unit** and $l > 0$ are all DI approachable.

(2) $\Diamond(X = 1)$ is DI approachable.

(3) $\sharp = 0$ is monotonic, but not DI approachable.

(4) $\sharp \leq 2$ is DI approachable, but not monotonic.

(5) $\mathbf{stb}(X)$ is neither DI approachable nor monotonic.   □

Define

$$\Phi_2(F) \ =_{df} \ (\sharp \leq 2) \backslash\backslash F$$

Theorem 4.9

F is DI approachable iff $F \ = \ \Phi_2(F)$ □

Corollary DI approachable formulae form a complete lattice.   □

Theorem 4.10

F is DI approachable iff it lies in the image set of Φ_2.

Proof $(\sharp \leq 2)\backslash\backslash(\sharp \leq 2)$ $\{(\backslash\backslash - 8) \text{ and } (\backslash\backslash - 3)\}$

$\quad = \quad (\sharp \leq 2)\backslash\backslash(\sharp = 1) \vee (\sharp \leq 2)\backslash\backslash(\sharp = 2)$ $\{(\backslash\backslash - 2), \ (\backslash\backslash - 9) \text{ and } (\backslash\backslash - 10)\}$

$\quad = \quad (\sharp \leq 2) \wedge (\sharp = 1) \vee (\sharp \leq 2) \wedge (l > 0)$ $\{(int - 1)\}$

$\quad = \quad \sharp \leq 2$

which together $(\backslash\backslash - 2)$ implies that Φ_2 is idempotent.   □

Theorem 4.11

(1) $\Phi_2(F \vee G) \ = \ \Phi_2(F) \vee \Phi_2(G)$

(2) $\Phi_2(F \wedge G) \ = \ \Phi_2(F) \wedge \Phi_2(G)$

(3) $\Phi_2(F \hat{\ } G) \ = \ \Phi_2(F)\hat{\ }\Phi_2(G)$

(4) $\Phi_2(\exists h \bullet F) \ = \ \exists h \bullet \Phi_2(F)$

(5) $\Phi_2(F^*) \ = \ (\Phi_2(F))^*$

(6) $\Phi_2(F \backslash\backslash G) \ = \ \Phi_2(F) \backslash\backslash G$

(7) $\Phi_2(F \triangleleft b(\overleftarrow{X}) \triangleright G) \ = \ \Phi_2(F) \ \triangleleft b(\overleftarrow{X}) \triangleright \ \Phi_2(G)$

Proof $\Phi_2(F \hat{\ } G)$ $\{(\backslash\backslash - 5)\}$

$\quad = \quad (\mathbf{unit}\backslash\backslash F)\hat{\ }\Phi_2(G) \ \vee \ \Phi_2(F)\hat{\ }\Phi_2(G) \vee$

$\qquad \Phi_2(F)\hat{\ }(\mathbf{unit}\backslash\backslash G)$ $\{(\backslash\backslash - 2) \text{ and } (int - 14)\}$

$\quad = \quad \Phi_2(F \wedge \mathbf{unit})\hat{\ }\Phi_2(G) \ \vee \ \Phi_2(F)\hat{\ }\Phi_2(G) \vee$

$\qquad \Phi_2(F)\hat{\ }\Phi_2(G \wedge \mathbf{unit})$ $\{(\backslash\backslash - 7)\}$

$\quad = \quad \Phi_2(F)\hat{\ }\Phi_2(G)$ □

Theorem 4.12 (Closure of DI-approachable formulae)

If F and G are DI-approachable, so are $F \vee G$, $F \wedge G$, $F \hat{\ } G$, F^*, $F \backslash\backslash H$ (for all H) and $\exists h \bullet F$.   □

4.3   Continuity

Definition 4.13
A formula F is continuous if for any model and for any time interval σ

$$\mathcal{M}_\sigma(F) \;=\; \bigvee\nolimits_{\rho \in DI \,\wedge\, \rho \leq \sigma} \mathcal{M}_\rho(F) \qquad\qquad \square$$

Examples 4.14
(1) **true** and **false** are continuous.
(2) Let x be a global variable. Then the predicate $p(x, l)$ is continuous.
(3) Let $E1$ and $E2$ be expressions of state variables. $\overrightarrow{E1}{=}\overleftarrow{E2}$ is continuous. $\square$

Define

$$\Phi_3(F) \;=_{df}\; \mathbf{true}\backslash\backslash F$$

Theorem 4.15
F is continuous **iff** $F \;=\; \Phi_3(F)$ $\qquad\qquad\qquad\qquad\qquad\qquad\qquad\quad \square$

Corollary Continuous formulae form a complete lattice. $\qquad\qquad\qquad\quad \square$

Theorem 4.16
F is continuous **iff** it is monotonic and DI approachable.

$$
\begin{array}{llll}
\textbf{Proof of } (\Rightarrow) & \Phi_2(F) & & \{F \;=\; \Phi_3(F)\}\\[2pt]
= & (\sharp \leq 2)\backslash\backslash(\mathbf{true}\backslash\backslash F) & & \{(\backslash\backslash - 1)\}\\[2pt]
= & ((\sharp \leq 2)\backslash\backslash\mathbf{true})\backslash\backslash F & & \{\text{Example } 4.7(1)\}\\[2pt]
= & \mathbf{true}\backslash\backslash F & & \{F \;=\; \Phi_3(F)\}\\[2pt]
= & F & & \{F \;=\; \Phi_3(F)\}\\[2pt]
= & F \;\vee\; \Phi_3(F) & & \{\text{Def of } \Phi_3\}\\[2pt]
= & F \;\vee\; (\mathbf{true}\backslash\backslash F) & & \{\text{Def of } \Phi_1\}\\[2pt]
= & \Phi_1(F) & &\\[6pt]
(\Leftarrow) & F & \{(\backslash\backslash - 1) \text{ and } F \;=\; \Phi_2(F) \;=\; \Phi_1(F)\} &\\[2pt]
= & ((\sharp \leq 2)\backslash\backslash\mathbf{true})\backslash\backslash F & \{\text{Example } 4.7(1)\} &\\[2pt]
= & \mathbf{true}\backslash\backslash F & \{\text{Def of } \Phi_3\} &\\[2pt]
= & \Phi_3(F) & & \square
\end{array}
$$

Theorem 4.17
F is continuous **iff** it lies in the image set of Φ_3.

Proof From the fact that $\mathbf{true}\backslash\backslash\mathbf{true} \;=\; \mathbf{true}$. $\qquad\qquad\qquad\qquad\quad \square$

Theorem 4.18
(1) $\Phi_3(F \vee G) \;=\; \Phi_3(F) \vee \Phi_3(G)$
(2) $\Phi_3(F \wedge G) \;\Rightarrow\; \Phi_3(F) \wedge \Phi_3(G)$
(3) $\Phi_3(F \,\hat{} \, G) \;=\; \Phi_3(F) \,\hat{} \, \Phi_3(G)$
(4) $\Phi_3(\exists h \bullet F) \;=\; \exists h \bullet \Phi_3(F)$

(5) $\Phi_3(F^*) = (\Phi_3(F))^*$

(6) $\Phi_3(F\backslash\backslash G) = \Phi_3(F)\backslash\backslash G$

(7) $\Phi_2(F \lhd b(\overleftarrow{X}) \rhd G) = \Phi_2(F) \lhd b(\overleftarrow{X}) \rhd \Phi_2(G)$ □

Theorem 4.19 (Closure of continuous formulae)
If F and G are continuous, so are $F \vee G$, $F \wedge G$, $F^\frown G$, F^*, $F\backslash\backslash H$ (for all H)
and $\exists h \bullet F$.   □

4.4   Temporal Programs

Let E be an expression of state variables. The formula $\mathbf{stb}(E)$ holds on
an interval σ if the value of E remains unchanged throughout that interval.

$$\mathbf{stb}(E) =_{df} \exists x \bullet \Box_t(\overleftrightarrow{E} = x)$$

The formula $\mathbf{stb}^-(E)$ is true on σ if the value of E remains changed except at
the end of that interval.

$$\mathbf{stb}^-(E) =_{df} \exists x \bullet \Box_t(l > 0 \Rightarrow (\overleftarrow{E} = x))$$

Let $\underline{E} = < E_1, \ldots, E_n >$ be a list of expressions. We define

$$\mathbf{stb}(\underline{E}) =_{df} \mathbf{stb}(E_1) \wedge \ldots \wedge \mathbf{stb}(E_n)$$

The formula $\mathbf{stb}^-(\underline{E})$ can be defined in a similar way.

(stb-1) $\mathbf{stb}(\underline{E}) \wedge \mathbf{unit} = \mathbf{unit} = \mathbf{stb}^-(\underline{E}) \wedge \mathbf{unit}$

(stb-2) $\mathbf{stb}(\underline{E}) = \mathbf{stb}^-(\underline{E}) \wedge (\overleftarrow{E}=\overrightarrow{E})$

(stb-3) $\mathbf{stb}(\underline{E}) \wedge (F^\frown G) = (\mathbf{stb}(\underline{E}) \wedge F)^\frown(\mathbf{stb}(\underline{E}) \wedge G)$

(stb-4) $\mathbf{stb}^-(\underline{E})\backslash\backslash\mathbf{stb}^-(\underline{E}) = \mathbf{stb}^-(\underline{E})$

(stb-5) $\mathbf{stb}^-(< X, Y, \ldots, Z >)^* = \mathbf{stb}^-(X)^* \wedge \mathbf{stb}^-(< Y, \ldots, Z >)^*$

(stb-6) $\mathbf{stb}^-(< X, Y, \ldots, Z >)\backslash\backslash\mathbf{stb}^-(\underline{E}(X, Y, \ldots, Z)) =$

$\qquad \mathbf{stb}^-(< X, Y, \ldots, Z >)^* \wedge \mathbf{stb}^-(\underline{E}(X, Y, \ldots, Z))$

Definition 4.20 (Program variable)
A state variable X is a *program variable* if it is identified as a right continuous
step function with finite variability, i.e.

$$\mathbf{stb}^-(X)^* = \mathbf{true}$$ □

Definition 4.21 (Program)
A formula F is said to be a *temporal program* of variables $X, Y \ldots, Z$ if

$$F = \mathbf{stb}^-(< X, Y, \ldots, Z >)\backslash\backslash F$$

We will use $\underline{VAR}$ to abbreviate the list $< X, Y, \ldots, Z >$ of state variables henceforth.   □

Examples 4.22
(1) **true** and **false** are temporal programs.
(2) From (stb-1) and $(\backslash\backslash - 2)$ it follows that **unit** is a program.

(3) Let p be a predicate, and x a global variable. From $(\backslash\backslash - 12)$ and Corollary of Theorem 3.1 we conclude that $p(l, x)$ is a temporal program.

(4) Let $E1$ and $E2$ be expressions of program variables $X, Y, \ldots, Z$. $\overrightarrow{E1}=\overleftarrow{E2}$ is a temporal program.

(5) $\mathbf{stb}^-(b)$ and $\mathbf{stb}(b)$ are temporal programs.   □

Theorem 4.23
A monotonic formula F is a temporal program of $X, Y, \ldots, Z$ **iff** F is continuous.

Proof of ($\Leftarrow$) F .... $\{F \text{ is continuous}\}$

$\quad = \quad \mathbf{true}\backslash\backslash F$ .... $\{(\mathbf{stb} - 6)\}$

$\quad = \quad (\mathbf{stb}^-(\underline{VAR})^*)\backslash\backslash F$ .... $\{\text{Corollary of Theorem 3.1}\}$

$\quad = \quad (\mathbf{stb}^-(\underline{VAR})\backslash\backslash\mathbf{true})\backslash\backslash F$ .... $\{(\backslash\backslash - 1)\}$

$\quad = \quad \mathbf{stb}^-(\underline{VAR})\backslash\backslash(\mathbf{true}\backslash\backslash F)$ .... $\{F \text{ is continuous}\}$

$\quad = \quad \mathbf{stb}^-(\underline{VAR})\backslash\backslash F$

$\quad (\Rightarrow) \quad F$ .... $\{F \text{ is monotonic}\}$

$\quad = \quad F \vee (\mathbf{true}\backslash\backslash F)$ .... $\{F \text{ is a program}\}$

$\quad = \quad (\mathbf{stb}^-(\underline{VAR})\backslash\backslash F) \vee (\mathbf{true}\backslash\backslash F)$ .... $\{(\backslash\backslash - 7)\}$

$\quad = \quad \mathbf{true}\backslash\backslash F$ □

Theorem 4.24
F is a temporal program **iff** there is a formula G such that

$$F = \mathbf{stb}^-(\underline{VAR})\backslash\backslash G$$

Proof $\mathbf{stb}^-(\underline{VAR})\backslash\backslash(\mathbf{stb}^-(\underline{VAR})\backslash\backslash G)$ .... $\{(\backslash\backslash - 1)\}$

$\quad = \quad (\mathbf{stb}^-(\underline{VAR})\backslash\backslash\mathbf{stb}^-(\underline{VAR}))\backslash\backslash G$ .... $\{(\mathbf{stb} - 4)\}$

$\quad = \quad \mathbf{stb}^-(\underline{VAR})\backslash\backslash G$ □

Theorem 4.25
(1) Temporal programs form a complete lattice.

(2) If F and G are temporal programs, so are $F \vee G$, $F\,\widehat{}\,G$, F^*, $F \triangleleft b \triangleright G$ and $\exists h \bullet F$.   □

Example 4.26 (Temporal assignment)
Let $E1$ and $E2$ be the expressions of program variables.
The notation $E1 \leftarrow E2$ denotes a *temporal assignment*, which holds on the interval σ if the final value of $E1$ and the initial value of $E2$ are the same.

$$E1 \leftarrow E2 \;=_{df}\; \overrightarrow{E1}=\overleftarrow{E2}$$

Example 4.22(3) indicates that $E1 \leftarrow E2$ is a temporal program.   □

Example 4.27 (Assignment)

Conventional programming language assignments $X := E$ usually incorporate additional assumptions that are not captured by temporal assignments. Typically, all program variables but X are assumed to remain unchanged, and the update on X occurs at the end of the interval.

$$X := E \ =_{df} \ (X \leftarrow E) \ \wedge \ (\mathbf{stb}^-(X) \wedge \mathbf{stb}(Y) \wedge \ldots \wedge \mathbf{stb}(Z)) \qquad \square$$

5   VERILOG Timing Controlled Statements

The VERILOG hardware description language [11] is widely used to model the structure and behaviour of digital systems ranging from simple hardware building blocks to complete systems. Its semantics is based on scheduling of events and the propagation of changes. In this section we are going to examine the VERILOG timing controlled statements and the delayed assignments.

Timing controls are used in VERILOG for scheduling. They are either delay (#e) or *guards*. Guards are either *level sensitive* ($\mathbf{wait}(b)$) or *edge sensitive* ($\Delta(b)$, $\Uparrow (b)$ or $\Downarrow (b)$).

Let P be a program, and e an expression. The VERILOG statement #$e \,\&P$ postpones the execution of P for e time units.

$$\#e \ P \ =_{df} \ (l = \overleftarrow{e})^\frown P$$

Let b be a Boolean expression of program variables. $\mathbf{wait}(b)\&P$ fires the program P whenever the guard b becomes true.

$$\mathbf{wait}(b) \,\& \, P \ =_{df} \ (\mathbf{unit} \lhd b \rhd \mathbf{stb}^-(b))^\frown (P \lhd b \rhd \mathbf{stb}(b))$$

$\Uparrow (b) \,\& \, P$ executes the program P whenever the value of b switches from ff to tt.

$$\Uparrow (b) \,\& \, P \ =_{df} \ (\mathbf{stb}^-(b)^\frown(\mathbf{stb}(b) \lhd b \rhd (\mathbf{wait}(b)\&P))) \ \lhd b \rhd \ (\mathbf{wait}(b)\&P)$$

Its dual, denoted by $\Downarrow (b) \,\& \, P$, executes P whenever the value of b goes back to ff.

$$\Downarrow (b) \,\& \, P \ =_{df} \ \Uparrow (\neg b) \,\&P$$

$\Delta(b) \,\& \, P$ executes the program P once the Boolean expression b changes its value.

$$\Delta(b) \,\& \, P \ =_{df} \ (\mathbf{wait}(\neg b) \,\& \, P) \lhd b \rhd (\mathbf{wait}(b) \,\& \, P)$$

The notation $X \ = \ \#e \, E$ denotes a delayed assignment which evaluates the value of E, and then assigns it to X after e time units delay.

$$X \ = \ \#e \, E \ =_{df} \ \exists c \bullet (\overleftarrow{E} = c) \ \wedge \ (\#e \, \&(X \leftarrow c))$$

The delayed assignment $X \ = \ \mathbf{wait}(b) \, E$ evaluates the value of E first, and assigns it to X whenever b becomes true.

$$(X \ = \ \mathbf{wait} \, b \, E) \ =_{df} \ \exists c \bullet (\overleftarrow{E} = c) \ \wedge \ (\mathbf{wait}(b) \,\&(X \leftarrow c))$$

From Theorem 4.25 it follows that all timing controlled statements and the delayed assignments are temporal programs. $\qquad \square$

6   Clock

In this section, we choose natural numbers as the end points of the intervals:

$$\mathcal{E} \ =_{df} \ Nat$$

As a result, every interval has integer length

$$\exists n \in Nat \bullet (l = n) \ = \ \textbf{true}$$

and $(\textbf{stb} - 4)$ can be strengthen to

$(\textbf{stb}\text{-4a})$ $(\textbf{stb}^-(\underline{E}) \wedge l \leq 1)\backslash\backslash\textbf{stb}^-(\underline{E}) \ = \ \textbf{stb}^-(\underline{E})$

Definition 6.1 (Register)
A state variable X is a register variable if its value changes only at the end points.

$$\textbf{stb}^-(X)^* \ = \ \textbf{true} \qquad\qquad \Box$$

Definition 6.2 (Fullness)
A time interval σ is *full* if it contains all the end points of $\mathcal{E}$ lying between $\sigma.b$ and $\sigma.e$, i.e.

$$\{n \mid n \in \mathcal{E} \ \wedge \ (\sigma.b \leq n \leq \sigma.e)\} \subseteq \sigma$$

All the intervals in CI are full. The discrete interval $< 0, 1, 2 >$ is full, but $< 0, 2 >$ is not.

Define

$$\textbf{full} \ =_{df} \ (\sharp = 0) \ \vee \ (\sharp = l + 1)$$

It is obvious that **full** holds on σ **iff** σ is full. Furthermore, if σ is full, so are its subintervals.

$(\textbf{full-1})$ $\Box\,\textbf{full} \ = \ \textbf{full}$

$(\textbf{full-2})$ $\Box_t\,\textbf{full} \ = \ \textbf{full}$ \qquad\qquad $\Box$

Theorem 6.3
If $\underline{VAR} =_{df} < X, Y, \ldots, Z >$ is a list of register variables then

$$(\textbf{stb}^-(\underline{VAR}) \wedge (l \leq 1))^* \ = \ \textbf{full} \qquad\qquad \Box$$

Definition 6.4 (Clocked program)
F is a *clocked program* of register variables of $\underline{VAR}$ if

$$F \ = \ (\textbf{stb}^-(\underline{VAR}) \wedge l \leq 1)\backslash\backslash F \qquad\qquad \Box$$

Theorem 6.5 (Additional healthiness condition)
F is a clocked program **iff** F is a temporal program satisfying $F \ = \ F \wedge \textbf{full}$

Proof of $(\Rightarrow)$ $\textbf{stb}^-(\underline{VAR})\backslash\backslash F$ \hfill $\{\text{Def. 6.4}\}$

$\ = \ (\textbf{stb}^-(\underline{VAR})\backslash\backslash(\textbf{stb}^-(\underline{VAR}) \wedge (l \leq 1)))\backslash\backslash F$ \hfill $\{(\backslash\backslash - 12)\}$

$\ = \ ((\textbf{stb}^-(\underline{VAR})\backslash\backslash\textbf{stb}^-(\underline{VAR})) \wedge (l \leq 1))\backslash\backslash F$ \hfill $\{(\textbf{stb} - 4)\}$

$\ = \ (\textbf{stb}^-(\underline{VAR}) \wedge (l \leq 1))\backslash\backslash F$ \hfill $\{\text{Def. 6.4}\}$

$\ = \ F$

which implies that F is a temporal program. From $(\backslash\backslash - 3)$ and the fact that

$$F = (\mathbf{stb}^-(VAR) \wedge (l \leq 1))\backslash\backslash F$$

we conclude that $F = F \wedge \mathbf{full}$.

$$
\begin{array}{lll}
(\Leftarrow)\quad F & & \{\text{Def. 5.2}\} \\
= (\mathbf{stb}^-(\underline{VAR})\backslash\backslash F) & & \{(\mathbf{stb} - 4a)\} \\
= ((\mathbf{stb}^-(\underline{VAR}) \wedge l \leq 1)\backslash\backslash\mathbf{stb}^-(\underline{VAR}))\backslash\backslash F & & \{(\backslash\backslash - 1)\} \\
= (\mathbf{stb}^-(\underline{VAR}) \wedge l \leq 1)\backslash\backslash F & & \square
\end{array}
$$

Theorem 6.6
If F is a clocked program then F is monotonic. $\square$

Corollary
F is a clocked program **iff** F is continuous and satisfies

$$F = F \wedge \mathbf{full}$$

Proof of $(\Rightarrow)$ From Theorems 6.5 and 6.6 it follows that F is a monotonic program satisfying $F = F \wedge \mathbf{full}$. The conclusion that F is also continuous follows directly from Theorem 4.23.

$(\Leftarrow)$ The conclusion follows from Theorems 4.23 and 6.5. $\square$

Theorem 6.7
(1) Clocked programs form a complete lattice.

(2) If F and G are clocked programs, so are $F^\frown G$, $F \vee G$, $F \wedge G$, $(\neg F \wedge \mathbf{full})$, $\exists x \bullet F$, $F \lhd b(\overleftarrow{X}) \rhd G$, $\square_t F$ and $\square F$. $\square$

Examples 6.8
(1) **false** and **full** are clocked programs.

(2) Let $p(\overleftarrow{X}, \overrightarrow{X}, l)$ be a predicate. Then $p(X, X', l) \wedge \mathbf{full}$ is a clocked program.

(3) Let X be a register variable. Then $\mathbf{stb}(X) \wedge \mathbf{full}$ is a clocked program. $\square$

TEMPURA [4, 9] is a computer programming language that is especially good at expression temporal behaviour. The following are several built-in operators for constructing TEMPURA programs.

The notation *empty* is used to mark termination.

$$empty =_{df} \mathbf{unit}$$

From the fact that

$$(\mathbf{stb}^-(\underline{VAR}) \wedge (l \leq 1))\backslash\backslash\mathbf{unit} = \mathbf{stb}^-(\underline{VAR}) \wedge \mathbf{unit} = \mathbf{unit}$$

it follows that *empty* is a clocked program.

The operator **next** is used to describe what happen next, where "next" means "after one unit of time".

$$\mathbf{next}\ F =_{df} (l = 1)^\frown F$$

From Theorem 6.7 it follows that **next** preserves clocked programs.

Something is considered to happen *always* if it happens immediately and then again after each time unit.

$$\textbf{always } F \ =_{df} \ \Box_t \, F$$

Clearly **always** also preserves clocked programs.

The formula **halt** F holds on the interval σ **iff** F holds on the interval $<\sigma.e>$.

$$\textbf{halt } F \ =_{df} \ \textbf{always } (\textbf{full} \ \wedge \ (empty \equiv F))$$

From Theorem 6.7 it follows that if F is a clocked program so is **halt** F.

The assignment **assign**(A, B) asserts that the final value of A is equal to the initial value of B.

$$\textbf{assign}(A, B) \ =_{df} \ (A \leftarrow B) \wedge \textbf{full}$$

From Example 6.8(2) we conclude that **assign**(A, B) is a clocked program.

Unit-assignment is an assignment which completes its execution in one time unit.

$$\textbf{uassign}(A, B) \ =_{df} \ (l = 1) \ \wedge \ \textbf{assign}(A, B)$$

Both $(l = 1)$ and **assign**(A, B) are clocked programs, so is their conjunction **uassign**(A, B).

Another kind of assignment that occurs frequently is initialisation. It can be achieved in zero-time.

$$\textbf{iassign}(A, B) \ =_{df} \ empty \wedge \textbf{assign}(A, B)$$

From Example 6.8(2) it follows that the initialisation is a clocked program.

TEMPERA statement **gets**(A, B) is used to express the repeated assignment.

$$\textbf{gets}(A, B) \ =_{df} \ \textbf{always} \ (empty \vee \exists x \bullet x = \overleftarrow{B} \ \wedge \ \textbf{next} \, (\overleftarrow{A} = x)))$$

From Theorem 6.7 it follows that **gets**(A, B) is also a clocked program.

References

[1] M. Abadi and Z. Manna. Temporal logic programming. Proc. IEEE Symposium on Logic Programming, (1987).

[2] M.R. Barbacci. Instruction Set Processor Specifications (ISPS): The notation and its application. IEEE Trans. Comp. 30: 24–40, (1981).

[3] M. Gordon. Proving a computer correct. Technical Report 42, University of Cambridge Computer Laboratory, (1983).

[4] R.W.S. Hale. Programming in Temporal Logic. Technical Report 173, Computing Laboratory, University of Cambridge, (1980).

[5] J. Halpern, Z. Manna and B. Moszkowski. A hardware semantics based on temporal intervals. In Proc. of 10th Internal Colloquium on Automata, Languages and Programming, 278–291, (1983).

[6] D. May and R. Shepherd. The transputer implementation of Occam. In Communication Process Architecture, 19–29, (1988).

[7] S. Mazor. A Guide to VHDL. Kluwer Publisher, (1992).

[8] B.C. Moszkowski. A Temporal Logic for multi-level reasoning about hardware. IEEE Computer 18(2): 10–19, (1985).

[9] B.C. Moszkowski. Executing Temporal Logic Programs. Cambridge University Press, Cambridge, (1986).

[10] A.C. Parker and J.J. Wallace. SLOIDE: An I/O hardware description language. IEEE Trans. Comp, 423–439, (1981).

[11] D.E. Thomas and P. Moorby. The VERILOG Hardware Description Language. Kluwer Publisher, (1991).

[12] Zhou Chaochen, C.A.R. Hoare and A.P. Ravn. A calculus of duration. Information Processing Letters 40(5): 269–275, (1991).

A Weakest Precondition Semantics for an Object-Oriented Language of Refinement

Ana Cavalcanti[1] and David A. Naumann[2]

[1] Departamento de Informática
Universidade Federal de Pernambuco, Po Box 7851 50740-540 Recife PE Brazil
Phone: +55 81 271 8430 Fax: +55 81 271 8438
alcc@di.ufpe.br   www.di.ufpe.br/~alcc
[2] Department of Computer Science
Stevens Institute of Technology, Hoboken NJ 07030 USA
naumann@cs.stevens-tech.edu   www.cs.stevens-tech.edu/~naumann

Abstract. We define a predicate-transformer semantics for an object-oriented language that includes specification constructs from refinement calculi. The language includes recursive classes, visibility control, dynamic binding, and recursive methods. Using the semantics, we formulate notions of refinement. Such results are a first step towards a refinement calculus.

Keywords: refinement calculi, semantic models, object-orientation, verification

1   Introduction

There has been extensive study of formal type-systems for object-oriented languages, and some study of formal specification, but formalization of development methods [BKS98, Lan95] lags behind both the language features and the informal methods presently used. This paper presents a semantic basis for formal development of programs in languages like Java and C++. Our language, called ROOL (for Refinement Object-oriented Language), is sufficiently similar to Java to be used in meaningful case studies and to capture some of the central difficulties, yet it is sufficiently constrained to make it possible to give a comprehensible semantics.

We assume the reader is familiar with basic concepts and terminology of object-oriented programming. We address the following challenging issues.

- Dynamic binding of methods means that the version of a method that will be invoked is determined only at run time. Such programs exhibit phenomena similar to higher-order imperative programs.
- Classes are important in practice for modularity, but they are complicated to model (for which reason many studies focus on instance-oriented subtyping).
- Object-oriented programs involve fine-grained control of visibility in terms of private, inherited, and public identifiers.

Our language has mutually recursive classes and recursive methods. We omit reference types, however. Pointers are ubiquitous in practice, but so are techniques

J. Wing, J. Woodcock, J. Davies (Eds.): FM'99, Vol. II, LNCS 1709, pp. 1439–1459, 1999.

to isolate deliberate sharing from the many situations where value semantics is preferable. Our object values are tuples with recursive nesting but no sharing. We leave pointers as an important but separate issue [AdB94].

Our work is part of a project that aims to extend to object-oriented programming the most widely-used and well-developed formal methods – those associated with Hoare logic and weakest preconditions. Because behavioural subclassing involves intermingled programs and specifications [LW94], it is natural to extend a refinement calculus [Mor94, BvW98]. As usual in refinement calculi, our semantics is based on weakest preconditions.

In the approach we adopt, commands denote functions on formulas. In isolation, purely syntactic transformer semantics is dubious. While our collaborators are developing a state-transformer semantics which will make it possible to prove operational soundness, we have taken the preliminary step of giving a set-theoretic semantics for predicate formulas and expressions, for the type-correctness results. Object states are represented by tuples of attribute values, and in general types denote sets of values. Methods are treated as procedures with a distinguished self parameter. Classes denote tuples of method meanings. Predicate formulas denote sets of states. The interplay between the value-oriented semantics of expressions and the formula-oriented semantics of commands is mediated by the semantics of formulas.

The semantics is based on a typing system. In the methodological literature simpler approaches are usually taken: there is a fixed global typing, or untyped variables are used and types are treated as predicates. A fixed global typing is unsuitable for formulating laws about subclasses and inheritance; and treating types as predicates risks inconsistency in the presence of higher-order phenomena. We employ techniques that have become standard in type theory and denotational semantics; the semantics is defined in terms of typing derivations, which provides convenient access to necessary contextual information.

We do not treat more advanced notions of subtyping than those in Java: we are interested in reasoning about type casts and tests as they are used in Java and its cousin languages. The typing system is similar to that of [Nau98b], and also to those used in typing algorithms, where subsumption is incorporated into rules for different constructs rather than being present as a general rule. Nonetheless, soundness of our definitions is not at all obvious, due to subtleties of modelling dynamic binding as well as mutually recursive classes. In this paper, we disallow mutually recursive methods, which lets us use a simpler, though non-trivial, well-ordering to show the semantics is well defined.

The main contribution of this paper is the extension of standard weakest precondition semantics to a Java-like language with classes, visibility, dynamic binding, and recursion. We give basic results on soundness of the definitions, define notions of program and class refinement, and show that the constructors of ROOL are monotonic with respect to refinement. Our semantics is being used in ongoing research on practical specification and verification. For reasons of space we omit many definitions and proofs that appear in [CN99].

$$
\begin{array}{lll}
e \in \mathit{Exp} & ::= \mathbf{self} \mid \mathbf{super} \mid \mathbf{null} \mid \mathbf{new}\ N & \\
& \mid x \mid f(e) & \text{variable, built-in application} \\
& \mid e\ \mathbf{is}\ N \mid (N)e & \text{type test, type cast} \\
& \mid e.x \mid (e;\ x : e) & \text{attribute selection and update} \\
\psi \in \mathit{Pred} & ::= e \mid e\ \mathbf{isExactly}\ N & \text{boolean expression, exact type test} \\
& \mid (\vee\ i \bullet \psi_i) \mid \psi \Rightarrow \psi \mid \forall\, x : T \bullet \psi & \\
c \in \mathit{Com} & ::= le := e \mid c;\ c & \text{multiple assignment, sequence} \\
& \mid x : [\psi, \psi] & \text{specification statement} \\
& \mid pc(e) & \text{parameterized command application} \\
& \mid \mathbf{if}\ []i \bullet \psi_i \rightarrow c_i\ \mathbf{fi} & \text{alternation} \\
& \mid \mathbf{rec}\ Y \bullet c\ \mathbf{end} \mid Y & \text{recursion, recursive call} \\
& \mid \mathbf{var}\ x : T \bullet c\ \mathbf{end} & \text{local variable block} \\
& \mid \mathbf{avar}\ x : T \bullet c\ \mathbf{end} & \text{angelic variable block} \\
pc \in \mathit{PCom} & ::= pds \bullet c & \text{parameterization} \\
& \mid m \mid le.m & \text{method calls} \\
pds \in \mathit{Pds} & ::= \varnothing \mid pd \mid pd;\ pds & \text{parameter declarations} \\
pd \in \mathit{Pd} & ::= \mathbf{val}\ x : T \mid \mathbf{res}\ x : T \mid \mathbf{vres}\ x : T & \\
\end{array}
$$

Table 1. Expressions, selected predicates, commands, and parameterized commands.

2   Language

The imperative constructs of ROOL are based on the language of Morgan's refinement calculus [Mor94], which extends Dijkstra's language of guarded commands. Specifications are regarded as commands; we use the word command to refer to specifications, commands in the traditional sense, and hybrids where programming structures and specifications are mixed.

Data types T are the types of attributes, local variables, method parameters, and expressions. They are either primitive (**bool**, **int**, and others) or class names N. Primitives may include functional types such as arrays of integers.

The expressions e are generated by a rule in Table 1. We assume that x stands for a variable identifier, and f for a literal or built-in function. Built-ins should include primitive predicates like equality. The update $(e_1;\ x : e_2)$ denotes a fresh object copied from e_1 but with the attribute x mapped to a copy of e_2. Attribute selection $e.x$ is a run-time error in states where e denotes **null**, and $(N)e$ is an error if the value of e is not of dynamic type N. The type test $e\ \mathbf{is}\ N$ checks whether non-null e has type N; it is false if e is **null**, like `instanceof` in Java. The predicates ψ of ROOL include formulas of first-order logic, program expressions of type **bool**, and exact type tests $e\ \mathbf{isExactly}\,N$.

We identify a subset Le of Exp; these left-expressions can appear as the target of assignments and method calls, and as result and value-result arguments.

$$
le \in \mathit{Le}\ ::=\ le1 \mid \mathbf{self} \mid \mathbf{self}.le1 \qquad\qquad le1 \in \mathit{Le}1\ ::=\ x \mid le1.x
$$

Assignments to **self** and method calls with **self** as a result or value-result argument would never appear in user programs, but they are used in the semantics. We allow le in $le := e$ to range over finite non-empty sequences of left-expressions, and e over corresponding lists.

For alternation we use an informal indexed notation for finite sets of guarded commands. Specification statements are as in [Mor94]. Methods are defined using procedure abstractions in the form of Back's parameterized commands **val** $x : T \bullet c$, **res** $x : T \bullet c$, or **vres** $x : T \bullet c$ [CSW99]. These correspond to parameter passing by copy: call-by-value, by-result, and by-value-result, respectively. In each case, x stands for a finite sequence of variable identifiers, T for a corresponding list of types, and c for a command. We use x to stand both for a single variable and for lists of variables; the context should make clear which one is meant. The same comment applies to our uses of e and T.

A parameterized command can be applied to a list of arguments to yield a command. A method call is a parameterized command. A call m refers to a method of the current object; a call $le.m$ refers to a method associated with the object that is the current value of le. We do not allow method calls $e_1.m(e)$ where e_1 is a general expression, because it is convenient in the semantic definitions that the object is named by a variable (the same is done in [AL97]). If e_1 is not a left-expression, $e_1.m(e)$ is equivalent to **var** $x : T \bullet x := e_1; \ x.m(e)$ **end**, where x is fresh. This is not an adequate replacement for $e_1.m(e)$, when e_1 is a left-expression, because it does not make persistent the changes to e_1. However, calls of the form $le.m(e)$ are available in ROOL.

A program is a sequence of class declarations followed by a command.

$$
\begin{aligned}
&Program \ ::= cds \bullet c \\
&cds \in Cds ::= \varnothing \mid cd \ cds \\
&cd \in Cd \quad ::= \textbf{class } N_1 \ [\textbf{extends } N_2] \\
&\qquad\qquad\qquad \textbf{pri } x_1 : T_1; \ \textbf{prot } x_2 : T_2; \ \{\textbf{meth } m \mathrel{\widehat{=}} (pds \bullet c) \ \textbf{end}\}^*; \\
&\qquad\qquad \textbf{end}
\end{aligned}
$$

A class declaration cd introduces a class named N_1. The optional **extends**-clause determines the immediate superclass of N_1. In its absence, N_1 extends **object**, which has no attributes or methods. The **pri** and **prot** clauses introduce the private and protected attributes of N_1 (recall that x_1 and x_2 can be lists). The visibility mechanism is similar to that of Java: private attributes are visible just inside the class, and protected attributes are visible in the class and in its subclasses. Following the **pri** and **prot** clauses, there is a list of method declarations. The method introduced by **meth** $m \mathrel{\widehat{=}} (pds \bullet c)$ **end** is named m; its body is the parameterized command $(pds \bullet c)$. All methods are considered to be public.

3   Typing

Besides the data types T, other phrase types θ are available for predicate formulas, commands, parameterized commands, and complete programs.

$$\theta ::= T \mid \textbf{pred} \mid \textbf{com} \mid \textbf{pcom}(pds) \mid \textbf{program}$$

The types of phrases, in the context of a collection of class declarations, a specific class, and some method parameter and local variable declarations, are given by the typing relation $\triangleright$. For example, $\Gamma, N \triangleright c : \mathbf{com}$ asserts that c is a command that can appear in the body of a method in class N. Here Γ is a typing environment; it records class declarations as well as locals for c: the attributes visible in N, and method parameters and local variables in scope. Similarly, $\Gamma, N \triangleright e : T$ asserts that in a method of N, e is an expression of type T.

3.1   Typing Environment

We assume the existence of two disjoint sets of names: the set *CName* of class names and the set *LName* of local names. A local may be either an attribute, a method, a method parameter, or a local variable. We also distinguish two class names: **object** and **main**. The former is the superclass of all classes. The latter does not refer to a class itself, but to the main part of a complete program.

A typing environment Γ is a record with six fields: *attr*, *meth*, *vis*, *cnames*, *supcls*, and *locals*. The first, *attr*, is a finite partial function $CName \nrightarrow LSignature$. An *LSignature* associates a local name with a type: $LSignature = LName \nrightarrow Type$. The field *attr* records the names and types of all declared and inherited attributes of every declared class. Similarly, *meth* records the names and signatures of all declared and inherited methods of the known classes: *meth* has type $CName \nrightarrow MDecs$ where $MDecs = LName \nrightarrow Pds$.

The third field of a typing environment, *vis*, records the visibility of the attributes of the declared classes: *vis* has type $CName \nrightarrow (LName \nrightarrow Visibility)$ where $Visibility = \{pri, prot, ipri\}$. If, we have that for an attribute x of a class N, $vis\ N\ x = pri$, then x is a private attribute of N that was declared (and not inherited) by N; the inherited private attributes of N are associated to *ipri*. Finally, *prot* refers to the protected (either inherited or declared) attributes.

The *cnames* field of a typing environment is a set containing the name of all declared classes: $cnames = \operatorname{dom} attr = \operatorname{dom} meth = \operatorname{dom} vis$. The distinguished class name **object** is supposed to be in *cnames*, while **main**, which does not refer to a class, is supposed not to be in *cnames*. Moreover, the class **object** is associated to the empty signature in both *attr* and *meth*.

The *supcls* field of a typing environment associates a class name to the name of its immediate superclass: *supcls* has type $CName \nrightarrow CName$. All declared classes have a direct superclass: either a class mentioned explicitly in their declarations or **object**. On the other hand, **object** itself does not have a superclass. Furthermore, a superclass is a declared class and the inheritance relationship is not allowed to have circularities. The subtype relation $\leq_\Gamma$ is defined by $T_1 \leq_\Gamma T_2 \Leftrightarrow (T_1, T_2) \in (\Gamma.supcls)^+ \vee T_1 = T_2$.

The last component of a typing environment, *locals*, is an *LSignature* that records the types of the visible atributes of the current class, and of any method parameter and local variables in scope. The attributes are also recorded in *attr*; this redundancy simplifies typing rules. The classes referred to in the signatures in the range of either *attr* or *meth* and in *locals* must be declared.

$$\frac{N \neq \mathbf{main}}{\Gamma, N \rhd \mathbf{self} : N} \qquad \frac{N' \in \Gamma.cnames}{\Gamma, N \rhd \mathbf{new}\ N' : N'} \qquad \frac{\Gamma, N \rhd e : N' \quad N'' \leq_\Gamma N'}{\Gamma, N \rhd e\ \mathbf{is}\ N'' : \mathbf{bool}}$$

$$\frac{\Gamma, N \rhd e : N' \quad N'' \leq_\Gamma N'}{\Gamma, N \rhd (N'')e : N''} \qquad \frac{\Gamma, N \rhd e : N' \quad \Gamma.attr\ N'\ x = T \quad visib\ \Gamma\ N'\ N\ x}{\Gamma, N \rhd e.x : T}$$

$$\frac{\Gamma \rhd e : \mathbf{bool}}{\Gamma \rhd e : \mathbf{pred}} \qquad \frac{\Gamma \rhd \psi_i : \mathbf{pred} \quad \text{for all } i}{\Gamma \rhd (\vee\ i \bullet \psi_i) : \mathbf{pred}} \qquad \frac{\Gamma;\ x : T \rhd \psi : \mathbf{pred}}{\Gamma \rhd \forall x : T \bullet \psi : \mathbf{pred}}$$

$$\frac{\Gamma, N \rhd e : N' \quad N'' \leq_\Gamma N'}{\Gamma, N \rhd e\ \mathbf{isExactly}\ N'' : \mathbf{pred}} \qquad \frac{(\Gamma;\ x : N'') \rhd \psi : \mathbf{pred} \quad N'' \leq_\Gamma N'}{(\Gamma;\ x : N') \rhd x\ \mathbf{isExactly}\ N'' \wedge \psi : \mathbf{pred}}$$

Table 2. Typing of selected expressions and predicates.

A typing $\Gamma, N \rhd$ *phrase* $: \theta$ holds just if it is well formed and is derivable using the rules to be presented in the sequel. Well formedness is characterised by three properties. First, Γ has to satisfy the conditions above for environments. Secondly, the current class must be declared: $N \neq \mathbf{main} \Rightarrow N \in \Gamma.cnames$. Thirdly, dom $\Gamma.locals$ should include all visible attributes of N, i.e. the declared private and the declared and inherited protected attributes – all but the inherited private ones. We assume that no parameter or local variable has the same name as an attribute of the class. If N is **main** there are no restrictions on $\Gamma.locals$, which contains only parameters and local variables.

3.2   Expressions and Predicates

Typing rules for some expressions and predicates are in Table 2. The boolean expression e **is** N'' is well-typed when the type of e is a superclass of N''. The type of $e.x$ is that of the x attribute of the class of e, provided this attribute is visible from the current class. In a hypothesis like $\Gamma.attr\ N'\ x = T$, which involves partial functions, we mean that the expressions are defined and equal. Visibility is considered in $visib\ \Gamma\ N'\ N\ x$, a condition stating that, according to Γ, x is an attribute of N' visible from inside N. We define $visib\ \Gamma\ N'\ N\ x$ to hold if and only if $N \leq_\Gamma N'$, $\Gamma.vis\ N\ x \neq ipri$, and $N \neq N' \Rightarrow \Gamma.vis\ N\ x \neq pri$. The attributes visible in N are those declared in N itself and those inherited from its superclasses that are not private.

A typing $\Gamma, N \rhd \psi : \mathbf{pred}$ is for a predicate on the state space of a method in class N, where $\Gamma.locals$ declares local variables, parameters, and attributes to which ψ may refer. We say ψ is typable in Γ, N, meaning $\Gamma, N \rhd \psi : \mathbf{pred}$ is derivable; similarly for command typings later. In some rules we omit the current class N because it does not change throughout the rule. The environment $\Gamma;\ x : T$, differs from Γ just in the *locals* field: we define $(\Gamma;\ x : T).locals$ to be $\Gamma.locals \oplus \{x \mapsto T\}$, where $\oplus$ denotes function overriding.

The rule for **isExactly** is similar to the rule for **is**, but we also need coercion rules for **is** and **isExactly** in combination with $\wedge$ and $\Rightarrow$. As an example, consider

$$\frac{(\Gamma;\ x:T) \rhd c : \mathbf{com} \quad par \in \{\mathbf{val}, \mathbf{res}, \mathbf{vres}\}}{\Gamma \rhd (par\ x:T \bullet c) : \mathbf{pcom}(par\ x:T)}$$

$$\frac{\Gamma.meth\ N\ m = pds}{\Gamma, N \rhd m : \mathbf{pcom}(pds)} \qquad \frac{\Gamma, N \rhd le : N' \quad \Gamma.meth\ N'\ m = pds}{\Gamma, N \rhd le.m : \mathbf{pcom}(pds)}$$

$$\frac{\Gamma \rhd le : T \quad \Gamma \rhd e : T' \quad T' \leq_\Gamma T \quad sdisjoint\ le}{\Gamma \rhd le := e : \mathbf{com}}$$

$$\frac{\Gamma \rhd pc : \mathbf{pcom}(\mathbf{val}\ x : T) \quad \Gamma \rhd e : T' \quad T' \leq_\Gamma T}{\Gamma \rhd pc(e) : \mathbf{com}}$$

$$\frac{\Gamma \rhd pc : \mathbf{pcom}(\mathbf{vres}\ x : T) \quad \Gamma \rhd le : T \quad sdisjoint\ le}{\Gamma \rhd pc(le) : \mathbf{com}}$$

$$\frac{\Gamma \rhd \psi_i : \mathbf{pred} \quad \Gamma \rhd c_i : \mathbf{com}}{\Gamma \rhd \mathbf{if}\ [\,]i \bullet \psi_i \rightarrow c_i\ \mathbf{fi} : \mathbf{com}} \qquad \frac{(\Gamma;\ x : T) \rhd c : \mathbf{com}}{\Gamma \rhd (\mathbf{var}\ x : T \bullet c\ \mathbf{end}) : \mathbf{com}}$$

Table 3. Typing of selected parameterized commands and commands.

a class Pt of points and an extended class Cpt with an added attribute *color*. The predicate $(x.color = red)$ is not typable in a context $(\Gamma;\ x : Pt), N$. However, if for instance $(\Gamma, x : Cpt), N \rhd x.color = red : \mathbf{pred}$, we would like the predicate x **is** $Cpt \Rightarrow x.color = red$ to be typable in a context where x has type Pt. Using only the separate rules for **is** and $\Rightarrow$, it is not typable as such; but it can be typed by a coercion rule for **is** like the one for **isExactly** in Table 2. Rules like this allow the derivation of typings in more than one way, but the semantic definitions ensure that the meaning is independent of derivation (Lemma 6).

Substitution on formulas and expressions is standard, but it is worth noting that the free variables of $e.x$ are those of e. This is because x is in the role of an attribute name.

3.3   Parameterized Commands, Commands, and Programs

Typing rules for selected commands and parameterized commands are presented in Table 3. The type of a parameterized command records its parameter declarations. In the cases of m and $le.m$, the declarations are recorded in the *meth* attribute of the typing environment. Of course, $le.m$ is well-typed only if the type of le is a class with a method m. An omitted rule deals with multiple parameters.

To preclude aliasing, the rule for assignment stipulates *sdisjoint le*. This means that, if le is a list, then no member of le is a prefix of another, after deleting **self**. For example, neither $x, x.y$ nor $x, \mathbf{self}.x$ is *sdisjoint*, but $x, y.x$ is. If pc is a parameterized command with parameter declaration **val** $x : T$, then $pc(e)$ is well-typed when the type of e is a subtype of T. If x is a result or a value-result parameter, then pc can only be applied to *sdisjoint* left-expressions. If x is a result parameter, $pc(le)$ is well-typed when T is a subtype of the type of le. When x is a value-result parameter, these types have to be the same.

A complete program $cds \bullet c$ is well-typed in an environment where only global variables x are in scope, just when c is well-typed in the environment Γ determined by cds and $x : T$, and considering that the current class is **main**.

$$
\frac{\Gamma, \textbf{main} \rhd c : \textbf{com} \qquad \Gamma = ((\textit{VDecs } cds \textbf{ main}); \ x : T)}{\textit{Vmeth } \Gamma \ cds \qquad \textit{nomrec } \Gamma \ cds}
$$
$$
(\varnothing; \ x : T) \rhd cds \bullet c : \textbf{program}
$$

The fields of the environment $\varnothing$ are all empty, so that in $(\varnothing; \ x : T)$ the only non-empty field is *locals*, which records the global variables $x : T$ of the program. The function *VDecs* extracts information from and checks a sequence of class declarations. In the environment determined by this function, the classes are associated with both its declared and inherited methods. The condition *Vmeth Γ cds* checks that the method bodies in cds are well-typed in the environment Γ. The method bodies are checked in an environment that includes their signatures, so recursive calls are appropriately dealt with. Mutually recursive calls, however, are not allowed. This is verified by the condition *nomrec Γ cds*.

The absence of mutual recursion between methods can not be checked as easily as the absence of mutual recursion between procedures of a traditional imperative program. By way of illustration, consider classes C, D and C'; the class C has an attribute a of type integer and a method $m1$ that, for instance, increments a by 1. The class D has an attribute c of class C, a method $m2$ with a call $c.m1()$, and some other methods. There is no mutual recursion, as $m1$ does not call $m2$. However, suppose that in a subclass C' of C we declare an attribute $d : D$ and redefine $m1$ introducing a call $d.m2()$. Now, if the private attribute c of D happens to have dynamic type C' when $m2$ is called, then mutual recursion will arise. To rule out mutual recursion, we require that if a method $m2$ calls a method $m1$ then neither $m1$ nor any of its redefinitions calls $m2$.

3.4   Properties of Typing

To a large extent, a context determines the type of an expression; an exception is **null**, for which we have $\Gamma, N \rhd \textbf{null} : N'$ for all N, N'. Some phrases, however, can be typed in many contexts. For example, considering again the class Pt and its subclass CPt, the command $x := \textbf{new } CPt$ can be typed in $\Gamma; \ x : Pt$ and also in $\Gamma; \ x : CPt$. Nonetheless, an expression typing does determine a derivation.

Lemma 1. *For all typings $\Gamma, N \rhd e : T$, there is at most one derivation.*

For predicates, the coercion rules make it possible to derive certain typings in more than one way. For example, if ψ is derivable in $(\Gamma; \ x : N'), N$, then $(\Gamma; \ x : N'), N \rhd x \textbf{ is } N' \Rightarrow \psi : \textbf{pred}$ can be derived using the rules for **is** and $\Rightarrow$, or using a coercion rule; more on this later.

To show type-correctness of method calls we need the following result. It is similar to the coercion rules, but in fact it does not depend on them.

Lemma 2. *The following rule is admissible, in the sense that the conclusion is derivable if the hypothesis are.*

$$\frac{\Gamma, N \rhd \psi_{N'} : \textbf{pred} \quad \textit{for all } N' \leq_\Gamma N \qquad N \neq \textbf{main}}{\Gamma, N \rhd (\vee_{N' \leq_\Gamma N} \bullet \textbf{ self isExactly } N' \wedge \psi_{N'}) : \textbf{pred}}$$

Many type systems include a rule of subsumption, but this would make coherence (Lemma 6) harder to prove. The useful effects of subsumption are built-in to the typing rules.

4   Semantics

Since ROOL includes infeasible (discontinuous) constructs, recursive class definitions cannot be interpreted by standard domain-theoretic techniques. We deal with recursive classes by separating attributes from methods, so the domain equations to be solved are simple "polynomials" involving first-order records.

The semantics $[\![\Gamma, N \rhd \textit{phrase} : \theta]\!]$ of each derivable typing, except method call, is defined as a function of the semantics of its constituent phrases. Most typing rules have a corresponding semantics which we present in a form that mimics the typing rule, to remind the reader of the typings for constituent phrases and any side conditions on those typings. Some phrases are treated indirectly through syntactic transformations described later.

Method calls are the most complicated part of the semantics, and they are discussed last. Semantics of method call goes beyond recursion on typing derivations. Moreover, we need the semantics to be defined for any phrase typable in an extended typing system defined as follows. The first change is that constraints involving the predicate *visib* are dropped. The second is that, in the rules for type tests and type casts, the subtyping constraint is dropped.

Semantically, e **is** N'', for example, can only hold if N'' is a subtype of the declared type of e. Nevertheless, this constraint is incompatible with the semantics of assignment, which as usual is interpreted by substitution. Consider, for instance, a context Γ with locals $x : Pt, z : SCPt$ where $SCPt \leq_\Gamma CPt \leq_\Gamma Pt$. In this context, both $x := z$ and x **is** CPt are typable, but substitution yields z **is** CPt which is not typable in the original system because $CPt \not\leq_\Gamma SCPt$.

All results in Section 3.4 hold for both typing systems. The constraints we drop are natural for user programs, but such constraints are not found in semantic studies. Although user specifications would not refer to non-visible attributes, such predicates can be used in proofs of laws.

4.1   Environments, Data Types, and States

An environment is a finite partial function $CName \nrightarrow (LName \nrightarrow PCom)$ that for a given class associates method names to parameterized commands. As formalized later on, the parameterized command corresponding to a method will be that given in its declaration, with an extra parameter *me*. This parameter is passed by value-result and provides the attributes of the object upon which the method is called. This facilitates interpretation of the method body in the context of its calls.

For a given typing environment Γ, we define the set $[\![\Gamma]\!]$ of environments compatible with Γ. The environments η in $[\![\Gamma]\!]$ are characterized by the following conditions. First, $\operatorname{dom}\eta = \Gamma.cnames$. Also, $\operatorname{dom}(\eta\ N) = \operatorname{dom}(\Gamma.meth\ N)$ for all $N \in \operatorname{dom}\eta$. Finally, the parameter declarations are those recorded in $\Gamma.meth$, along with the extra value-result parameter me; for all N, m there is some c such that $\eta\ N\ m = (\mathbf{vres}\ me : N;\ \Gamma.meth\ N\ m \bullet c)$. In the environments we construct later, c is derived from the declared body as a fixpoint.

In addition to the environment, the semantic function for expressions also takes a state as argument. A state assigns type-correct values to the attributes of the current object, and to the parameters and local variables. It also records the class of the current object. Object values, like states, assign values to attribute names. Our formalization begins with a universal set of untyped values, which are then used for the semantics of specific data types and state types.

The sets $Value$ and $ObjValue$ are the least solutions to the equations below. We assume the unions are disjoint. The symbol $\lhd$ means domain subtraction.

$$Value = \{\mathbf{error}, \mathbf{null}\} \cup \{\mathrm{true}, \mathrm{false}\} \cup \mathbb{Z} \cup ObjValue$$
$$ObjValue = \{f : (\{myclass\} \cup LName) \nrightarrow (CName \cup Value) \mid$$
$$myclass \in \operatorname{dom}f \wedge f\ myclass \in CName \wedge$$
$$(\{myclass\} \lhd f) \subseteq (LName \nrightarrow Value)\}$$

Values for other primitive types should also be included. An object value is a mapping from field names to values, with the distinguished name $myclass$ mapped to a class name.

The meanings of data types are parameterized by a typing environment. For primitives, we define $[\![\mathbf{bool}]\!]_\Gamma = \{\mathbf{error}, \mathrm{true}, \mathrm{false}\}$ and $[\![\mathbf{int}]\!]_\Gamma = \{\mathbf{error}\} \cup \mathbb{Z}$. For N in $\Gamma.cnames$, we define $[\![N]\!]_\Gamma$ to be the correctly-typed object values.

$$[\![N]\!]_\Gamma = \{\mathbf{error}, \mathbf{null}\} \cup$$
$$\{f : ObjValue \mid$$
$$\operatorname{dom}f = \operatorname{dom}(\Gamma.attr\ (f\ myclass)) \cup \{myclass\} \wedge$$
$$f\ myclass \leq_\Gamma N \wedge$$
$$\forall x : \operatorname{dom}(\Gamma.attr\ (f\ myclass)) \bullet f\ x \in [\![\Gamma.attr\ (f\ myclass)\ x]\!]_\Gamma\}$$

It is straightforward to prove that $N \leq_\Gamma N'$ implies $[\![N]\!]_\Gamma \subseteq [\![N']\!]_\Gamma$.

States are elements of $ObjValue$, although the "attributes" in a state include values of parameters and local variables. We write $[\![\Gamma, N]\!]$ for the set of states for class N and typing environment Γ. An state σ is in $[\![\Gamma, N]\!]$ just if it satisfies the following conditions. First, σ gives values to the attributes of the actual class, if it is not **main**, and to the variables in $\Gamma.locals$.

$$N \neq \mathbf{main} \Rightarrow \operatorname{dom}\sigma \setminus \{myclass\} = \operatorname{dom}(\Gamma.attr\ (\sigma\ myclass)) \cup \operatorname{dom}(\Gamma.locals)$$

The union is not disjoint: $\Gamma.locals$ declares the visible attributes and any local variables and method parameters; $\Gamma.attr(\sigma\ myclass))$ declares all attributes, including inherited private ones. If N is **main**, σ gives values just to the variables in $\Gamma.locals$. Also, if N is not **main**, then $myclass$ is a subclass of N; otherwise, $myclass$ is **main** itself. The last condition is that σ assigns values of the correct type. For $N \neq$ **main** and x in $\operatorname{dom}\sigma \setminus \{myclass\}$ we require $x \in \operatorname{dom}(\Gamma.attr\ N)$ to imply $\sigma\ x \in [\![\Gamma.attr\ N\ x]\!]_\Gamma$, and $x \in \operatorname{dom}\Gamma.locals$ to imply $\sigma\ x \in [\![\Gamma.locals\ x]\!]_\Gamma$. Just the latter implication applies if $N =$ **main**.

4.2 Expressions and Predicates

For $\eta \in [\![\Gamma]\!]$, $\sigma \in [\![\Gamma, N]\!]$, and derivable $\Gamma, N \rhd e : T$, we define $[\![\Gamma, N \rhd e : T]\!]\eta\ \sigma$, the value of e in state σ. It is an element of $[\![T]\!]_\Gamma$ (Lemma 5).

We assume that for built-in function $f : T \to U$ a semantics is given, as a total function $[\![T]\!]_\Gamma \to [\![U]\!]_\Gamma$. The semantics of **self** is as follows.

$$[\![\Gamma, N \rhd \textbf{self} : N]\!]\eta\ \sigma = (\{myclass\} \cup \operatorname{dom}(\Gamma.attr\ (\sigma\ myclass))) \lhd \sigma$$

This uses domain restriction ($\lhd$) of σ: the attributes and $myclass$ are retained; local variables and parameters are dropped. The similar definition for **super** and those for **null** and variables are omitted. We define $[\![\Gamma, N \rhd \textbf{new}\ N' : N']\!]\eta\ \sigma$ as $init\ \Gamma\ N'$ where $init\ \Gamma\ N'$ is an object initialized with default values: false for boolean attributes, 0 for integers and **null** for objects. For other primitive types a default initial value should be given.

The value of the boolean expression e **is** N'' is determined by whether the value of e is an object of class N''. We omit the **null** and **error** cases.

$$\frac{[\![\Gamma, N \rhd e : N']\!]\eta\ \sigma = v \qquad v \notin \{\textbf{null}, \textbf{error}\}}{[\![\Gamma, N \rhd e\ \textbf{is}\ N'' : \textbf{bool}]\!]\eta\ \sigma = (v\ myclass \leq_\Gamma N'')}$$

Semantics of attribute selection, update, and cast are straightforward; they yield **error** for **null**.

The semantics $[\![\Gamma, N \rhd \psi : \textbf{pred}]\!]\eta$ of a predicate ψ is a subset of $[\![\Gamma, N]\!]$ (Lemma 6). The semantics of expressions as formulas, and of the logical operations, is standard and omitted. The semantics of **isExactly** is similar to that of **is**.

$$\frac{[\![\Gamma, N \rhd e : N']\!]\eta = f}{\begin{array}{l}[\![\Gamma, N \rhd e\ \textbf{isExactly}\ N'' : \textbf{pred}]\!]\eta = \\ \{\sigma : [\![\Gamma, N]\!] \mid f\ \sigma \notin \{\textbf{null}, \textbf{error}\} \wedge (f\ \sigma)\ myclass = N''\}\end{array}}$$

The coercion rules have similar semantics; we consider that involving **is** and $\wedge$.

$$\frac{[\![(\Gamma;\ x : N''), N \rhd \psi : \textbf{pred}]\!]\eta = \Sigma \qquad N'' \leq_\Gamma N'}{\begin{array}{l}[\![(\Gamma;\ x : N'), N \rhd x\ \textbf{is}\ N'' \wedge \psi : \textbf{pred}]\!]\eta = \\ \{\sigma : [\![(\Gamma;\ x : N'), N]\!] \mid (\sigma\ x) \notin \{\textbf{null}, \textbf{error}\} \wedge (\sigma\ x)\ myclass \leq_\Gamma N'' \wedge \sigma \in \Sigma\}\end{array}}$$

This combines the interpretations of the combined operators.

$$(\textbf{val } x : T \bullet c)(e) \quad \longrightarrow \quad (\textbf{var } l : T \bullet l := e; \; c[l/x]) \qquad \text{if } l \notin (FV \; e) \cup (FV \; c)$$
$$(\textbf{res } x : T \bullet c)(le) \quad \longrightarrow \quad (\textbf{var } l : T \bullet c[l/x]; \; le := l) \qquad \text{if } l \notin (FV \; le) \cup (FV \; c)$$
$$(\textbf{vres } x : T \bullet c)(le) \quad \longrightarrow \quad (\textbf{var } l : T \bullet l := le; \; c[l/x]; \; le := l) \; \text{if } l \notin (FV \; le) \cup (FV \; c)$$
$$(pd; \; pds \bullet c)(e, e') \quad \longrightarrow \quad (pd \bullet (pds \bullet c)(e'))(e) \qquad \text{if } \alpha(pd) \notin (FV \; e')$$
$$(\bullet \; c)() \quad \longrightarrow \quad c$$
$$le.x := e \quad \longrightarrow \quad le := (le; \; x : e)$$
$$le.x, y := e, e' \quad \longrightarrow \quad le, y := (le; \; x : e), e'$$
$$le, le' := e, e' \quad \longrightarrow \quad le', le := e', e$$
$$m(e) \quad \longrightarrow \quad \textbf{self}.m(e)$$

Table 4. Syntactic transformations

4.3 Commands and Parameterized Commands

For command typing $\Gamma, N \rhd c : \textbf{com}$ and environment $\eta \in [\![\Gamma]\!]$, the semantics $[\![\Gamma, N \rhd c : \textbf{com}]\!]\eta$ is a total function on formulas (Theorem 1) which, when applied to a formula typable in Γ, N yields a result typable in Γ, N (Theorem 2).

Assignments to general left-expressions are dealt with using syntactic transformations that yield assignments of update expressions to simple variables and to **self**. Assignment to simple variables is interpreted using substitution.

$$\frac{\Gamma \rhd x : T \quad \Gamma \rhd e : T' \quad T' \leq_\Gamma T}{[\![\Gamma \rhd x := e : \textbf{com}]\!]\eta \; \psi = (e \neq \textbf{error} \wedge \psi[e/x])}$$

We use an expression "**error**". In this paper we omit **error** from the grammar because it has no other use; its typing rule and semantics are straightforward.

User programs should not include assignments to **self** and method calls where **self** is used as a result or value-result argument. Assignments to **self** are introduced only in the syntactic transformations for parameter passing, when the argument corresponding to the *me* parameter of a method is **self**. This guarantees that **self** is always assigned an object of the current class, but the semantics cannot depend on this assumption.

$$\frac{\Gamma, N \rhd e : N' \quad N' \leq_\Gamma N}{\begin{array}{l} [\![\Gamma, N \rhd \textbf{self} := e : \textbf{com}]\!]\eta \; \psi = \\ (\vee_{N' \leq_\Gamma N} \bullet \; e \; \textbf{isExactly} \; N' \wedge \psi[e, e.x/\textbf{self}, x]) \; \text{where } x = \text{dom}(\Gamma.attr \; N') \end{array}}$$

This uses a disjunction over the subclasses N' of N; each disjunct involves a substitution for appropriate attributes. There is no need to check that e is not **error** because **error isExactly** N' is false, for all N'. If the only assignments to **self** are those introduced in the semantics, **self** is always assigned an object of the current class, in which case the semantics simplifies to $\psi[e, e.x/\textbf{self}, x]$. We need not give an operational justification for the general case.

We define $[\![\Gamma; \; x : T \rhd x : [\psi_1, \psi_2] : \textbf{com}]\!]\eta \; \psi$ to be $\psi_1 \wedge (\forall x : T \bullet \psi_2 \Rightarrow \psi)$ as in Morgan's work. We also use the standard semantics for control constructs and blocks.

Parameter passing and various forms of assignment are reduced by the rule below to more basic constructs using the relation $\longrightarrow$ defined in Table 4.

$$\frac{c \longrightarrow^* c' \quad [\![\Gamma, N \rhd c' : \mathbf{com}]\!] \eta = g}{[\![\Gamma, N \rhd c : \mathbf{com}]\!] \eta = g}$$

If $\Gamma, N \rhd c : \mathbf{com}$ and $c \longrightarrow c'$ then $\Gamma, N \rhd c' : \mathbf{com}$ (Lemma 3). The reflexive-transitive closure $\longrightarrow^*$ of $\longrightarrow$ reduces every derivable command typing to one for which there is a direct semantic definition (Theorem 1). The first five transformations rewrite parameter passing in the usual way; $\alpha(pd)$ denotes the set of variables declared in pd, and FV gives free variables. The next three transformations rewrite assignments to left-expressions into assignments to simple variables or **self**. The last transformation inserts the missing object (**self**) in a method call $m(e)$.

4.4 Programs and Method Calls

The meaning of a complete program is the meaning of its main command, in an appropriate environment. The typing includes global variables x of c.

$$\frac{[\![\Gamma, \mathbf{main} \rhd c : \mathbf{com}]\!] \eta = f \quad \Gamma = ((VDecs\ cds\ \mathbf{main});\ x : T)}{Vmeth\ \Gamma\ cds \qquad \eta = Meths\ \Gamma\ cds}}{[\![\varnothing;\ x : T \rhd cds \bullet c : \mathbf{program}]\!] = f}$$

The environment η records the methods available for objects of each of the classes declared in cds; these methods are extracted from cds by the function $Meths$ which builds η as follows.

For each class N and method m, the parameterized command $\eta\ N\ m$ has an extra value-result parameter me, and in its body each occurrence of an attribute x of N or of a call to a method m of N is replaced by $me.x$ and $me.m$. Only "top level" occurrences of attributes are changed: if x is an attribute, then $x.x$ becomes $me.x.x$. For a class that inherits m, me must be given the more specific type; it always has exactly the type of the object, compatible with the typing rule for value-result parameters.

If the declared body of a method m contains recursive invocations, then $\eta\ N\ m$ is the least fixed point of the context determined by the body. This approach is also used in Back's work and [CSW98] to deal with recursive parameterized procedures. We forbid mutual recursion so that fixpoints can be taken separately for each method. We justify existence of the least fixed point by techniques used in the cited works; it depends on monotonicity (Theorem 3).

Finally we consider method calls $le.m(e)$. Even though $le.m$ is a parameterized command, typed for example as $\Gamma, N \rhd le.m : \mathbf{pcom}(\mathbf{val}\ x : T)$, no transformation rule is applicable. In a state where the dynamic type of le is N', $\eta\ N'\ m$ takes the form $(\mathbf{vres}\ me : N';\ \mathbf{val}\ x : T \bullet c)$, and if we define $f_{N'}$ as $[\![\Gamma, N \rhd (\mathbf{vres}\ me : N';\ \mathbf{val}\ x : T \bullet c)(le, e) : \mathbf{com}]\!] \eta$, then we should define $[\![\Gamma, N \rhd le.m(e) : \mathbf{com}]\!] \eta\ \psi$ to be $f_{N'}\ \psi$. The semantics of method call is the disjunction, over the possible classes N', of le **isExactly** $N' \wedge f_{N'} \psi$. Thus the semantics $f_{N'}$ is used just when it should be. The possible classes N' are the subclasses of the static type N'' of le, determined by the derivation of le.

$$\frac{[\![\Gamma, N \rhd (\eta\ N'\ m)(le, e) : \mathbf{com}]\!]\eta = f_{N'} \quad \text{all } N' \leq_\Gamma N'', \text{for } N'' \text{ the type of } le}{[\![\Gamma, N \rhd le.m(e) : \mathbf{com}]\!]\eta\ \psi = (\vee_{N' \leq_\Gamma N''}\bullet\ le\ \mathbf{isExactly}\ N' \wedge f_{N'}\psi)}$$

The hypothesis depends on $\eta\ N'\ m$ being typable in Γ, N. The free variables in the original declaration of m are attributes visible in the class, now accessed through the me parameter. Those attributes are not necessarily visible in the context of the call, so references $me.x$ are only typable in the extended system.

4.5   Example

The program below acts on a global variable c of type C. For clarity, we write the body of a method with no parameters as a command, instead of as a parameterized command with an empty declaration.

> **class** C **pri** $x : \mathbf{int}$; **meth** $Inc \mathrel{\widehat{=}} x := x + 1$; **meth** $Dec \mathrel{\widehat{=}} x := x - 1$ **end**
> $\bullet\ c.Inc()$

We calculate the weakest precondition for this program to establish $c.x > 0$. Writing CD to stand for the declaration of C above, we begin.

$$[\![\varnothing;\ c : C;\ \rhd CD \bullet c.Inc() : \mathbf{program}]\!]\ (c.x > 0)$$

$$= [\![\Gamma, \mathbf{main} \rhd c.Inc() : \mathbf{com}]\!]\eta\ (c.x > 0)$$

Here the typing environment $\Gamma = (VDecs\ CD\ \mathbf{main})$; $c : C$ is as follows.

> $(attr = \{\mathbf{object} \mapsto \varnothing, C \mapsto \{x \mapsto \mathbf{int}\}\ \},$
> $\quad meth = \{\mathbf{object} \mapsto \varnothing, C \mapsto \{Inc \mapsto \varnothing, Dec \mapsto \varnothing\}\ \},$
> $\quad vis = \{\mathbf{object} \mapsto \varnothing, C \mapsto \{x \mapsto pri\}\ \},$
> $\quad cnames = \{\mathbf{object}, C\},\ supcls = \{C \mapsto \mathbf{object}\},\ locals = \{c \mapsto C\})$

The environment $\eta = Meth\ \Gamma\ CD$ is shown below.

> $\{\mathbf{object} \mapsto \varnothing, C \mapsto \{Inc \mapsto (\mathbf{vres}\ me : C \bullet me.x := me.x + 1), Dec \mapsto \ldots\}\ \}$

We proceed as follows.

$$[\![\Gamma, \mathbf{main} \rhd c.Inc() : \mathbf{com}]\!]\eta\ (c.x > 0)$$

$$= (\vee_{N' \leq_\Gamma C}\bullet\ c\ \mathbf{isExactly}\ N' \wedge [\![\Gamma, \mathbf{main} \rhd (\eta\ N'\ Inc)(c) : \mathbf{com}]\!]\ (c.x > 0))$$
$$\text{[by the semantics of method call]}$$

$$= c \notin \{\mathbf{null}, \mathbf{error}\} \wedge [\![\Gamma, \mathbf{main} \rhd (\eta\ C\ Inc)(c) : \mathbf{com}]\!]\ (c.x > 0)$$
$$\text{[by } C \text{ has no proper subclasses and the semantics of } \mathbf{isExactly]}$$

$$= c \notin \{\mathbf{null}, \mathbf{error}\} \wedge \qquad\qquad\qquad \text{[by the definition of } \eta]$$
$$[\![\Gamma, \mathbf{main} \rhd (\mathbf{vres}\ me : C \bullet me.x := me.x + 1)(c) : \mathbf{com}]\!]\eta\ (c.x > 0)$$

$= c \notin \{\mathbf{null}, \mathbf{error}\} \wedge$ [by a syntactic transformation]
$[\![\Gamma, \mathbf{main} \rhd (\mathbf{var} \; l : C \bullet l := c; \; l.x := l.x + 1; \; c := l) : \mathbf{com}]\!]\eta \; (c.x > 0)$

$= c \notin \{\mathbf{null}, \mathbf{error}\} \wedge$ [by the semantics of variable blocks]
$\forall l \bullet [\![\Gamma; \; l : C, \mathbf{main} \rhd (l := c; \; l.x := l.x + 1; \; c := l) : \mathbf{com}]\!]\eta \; (c.x > 0)$

$= c \notin \{\mathbf{null}, \mathbf{error}\} \wedge c.x \neq \mathbf{error} \wedge (c.x > 0)[l/c][(l; \; x : l.x + 1)/l][c/l]$
                [by the semantics of sequence and assignment]

$= c \notin \{\mathbf{null}, \mathbf{error}\} \wedge c.x \neq \mathbf{error} \wedge c.x + 1 > 0$
              [by a properties of substitution and update expressions]

The result obtained is exactly what should be expected.

5 Properties of the Semantics

This section shows that the semantics is a well-defined function of typings, and that it is type-correct. Before presenting these theorems, however, we present auxiliary results.

Lemma 3. *The syntactic transformations preserve typing, in the sense that* $\Gamma, N \rhd c : \mathbf{com}$ *and* $c \longrightarrow c'$ *imply* $\Gamma, N \rhd c' : \mathbf{com}$*, for all* c, c'*.*

To prove the type-correctness theorem, we need typability to be preserved by substitution on formulas. This result holds only in the extended type system, where subtyping constraints are dropped from the rules for type tests and casts.

Lemma 4. *(a) Suppose* $\Gamma, N \rhd \psi : \mathbf{pred}$ *is derivable and* x *is free in* ψ*; let* T *be the type of* x *(which is uniquely determined by* Γ, N*). If* $T' \leq_\Gamma T$ *and* $\Gamma, N \rhd e : T'$ *is derivable then* $\Gamma, N \rhd \psi[e/x] : \mathbf{pred}$ *is derivable. (b) Same as part (a) but with* $\mathbf{self}$ *in place of* x*.*

The rules for assignment and result-parameter passing also involve subtyping constraints, but that does not invalidate Lemma 4 because predicate typings do not depend on command typings.

Because the semantics of ROOL is not defined by structural recursion on program texts, we need to show that the notation is coherent, in the sense that $[\![\Gamma, N \rhd phrase : \theta]\!]$ is a function of the typing $\Gamma, N \rhd phrase : \theta$. Expression typings have unique derivations (Lemma 1), and the semantics is defined directly in terms of the typing rules, so coherence for expressions is immediate. As a result, type-correctness for expressions is straightforward.

Lemma 5. *If* $\Gamma, N \rhd e : T$ *then* $[\![\Gamma, N \rhd e : T]\!]\eta \; \sigma \in [\![T]\!]_\Gamma$ *for all* $\eta \in [\![\Gamma]\!]$ *and* $\sigma \in [\![\Gamma, N]\!]$*.*

Due to the coercion rules, predicate typings are not unique. We need a coherence lemma.

Lemma 6. *The semantics $[\![\Gamma, N \rhd \psi : \mathbf{pred}]\!]$ of a predicate typing is a function of the typing $\Gamma, N \rhd \psi : \mathbf{pred}$, and $[\![\Gamma, N \rhd \psi : \mathbf{pred}]\!] \subseteq [\![\Gamma, N]\!]$.*

For command typings, derivations are unique except for derivations of predicates that occur within commands. Nevertheless, the semantics of commands does not depend on semantics of predicates, so there is no issue of coherence.

There are two parts of the semantics of commands, however, that are not simply defined by structural recursion on derivations. The first is that for some commands the semantics is given indirectly by syntactic transformation. Nonetheless, these transformations preserve typing (Lemma 3), and the derivations of the transformed phrases are built from the derivations of the original phrases in such a way that the semantics depends only on the semantics of subderivations.

Method calls are the second difficult part: $[\![\Gamma, N \rhd le.m(e) : \mathbf{com}]\!]\eta$ depends on the semantics of method calls $[\![\Gamma, N \rhd \eta\ N'\ m(e) : \mathbf{com}]\!]\eta$ where N' ranges over subtypes of the type N'' of le. The parameterized command $\eta\ N'\ m$ can contain method calls, so the semantics of a method call depends on the semantics of method calls, which are certainly not part of the derivation of $le.m(e)$.

However, we are only concerned recursion-free environments: those obtained from *Meth Γ cds*, in which recursion has been resolved already. The semantics of a method m of a class N depends only on methods N', m' that do not depend on N, m, and the relation "can call" on pairs N', m' is well founded. We combine this lexicographically with the order "is a subderivation" to obtain a well founded order. We define the notion of the semantics $[\![\Gamma, N \rhd phrase : \theta]\!]$ in the context of some method N', m'; this depends on subderivations of *phrase* : θ and also on semantics for phrases in context of methods N'', m'' smaller than N', m'.

Theorem 1. *For all derivable $\Gamma, N \rhd c : \mathbf{com}$ and all $\eta \in [\![\Gamma]\!]$, the semantics $[\![\Gamma, N \rhd c : \mathbf{com}]\!]\eta$ is a total function on all formulas, regardless of type, provided that η is recursion-free.*

Proof By induction with respect to the order discussed above.
Case assignment: for assignments to simple identifiers, and for assignments to **self**, the semantics is given directly. Others are reduced by syntactic transformations to the simple case. By Lemma 3 the transformed assignments are typable in Γ, N. Any assignment can be rewritten to a simple one which is unique up to the order in which variables are listed; and order does not affect the semantics.
Case specification statement: this has a single typing rule and the semantics is given directly.
Case application $pc(e)$ of an explicit parameterized command (not a method call): the transformation rules eliminate argument(s) e in favor of local variables and assignments. The result is typable (Lemma 3). Moreover, the derivation of the transformed command is composed of subderivations of the original command. Introducing local variables involves the choice of identifier l, but the semantics is independent of the choice because l is bound by $\forall$.
Case method call applied to parameters: a method call $m(e)$ is reduced to **self**.$m(e)$, which has the general form $le.m(e)$. Let ψ be any formula. The semantics for $le.m(e)$ is defined provided each $f_{N'}$, i.e. $[\![\Gamma, N \rhd \eta\ N'\ m(le, e) : \mathbf{com}]\!]\eta$,

is defined. By the conditions on environments, $\eta \, N' \, m(le, e)$ is typable. The methods on which $\eta \, N' \, m$ depends are smaller in our ordering, by the proviso that η is recursion-free. By induction, $[\![\Gamma, N \rhd \eta \, N' \, m(le, e) : \mathbf{com}]\!]\eta$ denotes a total function on formulas, and hence so does the semantics of the call.

Cases explicit recursion: this is defined using least fixpoints of program contexts. Because these are monotonic (Theorem 3), the least fixpoints are well defined.

Cases sequence, alternation and variable blocks: in each case there is a direct semantic definition and the result holds by induction. $\qquad \square$

Theorem 2. *If $\Gamma, N \rhd \psi : \mathbf{pred}$ and $\Gamma, N \rhd c : \mathbf{com}$ are derivable then so is $\Gamma, N \rhd ([\![\Gamma, N \rhd c : \mathbf{com}]\!]\eta \; \psi) : \mathbf{pred}$, provided η is recursion-free.*

Proof By induction, using the order defined above.

Case assignment: for simple variables, the semantics requires that the predicate $e \neq \mathbf{error} \wedge \psi[e/x]$ be typable in Γ provided that ψ is. Thus we need that $\Gamma \rhd x : T$ and $\Gamma \rhd e : T'$ and $T' \leq_\Gamma T$ imply $\Gamma \rhd \psi[e/x] : \mathbf{pred}$. That is by Lemma 4(a). To type $e \neq \mathbf{error}$, we use the typing rule for $\mathbf{error}$ (which gives it any type), and then the rule for built-in functions to type the equality. For assignments to $\mathbf{self}$, suppose ψ is typable in Γ, N. For each N', we have, by Lemma 4(b), $\psi[e, e.x/\mathbf{self}, x]$ typable in Γ, N'. Moreover, if an assignment to $\mathbf{self}$ is typable in Γ, N, then $\mathbf{self}$ is typable in Γ, N and so $N \neq \mathbf{main}$. Thus, by Lemma 2, $(\vee_{N' \leq_\Gamma N} \bullet \mathbf{self} \; \mathbf{isExactly} \; N' \wedge \psi[e, e.x/\mathbf{self}, x])$ is typable in Γ, N.

Case specification statement: for $\Gamma; \; x : T \rhd x : [\psi_1, \psi_2] : \mathbf{com}$ to be derivable, ψ_1 and ψ_2 are typable in $\Gamma; \; x : T$. For ψ with $\Gamma; \; x : T \rhd \psi : \mathbf{pred}$ the semantics yields $\psi_1 \wedge (\forall x : T \bullet \psi_2 \Rightarrow \psi)$, which can be typed for $\Gamma; \; x : T$ using the rules for $\wedge$, $\forall$, and $\Rightarrow$.

Cases sequence: straightforward use of induction.

Case alternation: by induction, each f_i in the semantics yields well-typed formulas, and the guards have to be typable predicates in Γ, N, so the formula $(\vee \, i \bullet \psi_i) \wedge (\wedge \, i \bullet \psi_i \Rightarrow f_i \; \psi)$ is also typable using the rules for $\wedge$, $\vee$, and $\Rightarrow$.

Case method call: for method calls $le.m(e)$, we have to show that the predicate $(\vee_{N'} \bullet le \; \mathbf{isExactly} \; N' \wedge f_{N'} \; \psi)$ is typable in Γ, N. By induction, each $f_{N'}$ applies to formulas typable in Γ, N, and each returns the same. Now le is typable in Γ, N, so by using the rules $\vee$, $\wedge$, and $\mathbf{isExactly}$ we obtain the desired result.

Case blocks: the weakest precondition $[\![\Gamma \rhd (\mathbf{var} \; x : T \bullet c \; \mathbf{end}) : \mathbf{com}]\!]\eta \; \psi$ is defined as $(\forall x : T \bullet f \; \psi)$, where $f = [\![\Gamma; \; x : T \rhd c : \mathbf{com}]\!]\eta$. If ψ is typable in Γ then it is also typable in $\Gamma; \; x : T$. Therefore f can be applied to ψ and by induction $f \; \psi$ is typable in $\Gamma; \; x : T$, and hence by the typing rule for $\forall$ we get $(\forall x : T \bullet f \; \psi)$ typable in Γ. Similar considerations apply to $\mathbf{avar}$ blocks. $\qquad \square$

It is straightforward to formulate and prove definedness and type-preservation for complete programs, using Theorems 1 and 2.

6   Refinement

In this section we define notions of refinement and give the basic result on monotonicity. To simplify definitions, we assume that all phrases are well-typed.

The fundamental refinement relationship $\sqsubseteq$ is between programs. This is based on pointwise order on predicate transformers, as usual, but restricted to healthy predicates just as in languages where procedures can be assigned to variables [Nau98b, HH98]. As an example, if class CPt suitably refines Pt we expect the refinement $x := \textbf{new } Pt \sqsubseteq x := \textbf{new } CPt$. But the postcondition x **isExactly** Pt is established only by the first assignment. The solution is to restrict attention to monotonic predicates. For our purposes, a predicate ψ is monotonic provided that for any object values $ov1, ov2$, if $ov1$ satisfies ψ and $ov2$ $myclass \leq_{\Gamma} ov1$ $myclass$, and $ov2$ agrees with $ov1$ on all the attributes of $ov1$ $myclass$, then $ov2$ satisfies ψ.

Definition 1. *For sequences of class declarations cds and cds', commands c and c' with the same free variables $x : T$, define $(cds \bullet c) \sqsubseteq (cds' \bullet c')$ if and only if, for all monotonic ψ,*

$$[\![\varnothing;\ x : T \rhd (cds \bullet c) : \textbf{program}]\!]\ \psi \Rightarrow [\![\varnothing;\ x : T \rhd (cds' \bullet c') : \textbf{program}]\!]\ \psi$$

The free variables of a program represent its input and output; therefore, it makes sense to compare only programs with the same free variables.

A program can be refined by refining its command part and its class declarations. Commands in ROOL apear in the context of a sequence of class declarations, so we first define relation $cds, N \rhd c \sqsubseteq c'$, which establishes that in the context of cds the command c occurring in the class N is refined by c'.

Definition 2. *For a sequence of class declarations cds, commands c and c', and a class N, define $cds, N \rhd c \sqsubseteq c'$ if and only if, for all monotonic predicates ψ,*

$$[\![\Gamma, N \rhd c : \textbf{com}]\!] \eta\ \psi \Rightarrow [\![\Gamma, N \rhd c' : \textbf{com}]\!] \eta\ \psi$$

where $\Gamma = (VDecs\ cds\ N)$; $x : T$, x are the method parameters and local variables in scope, and $\eta = Meths\ \Gamma\ cds$.

Because methods are parameterized commands, we need the analog of Definition 1 for them.

Definition 3. *For sequence of class declarations cds, parameterized commands pc and pc', which have the same parameters, and a class N, $cds, N \rhd pc \sqsubseteq pc'$ if and only if, for all (lists of) expressions e, $cds, N \rhd pc(e) \sqsubseteq pc'(e)$*

This is a straightforward extension Back's definition (see [CSW98]).

Using induction as in Theorems 1 and 2, the following can be proved.

Theorem 3. *Suppose we have a sequence of class declarations cds, a class N, a parameterized command pc, and a context $\mathcal{C}[\cdot]$ which is a parameterized command, and so, a function from parameterized commands to parameterized commands. If we have that $cds, N \rhd pc \sqsubseteq pc'$, then $cds, N \rhd \mathcal{C}[pc] \sqsubseteq \mathcal{C}[pc']$. Similarly, the command constructors are monotonic.*

This theorem justifies our treatment of recursion and recursive methods.

As a class is a data type, refinement of classes is related to data refinement [HHS87]. We define the relation $view, cds \rhd cds' \preceq cds''$, for a list of methods $view$ and sequences of class declarations cds, cds', and cds''. The meaning is that in the context of cds, if only methods listed in $view$ are used, then the class declaration cds' can be replaced by cds''.

Definition 4. *For a list of methods view, sequences of class declarations cds, cds', and cds'', $view, cds \rhd cds' \preceq cds''$ if and only if, for all commands c that uses only methods in view, $(cds; cds' \bullet c) \sqsubseteq (cds; cds'' \bullet c)$.*

Refinement between single classes cd' and cd'' is a special case. By considering a more general relation, we allow for restructuring a collection of class declarations. In practice, Definition 4 would not be used directly, but it is the fundamental notion with respect to which techniques such as downward and upward simulation must be proved sound [HHS87, Nau98a].

7   Discussion

We have shown how the standard predicate-transformer model can be extended to an object-oriented language. The semantics can be modified to allow arbitrary mutual recursion among methods, at the cost of taking a single fixpoint for the entire environment of methods. This makes it more complicated to prove refinement laws, so we have chosen the simpler approach at this stage.

Others [Lei98, MS97, BKS98] have extended existing refinement calculi with object-oriented features, but restricting inheritance or not dealing with classes and visibility. Those works, however, deal with sharing and concurrency. Another approach to objects is implicit in the parametricity semantics of Algol-like languages. It has been adapted to object-oriented programs by Reddy [Red98], with whom we are collaborating to give a semantics for ROOL.

The main shortcoming of our semantics is that it is not entirely compositional. Since our aim is to validate laws like those in [Bor98], for when one class is a behavioural subclass of another, within the context of some other classes, this is a potential problem. However, the touchstone criteria for behavioural refinement is that $cds_1 \bullet c \sqsubseteq cds_2 \bullet c$ should hold whenever cds_2 is obtained from cds_1 by behavioural refinement of some classes. Fortunately, this has a natural formulation with a single context that includes all relevant classes.

Our notion of class refinement corresponds to the notion of behavioural subtyping introduced by Liskov and Wing [LW94]. Definition 4 captures the essence of their subtype requirement. In our framework the property of interest is refinement of programs, which captures the notion of total correctness. The two ways of defining the subtype relation presented in [LW94] are based on the downward simulation technique [HHS87], specialized to the particular case of functional data refinement. We expect that particular techniques like these can be proved sound with respect to Definition 4. Similarly, Liskov and Wing claim, but do not formalize, that their definitions satisfy the subtype requirement.

By using a language of specification and programming, we do not need a distinction between specifications and implementations of classes. As already seen in traditional refinement calculi, this simplifies both the theory of refinement and the presentation and application of refinement laws.

Acknowledgement This work benefitted from discussions with our collaborators Augusto Sampaio, Uday Reddy, Paulo Borba, and Hongseok Yang. UFPE and Stevens provided generous support for travel.

References

[AdB94]   Pierre America and Frank de Boer. Reasoning about dynamically evolving process structures. *Formal Aspects of Computing*, 6:269–316, 1994.

[AL97]   Martín Abadi and K. Rustan Leino. A logic of object-oriented programs. In *Proceedings, TAPSOFT 1997*. Springer-Verlag, 1997. Expanded in DEC SRC report 161.

[BvW98]   R. J. R. Back and J. von Wright. *Refinement Calculus: A Systematic Introduction*. Graduate Texts in Computer Science. Springer-Verlag, 1998.

[BKS98]   Marcello M. Bonsangue, Joost N. Kok, and Kaisa Sere. An approach to object-orientation in action systems. In Johan Jeuring, ed., *Mathematics of Program Construction*, LNCS 1422, pages 68–95. Springer, 1998.

[Bor98]   Paulo Borba. Where are the laws of object-oriented programming? In *I Brazilian Workshop on Formal Methods*, pages 59–70, Porto Alegre, Brazil, 19th–21st October 1998.

[CN99]   A. L. C. Cavalcanti and D. A. Naumann. A Weakest Precondition Semantics for an Object-oriented Language of Refinement - Extended Version. Available at http://www.di.ufpe.br/~alcc

[CSW98]   A. L. C. Cavalcanti, A. C. A. Sampaio, and J. C. P. Woodcock. Procedures and Recursion in the Refinement Calculus. *Journal of the Brazilian Computer Society*, 5(1):1–15, 1998.

[CSW99]   A. L. C. Cavalcanti, A. Sampaio, and J. C. P. Woodcock. An inconsistency in procedures, parameters, and substitution in the refinement calculus. *Science of Computer Programming*, 33(1):87–96, 1999.

[HH98]   C. A. R. Hoare and J. He. *Unifying Theories of Programming*. Prentice Hall, 1998.

[HHS87]   C. A. R. Hoare and J. He and J. W. Sanders. Prespecification in data refinement. *Information Processing Letters*, 25(2), 1987.

[Lan95]   Kevin Lano. *Formal Object-Oriented Development*. Springer, 1995.

[Lei98]   K. Rustan M. Leino. Recursive object types in a logic of object-oriented programming. In Chris Hankin, ed., *7th European Symposium on Programming*, LNCS 1381. Springer, 1998.

[LW94]   Barbara H. Liskov and Jeannette M. Wing. A behavioral notion of subtyping. *ACM Transactions on Programming Languages and Systems*, 16(6), 1994.

[MS97]   A. Mikhajlova and E. Sekerinski, Class refinement and interface refinement in object-oriented programs. In *Proceedings of FME'97: Industrial Benefit of Formal Methods*. Springer, 1997.

[Mor94]   Carroll Morgan. *Programming from Specifications*, 2ed. Prentice Hall, 1994.

[Nau98a]   David A. Naumann. Validity of data refinement for a higher order impera-
            tive language. Submitted.
[Nau98b]   David A. Naumann. Predicate transformer semantics of a higher order im-
            perative language with record subtypes. *Science of Computer Programming*,
            1998. To appear.
[Red98]   U. S. Reddy.   Objects and classes in Algol-like languages.   In *Fifth
            Intern. Workshop on Foundations of Object-oriented Languages.* URL:
            http://pauillac.inria.fr/ remy/fool/proceedings.html, Jan 1998.

Reasoning About Interactive Systems

Ralph Back, Anna Mikhajlova, and Joakim von Wright

Turku Centre for Computer Science, Åbo Akademi University
Lemminkäisenkatu 14A, Turku 20520, Finland
phone: +358-2-215-4032, fax: +358-2-241-0154
backrj, amikhajl, jwright@abo.fi

Abstract. The unifying ground for interactive programs and component-based systems is the interaction between a user and the system
or between a component and its environment. Modeling and reasoning
about interactive systems in a formal framework is critical for ensuring the systems' reliability and correctness. A mathematical foundation
based on the idea of contracts permits this kind of reasoning. In this
paper we study an iterative choice contract statement which models an
event loop allowing the user to repeatedly choose from a number of actions an alternative which is enabled and have it executed. We study
mathematical properties of iterative choice and demonstrate its modeling capabilities by specifying a component environment which describes
all actions the environment can take on a component, and an interactive
dialog box permitting the user to make selections in a dialog with the
system. We show how to prove correctness of the dialog box with respect
to given requirements, and develop its refinement allowing more complex
functionality and providing wider choice for the user.

1 Introduction

Most of contemporary software systems are inherently interactive: desk-top applications interact with a user, embedded systems interact with the environment,
system integration software interacts with the systems it integrates, etc. In addition, in systems constructed using an object-oriented or a component-based
approach objects or components interact with each other.

To be able to verify the behavior of an interactive system in its entirety, it is
first necessary to capture this behavior in a precise specification. Formal methods
have been traditionally weak in capturing the intricacy of interaction. Probably
for this reason, the importance of specifying and verifying program parts describing interaction with the environment (especially in case of interacting with
a human user) is considered as secondary to the importance of establishing correctness of some "critical" parts of the program. However, in view of the growing
complexity and importance of various interactive systems, the need for verifying correctness of interaction becomes obvious. For instance, embedded systems,
which are intrinsically interactive and often used in safety-critical environments,
can lead to dramatic consequences if they ignore input from the environment or
deliver wrong output.

J. Wing, J. Woodcock, J. Davies (Eds.): FM'99, Vol. II, LNCS 1709, pp. 1460–1476, 1999.
© Springer-Verlag Berlin Heidelberg 1999

Component-oriented approach to software design and development is rapidly gaining popularity and stimulates research on methods for analysis and construction of reliable and correct components and their compositions. Component compositions consist of cooperating or interacting components, and for each component all the other components it cooperates with can be collectively considered as the environment. Although various standard methods can be used for reasoning about separate components, component environments present in this respect a challenge. The ability to model and reason about component environments is critical for reasoning about component-based systems. The designer of a component should be aware of the behavior of the environment in which the component is supposed to operate. Knowing the precise behavior of the environment, it is then possible to analyze the effect a change to the component will have on the environment, design an appropriate component interface, etc.

Interaction is often multifaceted in the sense that component-based systems can interact with the user and interactive programs can be component-based. Moreover, for components in a component-based system their environment can be transparent, they will interact with this environment in the same way regardless of whether it is another component or a human user.

To a large extent the weakness of verification techniques for interactive parts of programs can be explained by the lack of modeling methods capable of capturing interaction and the freedom of choice that the environment has. Accordingly, development of a specification and verification method in a formalism expressive enough to model interaction is of critical importance. The mathematical foundation for reasoning about interactive systems, based on the idea of contracts, has been introduced in [4, 6]. In particular, Back and von Wright proposed using an *iterative choice* contract statement which describes an event loop, allowing the user to repeatedly choose from a number of actions an alternative which is enabled and have it executed. In this paper we focus on the iterative choice statement, examine its modeling capabilities, and develop its mathematical properties. In particular, we present rules for proving correctness of iterative choice with respect to given pre- and postconditions, and rules for iterative choice refinement through refining the options it presents and adding new alternatives. We illustrate the expressive power and versatility of iterative choice by specifying a component environment which describes all actions the environment can take on a component, and an interactive dialog box permitting the user to make selections in a dialog with the system. We show how to prove correctness of the dialog box with respect to given requirements, and develop its refinement allowing more complex functionality and providing wider choice for the user.

Notation: We use *simply typed higher-order logic* as the logical framework in the paper. The type of functions from a type Σ to a type Γ is denoted by $\Sigma \to \Gamma$ and functions can have arguments and results of function type. Functions can be described using λ-abstraction, and we write $f . x$ for the application of function f to argument x.

2   Contracts and Refinement

A computation can generally be seen as involving a number of agents (programs, modules, systems, users, etc.) who carry out actions according to a document (specification, program) that has been laid out in advance. When reasoning about a computation, we can view this document as a contract between the agents involved. In this section we review a notation for *contract statements*. A more detailed description as well as operational and weakest precondition semantics of these statements can be found in [4, 6].

We assume that the world that contracts talk about is described as a *state* σ. The *state space* Σ is the set (type) of all possible states. The state has a number of *program variables* $x_1, \ldots, x_n$, each of which can be observed and changed independently of the others. A program variable x of type Γ is really a pair of the *value function* $valx : \Sigma \to \Gamma$ and the *update function* $setx : \Gamma \to \Sigma \to \Sigma$. Given a state σ, $valx. \sigma$ is the value of x in this state, while $\sigma' = setx. \gamma. \sigma$ is the new state that we get by setting the value of x to γ. An *assignment* like $x := x + y$ denotes a state changing function that updates the value of x to the value of the expression $x + y$, i.e. $(x := x + y). \sigma = setx. (valx. \sigma + valy. \sigma). \sigma$.

A *state predicate* $p : \Sigma \to$ Bool is a boolean function on the state. Since a predicate corresponds to a set of states, we use set notation ($\cup$, $\subseteq$, etc.) for predicates. Using program variables, state predicates can be written as boolean expressions, for example, $(x + 1 > y)$. Similarly, a *state relation* $R : \Sigma \to \Sigma \to$ Bool relates a state σ to a state σ' whenever $R. \sigma. \sigma'$ holds. We permit a generalized assignment notation for relations. For example, $(x := x' \mid x' > x + y)$ relates state σ to state σ' if the value of x in σ' is greater than the sum of the values of x and y in σ and all other variables are unchanged.

2.1   Contract Notation

Contracts are built from state changing functions, predicates and relations. The *update* $\langle f \rangle$ changes the state according to $f : \Sigma \to \Sigma$. If the initial state is σ_0 then the agent must produce a final state $f. \sigma_0$. An *assignment statement* is a special kind of update where the state changing function is an assignment. For example, the assignment statement $\langle x := x + y \rangle$ (or just $x := x + y$ when it is clear from the context that an assignment statement rather than a state changing function is intended) requires the agent to set the value of program variable x to the sum of the values of x and y.

The *assertion* $\{p\}$ of a state predicate p is a requirement that the agent must satisfy in a given state. For instance, $\{x + y = 0\}$ expresses that the sum of (the values of variables) x and y in the state must be zero. If the assertion does not hold, then the agent has *breached* the contract. The *assumption* $[p]$ is dual to an assertion; if the condition p does not hold, then the agent is released from any obligation to carry out his part of the contract.

In the *sequential action* $S_1; S_2$ the action S_1 is carried out first, followed by S_2. A *choice* $S_1 \sqcup S_2$ allows the agent to choose between carrying out S_1 or S_2.

In general, there can be a number of agents that are acting together to change the world and whose behavior is bound by contracts. We can indicate explicitly which agent is responsible for each choice. For example, in the contract

$$S = x := 0; ((y := 1 \sqcup_b y := 2) \sqcup_a x := x + 1); \{y = x\}_a$$

the agents involved are a and b. The effect of the update is independent of which agent carries it out, so this information can be lost when writing contract statements.

The *relational update* $\{R\}_a$ is a contract statement that permits an agent to choose between all final states related by the state relation R to the initial state (if no such final state exists, then the agent has breached the contract). For example, the contract statement $\{x := x' \mid x < x'\}_a$ is carried out by agent a by changing the state so that the value of x becomes larger than the current value, without changing the values of any other variables.

A *recursive contract statement* of the form $(\text{rec}_a \ X \bullet S)$ is interpreted as the contract statement S, but with each occurrence of statement variable X in S treated as a recursive invocation of the whole contract $(\text{rec}_a \ X \bullet S)$. A more convenient way to define a recursive contract is by an equation of the form $X =_a S$, where S typically contains some occurrences of X. The indicated agent is responsible for termination; if the recursion unfolds infinitely, then the agent has breached the contract.

2.2   Using Contracts

Assume that we pick out one or more agents whose side we are taking. These agents are assumed to have a common goal and to coordinate their choices in order to achieve this goal. Hence, we can regard this group of agents as a single agent. The other agents need not share the goals of our agents. To prepare for the worst, we assume that the other agents try to prevent us from reaching our goals, and that they coordinate their choices against us. We will make this a little more dramatic and call our agents collectively the *angel* and the other agents collectively the *demon*. We refer to choices made by our agents as *angelic choices*, and to choices made by the other agents as *demonic choices*.

Having taken the side of certain agents, we can simplify the notation for contract statements. We write $\sqcup$ for the angelic choice $\sqcup_{angel}$ and $\sqcap$ for the demonic choice $\sqcup_{demon}$. Furthermore, we note that if our agents have breached the contract, then the other agents are released from it, i.e. $\{p\}_{angel} = [p]_{demon}$, and vice versa. Hence, we agree to let $\{p\}$ stand for $\{p\}_{angel}$ and $[p]$ stand for $\{p\}_{demon}$. This justifies the following syntax, where the explicit indication of which agent is responsible for the choice, assertion or assumption has been removed:

$$S ::= \langle f \rangle \mid \{p\} \mid [p] \mid S_1; S_2 \mid S_1 \sqcup S_2 \mid S_1 \sqcap S_2$$

This notation generalizes in the obvious way to generalized choices: we write $\sqcup\{S_i \mid i \in I\}$ for the angelic choice of one of the alternatives in the set $\{S_i \mid i \in I\}$

and we write $\sqcap\{S_i \mid i \in I\}$ for the corresponding demonic choice. For relational update, we write $\{R\}$ if the next state is chosen by the angel, and $[R]$ if the next state is chosen by the demon. Furthermore, we write $(\mu X \bullet S)$ for $(\text{rec}_{angel} \, X \bullet S)$ and $(\nu X \bullet S)$ for $(\text{rec}_{demon} \, X \bullet S)$; this notation agrees with the predicate transformer semantics of contracts.

The notation for contracts allows us to express all standard programming language constructs, like sequential composition, assignments, empty statements, conditional statements, loops, and blocks with local variables.

2.3   User Interaction

Interactive programs can be seen as special cases of contracts, where two agents are involved, the *user* and the *computer system*. The user in this case is the angel, which chooses between alternatives in order to influence the computation in a desired manner, and the computer system is the demon, resolving any internal choices in a manner unknown to the user.

User input during program execution is modeled by an angelic relational assignment. For example, the contract

$$\{x, e := x', e' \mid x' \geq 0 \wedge e > 0\}; [x := x' \mid -e < x'^2 - x < e]$$

describes how the user gives as input a value x whose square root is to be computed, as well as the precision e with which the computer is to compute this square root.

This simple contract *specifies* the interaction between the user and the computing system. The first statement specifies the user's responsibility (to give an input value that satisfies the given conditions) and the second statement specifies the system's responsibility (to compute a new value for x that satisfies the given condition).

2.4   Semantics, Correctness, and Refinement of Contracts

Every contract statement has a weakest precondition predicate transformer semantics. A *predicate transformer* $S : (\Gamma \to \text{Bool}) \to (\Sigma \to \text{Bool})$ is a function from predicates on Γ to predicates on Σ. We write

$$\Sigma \mapsto \Gamma \,\,\widehat{=}\,\, (\Gamma \to \text{Bool}) \to (\Sigma \to \text{Bool})$$

to denote a set of all predicate transformers from Σ to Γ. A contract statement with initial state in Σ and final state in Γ determines a monotonic predicate transformer $S : \Sigma \mapsto \Gamma$ that maps any postcondition $q : \Gamma \to \text{Bool}$ to the weakest precondition $p : \Sigma \to \text{Bool}$ such that the statement is guaranteed to terminate in a final state satisfying q whenever the initial state satisfies p. Following an established tradition, we identify contract statements with the monotonic predicate transformers that they determine. For details of the predicate transformer semantics, we refer to [4, 6].

The *total correctness assertion* $p \, \{\!\| \, S \, \|\!\} \, q$ is said to hold if the user can use the contract S to establish the postcondition q when starting in the set of states p. The pair of state predicates (p, q) is usually referred to as the pre- and postcondition specification of the contract S. The total correctness assertion $p \, \{\!\| \, S \, \|\!\} \, q$, which is equal to $p \subseteq S. \, q$, means that the user can (by making the right choices) either achieve the postcondition q or be released from the contract, no matter what the other agents do.

A contract S is *refined by* a contract S', written $S \sqsubseteq S'$, if any condition that we can establish with the first contract can also be established with the second contract. Formally, $S \sqsubseteq S'$ is defined to hold if $p \, \{\!\| \, S \, \|\!\} \, q \Rightarrow p \, \{\!\| \, S' \, \|\!\} \, q$, for any p and q. Refinement is reflexive and transitive. In addition, the contract constructors are monotonic, so a contract can be refined by refining a subcomponent.

The refinement calculus provides rules for transforming more abstract program structures into more concrete ones based on the notion of refinement of contracts presented above. Large collections of refinement rules are given, for instance, in [6, 10].

3   Iterative Choice and Its Modeling Capabilities

3.1   Modeling Component Environment

To demonstrate how the iterative choice statement can be used to model a component environment, let us first introduce the notion of a component. We view a component as an abstract data type with internal state and methods that can be invoked on the component to carry out certain functionality and (possibly) change the component's state.

$$
\begin{aligned}
c \; = \; &\mathsf{component} \\
&x : \Sigma := x_0 \\
&m_1 \, (\mathsf{val} \; x_1 : \Gamma_1, \mathsf{res} \; y_1 : \Delta_1) \; = \; M_1, \\
&\quad \ldots \\
&m_n \, (\mathsf{val} \; x_n : \Gamma_n, \mathsf{res} \; y_n : \Delta_n) \; = \; M_n \\
\mathsf{end}&
\end{aligned}
$$

Here $x : \Sigma$ are the variables which carry the internal component's state. These variables have some initial values x_0. Methods named $m_1, \ldots, m_n$ are specified by statements $M_1, \ldots, M_n$ respectively. Invocation of a method on a component has a standard procedure call semantics, with the only difference that the value of the component itself is passed as a value-result argument. We will denote invocation of m_i on c with value and result arguments $v : \Gamma_i$ and $r : \Delta_i$ by $c.m_i(v, r)$.

An environment using a component c does so by invoking its methods. Every time the environment has a choice of which method to choose for execution. In general, each option is preceded with an assertion which determines whether the option is enabled in a particular state. While at least one of the assertions holds, the environment may repeatedly choose a particular option which is enabled and have it executed. The environment decides on its own when it is willing to stop choosing options. Such an iterative choice of method invocations, followed by arbitrary statements not affecting the component state directly, describes all the actions the environment program might undertake:

begin var $l : \Lambda \bullet p$; do $q_1 :: c.m_1(g_1, d_1); L_1 \lozenge \ldots \lozenge q_n :: c.m_n(g_n, d_n); L_n$ od end

Here the construct inside the keywords do .. od is the iterative choice statement. The alternatives among which the choice is made at each iteration step are separated by $\lozenge$. Variables $l : \Lambda$ are some local variables initialized according to p, predicates $q_1 \ldots q_n$ are the asserted conditions on the state, and statements L_1 through L_n are arbitrary. The initialization p, the assertions $q_1 \ldots q_n$, and the statements $L_1, \ldots, L_n$ do not refer to c, which is justified by the assumption that the component state is encapsulated.

The whole program statement is a contract between the component c and *any environment* using c. The method enabledness condition q_i corresponds to the assumptions made by the corresponding method m_i, as stated in its subcontract (the method body definition). For example, in a component *EntryField* a method *SetLength*(val l : Nat) can begin with an assumption that the length l does not exceed some constant value *lmax*. An environment invoking *SetLength* on *EntryField* will then have to assert that a specific *length* does indeed satisfy this requirement:

do $length \leq lmax :: EntryField.SetLength(length); \ldots$ od

The assumption of this condition in the body of *SetLength* will pass through, as $\{p\}; [p] = \{p\}$, for all predicates p.

3.2   Modeling an Interactive Dialog Box

Suppose that we would like to describe a font selection dialog box, where the user is offered the choice of selecting a particular font and its size. The user can select a font by typing the font name in the entry field; the selection is accepted if the entered font name belongs to the set of available fonts. The size of the font can also be chosen by typing the corresponding number in the entry field. The user may change the selections of both the font and the size any number of times before he presses the OK button, which results in closing the dialog box and changing the corresponding text according to the last selection. We can model this kind of a dialog box as shown in Fig. 1. In this specification *fentry* : String and *sentry* : Nat are global variables representing current selections of the font name and its size in the corresponding entry fields of the dialog box. The constants *Fonts* : set of String and *Sizes* : set of Nat represent sets of available font names and font sizes.

When the user opens the dialog box, he assumes that the default entries for the font name and size are among those available in the system, as expressed by the corresponding assumption in *DialogBoxSpec*. If this assumption is met by the system, the user may enter new font name, or new font size, or leave the current

$$DialogBoxSpec \; = \; [\mathit{fentry} \in \mathit{Fonts} \wedge \mathit{sentry} \in \mathit{Sizes}];$$
$$\textbf{do} \;\; \textbf{true} :: \{\mathit{fentry} := s \,|\, s \in \mathit{Fonts}\}$$
$$\lozenge \;\; \textbf{true} :: \{\mathit{sentry} := n \,|\, n \in \mathit{Sizes}\}$$
$$\textbf{od}$$

Fig. 1. Specification of a dialog box

selections intact. The user may select any alternative any number of times until he is satisfied with the choice and decides to stop the iteration. Note that to model dialog closing, we do not need to explicitly maintain a boolean variable *Ok_pressed*, have all the options enabled only when $\neg\mathit{Ok\_pressed}$ holds, and set it explicitly to **true** to terminate iteration: all this is implicit in the model.

This is a very general specification of *DialogBoxSpec*, but still it is a useful abstraction precisely and succinctly describing the intended behavior. In Sec. 4.3 we will show how one can check correctness of this specification with respect to a given precondition and postcondition. Also, this specification can be refined to a more detailed one, specifying an extended functionality, as we will demonstrate in Sec. 4.5.

4   Definition and Properties of Iterative Choice

We begin with studying mathematical properties of an *angelic iteration* operator, which is used to define iterative choice.

4.1   Angelic Iteration and Its Properties

Let S be a monotonic predicate transformer (i.e., the denotation of a contract). We define an iteration construct over S, *angelic iteration*, as the following fixpoint:

$$S^{\phi} \;\; \hat{=} \;\; (\mu X \bullet S; X \sqcup \textsf{skip}) \qquad\qquad \textit{(Angelic iteration)}$$

As such, this construct is a dual of the weak iteration S^{*} defined in [6] by $(\nu X \bullet S; X \sqcap \textsf{skip})$.

Theorem 1. *Let S be an arbitrary monotonic predicate transformer. Then*

$$S^{\phi} \; = \; ((S^{\circ})^{*})^{\circ}$$

Intuitively, the statement S^{ϕ} is executed so that S is repeated an angelically chosen (finite) number of times before the iteration is terminated by choosing skip. For example, $(x := x+1)^{\phi}$ increments x an angelically chosen finite number of times, and has, therefore, the same effect as the angelic update $\{x := x' \,|\, x \leq x'\}$.

A collection of basic properties of angelic iteration follows by duality from the corresponding properties of weak iteration proved in [5].

Theorem 2. *Let S and T be arbitrary monotonic predicate transformers. Then*

    (a) S^ϕ is monotonic and terminating

    (b) S^ϕ preserves termination, strictness, and disjunctivity

    (c) $S \sqsubseteq S^\phi$

    (d) $(S^\phi)^\phi = S^\phi$

    (e) $S^\phi; S^\phi = S^\phi$

    (f) $S \sqsubseteq T \Rightarrow S^\phi \sqsubseteq T^\phi$

Here, a predicate transformer S is said to be *terminating* if $S.\text{true} = \text{true}$, *strict* if $S.\text{false} = \text{false}$, and *disjunctive* if $S.(\cup i \in I \bullet q_i) = (\cup i \in I \bullet S.q_i)$, for $I \neq \emptyset$.

To account for tail recursion, angelic iteration can be characterized as follows:

Lemma 1. *Let S and T be arbitrary monotonic predicate transformers. Then*

$$S^\phi; T = (\mu X \bullet S; X \sqcup T)$$

This lemma provides us with general unfolding and induction rules. For arbitrary monotonic predicate transformers S and T,

    $S^\phi; T = S; S^\phi; T \sqcup T$ *(unfolding)*

    $S; X \sqcup T \sqsubseteq X \Rightarrow S^\phi; T \sqsubseteq X$ *(induction)*

From the unfolding rule with T taken to be skip we get the useful property that doing nothing is refined by angelic iteration:

$$\text{skip} \sqsubseteq S^\phi$$

Angelic iteration can also be characterized on the level of predicates:

Lemma 2. *Let $S : \Sigma \mapsto \Sigma$ be an arbitrary monotonic predicate transformer and $q : \mathcal{P}\Sigma$ an arbitrary predicate. Then*

$$S^\phi.q = (\mu x \bullet S.x \cup q)$$

When applied to monotonic predicate transformers, the angelic iteration operator has two interesting properties known from the theory of regular languages, namely, the *decomposition property* and the *leapfrog property*.

Lemma 3. *Let S and T be arbitrary monotonic predicate transformers. Then*

    $(S \sqcup T)^\phi = S^\phi; (T; S^\phi)^\phi$ *(decomposition)*

    $(S; T)^\phi; S \sqsubseteq S; (T; S)^\phi$ *(leapfrog)*

(if S is disjunctive, then the leapfrog property is an equality).

Lemma 1, Lemma 2, and Lemma 3 follow by duality from the corresponding properties of weak iteration as given in [6].

Let us now study under what conditions the total correctness assertion $p \{\!| S^\phi |\!\} q$ is valid. In lattice theory, the general least fixpoint introduction rule states that

$$\frac{t_w \sqsubseteq f.\, t_{<w}}{t \sqsubseteq \mu\, f}$$

where $\{t_w \mid w \in W\}$ is a ranked collection of elements (so that W is a well-founded set and $v < w \Rightarrow t_v \sqsubseteq t_w$), $t_{<w}$ is an abbreviation for $(\sqcup v \mid v < w \cdot t_v)$, and $t = (\sqcup w \in W \cdot t_w)$. When used for predicates, with $S^\phi.\, q = (\mu x \cdot S.\, x \cup q)$, this rule directly gives us the correctness rule for angelic iteration

$$\frac{p_w \subseteq (S.\, p_{<w}) \cup q}{p \{\!| S^\phi |\!\} q} \qquad\qquad \begin{array}{l} (\textit{angelic iteration} \\ \textit{correctness rule}) \end{array}$$

where $\{p_w \mid w \in W\}$ is a ranked collection of predicates and $p = (\cup w \in W \cdot p_w)$. If the ranked predicates are written using an invariant I and a termination function t, then we have

$$\frac{I \cap t = w \subseteq S.\, (I \cap t < w) \cup q}{I \{\!| S^\phi |\!\} q}$$

where w is a fresh variable. Intuitively, this rule says that at every step either the invariant I is preserved (with t decreasing) or the desired postcondition q is reached directly and the iteration can terminate. This corresponds to temporal logic assertions "I *until* q" and "*eventually not* I". Since t cannot decrease indefinitely, this guarantees that the program eventually reaches q if it started in I.

4.2 Iterative Choice and Its Properties

Now we consider a derivative of the angelic iteration S^ϕ, the *iterative choice* statement. This specification construct was defined in [6] as follows:

$$\textbf{do}\; \langle\rangle_{i=1}^n g_i :: S_i \; \textbf{od} \;\; \widehat{=} \qquad\qquad (\textit{Iterative choice})$$
$$(\mu\, X \cdot \{g_1\}; S_1; X \sqcup \ldots \sqcup \{g_n\}; S_n; X \sqcup \textbf{skip})$$

As such, iterative choice is equivalent to the angelic iteration of the statement $\sqcup_{i=1}^n \{g_i\}; S_i$,

$$\textbf{do}\; \langle\rangle_{i=1}^n g_i :: S_i \; \textbf{od} \;=\; (\sqcup_{i=1}^n \{g_i\}; S_i)^\phi$$

and its properties can be derived from the corresponding properties of the angelic iteration.

An angelic iteration is refined if every alternative in the old system is refined by the angelic choice of all the alternatives in the new system.

Theorem 3. *For arbitrary state predicates* $g_1, \ldots, g_n$ *and* $g'_1, \ldots, g'_m$, *and arbitrary contract statements* $S_1, \ldots, S_n$ *and* $S'_1, \ldots, S'_m$ *we have that*

$$(\forall i \mid 1 \leq i \leq n \bullet \{g_i\}; S_i \sqsubseteq \sqcup_{j=1}^{m} \{g'_j\}; S'_j) \Rightarrow$$
$$\text{do } \langle \rangle_{i=1}^{n} g_i :: S_i \text{ od} \sqsubseteq \text{do } \langle \rangle_{j=1}^{m} g'_j :: S'_j \text{ od}$$

This can be compared with the rule for Dijkstra's traditional do-loop, where every alternative of the new loop must refine the demonic choice of the alternatives of the old loop (and the exit condition must be unchanged).

Two useful corollaries state that whenever every option is refined, the iterative choice of these options is a refinement, and also that adding alternatives in the iterative choice is a refinement.

Corollary 1. *For arbitrary state predicates* $g_1, \ldots, g_n$ *and* $g'_1, \ldots, g'_n$, *and arbitrary contract statements* $S_1, \ldots, S_n$ *and* $S'_1, \ldots, S'_n$ *we have that*

$$g_1 \sqsubseteq g'_1 \wedge \ldots \wedge g_n \sqsubseteq g'_n \wedge \{g_1\}; S_1 \sqsubseteq S'_1 \wedge \ldots \wedge \{g_n\}; S_n \sqsubseteq S'_n \Rightarrow$$
$$\text{do } \langle \rangle_{i=1}^{n} g_i :: S_i \text{ od} \sqsubseteq \text{do } \langle \rangle_{i=1}^{n} g'_i :: S'_i \text{ od}$$

Corollary 2. *For arbitrary state predicates* $g_1, \ldots, g_{n+1}$ *and arbitrary contract statements* $S_1, \ldots, S_{n+1}$ *we have that*

$$\text{do } \langle \rangle_{i=1}^{n} g_i :: S_i \text{ od} \sqsubseteq \text{do } \langle \rangle_{i=1}^{n+1} g_i :: S_i \text{ od}$$

The correctness rule for iterative choice states that for each ranked predicate which is stronger than the precondition there should be a choice decreasing the rank of this predicate or the possibility of establishing the postcondition directly:

$$\frac{p_w \subseteq \cup_{i=1}^{n}(g_i \cap S_i. \, p_{<w}) \cup q}{p \, \{\!| \, \text{do } \langle \rangle_{i=1}^{n} g_i :: S_i \text{ od} \, |\!\} \, q} \qquad \begin{array}{l} \textit{(iterative choice} \\ \textit{correctness rule)} \end{array}$$

When the ranked predicates are written using an invariant I and a termination function t, this rule becomes

$$\frac{p \subseteq I \qquad I \cap t = w \subseteq \cup_{i=1}^{n}(g_i \cap S_i. \, (I \cap t < w)) \cup q}{p \, \{\!| \, \text{do } \langle \rangle_{i=1}^{n} g_i :: S_i \text{ od} \, |\!\} \, q}$$

From the correctness rule we immediately get the iterative choice introduction rule

$$\frac{p_w \subseteq \cup_{i=1}^{n}(g_i \cap S_i. \, p_{<w}) \cup q[x' := x]}{\{p\}; [x := x' \mid q] \sqsubseteq \text{do } \langle \rangle_{i=1}^{n} g_i :: S_i \text{ od}} \qquad \begin{array}{l} \textit{(iterative choice} \\ \textit{introduction rule)} \end{array}$$

where x does not occur free in q.

4.3   Proving Correctness of the Interactive Dialog Box

Suppose that the font "Times" belongs to the set of available fonts, *Fonts*, and the size 12 is in the set of available sizes, *Sizes*. Can the user, by making the right choices, select this font with this size? The answer to this question can be given by verifying the following total correctness assertion:

$$
\text{"Times"} \in Fonts \cap \atop 12 \in Sizes
\begin{array}{l}
\text{do} \; \text{true} :: \{fentry := s \mid s \text{ in } Fonts\} \\
\{| \quad \lozenge \quad \text{true} :: \{sentry := n \mid n \text{ in } Sizes\} \; |\} \\
\text{od}
\end{array}
\begin{array}{l}
fentry = \text{"Times"} \cap \\
sentry = 12
\end{array}
$$

Using the rule for the correctness of iterative choice with the invariant I and the termination function t such that

$$
\begin{aligned}
I &= \text{"Times"} \in Fonts \cap 12 \in Sizes \\
t &= \#(\{\,\text{"Times"}, 12\} \setminus \{fentry, sentry\})
\end{aligned}
$$

we then need to prove two subgoals:

1. "Times" $\in Fonts \cap 12 \in Sizes \subseteq I$
2. $I \cap t = w \subseteq$ true $\cap \{fentry := s \mid s \text{ in } Fonts\}. (I \cap t < w) \cup$
   true $\cap \{sentry := n \mid n \text{ in } Sizes\}. (I \cap t < w) \cup$
   $fentry = \text{"Times"} \cap sentry = 12$

The first subgoal states that the precondition is stronger than the invariant and is trivially true. The second subgoal states that, when the invariant holds, at least one of the alternatives will decrease the termination function while preserving the invariant. It can be proved by using the definition of angelic relational update and rules of logic.

Being very simple, this example nethertheless demonstrates the essence of establishing correctness in the presence of iterative choice. By verifying that this specification is correct with respect to the given pre- and postcondition, we can guarantee that any refinement of it will preserve the correctness.

4.4   Data Refinement of Iterative Choice

Data refinement is a general technique by which one can change data representation in a refinement. A contract statement S may begin in a state space Σ and end in a state space Γ, written $S : \Sigma \mapsto \Gamma$. Assume that contract statements S and S' operate on state spaces Σ and Σ' respectively, i.e. $S : \Sigma \mapsto \Sigma$ and $S' : \Sigma' \mapsto \Sigma'$. Let $R : \Sigma' \to \Sigma \to$ Bool be a relation between the state spaces Σ' and Σ. Following [3], the statement S is said to be *data refined* by the statement S' via the relation R, denoted $S \sqsubseteq_{\{R\}} S'$, if $\{R\}; S \sqsubseteq S'; \{R\}$. An alternative and equivalent characterization of data refinement using the inverse relation R^{-1} arises from the fact that $\{R\}$ and $[R^{-1}]$ are each others inverses, in the sense that $\{R\}; [R^{-1}] \sqsubseteq$ skip and skip $\sqsubseteq [R^{-1}]; \{R\}$. Abbreviating $\{R\}; S; [R^{-1}]$ by $S \downarrow \{R\}$ we have that

$$
S \sqsubseteq_{\{R\}} S' \equiv S \downarrow \{R\} \sqsubseteq S'
$$

We will call D an *abstraction statement* if D is such that $D = \{R\}$, for some R. In this case, our notion of data refinement is the standard one, often referred to as forward data refinement or downward simulation.

Data refinement properties of angelic iteration and iterative choice cannot be proved directly by a duality argument from the corresponding results for the traditional iteration operators. However, they can still be proved:

Theorem 4. *Assume that S and D are monotonic predicate transformers and that D is an abstraction statement. Then*

$$S^\phi \downarrow D \sqsubseteq (S \downarrow D)^\phi$$

As a consequence, the angelic iteration operator preserves data refinement:

Corollary 3. *Assume that S, S' and D are monotonic predicate transformers and that D is an abstraction statement. Then*

$$S \sqsubseteq_D S' \;\Rightarrow\; S^\phi \sqsubseteq_D S'^\phi$$

Proofs of Theorem 4 and Corollary 3 can be found in [2].

Data refinement rules for iterative choice also arise from the corresponding rules for angelic iteration. First, data refinement can be propagated inside iterative choice:

Theorem 5. *Assume that $g_1, \ldots, g_n$ are arbitrary state predicates, $S_1, \ldots, S_n$ are arbitrary contract statements, and D is an abstraction statement. Then*

$$\mathsf{do}\ \langle\!\rangle_{i=1}^n g_i :: S_i\ \mathsf{od} \downarrow D \;\sqsubseteq\; \mathsf{do}\ \langle\!\rangle_{i=1}^n D.\, g_i :: S_i \downarrow D\ \mathsf{od}$$

A more general rule shows how a proof of data refinement between iterative choices can be reduced to proofs of data refinement between the iterated alternatives.

Theorem 6. *Assume that $g_1, \ldots, g_n$ and $g'_1, \ldots, g'_m$ are arbitrary state predicates, $S_1, \ldots, S_n$ and $S'_1, \ldots, S'_m$ are arbitrary contract statements, and D is an abstraction statement. Then*

$$(\forall i \mid 1 \le i \le n \bullet \{g_i\}; S_i \sqsubseteq_D \sqcup_{j=1}^m \{g'_j\}; S'_j) \;\Rightarrow$$
$$\mathsf{do}\ \langle\!\rangle_{i=1}^n g_i :: S_i\ \mathsf{od} \sqsubseteq_D \mathsf{do}\ \langle\!\rangle_{j=1}^m g'_j :: S'_j\ \mathsf{od}$$

Proofs of Theorems 5 and 6 can be found in [2]. A useful special case of these theorems is when the number of choices is the same and they are refined one by one.

Corollary 4. *Assume that $g_1, \ldots, g_n$ and $g'_1, \ldots, g'_n$ are arbitrary state predicates, $S_1, \ldots, S_n$ and $S'_1, \ldots, S'_n$ are arbitrary contract statements, and D is an abstraction statement. Then*

$$D.\, g_1 \subseteq g'_1 \wedge \ldots \wedge D.\, g_n \subseteq g'_n \wedge \{g_1\}; S_1 \sqsubseteq_D S'_1 \wedge \ldots \wedge \{g_n\}; S_n \sqsubseteq_D S'_n \;\Rightarrow$$
$$\mathsf{do}\ \langle\!\rangle_{i=1}^n g_i :: S_i\ \mathsf{od} \sqsubseteq_D \mathsf{do}\ \langle\!\rangle_{i=1}^n g'_i :: S'_i\ \mathsf{od}$$

4.5   Data Refinement of Interactive Dialog Box

Let us now demonstrate how our original specification of a dialog box can be data refined to a more concrete one. Suppose that we would like to describe a dialog box, where the user can select a font by choosing it from the list of available fonts or by typing the font name in the entry field. The size of the font can also be chosen either from the list of sizes or by typing the corresponding number in the entry field. Using the iterative choice statement, we can model this kind of a dialog box as shown in Fig. 2.

In this specification the arrays *fonts* : array 1..*fmax* of **String** and *sizes* : array 1..*smax* of **Nat** are used to represent lists of the corresponding items. When the user opens the dialog box, the system initializes *fonts* and *sizes* to contain elements from the constant sets *Fonts* and *Sizes*. The function *array_to_set*, used for this purpose, is given as follows:

$$array\_to\_set = (\lambda(a,n). \{e \mid \exists i \bullet 1 \le i \le n \land a[i] = e\})$$

The initialization conditions #*Fonts* = *fmax* and #*Sizes* = *smax* state, in addition, that the arrays contain exactly as many elements as the corresponding constant sets. Indices *fpos* : **Nat** and *spos* : **Nat** represent the currently chosen selections in the corresponding arrays and are initialized to index some items in *fonts* and *sizes*; the variables *fentry* and *sentry* are initialized with values of these items. The implicit invariant maintained by *DialogBox* states that *fonts*[*fpos*] = *fentry* and *sizes*[*spos*] = *sentry*, i.e. the currently selected font in the list of available fonts is the same as the one currently typed in the font entry field, and similarly for font sizes.

The iterative choice statement is the contract stipulating the interaction between the user making choices and the system reacting to these choices. Consider,

---

$DialogBox$ = $[fentry, sentry, fonts, sizes, fpos, spos :=$
$\qquad fentry', sentry', fonts', sizes', fpos', spos' \mid$
$\qquad\quad array\_to\_set(fonts', fmax) = Fonts \land \#Fonts = fmax \land$
$\qquad\quad array\_to\_set(sizes', smax) = Sizes \land \#Sizes = smax \land$
$\qquad\quad fentry' = fonts'[fpos'] \land sentry' = sizes'[spos'] \land$
$\qquad\quad 1 \le fpos' \le fmax \land 1 \le spos' \le smax];$

$\qquad$ **do** true :: $\{fentry := fentry' \mid \exists i \bullet 1 \le i \le fmax \land fonts[i] = fentry'\};$
$\qquad\qquad\qquad [fpos := fpos' \mid fonts[fpos'] = fentry]$
$\qquad \Diamond$ true :: $\{sentry := sentry' \mid \exists i \bullet 1 \le i \le smax \land sizes[i] = sentry'\};$
$\qquad\qquad\qquad [spos := spos' \mid sizes[spos'] = sentry]$
$\qquad \Diamond$ true :: $\{fpos := fpos' \mid 1 \le fpos' \le fmax\}; fentry := fonts[fpos]$
$\qquad \Diamond$ true :: $\{spos := spos' \mid 1 \le spos' \le smax\}; sentry := sizes[spos]$
$\qquad$ **od**

Fig. 2. Specification of a dialog box refinement

for example, the case when the user wants to select a font by directly choosing it from the list of available fonts, as modeled by the third alternative. First, the user is offered to pick an index $fpos'$, identifying a certain font in the list of fonts, and then the system updates the variable $fentry$ to maintain the invariant $fonts[fpos] = fentry$.

The abstraction relation coercing the state of $DialogBox$ to the state of $DialogBoxSpec$ is essentially an invariant on the concrete variables:

$$array\_to\_set(fonts, fmax) = Fonts \land \#Fonts = fmax \land 1 \leq fpos \leq fmax \land$$
$$array\_to\_set(sizes, smax) = Sizes \land \#Sizes = smax \land 1 \leq spos \leq smax \land$$
$$fentry = fonts[fpos] \land sentry = sizes[spos]$$

Strictly speaking, we should distinguish between $fentry, sentry$ of $DialogBoxSpec$ and $fentry, sentry$ of $DialogBox$; the abstraction relation also includes the conditions $fentry = fentry_0$ and $sentry = sentry_0$, where $fentry_0$ and $sentry_0$ denote $fentry$ and $sentry$ of $DialogBoxSpec$. It can be shown that $DialogBoxSpec \sqsubseteq_{\{R\}} DialogBox$, where

$$R.\ concrete.\ abstract\ =\ array\_to\_set(fonts, fmax) = Fonts \land \#Fonts = fmax \land$$
$$array\_to\_set(sizes, smax) = Sizes \land \#Sizes = smax \land$$
$$1 \leq fpos \leq fmax \land 1 \leq spos \leq smax \land$$
$$fentry = fonts[fpos] \land sentry = sizes[spos] \land$$
$$fentry = fentry_0 \land sentry = sentry_0$$

with $concrete = fentry, sentry, fonts, sizes, fpos, spos$ and $abstract = fentry_0, sentry_0$.

5   Conclusions and Related Work

We have described an interactive computing system in terms of contracts binding participating agents and stipulating their obligations and assumptions. In particular, we have focused on the iterative choice contract and studied its algebraic properties and modeling capabilities. This work extends [4] where Back and von Wright introduced the notions of correctness and refinement for contracts and defined their weakest precondition semantics.

The notion of contracts is based on the fundamental duality between demonic and angelic nondeterminism (choices of different agents), abortion (breaching a contract), and miracles (being released from a contract). The notion of angelic nondeterminism goes back to the theory of nondeterministic automata and the nondeterministic programs of Floyd [8]. Broy in [7] discusses the use of demonic and angelic nondeterminism with respect to concurrency. Some applications of angelic nondeterminism are shown by Ward and Hayes in [12]. Adabi, Lamport, and Wolper in [1] study realizability of specifications, considering them as "determined" games, where the system plays against the environment and wins if it produces a correct behavior. Specifications are identified with the properties that they specify, and no assumptions are made about how they are written.

Moschovakis in [11] studies non-deterministic interaction in concurrent communication also considering it from the game-theoretic perspective.

Another direction of related work concentrates on studying the role of interaction in computing systems. Wegner in [13] proposes to use *interaction machines* as "a formal framework for interactive models". Interaction machines are described as extensions of Turing machines with unbounded input streams, which "precisely capture fuzzy concepts like open systems and empirical computer science". The main thesis of work presented in [13] and further developed in [14] is that "Logic is too weak to model interactive computation" and, instead, empirical models should be used for this purpose. Apparently, first-order logic is meant by the author, which is indeed too weak for modeling interaction. However, our formalization is based on an extension of higher-order logic and, as such, is perfectly suitable for this purpose. Also, it is claimed in [13] that "Interaction machines are incomplete in the sense of Gödel: their nonenumerable number of true statements cannot be enumerated by a set of theorems. [...] The incompleteness of interactive systems implies that proving correctness is not merely hard but impossible." We believe that our work presents a proof to the contrary.

As future work we intend to investigate modeling capabilities of iterative choice further. In particular, its application to modeling client and server proxies in distributed object-oriented systems appears to be of interest. Various architectural solutions, such as implicit invocation [9], can also be described in this framework, and the work on this topic is the subject of current research.

References

[1] M. Abadi, L. Lamport, and P. Wolper. Realizable and unrealizable specifications of reactive systems. In *Proceedings of 16th ICALP*, volume 372 of *LNCS*, pages 1–17, Stresa, Italy, 11–15 July 1989. Springer-Verlag.

[2] R. Back, A. Mikhajlova, and J. von Wright. Modeling component environments and interactive programs using iterative choice. Technical Report 200, Turku Centre for Computer Science, September 1998.

[3] R. J. R. Back. Changing data representation in the refinement calculus. In *21st Hawaii International Conference on System Sciences*. IEEE, January 1989.

[4] R. J. R. Back and J. von Wright. Contracts, games and refinement. In *4th Workshop on Expressiveness in Concurrency, EXPRESS'97*, volume 7 of *Electronic Notes in Theoretical Computer Science*. Elsevier, September 1997.

[5] R. J. R. Back and J. von Wright. Reasoning algebraically about loops. Technical Report 144, Turku Centre for Computer Science, November 1997.

[6] R. J. R. Back and J. von Wright. *Refinement Calculus: A Systematic Introduction*. Springer-Verlag, April 1998.

[7] M. Broy. A theory for nondeterminism, parallelism, communication, and concurrency. *Theoretical Computer Science*, 45:1–61, 1986.

[8] R. W. Floyd. Assigning meaning to programs. In J. T. Schwartz, editor, *Mathematical aspects of computer science*, volume 19, pages 19–31. American Mathematical Society, 1967.

[9] D. Garlan and D. Notkin. Formalizing design spaces: Implicit invocation mechanisms. In *VDM 91, Volume 1: Conference Contributions*, LNCS 551, pages 31–44. Springer-Verlag, Oct. 1991.

[10] C. C. Morgan. *Programming from Specifications*. Prentice–Hall, 1990.

[11] Y. N. Moschovakis. A model of concurrency with fair merge and full recursion. *Information and Computation*, 93(1):114–171, July 1991.

[12] N. Ward and I. Hayes. Applications of angelic nondeterminism. In P.A.C.Bailes, editor, *6th Australian Software Engineering Conference*, pages 391–404, Sydney, Australia, 1991.

[13] P. Wegner. Interactive software technology. In J. Allen B. Tucker, editor, *The Computer Science and Engineering Handbook*. CRC Press, in cooperation with ACM, 1997.

[14] P. Wegner. Interactive foundations of computing. *Theoretical Computer Science*, 192(2):315–351, Feb. 1998.

Non-atomic Refinement in Z

John Derrick and Eerke Boiten

Computing Laboratory, University of Kent, Canterbury, CT2 7NF, UK.
J.Derrick@ukc.ac.uk

Abstract. This paper discusses the refinement of systems specified in Z when we relax the assumption that the refinement will preserve the atomicity of operations. Data refinement is a well established technique for transforming specifications of abstract data types into ones which are closer to an eventual implementation. To verify a refinement a retrieve relation is used which relates the concrete to abstract states and allow the comparison between the data types to be made on a step by step basis by comparing an abstract operation with its concrete counterpart. A step by step comparison is possible because the two abstract data types are assumed to be *conformal*, i.e. there is a one-one correspondence between abstract and concrete operations, so each abstract operation has a concrete counterpart. In this paper we relax that assumption to discuss refinements where an abstract operation is refined by, not one, but a sequence of concrete operations. Such non-conformal or non-atomic refinements arise naturally in a number of settings and we illustrate our derivations with a simple example of a bank accounting system.

Keywords: Specification; Refinement; Z; Non-atomic refinement; Non-atomic operations.

1 Introduction

This paper discusses the refinement of systems specified in state-based specification languages such as Z [8] when we relax the assumption that refinements preserve the atomicity of operations.

State-based languages have gained a certain amount of acceptance in the software community as an industrial strength formal method. As a canonical example, we will concentrate on Z in this paper, although the methods we derive could be applied to other state-based languages. Z is a state-based language whose specifications are written using set theory and first order logic. Abstract data types are specified in Z using the so called "state plus operations" style, where a collection of operations describe changes to the state space. The state space, initialisation and operations are described as *schemas*, and the schema calculus has proved to be an enduring structuring mechanism for specifying complex systems. These schemas, and the operations that they represent, can be understood as (total or partial) relations on the underlying state space.

J. Wing, J. Woodcock, J. Davies (Eds.): FM'99, Vol. II, LNCS 1709, pp. 1477–1496, 1999.

In addition to specifying a system, we might also wish to develop, or *refine*, it further. This idea of data refinement is a well established technique for transforming specifications of abstract data types into ones which are closer to an eventual implementation. Such a refinement might typically weaken the precondition of an operation, remove some non-determinism or even alter the state space of the specification. The conditions under which a development is a correct refinement are encapsulated into two refinement (or simulation) rules: downward and upward simulations [10]. To verify a refinement the simulations use a retrieve relation which relates the concrete to abstract states and allow the comparison between the data types to be made on a step by step basis by comparing an abstract operation with its concrete counterpart. Versions of the simulation rules for Z are given in [10].

The step by step comparison that a simulation makes is possible because the two abstract data types are assumed to be *conformal* [6], i.e. there is a one-one correspondence between abstract and concrete operations, so each abstract operation has a concrete counterpart. In this paper we relax that assumption to discuss refinements where an abstract operation is refined by, not one, but a sequence of concrete operations. The motivation for such a refinement is twofold: we might wish to reflect the structure of the eventual implementation in a specification without having to make that choice at an initial abstract level, and going further, we might wish to allow interleavings of concrete operations for the sake of efficiency. For example, we might want to describe an abstract operation AOp in the first instance, but in a subsequent development describe how AOp is implemented as a sequence of concrete operations: COp_1 followed by COp_2.

Such non-conformal or non-atomic refinements arise naturally in a number of settings. For example, a protocol might be specified abstractly as a single operation, but in a later development refined into a sequence of operations describing the structure of how the protocol works in more detail. Another example might be a (coffee!) machine which has an operation that requires a sequence of inputs (or generates a sequence of outputs). At the abstract level this is described as a single atomic operation, but at the concrete level we may wish to dispense with this assumption and specify the process of entering the inputs (generating the outputs) one by one.

Such non-atomic refinements have been extensively studied in the context of process algebras, usually under the name of action refinement [2]. Examples of simple non-atomic refinements are beginning to emerge for state-based specifications, however, we are not aware of any systematic study of state-based non-atomic refinement. (Although there has been some study of hiding sets of actions in action systems [7].) The purpose of this paper is to contribute to such a discussion.

The simplest approach to non-atomic refinement is to introduce a *skip* operation in the abstract specification, such an operation produces no change in the abstract state. One of the concrete operations, say COp_1, can refine AOp whilst the other refines *skip*. Examples of applications of such an approach include protocol refinements in B [1], in Z [10] and buffers in B [4]. In Section 3 of this paper we derive the relational basis for refinements of this kind and give a Z formulation for the appropriate simulation conditions.

However, not all non-atomic refinements can be verified in such a manner. Consider a refinement where we would like to split a collection of inputs or outputs across several concrete operations. Because we are transforming the inputs/outputs in this fashion, such a refinement cannot in general be verified using abstract steps of *skips*. A more complex example which illustrates some of the problems will be given in Section 4.

In Section 5 we consider how such refinements can be verified in general. The initial condition we consider decomposes an abstract operation into a sequence of concrete operations $COp_1 \, \S \, COp_2$, where no requirement is made that either of the concrete operations refines *skip*. In order to distribute an abstract operation's inputs and outputs across a sequence of concrete operations we apply current work on I/O refinement described in [3, 9], extending it where necessary to provide the required generalisation. This generalisation is derived in Section 6. The resulting refinement rules are given in Z and we show how they can be applied to the example in Section 4. In Section 7 we summarise the rules and in Section 8 we make some concluding remarks. We begin by describing the traditional view of refinement in Z based upon the standard relational semantics, throughout the paper we will work at the relational level only using the Z schema calculus to give the final refinement conditions.

2   A Relational View of Refinement in Z

In this section we discuss the relational view of refinement and describe how it treats partiality, leading to the standard presentation of refinement in a language such as Z [8, 10]. In doing so we present a summary of results in [6, 10] to which the reader is directed for more detailed explanation if necessary.

The underlying model of a state based system is a relational model, where the components of an abstract data type (ADT) are relations (assumed total for the moment). An ADT is a quadruple $\mathcal{A} = (Astate, ai, \{aop_i\}_{i \in I}, af)$ which acts on a global state space G such that: $Astate$ is the space of values; $ai \in G \leftrightarrow Astate$ is an initialisation; $af \in Astate \leftrightarrow G$ is a finalisation; aop_i are operations in $Astate \leftrightarrow Astate$.

A program P is a sequence of operations upon a data type beginning with an initialisation and ending with a finalisation, e.g.

$$P(\mathcal{A}) = ai \, \S \, aop_1 \, \S \, aop_2 \, \S \, af$$

The standard derivation of refinement assumes that the abstract and concrete data types are conformal, i.e. they have the same global state space G and that the indexing sets for the operations coincide (so every abstract operation has a concrete counterpart and vice versa).

Definition 1. *A data type $\mathcal{C}$ refines a data type $\mathcal{A}$ if, for every program P, $P(\mathcal{C}) \subseteq P(\mathcal{A})$.*

This has the effect (for total relations) of refinement being the reduction of non-determinism. This definition of refinement involves quantification over all programs, and in order to verify such refinements, *simulations* are used which consider values produced at each step of a program's execution. Simulations are thus the means to make the verification of a refinement feasible. In order to consider values produced at each step we need a relation r between the two state spaces *Astate* and *Cstate*, this relation is known as the *retrieve* relation.

Partiality

In the relational framework we have described so far the relations were assumed to be total relations. However, not all operations are total, and the traditional meaning of an operation ρ specified as a partial relation is that ρ behaves as specified when used within its precondition (domain), and outside its precondition, anything may happen.

In order to deal with this partial relations are totalised, i.e. we add a distinguished element $\perp$ to the state space, denoting undefinedness, and we denote such an augmented version of X by $X^{\perp}$. Thus if ρ is a partial relation between X and Y, we add the following sets of pairs to ρ: $\{x : X^{\perp}, y : Y^{\perp} \mid x \notin \operatorname{dom} \rho \bullet x \mapsto y\}$, and call this new (total) relation $\overset{\bullet}{\rho}$.

We also require that the retrieve relation be strict, i.e., that r propagates undefinedness and we ensure this by considering the lifted form of $r \in X \leftrightarrow Y$:

$$\overset{\circ}{r} = r \cup (\{\perp\} \times Y^{\perp})$$

The retrieve relation gives rise to two types of step by step comparisons: downwards simulation and upwards simulation [10]. These simulation relations are the basis for refinement methods in Z and other state based languages. Their usefulness lies in the fact that they are sound and jointly complete [6].

In this paper we restrict our attention to the more commonly occurring downward simulations. A downward simulation is a relation r from *Astate* to *Cstate* such that

$$\overset{\bullet}{ci} \subseteq \overset{\bullet}{ai} \,\overset{\circ}{\,_9\,}\, \overset{\circ}{r}$$

$$\overset{\circ}{r} \,_9\, \overset{\bullet}{cf} \subseteq \overset{\bullet}{af}$$

$$\overset{\circ}{r} \,_9\, \overset{\bullet}{cop_i} \subseteq \overset{\bullet}{aop_i} \,_9\, \overset{\circ}{r} \qquad \text{for each index } i \in I$$

The simulation rules are defined in terms of augmented relations. We can extract the underlying rules for the original partial relations as follows. For example, for a downwards simulation these rules are equivalent to the following:

$$ci \subseteq ai \,_9\, r$$
$$r \,_9\, cf \subseteq af$$
$$(\operatorname{dom} aop_i \lhd r \,_9\, cop_i) \subseteq aop_i \,_9\, r$$
$$\operatorname{ran}((\operatorname{dom} aop_i) \lhd r) \subseteq \operatorname{dom} cop_i$$

The last two conditions (where $\lhd$ is domain restriction [8]) mean that: the effect of cop_i must be consistent with that of aop_i; and, the operation cop_i is defined for every value that can be reached from the domain of aop_i using r.

Inputs and Outputs

We can use this relational semantics to model systems in which operations have input and output (IO) by providing all inputs at initialisation and delaying outputs until finalisation. To do so we augment the state by adding two sequences, an input sequence and an output sequence. Initially, the output sequence is empty; in the final state, the input sequence is empty. Every time an operation is executed, (if the operation has an input) the first value is removed from the input sequence, and (if the operation has an output) a value is added to the end of the output sequence. The outcome of the operation does not (directly) depend on any other value in the input or output sequence.

Above conditions for a downward simulation were derived for use between operations that have no inputs or outputs. We can now derive similar downward simulation conditions for operations that do have inputs and outputs, by augmenting the state with extra components representing the sequence of inputs still to be dealt with and the sequence of outputs already computed.

Let operations aop and cop consume input and produce output. Let us denote the equivalent operations that expect input and output sequences by aop_s and cop_s. It is now possible to translate the conditions for a downwards simulation between aop_s and cop_s into conditions between aop and cop. Given a relation r between states without input and output sequences, we must construct an equivalent relation that acts on the enhanced form of the state. We use the following retrieve relation on the extended state

$$r_s = r \| id[Inp] \| id[Outp]$$

where $\|$ is a relational parallel composition (see [10]) and Inp and $Outp$ are the types of the input and output sequences of aop. $id[Inp]$ maps an abstract input sequence to an identical concrete input sequence, and similarly for the output (see figure 1).

Using such a retrieve relation, [10] derive equivalent simulation rules for aop and cop which are as follows (because any operation can produce output the finalisation condition is no longer required):

$$ci \subseteq ai \,\S\, r$$
$$(\text{dom } aop \lhd (r\|id) \,\S\, cop) \subseteq aop \,\S\, (r\|id)$$
$$\text{ran}((\text{dom } aop) \lhd (r\|id)) \subseteq \text{dom } cop$$

These rules can now be transformed from their relational setting to simulation rules for Z specifications by writing them in the Z schema calculus. This formalisation is the same as the rules given in standard presentations of refinement in Z, e.g. [8].

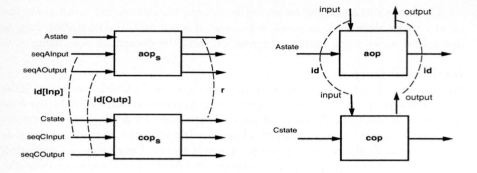

Fig. 1. Refinement of operations with input and output

Definition 1 *Let R be the retrieve relation between data types (Astate, Ainit,*
{AOp}) and (Cstate, Cinit, {COp}). Suppose that the operations have an input
x? : X and output y! : Y . R is a downwards simulation if the following hold.

$$\forall\, Cstate \bullet CInit \Rightarrow (\exists\, Astate \bullet AInit \wedge R)$$
$$\forall\, Astate;\ Cstate;\ x? : X \bullet pre\, AOp \wedge R \Rightarrow pre\, COp$$
$$\forall\, Astate;\ Cstate;\ Cstate';\ x? : X;\ y! : Y \bullet$$
$$pre\, AOp \wedge COp \wedge R \Rightarrow \exists\, Astate' \bullet R' \wedge AOp$$

In the subsequent sections of this paper we will relax two assumptions made
above. The starting point will be to consider the consequences of refining an
abstract operation into more than one concrete operation. In doing so we will
need the generality of IO refinement which assumes a general mapping between
the pairs of input and output streams as opposed to the identities $id[Inp]$ and
$id[Outp]$ used above.

3   Simple Non-atomic Refinement

We begin our derivation with the same definition of refinement, namely that for
every program P, $P(\mathcal{C}) \subseteq P(\mathcal{A})$. Let us now suppose that in the two data types
the indexes coincide except that abstract operation aop is refined by the sequence
cop_1; cop_2. We now have two sets of potential programs, those drawn from the
abstract indexes and those from the concrete indexes. Let us denote these P_A
and P_C respectively. So $ai \,\overset{\circ}{,}\, aop \,\overset{\circ}{,}\, af$ and $ci \,\overset{\circ}{,}\, cop_1 \,\overset{\circ}{,}\, cop_2 \,\overset{\circ}{,}\, cf$ are programs in $P_A(\mathcal{A})$
and $P_A(\mathcal{C})$ respectively, whereas $ci \,\overset{\circ}{,}\, cop_2 \,\overset{\circ}{,}\, cf$, $ci \,\overset{\circ}{,}\, cop_1 \,\overset{\circ}{,}\, cf$ and $ci \,\overset{\circ}{,}\, cop_2 \,\overset{\circ}{,}\, cop_1 \,\overset{\circ}{,}\, cf$
are programs in $P_C(\mathcal{C})$. Thus for non-atomic refinement there are two conditions
which can perhaps be considered as liveness and safety conditions respectively:

$$P_A(\mathcal{C}) \subseteq P_A(\mathcal{A}) \qquad \text{and} \qquad P_C(\mathcal{C}) \subseteq P_C(\mathcal{A})$$

The first requires that if we take abstract indexes then the equivalent concrete program reduces non-determinism, e.g. $ci \mathbin{\fatsemi} cop_1 \mathbin{\fatsemi} cop_2 \mathbin{\fatsemi} cf \subseteq ai \mathbin{\fatsemi} aop \mathbin{\fatsemi} af$. The second implies that to every concrete program there must be some abstract equivalent that it refines, e.g. there will be an abstract equivalent to $ci \mathbin{\fatsemi} cop_2 \mathbin{\fatsemi} cf$.

To begin we consider the case when both these conditions are required. Simulations can be used to make step-by-step comparisons as before. Quantification over all abstract programs leads to the requirement that

$$\mathring{r} \mathbin{\fatsemi} \overset{\bullet}{cop_1} \mathbin{\fatsemi} \overset{\bullet}{cop_2} \subseteq \overset{\bullet}{aop} \mathbin{\fatsemi} \mathring{r} \tag{1}$$

whilst quantification over all concrete programs requires that we find abstract counterparts to cop_1 and cop_2 which we denote p_A^1 and p_A^2 such that

$$\mathring{r} \mathbin{\fatsemi} \overset{\bullet}{cop_1} \subseteq p_A^1 \mathbin{\fatsemi} \mathring{r} \qquad \text{and} \qquad \mathring{r} \mathbin{\fatsemi} \overset{\bullet}{cop_2} \subseteq p_A^2 \mathbin{\fatsemi} \mathring{r}$$

The obvious choice for p_A^1 and p_A^2 are for one to be the original abstract operation $\overset{\bullet}{aop}$ and for the other to be $skip_R$ (the subscript R will be explained in a moment). Clearly these choices are sufficient, but not necessary, however whilst it is possible to construct examples where the concrete operations are refining different abstract operations it is difficult to construct realistic examples. Thus, without loss of generality taking cop_1 to refine aop, let us consider the requirement that

$$\mathring{r} \mathbin{\fatsemi} \overset{\bullet}{cop_1} \subseteq \overset{\bullet}{aop} \mathbin{\fatsemi} \mathring{r} \qquad \text{and} \qquad \mathring{r} \mathbin{\fatsemi} \overset{\bullet}{cop_2} \subseteq \overset{\bullet}{skip_R} \mathbin{\fatsemi} \mathring{r} \tag{2}$$

The abstract operation $skip_R$ can be chosen to be any operation satisfying (1) with the property that $\overset{\bullet}{aop} \mathbin{\fatsemi} skip_R = \overset{\bullet}{aop}$. For then if (2) holds we have

$$\mathring{r} \mathbin{\fatsemi} \overset{\bullet}{cop_1} \mathbin{\fatsemi} \overset{\bullet}{cop_2} \subseteq \overset{\bullet}{aop} \mathbin{\fatsemi} \mathring{r} \mathbin{\fatsemi} \overset{\bullet}{cop_2} \subseteq \overset{\bullet}{aop} \mathbin{\fatsemi} \overset{\bullet}{skip_R} \mathbin{\fatsemi} \mathring{r} = \overset{\bullet}{aop} \mathbin{\fatsemi} \mathring{r}$$

Thus (2) represents sufficient conditions for the action refinement of aop into cop_1; cop_2. We can now extract the underlying conditions on the partial relations in the usual manner. The first is the standard condition for refining aop by cop_1, namely that (we elide the identities over input and output streams for the moment)

(dom $aop \lhd r \mathbin{\fatsemi} cop_1) \subseteq aop \mathbin{\fatsemi} r$
ran((dom $aop) \lhd r) \subseteq$ dom cop_1

The requirement that $\overset{\bullet}{aop} \mathbin{\fatsemi} skip_R = \overset{\bullet}{aop}$ could be satisfied by $skip_R = skip$, however, this is unnecessarily restrictive and in fact we can take $skip_R = A \lhd skip$ for any A with ran $aop \subseteq A$. Possible choices for $skip_R$ then range from ran $aop \lhd skip$ to $skip$ itself. The second requirement in (2) is equivalent to

(dom $skip_R \lhd r \mathbin{\fatsemi} cop_2) \subseteq skip_R \mathbin{\fatsemi} r$
ran((dom $skip_R) \lhd r) \subseteq$ dom cop_2

Taking $skip_R = \text{ran } aop \lhd skip$ these become

$$(\text{ran } aop \lhd r \mathbin{\fatsemi} cop_2) \subseteq \text{ran } aop \lhd r$$
$$\text{ran}(\text{ran } aop \lhd r) \subseteq \text{dom } cop_2$$

and when $skip_R = skip$ they are: $r \mathbin{\fatsemi} cop_2 \subseteq r$ and $\text{ran } r \subseteq \text{dom } cop_2$.

These can be translated into Z in the usual manner. It is in this context that the non-atomic refinements given in [10, 4] are verified.

For example, in [4] a specification is given of an unordered buffer together with a refinement of it. The refinement introduces an additional operation, *mid*, which is a refinement of *skip* at the abstract level.

However, some desirable non-atomic refinements are more complex than this, and we illustrate the problem with an example which will motivate our need for more general refinement conditions.

4   Example - A Bank Account

We specify a bank consisting of a number of electronic booths where users may deposit money and check their balances. At an abstract level we are given a mapping from names to Money ($= \mathbb{N}$), and operations allowing money to be deposited and balances checked. The example illustrates nicely many of the issues involved in non-atomic refinement*.

$$ABank \mathrel{\widehat{=}} [act : Name \nrightarrow Money]$$
$$ABankInit \mathrel{\widehat{=}} [ABank' \mid act' = \varnothing]$$
$$AOpenAcct \mathrel{\widehat{=}} [\Delta ABank; \; n? : Name \mid act' = act \oplus \{n? \mapsto 0\}]$$

┌ *Deposit* ───────────	┌ *Balance* ───────────
$\Delta ABank$	$\Xi ABank$
$n? : Name$	$n? : Name$
$p? : Money$	$b! : Money$
───────────	───────────
$n? \in \text{dom } act$	$n? \in \text{dom } act$
$act' = act \oplus \{n? \mapsto act(n?) + p?\}$	$b! = act\ n?$

At the concrete level an atomic *Deposit* operation is unrealistic and we would like the amounts to be transferred coin by coin at every booth thus allowing interleaving of these operations with actions at other booths, where $Coin = \{1, 2, 5, 10\}$ say. To specify this we use a collection of temporary accounts *tct* and split the *Deposit* operation into a transaction consisting of a *Start*, a succession of *Next* operations transferring the amount coin by coin with a *Stop* operation ending the process. A temporary account is now represented by sequences of coins. The *Stop* operation takes this sequence and sums the coins entered, updating the concrete account with the result of this calculation

---

* and is adapted from an example in [10] which specifies a distributed file store.

(remember that $+/.$ represents distributed summation over a sequence). The concrete specification is as follows, where $\lhd$ is domain subtraction.

```
┌─ CBank ─────────────────────────────────────────────────────
│ cct : Name ↛ Money
│ tct : Name ↛ seq Coin
│─────────────────────
│ dom tct ⊆ dom cct
└──────────────────────────────────────────────────────────────
```

$$CBankInit \mathrel{\widehat{=}} [CBank' \mid cct' = tct' = \varnothing]$$

```
┌─ Start ──────────────────────┐   ┌─ Next ──────────────────────┐
│ ΔCBank                        │   │ ΔCBank                       │
│ n? : Name                     │   │ n? : Name                    │
│                               │   │ c? : Coin                    │
│─────────────────              │   │──────────                    │
│ n? ∈ dom cct                  │   │ n? ∈ dom tct                 │
│ tct' = tct ⊕ {n? ↦ ⟨⟩}        │   │ tct' = tct ⊕ {n? ↦ (tct n?) ⌢ ⟨c?⟩} │
│ cct' = cct                    │   │ cct' = cct                   │
└───────────────────────────────┘   └──────────────────────────────┘
```

```
┌─ Stop ─────────────────────┐   ┌─ Balance ──────────────────┐
│ ΔCBank                      │   │ ΞCBank                      │
│ n? : Name                   │   │ n? : Name                   │
│                             │   │ b! : Money                  │
│─────────────────            │   │──────────                   │
│ n? ∈ dom tct                │   │ n? ∈ dom cct                │
│ tct' = {n?} ⊲ tct           │   │ b! = cct n?                 │
│ cct' = cct⊕                 │   │                             │
│   {n? ↦ cct(n?) + (+/.(tct n?))} │ │                         │
└─────────────────────────────┘   └─────────────────────────────┘
```

The link between the abstract and concrete state spaces will be via the relation R

```
┌─ R ─────────────────────────────────────────────────────────
│ ABank
│ CBank
│─────────
│ act = cct
└──────────────────────────────────────────────────────────────
```

Clearly at some level the abstract *Deposit* operation is being refined by the sequence $Start \mathbin{\S} Next \ldots Next \mathbin{\S} Stop$. However, the refinement isn't simply a matter of one of the concrete operations corresponding to *Deposit* whilst the others correspond to *skip*.

At issue is the following. The retrieve relation links act and cct, therefore abstract *skip* operations can be refined by concrete operations which only change the temporary account tct. Therefore *Start* and *Next* look suitable candidates to refine *skip*. There are however two problems. The first is that although *Start* and *Next* do not alter *cct* they do consume input, conceptually taking values off the input stream. Therefore at the level of an augmented state complete with input stream they do not simply correspond to *skip*. The second, and related, problem is that if *Stop* corresponds to *Deposit* then pre *Deposit* $\wedge$ *R* needs to imply the precondition of *Stop*. However, the precondition of *Stop* is that $n? \in$ dom *tct*, which isn't a consequence of pre *Deposit* $\wedge$ *R*. The issue is that $n? \in$ dom *tct* is assuming that at least a *Start* operation has already happened, and that the system is now ready to *Stop*. *Stop* can in fact be amended to overcome this problem. However to do this you need to put sufficient functionality into it that the other concrete operations are then unnecessary.

As we can see there are many issues involved in such a refinement, not least is the problem that the inputs of *Deposit* are distributed throughout the concrete operations, this means that we must develop machinery in addition to that discussed in the last section. This is what we seek to do next.

5   General Non-atomic Refinement

In this section we will consider more general refinements than considered in Section 3, in particular we drop the requirement that $P_C(\mathcal{C}) \subseteq P_C(\mathcal{A})$. This means that we can consider decomposing an abstract operation into a sequence of concrete operations without requiring that any of these concrete operations refine an abstract operation of *skip*. This opens the way to providing methods of refinement that can tackle some of the issues highlighted in the previous section. In this section we also consider various properties of non-atomic refinement. In particular, we show that non-atomic refinement is transitive and we consider conditions on the concrete operations that will allow interleaving of the components of a non-atomic decomposition.

To verify a general non-atomic refinement we must also address in some detail how we treat inputs and outputs. The bank account example is particularly interesting in this respect because it has taken an input amount $p? : Money$ and broken it down into a single input $c? : Coin$ provided a number of times via the *Next* operation. To verify such refinements we will use the technique of IO-refinement and to apply it we extend current work in this area [3, 9]. These points are discussed in Section 6, we begin now with the general conditions for a non-atomic refinement.

5.1   Conditions for a Non-atomic Refinement

We begin by dropping the safety requirement that $P_C(\mathcal{C}) \subseteq P_C(\mathcal{A})$, so in particular the requirements of (2) disappear and the single requirement is that:

$$\overset{\circ}{r} \,\overset{\circ}{9}\, \overset{\bullet}{cop_1} \,\overset{\circ}{9}\, \overset{\bullet}{cop_2} \subseteq \overset{\bullet}{aop} \,\overset{\circ}{9}\, \overset{\circ}{r} \tag{3}$$

With this single requirement we can extract the underlying conditions on the partial relations as before to find that this is equivalent to three conditions, namely that

$$(\text{dom } aop \lhd r \, \mathbin{\mathring{,}} \, cop_1 \, \mathbin{\mathring{,}} \, cop_2) \subseteq aop \, \mathbin{\mathring{,}} \, r \tag{4}$$

$$\text{ran}((\text{dom } aop) \lhd r) \subseteq \text{dom } cop_1 \tag{5}$$

$$\text{ran}((\text{dom } aop) \lhd r \, \mathbin{\mathring{,}} \, cop_1) \subseteq \text{dom } cop_2 \tag{6}$$

If cop_1 is deterministic we can replace the last two (applicability) conditions by a single condition.

Proposition 1 *If cop_1 is deterministic then*

$ran((dom\ aop) \lhd r) \subseteq dom\ cop_1 \ \wedge$
$ran((dom\ aop) \lhd r \, \mathbin{\mathring{,}} \, cop_1) \subseteq dom\ cop_2$

is equivalent to the condition $ran((dom\ aop) \lhd r) \subseteq dom(cop_1 \, \mathbin{\mathring{,}} \, cop_2)$.

The requirement of cop_1 being deterministic is necessary to ensure that the resultant condition implies $\text{ran}((\text{dom } aop) \lhd r \, \mathbin{\mathring{,}} \, cop_1) \subseteq \text{dom } cop_2$, the other implications always hold.

Before we proceed any further it is important to check whether non-atomic refinement is transitive, that is further non-atomic or atomic refinements should give rise to an overall refinement. This is indeed the case.

Theorem 1. *Non-atomic refinement is transitive.*

Proof. There are four cases to consider which are illustrated in the following diagram.

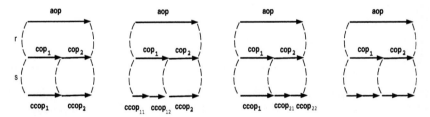

In each case it is easy to see that we have transitivity. □

Without considering any input and output transformations at this stage we can express the relational conditions given in (4-6) in the Z schema calculus. The formulation is as follows.

Definition 2 *R is a non-atomic downwards simulation if the following hold.*

$\forall Astate;\ Cstate;\ Cstate' \bullet$
$\quad\quad\quad pre\ AOp \wedge (COp_1 \, \mathbin{\mathring{,}} \, COp_2) \wedge R \Rightarrow \exists Astate' \bullet R' \wedge AOp$
$\forall Astate;\ Cstate \bullet pre\ AOp \wedge R \Rightarrow pre\ COp_1$
$\forall Astate;\ Cstate \bullet pre\ AOp \wedge R \wedge COp_1 \Rightarrow pre\ COp_2$

These conditions generalise to a non-atomic refinement with an arbitrary number of abstract and concrete operations in the obvious manner.

Let us consider the bank account example when the deposit p? consists of a single coin. We then have three operations $Start \, \text{\textcelsius} \, Next \, \text{\textcelsius} \, Stop$ in our concrete refinement (we will consider an arbitrary amount deposited later when we have a way to transform inputs). To verify such a refinement we have to demonstrate four conditions:

$\forall Astate; \ Cstate; \ Cstate' \bullet$
$\qquad \text{pre} \, Deposit \land (Start \, \text{\textcelsius} \, Next \, \text{\textcelsius} \, Stop) \land R \Rightarrow \exists Astate' \bullet R' \land Deposit$
$\forall Astate; \ Cstate \bullet \text{pre} \, Deposit \land R \Rightarrow \text{pre} \, Start$
$\forall Astate; \ Cstate \bullet \text{pre} \, Deposit \land R \land Start \Rightarrow \text{pre} \, Next$
$\forall Astate; \ Cstate \bullet \text{pre} \, Deposit \land R \land (Start \, \text{\textcelsius} \, Next) \Rightarrow \text{pre} \, Stop$

We will consider the three applicability conditions first. The predicate of pre $Deposit \land R$ will be the condition that $n? \in \text{dom} \, cct$, which is the precondition of $Start$. Similarly pre $Deposit \land R \land Start$ implies $n? \in \text{dom} \, tct$ which is the precondition of $Next$. The precondition of $Stop$ works in a similar way. Thus even without IO transformations the applicability conditions can be verified.

The correctness condition requires that we calculate the schema composition $(Start \, \text{\textcelsius} \, Next \, \text{\textcelsius} \, Stop)$ which results in

---
$\Delta CBank$
$n? : Name$
$c? : Coin$

$n? \in \text{dom} \, cct$
$tct' = \{n?\} \lhd tct$
$cct' = cct \oplus \{n? \mapsto cct(n?) + c?\}$

Given a very simple input transformation of a deposit p? into a single coin this can be seen to satisfy (at an intuitive level) the criteria for decomposing $Deposit$ into these three operations as long as we assume inputs correspond to a single coin. In the next section we will see how this intuition can be formalised and how we can verify the general case of an arbitrarily large deposit.

6   Input and Output Transformations

In this section we consider the input and output transformations that are needed to support non-atomic refinements. We begin with a discussion of IO refinement which generalises the standard refinement conditions by allowing inputs and outputs to alter under refinement. We apply this work to non-atomic refinement in Section 6.2 resulting in a set of conditions that allow inputs and outputs to be distributed throughout a concrete decomposition.

To understand the issues let us consider our running example again. In order to verify a refinement we have to prove a correctness condition between *Deposit* and the concrete decomposition. At the end of the previous section we considered the case when the input deposit was composed of a single coin, and we calculated the schema composition (*Start* $\S$ *Next* $\S$ *Stop*) to verify the correctness criteria.

Even at this point there is an issue to consider, for this composition has an input $c?$: *Coin* whereas *Deposit* has an input $p?$: *Money*. Although at an intuitive level we can see the correspondence between these schemas, a strict interpretation of standard refinement does not allow the inputs and outputs or their types to be changed**. This is a direct consequence of the use of the identities $id[Inp]$ and $id[Outp]$ in the retrieve relation

$$r_s = r \| id[Inp] \| id[Outp]$$

discussed in section 2. These identities map abstract input and output sequences to identical concrete input and output sequences, because they are identical, the types of the input and output cannot change.

6.1   IO Refinement

Recent work on IO refinement [3, 9] has tackled this issue, and provides a solution to this problem by generalising the retrieve relation r_s. Here we follow the formalisation of [3] although [9] provides an alternative characterisation.

IO refinement is a generalisation of standard (atomic) refinement. Let us consider the refinement of an abstract operation *aop* into a concrete one *cop*. Suppose further that r is the retrieve relation which links the abstract and concrete state spaces. In order to allow the types of inputs and outputs to change IO refinement replaces the identities with arbitrary relations *it* and *ot* between the input and output elements respectively. Thus *it* and *ot* are essentially retrieve relations between the inputs and outputs, hence allowing these to change under a refinement in a similar way to changing the state space. The full retrieve relation r_s between the enhanced state is then

$$r_s = r \| it^* \| ot^*$$

where it^* applies *it* along each element in the input sequence.

It is necessary to impose some conditions on *it* and *ot*. The first is that for r_s not to exclude combinations of states in r, we need to require that *it* and *ot* are total on the abstract input and output types. Secondly, *ot* must be injective. This condition guarantees that different abstract ("original") outputs can be distinguished in the concrete case because their concrete representations will be different as well.

** The file store example given in [10] contains another example of such a transformation where an input file is decomposed into a sequence of bytes.

The conditions for an IO refinement between aop_s and cop_s can be given an equivalent formulation in terms of aop and cop (see figure 2):

$$\text{dom } aop \lhd ((r\|it) \,{}_9^{\,\circ}\, cop) \subseteq aop \,{}_9^{\,\circ}\, (r\|ot)$$
$$\text{ran}(\text{dom } aop \lhd (r\|it)) \subseteq \text{dom } cop$$

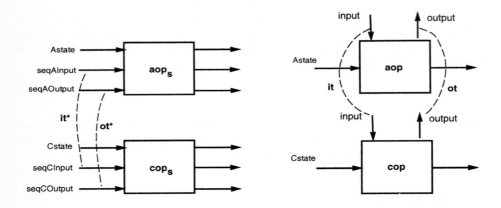

Fig. 2. IO refinement of operations

These conditions can be expressed as conditions on Z schemas as follows. The relations it and ot between the inputs and outputs become schemas called *input and output transformers*. An input transformer for a schema is an operation whose outputs exactly match the schema's inputs, and whose signature is made up of input- and output components only; similarly for output transformers. These are applied to the abstract and concrete operations using piping ($\gg$).

With these notions in place we can re-phrase the conditions of IO refinement in the Z schema calculus. We use an overlining operator, which extends componentwise to signatures and schemas: $\overline{x?} = x!, \overline{x!} = x?$. Thus $\overline{IT}$ denotes the schema where all inputs become outputs with the same basename, and all outputs inputs.

Definition 3 *Let IT be an input transformer for COp which is total on the abstract inputs. Let OT be a total injective output transformer for AOp. The retrieve relation R defines an IO refinement if:*

applicability $\forall\, Astate;\ Cstate \bullet pre(\overline{IT} \gg AOp) \wedge R \Rightarrow pre\, COp$

correctness *wherever AOp is defined, COp with the input transformation should produce a result related by R and the output transformation to one that AOp could have produced:*

$$\forall\, Astate;\ Cstate;\ Cstate' \bullet$$
$$pre\, AOp \wedge R \wedge (IT \gg COp) \Rightarrow \exists\, Astate' \bullet R' \wedge (AOp \gg OT)$$

IO refinement allows inputs and outputs to be refined in a controlled manner. Controlled because since inputs and outputs are observable we must be able to reconstruct the original behaviour from a concrete refinement. This reconstruction is achieved by using the input and output transformers which essentially act as wrappers to a concrete operation, converting abstract inputs to concrete ones and similarly for the output. Hayes and Sanders [5] use piping in much the same way: to represent the equivalent of relational composition for inputs and outputs in Z schemas. They use the term "representation schema" for what we call "transformers".

We can apply these ideas to our example. The input transformer schema that we need to use is thus given by

$$
\begin{array}{l}
\hline
\quad IT \underline{\hspace{7cm}} \\
\quad p? : Money \\
\quad c! : Coin \\
\quad n?, n! : Name \\
\hline
\quad c! = p? \land n! = n? \\
\hline
\end{array}
$$

Here $c!$ is an output so that it matches the input $c?$ of the composition ($Start \,\S\, Next \,\S\, Stop$), and no changes are made to the name so that is passed through unchanged. There are no outputs so the output transformer is the identity. With this in place it is easy to see that we have the correct transformations in place to deal with the change of input when each input $p?$ is entered as a sequence consisting of one single coin, and we can verify the condition

$$\text{pre } Deposit \land (IT \gg Start \,\S\, Next \,\S\, Stop) \land R \Rightarrow \exists\, Astate' \bullet R' \land Deposit$$

However, in reality deposits can be arbitrarily large (i.e. not provided by a single coin), and to deal with this we need further generalisations. The next subsection considers how to do this by integrating IO refinement into the non-atomic refinement conditions we have already derived.

6.2   General IO Transformations

Consider the case when the input deposit is given as two coins. We will now have to verify a correctness condition between $Deposit$ and the composition ($Start\,\S\,Next\,\S\,Next\,\S\,Stop$) to show that the non-atomic refinement holds. However, if we calculate this composition we result in

$$
\begin{array}{l}
\hline
\quad \Delta CBank \\
\quad n? : Name \\
\quad c? : Coin \\
\hline
\quad n? \in \text{dom } cct \\
\quad tct' = \{n?\} \lhd tct \\
\quad cct' = cct \oplus \{n? \mapsto cct(n?) + c? + c?\} \\
\hline
\end{array}
$$

We have lost the differentiation needed between the inputs of distinct applications of the *Next* operation. Furthermore, our input transformation is now not just between two operations, but a whole sequence of concrete operations, the length of which is only determined by the input $p?$ (the number of *Next* operations needed is in fact determined by the coins used as long as they sum to the correct amount $p?$), and this can continually vary.

To deal with this we will generalise IO refinement in the following way. IO refinement was derived as a condition between one abstract and one concrete operation, because of that a simple element by element mapping *it* sufficed. In our world of non-atomic refinement we wish to decompose one abstract operation into a sequence of concrete operations. Therefore we need a mapping between an abstract input and a sequence of concrete inputs representing the inputs needed in the decomposition. We thus replace the maps *it* and *ot* by r_{in} and r_{out} where

$$r_{in} : Ainput \longleftrightarrow \text{seq } Cinput$$
$$r_{out} : Aoutput \longleftrightarrow \text{seq } Coutput$$

and r_{in} is total on *Ainput*, and r_{out} is total on seq *Coutput*. For example, suppose that an amount $p?$ is entered as the sequence of coins $\langle c_1?, \ldots, c_m? \rangle$, then an abstract input $(n?, p?)$ for the *Deposit* operation will be mapped to the input sequence $\langle n?, (n?, c_1?), \ldots, (n?, c_m?), n? \rangle$ to be consumed by $(Start \,_\S$ *Next*, ..., *Next* $_\S$ *Stop*).

Given a decomposition of *aop* into $cop_1 \,_\S cop_2$ let us denote operations acting on the augmented state space be denoted by, as before, aop_s, cop_{1s} and cop_{2s}. With mappings r_{in} and r_{out} describing how the inputs and outputs of *aop* are turned into those for cop_1 and cop_2, and a retrieve relation r between the state spaces, the retrieve relation r_s on the augmented state will be given by

$$r_s = r \| \,\widehat{}/.r_{in}^* \| \,\widehat{}/.r_{out}^*$$

Here $\widehat{}/.r_{in}^*$ takes an input sequence seq *Ainput* and creates a concrete input sequence by concatenating together the effect of r_{in} for each item in seq *Ainput*. If there are two concrete operations in the refinement, then r_{in} maps each abstract input into a pair of concrete inputs, the first for consumption by cop_1 the second for cop_2 (see figure 3).

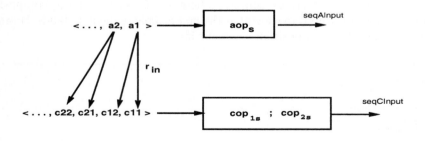

Fig. 3. Splitting the abstract input

We can now take the three non-atomic refinement conditions described in terms of an augmented state:

$$(\operatorname{dom} aop_s \lhd r_s \,\fatsemi\, cop_{1s} \,\fatsemi\, cop_{2s}) \subseteq aop_s \,\fatsemi\, r_s \qquad (7)$$

$$\operatorname{ran}((\operatorname{dom} aop_s) \lhd r_s) \subseteq \operatorname{dom} cop_{1s} \qquad (8)$$

$$\operatorname{ran}((\operatorname{dom} aop_s) \lhd r_s \,\fatsemi\, cop_{1s}) \subseteq \operatorname{dom} cop_{2s} \qquad (9)$$

and turn these into equivalent conditions on the operations with input and output at each step: aop, cop_1 and cop_2 in the usual way. It is easy to see that they become:

$$\operatorname{dom} aop \lhd (r\|r_{in}) \,\fatsemi\, (id\|cop_1) \,\fatsemi\, (cop_2\|id) \subseteq aop \,\fatsemi\, (r\|r_{out}) \qquad (10)$$

$$\operatorname{ran}(\operatorname{dom} aop \lhd (r\|r_{in})) \subseteq \operatorname{dom} cop_1 \qquad (11)$$

$$\operatorname{ran}(\operatorname{dom} aop \lhd (r\|r_{in}) \,\fatsemi\, (id\|cop_1)) \subseteq \operatorname{dom} cop_2 \qquad (12)$$

where again we require that r_{out}, like ot, is injective.

In the formalisation of these conditions we need to write $(id\|cop_1)$ and $(cop_2\|id)$ because a single abstract input has become a pair of concrete inputs, one for cop_1 and one for cop_2. In order to correctly select its input we need to write $(id\|cop_1)$ and $(cop_2\|id)$ in the relational formalisation. These manipulations will appear in a different form when we express these conditions in the Z schema calculus.

To illustrate how this is done let us return for the moment to our example. For an arbitrary large deposit the input transformer IT is something like

---
IT
___
$p? : Money$
$c! : \operatorname{seq} Coin$
$n?, n! : Name$
___
$+/.(c!) = p? \wedge n! = n?$

---

where now we will output the deposit as a sequence of coins $c!$. However, we need to represent one more bit of information, namely that expressed in $(id\|cop_1)$ which says the concrete operations take the transformed input one at a time. Let us suppose a deposit comprises m coins. Then the cleanest way to express this is to observe that $c! = \langle c_1, \ldots, c_m \rangle$, and describe the process explicitly as substitutions in the operations, i.e. as $(Start\,\fatsemi\,Next[c_1/c?]\,\fatsemi\,\ldots\,\fatsemi\,Next[c_m/c?]\,\fatsemi\,Stop)$. With this in place we can express the refinement conditions that have to be verified, e.g. we require

$$\operatorname{pre} Deposit \wedge (IT \gg Start \,\fatsemi\, Next[c_1/c?] \,\fatsemi\, \ldots \,\fatsemi\, Next[c_m/c?] \,\fatsemi\, Stop) \wedge R \Rightarrow$$
$$\exists\, Astate' \bullet R' \wedge Deposit$$

The general formalisation in Z effectively combines our three conditions needed for a non-atomic refinement of AOp into $COp_1 \,\fatsemi\, COp_2$ with the use of input and output transformers from IO refinement. Explicit substitutions (as in the *Next* operation) are only necessary when the decomposition of AOp involves more than one occurrence of the same concrete operation. If COp_1 and COp_2 are distinct operations then the formalisation is the following:

Definition 4 *Non-atomic refinement with IO transformations*
Let IT be an input transformer for $COp_1 \,\fatsemi\, COp_2$ which is total on the abstract inputs. Let OT be a total injective output transformer for AOp. The retrieve relation R defines a non-atomic IO refinement if:

$\forall\, Astate;\; Cstate;\; Cstate' \bullet$
$\quad pre\, AOp \wedge (IT \gg COp_1 \,\fatsemi\, COp_2) \wedge R \Rightarrow \exists\, Astate' \bullet R' \wedge (AOp \gg OT)$
$\forall\, Astate;\; Cstate \bullet pre(\overline{IT} \gg AOp) \wedge R \Rightarrow pre\, COp_1$
$\forall\, Astate;\; Cstate \bullet pre(\overline{IT} \gg AOp) \wedge R \wedge (IT \gg COp_1) \Rightarrow pre\, COp_2$

If COp_1 and COp_2 are not distinct (e.g. two *Next* operations) then explicit substitutions are needed to control the inputs and outputs together with a predicate in the input transformer describing which operation receives which input.

Finally consider the situation where deposits can be arbitrary large. Now we do not know the number of operations in the concrete decomposition at the outset, and we have to describe it as follows. Given the abstract *Deposit* operation we use the same input transformer IT as before and decompose *Deposit* into the sequence

$$Start \,\fatsemi\, (\fatsemi/\{(i, Next[c!.i/c?]) \mid i \in dom\, c!\}) \,\fatsemi\, Stop$$

Here $\fatsemi/$ denotes distributed schema composition along the sequence $\langle Next[c!.1/c?], \ldots, Next[c!.m/c?]\rangle$ where $m = \#c!$. This expression produces a schema composition of the correct number of *Next* operations according to the size of $c!$ as required ($c!$ can be any sequence that adds up to the correct amount). We can calculate such a schema composition, and it is easy to see that all the conditions for a non-atomic refinement are met.

7   Summary

It is worth summarising the criteria for non-atomic refinement as we have derived them gradually throughout the paper. In this summary we do not mention the initialisation condition which is identical to that of standard refinement. Let AOp be decomposed into the sequence $COp_1 \,\fatsemi\, COp_2$.

Simple non-atomic refinement requires that one of the concrete operations (COp_1 say) refines AOp and the other refines a restricted *skip*. The requirements on COp_1 refining AOp are the standard ones whilst those on COp_2 are that for some abstract state A with ran $AOp \Rightarrow A$ we have

$\quad \forall\, Astate;\; Cstate;\; A \bullet A \wedge R \Rightarrow pre\, COp_2$
$\quad \forall\, Astate;\; Cstate;\; Cstate';\; A \bullet A \wedge R \wedge COp_2 \Rightarrow \exists\, A' \bullet \Xi A \wedge R'$

For a general non-atomic refinement where we drop the requirement that concrete operations directly refine abstract counterparts we have three basic conditions. They are:

$$\forall Astate; \; Cstate; \; Cstate' \bullet$$
$$\text{pre} \, AOp \wedge (COp_1 \, \frac{\circ}{\circ} \, COp_2) \wedge R \Rightarrow \exists Astate' \bullet R' \wedge AOp$$
$$\forall Astate; \; Cstate \bullet \text{pre} \, AOp \wedge R \Rightarrow \text{pre} \, COp_1$$
$$\forall Astate; \; Cstate \bullet \text{pre} \, AOp \wedge R \wedge COp_1 \Rightarrow \text{pre} \, COp_2$$

These conditions do not allow any input or output transformations. If we require abstract inputs and outputs to be distributed over the concrete operations it is necessary to use input and output transformers IT and OT such that:

$$\forall Astate; \; Cstate; \; Cstate' \bullet$$
$$\text{pre} \, AOp \wedge (IT \gg COp_1 \, \frac{\circ}{\circ} \, COp_2) \wedge R \Rightarrow \exists Astate' \bullet R' \wedge (AOp \gg OT)$$
$$\forall Astate; \; Cstate \bullet \text{pre}(\overline{IT} \gg AOp) \wedge R \Rightarrow \text{pre} \, COp_1$$
$$\forall Astate; \; Cstate \bullet \text{pre}(\overline{IT} \gg AOp) \wedge R \wedge (IT \gg COp_1) \Rightarrow \text{pre} \, COp_2$$

where IT is total on the abstract inputs and is an input transformer for $COp_1 \, \frac{\circ}{\circ} \, COp_2$ and OT is a total and injective output transformer for AOp.

If the concrete decomposition involves more than one occurrence of the same concrete operation (as in *Next* above), then it may be necessary to use explicit schema substitutions for the input names in this last formalisation.

8   Conclusions

In this paper we have presented the beginnings of a study of state based non-atomic refinement. This led to a number of conditions for such a refinement given in the summary above. All of these conditions are derived from the basic definition of refinement as the reduction of non-determinism. Differences between the sets of conditions arise firstly from whether we require both $P_A(\mathcal{C}) \subseteq P_A(\mathcal{A})$ and $P_C(\mathcal{C}) \subseteq P_C(\mathcal{A})$ to hold, or just the former.

Considering just the former allowed us to consider how abstract inputs and outputs could be distributed over the sequence of concrete operations. To do so we applied the theory of IO refinement which extends standard refinement by allowing the retrieve relation to be extended to input and output types in addition to relating the state spaces.

The result is three sets of conditions. The first can be used when one of the concrete operations refines *skip* and the other refines the original abstract oper-ation. The second defines conditions for a general decomposition into a numbe of concrete operations where the inputs and outputs are not altered. The thi used IO transformers to relax this last condition. Although the use of IO tr formers looks at first sight complex, they are merely wrappers which e how an abstract input (or output) gets turned into its concrete counter though our illustrative example concentrated on input transformati transformations are feasible for the outputs of an operation.

Further work to be done in this area includes looking at the relationship between upward simulations and non-atomic refinement, where we expect similar rules could be developed. It would also be useful to develop syntactic support for non-atomic refinement. For example, if an abstract operation is specified at the abstract level as $AOp \cong AOp_1 \, \S \, AOp_2$ under what conditions is $AOp_1 \, \S \, AOp_2$ a non-atomic refinement of AOp.

References

[1] Jean-Raymond Abrial and Louis Mussat. Specification and design of a transmission protocol by successive refinements using B. In Manfred Broy and Birgit Schieder, editors, *Mathematical Methods in Program Development*, volume 158 of *NATO ASI Series F: Computer and Systems Sciences*, pages 129–200. Springer, 1997.

[2] L. Aceto. *Action refinement in process algebras*. CUP, London, 1992.

[3] E.A. Boiten and J. Derrick. IO - refinement in Z. In *3rd BCS-FACS Northern Formal Methods Workshop*, Electronic Workshops in Computing. Springer Verlag, September 1998.

[4] M. Butler. An approach to the design of distributed systems with B AMN. In J. P. Bowen, M. G. Hinchey, and D. Till, editors, *ZUM'97: The Z formal specification notation*, LNCS 1212, pages 223–241, Reading, April 1997. Springer-Verlag.

[5] I.J. Hayes and J.W. Sanders. Specification by interface separation. *Formal Aspects of Computing*, 7(4):430–439, 1995.

[6] He Jifeng and C.A.R. Hoare. Prespecification and data refinement. In *Data Refinement in a Categorical Setting*, Technical Monograph, number PRG-90. Oxford University Computing Laboratory, November 1990.

[7] J. Sinclair and J. Woodcock. Event refinement in state-based concurrent systems. *Formal Aspects of Computing*, 7:266–288, 1995.

[8] J. M. Spivey. *The Z notation: A reference manual*. Prentice Hall, 1989.

[9] S. Stepney, D. Cooper, and J. C. P. Woodcock. More powerful data refinement in Z. In J. P. Bowen, A. Fett, and M. G. Hinchey, editors, *ZUM'98: The Z Formal Specification Notation*, volume 1493 of *LNCS*, pages 284–307. Springer-Verlag, 1998.

[10] J. Woodcock and J. Davies. *Using Z: Specification, Refinement, and Proof*. Prentice Hall, 1996.

Refinement Semantics and Loop Rules

Eric C.R. Hehner[1], Andrew M. Gravell[2]

[1] Dep't Computer Science, University of Toronto,
Toronto ON M5S 3G4, Canada
hehner@cs.toronto.edu
[2] Electronics and Computer Science Dep't, University of Southampton,
Southampton SO9 5NH UK
amg@ecs.soton.ac.uk

Abstract. Refinement semantics is an alternative to least fixpoint semantics that is more useful for programming. From it we derive a variety of rules for **while**-loops, **for**-loops, and loops with intermediate and deep exits. We illustrate the use of these rules with examples.

1 Introduction

A specification is a boolean expression whose variables represent quantities of interest. By "boolean expression" we mean an expression of type boolean; we do not mean to restrict the types of variables and subexpressions, nor the operators, within a specification. Quantifiers, functions, terms from the application domain, and terms invented for one particular specification are all welcome. Here is an example specification using x and n as the initial values of two integer variables, x' and n' as their final values, t as the time when execution starts, and t' as the time when execution finishes.

$$n \geq 0 \implies x' = x \times 2^n \land t' \leq t + n$$

A specification is implemented on a computer when, for any initial values of the variables, the computer generates (computes) final values to satisfy the specification. A specification is implementable if, for any initial values of the variables, there are final values to satisfy the specification with nondecreasing time. In our example variables, a specification S is implementable if

$$\forall x, n, t \cdot \exists x', n', t' \cdot S \land t' \geq t$$

A program is a specification that has been implemented, so that a computer can execute it. The program notations we use include: ok (the empty program), $x := e$ (assignment), $P;Q$ (sequential composition), and **if** b **then** P **else** Q (conditional composition). In variables x, n, and t, they are defined as

$$ok = x' = x \land n' = n \land t' = t$$
$$x := e = x' = e \land n' = n \land t' = t$$
$$P;Q = \exists x'', n'', t'' \cdot \quad \text{(for } x', n', t' \text{ substitute } x'', n'', t'' \text{ in } P\text{)}$$
$$\land \text{ (for } x, n, t \text{ substitute } x'', n'', t'' \text{ in } Q\text{)}$$
$$\textbf{if } b \textbf{ then } P \textbf{ else } Q = b \land P \lor \neg b \land Q$$
$$= (b \implies P) \land (\neg b \implies Q)$$

J. Wing, J. Woodcock, J. Davies (Eds.): FM'99, Vol. II, LNCS 1709, pp. 1497-1510, 1999.

There are many useful laws that save us from having to use the definitions directly; for a list of laws see [4]. One such law is the Substitution Law

$$x := e; P \quad = \quad \text{(for } x \text{ substitute } e \text{ in } P \text{)}$$

which can be proven from the equations just given defining assignment and sequential composition.

Suppose we are given specification S. If S is a program, we can execute it. If not, we have some programming to do. That means building a program P such that $S \Leftarrow P$ is a theorem; this is called refinement. Since S is implied by P, all computer behavior satisfying P also satisfies S. We might refine in steps, finding specifications R, Q, ... such that $S \Leftarrow R \Leftarrow Q \Leftarrow ... \Leftarrow P$.

If S is a specification and P is a program, and $S \Leftarrow P$, then we have an implementation for S : to execute S just execute P. So we can consider S to be a program also. If S is implementable, and P would be a program but for occurrences of S, we still have an implementation of S : when S reoccurs (recursively), just reexecute P (recursively). So we can still consider S to be a program. For example,

$$n \geq 0 \quad \Rightarrow \quad x' = x \times 2^n \ \wedge \ t' \leq t + n$$
$$\Leftarrow \quad \textbf{if } n \neq 0 \textbf{ then } (x := x \times 2; \ n := n-1; \ t := t+1; \ n \geq 0 \Rightarrow x' = x \times 2^n \wedge t' \leq t + n) \textbf{ else } ok$$

In this context, we may pronounce $\Leftarrow$ as any of "is implied by", "is refined by", or "is implemented by". The occurrence of $t := t+1$ is not executed in the sense of having a value computed and stored, but only in the sense that it accounts for the time required to execute other instructions. We could have chosen different time increments and placed them differently; this choice simply counts iterations. Inside the brackets we use the Substitution Law three times (from right to left), and replace **if** and ok by their definitions, to obtain

$$n \geq 0 \quad \Rightarrow \quad x' = x \times 2^n \wedge t' \leq t + n$$
$$\Leftarrow \quad (n > 0 \Rightarrow x' = x \times 2^n \wedge t' \leq t + n) \ \wedge \ (n = 0 \Rightarrow x' = x \wedge n' = n \wedge t' = t)$$

which is clearly a theorem.

2   Notation

Here are all the notations used in this paper, arranged by precedence level.

0.	$0 \ 1 \ 2 \ \infty \quad \top \ \bot \quad x \ y \quad ( ) \quad [\ ]$	numbers, booleans, variables, brackets
1.	fx	application, indexing
2.	2^x	exponentiation
3.	$\times$	multiplication
4.	$+ \ -$	addition, subtraction
5.	$= \ \neq \ < \ > \ \leq \ \geq$	comparisons
6.	$\neg$	negation
7.	$\wedge$	conjunction
8.	$\vee$	disjunction
9.	$\Rightarrow \ \Leftarrow$	implications
10.	$:=$ **if then else** **while do** **for do**	assignment, conditional, loops
11.	$\forall \cdot \ \exists \cdot \ ;$	quantifications, sequential composition
12.	$= \ \Rightarrow \ \Leftarrow$	equation, implications

Superscripting serves to bracket all operations within it. The infix operator $-$ associates from left to right. The infix operators $\times$ $+$ $\wedge$ $\vee$; are associative (they associate in both directions). On levels 5, 9, and 12 the operators are continuing; for example, $a=b=c$ neither associates to the left nor associates to the right, but means $a=b \wedge b=c$. On any one of these levels, a mixture of continuing operators can be used. For example, $a \leq b < c$ means $a \leq b \wedge b < c$. The operators $=$ $\Rightarrow$ $\Leftarrow$ are identical to $=$ $\Rightarrow$ $\Leftarrow$ except for precedence. Square brackets [ ] universally quantify over all state variables (initial and final values), including time.

We use σ to stand for all the unprimed variables, σ' for primed versions of the same variables, and σ'' for double-primed versions. If e is an expression in unprimed variables, then e' is the same expression as e but with primes on all the variables, and e'' has double-primes on all the variables. If P is a specification (a boolean expression in unprimed and primed variables), then $P\sigma_{\sigma''}$ is the same as P but with all its unprimed variables replaced with the corresponding double-primed variables.

3 Least Fixpoints

Least fixpoints are a standard way to define the semantics of loop constructs. "Least" means least refined, so in the context of this paper it means least strong; to avoid confusion about the ordering, we shall say "weakest". The **while**-loop can be defined by the following two axioms.

$$\textbf{while } b \textbf{ do } S \;=\; \textbf{if } b \textbf{ then } (S; \textbf{while } b \textbf{ do } S) \textbf{ else } ok$$

$$[W = \textbf{if } b \textbf{ then } (S; W) \textbf{ else } ok] \;\Rightarrow\; [W \Rightarrow \textbf{while } b \textbf{ do } S]$$

The first axiom says that **while** b **do** S is a fixpoint of the function (in variable W)

$$\textbf{if } b \textbf{ then } (S; W) \textbf{ else } ok$$

The second axiom says that **while** b **do** S is weaker than or equal to any fixpoint of that function. Together, they say that **while** b **do** S is the weakest fixpoint.

In place of fixpoints, we can use prefixpoints to define the semantics of loop constructs. The **while**-loop can be defined by the following two axioms.

$$\textbf{while } b \textbf{ do } S \;\Rightarrow\; \textbf{if } b \textbf{ then } (S; \textbf{while } b \textbf{ do } S) \textbf{ else } ok$$

$$[W \Rightarrow \textbf{if } b \textbf{ then } (S; W) \textbf{ else } ok] \;\Rightarrow\; [W \Rightarrow \textbf{while } b \textbf{ do } S]$$

The weakest fixpoint and weakest prefixpoint definitions are equivalent, but the latter may be preferred because, from it, the former is easily proven (algebraically), but from the former the proof of the latter is harder (topological).

When we include time among the observable properties of a computation, we can strengthen our loop semantics by using the weakest progressive prefixpoint [9]. This time we define the **while**-loop as follows.

$$\textbf{while } b \textbf{ do } S \;\Rightarrow\; t' \geq t$$

$$\textbf{while } b \textbf{ do } S \;\Rightarrow\; \textbf{if } b \textbf{ then } (S; t:= t+1; \textbf{while } b \textbf{ do } S) \textbf{ else } ok$$

$$[W \Rightarrow t' \geq t] \wedge [W \Rightarrow \textbf{if } b \textbf{ then } (S; t:= t+1; W) \textbf{ else } ok]$$
$$\Rightarrow [W \Rightarrow \textbf{while } b \textbf{ do } S]$$

This definition is not equivalent to the previous two. With it we can prove

$$\textbf{while } \top \textbf{ do } ok \;=\; t' = \infty$$

which says sensibly that the loop takes infinite time, whereas the previous two say

$$\textbf{while } \top \textbf{ do } ok \ = \ \top$$

which tells us nothing useful. The only disadvantage of the weakest progressive prefixpoint is that it is tied to the particular measure of time that counts iterations, whereas the others can be used with a real-valued time variable that measures the real execution time.

4   Refinement Semantics

All three of the least fixpoint semantics (weakest fixpoint, weakest prefixpoint, weakest progressive prefixpoint) say what a loop is by saying how it can be implemented (or refined). For example, the axiom

$$[W \ \Rightarrow \ \textbf{if } b \textbf{ then } (S; W) \textbf{ else } ok] \ \Rightarrow \ [W \Rightarrow \textbf{while } b \textbf{ do } S]$$

says that **while** b **do** S can be implemented (refined) by W if

$$W \ \Rightarrow \ \textbf{if } b \textbf{ then } (S; W) \textbf{ else } ok$$

Refinement semantics says what a loop is by saying what it implements (or refines). Whereas a least fixpoint semantics tells the implementers what they want to know, refinement semantics tells programmers what they want to know in order to use loops as programming notations.

As a first effort at refinement semantics, we might try

$$\textbf{while } b \textbf{ do } S \ \Leftarrow \ \textbf{if } b \textbf{ then } (S; \textbf{while } b \textbf{ do } S) \textbf{ else } ok$$

$$[W \ \Leftarrow \ \textbf{if } b \textbf{ then } (S; W) \textbf{ else } ok] \ \Rightarrow \ [W \Leftarrow \textbf{while } b \textbf{ do } S]$$

making **while** b **do** S the greatest (strongest) postfixpoint. The second of these axioms says that **while** b **do** S implements (refines) W if

$$W \ \Leftarrow \ \textbf{if } b \textbf{ then } (S; W) \textbf{ else } ok$$

With this axiom alone, **while** b **do** S might just be $\bot$, but according to the first axiom it must be implemented (refined) by its first unrolling. Unfortunately, that definition sometimes makes **while** b **do** S unimplementable (even when S is implementable). Restricting W to be implementable and insisting that **while** b **do** S be implementable is unfortunately inconsistent. Dropping the first axiom and restricting W to be implementable in the second, we can still prove

$$x'=2 \wedge t'=\infty \ \Leftarrow \ \textbf{while } \top \textbf{ do } t:= t+1$$

By itself, this is not a problem. Although it may be strange to say that an infinite loop results in a final value of 2 for variable x, this final value is promised only at time ∞ when no-one can observe the contrary. But we can equally well prove

$$x'=3 \wedge t'=\infty \ \Leftarrow \ \textbf{while } \top \textbf{ do } t:= t+1$$

and hence, by boolean algebra,

$$\bot \ \Leftarrow \ \textbf{while } \top \textbf{ do } t:= t+1$$

and so, by transitivity,

$$x'=2 \wedge t'=t \ \Leftarrow \ \textbf{while } \top \textbf{ do } t:= t+1$$

which promises a final value of 2 for variable x at the present time, when we can easily observe the contrary. Greatest fixpoints just don't work.

To avoid all these problems and still provide a semantics oriented toward programming rather than implementation, we define the refinement semantics of **while** as follows. Let

$W \Leftarrow$ **while** b **do** S

be an abbreviation (syntactic sugar) for the refinement

$W \Leftarrow$ **if** b **then** $(S;\ W)$ **else** ok

Refinement semantics does not ascribe any meaning to the **while**-loop by itself, but only to the refinement.

As an example, we previously proved

$n{\geq}0 \implies x' = x{\times}2^n \wedge t' \leq t{+}n$

$\Leftarrow$ **if** $n{\neq}0$ **then** $(x:= x{\times}2;\ n:= n{-}1;\ t:= t{+}1;\ n{\geq}0 \implies x'{=}x{\times}2^n \wedge t'{\leq}t{+}n)$ **else** ok

hence refinement semantics says

$n{\geq}0 \implies x' = x{\times}2^n \wedge t' \leq t{+}n$

$\Leftarrow$ **while** $n{\neq}0$ **do** $(x:= x{\times}2;\ n:= n{-}1;\ t:= t{+}1)$

Programming constructs are required to be monotonic, which means for the **while**-loop

$[P{\Rightarrow}Q] \implies [\textbf{while } b \textbf{ do } P \implies \textbf{while } b \textbf{ do } Q]$

Since refinement semantics does not give a meaning to the **while**-loop, we cannot prove monotonicity in this form. Instead we can prove monotonicity in the form

$[W \Leftarrow \textbf{while } b \textbf{ do } P] \wedge [P \Leftarrow Q] \implies [W \Leftarrow \textbf{while } b \textbf{ do } Q]$

which is exactly the Law of Stepwise Refinement used by programmers to refine a specification in a sequence of steps. Similarly we can prove the Law of Partwise Refinement

$[W \Leftarrow \textbf{while } b \textbf{ do } P] \wedge [X \Leftarrow \textbf{while } b \textbf{ do } Q]$

$\implies [W{\wedge}X \Leftarrow \textbf{while } b \textbf{ do } P{\wedge}Q]$

which allows programmers to write a specification in parts, refine the parts separately (with the same structure), and then combine the refinements to get a solution to the combined specification.

5   Comparison of Least Fixpoint and Refinement Semantics

If the body of a loop does not decrease variable x , then the loop does not decrease x . The refinement

$x'{\geq}x \Leftarrow$ **while** b **do** $x:= x{+}1$

is an easy theorem by refinement semantics, but not a theorem at all by any of the least fixpoint semantics. The problem is that the loop condition b might be $\top$ and the loop execution is infinite. It may seem reasonable to refrain from concluding anything about final values after an infinite computation, but

$t'{\geq}t \Leftarrow$ **while** b **do** $t:= t{+}1$

is reasonable even if the computation is infinite. It is easily provable by refinement semantics. It is an axiom in weakest progressive prefixpoint semantics. It is not provable by weakest fixpoint semantics, nor (of course) by weakest prefixpoint semantics.

The next example

$x{<}0 \implies t'{=}\infty \Leftarrow$ **while** $x{\neq}0$ **do** $(x:= x{-}1;\ t:= t{+}1)$

informs us that for negative initial x , the computation is infinite. This too is easily provable by refinement semantics, provable with difficulty by weakest progressive prefixpoint semantics, but not provable by weakest fixpoint semantics, nor (of course) by weakest prefixpoint semantics.

The final example for the purpose of comparison

$$t'=3 \;\Leftarrow\; \textbf{while}\; \mathsf{T}\; \textbf{do}\; t:= t+1$$

says, unreasonably, that this computation will end at time 3. To their credit, it is not provable by any of the least fixpoint semantics. To its discredit, it is provable by refinement semantics. However, refinement semantics says that this is just an abbreviation for

$$t'=3 \;\Leftarrow\; \textbf{if}\; \mathsf{T}\; \textbf{then}\; (t:= t+1;\; t'=3)\; \textbf{else}\; ok$$

and as stated earlier, to consider that $t'=3$ is implemented by this recursion, it must first be implementable. Since it is not, it is excluded from consideration.

As a practical matter, it is convenient to be able to prove invariance (safety) properties without having to prove termination (or liveness) first. Refinement semantics allows this separation of concerns; the various least fixpoint semantics do not. With the addition of communication (input and output, not covered in this paper, see [4]), nonterminating executions can perform useful computation, so a semantics that does not insist on termination is useful.

6 Variant

A variant v is an expression in unprimed variables, together with an ordering $<$ satisfying the well-founded induction axiom:

$$[(v'<v;\; \neg P) \vee P] \Rightarrow [P]$$

or, more verbosely [2],

(0) $[(\forall \sigma''\cdot\; v''<v \Rightarrow P\sigma_{\sigma''}) \Rightarrow P] \Rightarrow [P]$

When specialized to the natural numbers,

$$(\forall n\cdot (\forall m\cdot\; m<n \Rightarrow Pm) \Rightarrow Pn) \;\Rightarrow\; (\forall n\cdot Pn)$$

it is sometimes called "course-of-values induction" or "Noetherian induction".

When the body of a loop decreases a variant, refinement semantics is a consequence of least fixpoint semantics. All we need is the prefixpoint axiom

(1) $\textbf{while}\; b\; \textbf{do}\; v'<v \;\Longrightarrow\; \textbf{if}\; b\; \textbf{then}\; (v'<v;\; \textbf{while}\; b\; \textbf{do}\; v'<v)\; \textbf{else}\; ok$

Now suppose

(2) $S \;\Leftarrow\; \textbf{if}\; b\; \textbf{then}\; (v'<v;\; S)\; \textbf{else}\; ok$

From (0), (1), and (2) we can prove

(3) $S \;\Leftarrow\; \textbf{while}\; b\; \textbf{do}\; v'<v$

Proof: We start with what we want to prove.

$\quad [S \;\Leftarrow\; \textbf{while}\; b\; \textbf{do}\; v'<v]$ \hfill use (0) with (3) as P

$\Leftarrow\quad [(\forall \sigma''\cdot\; v''<v \Rightarrow (S \;\Leftarrow\; \textbf{while}\; b\; \textbf{do}\; v'<v)\sigma_{\sigma''}) \Rightarrow (S \;\Leftarrow\; \textbf{while}\; b\; \textbf{do}\; v'<v)]$

To prove this, we prove the final implication, making use of its context (the other information on the same line) when necessary.

$\quad S$ \hfill use (2)

$\Leftarrow\quad \textbf{if}\; b\; \textbf{then}\; (v'<v;\; S)\; \textbf{else}\; ok$ \hfill expand the ;

$=\quad \textbf{if}\; b\; \textbf{then}\; (\exists \sigma''\cdot\; v''<v \;\wedge\; S\sigma_{\sigma''})\; \textbf{else}\; ok$ \hfill strengthen $S\sigma_{\sigma''}$ using context

$\Leftarrow\quad \textbf{if}\; b\; \textbf{then}\; (\exists \sigma''\cdot\; v''<v \;\wedge\; (\textbf{while}\; b''\; \textbf{do}\; v'<v'))\; \textbf{else}\; ok$ \hfill contract to ;

$=\quad \textbf{if}\; b\; \textbf{then}\; (v'<v;\; \textbf{while}\; b\; \textbf{do}\; v'<v)\; \textbf{else}\; ok$ \hfill use (1)

$\Leftarrow\quad \textbf{while}\; b\; \textbf{do}\; v'<v$

Thus, in the presence of a variant, refinement semantics is sound relative to fixpoint semantics. In fact, in the presence of a variant, there is exactly one fixpoint, and all postfixpoints are weaker than or equal to the fixpoint. Although the loop body $v'{<}v$ appears to do nothing but decrease the variant, the result generalizes to loops whose bodies do other work while decreasing the variant (the variant v and its relation $<$ can be defined so that $v'{<}v$ includes useful work). Although the result has been stated and proven for **while**-loops, it generalizes to any recursion in which each recursive call occurs in a monotonic context and the variant is decreased before the call.

7   Rule of Invariants and Variants

Since the least fixpoint semantics is oriented to implementation rather than programming, programmers are not able to use it directly. Instead, they have used rules that can be derived from it. The best-known rule for the use of **while**-loops is the Rule of Invariants and Variants. The version in [8] is as follows: Let I (the invariant) be a boolean expression in unprimed variables, and let v (the variant) be an integer expression in unprimed variables. Then

$$I \Rightarrow I' \wedge \neg b' \ \Longleftarrow \ \textbf{while } b \textbf{ do } I \wedge b \Rightarrow I' \wedge 0{\le}v'{<}v$$

If the body of the loop maintains the invariant and decreases the variant but not below 0 , then the loop maintains the invariant and negates the condition.

The Rule of Invariants and Variants is a special case of the refinement semantics. It is easy to prove

$$I \Rightarrow I' \wedge \neg b' \ \Longleftarrow \ \textbf{if } b \textbf{ then } (I \wedge b \Rightarrow I' \wedge 0{\le}v'{<}v; \ I \Rightarrow I' \wedge \neg b') \textbf{ else } ok$$

but that doesn't prove termination. To use refinement semantics to prove that the variant gives termination, we augment the specification with $0{\le}v \Rightarrow t' \le t{+}v$, and add $t{:=} t{+}1$ to the loop body. We prove

$$I \wedge 0{\le}v \Rightarrow I' \wedge \neg b' \wedge t' \le t{+}v$$
$$\Longleftarrow \quad \textbf{while } b \textbf{ do } (I \wedge 0{\le}v \wedge b \Rightarrow I' \wedge 0{\le}v'{<}v; \ t{:=} t{+}1)$$

by proving

$$I \wedge 0{\le}v \Rightarrow I' \wedge \neg b' \wedge t' \le t{+}v$$
$$\Longleftarrow \quad \textbf{if } b$$
$$\textbf{then } (I \wedge 0{\le}v \wedge b \Rightarrow I' \wedge 0{\le}v'{<}v; \ t{:=} t{+}1; \ I \wedge 0{\le}v \Rightarrow I' \wedge \neg b' \wedge t' \le t{+}v)$$
$$\textbf{else } ok$$

The proof is easy and is omitted.

It is well-known that the Rule of Invariants and Variants is incomplete; for example, it cannot be used as it stands to prove

$$x'{=}x \ \Longleftarrow \ \textbf{while } \bot \textbf{ do } \top$$

because $x'{=}x$ cannot be rewritten in the required form. The standard work-around is to allow a slightly different form of the rule, using so-called "logical constants". Instead of the preceding, we prove

$$x'{=}x \ \Longleftarrow \ \forall X{\cdot} \ x{=}X \Rightarrow x'{=}X$$
$$\forall X{\cdot} \ (x{=}X \Rightarrow x'{=}X \ \Longleftarrow \ \textbf{while } \bot \textbf{ do } \top)$$

Here is an example of the use of the Rule of Invariants and Variants.

$$n{\geq}0 \Rightarrow x'{=}2^n \quad \Longleftarrow \quad x{:=}1; \ n{\geq}0 \Rightarrow x' = x{\times}2^n$$

$$n{\geq}0 \Rightarrow x' = x{\times}2^n \quad \Longleftarrow \quad \textbf{while } n{\neq}0 \textbf{ do } (x{:=}x{\times}2; \ n{:=}n{-}1)$$

To put the specification $n{\geq}0 \Rightarrow x' = x{\times}2^n$ in the proper form to use the rule, we need to find an invariant and a variant. The variant is obvious: n . For the invariant, we need a "logical constant" C ; the invariant is then $0{\leq}n \wedge x{\times}2^n{=}C$.

$$n{\geq}0 \Rightarrow x'{=}2^n \quad \Longleftarrow \quad x{:=}1; \ \forall C{\cdot} \ \ 0{\leq}n \wedge x{\times}2^n{=}C \Rightarrow 0{\leq}n' \wedge x'{\times}2^{n'}{=}C \wedge n'{=}0$$

$$\forall C{\cdot} (\qquad 0{\leq}n \wedge x{\times}2^n{=}C \Rightarrow 0{\leq}n' \wedge x'{\times}2^{n'}{=}C \wedge n'{=}0$$

$$\Longleftarrow \ \textbf{while } n{\neq}0 \textbf{ do} \qquad 0{\leq}n \wedge x{\times}2^n{=}C \wedge n{\neq}0$$

$$\Rightarrow \ 0{\leq}n' \wedge x'{\times}2^{n'}{=}C \wedge 0{\leq}n'{<}n)$$

$$0{\leq}n \wedge x{\times}2^n{=}C \wedge n{\neq}0 \Rightarrow 0{\leq}n' \wedge x'{\times}2^{n'}{=}C \wedge 0{\leq}n'{<}n \quad \Longleftarrow \quad x{:=}x{\times}2; \ n{:=}n{-}1$$

For this very ordinary example, the Rule of Invariants and Variants has made the proof considerably harder than the refinement semantics proof.

There is a hidden subtlety in the Rule of Invariants and Variants: the body is unimplementable unless $I{\wedge}b \Rightarrow 0{<}v$. The rule is still sound without this constraint, but then the loop body cannot be implemented.

For further special cases of this rule worth mentioning see [3].

8 Terminating While-Loop Rule

Early work [5,1] presented semantics and proof rules by a pair of boolean expressions (then called "predicates"). One expression of the pair characterized initial states, and the other characterized final states. It was soon realized that most often the final state depends on the initial state, and "logical constants" were needed to relate the two states. All current work (VDM, Z, B, TLA, refinement calculus) uses two related sets of variables (undecorated and decorated) in the same boolean expression, making "logical constants" unnecessary. An invariant is a boolean expression about one state; it is a remnant of the early work. The Rule of Invariants and Variants is leftover from the days when the initial and final states had to be described separately and then related by "logical constants". There is no longer any need to do so. We now present a new rule, the terminating **while**-loop rule, which is simpler, more convenient, and more general.

At the same time as we get rid of invariants, independently we take the opportunity to relabel the variant as an upper bound on the remaining execution time, measured as a count of iterations. The Rule of Invariants and Variants uses this time bound (the variant) to imply termination, then throws it away; it does not appear in the loop specification $I \Rightarrow I' \wedge \neg b'$. But a time bound is interesting information in its own right, so we won't throw it away.

Let f be a nonnegative real-valued function of the state σ and let δ be a positive real constant. Then

$$W \wedge t'{\leq}t{+}f\sigma \ \Longleftarrow \ \textbf{while } b \textbf{ do } S$$

if

$$W \wedge t'{\leq}t{+}f\sigma \ \Longleftarrow \ \textbf{if } b \textbf{ then } (S; \ W \wedge t'{\leq}t{+}f\sigma{+}\delta) \textbf{ else } ok$$

To use this rule on our example problem we must restrict n to be a natural variable. Then

$$x' = x \times 2^n \ \wedge \ t' \leq t+n \ \Leftarrow \ \textbf{while} \ n \neq 0 \ \textbf{do} \ (x := x \times 2; \ n := n-1)$$

because

$$x' = x \times 2^n \ \wedge \ t' \leq t+n$$
$$\Leftarrow \quad \textbf{if} \ n \neq 0 \ \textbf{then} \ (x := x \times 2; \ n := n-1; \ x' = x \times 2^n \ \wedge \ t' \leq t+n+1) \ \textbf{else} \ ok$$

The terminating **while**-loop rule can be proven both by refinement semantics (trivially) and by least fixpoint semantics (harder).

9 Loops with Exits

Loops with intermediate or deep exits are awkward to define by least fixpoint semantics, but quite straightforward by refinement semantics. For example, to prove

$L \ \Leftarrow \ \textbf{loop}$
       P;
       $\textbf{exit} \ 1 \ \textbf{when} \ b$;   exit one level of loop
       Q;
       $\textbf{loop}$
           $\textbf{exit} \ 2 \ \textbf{when} \ c$;   exit two levels of loop
           R;
           $\textbf{exit} \ 1 \ \textbf{when} \ d$ exit one level of loop
       $\textbf{end}$
   $\textbf{end}$

find a specification M for the inner loop and prove

$L \ \Leftarrow \ P; \ \textbf{if} \ b \ \textbf{then} \ ok \ \textbf{else} \ (Q; \ M; \ L)$
$M \ \Leftarrow \ \textbf{if} \ c \ \textbf{then} \ ok \ \textbf{else} \ (R; \ \textbf{if} \ d \ \textbf{then} \ L \ \textbf{else} \ M)$

Refinement semantics requires a specification for every loop, which is recommended programming practice anyway.

10 For-Loops

The **for**-loop has usually been treated as a syntactic sugar for a **while**-loop, given neither a semantics of its own nor rules for its use. We now offer four rules for the use of **for**-loops; one of them is taken from [4], and is similar to [6]; the other three are new. Any of the three new rules can serve as the refinement semantics of the **for**-loop.

We shall use the syntax

    $\textbf{for} \ i := m, ..n \ \textbf{do} \ Si$

for controlled iteration, where i is a fresh identifier, not assignable within the loop body, m and n are integer expressions evaluated once, $m \leq n$, and Si is a specification indexed by i . The asymmetric notation $m, ..n$ indicates that m is included and n excluded, so there are $n-m$ iterations. This asymmetry simplifies the rules for the use of **for**-loops.

Rule I (Invariant).   Our first **for**-loop rule is taken from [4]. Let Ii be a boolean expression in unprimed variables indexed by i . Then

$$m{\le}n \wedge Im \Rightarrow I'n \quad \Leftarrow \quad \textbf{for } i{:=} m,..n \textbf{ do } m{\le}i{<}n \wedge Ii \ \Rightarrow \ I'(i{+}1)$$

Here is an example of the use of Rule I. Let $Ii = x{=}2^i$.

$$n{\ge}0 \Rightarrow x'{=}2^n \quad \Leftarrow \quad x:= 1; \ \ 0{\le}n \wedge x{=}2^0 \Rightarrow x'{=}2^n$$
$$0{\le}n \wedge x{=}2^0 \Rightarrow x'{=}2^n \quad \Leftarrow \quad \textbf{for } i{:=} 0,..n \textbf{ do } 0{\le}i{<}n \wedge x{=}2^i \Rightarrow x'{=}2^{i+1}$$
$$0{\le}i{<}n \wedge x{=}2^i \Rightarrow x'{=}2^{i+1} \quad \Leftarrow \quad x:= x{\times}2$$

Like the **while**-loop Rule of Invariants and Variants, Rule I is incomplete; for example, it cannot be used as it stands to prove

$$x'{=}x \quad \Leftarrow \quad \textbf{for } i{:=} 0,..0 \textbf{ do } \mathsf{T}$$

because $x'{=}x$ cannot be rewritten in the required form. However, Rule I becomes complete if we allow the use of "logical constants". Instead of the preceding, we prove

$$x'{=}x \quad \Leftarrow \quad \forall X{\cdot}\ x{=}X \Rightarrow x'{=}X$$
$$\forall X{\cdot}\ (x{=}X \Rightarrow x'{=}X \quad \Leftarrow \quad \textbf{for } i{:=} 0,..0 \textbf{ do } \mathsf{T})$$

As in the Rule of Invariants and Variants, the invariant is a vestige of earlier programming methods, and is completely superseded by the following three rules.

Rule F (Forward).   Let Fi be a specification indexed by i . Then
$$m{\le}n \Rightarrow Fm \quad \Leftarrow \quad \textbf{for } i{:=} m,..n \textbf{ do } m{\le}i{<}n \Rightarrow Si$$
if
$$\forall i{:}\ m,..n{\cdot}\ (Si;\ F(i{+}1)) \Rightarrow Fi$$
$$ok \Rightarrow Fn$$

Specification Fi describes what has yet to be done at iteration i . At the beginning, everything (Fm) has yet to be done. At iteration i , Fi will be done by doing Si and then $F(i{+}1)$. At the end, Fn will be done by doing nothing more (ok).

Here is an example of the use of Rule F. Define $Fi = x'{=}x{\times}2^{n-i}$. Then
$$n{\ge}0 \Rightarrow x'{=}2^n \quad \Leftarrow \quad x:= 1; \ \ 0{\le}n \Rightarrow x'{=}x{\times}2^n$$
$$0{\le}n \Rightarrow x'{=}x{\times}2^n \quad \Leftarrow \quad \textbf{for } i{:=} 0,..n \textbf{ do } x:= x{\times}2$$
because
$$\forall i{:}\ 0,..n{\cdot}\ (x:= x{\times}2;\ x'{=}x{\times}2^{n-(i+1)}) \ \Rightarrow \ x'{=}x{\times}2^{n-i}$$
$$ok \Rightarrow x'{=}x{\times}2^{n-n}$$

The soundness of Rule F can be demonstrated by correspondence with the following computation.

Fm where

$$Fi \quad \Leftarrow \quad \textbf{if } i{=}n \textbf{ then } ok \textbf{ else } (Si;\ F(i{+}1))$$

which says: execute procedure F with argument m , where procedure F with parameter i is implemented as **if** $i{=}n$ **then** ok **else** $(Si;\ F(i{+}1))$. This is the standard **while**-loop definition of a **for**-loop. If we accept that this execution is what we intended, then Rule F is sound.

To show the completeness of Rule F, let $Fi = Si;\ S(i{+}1);\ ...;\ S(n{-}1)$. Then Fm specifies the **for**-loop exactly.

Rule B (Backward).   Let Bi be a specification indexed by i. Then

$$m{\le}n \Rightarrow Bn \quad \Longleftarrow \quad \textbf{for } i{:=} m,..n \textbf{ do } m{\le}i{<}n \Rightarrow Si$$

if

$ok \Rightarrow Bm$

$\forall i\colon m,..n\cdot (Bi;\ Si) \Rightarrow B(i{+}1)$

Specification Bi describes what has been done up to iteration i. At the beginning, when we have done nothing (ok), we have done Bm. When we have done Bi and then we do Si, then we have done $B(i{+}1)$. At the end we have done everything (Bn).

Here is an example of the use of Rule B. Define $Bi\ =\ x'{=}x{\times}2^i$. Then

$n{\ge}0 \Rightarrow x'{=}2^n \quad \Longleftarrow \quad x{:=} 1;\ \ 0{\le}n \Rightarrow x'{=}x{\times}2^n$

$0{\le}n \Rightarrow x'{=}x{\times}2^n \quad \Longleftarrow \quad \textbf{for } i{:=} 0,..n \textbf{ do } x{:=} x{\times}2$

because

$ok \Rightarrow x'{=}x{\times}2^0$

$\forall i\colon 0,..n\cdot (x'{=}x{\times}2^i;\ x{:=} x{\times}2) \Rightarrow x'{=}x{\times}2^{i+1}$

The soundness of Rule B can be demonstrated by correspondence with the following computation.

Bn where

$Bi \quad \Longleftarrow \quad \textbf{if } i{=}m \textbf{ then } ok \textbf{ else } (B(i{-}1);\ S(i{-}1))$

This computation dives into its recursions from n down to m, executing the Si on the way back up. If we accept this as an execution of the **for**-loop, then Rule B is sound.

To show the completeness of Rule B, let $Bi\ =\ Sm;\ S(m{+}1);\ ...;\ S(i{-}1)$. Then Bn specifies the **for**-loop exactly.

Rule G (General).   Let Gik be a specification indexed by i and k. Then

$$m{\le}n \Rightarrow Gmn \quad \Longleftarrow \quad \textbf{for } j{:=} m,..n \textbf{ do } m{\le}j{<}n \Rightarrow Gj(j{+}1)$$

if

$m{=}n \wedge ok \Rightarrow Gmn$

$\forall i, j, k\cdot m{\le}i{<}j{<}k{\le}n \wedge (Gij;\ Gjk) \Rightarrow Gik$

Here is an example of the use of Rule G. Define $Gik\ =\ x'{=}x{\times}2^{k-i}$. Then

$n{\ge}0 \Rightarrow x'{=}2^n \quad \Longleftarrow \quad x{:=} 1;\ \ 0{\le}n \Rightarrow x'{=}x{\times}2^n$

$0{\le}n \Rightarrow x'{=}x{\times}2^n \quad \Longleftarrow \quad \textbf{for } j{:=} 0,..n \textbf{ do } 0{\le}j{<}n \Rightarrow x'{=}x{\times}2^{(j+1)-j}$

$0{\le}j{<}n \Rightarrow x'{=}x{\times}2^{(j+1)-j} \quad \Longleftarrow \quad x{:=} x{\times}2$

because

$m{=}n \wedge x'{=}x \Rightarrow x'{=}x{\times}2^{n-m}$

$\forall i, j, k\cdot 0{\le}i{<}j{<}k{\le}n \wedge (x'{=}x{\times}2^{j-i};\ x'{=}x{\times}2^{k-j}) \Rightarrow x'{=}x{\times}2^{k-i}$

The soundness of Rule G can be demonstrated by correspondence with the following computation.

$\textbf{if } m{=}n \textbf{ then } ok \textbf{ else } Gmn$ where

$Gik \quad \Longleftarrow \quad \textbf{if } i{+}1{=}k \textbf{ then } Si \textbf{ else } (i{<}j'{<}k;\ Gij;\ Gjk)$

If we accept this as an execution of the **for**-loop, then Rule G is sound.

To show the completeness of Rule G, let $Gik\ =\ Si;\ S(i{+}1);\ ...;\ S(k{-}1)$. Then Gmn specifies the **for**-loop exactly.

11   Comparison of the For-Loop Rules

Each rule asks us to think about the computation in a different way.

Rule I: what is true between iterations?

Rule F: what is true of a final segment of the iterations?

Rule B: what is true of an initial segment of the iterations?

Rule G: what is true of an arbitrary segment of the iterations?

Rules F and B require us to choose a direction; rules I and G are directionless. Rules F, B, and G are like the definition of lists: we may construct lists by appending items, prepending items, or catenation of lists.

Each of the rules F, B, and G is a special case of each of the other two, so all three of them are sound and complete if one of them is. In one respect, Rule G seems to demand more than necessary: it asks us to prove $(Gij; Gjk) \Rightarrow Gik$ for all j between i and k , when one such j is enough. Rules B and F are the special cases of Rule G when j is chosen to be either $i+1$ or $k-1$. But we have to specify the effect of the **for**-loop from m to n anyway, and so it may be easy to generalize the specification to an arbitrary segment.

Rules F and B ask us to specify a single step (Si) in addition to a segment (Fi or Bi); Rules I and G do not, since $Ii{\Rightarrow}I(i+1)$ and $Gi(i+1)$ are single steps. We can rewrite Rule F so that it does not require us to specify Si , as follows.

$$m{\le}n \Rightarrow Fm \quad \Leftarrow \quad \textbf{for } i{:=} m,..n \textbf{ do } m{\le}i{<}n \Rightarrow \neg(\neg Fi; F(i+1){\cup})$$

where $\cup$ is transposition (put primes on all unprimed variables and simultaneously remove primes from all primed variables). The expression $\neg(\neg Fi; F(i+1){\cup})$ is known as the weakest prespecification of Fi and $F(i+1)$ [7]. We can similarly rewrite Rule B so that it does not require us to specify Si , as follows.

$$m{\le}n \Rightarrow Bm \quad \Leftarrow \quad \textbf{for } i{:=} m,..n \textbf{ do } m{\le}i{<}n \Rightarrow \neg(Bi{\cup}; \neg B(i+1))$$

The expression $\neg(Bi{\cup}; \neg B(i+1))$ is the weakest postspecification of Bi and $B(i+1)$. We did not do so, judging that the specification of Si was the lesser evil.

For the record, the rules remain valid when $n{=}\infty$. Also for the record, the **for**-loop rules could be stated more simply as follows:

Rule I: $Im \Rightarrow I'n \quad \Leftarrow \quad \textbf{for } i{:=} m,..n \textbf{ do } Ii \Rightarrow I'(i+1)$

Rule F: $Fm \quad \Leftarrow \quad \textbf{for } i{:=} m,..n \textbf{ do } Si$

Rule B: $Bn \quad \Leftarrow \quad \textbf{for } i{:=} m,..n \textbf{ do } Si$

Rule G: $Gmn \quad \Leftarrow \quad \textbf{for } i{:=} m,..n \textbf{ do } Gi(i+1)$

The missing parts can be incorporated into the remaining parts. The way we have stated the rules is longer but more convenient for use.

12   Examples

In practice, the differences among the rules may be small. The most common use of a **for**-loop is to do something to every item (element) of a list (array). As an example, let's just add 1 to every item of list L . Formally,

$$\#L'{=}\#L \wedge (\forall j: 0,..\#L \cdot L'j = Lj + 1)$$

For Rule I we have to introduce "logical constant" M to be the initial value of L . The four rules require us to invent the following four specifications.

$$Ii = \#L=\#M \wedge (\forall j: 0,..i \cdot Lj = Mj + 1) \wedge (\forall j: i,..\#L \cdot Lj = Mj)$$
$$Fi = \#L'=\#L \wedge (\forall j: 0,..i \cdot L'j = Lj) \wedge (\forall j: i,..\#L \cdot L'j = Lj + 1)$$
$$Bi = \#L'=\#L \wedge (\forall j: 0,..i \cdot L'j = Lj + 1) \wedge (\forall j: i,..\#L \cdot L'j = Lj)$$
$$Gik = \#L'=\#L \wedge (\forall j: 0,..i \cdot L'j = Lj) \wedge (\forall j: i,..k \cdot L'j = Lj + 1)$$
$$\wedge (\forall j: k,..\#L \cdot L'j = Lj)$$

Our next example is cubing by addition.

$$x'=n^3$$
$$\Leftarrow \quad x:= 0; \quad y:= 1; \quad z:= 6; \quad \textbf{for } i:= 0;..n \textbf{ do } (x:= x+y; \quad y:= y+z; \quad z:= z+6)$$

The four rules require us to invent the following four specifications.

$$Ii = x=i^3 \wedge y = 3i^2+3i+1 \wedge z = 6i+6$$
$$Fi = x=i^3 \wedge y = 3i^2+3i+1 \wedge z = 6i+6 \Rightarrow x'=n^3 \wedge y' = 3n^2+3n+1 \wedge z' = 6n+6$$
$$Bi = x=0 \wedge y=1 \wedge z=6 \Rightarrow x' = i^3 \wedge y' = 3i^2+3i+1 \wedge z' = 6i+6$$
$$Gik = x' = x+k^3-i^3 \wedge y' = y+3(k^2-i^2)+3(k-i) \wedge z' = z+6(k-i)$$

In those two examples at least, there is little to help us decide which rule is best.

13   Conclusions

Refinement semantics is an alternative to least fixpoint semantics that is more useful for programming. From it we derived a variety of rules for **while**-loops, **for**-loops, and loops with intermediate and deep exits. We illustrated the use of these rules with examples.

The difficulty of finding invariants is one of the deterrents to wider adoption of formal methods. Invariants are a vestige of the earliest work on loop rules, which used two one-state expressions. The invariant rules are entirely superseded by simpler, more general, easier-to-use rules.

The variant, used to prove loop termination, is entirely superseded by the more general, easier-to-use time variable. A variant is equivalent to the special case of a time variable that counts loop iterations. With a time variable, we can measure time any way we want, including real time, and no special rule is required to prove time bounds.

Least fixpoint semantics quantifies over specifications, and so it is second order. Refinement semantics is absolutely first order. It achieves this by treating loop constructs as second-class citizens; they are merely a "syntactic sugar" for a recursive refinement. Whether by least fixpoint or refinement semantics, loop constructs are given meaning by translation to a recursive form. If we use formal methods for programming, it is easier to refine to the recursive form than to the loop constructs; a compiler can then compile the recursive form to an efficient machine code with branching. It is therefore appropriate to treat loop constructs as second-class: they are neither necessary nor convenient.

Acknowledgments

We thank Victor Kwan, Emil Sekerinski, and Michael Butler for substantive contributions to this paper. The first author thanks IFIP Working Groups 2.1 and 2.3 for being his research fora, and the University of Southampton for support and hospitality during the writing of this paper.

References

1. E.W.Dijkstra: *a Discipline of Programming*, Prentice-Hall, New Jersey, 1976
2. E.W.Dijkstra, A.J.M.vanGasteren: "a Simple Fixpoint Argument without the Restriction to Continuity", *Acta Informatica* v.13 p.1-7, 1986
3. A.M.Gravell: "Simpler Laws for the Introduction of Loops", ECS, University of Southampton, 1996
4. E.C.R.Hehner: *a Practical Theory of Programming*, Springer-Verlag, New York, 1993
5. C.A.R.Hoare: "an Axiomatic Basis for Computer Programming", *CACM* 12(10), 1969
6. C.A.R.Hoare: "a Note on the **for** statement", *BIT* v.12 n.3 p.334-341, 1972
7. C.A.R.Hoare, J.He: "the Weakest Prespecification", *Fundamenta Informaticae* v.9 p.51-84, 217-252, 1986
8. C.C.Morgan: *Programming from Specifications*, second edition, Prentice-Hall, London, 1994
9. T.S.Norvell: "Predicative Semantics of Loops", *Algorithmic Languages and Calculi*, Chapman-Hall, 1997

Lessons from the Application of Formal Methods to the Design of a Storm Surge Barrier Control System

Michel Chaudron[1], Jan Tretmans[2] & Klaas Wijbrans[1]

[1]CMG Public Sector B.V., Division Advanced Technology,
P.O. Box 187, 2501 CD The Hague, The Netherlands
{michel.chaudron, klaas.wijbrans}@cmg.nl

[2] University of Twente, Department of Computer Science,
Formal Methods & Tools group,
P.O. Box 217, 7500 AE Enschede, The Netherlands
tretmans@cs.utwente.nl

Abstract   We describe the experience of the industrial application of formal methods in the development of a mission critical system. We give a description of the system that was to be developed and the methods that were employed to realize the high level of reliability that was required. In this paper we will describe which formal techniques were used, how these techniques were used, the influence of formal methods on the development process and recommendations for managing the use of formal methods.

1. Introduction

The control of more and more processes that are critical to businesses and society are trusted to computer systems. This calls for methods for the engineering of systems with very high quality requirements such as reliability, safety and security. The developments in this area are aimed at improving the quality of the engineering process (such as ISO 9001, Capability Maturity Model (CMM) [Pau94]) as well as at improving the quality of the product (such as formal methods).

The application of formal methods in industrial software development projects is gaining maturity, but still raises a number of technical and managerial questions to which no definitive answers have been given. In this paper we will touch upon a number of technical and managerial questions related to the use of formal methods. These questions were encountered in the course of the engineering of a safety-critical system in a fixed-time, fixed-price project where the project members had had prior experience with software engineering, but hardly any experience with formal methods. The experiences described in this paper are based on interviews with the people involved in the development of the system. The issues raised in these interviews were mainly non-technical and are concerned with how engineers and managers experienced the use of formal methods. No attempts to quantification or measurements are made. For technical issues with respect to the formal techniques used we refer to [Kar97, Kar98].

J. Wing, J. Woodcock, J. Davies (Eds.): FM'99, Vol. II, LNCS 1709, pp. 1511-1526, 1999.
© Springer-Verlag Berlin Heidelberg 1999

This paper is organized as follows: in section 2 we describe the context of the system that was to be built, the systems high quality requirements and the approach used in the engineering of the system. In section 3 we describe our evaluation of the use of formal methods in this process. The lessons learned from this project are described in section 4 and conclusions in section 5.

2. Case Description: The BOS System

BOS (Dutch: *Beslis & Ondersteunend Systeem*, i.e., Decision & Support System) is the system that controls the storm surge barrier in the Nieuwe Waterweg near Rotterdam. BOS was developed by CMG, division Advanced Technology. In this section we describe the storm surge barrier that BOS has to control. This context of the project explains the very high requirements that were put on the reliability and safety of the BOS system. Because of the special nature of this system, a dedicated system engineering process was devised for the project. This dedicated engineering process was ISO 9001 certified.

2.1 The Battle with the Sea

The Netherlands are located in a low delta by the sea, into which important rivers such as the Rhine and IJssel flow. The history of The Netherlands has been shaped by the struggle against the sea. The great flood disaster of 1953 in Zeeland was a rude shock to the Netherlands, demonstrating yet again that the country was not safe. It was shortly after this flood disaster that the Delta Plan was drafted, with measures to prevent such calamities from occurring in the future. This Delta Plan was a defense plan which involved the building of a network of dams in Zeeland and upgrading the existing dikes to a failure rate of 10^{-4}, i.e., one flooding every 10,000 years.

The realization of the Delta Plan started soon after 1953 and in 1986 the impressive dam network in Zeeland was finished. The weak point in the defence was now the Nieuwe Waterweg. The Nieuwe Waterweg connects the main port of Rotterdam with the North Sea, hence it is an important shipping route. Because the Nieuwe Waterweg is completely open and large parts of Rotterdam are situated below sea level, it forms a major risk for flooding of Rotterdam. Moreover, the Nieuwe Waterweg is a major outlet for water coming from the Rhine.

To protect Rotterdam from flooding, a storm surge barrier, called the *Maeslant Kering*, was constructed in the Nieuwe Waterweg. An impression of the barrier is given in Figure 1.

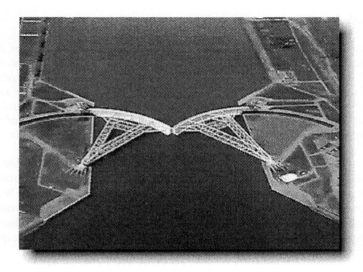

Fig. 1. Top view of the Maeslant Kering near Hoek van Holland. At the top of the figure the Nieuwe Waterweg flows to the North Sea; in the bottom direction is Rotterdam. The Nieuwe Waterweg is about 300m wide.

The requirements that Rotterdam should be protected from flooding, that its port should be reachable at all times (except at unacceptable weather conditions), and that the water coming from the Rhine should not cause Rotterdam to be flooded from the inside, has led to a design of a movable barrier. The barrier consists of two hollow floating walls, called sector doors, connected with steel arms to pivot points on both banks. Each sector door, which should resist the huge forces of the incoming water, is as large as the Eiffel Tower. During normal weather conditions the two sector doors rest in their docks. Only when storms are expected with danger of flooding the two sector doors are closed. The closing procedure consists of several steps. First the docks are filled with water, so the doors start to float, then the doors are moved to the centre of the Nieuwe Waterweg and then they are filled with water until they touch the bottom. A big advantage of the design of the movable barrier is that the construction and maintenance can be done without interfering with the ship traffic. For animation and more information, see the internet-site of the Dutch Ministry of Transport, Public Works and Water Management [RWS].

The main requirement on the barrier is that it is as reliable as a dike. Careful failure analysis showed that a manual control of this barrier would undermine the reliability. For complex tasks − like deciding when to close the barrier and then closing it − normal human beings have a failure probability of one in thousand. Therefore it was considered to be safer to let a computer control the barrier.

2.2 The BOS System

The BOS system decides autonomously about opening or closing the barrier. BOS has the responsibility for closing the barrier when predictions indicate that the expected water level in Rotterdam will be too high. But since Rotterdam is a major port with a lot of ship traffic, the barrier should be closed only when really necessary and as for as short a period as possible. An unnecessarily closed barrier will cost millions of guilders because of restricted ship traffic, while there is also the danger of flooding from the landside through the Rhine if its water cannot flow freely to the sea.

The design of the BOS system is an effort in linking several distinct disciplines. These include the organizational and global overview of the system functionality and requirements by *Rijkswaterstaat* (the Dutch Ministry of Transport, Public Works and Water Management), the hydrological knowledge and model-based water level predictions by the *Waterloopkundig Laboratorium* (independent research institute for water management and control), and the controlling and automation discipline and systems' integration knowledge by CMG.

2.3 Building a Safety Critical System

Because of the dangers and costs involved, very strict safety and reliability requirements are imposed on the BOS software. The failure probability for not closing the barrier when this is deemed necessary should be less than 10^{-4}, and the failure probability for not opening the barrier when requested should be less than 10^{-5}. The latter is seen as more critical because of the danger of destruction of the whole barrier if, due to water flowing from the Rhine, the pressure at the inside, i.e., landside, of the barrier is higher than the pressure from the seaside.

The high safety and reliability requirements make BOS a *mission critical system* (or safety critical system) for which special care, effort and precautions should be taken in order to guarantee its safe, reliable and correct operation. To this extent, the design and development of the BOS software was guided by the standard IEC1508 [IEC1508]. This standard is aimed at software development for safety critical systems. It is a best practices standard that categorizes systems according to their safety and reliability requirements into different *Safety Integrity Levels* (SIL). According to this categorization BOS belongs to the highest SIL level (SIL 4). IEC1508 denotes methodologies, techniques and activities as "not recommended", "recommended", "highly recommended", etc. depending on SIL level. For SIL 4 inspection and reviewing, use of an independent test team and the use of formal methods are "highly recommended".

None of the "highly recommended" techniques can completely assure the required safety, reliability and correctness [Bro95]. Only a carefully chosen combination of appropriate techniques can help to increase the confidence that the system has the required quality. This has led to the formulation of a dedicated system engineering process depicted in Figure 2. This Figure indicates which techniques have been used in the different phases of development.

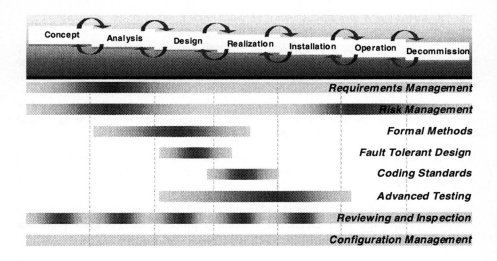

Fig. 2. The dedicated system engineering process combines different techniques.

An integral, risk oriented approach in the system development path identifies at an early stage the aspects of the system that are critical for carrying out the mission of the system. These risks are managed by carrying out both process and product measures. In the development path, a number of methods and techniques are integrated. These are mutually supporting and bring about an effectiveness of the whole that is greater than the sum of the parts. One of the techniques that is proposed in the system development process and that was used in the development of the BOS system is formal methods. The remainder of this paper concentrates on issues concerning the practical use of formal methods in the BOS project.

The BOS system was delivered on time and within budget and is fully operational since October 1998. Its development took three years and about 25 man-years of effort. It resulted in 20,000 lines of formal specification and in 450,000 lines of (a safe subset of) C++ code.

3. Putting Formal Methods into Practice

In this section we describe how formal methods were used in the engineering of the BOS system. It should be noted that a number of observations made here hold more generally for the use of new techniques, not only for formal methods. Moreover, not all benefits achieved within the project can be solely attributed to the use of formal methods because there appeared to be a synergetic effect between the different, quality improving techniques that were applied.

3.1 The Degree of Formality

On the grounds of the promises of formal methods and their recommendation by the IEC 1508 standard, it was decided to investigate their use for the engineering of the BOS system. It was thought that most benefits of the use of formal methods were to be gained if they would be used as an integral part of the system engineering process. This is a clear difference with many other projects where formal methods are used in a parallel or in a "shadow" project. Important consequences of integrating formal methods in the critical path of the engineering process are:

- All project members had to acquire working knowledge of formal methods. Hence a phase of learning and acceptance becomes an integral part of the engineering process.

- The degree of formality that is achieved is probably somewhat lower than is typically achieved in a parallel development process because such processes usually employ highly specialized team-members.

- At completion of the project, it is not possible to compare between processes with and without formal methods. This complicates the evaluation of the use of formal methods.

Central to the engineering process of the complete system was the reduction of risks. For the software system, the following risks were identified:

- The BOS system consists of multiple concurrent processes. This incurs the risks of deadlock or the use of 'bad data' due to synchronization issues.

- The incomplete specification of the behaviour of the system could lead to unexpected behaviour in situations that had not been foreseen. Experience had shown that situations that are typically overlooked are error handling and error recovery.

- Interface faults may occur if interfaces are not specified completely or when they lack robustness.

The use of formal methods was aimed at reducing the probability of the manifestation of these risks. To this end, the degree of formality used was adjusted to the degree of criticality of the different parts of the system. The following levels of formality were identified:

1. Formal annotation of "informal" specifications in order to increase precision and reduce ambiguity.

2. Formal definition of specifications: the purpose is to come to a complete, precise and unambiguous specification of a system.

3. Formal specifications as basis for informal reasoning about the system.

4. Formal specification and reasoning about system properties: mathematical reasoning, possibly supported by tools, is employed to deduce properties of the specification.

Most modules were specified at level 2, sometimes with informal reasoning (level 3). This level was deemed useful for prevention and early detection of faults introduced in the development process through miscommunication and misinterpretation between designers, implementers and testers. In particular, it was hoped that this would aid in reducing the faults that would occur in the integration test (when modules that have been coded and tested individually are composed). Less critical parts of the system were dealt with at level 1, for example, the graphical user interface. Some of the modules that could potentially contribute to the manifestation of one of the aforementioned risks were dealt with at a high level of formality (some at level 3 and some (almost) at level 4). This concerned the internal process scheduling and the communication protocols with the "outside world".

It is important to note that only very small parts of the BOS system were dealt with at level 4, and that for these parts only the design was considered at this level of formality. Not a single line of program code was completely proved correct. Hence, in the BOS approach formal methods do not guarantee complete correctness of code. Different levels of formality and, consequently, different levels of (expected) correctness, were considered. For some parts "a little bit of formal methods" was applied while for other parts "a bit more formality" was used.

3.2 The Selection of Formal Methods

Once it was decided that formal methods were to be used, a selection had to be made in favour of a (combination of) particular technique(s). The techniques had to be suitable for modelling the aspects of the system that were considered critical.

The aspects that are addressed by a formal technique are related to the view a technique takes on a software system. Formal techniques can be classified according to these different views of software systems:

- the *data view*: which data plays a role in a system

- the *functional* (or *input-output*) *view*: which functions play a role in the system and in what way do these transform the data

- the *dynamic* or *behaviour* view: in what order are functions executed

The BOS project focussed on the formalization of the behavioural and functional views. The main candidates considered for the behavioural aspects were CSP [Hoa85], Promela [Hol91] and LOTOS [ISO8807]. The main candidates for the functional view were Z [Spi92] and VDM [Jon90]. The choice in favour of these techniques was made on pragmatic grounds. The arguments that played a role in the selection procedure were: expected learning time, familiarity of the team with a technique and the availability (and price) of tools.

Because of its resemblance to C, it was expected that Promela was easy to learn. Furthermore, a free validation tool called Spin, is available for Promela and can be easily obtained [Spin]. (Free tools were important, in the first place, because there was only a restricted budget for formal methods tools. Moreover, free tools allow experimenting, playing and learning without bureaucracy and without having to convince managers of their necessity. Especially, in the more or less experimental starting phase, it helps if tools can be obtained easily. These advantages were considered to be more important than consistent and guaranteed level of support provided by commercial tools.)

For the functional view, Z seemed easier to learn than VDM. Furthermore there was some familiarity within the project team and some free tools for Z are available. Hence, the behavioural view was modelled using Promela and the functional view using Z.

Promela was used for modelling the interaction between processes and the interaction between the BOS system and the "outside" world. Verification using Promela was limited to the verification of standard properties such as the absence of deadlock and live-lock. Furthermore, the Promela specifications were simulated. This increased insight into system properties. The use of Promela and Spin has led to the identification of significant errors and omissions in early designs. The use of Promela and Spin is considered successful because (1) it helped in reducing defects and (2) it helped in detecting defects early in the development process which reduces the effort and cost required in later stages of development.

Z was used for specifying the functions performed by processes. A common critique on Z is the great diversity of mathematical symbols used. In practice, this was not considered to be a problem for learning Z. A more significant issue was the great degree of expressive freedom of Z. The bases for Z are set theory and predicate logic. These make Z a very powerful formalism with a great expressiveness. However, as a result, Z allows a great deal of freedom and offers little structure for the style in which it is to be used. In the initial phases of using Z, different people used different styles for writing schemas and schemas were not very comprehensible. A need arose for a common 'style' for using Z, which would be acceptable to all project members. The most important issues this style had to provide were guidelines and conventions for writing specifications and guidelines for choosing suitable (levels of) abstractions. But the style should also take into account the needs of implementers, testers and reviewers. Implementers prefer a style that is concrete and can be easily mapped onto programming language constructs. Testers need clearly distinguishable, testable constraints, and easy controllability (bringing the system in a desired state) and observability (observing that the system is in a required state). Reviews are most easily performed if there is a close relationship, preferably one-to-one, between the concepts of the document to be checked and the document with respect to which it is checked.

For the BOS project, a specification-standard – comparable to a coding-standard – was developed. This standard constrained the use of Z and contained heuristic and pragmatic rules for its use. Also very practical issues like layout of schemas and naming conventions were fixed by this standard. Examples of style are a clear separation between pre- and post-conditions for all operation schemas and a constructive style of writing Z constraints where the new value of a variable (primed variable) always appears at the left-hand side of an equation. The recognition of this style-problem and the development of the standards in such a way that they satisfied designers, reviewers, implementers and testers, have taken much time. We found that the literature on learning and using Z did not provide sufficient support for these issues. Moreover, the nature of these problems is such that learning by own experience is a necessity anyhow. After the introduction of the standards, the situation improved rapidly: specifications were written according to a similar structure and were more easily comprehensible by implementers, reviewers and testers. From this stage onward, it was found an important benefit of Z that programmers and testers could use the formal specifications as a clear, precise and indisputable basis for their work.

The tool used for Z was ZTC (Z Type Checker) [ZTC]. (The associated animator ZANS was not used.) ZTC can only verify static properties such as syntax, variable declarations and typing. Such a tool is essential for obtaining a reasonable level of completeness and consistency, in particular, since large portions of errors were simple type-errors. Other errors that were encountered were incomplete cases, i.e., not all combinations of predicates of an operation were covered, however, these errors could only be discovered by manual, laborious checking and not through the use of ZTC. It was felt that tools were lacking for rewriting specifications (for instance, for rewriting preconditions into a standard format such as disjunctive normal form) and for (simple) proofs such as checking pre- and post-conditions and invariant properties – which could have been used to find the incomplete cases of operations.

An important problem in the use of formal methods is the making of models, i.e., abstractions of reality. Choosing the level of abstraction seems to be inherently difficult. Although this problem occurs with all modelling methods, it is more manifest with Z than with Promela. This is probably because Promela is, as a language, less abstract than Z: the concepts of Promela (processes, messages, channels, etc.) are more concrete and closer to the concepts which software engineers usually use for thinking and reasoning. The best way of learning abstraction and modelling seems to be through practice.

3.3 Combining Promela and Z

In the BOS project, the behavioural view was modelled using Promela and the functional view using Z, hence there was a need for combining the specifications of the different views of the system. This was done in a fairly informal manner by using naming conventions in Promela and Z.

The use of multiple formalisms brings along advantages as well as disadvantages. An advantage is that the system is considered from different points of view and that special attention is paid to connecting these views. The confrontation of the different views increases the likelihood of finding problems or omissions in an early stage. On the other hand, disadvantages are that the different specifications may overlap, thus introducing possible inconsistency, or that the different specifications may leave certain systems parts unspecified, thus introducing incompleteness. Another disadvantage is that there is no tool support for the integrated use of Promela and Z. Although the use of one, integrated language would have been beneficial for the BOS project, the use of different formalisms was not considered to be a big hindrance.

3.4 Formal Methods in the Development Process

In the BOS project, formal methods were used in the technical design phase for the writing of formal specifications. The resulting formal specifications were used as basis for coding and testing. In this section we describe issues related to formal methods that arose in the different phases of the software development process.

Functional specification & technical design

A functional specification in natural language, combined with Hatley & Pirbhai kind of diagrams [HP87], was input to the project. On the basis of this specification a formal technical design was to be written. The formalization of the functional specification led to the detection and resolution of many ambiguities, omissions and errors in the functional specification. In hindsight, more errors were found through the process of formalization (making the formal description) than in a later stage through the validation of the formal specification. We conclude that the use of formal methods requires precision, structure and consistency, which help in the prevention and early detection of errors.

It takes more time to write a formal technical design than an "informal" design. This is because more thought has to be put into details of the design. Also it is more difficult to leave open (or hide) design decisions. The extra investment in the formalization of a technical design is easily compensated during the implementation, testing and maintenance phases.

Validation

Promela was used for a number of validations and simulations, in particular, of protocols for communication between BOS and its environment. Also, a formal model has been made of the interaction of the modules of the BOS system. These analyses have shown the absence of deadlock and live-lock. No formal validations were performed using Z. Only static checks and informal, manual reasoning about Z schemas was used.

The possibilities for validation were limited by the functionality (in particular for Z) and performance (mainly for Promela) of the available tools. For the Promela tool Spin the state-space explosion problem was the main bottleneck. For Z the possibility of rewriting a specification was missed; see also the discussion in section 3.2 about ZTC.

Design reviews

Reviews were performed based on formal specifications annotated with natural language descriptions. These reviews were found to be much more effective than reviews based solely on specifications in natural language. The increase in effectiveness was attributed to the fact that concepts, attributes and properties could be addressed, discussed and pointed to with more preciseness and less ambiguity. There were less disputes of the form "what do you exactly mean with that?"

Implementation

The implementations of the system modules in (a safe subset of) C++ were developed on the basis of the formal specifications of the technical design. However, no formal derivation of programming code was used because the benefits were estimated to be marginal in relation to the large efforts which would be needed for this. In hindsight, this estimation turned out to be valid. The number of defects introduced by the manual implementation process was relatively small.

An important lesson from the implementation phase is that programmers have to learn to be very precise in reading the formal specifications. They have to convert the specifications into program code without making their own interpretations and design decisions. This is different from what most programmers use to do and it implies the need for a change of mentality.

Testing

We previously reported on the benefits of formal methods for testing in [GWT98]. Although no formal derivation of tests was applied, the use of formal methods facilitated the systematic identification of test cases. The precise and formally specified requirements led to a clear and structured set of tests with a high degree of code coverage.

Testers appeared to be more rigorous than they would have been without formal specifications, in the sense that more detail-errors were found (but less major design errors were found, as expected). Furthermore, the formal specifications settled easily interpretation differences between testers and implementers. Future improvements of the testing phase are possible through increased automated support including automatic derivation of tests from formal specifications [Tre99].

General

Current formal methods focus on one of the views of software systems. It would be desirable to have a formal method which deals with the different views of software systems in an integrated fashion – preferably in combination with existing software development methods and techniques, such as data-flow diagrams, Ward & Mellor [WM85], Hatley & Pirbhai [HP87] or UML [BRJ98].

4. Lessons Learned

In this section we describe some of the important lessons we learned from our experience with formal methods.

4.1 Quality

The general conclusion of most project members is that the quality of the system is higher than could have been achieved without the use of formal methods. Once a working knowledge of formal methods had been acquired, the system modules produced were close to "first time right." Modules that were specified formally required less maintenance and rework. Most problems were encountered in modules where formal methods were not used or where the quality of the formal specification was low due to time-pressure.

4.2 Costs

Costs of formal development were estimated to be comparable with costs without the use of formal methods. It should be noted, however, that a large amount of these costs were related to learning and obtaining experience, hence it could be expected that a next formal project will save money.

4.3 The Learning Phase

On the first use of formal methods a training phase is unavoidable. Besides the learning of syntax and semantics of the formalisms, people had to learn how to use the formal methods effectively. In particular, people had to learn that a formal specification had to be read in a much more precise manner than a specification in natural language. Also, in the learning phase it was found that a specification "style" was needed to constrain the degrees of freedom of the specification methods.

In the process of getting acquainted with a formal method, it was found to be important to have an experimentation phase. In this phase people should be allowed to get a feeling for the possibilities, structure, constructions and the like of a formal method by making specifications and programs that are not part of the final product. This leaves opportunity for exploring and investigation and learning from making mistakes without the pressure of having to produce fault-free products. This learning phase is also a good time to explore the possible ways in which one formal method can be combined with other (formal) methods. The availability of tools helps in this learning phase. In particular, a formal-methods simulation tool is a good means for providing feedback to the student of a method. The use of the Promela simulator in Spin was profitable in this respect.

4.4 Support from Academia

During the development of BOS CMG was supported by the Formal Methods & Tools group of the University of Twente. It turned out that the expertise of the University of Twente was not completely sufficient for supporting the application of, mainly, Z in large projects such as BOS. The expertise was mainly oriented towards formal methods as formal (mathematical) languages and towards formal syntax, semantics and proof techniques. The problems encountered in BOS, however, were not formal (mathematical) problems, but mainly problems related to the use of formal methods in a large project: how to use formal methods effectively in a software development trajectory; how to combine formal methods with other software engineering techniques; and the identification and definition of the "specification standards" for Z. With these aspects there was little experience at the University of Twente. Also in the literature there is little known about these practical aspects of the use of formal methods. The combination of knowledge and experience of both practical software engineering and formal methods is still rare.

4.5 Tools

Although it is known for some time that the availability of tools is essential to the industrial acceptance of formal methods, the tools we used provide too little support. In particular, attention should be paid to scaling up tools to large applications and to the integration or compatibility of formal methods tools with existing software development methods and tools.

4.6 Planning and Monitoring

The use of formal methods in the development process had several consequences for the planning of the project. Firstly, formally specifying the functional design takes up more time than specifying in natural language. However, using a formal method for the design leads to the identification of omissions, ambiguities and inconsistencies that can be removed at a relatively early stage. We are confident that the effort invested in the design phase has been (more than) compensated by reductions of effort in subsequent phases.

A second consequence is that large parts of the testing phase can be performed concurrently with coding of the implementation. Whereas in many system development projects test suites are only developed and implemented after the system has been implemented, BOS shows that the level of detail provided by a formal design makes is possible to perform these phases concurrently. Starting from the formal design, implementers start coding, while at the same time testers start writing test plans, generating test suites and developing a test environment. Usually, testers are faster so that when the implementation is ready, test execution can start immediately. Clearly, this reduces the total project time by reducing the critical path for testing.

In the beginning, metrics from the design phase were not used for planning the coding and testing phase. After some time, it turned out that the number of lines of Z could be used as a rudimentary metrics for planning. Analysis showed a correlation between the number of lines of Z and the number of lines of C++ code or the testing effort, respectively. In particular, after some experience had been obtained and some data had been collected, module test execution could be planned relatively precisely based on this metrics. This effect was strengthened by the fact that test plans and test suites were developed concurrently with coding, see above. Further analysis is needed to explore the precise nature of the correlation between the size of the specification and the implementation and testing effort. Other metrics that could be explored are the number of Z schemas or the number of data items in a description.

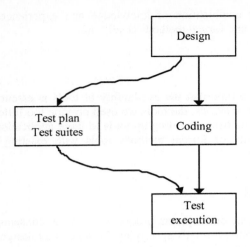

4.7 People Management

People are stimulated by the possibility of learning new skills and experiencing that they improve the quality of their work. This can be illustrated by the fact that at later stages of the project, some project members decided to write and analyse a module (GUI) at a higher level of formality than followed from its degree of criticality.

The different levels of formality require different skills in using formal techniques. Hence, the training of different project members may need to be aimed at different skill levels. Learning to read and review formal specifications requires less training than learning to write specifications, which, in turn, requires less training than necessary for doing model-checking. Of course, each person's tasks should be adapted to his or her capabilities and education, e.g., while almost all software engineers, after some training, can read formal specifications, model-checking is better performed by people having some mathematical background. Some team members did not have any affinity with formal methods. These persons left the project, to mutual benefit of both these persons and the project.

4.8 Communication with the Client

A common critique of formal methods is that they are not suitable for communication with clients. In the BOS project we have dealt with this issue in the following way. Firstly, all specifications consisted of a combination of formal text and accompanying text in natural language. In practice, the clients focussed mainly on the description in natural language. Secondly, it was found that the animations of Promela specifications using the Spin simulator were very helpful in communicating with the client, in order to have the client understand the design and to make the client aware of potential problems.

5. Conclusions and Recommendations

We have described some of our experiences with the use of formal methods in the commercial engineering of an industrial, safety-critical system. The system was delivered on time and within budget. It was found that formal methods had a positive contribution to the quality of the system. However, it should be noted that formal methods were used as one of a number of integrated techniques and that there is a synergetic effect between these techniques. Formal methods have the greatest added value when they are applied in combination with other quality improvement techniques. Hence, methods to improve the quality of the software product should be used in combination with methods for the improvement of the quality of the engineering process (such as are suggested by CMM). More about the other quality improving techniques used in BOS can be found in [WBG98].

On pragmatic grounds we used Promela for modelling the behavioural view of the system and Z for the functional view. The introduction of Promela went relatively easy because of its ease in use, among others, through its visualization using message sequence charts. A few early successes in finding major design errors stimulated its further use. Overall, it was found useful in exposing errors in interface design.

The use of Z in a professional software-engineering project requires more than a few courses in first-order predicate logic and Z-notation. A useful idiom and conventions have to be developed ranging from high-level structuring conventions to naming conventions. The developed set of conventions for Z together with extensive coding standards (implementation guidelines) proved to enhance efficiency in the coding phase. In [GWT98] we have reported the additional benefits of this approach to the independent test phase.

More errors were found through the process of formalization (making a formal description) than in later stages through the validation of the formal specifications. Formal derivation or proof of code was not used at all. Yet, we conclude that the use of formal methods was profitable. Their use provides precision, structure and consistency that help in the prevention and early detection of errors.

Acknowledgements

The authors would like to thank Eric Burgers, Wouter Geurts, Franc Buve, Rijn Buve, Sjaak de Graaf, Hedde van de Lugt, Peter Bosman, Peter van de Heuvel and Robin Rijkers, all of CMG Public Sector B.V. in The Hague, for their active participation during the interviews that form the basis of this paper. Annemieke van Wijk, CMG, for is thanked for her secretarial support. Ed Brinksma, Pim Kars, Wil Janssen, Job Zwiers and Theo Ruys from the University of Twente gave support and feedback during different phases of the BOS development. The second author acknowledges the financial support of CMG The Netherlands while performing part of the work underlying this paper. The anonymous referees are thanked for their constructive criticism, which helped in improving this paper.

References

[BRJ98]   G. Booch, J. Rumbaugh and I. Jacobsen. The Unified Modeling Language –
             User Guide. The Addison-Wesley Object Technology Series, Addison
             Wesley, 1998.
[Bro95]   F. P. Brookes. *The Mythical Man-Month: Essays on Software Engineering.*
             Anniversary edition. Addison Wesley, 1995.
[GWT98]   W. Geurts, K. Wijbrans and J. Tretmans. Testing and Formal Methods –
             BOS Project Case Study. In: *EuroSTAR'98*: 6th European Intl. Conference
             on Software Testing, Analysis & Review, pages 215 – 229, Munich,
             Germany, November 30 – December 1, 1998.
[Hoa85]   C. A. R. Hoare, *Communicating Sequential Processes,* Prentice-Hall, 1985.
[HP87]   D. J. Hatley and I.A. Pirbhai. *Strategies for Real Time System Specification.*
             Dorset House, 1987.
[Hol91]   G. J. Holzmann. *Design and Validation of Computer Protocols.* Prentice-
             Hall, 1991.
[IEC1508]   IEC (International Electrotechnical Commission), Functional Safety of
             Electrical/Electronic/Programmable Systems: Generic Aspects, IEC 1508,
             1995. (Now: IEC 61508).
[ISO8807]   ISO, Information Processing Systems Open Systems Interconnection,
             LOTOS – A Formal Description Technique based on the Temporal
             Ordering of Observational Behaviour, International Standard IS8807, ISO,
             Geneva, 1989.
[Jon90]   C. B. Jones, *Systematic Software Development using VDM* (2nd edition),
             Prentice Hall, 1990.
[Kar97]   P. Kars, The Application of Promela and SPIN in the BOS Project, in J.-C.
             Grégoire, G. J. Holzmann and D. Peled (eds), *The Second Workshop on the
             SPIN Verification System; Proceedings of a DIMACS workshop,* August 5,
             1996, volume 32 of DIMACS series in Discrete Mathematics and
             Theoretical Computer Science, pages 51-63. American Mathematical
             Society, 1997.
[Kar98]   P. Kars, Formal Methods in the Design of a Storm Surge Barrier Control
             System. In: G. Rozenberg and F. W. Vaandrager (eds.) *Lectures on
             Embedded Systems*, pages 353 – 367, Lecture Notes in Computer Science
             1494, Springer-Verlag, 1998.
[Pau94]   M. C. Paulk et al., *The Capability Maturity Model: Guidelines for
             Improving the Software Process,* Addison-Wesley, 1994.
[RWS]   Dutch Ministry of Transport, Public Works and Water Management.
             URL: http://www.minvenw.nl/rws/dzh/svk/engels/index.html
[Spin]   Spin. On-the-fly, LTL Model Checking with Spin.
             URL: http://netlib.bell-labs.com/netlib/spin/whatispin.html
[Spi92]   J. M. Spivey. *The Z notation: a Reference Manual* (2nd edition). Prentice-
             Hall, 1992.
[Tre99]   J. Tretmans. Testing Concurrent Systems: A Formal Approach. In: J.
             Baeten and S. Mauw, *Concur'99.* Lecture Notes in Computer Science,
             Springer-Verlag, 1999.
[WBG98]   K. C. J. Wijbrans, F. Buve and W. Geurts. Practical Experiences in the BOS
             Project. In: *Proceedings of the Embedded Systems Symposium*, May 19,
             1998, Eindhoven University of Technology, Eindhoven, The Netherlands.
[WM85]   P.T. Ward and S.J. Mellor. *Structured Development for Real Time Systems.*
             Volume 1: Introduction & Tools. Yourdon Press Computing Series.
             Prentice Hall, 1985.
[ZTC]   ZTC. Z Type Checker. URL: http://saturn.cs.depaul.edu/~fm/ztc.html

The Value of Verification: Positive Experience of Industrial Proof

Steve King[1], Jonathan Hammond[2], Rod Chapman[2], and Andy Pryor[2]

[1] Department of Computer Science, University of York,
Heslington, York, YO10 5DD, UK
king@cs.york.ac.uk
[2] Praxis Critical Systems, 20 Manvers St, Bath, BA1 1PX, UK
{jarh,rod,aap}@praxis-cs.co.uk

Abstract. This paper describes the use of formal development methods on an industrial safety-critical application. The Z notation was used for documenting the system specification and part of the design, and the SPARK subset of Ada was used for coding. However, perhaps the most distinctive nature of the project lies in the amount of proof which was carried out: proofs were carried out both at the Z level — approximately 150 proofs in 500 pages — and at the SPARK code level — approximately 9000 verification conditions generated and discharged. The project was carried out under UK Interim Defence Standards 00-55 and 00-56, which require the use of formal methods on safety-critical applications. It is believed to be the first to be completed against the rigorous demands of the 1991 version of these standards.

The paper includes a comparison of proof with the various types of testing employed, in terms of their efficiency at finding faults. The most striking result is that the Z proof was substantially more efficient at finding faults than the most efficient testing phase. Given the importance of early fault detection, this helps to demonstrate the significant benefit and practicality of large-scale proof on projects of this kind.

1 Introduction

When early drafts of the UK Defence Standard 00-55[1] were produced, there was a certain amount of controversy among software suppliers because of the perceived emphasis on formal methods: a formal specification and design were required, as well as formal arguments to link the specification to the design, and the design to the code, and even to support the production of an executable prototype. It was claimed that the level of formality required was unrealistic given current technology. The work reported in this paper shows that developing software using such formal techniques is indeed possible. It is now becoming more common for projects to use formal notations to document specifications and even designs, but this project is unusual in the scale of the proof work that has been carried out. The particular notations used were Z [24, 28] for specification and design, and

---

[1] The procurement of Safety Critical Software in Defence Equipment [18, 19]

J. Wing, J. Woodcock, J. Davies (Eds.): FM'99, Vol. II, LNCS 1709, pp. 1527–1545, 1999.
© Springer-Verlag Berlin Heidelberg 1999

the SPARK [3, 23] subset of Ada for code, together with its associated toolset. The proof work on Z covered about 500 pages, while over 9,000 verification conditions were generated and discharged in the SPARK proof work.

During the project, many metrics were recorded, and a selection are reported in this paper. It is interesting to compare the numbers of faults found at various stages of the process with the amount of effort spent on the stage. These figures seem to show the value of the proofs that were carried out on the Z documents.

The structure of the paper is as follows: after a brief description of the application, the SPARK programming language and toolset are described. (It is assumed that the reader is familiar with the Z notation: if not, there are several good text books available [28, 16], and a glossary is provided in Appendix A for a few key Z terms.) We then describe in some detail how proof was used in the development process, and look at both quantitative and subjective results before drawing some conclusions.

2   The Application: SHOLIS

The application we describe in this paper is called SHOLIS — the Ship Helicopter Operating Limits Information System. This is a new safety-critical system, which aids the safe operation of helicopters on naval vessels. It is essentially an information system, giving advice on the safety of helicopter flying operations. The SHOLIS programme is on-going but, after evaluation (if successful), it is intended that SHOLIS will be used on UK Royal Navy and Royal Fleet Auxiliary vessels. SHOLIS is developed for the UK Ministry of Defence (MoD) by PMES[2], with Praxis Critical Systems as the subcontractor responsible for the development of all the application software.

Brief System Description SHOLIS contains a database of Ship Helicopter Operating Limits (SHOLs). Each SHOL specifies the allowed limits for performing a given operation, e.g. takeoff or land, for a particular type of helicopter. One of the main safety-critical functions of SHOLIS is to make continual comparisons of sensor information against a selected SHOL. Audible and visual alarms are given whenever the current environmental conditions exceed the allowed limits.

The SHOLIS functions are grouped on a number of pages. These are viewed on plasma displays on the flight deck and bridge of a ship. Operators at each display can use buttons to view the pages independently. The buttons are also used to enter information, although certain functions, e.g. the selection of a SHOL, are only available to one display at any given time.

Due to its critical nature the system is developed to stringent standards, including the MoD Interim Defence Standards 00-55 [18, 19] and 00-56 [17], as discussed above. High availability requirements necessitate the use of dual redundant hardware.

---

[2] Power Magnetics and Electronic Systems Limited

Safety Requirements SHOLIS has a number of catastrophic hazards, which, if they occurred, could lead to the loss of an aircraft and/or damage to a ship. Any software with the potential to cause such a hazard, as identified by the software safety analysis, is classed as safety-critical and developed to SIL4[3]. The remaining software is classed as non-safety critical, although it is still developed to a stringent standard (roughly equivalent to SIL3).

3 The Programming Language: SPARK

SPARK is a high-level programming language, designed for writing software for high integrity systems. The executable part of the language is a subset of Ada [20], but there are additional annotations permitted which make it possible to carry out data and information flow analysis [4], and to prove partial code correctness, using the commercial toolset associated with the language: the SPARK Examiner, Simplifier and Proof Checker.[4]

There were several design drivers behind the choices as to what parts of Ada should be removed from the SPARK programming language:

- logical soundness: there should be no ambiguities in the language;
- simplicity of formal description: it should be possible to describe the whole language in a relatively simple way;
- expressive power: notwithstanding the previous two factors, the language should be rich enough to describe real systems;
- security: it should be possible to determine statically whether a program conforms to the language rules;
- verifiability: program verification should be not only theoretically possible, but also tractable for industrial-sized systems;
- bounded time and space requirements: in order to avoid the possibility of run-time errors caused by exhausting finite resources such as time and space, the resource requirements of a program should be determinable statically.

Together, these considerations led to decisions to omit several features of Ada: gotos, aliasing, default parameters for subprograms (i.e. procedures and functions), side-effects in functions, recursion, tasks, exceptions and generics. In addition, several other features, such as the type model, are simplified: no access types (pointers), type aliasing, derived types or anonymous types. Apart from these exclusions and restrictions, the normal Ada package structure is used for programming, with its distinction between package interfaces (or specifications) and package bodies. Within a package, further structuring is possible using procedures and functions and it is at this level that we can see the first of the new annotations.

---

[3] Interim Defence Standard 00-56 defines four Safety Integrity Levels (SILs), of which SIL4 is the most critical, and SIL1 is the least critical.

[4] SPARK and its toolset were originally developed by Program Validation Limited (PVL), which was incorporated into Praxis Critical Systems in 1994.

Annotations are comments which are ignored by an Ada compiler, but processed by the SPARK tools. The first group of annotations is concerned with data and information flow analysis[5]:

- --# global
- --# derives
- --# own
- --# inherit

The --# global and --# derives annotations between them specify the information needed for data and information flow analysis of individual subprograms. Data-flow analysis involves checking that global variables and parameters are used in the expected way: imported variables can only be read from, exported variables can be written to, and variables that are both imported and exported can be read from and written to. There are also checks that variables are not being read before being initialised with a value, that values are not overwritten before being read, that all imported variables are actually used somewhere, and so on.

Information-flow analysis uses the --# derives annotation where, for each output variable, a list is given of the imported variables on which its final value depends. These dependencies are checked by making an analysis of the expressions assigned to variables in the subprogram body. Both data- and information-flow analyses are decidable, and entirely automated by the SPARK Examiner.

The own and inherit annotations are used for scoping and structuring. The own annotation is used to declare the existence of state variables inside a package: the values of these variables are preserved between calls of subprograms in the package. The inherit annotation makes visible the items from another package scope, e.g. it allows the annotations in a package to refer to the own variables of the inherited package.

The second group of annotations is used for code verification:

- --# pre
- --# post
- --# assert
- --# return

The pre and post annotations are found in the specification of a procedure, and are used for the traditional precondition and postcondition of the procedure — pre gives a predicate on the input parameters and initial state (imported) variables, while post relates input and output parameters and initial and final state (exported) variables. On non-looping programs, the SPARK Examiner produces proof obligations by 'hoisting' the postcondition through the procedure body and checking that the supplied precondition implies this transformed postcondition. For looping programs, the assert annotation is used to specify the loop invariant. The verification conditions (VCs) generated by the Examiner for looping programs check for *partial* correctness: separate arguments are needed

---

[5] All annotations are prefixed by --#, with -- being the Ada comment prefix

to consider loop termination, if total correctness is required. Finally, the `return` annotation is used to define (explicitly or implicitly) the result of a function, thus allowing checking of functions to be carried out at a more abstract level.

The SPARK Examiner has a mode of operation where, in addition to the VCs generated by the flow analysis and proof annotations, it also generates VCs which, if discharged, would guarantee that the SPARK program could not raise any run-time exceptions. The design of the SPARK language itself ensures that the Ada exceptions `Tasking_Error` and `Program_Error` can never arise in a SPARK program. In addition, since SPARK is designed so that the space requirements can be computed statically, it is possible to guarantee that `Storage_Error` cannot be raised. The only remaining possible exception is `Constraint_Error`, and the restrictions on the SPARK language mean that this can only be caused by a division check, an index check, a range check or an overflow check. When invoked with the run-time check (RTC) option, the SPARK Examiner generates VCs for the first three of these checks, and the VCs for the overflow check can be generated by the RTC plus Overflow option.

There are two possible routes for discharging the VCs produced by the Examiner: the Simplifier and the Proof Checker. The Simplifier is an automatic tool which carries out routine simplification using a collection of rules. If a VC cannot be discharged by the Simplifier, then a developer can invoke the Proof Checker, which is an interactive assistant allowing exploration of the problem and (it is hoped) the construction of a proof.

4   Proof in the SHOLIS Development Process

4.1   The Development Process

The development process used for SHOLIS was a fairly standard one, following the requirements of IDS 00-55. In simplified form, it comprised:

- Requirements, written in English;
- Software Requirement Specification (SRS), written in Z and English;
- Software Design Specification (SDS), written in SPARK, Z and English;
- Code, written in SPARK;
- Testing.

The Requirements documents consisted of over 4,000 statements of system requirements, most of which were software-related, while the SRS was about 300 pages long, containing Z, English and some additional mathematical definitions (of vector geometry). The purpose of the SDS was to add implementation details to the SRS: software architecture, 'refinement' of one part of the Z specification (where an intermediate level of design was needed), scheduling design, resource usage, SPARK package specifications and so on. The software itself totalled about 133,000 lines of code, made up of 13,000 lines of Ada declarations, 14,000 lines of Ada statements, 54,000 lines of SPARK flow annotations,[6] 20,000 lines of SPARK proof annotations and 32,000 blank or comment lines.[7]

4.2   Proof Activities

The proof activities on SHOLIS can be divided into two areas: Z proof and SPARK proof. Proof of various Z properties took place at both SRS and SDS level. The SRS, containing the abstract Z specification, has several standard opportunities for proof: consistency of global variables and constants, existence of initial states and checking of preconditions. It is interesting to see how the structure of the Z specification was exploited in these proofs. The main structuring of the Z specification was by what were called 'subsystems', i.e. the state was partitioned into a number of pieces that were separately specified, together with 'local' operations. Subsystems included such things as sensors, alarms, faults, and the currently selected SHOL, etc. Each main display page selectable by the user also had its own subsystem. In general, the complete SHOLIS state was simply the conjunction of all the subsystems, with appropriate additional invariants.

The notable exception to this involved the pages, as SHOLIS has two displays. So a display state schema was defined (which included the various pages as schema types), and a standard functional promotion carried out to the complete multiple displays state. Thus an individual page's state schema is effectively promoted twice (once to the 'display level' and again to the 'multiple displays level').

Each of the 14 top-level (system) operations had a precondition proof. At the top level this consisted of manual rigorous argument to remove Ξ schemas (on unaffected subsystems) and associated top-level invariants. The rigorous arguments continued until the precondition proof had been 'factored down' to precondition proofs of the constituent subsystem operations. Sometimes top-level invariants (which were not obviously preserved) were also 'factored down', so the subsystem precondition proofs were sometimes stronger than the 'standard' Z precondition proofs (in that there was an additional 'factored down' invariant to preserve). In general, schema expansion was not performed until the subsystem level was reached. Proofs were only carried out for subsystems that had been identified as SIL4. This structuring did not apply to the initial state proof. Here the top-level obligation was mechanically fully expanded and then simplified.

Each subsystem was a separate chapter in the SRS and mapped to a different Ada package in the design.

---

[6] The SPARK flow annotations are deliberately written in a very 'spread-out' way which uses a large number of lines, for ease of maintenance. Furthermore the need to do code proof, coupled with the current lack of abstract proof support, meant that the SPARK concept of own variable refinement could not be exploited to reduce substantially the size of the annotations (see section 5.2).

[7] There was a little non-SPARK code: some assembler, used only in booting up SHOLIS, and some non-SPARK Ada, used for interfacing to hardware devices.

The key safety properties of SHOLIS were also formalised in Z, and proved. These properties were expressed in terms of a sequence of operations. Clearly, for this application, the most important safety properties involved ensuring that when certain sensor values were outside the current SHOL, a warning had to be given, and also that when the values were inside the SHOL, no alarm would be given.[8] Thus the proofs of safety properties involved checks of the form

$$In \, _9^0 \ Calc \, _9^0 \ Out \qquad \text{gives the correct warning} \ ,$$

where the schema In verified and stored the input values, $Calc$ performed the comparison with the current SHOL and updated the alarm state, and Out gave the output processing. Each of these schemas represents one of the 14 top-level system operations, and thus the safety properties could not be expressed as part of the main specification, as they cover sequences of system operations.

At the SDS level there were further proof opportunities, demonstrating the consistency and correctness of the part of the design written in Z.

All of the proofs at the Z level were carried out by a form of 'rigorous argument', with some assistance from tools — particularly the CADiZ tool [26], for schema expansion. For the SPARK proof work, on the other hand, all of the work was carried out with machine assistance: the Examiner, Simplifier and Proof Checker were used.

Data- and information-flow analysis was carried out for all of the code in SHOLIS. The intention had been to do only data-flow analysis for the main control loop, and parts of the event scheduler called from this control loop. This is because, at that level, almost every variable has an effect on every other variable, so the information-flow annotations would be both lengthy and uninformative. However, the SHOLIS application software is a single process running on a single processor (modulo redundant hardware), containing software of different integrity levels. Hence, full information-flow analysis was needed at the top level to demonstrate functional separation between the SIL4 and non-SIL4 code, e.g. to show that the non-SIL4 code did not incorrectly interfere with critical data on the same processor.

The demonstration of functional separation also justified only constructing SPARK program correctness proofs on the SIL4 parts of the software. For every subprogram of this sort, SPARK pre and post annotations were produced from the Z descriptions. The SPARK names were kept as close as possible to the Z names, but there were inevitable small differences, for instance package names. There were also simple type translations: Z sequences became arrays with a slightly different syntax, partial functions also became arrays and so on. Although this could be seen as a 'weak link' in the formal development process, experience showed that it was actually relatively simple to produce these SPARK annotations, and very few detected errors were introduced at this point. The Z state invariants were incorporated into both pre and post annotations of procedures, which produced one or two interesting difficulties: the annotations could only refer to variables which were visible according to the SPARK rules,

---

[8] Otherwise safe recovery of aircraft might not be possible.

but sometimes the invariants referred to variables which were not visible. The solution was to write the strongest condition possible using the visible variables, so that, at the next level 'up', this condition together with the frame knowledge that other variables were unchanged would establish the invariant.

Although the intention had originally been to generate the proof annotations along with the code, time pressures — caused by the need to pass the code to the IV&V team[9] — meant that many proof annotations were actually added slightly later. Having produced the necessary annotations, the SPARK Examiner was then used to generate the proof obligations to show that the code did indeed satisfy its specification. These proof obligations were first submitted to the SPARK Simplifier, which managed to discharge about 75% of them automatically. The remaining ones were virtually all proved using the SPARK Proof Checker, the exceptions being:

- proof obligations that depended on formal descriptions of hardware devices which were not available; and
- proof obligations for a few subprograms, that involved a lot of effort to prove, but which, by symmetry, were merely further examples of code that had already been proved.

The final group of SPARK proof activities concerned the run-time checks (RTCs). Since it was clear that a run-time failure — be it invalid range or index, division by zero, or overflow — would be a danger to the safety-critical parts of SHOLIS whether it occurred in SIL4 code or not, the whole of the software was subjected to the SPARK Examiner's RTC (plus Overflow) facility. Again, all of the generated proof obligations were proved, either by the Simplifier or using the Proof Checker.

4.3   Proof Personnel

The proof activity on the SHOLIS project was carried out by four engineers. Two were responsible for the Z proofs, and one of these also worked with the other two engineers on the generation of SPARK proof annotations corresponding to the Z specifications, and all the SPARK proof activity. The data- and information-flow analysis was carried out by the two coders. All of the proof engineers were experienced mathematicians and software engineers who had worked for several years in various formal methods, including Z and CSP. However, only one had experience with the SPARK Simplifier and Proof Checker before the project started.

It is also interesting to consider, with hindsight, the skills which seem to be *necessary* for such a project. For the Z proof work, significant experience (either academic or industrial) of Z and at least some exposure to proof are necessary to be productive enough to be commercially cost-effective (e.g. familiarity with concepts such as proof by cases and proof by contradiction). For the *formal*

---

[9] Independent Verification and Validation team: part of Praxis Critical Systems, but independent of the development team.

SPARK proofs, a good (informal) understanding of the meaning of imperative programming constructs is essential, together with some familiarity with relevant proof concepts such as loop invariants. However, previous experience with the tools is not thought necessary. Interestingly, the proofs of absence of run-time errors are much more accessible, since the tools can generate the VCs without any additional proof annotations (although annotations may be needed to enable the VCs to be proved). Also, a large proportion of these VCs are typically proved automatically using the Simplifier. This enables effort to be quickly focussed on potential problem areas and/or the more complex code, where it may not be straightforward to prove the code error-free.

4.4   Proof Validation

The Z proofs were subject to a formal peer-review process, when the proofs produced by each engineer were formally reviewed by the other. In addition, the IV&V team reviewed a sample (selected by them) of the proofs, and found only typographical errors. The SPARK code proofs were also reviewed by the IV&V team, and are replayable on the SPARK toolset. The team also reviewed the additional proof rules that had been inserted to discharge the VCs.[10] However, none of the proofs was inspected or reviewed by the customer.

4.5   Timing and Resource Usage

As already discussed, the SHOLIS application consists of both SIL4 and non-SIL4 code. Although the information-flow analysis demonstrated functional separation, non-functional interactions (e.g. slow performance of non-SIL4 code preventing the timely execution of SIL4 code) could still have had an unacceptable impact on safety. So, in addition to functional correctness, significant effort was spent on non-functional aspects of the behaviour of *all* the SHOLIS code.

Timing: An in-house static timing analysis tool was used, which was based on programmer-supplied annotations in the source code. This did not read or analyse the object code at all — it merely computed a worst-case number of "statements" for each subprogram, and used a constant "number of statements per second" (determined by hand analysis and actual timing of a "typical" portion of the code) to make a crude estimate of an upper-bound on the timing of a subprogram.

Memory: Care was taken never to allocate memory dynamically: SPARK ensures this 99% of the time, but there were a few cases where careful coding was necessary to take into account the compiler's allocation policy.[11] SPARK is non-recursive, so a simple static analysis of object code is sufficient to determine worst-case stack usage, which was done.

---

[10] These rules were either the necessary definitions of SPARK proof functions, or more generally useful rules which are not part of the Proof Checker's rulebase.

[11] Section 5.2 contains more details on this topic.

I/O bandwidth: This was a crucial aspect of SHOLIS, since the available bandwidth to the displays was a limiting factor. Again, programmer-supplied annotations in the source (actually PERL expressions!) were used to indicate the worst-case number of characters that could be sent to the display by each subprogram. A simple PERL tool collected and evaluated the results.

The above systematic estimation/calculation was backed up in all cases with targetted testing, based on known worst-case application behaviour, to measure actual timing and resource usage (e.g. a dynamic "high water mark" test of stack usage). These tests provided additional confidence in the accuracy/conservative nature of the systematically produced figures.

5   Results, Experiences, and Lessons Learnt

Having described what was carried out in the way of proof on the SHOLIS project, we can now look at the results of this work, both in terms of quantitative results and in terms of more subjective feelings about the work.

5.1   Quantitative Results

In the Z proof work, approximately 150 proofs were carried out, of which about 130 were at the SRS level and the remainder at the SDS level. These proofs covered about 500 pages. In the SPARK proof work, approximately 9,000 verification conditions (VCs) were generated, of which 3,100 were proofs of functional and safety properties, and the remaining 5,900 came from the RTC generator. Of these 9,000 VCs, 6,800 were discharged automatically by the Simplifier and the remainder were discharged by the SPARK Proof Checker, or by the 'rigorous argument' referred to above, in a few cases. Indeed, subjective feedback from the project team emphasised the importance of using the most powerful workstations possible for the computationally intensive work of the Simplifier: 'a big computer is far cheaper than the time of the engineers using it'!

The project team kept track of faults found at different stages during the development process, and the rounded percentages are shown in Figure 1. The definition of a fault for these purposes is simply an error which required something to be changed. It could therefore range from a simple clerical error to an observable system failure. However, these figures exclude faults which were not faults in the actual system development (specification, design, code etc). Thus, for instance, errors in test scripts are not included. Figure 1 also shows how much of the total effort on SHOLIS (19 person-years) was spent on each phase.

Note that Figure 1 lists the project phases in approximately the order in which they occurred. However, there was some parallelism between phases. In particular, code proof overlapped with unit and integration testing, and especially with system validation testing.

For comparison, [13] contains figures on effort and size metrics for another safety-related real-time project, but for a much larger system than SHOLIS. This

Project phase	Faults found (%)	Effort (%)
Specification	3.5	5
Z proof	16	2.5
High-level design	1.5	2
Detailed design, code & informal test	26.5	17.5
Unit test	16	25
Integration test	1	1
Code proof	5.5	4
System validation test	21.5	9.5
Acceptance test	0.5	1.5
Other[12]	8	32

Fig. 1. Faults found and effort spent during phases of the project

other project also used formal methods, although there was only a very small amount of proof.

Informal feedback from the SHOLIS team indicated a feeling that the most cost-effective phases for fault-finding were Z Proof and System Validation Tests. The Z Proof phase in particular was felt to be effective at finding a significant number of faults, with relatively little effort, early in the development process. Figure 2 gives a graphical representation of the exact figures, where the dark bars show the actual number of faults found by each phase. For the verification phases, i.e. those phases whose main purpose was the detection of faults, Figure 2 also shows the efficiency with which faults were found (the lighter bars), by dividing the number of detected faults by the effort expended.

These figures clearly show that the Z Proof was, by a significant margin, the most efficient phase at finding faults, followed by the System Validation Test phase. It is perhaps even more surprising that Code Proof was more efficient than Unit Testing, despite the fact that substantial amounts of unit testing were completed before the bulk of code proof started.

One word of caution: it has not yet been possible to conduct a serious analysis of the nature of the faults (e.g. severity) found by different project phases. However, some initial impressions are described here.

The faults found during System Validation often originated from the requirements, or from incorrectly capturing the requirements in Z, rather than being instances of code not being a correct implementation of the Z specification. The faults found during the Code Proof phase were mostly cases of very subtle problems revealed by the RTCs — in particular circumstances (usually very unlikely ones), it might have been possible for a run-time error to have occurred. On the other hand, the traditional Unit and Integration Testing phases did find a number of faults that could have manifested themselves in realistic use of the final system. This included faults in two small, but critical, numerical calculations

---

[12] Staff familiarisation (1%), project management and planning (20%), safety management and engineering (7%) and IV&V non-testing activities (4%).

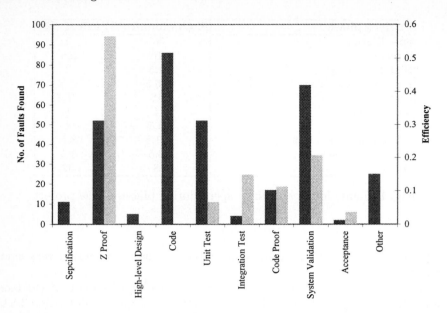

Fig. 2. Faults found and 'efficiency' of the phases of development

involving real (Ada fixed-point) arithmetic, where the SPARK proof model is not rich enough to allow precise reasoning about rounding and accuracy errors.[13] By sampling a few of the other faults found during unit testing, it has been confirmed that code proof should also have found the faults (since unprovable VCs are generated from the faulty code) if proof had occurred before testing. Even given the ordering of phases, the Code Proof phase did reveal one significant bug: the proof of the safety properties involved checking that certain invariants were maintained at the control loop level, but it was found that there was a path through the system which invalidated one of these invariants. Once this was understood, it was relatively easy for the developer to go to the test installation, press a few buttons and show that the system was in a clearly invalid state.

5.2   Subjective Feedback on the Use of Proof

Since this project was unique, in our experience, in the amount of Z/SPARK proof carried out, there were many lessons learnt, both about the advantages of doing these sorts of proofs, and about their drawbacks. One of the most important ideas to appreciate was the limit of formality. Figure 3 gives a representation of the call-tree of the main program: procedure Main is at the top of the tree, followed closely by the scheduler and event handler, while the subprograms and packages at the bottom include device drivers for the I/O devices.

---

[13] In these cases, manual numerical analysis was carried out to confirm the accuracy of the code.

Although the 'middle' part of the system could be neatly described by Z and SPARK, there were problems with both the 'top' and 'bottom' parts of the system. At the very top level, experience showed that the proof annotations were often simply too large to be manageable. This was exacerbated by the current lack of abstract proof support in SPARK, unlike the existing abstraction support for data and information flow analysis.[14]

Thus a decision was taken to prove only 'interesting properties' — such as the safety invariants — at the very top level of the SPARK. On the other hand, at the 'bottom' of the architecture, there was a need to interface with other software, such as device drivers, for which there was no formal specification at all. In this case, the solution adopted was often to supply a very abstract formal specification but no more. This usually took the form of a specification such as

$$o! = f(x) \quad ,$$

where the function f, acting on the state variables x to produce outputs $o!$, is left entirely nondeterministic. However, by naming f, it is possible to express the proof annotations, and to show exactly what properties of the supplied device driver are being relied on.

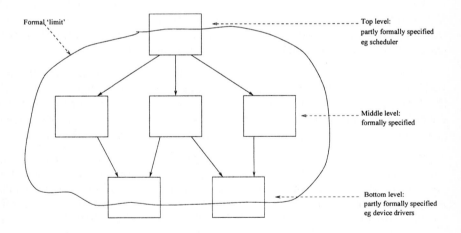

Fig. 3. The limits of formality

---

[14] SPARK includes the concept of an abstract own variable, where a single own variable (declared in a package specification) may represent a set of variables used in the implementation. Although the SPARK toolset fully supports abstract own variables in all types of flow analysis, there is currently no support for reasoning about such variable 'refinements'.

It was also important to remember that, of course, the development process did not stop when SPARK source code was produced: the code had to be compiled into object code. However good the development process had been in order to produce the source code, if the compiler had bugs, then the delivered system might be unacceptable due to compiler-introduced errors. A commercial, validated Ada compiler was used since that would bring some guarantees of quality through its years of service and the hope that any compiler bugs had been found by other users. In fact, the only compiler bug found during the project was in the optimiser, which was then switched off — the necessary performance was achieved by having the Ada run-time checks turned off in the compiled code. However, one difficulty with using a compiler for the full Ada language was that of course it did not understand the philosophy behind SPARK: on one occasion, it was realised that the compiler was using a perfectly valid code-generation strategy involving dynamic allocation of a large temporary variable, contrary to all of the SPARK ideas of predictability of resource usage, no dynamic memory allocation and so on. Here the solution involved a member of the project team using his ability to read the object code to write a script which checked the generated object code for dynamic memory allocation calls. There were also one or two problems in ensuring that the SPARK code was both provable and obeyed the timing requirements of the system. The fact that there was an expert in timing analysis [6] in the team was invaluable here.

In the Z proofs, it was found that the choice of state invariants was particularly important for finding errors: if the invariants were not strong enough, then it was quite possible to discharge the precondition proof obligation for an operation that had a postcondition which did not correspond to the desired outcome. (Some details of errors found by Z proofs are given below.)

There were several lessons learnt about coding styles which made the proof task easier: these are to be recorded in an internal 'Coding Style Guide' for future SPARK proof projects. For instance, if it is necessary to perform some action for every value of a small discrete type, it is sometimes easier to prove correct a sequence of statements rather than a loop over all of the possible values.

It is too early for there to be evidence yet about the cost of future changes to the system, though this is clearly an important question given the fairly novel and extensive use of proof on SHOLIS. Although there is limited experience of using tools to maintain proofs, it should be noted that the proportion of effort spent producing the proofs was fairly low (6.5%). One of the SHOLIS developers has remarked that he believes, as for most developments, that it is the design structure which is likely to have the most significant effect on the cost of future changes. There is also evidence [22], from an independent analysis of the project described in [13], that the use of a formal specification leads to simpler code which is easier to understand, and therefore to maintain.

Finally, at least one of the developers/provers remarked that it was from the VCs which *didn't* go straight through the Simplifier that most was learnt. In fact the code proof stage provided confidence that the code did actually implement the Z specification, and the RTC proofs gave confidence that the Ada run-time check options on the compiler could be turned off safely.

5.3   The Types of Errors Found by Z Proofs

Approximately 70% of the Z proofs concerned preconditions, and they found approximately 75% of the total faults found by Z proof. An initial analysis of the faults reveals a number of different types (in approximately decreasing order of significance).

Incorrect functionality specified: there were several cases where, although the Z was well-defined and had the expected precondition, the actual functionality specified did not meet the requirements. These instances were found as a side-effect of the (human) prover having to understand precisely what the Z meant, in order to construct the proof, and realising that this did not correspond with their informal understanding of the required behaviour.

Lack of mode/history information modelled: as already described, SHO-LIS has a number of different types of information pages. Certain pages and/or associated system functions are only available in particular circumstances, e.g. after a selection has been made. A number of precondition proofs revealed that the Z model did not adequately capture these ordering dependencies.[15] In each case, the solution was to add invariants to encode 'history' information, e.g. if this button (and hence system function) is available to the user then this selection state must be defined.

Contradictory operations: for a couple of operations, there were overlapping cases that specified conflicting behaviour, resulting in a contradiction. Perhaps more interesting were operations whose explicit postcondition predicates contradicted (implicitly included) invariants. In about four cases it turned out that the invariant was too strong, i.e. when the invariant was originally formulated, it was not noticed that there were legitimate situations where the invariant would not hold. Typically, these situations could be characterised and the invariant 'weakened' by the addition of an 'or'-case.

Missing cases: there were a number of instances of missing cases (e.g. not covering all possible combinations of input values). These typically resulted from either undefined function-applications (i.e. a value not being in a function's domain), or from the result of a calculation being outside an allowed range (e.g. to trying to increase a value beyond a fixed upper limit).

Incorrectly loose specifications: there were three or four examples where the prover spotted that the postcondition did not specify a value for one or more state components. Since Z has no 'rest unchanged' convention, for any variables which are to be left unchanged, this must be explicitly specified. As with the incorrect functionality case, it was not the precondition itself which showed the problem, but the thorough consideration of the operation required to produce the proof.

---

[15] Z has no explicit mechanism for specifying dependencies on the ordering of operations.

5.4   SPARK 83 versus SPARK 95

Since the SHOLIS project started in 1993, it was obviously not possible to use SPARK 95, the later version of SPARK derived from Ada 95, together with an updated toolset. However, it is clear that several features of SPARK 95 would have made life easier on the SHOLIS project: use type clauses, the ability to read out parameters, moded globals and the changes to static expressions. Some details of a later trial port of SHOLIS to SPARK 95 can be found in [7].

6   Related Work

While there has been an increasing use of formal methods for specification in industry — see, for example, [11, 12, 15] — there is less evidence for the use of refinement and proof. However, [25] offers a recent example of the use of Z refinement on an industrial scale. This work led to some improvements in the formulation of the Z refinement rules, and to a better understanding of the Z/CSP relationship [5].

On the SPARK proof front, [10] reports the use of SPARK with an extension to SPC's CoRE (Consortium Requirements Engineering) modelling method [8], which in turn is based on Parnas tables[1]. The specifications in these tables were converted to SPARK postconditions. Parnas tables were used successfully on the Darlington shutdown system [21, 9], but would not have been as appropriate as Z for the SHOLIS work, since Z has a much richer state-modelling capability. This was necessary for areas like maintaining a history of input sensor values.

7   Conclusions

The SHOLIS project made extensive use of formal methods, including both Z and SPARK proof, and it is believed to be the first to be completed under the 1991 version of UK MoD Interim Defence Standards 00-55 and 00-56.

The overall experience of industrial-scale proof has been very positive and obtained significantly better results than were originally expected. In terms of faults found for effort expended, the Z Proof phase was by far the most efficient phase of the project. One reason for this may be because the Z Proof was the first verification phase on the project. Proofs at the SPARK code level were not as efficient at finding faults, but this was to be expected since significant testing — both informal and formal — had already been completed before the code proofs took place. However, the code proofs were still more efficient at error detection than unit testing, and provided crucial assurance that the code was free of run-time exceptions.

The results of the different types of testing are also quite revealing. In particular, system validation testing was substantially more efficient at finding faults than unit testing. In our experience this is consistent with anecdotal evidence from other high-integrity projects. As a result we have significantly refined our testing strategy on more recent projects.

There are some important constraints to remember when attempting proof on a large-scale. Part of the success of proof on SHOLIS is due to the simple system architecture, and hence the straightforward mapping that is possible between the specification, design and code. If SHOLIS were a heavily distributed system, it is not believed that as much could have been achieved. (Further discussion of practical issues concerning the use of formal methods in large-system design can be found in [13, 14].) The limits of formality must also be considered. For the foreseeable future, testing is likely to have an important role in gaining necessary assurance of compilers, hardware, timing issues etc.

On the Z side, further support is needed (in terms of both proof techniques and tools) for reasoning about subsystems coupled by invariants, other than by brute force expansion. Some large-scale SPARK reasoning mechanisms are also needed, including some support for abstract proof, before the technology can be extensively used at the highest levels of large systems. The next release of the SPARK toolset is very likely to contain such mechanisms, as a result of experiences on SHOLIS and other projects.

In summary, proof was an important part of the SHOLIS development process, and an important factor in contributing to the quality of the delivered product. We believe our success shows both the significant benefit and practicality of large-scale proof on projects of this kind.

Acknowledgements

This paper reports the work of the entire SHOLIS proof and coding team: Janet Barnes, Rod Chapman, Jonathan Hammond, Andy Pryor and Neil White. The permission of PMES and MoD to publish this paper is gratefully acknowledged. The FM99 referees and Anthony Hall gave useful feedback on earlier versions of the paper.

A   Z Glossary

This glossary gives brief definitions for the Z terms used in the paper. Readers are referred to the many text books on Z for a more extensive introduction.

Schema expansion: one of the key features of Z is the schema, a named collection of variable declarations and invariants linking them. The schema name can be used as a declaration, and this technique is widely used to control complexity. Schema expansion involves replacing schema names with the corresponding declarations and invariants. This can either be carried out 'all-in-one', when expansion continues until there are no schema names left, or 'one-level-at-a-time', when only the immediately-visible schema names are expanded — of course, this may introduce further schema names.

Ξ **schema:** a Ξ schema is used to describe operations which do not change the state of a system. It is a shorthand for the inclusion of a state before, a state after and an equality predicate stating that all state components are unchanged. It is typically used in 'enquiry' operations, where the purpose of the operation is to give an output depending on the current state, rather than to change the state.

Promotion: this is a technique for specifying the behaviour of systems which consist of several copies of a smaller subsystem. The state of the subsystem is first described, together with operations on it. This 'local' state is then used in the description of the larger 'global' state, and the 'local' operations are combined with a *framing schema* to describe the operations on the global state. A 'functional promotion' is one where the local state is included in the global state by introducing a variable which is a function from an indexing set to the local state. Further details may be found in [28, 27, 2].

Precondition proof: in Z, operations are described with a single predicate, encapsulating both the precondition and the postcondition. The precondition can be extracted from this by applying the *pre* operator, which hides the after-state and outputs. The 'precondition proof' is then a check that the specifier's view of the operation's precondition — obtained by consideration of the environment in which the operation is executed — is strong enough to imply the real precondition, as expressed with *pre*.

Initial state proof: this is a proof that a valid initial state for the system does exist. In this context, 'valid' means 'obeying the state invariant'.

References

[1] T. Alspaugh, S. Faulk, K. Heninger Britton, R. Parker, D. Parnas, and J. Shore. Software requirements for the A7-E aircraft. Technical Report NRL/FR/5530-92-9194, Naval Research Laboratory, Washington, D.C., 1992.

[2] R. Barden, S. Stepney, and D. Cooper. *Z in practice*. BCS Practitioner Series. Prentice-Hall, 1994.

[3] J. Barnes. *High integrity Ada: The SPARK approach*. Addison-Wesley, 1997.

[4] J-F. Bergeretti and B.A. Carré. Information-flow and data-flow analysis of while-programs. *ACM Trans. Prog. Lang. Sys.*, 7(1), January 1985.

[5] C. Bolton, J. Davies, and J.C.P. Woodcock. On the refinement and simulation of data types and processes. In K. Araki, A. Galloway, and K. Taguchi, editors, *IFM99: Proceedings of the 1st International Conference on Integrated Formal Methods*, pages 273–292. Springer-Verlag, 1999.

[6] R.C. Chapman, A. Burns, and A.J. Wellings. Combining static worst-case timing analysis and program proof. *Real-Time Systems Journal*, 11(2):145–171, September 1996.

[7] R.C. Chapman and R. Dewar. Re-engineering a safety-critical application using SPARK 95 and GNORT. In M.H. Harbour and J.A. de la Puente, editors, *Reliable Software Technology: Proceedings of the 1999 Ada Europe Conference, Santander, Spain*, number 1622 in Lecture Notes in Computer Science, pages 39–51. Springer-Verlag, 1999.

[8] Consortium Requirements Engineering Guidebook. Technical Report SPC-92060-CMC Version 01.00.09, Software Productivity Consortium, Herndon, VA, USA, 1993.

[9] D. Craigen, S. L. Gerhart, and T. J. Ralston. An international survey of industrial applications of formal methods. Technical Report NIST GCR 93/626-V1 & 2,

Atomic Energy Control Board of Canada, US National Institute of Standards and Technology, and US Naval Research Laboratories, 1993.

[10] M. Croxford and J.M. Sutton. Breaking through the V and V bottleneck. In M. Toussaint, editor, *Ada in Europe 1995*, volume 1031 of *Lecture Notes in Computer Science*, pages 344–354. Springer-Verlag, 1995.

[11] J. Fitzgerald, C. B. Jones, and P. Lucas, editors. *FME'97: Industrial Application and Strengthened Foundations of Formal Methods*, volume 1313 of *Lecture Notes in Computer Science*. Formal Methods Europe, Springer-Verlag, 1997.

[12] M.-C. Gaudel and J. C. P. Woodcock, editors. *FME'96: Industrial Benefit and Advances in Formal Methods*, volume 1051 of *Lecture Notes in Computer Science*. Formal Methods Europe, Springer-Verlag, 1996.

[13] A. Hall. Using formal methods to develop an ATC information system. *IEEE Software*, 13(2):66–76, March 1996.

[14] A. Hall. Keynote speech: What does industry need from formal specification techniques? In *2nd IEEE Workshop on Industrial-Strength Formal Specification Techniques*, 1998.

[15] M.G. Hinchey and Bowen J.P., editors. *Applications of Formal Methods*. Prentice-Hall International series in computer science / C.A.R. Hoare, series editor. Prentice-Hall International, Englewood Cliffs, N.J. ; London, 1996.

[16] J. Jacky. *The way of Z: Practical programming with formal methods*. Cambridge University Press, Cambridge, UK, 1997.

[17] MOD. *Hazard analysis and safety classification of the computer and programmable electronic system elements of defence equipment*. UK Ministry of Defence, April 1991. INTERIM DEF STAN 00-56.

[18] MOD. *The procurement of safety critical software in defence equipment*. UK Ministry of Defence, April 1991. INTERIM DEF STAN 00-55 (Part 1: Requirements).

[19] MOD. *The procurement of safety critical software in defence equipment*. UK Ministry of Defence, April 1991. INTERIM DEF STAN 00-55 (Part 2: Guidance).

[20] K.A. Nyberg, editor. *The annotated Ada Reference Manual*. ANSI, 1983. ANSI/MIL-STD-1815A-1983.

[21] D.L. Parnas, G.J.K. Asmis, and J.D. Kendall. Reviewable development of safety critical software. In *Proceedings of the International Conference on Control and Instrumentation in Nuclear Installations*, 1990.

[22] S.L. Pfleeger and Hatton L. Investigating the influence of formal methods. *IEEE Computer*, 30(2):33–43, February 1997.

[23] *SPARK — The SPADE Ada Kernel*. Praxis Critical Systems, August 1997. Edition 3.3.

[24] J.M. Spivey. *The Z Notation: A Reference Manual*. Prentice Hall International Series in Computer Science, 2nd edition, 1992.

[25] S. Stepney, D. Cooper, and J.C.P. Woodcock. More powerful Z data refinement: Pushing the state of the art in industrial refinement. In J.P. Bowen, A. Fett, and M.G. Hinchey, editors, *ZUM'98: the Z formal specification notation*, volume 1493 of *Lecture Notes in Computer Science*, pages 284–307. Springer-Verlag, 1998.

[26] I. Toyn and J.A. McDermid. CADiZ: An architecture for Z tools and its implementation. *Software — Practice and Experience*, 25(3):305–330, March 1995.

[27] J.C.P. Woodcock. Mathematics as a management tool: Proof rules for promotion. In B.A. Kitchenham, editor, *Software Engineering for Large Software Systems*. Elsevier, 1990.

[28] J.C.P. Woodcock and J. Davies. *Using Z: specification, refinement and proof*. Prentice-Hall International series in computer science / C.A.R. Hoare, series editor. Prentice Hall, 1996.

Formal Development and Verification of a Distributed Railway Control System

Anne E. Haxthausen[1] and Jan Peleska[2]

[1] Dept. of Information Technology, Techn. University of Denmark, DK-2800 Lyngby,
ah@it.dtu.dk
[2] BISS, Universität Bremen, P.O. Box 330440, D-28334 Bremen,
jp@informatik.uni-bremen.de

Abstract. In this article we introduce the concept for a distributed railway control system and present the specification and verification of the main algorithm used for safe distributed control. Our design and verification approach is based on the RAISE method, starting with highly abstract algebraic specifications which are transformed into directly implementable distributed control processes by applying a series of refinement and verification steps. Concrete safety requirements are derived from an abstract version that can be easily validated with respect to soundness and completeness. Complexity is further reduced by separating the system model into a domain model describing the physical system in absence of control and a controller model introducing the safety-related control mechanisms as a separate entity monitoring observables of the physical system to decide whether it is safe for a train to move or for a point to be switched.

1 Introduction

The present modernisation of European railway networks raises a large variety of issues related to the design and verification of railway control systems. One of these problems is the question how to design control systems for small local networks that can only operate effectively if the costs for initial installation, operation and maintenance of the control system are low. Today's centralised interlocking systems – at least those which are available in Germany – are far too expensive for such small (possibly privatised) networks. A promising approach is to *distribute* the tasks of train control, train protection and interlocking over a network of cooperating components using the standard communication facilities offered by mobile telephone providers. On the other hand, a distributed control concept also introduces new safety issues that could be disregarded as long as centralised control was applied: First, the new communication medium requires security and reliability mechanisms that were unnecessary for centralised systems transmitting control commands to signals and points over wires. Second, the distribution of a control algorithm over several components raises new design and verification issues, since the concept of a global state space as available in a centralised interlocking system can no longer be implemented.

J. Wing, J. Woodcock, J. Davies (Eds.): FM'99, Vol. II, LNCS 1709, pp. 1546–1563, 1999.
© Springer-Verlag Berlin Heidelberg 1999

In this article, we will describe the concept of a distributed railway control system consisting of *switch boxes (SB)*, each one locally controlling a point, and *train control computers (TCC)* residing in the train engines and collecting the local state information from switch boxes along the track to derive the decision whether the train may enter the next track segment. The system concept does not require signals along the track, since the "go/no-go" decisions are performed and indicated in the train control computers. We give an overview over the formal specification and verification of the main control algorithm executed by the distributed cooperating control components. The system is designed to operate on *simple networks*, which means in our context that there are two distinguished destinations A and B, such that at each track segment of the network there is a uniquely defined direction to reach A and B, respectively. Typically, this definition applies to networks which are not highly frequented by trains and connect two main stations with small intermediate stations (Figure 1).

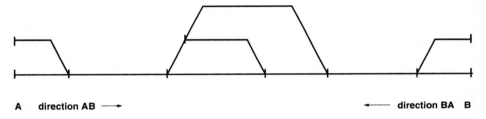

A   direction AB ⟶   ⟵ direction BA   B

Fig. 1. Simple railway network.

Our specification and verification approach is based on the RAISE formal method and tool set [6, 7] and follows the *invent-and-verify paradigm*. To address safety issues in a systematic way the standard procedure (see [8]) separating the *equipment under control* – that is, the railway network with its trains – from the *control system* – in our case, the set of TCCs and SBs – is applied. To this end, we first develop abstract algebraic specifications for the *domain model*, i.e., the railway network and the trains to be controlled, and the *safety requirements* stating that the system must not perform a transition into a hazardous state where trains may collide or derailing might occur. These requirements are expressed as conditions about the *observables* of the domain model. Using stepwise refinement and accompanying verification steps, we introduce additional observables that may be monitored by a *controller* giving the "can move/cannot move" conditions for each train and the "can be switched/cannot be switched" conditions for each point. The completeness and consistency of these conditions is verified by proving refinement relations to the higher-level specifications which already have been proved to be consistent with the initial safety requirements. The first stage of the invent-and-verify development ends when the observables of the last refinement needed to control the safety of train movements and point switching are implementable in the sense that they can be transformed into a concrete state space that may be conveniently partitioned among a set of distributed cooperating processes. The second stage specifies and verifies the concrete – i.e., implementable – distributed *controller model* by introducing communicating processes which represent train control computers and switch boxes. The TCC processes collect state information from the SB processes to make the "can move/cannot move" decisions. The SB processes store the relevant state information to take the "can be switched/cannot be switched" decisions for their local points. The resulting controller is a distributed program which is underspecified with respect to application-dependent control decisions – like defining the order in which trains may pass along a single-track section – which can be made without violating the safety requirements. Concrete controller implementations will resolve this underspecification by choosing a specific solution for application-dependent control decisions.

The work presented here originated from a collaboration of the authors with INSY GmbH Berlin, who developed the distributed systems design described in the next section for their railway control system RELIS 2000 designed for local railway networks. In this collaboration, the authors focus on the generalisation and verification of the control concepts used in RELIS 2000. Furthermore, the second author is cooperating with Transnet (South African Railways) in the field of development, verification, validation and test of safety-critical systems.

In Section 2, we introduce the general concept for the distributed railway control system discussed in this article. Similar approaches of "Funkbasierter Fahrbetrieb (FFB)" – that is, train control based on radio transmission – are presently investigated by German Railways [3]. Our verification concept described in the following sections applies to all of these approaches. Section 3 presents the formal specification of the system's domain model. In Section 4, an abstract version of the safety requirements is introduced. The subsequent sections are concerned with the development of the control system as a series of refinement and verification steps. In the discussion (Section 7) we sketch the more general issues of our concept for the development, verification, validation and test of safety-critical systems.

2   Engineering Concept

In this section, we introduce the technical concept of the distributed railway control system to be formally specified and verified below. The technical concept is based on the RELIS 2000 system of INSY GmbH with generalisations and modifications performed by the authors.

Consider the system configuration depicted in Figure 2. The tasks of train control, train protection and interlocking are distributed on train control computers (TCC) residing in each train T1, T2 and switch boxes (SB) SB1, SB2, SB3, each one controlling a single point, the boundary between two segments (e.g. blocks) of a single track or a railway crossing. The basic principle of the control algorithm is as follows:

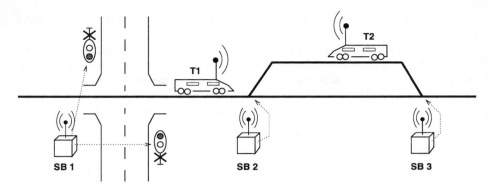

Fig. 2. Distributed railway control system – trains communicating with switch boxes.

- Each switch box stores the local safety-related information in its state space. For example, this information contains the actual state of the traffic lights guarding the railway crossing, whether a train is approaching the switch box or the track segments that are presently connected by the local point. The switch boxes use sensors to detect approaching trains and to decide whether a train has left the critical area close to a point or a crossing.
- To pass a railway crossing or to enter a new track segment, a train's TCC communicates with the relevant switch boxes to make a request for blocking a crossing, switching a point or just reserving the relevant track segments at the SB for the train to pass. The decision which switch boxes to address is based on the location of the train which is determined by means of the Global Positioning System (GPS) or by using track components signalling their location to the passing train.
- Depending on their local state, the switch boxes may or may not comply with the request received from a TCC. In any case, each SB returns its (possibly updated) local state information to the requesting TCC. After having collected the response from each relevant SB, the TCC evaluates the SB states to decide whether it is safe to approach the crossing or to enter the next track segment.
- For train protection, each TCC blocks the train engine if it is not allowed to leave a station and triggers the emergency brake if the train approaches a railway crossing or enters a new track segment without permission from the associated switch boxes. Furthermore, each TCC monitors the speed of the train and gives warning messages or triggers the emergency brakes if the actual speed exceeds the maximum velocity admitted for the type of train at its actual location in the network.

Observe that in principle, the concept sketched above would admit completely automatic train control without train engine drivers being present. However, in the possible realisations presently discussed, this is not intended: The train engine driver has the ultimate responsibility to decide whether it is safe to leave a station, enter a new track segment or pass a crossing.

In the subsequent sections we will focus on the formal specification and verification of the control algorithm concerned with "can move/cannot move" decisions for trains and "can be switched/cannot be switched" decisions for points. To introduce the principles of this algorithm, consider Figure 3 which shows the local state spaces of two switch boxes SB1, SB2 and trains T1, T2.

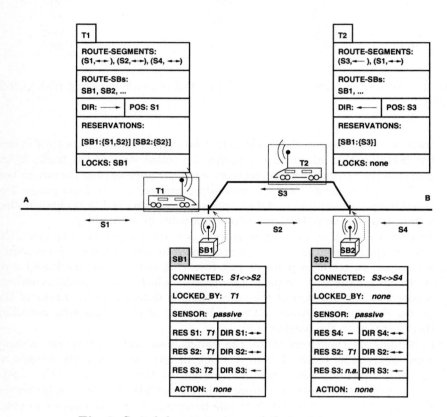

Fig. 3. Switch boxes, trains and their state spaces.

In state component CONNECTED, the switch box stores which track segments are presently connected by the local point. (If the SB just separates two blocks on a single track, this information is static.) In the components DIR S1, DIR S2,... the directions associated with each track segment are stored: A segment can either be used only for trains going in direction $A \rightarrow B$, or for trains going in direction $B \rightarrow A$ or in both directions $(A \leftrightarrow B)$. Typically, this information is fairly static and will only be changed if deviations from the ordinary train schedule occur, for example when constructions are going on or when a train arrives late. As explained below, the segment direction will be evaluated to decide whether a train may reserve a switch box. The LOCKED_BY state component indicates whether a specific train has the right to pass the switch box. If such a train is registered in this component, it is impossible to switch the local point to another direction until the train has passed. For the detection of passing trains, a state component SENSOR is activated by a set of sensors attached to the track when a train approaches the point. The component is returned to state "passive" as soon as the sensors indicate that the last waggon of the train has passed the point. To decide whether a train may get a reservation for a segment approaching the switch box and whether a point may be locked for a train, additional state components RES S1, RES S2,... are maintained at each switch box for every track segment whose segment direction is approaching the SB. The ACTION component of the state space is used as a "transaction flag" for commands which have to be executed on several switch boxes in a synchronised manner: The switch box will refuse new commands, as long as the ACTION flag indicates such a transaction. Observe that this flag is unnecessary for the standard reservation commands described next.

The state space of each TCC contains the lists ROUTE-SEGMENTS and ROUTE-SBs of track segments and switch boxes along the train route. When leaving a segment and passing a switch box, these entries are removed from the head of each list. Again, segments are stored together with their directions $\rightarrow, \leftarrow, \leftrightarrow$. State component DIR stores the direction where the train is heading to. A train may only move along segments whose direction is compatible with DIR. In POS, the actual position is stored. In the abstraction presented here, positions are specified by one or two segments, the former indicating that the train is on the segment without touching neighbouring segments, the latter indicating that the train is in the critical area of a point (potentially) connecting the two segments. State component RESERVATIONS stores the switch boxes and associated segments which have been reserved by the train. LOCKS is a list of switch boxes whose points have been switched in the direction of the train route and are locked for the train. Whenever a train is allowed to proceed into the next segment, this information must be consistent with the corresponding RES- and LOCKED_BY-components of the switch boxes involved.

To determine, whether a train T1 may enter a new segment S2 (cf. Figure 3), the train control computer and the relevant switch boxes evaluate the state space described above as follows:

– To guarantee safety for the train at its local position, two conditions must be fulfilled:

  1. The train direction must be consistent with the direction associated with the local track segment. (Train T1 going in direction $A \rightarrow B$ cannot have its position on segment S3, since the latter has associated direction $B \rightarrow A$.)
  2. Each train must have a reservation for its local track segment at the next switch box to be approached by the train (S1 must be reserved for train T1 at switch box SB1).

- To enter the next segment (S2 for train T1), three safety conditions must be fulfilled:
    1. The train direction must be consistent with the direction of the segment to be entered. (S1 has direction $A \leftrightarrow B$, so this is consistent with T1's train direction $A \rightarrow B$.)
    2. The next SB must be locked for the train (SB1 is locked by T1, so this condition is fulfilled for T1).
    3. The train must have a reservation for the next segment S2 at every switch box where S2 is an approaching segment. (In Figure 3, S2 approaches both SB1 and SB2, so T1 must reserve S2 at both switch boxes. In contrast to that, T2 only needed to reserve S3 at SB1 before entering S3 from S4.)
- In order to fulfil these three conditions, the train signals its wish to enter the next segment to the associated switch boxes. Each switch box enters the train's reservation for the next segment if this is not already reserved for another train. If reservation is possible and the SB is not locked by another train, it will switch its point into the required direction if necessary and lock the point for the requesting train.
- If the three conditions are fulfilled the train may enter the next segment. As soon as the train has passed the next SB, the SB will delete the lock and all reservations made by the train. (In Figure 3, SB1 will unlock its point and delete all references to T1, as soon as the train has passed the point and entered S2. Note that T1 is still completely safe at its new location, since each train wishing to enter S2 from either S1 or S4 also needs a reservation of S2 at SB2, and this is still blocked by T1.) The train will update its own state space accordingly.

In the sections below, this informal system concept is described and verified in a formal way. Observe that in this article we deal with untimed control and safety mechanisms only. Time-dependent conditions – for example, "when is last time point (depending on speed and position) to trigger the emergency brakes in order to prevent the train from entering the next segment ?" – are imported into the specifications at a later stage as a "timed refinement" of the untimed control mechanisms discussed here.

3   Domain Model

In this section we show (parts of) a domain model capturing those physical objects and events of the uncontrolled railway system which are relevant for the development of the railway control system. We divide the model into a static part and a dynamic (state based) part. Other authors have established similar railway domain models [1, 4, 5].

3.1   Static Part of the Model

The static part of the model comprise definitions of data types for objects. The physical objects we consider include the trains, the points (switch boxes) and the railway network.

Trains

Each train has a unique identification belonging to the following, not further specified type:

type TrainId

Points

Each point has a unique identification belonging to the following, not further specified type:

type PointId

Railway Network

A railway network consists of segments connected according to the network topology.

Each segment has a unique identification belonging to the following, not further specified type:

type Segment

In our model, the network topology is specified by a predicate (*are_neighbours*) which defines which segment ends are neighbours:

value
    are_neighbours : SegmentEnd × SegmentEnd → **Bool**

where a segment end is a pair consisting of a segment identification and one of two possible ends:

type
    SegmentEnd = Segment × End, End == a_end | b_end

The *are_neighbours* predicate must satisfy a number of axioms (not presented here) ensuring that the network is directed.

3.2   Dynamic Part of the Model

As trains move along the segments of the network and points are switched, the *state* of the railway may change over time. We use a discrete, event-based model to describe state transitions.

The State Space

At this early phase of development, we do not yet know, what the exact state space is, but only that the state space should contain information about some dynamic properties of objects which we will explain below. Therefore, we just introduce a name for the type of states without giving any datatype representation:

> **type** State

and characterise this type implicitly by specifying state observer functions of the form *obs : State* × ... → *T* which can be used to capture information (of type *T*) about the state.

Dynamic Properties of Trains

Each train has a *position* and a *direction* which may change over time.

We assume that the length of segments is chosen such that any train has a position on one or two neighbouring segments[1] or it has passed an end point of the network:

> **type**
>   Position ==
>   single(seg_of : Segment) | double(fst : Segment, snd : Segment) | error

A position of the form *single(s)* indicates that the train is residing on a single segment *s*, a position of the form *double(s1, s2)*, where *s1* and *s2* are two neighbouring segments, indicates that the train is residing on one or both segments in the critical area of the point potentially connecting these segments. The *error* position is used to model the case where a train has passed an end point of the network.

Since the railway network is directed according to our *simple network* assumption described in the introduction, there are two possible train directions:

> **type** Direction == dirAB | dirBA

We introduce the following functions to observe the mentioned properties:

> **value** /∗ state observers ∗/
>   position : State × TrainId → Position,
>   direction : State × TrainId → Direction

---

[1] Our engineering concept can be adapted to railway systems for which this assumption does not hold by using lists of segments for train positions instead of the here proposed representation.

Dynamic Properties of Points

Points may be switched. Hence, the connections between segment ends of the railway network may change over time. We introduce the following function to observe this:

value /∗ state observer ∗/
    are_connected : State × SegmentEnd × SegmentEnd → **Bool**

The *are_connected* observer must satisfy some axioms (not presented here) ensuring that some *physical laws* are satisfied, e.g. that only neighbouring segments are connected and there is exactly one connection in each point.

Events

We consider the following events:

− trains move from one position to their next position
− points are switched

It should be noted that in this uncontrolled model, events may lead to unsafe states.

For each kind of event we introduce a state constructor which can be used to make the associated state changes:

value /∗ state constructors ∗/
    move : State × TrainId → State,
    switch : State × PointId × SegmentEnd → State

Their behaviour is defined by observer axioms. For instance, the following axiom states that moving a train does not change how segment ends are connected

axiom /∗ observer axioms ∗/
    [are_connected_move]
        ∀ σ : State, t : TrainId, se1, se2 : SegmentEnd •
            are_connected(move(σ, t), se1, se2) ≡ are_connected(σ, se1, se2)

and the following axiom states that moving a train affects the position of the train itself:

    [position_move]
        ∀ σ : State, t1, t2 : TrainId •
            position(move(σ, t1), t2) ≡
                if t2 = t1 **then**
                    next_position(σ, position(σ, t2), direction(σ, t2))
                else position(σ, t2) **end**
            pre safe(σ)

where *safe* is a function defined in next section, and *next_position(σ, pos, dir)* is an auxiliary function defined below. It gives the next position after *pos* in direction *dir*.

value
$\quad$ next_position : State × Position × Direction → Position

axiom
$\quad$ ∀ σ : State, s1, s2 : Segment, dir : Direction •
$\qquad$ next_position(σ, double(s1, s2), dir) ≡ single(s2),

$\quad$ ∀ σ : State, s1, s2 : Segment, dir : Direction •
$\qquad$ are_connected(to_end(s1, dir), from_end(s2, dir)) ⇒
$\qquad$ next_position(σ, single(s1), dir) ≡ double(s1, s2),

$\quad$ ∀ σ : State, s1 : Segment, dir : Direction •
$\qquad$ (∀ s2 : Segment •
$\qquad\quad$ ∼ are_connected(to_end(s1, dir), from_end(s2, dir))
$\qquad$) ⇒
$\qquad$ next_position(σ, single(s1), dir) ≡ error

The first axiom states that the next possible position of a train having a position on two segments, $s1$ and $s2$, is its front segment $s2$. The second and the third axiom define the next possible position for trains in direction dir having a position on a single segment $s1$. If the "to-end" in direction dir of segment $s1$ is connected to the "from-end" in direction dir of some segment $s2$ then the train will have its next possible position on $s1$ and $s2$, otherwise the train is at an end point of the railway network and will have *error* (modelling derailing) as its next possible position. The "to-end" in direction dir of segment s is defined as follows

value
$\quad$ to_end : Segment × Direction → SegmentEnd
$\quad$ to_end(s, dir) ≡ **if** dir = dirAB **then** (s, b_end) **else** (s, a_end) **end**

The "from-end" is the opposite end of the "to-end".
$\quad$ There are similar observer axioms for switch.

4   Safety Requirements

Our goal is to develop a *train control & interlocking system* satisfying the following two safety requirements:

No collision: Two trains must not reside on the same segment.
No derailing: Trains must not derail (by passing an end point of the network or by entering a point from a segment which is not connected with the next segment).

The notion of safety can be formalised by defining a predicate which can be used to test whether a state is safe:

value
    safe : State → **Bool**
    safe(σ) ≡ no_collision(σ) $\land$ no_derailing(σ),

    no_collision : State → **Bool**
    no_collision(σ) ≡
        ($\forall$ t1, t2 : TrainId • t1 $\neq$ t2 $\Rightarrow$
            segments(position(σ, t1)) $\cap$ segments(position(σ, t2)) = {}
        ),

    no_derailing : State → **Bool**
    no_derailing(σ) ≡
        ($\forall$ t : TrainId •
            position(σ, t) $\neq$ error $\land$
            ($\forall$ s1, s2 : Segment • position(σ, t) = double(s1, s2) $\Rightarrow$
               are_connected
                   (σ, to_end(s1, direction(σ, t)), from_end(s2, direction(σ, t))))))

Here *segments* is an auxiliary function giving the segments of a position.

5 Development of the Railway Control System: First Stage

The purpose of the railway control system is to prevent events to happen when they may lead to an unsafe state. We develop an implementable controller model by stepwise refinement following the *invent-and-verify paradigm*. The development is divided into two major stages of which we describe the first in this section.

In the first major stage of development we design a full state space keeping information not only about the dynamic properties described in the domain model, but also about new dynamic data (observables) like segment reservations which may be monitored by the controller to evaluate the "can move/cannot move" and "can be switched/cannot be switched" conditions. New data like segment reservations also give rise to new state constructors modelling events like making a reservation.

Our strategy for fulfilling the safety requirements is to invent

1. a *state invariant consistent(σ)*, and
2. for each constructor *con*, a *guard* (condition) *can_con(σ, ...)* which can be used by the controller to decide whether it should allow events (corresponding to application of that constructor) to happen

such that the following *strong safety requirements* are fulfilled:

1. States satisfying the state invariant must also be safe.
2. Any state transition made by a state constructor must preserve the state invariant when the associated guard is true.

3. If the guards for two different events are both true in a state satisfying the state invariant, then a state change made by one of the events must not make the guard for the other event false.

These requirements ensure that if the initial state satisfies the state invariant, and the railway control system only allows events to happen when the corresponding guards are true then the system will stay safe.

The first strong safety requirement can be formalised by the following theory:

[consistent_is_safe]
    $\forall \sigma : \text{State} \bullet \text{consistent}(\sigma) \Rightarrow \text{safe}(\sigma)$

The second strong safety requirement can be formalised by a theory

[safe_con]
    $\forall \dots \bullet \text{consistent}(\sigma) \wedge \text{can\_con}(\sigma, \dots) \Rightarrow \text{consistent}(\text{con}(\sigma, \dots))$

for each constructor *con*, and the third strong safety requirement can be formalised by a theory typically of the form

[safe_con1_con2]
    $\forall \dots \bullet$
        $\text{consistent}(\sigma) \wedge \text{can\_con1}(\sigma, x) \wedge \text{can\_con2}(\sigma, y)$
            $\Rightarrow \text{can\_con2}(\text{con1}(\sigma, x), y)$

for each pair of constructors, *con1* and *con2*.

The state space, state invariant, guards etc. are found by stepwise refinement and verification.

5.1   First Specification

The first specification is an abstract, algebraic specification extending the domain model with the following declarations:

value /* state invariant */
    consistent : State $\rightarrow$ **Bool**
value /* guards for constructors */
    can_move : State $\times$ TrainId $\rightarrow$ **Bool**,
    can_switch : State $\times$ PointId $\times$ SegmentEnd $\rightarrow$ **Bool**

As the *State* is not yet explicit, and the set of observers is not complete, we cannot yet give complete explicit definitions of the state invariant and guards. Instead we specify requirements to the guards by implications of the form

axiom /* requirements to guard can_con */
    [can_con_implication1]
        $\forall \dots \; \text{can\_con}(\sigma, \dots) \wedge \text{consistent}(\sigma) \Rightarrow \dots$

and requirements to the state invariant by an implication of the form:

axiom /∗ requirements to consistent ∗/
   [consistent_implication1]
     ∀ σ : State • consistent(σ) ⇒ p1(σ)

We use implications so that we can enrich the requirements in later steps with additional constraints.

5.2 Second to Fourth Specification

Each of the next three specifications are algebraic and obtained from the previous specification by adding declarations of new observers, state constructors and guards, observer-constructor axioms for new observers and/or constructors and requirement axioms (in form of implications) for new guards. Furthermore, the requirements to the state invariant is enriched in specification number i by adding the axiom

axiom /∗ requirements to consistent ∗/
   [consistent_implicationi]
     ∀ σ : State • consistent(σ) ⇒ pi(σ)

(where $pi(\sigma)$ is a predicate), and the requirements to some of the previous guards can_con are refined by making the predicate of the right-hand side of the [can_con_implication] axioms stronger.

    Below, we give a short survey of which concepts are added in the second to fourth specification.

Second Specification
In the second specification, two new concepts are introduced:

- segment registrations for trains, and
- segment directions

The idea is, that a train must only be allowed to move to a segment if it is registered on that segment and if its direction is consistent with the direction of that segment.

Third Specification
In the third specification, segment reservations at switch boxes is introduced and segment registrations is defined in terms of that. Furthermore, a concept of locking of points is introduced. The idea is that a train must lock a point in order to pass it, and when a train has locked a point, the point cannot be switched before the train has passed the point.

Fourth Specification
In the fourth specification, a notion of train routes is introduced, and sensors at the switch boxes sense when trains are passing.

5.3   Fifth Specification

Finally, in the fifth specification we are able to define a concrete state space consisting of a state space for each train and a state space for each switch box:

type
   State = {| σ : State' • is_wff(σ) |},
   State' = (TrainId $\underset{m}{\rightarrow}$ TrainState) × (SwitchboxId $\underset{m}{\rightarrow}$ SwitchboxState)

where *TrainState* and *SwitchboxState* are given explicit formal representations for the local train state and switch box state, respectively. These representations correspond to the informal descriptions in Figure 3. We only consider states (defined by a predicate *is_wff*) which satisfy the axioms of physical laws (like "only neighbouring segments are connected") of the domain model.

With this explicit definition of *State*, it is now possible to replace all axioms with explicit function definitions in terms of functions defined for the two new types *TrainState* and *SwitchboxState*. For instance, the observer function *direction* can be defined as follows

direction : State × TrainId → Direction
direction((σ_t, σ_s), t) ≡ T.direction(σ_t(t))

where *T.direction* is an observer function defined for train states (of type Train-State), and the state invariant can be given a definition of the form

consistent : State → **Bool**
consistent(σ) ≡ p1(σ) ∧ ... ∧ p5(σ)

5.4   Verification

Implementation Relations
In each of the development steps (from specification number i to specification number $i + 1$, $i = 1, ..., 4$) above, we have used the RAISE justification tools to prove that the new specification is a *refinement* of the previous specification, i.e. the new specification provides declarations of at least all the types and functions provided by the previous specification, and that all the axioms of the previous specification are consequences of the axioms of the new specification.

Satisfaction of Safety Requirements
For each of the first four specifications we prove that it is consistent with the strong safety requirements stated in the beginning of this section, and finally for the fifth specification we prove that it fully satisfies these requirements.

The *[consistent_is_safe]* theory is verified to hold already for the first specification. Then, since refinements preserve theories, we know that it also holds for the second to fifth specification.

Verification of the *[can_con]* theories is done stepwise: For specification number i we prove

$\forall \ldots \bullet \; \mathrm{consistent}(\sigma) \wedge \mathrm{can\_con}(\sigma, \ldots\,) \Rightarrow \mathrm{pi}(\mathrm{con}(\sigma, \ldots))$

Then, since refinements preserve theories, the fifth specification satisfies

$$\forall \ldots \bullet \; \mathrm{consistent}(\sigma) \wedge \mathrm{can\_con}(\sigma, \ldots\,) \Rightarrow$$
$$(\mathrm{p1}(\mathrm{con}(\sigma, \ldots)) \wedge \ldots \wedge \mathrm{p5}(\mathrm{con}(\sigma, \ldots)))$$

which is equivalent to the *[can_con]* theory, cf. the definition of *consistent* in the fifth specification.

Verification of the *[can_con1_con2]* theories is done similarly.

6   Development of the Railway Control System: Second Stage

The fifth specification presented above introduced explicit implementable states for trains and switch boxes. However, at that stage no architectural requirements were present, so that different centralised or distributed system designs may be elaborated as correct implementations of this specification. The second stage of our development introduces a concrete architectural design and communication protocol for a distributed railway controller consisting of concurrent communicating processes

value
   controller : State $\overset{\sim}{\to}$ **in any out any Unit**
   controller(σ_t, σ_s) $\equiv$
      ($\|$ { TCC[t].main($\sigma\_t(t)$) | t : TrainId})
      $\|$
      ($\|$ { SB[s].main($\sigma\_s(s)$) | s : SwitchboxId})

where $TCC[t].main(\sigma_t(t))$ is a process representing the train control computer in train t, and $SB[s].main(\sigma_s(s))$ is a process representing switch box s. These processes are defined in terms of the guards, state constructors and observers defined in the first major stage, and follow the protocol described in section 2. The transition from the last specification stage to the distributed design stage is performed according to a standardised procedure resulting in designs which are consistent to the specification in a natural way (cf. Figure 4):

- The global specification state is mapped in one-one correspondence to the distributed components: For global state (σ_t, σ_s), train tid and switch box bid, $\sigma\_t(\text{tid})$ is mapped to TrainState[tid] and $\sigma\_s(\text{bid})$ is mapped to SwitchboxState[bid].
- Application of each constructor *con* on a train state and/or a switch box state is guarded by a channel command and the corresponding *can_con* guard defined in the fifth specification layer. Observe that the train and switch box state spaces have been designed in such a way that each guard evaluation can be based on the local state space only. For example, a train control computer will allow the train to move if it is triggered by the do_move channel and the *can_move* guard evaluates to *true* on the local state space.

– For correct implementation of the fifth specification layer, corresponding state components in trains and switch boxes (for example, the reservation state and the lock state described in section 2) must be consistent, whenever a guard using this state information is evaluated. To ensure this, a communication protocol between trains and switch boxes is designed to implement the reservation constructor introduced in the specifications: Train tid sends a reservation request on channel C[tid,bid].res to switch box bid. The switch box evaluates a local guard and responds by returning its possibly updated state space to the train via channel C[tid,bid].SBstate. This information is used by the TCC to update its local information about reservations and locks.

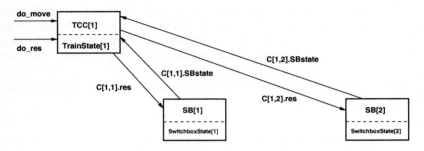

Fig. 4. Distributed architecture with train control computers, switch boxes and communication channels.

7   Discussion

In this article, we have presented the engineering concept and the design and verification of a control algorithm for a distributed railway control system. We consider the following aspects of our work to be the main advantages in comparison to other work that has been performed in the field of design and verification of similar systems (see [2] as an example of another practically relevant approach to formal specification and verification in the railway domain):

– Our refinement approach starting with highly abstract algebraic specifications and ending with concrete distributed programs helps to separate general aspects of train control mechanisms and their safety from concrete application-specific design decisions.
– Our verification concept is independent on the size of the underlying network topology. In contrast to that, experiments with model checking have led to unmanageable explosions of the state space, as soon as more complex networks were involved or a larger number of trains had to be controlled.

- Within the restrictions of the *simple network* definition given above, the network topologies covered by our algorithm are fairly general: There are no limits regarding the size of the network, the number tracks involved or the places where points may occur. In contrast to that, approaches using compositional reasoning and structural induction over the underlying network topologies only seem to work for unrealistically simplified networks.
- Starting with a most abstract version of safety requirements, our approach allows to verify their completeness and trace their "implementation" in the more concrete refinements of the abstract control algorithm in a straight-forward manner. For approaches defining only implementation-specific safety requirements without reference to a more abstract safety concept, it is nearly infeasible to check safety requirements with respect to completeness.

We would like to emphasise that the control algorithm presented here represents just a building block in a more general approach for the development, verification, validation and test (VVT) of safety-critical systems which is investigated by the authors' research groups at DTU and the Bremen Institute of Safe Systems (BISS). In this wider context, our research work covers

- A systems engineering approach for safety-critical systems which is driven by hazard analysis, risk analysis and a design approach taking VVT issues into consideration right from the beginning of the development life cycle,
- Software-architectures for safety controllers,
- Automated real-time testing for embedded hardware/software components,
- An integrated standardised concept for verification, validation and test of safety-critical embedded controllers, applying combinations of VVT methods, each one optimised for a specific step in the system development life cycle.

References

[1] D. Bjørner, C.W. George, B. Stig Hansen, H. Laustrup, and S. Prehn. A railway system, coordination'97, case study workshop example. Technical Report 93, UNU/IIST, P.O.Box 3058, Macau, 1997.
[2] B. Dehbonei and F. Mejia. Formal development of safety-critical software systems in railway signalling. In M. G. Hinchey and J. P. Bowen, editors, *Applications of Formal Methods*, pages 227–252. Prentice Hall Int., 1995.
[3] Regionalstrecken. Eisenbahntechnische Rundschau (ETR) 46 (1997), Heft 6, 323-331.
[4] K. Mark Hansen. *Linking Safety Analysis to Safety Requirements — exemplified by Railway Interlocking Systems*. PhD thesis, Department of Information Technology, Technical University of Danmark, Lyngby, 1996.
[5] K. Mark Hansen. Formalising railway interlocking systems. In *Proceedings of Second FMERail Workshop*, October 1998.
[6] The RAISE Language Group. *The RAISE Specification Language*. The BCS Practitioners Series. Prentice Hall Int., 1992.
[7] The RAISE Method Group. *The RAISE Development Method*. The BCS Practitioners Series. Prentice Hall Int., 1995.
[8] N. Storey. *Safety-Critical Computer Systems*. Addison Wesley, 1996.

Safety Analysis in Formal Specification

Kaisa Sere and Elena Troubitsyna

Department of Computer Science, Åbo Akademi University,
Turku Centre for Computer Science (TUCS),
Lemminkäisenkatu 14 A, FIN-20520 Turku, Finland,
{Kaisa.Sere, Elena.Troubitsyna}@abo.fi

Abstract. Formal methods give us techniques to specify the functionality of a system, to verify its correctness or to develop the system stepwise from an abstract specification to its implementation. These aspects are important when designing safety-critical systems. Safety analysis is a vital part of the development of such systems. However, formal methods seldom interface well with the more informal techniques developed for safety analysis. Action systems is a formal approach to distributed computing that has proven its worth in the design of safety-critical systems. The approach is based on a firm mathematical foundation within which the reasoning about the correctness and behaviour of the system under development is carried out. The purpose of this paper is to show how we can incorporate the results of safety analysis into an action system specification by encoding this information via available composition operators for action systems in order to specify robust and safe controllers.

1 Introduction

Formal methods give us techniques to formally specify the functionality of a system, to verify its correctness or to develop the system stepwise from an abstract specification to its implementation. These aspects are important when designing safety-critical systems. Safety analysis is a vital part of the development of such systems. However, formal methods seldom interface well with the more informal techniques developed for safety analysis [13, 6]. Hansen et al. [5] spotted the problem of the semantic gap between the abstract level of the hazard analysis and the way of software specification. They suggest to use the results of Fault Tree Analysis as a source of the formulation of requirements which embedded software should meet. In their approach a description of fault trees is given in terms of real-time temporal logic. Their goal is to obtain a safety invariant which embedded software should preserve. Wong and Joyce [16] show how safety-related hazards are expressed in terms of source code for embedded software in order to verify this with respect to the hazards. The purpose of this paper is to develop a theory on how safety analysis techniques are used hand-in-hand with formal specification methods and how the results of the analysis are stepwise adopted by the specification in order to produce safe and robust systems consisting of both hardware and software.

J. Wing, J. Woodcock, J. Davies (Eds.): FM'99, Vol. II, LNCS 1709, pp. 1564–1583, 1999.
© Springer-Verlag Berlin Heidelberg 1999

We use the action system formalism [1] as our formal design technique. This formalism is a state-based approach to system design. It provides a completely rigorous foundation for the stepwise development of system specifications and implementations. It has found many applications especially among parallel and distributed systems among which many are safety-critical [3, 10]. Our target systems are reactive, i.e., usually concurrent systems that interact with their environment and respond to not only normal safe situations, but to the occurred hazardous situations as well. We often call this environment a plant. Examples of such systems are embedded control systems.

In our earlier work [9, 14] we have proposed methods to reason about the impact of probabilistic behaviour of components on the overall safety of a control system. We concentrated on the probabilistic extension of the specification language developing tools to reason quantitatively about the systems' reliability and safety. Here we use the available modularization operators, most notably the prioritising composition [11], to capture the idea of safety related hazards. Our preliminary work [12] shows that the approach seems promising. We show in this paper how to embed the results of a hazard analysis into an action systems specification in a stepwise manner. The embedding is carried out within a formal calculus, the refinement calculus for action systems [1]. Our approach is similar to that of Hansen et al. in the sense that we can also obtain a safety invariant as a result of the safety analysis as they do. In addition, our approach allows the identified hazards to be specified and handled by the controller software. Hence, we focus on the specification aspect here.

Overview. In Section 2, we briefly describe action systems concentrating on the language issues and refinement as well as defining the important composition operators. In Section 3, we outline the way control systems are specified in the action systems framework. In Section 4, we show how the results of the Fault Tree Analysis can be encoded into the formalism. We exemplify the approach in Section 5. In Section 6, we concentrate on hazard analysis in a more general setting. We end in Section 7 with some concluding remarks.

2   Action Systems

An action system $\mathcal{A}$ is a set of actions operating on local and global variables:

$$\mathcal{A} \mathrel{\widehat{=}} \textbf{const } c; \textbf{ global } z; \; |[\textbf{ var } a \; ; A_0 \; ; \textbf{ do } A_1 \;] \; \dots \;] \; A_n \textbf{ od }]|$$

The system $\mathcal{A}$ describes a computation, in which local variables a are first created and initialised in A_0. Then repeatedly any of the enabled actions $A_1, \dots, A_n$ is non-deterministically selected for execution. The computation terminates if no action is enabled, otherwise it continues infinitely. Actions operating on disjoint sets of variables can be executed in any order or in parallel.

Actions are taken to be *atomic*, meaning that only their input-output behaviour is of interest. They can be arbitrary sequential statements. Their behaviour can therefore be described by the weakest precondition predicate transformer of Dijkstra [4]: $wp(A, p)$ is the weakest precondition such that action A

terminates in a state satisfying predicate p. In addition to the statements considered by Dijkstra, we allow pure guarded commands $g \to A$, non-deterministic choice $A \parallel B$ between actions A, B, and nondeterministic assignment $v := v'.Q$ which assigns to variables v such a value v' that the predicate Q holds.

$$
\begin{aligned}
&wp(abort, p) \mathrel{\widehat{=}} false && wp((A \; ; \; B), p) \mathrel{\widehat{=}} wp(A, wp(B, p)) \\
&wp(skip, p) \mathrel{\widehat{=}} p && wp((A \parallel B), p) \mathrel{\widehat{=}} wp(A, p) \wedge wp(B, p) \\
&wp(v := e, p) \mathrel{\widehat{=}} p[v := e] && wp((g \to A), p) \mathrel{\widehat{=}} g \Rightarrow wp(A, p) \\
& && wp(v := v'.Q, p) \mathrel{\widehat{=}} (\forall v'.Q \Rightarrow p[v := v'])
\end{aligned}
$$

Generally, an action that establishes any postcondition is said to be miraculous. We take the view that an action is only enabled in those initial states in which it behaves non-miraculously. The guard of an action characterises those states for which the action is enabled:

$$
gd\ A \mathrel{\widehat{=}} \neg\ wp(A, false)
$$

The body S of an action $A = g \to S$ is denoted by sA.

Let A and B be actions. The prioritising composition $A \mathbin{/\!/} B$ selects the first operand if it is enabled, otherwise the second, the choice being deterministic.

$$
A \mathbin{/\!/} B \mathrel{\widehat{=}} A \parallel (\neg gd\ A \to B)
$$

The prioritising composition of two actions is enabled if either operand is.

$$
gd(A \mathbin{/\!/} B) = gd\ A \vee gd\ B
$$

Let us now study different notions of refinement for action systems [2]. We say that action A is refined by action C, written $A \le C$, if, whenever A establishes a certain postcondition, so does C:

$$
A \le C \text{ iff for all } p: wp(A, p) \Rightarrow wp(C, p)
$$

Together with the monotonicity of wp this implies that for a certain precondition, C might establish a stronger postcondition than A (reduce nondeterminism of A) or even establish postcondition *false* (behave miraculously).

A variation of refinement is if A is (data-) refined by C via a relation R, written $A \le_R C$. For this, assume A operates on variables a, u and C operates on variables c, u. Let R be a predicate over a, c, u:

$$
A \le_R C \text{ iff for all } p: R \wedge wp(A, p) \Rightarrow wp(C, (\exists\, a \cdot R \wedge p))
$$

Data refinement allows the local variables of an action system to be replaced. We have the following theorem to prove data refinement between actions:

Theorem 1. $A \le_R C$ *holds iff*

(i) $R \wedge gd\ C \Rightarrow gd\ A$
(ii) *for all* p: $R \wedge gd\ C \ \wedge\ wp(sA, p) \Rightarrow wp(sC, (\exists a \cdot R \wedge p))$

Rule 1 $a{:}=? \leq a{:}=a'.Q$,where $a{:}=? \mathrel{\widehat{=}} a{:}=a'.true$

Rule 2   For two actions A, B: $A \parallel B \leq A /\!/ B$

Rule 3 $g1 \lor g2 \to abort /\!/ g(A) \to A \leq g1 \to abort /\!/ g2 \to B \parallel g(A) \to A$
          where A and B can also be abortive

Rule 4 $a{:}=? \leq_R c{:}=c'.Q$ if $Q \land R \Rightarrow (\exists a'{\cdot}R[a, c{:}=a', c'])$

Rule 5 $A1;A2 \leq_R C1;C2$ if $A1 \leq_R C1$ and $A2 \leq_R C2$

Rule 6 $A1 /\!/ A2 \leq_R C1 /\!/ C2$ if $A1 \leq_R C1$ and $A2 \leq_R C2$
          and $R \land gd\,A1 \Rightarrow gd\,C1$

Fig. 1. Refinement rules

The next theorem presents conditions to be verified in order to establish refinement between action systems.

Theorem 2. $\mathcal{A} \leq_R \mathcal{C}$ *holds iff*

(i) $C0 \Rightarrow (\exists a{\cdot}R \land A0)$
(ii) $A \leq_R C$
(iii) $R \land gd\,A \Rightarrow gC$

The proofs of Theorem 1 and Theorem 2 can be found elsewhere [2].

When carrying out refinement in practice one seldom appeals to the general definition of refinement. Instead certain pre-proven refinement rules are used. Figure 1 presents a number of rules [12] that are especially useful when working with hazards as will be seen later.

3   Specifying Control Systems with Safety Consideration

Let us now sketch a way to specify control systems within action systems formalism. Rather than embody all the requirements in the initial specification, we introduce some of them in successive refinement steps. Usually, refinement is used as a way of verifying the correctness of an implementation with respect to a specification, but is it can also be used as a way of structuring the requirements such that they are easier to validate [3, 10]. In this paper we develop mechanisms to handle failure situations by the refinement activity.

Our initial action system is intended to model the behaviour of the overall system, that is, the physical environment and the controller together. It allows us to use assumptions that we make about how the environment behaves. The initial specification of the system is very abstract. Usually it is built in such a way that all the details concerning interaction between the plant and the controller (via sensors and actuators) as well as details of failures are omitted.

Below a control system is modelled as an interleaving between the plant P and the controller C

$$System \mathrel{\widehat{=}} \textbf{const } c;\ \textbf{global } z;\ \|[\ \textbf{var } pv, cv, fail;\ I;\ \textbf{do } P\ ;\ C\ \textbf{od }\,]\| \qquad (1)$$

The action I initialises the system. Both P and C are actions and they might share variables. This initial specification of the plant action P is

$$P \cong pv, z, fail: =?, ?, ?$$

where pv are the state variables needed to model the local state of the plant, and the controller action C is

$$C \cong Failure \mathbin{/\!/} (Unit_1 \,\|\, Unit_2 \,\|\, \ldots \,\|\, Unit_M)$$

The controller consists of a prioritising composition of the action *Failure*

$$Failure \cong fail \to Emergency$$

which shuts down the system if a failure occurs, i.e., the action *Emergency* is equivalent to *abort*, and the actions $Unit_i$, $i = 1..M$, which have the form

$$Unit_i \cong g_i \to control\ action_i$$

Here for simplicity we assume that the occurrence of a global system failure is modelled by a local variable *fail*. Later we drop this simplification and consider the action *Failure* guarded by a predicate over the global and the local variables of the system. Each of the actions $Unit_i$ specifies the control required to operate a certain plant device (we call it a plant unit) in absence of failures. They can refer to the variables pv, z, and normally some other variables, too, denoted as cv in (1) . Observe that we can be certain that there are no failures present when an action $Unit_i$ is executed as the prioritising composition between the faulty behaviour and the control actions ensures this. Without this operator, i.e., using the choice operator between these actions, the control actions would require a more elaborate guard, namely $g_i \wedge \neg fail$. This latter approach is taken for instance by Liu and Joseph [8].

In our initial specification *System* we assume that the state of the plant can be directly observed by the controller. Further refinement of the initial specification leads to the introduction of implementation details which make the specification more realistic: the controller cannot observe the real state of the plant any more but rather makes assumptions about it based on sensor readings. Control is performed by means of actuators which, like the sensors, are modelled as state variables [3]. Eventually, we arrive at the representation of the system in the form presented in Fig. 2.

In our previous work on action systems for safety-critical systems [3, 10], failure modes of the components together with the safety invariant imposed on the system were given a priori. The task was to capture these requirements into a specification. In the industrial practice, however, the design of a safety-critical system assumes that this information is unavailable and should be obtained as a result of a safety analysis of the system. On the base of the safety analysis the designer should build the controller so that it is able to withstand faults appearing in the fault-prone units. To obtain the failure modes for the controlling program we show how the specification and refinement of the system under construction can proceed hand-in-hand with the safety analysis.

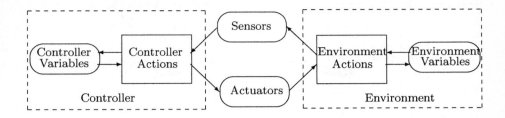

Fig. 2. Structure of the system specification

Observe, that both the safety analysis and the stepwise program development conduct reasoning from an abstract level to a concrete level. The safety analysis starts by identifying hazards which are potentially dangerous, and proceeds by producing detailed descriptions of them together with finding the means to cope with these hazards. We incorporate the information that becomes available at each stage of the safety process by performing corresponding refinements of the initial specification, as shown in Fig. 3.

With such an approach the preliminary hazard identification gives the semantics to the action *Failure*: it is a reaction on the occurrence of the identified hazard. When the system enters a hazardous state it violates the safety invariant and therefore, should be shut down. Safe operation of the action system *System* (1) can be expressed via a safety invariant *safety* on the state variables of the system:

$$safety \; \widehat{=} \; \neg fail \; \Rightarrow \; safety\ condition$$

Safety is checked within the weakest precondition calculus by ensuring that the initial state establishes *safety*, and that $wp(C, safety)$ holds, i.e. the actions of the controller preserve *safety*. As the safety analysis proceeds more information on the failures causing hazardous situations becomes available and allows us to weaken the safety invariant by expressing this new information.

4   Representing a Fault Tree in a Specification

There are a number of standard techniques for producing detailed description of the identified hazards [6, 13]. In this paper we choose the Fault Tree Analysis and show next, how to incorporate the information obtained as a result of the fault tree analysis in the initial system specification (1) given in form of an action system. The Fault Tree Analysis (FTA) is a deductive safety analysis technique. It is a top-down approach applied during the entire design stage. A preliminary hazard identification provides information about functions of the system and the possible failures (see Fig. 3). This information is taken as an input for the FTA. The result of the FTA is an identification of those component faults that result in different hazardous situations. Each fault tree has a root representing

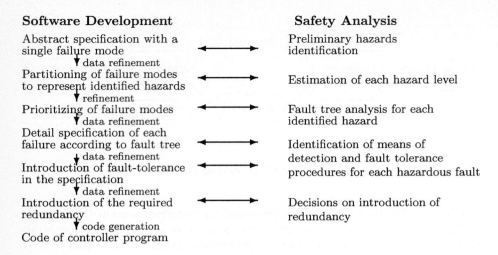

Fig. 3. Interaction of software development process with safety analysis

a hazardous failure. The tree traces the system to the lower component level revealing the possible causes of the failure.

A fault tree consists of two main entities, leaves and gates. The leaves, often called events, represent the system states which in combination with other events lead to the occurrence of the hazardous fault represented by the root of the tree. The gates are logical connectives which join the leaves. They describe which particular combination of events results in the occurrence of the hazard. In this paper we consider two basic logical gates, namely disjunction and conjunction. Below we present the rules which allow us to embed the information about failures given in the form of a fault tree in the specification of the system given in the form of an action system.

A leaf of a fault tree describes a certain set of system states. It, therefore, can be expressed as a predicate over the state variables of the system. In the system specification the leaves, or more precisely the predicates representing the leaves, appear as the guards of the actions which specify the reaction of the system on the occurred faults. With each event we also associate a certain level of criticality defined by the level of the fault tree at which that particular event appears. The root of the tree, therefore, is the event of the first level of criticality, the events directly connected to the root by means of a logical gate have the second level of criticality etc. It is clear, that the occurrence of an event which is close to the root might lead to an inevitable catastrophe, and therefore, should be dealt with urgently.

A gate of a fault tree defines the logical operator (conjunction or disjunction) over the predicates representing the leaves which the gate connects. Therefore, if an action specifies a reaction of the controller on the combination of certain events we define its guard on the base of the gate which conjoins these events.

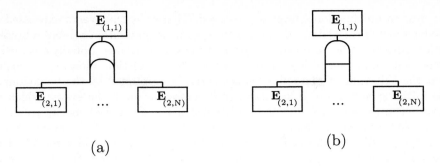

Fig. 4. Basic fault trees

The approach we advocate in this paper suggests to analyse a fault tree in a stepwise manner. Namely, we start from the specification of the system in form (1) where the value *true* of the boolean *fail* represents the root of the fault tree. Here for simplicity, we assume that there is only one hazard identified for a given system. In the next section we extend the technique to reason about systems with several hazards. Analysing the fault tree level after level we stepwise embed detailed representation of the faults and model the reaction of the controller in the specification. As a result, we obtain a specification of the system within which both faults and reactions on them are specified in terms of the state variables. Moreover, the faults are treated according to their criticality which is defined by the levels of the fault tree. Below we describe a number of generic rules which allow us to specify faults preserving the structure of the fault tree.

Consider the fault tree (a) in Fig. 4, where events $E_{(2,1)}, \ldots, E_{(2,N)}$ are caused by failures of sensors and actuators (see Fig.2) or represent certain events over globally observed system states (e.g. the states of the physical environment). The event $E_{(i,j)}$ stands for the $j - th$ event on the $i - th$ level of the fault tree. Even though we consider here only two levels, the results can be applied recursively to an arbitrary number of levels. We show an example of this in the next section.

The occurrence of the failure $E_{(1,1)}$ and the system reaction on that can be specified by the action *Failure* of the following form:

$$Failure \ \widehat{=}\ E_{(2,1)} \vee \ldots \vee E_{(2,N)} \ \rightarrow\ Reaction\ on\ E_{(1,1)}$$

where $E_{(2,1)}, \ldots, E_{(2,i)}$ are predicates over the local variables of the system representing sensor and actuator failures and $E_{(2,i+1)}, \ldots, E_{(2,N)}$ are predicates over the global variables representing events over globally observed system states. Moreover,

$$E_{(1,1)} = E_{(2,1)} \vee \ldots \vee E_{(2,N)}$$

Data refinement allows us to change the local part of the state space (i.e. to manipulate the local variables of the specification) provided the behaviour of the system on the global level is preserved. Therefore, the events expressed as predicates over the global variables of the system should obtain a detail representation already in the initial specification of the system as new globally observable behaviour cannot be added via refinement. This restriction allows us to ensure that the behaviour of the refined specification is subsumed by the behaviour of the initial specification. In contrary, the representation of the events which do not refer to the global state can be very abstract in the initial specification.

Consider again the fault tree (a) in Fig. 4 where none of the events $E_{(2,1)}$, ..., $E_{(2,N)}$ refers to the global state and hence are for simplicity modelled by the local variables $E_{(2,1)}, \ldots, E_{(2,N)}$ in the system specification. For that case we have the following result:

Theorem 3. *The action system $\mathcal{A}$ of the form (1) such that $E_{(1,1)} = fail$ in the fault tree (a) in Fig. 4 is refined by the action system $\mathcal{A}'$:*

$$\mathcal{A}' \mathrel{\hat{=}} \textbf{const } c; \textbf{ global } z; \ [\![\textbf{ var } v, E_{(2,1)}, ..., E_{(2,N)}; \ I'; \textbf{ do } P \ ; \ C' \textbf{ od }]\!]$$

where I' initialises the variables and the controller action C' is a prioritising composition of the reaction on the occurred failure $E_{(1,1)}$ specified by the action Failure'

$$Failure' \mathrel{\hat{=}} E_{(2,1)} \vee \ldots \vee E_{(2,N)} \to Emergency$$

with the control actions:

$$C' \mathrel{\hat{=}} Failure' \ /\!/ \ (Unit_1 \ [\!] \ Unit_2 \ [\!] \ldots [\!] \ Unit_M)$$

Proof. The refinement relation $R \mathrel{\hat{=}} fail = (E_{(2,1)} \vee \ldots \vee E_{(2,N)})$ allows us to prove that $\mathcal{A} \leq_R \mathcal{A}'$ appealing to Theorem 2, hence, proving the theorem.

Next we develop a similar rule for specifying the fault tree (b) in Fig. 4 which contains the logical gate conjunction. Assume that events $E_{(2,1)}, \ldots, E_{(2,i)}$ are caused by failures of sensors and actuators (see Fig.2) and events $E_{(2,i+1)}, \ldots, E_{(2,N)}$ represent certain events over globally observed system states. The occurrence of the failure $E_{(1,1)}$ is caused by the conjunction of these events as specified by the fault tree. We specify the occurrence of the event $E_{(1,1)}$ and the reaction of the controller on that by the action *Failure* of the following form:

$$Failure \mathrel{\hat{=}} E_{(2,1)} \wedge \ldots \wedge E_{(2,N)} \to Reaction \ on \ E_{(1,1)}$$

where $E_{(2,1)}, \ldots, E_{(2,i)}$ are again predicates over the local variables of the system and $E_{(2,i+1)}, \ldots, E_{(2,N)}$ are predicates over the global variables and

$$E_{(1,1)} = E_{(2,1)} \wedge \ldots \wedge E_{(2,N)}$$

Note, that in case a failure is caused by disjunction of a set of events (the fault tree (a) in Fig. 4) the controller is intolerant to the occurrence of any single event from this set. In case of conjunction (the fault tree (b) in Fig. 4) the situation is different: the controller can cope with each particular event to preclude the occurrence of the more critical failure caused by the conjunction of these events.

Again for simplicity assume that none of the events $E_{(2,1)}, \ldots, E_{(2,N)}$ of the fault tree (b) in Fig. 4 refers to the global states and are therefore modelled by local variables of the same name in the system specification. Then the following theorem provides us with a formal technique to represent such a fault tree in the specification as a refinement of the initial system specification.

Theorem 4. *The action system $\mathcal{A}$ of the form (1) such that $E_{(1,1)} = fail$ in the fault tree (b) in Fig. 4 is refined by the action system $\mathcal{A}'$:*

$$\mathcal{A}' \,\hat{=}\, \textbf{const } c; \, \textbf{global } z; \,\, \lVert \, \textbf{var } v, E_{(2,1)}, \ldots, E_{(2,N)}; \, I'; \,\, \textbf{do } P \, ; \, C' \, \textbf{od } \rVert$$

where I' is the new initialisation and the controller action C'

$$C' \,\hat{=}\, Failure' \, /\!/ \, (Unit_1 \, \lVert \, Unit_2 \, \lVert \ldots \rVert \, Unit_M)$$

is a prioritising composition between the control actions $Unit_1, Unit_2, \ldots, Unit_M$ and the action $Failure'$

$$
\begin{aligned}
Failure' \,\hat{=}\,\, & E_{(2,1)} \wedge \ldots \wedge E_{(2,N)} \rightarrow Emergency \\
/\!/ \,\, & E_{(2,1)} \rightarrow Rescue_{E_{(2,1)}} \\
\lVert \,\, & \ldots \\
\lVert \,\, & E_{(2,N)} \rightarrow Rescue_{E_{(2,N)}}
\end{aligned}
$$

which specify the reaction $Emergency$ of the controller on the occurrence of the hazardous failure $E_{(1,1)}$, together with the reaction statements $Rescue_{E_{(2,1)}}, \ldots, Rescue_{E_{(2,N)}}$ on the local variables $E_{(2,1)}, \ldots, E_{(2,N)}$.

Proof. The refinement relation $R \,\hat{=}\, fail = (E_{(2,1)} \vee \ldots \vee E_{(2,N)})$ allows us to prove that $\mathcal{A} \leq_R \mathcal{A}'$ on the base of Theorem 2. This results in proving the theorem.

The statements $Rescue_{E_{(2,1)}} \ldots, Rescue_{E_{(2,N)}}$ specify invocations of the maintenance procedures as the responses on the occurred failures of the sensors and the actuators (see Fig.2).

The treatment of a more general case where the events $E_{(2,1)}, \ldots, E_{(2,N)}$ can refer to both global and local states is different in the sense that we have to give a detailed description of the events over the global system state already in the initial specification. The reasoning about the events referring to the local part of the state space is, however, still conducted as above.

Below we present a general form of the initial specification of the action *Failure* for this case which additionally specifies controller reactions on combined events caused by multiple failures. In that case the action representing the occurrence of failure $E_{(1,1)}$ of the fault tree (b) in Fig. 4 contains also the actions specifying the reactions on these combined events. The specification of the occurrence of the failure $E_{(1,1)}$ as well as the occurrences of the combinations of the events $E_{(2,1)}, \ldots, E_{(2,N)}$ with the reactions of the controller are represented by the action *Failure* below

$$Failure \mathrel{\widehat{=}} E_{(2,1)} \wedge ... \wedge E_{(2,N)} \to Emergency$$

$$/\!/ \bigwedge_{i\in[1..N]} E_{(2,i)} \to Resque_1$$

$$\| \ ...$$

$$\| \bigwedge_{i\in[1..N]} E_{(2,i)} \to Resque_l$$

(2)

where $E_{(2,1)}, \dots, E_{(2,N)}$ are predicates over the local and the global variables. Here the statements $Resque_1, \dots, Resque_l$ specify the invocations of the maintenance procedures as the responses on the occurred events. The guards of these actions are formed from arbitrary event combinations and might describe reactions on each of the events $E_{(2,1)}, \dots, E_{(2,N)}$ separately as well.

5   Example: A Heater Controller

To illustrate both construction of a fault tree and building of the corresponding specification we consider an example — a heater controller for a tank of toxic liquid. A computer controls the heater using a power switch on the basis of information obtained from a temperature sensor. The controller tries to maintain the temperature between certain limits. If the temperature exceeds a critical threshold the toxic liquid can harm its environment in a certain way (we leave it unspecified).

We start the safety analysis of our system (see Fig. 3) by the preliminary hazard identification. Since the system can harm its environment as a result of overheating of the toxic liquid, we identify the hazard *overheating* and proceed the analysis by constructing the corresponding fault tree. The fault tree in Fig. 5 identifies the faults of the system components and their logical combinations which lead to overheating.

Overheating of the toxic liquid, the event $E_{(1,1)}$ takes place if the temperature reaches a predefined threshold, heat is supplied, and a failure to switch off the heater takes place. Therefore, $E_{(1,1)} = E_{(2,1)} \wedge E_{(2,2)} \wedge E_{(2,3)}$. The failure to switch of the heater, the event $E_{(2,3)}$ is a result of the failure to issue the switch off signal or a primary switch failure, $E_{(2,3)} = E_{(3,1)} \vee E_{(3,2)}$. Finally, the failure $E_{(3,1)}$ occurs if either the controller fails or the temperature sensor fails and indicates a wrong (lower than the real) temperature, $E_{(3,1)} = E_{(4,1)} \vee E_{(4,2)}$.

Designing a formal specification of the system according to the approach proposed in this paper, we depict the information obtained from the construction of the fault tree. Our initial specification of the system below:

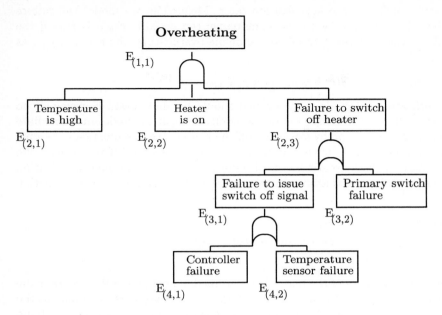

Fig. 5. Fault tree of overheating

$\mathcal{A} \,\hat{=}\, \textbf{const}$ tr: $Real$ / * $critical$ $threshold$ * /
         ht: $Real$ / * $high$ $temperature$ $limit$ * /
         lt: $Real$ / * low $temperature$ $limit$ * /
         $maxd$: $Real$ / * $maximal$ $temperature$ $decrease$ per $unit$ of $time$ * /
         $maxi$: $Real$ / * $maximal$ $temperature$ $increase$ per $unit$ of $time$ * /
         $maxt$: $Real$ / * $maximal$ $feasible$ $temperature$ * /
         $lt < ht < tr$;
    $\textbf{global}$ t: $Real$ / * $temperature$ * /
         $heat$: $on|off$ / * $supply$ of $heating$ * /
    $[\![$ $\textbf{var}$ $E_{(2,3)}$:$Bool$; I ; $\textbf{do}$ $Environment$; $Controller$ $\textbf{od}$ $]\!]$

has the form (1) where $Controller$ $=$ $Failure$ $/\!/$ $Switch$.

As described previously, the action $Failure$ specifies the occurrence of overheating and the rescue procedures undertaken by the controller as responses to
the occurred failures. Overheating is the result of the conjunction of the events
$E_{(2,1)}$, $E_{(2,2)}$, $E_{(2,3)}$. We express the event $E_{(2,1)}$ by the predicate $t \geq tr$, where t
is a global variable modelling the temperature of the liquid and tr is the critical
temperature threshold defined by the corresponding constant in our specification. Similarly, the event $E_{(2,2)}$ is represented by the predicate $heat = on$. The
global variable $heat$ evaluates to on if the heater is switched on and to off otherwise. The event $E_{(2,3)}$ is caused by the failures of the sensor and the actuator,

which will appear in the specification later. Meanwhile we model the failure $E_{(2,3)}$ by a local variable with the same name: the variable $E_{(2,3)}$ is *true* if the event $E_{(2,3)}$ takes places. Therefore, we define overheating, the event $E_{(1,1)}$, as follows:

$$overheating = t \geq tr \wedge heat = on \wedge E_{(2,3)}$$

If overheating takes place the system should be shut down. However, if no failure to switch off heating occurs the controller can preclude an immediate occurrence of overheating by switching off the heater. We pessimistically assume that the system is shut down if there is a failure to switch off the heater. We specify a more realistic treatment of this failure as soon as a detailed specification of the sensor and the actuator becomes available. The specification of the action *Failure*

$$Failure \mathrel{\widehat{=}} overheating \rightarrow abort$$
$$// \ t \geq tr \wedge heat = on \rightarrow heat \colon = off$$
$$[\!] \ \ E_{(2,3)} \rightarrow abort$$

is obtained on the basis of the reasoning described in Section 4. Observe, that the structure of the part of the fault tree in Fig. 5 we analyse here is similar to the structure of the fault tree (*b*) in Fig. 4. The general form of an action specifying the responses of the system to combined events was given by the action (2). Here we applied the same kind of reasoning to obtain the action *Failure*.

The rest of the system specification is rather typical for control systems treated within the action system formalism. Specifying the initialisation we assume that the system starts its operation in a state where no failures have occurred: $I \mathrel{\widehat{=}} E_{(2,3)} \colon = false$.

We specify the environment very abstractly: we merely describe an arbitrary temperature change and a non-deterministic occurrence of a fault.

$$\begin{aligned} Environment &= Env_p; Env_f \\ Env_p &= t \colon =? \\ Env_f &= E_{(2,3)} \colon =? \end{aligned}$$

The control action *Switch* specifies the switching off and on the heater in order to maintain the liquid temperature in the safe region:

$$Switch \mathrel{\widehat{=}} t \geq ht \wedge heat = on \rightarrow heat \colon = off$$
$$[\!] \ \ t \leq lt \wedge heat = off \rightarrow heat \colon = on$$

The analysis of the next level of the fault tree is based on the application of Theorem 3: the occurrence of the event $E_{(2,3)}$ results from the disjunction of the events $E_{(3,1)}$ and $E_{(3,2)}$. To specify the event $E_{(3,1)}$ we introduce a local variable $E_{(3,1)}$ which is *true* if the event occurs. The event $E_{(3,2)}$ results from the failure of the actuator — the power switch. To specify this we introduce the local variable *sw_stat* modelling the status of the switch in our specification. To simplify the reasoning we omit the detailed specification of an invocation of a switch repair procedure and present only its effect: the repaired power switch. The specification of the response on the event $E_{(3,1)}$ is similar to that of the event $E_{(2,3)}$.

The specification of the system $\mathcal{A}'$ is as follows

$$\mathcal{A}' \; \widehat{=} \; \dots \; |[\; \textbf{var} \; sw\_stat{:}ok|failed \; ; \; E_{(3,1)}{:}Bool \; ; \; I'; $$
$$\textbf{do} \; Environment'; Controller' \; \textbf{od} \;]|$$

where $Controller' = Failure' \mathbin{/\!/} Switch$ is obtained by taking into account information obtained from the analysis of the second and the third levels of the fault tree in Fig. 5 as specified by the action $Failure'$

$$Failure' \; \widehat{=} \; overheating' \rightarrow abort$$
$$\mathbin{/\!/} \; t \geq tr \wedge heat = on \rightarrow heat{:} = off$$
$$\mathbin{/\!/} \; sw\_stat = failed \rightarrow sw\_stat{:} = ok$$
$$\mathbin{[\!\!|} \; E_{(3,1)} \rightarrow abort$$

Here $overheating' = t \geq tr \wedge heat = on \wedge (sw\_stat = failed \vee E_{(3,1)})$.

Also in this step we refine the environment action by considering maximal system dynamics and by modelling the occurred failures over the introduced local variables:

$$Environment' \; \widehat{=} \; Env'_p; Env'_f$$
$$Env'_p \qquad \widehat{=} \; t{:} = t'.t - maxd \leq t' \leq t + maxi \wedge 0 \leq t \leq maxt$$
$$Env_f \qquad \widehat{=} \; sw\_stat{:} =? \; ; \; E_{(3,1)}{:} =?$$

The new initialisation is $I' \; \widehat{=} \; sw\_stat{:} = ok \; ; \; E_{(3,1)}{:} = false$

On the base of Theorem 3 and the refinement rules given in Fig.1 it can be shown that the action system $\mathcal{A}'$ refines the action system $\mathcal{A}$ with the refinement relation R_1

$$R_1 \; \widehat{=} \; E_{(2,3)} = (sw\_stat = failed \vee E_{(3,1)})$$

Analysing the last level of the fault tree in Fig. 5, we observe that the event $E_{(4,1)}$ cannot be expressed in the specification of the controller. The failure of the controller is caused by the hardware or software error. However, it points out the necessity to introduce a controller independent device in the system design, a watch dog. Such a device periodically checks the status of the controller and shuts down the system or activates a stand-by controller if the main controller fails. Therefore, we consider the event $E_{(4,2)}$ which specifies a failure of the temperature sensor. The introduction of a representation of the sensor in the system specification transforms the specification of the controller in such a way that the controller relies on the sensor readings to perform its duties. The real state of the environment becomes inaccessible to the controller. Applying Theorem 3 we perform data refinement of the system obtaining the specification $\mathcal{A}''$.

$$\mathcal{A}'' \; \widehat{=} \; \dots \; |[\; \textbf{var} \; sw\_stat, sen\_stat{:}ok|failed \; ; \; t\_tr, t\_est_1, t\_est_2{:}Real \; ; \; I''; $$
$$\textbf{do} \; Environment''; Controller'' \; \textbf{od} \;]|$$

where $Controller'' = Failure'' /\!/ Switch'$. The initialisation establishes a state where both the temperature sensor and the power switch function properly.

$$I'' \mathrel{\widehat{=}} sw\_stat\!: = ok \; ; \; sen\_stat\!: = ok; t\_tr\!: = t; t\_est_1, t\_est_2\!: = t\_tr, t\_tr$$

The environment models a change of the temperature, independent occurrences of the sensor and the actuator failures, and an estimate of the temperature made by the controller:

$$
\begin{aligned}
Environment'' &\mathrel{\widehat{=}} Env'_p \; ; \; Env''_f \; ; \; T\_Estim \\
Env''_f &\mathrel{\widehat{=}} sw\_stat\!: =? \; ; \; sen\_stat\!: =?; \\
&\quad t\_tr\!: = t\_tr'.sen\_stat = ok \Rightarrow t\_tr' = t \wedge \\
&\qquad\qquad\qquad sen\_stat = failed \Rightarrow t\_tr' = t\_tr \\
T\_Estim &\mathrel{\widehat{=}} t\_est_1, t\_est_2\!: = t\_est'_1, t\_est'_2.Q
\end{aligned}
$$

where

$$
\begin{aligned}
Q = \;&(sen\_stat = ok \Rightarrow t\_est'_1 = t\_tr \wedge t\_est'_2 = t\_tr) \wedge (sen\_stat = failed \Rightarrow \\
&(t\_est'_1 = (if \; t\_est_1 + maxi < maxt \; then \; t\_est_1 + maxi \; else \; maxt) \wedge \\
&t\_est'_2 = (if \; t\_est_2 - maxd > 0 \; then \; t\_est_2 - maxd \; else \; 0)))
\end{aligned}
$$

Compared to the action $Failure'$, the action $Failure''$ introduces additionally a reaction to the failure of the sensor. Moreover, it defines overheating by tracing the whole fault tree (Fig. 5):

$$
\begin{aligned}
Failure'' = \;&overheating'' \rightarrow abort \\
/\!/ \; &t\_est_1 \geq tr \wedge heat = on \rightarrow heat\!: = off \\
/\!/ \; &sw\_stat = failed \rightarrow sw\_stat\!: = ok \\
/\!/ \; &sen\_stat = failed \rightarrow sen\_stat\!: = ok
\end{aligned}
$$

with $overheating'' = t\_est_1 \geq tr \wedge heat = on \wedge (sw\_stat = failed \vee sen\_stat = failed)$.

In the specification of the controller we change the access to the real temperature and substitute it by the temperature estimate of the controller:

$$
\begin{aligned}
Switch' \mathrel{\widehat{=}} \;&t\_est_1 \geq ht \wedge heat = on \rightarrow heat\!: = off \\
\| \; &t\_est_2 \leq lt \wedge heat = off \rightarrow heat\!: = on
\end{aligned}
$$

Data refinement between the action systems $\mathcal{A}'$ and $\mathcal{A}''$, $\mathcal{A}' \leq_{R2} \mathcal{A}''$, is proved with the refinement relation

$$
\begin{aligned}
R2 \mathrel{\widehat{=}} \;&E_{(3,1)} = sen\_stat \wedge \\
&(sen\_stat = ok \Rightarrow t = t\_tr \wedge t\_est_1 = t\_tr \wedge t\_est_2 = t\_tr) \wedge \\
&(sen\_stat = failed \Rightarrow t\_est_2 \leq t \leq t\_est_1)
\end{aligned}
$$

6   Prioritising Hazards

Section 4 provided us with techniques that allow us to represent a single hazard in a specification. Often, however, there are several hazards identified for a system under construction. We need, therefore, to generalise the presented approach to reasoning about system hazards in general.

We assume that a set of hazards $\mathcal{H}$ is obtained as a result of the hazard identification. For each hazard $H_i \in \mathcal{H}$ an appropriate fault tree FT_i is constructed. The obtained fault trees form a set $\mathcal{FT}$: each tree from the set can be represented in the system specification as described in Section 4. Here we focus on the interaction between the representation of hazards in the specification.

Analysing the set of hazards $\mathcal{H}$ we assess the risk associated with each hazard from this set. The assessment is based on available quantitative information about component reliabilities or on expert judgements about the likelihood and severity of each hazard. Having assessed the risks associated with the identified hazards we can classify them. There are a number of methods and standards providing guidance for the classification of risks [13]. Without going into details we assume without loss of generality that there are three disjoint classes of hazards formed on the basis of the classification of risks associated with the hazards.

$$Class\ I\text{:}\quad \{H_1, \ldots, H_{c_1}\}$$
$$Class\ II\text{:}\quad \{H_{c_1+1}, \ldots, H_{c_2}\}$$
$$Class\ III\text{:}\quad \{H_{c_2+1}, \ldots, H_{c_3}\}$$

Let us make this more concrete by giving a potential interpretation to the classes. Assume that on the base of the performed classification we formulate failure modes of the system to be designed. The system enters *Emergency* mode if any of the hazardous situations from *Class I* occurred. Hence, these are the hazards that are intolerable and have a high risk associated with them. The mode *Resque* is caused by hazards belonging to class *Class II*. These are less severe hazards but still critical. They should be avoided or their effect should be mitigated. An occurrence of a hazard from *Class III* transforms the system into the *Degraded* mode. Here the failures can be tolerated as the risks associated with the corresponding hazards are negligible.

Now we return to the specification of the system from the software point of view. Developing the specification of the controller which should withstand several types of hazardous failures it is desirable to carry out the development process in such a way that the produced classification of hazards is preserved.

Consider again the general form of the system specification (1). As we described previously the guard of the action *Failure*, *fail* is in general a predicate over the global and the local variables. It expresses the occurrence of the identified hazardous failure. Since we now consider a set of hazardous failures the predicate *fail* should express the occurrence of any of them, i.e.

$$fail = \bigvee_{i=1}^{N} H_i$$

where each of the predicates H_i, $H_i \in \mathcal{H}$ for $i = 1..N$ describes a corresponding hazard in terms of the state variables as explained in Section 4. In the initial system specification we assume pessimistically, that each of the hazardous faults is treated equally by *Emergency* statement.

To introduce the different failure modes in the general specification of failures given by the action *Failure* we partition it as shown below:

$$Failure = Fail1 \parallel Fail2 \parallel Fail3$$

The three actions *Fail1, Fail2, Fail3* which describe the different classes of hazards:

$$Fail1 \,\hat{=}\, gFail1 \rightarrow Emergency$$
$$Fail2 \,\hat{=}\, gFail2 \rightarrow Resque$$
$$Fail3 \,\hat{=}\, gFail3 \rightarrow Degraded$$

The action *Fail1* specifies the reaction of the system on hazards from *Class I* which is *Emergency*, shut down of the system. The occurrence of a hazard or several of them is modelled by the guard of the action, which is defined to be disjunction of hazards from *Class I*:

$$gFail1 \,\hat{=}\, \vee_{i=1}^{c_1} H_i$$

The hazards belonging to *Class II* are specified by the action *Fail2*. Since a hazard from *Class II* does not lead to the imminent catastrophe, some actions to bring the system back to a non-hazardous state should be undertaken. Generally, the action has the form

$$Fail2 \,\hat{=}\, H_{c_1+1} \rightarrow Resque_{c_1+1} \parallel \ldots \parallel H_{c_2} \rightarrow Resque_{c_2}$$

Here each of the individual actions becomes enabled if a corresponding hazard from *Class II* occurs. The body of each action is an invocation of some *Resque* procedure. The structure of the action *Fail3* is similar to the action *Fail2*, but has the hazards of *Class III* as the guards and corresponding corrective procedures as the bodies.

Another safety requirement which we capture in the specification is a necessity to cope with the failures according to their criticality: we give priority to failures with high risks associated to them. Hence, *Fail1* should be executed immediately when enabled. Also *Fail2* and *Fail3* will be taken whenever enabled provided no action in a higher priority class is enabled. A normal control action $Unit_i$ is only taken when there are no failures detected in the system. Therefore, the most severe hazards — hazards belonging to *Class I* should be handled by the controller with highest priority. They form the class of highest priority in the specification of the controller. Consequently, the priority of the class decreases with increasing its priority index. The non-deterministic choice between the failure actions cannot guarantee this. The effect is obtained by prioritising the failure actions:

$$Fail1 \parallel Fail2 \parallel Fail3 \leq Fail1 \;/\!/\; Fail2 \;/\!/\; Fail3$$

The generalisation of the made observations from the perspective of the program refinement is given by the following theorem:

Theorem 5. *The action system*

$$\mathcal{A} \mathrel{\widehat=} \textbf{const } c; \textbf{ global } z; \; [\![\textbf{ var } pv, cv; \; I; \; \textbf{do } P \; ; (Failure \; /\!/ \; C) \textbf{ od }]\!]$$

such that

$$Failure \mathrel{\widehat=} fail \rightarrow Emergency$$

where fail is a predicate over the local and the global system variables and Emergency is equivalent to abort is refined by the action system

$$\mathcal{A}' \mathrel{\widehat=} \textbf{const } c; \textbf{ global } z; \; [\![\textbf{ var } pv, cv; \; I; \; \textbf{do } P \; ; (Failure' \; /\!/ \; C) \textbf{ od }]\!]$$

where

$$Failure' \mathrel{\widehat=} fail_1 \rightarrow Emergency$$
$$/\!/ \; fail_2 \rightarrow Rescue$$
$$/\!/ \; fail_3 \rightarrow Degraded$$

and

$$fail_1 \mathrel{\widehat=} \bigvee_{i=1}^{c_1} H_i$$
$$fail_2 \mathrel{\widehat=} \bigvee_{i=c_1+1}^{c_2} H_i$$
$$fail_3 \mathrel{\widehat=} \bigvee_{i=c_2+1}^{N} H_i$$

and where H_i for $i = 1..N$ are the predicates over the local and the global variables such that $fail = \bigvee_{i=1}^{N} H_i$

Proof. The theorem follows from the observation that an action guarded by the disjunction of predicates can be partitioned to actions guarded by separate disjuncts. Moreover, the application of Rule 2 in Fig. 1 allows us to prioritise these actions. Finally, *abort* statement is trivially refined by any statement (by itself also as follows from the reflexivity of the refinement).

7   Concluding Remarks

We have shown how information about hazardous situations occurring in a plant can be embedded in the formal specification of a control program. Via this embedding the hazardous situations are treated according to their criticality and urgency. This allows to enhance safety of the overall system by ensuring that in case some marginal failure occurred simultaneously with a more critical failure the latter one will be treated with the highest priority. The development of the heater controller in Section 5 illustrated the application of the approach.

We have chosen to model the plant with the controlling software within the action system formalism. Our approach to embed safety analysis within the system development was based on using the refinement calculus associated with action systems. The creation of the system specification was carried out in the stepwise manner: each refinement step incorporated information supplied by the corresponding level of the fault tree. Our example on the heater controller in Section 5 confirmed that the stepwise program refinement can naturally proceed hand-in-hand with the safety analysis. Observe also, the benefits of such an incorporation: the final form of the action modelling failures correctly prioritises the failures according to their criticality by the construction. A more elaborate case study on the approach is given in an accompanying paper [15] where we design a mine pump control system.

Further refinement steps are concentrated on the introduction of detailed specification of each identified hazard as illustrated in Section 5. Observe that applying the results of Theorem 5 we obtain a possibility to reason about each hazard in context of its own class. The reasoning structured in this way ensures a correct prioritising of failures causing hazards of different criticality. Therefore, when applying the techniques from Section 4 to elaborate on each of the identified hazards we do not only preserve the structure of the corresponding fault trees, but also the criticality of faults constituting the hazards from different classes.

Even though we in this paper concentrated on safety analysis and faulty behaviour of a system, the system itself is developed in a modular fashion, concentrating first on the normal behaviour of the system stating both the plant and the controller requirements within a single framework. Thereafter the different failure mechanisms are incorporated into the specification. Hence, we can separate the concerns, concentrate on parts of the system separately as well as use and state assumptions about the physical plant itself. This is an approach traditionally advocated by action systems [3, 10]. We as well as other researchers [7] argue that only such an approach makes a formal analysis of a system feasible, easily adjustable and less redundant.

Acknowledgements. The work reported here was supported by the Academy of Finland. The authors are grateful to the anonymous referees for their comments on the paper.

References

[1] R. J. R. Back and K. Sere. From modular systems to action systems. Proc. of *Formal Methods Europe'94*, Spain, October 1994. *Lecture Notes in Computer Science*. Springer–Verlag, 1994.

[2] R. J. R.Back and J. von Wright. Trace Refinement of Action Systems. In Proc. of *CONCUR-94*, Sweden, August 1994. *Lecture Notes in Computer Science*. Springer–Verlag, 1994.

[3] M. Butler, E. Sekerinski, and K. Sere. An Action System Approach to the Steam Boiler Problem. In Jean-Raymond Abrial, Egon Borger and Hans Langmaack, editors, *Formal Methods for Industrial Applications: Specifying and Programming the Steam Boiler Control*, Lecture Notes in Computer Science Vol. 1165. Springer-Verlag, 1996.

[4] E.W. Dijkstra. A Discipline of Programming. Prentice Hall International, Englewood Cliffs, N.J., 1976.

[5] K.M. Hansen, A. P. Ravn and V. Stavridou. From Safety Analysis to Software Requirements. In *IEEE Transactions on Software Engineering*, Vol.24, No.7, July 1998

[6] N.G. Leveson. Safeware: System Safety and Computers, Addison-Wesley, 1995.

[7] N.G. Leveson, M.P.E. Heimdahl, H. Hildreth, and J.D. Reese. Requirements Specification for Process-Control Systems. In *IEEE Transactions on Software Engineering*, 1994.

[8] Z. Liu and M. Joseph. Transformations of programs for fault-tolerance. In *Formal Aspects of Computing*, Vol 4, No. 5 1992, pp. 442-469

[9] A. McIver, C.C. Morgan and E. Troubitsyna. The probabilistic steam boiler: a case study in probabilistic data refinement. In *Proc. of IRW/FMP'98*, Australia, 1998.

[10] E. Sekerinski and K. Sere (Eds.). Program Development by Refinement - Case Studies Using the B Method. Springer Verlag 1998.

[11] E. Sekerinski and K. Sere. A Theory of Prioritizing Composition . The Computer Journal, VOL. 39, No 8, pp. 701-712. The British Computer Society. Oxford University Press.

[12] K. Sere and E. Troubitsyna. Hazard Analysis in Formal Specification. In *Proc. of SAFECOMP'99*, France, 1999. To appear.

[13] N. Storey. Safety-critical computer systems. Addison-Wesley, 1996.

[14] E. Troubitsyna. Refining for Safety. TUCS Technical Report No.237, February 1999.

[15] E. Troubitsyna. Specifying Safety-Related Hazards Formally. In *Proc. of ISSC'99*, USA, 1999. To appear.

[16] K. Wong and J. Joyce. Refinement of Safety-Related Hazards into Verifiable Code Assertions. in *Proceedings of SAFECOMP'98,*, Heidelberg, Germany, October, 1998.

Formal Specification and Validation of a Vital Communication Protocol*

A. Cimatti[1], P.L. Pieraccini[2], R. Sebastiani[1], P. Traverso[1], and A. Villafiorita[1]

[1] ITC-IRST, Via Sommarive 18, 38055 Povo, Trento, Italy
{cimatti,leaf,rseba,adolfo}@irst.itc.it
[2] Ansaldo Segnalamento Ferroviario, Via dei Pescatori 35, Genova, Italy
pieraccini@ansaldo.it

Abstract. Formal methods have a great potential of application as powerful specification and early debugging methods in the development of industrial systems. In certain application fields, formal methods are even becoming part of standards. However, the application of formal methods in the development of industrial products is by no means trivial. Indeed, formal methods can be costly, slow down the process of development, and require changes on the development cycle, and training. This paper describes a project developed by Ansaldo Segnalamento Ferroviario with the collaboration of IRST. Formal methods have been successfully applied to the development of an industrial communication protocol for distributed, safety critical systems. The project used a formal language to specify the protocol, and model checking techniques to validate the model.

1 Introduction

Formal methods have a great potential of application as powerful specification and early debugging methods in the development of industrial systems [2]. In certain application fields, formal methods are even becoming part of standards [1, 4]. However, the application of formal methods in the development of industrial products is by no means trivial. Indeed, formal methods can be costly, slow down the process of development, and require changes on the development cycle, and training.

This paper describes a project developed by Ansaldo Segnalamento Ferroviario (Asf) with the collaboration of IRST, where formal methods have been successfully applied to the development of an industrial communication protocol, called Safety Layer. The Safety Layer is used to present to safety-critical applicative software point-to-point, dependable channels, implemented over a double field bus. The design of such a protocol is a very complex task. A previous implementation, developed without the assistance of formal methods, required an expensive activity of debugging on the field, and was difficult to maintain

---

* The work described in this paper was founded under contracts 1607/249958(NA) and 4508/324731(GE).

J. Wing, J. Woodcock, J. Davies (Eds.): FM'99, Vol. II, LNCS 1709, pp. 1584–1604, 1999.
© Springer-Verlag Berlin Heidelberg 1999

and extend. On the other hand, the protocol was chosen (for its good qualities in safety and dependability) as the communication basis of several computer-based, distributed safety-critical products under development in ASF. Formal methods were thus applied to develop a high-quality product. The goal of the project described in this paper was to produce and validate a detailed design specification of the Safety Layer, which could be used as a basis for newly developed, well documented and highly maintainable software. Besides the technical difficulties, the project was subject to strict timing constraints. Furthermore, it was necessary to make the specification easily understandable also by software developers which were not expert in formal methods. Finally, the specification had to be as simple as possible to allow for a clean implementation.

The project started from informal requirements of previous implementations, from informal descriptions and from the knowledge internal to the company. During the project, the protocol was completely redesigned and formally specified and validated. The activity was carried out with OBJECTGEODE [10], a tool for the formal development of concurrent systems. The SDL [6] graphical specification language was used to provide an operational specification of the protocol. The model checker of OBJECTGEODE was heavily used to interactively simulate and exhaustively analyze the protocol. Several anomalous behaviors and incompletenesses in intermediate versions of the specifications were detected by simulation, and conveniently displayed in form of (automatically generated) Message Sequence Charts (MSC's) [7].

The final document specifying the Safety Layer [3] combines the formal model with informal explanations and annotations. It is currently being used as the basis for the implementation, and will be used as the basis for the interface specification of a stand-alone product. The executable formal model will be available for the analysis of possible modifications, and for the generation of the test cases.

This paper is structured as follows. In section 2 we describe the Safety Layer protocol. In section 3 we outline the project requirements, phases, and methodology. In section 4 we describe the specification of the Safety Layer, highlighting the technical details and the interaction of informal and formal specification. In section 5 we discuss the process of formal validation. Finally, in section 6 we discuss the impact of the project and we draw some conclusions.

2   Informal Description of the Safety Layer

The Safety Layer is a communication protocol intended to provide reliable communication for distributed safety critical systems, e.g. Automatic Train Control systems, track-to-train communication systems, interlocking systems. Typically, such systems are based on several computing stations connected via field bus.

The Safety Layer provides applicative programs (running on different units) with point to point communication channels. Figure 1 depicts applicative programs A, B and C, running on different units, connected by point-to-point bidirectional channels AB and BC. Such channels are protected against data

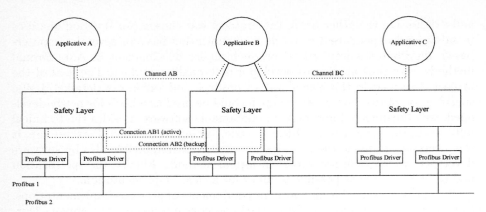

Fig. 1. The Safety Layer

corruption and out-of-order reception by means of CRC (Cyclic Redundancy Checksum) protection, authentication mechanisms, sequence numbering and final shutdown in presence of repeated errors. The interface to the application program is extremely simple, i.e. only send and receive primitives are available. The Safety Layer is configured off-line, i.e. the applicative-level channels are fixed at design time.

Besides guaranteeing the *safety* of communication channels to the applicative programs, the role of the Safety Layer is to enhance *dependability*, i.e. to make the channels available for the applicative programs as much as possible. Therefore, each unit running the Safety Layer is connected to two independent field buses. The PROFIBUS [8] drivers provide the Safety Layer with connection-oriented communication primitives. The role of the Safety Layer is to hide this redundancy from the application program, which only can see a reliable communication channel. The Safety Layer tries to maintain two connections, one per PROFIBUS, for each point-to-point channel to the application level. In Figure 1, the channel AB between applicatives A and B is realized through the two connections AB1 and AB2. In the case of nominal behavior of the protocol, one connection is active, through which data can be transmitted, while the other is in standby. (Notationally, the former is called the *active* connection, while the latter is called the *backup* connection.) Even when no data is transmitted, a minimum rate of transmission is guaranteed on both connections, by means of special control telegrams, called connection monitoring. This mechanism is used to reduce the time needed to detect problems, such as disturbance on the bus, or malfunctioning of hardware components. Such problems may be revealed by messages with corrupted CRC or out-of-order sequence numbers, or by time-outs.

When a problem arises on the backup bus, the backup connection is reset, and the reconnection procedure is retried. The active connection is not affected. The protocol can thus work properly in a degraded mode, when only one connection is available, but this is completely hidden to the applicative program.

If a problem arises on the active connection, and the backup connection is working properly, then the *switch-over* procedure is undertaken. The switch-over is a distinguishing mechanism of the protocol. When a switch-over occurs, the backup connection becomes active, and will be used to transmit applicative data, while the (previously) active connection is reset and restarted in standby.

3   The Project

The Safety Layer is a very complicated protocol. A previous implementation had been built with traditional software development methods, for a particular redunded architecture. This activity had been troublesome, and had resulted in high costs in development and maintainability.

3.1   Requirements

The Safety Layer protocol, presented in previous section, is the basis for several computer-based, distributed safety-critical products under development in ASF. The main requirement of the project was to provide a detailed, operational specification of the Safety Layer, describing the state machines realizing the protocol. This specification is a direct input to the implementation of the protocol, and the state variables specified in the model are to be implemented exactly as specified. This direct link between specification and implementation was required to enhance the maintainability of the protocol, and its reusability in subsequent applications. Furthermore, the specification should consider as legal the behaviors generated by the previous implementation of the Safety Layer. Finally, it was required that the time for the specification of the Safety Layer should not be too long, in order not to delay the implementation and thus impact on the projects where the Safety Layer had to be used.

3.2   Phases

The project was carried out in 10 months, along the following stages. First, an analysis of the protocol requirements was carried out. This task was particularly heavy, due to the large incompleteness in the documentation of the first implementation, and its dependence on the hardware architecture. As a result of this phase, a distinction was carried out between the aspects which should be formally analyzed, and the ones which were clear enough to be informally specified. Then, a preliminary model was developed, where the PROFIBUS was assumed not to corrupt but only lose data, i.e. transmission errors were not taken into account. In this stage, a crucial design choice was taken to structure the Safety Layer by introducing an intermediate level. This choice allowed to partition the complexity of the design problem, and resulted in a much clearer and manageable design. In the final stage, the protocol specification was extended to take into account the details of the transmission error. This phase required a substantial complication of (some of) the state machines. However, the modification to be applied to the model generated in the previous phase were uniform, and thus simple to realize.

3.3   Methodology

The methodology applied in this project was heavily based on formal methods. The OBJECTGEODE tool was thoroughly applied in the project. OBJECT-GEODE is a commercial tool for the development of real-time distributed systems, based on formal methods. It allows to specify the system to be analyzed by means of SDL. A translator from StateCharts to SDL allows to obtain skeletons for SDL programs from high-level description of state machines. Requirements can be expressed by means of MSC's, or via observer automata expressed in a programming language. An explicit state model checker is directly connected to the SDL, and allows to exhaustively analyze finite state systems.

In this project, StateCharts were used to provide high level, pictorial representation of the finite state machines realizing the protocol. SDL was used to provide a precise, executable specification of the machines. The OBJECTGEODE model checker was applied to reduce the development time, by pointing out a large number of problems in intermediate versions of the design. MSC were generated via simulation to provide an easy-to-understand description of behaviors.

4   Formal Specification of the Safety Layer

The design specifications were produced in form of an SDL model. An SDL model of a system is described by a hierarchy of diagrams. In the top diagram (*interconnection diagram*) the system is decomposed into building *blocks*; each block is connected to other blocks and to the environment by *channels*; channels and blocks are interfaced by *gates*; each SDL channel is labeled by a couple of *message lists*, which describe the sets of messages which can be sent in the two directions. In a lower level of interconnection diagrams, each block is decomposed into a set of *processes*, which are interconnected by *routes*. In the further lower level of the hierarchy, each process is exploded into a set of *transition diagrams*, which represents (the SDL code of) the state machine of the process. This code can be executed by the OBJECTGEODE simulator.

4.1   Safety Layer = CM + 2 · SL

The Safety Layer allows in principle to handle several channels to different units. For instance, channels AB and BC are handled by the central Safety Layer block in Figure 1. However, since there are no interactions between different channels on the same Safety Layer, it is possible to consider only the problem of specifying the management of a single channel. This means to "fill" a box with a port to the applicative program, and two ports to the PROFIBUS drivers. The internal

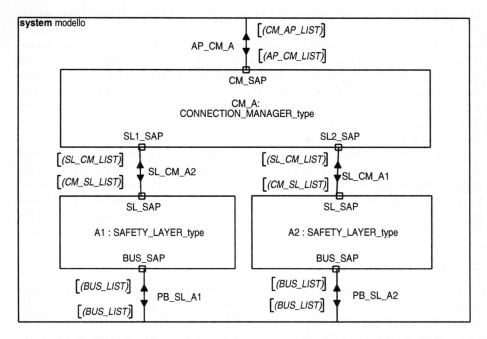

Fig. 2. The SDL diagram of the model of the Safety Layer.

structure of such box is presented in Figure 2, in the form of SDL interconnection diagram.

The system is decomposed into three blocks: an upper block "Connection Manager" (CM) CM_A and two lower identical blocks "Safety Layer" (SL) A1 and A2. (For compatibility with the notation used in other ASF documents, the expression "Safety Layer" has been used to denote both the whole system and the lower blocks; to avoid ambiguities, from now on we will denote the latter ones simply by "SL".) CM_A communicates with the application by means of channel AP_CM_A through gate CM_SAP, exchanging in the two directions messages belonging to CM_AP_LIST and CM_AP_LIST respectively. CM_A also communicates with the two SL's A1, A2 by means of channels SL_CM_A1, SL_CM_A1 through gates SL1_SAP, SL1_SAP, exchanging messages belonging to CM_AP_LIST and CM_AP_LIST. A1 (resp. A2) communicates with its own PROFIBUS driver by means of channel PB_SL_A1 (resp. PB_SL_A2) through gate BUS_SAP, exchanging messages belonging to BUS_LIST.

The idea is thus to hierarchically decompose the protocol in three components. The rationale behind the decomposition is that each SL machine is able to handle a single connection, and is not even aware of the existence of the other SL machine. The CM is not aware of the details of the status of the SL machines. On the other hand, the CM has a clear view of the redundancy of the channel, and enforces control on the SL machines according to the events which are signaled by them.

In this way, it was possible to specify independently the SL and CM machines. This allowed to partition the specification problem, and make it possible to contain the number of states in each machine. The model checker was invaluable in the task of pointing out the bad interactions between them. Furthermore, the blocks A1 and A2 are implemented as two instances of the same process type. This means that the resulting system is conceptually simpler, the code can be heavily factored, and thus it is easier to maintain.

Finally, the SL and CM machines are asynchronously composed in the final system. This is a precise design choice of the model. Once the protocol is validated without constraints on the order of execution of its component machines, it is possible to choose, in the implementation phase, any possible algorithm of activation of the SL and CM machines. The model has been designed to reduce as much as possible the unnecessary constraints on the implementation level.

4.2   Overview of the CM Machine

The executable SDL model of the machines was integrated with a set of high level, abstract StateCharts, which were used as a graphical roadmap for the specification. Figure 3 represents (a simplified view of) the CM machine. The name of each state is in the form `<s1>A_<s2>R`, where `<s1>` represents the state of the active connection and `<s2>` represents the state of the backup one. A couple of pointers keep track of which is the active SL and which is the backup one. The states are grouped into three distinct macro-states, each representing an operating mode of the channel.

Non-operative. It involves the states `IdleA_IdleR`, `SyncA_IdleR` (synchronization of the active connection), `StartA_IdleR`, `WcA_IdleR` (setup of the active connection), `IdleA_WsoR` and `WdisA_WsoR` (switch-over). No connection is currently set; the two stations cannot exchange data; the CM tries to setup the active connection.

Operative (without backup). It involves the states `DataA_IdleR`, `DataA_SyncR` (synchronization of the backup connection), `DataA_StartR` and `dataA_WcR` (setup of the backup connection). Only the active connection is set; the CM tries to set up also the backup connection. The two stations can exchange data along the active connection; if no data telegram is to be sent, the active connection is monitored by sending connection monitoring (CM) telegrams. If the active connection is dropped, the channel becomes non-operative, as there is no backup connection.

Operative (with backup). It involves only the state `DataA_StandbyR`. Both the active and backup connection are set. The two stations can exchange data along the active connection; if no data are to be sent, the active connection is monitored by sending connection monitoring (CM) telegrams; the backup connection is also periodically monitored by sending CM telegrams. If the active connection is dropped, the backup connection becomes active (switch-over) and the channel keeps operative (without backup).

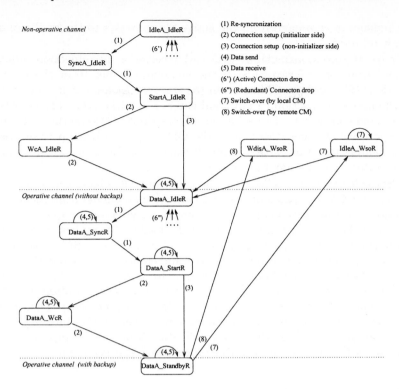

Fig. 3. A simplified view of the CM machine.

The transitions are grouped into eight main functionalities:

(1) Re-synchronization of the active (resp. backup) connection. From the initial state IdleA_IdleR (resp. DataA_IdleR), before starting the setup of the active (resp. backup) connection, the CM enters the state SyncA_IdleR (resp. DataA_SyncR) where it waits for a fixed amount of time. During this period all the commands coming from both connections (resp. from the backup connection) are discharged. This removes all the information related to the previous connection and leaves enough time to the remote station to detect the disconnection and to drop the connection too. After the re-synchronization period, the CM enters the state StartA_IdleR (resp. DataA_StartR).

(2,3) Connection Setup These transitions allow the CM to set up new connections. The modalities depend on the CM (whether it is initializer or not), and on the connection (whether it is to be active or backup).

(4,5) Data send and receive. The CM is in one of the operative channel states (DataA_XxxxR) When it receives a data slot to send from the application, it sends a data command to the active SL and waits. When the CM receives the data confirm command, it provides a confirmation to the application. When it receives a data indication command from the active SL, it passes to the application the data slot received.

(6) Drop of one connection. The CM receives a disconnection indication command from one of two SL's. If the command comes from the active SL (Transitions (6')) and the CM is not in the state DataA_StandbyR, then the CM drops the active connection (if any) and enters the initial state IdleA_IdleR. If the command comes from the backup SL (Transitions (6")) and the CM is in one of the operative channel states, then the CM drops the backup connection (if any) and enters the state DataA_IdleR; if the CM is not in one of the operative channel states, the command is ignored.

(7,8) Switch-over. The CM is in DataA_StandbyR (channel operative with backup). If the CM receives a disconnect indication command from the active SL (Transitions 7), then it sends to the backup SL a switch-over request command and waits in the state IdleA_WsoR. When the backup SL replies with a switch-over confirm command, the CM swaps the roles of the two SL's —so that the former backup connection becomes active— and enters the state DataA_IdleR. In the state IdleA_WsoR the CM may also receive from the backup SL a switch-over indication command; this happens whenever also the other station detects the disconnection and initiates the switch-over (double switch-over). Then the CM replies with a switch-over response command, remaining in the state IdleA_WsoR. The CM can also receive a switch-over indication from the backup SL, in which case activates the suitable switch-over procedure (Transitions 8).

4.3   Overview of the SL Machine

Figure 4 represents (a simplified view of) each SL machine. The transitions are grouped into eight main functionalities:

(1) Connection setup (initializer side). The SL is in the state IDLE (non connected). When it receives from its CM a connection request command — indicating the role of the connection: active or backup— it sends via PROFIBUS a telegram CR (connection request) and waits for a reply in the state WFCC. When it receives back the telegram CC (connection confirm), it sends via PROFIBUS a telegram A1 (authentication) and waits for a reply in the state WFA2. When it receives back the telegram A2 (authentication acknowledge) it performs an authentication test: if everything is correct, the connection is setup, and the SL enters the state DATA (active) or STANDBY (backup) depending to the role assigned.

(2) Connection setup (non-initializer side). The SL is in the state IDLE (non connected). When it receives via PROFIBUS a telegram CR, it replies with a telegram CC and waits in the state WFA1. When it receives via PROFIBUS a telegram A1, it replies with a telegram CC and waits in the state WFA1. When it receives back the telegram A1 it performs an authentication test: if everything is correct, it informs its own CM by a connection indication command and waits in the state WFC_RESP. When it receives back a connection response confirm — indicating the role of the connection: active or backup— it sends via PROFIBUS

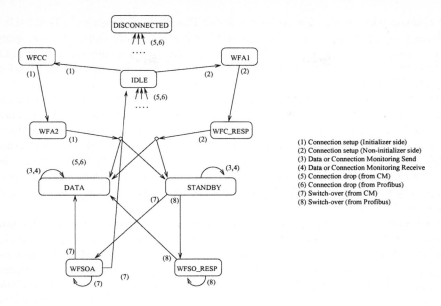

Fig. 4. A simplified view of the SL machine.

the telegram A2. The connection is setup, and the SL enters the state DATA (active) or STANDBY (backup) depending to the role assigned.

(3) Data and Connection Monitoring send. In case of active connection, the SL handles each send data request command received from its CM by sending a data telegram (DT) via PROFIBUS containing the data received; the acknowledge received from the PROFIBUS is passed to the CM by a data confirm command; when there is no data to be sent within a certain time slot, the SL sends a connection monitoring telegram (CM). In case of backup connection, the SL sends CM telegrams at fixed intervals.

(4) Data and Connection Monitoring receive. In case of active connection, the SL handles each data telegram DT received via PROFIBUS by sending to the CM a data send confirm command containing the data received; moreover, the SL monitors the receipt of at least one DT or CM every time slot. In case of backup connection, the SL just monitors the receipt of at least one CM every time slot. In both cases, if the connection monitoring test fails, the connection is dropped.

(5) Connection drop (from CM) The SL may receive from its CM a disconnect request command. If so, the SL drops the connection. Depending on some information contained in the command and on the current state, the SL can enter either the state IDLE (temporary disconnection: another connection can be setup) or the state DISCONNECTED (permanent disconnection: no new connection is possible); it can either send via PROFIBUS a disconnect telegram (DI) or not; it can either acknowledge the disconnection by a disconnection indication command or not.

(6) Connection drop (from PROFIBUS) The SL may receive via PROFIBUS a disconnect telegram DI. If so, the SL drops the connection. Depending on some information contained in the telegram, the SL can enter either the states IDLE or DISCONNECTED; it can either inform the CM by a disconnection indication command or not.

(7) Switch-over (from CM). The SL is in the state STANDBY (backup connection). If it receives from the CM a switch-over request command then it sends via PROFIBUS a switch-over indication telegram (SOI) and waits for a reply in the state WFSOA. When it receives back a switch-over acknowledgment telegram (SOA), it informs the CM with a switch-over confirm command and enters the state DATA: the new active connection is set. In the state WFSOA the SL may also receive via PROFIBUS a SOI telegram (double switch-over). If so, the SL simply replies with a SOA telegram, remaining in the state WFSOA.

(8) Switch-over (from PROFIBUS). The SL is in the state STANDBY (backup connection). If it receives via PROFIBUS a switch-over indication telegram (SOI), then it informs its CM with a switch-over indication command and waits for a reply in the state WFSO_RESP. When it receives back a switch-over response command, it sends via PROFIBUS a switch-over acknowledgment telegram (SOA) and enters the state DATA. In the state WFSO_RESP the SL handles the situations of double switch-over; if it receives from the CM a switch-over request command, then it sends via PROFIBUS a switch-over indication telegram (SOI) and remains in WFSO_RESP; if it receives back a switch-over acknowledgment telegram (SOA), it informs the CM with a switch-over confirm command, and remains in WFSO_RESP; the same happens if the SL is already in the state DATA.

The telegrams CR, CC, A1 and SOI are acknowledged by the receipt of the telegrams CC, A1, A2 and SOA respectively: if one telegram is not acknowledged within a certain time slot, the connection is dropped.

In order to send telegram to the partner station, each SL uses the PROFIBUS service "Send Data with Acknowledgment" [8], which provides a positive (resp. negative) acknowledgment whenever the telegram sent is successfully delivered (resp. is not delivered) to the remote SL. Thus, each time a SL sends a telegram via PROFIBUS, it waits for the acknowledgment in a proper intermediate state: if the acknowledgment is positive, the remaining part of the transition is processed, otherwise the connection is dropped. Notice that the intermediate states can not be interleaved: when the SL is in a intermediate state, any event incoming is temporarily saved and its processing is postponed to the next state. This corresponds to consider the "send with acknowledge" phase as an atomic operation. (Notationally, the positive and negative acknowledgment are denoted by pb_ack and pb_nak respectively; the intermediate states are called *acknowledgment states*, and are denoted by the suffix "_ACK"; the states represented in Figure 4 are called instead the *main states*.)

4.4   An Example of Transition Diagram

To provide an example of an SDL process diagram, in Figure 5 we report the SDL description of the functionality (8) of the SL "Switch-over from PROFIBUS".

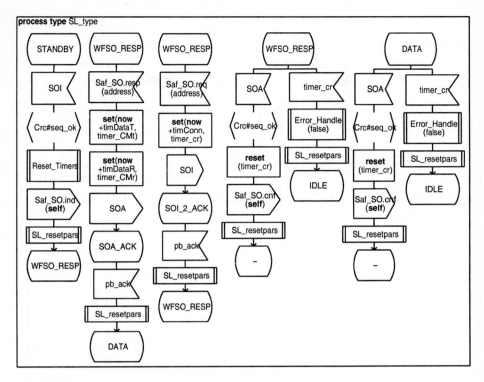

Fig. 5. An example of the SDL specification of SL transitions: (8) Switch-over from PROFIBUS.

(Notationally, as it is standard practice in protocol theory [9], the service primitives of the protocols —called "commands" here— have been classified into *request* (.req), *indication* (.ind), *response* (.resp) and *confirm* (.cnf) commands. The SDL notation is rather intuitive and will be clear in the description below.) By "the SL receives correctly a telegram" we will mean that the SL receives a telegram, it tests both the CRC and the sequence number of the telegram and the result is positive (condition Crc#seq_ok); by "the SL sends correctly a telegram" we will mean that the SL sends the telegram and waits in a proper acknowledgment state "_ACK" until it receives a pb_ack. (The unsuccessful send and receipt of telegrams are described in other diagrams.) The procedure call SL_resetpars at the end of the transitions resets the values of the fields of input telegrams and commands; it will be ignored in the description. A state labeled with "–" means "the previous state". The timers timer_CMt, timer_CMr and timer_cr check respectively the connection monitoring —transmission and reception— and the acknowledgment of the telegrams CR, CC, A1 and SOI, as described above.

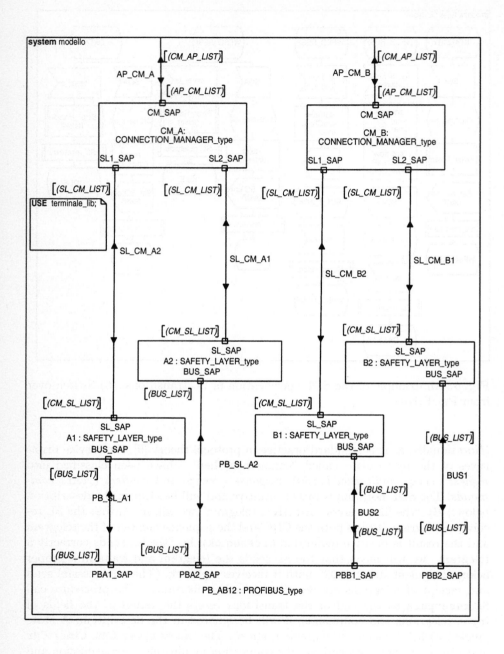

Fig. 6. The SDL interconnection diagram of the simulated model.

The transitions represented in Figure 5 can be described as follows:

1. The SL is in the state STANDBY (backup connection) and receives correctly via PROFIBUS a switch-over indication telegram SOI. Thus it resets all timers (procedure call Reset_Timers), it sends to the CM a switch-over indication command Saf_SO.ind and waits for a reply in the state WFSO_RESP.

2. When the CM replies with a switch-over response command Saf_SO.resp, the SL sets the timers timer_CMt and timer_CMr to some proper values, sends successfully via PROFIBUS a switch-over acknowledgment telegram SOA and enters the state DATA. (The new active connection is now set, so that the SL can send and receive data and connection monitoring telegrams.)

3. It may be the case that, in the state WFSO_RESP, the SL receives from the CM a switch-over request command Saf_SO.resp (double switch-over). If so, the SL sets timer_cr to a proper value, it sends successfully the switch-over indication telegram SOI waiting in WFSO_RESP both the switch-over response command from the CM and the telegram SOA from the remote SL.

4. The SL can receive via PROFIBUS a telegram SOA in the state WFSO_RESP. (This happens in case of double switch-over, if the telegram SOA is received before the command Saf_SO.resp.) If so, it simply sends to the CM a switch-over indication command Saf_SO.ind and remains in the same state. If timer_cr triggers before the reception of the telegram SOA, the SL considers it as an error, invokes the procedure Error_handle and drops the connection, entering the state IDLE.

5. The SL can receive via PROFIBUS a telegram SOA also in the state DATA. (This happens in case of double switch-over, if the telegram SOA is received after the command Saf_SO.resp.) If so, the SL behaves exactly as in the previous situation.

5   Formal Validation

During the project, interactive and exhaustive simulations were performed on the model configured as depicted in Figure 6. (In this model each block is built by one single process; thus from now on we will use the words "block" and "process" as synonyms.) The model represents a point-to-point channel AB between two partner stations A and B. The station A consists on a CM block CM_A and two SL blocks A1 and A2; the station B consists on a CM block CM_B and two SL blocks B1 and B2. (The names of the gates and of the message lists are analogous to the ones in Figure 2.) A1 and B1 (resp. A2 and B2) exchange telegrams through the connection AB1 (resp. AB2), which they setup and monitor. A1 and A2 exchange telegrams with B1 and B2 respectively by means of a block PB_AB12 representing the PROFIBUS layer. PB_AB12 is a non-deterministic process: when one of the SL process sends a telegram, PB_AB12 can either send the telegram to the partner SL process and return pb_ack to the source SL, or return pb_nak to the source SL without sending the telegram to the partner SL.

The development and validation of the model has been a cyclic process: at each cycle the model was simulated by running the simulator/model checker of

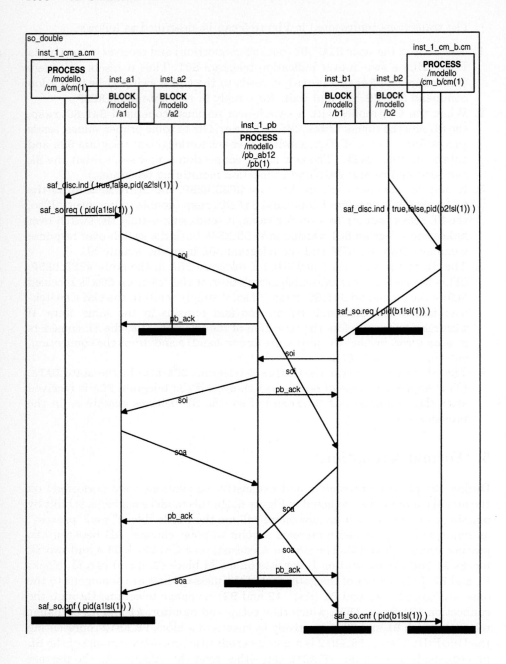

Fig. 7. The MSC of the double switch-over.

OBJECTGEODE in both interactive and exhaustive mode; the errors or anomalous behaviors revealed were traced by means of MSC's and analyzed; then a new version of the model was produced which included the modifications suggested by the analysis. All simulations have been performed on a SUN SPARC10 workstation with 128MB RAM.

5.1 Interactive Simulation

The first step of every simulation cycle was to run the simulator in interactive mode, in order to verify by hand the nominal behavior of the system and some typical scenarios. For instance, we have simulated interactively standard situations like setup of both active and backup connection, data and connection monitoring exchange, drop of active and/or backup connection, single and double switch-over, plus some scenarios of typical error handling (CRC errors, PROFIBUS errors, channel delays, etc.). The corresponding MSC's have been produced and analyzed.

As an example, the MSC so_double of Figure 7 describes the execution of a scenario of double switch-over. The MSC notation is rather intuitive: the vertical lines represent, from left to right, the seven blocks/processes CM_A, A1, A2, PB_AB12, B1, B2 and CM_B; the arrows represent the messages exchanged. The MSC has been obtained by simulating interactively the final version of the model. At the starting point, the channel is operative with backup, AB2 is the active connection and AB1 the backup one, so that CM_A, CM_B are in DataA_StandbyR, A2, B2 are in DATA and A1, B1 are in STANDBY. (In the following description all telegrams are sent with success, so that we omit to mention the pb_ack messages; we also omit the description of the values of the fields of the commands and telegrams because they are not relevant in this context.) Each active SL A2 and B2 reveals a problem on the active connection (e.g., a failed connection monitoring). Then it informs its own CM with a disconnection indication command Saf_DISC.ind. Each CM starts the switch-over phase by sending a switch-over request command Saf_SO.req to its own backup SL. The latter sends via PROFIBUS a switch-over indication telegram SOI and waits for the switch-over acknowledge telegram SOA. Instead it receives first the SOI telegram from the other SL (double switch-over) and simply replies with a SOA. When it finally receives the SOA, it informs its own CM by a switch-over confirm command saf_SO.cnf. Then each CM swaps the roles of its SL's. The connection AB1 is now the active one, and the CM can start the setup of the backup connection AB2.

5.2 Model Checking

The second step of every simulation cycle was to run the simulator in exhaustive mode (model checking). This was a very effective form of *early debugging* for the system, as the model checker found automatically a large number of errors or unexpected behaviors. Furthermore, most of these problems were of such a complicate nature to be nearly impossible for a human analyst to conceive.

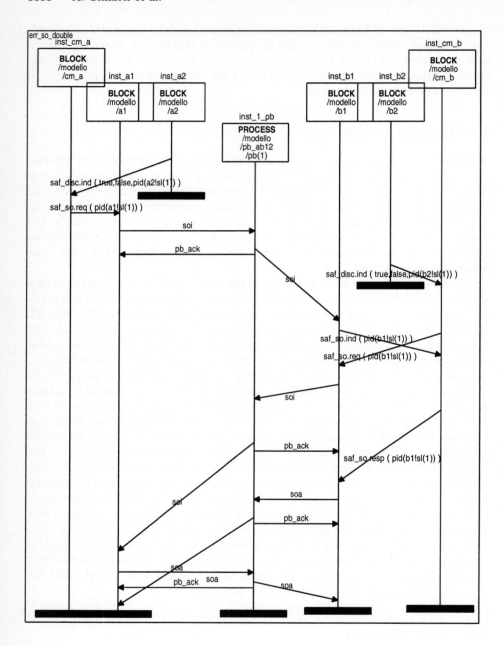

Fig. 8. The MSC of an error occurred during a double switch-over (revealed in an intermediate version of the model).

During this phase, we have pervasively used most of the optional features of the simulator/model checker of OBJECTGEODE, in particular:

- different choices of search strategy. For instance, depth-first search allows for detecting strongly connected cycles, while breadth-first search allows for generating error scenarios of minimal length;
- state compression, to reduce memory occupation;
- *filtering*, to hinder the execution of some selected transitions, thus allowing for a selective analysis of the various functionalities of the model.

An Example of Early Debugging In an intermediate version of the SDL model, the last couple of transitions of the diagram in Figure 5 —input of SOA and timer_cr in the state DATA— was not there, and timer_cr was not used in WFSO_RESP. (Intuitively, this was due to the assumption —which revealed incorrect— that no switch-over telegram could ever be received by an active SL.) During an exhaustive simulation, the model checker stopped for a "false input" error: the SL B1 had received an unexpected input of a SOA telegram while it was in the state DATA.

The MSC derived from the error scenario generated is reported in the MSC of Figure 8. (The starting conditions and the assumptions are the same as for the MSC so_double of Figure 7.) The active SL A2 reveals a problem on the active connection and informs CM_A with a disconnection indication command Saf_DISC.ind. CM_A sends a switch-over request command Saf_SO.req to its own backup SL A1, which sends via PROFIBUS a switch-over indication telegram SOI to the remote SL B1. B1 informs CM_B by a switch-over indication command Saf_SO.ind, and waits for the switch-over response command Saf_SO.resp in the state WFSO_RESP (first transition of Figure 5). In the meanwhile also the SL B2 reveals a problem on the active connection and informs CM_B with a disconnection indication command Saf_DISC.ind; CM_B reacts by sending a switch-over request command Saf_SO.req to B1. B1 receives the Saf_SO.req and sends via PROFIBUS a telegram SOI to A1 (third transition of Figure 5). CM_B replies to the command Saf_SO.ind with a switch-over response command Saf_SO.resp. B1 receives it, sends via PROFIBUS a telegram SOA and enters the state DATA (second transition of Figure 5). A1 replies to the SOI with a telegram SOA. Unfortunately —as the last couple of transitions of Figure 5 is missing— B1 is not prepared to receive a telegram SOA in the state DATA. This causes an error.

Notice that the error happens because the Saf_SO.ind and the Saf_SO.req "cross" between B1 and CM_B, so that B1 receives the Saf_SO.req in between the exchange Saf_SO.ind/Saf_SO.resp. In an implemented version of the system, it is reasonable to assume that the communications between CM and SL are much faster than those via PROFIBUS, so that the probability of a similar crossing is very low. Therefore this error would have been extremely hard to detect during the testing phase of the implemented system.

Final Validation

We focus now on three very intensive exhaustive simulations we performed of the final version of the model. No transition has been filtered, so that all functionalities are analyzed. Using the state compression allowed by the model checker, we could impose a bound of $3 \cdot 10^6$ reachable states. [1] In the first two simulations the model checker was run with a breadth-first search strategy, starting from the situations "channel non operative" and "channel operative with backup" respectively; in the third simulation the model checker was run with a depth-first search strategy. Each simulation required several hours of CPU time.

The three simulations shared the following results. [2]

```
verify stopped by states limit
Number of exceptions: 0
Number of deadlocks: 0
Number of stop conditions: 0
Transitions coverage rate: 75.00 (94 transitions not covered)
States coverage rate: 100.00 (0 states not covered)
(...)
```

None of the three simulations has been able to cover the whole state space (that is, the number of reachable states is greater than $3 \cdot 10^6$). They have covered respectively 9, 10 and 13 million transitions. However, it is worth remarking that, when an error was detected in intermediate versions of the model, this was always done within up to a few thousands states analized. Since the final runs signaled no exception (dynamic error), deadlock, or stop condition (unexpected inputs, role incongruences of the SL's), the degree of confidence on the correctness of the design was considered to be rather high.

All simulations have covered the 100% of the control states and about 75% of the transitions. Furthermore, all the uncovered transitions of the CM's had been introduced to fill the matrix event/state, and were not expected to be covered:

```
from_wdisa_wsor_input_all: 0
from_idlea_wsor_input_all: 0
from_idlea_idler_synca_idler_starta_idler_wca_idler_wdisa_wsor_
idlea_wsor_input_cm_put.req: 0
from_dataa_startr_dataa_wcr_input_all: 0
from_starta_idler_wca_idler_input_all: 0
from_dataa_syncr_input_all: 0
from_dataa_idler_input_all: 0
from_idlea_idler_input_all: 0
(...)
```

(The SL's filtered the unexpected telegrams and thus they did not send anomalous commands to their CM.)

---

[1] Empirically, $3 \cdot 10^6$ was the biggest number of states we could handle with 128M RAM.

[2] The simulator's outputs have been slightly reformatted in order to fit into the page frame.

The explosion of the state space was to be expected: industrial systems tend to explode. Although several tricks were used to contain the state explosion — like, e.g., filtering and state compression— it was impossible to complete the exploration because the model is actually infinite state in principle. This is due to the fact that no rigid synchronization is imposed on the blocks of the system, and that the length of the queues is not limited. Another fancier model checker (e.g., SPIN [5]) could be applied with profit. In particular, the partial order reduction appear to be particularly promising in case of asynchronous composition of processes in the same site.

6   Conclusions

In this paper we presented an application of formal methods to the design of a complex communication protocol for distributed, safety critical systems. During the project, the protocol was formally specified as composition of several finite state machines. Model checking techniques were used to automatically analyze the specifications, and pinpoint several subtle errors and unexpected behaviours in early stages of the design.

It is well known that formal methods are not a panacea, and may have drawbacks if not applied in the right way. The quantification of the costs and benefits of formal methods is not easy. For this particular project, however, it is fair to say that the application of formal methods was effective. The specification of the protocol has been judged to be of high quality, it is independent of the architecture, and imposes very weak constraints on the particular combination of the SL and CM machines, thus allowing for different architectural choices at implementation time. An informal specification of the protocol would have been hard, and its manual validation would have been nearly impossible without the support of model checking. The pay-off from the application of formal methods is also in the further availability of an executable model. This can be used for mechanically assisted test design, and provides a basis for an easy and early validation of future modifications. The impact of the use of formal methods in this project is very significant. The formal specifications are currently used to implement two different versions of the safety layer, running on two different hardware platforms.

References

[1] J. Bowen. Formal Methods in Safety-Critical Standards. Oxford University Computing Laboratory Technical Report, 1995.
[2] J. Bowen. The Industrial Take-Up of Formal Methods. Oxford University Computing Laboratory Technical Report, 1995.
[3] A. Cimatti, R. Sebastiani, and P. Traverso. Specifica formale dei protocolli Safety Layer e Connection Manager (Formal specification of the Safety Layer and Connection Manager protocols). In italian. ITC-IRST deliverable 9808-02, project Safety Critical Applications III - SCAPIII, January 1999.

[4] European Commitee for Electrotechnical Standardization. European Standard - Railway Applications: Software for Railways Control and Protection Systems. EN 50128, 1995.

[5] G.J. Holzmann. *Design and Validation of Computer Protocols.* Prentice Hall, 1991.

[6] ITU-T. *CCITT specification and description language (SDL)*, March 1993. ITU-T Recommendation Z.100.

[7] ITU-T. *Message Sequence Chart (MSC)*, October 1996. ITU-T Recommendation Z.120.

[8] Profibus Nutzerorganization. *Profibus Standard*, July 1996. DIN 19 245.

[9] A. Tanenbaum. *Computer Networks.* Prentice Hall, 1989.

[10] VERILOG. *ObjectGEODE Documentation.* Available at *www.verilogusa.com.*

Incremental Design of a Power Transformer Station Controller using a Controller Synthesis Methodology*

Hervé Marchand[1] and Mazen Samaan[2]

[1] IRISA / INRIA - Rennes,
F-35042 RENNES, France
e-mail: hmarchan@irisa.fr
[2] EDF/DER, EP, dept. CCC,
6 quai Watier, 78401 CHATOU, France
e-mail: Mazen.Samaan@der.edf.fr

Abstract. In this paper, we describe the incremental specification of a power transformer station controller using a *controller synthesis methodology*. We specify the main requirements as simple properties, named *control objectives*, that the controlled plant has to satisfy. Then, using algebraic techniques, the controller is automatically derived from these set of control objectives. In our case, the plant is specified at a high level, using the data-flow synchronous SIGNAL language and then by its logical abstraction, named polynomial dynamical system. The control objectives are specified as *invariance, reachability, attractivity* properties, as well as *partial order relations* to be checked by the plant. The control objectives equations are then synthesized using algebraic transformations.

Key-words: Discrete Event Systems, Polynomial Dynamical System, Supervisory Control Problem, SIGNAL, Power Plant.

1 Introduction & Motivations

The SIGNAL language [8] is developed for precise specification of real-time reactive systems [2]. In such systems, requirements are usually checked *a posteriori* using property verification and/or simulation techniques. Control theory of Discrete Event Systems (DES) allows to use constructive methods, that ensure, *a priori*, required properties of the system behavior. The validation phase is then reduced to properties that are not guaranteed by the programming process.

There exist different theories for control of Discrete Event Systems since the 80's [14, 1, 5, 13]. Here, we choose to specify the plant in SIGNAL and the control synthesis as well as verification are performed on a logical abstraction of this program, called a polynomial dynamical system (PDS) over $\mathbb{Z}/_{3\mathbb{Z}}$. The control

---

* This work was partially supported by Électricité de France (EDF) under contract number M64/7C8321/E5/11 and by the Esprit SYRF project 22703.

of the plant is performed by restricting the controllable input values with respect to the control objectives (logical or optimal). These restrictions are obtained by incorporating new algebraic equations into the initial system. The theory of PDS uses classical tools in algebraic geometry, such as ideals, varieties and morphisms. This theory sets the basis for the verification and the formal calculus tool, SIGALI built around the SIGNAL environment. SIGALI manipulates the system of equations instead of the sets of solutions, avoiding the enumeration of the state space. This abstract level avoids a particular choice of set implementations, such as BDDs, even if all operations are actually based on this representation for sets.

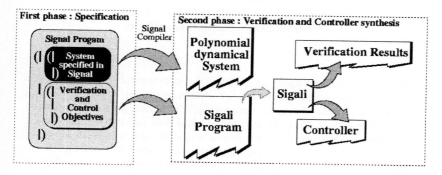

Fig. 1. Description of the tool

The methodology is the following (see Figure 1). The user first specifies in SIGNAL both the physical model and the control/verification objectives to be ensured/checked. The SIGNAL compiler translates the SIGNAL program into a PDS, and the control/verification objectives in terms of polynomial relations/operations. The controller is then synthesized using SIGALI. The result is a controller coded by a polynomial and then by a Binary Decision Diagram.

To illustrate our approach, we consider in this paper the application to the specification of the automatic control system of a power transformer station. It concerns the response to electric faults on the lines traversing it. It involves complex interactions between communicating automata, interruption and preemption behaviors, timers and timeouts, reactivity to external events, among others. The functionality of the controller is to handle the power interruption, the redirection of supply sources, and the re-establishment of the power following an interruption. The objective is twofold: the safety of material and uninterrupted best service. The safety of material can be achieved by (automatic) triggering circuit-breakers when an electric fault occurs on lines, whereas the best quality service can be achieved by minimizing the number of costumers concerned by a power cut, and re-establishment of the current as quickly as possible for the customers hit by the fault (i.e, minimizing the failure in the distribution of power in terms of duration and size of the interrupted sub-network).

2   Overview of the power transformer station

In this section, we make a brief description of the power transformer station network as well as the various requirements the controller has to handle.

2.1   The power transformer station description

Électricité de France has hundreds of high voltage networks linked to production and medium voltage networks connected to distribution. Each station consists of one or more power transformer stations to which circuit-breakers are connected. The purpose of an electric power transformer station is to lower the voltage so that it can be distributed in urban centers to end-users. The kind of transformer (see Figure 2) we consider, receives high voltage lines, and feeds several medium voltage lines to distribute power to end-users.

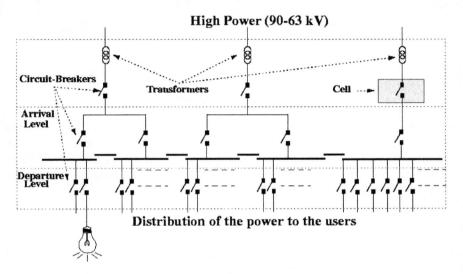

Fig. 2. The power transformer station topology.

For each high voltage line, a transformer lowers the voltage. During operation of this system, several faults can occur (three types of electric faults are considered: phase PH, homopolar H, or wattmetric W), due to causes internal or external to the station. To protect the device and the environment, several circuit breakers are placed in a network of *cells* in different parts of the station (on the arrival lines, link lines, and departure lines). These circuit breakers are informed about the possible presence of faults by sensors.

Power and Fault Propagation: We discuss here some physical properties of the power network located inside the power transformer station controller. It is obvious that the power can be seen by the different cells if and only if all the upstream circuit-breakers are closed. Consequently, if the link circuit-breaker is opened, the power is cut and no fault can be seen by the different cells of the power transformer station. The visibility of the fault by the sensors of the cells is less obvious. In fact, we have to consider two major properties:

- On one hand, if a physical fault, considered as an input of our system, is seen by the sensors of a cell, then all the downstream sensors are not able to see some physical faults. In fact, the appearance of a fault at a certain level (the departure level in Figure 3(a) for example) increases the voltage on the downstream lines and masks all the other possible faults.

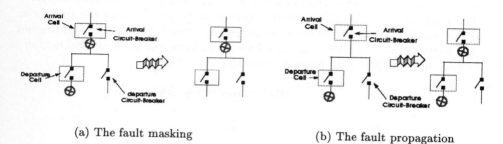

(a) The fault masking   (b) The fault propagation

Fig. 3. The Fault properties

- On the other hand, if the sensors of a cell at a given level (for example the sensors of one of the departure cells as illustrated in Figure 3(b)) are informed about the presence of a fault, then all the upstream sensors (here the sensors of the arrival cell) detect the same fault. Consequently, it is the arrival cell that handle the fault.

2.2   The controller

The controller can be divided into two parts. The first part concerns the local controllers (*i.e.*, the cells). We chose to specify each local controller in SIGNAL, because they merge logical and numerical aspects. We give here only a brief description of the behavior of the different cells (more details can be found in [12,7]). The other part concerns more general requirements to be checked by the global controller of the power transformer station. That specification will be described in the following.

The Cells: Each circuit breaker controller (or cell) defines a behavior beginning with the confirmation and identification of the type of the fault. In fact, a variety of faults are transient, i.e., they occur only for a very short time. Since their duration is so short that they do not cause any danger, the operation of the circuit-breaker is inhibited. The purpose of this confirmation phase is let the transient faults disappear spontaneously. If the fault is confirmed, the handling consists in opening the circuit-breaker during a given delay for a certain number of periods and then closing it again. The circuit-breaker is opened in consecutive cycles with an increased duration. At the end of each cycle, if the fault is still present, the circuit-breaker is reopened. Finally, in case the fault is still present at the end of the last cycle, the circuit-breaker is opened definitively, and control is given to the remote operator.

The specification of a large part of these local controllers has been performed using the SIGNAL synchronous language [12] and verified using our formal calculus system, named SIGALI [7].

Some global requirements for the controller: Even if is quite easy to specify the local controllers in SIGNAL, some other requirements are too informal, or their behaviors are too complex to be expressed directly as programs.

1. One of the most significant problems concerns the appearance of two faults (the kind of faults is not important here) at two different departure cells, at the same time. Double faults are very dangerous, because they imply high defective currents. At the place of the fault, this results in a dangerous path voltage that can electrocute people or cause heavy material damages. The detection of these double faults must be performed as fast as possible as well as the handling of one of the faults.
2. Another important aspect is to know which of the circuit breakers must be opened. If the fault appears on the departure line, it is possible to open the circuit breaker at departure level, at link level, or at arrival level. Obviously, it is in the interest of users that the circuit be broken at the departure level, and not at a higher level, so that the fewest users are deprived of power.
3. We also have to take into account the importance of the departure circuit-breaker. Assume that some departure line, involved in a double faults problem, supplies a hospital. Then, if the double faults occur, the controller should not open this circuit-breaker, since electricity must always delivered to a hospital.

The transformer station network as well as the cells are specified in SIGNAL. In order to take into account the requirements (1), (2) and (3), with the purpose of obtaining an optimal controller, we rely on automatic controller synthesis that is performed on the logical abstraction of the global system (network + cells).

3   The SIGNAL equational data flow real-time language

SIGNAL [8] is built around a minimal kernel of operators. It manipulates *signals* X, which denote unbounded series of typed values $(x_t)_{t \in T}$, indexed by time t in a time domain T. An associated clock determines the set of instants at which values are present. A particular type of signals called event is characterized only by its presence, and has always the value *true* (hence, its negation by not is always *false*). The clock of a signal X is obtained by applying the operator event X. The constructs of the language can be used in an equational style to specify the relations between signals i.e. , between their values and between their clocks. Systems of equations on signals are built using a composition construct, thus defining *processes*. Data flow applications are activities executed over a set of instants in time. At each instant, input data is acquired from the execution environment; output values are produced according to the system of equations considered as a network of operations.

3.1   The SIGNAL language.

The kernel of the SIGNAL language is based on four operations, defining primitive processes or equations, and a composition operation to build more elaborate processes in the form of systems of equations.

Functions are instantaneous transformations on the data. The definition of a signal Y_t by the function f: $\forall t$, $Y_t = f(X_{1_t}, X_{2_t}, \ldots, X_{n_t})$ is written in SIGNAL: Y := f{ X1, X2, ... , Xn}. Y, X1, ... , Xn are required to have the same clock.

Selection of a signal X according to a boolean condition C is: Y := X when C. If C is present and *true*, then Y has the presence and value of X. The clock of Y is the *intersection* of that of X and that of C at the value *true*.

Deterministic merge noted: Z := X default Y has the value of X when it is present, or otherwise that of Y if it is present and X is not. Its clock is the *union* of that of X and that of Y.

Delay gives access to past values of a signal. E.g., the equation $ZX_t = X_{t-1}$, with initial value V_0 defines a *dynamic process*. It is encoded by: ZX := X$1 with initialization ZX init V0. X and ZX have equal clocks.

Composition of processes is noted "|" (for processes P_1 and P_2, with parenthesizing: (| P_1 | P_2 |)). It consists in the composition of the systems of equations; it is associative and commutative. It can be interpreted as parallelism between processes.

The following table illustrates each of the primitives with a trace:

n	3	2	1	0	3	2	...
zn := n$ 1 init 0	0	3	2	1	0	3	...
p := zn-1	-1	2	1	0	-1	2	...
x := true when (zn=0)	t				t		
y := true when (n=0) default (not x)	f			t	f		

Derived features: Derived processes have been defined on the base of the primitive operators, providing programming comfort. E.g., the instruction X ^= Y specifies that signals X and Y are synchronous (i.e., have equal clocks); when B gives the clock of *true*-valued occurrences of B.

For a more detailed description of the language, its semantic, and applications, the reader is referred to [8]. The complete programming environment also features a block-diagram oriented graphical user interface and a proof system for dynamic properties of SIGNAL programs, called SIGALI (see Section 4).

3.2 Specification in SIGNAL of the power transformer station

The transformer station network we are considering contains four departure, two arrival and one link circuit-breakers as well as the cells that control each circuit-breaker [7]. The process Physical_Model in Figure 4 describes the power and fault propagation according to the state of the different circuit-breakers. It is composed of nine subprocesses. The process Power_Propagation describes the propagation of power according to the state of the circuit-breakers (Open/Closed). The process Fault_Visibility describes the fault propagation and visibility according to the other faults that are potentially present. The remaining seven processes encode the different circuit-breakers.

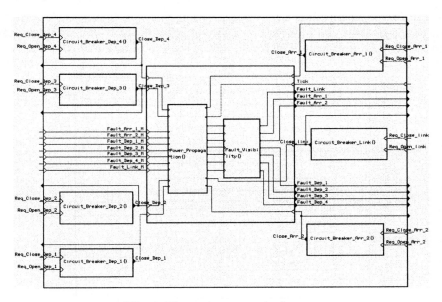

Fig. 4. The main process in SIGNAL

The inputs of this main process are booleans that encode the physical faults: Fault_Link_M, Fault_Arr_i_M (i=1,2), Fault_Dep_j_M (j =1,..,4). They encode faults that are really present on the different lines. The event inputs req_close_... and req_open_... indicate opening and closing requests of the various circuit-breakers. The outputs of the main process are the booleans Fault_Link, Fault_Arr_i, Fault_Dep_j, representing the signals that are sent to the different cells. They indicate whether a cell is faulty or not. These outputs represents the knowledge that the sensors of the different cells have.

We will now see how the subprocesses are specified in SIGNAL.

The circuit-breaker: A circuit-breaker is specified in SIGNAL as follows: The process Circuit-Breaker takes two sensors inputs: Req_Open and Req_Close. They represent opening and closing requests. The output Close represents the status of the circuit-breaker.

```
(| Close := (Req_Close default (false when Req_Open) default Z_Close
 | Z_Close := Close $1 init true
 | Close ^= Tick
 | (Req_Close when Req_Open) ^= when (not Req_Open) |)
```

Fig. 5. The Circuit-breaker in SIGNAL

The boolean Close becomes *true* when the process receives the event req_close, and *false* when it receives the event Req_open, otherwise it is equal to its last value (i.e. Close is *true* when the circuit-breaker is closed and *false* otherwise). The constraint Req_Close when Req_Open ^= when not Req_Close says that the two events Req_Close and Req_Open are exclusive.

Power Propagation: It is a filter process using the state of the circuit-breakers. Power propagation also induces a visibility of possible faults. If a circuit-breaker is open then no fault can be detected by the sensors of downstream cells.

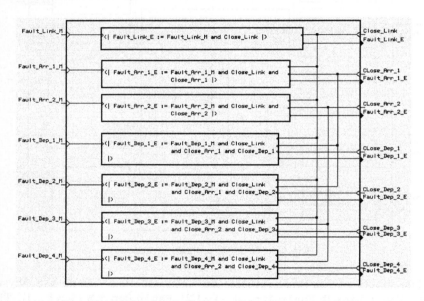

Fig. 6. specification in SIGNAL of the power propagation

This is specified in the process Power_Propagation shown in Figure 6. The inputs are booleans that code the physical faults and the status of the circuit-breakers. For example, a fault could be detected by the sensor of the departure cell 1 (i.e. Fault_Dep_1_E is *true*) if there exists a physical fault (Fault_Dep_1_M=*true*) and if the upstream circuit-breakers are closed (ie, Close_Link=*true* and Close_Arr_1=*true* and Close_Dep_1=*true*).

Fault visibility and propagation: The Fault_Visibility process in Figure 7, specifies fault visibility and propagation. As we explained in Section 2.1, a fault could be seen by the sensors of a cell only if no upstream fault is present.

```
(| Fault_Link_K := Fault_Link_E
 | Fault_Arr_1_K := (not (when Fault_Link_K)) default Fault_Arr_1_E
 | Fault_Arr_2_K := (not (when Fault_Link_K)) default Fault_Arr_2_E
 | Fault_Dep_1 := (not (when Fault_Link_K)) default (not (when Fault_Arr_1_K)) default Fault_Dep_1_E
 | Fault_Dep_2 := (not (when Fault_Link_K)) default (not (when Fault_Arr_1_K)) default Fault_Dep_2_E
 | Fault_Dep_3 := (not (when Fault_Link_K)) default (not (when Fault_Arr_2_K)) default Fault_Dep_3_E
 | Fault_Dep_4 := (not (when Fault_Link_K)) default (not (when Fault_Arr_2_K)) default Fault_Dep_4_E
 | Fault_Arr_1 := (when (Fault_Dep_1 default Fault_Dep_2)) default Fault_Arr_1_K
 | Fault_Arr_2 := (when (Fault_Dep_3 default Fault_Dep_4)) default Fault_Arr_2_K
 | Fault_Link := (when (Fault_Arr_1 default Fault_Arr_2)) default Fault_Link_K
 | Fault_Link ^= Fault_Arr_2 ^= Fault_Arr_1 ^= Fault_Dep_4 ^= Fault_Dep_3 ^= Fault_Dep_2 ^=
   Fault_Dep_1 ^= Tick
 |)
```

Fig. 7. Specification in SIGNAL of the fault propagation and visibility

For example, a fault cannot be detected by the sensor of the departure cell 1 (i.e. Fault_Dep_1 is *false*), even if a physical fault exists at this level (Fault_Dep_1_E=*true*[1]), when another physical fault exists at the link level (Fault_Link_1_K=*true*) or at the arrival level 1 (Fault_Arr_1_K=*true*). It is thus, *true* just when the departure cell 1 detects a physical fault (Fault_Dep_1_E) and no upstream fault exists. *A contrario*, if a fault is picked up by a cell, then it is also picked up by the upstream cells. This is for example the meaning of Fault_Link := (when (Fault_Arr_1 default Fault_Arr_2)) default Fault_link_K.

4   Verification of SIGNAL programs

The SIGNAL environment contains a verification and controller synthesis toolbox, SIGALI. This tool allows us to prove the correctness of the dynamical behavior of the system. The equational nature of the SIGNAL language leads to the use of polynomial dynamical equation systems (PDS) over $\mathbb{Z}/3\mathbb{Z}$, *i.e.* integers modulo 3: $\{-1,0,1\}$, as a formal model of program behavior. The theory of PDS uses classical concepts of algebraic geometry, such as ideals, varieties and comorphisms [6]. The techniques consist in manipulating the system of equations instead of the sets of solutions, which avoids enumerating state spaces.

To model its behavior, a SIGNAL process is translated into a system of polynomial equations over $\mathbb{Z}/3\mathbb{Z}$ [7]. The three possible states of a boolean signal X (*i.e.* , *present* and *true*, *present* and *false*, or *absent*) are coded in a *signal variable* x by (*present* and *true* $\to 1$, *present* and *false* $\to -1$, and *absent* $\to 0$). For the non-boolean signals, we only code the fact that the signal is *present* or *absent*: (*present* $\to 1$ and *absent* $\to 0$).

Each of the primitive processes of SIGNAL are then encoded as polynomial equations. Let us just consider the example of the *selection* operator. C := A when B means "*if* $b = 1$ *then* $c = a$ *else* $c = 0$". It can be rewritten as a polynomial equation: $c = a(-b - b^2)$. Indeed, the solutions of this equation are the set of possible behaviors of the primitive process when. For example, if the signal B is *true* (*i.e.* , b=1), then $(-b - b^2) = (-1 - 1) = 1$ in $\mathbb{Z}/3\mathbb{Z}$, which leads to $c = a$.

---

[1] Note that this fault has already be filtered. It can only be present if all the upstream circuit-breakers are closed

The delay \$, which is dynamical, is different because it requires memorizing the past value of the signal into a *state variable* x. In order to encode B := A\$1 init B0, we have to introduce the three following equations:

$$\begin{cases} x' = a + (1 - a^2)x & (1) \\ b = xa^2 & (2) \\ x_0 = b_0 & (3) \end{cases}$$

where x' is the value of the memory at the next instant. Equation (1) describes what will be the next value x' of the state variable. If a is *present*, x' is equal to a (because $(1 - a^2) = 0$), otherwise x' is equal to the last value of a, memorized by x. Equation (2) gives to b the last value of a (*i.e.* the value of x) and constrains the clocks b and a to be equal. Equation (3) corresponds to the initial value of x, which is the initial value of b.

Table 1 shows how all the primitive operators are translated into polynomial equations. Remark that for the non boolean expressions, we just translate the synchronization between the signals.

Boolean expressions	
B := not A	$b = -a$
C := A and B	$c = ab(ab - a - b - 1)$ $a^2 = b^2 = c^2$
C := A or B	$c = ab(1 - a - b - ab)$ $a^2 = b^2 = c^2$
C := A default B	$c = a + (1 - a^2)b$
C := A when B	$c = a(-b - b^2)$
B := A \$1 (init b_0)	$x' = a + (1 - a^2)x$ $b = a^2 x$ $x_0 = b_0$
non-boolean expressions	
B := $f(A_1, \ldots, A_n)$	$b^2 = a_1^2 = \cdots = a_n^2$
C := A default B	$c^2 = a^2 + b^2 - a^2 b^2$
C := A when B	$c^2 = a^2(-b - b^2)$
B := A \$1 (init b_0)	$b^2 = a^2$

Table 1. Translation of the primitive operators.

Any SIGNAL specification can be translated into a set of equations called polynomial dynamical system (PDS), that can be reorganized as follows:

$$S = \begin{cases} X' = P(X, Y) \\ Q(X, Y) = 0 \\ Q_0(X) = 0 \end{cases} \quad (1)$$

where X, Y, X' are vectors of variables in $\mathbb{Z}/3\mathbb{Z}$ and $dim(X) = dim(X')$. The components of the vectors X and X' represent the states of the system and are called *state variables*. They come from the translation of the delay operator. Y is a vector of variables in $\mathbb{Z}/3\mathbb{Z}$, called *event variables*. The first equation is the *state transition equation*; the second equation is called the *constraint equation* and specifies which events may occur in a given state; the last equation gives the initial states. The behavior of such a PDS is the following: at each instant t, given a state x_t and an admissible y_t, such that $Q(x_t, y_t) = 0$, the system evolves into state $x_{t+1} = P(x_t, y_t)$.

Verification of a SIGNAL program: We now explain how verification of a SIGNAL program (in fact, the corresponding PDS) can be carried out. Using algebraic operations, it is possible to check properties such as *invariance, reachability* and *attractivity* [7]. Note that most of them will be used in the sequel as control objectives for controller synthesis purposes. We just give here the basic definitions of each of this properties.

Definition 1.   *1. A set of states E is* **invariant** *for a dynamical system if for every x in E and every y admissible in x, $P(x, y)$ is still in E.*

2. A subset F of states is **reachable** *if and only if for every state $x \in F$ there exists a trajectory starting from the initial states that reaches x.*

3. A subset F of states is **attractive** *from a set of states E if and only if every state trajectory initialized in E reaches F.*   •

For a more complete review of the theoretical foundation of this approach, the reader may refer to [6, 7].

Specification of a property: Using an extension of the SIGNAL language, named SIGNAL+, it is possible to express the properties to be checked, as well as the control objectives to be synthesized (see section 5.2), in the SIGNAL program. The syntax is

```
(| Sigali(Verif_Objective(PROP)) |)
```

The keyword `Sigali` means that the subexpression has to be evaluated by SIGALI. The function `Verif_Objective` (it could be `invariance`, `reachability`, `attractivity`, etc) means that SIGALI has to check the corresponding property according to the boolean `PROP`, which defines a set of states in the corresponding PDS. The complete SIGNAL program is obtained composing the process specifying the plant and the one specifying the verification objectives in parallel. Thus, the compiler produces a file which contains the polynomial dynamical system resulting from the abstraction of the complete SIGNAL program and the algebraic verification objectives. This file is then interpreted by SIGALI. Suppose that, for example, we want, in a SIGNAL program named "`system`", to check the attractivity of the set of states where the boolean `PROP` is *true*. The corresponding SIGNAL+ program is then:

```
(| system() (the physical model specified in Signal)
 | PROP: definition of the boolean PROP in Signal
 | Sigali(Attractivity(True(PROP))) |)
```

The corresponding SIGALI file, obtained after compilation of the SIGNAL program, is:

```
read(''system.z3z'');  => loading of the PDS
Set_States : True(PROP); => Compute the  states where PROP is true
Attractivity(S,Set_States);
 => Check for the attractivity of Set_States from the initial states
```

The file "system.z3z" contains in a coded form the polynomial dynamical system that represents the system. Set_States is a polynomial that is equal to 0 when the boolean PROP is *true*. The methods consist in verifying that the set of states where the polynomial Set_States takes the value 0 is attractive from the initial states (the answer is then *true* or *false*): Attractivity(S, Set_States). This file is then interpreted by SIGALI that checks the verification objective.

4.1   Verification of the power transformer network

In this section, we apply the tools to check various properties of our SIGNAL implementation of the transformer station. After the translation of the SIGNAL program, we obtain a PDS with 60 state variables and 35 event variables. Note that the compiler also checks the causal and temporal concurrency of our program and produces an executable code. We will now describe some of the different properties, which have been proved.

(**1**) *"There is no possibility to have a fault at the departure, arrival and link level when the link circuit-breaker is opened."* In order to check this property, we add to the original specification the following code

```
(| Error:= ((Fault_Link or Fault_Arr_1 or Fault_Arr_1 or
        Fault_Dep_1 or Fault_Dep_2 or Fault_Dep_3 or Fault_Dep_4)
            when Open_Link)  default false
 | Error ^= Tick
 | Sigali(Reachable(True(Error))) |)
```

The Error signal is a boolean which takes the value *true* when the property is violated. In order to prove the property, we have to check that there does not exist any trajectory of the system which leads to the states where the Error signal is *true* (Reachable(True(Error))). The produced file is interpreted by SIGALI that checks whether this set of states is reachable or not. In this case, the result is *false*, which means that the boolean Error never takes the value *true*. The property is satisfied[2] . In the same way, we proved similar properties when one of the arrival or departure circuit-breakers is open.

(**2**) *"If there exists a physical fault at the link level and if this fault is picked up by its sensor then the arrival sensors can not detect a fault"*. We show here the property for the arrival cell 1. It can be expressed as an invariance of a set of states.

```
(| Error:= (Fault_Arr_1 when Fault_Link_E) default false
 | Error ^= Tick
 | Sigali(Invariance(False(Error))) |)
```

---

[2] Alternatively, this property could be also expressed as the invariance of the boolean False(Error), namely Sigali(Invariance(False(Error))).

We have proved similar properties for a departure fault as well as when a physical fault appears at the arrival level and at the departure level at the same time.

(3) We also proved using the same methods the following property: *"If a fault occurs at a departure level, then it is automatically seen by the upstream sensors when no other fault exists at a higher level."*

All the important properties of the transformer station network have been proved in this way. Note that the cell behaviors have also been proved (see [7] for more details).

5   The automatic controller synthesis methodology

5.1   Controllable polynomial dynamical system

Before speaking about control of polynomial dynamical systems, we first need to introduce a distinction between the events. From now on, we distinguish between the *uncontrollable* events which are sent by the system to the controller, and the *controllable* events which are sent by the controller to the system.

A polynomial dynamical system S is now written as:

$$S : \begin{cases} Q(X,Y,U) = & 0 \\ X' & = P(X,Y,U) \\ Q_0(X_0) & = 0 \end{cases} \tag{2}$$

where the vector X represents the state variables; Y and U are respectively the set of *uncontrollable* and *controllable event variables*. Such a system is called a controllable polynomial dynamic system. Let n, m, and p be the respective dimensions of X, Y, and U. The trajectories of a controllable system are sequences (x_t, y_t, u_t) in $(\mathbb{Z}/3\mathbb{Z})^{n+m+p}$ such that $Q_0(x_0) = 0$ and, for all t, $Q(x_t, y_t, u_t) = 0$ and $x_{t+1} = P(x_t, y_t, u_t)$. The events (y_t, u_t) include an uncontrollable component y_t and a controllable one u_t[3]. We have no direct influence on the y_t part which depends only on the state x_t, but we observe it. On the other hand, we have full control over u_t and we can choose any value of u_t which is admissible, *i.e.* , such that $Q(x_t, y_t, u_t) = 0$. To distinguish the two components, a vector $y \in (\mathbb{Z}/3\mathbb{Z})^m$ is called an *event* and a vector $u \in (\mathbb{Z}/3\mathbb{Z})^p$ a *control*. From now on, an event y is *admissible* in a state x if there exists a control u such that $Q(x,y,u) = 0$; such a control is said *compatible* with y in x.

The controllers: A PDS can be controlled by first selecting a particular initial state x_0 and then by choosing suitable values for $u_1, u_2, \ldots, u_n, \ldots$. We will here consider control policies where the value of the control u_t is instantaneously computed from the value of x_t and y_t. Such a controller is called a *static controller*. It is a system of two equations: $C(X,Y,U) = 0$ and $C_0(X) = 0$, where

---

[3] This particular aspect constitutes one of the main differences with [14]. In our case, the events are partially controllable, whereas in the other case, the events are either controllable or uncontrollable.

the equation $C_0(X) = 0$ determines initial states satisfying the control objectives and the other one describes how to choose the instantaneous controls; when the controlled system is in state x, and when an event y occurs, any value u such that $Q(x, y, u) = 0$ and $C(x, y, u) = 0$ can be chosen. The behavior of the system S composed with the controller is then modeled by the system S_c:

$$S_c = \begin{cases} X' = P(X, Y, U) \\ Q(X, Y, U) = 0 \quad C(X, Y, U) = 0 \\ Q_0(X_0) = 0 \qquad C_0(X_0) = 0 \end{cases} \tag{3}$$

However, not every controller (C, C_O) is acceptable. First, the controlled system S_C has to be initialized ; thus, the equations $Q_0(X) = 0$ and $C_0(X) = 0$ must have common solutions. Furthermore, due to the uncontrollability of the events Y, any event that the system S can produce must be admissible by the controlled system S_C. Such a controller is said to be *acceptable*.

5.2   Traditional Control Objectives

We now illustrate the use of the framework for solving a traditional control synthesis problem we shall reuse in the sequel.

Suppose we want to ensure the *invariance* of a set of states E. Let us introduce the operator $\widetilde{pre}$, defined by: for any set of states F,

$$\widetilde{pre}\,(F) = \{x \in (\mathbb{Z}/{}_{3\mathbb{Z}})^n \mid \forall y \text{ admissible}, \exists u, Q(x, y, u) = 0 \text{ and } P(x, y, u) \in F\}$$

Consider now the sequence $(E_i)_{i \in \mathbb{N}}$ defined by:

$$\begin{cases} E_0 = E \\ E_{i+1} = E_i \cap \widetilde{pre}\,(E) \end{cases} \tag{4}$$

The sequence (4) is decreasing. Since all sets E_i are finite, there exists a j such that $E_{j+1} = E_j$. The set E_j is then the greatest control-invariant subset of E. Let g_j be the polynomial that has E_j as solution, then $C_0(X) = g_j$ and $C(X, Y, U) = P^*(g_j)^4$ is an admissible feed-back controller and the system S_C : $S + (C_0, C)$ verifies the invariance of the set of states E.

Using similar methods, we are also able to to compute controllers (C, C_0) that ensure

- the *reachability* of a set of states from the initial states of the system,
- the *attractivity* of a set of states E from a set of states F.
- the *recurrence* of a set of states E.

We can also consider control objectives that are conjunctions of basic properties of state trajectories. However, basic properties cannot, in general, be combined in a modular way. For example, an invariance property puts restrictions on the

---

[4] the solutions of the polynomial $P^*(g)$ are the triples (x, y, u) that satisfy the relation "$P(x, y, u)$ is solution of the polynomial g".

set of state trajectories which may be not compatible with an attractivity property. The synthesis of a controller insuring both properties must be effected by considering both properties *simultaneously* and not by combining a controller insuring safety with a controller insuring attractivity independently. For more details on the way controllers are synthesized, the reader may refer to [4].

Specification of the control objectives: As for verification (Section 4), the control objectives can be directly specified in SIGNAL+ program, using the key-word Sigali. For example, if we add in the SIGNAL program the line Sigali(S_Attractivity(S,PROP)), the compiler produces a file that is interpreted by SIGALI which computes the controller with respect to the control objective. In this particular case, the controller will ensure the attractivity of the set of states Set_States, where Set_States is a polynomial that is equal to zero when the boolean PROP is *true*. The result of the controller synthesis is a polynomial that is represented by a Binary Decision Diagram (BDD). This BDD is then saved in a file that could be used to perform a simulation [11].

Application to the transformer station: We have seen in the previous section, that one of the most critical requirements concerns the double fault problem. We assume here that the circuit-breakers are ideal, i.e. they immediately react to actuators (*i.e.* , when a circuit-breaker receives an opening/closing request, then at the next instant the circuit-breaker is opened/closed). With this assumption, the double fault problem can be rephrased as follows:

"if two faults are picked up at the same time by two different departure cells, then at the next instant, one of the two faults (or both) must disappear."

In order to synthesize the controller, we assume that the only controllable events are the opening and closing requests of the different circuit-breakers. The other events concern the appearance of the faults and cannot be considered controllable. The specification of the control objective is then:

```
(| 2_Fault :=          when (Fault_Dep_1 and Fault_Dep_2)
              default  when (Fault_Dep_1 and Fault_Dep_3)
              default  when (Fault_Dep_1 and Fault_Dep_4)
              default  when (Fault_Dep_2 and Fault_Dep_3)
              default  when (Fault_Dep_2 and Fault_Dep_4)
              default  when (Fault_Dep_3 and Fault_Dep_4) default false
  | Z_2_Fault := 2_Fault $1 init false
  | Error := 2_Fault and Z_2_Fault
  | Sigali(S_Invariance(S,False(Error))) |)
```

The boolean 2_Fault is *true*, when two faults are present at the same time and is *false* otherwise. The boolean Error is *true* when two faults are present at two consecutive instants. We then ask SIGALI to compute a controller that forces the boolean Error to be always *false* (i.e., whatever the behavior, there is no possibility for the controlled system to reach a state where Error is *true*).

The SIGNAL compiler translates the SIGNAL program into a PDS, and the control objectives in terms of polynomial relations and polynomial operations. Applying the algorithm, described by the fixed-point computation (4), we are able to synthesize a controller (C_1, C_0), that ensures the invariance of the set of states where the boolean *Error* is *true*, for the controlled system $S_{C_1} = S + (C_1, C_0)$. The result is a controller coded by a polynomial and a BDD.

Using the controller synthesis methodology, we solved the double fault problem. However, some requirements have not been taken into account (importance of the lines, of the circuit-breakers,...). This kind of requirements cannot be solved using traditional control objectives such as invariance, reachability or attractivity. In the next section, we will handle this kind of requirements, using control objectives expressed as order relations.

5.3   Numerical Order Relation Control Problem

We now present the synthesis of control objectives that considers the way to reach a given logical goal. This kind of control objectives will be useful in the sequel to express some properties of the power transformer station controller, as the one dealing with the importance of the different circuit-breakers. For this purpose we introduce cost functions on states. Intuitively speaking, the cost function is used to express priority between the different states that a system can reach in one transition. Let S be a PDS as the one described by (2). Let us suppose that the system evolves into a state x, and that y is an admissible event at x. As the system is generally not deterministic, it may have several controls u such that $Q(x, y, u) = 0$. Let u_1 and u_2 be two controls compatible with y in x. The system can evolve into either $x_1 = P(x, y, u_1)$ or $x_2 = P(x, y, u_2)$. Our goal is to synthesize a controller that will choose between u_1 and u_2, in such a way that the system evolves into either x_1 or x_2 according to a given choice criterion. In the sequel, we express this criterion as a cost function relation.

Controller synthesis method: Let $X = (X_1, \ldots, X_n)$ be the state variables of the system. Then, a cost function is a map from $(\mathbb{Z}/3\mathbb{Z})^n$ to $\mathbb{N}$, which associates to each x of $(\mathbb{Z}/3\mathbb{Z})^n$ some integer k.

Definition 2. *Given a PDS S and a cost function c over the states of this system, a state x_1 is said to be c-better than a state x_2 (denoted $x_1 \succeq_c x_2$), if and only if, $c(x_2) \geq c(x_1)$.*   ●

In order to express the corresponding order relation as a polynomial relation, let us consider $k_{max} = sup_{x \in (\mathbb{Z}/3\mathbb{Z})^n}(c(x))$. The following sets of states are then computed $A_i = \{x \in (\mathbb{Z}/3\mathbb{Z})^n \mid c(x) = i\}$. The sets $(A_i)_{i=0..k_{max}}$ form a partition of the global set of states. Note that some A_i could be reduced to the empty set. The proof of the following property is straightforward:

Proposition 1. $x_1 \succeq_c x_2 \Leftrightarrow \exists i \in [0, .., k_{max}], \ x_1 \in A_i \wedge x_2 \in \bigcup_{j=i}^{k_{max}} A_j$ ○

Let $g_0, \ldots, g_{k_{max}}$ be the polynomials that have the sets $A_1, \ldots, A_{k_{max}}$ as solutions[5]. The order relation $\succeq_c$ defined by the proposition 1 can be expressed as polynomial relation:

Corollary 1. $x \succeq_c x' \Leftrightarrow R_{\succeq_c}(x, x') = 0$, where

$$R_{\succeq_c}(X, X') = \prod_{i=1}^{n} \{g_i^2(X) \oplus (\prod_{j=i}^{n}(g_j^2(X')))\} \ with \ f \oplus g = (f^2 + g^2)^2.$$

As we deal with a non strict order relation, from $\succeq_c$, we construct a strict order relation, named $\succ_c$ defined as: $x \succ_c x' \Leftrightarrow \{x \succeq_c x' \wedge \neg(x' \succeq_c x)\}$. Its translation in terms of polynomial equation is then given by:

$$R_{\succ_c}(X, X') = R_{\succeq_c}(X, X') \oplus (1 - R_{\succeq_c}^2(X', X)). \tag{5}$$

We now are interested in the direct control policy we want to be adopted by the system; *i.e.*, how to choose the right control when the system S has evolved into a state x and an uncontrollable event y has occurred.

Definition 3. *A control u_1 is said to be* better *compared to a control u_2, if and only if $x_1 = P(x, y, u_1) \succ_c x_2 = P(x, y, u_2)$. Using the polynomial approach, it gives $R_{\succ_c}(P(x, y, u_1), P(x, y, u_2)) = 0$.* •

In other words, the controller has to choose, for a pair (x, y), a compatible control with y in x, that allows the system to evolve into one of the states that are maximal for the relation $R_{\succ_c}$. To do so, let us introduce a new order relation $\sqsupset_c$ defined from the order relation $\succ_c$.

$$(x, y, u) \sqsupset_c (x', y', u') \Leftrightarrow \begin{cases} x = x' \\ y = y' \\ P(x, y, u) \succ_c P(x, y, u') \end{cases} \tag{6}$$

In other words, a triple (x, y, u) is "better" than a triple (x, y, u') whenever the state $P(x, y, u)$ reached by choosing the control u is better than the state $P(x, y, u')$ reached by choosing the control u'.

We will now compute the maximal triples of this new order relation among all of the triples. To this effect, we use $I = \{(x, y, u) \in (\mathbb{Z}/3\mathbb{Z})^{n+m+p} \mid Q(x, y, u) = 0\}$ the set of admissible triples (x, y, u). The maximal set of triples I_{max} is then provided by the following relation:

$$I_{max} = I - \{(x, y, u) \mid \exists (x, y, u') \in I, (x, y, u') \sqsupset_c (x, y, u)\} \tag{7}$$

The characterization of the set of states I_{max} in terms of polynomials is the following:

---

[5] To compute efficiently such polynomials, it is important to use the Arithmetic Decision Diagrams (ADD) developed, for example, by [3].

Proposition 2. *The polynomial C that has I_{max} as solutions is given by:*

$$C(X, Y, U) = Q(X, Y, U) \oplus (1 - \exists elim_{U'}(Q(X, Y, U') \oplus R_{\succ_c}(P(X, Y, U'), P(X, Y, U))))$$

where the solutions of $\exists elim_{U'}(Q(X, Y, U')$ are given by the set $\{(x, y)/\exists u', Q(x, y, u') = 0\}$.

Using this controller, the choice of a control u, compatible with y in x, is reduced such that the possible successor state is maximal for the (partial) order relation $\succ_c$. Note that if a triple (x, y, u) is not comparable with the maximal element of the order relation $\sqsupset_c$, the control u is allowed by the controller (*i.e.* , u is compatible with the event y in the state x).

Without control, the system can start from one of the initial states of $I_0 = \{x \ / \ Q_0(x) = 0\}$. To determine the new initial states of the system, we will take the ones that are the maximal states (for the order relation $R_{\succ_c}$) among all the solutions of the equation $Q_0(X) = 0$. This computation is performed by removing from I_0 all the states for which there exist at least one smaller state for the strict order relation $\succ_c$. Using the same method as the one previously described for the computation of the polynomial C, we obtain a polynomial C_0. The solutions of this polynomial are the states that are maximal for the order relation $\sqsupset_c$.

Theorem 1. *With the preceding notations, (C, C_0) is an acceptable controller for the system S. Moreover, the controlled system $S_C = (S + (C, C_0))$ adopts the control policy of Definition 3.*   o

Some others characterization of order relations in terms of polynomials can be found in [10]. Finally, note that the notion of numerical order relation has been generalized over a bounded states trajectory of the system, retrieving the classical notion of *Optimal Control* [9].

Application to the power transformer station controller: We have seen in Section 5.2 how to compute a controller that solves the double fault problem. However, even if this particular problem is solved, other requirements had not been taken into account. The first one is induced by the obtained controller itself. Indeed, several solutions are available at each instant. For example, when two faults appear at a given instant, the controller can choose to open all the circuit-breakers, or at least the link circuit-breaker. This kind of solutions is not admissible and must not be considered. The second requirements concerns the importance of the lines. The first controller (C_1, C_0) does not handle this kind of problems and can force the system to open the bad circuit-breakers.

As consequences, two new requirements must be added in order to obtain a real controller:

1. The number of opened circuit-breaker must be minimal
2. The importance of the lines (and of the circuit-breakers) has to be different.

These two requirements introduce a quantitative aspect to the control objectives. We will now describe the solutions we proposed to cope with these problems.

First, let us assume that the state of a circuit-breaker is coded with a state variable according to the following convention: the state variable i is equal to 1 if and only if the corresponding circuit-breaker i is closed. CB is then a vector of state variables which collects all the state variables encoding the states of the circuit-breakers. To minimize the number of open circuit-breaker and to take into account the importance of the line, we use a cost function . We simply encode the fact that the more important is the circuit-breaker, the larger is the cost allocated to the state variable which encodes the circuit-breaker. The following picture summarizes the way we allocate the cost.

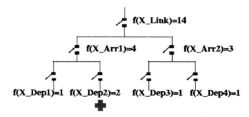

The cost allocated to each state variable corresponds to the cost when the corresponding circuit-breaker is opened. When it is closed, the cost is equal to 0. The cost of a global state is simply obtained by adding all the circuit-breaker costs. With this cost function, it is always more expensive to open a circuit-breaker at a certain level than to open all the downstream circuit-breakers. Moreover, the cost allocated to the state variable that encodes the second departure circuit-breaker (encoded by the state variable X_{dep2})) is bigger than the others because the corresponding line supplies a hospital (for example). Finally note that the cost function is minimal when the number of open circuit-breaker is minimal.

Let us consider the system S_{C_1}. We then introduce an order relation over the states of the system: a state x_1 is said to be better compared to a state x_2 ($x_1 \sqsupseteq x_2$) if and only if for their corresponding sub-vectors CB_1 and CB_2, we have $CB_1 \sqsupseteq_c CB_2$. This order relation is then translated in an algebraic relation $R_{\sqsupseteq_c}$, following Equation (5) and by applying the construction described in proposition 2 and 1, we obtain a controller (C_2, C'_0) for which the controlled system $S_{C_2} = (S_{C_1} + (C_2, C'_0))$ respects the control strategy.

6 Conclusion

In this paper, we described the incremental specification of a power transformer station controller using the control theory concepts of the class of polynomial dynamical systems over $\mathbb{Z}/3\mathbb{Z}$. As this model results from the translation of a SIGNAL program [8], we have a powerful environment to describe the model for a synchronous data-flow system. Even if classical control can be used, we have shown that using the algebraic framework, optimal control synthesis problem is possible. The order relation controller synthesis technique can be used to synthesize control objectives which relate more to the way to get to a logical goal, than to the goal to be reached.

Acknowledgment: The authors gratefully acknowledge relevant comments from the anonymous reviewers of this paper.

References

1. S. Balemi, G. J. Hoffmann, H. Wong-Toi, and G. F. Franklin. Supervisory control of a rapid thermal multiprocessor. *IEEE Transactions on Automatic Control*, 38(7):1040–1059, July 1993.
2. A. Benveniste and G. Berry. Real-time systems designs and programming. *Proceedings of the IEEE*, 79(9):1270–1282, September 1991.
3. R.E. Bryant and Chen Y. Verification of Arithmetic Functions with Binary Diagrams. Research Report, School of Computer Science CMU, May 1995.
4. B. Dutertre and M. Le Borgne. Control of polynomial dynamic systems: an example. Research Report 798, IRISA, January 1994.
5. L.E. Holloway, B.H. Krogh, and A. Giua. A survey of Petri net methods for controlled discrete event systems. *Discrete Event Dynamic Systems: Theory and Application*, 7:151–190, 1997.
6. M. Le Borgne, A. Benveniste, and P. Le Guernic. Polynomial dynamical systems over finite fields. In *Algebraic Computing in Control*, volume 165, pages 212–222. LNCIS, G. Jacob et F. Lamnabhi-lagarrigue, March 1991.
7. M. Le Borgne, H. Marchand, E. Rutten, and M. Samaan. Formal verification of signal programs: Application to a power transformer station controller. In *Proceedings of AMAST'96*, pages 271–285, Munich, Germany, July 1996. Springer-Verlag, LNCS 1101.
8. P. Le Guernic and T. Gautier. Data-flow to von Neumann: the SIGNAL approach. In Jean-Luc Gaudiot and Lubomir Bic, editors, *Advanced Topics in Data-Flow Computing*, chapter 15, pages 413–438. Prentice-Hall, 1991.
9. H. Marchand and M. Le Borgne. On the optimal control of polynomial dynamical systems over $\mathbb{Z}/p\mathbb{Z}$. In *4th International Workshop on Discrete Event Systems*, pages 385–390, Cagliari, Italy, August 1998.
10. H. Marchand and M. Le Borgne. Partial order control of discrete event systems modeled as polynomial dynamical systems. In *1998 IEEE International Conference On Control Applications*, Trieste, Italia, September 1998.
11. H. Marchand, Bournai P., M. Le Borgne, and P. Le Guernic. A design environment for discrete-event controllers based on the signal language. In *1998 IEEE International Conf. On Systems, Man, And Cybernetics*, pages 770–775, San Diego, California, USA, October 1998.
12. H. Marchand, E. Rutten, and M. Samaan. Synchronous design of a transformer station controller with Signal. In *4th IEEE Conference on Control Applications*, pages 754–759, Albany, New-York, September 1995.
13. H. Melcher and K. Winkelmann. Controller synthesis for the production cell case study. In *Proceedings of the 2nd Workshop on Formal Methods in Software Practice (FMSP-98)*, pages 24–33, New YOrk, March 4–5 1998. ACM Press.
14. P. J. Ramadge and W. M. Wonham. The control of discrete event systems. *Proceedings of the IEEE; Special issue on Dynamics of Discrete Event Systems*, 77(1):81–98, 1989.

Verifying Behavioural Specifications in CafeOBJ Environment

Akira Mori and Kokichi Futatsugi

Japan Advanced Institute of Science and Technology, Hokuriku
1-1 Asahidai Tatsunokuchi Nomi Ishikawa, 923-1292, JAPAN
{amori,kokichi}@jaist.ac.jp

Abstract. In this paper, we present techniques for automated verification of behavioural specifications using hidden algebra. Two non-trivial examples, the Alternating Bit Protocol and a snooping cache coherence protocol, are presented with complete specification code and proof scores for CafeOBJ verification system. The refinement proof based on behavioural coinduction is given for the first example, and the coherence proof based on invariance is given for the second.

1   Introduction

The promise of formal methods has been heard for a long time, but with a few exceptions, they have not lived up to expectations. The shortcomings are due to:

- gap between specification and implementation, leading to the overspecification problem, and
- lack of unified logical systems that cover entire software design/development process, necessitating human intervention.

In other words, there have not been appropriate logical foundations for software specification. Overpopulation of specification languages has led to idiosyncrasy that is so difficult to see through. If formal methods are to have industrial impact on software productivity, they have to offer seamless integrated support throughout specification, verification, and transformation.

In this paper, we report on several techniques developed for behavioural specification based on hidden algebra to demonstrate its potential to be an industrial-strength specification method in the future. Hidden algebra was developed in an attempt to give a semantics for software engineering, and for the object paradigm in particular, supporting correctness proofs that are as simple and mechanical as possible [1]. It distinguishes *hidden* sorts from visible sorts. As hidden sorts model states of the system, equations of hidden sorts need to be interpreted in a different manner. For this, hidden algebra formalises a notion of **behavioural abstraction,** by defining *behavioural satisfaction* of equations. An effective proof method for behavioural equation has been developed, called *behavioural coinduction*, and used for various refinement proofs.

J. Wing, J. Woodcock, J. Davies (Eds.): FM'99, Vol. II, LNCS 1709, pp. 1625–1643, 1999.
© Springer-Verlag Berlin Heidelberg 1999

The development of hidden algebra is not an isolated event. There are many other proposed methods for *behavioural specification*, whose purpose is to characterise how systems behave instead of how they are implemented, but very few computer support systems exist. The CafeOBJ [2] system offers an integrated environment for specification and verification in the tradition of the OBJ languages, and is the only system that supports behavioural specification based on hidden algebra. As part of an effort to show the capability of behavioural specification, we report on some of the new features of CafeOBJ by means of two non-trivial examples, the Alternating Bit Protocol and a snooping cache coherence protocol. Specification code and correctness proof scores for CafeOBJ are presented for a complete explanation.

The organisation of the paper is as follows: Section 2 briefly summarises theoretical backgrounds of hidden algebra, Section 3 and 4 detail the specification and verification of the Alternating Bit Protocol and snooping cache coherence protocol respectively, and Section 5 concludes with comparisons with other approaches and future plans.

2   Hidden Algebra

This section presents basic definitions of hidden algebra. See [1, 3] for more details.

Hidden algebra distinguishes **hidden** state values from **visible** data values. Data values are defined as elements of a fixed (ordinary) algebra D with signature Ψ and sort set V such that for each $d \in D_v$ with $v \in V$ there is some $\psi \in \Psi_{[],v}$ interpreted as d in D. On the other hand, (hidden) state values are defined as elements of a special algebra with syntactic restrictions on its signature.

Definition 1. *A **hidden signature (over** (V, Ψ, D)) is a triple (H, Σ, Σ^b), where H is a set of **hidden sorts** disjoint from V, Σ is an $(H \cup V)$-sorted signature with $\Psi \subseteq \Sigma$, and $\Sigma^b \subseteq \Sigma$ is a set of **behavioural operations** disjoint from Ψ, such that*

- *each $\sigma \in \Sigma_{w,s}$ with $w \in V^*$ and $s \in V$ lies in $\Psi_{w,s}$, and,*
- *each $\sigma \in \Sigma^b_{w,s}$ has exactly one element of H in w.*

(H, Σ, Σ^b) *may be abbreviated to Σ leaving Σ^b implicit. An operation σ in $\Sigma^b_{w,s}$ is called a **method** if $s \in H$ and an **attribute** if $s \in V$. $\sigma \in \Sigma_{w,s}$ is called a **hidden constant** if $w \in V^*$ and $s \in H$.*

Note that operations in $\Sigma_{w,s} - \Sigma^b_{w,s}$ may have more than one elements of H in w. These **non-behavioural operations** were not considered in the original definition of hidden algebra [1]. They have been introduced to increase expressiveness of hidden algebra [4, 5]. The above definition is due to [4] and is supported in the current CafeOBJ system.

Definition 2. *Given a hidden signature (H, Σ, Σ^b), a **hidden Σ-algebra** A is a (many sorted) Σ-algebra A such that $A\restriction_\Psi = D$.*

As mentioned above, the elements of A_v where $v \in V$ is thought of as data values and the elements of A_h where $h \in H$ as state values.

Definition 3. *A **hidden** (or **behavioural**) **theory** (or **specification**) is a quadruple (H, Σ, Σ^b, E), where (H, Σ, Σ^b) is a hidden signature and E is a set of Σ-(conditional) equations; we may write (Σ, E) for short.*

Example 1. We present a behavioural specification of a flag object using CafeOBJ notations [3]. A flag object is either up or down, and there are methods to put it up, to put it down, and to reverse its state:

```
mod* FLAG {
  *[ Flag ]*
  bops (up_) (dn_) (rev_) : Flag -> Flag   -- methods
  bop up?_ : Flag -> Bool                  -- attribute
  var F : Flag
  eq up? up F = true .
  eq up? dn F = false .
  eq up? rev F = not up? F .
}
```

A CafeOBJ keyword `mod*` means that the module has a **loose** behavioural semantics in contrast with a **tight** (initial algebra) semantics specified by the keyword `mod!`. A pair of starred brackets `*[ ... ]*` is used for sort declaration and `*` indicates that the declared sort is a hidden sort. For visible sorts, `[ ... ]` is used. The keyword `bop` declares behavioural operations in Σ^b (i.e., attributes and methods).

The meaning of the `FLAG` specification should be clear, however, some of the intended behaviours of the flag object, for example, a behavioural equation `rev rev F = F` cannot be deduced from the `FLAG` specification using ordinary equational reasoning[1]. This means that ordinary satisfaction of equations is too strict for behavioural equations and a weaker notion of satisfaction based on *indistinguishability*[2] is needed. In hidden algebra, it is formalised using *contexts* as follows.

Definition 4. *Given a hidden signature (H, Σ, Σ^b), a **behavioural context** is a term having a single occurrence of a special variable of hidden-sort denoted by z and is formed by the following rules:*

- *any variable z (of any sort) is a behavioural context,*
- *for any $\sigma \in \Sigma^b_{vh,s}$, any behavioural context c of sort h, and any tuple of ground terms $t \in (T_\Sigma)_v$, $\sigma(t, c)$ is a behavioural context, where $v \in V^*$ and $h \in H$. If $s \in V$, then $\sigma(t, c)$ is called **visible**, otherwise it is called **hidden**.*

---

[1] Not to mention induction.

[2] By means of method application and attribute observation.

*Given a hidden Σ-algebra A, two elements a and a' of the same carrier set A_s are said to be **behaviourally equivalent**, denoted by $a \sim_s a'$ (or just $a \sim a'$) iff $A_c(a) = A_c(a')$ for all visible behavioural contexts c, where A_c denotes the function interpreting the context c as an operation on A.*

*A hidden Σ-algebra A **behaviourally satisfies** a (conditional) equation e of the form $(\forall X) t = t'$ **if** $t_1 = t'_1, ..., t_m = t'_m$ iff*

$$\theta^*(t) \sim \theta^*(t') \text{ whenever } \theta^*(t_j) \sim \theta^*(t'_j) \text{ for all } j = 1, ..., m$$

for every valuation $\theta : X \to A$. In this case, we write $A \models_\Sigma e$. We may drop the subscript Σ.

Note that for visible sorted equations, there is no difference between ordinary satisfaction and behavioural satisfaction. We will use the symbol $\sim$ instead of $=$ when the equation should be interpreted by behavioural satisfaction. Such equations are called **behavioural equations** and specified by keywords beq, bceq in CafeOBJ, instead of eq, ceq where ceq stands for conditional equations.

The first effective algebraic proof technique for behavioural equivalence was context induction [6], however, a more comprehensive technique based on *maximality* has been developed.

Definition 5. *Given a hidden signature Σ, and a hidden Σ-algebra A, **behavioural congruence** on A is a Σ^b-congruence which is identity on visible sorts.*

Theorem 1. *Given a hidden signature Σ and a hidden Σ-algebra A, then behavioural equivalence is the largest behavioural congruence on A.*

See [1, 4, 5] for the proof.

Thanks to this theorem, one can show $a \sim a'$ by finding some behavioural congruence that relates a and a' [3]. This is what is called **behavioural** (or **hidden) coinduction** and justifies a variety of techniques for proving behavioural equivalence. For example, to show that every FLAG-algebra satisfies the equation $(\forall F : \text{Flag}) \text{ rev rev } F = F$, one only needs to show that up? rev rev F = up? F. This is a special case of **attribute coherent** theory, where the equivalence on attributes is behavioural equivalence [4]. CafeOBJ system automatically checks if this happens every time a new module is loaded. When this is the case, showing behavioural satisfaction is automatic.

Non-behavioural operations have been introduced to enhance the expressive power of hidden algebra [4], for example for modular construction of behavioural specifications. However, non-behavioural constructors may not preserve behavioural equivalence and therefore may ruin the soundness of equational reasoning (specifically the congruence rule substituting equal with equal). The next definition gives a sufficient condition for sound equational deduction.

---

[3] Note that the situation is very much similar to the technique in process algebra for demonstrating (strong) bisimilarity through bisimulation [7].

[4] Visit the website at UCSD, http://www.cs.ucsd.edu/groups/links.

Definition 6. *Given a hidden signature Σ and a hidden Σ-algebra A, an operation $\sigma \in \Sigma_{w,s} - \Sigma_{w,s}^b$ is said to be **behaviourally coherent** iff it preserves the behavioural equivalence on A, that is, $A_\sigma(a_1, a_2, \ldots, a_n) \sim_s A_\sigma(a_1', a_2', \ldots, a_n')$ if $a_1 \sim_{s_1} a_1', a_2 \sim_{s_2} a_2', \ldots, a_n \sim_{s_n} a_n'$ for all $(a_1, a_2, \ldots, a_n)$ and $(a_1', a_2', \ldots, a_n')$ in $A_{s_1} \times A_{s_2} \times \cdots \times A_{s_n}$, where $w = s_1 s_2 \cdots s_n$.*

The next theorem is due to [4]. See also [5] for another proof (in a slightly different setting) and examples.

Theorem 2. *If all operations in $\Sigma - \Sigma^b$ are behaviourally coherent, then ordinary equational deduction is sound for behavioural equations.*

3   The Alternating Bit Protocol

Now that we have introduced all necessary concepts, let us turn to some interesting specifications and their verification.

The first example is the classic Alternating Bit Protocol (ABP) [8]. The protocol is designed to achieve secure communication through unreliable channels that may lose or duplicate packets. The model of the protocol consists of four agents, the sender, the receiver, the message (msg) channel from the sender to the receiver, and the acknowledgement (ack) channel from the receiver to the sender.

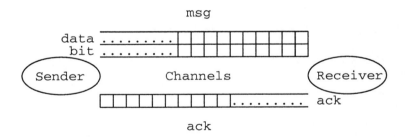

Fig. 1. The Alternating Bit Protocol

In addition to data that are transmitted, the protocol uses extra bits to recover potential errors (loss and duplication) in the channels. The sender sends messages, each of which consists of a data and a bit, along the msg channel, and receives acknowledgement bits from the ack channel. The receiver receives messages from the msg channel and sends back acknowledgements along the ack channel. The channel is modeled as a simple unbounded queue that may lose or duplicate packets, but does not alter the order of packets. As its name suggests, the key trick of the protocol is the bit alternation that takes place when a packet having the *right* bit is received. This is a good example for formal specification and verification methods, since its procedure is extremely simple, yet very sophisticated.

We model the protocol in terms of actions taken by the sender and the receiver. Each agent maintains three types of information, a data, a bit, and a timer. Each checks the incoming bit with the bit it has and then determines the next action. We have included the timer since it is necessary to prevent deadlocks[5].

Sender:

- receives a right ack (the same bit as it has) from the ack channel, accepts and keeps a new data, alternates the bit, sends a couple of the new data and the new bit along the msg channel, sets a timer;
- receives a wrong ack (does nothing);
- resends a couple of the current data and bit when the timer goes off.

Receiver:

- receives a message with a right bit (the *opposite* bit of the one it has) from the msg channel, keeps the new data (for future delivery), alternates the bit, sends the new bit along the ack channel, sets a timer;
- receives a message with a wrong bit (does nothing);
- resends the current bit when the timer goes off.

Below is a more or less faithful behavioural specification of the descriptions above.

```
mod! DATA { protecting(BOOL) [ Nat Bool < Data ] }

mod! QUEUE(X :: TRIV) {
  [ NeQueue < Queue ]
  op nil : -> Queue
  op front : NeQueue -> Elt
  op enq : Elt Queue -> NeQueue
  op deq : NeQueue -> Queue
  vars D E : Elt    var Q : Queue
  eq deq(enq(E,nil)) = nil .
  eq deq(enq(E,enq(D,Q))) = enq(E,deq(enq(D,Q))) .
  eq front(enq(E,nil)) = E .
  eq front(enq(E,enq(D,Q))) = front(enq(D,Q)) .
}
mod* SENDER {
  protecting(DATA)
  *[ Sender ]*
  bop bit : Sender -> Bool
  bop val : Sender -> Data
```

---

[5] However, the timer does not appear in the behavioural specification.

```
  bop in : Data Bool Sender -> Sender
  op init : -> Sender
  var D : Data    var B : Bool    var S : Sender
  eq bit(init) = true .    -- valid initial state
  ceq val(in(D,B,S)) = D if bit(S) == B.--new data for right ack
  ceq bit(in(D,B,S)) = not bit(S) if bit(S) == B.--alternates bit
  bceq in(D,B,S) = S if bit(S) =/= B .   -- stays put for wrong ack
}
mod* RECEIVER {
  protecting(DATA)
  *[ Receiver ]*
  bop bit : Receiver -> Bool
  bop val : Receiver -> Data
  bop get : Data Bool Receiver -> Receiver
  op init : -> Receiver
  var D : Data    var B : Bool    var R : Receiver
  eq bit(init) = true .    -- valid initial state
  ceq val(get(D,B,R)) = D if bit(R) =/= B . -- output value
  ceq bit(get(D,B,R)) = not bit(R) if bit(R)=/=B.--alternates bit
  bceq get(D,B,R) = R if bit(R) == B . -- stays put for wrong bit
}
mod* ABP {
  protecting(SENDER + RECEIVER + QUEUE[DATA])
  *[ Abp ]*
  op Init : -> Abp
  op Protocol: Sender Receiver Queue Queue Queue->Abp {coherent}
  bop In : Data Abp -> Abp
  bop Out : Abp -> Abp
  bop Val : Abp -> Data
  vars D E : Data    var B : Bool    var A : Abp    var S : Sender
  var R : Receiver    vars L L1 L2 : Queue
  beq Init = Protocol(init,init,nil,nil,nil) .
  bceq In(D,Protocol(S,R,L1,L2,enq(B,L)))
      = Protocol(in(D,front(enq(B,L))),S),R,enq(D,L1),
                enq(not bit(S),L2),deq(enq(B,L)))
        if bit(S) == front(enq(B,L)) .
  beq In(D,Protocol(S,R,enq(E,L1),enq(B,L2),nil))
      = Protocol(S,R,enq(E,L1),enq(B,L2),nil) .
  bceq [ 1 ] : Protocol(S,R,L1,L2,enq(B,L))
              = Protocol(S,R,L1,L2,deq(enq(B,L)))
                if bit(S) =/= front(enq(B,L)) .
  bceq Out(Protocol(S,R,enq(D,L1),enq(B,L2),L))
      = Protocol(S,get(front(enq(D,L1)),front(enq(B,L2)),R),
        deq(enq(D,L1)),deq(enq(B,L2)),enq(not bit(R),L))
        if bit(R) =/= front(enq(B,L2)) .
```

```
bceq [ 2 ] : Protocol(S,R,enq(D,L1),enq(B,L2),L)
              = Protocol(S,R,deq(enq(D,L1)),deq(enq(B,L2)),L)
              if bit(R) == front(enq(B,L2)) .
beq Out(Protocol(S,R,nil,nil,enq(B,L)))
    = Protocol(S,R,nil,nil,enq(B,L)) .
beq [ 3 ] : Protocol(S,R,L1,L2,L)
              = Protocol(S,R,enq(val(S),L1),enq(bit(S),L2),L) .
beq [ 4 ] : Protocol(S,R,L1,L2,L)
              = Protocol(S,R,L1,L2,enq(bit(R),L)) .
eq Val(Protocol(S,R,L1,L2,L)) = val(R) .
}
```

A few remarks about the specification are in order.

— Transmitted data and alternation bits are specified using CafeOBJ's default built-in modules Nat (the natural numbers) and Bool (the Booleans).
— A parameterised module QUEUE and subsorts Nat and Bool are used to avoid multiple presence of QUEUE modules. Also subsort NeQueue is used to avoid introducing user-defined error elements.
— Modules are imported by protecting declaration. It instructs that the semantics of imported modules should not be altered. There are other importation modes than protecting. See [3] for details and semantics.
— Initial states are defined as hidden constants. Attribute values for initial states can be defined by visible equations. The initial state of ABP may look strange since the data transmission can only be started by the Receiver taking a time-out action[6]. This is rather a syntactic convenience, i.e., one could have put an appropriate acknowledgement bit in the ack channel.
— Module expressions such as SENDER + RECEIVER + QUEUE[DATA] avoid multiple internal copies of shared modules.
— A non-behavioural operation Protocol is declared **coherent** in the ABP module. Thus one can freely use equational reasoning through reduction commands reduce or red in CafeOBJ. The coherence of Protocol needs to be proved separately, however, it is trivial and omitted here. One can think of coherent operations as *behavioural constructors* just like ordinary data type constructors. They are used to define legitimate system configurations in terms of behavioural sub-modules.

CafeOBJ keywords appearing in the specification should be easily interpreted by corresponding hidden algebra notions. Interested readers are referred to [3] for CafeOBJ specific details.

Interpreting equations [1], [2], [3], and [4] with (ordinary) strict satisfaction of equations will not make sense. For example, one might think that equations [3] and [4] bring about inconsistency since the operation Protocol acts as a constructor. One has to remember, however, that they are behavioural equations that only need to be satisfied behaviourally. By virtue of

---

[6] Not by the Sender.

behavioural satisfaction, equations [1] and [2] state that wrong packets are removed without making any trace while [3] and [4] state that time-out events are invisible and resending actions should not affect the following behaviour of the protocol. Writing behavioural equations always runs a risk of producing inconsistent specifications since they imply infinite number of visible equations. This is probably the most difficult aspect of behavioural specification.

We define the notion of behavioural refinement first.

Definition 7. *A **hidden signature map** $\varphi : (H, \Sigma) \to (H', \Sigma')$ is a signature morphism $\varphi : \Sigma \to \Sigma'$ that preserves hidden sorts and behavioural operations, and that is the identity on (V, Ψ). A hidden signature map $\varphi : (\Sigma, E) \to (\Sigma', E')$ is a **refinement** iff for every (Σ', E')-algebra M' we have $\varphi M' \models_\Sigma E$. ($\varphi M'$ denotes M' viewed as a Σ-algebra.)*

It can be shown that φ is a refinement iff all visible consequences of the abstract specification hold in the concrete specification [9]:

Proposition 1. *A hidden signature map $\varphi : (\Sigma, E) \to (\Sigma', E')$ is a refinement iff $E' \models \varphi(c[e])$ for each $e \in E$ and each visible Σ-context c, where if e is the equation $(\forall X)\ t = t'$, then $c[e]$ denotes the equation $(\forall X)\ c[t] = c[t']$.*

Now we want to show that ABP is a refinement of the following behavioural specification BUF of a buffer of capacity one.

```
mod* BUF {
  [ Nat ]   *[ Buf ]*
  op init :   -> Buf
  bop in : Nat Buf -> Buf
  bop val : Buf -> Nat
  bop out : Buf -> Buf
  bop empty? : Buf -> Bool
  var N : Nat    var B : Buf
  eq empty?(init) = true .
  ceq empty?(out(B)) = true if not empty?(B) .
  eq empty?(in(N,B)) = false .
  ceq val(out(in(N,B))) = N if empty?(B) .
  bceq in(N,B) = B if not empty?(B) .
  bceq out(B) = B if empty?(B) .
}
```

The meaning of this specification should be clear, however, note that the output value is secure only after the out operation.

In order to demonstrate[7] refinement from BUF to ABP, we first need to find an underlying signature map. For this, we define an ABP counterpart Empty? of empty? as follows.

---

[7] Before starting formal verification, one can check how ABP works via symbolic execution. See Appendix A for a CafeOBJ session of simple ABP reductions.

```
bop Empty? : Abp -> Bool .
var S : Sender    var R : Receiver    vars L L1 L2 : Queue
eq Empty?(Protocol(S,R,L1,L2,L)) = bit(S) == bit(R) .
```

Then the refinement proof requires us to show all equations from **BUF** are valid in **ABP** as well. This is done by finding an appropriate candidate relation R on **Abp** and showing that it is a behavioural congruence. In general, this is highly non-trivial. However, a closer look at behavioural equations [1] – [4] of **ABP** leads to the observation that for any **reachable state** of the protocol there is a behaviourally equivalent state whose channels are all empty. This is the ingenious aspect of the protocol that achieves robust communication against loss and duplication in the channels.

We are going to make this observation precise by creating CafeOBJ scores. However, since CafeOBJ does not have full theorem proving capability (only reductions), we need some maneuvers for quantified variables and conditionals, and also for rewriting directions and orders. The CafeOBJ commands for controlling these are omitted from the following proof score.

We define the candidate relation R to be

```
op _R_ : Abp Abp -> Bool .
vars S1 S2 : Sender    vars R1 R2  : Receiver
ceq Protocol(S1,R1,nil,nil,nil) R Protocol(S2,R2,nil,nil,nil)=true
    if val(S1) == val(S2) and val(R1) == val(R2) and
       ((bit(S1) == bit(R1)) == (bit(S2) == bit(R2))) .
```

It suffices to define R on states with empty channels since behavioural equations in **ABP** are closed within *reachable* states `Protocol(S,R,L1,L2,L)` where

$$L2 = a^*b^*, L = b^*\overline{a}^*, a = \text{bit}(S), b = \text{bit}(R).$$

(The head of the queue is placed to the right, and $\overline{a}$ stands for the opposite bit of a.) It is very interesting to note that only one bit change occurs in the concatenation of $L2$ and L, depending upon whether $a = b$ or $a \neq b$. The $a = b$ case corresponds to the *empty* state ready to accept a new data, and $a \neq b$ to the *full* state having an accepted data waiting to be delivered. Identifying these two groups of states is essential for any attempt at formal verification of the ABP. It is also noted that the use of a coherent non-behavioural operation (that is, `Protocol`) simplifies the specification together with the enabled power of equational reasoning.

Now to check congruence of R.

```
-- universally quantified variables
-- i.e., Theorem of (Hidden) Constants
ops s s1 s2 s3 : -> Sender .   ops r r1 r2 r3 : -> Receiver .
ops a a1 a2 a3 : -> Abp .   op e : -> Nat .

-- a matches a2 while a1 matches a3,
eq a = Protocol(s,r,nil,nil,nil) .
```

```
eq a1 = Protocol(s1,r1,nil,nil,nil) .
eq a2 = Protocol(s2,r2,nil,nil,nil) .
eq a3 = Protocol(s3,r3,nil,nil,nil) .

-- relational expansion of R for "a R a2" and "a1 R a3"
eq bit(r) = not bit(s) .   eq bit(r2) = not bit(s2) .
eq val(r) = val(r2) .   eq val(s) = val(s2) .
eq bit(r1) = bit(s1) .   eq bit(r3) = bit(s3) .
eq val(r1) = val(r3) .   eq val(s1) = val(s3) .

-- check if R is a behavioural congruence
red In(e,a) R In(e,a2) . -- should be true
red Out(a) R Out(a2) . -- should be true
red In(e,a1) R In(e,a3) . -- should be true
red Out(a1) R Out(a3) . -- should be true
```

CafeOBJ gives true for all reductions.

We have used the Theorem of (Hidden) Constants to perform proof rules for universal quantifiers by introducing fresh constant operations. The soundness of the method is proved in [1, 5]. We have also used implication elimination and case analysis. One can mimic proof rules of first order logic with equality in a similar manner. An automated proof support tool called **Kumo** has been developed for OBJ3 and CafeOBJ systems [10]. Kumo is not just a proof checking tool, but also helps to publish proofs over the internet, i.e., Kumo creates webpages for proofs as it checks proofs given in the proof scripts.

Now that we have established a behavioural congruence, we can use behavioural coinduction to prove behavioural equations. The general case is rather complicated, however, if we restrict attention to ABP states with empty channels as the representatives of equivalent classes modulo R, the coinduction proof becomes manageable using reduction. The following CafeOBJ score does this by unfolding conditionals. Note that the constants a and a1 are the same as defined earlier.

```
var B : Bool
eq not(not(B)) = B . -- necessary!  inductive theorem on Bool

red Empty?(init) .   -- should be true
red Empty?(Out(a)) == true .   -- should be true

red Empty?(In(e,a)) == false . -- should be true
red Empty?(In(e,a1)) == false . -- should be true

red Val(Out(In(e,a1))) == e . -- should be true
red In(e,a) R a .  -- should be true
red Out(a1) R a1 . -- should be true
```

Again, CafeOBJ returns `true` for all reductions [8]. We can now claim that

"ABP implements BUF when there are no errors in channels."

However, the error recovering capability of ABP is automatic since any loss or duplication in the channel does not affect the (now proved) behavioural congruence of R. Therefore, we arrive at the following correctness theorem for ABP.

Theorem 3. *As far as the reachable states are concerned, errors in channels do not affect the behaviour of the protocol. In other words, the ABP is a robust implementation of a buffer BUF of capacity one.*

Mechanising the whole process should be possible by defining an appropriate merge operation on queues and the filter that checks bit changes. However, it is going to be an induction flood. We do not feel it necessary to completely mechanise proofs when human can do a much better job. We will see a fully automated verification example using a theorem prover in the next section.

4   Cache Coherence Protocol

In this section, we present a somewhat more implementation-oriented example of a cache coherence protocol.

A number of computation units share a main memory through a common access bus. Each unit issues access requests through the bus and maintains its own cached copy. In order to assure consistency among cached copies, the protocol watches (snoops) requests on the bus and takes appropriate actions depending on the flag values that tracks cache states. A coherence condition we consider is the following.

"If there are two shared copies, they must be of the same value."

We model the Illinois cache protocol [11] following [12]. There are three types of requests, (`read`, `write`, and `replacement`), and four different flag values (cache states):

- `invalid` – obsolete;
- `shared` – not modified, possible copies in other caches;
- `valid-exclusive` – not modified, only copy in caches;
- `dirty` – modified, only copy in caches.

Coherence actions are taken as follows, depending on the cache state of the requesting unit and the existence of other cached copies.

Read Hit. the cache (in the requesting unit) is not `invalid`, no extra action;
Read Miss. the cache is `invalid`, look for other cached copies;

---

[8] The *double negation* equation is necessary. The situation is frequently encountered, in which coinduction (or invariance proof) on hidden sorts requires induction on visible sorts.

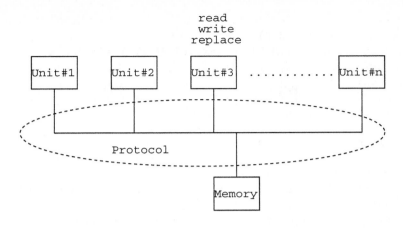

Fig. 2. The Illinois Cache Protocol

- dirty cache provides the latest value, both end up shared;
- any other valid-exclusive or shared cache provides the latest value, all caches having a copy end up shard;
- no cached copy, get a valid-exclusive copy from the main memory;

Write Hit. the cache is not invalid;
- the cache is dirty, no extra action;
- valid-exclusive turns dirty;
- shared turns dirty, all other shared copies are invalid-ated;

Write Miss. invalid turns dirty, all cached copies are invalid-ated;

Replacement. dirty copy is written back to the main memory, stays dirty;

Below is a behavioural specification PROTOCOL of the above procedure.

```
mod! FLAG {
  [ Flag ]
  ops invalid valid-exclusive dirty shared : -> Flag
}
mod* PROTOCOL {
  protecting(NAT + BOOL + FLAG)
  *[ Protocol ]*
  bop flag : Nat Protocol -> Flag -- cache state
  bop cdata : Nat Protocol -> Nat -- cache value
  bop mdata : Protocol -> Nat -- memory value
  bop read : Nat Protocol -> Protocol
  bop write : Nat Nat Protocol -> Protocol
  op init : -> Protocol
  vars I J K M N : Nat    var P : Protocol
-- initial state
  eq flag(I,init) = invalid .
```

```
-- write
  eq cdata(I,write(I,M,P)) = M .
  ceq cdata(J,write(I,M,P)) = cdata(J,P) if I =/= J .
  eq flag(I,write(I,M,P)) = dirty .
  -- invalidation
  ceq flag(J,write(I,M,P)) = invalid if I =/= J .
  ceq mdata(write(I,M,P)) = mdata(P) .
-- read
  -- read hit
  bceq read(I,P) = P if flag(I,P) =/= invalid .
  -- if there is a dirty copy Cj then
  eq cdata(I,read(I,write(J,M,P)))=M.--Cj provides missing block
  eq mdata(read(I,write(J,M,P))) = mdata(P) .
  ceq flag(I,read(I,write(J,M,P))) = shared -- and Ci, Cj
      if I =/= J .
  ceq flag(J,read(I,write(J,M,P))) = shared -- end up shared.
      if I =/= J .
  -- if there is a clean copy Cj then
  ceq cdata(I,read(I,read(J,P))) = cdata(J,read(J,P)) if I =/= J .
      -- Cj provides the missing block
  ceq flag(I,read(I,read(J,P)))=shared if I =/= J.--and Ci,Cj
  ceq flag(J,read(I,read(J,P)))=shared if I =/= J.--end up shared.
  -- independence
  beq read(I,read(I,P)) = read(I,P) .
  ceq flag(I,read(J,read(K,P))) = flag(I,read(K,P))
      if I =/= J and I =/= K .
  ceq cdata(I,read(J,P)) = cdata(I,P) if I =/= J .
  eq mdata(read(I,P)) = mdata(P) .
  -- if there is no cached copy (i.e., only in initial state)
  eq cdata(I,read(I,init)) = mdata(init) .
  eq flag(I,read(I,init)) = valid-exclusive .
  eq mdata(read(I,init)) = mdata(init) .
}
```

A few remarks on the specification.

- It does not have any non-behavioural operations, thus equational reasoning is trivially sound.
- Unlike ABP, it handles arbitrary number of units, which is modeled by operations having an index argument for the unit.
- It only models a single memory block since multiple blocks can be modeled by an extra argument of each operation.
- It does not model **replacement** since it has little effect on the coherence property (and due to the limit of space).
- It is written in a deterministic fashion to allow symbolic execution with term rewriting (reduction) in CafeOBJ. It is based on the following decision and observation.

- The unit that made a `read` request most recently is the one who provides the value.
- `write` always gets a `dirty` copy and invalidates other copies.

As we mentioned earlier, getting inconsistent specifications is much more likely in behavioural specification. We had great help from a resolution / paramodulation theorem prover that was implemented on CafeOBJ, in finding subtle inconsistencies among attribute values in the earlier versions.

Now we want to show the following coherence condition.

In all reachable states `S:Protocol`,
`∀I,J:Nat flag(I,S)=flag(J,S)=shared ⇒ cdata(I,S)=cdata(J,S) .`

Equational reasoning cannot prove this because it cannot trace all reachable states with respect to behavioural equivalence. The proof requires a technique similar to coinduction, known as **invariance proof**. (See [13] for a category-theoretic characterisation of invariants including relation to bisimulation, and [14] for a fixed-point characterisation.) It is a well-studied topic in the field of program verification and is also a prototype of (safety) model checking. There are two equivalent ways of proving invariance, forward and backward. Backward calculation of largest invariants (also known as *weakest preconditions*) is particularly suitable for behavioural specification. Making a long story short, to prove that a predicate $P(S : h)$ on a hidden sort h is an invariant for all reachable states, it suffices to show that the initial state satisfies P and that P is closed under all methods, that is, $\forall S : h \ \forall X : v \ P(S) \Rightarrow P(m(X, S))$ for all method $m \in \Sigma^b_{vh,h}$ (e.g., [13]). In our case, the predicate on `Protocol` is defined as follows.

`P(S:Protocol)=`
`∀I,J:Nat flag(I,S)=flag(J,S)=shared ⇒ cdata(I,S)=cdata(J,S).`

Thus, in order to prove the invariance of P, we have to prove the following formulas.

`P(init).`
`∀S:Protocol ∀N:Nat P(S) ⇒ P(read(N,S)) .`
`∀S:Protocol ∀N,M :Nat P(S) ⇒ P(write(N,M,S)) .`

It took about five minutes for our resolution/paramodulation theorem prover to get the proofs of these on a Pentium 266MHz PC [9]. The process is completely automatic except for the inductive theorems on visible sort (in our case, `Flag`) mentioned below. The user gives a predicate and the system generates all proof obligations in clausal form, which are then passed to the prover. Taking five minutes may not sound great. However, the proof is not easy for a human either. One of the authors tried the proof and it took more than five minutes. It is a straight-forward case analysis and we believe that resolution is particularly

---

[9] The first one is trivial, the third one is easy, and the second one took almost the entire execution time.

useful for this type of theorem proving. Although this proof is probably close to the practical limit of automated theorem provers, we see many interesting applications to behavioural specifications.

For example, the above proof requires inductive theorems on the `FLAG` specification[10].

```
∀F:Flag (F=invalid ∨ F=valid-exclusive ∨ F=dirty ∨ F=shared) .
invalid ≠ valid − exclusive .
invalid ≠ dirty .
...
```

It is an interesting challenge to work with full-fledged inductive theorem provers so that these inductive theorems are discovered automatically when needed.

The example here may be interesting as a cache coherence proof in its own right since there are very few examples that are: 1) fully automated (no human intervention), 2) ready for implementation , 3) free of syntactic translation, and 4) machine supported, despite the large volume of research devoted to the topic.

The invariance proof is too simple when regarded as model checking. However, by combining iterative calculations of largest fixed-points, one can perform full-scale model checking. We are currently working on a so-called *behavioural model checker* that manages predicate representations, obligation generation, and theorem prover (resolution + induction) control. This is an interesting area of study, i.e., the combination of deductive and model-theoretic methods for software verification.

5   Concluding Remarks

In this paper, we have presented methods for verifying behavioural specifications based on hidden algebra. We have reported on CafeOBJ's automation support with a couple of non-trivial examples, the Alternating Bit Protocol and a snooping cache coherence protocol. The refinement proof based on behavioural coinduction is given for the first example, and the coherence proof based on invariance is given for the second. We have included almost complete specification code and proof scores since they are much more valuable and effective sometimes than verbal descriptions and explanations.

Since the hidden algebra (or behavioural) approach is a relatively new branch of formal methods, we compare its characteristics with other well-established[11] methods.

Process algebra treats observability based on events (rather than values) and is very suitable for defining process interaction and evolution, which is one of the unexplored fields of study in hidden algebra. On the other hand, hidden algebra fits very well the notion of object orientation (methods/ attributes, encapsulated states, inheritance, overloading, and so on). The

---

[10] These were given to the system in advance.
[11] Thus some references are omitted.

examples presented in the paper are ready for implementation in Java, for instance. Also hidden algebra fully inherits the power of abstract data type specification, by which one can define static, architectural aspects of software systems (by modules expressions) as well as basic data types within them.

Temporal logic enjoys the rigor of mathematical logics and has made considerable impact on formal verification through model checking technologies. We are afraid, however, that it may not support software design process (via refinement) very well since implementing temporal formulas (again for example in Java) can be very difficult. We are developing techniques for model checking behavioural specifications, which is briefly touched upon in Section 4, and planning to use temporal formulas as an input language.

I/O Automata [15] and evolving algebra [16] are probably the closest to the hidden algebra approach. This is not surprising since hidden algebra stems from early formalisation efforts for automata. We feel that these techniques are more or less compatible. However, hidden algebra has a clear relation with ordinary algebra via behavioural equivalence and can rely on equational reasoning with machine support systems such as CafeOBJ.

Coalgebra [13] stresses duality with algebra and has produced many nice theoretical (mostly category-theoretic) results including the construction of terminal coalgebra, Birkhoff like axiomatisability results, and so on. Hidden algebra (without non-behavioural operations) is actually a concrete case of coalgebra (e.g.,[17]) just like many-sorted algebra is a concrete case of algebra (of endo-functors). Coalgebra provides strong supports for hidden algebra in the area of theoretical development.

We like to mention briefly a couple of related techniques that we think are effective if used with behavioural specification.

Abstract interpretation [14] can go beyond the limit of refinement-based verification as it goes in the other direction. However, giving a *right* abstraction can be very difficult. Combining these two (refinement and abstraction) seems very promising. Various safety properties can be proved in this way.

Model checking has become a major topic in automated verification because of the increased computational capability enabled by binary decision diagrams (BDD) techniques. Application is still limited to hardware since the BDD techniques only apply to finite state systems. It is now a common perception that model checking for software systems requires a combined use of deductive and model-theoretic techniques. We feel behavioural specification offers a very good common ground for this. The example in Section 4 is the first step toward this.

We are building an integrated specification/verification environment on top of the CafeOBJ system. The planned features include a more efficient built-in resolution engine, an inductive theorem prover, and a behavioural model checking system. We also plan to have more substantial examples of distributed algorithms, fault-tolerant protocols, and security protocols. This is very important not just for theoreticians to get feedback, but also for practitioners to enhance the applicability of the method.

Acknowledgement. We thank Prof. Joseph Goguen for his pioneering work in algebraic specification theory and for creating a new exciting field of study for us.

References

[1] Goguen, J., Malcolm, G.: A Hidden Agenda. To appear in *Theoretical Computer Science*, also available as Technical Report CS97-538, Computer Sci.& Eng. Dept., Univ. of Calif. at San Diego (1997)

[2] Futatsugi, K., Nakagawa, A.: An Overview of CAFE Specification Environment: an algebraic approach for creating, verifying, and maintaining formal specification over networks, Proc. of *First IEEE Int'l. Conf. on Formal Engineering Methods* (1997)

[3] Diaconescu, R., Futatsugi, K.: CafeOBJ *Report.* World Scientific (1998)

[4] Diaconescu, R: Behavioural Coherence in Object-oriented Algebraic Specification. Technical Report IS-RR-98-0017F, Japan Advanced Institute of Science and Technology (1998)

[5] Roşu, G., Goguen, J.: Hidden Congruent Deduction. To appear in *Lecture Notes in Artificial Intelligence* (1999)

[6] Bidoit, M., Hennicker, R., Wirsing, M.: Behavioural and Abstractor Specifications. *Science of Computer Programming* **25(2-3)** (1995) 149–186

[7] Milner, R.: *Communication and Concurrency.* Prentice-Hall (1989)

[8] Bartlett, K., Scantlebury, R., Wilkinson, P.: A Note on Reliable Full-duplex Transmission over Half-duplex Links. *Communication of the ACM* **12(5)** (1969) 260–261

[9] Malcolm, G., Goguen, J.: Proving Correctness of Refinement and Implementation. Technical Monograph PRG-114, Programming Research Group, University of Oxford (1994)

[10] Goguen, J.. Mori, A., Lin, K, Roşu, G., Sato, A.: Distributed Cooperative Formal Methods Tools. Proc. of *IEEE First Int'l Conf. on Automated Software Engineering* (1997) 55–62

[11] Paramarcos, M., Patel, J.: A Low-Overhead Coherence Solution for Multiprocessors with Private Cache Memories. Proc. of *Eleventh Int'l. Symp. on Computer Architecture* (1984) 348–354

[12] Pong, F.: Symbolic State Model: A New Approach for the Verification of Cache Coherence Protocols. Ph.D. Thesis, Dept. of Electrical Engineering-Systems, Univ. of Southern California (1995)

[13] Jacobs, B.: Invariants, Bisimulations and the Correctness of Coalgebraic Refinements. *Lecture Notes in Computer Science* **1349** (1998) 276–291

[14] Cousot, P., Cousot, R.: Refining Model Checking by Abstract Interpretation. To appear in *Automated Software Engineering Journal* **6(1)** (1999) 69–95

[15] Lynch, N.: Distributed Algorithms. Morgan Kaufman Pub. Inc. (1996)

[16] Gurevich, Y.: Evolving Algebras 1993: Lipari Guide. In Börger, ed. *Specification and Validation Methods*, Oxford University Press (1995) 9–36

[17] Cîrstea, C.: Coalgebra Semantics for Hidden Algebra: Parameterised Objects and Inheritance. *Lecture Notes in Computer Science* **1376** (1998)

A   A CafeOBJ Session for the Alternating Bit Protocol

```
mori(d194-054)[1024]cafeobj
-- loading standard prelude
Loading /usr/local/cafeobj-1.4/prelude/std.bin
Finished loading /usr/local/cafeobj-1.4/prelude/std.bin


             -- CafeOBJ system Version 1.4.2(b3+) --
                 built: 1998 Nov 28 Sat 6:29:00 GMT
                     prelude file: std.bin
                            ***
                  1999 Feb 10 Mon 16:46:26 GMT
                      Type ? for help
                          ---
                 uses GCL (GNU Common Lisp)
           Licensed under GNU Public Library License
              Contains Enhancements by W. Schelter
CafeOBJ> in abp
processing input : ./abp.mod
-- defining module! DATA_*.._* done.
-- defining module! QUEUE_*_*............._....* done.
-- defining module* SENDER............._...*
** system already proved =*= is a congruence of SENDER done.
-- defining module* RECEIVER............._...*
** system already proved =*= is a congruence of RECEIVER done.
-- defining module* ABP,,,,,,,*_*............._.
** system failed to prove =*= is a congruence of ABP done.
CafeOBJ> in test
processing input : ./test.mod
-- opening module ABP.. done.
-- reduce in % : Val(Out(In(2,Out(In(1,Init)))))
2 : NzNat
(0.000 sec for parse, 99 rewrites(0.020 sec), 142 matches)
-- reduce in % : Val(Out(In(2,In(1,Init))))
1 : NzNat
(0.000 sec for parse, 46 rewrites(0.000 sec), 78 matches)
-- reduce in % : Val(Out(In(3,In(2,In(1,Init)))))
1 : NzNat
(0.000 sec for parse, 53 rewrites(0.010 sec), 96 matches)
-- reduce in % : Val(Out(In(3,In(2,Out(In(1,Init))))))
2 : NzNat
(0.000 sec for parse, 114 rewrites(0.010 sec), 170 matches)
-- reduce in % : Val(Out(In(3,Out(Out(In(2,Out(In(1,Init))))))))
3 : NzNat
(0.000 sec for parse, 250 rewrites(0.020 sec), 354 matches)
CafeOBJ>
```

Component-Based Algebraic Specification and Verification in CafeOBJ

Răzvan Diaconescu*, Kokichi Futatsugi, and Shusaku Iida

Japan Advanced Institute of Science and Technology

Abstract. We present a formal method for component-based system specification and verification which is based on the new algebraic specification language CafeOBJ, which is a modern successor of OBJ incorporating several new developments in algebraic specification theory and practice.

We first give an overview of the main features of CafeOBJ, including its logical foundations, and then we focus on the behavioural specification paradigm in CafeOBJ, surveying the object-oriented CafeOBJ specification and verification methodology based on behavioural abstraction.

The last part of this paper further focuses on a component-based behavioural specification and verification methodology which features high reusability of both specification code and verification proof scores. This methodology constitutes the basis for an industrial strength formal method around CafeOBJ.

1 Overview of CafeOBJ

CafeOBJ (whose definition is given by [7]) is a modern successor of the OBJ language [18, 10] incorporating several new major developments in algebraic specification theory and practice. It is aimed to be an industrial strength language, suitable both for researchers and for practitioners. This section is devoted to a brief overview of CafeOBJ, including its main features, its specification and verification environment, and its logical foundations.

1.1 CafeOBJ Main Features

Equational Specification and Programming. This is inherited from OBJ [18, 10] and constitutes the basis of the language, the other features being somehow built on top of it. As with OBJ, CafeOBJ is *executable* (by term rewriting), which gives an elegant declarative way of functional programming, often referred as *algebraic programming*.[1]
As with OBJ, CafeOBJ also permits equational specification modulo several equational theories such as associativity, commutativity, identity, idempotence, and combinations between all these. This feature is reflected at the execution level by term rewriting *modulo* such equational theories.

---

* On leave from the Institute of Mathematics of the Romanian Academy, PO Box 1-764, Bucharest 70700, ROMANIA.
[1] Please notice that although this paradigm may be used as programming, this aspect is still secondary to its specification side.

J. Wing, J. Woodcock, J. Davies (Eds.): FM'99, Vol. II, LNCS 1709, pp. 1644–1663, 1999.
© Springer-Verlag Berlin Heidelberg 1999

Behavioural Specification. Behavioural specification [13, 14, 4] provides another novel generalization of ordinary algebraic specification but in a different direction. Behavioural specification characterizes how objects (and systems) *behave*, not how they are implemented. This new form of abstraction can be very powerful in the specification and verification of software systems since it naturally embeds other useful paradigms such as concurrency, object-orientation, constraints, nondeterminism, etc. (see [14] for details). Behavioural abstraction is achieved by using specification with hidden sorts and a behavioural concept of satisfaction based on the idea of indistinguishability of states that are observationally the same, which also generalizes process algebra and transition systems (see [14]).

CafeOBJ directly supports behavioural specification and its proof theory through special language constructs, such as

- hidden sorts (for states of systems),
- behavioural operations (for direct "actions" and "observations" on states of systems),
- behavioural coherence declarations for (non-behavioural) operations (which might be either derived (indirect) "observations" or "constructors" on states of systems), and
- behavioural axioms (stating behavioural satisfaction).

The advanced coinduction proof method receives support in CafeOBJ via a default (candidate) coinduction relation (denoted $=*=$). In CafeOBJ, coinduction can be used either in the classical HSA sense [14] for proving behavioural equivalence of states of objects, or for proving behavioural transitions (which appear when applying behavioural abstraction to RWL).[2]

Besides language constructs, CafeOBJ supports behavioural specification and verification by several methodologies.[3] CafeOBJ currently highlights a methodology for concurrent object composition which features high reusability not only of specification code but also of verifications [7, 8]. Behavioural specification in CafeOBJ might also be effectively used as an object-oriented (state-oriented) alternative for traditional ADT specifications. Experiments seem to indicate that an object-oriented style of specification even of basic data types (such as sets, lists, etc.) might lead to higher simplicity of code and drastic simplification of verification process [7].

Behavioural specification is reflected at the execution level by the concept of *behavioural rewriting* [7, 4] which refines ordinary rewriting with a condition ensuring the correctness of the use of behavioural equations in proving strict equalities.

Rewriting Logic Specification. Rewriting logic specification in CafeOBJ is based on a simplified version of Meseguer's *rewriting logic* [20] specification framework for concurrent systems which gives a non-trivial extension of traditional algebraic specification towards concurrency. RWL incorporates many different models of concurrency

---

[2] However, until the time this paper was written, the latter has not been yet explored sufficiently, especially practically.

[3] This is still an open research topic, the current methodologies might be developed further and new methodologies might be added in the future.

in a natural, simple, and elegant way, thus giving CafeOBJ a wide range of applications. Unlike Maude [2], the current CafeOBJ design does not fully support *labelled* RWL which permits full reasoning about multiple transitions between states (or system configurations), but provides proof support for reasoning about the *existence* of transitions between states (or configurations) of concurrent systems via a built-in predicate (denoted ==>) with dynamic definition encoding both the proof theory of RWL and the user defined transitions (rules) into equational logic.

From a methodological perspective, CafeOBJ develops the use of RWL transitions for specifying and verifying the properties of *declarative encoding of algorithms* (see [7]) as well as for specifying and verifying transition systems.

Module System. The principles of the CafeOBJ module system are inherited from OBJ which builds on ideas first realized in the language Clear [1], most notably institutions [11, 9]. CafeOBJ module system features

- several kinds of imports,
- sharing for multiple imports,
- parameterized programming allowing
  - multiple parameters,
  - views for parameter instantiation,
  - integration of CafeOBJ specifications with executable code in a lower level language
- module expressions.

However, the theory supporting the CafeOBJ module system represents an updating of the original Clear/OBJ concepts to the more sophisticated situation of multi-paradigm systems involving theory morphisms across institution embeddings [5], and the concrete design of the language revise the OBJ view on importation modes and parameters [7].

Type System and Partiality. CafeOBJ has a type system that allows subtypes based on *order sorted algebra* (abbreviated **OSA**) [17, 12]. This provides a mathematically rigorous form of runtime type checking and error handling, giving CafeOBJ a syntactic flexibility comparable to that of untyped languages, while preserving all the advantages of strong typing.

Since at this moment there are many order sortedness formalisms, many of them very little different from others, and each of them having its own technical advantages and disadvantages and being most appropriate for a certain class of applications, we decided to keep the concrete order sortedness formalism open at least at the level of the language definition. Instead we formulate some basic simple conditions which any concrete CafeOBJ order sorted formalism should obey. These conditions come close to Meseguer's OSA^R [21] which is a revised version of other versions of order sortedness existing in the literature, most notably Goguen's OSA [12].

CafeOBJ does not directly do partial operations but rather handles them by using error sorts and a sort membership predicate in the style of *membership equational logic* (abbreviated **MEL**) [21]. The semantics of specifications with partial operations is given by MEL.

1.2   The CafeOBJ Specification and Verification Environment

Although this is rather a feature of the current system rather than of the language, due to its importance for the effective use of the current CafeOBJ system, we briefly survey it here.

The CafeOBJ system includes an environment supporting specification documents with formal contents over networks and enabling formal verifications of specifications. The CafeOBJ environment takes advantage of current InterNet technologies and can be thought as consisting of four parts:

- The **interpreter** in isolation acts very much like the OBJ3 interpreter by checking syntax and evaluating (reducing) terms. In addition, the CafeOBJ interpreter incorporates an abstract TRS machine and a compiler.
- The **proof assistant** extends the theorem proving capabilities of the interpreter with more powerful, dedicated provers.
- The **document manager** takes care of processing of specification documents over networks.
- **Specification libraries** focus on several specific problem domains, such as object-oriented programming, database management, interactive systems, etc.

1.3   CafeOBJ Logical Foundations

CafeOBJ is a declarative language with firm mathematical and logical foundations in the same way as other OBJ-family languages (OBJ, Eqlog [15, 3], FOOPS [16], Maude [20]) are. The reference paper for the CafeOBJ mathematical foundations is [6], while the book [7] gives a somehow less mathematical easy-to-read (including many examples) presentation of the semantics of CafeOBJ. In this section we give a very brief overview of the CafeOBJ logical and mathematical foundations, for a full understanding of this aspect of CafeOBJ the reader is referred to [6] and [7].

The mathematical semantics of CafeOBJ is based on state-of-the-art algebraic specification concepts and results, and is strongly based on category theory and the theory of institutions [11, 5, 9]. The following are the principles governing the logical and mathematical foundations of CafeOBJ:

P1. there is an underlying logic[4] in which all basic constructs and features of the language can be rigorously explained.
P2. provide an integrated, cohesive, and unitary approach to the semantics of specification in-the-small and in-the-large.
P3. develop all ingredients (concepts, results, etc.) at the highest appropriate level of abstraction.

The CafeOBJ Cube. CafeOBJ is a multi-paradigm language. Each of the main paradigms implemented in CafeOBJ is rigorously based on some underlying logic; the paradigms resulting from various combinations are based on the combination of

---

[4] Here "logic" should be understood in the modern relativistic sense of "institution" which provides a mathematical definition for a logic (see [11]) rather than in the more classical sense.

logics. The structure of these logics is shown by the following **CafeOBJ cube** , where the arrows mean embedding between the logics, which correspond to institution embeddings (i.e., a strong form of institution morphisms of [11, 9]) (the orientation of arrows correspond to embedding "less complex" into "more complex" logics).

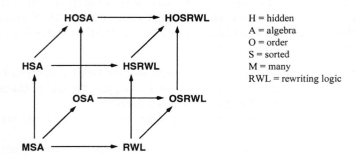

H = hidden
A = algebra
O = order
S = sorted
M = many
RWL = rewriting logic

The mathematical structure represented by this cube is that of a *lattice of institution embeddings* [5, 6]. By employing other logical-based paradigms the CafeOBJ cube may be thought as a hyper-cube (see [6, 7] for details). It is important to understand that th CafeOBJ logical foundations are based on the CafeOBJ cube rather than on its flattening represented by HOSRWL.[5]

The design of CafeOBJ lead to several important developments in algebraic specification theory. One of them is the concept of *extra theory morphism* [5], which is a concept of theory morphism across institution embeddings, generalizing the ordinary (intra) theory morphisms to the multi-paradigm situation. Another important theoretical development is constituted by the formalism underlying behavioural specification in CafeOBJ which is a non-trivial extension of classical hidden algebra [14] in several directions, most notably permitting operations with several hidden arguments via the crucial *coherence* property. This extension is called "coherent hidden algebra" in [4] and comes very close to the "observational logic" of Bidoit and Hennicker [19]. The details of the "coherent hidden algebra" institution can be found in [6].

2   Behavioural Specification in CafeOBJ

Behavioural specification might be the most distinctive feature of CafeOBJ within the broad family of algebraic specification languages. As mentioned above, behavioural specification paradigm is incorporated into the design of the language in a rather direct way. Also, this paradigm constitutes the core of the current CafeOBJ object-oriented specification and verification methodologies. We devote this section to a methodological presentation of the behavioural specification paradigm in CafeOBJ, trying also to explain the main concepts behind this paradigm.

---

[5] The technical reason for this is that model reducts across some of the edges (i.e., the left-to-right ones) of the CafeOBJ cube involve both an ordinary model reduct and a non-trivial reduct along the corresponding institution embedding, see [6, 5, 7] for details.

2.1 Basic Behavioural Specification

Basic behavioural specification is the simplest level of behavioural specification in which the operations are either *actions* or *observations* on the states of the objects. Let us consider an object-oriented (or "state-oriented") CafeOBJ specification for lists:

```
mod! TRIV+ (X :: TRIV) {
  op err :  -> ?Elt
}
mod* LIST  {
  protecting(TRIV+)
  *[ List ]*
  op nil : -> List
  bop cons : Elt List-> List  -- action
  bop car : List -> ?Elt      -- observation
  bop cdr : List -> List      -- action
  vars E E' : Elt
  var L : List
  eq car(nil) = err .
  eq car(cons(E, L)) = E .
  beq cdr(nil) = nil .
  beq cdr(cons(E, L)) = L .
}
```

This is quite different from the usual data-oriented specification of lists. In our behavioural specification, lists are treated as *objects* with states (the sort of states is the *hidden* sort List), and the usual list operations (*cons* and *cdr*) *act* on the states of the list object or (*car*) *observe* the states. Actions and observations are specified as *behavioural* operations. In general, a behavioural operation is called *action* iff its sort is hidden (i.e., state type), and is called *observation* iff its sort is visible (i.e., data type). Behavioural operations are restricted to have *exactly* one hidden sort in their arity, this monadicity property being characteristic to behavioural operations (either actions or observations). Behavioural operations define the *behavioural equivalence* relation between the states of the object, denoted as $\sim$:

$$s \sim s' \ \text{ iff } \ [c(s) = c(s') \ \text{ for all } \textit{visible behavioural contexts } c]$$

A behavioural context c is any string of behavioural operations (this makes sense because of the monadicity property on hidden sorts of the behavioural operations). c is visible iff its sort is visible; this is the same as saying that c has an observation at the top. It is important to notice that behavioural equivalence is a semantic notion; this means that whenever we consider a behavioural equivalence relation we need to consider a model (i.e., an implementation) for the specification[6].

CafeOBJ methodologies introduce a graphical notation extending the classical ADJ-diagram notation for data types for behavioural specification in which

G1. *Sorts are represented by ellipsoidal disks with visible (data) sorts represented in white and hidden (state) sorts represented in grey, and with subsort inclusion represented by disk inclusion, and*

---

[6] Which needs not to be a concrete one.

G2. *Operations are represented by multi-source arrows with the monadic part from the hidden sort thickened in case of behavioural operations.*

The list specification can be therefore visualised as follows:

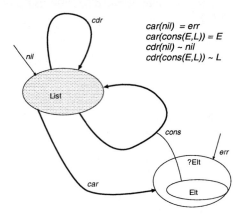

$$
\begin{aligned}
car(nil) &= err \\
car(cons(E,L)) &= E \\
cdr(nil) &\sim nil \\
cdr(cons(E,L)) &\sim L
\end{aligned}
$$

Several other aspects of this specifications need special attention. The first one concerns the data of this specification and the error handling aspect of this methodology. LIST specifies a list object over any set of elements. "Any set of elements" is specified by the built-in module TRIV which specifies one sort (Elt) with loose denotation (hence its denotation is given by all sets); this is used as a parameter of the specification LIST and can be instantiated to any concrete data type. The error handling aspect arises because of the partiality of *car*. TRIV+ just introduces a new error element (*err*). The error supersort ?Elt is built-in[7] and *err* is the only new element belonging to [the denotation of] ?Elt; this is ensured by the free extension of [the loose denotation of] TRIV which is specified by giving TRIV+ initial denotation (**mod!**). Notice that this style of error handling contrasts the more complex data-oriented approach which uses a subsort for the non-empty lists and overloads the list operations on this subsort. This methodological simplification is mainly possible because of the loose denotation of behavioural specification (with the adequate "loose" behavioural equality) which avoids the strictness of the initial denotation of the data-oriented approach.

Another aspect is given by the use of behavioural equations in the specification LIST. Behavioural equations represent behavioural equivalence relations between states rather than strict equalities. Therefore each model (implementation) of LIST does not need to interpret *cdr(cons(e,l))* as *l*, where *e* is an element and *l* is a list[8], but rather as a state behavioural equivalent to *l*. For example, if one implements the list object as an array with pointer, in this model (implementation) this equality does not hold strictly, but it holds behaviourally. Generally speaking, behavioural equality is the meaningful equality on hidden sorts, while the strict equality is the meaningful equality for the visible (data) sorts. However, there are situations when the strict equality on hidden sorts is also necessary. Behavioural abstraction also provides a nice way of error handling for

---

[7] It is provided by the system.

[8] Better said, a state of the list object.

hidden sorts, as shown by the other behavioural equation. Thus instead of introducing a (hidden) error for *cdr(nil)*, we rather shift the error handling to the data type by saying this is behaviourally equivalent to *nil*.[9] A finer analysis of the behavioural equivalence on the list object (see the section below) tells us that the behavioural equality between *cdr(nil)* and *nil* is exactly the same with saying that $car(cdr^n(nil)) = err$ for all natural numbers *n*, which is the natural minimal condition for the behaviour of *nil*.

2.2 Behavioural Specification with Hidden Constructors

Behavioural specification with hidden constructors is a more advanced level of behavioural specification which relies on the important novel concept of *behavioural coherence* first defined and studied in [7, 4] and which was first realized by the CafeOBJ language [7].

At the general level, a *hidden constructor* is an operation on hidden sorts[10] whose sort is also hidden and which is not declared behavioural. This means that such operation does *not* take part in the definition of the behavioural equivalence relation. Also (and related to the above), a hidden constructor need not be monadic on the hidden sorts, thus it may admit several hidden sorts in the arity.

In the data-oriented specification of lists there is a difference in nature between *cons* and *cdr*, in that *cons* is a "constructor" and *cdr* is a "destructor". This different nature of *cons* and *cdr* reflects in the behavioural specification too and is formally supported by the fact that one may prove (from the specification LIST) that for all lists *l* and *l'*,

$$l \sim l' \text{ iff } [car(cdr^n(l)) = car(cdr^n(l')) \text{ for all natural numbers } n]$$

Technically this means that for the purpose of defining the appropriate behavioural equivalence for lists, *cons* does not play any rôle, therefore it may be specified as an ordinary operation, hence *cons* is a hidden constructor. Consequently, the only *real* behavioural operations are the observation *car* and the action *cdr*. This new specification for lists can be visualized by the following CafeOBJ diagram:

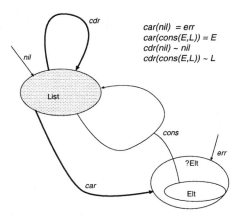

---

[9] Recall that in LISP *cdr(nil)* is also equal to *nil* but under a LISP concept of equality; it may be worthwhile trying to think LISP equality in behavioural abstraction terms.

[10] Which may also have visible sorts in the arity.

This "neutrality" of *cons* with respect to the behavioural equivalence may be understood by the fact that *cons preserves* the behavioural equivalence defined by *cdr* and *car* only. This basic property of hidden constructors is called *coherence* [7, 4], which in general means the preservation of the behavioural equivalence relation by the hidden constructors. In CafeOBJ the coherence property is user specified as an operation attribute:

op *cons* : Elt List -> List   {coherent}

The semantic meaning of a coherence declaration is that the corresponding specification admits only models for which the operation is coherent (i.e., it preserves the behavioural equivalence). For methodological reason CafeOBJ admits potentially non-coherent operations (in the absence of the coherence declaration), however in the final version of the specification all hidden constructors should be declare coherent both for semantical and operational reasons.[11]

2.3   Behavioural Coherence Methodologies

In the above list example the coherence of *cons* can be proved as a formal property of the specification [12]. This means that in any model of this specification the interpretation of *cons* automatically preserves the behavioural equivalence, so the class of models (implementations) of the specification with *cons* not specified as coherent coincides with its subclass of models for the case when *cons* is specified as coherent. Such constructors, which occurs frequently and which are practically desirable are called the *conservative*.

The opposite case is represented by the *non-conservative* constructors, which corresponds to the situation when the class of models for the case when the operation is specified as coherent is a strict subclass of the class of models when the operation is not specified as coherent. Proof-theoretically, this means the coherence property of the operation cannot be formally proved as a consequence property of the [rest of the] specification. Because of its semantical aspect, the methodology of non-conservative constructors is more advanced and sophisticated than the conservative one. However it might be very useful in dealing with non-terminating computations, in a way similar to the the use of commutativity attribute for operations in classical algebraic specification (see [4] for more details).

Proving Behavioural Coherence. We now concentrate to an example illustrating the behavioural coherence methodology of conservative constructors. Consider the following behavioural specification of sets:

---

[11] A simple example is given by the coherence proof scores, when one needs to start with the absence of the coherence declaration for the operation. The coherence declaration is added to the specification only after its proof.

[12] The CafeOBJ proof score for this is rather simple; we leave it as exercise for the reader.

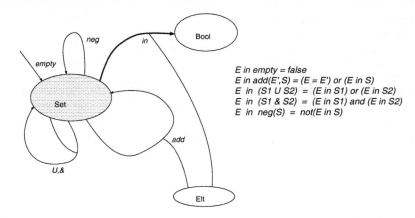

E in empty = false
E in add(E',S) = (E = E') or (E in S)
E in (S1 U S2) = (E in S1) or (E in S2)
E in (S1 & S2) = (E in S1) and (E in S2)
E in neg(S) = not(E in S)

This specification has only one behavioural operation, namely the observation _in_. The hidden constructors *add*, _U_, _&_, and *neg* can be proved coherent by the following CafeOBJ proof score:

open .
    ops *s1 s2 s1' s2'* : -> Set . -- arbitrary sets as temporary constants
    ops *e e'* : -> Elt . -- arbitrary elements as temporary constants
    ceq *S1* =*= *S2* = true if (*e* in *S1*) == (*e* in *S2*) . -- definition of behavioural equivalence
    beq *s1* = *s1'* . -- hypothesis
    beq *s2* = *s2'* . -- hypothesis
    red *add(e, s1)* =*= *add(e, s1')* . -- beh coherence of *add(_)* for variable clash at Elt
    red *add(e', s1)* =*= *add(e', s1')* . -- beh coherence of *add(_)* for no variable clash at Elt
    red (*s1 U s2*) =*= (*s1' U s2'*) . -- beh coherence of _U_
    red (*s1 & s2*) =*= (*s1' & s2'*) . -- beh coherence of _&_
    red *neg(s1)* =*= *neg(s1')* . -- beh coherence of *neg_*
    close
where

Notice the simplicity of this proof score which uses the built-in default coinduction relation =*= which in practice is oftenly the behavioural equivalence. Once the coherence of the hidden constructors is formally proved, their coherence declarations are added to the specification, thus obtaining the final version of the specification under the methodology of conservative hidden constructors.

2.4   Behavioural Verification

One of the great advantages of behavioural specification lies in the simplicity of the verification stage which sometimes contrasts sharply with the complexity of corresponding data type verifications. Sets are one of the examples showing clearly the greater simplicity of behavioural verifications. While the verification of set-theoretic properties in the data approach gets into a very complex induction process, behavioural properties of sets can be proved almost immediately. The following is the very simple CafeOBJ proof score for one of De Morgan laws:

open .
    op *e* : -> Elt .

```
ops s1 s2 s3 : -> Set .
```
-- definition of behavioural equivalence
```
ceq S1:Set =*= S2:Set = true if (e in S1) == (e in S2) .
red neg(s1 U s2) =*= (neg(s1) & neg(s2)) . -- proof of de Morgan law
close
```
Notice that CafeOBJ proof scores follow a certain pattern. Firstly, one "opens" an working module for adding temporary entities; this is the command **open**. The command **close** "closes" the module, thus resetting it to its original content. After opening, one introduces temporary constants which, due to the fact that they are arbitrary, have the meaning of variables local to the proof score. The next step consists of setting up the proof context, involving declaring the hypotheses, etc. The proofs are effectively done by CafeOBJ reduction mechanism (the command red). The inputs of red are usually logical atomic properties which are encoded as Boolean terms, so in general one expects a true answer from the CafeOBJ interpreter for each of such reductions. In case of more complex proofs, a CafeOBJ proof score flatten the corresponding proof tree to a sequence of hypotheses and reductions. In this flattening, properties proved by reductions might be lemmas which might be later used as hypotheses for other reductions.

Behavioural Rewriting. The execution of behavioural specifications is done by behavioural rewriting, which is a refinement of ordinary (term) rewriting that ensures the correctness of rewriting when using behavioural equations as rewrite rules. The basic condition of behavioural rewriting requires the existence of a path formed by behavioural or coherent operations on top of the redex. When inferring strict equalities, it is required in addition that the top of such path is of visible sort. For example, when proving the behavioural coherence of *add*,
```
red add(e, s1) =*= add(e, s1') .
```
means a strict equality reduction. In this case the first behavioural equation of the corresponding proof score cannot be used as a first rewriting step since the condition of behavioural rewriting is not fulfilled. This triggers the use of the conditional equation instead as a first rewriting step, and only after this the use of behavioural equations of the proof score fall under the required condition.

2.5   Behavioural Refinement

Object refinement in behavioural specification is a relaxed form of behavioural specification morphism (see [7] for more details). As an example we show how behavioural lists refine behavioural sets, which corresponds to the basic intuition of sets implemented as lists. For simplicity of presentation we consider here only the case of basic sets, without union, intersection, and negation[13]. The refinement of behavioural basic sets to lists was represented above by extending the graphical notation previously introduced with:

G3. *Refinement of sorts and operations is written by ⫫ and sharing the same figure (disk or arrow) in the diagram.*
G4. *Newly introduced sorts and operations are represented by dotted lines.*

---

[13] Our example can be easily extended to union and intersection, but not so easily to negation.

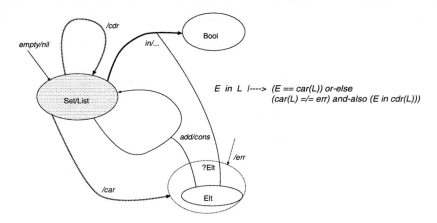

In this refinement, the hidden sort Set is refined to the hidden sort List (this means that any state of the set object and be implemented by a state of the list object), *add* is refined to *cons*. The list object has the observation *car* and the action *cdr* as new behavioural operations and also adds the error handling. The set object observation *_in_* is refined to a derived observation (using some operational versions of the Boolean connectives). This refinement can be encoded in CafeOBJ by the following module import:

> **mod*** LIST' {   protecting(LIST)
> op _in_ : Elt List -> Bool {coherent} -- coherence provable from the rest of spec
> vars *E E'* : Elt
> var *L* : List
> eq *E in L = (E == car(L)) or-else (car(L) =/= err and-also E in cdr(L))* . }

The following is the proof score for the fact that the mapping defined above is indeed a refinement, i.e., the property of *add* holds for *cons*:[14]

> **open** LIST' .
> ops *e e1 e2* : -> Elt . -- arbitrary elements as temporary constants
> op *l* : -> List . -- arbitrary list as temporary constant
> eq *e1 in l* = true . -- the basic case when the element does belong to the list
> eq *e2 in l* = false . -- the basic case when the element does not belong to the list
> red *e in nil*   == false . -- the *nil* case
> red *e1 in cons(e,l)* == true .
> red *e2 in cons(e,l)* == false .
> red *e in cons(e,l)* == true . -- the element clash case
> **close**

3   Concurrent Object Composition in CafeOBJ

In this section we present the object composition method of CafeOBJ based on the behavioural specification paradigm. We present here a simplified method which does not use behavioural coherence. We use UML to represent object composition:

---

[14] This involves a small case analysis.

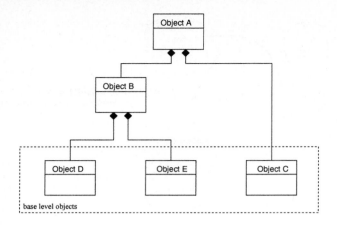

In the above UML figure, B is composed of D and E, A of B and C, and non-compound objects (i.e., objects with no components) are called *base level objects*. A composition in UML is represented by line tipped by a diamond, and if necessary, qualified by the numbers of components (**1** for one and * for many).

Projection operations from the hidden sort of the states of the compound object to the hidden sorts of the states of the component objects constitute the main technical concept underlying the CafeOBJ composition method; projection operations are related to the lines of UML figures. Projection operations are subject to the following mathematical conditions [8, 7]. Given a compound object O (with signature $(V \cup H, \Sigma)$ for which V is a set of visible sorts and H is a set of hidden sorts), a set of the labels of its components Obj, and the components $\{O_n\}_{n \in Obj}$ of O (with signatures $(V_n \cup H_n, \Sigma_n)$), the projection operations $\pi_n : h \to h_n$ (with $h \in H$ and $h_n \in H_n$) for each $n \in Obj$ satisfy the following conditions:

1. for each observation o of O, there exists $n \in Obj$ and a data (possibly derived) operation $f : v_{n_1}...v_{n_i} \to v$ ($v_{n_i} \in V_n$ and $v \in V$ where i is a natural number), and for each n_k with $k \in \{1,...,i\}$ a visible O_{n_k}-context c_{n_k} (i.e., made only of operations of the signature of O_{n_k}) such that $o(X) = f((c_{n_1} \circ \pi_{n_1})(X),...,(c_{n_i} \circ \pi_{n_i})(X))$ for all states X,

2. for each action a of O, and for each $n \in Obj$, there exists a sequence of actions a_n such that $\pi_n \circ a = a_n \circ \pi_n$, and

3. for each constant *const* of O, and for each $n \in Obj$, there exists a constant $const_n$ such that $\pi_n(const) = const_n$ (i.e., the initial state of a compound object should be is related to the initial state of each component.)

In the compound objects we only define communication between the components; this means that the only equations at the level of the specification of the compound objects are the ones relating the actions and observations of the compound objects to those of the components as described above. In the case of synchronized compositions, the equations of the previous definition are conditional rather than unconditional. Their conditions are subject to the following:

- each condition is a finite conjunction of equalities between terms of the form $c_n \circ \pi_n$ (where π_n is a projection operator and c_n is an O_n-context) and terms in the data signature, and
- disjunction of all the conditions corresponding to a given left hand side (of equations regarded as a rewrite rule) is true.

3.1   Parallel Connection

The components of a composite object are connected (unsynchronized) in parallel if there is no synchronization between them. In order to define the concept of synchronization, we have to introduce the concept of *action group*. Two actions of a compound object are in the same action group when they change the state of the same component object via a projection operation. Synchronization appears when:

- there exists an overlapping between some action groups, or
- the projected state of the compound object (via a projection operation) depends on the state of a different (from the object corresponding to the projection operation) component.

The first case is sometimes called *broadcasting* and the second case is sometimes called *client-server computing*. In the unsynchronized case, we have full concurrency between all the components, which means that all the actions of the compound object can be applied concurrently, therefore the components can be implemented as distributed processes or concurrent processes with multi-thread which are based on asynchronous communications.

For unsynchronized parallel connection, we consider a bank account system example. Firstly, we consider a very simple bank account system which consists of a fixed numbers of individual accounts, lets actually consider the case of just two accounts. The specification of an account can be obtained just by renaming the specification COUNTER1 of a counter object with integers as follows

    mod* ACCOUNT1 { protecting(COUNTER1 *{ hsort Counter -> Account1,
                                    op init-counter -> init-account1 })}
    mod* ACCOUNT2 { protecting(COUNTER1 *{ hsort Counter -> Account2,
                                    op init-counter -> init-account2 })}

where COUNTER1 is represented in CafeOBJ graphical notation as follows:

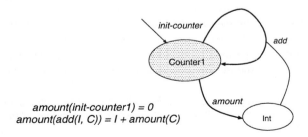

$$amount(init\text{-}counter1) = 0$$
$$amount(add(I, C)) = I + amount(C)$$

We then compose these two account objects as in the following double figure containing both the UML and the CafeOBJ graphical[15] representation of this composition, where *deposit1* and *withdraw1* are the actions for the first account, *balance1* is the observation for the first account, *account1* is the projection operation for the first account, and *deposit2, withdraw2, balance2,* and *account2* are the corresponding actions, observation, and projection operation for the second account:

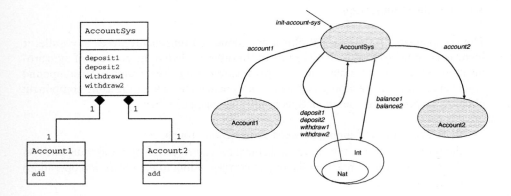

The equations for this parallel connection (composition) are as follows:

eq *balance1(AS) = amount(account1(AS))* .
eq *balance2(AS) = amount(account2(AS))* .
eq *account1(init-account-sys) = init-account1* .
eq *account1(deposit1(N, AS)) = add(N, account1(AS))* .
eq *account1(deposit2(N, AS)) = account1(AS)* .
eq *account1(withdraw1(N, AS)) = add(-(N), account1(AS))* .
eq *account1(withdraw2(N, AS)) = account1(AS)* .
eq *account2(init-account-sys) = init-account2* .
eq *account2(deposit1(N, AS)) = account2(AS)* .
eq *account2(deposit2(N, AS)) = add(N, account2(AS))* .
eq *account2(withdraw1(N, AS)) = account2(AS)* .
eq *account2(withdraw2(N, AS)) = add(-(N), account2(AS))* .

Notice that besides the first two equations relating the observations on the compound object to those on the components, the other equations relate the actions of the account system to the actions of the components. Remark that the actions corresponding to one component do not change the state of the second component (via the projection operation), hence this composition is unsynchronized. In fact these equations expressing the concurrency of composition need not be specified by the user, in their absence they may be generated internally by the system, thus reducing the specification of the composition to the essential information which should be provided by the user.

---

[15] The CafeOBJ graphical representation corresponds to the module defining this object composition rather than to the "flattened" specification, hence the operations of the components are not included in the figure.

3.4   Compositionality of Verifications

In object-oriented programming, reusability of the source code is important, but in object-oriented specification, reusability of the proofs is also very important because of the verification process. We call this *compositionality of verifications* of components. In the CafeOBJ object composition method this is achieved by the following fundamental Theorem (for its proof see [8]):

Theorem 1. *Given the states s and s' of a compound object then the behavioural equivalence $\sim$ of the compound object is defined as follows:*

$$s \sim s' \ iff \ \pi_n(s) \sim_n \pi_n(s') \ for \ all \ n \in Obj$$

where Obj is a set of the labels for the components (you can consider these labels as the names of the component modules), π_n is the projection operation corresponding to the component object n, and $\sim_n$ is the behavioural equivalence of the component. $\square$

Therefore, in the case of a hierarchic object composition, the behavioural equivalence for the whole system is just the conjunction of the behavioural equivalences of the base level objects, which are generally rather simple.

For example, the behavioural equivalence for the bank account system is a conjunction of the behavioural equivalence Account (indexed by the user identifiers) and UserDB, and these two are checked automatically by the CafeOBJ system. This means that behavioural proofs for the bank account system are almost automatic, without having to go through the usual coinduction process. Therefore, the behavioural equivalence _R[_]_ of AccountSys can be defined by the following CafeOBJ code:

```
mod BEQ-ACCOUNT-SYSTEM {  protecting(ACCOUNT-SYSTEM)
 op _R[_]_ : AccountSys Uid AccountSys -> Bool
 vars AS1 AS2 : AccountSys
 var U : Uid
 eq AS1 R[U] AS2 = account(U, AS1) =*= account(U, AS2) and
                   user-db(AS1) =*= user-db(AS2) . }
```

Notice the use of the parameterized relation for handling the conjunction indexed by the user identifiers.

Now, we will prove the true concurrency of withdrawals of two different users, which can be considered as a safety property for this system of bank accounts and which is formulated as the following commutativity behavioural property:

$$withdraw(u1, n1, withdraw(u2, n2, as)) \sim withdraw(u2, n2, withdraw(u1, n1, as))$$

The following CafeOBJ code builds the proof tree containing all possible cases formed by orthogonal combinations of atomic cases for the users with respect to their membership to the user accounts data base. The basic proof term is *TERM*. The automatic generation of the proof tree (*RESULT*)is done by a meta-level encoding in CafeOBJ by using its rewrite engine for one-directional construction of the proof tree (this process uses the rewriting logic feature of CafeOBJ, hence the use of transitions (trans) rather than equations).

```
mod PROOF-TREE {  protecting(BEQ-ACCOUNT-SYSTEM)
 ops n1 n2 : -> Nat  -- arbitrary amounts for withdrawal
```

ops *u u1 u1' u2 u2'* : -> UId -- arbitrary user identifiers
op *as* : -> AccountSys -- arbitrary state of the account system
eq *u1 in user-db(as)* = true . -- first user is in the data base
eq *u2 in user-db(as)* = true . -- second user is in the data base
eq *u1' in user-db(as)* = false . -- first user is not in the data base
eq *u2' in user-db(as)* = false . -- second user is not in the data base
vars *U U1 U2* : UId
op *TERM* : UId UId UId -> Bool -- basic proof term
trans *TERM(U, U1, U2)* => *withdraw(U1, n1, withdraw(U2, n2, as)) R[U]*
                          withdraw(U2, n2, withdraw(U1, n1, as)) .
op *TERM1* : UId UId -> Bool
trans *TERM1(U, U1)* => *TERM(U, U1, u2) and TERM(U, U1, u2')* .
op *TERM2* : UId -> Bool
trans *TERM2(U)* => *TERM1(U, u1) and TERM1(U, u1')* .
op *RESULT* : -> Bool -- final proof term
trans *RESULT* => *TERM2(u1) and TERM2(u1') and TERM2(u)* . }

The execution of the proof term *RESULT* gives true after the system performs 233
rewrites.

4   Conclusions and Future Work

In this paper we presented the CafeOBJ object-oriented methodology for component-
based specification and verification which is based on the CafeOBJ behavioural abstraction paradigm. We also presented the basic behavioural specification methodology
in CafeOBJ and gave a brief overview of the CafeOBJ language, system and specification environment.

Future work in this area will further explore and refine the current CafeOBJ methodologies exposed here with the aim of creating an industrial tool around these methodologies containing an industrial-oriented tutorial, a GUI interface probably based on
the current CafeOBJ graphical notation, a graphical proof environment supporting distributed proofs over networks, etc.

Also, the power and sophistication of CafeOBJ gives the possibility to develop alternative behavioural specification and verification methodologies, including component-
based ones. We plan to study such alternative methodologies and their relationship to
the current one.

References

[1] Rod Burstall and Joseph Goguen. The semantics of Clear, a specification language. In
    Dines Bjorner, editor, *Proceedings, 1979 Copenhagen Winter School on Abstract Software
    Specification*, pages 292–332. Springer, 1980. Lecture Notes in Computer Science, Volume
    86.
[2] Manuel Clavel, Steve Eker, Patrick Lincoln, and Jose Meseguer. Principles of Maude.
    Electronic Notes in Theoretical Computer Science, 4, 1996. Proceedings, First International
    Workshop on Rewriting Logic and its Applications. Asilomar, California, September 1996.
[3] Răzvan Diaconescu. Category-based semantics for equational and constraint logic pro-
    gramming, 1994. DPhil thesis, University of Oxford.

[4] Răzvan Diaconescu. Behavioural coherence in object-oriented algebraic specification. Technical Report IS-RR-98-0017F, Japan Advanced Institute for Science and Technology, June 1998. Submitted to publication.
[5] Răzvan Diaconescu. Extra theory morphisms for institutions: logical semantics for multi-paradigm languages. *J. of Applied Categorical Structures*, 6(4):427–453, 1998.
[6] Răzvan Diaconescu and Kokichi Futatsugi. Logical foundations of CafeOBJ. 1998. Submitted to publication.
[7] Răzvan Diaconescu and Kokichi Futatsugi. *CafeOBJ Report: The Language, Proof Techniques, and Methodologies for Object-Oriented Algebraic Specification*, volume 6 of *AMAST Series in Computing*. World Scientific, 1998.
[8] Răzvan Diaconescu, Kokichi Futatsugi, and Shusaku Iida. Component-based algebraic specifications: – behavioural specification for component based software engineering –. In *Behavioural Semantics of Object-oriented Business and System Specification*. Kluwer, 1999.
[9] Răzvan Diaconescu, Joseph Goguen, and Petros Stefaneas. Logical support for modularisation. In Gerard Huet and Gordon Plotkin, editors, *Logical Environments*, pages 83–130. Cambridge, 1993. Proceedings of a Workshop held in Edinburgh, Scotland, May 1991.
[10] Kokichi Futatsugi, Joseph Goguen, Jean-Pierre Jouannaud, and Jose Meseguer. Principles of OBJ2. In *Proceedings of the 12th ACM Symposium on Principles of Programming Languages*, pages 52–66. ACM, 1985.
[11] Joseph Goguen and Rod Burstall. Institutions: Abstract model theory for specification and programming. *Journal of the Association for Computing Machinery*, 39(1):95–146, January 1992.
[12] Joseph Goguen and Răzvan Diaconescu. An Oxford survey of order sorted algebra. *Mathematical Structures in Computer Science*, 4(4):363–392, 1994.
[13] Joseph Goguen and Răzvan Diaconescu. Towards an algebraic semantics for the object paradigm. In Harmut Ehrig and Fernando Orejas, editors, *Recent Trends in Data Type Specification*, volume 785 of *Lecture Notes in Computer Science*, pages 1–34. Springer, 1994.
[14] Joseph Goguen and Grant Malcolm. A hidden agenda. Technical Report CS97-538, University of California at San Diego, 1997.
[15] Joseph Goguen and José Meseguer. Eqlog: Equality, types, and generic modules for logic programming. In Douglas DeGroot and Gary Lindstrom, editors, *Logic Programming: Functions, Relations and Equations*, pages 295–363. Prentice-Hall, 1986.
[16] Joseph Goguen and José Meseguer. Unifying functional, object-oriented and relational programming, with logical semantics. In Bruce Shriver and Peter Wegner, editors, *Research Directions in Object-Oriented Programming*, pages 417–477. MIT, 1987.
[17] Joseph Goguen and José Meseguer. Order-sorted algebra I: Equational deduction for multiple inheritance, overloading, exceptions and partial operations. *Theoretical Computer Science*, 105(2):217–273, 1992.
[18] Joseph Goguen, Timothy Winkler, José Meseguer, Kokichi Futatsugi, and Jean-Pierre Jouannaud. Introducing OBJ. In Joseph Goguen, editor, *Algebraic Specification with OBJ: An Introduction with Case Studies*. Cambridge. To appear.
[19] Rolf Hennicker and Michel Bidoit. Observational logic. In A. M. Haeberer, editor, *Algebraic Methodology and Software Technology*, number 1584 in LNCS, pages 263–277. Springer, 1999. Proc. AMAST'99.
[20] José Meseguer. Conditional rewriting logic as a unified model of concurrency. *Theoretical Computer Science*, 96(1):73–155, 1992.
[21] José Meseguer. Membership algebra as a logical framework for equational specification. In F. Parisi-Pressice, editor, *Proc. WADT'97*, number 1376 in Lecture Notes in Computer Science, pages 18–61. Springer, 1998.

Using Algebraic Specification Techniques in Development of Object-Oriented Frameworks

Shin Nakajima

NEC C&C Media Research Laboratories, Kawasaki, Japan

Abstract. This paper reports experience in using CafeOBJ (a multi-paradigm algebraic specification language) in the development of object-oriented frameworks of the ODP trader that is implemented with Java and JavaIDL. We first identify several aspects in the target problem before applying the known techniques of developing object-oriented frameworks. We use CafeOBJ to describe each aspect solution to mechanically check the integrity of the descriptions when all the aspects are put together. Although the experience is based on a particular problem only, the proposed method is clear enough to give a systematically and sharply focused help in reaching the solution, and to illustrate practice of using formal methods in the process.

1   Introduction

Formal methods are finding increasingly widespread use in the development of complex software systems and several notable projects are reported that have used the technology successfully [9]. The technology, however, has not yet reached the level where most software engineers use formal methods in their daily work. The basis of formal methods is mathematically-based languages for specifying and verifying software systems. Generally a specification language is used for writing functional properties and is able to handle only one aspect of the system. Thus, we often rest satisfied with specifying essential or critical properties of the system even when we use formal methods.

In real world software systems, however, characteristics other than functional properties such as ease of customization or maintenance are equally important. Software system, at the same time, can be viewed as an aggregate of various heterogeneous, often interrelated, subproblems [17]. Identifying aspects that can be tackled with a formal specification language is sometimes the most difficult task. Establishing the methodological principles of selecting and applying formal software development techniques is important[7].

This paper reports experience in using an algebraic specification language CafeOBJ [11][13] in the development of the ODP trading service [1], and in particular focuses on the design method. The trading server is implemented as object-oriented frameworks [10][18] so that it has a well-organized architecture making it easy to customize. We first identify a set of distinct aspects in the problem. Next, we refine and elaborate each aspect by using various specification

J. Wing, J. Woodcock, J. Davies (Eds.): FM'99, Vol. II, LNCS 1709, pp. 1664–1683, 1999.
© Springer-Verlag Berlin Heidelberg 1999

techniques for each one. Because the basic idea of identifying distinct aspects is decomposition, completing the system requires an integration of all. We use CafeOBJ to write solutions of each aspect, and thus checking the integrity is made possible when all the aspect descriptions are put together.

The present paper is organized as follows: section 2 explains the ODP trading service server. Section 3 reports on our experience in design and implementation of the ODP trading service server. Section 4 concludes the paper, and the appendix gives small example CafeOBJ specifications as an introduction to the language.

2   Trading Service Server

To facilitate the construction of distributed application systems, common service objects for distributed computing environments are being established [2]. The ODP trader provides functionalities to manage service in an open globally distributed environment [1].

2.1   The ODP Trader

The ODP trader is widely accepted because it is defined following the RM-ODP [24] (a result of a longterm joint effort by ISO and ITU-T) that aims to provide a general architectural framework for distributed systems in a multi-vendor environment. The standard document of the ODP trading function follows the guideline of the RM-ODP, and describes three viewpoints: enterprise (requirement capture and early design), information (conceptual design and information modeling), and computational (software design and development). The information viewpoint uses the Z notation to define basic concepts, the trader state, and a set of top-level operations visible from the outside. The computational viewpoint provides a decomposition of the overall functionality into several components and their interactions. It uses IDL [2] to describe the basic datatypes and the top-level operation interfaces, and it supplements the descriptions of all functional properties by using natural language. Actually, the specification written in IDL comprises five major functional interfaces: Lookup, Register, Admin, Link, and Proxy. The computational viewpoint is technically aligned with the OMG trading object service [3], although the OMG trader is restricted to manage service implemented as CORBA objects[1].

2.2   Trading Functions and Design Aspects

Figure 1 shows a trader and the participants in a trading scenario. The Exporter exports a service offer. The Importer imports the service offer and then becomes

---

[1] In this paper, the ODP/OMG trader refers to the computational viewpoint specification.

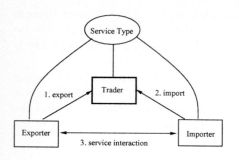

Fig. 1. Trading Scenario

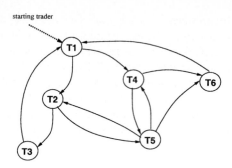

Fig. 2. Federated Trader Group

Aspect (example)	Specification Technique
common concept (service type)	abstract datatype
policy (scoping policy)	functional programming
algorithm (query, federation)	stream-style programming
language (constraint language)	denotational semantics style
functional object (Lookup)	concurrent object
architecture	concurrent object

Table 1. Aspects and Specification techniques

a client of the service. The `Trader` mediates between the two by using the exported service offers stored in its own repository which is ready for import requests. Every service offer has a service type and is considered to be its instance. The service type holds the interface type of the object being advertised and a list of property definitions. A property is a triple of name, type of the value and mode which indicates whether the property is mandatory or optional. Further, a subtype relation is defined between service types. The relation is useful both in importing offers that do not exactly match the request and in defining a new derived service type from the existing ones. The common concept defined in the ODP/OMG trader specification document, such as the service type, the service offer or the property definition, plays a central role in the trading scenario, and thus proper understanding of the concepts is important in designing the trader server.

Because importing, implemented as the `Lookup` interface, is the most complex and interesting function, this paper focuses on its design and implementation. The following IDL fragment shows a portion of a `query` operation of the `Lookup` interface. It is the operation for importing.[2]

```
typedef Istring ServiceTypeName;
typedef Istring Constraint;
typedef Istring Preference;
```

---

[2] Parameters not relevant here are omitted for brevity.

```
void query(
  in ServiceTypeName type,
  in Constraint constr,
  in Preference pref,
  ...
  out OfferSeq offers,
  out OfferIterator offer_itr,
  ...
) raises ( ... )
```

The first parameter `type` specifies the service type name of requested offers. The parameter `constr` is a condition that the offers should satisfy and is a *constraint language* expression that specifies the condition in a concise manner. The expression describes semantically a set of property values of service offers that the client tries to import. The trader searches its repository to find service offers whose property values satisfy the constraint expression. Understanding the search process requires an explicit formulation of the constraint language, and its formal definition would be valuable.

The parameter `pref` is preference information that specifies that the matched offers are sorted according to the preference rule. The sorted offers are returned to the importer in the `out` parameters: `offers` and `offer_itr`. The standard specification also defines a set of *scoping policies* to provide the upper bounds (cardinalities) of offers to be searched at various stages of the search process. Actual values of the cardinalities are determined by a combination of the importer's policies and the trader's policies. Understanding the role of each scoping policy requires grasping the global flow of the base query algorithm.

The ODP/OMG trader defines the specification for interworking or federation of traders to realize scalability. The use of a federated trader group enables a large number of service offers to be partitioned into a set of small offer sets of manageable size. One trader is responsible for each partition and works with the other traders when necessary. Figure 2 shows an example of a federated trader group. The traders T1 to T6 are linked as indicated by the curved arrows. When a `query` is issued on the starting trader T1 and a federated search is requested, traders T2 to T6 also initiate local searches. All the matching offers are collected and returned to the client importer.

The federation process uses a set of policies controlling the graph traversal. A simple one is the `request_id` that cuts out unnecessary visits to the same trader, and another is the `hop_count` that restricts the number of traders to visit. A set of policies called the *FollowOption* controls the traversal semantically. For example, a link marked with `if_no_local` is followed only if no matched offer is found in a trader at the source of the link. Again, the role of each policy is hard to understand without referring to the global flow of the base federation algorithm.

The ODP/OMG standard describes the query and federation algorithm and the role of each policy by using illustrative examples. In particular, the explanation adapts a stream processing style of selecting appropriate offers from an initial candidate set. The overall picture, however, is hard to grasp because the descriptions are informal and scattered over several pages of the document [1][3]. A concise description is needed to prepare a precise design description of the algorithm, and functional programming style is a good candidate.

After the analysis of the trader specification mentioned above, we come to a conclusion that the six aspects in table 1 are mixed together to form the whole system. Table 1 shows the aspects and the accompanying specification techniques. In summary, the ODP/OMG trader is a medium scale, non-trivial problem that has six heterogeneous subproblems. Since the aspects are quite distinct in nature, no general-purpose methodology is adequate. Using specification techniques suitable for each aspect is a better approach to a systematically and sharply focused help in reaching the solution.

3   Design and Implementation

We use Java [5] as the implementation language and JavaIDL [19] as the ORB (Object Request Broker) to implement the trading service server. We also adapt the object-oriented framework technology to construct a highly modular system that aims to allow future customizations and ease of maintenance.

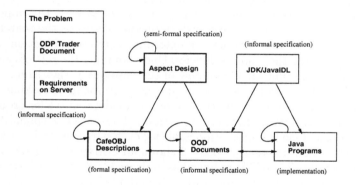

Fig. 3. Development Process

3.1   Overview of Development Process

Figure 3 summarizes the development process, which is one adapted from a process based on the parallel-iterative model of software development [26].

The aspect-centered design phase starts with the analysis of the ODP document and of what is required on the target system. Then the specification techniques that best describe the characteristics of each of the aspects are selected (Table 1). From the semi-formal description of the aspect design, informal specification descriptions are obtained with the help of standard techniques using collaboration-based design [6][8][22] and design patterns [14][18]. In particular, the collaboration-based design, sometimes called scenario-based design, focuses on the analysis of interaction patterns between participant objects, and promotes to use notations such as MSC (Message Sequence Chart). During this phase, the specifications of the JDK library and JavaIDL are referred to. While the informal specifications and the implementation are being prepared, CafeOBJ descriptions of the aspects are also being prepared as the formal specification documents.

The aspect-centered design is quite useful because the ODP/OMG trading service server is a complicated specification. Identifying six important aspects and refining and elaborating each one with an appropriate design technique individually facilitates the design and implementation of the object-oriented frameworks. Aspect design alone, however, comes with one drawback.

The basic idea of the aspect design is decomposition of a complicated problem into a set of various aspects. Conversely, completing the system requires integration of the solutions of each aspect. Without the formal specification descriptions that can be mechanically analyzable, we only have a combination of mostly analyzable functional programs and unanalyzable graphical notations such as MSC. What could do is human design review only. Instead we use a specification language to describe solution descriptions of each aspect, and thus make it easy to check integrity when all the aspect descriptions are put together.

Our choice is a multiparadigm algebraic specification language CafeOBJ, which has clear semantics based on hidden order-sorted rewriting logic [11][13]. The logic subsumes order-sorted equational logic [12][15], concurrent rewriting logic [20], and hidden algebra [16].[3] Being an algebraic specification language, CafeOBJ promotes a property-oriented specification style: the target system is modeled as *algebra* by describing a set of properties to be satisfied. By introducing suitable specification modules (*algebra*), various computational models ranging from MSC[4] to functional programming and concurrent objects can be encoded in CafeOBJ. Further because CafeOBJ has clear operational semantics, specifications written in it are executable. It helps much to validate functionality of the system. The appendix provides a brief introduction to CafeOBJ.

3.2   CafeOBJ Descriptions of Aspect Solutions

This section deals with some example CafeOBJ descriptions of the aspect solution.

Common Concepts Of the entries in Table 1, the common concepts such as `ServiceType` and `PropertyDefinition` are easily translated into CafeOBJ modules because abstract datatype technique provides a concise way to model such basic vocabularies.

---

[3] We will not consider hidden algebra in this paper.

[4] Basically a transition system. The use of MSC in object-oriented modeling and its encoding method in CafeOBJ are described in [22].

The module SERVICE-TYPE-NAME introduces a new sort ServiceTypeName that specifies a set of service type name.

```
mod! SERVICE-TYPE-NAME { [ ServiceTypeName ] }
```

Service type is defined as an abstract data type. The module SERVICE-TYPE provides a concise notation to represent record-like terms and accessor functions. The module SERVICE-SUBTYPING defines the service subtyping relationship. Actually _is-subtype-of_ is a predicate used to calculate whether the operand service types satisfy the subtyping relationship.

```
mod! SERVICE-TYPE {
  [ ServiceType ]
  protecting (PROPERTY-DEFINITION)
  protecting (INTERFACE)
  protecting (SERVICE-TYPE-NAME)
  signature {
   op [name=_, interface=_, properties=_] :
       ServiceTypeName Interface PropertyDefinition -> ServiceType
   op _.name : ServiceType -> ServiceTypeName
   op _.interface : ServiceType -> Interface
   op _.properties : ServiceType -> PropertyDefinition
   op _.property(_) : ServiceType PropertyName -> ModeAndType
   op _.names : ServiceType -> Seq<PropertyName>
  }
  axioms {
    var S : ServiceTypeName  var T : ServiceType
    var N : PropertyName  var I : Interface  var PS : PropertyDefinition

  eq ([name=(S), interface=(I), properties=(PS)]).name = S .
  eq ([name=(S), interface=(I), properties=(PS)]).interface = I .
  eq ([name=(S), interface=(I), properties=(PS)]).properties = PS .
  eq ([name=(S), interface=(I), properties=(PS)]).property(N) =
                                                lookup(PS,N) .
  eq (T).names = names((T).properties) .
  }
}


mod! SERVICE-SUBTYPING {
  protecting (SERVICE-TYPE)
  signature { op _is-subtype-of_ : ServiceType ServiceType -> Bool }
  axioms {
    vars T1 T2 : ServiceType

  eq (T1) is-subtype-of (T2)
  =    (((T1).interface is-subinterface-of (T2).interface)
  and ((T1).names includes (T2).names))
  and (mode-strength((T2).names,(T1).properties,(T2).properties)) .
  }
}
```

Query Algorithm and Policy The *policy* of the ODP/OMG trader is just a parameter that modifies the behavior of both local and federated query algorithms. It is hard to understand the meaning of policies without referring to the basic algorithm. Additionally in order to grasp the global behavior of the algorithm at a glance, a concise notation is needed. Notation borrowed from the functional programming language StandardML[21] is used, and some symbols for describing and handling set-like collections of data are added. The query processing is in particular viewed from a stream-based functional programming style. This viewpoint is in accordance with the informal presentation in the ODP/OMG document [1][3]. Below CafeOBJ modules are explained with referring to the pseudo StandardML descriptions.

The top-level function IDLquery(T,I), which is invoked as an IDL request takes the following form. All the function definitions are supposed to come in the lexical context (as fun ⋯) of the IDLquery(T,I). They use T and I freely as global constants, where T refers to the trader state and trader's policy and I is the importer's request and policy.

```
fun IDLquery(T,I) =
  fun query() = if valid-trader()
    then if valid_id() then (select ∘ federation ∘ search)(T.offers) else φ
    else IDLquery(remote_trader(T),I)
  fun ⋯
  in
    query()
  end
```

IDLquery(T,I) calls query to check whether the request is on the trader itself. Then, it invokes the body of query function, which is a stream-style processing consisting of search, federation, and select. The module QUERY-ALGORITHM is a CafeOBJ description of IDLquery(T,I).

```
mod! QUERY-ALGORITHM [X :: TH-TRADER-STATE, Y :: TH-IMPORTER-REQUEST ] {
  signature {
    op query' : TraderState Request Set<Offer> -> Seq<Offer>
    op valid-trader : TraderState TraderName  -> Bool
    op valid-request-id : TraderState RequestId -> Bool
  }
  axioms {
    var T : TraderState  var I : Request var S : Set<Offer>

    eq query'(T,I,S) = if valid-trader(T,(I).starting-trader)
                then (if valid-request-id(T,(I).request-id)
                        then select(T,I,federation(T,I,search(T,I,S)))
                        else empty<Offer> fi)
                    else delegate(T,I) fi .
  }
}
```

The function **search** collects candidate offers. The candidate space is then truncated according to appropriate policies on cardinality. The **search** uses two such cardinality filters. The functions **select** and **order** describe the specifications for the preference calculation.

fun search(R) = (match_cardinality_filter ∘ match
$\qquad\qquad$ ∘ search_cardinality_filter ∘ gather)(R)
fun select(R) = (return_cardinality_filter ∘ order)(R)
fun order(R) = order_on_preference(R,I.preference)

The module **SEARCH-CARDINALITY**, for example, defines the way that the *search cardinality* is calculated by using a trader's policy and an importer's policy.

```
mod! SEARCH-CARDINALITY [X :: TH-TRADER-POLICY, Y :: TH-IMPORTER-POLICY]{
  signature {
    op search-cardinality : TraderPolicy ImporterPolicy -> Cardinality
  }
  axioms {
    var T : TraderPolicy    var I : ImporterPolicy

    eq search-cardinality(T,I)
    = if exist((I).search-card)
        then min((I).search-card,(T).max-search-card)
        else (T).def-search-card fi .
  }
}
```

The function **federation(R)** controls a federated query process. It first checks whether further IDL query requests to the linked traders are necessary by consulting the trader's policy on the **hop_count**.

fun federation(R)
= let val new_count = new_hop_count()
$\quad$ in
$\qquad$ if new_count ≥ 0 then traversal((I with new_count),R) else R
$\quad$ end

The function **traversal** is invoked with a modified importer policy (J) and the offers obtained locally (R), and it controls invocations on the target trader located at the far end of the specified link. The control again requires a scoping policy calculation, which involves the link policies as well as the trader's and the importer's policies. The two functions **new_importer_follow_rule(L,J)** and **current_link_follow_rule(L,J)** show how to use the **FollowOption** policy. Finally, the function **dispatch** shows the use of the **FollowOption** rule. The rule defines three cases – **local_only**, **if_no_local**, and **always** –. And how the final offers are constructed depends on the case.

fun traversal(J,R)
= $\bigcup_{\forall L \in T.\text{links}}$ dispatch_on(current_link_follow_rule(L,J), L,
$\qquad\qquad\qquad$ (I with new_importer_follow_rule(L,J)),R)

fun current_link_follow_rule(L,J)
= if exist(J.link_follow_rule)
   then min(J.link_follow_rule, L.limiting_follow_rule, T.max_follow_policy)
   else min(L.limiting_follow_rule, T.max_follow_policy, T.def_follow_policy)
fun dispatch_on(local_only,L,J,R) = R
  | dispatch_on(if_no_local,L,J,R) = if empty(R) then follow(L,J) else R
  | dispatch_on(always,L,J,R) = follow(L,J) ∪ R

The module FOLLOW-OPTION describes *FollowOption* policy. Basically it provides min functions, and other functions are omitted for brevity. The module NEW-LINK-OPTION shows an example of calculating the *FollowOption* policy, which is used in the federation process.

```
mod! FOLLOW-OPTION {
  [ FollowOption ]
  signature {
    ops local-only if-no-local always : -> FollowOption
    op min : FollowOption FollowOption -> FollowOption
    op min : FollowOption FollowOption FollowOption -> FollowOption
    op _<_ : FollowOption FollowOption -> Bool
    ... (omitted) ...
  }
  axioms {
    vars F1 F2 F3 : FollowOption

    eq (F1) < (F2) =  (((F1 == local-only) and (not (F2 == local-only)))
                        or ((F1 == if-no-local) and (F2 == always)))) .
    ceq min(F1,F2) = F1  if (F1)<(F2) .
    ... (omitted) ...
  }
}


mod! NEW-LINK-OPTION [X :: TH-TRADER-POLICY, Y :: TH-IMPORTER-POLICY,
                      Z :: TH-LINK-POLICY ] {
  protecting (FOLLOW-OPTION)
  signature {
    op current-link-follow-rule :
        TraderPolicy ImporterPolicy LinkPolicy -> FollowOption
  }
  axioms {
    var T : TraderPolicy    var I : ImporterPolicy   var L : LinkPolicy

    eq current-link-follow-rule(T,I,L)
    = if exist((I).link-follow-rule)
      then min((I).link-follow-rule, (L).limiting-follow-rule,
              (T).max-follow-policy)
      else min((L).limiting-follow-rule, (T).max-follow-policy,
              (T).def-follow-policy) fi .
  }
}
```

Constraint Language Two functions (`match` and `order_on_preference`) used in the query algorithm involve evaluation of a constraint expression and a preference expression. Each function is defined in such a way that it calls an evaluation function (either $\mathcal{CE}$ or $\mathcal{PE}$).

> fun match(R) = $\mathcal{CE}$ ⟦ I.constraint ⟧ R
> fun order_on_preference(R,X) = $\mathcal{PE}$ ⟦ X ⟧ R

The constraint language is defined in a standard way according to the denotational description of language semantics. First, the abstract syntax of the language, a portion of which is shown below, is defined.

```
CExp ::= Pred
Pred ::=  L  | Exp == Exp  | exist L      | not Pred
         | Pred and Pred   | Pred or Pred  | ...
```

Then, a valuation function for each syntax category is introduced; $\mathcal{CE}$ is an example one for constraint expressions (`CExp`) and it further calls $\mathcal{LE}$ of the valuation function for predicates (`Pred`). R stands for a set of offers and O is an offer.

> $\mathcal{CE}$: CExp → R → R
> $\mathcal{LE}$: Pred → O → Bool

The specifications of the constraint language interpreter or evaluator are given by the definitions of the valuation function. It can be defined systematically by studying the meaning of each abstract syntax construct.

> $\mathcal{CE}$ ⟦ E ⟧ R = { O ∈ R | $\mathcal{LE}$⟦ E ⟧ O }
> $\mathcal{LE}$⟦ L ⟧ O = prop-val(O,L)$\downarrow_{Bool}$
> $\mathcal{LE}$⟦ E1 == E2 ⟧ O = $\mathcal{AE}$⟦ E1 ⟧ O == $\mathcal{AE}$⟦ E2 ⟧ O
> ...

The CafeOBJ description is straightforward because the denotational-style description of language definition is translated easily in a standard way into CafeOBJ. The module `PRED-SYNTAX` defines the abstract syntax tree and the module `PRED-EVAL` provides the valuation function.

```
mod! PRED-SYNTAX {
  protecting (EXP-SYNTAX)
  [ Pred,  Exp < Pred ]
  signature {
    op  _==_  : Exp Exp -> Pred
    op  exist : Exp -> Pred
    op  not   : Pred -> Pred
    ... (omitted) ...
  }
}
```

```
mod! PRED-EVAL {
  protecting (PRED-SYNTAX)
  protecting (EXP-EVAL)
  signature { op EP(_)_ : Pred ServiceOffer -> Bool }
  axioms {
    vars E1 E2 : Exp  var P : Pred  var N : PropertyName
    var  O : ServiceOffer

  eq EP(label(N)) O = EE(label(N)) O .
  eq EP(E1 == E2) O = (EE(E1) O) == (EE(E2) O) .
  eq EP(exist E) O  = exist-property(O,(EE(E) O)) .
  eq EP(not P) O    = not(EP(P) O) .
  ... (omitted) ...
  }
}
```

Functional Objects and Architecture A functional object describes the behavior of interfaces such as the Lookup and Register, while the architecture here refers to a global organization of functional objects. We use collaboration-based design methods to refine and elaborate these aspects in order to identify the responsibilities of constituent objects, each of which is then translated into a Maude concurrent object [20]. The Maude model is a standard encoding of concurrent objects in algebraic specification languages [22][27]. Please refer to the appendix for a brief explanation on how to encode the Maude concurrent object model in CafeOBJ.

The module IDL-LOOKUP represents the CORBA object implementing the Lookup interface with its behavioral specification written in CafeOBJ. Other functional objects are IDL-REGISTER, IDL-LINK, IDL-ADMIN, TRADER-STATE, TYPE-REPOSITORY, and OFFER-REPOSITORY. The architecture is just a collection of the concurrent objects (Configuration), each of which is described by the corresponding module such as IDL-LOOKUP.

A Lookup object receiving a query(O,N,C,P,Q,D,H,R) message converts the input parameters into the representation that the part of the algorithm assumes, then invokes the body of the query algorithm (query'), and finally translates the result to match the IDL interface specifications.

```
mod! IDL-LOOKUP[X :: TH-LOOKUP-AID, Y :: TH-LOOKUP-MSG] {
  extending (ROOT)
  protecting (LOOKUP-VALUE)
  [ LookupTerm < ObjectTerm , CIdLookup < CId ]
  signature {
    op <(_:_)|_> : OId CIdLookup Attributes -> LookupTerm
    op Lookup : -> CIdLookup
    op invoke-query : TraderState ServiceTypeName Constraint Preference
              Seq<Policy> Seq<PolicyName> Nat Set<Offer> -> Seq<Offer>
  }
  axioms {
    vars O R R' : OId        var REST : Attributes   vars T U : OId
    var N : ServiceTypeName  var C : Constraint       var H : Nat
```

```
      var P : Preference        var Q : Seq<Policy>
      var D : Seq<PolicyName>    var X : TraderState    var S : Set<Offer>

  trans query(O,N,C,P,Q,D,H,R)
      <(O : Lookup)|(offers=(U)),(state=(T)),(client=(R')),(REST)>
  => trader-state(T,O) initial-offers(U,O) m-wait(O,U,T)
      <(O : Lookup)|(offers=(U)),(state=(T)),(client=(R)),(REST)> .

  trans m-wait(O,U,T) return(O,U,S) return(O,T,X)
      <(O : Lookup)|(client=(R)),(REST)>
  => void(R) outArgs(invoke-query(X,N,C,P,Q,D,H,S))
      <(O : Lookup)|(client=(R)),(REST)> .

  eq invoke-query(X,N,C,P,Q,D,H,S) = query'(X,request(N,C,P,Q,D,H),S) .
  }
}
```

On receiving a query message, the Lookup object sends messages to the
OfferRepository object (U) and the TraderState object (T) to obtain a set of
potential offers and the trader state. The Lookup object, then, invokes query'.
As shown before in the module QUERY-ALGORITHM, query' is defined algorithmically. The above module assumes that the module LOOKUP-VALUE imports *library*
modules such as QUERY-ALGORITHM.

Putting Together The last step is to put together all the aspect solutions to
have a whole design artifact of the ODP/OMG trader. Each solution consists
of one or more CafeOBJ module(s), and the integration is just to introduce a
top level module that imports all the necessary ones. The following CafeOBJ
module illustrates a way of integrating what is necessary to describe the whole
system.

```
mod! WHOLE-SYSTEM {
  protecting (IDL-LOOKUP[TRADER-AID, TRADER-MSG])
  protecting (IDL-REGISTER[TRADER-AID, TRADER-MSG])
  protecting (IDL-LINK[TRADER-AID, TRADER-MSG])
  protecting (IDL-ADMIN[TRADER-AID, TRADER-MSG])
  protecting (TRADER-STATE[TRADER-AID, TRADER-MSG])
  protecting (TYPE-REPOSITORY[TRADER-AID, TRADER-MSG])
  protecting (OFFER-REPOSITORY[TRADER-AID, TRADER-MSG])
}
```

For example, instantiating the parameterized module IDL-LOOKUP with the appropriate modules produces a *algebraic model* of the Lookup object. The CAFE
environment automatically imports all the modules by recursively traversing the
module import relations of each module such as protecting(LOOKUP-VALUE) or
extending(ROOT). The process automatically involves syntax and sort checking.

3.3   Resultant Frameworks Written in Java

The trading server consists of several object-oriented frameworks (subsystems) that are refined and elaborated from the aspect solutions. This section focuses on two such subsystems. Figures 4 and 5 show the resultant frameworks written in Java.

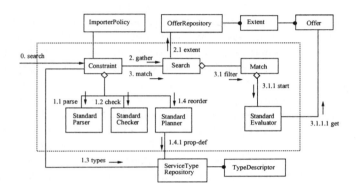

Fig. 4. Query Processing Framework

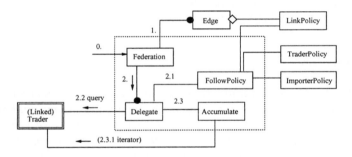

Fig. 5. Federation Framework

Based on the formal language definition presented early, designing the framework for constraint-language processing is straightforward (figure 4). This framework is a representative of using design patterns [14]: the composite pattern for representing the abstract syntax tree (AST) and the visitor pattern for representing the tree walkers such as a light semantic checker (`StandardChecker`), a filtering condition reorder planner (`StandardPlanner`), and an interpreter (`StandardEvaluator`).

Two offline support tools are used in implementing the constraint language processor: JavaCC [4](a public domain Java-based parser generator) and ASTG (a visitor-skeleton generator). ASTG accepts BNF descriptions of abstract syntax similar to the one in [25], and generates Java class definitions implementing both the AST node objects and skeleton codes for tree-walking. The skeleton code follows a convention of the visitor design pattern. Completing the program is not difficult because the program code fragment that need to be written in the body part of the skeleton corresponds to the clauses of the valuation functions,

Figure 5 shows the object-oriented framework that implements the federation process. This subsystem is an example of using the collaboration-based design technique with an algorithmic representation of the aspect design as its input specification. The collaboration-based design focuses on the analysis of the interaction patterns or a sequence of messages between objects, and the algorithm expressed in the functional programming style can be considered to provide an abstract view of a sequence of messages between (potential) participant objects.

The design step involves (1) identifying participant objects in a heuristic manner, and (2) determining responsibility of each object [6][8] to be consistent with the algorithm description. For example, the algorithm described by the function `federation(R)` is divided into `Federation` and `Delegate`. Class `Delegate` corresponds to the body of the function `traversal(J,R)` and thus implements details of the algorithm. Class `Federation` is responsible for controlling the whole federation process and thus plays the role of Façade [14], which decouples the federation subsystem from the rest of the program and thus makes it easy for testing. Another example of the important design decision is encapsulating FollowOption calculation functions in class `FollowOption`, which aims to allow future customization of the policy.

3.4   Discussions

Reflection on Development Process The main development process consisted of three steps: the aspect design, the functional design, and the coding and testing. The aspect design step started with the study of the system requirements and ended with the semi-formal description of each aspects. The functional design step was one in which the collaboration-based object-oriented design method and the design pattern technique were used to produce design documents describing specifications of Java classes. It was followed by the coding and testing. We assigned one person (this author) to the aspect design and two engineers to the coding and testing. All three persons worked together to produce the design documents at the intermediate step. The engineers were not familiar with the collaboration-based object-oriented design technique and required *on the job* training. The functional design step involved technology transfer, and took far longer than initially planned. The time needed for coding and testing, however, was short for a program of this size.[5]

One advantage of the aspect design is that the resultant solutions contribute to provide a guideline for elaborating the design into object-oriented frameworks written in Java. Especially, the design is helpful to identify *hot spots* (program

---

[5] Roughly 25 K lines of Java, but the size is not constant because the program code is updated periodically.

points to be customized) and to determine the structure or the architecture of the Java program.

We could start to use CafeOBJ only when we almost reached a code complete stage of the first working prototype. It is partly because we had to finish most of the coding work as early as possible due to the time constraint of the financial support. We used the CafeOBJ descriptions to check the conformance of the informal design and the implementation against the ODP document.

Additionally, we think that most of the engineers would not accept CafeOBJ descriptions as their input source information because the engineers resisted even the semi-formal descriptions of the aspect design. Proper division of labor between project members is thus important when formal methods are used in real world projects.

Relation to Information Viewpoint As mentioned in section 2.1, the ODP trader recommendation follows the RM-ODP and presents three viewpoints: enterprise, information, and computational. Because the information and computational viewpoints deal with the ODP trader specification formally, establishing the relationship between the two viewpoints is also desirable. However, since the current recommendation uses more than one technique to specify essentially one functionality (the ODP trading function), there are some gaps between descriptions of the two viewpoints. Actually, the Z specification and the IDL specification define one concept through the use of respective language constructs. Since each language has different underlying computational models, the two kinds of specification are not easy to compare to see how both viewpoint specifications are really related. This is partly because each specification uses a lot of language-specific *idioms*.

We have presented CafeOBJ descriptions of the information viewpoint of the ODP trader elsewhere [23]. Together with the CafeOBJ descriptions in the present paper, these descriptions show that CafeOBJ can represent different abstract levels for different aspects of the specificand while providing the same specification fragments for a set of the common vocabulary such as `ServiceType` or `PropertyDefinition`. The CafeOBJ descriptions of the information viewpoint were used as *data dictionaries* in writing the present CafeOBJ descriptions.

Role of CafeOBJ Descriptions The basic idea of the aspect-centered design is to break a whole problem into a set of manageable subproblems that can be solved individually. Each aspect may have its own notation such as functional-style descriptions or message-sequence charts, and the descriptions of each aspect can be validated separately. On the other hand, the overall system cannot be described without integrating all the solution descriptions, and this is difficult when each aspect and its solution have a different notation.

We use CafeOBJ to write each aspect solution, and thus make it possbile to check the integrity when all the aspect descriptions are put together. First, we can get benefits from syntax and sort checking. This helps to identify what is missing. Second, with appropriate input test terms, we can validate the design by test execution (specification animation). It also helps uncover logical inconsistency spreading over different aspect descriptions.

The CafeOBJ descriptions themselves form an artifact. It is an *analogic* model [17] in the sense that the artifact does not represent the Java program faithfully, but instead elucidates essential design in an abstract manner. We plan to use the model as a reusable design artifact when we develop a product line (a family of systems having similar functionalities) in future.

One of methodological advantages of CafeOBJ is to provide hidden algebra or behavioral equations[11][13][16]. Specifications using hidden algebra are basically statemachines, where sequences of allowable *events* describe the properties of the statemachine without defining the constituting states explicitly. The technique is adequate when certain properties are verified by using observational equivalence.

Contrarily, writing specifications in a constructive and operational manner is significant in the present development process. The CafeOBJ descriptions focus on the design aspects and the solutions such as the query and federation algorithm in detail. Such a detailed description acts as a starting point for the further refinement and elaboration. In summary, the CafeOBJ description is an *abstract* implementation in the present approach. It is worth investigating to compare the pro and cons of the two approaches (the present one and the hidden algebra approach) and to study their roles in the development process of object-oriented frameworks.

4   Conclusion

We have reported our experience in using CafeOBJ (a multiparadigm algebraic specification language) in developing object-oriented frameworks of the ODP/OMG trader that is implemented with Java and JavaIDL.

We have discussed the ways in which the introduction of an explicit design phase for the aspect analysis greatly helped us develop object-oriented frameworks for the trading server object. In addition, the use of a single specification language (CafeOBJ) made it possible to check integrity after all the aspect descriptions were put together. The formal descriptions in CafeOBJ contributed to raising credibility of the design description. Although our experience is based on the ODP/OMG trader only, the idea of the aspect design with a proper use of CafeOBJ is clear enough to illustrate practice of using formal methods in the development of object-oriented frameworks.

Acknowledgements

Discussions with Prof. Kokichi Futatsugi (JAIST) and Prof. Tetsuo Tamai (Univ. of Tokyo) were helpful in forming the idea presented in this paper. The comments from the anonymous reviewers helped much to improve the presentation.

References

[1] ITU-T Rec. X.950-1 : Information Technology - Open Distributed Processing - Trading Function - Part 1: Specification (1997).

[2] OMG : OMG CORBA (http://www.omg.org).

[3] OMG : CORBAservices, Trading Object Service Specification (1997).

[4] Sun Microsystems : JavaCC Documentation (http://www.suntest.com/JavaCC/).

[5] Arnold, K. and Gosling, J. : *The Java^{TM} Programming Language*, Addison-Wesley 1996.

[6] Beck, K. and Cunningham, W. : A Laboratory for Teaching Object-Oriented Thinking, Proc. OOPSLA'89, pp.1-6 (1989).

[7] Bjørner, D., Koussoube, S., Noussi, R., and Satchok, G. : Michael Jackson's Problem Frames: Towards Methodological Principles of Selecting and Applying Formal Software Development Techniques and Tools, Proc. 1st IEEE ICFEM (1997).

[8] Carroll, J.M. (ed.) : *Scenario-Based Design*, John Wiley & Sons 1995.

[9] Clarke, E.M. and Wing, J.M. : Formal Methods: State of the Art and Future Directions, ACM Computing Surveys (1996).

[10] Deutsch, L.P. : Design Reuse and Frameworks in the Smalltalk-80 Programming System, in *Software Reusability vol.2 (Biggerstaff and Perlis, ed.)*, pp.55-71, ACM Press 1989.

[11] Diaconescu, R. and Futatsugi, K. : *The CafeOBJ Report*, World Scientific 1998.

[12] Futatsugi, K., Goguen, J., Jouannaud, J-P., and Meseguer, J. : Principles of OBJ2, Proc. 12th POPL, pp.52-66 (1985).

[13] Futatsugi, K. and Nakagawa, A.T. : An Overview of CAFE Specification Environment, Proc. 1st IEEE ICFEM (1997).

[14] Gamma, E., Helm, R., Johnson, R. and Vlissides, J. : *Design Patterns: Elements of Reusable Object-Oriented Software*, Addison-Wesley 1994.

[15] Goguen, J. and Malcolm, G. : *Algebraic Semantics of Imperative Programs*, The MIT Press 1996.

[16] Goguen, J. and Malcolm, G. : A Hidden Agenda, UCSD CS97-538 (1997).

[17] Jackson, M. : *Software Requirements & Specifications*, Addison-Wesley 1995.

[18] Johnson, R. : Documenting Frameworks using Patterns, Proc. OOPSLA'92, pp.63-76 (1992).

[19] Lewis, G., Barber, S., and Siegel, E. : *Programming with Java IDL*, John Wiley & Sons 1998.

[20] Meseguer, J. : A Logical Theory of Concurrent Objects and its Realization in the Maude Language, in *Research Directions in Concurrent Object-Oriented Programming (Agha, Wegner and Yonezawa ed.)*, pp.314-390, The MIT Press 1993.

[21] Milner, R., Tofte, M., Harper, R., and MacQueen, D. : *The Definition of Standard ML (revised)*, The MIT Press 1997.

[22] Nakajima, S. and Futatsugi, K. : An Object-Oriented Modeling Method for Algebraic Specifications in CafeOBJ, Proc. 19th ICSE, pp.34-44 (1997).

[23] Nakajima, S. and Futatsugi, K. : An Algebraic Approach to Specification and Analysis of the ODP Trader, Trans. IPS Japan Vol.40 No.4, pp.1861-1873(1999).

[24] Raymond, K. : Reference Model of Open Distributed Processing (RM-ODP) : Introduction, Proc. ICODP'95 (1995).

[25] Wang, D.C., Appel, A.W., and Korn, J.L. : The Zephyr Abstract Syntax Description Language, Proc. USENIX DSL, pp.213-227 (1997).

[26] Wing, J. and Zaremski, A.M. : Unintrusive Ways to Integrate Formal Specifications in Practice, CMU-CS-91-113 (1991).

[27] Wirsing, M. and Knapp, A. : A Formal Approach to Object-Oriented Software Engineering, Proc. 1st Workshop on Rewriting Logic and its Applications (1996).

A   CafeOBJ: The Specification Language

CafeOBJ has two kinds of axioms[6] to describe functional behavior [11][13]. An equational axiom (*eq*) is based on equational logic and thus is suitable for representing static relationships, whereas a rewriting axiom (*trans*) is based on concurrent rewriting logic and is suitable for modeling changes in some states.

Here is a simple example, a CafeOBJ specification of LIST. The module LIST defines a generic abstract datatype List. _ _ (juxtaposing two data of the specified sorts) is a List constructor. |_| returns the length of the operand list data and is a recursive function over the structure of the list. The module LIST also defines some utility functions such as n-hd and n-tl.

```
mod! LIST[X :: TRIV] {
  [ NeList, List ]    [ Elt < NeList < List ]
  protecting (NAT)
  signature {
    op nil : -> List
    op __ : List List -> List {assoc id: nil}
    op __ : NeList List -> NeList
    op __ : NeList NeList -> NeList
    op |_| : List -> Nat
    op n-hd : Nat NeList -> NeList
    op n-tl : Nat NeList -> List
  }
  axioms {
    var X : Elt      var L : List

    eq | nil | = 0 .
    eq | X   | = 1 .
    eq | X L | = 1 + | L | .
    ... (omitted) ...
  }
}
```

The Maude concurrent object [20] can easily be encoded in CafeOBJ. The Maude model relies on a Configuration and rewriting rules based on concurrent rewriting logic. Configuration is a snapshot of global states consisting of objects and messages at some particular time. Object computation (sending messages to objects) proceeds as rewriting on Configuration. In addition, Maude has a concise syntax to represent the object term (<(_:_)|_>) and some encoding techniques to simulate *inheritance*. We regard the Maude model to be a standard encoding for concurrent objects in algebraic specification languages [22][27].

Below is an example of object definition: the module ITERATOR defines an Iterator object, which maintains a list of data and returns the specified number of data when requested by a next-n message. Actually, it is CafeOBJ encoding of the IDL iterator interface with functional behavior at an abstract level.

---

[6]   We do not consider hidden algebra here.

```
mod! ITERATOR[X :: TH-ITERATOR-AID, Y :: TH-ITERATOR-MSG] {
  extending (ROOT)
  protecting (ITERATOR-VALUE)
  [ IteratorTerm < ObjectTerm ]
  [ CIdIterator < CId ]
  signature {
    op <(_:_)|_> : OId CIdIterator Attributes -> IteratorTerm
    op Iterator : -> CIdIterator
  }
  axioms {
    vars O R : OId    var L : List    var N : NzNat
    var REST : Attributes

  ctrans next-n (O,N,R) <(O : Iterator)|(body = L), (REST)>
  => <(O : Iterator)|(body = n-tl(N,L)), (REST)>
     return(R,true) outArgs(R,n-hd(N,L))      if N <= |L| .

  ctrans next-n (O,N,R) <(O : Iterator)|(body = L), (REST)>
  => <(O : Iterator)|(body = L), (REST)> return(R,false)  if N > |L| .

  trans destroy(O,R)  <(O : Iterator)|(REST)> => void(R) .
  }
}
```

The module ITERATOR imports two other modules ROOT and ITERATOR-VALUE.
The module ROOT is a runtime module that provides the symbols necessary to
represent Maude concurrent objects. That is, it provides the following sort symbols: Configuration to represent the snapshot, Message for messages,
ObjectTerm for the body of objects which consists of Attributes (a collection of attribute name and value pairs), CId for class identifiers, and OId for
identifiers of object instances.

As shown in the example, a user-defined class should define a concrete rep-
resentation of the object term (<(_:_)|_>) in a new sort (IteratorTerm) and
a class identifier constant (Iterator) in another new sort (CIdIterator). The
axioms part has a set of rewriting rules (either trans or ctrans), each of which
defines a method body. In writing the method body, we often refer to symbols defined in other modules, for example the sort List and the related utility
functions. The module ITERATOR-VALUE is supposed to import all the modules
necessary for the ITERATOR such as LIST[NAT].

Maude as a Formal Meta-tool[*]

M. Clavel[1], F. Durán[2], S. Eker[2], J. Meseguer[2], and M.-O. Stehr[2]

[1] Department of Philosophy, University of Navarre, Spain
[2] SRI International, Menlo Park, CA 94025, USA

Abstract. Given the different perspectives from which a complex software system has to be analyzed, the multiplicity of formalisms is unavoidable. This poses two important technical challenges: how to rigorously
meet the need to interrelate formalisms, and how to reduce the duplication of effort in tool and specification building across formalisms. These
challenges could be answered by adequate *formal meta-tools* that, when
given the specification of a formal inference system, generate an efficient inference engine, and when given a specification of two formalisms
and a translation, generate an actual translator between them. Similarly,
module composition operations that are logic-independent, but that at
present require costly implementation efforts for each formalism, could
be provided for logics in general by module algebra generator meta-tools.
The foundations of meta-tools of this kind can be based on a metatheory
of general logics. Their actual design and implementation can be based
on appropriate logical frameworks having efficient implementations. This
paper explains how the reflective logical framework of rewriting logic can
be used, in conjunction with an efficient reflective implementation such
as the Maude language, to design formal meta-tools such as those described above. The feasibility of these ideas and techniques has been
demonstrated by a number of substantial experiments in which new formal tools and new translations between formalisms, efficient enough to
be used in practice, have been generated.

1 Introduction

At present, formal methods for software specification and verification tend to
be monolithic, in the sense that in each approach only one formal system or
specification language is used to formalize the desired system properties. For
this reason, formal systems, and the tools based on them, can be as it were
autistic, because they lack the meta-tools and methods necessary for relating
them to other formalisms and to their supporting tools.

As a consequence, it is at present very difficult to integrate in a rigorous
way different formal descriptions, and to reason across such descriptions. This
situation is very unsatisfactory, and presents one of the biggest obstacles to the

[*] Supported by DARPA and NASA through Contract NAS2-98073, by Office of Naval
Research Contract N00014-96-C-0114, and by National Science Foundation Grant
CCR-9633363.

J. Wing, J. Woodcock, J. Davies (Eds.): FM'99, Vol. II, LNCS 1709, pp. 1684–1703, 1999.

use of formal methods in software engineering because, given the complexity of large software systems, it is a fact of life that no single perspective, no single formalization or level of abstraction suffices to represent a system and reason about its behavior. We use the expression *formal interoperability* to denote this capacity to move in a mathematically rigorous way across the different formalizations of a system, and to use in a rigorously integrated manner the different tools supporting such formalizations [52, 49].

By transforming problems in a formalism lacking tools into equivalent problems in a formalism that has them, formal interoperability can save much time and effort in tool development. Also, libraries of theories and specifications can in this way be amortized across many formalisms, avoiding much duplication of effort. One would similarly like to have rigorous meta-methods and tools making it easy to solve different parts of a complex problem using different formal tools, and to then integrate the subproblem solutions into an overall solution.

These considerations suggest that it would be very fruitful to investigate and develop new *formal meta-tools*, that is, tools in which we can easily and rigorously develop many formal tools at a very high level of abstraction; and also tools through which we can rigorously interoperate existing and future tools. Specifically, it would be very useful to have:

- *Formal Tool Generators*, that given a formal description of an inference system, generate an *inference engine* for it that is sufficiently efficient to be used in practice as a tool.
- *Formal Translation Generators*, that given formal descriptions of two formalisms and of a translation between them, generate an actual *translator* that can be used to translate specifications and to interoperate tools across the given formalisms.
- *Module Algebra Generators*, that given a formalism with appropriate metalogical properties, extend its language of basic specifications into a much richer algebra of specification-combining operations, including specification hierarchies, parameterized specifications, and many other specification transformations.

But where will the metatheory supporting such meta-tools come from? To make such tools mathematically rigorous, the first thing obviously needed is to have a mathematical metatheory of logics and of translations between logics. We have been investigating the theory of general logics [47, 44, 52, 11, 16] for this purpose. This theory axiomatizes the proof-theoretic and model-theoretic facets of logics and their translations, includes the theory of institutions as its model-theoretic component [30], and is related to other similar metatheories (see the survey [52]).

But meta-tools need more than a metatheory. They have to "run" and therefore they need an *executable* metatheory. This can be provided by an adequate *logical framework*, that is, by a logic with good properties as a metalogic in which other logics can be naturally represented, and that, in addition, is executable with good performance. Then, an implementation of such a framework logic could serve as a basis for developing the meta-tools.

This paper reports on our results and experiments in using the Maude language [15, 13] as a formal meta-tool in the senses described above. Maude is a reflective language based on rewriting logic [48] that essentially contains the OBJ3 language as an equational sublanguage. Rewriting logic extends equational logic and has very good properties as a logical framework, in which many other logics and many semantic formalisms can be naturally represented [43, 51]. A very important property of the rewriting logic framework is its being *reflective* [17, 12]. Reflection is efficiently supported by the Maude implementation and, together with the high-performance of Maude, is the key feature making possible the use of Maude as a meta-tool.

The rest of the paper is organized as follows. Section 2 explains in more detail in which sense rewriting logic is a reflective logical framework, and some basic principles and methods underlying the use of a rewriting logic implementation as a formal meta-tool. Section 3 describes the key features of Maude allowing it to be used as a meta-tool. Our experience in building formal tools in Maude is described in Section 4, where we report on several formal tool generator and formal translation generator uses, and on the beginnings of a module algebra generator capability. We finish the paper with some concluding remarks and future research directions.

2   A Reflective Logical Framework

A *formal* meta-tool must both rely on, and support, a precise axiomatization of different logics. That is what makes it formal, and what distinguishes it from tool implementations in conventional languages, say Java, in which the implementation itself is not a suitable formal axiomatization of the tool being implemented.

This leads us to the need for a metatheory of logics, as a necessary foundation for the design of formal meta-tools. In our work we have used the theory of *general logics* proposed in [47], which provides an axiomatic framework to formalize the proof theory and model theory of a logic, and which also provides adequate notions of *mapping* between logics, that is, of logic translations. This theory contains Goguen and Burstall's theory of institutions [30] as its model-theoretic component.

The theory of general logics allows us to define the space of logics as a *category*, in which the objects are the different logics, and the morphisms are the different mappings translating one logic into another. We can therefore axiomatize a translation Φ from a logic $\mathcal{L}$ to a logic $\mathcal{L}'$ as a morphism

$$(\dagger)\quad \Phi : \mathcal{L} \longrightarrow \mathcal{L}'$$

in the category of logics. A *logical framework* is then a logic $\mathcal{F}$ such that a very wide class of logics can be mapped to it by maps of logics

$$(\ddagger)\quad \Psi : \mathcal{L} \longrightarrow \mathcal{F}$$

called *representation maps*, that have particularly good properties such as conservativity[1].

A number of logics, particularly higher-order logics based on typed lambda calculi, have been proposed as logical frameworks, including the Edinburgh logical framework LF [35, 2, 27], generic theorem provers such as Isabelle [56], λProlog [54, 25], and Elf [57], and the work of Basin and Constable [4] on metalogical frameworks. Other approaches, such as Feferman's logical framework FS_0 [24]—that has been used in the work of Matthews, Smaill, and Basin [46]—earlier work by Smullyan [59], and the 2OBJ generic theorem prover of Goguen, Stevens, Hobley, and Hilberdink [33] are instead first-order. Our work should of course be placed within the context of the above related work, and of experiments carried out in different frameworks to prototype formal systems (for more discussion see the survey [52]).

2.1   Rewriting Logic and Reflection

We and other researchers (see references in [51]) have investigated the suitability of rewriting logic [48] as a logical framework and have found it to have very good properties for this purpose. One important practical advantage is that, what might be called the *representational distance* between a theory T in the original logic and its rewriting logic representation $\Psi(T)$ is often practically zero. That is, both T's original syntax and its rules of inference are faithfully mirrored by the rewrite theory $\Psi(T)$.

A rewrite theory (Ω, E, R) is an equational theory (Ω, E) with signature of operations Ω and equations E together with a collection R of labeled rewrite rules of the form

$$r : t \longrightarrow t'.$$

Logically, such rules mean that we can derive the formula t' from the formula t. That is, the logical reading of a rewrite rule is that of an *inference rule*.

Since the syntax Ω and the equational axioms E of a rewrite theory are entirely *user-definable*, rewriting logic can represent in a direct and natural way the formulas of any finitary logic as elements of an algebraic data type defined by a suitable equational theory (Ω, E). Furthermore, the *structural axioms* satisfied by such formulas—for example, associativity and commutativity of a conjunction operator, or of a set of formulas in a sequent—can also be naturally axiomatized as equations in such an equational theory. Each inference rule in the logic is then naturally axiomatized as a rewrite rule, that is applied *modulo* the equations E. If there are *side conditions* in the inference rule, then the corresponding rewrite rule is *conditional* [48]. Rewriting logic has then very simple (meta-) rules of deduction [48], allowing it to mirror deduction in any finitary logic as rewriting inference. In earlier work with Narciso Martí-Oliet we have shown how this general method for representing logics in the rewriting logic framework allows

---

[1] A map of logics is *conservative* [47] if the translation of a sentence is a theorem if and only if the sentence was a theorem in the original logic. Conservative maps are sometimes said to be *adequate* and *faithful* by other authors.

very natural and direct representations for many logics, including also a general method for representing quantifiers [43, 44, 45].

Besides these good properties, there is an additional key property making rewriting logic remarkably useful as a metalogic, namely *reflection*. Rewriting logic is reflective [17, 12] in the precise sense that there is a finitely presented rewrite theory U such that for any finitely presented rewrite theory T (including U itself) we have the following equivalence

$$T \vdash t \longrightarrow t' \iff U \vdash \langle \overline{T}, \overline{t} \rangle \longrightarrow \langle \overline{T}, \overline{t'} \rangle,$$

where $\overline{T}$ and $\overline{t}$ are terms representing T and t as data elements of U, of respective types *Theory* and *Term*. Since U is representable in itself, we can achieve a "reflective tower" with an arbitrary number of levels of reflection, since we have

$$T \vdash t \longrightarrow t' \iff U \vdash \langle \overline{T}, \overline{t} \rangle \longrightarrow \langle \overline{T}, \overline{t'} \rangle \iff U \vdash \langle \overline{U}, \overline{\langle \overline{T}, \overline{t} \rangle} \rangle \longrightarrow \langle \overline{U}, \overline{\langle \overline{T}, \overline{t'} \rangle} \rangle \dots$$

The key advantage of having a reflective logical framework logic such as rewriting logic is that we can represent—or as it is said *reify*—within the logic in a computable way maps of the form (†) and (‡). We can do so by extending the universal theory U with equational abstract data type definitions for the data type of theories *Theory*$_\mathcal{L}$ for each logic $\mathcal{L}$ of interest. Then, a map of the form (†) can be reified as an equationally-defined function

$$\overline{\Phi} : Theory_\mathcal{L} \longrightarrow Theory_{\mathcal{L}'}.$$

And, similarly, a representation map of the form (‡), with $\mathcal{F}$ rewriting logic, can be reified by a function

$$\overline{\Psi} : Theory_\mathcal{L} \longrightarrow Theory.$$

If the maps Φ and Ψ are computable, then, by a metatheorem of Bergstra and Tucker [5] it is possible to define the functions $\overline{\Phi}$ and $\overline{\Psi}$ by means of corresponding finite sets of Church-Rosser and terminating equations. That is, such functions can be effectively defined and executed within rewriting logic.

2.2   Formal Meta-tool Techniques

How can we systematically exploit all these properties to use a reflective implementation of rewriting logic as a meta-tool? *Formal tool generator* uses can be well supported by defining representation maps Ψ that are conservative. In conjunction with a reflective implementation of rewriting logic, we can reify such representation maps as functions of the form $\overline{\Psi}$ that give us a systematic way of executing a logic $\mathcal{L}$ by representing each theory T in $\mathcal{L}$—which becomes a data element $\overline{T}$ of *Theory*$_\mathcal{L}$—by the rewrite theory that $\overline{\Psi}(\overline{T})$ metarepresents. By executing such a rewrite theory we are in fact executing the (representation of) T. In our experience, the maps Ψ are essentially identity maps, preserving the original structure of the formulas, and mirroring each inference rule by a corresponding rewrite rule. Therefore, a user can easily follow and understand the rewriting logic execution of the theory T thus represented.

But how well can we *execute* the representation of such a theory T? In general, the inference process of T may be highly nondeterministic, and may have to be guided by so-called *strategies*. Will the status of such strategies be logical, or extra-logical? And will strategies be representable at all in the framework logic? Rewriting logic reflection saves the day, because strategies have a *logical* status: they are computed by rewrite theories at the metalevel. That is, in the reflective tower they are always one level above the rewrite theory whose execution they control. Furthermore, there is great freedom for creating different *internal strategy languages* that extend rewriting logic's universal theory U to allow a flexible logical specification of strategies [17, 12, 13].

Formal translator generator uses are of course supported by formally specifying the algebraic data types *Theory*$_\mathcal{L}$ and *Theory*$_{\mathcal{L}'}$ of the logics in question and the translation function $\overline{\Phi}$. *Module algebra generator* uses can be supported by defining a *parameterized* algebraic data type, say *ModAlg*$[X]$, that, given a logic $\mathcal{L}$ having good metalogical properties, extends the data type *Theory*$_\mathcal{L}$ of theories to an algebra of theory-composition operations *ModAlg*$[\textit{Theory}_\mathcal{L}]$.

Section 3 explains the reflective metalanguage features of Maude that make meta-tool uses of this kind possible, and Section 4 summarizes our practical meta-tool experience with Maude.

3   Maude's Metalanguage Features

Maude [15, 13] is a reflective language whose modules are theories in rewriting logic. The most general Maude modules are called *system modules*. Given a rewrite theory $T = (\Omega, E, R)$, a system module has essentially the form mod T endm, that is, it is expressed with a syntax quite close to the corresponding mathematical notation for its corresponding rewrite theory.[2] The equations E in the equational theory (Ω, E) underlying the rewrite theory $T = (\Omega, E, R)$ are presented as a union $E = A \cup E'$, with A a set of *equational axioms* introduced as *attributes* of certain operators in the signature Ω—for example, a conjunction operator $\wedge$ can be declared associative and commutative by keywords assoc and comm—and where E' is a set of equations that are assumed to be Church-Rosser and terminating *modulo* the axioms A. Maude supports rewriting modulo different combinations of such equational attributes: operators can be declared associative, commutative, with identity, and idempotent [13]. Maude contains a sublanguage of *functional modules* of the form fmod (Ω, E) endfm, with the equational theory (Ω, E) satisfying the conditions already mentioned. A system module mod T endm specifies the initial model [48] of the rewrite theory T. Similarly, a functional module fmod (Ω, E) endfm specifies the initial algebra of the equational theory (Ω, E).

---

[2] See [13] for a detailed description of Maude's syntax, which is quite similar to that of OBJ3 [32].

3.1   The Module META-LEVEL

A naive implementation of reflection can be very expensive both in time and in memory use. Therefore, a good implementation must provide efficient ways of performing reflective computations. In Maude this is achieved through its predefined META-LEVEL module, in which key functionality of the universal theory U of rewriting logic has been efficiently implemented. In particular, META-LEVEL has sorts Term and Module, so that the representations $\bar{t}$ and $\overline{T}$ of a term t and a module (that is, a rewrite theory) T have sorts Term and Module, respectively. As the universal theory U that it implements in a built-in fashion, META-LEVEL can also support a reflective tower with an arbitrary number of levels of reflection. We summarize below the key functionality provided by META-LEVEL:

- Maude terms are reified as elements of a data type Term of terms;
- Maude modules are reified as terms in a data type Module of modules;
- the process of reducing a term to normal form is reified by a function meta-reduce;
- the process of applying a rule of a system module to a subject term is reified by a function meta-apply;
- the process of rewriting a term in a system module using Maude's default strategy is reified by a function meta-rewrite; and
- parsing and pretty printing of a term in a module are also reified by corresponding metalevel functions meta-parse and meta-pretty-print.

Representing Terms. Terms are reified as elements of the data type Term of terms, with the following signature

```
subsort Qid < Term .
subsort Term < TermList .
op {_}_ : Qid Qid -> Term .
op _[_] : Qid TermList -> Term .
op _,_ : TermList TermList -> TermList [assoc] .
```

The first declaration, making the sort Qid of quoted identifiers a subsort of Term, is used to represent variables in a term by the corresponding quoted identifiers. Thus, the variable N is represented by 'N. The operator {_}_ is used for representing constants as pairs, with the first argument the constant, in quoted form, and the second argument the sort of the constant, also in quoted form. For example, the constant 0 in the module NAT discussed below is represented as {'0}'Nat. The operator _[_] corresponds to the recursive construction of terms out of subterms, with the first argument the top operator in quoted form, and the second argument the list of its subterms, where list concatenation is denoted _,_. For example, the term s s 0 + s 0 of sort Nat in the module NAT is metarepresented as

$$'\_+\_['s\_['s\_[\{'0\}'Nat]],'s\_[\{'0\}'Nat]].$$

Representing Modules. Functional and system modules are metarepresented in a syntax very similar to their original user syntax. The main differences are that: (1) terms in equations, membership axioms (see [50, 13] for more on membership axioms) and rules are now metarepresented as explained above; and (2) sets of identifiers—used in declarations of sorts—are represented as sets of quoted identifiers built with an associative and commutative operator _;_.

To motivate the general syntax for representing modules, we illustrate it with a simple example—namely, a module NAT for natural numbers with zero and successor and with a commutative addition operator.

```
fmod NAT is
   sorts Zero Nat .
   subsort Zero < Nat .
   op 0 : -> Zero .
   op s_ : Nat -> Nat .
   op _+_ : Nat Nat -> Nat [comm] .
   vars N M : Nat .
   eq 0 + N = N .
   eq s N + M = s (N + M) .
endfm
```

The syntax for the top-level operator representing functional modules is as follows.

```
sorts FModule Module .
subsort FModule < Module .

op fmod_is_____endfm : Qid ImportList SortDecl
      SubsortDeclSet OpDeclSet
      VarDeclSet MembAxSet EquationSet -> FModule .
```

The representation $\overline{\text{NAT}}$ of NAT in META-LEVEL is the term

```
fmod 'NAT is
   nil
   sorts 'Zero ; 'Nat .
   subsort 'Zero < 'Nat .
   op '0 : nil -> 'Zero [none] .
   op 's_ : 'Nat -> 'Nat [none] .
   op '_+_ : 'Nat 'Nat -> 'Nat [comm] .
   var 'N : 'Nat .
   var 'M : 'Nat .
   none
   eq '_+_[{'0}'Nat, 'N] = 'N .
   eq '_+_['s_['N], 'M] = 's_['_+_['N, 'M]] .
endfm
```

Since NAT has no list of imported submodules and no membership axioms those fields are filled by the nil import list, and the none set of membership axioms.

Similarly, since the zero and successor operators have no attributes, they have the **none** set of attributes.

Note that—just as in the case of terms—terms of sort **Module** can be metarepresented again, yielding then a term of sort **Term**, and this can be iterated an arbitrary number of times. This is in fact necessary when a metalevel computation has to operate at higher levels. A good example is the inductive theorem prover described in Section 4.1, where modules are metarepresented as terms of sort **Module** in the inference rules for induction, but they have to be metametarepresented as terms of sort **Term** when used in strategies that control the application of the inductive inference rules.

There are many advanced applications that the **META-LEVEL** module makes possible. Firstly, strategies or tactics to guide the application of the rewrite rules of a theory can be defined by rewrite rules in *strategy languages* [17, 12, 13], which are Maude modules extending **META-LEVEL** in which the more basic forms of rewriting supported by functions like **meta-apply** and **meta-reduce** can be extended to arbitrarily complex rewrite strategies defined in a declarative way within the logic. Secondly, as further explained in Section 4.5, an extensible *module algebra* of module composition and transformation operations can be constructed by defining new functions on the data type **Module** and on other data types extending it. Thirdly, as explained in Section 4, many uses of Maude as a *metalanguage* in which we can implement other languages, including formal specification languages and formal tools, are naturally and easily supported.

3.2   Additional Metalanguage Features

Suppose that we want to build a theorem prover for a logic, or an executable formal specification language. We can do so by representing the logic $\mathcal{L}$ of the theorem prover or specification language in question in rewriting logic by means of a representation map

$$\Psi : \mathcal{L} \longrightarrow RWLogic.$$

Using reflection we can, as already explained in Section 2, *internalize* such a map as an equationally defined function $\overline{\Psi}$. In Maude this is accomplished using the module **META-LEVEL** and its sort **Module**. We can reify the above representation map Ψ by defining an abstract data type $\text{Module}_{\mathcal{L}}$ representing theories in the logic $\mathcal{L}$ and specifying $\overline{\Psi}$ as an equationally-defined function

$$\overline{\Psi} : \text{Module}_{\mathcal{L}} \longrightarrow \text{Module}$$

in a module extending **META-LEVEL**. We can then use the functions **meta-reduce**, **meta-apply**, and **meta-rewrite**, or more complex strategies that use such functions, to execute in Maude the metarepresentation $\overline{\Psi}(T)$ of a theory T in $\mathcal{L}$. In other words, we can in this way *execute* $\mathcal{L}$ in Maude.

But we need more. To build a usable formal tool we need to build an *environment* for it, including not only the execution aspect just described, but parsing, pretty printing, and input/output. If we had instead considered formal translator generator uses of Maude, we would have observed entirely similar needs, since we need to get the specifications in different logics—originating from, or going to, different tools—in and out of Maude by appropriate parsing, pretty printing, and input-output functions. In Maude, these additional metalanguage features are supported as follows:

- The *syntax definition* for $\mathcal{L}$ is accomplished by defining the data type $\texttt{Module}_{\mathcal{L}}$. In Maude this can be done with very flexible user-definable *mixfix* syntax, that can mirror the concrete syntax of an existing tool supporting $\mathcal{L}$.
- Particularities at the *lexical* level of $\mathcal{L}$ can be accommodated by user-definable *bubble sorts*, that tailor the adequate notions of token and identifier to the language in question (see [13]).
- Parsing and pretty printing for $\mathcal{L}$ is accomplished by the $\texttt{meta-parse}$ and $\texttt{meta-pretty-print}$ functions in $\texttt{META-LEVEL}$, in conjunction with the bubble sorts defined for $\mathcal{L}$.
- Input/output of theory definitions, and of commands for execution in $\mathcal{L}$ is accomplished by the predefined module $\texttt{LOOP-MODE}$, that provides a generic read-eval-print loop (see [13]).

In Section 4 we describe our experience in using the $\texttt{META-LEVEL}$ and the above metalanguage features of Maude as a meta-tool to build formal tools.

4   Using Maude as a Formal Meta-tool

This section summarizes our experience using Maude as a formal meta-tool. Specifically, we report on three formal tool generator uses—an inductive theorem prover and a Church-Rosser Checker for membership equational logic, and a proof assistant for the open calculus of constructions—four formal translator generator uses, several specification language environment-building uses, and on the beginnings of a module algebra generator use.

4.1   An Inductive Theorem Prover

Using the reflective features of Maude's $\texttt{META-LEVEL}$ module, we have built an inductive theorem prover for equational logic specifications [14] that can be used to prove inductive properties of both CafeOBJ specifications [26] and of functional modules in Maude.

The specifications we are dealing with are equational theories T having an initial algebra semantics. The theory T about which we want to prove inductive properties is at the object level. The rules of inference for induction can be naturally expressed as a rewrite theory $\mathcal{I}$. For example, one of the inference rules is the following *constants lemma* rule, that reduces universally quantified goals with variables to ground goals in which the variables have been declared as constants

$$\frac{T \vdash (\forall \{x_1, \ldots, x_n\}).p}{T \cup \{\texttt{op } c_1 \colon \texttt{-> } s_1. \cdots \texttt{op } c_n \colon \texttt{-> } s_n.\} \vdash p[c_1/x_1, \ldots, c_n/x_n]}$$

where x_i has sort s_i and the constants $c_1, \ldots, c_n$ do not occur in T. Its expression as a rewrite rule in Maude—that rewrites the current set of goals modulo associativity and commutativity—is as follows

```
rl [constantsLemma]:
     goalSet(proveinVariety(IS,T,VQuantification(XS,P)), G)
  => --------------------------------------------------------
     goalSet(proveinVariety(IS,addNewConstants(XS, T),
                        varsToNewConstants(XS,P)), G) .
```

where the function `addNewConstants(XS, T)` adds a new constant of the appropriate sort to the theory T for each variable in XS. (The dashes in the rule are a, notationally convenient, Maude comment convention).

Note that, since this rewrite theory uses T as a data structure—that is, it actually uses its representation $\overline{T}$—the theory $\mathcal{I}$ should be defined at the metalevel. Proving an inductive theorem for T corresponds to applying the rules in $\mathcal{I}$ with some *strategy*. But since the strategies for any rewrite theory belong to the metalevel of such a theory, and $\mathcal{I}$ is already at the metalevel, we need *three levels* to clearly distinguish levels and make our design entirely *modular*, so that, for example, we can change the strategy without any change whatsoever to the inference rules in $\mathcal{I}$. This is illustrated by the following picture, describing the modular architecture of our theorem prover.

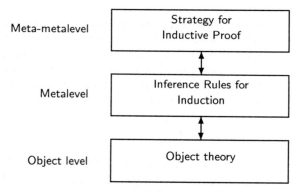

This tool uses several levels of reflection and associative-commutative rewriting, and expresses the inference rules at a very high level of abstraction. However, thanks to the efficient implementation of Maude—that can reach more than 1,300,000 rewrites per second on a 450 MHz Pentium II for some applications—the resulting implementation is a tool of competitive performance that can be used in practice in interactive mode with typically fast response times. Furthermore, our tool-building experience has been very positive, both in terms of how quickly we were able to develop the tool, and how easily we can extend it and maintain it. We are currently extending this theorem prover by extending both its logic, from equational to rewriting logic, and its inference rules, to support more powerful reasoning methods, including metalogical reasoning.

4.2   A Church-Rosser Checker

We have also built a Church-Rosser checker tool [14] that analyzes equational specifications to check whether they satisfy the Church-Rosser property. This tool can be used to analyze order-sorted [31] equational specifications in CafeOBJ and in Maude. The tool outputs a collection of proof obligations that can be used to either modify the specification or to prove them.

The Church-Rosser Checker has a reflective design similar to that of the inductive theorem prover, but somewhat simpler. Again, the module T, that we want to check is Church-Rosser, is at the object level. An inference system C for checking the Church-Rosser property uses $\overline{T}$ as a data structure, and therefore is a rewrite theory at the metalevel. However, since the checking process can be described in a purely functional way, there is no need in this case for an additional strategy layer at the meta-metalevel: two levels suffice.

Maude does not yet have built-in support for unification, but only for matching. Therefore, we implemented the order-sorted unification algorithm using rewrite rules which—with unification being the real workhorse of the tool—is of course inefficient. However, in spite of this inefficiency, of using reflection, and of making heavy use of associative-commutative rewriting—which is NP-complete—our tool has competitive performance. For example, it generates a long list of proof obligations for a substantial example, namely the number hierarchy from the natural to the rational numbers, after 2,091,898 rewrites in 12 seconds running on a 450 MHz Pentium II.

We are currently extending this tool in several ways. Firstly, unification will be performed by Maude in a built-in way. This will greatly improve performance, and will enhance the general capabilities of Maude as a formal meta-tool. Secondly, besides Church-Rosser checking we will support Knuth-Bendix completion of membership equational logic specifications [7] and coherence completion of rewrite theories [62].

4.3   Formal Interoperability Experiments

Using the general methods explained in Section 2.2, Maude can be used as a "logical bus" to interoperate in a systematic and rigorous way different formalisms and their associated tools.

The goal is twofold. Firstly, the mappings relating different formalisms should themselves be formalized in a metalogic, so that they are rigorously defined and it becomes possible to subject them to formal metalogical analysis to verify their correctness. Secondly, the formal definition of a mapping between two logics should be *executable*, so that it can be used to carry out the translation and to interoperate in practice different formal tools. This is precisely what defining such mappings in Maude makes possible.

Maps of logics can relate any two logics of interest. In particular, when the target logic is rewriting logic, we can execute in Maude the translated theories. However, in other cases the goal may be to relate two different formalisms which may have tools of their own. We describe below some formal interoperability experiments—carried out in cooperation with several colleagues—that illustrate the different uses just discussed and some combined uses.

HOL → Nuprl. The HOL theorem proving system [34] has a rich library of theories that can save a lot of effort by not having to specify from scratch many commonly encountered theories. Potentially, this is a very useful resource not only for HOL, but for other theorem proving systems based on other logics. Howe [37] defined a map of logics mapping the HOL logic into the logic of Nuprl [19], and implemented such a mapping to make possible the translation from HOL theories to Nuprl theories. In this way, the practical goal of relating both systems and making the HOL libraries available to Nuprl was achieved. However, the translation itself was carried out by conventional means, and therefore was not in a form suitable for metalogical analysis.

After studying this mapping with the kind help of D. Howe and R. Constable, Stehr and Meseguer have recently formally specified it in Maude. The result is an *executable formal specification* of the mapping that translates HOL theories into Nuprl theories. Large HOL libraries have already been translated into Nuprl this way.

In order to verify the correctness of the translation, we have investigated, in parallel with the work summarized above, an *abstract version of the mapping* in the categorical framework of general logics [47]. Stehr and Meseguer have proved a strong correctness result, namely, that the mapping is actually a mapping between the entailment systems of HOL and a classical variant of Nuprl. This result is of a proof-theoretic nature and hence complementary to the semantical argument given in [37]. Beyond its role as a direct justification for the translator, this result suggests an interesting new direction, namely, extending the mapping between entailment systems to a mapping between proof calculi, which would mean in practice that theorems could be translated together with their proofs.

LinLogic → RWLogic. As an illustration of the naturalness and flexibility with which rewriting logic can be used as a logical framework to represent other logics, Martí-Oliet and Meseguer defined two simple mappings from linear logic [29] to rewriting logic: one for its propositional fragment, and another for first-order linear logic [43]. In addition, they explained how—using the fact that rewriting logic is reflective and the methods discussed in Section 2.2—these mappings could be specified and executed in Maude, thus endowing linear logic with an executable environment. Based on these ideas, Clavel and Martí-Oliet have specified in Maude the mapping from propositional linear logic to rewriting logic [12].

Wright → CSP → RWLogic. Architectural description languages (ADLs) can be useful in the early phases of software design, maintenance, and evolution. Furthermore, if architectural descriptions can be subjected to formal analysis, design flaws and inconsistencies can be detected quite early in the design process. The Wright language [1] is an ADL with the attractive feature of having a formal semantics based on CSP [36].

Meseguer, Nodelman, and Talcott have recently developed in Maude a prototype executable environment for Wright using two mappings. The first mapping gives an executable formal specification of the CSP semantics of Wright, that is, it associates to each Wright architectural description a CSP process. The second mapping gives an executable rewriting logic semantics to CSP itself. The composition of both mappings provides a prototype executable environment for Wright, which can be used—in conjunction with appropriate rewrite strategies—to both animate Wright architectural descriptions, and to submit such descriptions to different forms of formal analysis.

PTS → ***RWLogic.*** *Pure type systems* (PTS) [3] generalize the λ-cube [3], which already contains important systems, like the simply typed and the (higher-order) polymorphic lambda calculi, a system λP close to the logical framework LF [35], and their combination, the calculus of constructions CC [20]. PTS systems are considered to be of key importance, since their generality and simplicity makes them an ideal basis for representing higher-order logics either directly, via the propositions-as-types interpretation [28], or via their use as a logical framework [27].

In [61] we show how the definition of PTS systems can be formalized in membership equational logic. It is noteworthy that the representational distance between the informal mathematical presentation of PTS systems with identification of α-equivalent terms and the membership equational logic specification of PTS systems is close to zero. In contrast to a higher-order representation in LF [35] or Isabelle [56], this first-order inductive approach is closer to mathematical practice, and the adequacy of the representation does not require complex metalogical justifications. It has also greater explanational power, since we explain higher-order calculi in terms of a first-order system with a very simple semantics.

We have also defined *uniform pure type systems* (UPTS) a more concrete variant of PTS systems that do not abstract from the treatment of names, but use a uniform notion of names based on CINNI [60], a new first-order calculus of names and substitutions. UPTS systems solve the problem of closure under α-conversion [58][42] in a very elegant way. A membership equational logic specification of UPTS systems can be given that contains the equational substitution calculus and directly formalizes the informal presentation.

Furthermore, [61] describes how meta-operational aspects of UPTS systems, like type checking and type inference, can be formalized in rewriting logic. For this purpose the inference system of a UPTS system is specified as a rewrite theory. The result of this formalization is an executable specification of UPTS systems that is correct w.r.t. the more abstract specification in an obvious way.

4.4   A Proof Assistant for the Open Calculus of Constructions

Rewriting logic favors the use of abstract specifications. It has a flexible computation system based on conditional rewriting modulo equations, and it uses a very liberal notion of inductive definitions. PTS systems, in particular CC, provide higher-order (dependent) types, but they are based on a fixed notion of computation, namely β-reduction. This unsatisfying situation has been addressed by addition of inductive definitions [55][40] and algebraic extensions in the style of abstract data type systems [6]. Also, the idea of overcoming these limitations using some combination of membership equational logic with the calculus of constructions has been suggested as a long-term goal in [39].

To close the gap between these two different paradigms of equational logic and higher-order type theory we are currently investigating the *open calculus of constructions* (OCC) an equational variant of the calculus of constructions with an open computational system and a flexible universe hierarchy. Using Maude and the ideas on CINNI and UPTS systems mentioned above, we have developed an experimental proof assistant for OCC that has additional features such as definitions and meta-variables. Maude has been extremely useful to explore the potential of OCC from the very early stage of its design. In addition, the formal executable specification of OCC exploits the reflective capabilities of Maude, yielding orders of magnitude speedups over Lego [41] and Coq [38] in the evaluation of functional expressions.

4.5   Implementing Formal Specification Languages

The efforts required for building adequate tools for formal specification languages are considerable. Such efforts can be particularly intense when such languages are *executable*, since a good execution engine must also be developed. The methods described in this paper can be used in practice to develop tools and environments for formal specification languages, including executable ones, and to endow such languages with a powerful module algebra of specification-combining operations.

We have applied these methods to the design and implementation of Maude itself. The most basic parts of the language—supporting module hierarchies of functional and system modules and some predefined modules—are implemented in C++, giving rise to a sublanguage called Core Maude. This is extended by special syntax for object-oriented specifications, and by a rich *module algebra* of parameterized modules and module composition in the Clear/OBJ style [10, 32] giving rise to the Full Maude language.

All of Full Maude has been formally specified in Core Maude [23, 22]. This formal specification—about 7,000 lines—is in fact its implementation, which is available in the Maude web page (`http://maude.csl.sri.com`). Our experience in this regard is very encouraging in several respects. Firstly, because of how quickly we were able to develop Full Maude. Secondly, because of how easy it will be to maintain it, modify it, and extend it with new features and new module operations. Thirdly, because of the competitive performance with which we can carry out very complex module composition and module transformation operations, that makes the interaction with Full Maude quite reasonable.

The reflective methods described in this paper, that underly our development of Full Maude, are much more general. They can equally be used to develop high-performance executable environments for other formal specification languages with much less effort and much greater flexibility, maintainability, and extensibility than what would be required in conventional implementations.

For example, Denker and Millen have specified in Maude their Common Authentication Specification Language (CAPSL) its CIL intermediate language, and a CAPSL to CIL translator [21], and plan to translate CIL into Maude to execute CAPSL specifications. Similarly, Braga and Mosses are using Maude to develop executable environment for Structural Operational Semantics and for Action Semantics [53]; and Bruni, Meseguer and Montanari have defined a mapping from Tile Logic to Rewriting Logic [9] and have used it as a basis for executing tile logic specifications in Maude [8]. It would be quite interesting to explore Maude implementations for other specification languages such as a next-generation CafeOBJ [26] and CASL [18].

Furthermore, we plan to generalize the module algebra that we have developed for Maude into a module algebra *generator*, that could endow many other specification languages with powerful and extensible algebras for combining and transforming specifications. As explained in Section 2.2, this can be done by defining such a module algebra as a *parameterized* algebraic data type. The module algebra of Maude provided by the Full Maude specification should then be regarded as the particular instance of such a generic construction, namely, for the case in which the underlying logic $\mathcal{L}$ is rewriting logic.

5   Conclusions

We have argued that, given the different perspectives from which a complex software system has to be analyzed, the multiplicity of formalisms is unavoidable. We have also argued that the technical challenges posed by the need to interrelate formalisms require advances in formal interoperability and in meta-tool design that can be based on a metatheory of general logics and on appropriate logical frameworks having efficient implementations. We have explained how the reflective logical framework of rewriting logic can be used, in conjunction with an efficient reflective implementation such as Maude, to design formal meta-tools and to rigorously support formal interoperability. The feasibility of these ideas and techniques has been demonstrated by a number of substantial experiments in which new formal tools and new translations between formalisms, efficient enough to be used in practice, have been generated.

Much work remains ahead to further advance these ideas. Maude 1.0 was made publicly available on the web in January 1999. It is well documented [13] and already supports all the formal meta-tool uses described in this paper. We are currently working towards version 2.0. In that new version we plan to enhance the formal meta-tool features of Maude. Specifically, we plan to increase Maude's flexibility in tailoring the lexical level of any language, to enhance its input/output capabilities by means of built-in objects, to provide efficient built-in support for unification modulo different equational theories, to support efficient search in the space of rewrite paths, and to further extend the expressiveness of Maude and of its META-LEVEL module.

We also plan to develop a module algebra generator by generalizing the current module algebra of Full Maude to a parameterized algebraic data type. The further development of Maude's theorem proving tools will also be very important, because it will allow carrying out proofs of *metalogical* properties about the formalisms and translations represented in Maude.

Finally, more experience on using Maude as a formal meta-tool is needed. We hope that the recent release of Maude, and the positive experience already gained will help us and others gain a broader experience in the future.

5.1   Acknowledgments

We thank: Stuart Allen, Robert Constable, and Douglas Howe for their help in understanding the *HOL → Nuprl* translation; Uri Nodelman and Carolyn Talcott for their work on the *Wright → CSP → RWLogic* translation; Grit Denker and Jon Millen for their work on the CAPSL to CIL translation; Christiano Braga and Peter Mosses for their work on building executable environments for SOS and Action Semantics; and Roberto Bruni and Ugo Montanari for their work on the translation from Tile Logic to Rewriting Logic, all of which are important experiments discussed in this paper. We also thank our fellow Maude team members Grit Denker, Patrick Lincoln, Narciso Martí-Oliet and José Quesada for their contributions to the theory and practice of Maude, and Carolyn Talcott for many discussions and extensive joint work on formal interoperability. We are also grateful to David Basin, Narciso Martí-Oliet, and the referees for their constructive criticism.

References

[1] R. Allen and D. Garlan. A formal basis for architectural connection. *ACM Trans. Soft. Eng. and Meth.*, July 1997.

[2] A. Avron, F. Honsell, I. A. Mason, and R. Pollack. Using typed lambda calculus to implement formal systems on a machine. *Journal of Automated Reasoning*, 9(3):309–354, December 1992.

[3] H. P. Barendregt. Lambda-calculi with types. In S. Abramsky, D. M. Gabbay, and T. Maibaum, editors, *Background: Computational Structures*, volume 2 of *Handbook of Logic in Computer Science*. Oxford: Clarendon Press, 1992.

[4] D. A. Basin and R. L. Constable. Metalogical frameworks. In G. Huet and G. Plotkin, editors, *Logical Environments*, pages 1–29. Cambridge University Press, 1993.

[5] J. Bergstra and J. Tucker. Characterization of computable data types by means of a finite equational specification method. In J. W. de Bakker and J. van Leeuwen, editors, *Automata, Languages and Programming, Seventh Colloquium*, pages 76–90. Springer-Verlag, 1980. LNCS, Volume 81.

[6] F. Blanqui, J. Jouannaud, and M. Okada. The calculus of algebraic constructions. In *Proc. RTA'99: Rewriting Techniques and Applications*, Lecture Notes in Computer Science. Springer-Verlag, 1999.

[7] A. Bouhoula, J.-P. Jouannaud, and J. Meseguer. Specification and proof in membership equational logic. To appear in *Theoretical Computer Science*, http://maude.csl.sri.com.

[8] R. Bruni, J. Meseguer, and U. Montanari. Internal strategies in a rewriting implementation of tile systems. *Proc. 2nd Intl. Workshop on Rewriting Logic and its Applications*, ENTCS, North Holland, 1998.

[9] R. Bruni, J. Meseguer, and U. Montanari. Process and term tile logic. Technical Report SRI-CSL-98-06, SRI International, July 1998.

[10] R. Burstall and J. A. Goguen. The semantics of Clear, a specification language. In D. Bjorner, editor, *Proceedings of the 1979 Copenhagen Winter School on Abstract Software Specification*, pages 292–332. Springer LNCS 86, 1980.

[11] M. Cerioli and J. Meseguer. May I borrow your logic? (Transporting logical structure along maps). *Theoretical Computer Science*, 173:311–347, 1997.

[12] M. Clavel. Reflection in general logics and in rewriting logic, with applications to the Maude language. Ph.D. Thesis, University of Navarre, 1998.

[13] M. Clavel, F. Durán, S. Eker, P. Lincoln, N. Martí-Oliet, J. Meseguer, and J. Quesada. Maude: specification and programming in rewriting logic. SRI International, January 1999, http://maude.csl.sri.com.

[14] M. Clavel, F. Durán, S. Eker, and J. Meseguer. Building equational proving tools by reflection in rewriting logic. In *Proc. of the CafeOBJ Symposium '98, Numazu, Japan*. CafeOBJ Project, April 1998. http://maude.csl.sri.com.

[15] M. Clavel, S. Eker, P. Lincoln, and J. Meseguer. Principles of Maude. In J. Meseguer, editor, *Proc. First Intl. Workshop on Rewriting Logic and its Applications*, volume 4 of *Electronic Notes in Theoretical Computer Science*. Elsevier, 1996. http://www.elsevier.nl/cas/tree/store/tcs/free/noncas/pc/volume4.htm.

[16] M. Clavel and J. Meseguer. Axiomatizing reflective logics and languages. In G. Kiczales, editor, *Proceedings of Reflection'96, San Francisco, California, April 1996*, pages 263–288, 1996. http://jerry.cs.uiuc.edu/reflection/.

[17] M. Clavel and J. Meseguer. Reflection and strategies in rewriting logic. In J. Meseguer, editor, *Proc. First Intl. Workshop on Rewriting Logic and its Applications*, volume 4 of *Electronic Notes in Theoretical Computer Science*. Elsevier, 1996. http://www.elsevier.nl/cas/tree/store/tcs/free/noncas/pc/volume4.htm.

[18] CoFI Task Group on Semantics. CASL—The CoFI algebraic specification language, version 0.97, Semantics. http://www.brics.dk/Projects/CoFI, July 1997.

[19] R. Constable. *Implementing Mathematics with the Nuprl Proof Development System*. Prentice Hall, 1987.

[20] T. Coquand and G. Huet. The calculus of constructions. *Information and Computation*, 76(2/3):95–120, 1988.

[21] G. Denker and J. Millen. CAPSL intermediate language. In N. Heintze and E. Clarke, editors, *Proc. of Workshop on Formal Methods and Security Protocols, July 1999, Trento, Italy*, 1999. www.cs.bell-labs.com/who/nch/fmsp99/program.html.

[22] F. Durán. A reflective module algebra with applications to the Maude language. Ph.D. Thesis, University of Malaga, 1999.

[23] F. Durán and J. Meseguer. An extensible module algebra for Maude. *Proc. 2nd Intl. Workshop on Rewriting Logic and its Applications*, ENTCS, North Holland, 1998.

[24] S. Feferman. Finitary inductively presented logics. In R. Ferro et al., editors, *Logic Colloquium'88*, pages 191–220. North-Holland, 1989.

[25] A. Felty and D. Miller. Encoding a dependent-type λ-calculus in a logic programming language. In M. Stickel, editor, *Proc. 10th. Int. Conf. on Automated Deduction, Kaiserslautern, Germany, July 1990*, volume 449 of *LNCS*, pages 221–235. Springer-Verlag, 1990.

[26] K. Futatsugi and R. Diaconescu. CafeOBJ report. AMAST Series in Computing, Vol. 6, World Scientific, 1998.

[27] P. Gardner. *Representing Logics in Type Theory*. PhD thesis, Technical Report CST-93-92, Department of Computer Science, University of Edinburgh, 1992.

[28] H. Geuvers. *Logics and Type Systems*. PhD thesis, University of Nijmegen, 1993.

[29] J.-Y. Girard. Linear Logic. *Theoretical Computer Science*, 50:1–102, 1987.

[30] J. Goguen and R. Burstall. Institutions: Abstract model theory for specification and programming. *Journal of the ACM*, 39(1):95–146, 1992.

[31] J. Goguen and J. Meseguer. Order-sorted algebra I: Equational deduction for multiple inheritance, overloading, exceptions and partial operations. *Theoretical Computer Science*, 105:217–273, 1992.

[32] J. Goguen, T. Winkler, J. Meseguer, K. Futatsugi, and J.-P. Jouannaud. Introducing OBJ. Technical Report SRI-CSL-92-03, SRI International, Computer Science Laboratory, 1992. To appear in J.A. Goguen and G.R. Malcolm, editors, *Applications of Algebraic Specification Using OBJ*, Academic Press, 1999.

[33] J. A. Goguen, A. Stevens, K. Hobley, and H. Hilberdink. 2OBJ: A meta-logical framework based on equational logic. *Philosophical Transactions of the Royal Society, Series A*, 339:69–86, 1992.

[34] M. Gordon. *Introduction to HOL: A Theorem Proving Environment*. Cambridge University Press, 1993.

[35] R. Harper, F. Honsell, and G. Plotkin. A framework for defining logics. *Journal of the Association Computing Machinery*, 40(1):143–184, 1993.

[36] C. Hoare. *Communicating Sequential Processes*. Prentice Hall, 1985.

[37] D. J. Howe. Semantical foundations for embedding HOL in Nuprl. In M. Wirsing and M. Nivat, editors, *Algebraic Methodology and Software Technology*, volume 1101 of *Lecture Notes in Computer Science*, pages 85–101, Berlin, 1996. Springer-Verlag.

[38] G. Huet, C. Paulin-Mohring, et al. The Coq Proof Assistant Reference Manual, Version 6.2.4, Coq Project. Technical report, INRIA, 1999. http://pauillac.inria.fr/coq/.

[39] J. P. Jouannaud. Membership equational logic, calculus of inductive constructions, and rewrite logic. In *2nd Workshop on Rewrite Logic and Applications*, 1998.

[40] Z. Luo. *Computation and Reasoning: A Type Theory for Computer Science*. International Series of Monographs on Computer Science. Oxford University Press, 1994.

[41] Z. Luo and R. Pollack. Lego proof development system: User's manual. LFCS Technical Report ECS-LFCS-92-211, University of Edinburgh, 1992.

[42] L. Magnussen. *The Implementation of ALF – a Proof Editor based on Martin-Löf's Monomorphic Type Theory with Explicit Substitutions*. PhD thesis, University of Göteborg, Dept. of Computer Science, 1994.

[43] N. Martí-Oliet and J. Meseguer. Rewriting logic as a logical and semantic framework. Technical Report SRI-CSL-93-05, SRI International, Computer Science Laboratory, August 1993. To appear in D. Gabbay, ed., *Handbook of Philosophical Logic*, Kluwer Academic Publishers.

[44] N. Martí-Oliet and J. Meseguer. General logics and logical frameworks. In D. Gabbay, editor, *What is a Logical System?*, pages 355–392. Oxford University Press, 1994.

[45] N. Martí-Oliet and J. Meseguer. Rewriting logic as a logical and semantic framework. In J. Meseguer, editor, *Proc. First Intl. Workshop on Rewriting Logic and its Applications*, volume 4 of *Electronic Notes in Theoretical Computer Science*. Elsevier, 1996. http://www.elsevier.nl/cas/tree/store/tcs/free/noncas/pc/volume4.htm.

[46] S. Matthews, A. Smaill, and D. Basin. Experience with FS_0 as a framework theory. In G. Huet and G. Plotkin, editors, *Logical Environments*, pages 61–82. Cambridge University Press, 1993.

[47] J. Meseguer. General logics. In H.-D. E. et al., editor, *Logic Colloquium'87*, pages 275–329. North-Holland, 1989.

[48] J. Meseguer. Conditional rewriting logic as a unified model of concurrency. *Theoretical Computer Science*, 96(1):73–155, 1992.

[49] J. Meseguer. Formal interoperability. In *Proceedings of the 1998 Conference on Mathematics in Artificial Intelligence, Fort Laurerdale, Florida, January 1998*, 1998. http://rutcor.rutgers.edu/~amai/Proceedings.html.

[50] J. Meseguer. Membership algebra as a semantic framework for equational specification. In F. Parisi-Presicce, ed., *Proc. WADT'97*, 18–61, Springer LNCS 1376, 1998.

[51] J. Meseguer. Research directions in rewriting logic. In U. Berger and H. Schwichtenberg, editors, *Computational Logic, NATO Advanced Study Institute, Marktoberdorf, Germany, July 29 – August 6, 1997*. Springer-Verlag, 1999.

[52] J. Meseguer and N. Martí-Oliet. From abstract data types to logical frameworks. In E. Astesiano, G. Reggio, and A. Tarlecki, editors, *Recent Trends in Data Type Specification, Santa Margherita, Italy, May/June 1994*, pages 48–80. Springer LNCS 906, 1995.

[53] P. Mosses. *Action Semantics*. Cambridge University Press, 1992.

[54] G. Nadathur and D. Miller. An overview of λProlog. In K. Bowen and R. Kowalski, editors, *Fifth Int. Joint Conf. and Symp. on Logic Programming*, pages 810–827. The MIT Press, 1988.

[55] C. Paulin-Mohring. Inductive Definitions in the system Coq – Rules and Properties. In M. Bezem and J. . F. Groote, editors, *Typed Lambda Calculi and Applications, International Conference on Typed Lambda Calculi and Applications, TLCA 93*, volume 664 of *Lecture Notes in Computer Science*. Springer Varlag, 1993.

[56] L. C. Paulson. *Isabelle*, volume 828 of *Lecture Notes in Computer Science*. Springer Verlag, 1994.

[57] F. Pfenning. Elf: A language for logic definition and verified metaprogramming. In *Proc. Fourth Annual IEEE Symp. on Logic in Computer Science*, pages 313–322, Asilomar, California, June 1989.

[58] R. Pollack. Closure under alpha-conversion. In H. Barendregt and T. Nipkow, editors, *Types for Proofs and Programs: International Workshop TYPES'93, Nijmegen, May 1993, Selected Papers.*, volume 806 of *Lecture Notes in Computer Science*, pages 313–332. Springer-Verlag, 1993.

[59] R. M. Smullyan. *Theory of Formal Systems*, volume 47 of *Annals of Mathematics Studies*. Princeton University Press, 1961.

[60] M.-O. Stehr. CINNI - A New Calculus of Explicit Substitutions and its Application to Pure Type Systems. Manuscript, SRI-International, CSL, Menlo Park, CA, USA.

[61] M.-O. Stehr and J. Meseguer. Pure type systems in rewriting logic — meta-logical and meta-operational views. Submitted for publication.

[62] P. Viry. Rewriting: An effective model of concurrency. In C. Halatsis et al., editors, *PARLE'94, Proc. Sixth Int. Conf. on Parallel Architectures and Languages Europe, Athens, Greece, July 1994*, volume 817 of *LNCS*, pages 648–660. Springer-Verlag, 1994.

Hiding More of Hidden Algebra

Joseph Goguen and Grigore Roşu*

Department of Computer Science & Engineering
University of California at San Diego

1 Introduction

Behavioral specification is a rapidly advancing area of algebraic semantics that
supports practical applications by allowing models (implementations) that only
behaviorally satisfy specifications, infinitary data structures (such as streams),
behavioral refinements, and coinduction proof methods. This paper generalizes
the hidden algebra approach to allow: (P1) operations with multiple hidden arguments, and (P2) defining behavioral equivalence with a subset of operations,
in addition to the already present (P3) built-in data types, (P4) nondeterminism, (P5) concurrency, and (P6) non-congruent operations. All important results
generalize, but more elegant formulations use the new institution in Section 5.
Behavioral satisfaction appeared 1981 in [20], hidden algebra 1989 in [9], multiple
hidden arguments 1992 in [1], congruent and behavioral operations in [1, 18], behavioral equivalence defined by a subset of operations in [1], and non-congruent
operations in [5]; all this was previously integrated in [21], but this paper gives
new examples, institutions, and results relating hidden algebra to information
hiding. We assume familiarity with basics of algebraic specification, e.g., [11, 13].

2 Basic Hidden Algebra

Definition 1. A *hidden signature* is (Ψ, D, Σ), often written just Σ, where Ψ is a
V-sorted signature, D is a Ψ-algebra called the *data algebra*, Σ is a $(V \cup H)$-sorted
signature extending Ψ such that each operation in Σ with both its arguments
and result in V lies in Ψ, and V and H are disjoint sets, called *visible sorts* and
hidden sorts, respectively. For technical reasons (e.g., see [12]), we assume each
element d in D is denoted by exactly one constant in Ψ, also denoted d.

A *hidden subsignature of* Σ is a hidden signature (Ψ, D, Γ) with $\Gamma \subseteq \Sigma$. A
behavioral, or *hidden*, Σ-*specification* or *theory* is (Σ, Γ, E), where Σ is a hidden
signature, Γ is a hidden subsignature of Σ, and E is a set of Σ-equations.
Operations in $\Gamma - \Psi$ may be called *behavioral* [6] or *observational* [1, 2].

A *hidden Σ-algebra* is a many sorted Σ-algebra A such that $A|_\Psi = D$. □

An adequate discussion of the complex historical and technical relations
among the many approaches to behavioral specification is not possible in this

---

* On leave from Fundamentals of Computer Science, Faculty of Mathematics, University of Bucharest, Romania.

J. Wing, J. Woodcock, J. Davies (Eds.): FM'99, Vol. II, LNCS 1709, pp. 1704–1719, 1999.
© Springer-Verlag Berlin Heidelberg 1999

short paper, but we do our best to be accurate, if not comprehensive. We drop
the restriction of [9, 12] to operations with at most one hidden argument. Operations with hidden arguments may be called *attributes* if the result is visible,
and *methods* if it is hidden; those with visible arguments and hidden result are
called *hidden constants*. Behavioral operations are used in experiments to distinguish states; i.e., they define behavioral equivalence. Note that our models
do not require all operations to be congruent (see Definition 5) as in [15, 18],
since non-congruent operations are needed for applications like length for lists
implemented as sets, and the push operation in Example 2. Example 3 gives a
spec equivalent to that in Example 1, with in as its only behavioral operation,
thus illustrating the need for (P2). Our models also satisfy (P3), having a fixed
subalgebra of data values, as distinct from observational logic ([1, 2], etc.) and
CafeOBJ [6]. This is desirable because real applications use standard Booleans
and integers rather than arbitrary models of some theory; however, all results
of this paper still hold for the fully loose semantics, and there are applications
where it is useful, although we feel these are better handled by parameterization.
Coalgebra is an elegant related approach (e.g., [16]) that lacks nondeterminism,
multiple hidden arguments, and other features; one symptom of the difference is
that final algebras no longer exist for our generalization. Set union is one natural
example motivating (P1); there are many others. If sets are objects with hidden
state, then operations like union have two hidden arguments:

Example 1. We can specify sets using CafeOBJ syntax[1] [6] as follows:

```
mod* SET { *[ Set ]*  pr(NAT)
   bop _in_   : Nat Set -> Bool ** attribute
   op empty   : -> Set           ** hidden const
   bop add    : Nat Set -> Set   ** method
   bop _U_    : Set Set -> Set   ** 2 hidden args
   bop _&_    : Set Set -> Set   ** 2 hidden args
   bop neg    : Set -> Set       ** method
   vars N N' : Nat   vars X X' : Set
   eq N in empty = false .
   eq N in add(N',X) = (N == N') or (N in X) .
   eq N in (X U X')  = (N in X)  or (N in X') .
   eq N in (X & X')  = (N in X) and (N in X') .
   eq N in neg(X)    =  not (N in X) . }
```

Here "*[Set]*" declares Set a hidden sort, "bop" declares behavioral operations, and "pr(NAT)" imports the module NAT of natural numbers in "protecting" mode, i.e., so that the naturals are not compromised. The constant empty
is the only non-behavioral operation, indicated by the keyword "op", and neg is
complement with respect to the set of all natural numbers. □

Definition 2. Given an equivalence $\sim$ on A, an operation σ in $\Sigma_{s_1...s_n,s}$ is
congruent for $\sim$ iff $A_\sigma(a_1,...,a_n) \sim A_\sigma(a_1',...,a_n')$ whenever $a_i \sim a_i'$ for $i = 1,...,n$. A *hidden Γ-congruence on* A is an equivalence on A which is the identity
on visible sorts and is congruent for each operation in Γ. □

---

[1] But CafeOBJ prohibits behavioral operations with more than one hidden argument.

The following result from [21] is the basis for generalizing coinduction and other results to operations with multiple hidden arguments:

Theorem 3. *Given a hidden subsignature Γ of Σ and a hidden Σ-algebra A, there exists a largest hidden Γ-congruence on A, called Γ-behavioral equivalence and denoted $\equiv_\Sigma^\Gamma$.* □

Definition 4. A hidden Σ-algebra A Γ-*behaviorally satisfies* a conditional Σ-equation $e = (\forall X)\ t = t'$ if $t_1 = t_1', ..., t_n = t_n'$ iff for each $\theta: X \rightarrow A$, if $\theta(t_i) \equiv_\Sigma^\Gamma \theta(t_i')$ for $i = 1, ..., n$, then $\theta(t) \equiv_\Sigma^\Gamma \theta(t')$; in this case we write $A \models_\Sigma^\Gamma e$. If E is a set of Σ-equations, we write $A \models_\Sigma^\Gamma E$ if A Γ-behaviorally satisfies each equation in E. When Σ and Γ are clear from context, we may write $\equiv$ and $\models$ instead of $\equiv_\Sigma^\Gamma$ and $\models_\Sigma^\Gamma$ respectively. We say that A *behaviorally satisfies* (or *is a model of*) a behavioral specification $\mathcal{B} = (\Sigma, \Gamma, E)$ iff $A \models_\Sigma^\Gamma E$, and in this case we write $A \models \mathcal{B}$; also $\mathcal{B} \models e$ means $A \models \mathcal{B}$ implies $A \models_\Sigma^\Gamma e$. □

Example 2. <u>Nondeterministic Stack:</u> The following example after [12] motivates non-congruent operations. We specify a random number generator for a distributed system, as a process that puts generated numbers on a stack, where numbers are consumed with exactly one call by one process, since multiple access to a single number is wrong. We consider two stack states equivalent iff they have the same numbers in the same order; then top and pop are congruent for this equivalence, but push is not, since its behavior should not be determined by what is on the stack.

```
mod* NDSTACK { *[ Stack ]*  pr(NAT)
    bop top   : Stack -> Nat      ** attribute
    bop pop   : Stack -> Stack    ** method
    op empty  : -> Stack          ** hidden constant
    op push   : Stack -> Stack    ** not congruent!
    var S : Stack
    beq pop(empty)    = empty .
    beq pop(push(S))  = S . }
```

An implementation might use a function $f: \text{Nat} \rightarrow \text{Nat}$ where $f(n)$ is the nth randomly generated number. To ensure that n changes with each new call, we can keep it as a variable with the stack, incremented whenever a new number is pushed. Such an implementation is equivalent to the following model: Let $A_{\text{Nat}} = \omega$, where ω is the natural numbers, and let $A_{\text{Stack}} = \omega \times \omega^*$, where ω^* is lists of naturals. Using [head,tail] list notation with $[]$ for the empty list, let $A_{\text{empty}} = (0, [])$, $A_{\text{top}}((n, [])) = 0$, $A_{\text{top}}((n, [h, t])) = h$, $A_{\text{pop}}((n, [])) = (n, [])$, $A_{\text{pop}}((n, [h, t])) = (n, t)$, and $A_{\text{push}}((n, l)) = (n + 1, [f(n), l])$. Then two states are behaviorally equivalent iff for every sequence of pops followed by a top they give the same number, that is, they store the same elements in the same order; in other words, $(n, l) \equiv (n', l')$ iff $l = l'$. push is not behaviorally congruent for this model, because $f(n)$ can be different from $f(n')$. □

2.1   Coinduction

Example 3. We prove that union in Example 1 is commutative, i.e., that
$$(\forall X, X')\ X \cup X' = X' \cup X$$
is behaviorally satisfied by all models of SET. For A a model of SET, we use infix
notation, $\_ \in \_$ instead of A_{in} and $\_ \cup \_$ instead of $A_{\_\cup\_}$.

Let $\_R\_$ be a binary relation on A, called the *candidate relation*, defined by
$a\ R\ a'$ if and only if $n \in a$ iff $n \in a'$ for all natural numbers n. We claim R
is a hidden congruence. We show only that union is congruent for R, the other
cases being similar. Suppose $a_1\ R\ a_1'$ and $a_2\ R\ a_2'$, i.e., $(n \in a_1$ iff $n \in a_1')$ and
$(n \in a_2$ iff $n \in a_2')$ for all natural numbers n. Then $n \in a_1 \cup a_2$ iff $n \in a_1' \cup a_2'$,
i.e., $a_1 \cup a_2\ R\ a_1' \cup a_2'$.

Since R is a hidden congruence, it is included in behavioral equivalence.
We now show $(a \cup a')\ R\ (a' \cup a)$ for all $a, a' \in A$. This is equivalent to $n \in$
$a \cup a'$ iff $n \in a' \cup a$, i.e., to $(n \in a$ or $n \in a')$ iff $(n \in a'$ or $n \in a)$, which
is obvious. Thus we conclude that $a \cup a'$ is behaviorally equivalent to $a' \cup a$
for all $a, a' \in A$. Therefore $A \models_{\Sigma}^{\Sigma} (\forall X, X')\ X \cup X' = X' \cup X$, and since A was
arbitrary, SET $\models (\forall X, X')\ X \cup X' = X' \cup X$. Here is a CafeOBJ proof score for
this reasoning (but see footnote 2):

```
mod* COINDUCTION { pr(SET)
  op _R_ : Set Set -> Bool
  op n : -> Nat
  vars X X' : Set
  eq X R X' = (n in X) == (n in X') . }
open COINDUCTION .
  ops a1 a1' a2 a2' : -> Set .
  eq n in a1 = n in a1' .          ** assume that a1 R a1'
  eq n in a2 = n in a2' .          ** assume that a2 R a2'
  red (a1 U a2) R (a1' U a2') .    **> should be true
  red (a1 & a2) R (a1' & a2') .    **> should be true
  red neg(a1) R neg(a1) .          **> should be true
  op m : -> Nat .
  red add(m, a1) R add(m, a1') .   **> should be true
  eq m = n .
  red add(m, a1) R add(m, a1') .   **> should be true
close
open COINDUCTION .
  ops a a' : -> Set .
  red (a U a') R (a' U a) .        **> should be true
close
```
□

3   Eliminating Behavioral Operations

The fewer operations in Γ, the easier it is to do coinduction, because fewer operations need be shown congruent for the candidate relation. This section follows
[21], using the notion of behaviorally equivalent specifications and conditions
for a specification to be behavioral equivalent to another with fewer behavioral

operations. The first definition of operations congruent over behavioral equivalence defined by a subset of operations seems to have been [1]; similar ideas also appear in [18, 19, 21], and in [6, 5] as well as in [15], which use the term *behavioral coherence*. We prefer the term "congruent" because the congruence rule of equational deduction is sound in hidden logic for an operation iff that operation is behaviorally congruent.

Definition 5. An operation σ is Γ-*behaviorally congruent* for A iff σ is congruent for $\equiv_\Sigma^\Gamma$ on A; we will often say just "congruent". An operation $\sigma \in \Sigma$ is *behaviorally congruent* for a specification $\mathcal{B}$ iff it is behaviorally congruent for every $A \models \mathcal{B}$. □

Proposition 6. *If $\mathcal{B} = (\Sigma, \Gamma, E)$ is a behavioral specification, then all operations in Γ and all hidden constants are behaviorally congruent for $\mathcal{B}$.* □

Corollary 7. Congruence Criterion: *Let $\mathcal{B} = (\Sigma, \Gamma, E)$ be a hidden specification and let $\sigma : v_1...v_m h_1...h_k \to h$ be an operation in Σ, where $v_1, ..., v_m$ are visible sorts and $h_1, ..., h_k, h$ are hidden sorts. If $W = \{y_1 : v_1, ..., y_m : v_m, x_1 : h_1, ..., x_k : h_k\}$ is a set of variables, then let $\sigma(W)$ denote the term $\sigma(y_1, ..., y_m, x_1, ..., x_k)$. If for each appropriate $\delta : s_1...s_n \to s$ in Γ and each $j = 1, ..., n$ such that $s_j = h$ there is some γ in $T_\Gamma(Z_j \cup W)$ such that the Σ-equation $(\forall Z_j, W)\ \delta(Z_j, \sigma(W)) = \gamma$ is in E (modulo renaming of variables), then σ is behaviorally congruent for $\mathcal{B}$.* □

Example 4 uses this criterion to show all the set operations congruent for the behavioral equivalence generated by `in`. The above is a special case of Theorem 16 of [21], which is further generalized in [4], although the result in [4] also follows from Theorem 16 of [21].

Definition 8. Hidden specifications $\mathcal{B}_1 = (\Sigma, \Gamma_1, E_1)$ and $\mathcal{B}_2 = (\Sigma, \Gamma_2, E_2)$ over the same hidden signature are *equivalent* iff for any hidden Σ-algebra A, $A \models \mathcal{B}_1$ iff $A \models \mathcal{B}_2$, and in this case $\equiv_\Sigma^{\Gamma_1} = \equiv_\Sigma^{\Gamma_2}$ on A. □

The rest of this section assumes $\mathcal{B}_1 = (\Sigma, \Gamma_1, E)$ and $\mathcal{B}_2 = (\Sigma, \Gamma_2, E)$ are two hidden specifications over the same signature with the same equations and with $\Gamma_1 \subseteq \Gamma_2$; we also assume that the Σ-equations in E have no conditions of hidden sort. The result below gives a method for eliminating behavioral operations from a specification. If a behavioral operation can be shown congruent for the behavioral specification that takes that operation as non-behavioral, then the two specs are equivalent.

Theorem 9. *$\mathcal{B}_1$ and $\mathcal{B}_2$ are equivalent iff all operations in Γ_2 are behaviorally congruent for $\mathcal{B}_1$.* □

Example 4. We modify the specification SET so that its only behavioral operation is `in`, and call the result SETH. By the congruence criterion (Corollary 7), `add`, `_U_`, `_&_` and `neg` are all behaviorally congruent for SETH. Thus by Theorem 9, SET and SETH are equivalent. This greatly simplifies the coinductive proof in Example 3:

```
mod* COINDUCTION { pr(SETH)
  op _R_ : Set Set -> Bool
  op n : -> Nat
  vars X X' : Set
  eq X R X' = (n in X) == (n in X') . }
open COINDUCTION .
  ops a a' : -> Set .
  red (a U a') R (a' U a) .  **> should be true
close
```
□

Example 5. Lists of Semaphores: The use of semaphores for scheduling and protecting resources is well known. A flag is associated with each non-preemptive
resource. When the resource is allocated to a process, its semaphore is put up,
and access is prohibited. When the process releases the resource, its semaphore
is put down and it can be allocated to another process. Many modern processors
support semaphores to speed up operating systems, and often include a function
to reverse a flag. Here is a CafeOBJ specification:

```
mod* FLAG { *[ Flag ]* pr(QID)
  bop resource_ : Flag -> Id
  bop up?_ : Flag -> Bool
  ops up down rev : Flag -> Flag
  var F : Flag
  eq up? up(F)   = true .     eq resource up(F)   = resource F .
  eq up? down(F) = false .    eq resource down(F) = resource F .
  eq up? rev(F)  = not up? F . eq resource rev(F)  = resource F . }
```

It is intended that all operations are behavioral, but by the congruence criterion
(Corollary 7) and Theorem 9, the spec with only up? and resource declared
behavioral is equivalent, because the others are obviously congruent.

When many resources of the same type are available (e.g., printers), their flags
are kept in a list (an array is undesirable since the number of resources varies
dynamically) from which the scheduler chooses the first unallocated resource
when a request is received. We want all operations behavioral, that is, to preserve
the intended behavior of flags and lists of flags. Here is a CafeOBJ spec (but see
footnote 2, noting that cons has two hidden arguments):

```
mod* FLAG-LIST { *[ List ]* pr(FLAG)
  bop car_ : List -> Flag
  bop cdr_ : List -> List
  bop cons : Flag List -> List
  var F : Flag    var L : List
  beq car cons(F, L) = F .
  beq cdr cons(F, L) = L . }
```

The behavioral equations here allow more flexible implementation. For example,
an operating system can allocate at its discretion software or hardware implementations for flags, so that car cons(F, L) is only behaviorally equivalent to
F. The congruence criterion can again be applied with Theorem 9 to show that
FLAG-LIST is equivalent to the spec where cons is not behavioral. (We have left

some details unspecified, such as car and cdr of the empty list, to make the spec easier to understand.)

Now consider a new spec where lists of flags can be put up and down. This is useful for operating systems to put resources in a safe state for system shutdown, or when hardware or software anomalies are detected.

```
mod* FLAG-LIST'{ *[ Flag < List ]*  pr(FLAG)
   bop car_ : List -> Flag
   bop cdr_ : List -> List
   op cons : Flag List -> List
   var F : Flag      var L : List
   beq car cons(F, L) = F .    beq cdr cons(F, L) = L .
   ops up down : List -> List
   beq car up(L)   =   up(car L) .    beq cdr up(L)   = up(cdr L) .
   beq car down(L) = down(car L) .    beq cdr down(L) = down(cdr L) . }
```

The congruence criterion and Theorem 9 again justify having only car and cdr behavioral. Now we use coinduction to prove that up(cons(F, L)) is behaviorally equivalent to cons(up(F), up(L)) for all flags F and lists of flags L:

```
mod* COINDUCTION { pr(FLAG-LIST')
   op _R_ : Flag Flag -> Bool
   op _R_ : List List -> Bool
   vars F F' : Flag    vars L L' : List
   eq F R F = true .  eq L R L = true .
   eq F R F' = (up? F == up? F') and (resource F == resource F') .
   eq L R L' = ((car L) R (car L')) and ((cdr L) R (cdr L')) . }
```

Notice that we didn't completely define the candidate relation, but rather gave axioms it should satisfy, saying R is a hidden congruence (but without symmetry and transitivity, since we don't need these properties); we know such relations exist, because behavioral equivalence is one. This code is a bit dangerous, because of its (co)recurrent definition of the candidate relation, which can lead to non-terminating rewriting; but it works in this case, because the equation eq L R L = true is applied before the last equation. We now demonstrate two interesting properties:

```
open COINDUCTION .
   op f : -> Flag .  op l : -> List .
   red up(cons(f, l))   R cons(up(f), up(l)) .     **> should be true
   red down(cons(f, l)) R cons(down(f), down(l)) . **> should be true
close
```

CafeOBJ does 29 rewrites and 114 matches for each reduction. □

4   Behavioral Abstraction Is Information Hiding

This section shows that any behavioral specification B over a hidden signature Σ can be translated to an ordinary algebraic specification $\tilde{B}$ over a signature $\tilde{\Sigma}$ containing Σ, such that a hidden Σ-algebra behaviorally satisfies B iff it strictly satisfies $\Sigma \Box \tilde{B}$ (which is the set of all Σ-theorems of $\tilde{B}$, see [7] for more detail). The specification $\tilde{B}$ can be generated automatically from B. This result allows using an equational logic theorem prover (such as OBJ3) for behavioral equations. Constructions in Definitions 12, 13 and 17 were inspired by work in [2, 3, 17].

Definition 10. For each hidden sort h, let $\star_h$ be a special variable of sort h different from every other variable appearing in this paper. Given a hidden Σ-algebra A and an element a_h of sort h of A, let $\tilde{a}_h : T_\Gamma(A \cup \{\star_h\}) \to A$ denote the unique extension of the function from $A \cup \{\star_h\}$ to A which is the identity on A and takes $\star_h$ to a_h. If t, t' are terms in $T_\Gamma(A \cup \{\star_h\})$ and $T_\Sigma(A \cup X)$ respectively, let $t[t']$ denote the term in $T_\Sigma(A \cup X)$ obtained by substituting $\star_h$ for t' in t. Let $LT_\Gamma(A \cup \{\star_h\})$ be the $(V \cup H)$-sorted subset of terms in $T_\Gamma(A \cup \{\star_h\})$ over the behavioral operations in Γ having exactly one occurrence of $\star_h$, whose proper subterms are either elements of A or else hidden terms in $LT_\Gamma(A \cup \{\star_h\})$. $\square$

In other words, there are only hidden valued operations on the path from $\star_h$ to the root of any term in $LT_\Gamma(A\cup\{\star_h\})$, except that the operation at the top may be visible, and all other proper subterms which do not contain $\star_h$ are elements of A. The following can be seen as an alternative proof of Theorem 3:

Proposition 11. *Given a hidden Σ-algebra A and $a, a' \in A_h$ then $a \equiv^\Gamma_{\Sigma,h} a'$ iff $\tilde{a}(c) = \tilde{a}'(c)$ for each $v \in V$ and each $c \in LT_{\Gamma,v}(A \cup \{\star_h\})$.*

Proof. We show that the relation $\sim$ defined by $a \sim_h a'$ iff $\tilde{a}(c) = \tilde{a}'(c)$ for each $v \in V$ and each $c \in LT_{\Gamma,v}(A \cup \{\star_h\})$ is the largest hidden Γ-congruence.

Let $\sigma : h_1...h_k v_{k+1}...v_n \to s$ be any operation in Γ (with its first k arguments hidden), let $a_i, a'_i \in A_{h_i}$ such that $a_i \sim_{h_i} a'_i$ for $i = 1, ..., k$, let $d_i \in A_{v_i}(= D_{v_i})$ for $i = k+1, ..., n$, and let $v \in V$ and $c \in LT_{\Gamma,v}(A \cup \{\star_s\})$ (if the sort s is visible, delete all occurrences of c in the proof that follows and replace terms of the form $c[t]$ by just t). Let c_i be the term $c[\sigma(a'_1, ..., a'_{i-1}, \star_{h_i}, a_{i+1}, ..., a_k, d_{k+1}, ..., d_n)]$ for each $i = 1, ..., k$. Because $a_i \sim_{h_i} a'_i$ one gets $\tilde{a}_i(c_i) = \tilde{a}'_i(c_i)$. Letting a and a' denote the elements $A_\sigma(a_1, ..., a_k, d_{k+1}, ..., d_n)$ and $A_\sigma(a'_1, ..., a'_k, d_{k+1}, ..., d_n)$ respectively, notice that $\tilde{a}(c) = \tilde{a}_1(c_1)$, $\tilde{a}'_i(c_i) = \tilde{a}_{i+1}(c_{i+1})$ for $i = 1, ..., k-1$, and $\tilde{a}'_k = \tilde{a}'(c)$. Therefore $\tilde{a}(c) = \tilde{a}'(c)$, and since c is arbitrary, we obtain $a \sim_s a'$, i.e., $\sim$ is preserved by σ, and so $\sim$ is a hidden Γ-congruence.

Because all operations in Γ preserve hidden Γ-congruences, so do the terms in $LT_\Gamma(A \cup \{\star_h\})$. In particular, terms in $LT_{\Gamma,v}(A \cup \{\star_h\})$ take congruent elements to identities. Therefore any hidden Γ-congruence is included in $\sim$. $\square$

Definition 12. Given a hidden signature (Ψ, D, Σ) (where $S = V \cup H$), let $(\tilde{S}, \tilde{\Sigma})$ be the ordinary signature with $\tilde{S} = S \cup (H \to S)$, where $(H \to S) = \{(h \to s) \mid s \in S, h \in H\}$ is a set of new sorts, and where $\tilde{\Sigma}$ adds to Σ:

- a new operation $\diamond_h : \to (h \to h)$ for each $h \in H$,
- a new operation $\sigma^k_h : s_1 \ ... \ s_{k-1} \ (h \to h_k) \ s_{k+1} \ ... \ s_n \to (h \to s)$ for each behavioral operation $\sigma : s_1 \ ... \ s_{k-1} \ h_k \ s_{k+1} \ ... \ s_n \to s$ in Γ, for each $k = 1, ..., n$ such that $h_k \in H$ and each $h \in H$, and
- a new operation $\_[\_] : (h \to s) \ h \to s$ for each $h \in H$ and $s \in S$.

$\square$

Definition 13. Given hidden Σ-algebra A, define an ordinary $\tilde{\Sigma}$-algebra $\tilde{A}$ by:

1. $\tilde{A}|_\Sigma = A$, so $\tilde{A}$ extends A,
2. $\tilde{A}_{(h \to s)} = LT_{\Gamma,s}(A \cup \{\star_h\})$,

3. $\tilde{A}_{\diamond_h} = \star_h$,
4. $\tilde{A}_{\sigma_h^k}: A_{s_1} \times \cdots A_{s_{k-1}} \times \tilde{A}_{(h \to h_k)} \times A_{s_{k+1}} \times \cdots \times A_{s_n} \to \tilde{A}_{(h \to s)}$ for each behavioral operation $\sigma : s_1 \ldots s_{k-1} \, h_k \, s_{k+1} \ldots s_n \to s$ in Γ and $h \in H$, by $\tilde{A}_{\sigma_h^k}(a_1, ..., a_{k-1}, t, a_{k+1}, ..., a_n) = \sigma(a_1, ..., a_{k-1}, t, a_{k+1}, ..., a_n)$ for $a_i \in A_{s_i}$ for $i \in \{1, ..., k-1, k+1, ..., n\}$, $t \in LT_{\Gamma, h_k}(A \cup \{\star_h\})$, and
5. $\tilde{A}_{\_[\_]}: \tilde{A}_{(h \to s)} \times A_h \to A_s$ for $s \in S$ and $h \in H$, by $\tilde{A}_{\_[\_]}(t, a_h) = \tilde{a}_h(t)$.
□

Proposition 14. *Given a hidden Σ-algebra A, then*

1. $\tilde{A} \models_{\tilde{\Sigma}} (\forall x : h) \diamond_h[x] = x$ *for each $h \in H$, and*
2. $\tilde{A} \models_{\tilde{\Sigma}} (\forall Y_k, z : (h \to h_k), x : h) \, \sigma_h^k(Y_k, z)[x] = \sigma(Y_k, z[x])$, *where Y_k is the set of variables $\{y_1 : s_1, ..., y_{k-1} : s_{k-1}, y_{k+1} : s_{k+1}, ..., y_n : s_n\}$, $\sigma_h^k(Y_k, z)$ is a shorthand for the term $\sigma_h^k(y_1, ..., y_{k-1}, z, y_{k+1}, ..., y_n)$ and $\sigma(Y_k, z[x])$ for the term $\sigma(y_1, ..., y_{k-1}, z[x], y_{k+1}, ..., y_n)$, for all behavioral operations $\sigma : s_1 \ldots s_{k-1} \, h_k \, s_{k+1} \ldots s_n \to s$ in Γ and all $h \in H$.*

Proof. 1. Let $\theta : \{x\} \to \tilde{A}$ be any assignment and let a_h be $\theta(x)$. Then
$$\tilde{\theta}(\diamond_h[x]) = \tilde{A}_{\_[\_]}(\tilde{A}_{\diamond_h}, a_h) = \tilde{a}_h(\star_h) = a_h = \tilde{\theta}(x) \, ,$$
where $\tilde{\theta} : T_{\tilde{\Sigma}}(\{x\}) \to \tilde{A}$ is the unique $\tilde{\Sigma}$-algebra morphism extending θ.

2. Let $\theta : Y_k \cup \{s : (h \to h_k), x : h\} \to \tilde{A}$ be any assignment and let $a_i = \theta(y_i)$ for all $i \in \{1, ..., k-1, k+1, ..., n\}$, $t = \theta(z)$, and $a_h = \theta(x)$. Then
$$\begin{aligned}
\tilde{\theta}(\sigma_h^k(Y_k, z)[x]) &= \tilde{A}_{\_[\_]}(\tilde{A}_{\sigma_h^k}(a_1, ..., a_{k-1}, t, a_{k+1}, ..., a_n), a_h) \\
&= \tilde{a}_h(\sigma(a_1, ..., a_{k-1}, t, a_{k+1}, ..., a_n)) \\
&= A_\sigma(a_1, ..., a_{k-1}, \tilde{a}_h(t), a_{k+1}, ..., a_n) \\
&= \tilde{A}_\sigma(a_1, ..., a_{k-1}, \tilde{A}_{\_[\_]}(t, a_h), a_{k+1}, ..., a_n) \\
&= \tilde{\theta}(\sigma(Y_k, z[x])) \, .
\end{aligned}$$
□

The rest of this section assumes equations have no conditions of hidden sort.

Definition 15. For each Σ-equation $e = (\forall X) \, t = t'$ if $t_1 = t'_1, .., t_n = t'_n$, let $\tilde{e}$ be the set of $\tilde{\Sigma}$-equations where $\tilde{e}$ is either the set containing only e regarded as a $\tilde{\Sigma}$-equation if the sort of t and t' is visible, or the set
$$\{(\forall X, z : (h \to v)) \, z[t] = z[t'] \text{ if } t_1 = t'_1, .., t_n = t'_n \mid v \in V\}$$
if the sort h of t and t' is hidden. □

Proposition 16. *Given a hidden Σ-algebra A and Σ-equation e, then $\tilde{A} \models_{\tilde{\Sigma}} \tilde{e}$ iff $A \models_{\Sigma}^{\Gamma} e$.*

Proof. Let e be the Σ-equation $(\forall X) \, t = t'$ if $t_1 = t'_1, .., t_n = t'_n$. If the sort of t, t' is visible then the result is easy, so we assume the sort h of t, t' is hidden.
    Suppose $\tilde{A} \models_{\tilde{\Sigma}} \tilde{e}$ and let $\theta : X \to A$ be any assignment such that $\theta(t_i) = \theta(t'_i)$ for $i = 1, ..., n$. Let $v \in V$ and $c \in LT_{\Gamma, v}(A \cup \{\star_h\})$. Define $\varphi : X \cup \{z : (h \to v)\} \to \tilde{A}$ to be θ on X, with $\varphi(z) = c$. Then $\tilde{A} \models_{\tilde{\Sigma}} \tilde{e}$ implies $\tilde{\varphi}(z[t]) = \tilde{\varphi}(z[t'])$, where

$\tilde{\varphi}\colon T_{\tilde{\Sigma}}(X \cup \{z : (h \to v)\}) \to \tilde{A}$ *is the unique extension of* φ *to a* $\tilde{\Sigma}$-*homomorphism. But* $\tilde{\varphi}(z[t]) = \tilde{A}_{\_[\_]}(\varphi(z), \theta(t)) = \theta(\tilde{t})(c)$ *and similarly* $\tilde{\varphi}(z[t']) = \theta(\tilde{t'})(c)$, *so by Proposition 11,* $\theta(t) \equiv_{\Sigma,h}^{\Gamma} \theta(t')$. *Thus* $A \models_{\Sigma} e$.

Conversely, suppose $A \models_{\Sigma} e$ *and let* $v \in V$ *and* $\varphi\colon X \cup \{z : (h \to v)\} \to \tilde{A}$ *such that* $\varphi(t_i) = \varphi(t_i')$ *for* $i = 1, ..., n$. *Then* $A \models_{\Sigma} e$ *implies* $\varphi(t) \equiv_{\Sigma,h}^{\Gamma} \varphi(t')$, *so by Proposition 11,* $\varphi(\tilde{t})(\varphi(z)) = \varphi(\tilde{t'})(\varphi(z))$. *But* $\varphi(\tilde{t})(\varphi(z)) = \tilde{\varphi}(z[t])$ *and* $\varphi(\tilde{t'})(\varphi(z)) = \tilde{\varphi}(z[t'])$, *so* $\tilde{\varphi}(z[t]) = \tilde{\varphi}(z[t'])$. *Therefore* $\tilde{A} \models_{\tilde{\Sigma}} \tilde{e}$. $\square$

Definition 17. Given $B = (\Gamma, \Sigma, E)$, let $\tilde{B} = (\tilde{\Sigma}, \tilde{E})$ be the ordinary specification with $\tilde{E}$ adding to $\bigcup_{e \in E} \tilde{e}$ the equations, for each $h \in H$

$(\forall x : h) \diamond_h[x] = x,$

$(\forall Y_k, z : (h \to h_k), x : h) \; \sigma_h^k(Y_k, z)[x] = \sigma(Y_k, z[x]) \,,$

for all behavioral operations $\sigma : s_1 \dots s_{k-1} \; h_k \; s_{k+1} \dots s_n \to s$ in Γ. (See the notation of Proposition 14). $\square$

Notice that $\tilde{B}$ is finite whenever B is finite, and that if B has no conditional equations then neither does $\tilde{B}$.

Example 6. If B is the specification SETH of Example 4, then $\tilde{B}$ is:

```
mod! SET! { [ Set ]   pr(NAT)
   op _in_  : Nat Set -> Bool
   op empty :  -> Set
   op add   : Nat Set -> Set
   op _U_   : Set Set -> Set
   op _&_   : Set Set -> Set
   op neg   : Set -> Set
   vars N N' : Nat   vars X X' : Set
   eq N in empty = false .
   eq N in add(N',X) = (N == N') or (N in X) .
   eq N in (X U X') = (N in X)  or (N in X') .
   eq N in (X & X') = (N in X) and (N in X') .
   eq N in neg(X)   = not (N in X) . }
mod! SET~ { [ Set->Set Set->Bool ]   pr(SET!)
   op <>  :  -> Set->Set
   op _IN_ : Nat Set->Set  -> Set->Bool
   op _[_] : Set->Set Set  -> Set
   op _[_] : Set->Bool Set  -> Bool
   var Z : Set->Set   var X : Set   var N : Nat
   eq       <> [ X ] = X .
   eq (N IN Z) [ X ] = N in Z [ X ] . }
```

Here SET! is just SETH with behavioral features removed, extended with sorts Set->Set and Set->Bool (we don't add the sort Set->Nat because there is no behavioral operation of sort Nat in SETH), a constant <> of sort Set->Set which stands for $\diamond_{\text{Set}} : \; \to (\text{Set->Set})$, an operation _IN_ which stands for $(\_in\_)_{\text{Set}}^2 : \text{Nat (Set->Set)} \to (\text{Set->Bool})$, two operations _[_] defined from Set->Set and Set to Set and from Set->Bool and Set to Bool respectively, and the two equations required by Definition 17. $\square$

Corollary 18. *For any hidden Σ-algebra A, $\tilde{A} \models \tilde{B}$ iff $A \models B$.*

Proof. From Propositions 14 and 16. □

Example 7. Proposition 16 and Corollary 18 can help prove behavioral properties equationally, such as commutativity of union in the spec SETH of Example 4. We claim it suffices to show that SET˜ satisfies

$(\star)$ $(\forall X, X' : \mathsf{Set}, Z : (\mathsf{Set} - > \mathsf{Bool}))\ Z[X\ \mathsf{U}\ X'] = Z[X'\ \mathsf{U}\ X]$.

Indeed, if A behaviorally satisfies SETH, then Corollary 18 implies $\tilde{A}$ satisfies $(\star)$, so by Proposition 16, A behaviorally satisfies $(\forall X, X' : \mathsf{Set})\ X\ \mathsf{U}\ X' = X'\ \mathsf{U}\ X$.

We prove that $(\forall X, X' : \mathsf{Set}, Z : \mathsf{Set} - > \mathsf{Bool})\ Z[X\ \mathsf{U}\ X'] = Z[X'\ \mathsf{U}\ X]$ is an equational consequence of SET˜. First open SET˜ and introduce two constants of sort Set and another of sort Set->Bool:

```
open SET~ .
  ops x x' : -> Set .   op  z : -> Set->Bool .   op  p : -> Bool .
  eq p = (z [ x U x' ] == z [ x' U x ]) .
```

Our goal is to prove that p reduces to **true**. Since _IN_ is the only operation of sort Set->Bool, the only way for z as above to exist is for it to be a term of the form n IN s, where n is a natural number and s is of sort Set->Set:

```
  op n : -> Nat .   op s : -> Set->Set .
  eq z = n IN s .
```

Because the only operation of sort Set->Set is <>, we can reduce p as follows:

```
  eq s = <> .
  red p .    **> should be true
```

CafeOBJ does 12 rewrites and 64 matches. This proof was simple because there were no behavioral operations of hidden sort, but in general such proofs would need induction on the structure of terms of sorts $(h \to h')$, and thus would be as awkward as are proofs by context induction [14]. □

Proposition 19. *If A is a Σ-algebra (not necessary hidden) such that $A \models_\Sigma (\forall X)\ t = t'$ if C, then:*

1. *$A \models_\Sigma (\forall X')\ t = t'$ if C for each $X \subseteq X'$;*
2. *$A \models_\Sigma (\forall X)\ t' = t$ if C;*
3. *$A \models_\Sigma (\forall X)\ t = t''$ if C whenever $A \models_\Sigma (\forall X)\ t' = t''$;*
4. *$A \models_\Sigma (\forall Y)\ \rho(t) = \rho(t')$ if $\rho(C)$ for any substitution $\rho \colon X \to T_\Sigma(Y)$, where $\rho(C)$ is the set $\{\rho(t_i) = \rho(t'_i) \mid t_i = t'_i \in C\}$.*

□

Theorem 20. *For any hidden Σ-algebra A and any behavioral specification B, $A \models B$ iff $A \models \Sigma \Box \tilde{B}$.*

Proof. If $A \models B$ then Corollary 18 gives $\tilde{A} \models \tilde{B}$, so that $\tilde{A} \models \Sigma \Box \tilde{B}$, and thus $A \models \Sigma \Box \tilde{B}$.

Suppose $A \models \Sigma \Box \tilde{B}$, let e be any Σ-equation $(\forall X)\ t = t'$ if C in B, and let $\theta \colon X \to A$ be any assignment such that $\theta(C)$. If the sort of t, t' is visible then $A \models_\Sigma e$, so $A \models_\Sigma^\Gamma e$. If the sort h of t, t' is hidden then let $v \in V$

and $c \in LT_{\Gamma,v}(A \cup \{\star_h\})$. *Then c has the form $\sigma_1(\alpha_1, \sigma_2(\alpha_2, ..., \sigma_m(\alpha_m, \star_h)...))$, where $\sigma_j(\alpha_j, t)$ indicates $\sigma_j(a_{1,j}, ..., a_{k-1,j}, t, a_{k+1,j}, ..., a_{n_j,j})$ for some appropriate elements $a_{1,j}, ..., a_{k-1,j}, a_{k+1,j}, ..., a_{n_j,j}$ in A, such that the sort of σ_1 is v and the sorts of $\sigma_2, ..., \sigma_m$ are hidden. Let $c_h \in T_{\tilde{\Sigma},(h \to v)}(A)$ be the term $(\sigma_1)_h^{k_1}(\alpha_1, \sigma_2)_h^{k_2}(\alpha_2, ..., (\sigma_m)_h^{k_m}(\alpha_m, \diamond_h)...))$. Using the special equations in $\tilde{B}$ (see Definition 17) and Proposition 19, it can be shown that $\tilde{B} \models (\forall X, A)\ c_h[t] = c[t]$ and $\tilde{B} \models (\forall X, A)\ c_h[t'] = c[t']$. On the other hand, since the equation*

$(\forall X, z : (h \to v))\ z[t] = z[t']$ **if** C

*is in $\tilde{E}$ and c_h is a $\tilde{\Sigma}$-term, Proposition 19 gives $\tilde{B} \models (\forall X, A)\ c_h[t] = c_h[t']$ **if** C. Also Proposition 19 gives $\tilde{B} \models (\forall X, A)\ c[t] = c[t']$ **if** C, i.e., $(\forall X, A)\ c[t] = c[t']$ **if** C belongs to $\Sigma \square \tilde{B}$. Therefore $A \models_{\Sigma} (\forall X, A)\ c[t] = c[t']$ **if** C. Letting $\varphi \colon X \cup A \to A$ be θ on X and the identity on A, we get $\theta(\tilde{t})(c) = \theta(\tilde{t'})(c)$. Since c was arbitrary, Proposition 11 gives $\theta(t) \equiv_{\Sigma}^{\Gamma} \theta(t')$. Thus $A \models_{\Sigma}^{\Gamma} e$, so that $A \models B$.* $\square$

5   Two Institutions for Hidden Algebra

We give two institutions [10] for the generalization of hidden algebra to multiple hidden arguments and fewer behavioral operations. The first follows the institution of basic hidden algebra [9] and the approach earlier in this paper, while the second seems more promising for future research. A similar adaptation (but without the citation) of the result in [9] to the observational logic framework appears in [15]; our approach also avoids the infinitary logic used in observational logic. We fix a data algebra D, and proceed as follows:

Signatures: The category **Sign** has hidden signatures over D as objects. A morphism of hidden signatures $\phi \colon (\Gamma_1, \Sigma_1) \to (\Gamma_2, \Sigma_2)$ is the identity on the visible signature Ψ, takes hidden sorts to hidden sorts, and if a behavioral operation δ_2 in Γ_2 has an argument sort in $\phi(H_1)$ then there is some behavioral operation δ_1 in Γ_1 such that $\delta_2 = \phi(\delta_1)$. **Sign** is indeed a category, and the composition of two hidden signature morphisms is another. Indeed, let $\psi \colon (\Gamma_2, \Sigma_2) \to (\Gamma_3, \Sigma_3)$ and let δ_3 be an operation in Γ_3 having an argument sort in $(\phi; \psi)(H_1)$. Then δ_3 has an argument sort in $\psi(H_2)$, so there is an operation δ_2 in Γ_2 with $\delta_3 = \psi(\delta_2)$. Also δ_2 has an argument sort in $\phi(H_1)$, so there is some δ_1 in Γ_1 with $\delta_2 = \phi(\delta_1)$. Therefore $\delta_3 = (\phi; \psi)(\delta_1)$, i.e., $\phi; \psi$ is a morphism of hidden signatures.

Sentences: Given a hidden signature (Γ, Σ), let $\mathbf{Sen}(\Gamma, \Sigma)$ be the set of all Σ-equations. If $\phi \colon (\Gamma_1, \Sigma_1) \to (\Gamma_2, \Sigma_2)$ is a hidden signature morphism, then $\mathbf{Sen}(\phi)$ is the function taking a Σ_1-equation $e = (\forall X)\ t = t'$ **if** $t_1 = t_1', ..., t_n = t_n'$ to the Σ_2-equation

$\phi(e) = (\forall X')\ \phi(t) = \phi(t')$ **if** $\phi(t_1) = \phi(t_1'), ..., \phi(t_n) = \phi(t_n')$,

where X' is $\{x : \phi(s) \mid x : s \in X\}$. Then $\mathbf{Sen} \colon \mathbf{Sign} \to \mathbf{Set}$ is indeed a functor.

Models: Given a hidden signature (Γ, Σ), let $\mathbf{Mod}(\Gamma, \Sigma)$ be the category of hidden Σ-algebras and their morphisms. If $\phi \colon (\Gamma_1, \Sigma_1) \to (\Gamma_2, \Sigma_2)$ is a hidden signature morphism, then $\mathbf{Mod}(\phi)$ is the usual reduct functor, $-|_{\phi}$. Unlike [1, 15], etc., this allows models where not all operations are congruent.

Satisfaction Relation: behavioral satisfaction, i.e., $\models_{(\Gamma,\Sigma)} = \models_\Sigma^\Gamma$.

Theorem 21. Satisfaction Condition: *Given* $\phi\colon (\Gamma_1, \Sigma_1) \to (\Gamma_2, \Sigma_2)$ *a hidden signature morphism,* $e = (\forall X)\ t = t'$ *if* $t_1 = t_1', ..., t_n = t_n'$ *a* Σ_1-*equation, and* A *a hidden* Σ_2-*algebra, then* $A \models_{\Sigma_2}^{\Gamma_2} \phi(e)$ *iff* $A|_\phi \models_{\Sigma_1}^{\Gamma_1} e$.

Proof. There is a bijection between $(A|_\phi)^X$ and $A^{X'}$ that takes $\theta\colon X \to A|_\phi$ to $\theta'\colon X' \to A$ defined by $\theta'(x : \phi(s)) = \theta(x : s)$, and takes $\theta'\colon X' \to A$ to $\theta\colon X \to A|_\phi$ defined by $\theta(x : s) = \theta'(x : \phi(s))$. Notice that for every term t in $T_{\Sigma_1}(X)$, we have $\theta(t) = \theta'(\phi(t))$ where $\phi(t)$ is the term t with each $x : s$ replaced by $x : \phi(s)$ and each operation σ replaced by $\phi(\sigma)$. It remains to prove that $a \equiv_{\Sigma_1,h}^{\Gamma_1} a'$ iff $a \equiv_{\Sigma_2,\phi(h)}^{\Gamma_2} a'$ for each $a, a' \in A_{\phi(h)}$, where $\equiv_{\Sigma_1}^{\Gamma_1}$ is behavioral equivalence on $A|_\phi$ and $\equiv_{\Sigma_2}^{\Gamma_2}$ is behavioral equivalence on A. Since $\phi(c_1) \in LT_{\Gamma_2}(A|_\phi \cup \{\star_{\phi(h)}\})$ whenever $c_1 \in LT_{\Gamma_1}(A|_\phi \cup \{\star_h\})$, one gets $a \equiv_{\Sigma_2,\phi(h)}^{\Gamma_2} a'$ implies $a \equiv_{\Sigma_1,h}^{\Gamma_1} a'$. Now if $c_2 \in LT_{\Gamma_2}(A \cup \{\star_{\phi(h)}\})$ then because for every operation δ_2 in Γ_2 having an argument sort in $\phi(H_1)$ there is some δ_1 in Γ_1 with $\delta_2 = \phi(\delta_1)$, we iteratively get a term $c_1 \in LT_{\Gamma_1}(A|_{phi} \cup \{\star_h\})$ such that $c_2 = \phi(c_1)$. Therefore $a \equiv_{\Sigma_1,h}^{\Gamma_1} a'$ implies $a \equiv_{\Sigma_2,\phi(h)}^{\Gamma_2} a'$. $\square$

Our second institution views the declaration of a behavioral operation as a new kind of sentence, rather than part of a hidden signature. The notion of model also changes, adding an equivalence relation as in [1]. This is natural for modern software engineering, since languages like Java provide classes with an operation denoted `equals` which serves this purpose. Sentences in [1] are pairs $\langle e, \Delta \rangle$, where Δ is a set of terms (pretty much like a cobasis over the derived signature), which are satisfied by $(A, \sim)$ iff $(A, \sim)$ satisfies e as in our case below (actually e is a first-order formula in their framework) and $\sim \subseteq \equiv_\Delta$. Fix a data algebra D, and proceed as follows:

Signatures: The category **Sign** has hidden signatures over D as objects. A morphism of hidden signatures $\phi\colon \Sigma_1 \to \Sigma_2$ is identity on the visible signature Ψ and takes hidden sorts to hidden sorts.

Sentences: Given a hidden signature Σ, let **Sen**(Σ) be the set of all Σ-equations unioned with Σ. If $\phi\colon \Sigma_1 \to \Sigma_2$ is a hidden signature morphism, then **Sen**(ϕ) is the function taking a Σ_1-equation $e = (\forall X)\ t = t'$ if $t_1 = t_1', ..., t_n = t_n'$ to the Σ_2-equation $\phi(e) = (\forall X')\ \phi(t) = \phi(t')$ if $\phi(t_1) = \phi(t_1'), ..., \phi(t_n) = \phi(t_n')$, where X' is the set $\{x : \phi(s) \mid x : s \in X\}$, and taking $\sigma\colon s_1 \ldots s_n \to s$ to $\phi(\sigma)\colon \phi(s_1) \ldots \phi(s_n) \to \phi(s)$. Then **Sen**$\colon$ **Sign** $\to$ **Set** is indeed a functor.

Models: Given a hidden signature Σ, let **Mod**(Σ) be the category of pairs $(A, \sim)$ where A is a hidden Σ-algebra and $\sim$ is an equivalence relation on A which is identity on visible sorts, with morphisms $f\colon (A, \sim) \to (A', \sim')$ with $f\colon A \to A'$ a Σ-homomorphism such that $f(\sim) \subseteq \sim'$. If $\phi\colon \Sigma_1 \to \Sigma_2$ is a hidden signature morphism, then **Mod**(ϕ), often denoted $\_|_\phi$, is defined as $(A, \sim)|_\phi = (A|_\phi, \sim|_\phi)$ on objects, where $A|_\phi$ is the ordinary many-sorted algebra reduct and $(\sim|_\phi)_s = \sim_{\phi(s)}$ for all sorts s of Σ_1, and as $f|_\phi\colon (A, \sim)|_\phi \to (A', \sim')|_\phi$ on morphisms. Notice that indeed $f|_\phi(\sim|_\phi) \subseteq \sim'|_\phi$, so **Mod** is well defined.

Satisfaction Relation: A Σ-model $(A, \sim)$ satisfies a conditional Σ-equation $(\forall X)\ t = t'$ **if** $t_1 = t_1', ..., t_n = t_n'$ iff for each $\theta\colon X \to A$, if $\theta(t_1) \sim \theta(t_1')$, ..., $\theta(t_n) \sim \theta(t_n')$ then $\theta(t) \sim \theta(t')$. Also $(A, \sim)$ satisfies a Σ-sentence $\gamma \in \Sigma$ iff γ is congruent for $\sim$.

Theorem 22. Satisfaction Condition: *Let $\phi\colon \Sigma_1 \to \Sigma_2$ be a morphism of hidden signatures, let e be a Σ_1-sentence and let $(A, \sim)$ be a model of Σ_2. Then $(A, \sim) \models_{\Sigma_2} \phi(e)$ iff $(A, \sim)|_\phi \models_{\Sigma_1} e$.*

*Proof. First suppose e is a Σ-equation $(\forall X)\ t = t'$ **if** $t_1 = t_1', ..., t_n = t_n'$. Notice that there is a bijection between functions from X to $(A|_\phi)$ and functions from X' to A taking $\theta\colon X \to A|_\phi$ to $\theta'\colon X' \to A$ defined by $\theta'(x : \phi(s)) = \theta(x : s)$ and taking $\theta'\colon X' \to A$ to $\theta\colon X \to A|_\phi$ defined by $\theta(x : s) = \theta'(x : \phi(s))$. Because for every term t in $T_{\Sigma_1}(X)$ we have $\theta(t) = \theta'(\phi(t))$ where $\phi(t)$ is the term t with each $x : s$ replaced by $x : \phi(s)$ and each operation σ replaced by $\phi(\sigma)$, the result is immediate.*

Second, suppose e is an operation $\gamma \in \Sigma$. Then $(A, \sim)$ satisfies $\phi(\gamma)$ iff $\phi(\gamma)$ is congruent for $\sim$, which is equivalent to γ being congruent for $\sim|_\phi$. $\square$

This institution justifies our belief that asserting an operation behavioral is a kind of sentence, not a kind of syntactic declaration as in the "extended hidden signatures" of [5][2]. Coinduction now appears in the following elegant guise:

Proposition 23. *Given a hidden subsignature Γ of Σ, a set of Σ-equations E and a hidden Σ-algebra A, then*

- $(A, \sim) \models_\Sigma E, \Gamma$ *implies* $(A, \equiv_\Sigma^\Gamma) \models_\Sigma E, \Gamma$.
- $(A, \equiv_\Sigma^\Gamma) \models_\Sigma \Gamma$.
- $A \models_\Sigma^\Gamma E$ *iff* $(A, \equiv_\Sigma^\Gamma) \models_\Sigma E$ *iff* $(A, \equiv_\Sigma^\Gamma) \models_\Sigma E, \Gamma$.

$\square$

There is a natural relationship between our two institutions:

- since congruent operations are declared with sentences, any signature in the first institution translates to a specification in the second;
- any model A of (Σ, Γ) in the first institution gives a model of the second, namely $(A, \equiv_\Sigma^\Gamma)$;
- any (Σ, Γ)-sentence is a Σ-sentence;

and we can see that for any (Σ, Γ)-sentence e and any hidden Σ-algebra A, we get $A \models_\Sigma^\Gamma e$ iff $(A, \equiv_\Sigma^\Gamma) \models_\Sigma e$. This relationship suggests a new (as far as we know) kind of relationship between institutions (here $\mathbf{Th}(\mathcal{I})$ denotes the category of theories over $\mathcal{I}$, see [10]):

Definition 24. Given two institutions $\mathcal{I} = (\mathbf{Sign}, \mathbf{Mod}, \mathbf{Sen}, \models)$ and $\mathcal{I}' = (\mathbf{Sign}', \mathbf{Mod}', \mathbf{Sen}', \models')$, then an *institution theoroidal forward morphism*[3], *from $\mathcal{I}$ to $\mathcal{I}'$ is (Φ, β, α) where:*

---

[2] However, the most recent version of [8] treats coherence assertions as sentences.

[3] This terminology is a preliminary attempt to bring some order to the chaos of relationships among institutions, by using names that suggest the nature of the relationship involved.

- Φ: **Sign** → **Th**$(\mathcal{I}')$ is a map such that $\Phi; \mathcal{U}'$: **Sign** → **Sign**$'$ is a functor, where $\mathcal{U}'$: **Th**$(\mathcal{I}')$ → **Sign**$'$ is the forgetful functor; we ambiguously let Φ also denote the functor $\Phi; \mathcal{U}'$,
- β: **Mod** $\Rightarrow \Phi$; **Mod**$'$ is a natural transformation, and
- α: **Sen** $\Rightarrow \Phi$; **Sen**$'$ is a natural transformation,

such that for any signature $\Sigma \in$ **Sign**, any sentence $e \in$ **Sen(Sign)** and any model $m \in$ **Mod(Sign)**, the *satisfaction condition*, $m \models_\Sigma e$ iff $\beta(m) \models_{\Phi(\Sigma)} \alpha(e)$, holds. $\square$

Proposition 25. *There is an institution theoroidal forward morphism from the first to the second institution defined above.* $\square$

We thank the anonymous referees for their comments, which have helped us to piece together aspects of the relationship of our work with that of other groups, and to conclude that a convergence of viewpoints may be occurring within the broad area that might be called behavioral algebra.

References

[1] Gilles Bernot, Michael Bidoit, and Teodor Knapik. Observational specifications and the indistinguishability assumption. *Theoretical Computer Science*, 139(1-2):275–314, 1995. Submitted 1992.

[2] Michael Bidoit and Rolf Hennicker. Behavioral theories and the proof of behavioral properties. *Theoretical Computer Science*, 165(1):3–55, 1996.

[3] Michael Bidoit and Rolf Hennicker. Modular correctness proofs of behavioural implementations. *Acta Informatica*, 35(11):951–1005, 1998.

[4] Michael Bidoit and Rolf Hennicker. Observer complete definitions are behaviourally coherent. Technical Report LSV-99-4, ENS de Cachan, 1999.

[5] Răzvan Diaconescu. Behavioral coherence in object-oriented algebraic specification. Technical Report IS–RR–98–0017F, Japan Advanced Institute for Science and Technology, June 1998. Submitted for publication.

[6] Răzvan Diaconescu and Kokichi Futatsugi. *CafeOBJ Report: The Language, Proof Techniques, and Methodologies for Object-Oriented Algebraic Specification*. World Scientific, 1998. AMAST Series in Computing, volume 6.

[7] Răzvan Diaconescu, Joseph Goguen, and Petros Stefaneas. Logical support for modularization. In Gerard Huet and Gordon Plotkin, editors, *Logical Environments*, pages 83–130. Cambridge, 1993.

[8] Răzvan Diaconescu and Kokichi Futatsugi. Logical foundations of CafeOBJ. Submitted for publication.

[9] Joseph Goguen. Types as theories. In George Michael Reed, Andrew William Roscoe, and Ralph F. Wachter, editors, *Topology and Category Theory in Computer Science*, pages 357–390. Oxford, 1991. Proceedings of a Conference held at Oxford, June 1989.

[10] Joseph Goguen and Rod Burstall. Institutions: Abstract model theory for specification and programming. *Journal of the Association for Computing Machinery*, 39(1):95–146, January 1992.

[11] Joseph Goguen and Grant Malcolm. *Algebraic Semantics of Imperative Programs*. MIT, 1996.

[12] Joseph Goguen and Grant Malcolm. A hidden agenda. *Theoretical Computer Science*, to appear 1999. Also UCSD Dept. Computer Science & Eng. Technical Report CS97–538, May 1997.

[13] Joseph Goguen, James Thatcher, and Eric Wagner. An initial algebra approach to the specification, correctness and implementation of abstract data types. In Raymond Yeh, editor, *Current Trends in Programming Methodology, IV*, pages 80–149. Prentice-Hall, 1978.

[14] Rolf Hennicker. Context induction: a proof principle for behavioral abstractions. *Formal Aspects of Computing*, 3(4):326–345, 1991.

[15] Rolf Hennicker and Michel Bidoit. Observational logic. In *Algebraic Methodology and Software Technology (AMAST'98)*, volume 1548 of *Lecture Notes in Computer Science*, pages 263–277. Springer, 1999.

[16] Bart Jacobs and Jan Rutten. A tutorial on (co)algebras and (co)induction. *Bulletin of the European Association for Theoretical Computer Science*, 62:222–259, 1997.

[17] Seikô Mikami. Semantics of equational specifications with module import and verification method of behavioral equations. In *Proceedings, CafeOBJ Symposium*. Japan Advanced Institute for Science and Technology, 1998. Numazu, Japan, April 1998.

[18] Peter Padawitz. Swinging data types: Syntax, semantics, and theory. In *Proceedings, WADT'95*, volume 1130 of *Lecture Notes in Computer Science*, pages 409–435. Springer, 1996.

[19] Peter Padawitz. Towards the one-tiered design of data types and transition systems. In *Proceedings, WADT'97*, volume 1376 of *Lecture Notes in Computer Science*, pages 365–380. Springer, 1998.

[20] Horst Reichel. Behavioural equivalence – a unifying concept for initial and final specifications. In *Proceedings, Third Hungarian Computer Science Conference*. Akademiai Kiado, 1981. Budapest.

[21] Grigore Roşu and Joseph Goguen. Hidden congruent deduction. In Ricardo Caferra and Gernot Salzer, editors, *Proceedings, First-Order Theorem Proving - FTP'98*, pages 213–223. Technische Universitat Wien, 1998. Full version to appear in Lecture Notes in Artificial Intelligence, 1999.

A Termination Detection Algorithm: Specification and Verification

Robert Eschbach

Department of Computing Sciences,
University of Kaiserslautern, PO 3049
D-67653 Kaiserslautern, Germany

Abstract. We propose a methodology for the specification and verification of distributed algorithms using Gurevich's concept of Abstract State Machines. The methodology relies on a distinction between a higher-level specification and a lower-level specification of an algorithm. The algorithm is characterized by an informal problem description. A justification assures the appropriateness of the higher-level specification for the problem description. A mathematical verification assures that the lower-level specification implements the higher-level one and is based on a refinement-relation. This methodology is demonstrated by a well-known distributed termination detection algorithm originally invented by Dijkstra, Feijen, and van Gasteren.

1 Introduction

In this paper we propose a methodology for the specification and verification of distributed algorithms using Gurevich's concept of Abstract State Machines (cf. [Gur95], [Gur97], [Gur99]). The development of distributed algorithms usually starts with an informal *problem description* (see figure 2). In order to get a mathematical model of the problem description at the starting point of construction one has to choose what often is called a ground model (cf. [Bör99]) or a *higher-level specification* for the problem description. In this paper the higher-level specification is an Abstract State Machine (ASM) and as such it constitutes a well-defined mathematical object. An *informal justification*[1] shows the appropriateness of the higher-level specification for the problem description (cf. [Bör99]). A so-called *lower-level specification* represents the algorithm on a more concrete abstraction level as the higher-level specification. The *mathematical verification* guarantees that the lower-level specification implements the higher-level specification and is usually based on refinement relations. In this paper we focus mainly on the mathematical verification.

We use a well-known distributed algorithm, namely a *termination detection algorithm* originally invented by Dijkstra, Feijen and van Gasteren in [DFvG83] as an example to show how such an algorithm can be specified and verified within this methodology using Abstract State Machines. We give in this paper

---

[1] Since the problem description is informal, a mathematical proof is not possible.

J. Wing, J. Woodcock, J. Davies (Eds.): FM'99, Vol. II, LNCS 1709, pp. 1720–1737, 1999.

a *correctness proof* for a variation[2] of the algorithm presented in [DFvG83]. As in [BGR95] our correctness proof relies on a distinction between a higher-level view and a lower-level view of the algorithm. The proof itself is given on a detailed mathematical level using thereby standard techniques from mathematics like case distinction or induction. We introduce for both the higher-level specification and the lower-level specification a kind of *stuttering steps*. The concept of stuttering is well-known from TLA (cf. [Lam94]). Stuttering steps represent steps in which a machine changes its local state. These changes are invisible. The stuttering itself leads to a simple and natural refinement relation which eases the construction of our correctness proof.

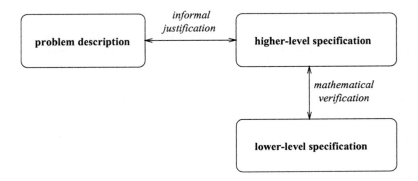

Fig. 1. Underlying Methodology

We specify and verify the termination detection algorithm of Dijkstra, Feijen, van Gasteren on a detailed mathematical level. The reader who is interested in a more intuitive explanation and an excellent derivation of this algorithm is referred to [Dij99] (or [DFvG83] for the original version). We start with a description of the *problem of termination detection* [Dij99]:

> We consider N machines, each of which is either active or passive. Only active machines send what are called "messages" to other machines; each message sent is received some finite period of time later. After having received a message a machine is active; the receipt of a message is the only mechanism that triggers for a passive machine its transition to activity. For each machine, the transition from the active to the passive state may occur "spontaneously". From the above it follows that the state in which

---

[2] The variation itself stems from Shmuel Safra. The variation is that message transmission no longer needs to be instantaneous and is described in [Dij99]. In [Dij99] Safra's algorithm is derived along the very same lines as in [DFvG83]. Note also that in [DFvG83] the authors present a [DS80]-algorithm for the detection of the termination of a distributed computation.

all machines are passive and no messages are on their way is stable: the distributed computation with which the messages are associated is said to have terminated. The purpose of the algorithm to be designed is to enable one of the machines, machine nr. 0 say, to detect that this stable state has been reached.

We denote the process by which termination is detected as "the probe". In addition to messages, machines can send what are called "signals" to other machines. We adopt a circular arrangement of the machines, more precisely, we assume that machine nr. 0 can send a signal to machine nr. N-1 and that machine nr. i+1 can send a signal to machine nr. i. Note that a machine can send a signal irrespective of its activity state. Especially this means that a passive machine can send a signal but cannot send a message.

This paper is organized as follows. In section 2 we construct the higher-level specification $\mathcal{A}$. This ASM represents the problem of termination detection stated above. We present domains, functions, modules, runs, and constraints of $\mathcal{A}$. In section 3 we construct the lower-level specification $\mathcal{A}'$. This ASM represents the termination detection algorithm presented in [Dij99]. In the lower-level specification the probe is implemented by adding new rules and refining old ones of $\mathcal{A}$, respectively. We present the lower-level specification in the same way as the higher-level one. Section 4 presents the correctness proof for the termination detection algorithm. First we define what it means for the lower-level ASM $\mathcal{A}'$ to implement the higher-level ASM $\mathcal{A}$. Then we prove that $\mathcal{A}'$ implements $\mathcal{A}$. In section 5 we give some concluding remarks.

Throughout this paper we assume the reader to be familiar with Gurevich's ASMs, especially with distributed ASMs, cf. [Gur95].

2   Higher-Level Specification

This section presents a higher-level specification for the problem description given in the introduction. The higher-level specification is given as a distributed ASM. In the following we describe a distributed ASM by its

1. domains,
2. functions,
3. modules,
4. runs,
5. constraints.

Domains (i.e., sets) can be classified into static and dynamic domains, i.e., domains which are changeable during a run or not changeable, respectively. *Functions* can be classified into internal, shared, and external functions. Our classification is based on a broad distinction between ASM agents and the environment. A more detailed classification can be found in [Bör99]. Internal functions can be changed by ASM agents only. A shared function can be affected by both ASM agents and the environment. External functions can be changed by the environment only. Furthermore functions can be classified into static or dynamic functions, i.e., functions which are changeable during a run or not changeable, respectively. *Modules* are ASM rules (programs) which are associated with ASM agents. In a run an agent executes its associated module. In this paper a *run* is essentially an infinite sequence of states S_k and an infinite sequence of ASM agents A_k such that S_k can be transformed by agent A_k and the environment into state S_{k+1}. *Constraints* can be used to impose conditions upon functions, e.g. external functions.

2.1   Domains of $\mathcal{A}$

We define Machine to be the static universe of machine identifiers $\{0, \ldots, N-1\}$. We assume each machine identifier to be associated with an agent in the distributed ASM $\mathcal{A}$. In the following instead of agents we simply speak of machines of $\mathcal{A}$. Bool denotes the domain $\{$true, false$\}$ of boolean values, Nat the universe of natural numbers, and Int the universe of integers. The set $\{$SM, RM, P, S$\}$ represents the set of so-called execution-modes.

2.2   Functions of $\mathcal{A}$

Let τ be the *vocabulary* of $\mathcal{A}$. Besides some standard functions on Bool, Nat, and Int the vocabulary τ is defined by the following functions. Messages are realized by an internal, dynamic function

$$\texttt{messages : Machine -> Nat.}$$

We assume that initially messages has value 0 for all machines. A machine can send a message (SM), receive a message (RM), execute the probe (P), or execute a skip (S). For this purpose we introduce an external, dynamic function

$$\texttt{mode : Machine -> \{SM,RM,P,S\},}$$

which determines the execution mode for each machine. A machine can either be active or be passive. The shared, dynamic function

$$\texttt{active: Machine -> Bool,}$$

determines the activity state for each machine. Active machines can send messages to other machines. The external, dynamic function

$$\texttt{receivingMachine: -> Machine}$$

determines the destination of a message transmission. In order to detect termination we introduce the external, dynamic function

$$\texttt{terminationDetected : -> Bool.}$$

We assume terminationDetected initially to be false.

2.3   Modules of $\mathcal{A}$

Each machine executes a module consisting of the rules SendMessage, Receive-Message, and Skip.
Sending a message to machine j is realized by incrementing `messages(j)`, receiving a message by machine i by decrementing `messages(i)`. Note that only active machines can send messages.

SENDMESSAGE

```
if mode(me) = SM and active(me) = true then
   messages(receivingMachine) := messages(receivingMachine) + 1
```

On receipt of a message, the receiving machine becomes active. Note that machines can receive messages irrespective of their activity state.

RECEIVEMESSAGE

```
if mode(me) = RM and messages(me) > 0 then
   messages(me) := messages(me) - 1, active(me) := true
```

The rule Skip realizes stuttering steps, i.e., steps in which machines invisibly change their local states. In $\mathcal{A}$ the probe is specified by execution-mode P, rule Skip, and the external, dynamic function `terminationDetected` constrained by properties given in section 2.5. An executing machine in mode P performs a stuttering step. Stuttering steps in a run can be replaced by concrete transitions in the lower-level specification. In this way we obtain a simple and natural refinement relation.

SKIP

```
if mode(me) = S or mode(me) = P then skip
```

2.4   Runs of $\mathcal{A}$

We rely on the notion of *partially ordered runs* of [Gur95] generalized to external and shared functions and specialized to the linear ordered set of moves (Nat, $<$). We consider only infinite runs. Since the only agents in $\mathcal{A}$ are machines, the function A which determines for each $k \in$ Nat an agent performing move k, is a mapping from the natural numbers to machine identifiers. The state function S is a mapping from the natural numbers to the states of $\mathcal{A}$. We define a *possible run* of $\mathcal{A}$ to be a tuple (A, S) with $A :$ Nat $\to$ Machine and $S :$ Nat $\to$ State such that

1. $S(0)$ is an initial state of $\mathcal{A}$, i.e., $S(0)$ fulfills the initial conditions given in section 2.2, and

2. state $S(k+1)$ is obtained from $S(k)$ by executing the module of machine $A(k)$ at $S(k)$ and then executing an action of the environment, i.e. by changing shared and external functions in an arbitrary way.

Instead of $S(k)$ (or $A(k)$) we sometimes write S_k (or A_k). In the following we simply say S_{k+1} is obtained from S_k by executing machine A_k, i.e., the action of the environment is omitted. We speak of move k or of step $(k, k+1)$ in run ρ. We say ρ is a *run* of $\mathcal{A}$ if ρ satisfies the constraints given in the following section 2.5.

Remark. We could use real-time semantics with either instantaneous or durative actions, like in [BGR95], but the algorithm can be formulated naturally and adequately in this simpler semantics.

2.5   Constraints of $\mathcal{A}$

We present the constraints of $\mathcal{A}$ using the standard temporal operators $\Box$ and $\Diamond$. We denote the value that a term t takes at time k in a run ρ by t_k. In the following let $\rho = (A, S)$ be a possible run of $\mathcal{A}$.

C0: $\forall i \in \text{Machine} : \Box\Diamond(A = i \land \text{mode}(i) = \text{RM})$

Intuitively, constraint C0 assures that a message sent is received a finite period of time later. Note that a machine may never send a message but must receive a sent message. Suppose one of the machines sends machine i a message. Thus there exists a time point, say k, with $messages(i)_k > 0$. From C0 we know there exists a time point, say l, with $k \leq l$ such that machine i is executed in step $(l, l+1)$ with $mode(i)_l = \text{RM}$. In this step machine i receives a sent message.

C1: The environment can change the function `active` in step $(k, k+1)$ only from true to false and this only if $\text{mode}(A_k)_k \neq \text{RM}$.

The receipt of a message is the only way for a passive machine to become active. Constraint C1 guarantees that the environment cannot change the activity state of an active machine which tries to receive a message. This avoids "inconsistencies" between receipt of a message and "spontaneous" transitions from the active to the passive state by the environment. Note that constraints C0 and C1 ensure a kind of "fair" runs. The ASM $\mathcal{A}$ together with C0 and C1 model the distributed system in the problem description.

Let $B_k = \sum i : 0 \leq i < N : messages(i)_k$ denote the number of messages on their way at time k. Termination at time k can then be characterized by:

Termination$_k \triangleq B_k = 0 \land (\forall i \in \text{Machine} : \text{active}(i)_k = false)$.

Now we pose some constraints on terminationDetected. These constraints are an essential part of the higher-level specification.

C2: □(terminationDetected → Termination)

Constraint C2 assures that the value of terminationDetected is correct, i.e., if termination is detected in ρ then there is termination.

C3: □(Termination → ◇ terminationDetected)

Constraint C3 makes sure that if there is termination in ρ then terminationDetected eventually becomes true.

C4: □(terminationDetected → □ terminationDetected)

Constraint C4 guarantees that terminationDetected remains true if it is once set to true. Constraints C2, C3, and C4 ensure "good" runs, i.e., runs in which the value of terminationDetected is true. Constraints C2, C3, and C4 essentially specify correctness of the termination detection problem. Note that constraints C3 and C4 implies □(Termination → ◇□ terminationDetected). The converse implication does not hold.

Remark. We think the higher-level specification $\mathcal{A}$ represents faithfully the problem description given in section 1 and hence can be seen as an adequate mathematical model of the informal problem description. Nevertheless a justification for this ASM is necessary. We refer the reader to [Bör99] for further information on the problem of justification. We concentrate in this paper mainly on the mathematical verification. A detailed justification is beyond the scope of this paper.

3   Lower-Level Specification

This section presents a lower-level specification for the algorithm presented in [DFvG83]. The lower-level specification is given as a distributed ASM. We describe $\mathcal{A}'$ in the same way as $\mathcal{A}$.

3.1   Domains of $\mathcal{A}'$

The abstract state machine $\mathcal{A}'$ has the same domains as $\mathcal{A}$.

3.2   Functions of $\mathcal{A}'$

Let τ' be the *vocabulary* of $\mathcal{A}'$. We do not mention standard functions on `Bool`, `Nat`, and `Int`. Vocabulary τ is a subvocabulary of τ', i.e., $\tau \subseteq \tau'$. The following functions of $\mathcal{A}'$ coincides on declaration, classification and initial conditions with the ones given in $\mathcal{A}$.

1. `messages : Machine -> Nat` (internal, dynamic)
2. `mode : Machine -> {SM,RM,P,S}` (external, dynamic)
3. `active: Machine -> Bool` (shared, dynamic)
4. `receivingMachine: -> Machine` (external, dynamic)

In $\mathcal{A}$ the function `terminationDetected` is an *external*, dynamic function. In $\mathcal{A}'$ the function `terminationDetected` is an *internal*, dynamic function.

$$\text{terminationDetected : -> Bool.}$$

We assume `terminationDetected` initially to be `false`.
Now we present new functions of $\mathcal{A}'$, i.e., functions of $\mathcal{A}'$ which are not part of the signature of $\mathcal{A}$. Each machine has a local message counter which is modeled by an internal dynamic function

$$\text{c: Machine -> Int.}$$

This local message counter can be incremented (sending a message) or decremented (receiving a message) by each machine. The intention is that counter `c(i)` represents local knowledge which can be used and changed only by machine i, i.e., `c(i)` can be seen as an internal location for machine i. We assume that initially all local message counters have value 0.
Each machine can turn either white or black. The color of a machine is realized by an internal, dynamic function

$$\text{color: Machine -> {black, white}.}$$

We assume each machine initially to be white.
We describe the probe as a token being sent around the ring using signalling facilities. The token is realized by an internal, dynamic function

$$\text{token: Machine -> Bool.}$$

Initially `token` is `false` for all machines. Like machines the token can turn either white or black. Since there is at most one token propagated through the ring we use nullary, internal, dynamic functions to model color and value of the token, respectively.

$$\text{tokenColor: -> {black, white}}$$
$$\text{tokenValue: -> Int}$$

The function `tokenColor` is assumed initially to be `white` and the function `tokenValue` initially to be 0. Note that M_0 initiates the probe by transmitting the token to M_{N-1} and each M_{i+1} transmits the token to M_i. We use the internal, static function

$$\texttt{next: Machine -> Machine,}$$

to model this circular arrangement of machines[3].
The internal, static function

$$\texttt{id: Machine -> Machine,}$$

returns for each machine its machine identifier.
We assume that machine M_0 can initiate the probe. We realize the initiation of the probe by a shared function

$$\texttt{initiateProbe : -> Bool.}$$

We assume `initiateProbe` initially to be `false`.

3.3   Modules of $\mathcal{A}'$

Each machine executes a module consisting of the rules SendMessage, ReceiveMessage, TransmitToken, InitiateProbe, NextProbe, and Skip.
Rule SendMessage of $\mathcal{A}'$ is a refined version of the one of $\mathcal{A}$. In the refined version additionally the local message counter c(me) is affected.

SENDMESSAGE

```
if mode(me) = SM and active(me) = true then
   messages(receivingMachine) := messages(receivingMachine) + 1,
   c(me) := c(me) + 1
```

On receipt of a message, the receiving machine is active and turns black. Note that machines can receive messages irrespective of their activity state. Note further that rule ReceiveMessage is a refined version of the one of $\mathcal{A}$ since it coincides with the latter on vocabulary τ.

RECEIVEMESSAGE

```
if mode(me) = RM and messages(me) > 0 then
   messages(me) := messages(me) - 1, active(me) := true,
   c(me) := c(me) - 1, color(me) := black
```

---

[3] $\text{next}(0) = N - 1$, $\text{next}(N - 1) = N - 2$, ..., $\text{next}(1) = 0$

In $\mathcal{A}$ the probe is realized by stuttering steps (rule Skip) and the external, dynamic function `terminationDetected` constrained by C2, C3, C4. In $\mathcal{A}'$ the probe is realized by the rules TransmitToken, InitiateProbe and NextProbe and the *internal*, dynamic function `terminationDetected`. Upon token transmission[4] the executing machine is passive and turns white. The value of the token is changed according to the local message counter. Note also that in the following rule only machines M_{i+1} can transmit the token.

TRANSMITTOKEN

```
if mode(me) = P and token(me) = true and
   active(me) = false and id(me) <> 0 then
   token(me) := false, token(next(me)) := true,
   if color(me) = black then tokenColor := black,
   tokenValue := tokenValue + c(me), color(me) := white
```

If machine 0 is executed in mode P and *initiateProbe = true* holds then a new token is created and transmitted to machine $N-1$. The token itself is white and has value 0. Furthermore machine 0 turns to white and sets `initiateProbe` to `false`. The latter avoids "nested" probes.

INITIATEPROBE

```
if mode(me) = P and id(me) = 0 and initiateProbe = true then
   token(next(me)) := true, tokenValue := 0,
   tokenColor := white, color(me) := white,
   initiateProbe := false
```

At token return machine 0 investigates whether the stable state of termination has been reached or not. We say, the probe has been *successful* if at token return `c(0)` + `tokenValue` = 0, machine 0 is white and passive, and the token is white. After an successful probe machine 0 sets `terminationDetected` to `true`. After an unsuccessful probe machine 0 initiates a next probe by setting `initiateProbe` to `true`.

NEXTPROBE

```
if mode(me) = P and id(me) = 0 and token(me) = true then
   if c(me) + tokenValue = 0 and color(me) = white and
      tokenColor = white and active(me) = false then
      terminationDetected := true
   else
      initiateProbe := true, token(me) := false
```

---

[4] via signal communication facilities which are available irrespective of facilities for message transmission, cf. section 1

As in $\mathcal{A}$ we realize stuttering by a rule Skip. Note also that in $\mathcal{A}$ an executing machine in mode P performs a stuttering step (cf. rule Skip of $\mathcal{A}$).

SKIP

```
if mode(me) = S then skip
```

3.4   Runs of $\mathcal{A}'$

We use the same notion of *possible run* of $\mathcal{A}'$ as for $\mathcal{A}$. We say ρ' is a *run* of $\mathcal{A}'$ if ρ' satisfies constraints C0, C1, and the constraints given in the following section 3.5.

3.5   Constraints of $\mathcal{A}'$

In the following let $\rho' = (A', S')$ be a possible run of $\mathcal{A}'$. Besides constraints C0 and C1 (stated for $\mathcal{A}'$) a run of $\mathcal{A}'$ has to fulfill the following constraints.

C5: $\forall i \in \text{Machine} : \Box\Diamond(A' = i \wedge \text{mode}(i) = P)$

Intuitively, constraint C5 assures that token transmission proceeds. More precisely, constraint C5 assures that each machine is executed infinite many times in mode P.

C6: The environment sets initiateProbe in ρ' exactly once to true.

Intuitively, constraint C6 assures that in each run the first probe is initiated by the environment. Note that initially initiateProbe is false and cannot changed by a machine until it is set to true by the environment.

4   Verification

In this section we show that the lower-level ASM $\mathcal{A}'$ is an implementation of $\mathcal{A}$. In the first subsection we define what it means for $\mathcal{A}'$ to implement $\mathcal{A}$. In the second subsection we prove that $\mathcal{A}'$ implements $\mathcal{A}$.

4.1   Implementation

In this subsection we define what it means for the lower-level ASM $\mathcal{A}'$ to *implement* the higher-level ASM $\mathcal{A}$.

There exists two distinct approaches to specification which Lamport calls in [Lam86] the *prescriptive* and *restrictive* approaches. In the prescriptive approach an implementation must exhibit all the same possible behaviors as the specification. In the restrictive approach, it is required that every possible lower-level behavior is represented by a higher-level behavior. In this paper the intention is that the lower-level specification $\mathcal{A}'$ should satisfy constraints C2, C3, C4, i.e., each run of $\mathcal{A}'$ should satisfy C2, C3, C4. We do not require that all higher-level runs are implemented in a single implementation. Otherwise an implementation has to detect termination in the moment it occurred (cf. constraint C3). We adopt here the restrictive approach.

As in first-order logic, the *reduct* of an τ'-state S' to the vocabulary τ is the state S denoted by $S'|\tau$ obtained from S' by restricting the interpretation of function names on τ' to τ. Note that τ is a subvocabulary of τ'.

Now we define a *refinement-relation*, more precisely, we define a refinement-relation between $\mathcal{A}$ and $\mathcal{A}'$ which is sufficient to give the corresponding correctness proof. We say a run $\rho' = (A', S')$ of $\mathcal{A}'$ *implements* a run $\rho = (A, S)$ of $\mathcal{A}$ if

1. $S_k \cong S'_k|\tau$, and
2. $A_k = A'_k$

for all $k \in \text{Nat}$. Call a run ρ of $\mathcal{A}$ a *higher-level run* and a run ρ' of $\mathcal{A}'$ a *lower-level run*, respectively. We say that ASM $\mathcal{A}'$ *implements* $\mathcal{A}$ iff each lower-level run implements a higher-level run. If $\text{Run}(\mathcal{A})$ denotes the collection of runs of $\mathcal{A}$ and $\text{Run}(\mathcal{A}')$ the collection of runs of $\mathcal{A}'$, respectively, then this refinement-relation can be characterized by

$$\text{Run}(\mathcal{A}')|\tau \subseteq \text{Run}(\mathcal{A}),$$

where $\text{Run}(\mathcal{A}')|\tau$ denotes the collection of runs of $\mathcal{A}'$ restricted to the vocabulary τ of $\mathcal{A}$ (cf. the construction of ρ in the following section 4.2). Look at [AL91] for a detailed discussion under which assumptions the existence of a refinement-relation can be guaranteed.

4.2 $\mathcal{A}'$ Implements $\mathcal{A}$

Now we will prove that $\mathcal{A}'$ implements $\mathcal{A}$. We have to show that each lower-level run is an implementation of a higher-level run. Let $\rho' = (A', S')$ be an arbitrary run of $\mathcal{A}'$. We define a tuple $\rho = (A, S)$ by:

1. $A_k := A'_k$
2. $S_k := S'_k|\tau$

We show that ρ is a run of $\mathcal{A}$. We make the following observations: (i) constraints C0 and C1 are satisfied in ρ (denoted by $\rho \models C0 \wedge C1$), (ii) $S_k \cong S'_k|\tau$ and $A_k = A'_k$ hold for all $k \in \text{Nat}$. It remains to show that (i) ρ is a possible run of $\mathcal{A}$, and (ii) $\rho \models C2 \wedge C3 \wedge C4$. In this case ρ is a run of $\mathcal{A}$. From this we can conclude that ρ' is an implementation of ρ and hence that $\mathcal{A}'$ implements $\mathcal{A}$. Since $\mathcal{A}$ and $\mathcal{A}'$ require the same initial conditions for functions from τ we know that $S'_0|\tau$ is an initial state of $\mathcal{A}$. It remains to show that S_{k+1} can be obtained from S_k by executing machine A_k in $\mathcal{A}$, i.e., that the so-called reduct property depicted in Fig. 2 holds. Note that in $\mathcal{A}'$ (and in $\mathcal{A}$) for each time point at most one guard of the rules is satisfied.

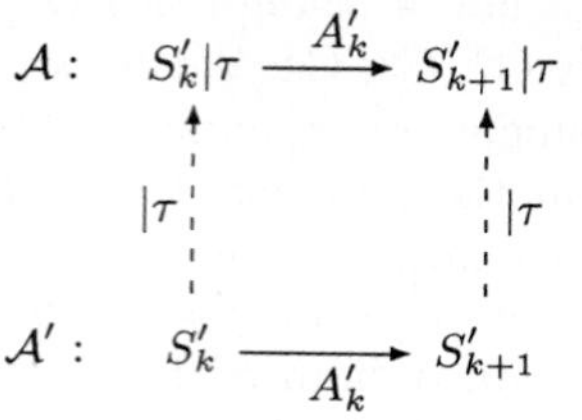

$$\mathcal{A}: \quad S_k'|\tau \xrightarrow{\quad A_k' \quad} S_{k+1}'|\tau$$

$$\mathcal{A}': \quad S_k' \xrightarrow{\quad A_k' \quad} S_{k+1}'$$

Fig. 2. Reduct Property

Lemma 1. *For all* $k \in$ Nat *state* S_{k+1} *can be obtained from* S_k *by executing machine* A_k *in* $\mathcal{A}$.

Proof. Let $k \in$ Nat. We simply say R_k holds, if the reduct property holds for k, i.e. if $S_{k+1}'|\tau$ is obtained from $S_k'|\tau$ by executing machine A_k'. (1) Assume mode$(A_k)_k \neq$ P. Rules SendMessage and ReceiveMessage of $\mathcal{A}'$ are refined versions of the corresponding rules of $\mathcal{A}$. Mode S leads in both $\mathcal{A}'$ and $\mathcal{A}'$ to stuttering steps. Hence we can conclude R_k. (2) Assume mode$(A_k)_k =$ P. Rules TransmitToken and InitiateProbe of $\mathcal{A}'$ change only functions from $\tau' \setminus \tau$. Rule NextProbe of $\mathcal{A}'$ changes function terminationDetected. This function is an external function of $\mathcal{A}$, i.e., can be changed by the environment in an arbitrary way. *q.e.d.*

With lemma 1 we can now conclude that ρ is a possible run of $\mathcal{A}$. It remains to show that ρ fulfills constraints C2, C3, and C4. Let $t :$ Nat $\rightarrow$ Machine be a partial function which is defined for all time points k, denoted by Def$(t(k))$, at which a token exists and which returns for such time points the machine at which the token resides. For the sake of brevity let q_k denote tokenValue$_k$. The following property P is taken from [Dij99] and is defined as

P: $\Box(\text{Def}(t) \rightarrow (\text{P0} \wedge (\text{P1} \vee \text{P2} \vee \text{P3} \vee \text{P4})))$

where:

P0: $B = (\sum i : 0 \leq i < N : c(i))$

Informally, property P0 says that the sum of all local message counters is the number of all messages on their way.

P1: $(\forall i : \text{t} < i < N : \text{active}(i) = \text{false}) \wedge (\sum i : \text{t} < i < N : c(i)) = q)$

Call machines $i : \text{t} < i < N$ visited machines. Informally, property P1 says that all visited machines are passive and that the tokenValue is the sum of the local message counters of these machines.

P2: $(\sum i : 0 \leq i \leq t : c(i)) + q > 0$

Informally, property P2 means that the sum of all local message counters of the unvisited machines plus the value of the token is greater than 0.

P3: $\exists i : 0 \leq i \leq t : \text{color}(i) = \text{black}$

Informally, property P3 means that there exists an unvisited machine i which is black.

P4: tokenColor $= \text{black}$

The meaning of property P4 is clear. We write $\mathcal{A}' \models P$ if each run of $\mathcal{A}'$ satisfies property P.

Lemma 2. P *is an invariant of* $\mathcal{A}'$, *i.e.,* $\mathcal{A}' \models P$.

Proof. Let $\rho' = (A', S')$ be a run run of $\mathcal{A}'$. We simply say Q_k holds for a state property Q if $S'_k \models Q$ is true.

The message counter of a machine will be incremented when sending a message and decremented when receiving a message. Thus we can immediately conclude $\forall k : P0_k$ or equivalently $\square P0$.

Let $\widehat{k}$ be an arbitrary natural number such that $t(\widehat{k})$ is defined. From the rules of $\mathcal{A}'$ follows that there must be at least one probe starting before $\widehat{k}$. More precisely, there exists a maximal $k_0 \leq \widehat{k}$ such that at time $k_0 - 1$ no machine has the token and at time k_0 machine M_{N-1} has the token.

We show:

1. the conjecture holds for k_0, and
2. if the conjecture holds for a $k < \widehat{k}$ so it holds for $k + 1$.

We start with $k = k_0$. At step $(k_0 - 1, k_0)$ the token is created. Thus M_0 executes in this move rule InitiateProbe. Hence $t(k_0) = N - 1$ and $P1_{k_0}$. Assume the conjecture to be true for $k < \widehat{k}$. Thus at least one of the properties $P1_k, ..., P4_k$ holds.

(1) Assume $P1_k$ holds.

    (1.1) Assume that there exists $i_0 : t(k) < i_0 < N$ such that M_{i_0} receives a message in step $(k, k + 1)$. Since M_{i_0} executes rule ReceiveMessage in step $(k, k + 1)$ the message counter of M_{i_0} is decremented and M_{i_0} becomes active (cf. C1). Token location, token color, and token value do not change. We know that $c(i_0)_{k+1} = c(i_0)_k - 1$, active$(i_0)_{k+1} = true$, and $t(k) = t(k + 1)$ hold. Since machine i_0 receives a message we get $B_k > 0$. With $P1_k$ we can conclude $(\sum i : t(k + 1) < i < N : c(i)_{k+1}) = q_k - 1$. With $P0_{k+1}$ and $B_{k+1} \geq 0$ we get $P2_{k+1}$.

(1.2) Assume that for all $i : t(k) < i < N$ machine M_i does not receive a message in step $(k, k+1)$. At time k all machines M_i with $t(k) < i < N$ are passive, thus they can not send a message and hence their message counters do not change. Their activity state does not change, too.

(1.2.1) Assume the token is not transmitted in step $(k, k+1)$. Then $P1_{k+1}$ holds.

(1.2.2) Assume the token is transmitted in step $(k, k+1)$. We can conclude that rule TransmitToken is executed by machine $M_{t(k)}$ and $t(k) > 0$. Hence machine $M_{t(k)}$ is passive both at time k and at time $k+1$ (cf. C1). The message counter of $M_{t(k)}$ does not change. When $M_{t(k)}$ executes rule TransmitToken it increases the token value by $c(t(k))$. Hence $P1_{k+1}$ holds.

(2) Assume $P2_k$ holds.

(2.1) Assume there exists $i_0 : 0 \le i_0 \le t(k)$ such that M_{i_0} receives a message in step $(k, k+1)$. Then $color(i_0)_{k+1} = black$ and $t(k+1) = t(k)$ holds. Thus $P3_{k+1}$ holds.

(2.2) Assume for all $i : 0 \le i \le t(k)$ M_i receives no message in step $(k, k+1)$. Thus we get $\sum i : 0 \le i \le t(k) : c(i)_{k+1} \ge \sum i : 0 \le i \le t(k) : c(i)_k$.

(2.2.1) Assume there is token transmission in step $(k, k+1)$. In this case $P2_{k+1}$ holds.

(2.2.2) Assume there is no token transmission in step $(k, k+1)$. In this case we know that rule TransmitToken is executed by machine $M_{t(k)}$. Furthermore we know that $t(k) > 0$ holds. We get immediately $\sum i : 0 \le i \le t(k) : c(i)_{k+1} = \sum i : 0 \le i \le t(k) : c(i)_k$. Using $t(k+1) = t(k) - 1$ and $q_{k+1} = q_k + c(t(k))_k$ we get $(\sum i : 0 \le i \le t(k+1) : c(i)_{k+1}) + q_{k+1} = (\sum : 0 \le i \le t(k) : c(i)_k) + q_k$. The assumption $P2_k$ gives $P2_{k+1}$.

(3) Assume $P3_k$ holds.

(3.1) Assume $t(k+1) = t(k)$ holds. We get immediately $P3_{k+1}$.

(3.2) Assume $t(k+1) \neq t(k)$ holds.

(3.2.1) Assume $M_{t(k)}$ is black at time k. The token will be blackened and transmitted to machine $M_{t(k+1)}$ in step $(k, k+1)$. Thus, we get $P4_{k+1}$.

(3.2.2) Assume $M_{t(k)}$ is white at time k. There exists i with $0 \le i \le t(k+1)$ such that M_i is black at time $k+1$. Thus, we get $P3_{k+1}$.

(4) Assume $P4_k$ holds. If Machine 0 initiates the probe it creates a new token (cf. rule InitiateProbe). This token is transmitted to machine $N-1$. The token is white and has value 0. Within a probe the token can only turn black (cf. rule TransmitToken). Thus we can conclude that $P4_{k+1}$ holds.

q.e.d.

This invariant is now used to prove $\rho \models C2 \wedge C3 \wedge C4$. Note that $\rho' \models C2 \wedge C3 \wedge C4$ implies $\rho \models C2 \wedge C3 \wedge C4$. We start with a simple lemma.

Lemma 3. $\rho \models C4$

Proof. There exists no rule in $\mathcal{A}'$ which sets terminationDetected to false. Thus we get $\rho' \models C4$ and hence $\rho \models C4$.   *q.e.d.*

Now we show that the value of terminationDetected in ρ is "correct".

Lemma 4. $\rho \models C2$

Proof. Assume in ρ' that there exists a time point k with terminationDetected$_k$ = true. Let k_1 be the smallest number with this property. This means that at time $k_0 := k_1 - 1$ terminationDetected is false. Hence M_0 sets in step (k_0, k_1) terminationDetected to true. Thus $c(0)_{k_0} + $ tokenValue$_{k_0} = 0$, color$(0)_{k_0} = $ white, active$(0)_{k_0} = $ false, and tokenColor$_{k_0} = $ white. With lemma 2 we know that $P1_{k_0} \vee P2_{k_0} \vee P3_{k_0} \vee P4_{k_0}$. From the above follows $\neg(P2_{k_0} \vee P3_{k_0} \vee P4_{k_0})$. Hence $P1_{k_0}$ holds. We can conclude that Termination$_{k_0}$ holds. Since terminationDetected remains true and the termination situation is stable this leads to $\rho' \models C2$ and hence $\rho \models C2$.   *q.e.d.*

Note that in each probe the token returns to machine 0 after a finite period of time if ρ' contains termination. In the following we simply say that in this case the probe ends after a finite period of time. This can be seen by constraint C5 and the rules realizing the probe, i.e., InitiateProbe, TransmitToken, and NextProbe, respectively.

Lemma 5. $\rho \models C3$

Proof. Assume there exists in ρ' a time point k such that Termination$_k$ holds. We know that in this case each probe ends after a finite period of time. If a probe ends at a point with no termination machine 0 initiates a new probe. Otherwise machine 0 would detect termination at a point with no termination. This is in contradiction with lemma 4. Hence lemma 4 guarantees the initiation of a new probe. Thus there exists a probe, say Pr_0, which ends within the termination.

(1) Assume M_0 detects in probe Pr_0 termination. Then we are finished.
(2) Assume M_0 detects not termination in probe Pr_0. Then a new probe Pr_1 is initiated by M_0. The token returns in probe Pr_1 with tokenValue $= 0$. Since upon token transmission machines whitens itself we know that all machines are white when the token returns to M_0.
(2.1) Assume the token returns white to M_0 in Pr_1. Then M_0 detects termination.
(2.2) Assume the token returns black to M_0 in Pr_1. Then M_0 initiates a new probe Pr_2. In this probe the token returns white to M_0 and M_0 detects termination.

q.e.d.

We can conclude that ρ is a run of $\mathcal{A}$. We have shown that each lower-level run is an implementation of a higher-level run. This subsection is summarized in the following theorem.

Theorem 1. $\mathcal{A}'$ *implements* $\mathcal{A}$

5   Conclusions

In this paper we have presented a methodology for the specification and verification of distributed algorithms using Gurevich's concept of Abstract State Machines. Starting with an informal *problem description* one constructs a *higher-level specification*, which should be an appropriate mathematical model of the problem description. The appropriateness is established by a *justification*. A *lower-level specification* represents the algorithm on a more concrete abstraction level. The *mathematical verification* guarantees that the lower-level specification implements the higher-level specification. This methodology was presented by a well-known distributed algorithm, namely the termination detection algorithm originally invented by Dijkstra, Feijen and van Gasteren in [DFvG83] in a slight variation presented in [Dij99].

In this paper we have mainly stressed on the mathematical verification. The verification is given on a detailed mathematical level. Note that the presented proofs are *not formal*, i.e., they are not based on a proof calculus. The goal of these informal proofs is to give the underlying ideas. They can be seen as abstractions from detailed and rigor formal proofs based on a proof calculus. Future research will emphasize on a *formal, mathematical verification*.

The *justification* that the higher-level specification is appropriate for the problem description is beyond the scope of this paper. Future research will emphasize on *methods for justification*. More precisely, we will investigate the FOREST-approach presented at web page [KP] (cf. [PGK97] for the underlying idea).

Acknowledgment. I would like to thank Thomas Deiß, Martin Kronenburg, and Klaus Madlener for their constructive criticism on this paper. Furthermore I would like to thank the anonymous referees for their useful and detailed comments and suggestions on the previous version of this paper.

References

[AL91]   Martín Abadi and Leslie Lamport. The existence of refinement mappings. *Theoretical Computer Science*, 82(2):253–284, May 1991.

[BGR95]   Egon Börger, Yuri Gurevich, and Dean Rosenzweig. The bakery algorithm: Yet another specification and verification. In E. Börger, editor, *Specification and Validation Methods*, pages 231–243. Oxford University Press, 1995.

[Bör99]   Egon Börger. High level system design and analysis using abstract state machines. In Hutter, Stephan, Traverso, and Ullman, editors, *Current Trends in Applied Formal Methods (FM-Trends 98)*, LNCS. Springer, 1999. to appear.

[DFvG83]   Edsger W. Dijkstra, W.H.J. Feijen, and A.J.M. van Gasteren. Derivation of a termination detection algorithm for distributed computations. *Information Processing Letters*, 16(5):217–219, 1983.

[Dij99]   Edsger W. Dijkstra. Shmuel Safra's version of termination detection. In M. Broy and R. Steinbrüggen, editors, *Proceedings of the NATO Advanced Study Institute on Calculational System Design, Marktoberdorf, Germany, 28 July - 9 August 1998*, pages 297–301, 1999.

[DS80]   Edsger W. Dijkstra and C.S. Scholten. Termination detection for diffusing computations. *Information Processing Letters*, 11(1):1–4, 1980.

[Gur95]   Yuri Gurevich. Evolving algebras 1993: Lipari guide. In E. Börger, editor, *Specification and Validation Methods*, pages 9–36. Oxford University Press, 1995.

[Gur97]   Yuri Gurevich. May 1997 draft of the ASM guide. Technical Report CSE-TR-336-97, University of Michigan, 1997.

[Gur99]   Yuri Gurevich. The sequential ASM thesis. *Bulletin of the European Association for Theoretical Computer Science*, 67:93–124, February 1999. Columns: Logic in Computer Science.

[KP]   Martin Kronenburg and Christian Peper. The FOREST Approach: World Wide Web page at `http://rn.informatik.uni-kl.de/~forest/`.

[Lam86]   Leslie Lamport. On interprocess communication. *Distributed Computing*, 1:77–101, 1986.

[Lam94]   Leslie Lamport. The temporal logic of actions. *ACM Transactions on Programming Languages and Systems*, 16(3):872–923, May 1994.

[PGK97]   Christian Peper, Reinhard Gotzhein, and Martin Kronenburg. A generic approach to the formal specification of requirements. In *1st IEEE International Conference on Formal Engineering Methods 1997 (ICFEM'97), Hiroshima, Japan*. IEEE Computer Society, 1997.

Logspace Reducibility via Abstract State Machines

Erich Grädel and Marc Spielmann

Mathematische Grundlagen der Informatik,
RWTH Aachen, D-52056 Aachen, Germany
{graedel, spielmann}@informatik.rwth-aachen.de

Abstract. We present a notion of logspace reducibility among structures that is based on abstract state machines (ASM). Our reductions are logspace computable (due to the syntactic restrictions we impose on ASM-programs) and are equally expressive as the logic (FO+DTC) enriched with the ability to handle sets. On ordered structures they precisely capture LOGSPACE. Our work continues that of Blass, Gurevich and Shelah on the choiceless fragment of PTIME. Indeed, our reductions can be seen as the choiceless fragment of LOGSPACE.

1 Introduction

Abstract State Machines (ASM) have become a successful methodology for the specification and verification of hardware and software systems. Aside this, ASM provide a computation model which is also very interesting under theoretical aspects. In this paper we study *applications of ASM to the theory of computation.* More precisely, we investigate logspace computability via ASM.

Logspace computability is an important level of complexity, for several reasons:

- It can be viewed as the natural notion of computability with 'very little' memory.
- Logspace computable functions can be computed in parallel very efficiently (i.e., in polylogarithmic time) with a reasonable amount of hardware (i.e., by circuits of polynomial size).
- Logspace reductions are widely accepted as a natural basis for completeness results for important complexity classes like P, NP, and PSPACE. Indeed, most of the complete problems for these classes are complete with respect to logspace reductions [Pap94, GHR95].

The standard computation model in complexity theory is the Turing machine. By definition, a function is logspace computable if it is computable by a Turing machine using on inputs of length n at most $O(\log n)$ cells of its work tapes. However, Turing machines work on strings, whereas many problems arising in computer science and logic have inputs that are naturally viewed as structures rather than strings. Furthermore, in most cases algorithms on structures should

J. Wing, J. Woodcock, J. Davies (Eds.): FM'99, Vol. II, LNCS 1709, pp. 1738–1757, 1999.
© Springer-Verlag Berlin Heidelberg 1999

treat isomorphic structures in the same way. Although we can encode structures by strings, there is no easily computable string representation of *isomorphism classes* of structures. (This problem was addressed by Chandra and Harel in the context of database queries [CH82]. It disappears when the structures are linearly ordered.). The situation calls for computation models that work directly on structures rather than strings, and in particular, for a notion of *logspace computability on structures* and for a *reduction theory among structures* that is based on such a notion.

There are several computation models on structures in the literature. Some of them have been developed in the context of database theory (see [AHV95]), most notably the *generic machines* of Abiteboul and Vianu. Another model, which we will use in this paper, is provided by *abstract state machines*, formerly known as *evolving algebras* [Gur91, Gur95, Gur97], which has become the foundation of a successful methodology for specification and verification of software and hardware systems [BH98]. One can view a Turing machine program as a description of how to modify the current configuration of a Turing machine to obtain the next configuration. Similarly, an ASM-program describes how to modify the current state of an ASM to obtain the next state. The main difference is that the states of an ASM are mathematical structures rather than strings. Thus, an ASM takes a structure as input and modifies it step by step, until it stops and outputs the resulting structure. (Aside from this basic model, there do exist more general types of ASM, e.g., real-time ASM and recursive ASM, which have been proved useful for specifying and verifying dynamic systems. These will not be considered in the present paper.)

Both generic machines and ASM (and a number of other models as well) are *computationally complete*: they can calculate all computable (isomorphism-invariant) functions on finite structures. Hence, the notion of (isomorphism-invariant) computable functions on structures is well-understood. The situation becomes much more intriguing when we impose complexity bounds. It is not at all clear whether there exists a computation model on structures (for instance a subclass of abstract state machines) that describes precisely the class of all polynomial-time computable functions, or the class of all logspace computable functions on structures. The straightforward approach, namely to impose appropriate time and space restrictions on one of the known (computationally complete) machine model on structures, does not work. The first problem is that honest time measures for such a model are not always obvious and (natural) space measures may not exist at all. But more importantly, the computational completeness of generic machines or ASM does not scale down to lower complexity levels. For instance, the class of functions computable by ASM in honest polynomial time is a strict subclass of the class of isomorphism-invariant functions that are polynomial-time computable in the usual sense, i.e. on string encodings of structures.

The problem of whether there exists a computation model describing precisely the logspace computable isomorphism-invariant functions has been formulated in different terms as the problem of whether there exists a logic for

LOGSPACE, one of the main open problems of finite model theory. This problem has been made precise by Gurevich [Gur88] (for polynomial time rather than logarithmic space, but the situation is similar). Let us briefly review the situation for LOGSPACE.

It is a well-known result due to Immerman [Imm87] that logspace computability is closely related to the logic (FO+DTC), first-order logic (FO) augmented with the deterministic transitive closure operator DTC. A query on ordered finite structures is logspace computable iff it is expressible in (FO+DTC). The DTC operator assigns to any definable binary relation E the transitive closure of the deterministic part E_{det} of E; E_{det} is obtained by removing all edges from E that start at a point with out-degree > 1. An advantage of this description of logspace computability is that once a query is formulated in (FO+DTC), it is guaranteed to be computable in logspace. There is no need to analyze the storage requirements of an algorithm.

On the other side, handling (FO+DTC) is not as straightforward as, say, a programming language and requires a certain familiarity with logic. Moreover, expressions in (FO+DTC) tend to be rather complex and hard to read when describing non-trivial queries. More to the point, if no linear order is available, (FO+DTC) fails to express all logspace queries. In fact, some very simple problems, which are obviously logspace computable, are not expressible in (FO+DTC). A standard example of such a problem, often called PARITY, is the question whether the cardinality of a given structure is even. Gurevich [Gur88] conjectured that there is no logic (and hence no computation model on structures) that captures PTIME or LOGSPACE on arbitrary finite structures.

A natural model-theoretic notion of reductions among structures is provided by (first-order) interpretations (see [Hod93, Chapter 5]). Informally, a structure $\mathcal{A}$ is interpreted in a structure $\mathcal{B}$ by a sequence of first-order formulae that define an isomorphic copy of $\mathcal{A}$ inside $\mathcal{B}$. It is well-known that first-order interpretations are weaker than logspace reductions. One way to enhance their power is to consider (FO+DTC)-interpretations instead. While these still do not capture all logspace computable functions from structures to structures they give us a better lower bound for the desired class of logspace reductions among structures.

After these introductory remarks, we are now in a position to formulate some necessary conditions for the notion of reductions among structures that we want to put forward:

1. Reductions should be computable in logarithmic space.
2. Reasonable closure properties should be satisfied. In particular, the class of reductions should be closed under composition.
3. On ordered structures, our notion should capture all logspace computable functions from structures to structures.
4. On unordered structures, our reductions should have at least the power of (FO+DTC)-interpretations.

Our work is based on a recent paper by Blass, Gurevich, and Shelah [BGS97], who introduced and investigated the *choiceless fragment of* PTIME, denoted ČPTIME. An important feature of algorithms on ordered structures (or strings) is the ability to make choices. Out of any set of (otherwise indistinguishable) elements the algorithm can select, say, the smallest, and proceed from there. Typical examples are graph algorithms. Consider, for instance, an algorithm deciding reachability in digraphs. A common way to determine whether a target node t is reachable from a source node s in a given digraph G is to construct the set of all reachable nodes from s. To this end the algorithm maintains an auxiliary set X of 'endpoints'. Initially, $X := \{s\}$. At each iteration step the algorithm 'chooses' a node in X, e.g., by selecting the smallest one, adds its neighbors to the set of reachable nodes, and updates the set of endpoints accordingly. The algorithm terminates once the target node has been found reachable, or the set of reachable points has become stable. It is easy to see that in this example explicit choice is not really needed. Instead of choosing one particular endpoint one can process all of them in parallel. But this seems not always possible. For example, in matching algorithms choice is used in a much more sophisticated way, and there is no known efficient algorithm for perfect matching that avoids explicit choice.

The main idea in [BGS97] is to use hereditarily finite sets and parallel execution to replace explicit choice. Abstract state machines serve as a convenient vehicle to define the choiceless fragment of PTIME in a precise and convincing way. The clean description via ASM makes the class amenable to combinatorial and model-theoretic tools that are used in [BGS97] to determine the power of C̃PTIME.

In this paper we continue the work of Blass, Gurevich and Shelah. We study reductions among structures that are defined by means of ASM-programs. Motivated by the approach in [BGS97], we equip our model with the ability to handle small sets, which, for instance, serve as a convenient reservoir for new elements. (Notice that while reducing an instance of one problem to an instance of another problem one often has to invent new elements, e.g., new nodes in a graph.) The syntactic restrictions we impose on ASM-programs will guarantee that all functions computed by such programs are logspace computable (by a Turing machine). On ordered structures, moreover, a function is logspace computable iff it can be computed by such a program. Due to the ability to handle sets, our programs are 'choiceless': they can form a set without ever actually choosing one *particular* element of the set. Indeed, the class of properties computable by our programs can be seen as the *choiceless fragment of* LOGSPACE, which we denote C̃LOGSPACE. Taking the results of [BGS97] into account, we obtain the following relations between standard, choiceless, and descriptive complexity classes:

$$
\begin{array}{ccc}
\text{LOGSPACE} & \subseteq & \text{PTIME} \\
\cup^1 & & \cup^1 \\
\text{C̃LOGSPACE} & \subset^2 & \text{C̃PTIME} \\
\cup^3 & & \cup^2 \\
(\text{FO+DTC}) & \subset^3 & (\text{FO+LFP})
\end{array}
$$

where the inclusions marked 1, 2, and 3 are proper due to the following problems:

(1) PARITY
(2) SMALL SUBSET PARITY (see Corollary 24)
(3) Reachability in double graphs (see Lemma 11)

We introduce two different variants of ASM-programs to define reductions among structures. Programs of the basic variant, which we call *nullary programs*, are essentially just basic ASM-programs (in the sense of [Gur97]) where every dynamic function is nullary. Nullary programs suffice to capture LOGSPACE on ordered input, but are fairly weak without access to an ordering. Programs of the more powerful variant, called *bounded memory programs*, are sequences of nullary programs where the nullary programs may also occur parameterized by means of `do-forall`-clauses (see [Gur97]). Bounded memory programs have two main advantages over nullary programs. Firstly, even for functions that can be computed by means of nullary programs, bounded memory programs admit presentations that are more succinct and easier to understand. Secondly, bounded memory programs are strictly more expressive than both nullary programs and the logic (FO+DTC).

At this point, the reader may wonder why we use the term "bounded memory programs" rather than, say, "logspace programs". Recall that ASM have been put forward as a model for describing algorithms *on their natural level of abstraction* [Gur95]. The term "logspace" refers to the bit-level. When we describe common logspace algorithms at their natural abstraction level (e.g., by ASM), we see that most of them actually use a bounded number of memory locations (variables) each of which stores an object that is identified by a logarithmic number of bits (e.g., an element of the input structure or a natural number polynomially bounded in the cardinality of the input structure). Hence we find 'bounded memory' programs more adequate for the spirit of ASM.

The contents of the paper is as follows: In Section 2 we recall some terminology from finite model theory and set theory, latter mostly adopted from [BGS97]. In Section 3 we introduce *nullary programs*, our basic variant of programs. In Section 4 we prove that all functions computable by nullary programs are logspace computable. To this end, we describe computations of nullary programs in terms of a set-theoretic extension of the logic (FO+DTC). *Bounded memory programs*, our more powerful variant of programs, are defined in Section 5. In Section 6 we introduce the complexity class $\tilde{\mathrm{C}}$LOGSPACE and show that it is a robust class which also has a logical characterization. Finally, we separate PTIME and LOGSPACE on the choiceless level.

2   Preliminaries

Global relations. Let C be a class of structures over some vocabulary σ. A k-ary *global relation* (or *query*) ρ on C is a mapping that assigns to every structure $\mathcal{A} \in C$ a (local) relation $\rho^{\mathcal{A}} \subseteq A^k$ (where A is the universe of $\mathcal{A}$), such that isomorphisms between structures in C are preserved, i.e., every isomorphism between two structures $\mathcal{A}$ and $\mathcal{B}$ in C is also an isomorphism between $(A, \rho^{\mathcal{A}})$ and $(B, \rho^{\mathcal{B}})$. For example, every first-order formula $\varphi(x_1, \ldots, x_k)$

over σ (all of whose free variables occur among $x_1, \ldots, x_k$) defines a k-ary global relation on the class of all σ-structures: φ maps a σ-structure $\mathcal{A}$ to $\varphi^{\mathcal{A}} := \{(a_1, \ldots, a_k) \in A^k : \mathcal{A} \models \varphi[a_1, \ldots, a_k]\}$.

Deterministic transitive closure logic. Let FO denote first-order logic with equality. *Deterministic transitive closure logic*, (FO+DTC), is obtained from FO by adding to the usual formula-formation rules of FO the rule

- If φ is a formula, $\bar{x}$ and $\bar{y}$ are two k-tuples of variables, and $\bar{u}$ and $\bar{v}$ are two k-tuples of terms, then $[\mathrm{DTC}_{\bar{x},\bar{y}}\,\varphi](\bar{u},\bar{v})$ is a formula.

For any $2k$-ary relation R, let $DTC(R)$ denote the transitive reflexive closure of the deterministic part R_{det} of R. (R_{det} is the $2k$-ary relation obtained from R by removing all edges $(\bar{a}, \bar{b}) \in R$ for which there exists an edge $(\bar{a}, \bar{b}') \in R$ such that $\bar{b} \neq \bar{b}'$.) The semantics of $[\mathrm{DTC}_{\bar{x},\bar{y}}\,\varphi](\bar{u},\bar{v})$ is as follows. Regard $[\mathrm{DTC}_{\bar{x},\bar{y}}\,\varphi]$ as a new $2k$-ary relation symbol whose interpretation is $DTC(R)$, where R is the $2k$-ary relation defined by $\varphi(\bar{x}, \bar{x}')$. As an example, consider a finite digraph $G = (V, E)$ with two distinguished nodes s and t. $G \models [\mathrm{DTC}_{x,y}\,E(x,y)][s,t]$ iff there exists a path in G (composed from E-edges) that starts at node s, ends at node t, and each node on the path (except t) has out-degree 1. For a more formal definition of the semantics of DTC-formulas the reader is referred to [EF95].

Fact 1 ([Imm87]). *A global relation on ordered structures is definable in the logic (FO+DTC) iff it is logspace computable.*

Hereditarily finite sets. Let A be a finite set of atoms (i.e., elements that are not sets, also called urelements in set theory). The set $\mathrm{HF}(A)$ of all *hereditarily finite objects* built from the atoms in A is the least set such that

- $A \subseteq \mathrm{HF}(A)$,
- every finite subset of $\mathrm{HF}(A)$ is an element of $\mathrm{HF}(A)$.

Thus, an object $X \in \mathrm{HF}(A)$ is either a finite set or an atom from A. A set X is *transitive*, if whenever $Z \in Y \in X$, then $Z \in X$. The transitive closure $\mathrm{TC}(X)$ of an object X is the least transitive set with $X \in \mathrm{TC}(X)$. For instance, $\mathrm{TC}(A) = A \cup \{A\}$. Observe that for every object $X \in \mathrm{HF}(A)$, $\mathrm{TC}(X)$ is finite and in $\mathrm{HF}(A)$. By the *size* of an object X we mean the cardinality of $\mathrm{TC}(X)$. For example, the size of A is $|A|+1$. Notice that the size of X is a bound for both the cardinality of $A \cap \mathrm{TC}(X)$ and the length k of chains $Y_1 \in Y_2 \in \ldots \in Y_k \in X$. The maximum k is also called the *rank* of X. We write $\mathrm{HF}_s(A)$ for the restriction of $\mathrm{HF}(A)$ to objects of size at most s.

3 Nullary Programs

In this section we introduce *nullary programs*, a restricted model for logspace computability on structures. On *ordered* input structures nullary programs suffice to describe all logspace computable functions.

States. Let σ and τ be disjoint finite relational vocabularies. We extend $\sigma \cup \tau$ to a *program vocabulary* $\Upsilon(\sigma, \tau)$ containing, in addition to $\sigma \cup \tau$,

- a unary relation symbol *Universe*,
- the set theoretic symbols $\in$, *Atoms*, *unique*, $\varnothing$, where $\in$ is a binary relation symbol, *Atoms* is a unary relation symbol, *unique* is a unary function symbol, and $\varnothing$ is a constant symbol,
- a number of constant symbols $f_1, \ldots, f_d$.

Our programs will take finite σ-structures as inputs and compute finite τ-structures as outputs. Therefore, we refer to σ as the *input vocabulary* and to τ as the *output vocabulary*. The universe of the output will be determined by the interpretation of the symbol *Universe*, and may grow during the course of a computation by writing to *Universe*. In the following we treat *Universe* as a special kind of output symbol.

Definition 2. Let $\mathcal{A}$ be a finite σ-structure whose universe A is a set of atoms. On input $\mathcal{A}$ every nullary program over $\Upsilon(\sigma, \tau)$ (defined below, see Definition 6) starts its computation in the *initial state* $\mathcal{S}(\mathcal{A})$, which is a $\Upsilon(\sigma, \tau)$-structure defined as follows:

- the universe of $\mathcal{S}(\mathcal{A})$ is $\mathrm{HF}(A)$,
- $\mathcal{A}$ is embedded in $\mathcal{S}(\mathcal{A})$, i.e., $R^{\mathcal{S}(\mathcal{A})} = R^{\mathcal{A}}$ for every input relation $R \in \sigma$,
- the interpretation of $\in$ and $\varnothing$ are the obvious ones; *Atoms* is interpreted as the set A; for every singleton $X \in \mathrm{HF}(A)$, *unique*(X) is the unique $Y \in X$; for all other $X \in \mathrm{HF}(A)$, *unique*$(X) := \varnothing$,
- every output relation (including *Universe*) is empty,
- each f_i is interpreted as $\varnothing$.

$\square$

Definition 3. Every *state* $\mathcal{S}$ of a nullary program over $\Upsilon(\sigma, \tau)$ on input $\mathcal{A}$ is a $\Upsilon(\sigma, \tau)$-structure with universe $\mathrm{HF}(A)$. During a computation the universe $\mathrm{HF}(A)$ and the interpretations of the input symbols and the set-theoretic symbols remain unchanged; these symbols are static. In contrast, $f_1, \ldots, f_d$ and all output symbols (including *Universe*) are dynamic in the sense that their interpretation may or may not change from one state to the next. While there are few restrictions on how to change the interpretation of $f_1, \ldots, f_d$, every output relation is write-only. Once a tuple is put into an output relation it remains there for the rest of the computation. We call $f_1, \ldots, f_d$ *dynamic functions*. $\square$

Notice that because tuples cannot be removed from the output, the output is in general relational. Since we will later also consider composition of programs, it is natural to restrict attention to relational input and output vocabularies. However, this restriction has no practical impact. For instance, if you like your favorite function F to be part of the input structure, simply include the graph G_F of F. Your program may then contain a term of the form *unique*$\{y \in Atoms : G_F(x, y)\}$ whose semantics will be $F(x)$.

The logic (FO+BS). The ASM-programs that we will put forward are based on a restricted variant of first-order definability over states. Below we define a fragment of FO over states which is not as expressive as full FO over states. The fragment is nevertheless strictly more expressive than FO over the input structures, as it can handle 'bounded' sets. To emphasize this, we denote the fragment (FO+BS) where "BS" alludes to "bounded sets".

For any vocabulary σ let $\sigma^+ := \sigma \cup \{\in, Atoms, unique, \varnothing\}$.

Definition 4. The *terms* and *formulae* of (FO+BS) over σ are defined by simultaneous induction:

T1 As usual, terms are built from variables and constants, and are closed under application of function symbols (from σ^+).

T2 If $t_1, \ldots, t_k$ are terms and s is a natural number, then $\{t_1, \ldots, t_k\}_s$ is a term. ($\{t_1, \ldots, t_k\}_s$ denotes the set whose elements are denoted by $t_1, \ldots, t_k$, provided that this set has size $\leq s$).

T3 Choose a term t, a variable x, a formula φ, and a natural number s. Let r be either a set symbol in σ^+ or a term with no free occurrence of x. Then $\{t : x \in r : \varphi\}_s$ is a term (denoting the set of all $t(x)$ with x from range r satisfying condition $\varphi(x)$, provided that this set has size $\leq s$).

F Atomic formulae are defined as usual (from $=$ and the relations in σ^+). Formulae are either atomic formulae or built from previously defined formulae by means of negation and disjunction.

The free and bound variables of terms and formulae are defined in the obvious way. In particular, a variable occurs free in $\{t : x \in r : \varphi\}_s$ if it occurs free in t, r or φ and is different from x. x itself occurs bound. □

The semantics of a term t with respect to a state $\mathcal{S}$ with universe HF(A) is clear in the case where t is of type T1. If $t = \{t_1, \ldots, t_k\}_s$ and the set $\{t_1^{\mathcal{S}}, \ldots, t_k^{\mathcal{S}}\}$ has size $\leq s$, then $t^{\mathcal{S}}$ is this set. Otherwise, $t^{\mathcal{S}} := \varnothing$. When $t = \{t_0 : x \in r : \varphi\}_s$ and the set $\{t_0^{\mathcal{S}}[X] : X \in r^{\mathcal{S}} : \mathcal{S} \models \varphi[X]\}$ has size $\leq s$, let $t^{\mathcal{S}}$ be this set. Otherwise, $t^{\mathcal{S}} := \varnothing$. The semantics of a formula φ with respect to $\mathcal{S}$ is standard.

We did not mention quantification in the definition of (FO+BS). But note that (FO+BS) can define a guarded form of quantification. For example, let $(\exists x \in r)\varphi$ abbreviate the formula $\varnothing \in \{\varnothing : x \in r : \varphi\}$. (Technically, the set term in this formula needs a subscript to bound its size; 2 will do. To ease notation we frequently omit the subscript at a set term when the set's description implies an obvious bound on its size.) By using *Atoms* for the guard r in $(\exists x \in r)\varphi$, we can simulate in (FO+BS) quantification over elements of the input structure. This implies that, with respect to definability over the input structures, (FO+BS) indeed extends FO.

Lemma 5. *For every FO-formula $\psi(\bar{x})$ over σ there exists a (FO+BS)-formula $\varphi(\bar{x})$ over σ such that for every finite σ-structure $\mathcal{A}$ and all $\bar{a} \in A^k$, $\mathcal{A} \models \psi[\bar{a}]$ iff $\mathcal{S}(\mathcal{A}) \models \varphi[\bar{a}]$.*

Syntax and semantics of nullary programs.

Definition 6. Fix a program vocabulary $\Upsilon = \Upsilon(\sigma, \tau)$ with dynamic functions $f_1, \ldots, f_d$. We define *nullary rules* over Υ inductively:

- **Updates:** For every dynamic function $f \in \Upsilon$, every k-ary output relation $R \in \Upsilon$, and all (FO+BS)-terms $t_0, t_1, \ldots, t_k$ over $\sigma \cup \{f_1, \ldots, f_d\}$ the two assignments $f := t_0$ and $R(t_1, \ldots, t_k) := \textit{true}$ are (*atomic*) nullary rules. (Frequently, we will abbreviate $R(t_1, \ldots, t_k) := \textit{true}$ to $R(t_1, \ldots, t_k)$.)
- **Conditional:** If φ is a (FO+BS)-formula over $\sigma \cup \{f_1, \ldots, f_d\}$ and Π a nullary rule, then (if φ then Π) is a nullary rule (with *guard* φ).
- **Parallel execution:** If Π_0 and Π_1 are nullary rules, then $\frac{\Pi_0}{\Pi_1}$ is a nullary rule (for brevity sometimes written as $\Pi_0 \| \Pi_1$).

The free and bound variables of a nullary rule are defined in the obvious way. A *nullary program* is a nullary rule without free variables. □

The semantics of nullary programs is (almost) standard. Consider a nullary program Π over $\Upsilon(\sigma, \tau)$ and let $\mathcal{S}$ be a state of Π. We denote the *sequel of $\mathcal{S}$ with respect to Π* (see [Gur97]) by $\Pi(\mathcal{S})$. The *run of Π on $\mathcal{S}$* is the maximal sequence $\mathcal{S}_0, \mathcal{S}_1, \mathcal{S}_2, \ldots$ of states such that $\mathcal{S}_0 = \mathcal{S}$, $\mathcal{S}_{i+1} = \Pi(\mathcal{S}_i)$, and $\mathcal{S}_{i+1} \neq \mathcal{S}_i$ for every state $\mathcal{S}_{i+1}$ in the sequence. Note that a run is either finite or infinite, and that a finite run ends with a state $\mathcal{S}_i$ satisfying $\mathcal{S}_i = \Pi(\mathcal{S}_i)$. The run of Π on a finite σ-structure $\mathcal{A}$ is the run of Π on $\mathcal{S}(\mathcal{A})$. In case the latter is finite and ends with a state $\mathcal{S}$, the *output* of Π on $\mathcal{A}$ is, by definition, the τ-reduct of the substructure of $\mathcal{S}$ induced by *Universe*$^{\mathcal{S}}$. This convention enables us to define the universe of the output by throwing into the unary output relation *Universe* all those objects which we want to be present.

Obviously, the output of Π on $\mathcal{A}$ is—if it exists—a τ-structure. But is it finite? To see this, observe that for every nullary program Π there exists an upper bound s of the size of the objects that Π can touch. ($s \geq 1$ is the maximum of all explicit size bounds of set terms occurring in Π.) Thus, the universe of the output structure is a subset of $\mathrm{HF}_s(A)$. For every finite A, $\mathrm{HF}_s(A)$ is finite.

Note also that the output of a nullary program in general cannot serve as input to another program, because its universe may contain elements that are sets. To avoid problems when composing programs later on we will from now on tacitly assume that the output of a nullary program has its non-atomic elements converted to genuine atoms.

Example 7. Consider the binary global relation ρ_{DTC} which maps every finite ordered digraph $G = (V, E, <)$ to $DTC(E)$. (Recall that $DTC(E)$ denotes the deterministic transitive closure of G's edge relation E.) We present a nullary program Π_{DTC} with input vocabulary $\{E, <\}$ and output vocabulary $\{DTC\}$ that computes ρ_{DTC}. On input G, Π_{DTC} outputs the graph $(V, DTC(E))$.

Let us first concentrate on an instance of the problem: write a nullary program Π which, given a node *start_node* $\in V$, outputs all nodes on the deterministic E-path that starts at *start_node*. Here is a possible solution. In the first step, Π initializes a nullary dynamic function *pebble* with *start_node*. Then, in every following step, Π outputs *pebble* and moves *pebble* along the deterministic path by executing the update *pebble* := *succ(pebble)*, where *succ(x)* abbreviates the term *unique*$\{y \in Atoms : Exy\}$.

But how do we ensure termination of this process if the path leads into a cycle? Every cycle in G has at most $|V|$ nodes. Thus it suffices to set up a counter which triggers termination after $|V|$ steps. Let *counter* be a nullary dynamic function and let *least* denote the least node in G w.r.t. to the ordering $<$ of the nodes. (Note that *least* is definable as *unique*$\{x \in Atoms : \neg(\exists y \in Atoms)\, y < x\}$.) Π initializes *counter* with *least* and executes in every step the update *counter* := *counter* + 1, where *counter* + 1 stands for the term *unique*$\{x \in Atoms : x > counter \wedge (\forall y \in Atoms)(y > counter \rightarrow y \geq x)\}$.

Π as defined below outputs a pair (*start_node*, *a*) for every node a on the deterministic path that starts at *start_node*. It becomes idle (i.e., it stops) when *pebble* has no unique E-successor or when *counter* assumes $\varnothing$ after $|V|$ steps.

```
Π := if  mode = initialize_pebble then
         pebble := start_node
         counter := least
         mode := move_pebble
     if  mode = move_pebble then
         if  pebble ≠ ∅ ∧ counter ≠ ∅ then
             DTC(start_node, pebble)
             pebble := succ(pebble)
             counter := counter + 1
     else
             mode := next_path
```

From Π one easily obtains the desired nullary program Π_{DTC}. Π_{DTC} systematically varies *start_node* over all nodes in V and calls for each instance the above program Π (see line (1) below). When Π terminates, Π_{DTC} resumes its computation in line (2).

```
Π_DTC := if  mode = initial then
             start_node := least
             mode := initialize_pebble
         Π                                                    (1)
         if  mode = next_path ∧ start_node ≠ ∅ then           (2)
             Universe(start_node)
             start_node := start_node + 1
             mode := initialize_pebble
```

$\square$

It is worth noticing that there is no obvious way to define a nullary program computing $DTC(E)$ without access to an ordering of the nodes. Without such an ordering we can neither count—and this way detect a cycle—nor search systematically through all nodes. The example reveals two defects of nullary programs when no order is available: (1) How can we ensure **termination** of nullary programs? (2) How do we perform **systematic search** of the universe? In Section 5 we are going to cure both defects by upgrading nullary programs to bounded memory programs.

4   Logical Description of Computations

In this section we prove that nullary programs are logspace computable. To this end we describe computations of nullary programs in terms of (FO+BS+DTC), i.e., the closure of (FO+BS) under (a bounded version of) the DTC-operator. Logspace computability of nullary programs then follows from the observation that every sentence in (FO+BS+DTC) can be evaluated in logarithmic space. On ordered input structures the other direction holds also: every logspace computable function can be computed by a nullary program. Thus, on ordered input nullary programs are as powerful as logspace Turing machines.

In the remainder of this section let σ denote a finite relational vocabulary.

Definition 8. The *hereditarily finite extension* $\mathcal{A}^+$ of a finite σ-structure $\mathcal{A}$ is a σ^+-structure defined as follows:

- the universe of $\mathcal{A}^+$ is $\mathrm{HF}(A)$,
- $R^{\mathcal{A}^+} = R^{\mathcal{A}}$ for every $R \in \sigma$, and
- the interpretation of $\in$, *Atoms*, *unique*, $\varnothing$ are as in Definition 2.

Let $\varphi(x_1, \dots, x_k)$ be a (FO+BS)-formula over σ. The *global relation defined by* φ, also denoted φ, maps the hereditarily finite extension $\mathcal{A}^+$ of a finite σ-structure $\mathcal{A}$ to the (possibly infinite) relation $\varphi^{\mathcal{A}^+} := \{(X_1, \dots, X_k) \in \mathrm{HF}(A)^k : \mathcal{A}^+ \models \varphi[X_1, \dots, X_k]\}$. For any finite σ-structure $\mathcal{A}$, let $\varphi^{\mathcal{A}}$ denote $\varphi^{\mathcal{A}^+}$.   □

We extend the logic (FO+BS) to the logic (FO+BS+DTC) by adding a new formula-formation rule to Definition 4:

F2 If s is a natural number, φ is a formula, $\bar{x}$ and $\bar{y}$ are two k-tuples of variables, and $\bar{u}$ and $\bar{v}$ are two k-tuples of terms, then $[\mathrm{DTC}_{\bar{x},\bar{y}}\, \varphi]_s(\bar{u},\bar{v})$ is a formula.

The semantics of a DTC-formula $[\mathrm{DTC}_{\bar{x},\bar{y}}\, \varphi]_s(\bar{u},\bar{v})$ is similar to that of a DTC-formula in (FO+DTC), except that now, in order to reach $\bar{v}$ from $\bar{u}$ via a deterministic φ-path, we may compose this path from φ-edges which connect points in $\mathrm{HF}_s(A)^k$ rather than A^k only. (Recall that $\mathrm{HF}_s(A)$ is the set of objects in $\mathrm{HF}(A)$ of size $\leq s$.) More precisely, consider a hereditarily finite extension $\mathcal{A}^+$ of some finite σ-structure $\mathcal{A}$ and interpretations $\bar{X} \in \mathrm{HF}(A)$ of the free variables in $[\mathrm{DTC}_{\bar{x},\bar{y}}\, \varphi]_s(\bar{u},\bar{v})$. Let R_s denote the restriction of $\varphi^{(\mathcal{A}^+,\bar{X})}$ to $\mathrm{HF}_s(A)$, where the $2k$-ary relation $\varphi^{(\mathcal{A}^+,\bar{X})}$ is the image of $(\mathcal{A}^+, \bar{X})$ under the global relation φ. By definition, $(\mathcal{A}^+, \bar{X}) \models [\mathrm{DTC}_{\bar{x},\bar{y}}\, \varphi]_s(\bar{u},\bar{v})$ iff $(\bar{u}^{(\mathcal{A}^+,\bar{X})}, \bar{v}^{(\mathcal{A}^+,\bar{X})}) \in DTC(R_s)$.

Definition 9. Let C be a class of finite σ-structures and let Π be a nullary program over $\Upsilon(\sigma, \{R\})$ that halts on all $\mathcal{A} \in C$. The *global relation computed by* Π *on* C, also denoted Π, maps every $\mathcal{A} \in C$ to the relation $\Pi^{\mathcal{A}} := R$, where (U, R) is the output of Π on input $\mathcal{A}$.   □

Lemma 10. *Every global relation computable by a nullary program is definable in* (FO+BS+DTC).

Lemma 11. *There is a class C of finite graphs and a nullary program Π so that the global relation computed by Π on C is not definable in* (FO+DTC).

Proof. (Sketch.) For every finite digraph $G = (V, E)$ let $2G := (2V, 2E)$ be its doubled version, where $2V := V \times \{0, 1\}$ and $2E := \{((a, i), (b, j)) : (a, b) \in E, 0 \le i, j \le 1\}$. Consider a graph G consisting of two disjoint (directed) cycles of the same even diameter. Suppose that in only one of the cycles there is a node labeled *start* and a node labeled *goal*. The distance between *start* and *goal* is maximal. Let C_1 be the collection of all $2G$. Now, modify G to G' by moving the label *goal* to the other cycle. Let C_2 be the collection of all $2G'$. There is a path from node $(start, 0)$ to node $(goal, 0)$ in every graph in C_1. No graph in C_2 has this property. Due to Immerman [Imm92] (see also [GM95]) there is no (FO+DTC)-sentence φ such that $2G \models \varphi$ for all $2G \in C_1$ and $2G' \not\models \varphi$ for all $2G' \in C_2$. Nevertheless, the nullary program Π displayed below accepts every graph in C_1 and rejects every graph in C_2. Hence, let $C := C_1 \cup C_2$.

$\Pi :=$ **if** *mode = initial* **then**
$\qquad\qquad$ *pebbles* := $\{(start, 0)\}_2$
$\qquad\qquad$ *mode* := *move_pebble*
$\qquad$ **if** *mode = move_pebble* **then**
$\qquad\qquad$ **if** $(goal, 0) \notin pebbles \land (start, 1) \notin pebbles$ **then**
$\qquad\qquad\qquad$ *pebbles* := $\{x \in Atoms : (\exists y \in pebbles)2E(y, x)\}_3$
$\qquad\qquad$ **if** $(goal, 0) \in pebbles$ **then** *Accept*
$\qquad\qquad$ **if** $(start, 1) \in pebbles$ **then** *Reject* $\qquad\qquad\qquad\qquad$ $\square$

The last two lemmas imply that (FO+BS+DTC) is more expressive than (FO+DTC). The next lemma shows that (FO+BS+DTC) is not too expressive.

Lemma 12. *Every nullary global relation definable by a sentence in the logic* (FO+BS+DTC) *is logspace computable.*

Logspace computability of every nullary program now follows by Lemma 10. The converse, i.e., that every logspace computable global relation is computable by a nullary program, does not hold in general (see Theorem 22). The situation changes if we restrict attention to ordered structures.

On ordered input structures.

Lemma 13. *Every logspace computable global relation on ordered structures can be computed by a nullary program.*

Proof. (Sketch.) Due to Fact 1 it suffices to show that every global relation definable in (FO+DTC) can be computed by a nullary program. We did most of the work in Example 7. By induction on the construction of a (FO+DTC)-formula $\varphi(\bar{x})$ one can define a nullary rule Π_φ which accepts an input $(\mathcal{A}, \bar{a})$ iff $\mathcal{A} \models \varphi[\bar{a}]$. The desired nullary program computing $\varphi^{\mathcal{A}}$ on input $\mathcal{A}$ then simply runs Π_φ for all possible $\bar{a} \in A^k$ and writes the accepted $\bar{a}$ into an output relation R. The details are left to the reader.   □

As pointed out in the discussion following Example 7, there is no obvious way to tell whether a given nullary program Π halts on all structures of a given class C. However, if the input is ordered then one can set up a counter (like *counter* in Example 7) that terminates Π once the maximal number of possible configurations of Π has been reached.

Lemma 14. *Every nullary program can be altered by a syntactic manipulation so that it halts on all ordered inputs and computes exactly the same output as the original program, whenever the latter halts.*

In the next section we will upgrade nullary programs to bounded memory programs. This will improve the handling of programs in practice as well as their expressive power (when no order is present).

5   Bounded Memory Programs

Nullary programs considered so far do not properly reflect two important properties of logspace computable functions, namely that such functions are closed under composition and 'distributed execution'. Nullary programs cannot simply be composed, because output relations must not occur in guards. But what do we mean with distributed execution? Consider, e.g., a logspace Turing machine $M(x)$ which takes (encodings of) finite structures as input together with a node x of the input structure as parameter. For two different nodes a and b of the input structure the computations of $M(a)$ and $M(b)$ do not interfere with each other. Thus, in order to compute $M(a)$ for every node a of the input structure, we may execute all the instances of $M(x)$ in parallel on distributed processors. This distributed execution is still in (sequential) logspace. We obtain the same result with a logspace Turing machine N that enumerates all nodes a in some order and simulates $M(x)$ with $x = a$.

We add both composition and distributed execution to nullary programs.

Definition 15. Let $\Upsilon^*(\sigma, \tau)$ denote a program vocabulary where σ and τ are not necessarily disjoint, i.e., where some relation symbols may be input and output at the same time. We define *distributed programs* over $\Upsilon^*(\sigma, \tau)$ inductively:

- Every nullary program is a distributed program.
- **Distributed execution:** Let $\bar{x}$ be a tuple of variables and let Π be a nullary rule all of whose free variables but none of whose bounded variables occur among $\bar{x}$. For each x_i in $\bar{x}$ choose a closed range term r_i, i.e., either a closed (FO+BS)-term over σ or a set symbol in σ^+. Let $\Pi_{\bar{x}}$ denote the result of replacing in Π every occurrence of a dynamic function f with the term $f(\bar{x})$. Then (do forall $\bar{x} \in \bar{r} \; \Pi_{\bar{x}}$) is a distributed program.

– **Guarded distributed execution:** Let $\bar{x}, \bar{r}$, and Π be as in the previous rule. In addition, let $\alpha_1, \ldots, \alpha_n$ be atomic FO-formulae over τ all of whose free variables occur among $\bar{x}$. Suppose that Π satisfies for each α_i, if $\alpha_i = R(\bar{t})$ and $R(\bar{t}')$ is an atomic subrule of Π then $\bar{t} = \bar{t}'$. (This ensures that all updates in Π of an output relation R occurring in some α_i affect only the tuple $\bar{t}$ specified by α_i.) Then the following is a distributed program:

```
do forall x̄ ∈ r̄
unless α₁ ∨ ... ∨ αₙ
    Πx̄
```

– If Π_0 and Π_1 are distributed programs, then $\Pi_0||\Pi_1$ is a distributed program.

(Observe that a distributed program obtained from a nullary rule Π by applying (guarded) distributed execution may have a different vocabulary than Π. This is because transforming Π to $\Pi_{\bar{x}}$ increases the arity of every dynamic function. Notice also that every distributed program has the form $\Pi_1||\ldots||\Pi_p$, where each Π_i is either a nullary program or a (guarded) distributed execution of a nullary rule. Since $||$ is associative and commutative, we can view every distributed program as a set of programs Π_i.)

Let $\Pi = \{\Pi_1, \ldots, \Pi_p\}$ be a distributed program over some vocabulary $\Upsilon^*(\sigma', \tau')$ and let σ and τ be disjoint finite relational vocabularies. A (σ, τ)-stratification of Π is a partition $(\Pi_1^*, \ldots, \Pi_q^*)$ of Π such that

– each Π_i^* is a distributed program over some vocabulary $\Upsilon^*(\sigma_i, \tau_i)$ where σ_i and τ_i are disjoint,
– $\sigma_i = \sigma \cup \tau_1 \cup \ldots \cup \tau_{i-1}$,
– $\tau \subseteq \tau_1 \cup \ldots \cup \tau_q$,
– if $\Pi_k \in \Pi_i^*$ is a guarded distributed execution then $\Pi_i^* = \{\Pi_k\}$.

A *bounded memory program* Π over (σ, τ) is a (σ, τ)-stratified distributed program $(\Pi_1^*, \ldots, \Pi_q^*)$. Each Π_i^* is called a *stratum* of Π. □

Let us first concentrate on bounded memory programs definable without using guarded distributed execution. One can show that every stratum Π_i^* of such a program is equivalent to a distributed program of the form (do forall $\bar{x} \in \bar{r}$ $\Pi_{\bar{x}}$), where $\Pi_{\bar{x}}$ was obtained from some nullary rule Π by replacing in Π every occurrence of a nullary dynamic function symbol f with the term $f(\bar{x})$ (proof omitted). We will often write $f_{\bar{x}}$ instead of $f(\bar{x})$ to indicate that f originated from a nullary function.

Informally, the semantics of a bounded memory program $\Pi = (\Pi_1^*, \ldots, \Pi_q^*)$ is the sequential execution of its strata. Stratum Π_{i+1}^* starts on the halting state of Π_i^* and uses, aside from the input structure, the output relations of all previous strata as input. To get an idea of the semantics of a single stratum Π_i^* assume that

```
Πᵢ* = do forall x ∈ rₓ, y ∈ r_y
          Πₓᵧ
```

The semantics of Π_i^* is the parallel execution of instances of Π_{xy}, where there is one instance Π_{XY} for each pair $(X, Y) \in r_x^{\mathcal{S}} \times r_y^{\mathcal{S}}$. That is, if Π_{XY} denotes the 'nullary program' Π_{xy}, where x and y are interpreted as the objects X and Y, respectively, then one step of Π_i^* can be thought of as one step of $\|_{X,Y} \Pi_{XY}$, where X varies in $r_x^{\mathcal{S}}$ and Y varies in $r_y^{\mathcal{S}}$. There is no direct interference between different instances of Π_{xy} because each instance Π_{XY} got its dynamic functions 'tagged' with X, Y. Π_i^* halts when either all instances halt or one instance produces an inconsistency.

To define the semantics of bounded memory programs formally, we first define the semantics of distributed programs. Suppose that Π is a distributed program over $\Upsilon^*(\sigma, \tau)$, where $\Upsilon^*(\sigma, \tau)$ may now contain dynamic function symbols of arity > 0. As in the case of nullary programs, a state $\mathcal{S}$ of Π is a $\Upsilon^*(\sigma, \tau)$-structure with universe $\mathrm{HF}(A)$ for some finite set A of atoms. The sequel $\Pi(\mathcal{S})$ of $\mathcal{S}$ with respect to Π is defined as usual (see [Gur97]). The only new case is when Π was obtained by means of guarded distributed execution.

$$
\begin{pmatrix}
\texttt{do forall } \bar{x} \in \bar{r} \\
\texttt{unless } \varphi \\
\Pi_{\bar{x}}
\end{pmatrix} (\mathcal{S}) \quad := \quad
\begin{pmatrix}
\texttt{do forall } \bar{x} \in \bar{r} \\
\texttt{if } \neg\varphi \texttt{ then} \\
\Pi_{\bar{x}}
\end{pmatrix} (\mathcal{S})
$$

Now consider a bounded memory program $\Pi = (\Pi_1^*, \ldots, \Pi_q^*)$ over (σ, τ), where $\Pi_1^* \cup \ldots \cup \Pi_q^*$ is a distributed program over $\Upsilon^*(\sigma', \tau')$. Like a nullary program, Π takes a finite σ-structure as input and, in case it halts, yields a finite τ-structure as output. W.l.o.g., we can assume that $\sigma \subseteq \sigma'$ (since any $R \in \sigma - \sigma'$ does not appear in Π). In the initial state $\mathcal{S}(\mathcal{A})$ of Π on an input $\mathcal{A}$ all symbols in $\sigma' - \sigma$ are considered to be output symbols. Hence, $\mathcal{S}(\mathcal{A})$ is a $\Upsilon^*(\sigma, \tau' - \sigma)$-structure and is defined as in Definition 2. In order to define the run of Π on $\mathcal{A}$, let us first consider the case $q = 2$, i.e., $\Pi = (\Pi_1^*, \Pi_2^*)$. For simplicity, let us also assume that no dynamic function of stratum Π_1^* occurs in stratum Π_2^*, and vice versa. (This can be achieved by renaming dynamic functions in a suitable way.) The *run of* (Π_1^*, Π_2^*) *on* $\mathcal{A}$ is either

- the infinite run of Π_1 on $\mathcal{S}(\mathcal{A})$, or otherwise
- the composed run $\mathcal{S}_0, \mathcal{S}_1, \ldots, \mathcal{S}_k, \mathcal{S}_{k+1}, \ldots$, where $\mathcal{S}_0, \mathcal{S}_1, \ldots, \mathcal{S}_k$ is the finite run of Π_1 on $\mathcal{S}_0 := \mathcal{S}(\mathcal{A})$, and $\mathcal{S}_k, \mathcal{S}_{k+1}, \ldots$ is the run of Π_2 on $\mathcal{S}_k$.

This generalizes to the case $q > 2$ in the obvious way. If the run of Π on $\mathcal{A}$ is finite, then the output of Π is defined as for nullary programs.

Lemma 16. *The class of partial functions computed by bounded memory programs is closed under composition.*

Why use guarded distributed quantification? In the introduction we formulated four necessary conditions for reductions among structures. One of them was that on unordered structures our reductions should have at least the power of (FO+DTC)-interpretations. The question is whether we can compute any (FO+DTC)-definable global relation on unordered structures with a bounded memory program. Recall Example 7 and the subsequent discussion concerning the two shortcomings of nullary programs on unordered structures, namely the problems of *termination* and *systematic search*. We already fixed the problem of systematic search by adding `do-forall` to nullary programs. For example, the following bounded memory program (resembling Π in Example 7) computes $DTC(E)$ on unordered graphs (V, E), although it may not terminate.

$$\Pi_{DTC} := \text{do forall } x \in V$$
$$\quad \text{if } mode_x = initial \text{ then}$$
$$\quad\quad pebble_x := x$$
$$\quad\quad mode_x := move\_pebble$$
$$\quad \text{if } mode_x = move\_pebble \land pebble_x \neq \varnothing \text{ then}$$
$$\quad\quad DTC(x, pebble_x)$$
$$\quad\quad pebble_x := succ(pebble_x)$$

Observe that an instance of the nullary body of Π_{DTC} may run into a cycle, thus prevent Π_{DTC} from halting. It is still not clear how to ensure termination without counting configurations.

Let us modify Π_{DTC} a little bit. The resulting program $\bar{\Pi}_{DTC}$ (see below) is a bounded memory program which uses guarded distributed execution to detect and terminate every instance of the nullary body of Π_{DTC} that 'hangs' in a cycle. In particular, $\bar{\Pi}_{DTC}$ halts on all inputs. We assume that *Cycle* is a new unary output relation.

$$\bar{\Pi}_{DTC} := \text{do forall } x \in V, y \in V$$
$$\quad \text{unless } Cycle(x)$$
$$\quad\quad \text{if } mode_{xy} = initial \text{ then}$$
$$\quad\quad\quad pebble_{xy} := x$$
$$\quad\quad\quad mode_{xy} := move\_pebble$$
$$\quad\quad \text{if } mode_{xy} = move\_pebble \land pebble_{xy} \neq \varnothing \text{ then}$$
$$\quad\quad\quad DTC(x, pebble_{xy})$$
$$\quad\quad\quad pebble_{xy} := succ(pebble_{xy})$$
$$\quad\quad \text{if } pebble_{xy} = y \land \neg reached_{xy} \text{ then } reached_{xy} := true$$
$$\quad\quad \text{if } pebble_{xy} = y \land \ reached_{xy} \text{ then } Cycle(x)$$

Let Π_{xy} denote the nullary body of $\bar{\Pi}_{DTC}$. The new guard "`unless` $Cycle(x)$" for Π_{xy} in $\bar{\Pi}_{DTC}$ ensures that only those instances of Π_{xy} contribute in the next computation step, for which $Cycle(x)$ does **not** hold. All other instances of Π_{xy} are *disabled*. Here is the idea behind $\bar{\Pi}_{DTC}$. Fix a node $a \in V$ and concentrate on the deterministic E-path starting at a. We run Π_{ab} for every node $b \in V$ in parallel. Each b can be seen as a probe. When $pebble_{ab}$ is placed on b the first time, we set a dynamic function $reached_{ab}$ to *true*, indicating that b has been touched once. If b is pebbled a second time we know that the deterministic path starting at a leads to a cycle through b. In that case there will be no further new output to $DTC(a, y)$, so that we can stop all Π_{ac} whose first subscript a is the same as that of Π_{ab}, which detects the cycle. As a stop signal for each Π_{ac} we set $Cycle(a)$ to *true*. On the other hand, if there is no b such that Π_{ab} places $pebble_{ab}$ on b twice, then the deterministic path starting at a does not lead to a cycle. All Π_{ac} will come to a halt simultaneously when the path ends.

The cycle detection technique described above is also the main crux in the proof of the following lemma.

Lemma 17. *Every global relation definable in* (FO+DTC) *is computable by a bounded memory program.*

6   Choiceless Logspace

In this section we define Choiceless Logarithmic Space ($\tilde{\text{C}}$LOGSPACE) as the class of graph properties decidable by means of bounded memory programs. $\tilde{\text{C}}$LOGSPACE is a fragment of all logspace computable graph properties and can be seen as the LOGSPACE counterpart of Choiceless Polynomial Time ($\tilde{\text{C}}$PTIME), the choiceless fragment of all polynomial-time computable graph properties. $\tilde{\text{C}}$PTIME was recently defined by Blass, Gurevich, and Shelah [BGS97] using polynomial-time bounded ASM-programs. Our programs are 'choiceless' in the sense that they can form and handle bounded sets of objects (like nodes in an input graph) without ever actually choosing one particular element of a set. Essentially this capability makes bounded memory programs more expressive than the logic (FO+DTC) (cf. the proof of Lemma 11). We conclude the section with the observation that bounded memory programs are not as powerful as the polynomial-time bounded programs of [BGS97]. This separates PTIME and LOGSPACE on the choiceless level.

There are two points to clarify in order to make the upcoming definition of $\tilde{\text{C}}$LOGSPACE reasonable:

- $\tilde{\text{C}}$LOGSPACE is supposed to be fragment of LOGSPACE. Thus we have to show that every bounded memory program actually is logspace computable.
- We cannot simply define $\tilde{\text{C}}$LOGSPACE by means of *all* bounded memory programs (which use, e.g., a Boolean output constants *Accept* to indicate acceptance), since some of these programs may not halt on all inputs and thus do not decide their input. The question is (still) how to ensure termination of bounded memory programs?

We will first solve the problem of termination by describing a syntactic manipulation of arbitrary bounded memory programs, so that the resulting "standard" bounded memory programs halt on all inputs.

Termination of bounded memory programs. We lift the cycle-detection construction leading from Π_{DTC} to $\bar{\Pi}_{DTC}$ in the previous section to arbitrary strata of the form

$$\Pi^* := \texttt{do forall } \bar{x} \in \bar{r}$$
$$\texttt{unless } \varphi$$
$$\Pi_{\bar{x}}$$

where $\Pi_{\bar{x}}$ was obtained from some nullary rule Π. (On can show that every stratum of a bounded memory program can be replaced with a stratum of that form.) Let $f_1, \ldots, f_d$ be an enumeration of the dynamic functions in Π. Consider an instance $\Pi_{\bar{X}}$ of $\Pi_{\bar{x}}$. The sequel of a state $(\mathcal{S}, \bar{X})$ of $\Pi_{\bar{X}}$ is entirely determined by the input embedded in $\mathcal{S}$ and the *dynamic part* $f_1^{\mathcal{S}}(\bar{X}), \ldots, f_d^{\mathcal{S}}(\bar{X})$ of $(\mathcal{S}, \bar{X})$. We can detect a cycle in the computation of $\Pi_{\bar{X}}$ if we run $\Pi_{\bar{X}}$ in parallel for every possible dynamic part, and stop the computation once we pass the same dynamic part twice. That is, for all possible values $Y_1, \ldots, Y_d$ of $f_1^{\mathcal{S}}(\bar{X}), \ldots, f_d^{\mathcal{S}}(\bar{X})$ in all possible states of $\Pi_{\bar{X}}$ we run an instance of $\Pi_{\bar{X}, y_1, \ldots, y_d}$ in parallel. ($\Pi_{\bar{x}, y_1, \ldots, y_d}$ is obtained from $\Pi_{\bar{x}}$ by replacing every occurrence of a $f_i(\bar{x})$ with $f_i(\bar{x}, y_1, \ldots, y_d)$.) If one of these instances, say, $\Pi_{\bar{X}, Y_1, \ldots, Y_d}$, finds for the second time that the current values of $f_1, \ldots, f_d$ match its private values $Y_1, \ldots, Y_d$, then $\Pi_{\bar{X}, Y_1, \ldots, Y_d}$ may stop all other instances of $\Pi_{\bar{X}, y_1, \ldots, y_d}$. Here is the standard form of stratum Π^* that detects repeating configurations and thus terminates on all inputs:

$$\bar{\Pi}^* := \textbf{do forall } \bar{x} \in \bar{r}, y_1, \ldots, y_d \in t$$
$$\quad \textbf{unless } \varphi \vee Cycle(\bar{x})$$
$$\quad \quad \Pi_{\bar{x}\bar{y}}$$
$$\quad \quad \textbf{if } \bigwedge_i f_{i\bar{x}\bar{y}} = y_i \wedge \neg reached_{\bar{x}\bar{y}} \textbf{ then } reached_{\bar{x}\bar{y}} := true$$
$$\quad \quad \textbf{if } \bigwedge_i f_{i\bar{x}\bar{y}} = y_i \wedge \ reached_{\bar{x}\bar{y}} \textbf{ then } Cycle(\bar{x})$$

where the range term t is such that $f_1^{\mathcal{S}}(\bar{X}), \ldots, f_d^{\mathcal{S}}(\bar{X}) \in t^{\mathcal{S}}$ for all possible states $(\mathcal{S}, \bar{X})$ of $\Pi_{\bar{X}}$ (on any input).

Unfortunately, we may not be able to find such a range term t for every stratum Π^*. This is because the range of a dynamic function f_i can in general be any subset of $\mathrm{HF}_s(A)$, where $s \geq 1$ is the maximum of all explicit size bounds of set terms occurring in Π^*. For instance, the range of f_i might be $\{\{a\} : a \in A\} \subseteq \mathrm{HF}_2(A)$ and it is easy to see that there is no (FO+BS)-term denoting (a superset of) $\{\{a\} : a \in A\}$. The next lemma provides a way out of this dilemma.

Lemma 18. *For every $s \geq 1$ there exist* (FO+BS)-*terms* $object_s(x, y_1, \ldots, y_s)$ *and* $Forms_s$ *over* $\{\varnothing\}$ *such that for every state $\mathcal{S}$ with universe* $\mathrm{HF}(A)$, $\mathrm{HF}_s(A) = \{object_s(F, \bar{m})^{\mathcal{S}} : F \in Forms_s^{\mathcal{S}}, \bar{m} \in A^s\}$.

Proceeding toward a standard form of stratum Π^* that does not depend on the existence of a range term t, modify the definition of $\bar{\Pi}^*$ as follows: (1) Replace "$y_1, \ldots, y_d \in t$" with "$F_1, \ldots, F_d \in Forms_s, \bar{m}_1, \ldots, \bar{m}_d \in Atoms$", where each F_i is a new variable and each $\bar{m}_i$ is a tuple of s new variables. (2) Replace "$\bigwedge_i f_{i\bar{x}\bar{y}} = y_i$" with "$\bigwedge_i f_{i\bar{x}\bar{y}} = object_s(F_i, \bar{m}_i)$", where $\bar{y}$ now abbreviates the tuple $F_1, \ldots, F_d, \bar{m}_1, \ldots, \bar{m}_d$ of variables. The newly defined $\bar{\Pi}^*$ halts on all inputs and computes the same output as Π^*.

Lemma 19. *Every bounded memory program can be altered by a syntactic manipulation so that it halts on all inputs and computes exactly the same output as the original program, whenever the latter halts.*

Using Lemma 18 we can also show the next theorem, which in turn implies logspace computability of bounded memory programs (recall Lemma 12).

Theorem 20. *A nullary global relation is definable by a sentence in the logic* (FO+BS+DTC) *iff it is computable by a bounded memory program.*

Choiceless Logarithmic Space. We call bounded memory programs altered according to Lemma 19 *standard*. A *bounded memory acceptor* Π is a standard bounded memory program over $(\sigma, \{Accept\})$. Π *accepts* a finite σ-structure $\mathcal{A}$ if Π outputs *Accept* on input $\mathcal{A}$. Otherwise Π *rejects* $\mathcal{A}$.

Definition 21. A class C of finite σ-structures is in $\tilde{\text{C}}$LOGSPACE iff it is closed under isomorphisms and there exists a bounded memory acceptor Π such that Π accepts every structure in C and rejects every finite σ-structure not in C. $\square$

The following theorem summarizes our main results of last three sections (taking into account the main result of [BGS97]).

Theorem 22. (FO+DTC) $\subsetneq$ (FO+BS+DTC) = $\tilde{\text{C}}$LOGSPACE $\subsetneq$ LOGSPACE.

We conclude this section by showing that the same problem which separates $\tilde{\text{C}}$PTIME and (FO+LFP) also separates $\tilde{\text{C}}$PTIME and $\tilde{\text{C}}$LOGSPACE. This problem, which we call SMALL SUBSET PARITY, is the following one. Given a finite structure $\mathcal{A} = (A, S)$ with S a subset of A such that $|S|! \leq |A|$, decide whether $|S|$ is even. It is easy to see that SMALL SUBSET PARITY is in $\tilde{\text{C}}$PTIME [BGS97]. Here we prove that SMALL SUBSET PARITY is not in $\tilde{\text{C}}$LOGSPACE, implying that $\tilde{\text{C}}$LOGSPACE is a proper subclass of $\tilde{\text{C}}$PTIME.

First, let us recall some definitions from [BGS97]. Consider a finite relational σ-structure $\mathcal{A}$ whose universe A consists of atoms.

- A set X of atoms is called a *support* of an object $Y \in \text{HF}(A)$, if every automorphism of $\mathcal{A}$ that pointwise fixes X also fixes Y. For example, $A_Y :=$ $A \cap \text{TC}(Y)$ is the *trivial support* of Y.
- Let $k \geq 1$ be a natural number. Call an object $Y \in \text{HF}(A)$ k-*symmetric*, if every $Z \in \text{TC}(Y)$ has a support of cardinality $\leq k$. Obviously, any Y is $|A_Y|$-symmetric.
- Let $\bar{\mathcal{A}}$ denote the $(\sigma \cup \{\in, \varnothing\})$-reduct of $\mathcal{A}^+$ (see Definition 8) and $\bar{\mathcal{A}}_k$ the restriction of $\bar{\mathcal{A}}$ to all k-symmetric objects.

Suppose that σ contains only unary relation symbols, say, $P_1, \dots, P_c$. A finite σ-structure $\mathcal{A}$ is called a *colored set*, if the colors $P_1, \dots, P_c$ partition the universe of $\mathcal{A}$.

Fact 23 ([BGS97]). *Fix some positive integers c, k, m. If $\mathcal{A}$ and $\mathcal{B}$ are colored sets, in each of which all the colors $P_1, \dots, P_c$ are sufficiently large, then $\bar{\mathcal{A}}_k$ and $\bar{\mathcal{B}}_k$ are $L^m_{\infty,\omega}$-equivalent.*

Corollary 24. SMALL SUBSET PARITY $\notin \tilde{\text{C}}$LOGSPACE.

Proof. (Sketch.) Towards a contradiction assume that there is a sentence φ in (FO+BS+DTC) over vocabulary $\{S\}$ which defines SMALL SUBSET PARITY. That is, for every finite structure $\mathcal{A} = (A, S)$ satisfying $|S|! \leq |A|$, $\mathcal{A}^+ \models \varphi$ iff $|S|$ is even. From φ we can extract a size bound s, such that the above relation still holds if we restrict $\mathcal{A}^+$ to any $U \supseteq \text{HF}_s(A)$. φ can be translated into an equivalent $L^m_{\infty,\omega}$-sentence φ' over $\{S, \in \varnothing\}$ (for some m) by unfolding DTC-subformulae. If $|S|! \leq |A|$ and $U \supseteq HF_s(A)$, then $(U, S, \in, \varnothing) \models \varphi'$ iff $|S|$ is even. Now choose a positive instance $\mathcal{A}$ and a negative instance $\mathcal{B}$ of SMALL SUBSET PARITY, in each of which the colors S and S^C (the complement of S) are so large, such that $\bar{\mathcal{A}}_s$ and $\bar{\mathcal{B}}_s$ are $L^m_{\infty,\omega}$-equivalent. Since for every object $Y \in HF_s(A)$ the trivial support A_Y has cardinality at most s, every such Y is s-symmetric. Hence, $HF_s(A)$ is a subset of the set of all s-symmetric objects and $\bar{\mathcal{A}}_s \models \varphi'$. A similar argument shows $\bar{\mathcal{B}}_s \not\models \varphi'$. But this contradicts $\varphi' \in L^m_{\infty,\omega}$.   □

Acknowledgements. We are grateful to Andreas Blass, Yuri Gurevich and Eric Rosen for numerous discussions and suggestions. In particular Yuri suggested the development of a logspace reduction theory among structures and proposed nullary ASM-programs as an initial model. Yuri's persistent propaganda for the ASM-model kept our interest alive.

References

[AHV95]   S. Abiteboul, R. Hull, and V. Vianu. *Foundations of Databases*. Addision-Wesley, 1995.

[BGS97]   A. Blass, Y. Gurevich, and S. Shelah. Choiceless Polynomial Time. Technical Report CSE-TR-338-97, University of Michigan, May 1997.

[BH98]   E. Börger and J. Huggins. Abstract State Machines 1988–1998: Commented ASM Bibliography. *Bulletin of the EATCS*, 64:105–127, February 1998.

[CH82]   A. Chandra and D. Harel. Structure and Compexity of Relational Queries. *Journal of Computer and System Sciences*, 25:99–128, 1982.

[EF95]   H. D. Ebbinghaus and J. Flum. *Finite Model Theory*. Springer-Verlag, 1995.

[GHR95]   R. Greenlaw, H. J. Hoover, and W. L. Ruzzo. *Limits to Parallel Computation – P-Completeness Theory*. Oxford University Press, 1995.

[GM95]   E. Grädel and G. McColm. On the Power of Deterministic Transitive Closures. *Information and Computation*, 119:129–135, 1995. See also: Deterministic versus Nondeterministic Transitive Closure Logic, in *Proceedings of 7th IEEE Symposium on Logic in Computer Science (LICS '92)*, 58–63.

[Gur88]   Y. Gurevich. Logic and the Challenge of Computer Science. In E. Börger, editor, *Current Trends in Theoretical Computer Science*, pages 1–57. Computer Science Press, 1988.

[Gur91]   Y. Gurevich. Evolving Algebras: An attempt to discover semantics. *Bulletin of the EATCS*, 43:264–284, 1991. a slightly revised version in G. Rozenberg and A. Salomaa, editors, *Current Trends in Theoretical Computer Science*, pages 266–292, World Scientific, 1993.

[Gur95]   Y. Gurevich. Evolving Algebras 1993: Lipari Guide. In E. Börger, editor, *Specification and Validation Methods*, pages 9–36. Oxford University Press, 1995.

[Gur97]   Y. Gurevich. May 1997 Draft of the ASM Guide. Technical Report CSE-TR-336-97, University of Michigan, May 1997.

[Hod93]   W. Hodges. *Model Theory*. Cambridge University Press, 1993.

[Imm87]   N. Immerman. Languages that capture complexity classes. *SIAM Journal of Computing*, 16:760–778, 1987.

[Imm92]   N. Immerman. Personal communication, 1992.

[Pap94]   C. H. Papadimitriou. *Computational Complexity*. Addison-Wesley Publishing Company, 1994.

Formal Methods for Extensions to CAS

Martin N. Dunstan*, Tom Kelsey, Ursula Martin, and Steve Linton

Division of Computer Science,
University of St Andrews,
North Haugh, St Andrews, UK
{mnd,tom,um,sal}@dcs.st-and.ac.uk

Abstract. We demonstrate the use of formal methods tools to provide a semantics for the type hierarchy of the AXIOM computer algebra system, and a methodology for Aldor program analysis and verification. We give a case study of abstract specifications of AXIOM primitives, and provide an interface between these abstractions and Aldor code.

1 Introduction

In this paper we report on the status of our work at St Andrews on the application of formal methods and machine assisted theorem proving techniques to improve the robustness and reliability of computer algebra systems (CAS). We present a case study which demonstrates the use of formal methods for extending existing CAS code. This paper is an extension of the work described in [9]. We have adopted the Larch [16] system of formal methods languages and tools, and applied them to the AXIOM [19] computer algebra system. NAG Ltd, who develop AXIOM and partially fund this project, are optimistic that our formal methods approach will aid system users.

We have constructed a formal model of the AXIOM algebraic category hierarchy, and developed a methodology for formally verifying type assertions contained in the AXIOM library. We have also created a Larch behavioural interface specification language (BISL) called Larch/Aldor and a prototype verification condition generator for the AXIOM compiled language, Aldor (see Section 2.4). This work enables interface specifications (also known as annotations) to be added to Aldor programs. These can be used for

- clear, concise, unambiguous and machine checkable documentation.
- lightweight verification (described in more detail in Section 3): helps users to identify mistakes in programs which compilers are unable to detect.
- compiler optimisations: specifications could be used to select between different function implementations, as described in [29].
- method selection: users could interrogate libraries for functions which perform a particular task under specific conditions, as described in [31].

---

* Funded by NAG Ltd

J. Wing, J. Woodcock, J. Davies (Eds.): FM'99, Vol. II, LNCS 1709, pp. 1758–1777, 1999.
© Springer-Verlag Berlin Heidelberg 1999

Although we have chosen to follow the Larch methodology which is based on a two-tiered specification system, we do not preclude the use of other formal methods such as VDM [20], or Z [27]. Other proof tools, especially those with higher order functionality such as PVS [25] or HOL [14], could be used. Nor do we rule out the application to other CAS such as Maple [4] and Mathematica [32]; in fact the weaker type systems of these and other CAS may benefit more from our approach than AXIOM has. Our approach is to use an automated theorem prover as a tool for debugging formal specifications used in the design and implementation of libraries for CAS. Our goal is to increase the robustness of CAS.

In the rest of this introduction we motivate our work and discuss the uses of verification conditions (VC's) generated from annotations. In Section 2 we introduce Larch and its algebraic specification language LSL. Then in Section 2.2 we explain how proofs of LSL specifications can be used to investigate claims made in the documentation of AXIOM categories and domains. This is followed by Sections 2.3 and 2.4 which describe Larch BISL's, with particular reference to Larch/Aldor. In Section 3 we describe the application of our technique of specification lightweight verification and condition generation to CAS in general, and to AXIOM in particular. Section 4 is a case study concerning AXIOM complex numbers, which illustrates how incorrect behaviour within AXIOM can be corrected both by abstract specification and the use of annotations. The final section is an outline of our conclusions and related work.

1.1   Motivation

Computer algebra systems are environments for symbolic calculation, which provide packages for the manipulation of expressions involving symbols. These symbols may, at some point, be assigned concrete numeric values. General purpose computer algebra systems, such as AXIOM [19], Maple [4], or Mathematica [32], as well as more specialised tools such as GAP [12] for computational discrete mathematics or the AXIOM/PoSSo library for high-performance polynomial system solving, are used by many different communities of users including educators, engineers, and researchers in both science and mathematics. The specialised systems in particular are extremely powerful. The PoSSo library has been used to compute a single Gröbner basis, used to obtain a solution of a non-linear system, which (compressed) occupies more than 5GB of disk space, while GAP is routinely used to compute with groups of permutations on millions of points.

After pioneering work in the 1960s CAS have become mainstream commercial products: everyday tools not only for researchers but also for engineers and scientists. For example Aerospatiale use a Maple-based system for motion planning in satellite control. The systems have become more complicated, providing languages, graphics, programming environments and diverse sophisticated algorithms for integration, factorisation and so on, to meet the needs of a variety of users, many not expert in mathematics. All the usual software engineering issues arise, such as modularity, re-use, interworking and HCI. NAG's AXIOM [19] is a sophisticated, strongly typed CAS: user and system libraries are written in the Aldor language which supports a hierarchy of built-in parameterised types and algorithms for mathematical objects such as rings, fields and polynomials. Aldor is interpreted in the AXIOM kernel which provides basic routines such as simplification and evaluation: code developed in Aldor may also be compiled to C for export to other products. Because such systems are large and complicated (and the algorithms are often developed by domain experts with considerable specialist knowledge) a body of library material has accrued, much of which is widely used even if not necessarily well documented or even entirely understood. For example, it may be known to experts that a certain routine is correct if the input is a continuous function, but because continuity is undecidable this may never be checked at run-time, and it may not even be noted in any obvious way in the documentation, so that an inexpert user may easily make mistakes.

AXIOM/Aldor users can be grouped into three types:

- command line users, who have access to a comprehensive graphical hypertext system of examples and documentation
- system developers, who may be expected to know about any pitfalls involving the libraries
- library developers (writing Aldor programs), who need more support than the description of routines in isolation, and who may be unaware of the subtle dependencies and conditions contained in the AXIOM type system.

Our project aims to improve the provision of support for this third group of users. It also encourages the reuse of software by providing unambiguous documentation for functions. We do not address the accuracy of the results of procedures; computer algebra algorithms have been developed by experts and are generally sound when applied correctly. However there can be hidden dependencies and implicit side conditions present which can lead to erroneous or misinterpreted results. Examples include inconsistent choice of branch cuts in integration algorithms [7], invalid assumptions for the types of arguments of a function or poorly documented side-conditions. Moreover CAS often contain several procedures which perform the same task, but which are optimised for a particular input domain. It is often not easy to select the best procedure without either a detailed knowledge of the system or a lengthy perusal of the documentation.

1.2   Using Verification Conditions

Part of our work is concerned with the generation of verification conditions (VC's) from Aldor programs which have been annotated with Larch/Aldor specifications. VC's are logical statements that describe the conditions under which a program satisfies its specification; they may be created during attempts of correctness proofs (see Section 3.1). However, once VC's have been generated one might ask what can we do with them? Ideally we would attempt to prove or disprove them but in practice this may be infeasible. For example, the GAP4 CAS [12] contains a small module which would generate an apparently simple verification condition. However, the proof of this VC relies on the "Odd Order

Theorem" whose proof occupied an entire 255 page issue of the Pacific Journal of Mathematics [11]. Other examples might include statements about continuity of mathematical functions or computational geometry. Generating verification conditions by hand is tedious even for tiny programs and so a mechanical program would normally be used. Once the verification conditions have been generated there are several options:

- trivial VC's might be automatically discharged by the generator
- theorem provers or proof assistants might be utilised
- hand-proofs might be attempted
- the user may appeal to their specialist knowledge or authoritative sources
- VC's may be ignored unless they are obviously unsatisfiable
- VC's can be noted in the documentation as extra requirements

We believe that our suggestion that the user may wish to ignore VC's unless they are clearly invalid is justified because obvious mistakes can sometimes be detected more quickly by inspection than by attempting to formally prove/disprove them. For example the VC

$$(\tan x) \; \textit{is-continuous-on} \; (0, \pi)$$

is clearly false and this can be easily seen from the graph of $\tan x$ over the specified interval $(0, \pi)$. However, attempting to show that this is false within a theorem prover is very difficult, requiring a model of the real numbers which is a topic of active research [17, 18].

Proof attempts which fail to show whether a VC is valid or invalid may indicate that the program annotations and/or the background theory needs to be extended. VC's which are found to be invalid mean that there is a mistake, probably in the program or the annotations but possibly in the theory used during the proof. If all VC's can be proved then the program satisfies its specification and the user will have increased confidence that it will behave as expected.

2   Specification and the Larch Approach

In this section we describe the languages and tools which comprise the Larch formal specification system, and propose a methodology for using Larch to specify AXIOM and Aldor components. Examples of specifications which relate directly to the AXIOM/Aldor CAS are provided.

Larch [16] is based on a two-tiered system. In the first tier users write algebraic specifications in a programming-language independent algebraic specification language called the Larch Shared Language (LSL). These specifications provide the background theory for the problem domain and allow the investigation of design options. The second tier consists of a family of behavioural interface specification languages (BISL's), each tailored to a particular programming language. User programs are annotated in the BISL of their choice. BISL specifications are primarily concerned with implementation details such as side-conditions on functions, memory allocation and pointer dereferencing. The Larch philosophy is to do as much work as possible at the LSL level, leaving implementation-specific details to be described using the BISL. This allows BISL specifications to be both concise and unambiguous.

2.1   The Larch Shared Language

The LSL tier allows the user to define operators and sorts (types) which provide semantics for terms appearing in the BISL annotations. The basic unit of LSL specification is a trait. The following example provides a basic abstraction of complex numbers (providing a constructor of ordered pairs from a commutative ring, and observers for the real and imaginary parts of a complex entity) which will be used in the case study:

```
RequirementsForComplex (CR) : trait
  assumes CommRingCat (CR)
  introduces
    complex : CR,CR → T
    imag, real : T → CR
  asserts
    T partitioned by real, imag
    T generated by complex
    ∀ x,y : CR
      complex(x,y) = complex(u,v) ⇒ x = u ∧ y = v;
      imag(complex(x,y)) == y;
      real(complex(x,y)) == x;
  implies
    ∀ z : T
      z == complex(real(z),imag(z))
```

The sections of the trait have the following meanings:

- assumes—textually include other traits (with renaming)
- introduces—declare new mix-fix operators
- asserts—define a set of axioms
- implies—statements implied by the axioms of this trait

The trait defines values of sort T, and is parameterized by the sort name CR. The partitioned by clause states that all distinct values of sort T can be distinguished using real and imag. The generated by clause states that all T values can be obtained using complex. What it means to be a value of sort CR is defined in the assumed trait CommRingCat. This assumption generates a proof obligation: any supplied argument must be shown to satisfy the axioms of a commutative ring (the LSL includes command is used to inherit properties without justification). LATEX is used for graphical symbols/operators, e.g. ∀ is written \forall. The first assertion formalises equality for complex values; the reverse implication is automatically true, since LSL operators always return equal results for equal arguments. The remaining assertions provide straightforward semantics for the observers in terms of the constructor. The `implies` section is used as checkable redundancy; proving the statements provides confidence that the axioms defined are specified correctly. Failed proof attempts may indicate the presence of errors or omissions in the original traits. This section can also provide extra information and lemmas which might not be obvious from the rest of the trait, but are useful properties for another trait to inherit.

A tool called `lsl` can be used to perform syntax and type checking of LSL specifications. It can also convert LSL specifications into the object language of the Larch Prover (LP), a proof assistant for a many-sorted first order logic with induction which can be used to check properties of LSL specifications.

2.2   Specifying AXIOM Using LSL and LP

The specification of AXIOM categories in LSL was described in [9]. The next stage is to specify AXIOM functors and debug these specifications using the Larch Prover. The resulting abstract specifications provide concrete definitions of the primitives which are used in interface specifications (annotations) to produce verification conditions.

An AXIOM category is a set of operator names, signatures and methods which provide an abstract framework for the definition of computer algebra types. A category will, in general, have many models; each implemented model is an AXIOM domain. For example, the AXIOM domains `Matrix Integer` and `Polynomial Integer` are both implementations of the AXIOM category `Ring`. We say that these domains have type `Ring`; their basic operators were defined in the `Ring` category.

AXIOM domains are constructed by functors. These take domains as argument, and return a domain as output. In the above examples `Matrix` and `Polynomial` are the functors, each taking the domain `Integer` as argument. AXIOM assigns a type to each domain returned by a functor. This assignment follows informal inbuilt rules which are not always valid. Thus AXIOM can assign an incorrect type to a functor, and hence obtain incorrect results. We give an example of this incorrect typing behaviour in our case study: AXIOM axioms asserts that a domain with non-zero zero divisors is a field. Prior to our work, the only method of checking the correctness of these assignments was experimentation with AXIOM code in conjunction with detailed examination of AXIOM documentation. This method is unsatisfactory: even if each existing AXIOM domain is tested, there remains the problem of testing domains not yet implemented.

Our approach is to provide a generic methodology, applicable both to existing and potential implementations. We supply LSL specifications of functors which allow us to formally verify that a given implementation is a model of the categories which define the type of a resulting domain. These proofs can be thought of as providing enhanced type-checking. Proof obligations are obtained by adding the clause

```
implies TypeTrait(Sortname, Opnames for names)
```

to the functor trait, where `TypeTrait` is a trait representing an AXIOM category, `Sortname` is the sort name for the domain produced by the functor, and `Opnames for names` replaces high level operator names with appropriate implementation level operator names.

The specifications also allow formal checks that implementations of operators act as expected in the model. For example we can check that abstract algebraic properties hold at the domain level, or that the implementation operators combine together in a satisfactory manner. Moreover an LSL clause of the form `assumes CategoryName(CN)` generates a proof obligation that a specification of an argument domain (with sort name `CN)`) is a model of the specification of `CategoryName`. Hence we can verify that argument domains are of the intended type. Examples of enhanced type-checking, operator suitability proofs, and argument correctness verification are given in Section 4.1

2.3 Larch BISL's

Once the necessary theories have been defined in LSL (and checked with LP), the user can proceed to write their program. In the ideal world implementations would be developed in conjunction with the annotations but in the case of legacy systems this may not be possible. For such systems specifying their behaviour as it has been implemented may be the only option, at least as the first step.

To date there are around 14 different Larch BISL'S for languages ranging from CLU [30] and Modula-3 [21] to C [16] and C++ [23]. Each has been designed to investigate various aspects of imperative programming such as inheritance [23] and concurrency [21] as well as different development methodologies such as specification browsing [5] and interactive program verification [15]. The syntax and use of BISL specifications is essentially the same in all languages. Functions and procedures can be annotated with statements defining their pre- and post-conditions as well as indicating any client-visible state which *might* be modified when the function is executed.

Below is a simple example of an annotated Aldor function declaration for `iqsrt` which computes the integer square root of a positive number:

```
++} requires  ¬ (x < 0);
++} ensures  (r*r ≤ x) ∧ (x < (r+1)*(r+1));
++} modifies nothing;
iqsrt(x:Integer):(r:Integer);
```

Annotations are embedded in the program source code and appear as special comments marked by lines beginning with "++}". In the example above the **requires** clause defines the pre-condition of the function and states that the argument must be a non-negative integer. The **ensures** clause defines the post-condition in terms of the return value "r" and places restrictions on the possible set of values that "r" may hold such that

$$\forall x \bullet x \geq 0 \Rightarrow \texttt{isqrt}(x) = \lfloor \sqrt{x} \rfloor$$

The **modifies** clause specifies which parts of the client-visible state (such as global variables) *might* be modified when this function is executed. A function is permitted to mutate *at most* the objects listed in the **modifies**—it may alter some or none of them if appropriate.

2.4   Larch/Aldor

As part of our work we have designed a Larch BISL for Aldor, the extension programming language for AXIOM, which we are using to investigate how program annotations can improve the reliability and robustness of computer algebra routines. Aldor programs may be annotated with Larch BISL specifications which can be used as clear, concise and machine-checkable documentation; they may also be used for verification condition generation (see Section 3). An example of a Larch/Aldor program which implements the integer division algorithm is given below.

```
++} requires  ¬(g = 0);
++} ensures   (f = ((result.q)*g + result.r))
++}            ∧ (abs(result.r) < abs(g));
++} modifies nothing;
integerDivide(f:INT, g:INT):Record(q:INT, r:INT) == {
    local quo:INT := 0;
    local rem:INT := f;

    ++} requires   ¬(g = 0) ∧ (quo^ = 0) ∧ (rem^ = f);
    ++} ensures    (f = (quo'*g + rem')) ∧ (abs(rem') < abs(g));
    ++} invariant  f = (quo*g + rem);
    ++} measure    abs(rem);
    ++} modifies   quo, rem;
    while (abs(rem) ≥ abs(g)) repeat {
        quo := quo + sign(f)*sign(g);
        rem := rem - sign(f)*abs(g);
    }

    record(quo, rem);
}
```

In the annotations of the example above, identifiers represent *logical* values of the corresponding Aldor variables. The identifiers marked with a caret (^) indicate that the value is with respect to the state of the program before the function is executed (the pre-state) while the primed identifiers correspond to values in the post-state. Unadorned identifiers are interpreted according to the context and usually have the same value in the pre- and post-states. The identifier **result** is known as a specification or ghost-variable and its value is the return value of the function. It is important to note that operators and functions that appear in the annotations are LSL operators and *not* Aldor functions.

3   Application of the Larch Method to CAS

The AXIOM computer algebra system has a large library containing numerous functors, as described in Section 2.2. Although a few of these can be applied to any type, such as List(T:Type), many have restrictions on the types of domains which they can accept as arguments and which they will return. As shown in the case study in Section 4, the functor Complex can only be applied to domains CR which are of type CommutativeRing. This means that the operations defined by Complex are able to rely on the fact that CR is a CommutativeRing, irrespective of the concrete instance of CR. This creates the risk that functors may contain errors that are not revealed by their application to any domain in the existing library, but may appear when new domains are added.

3.1   Lightweight Verification Condition Generation

Our proposal is to formally specify the requirements of the categories and the behaviour of functors, to allow checks that do not depend on specific domains. The diagram below is intended to describe the development used for Larch/Aldor programs. Users begin by writing LSL specifications which provide the theory for their problem. Next the interface specifications and Aldor source are produced, perhaps leaving some functions as stubs without a proper implementation. A separate tool can then generate verification conditions which can be analysed using LP, by hand or by some other theorem prover as appropriate. A prototype VC generator for Larch/Aldor has been implemented in Aldor by the authors.

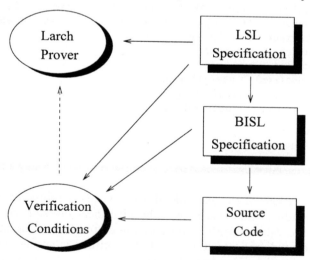

We use the notation $\{P\}\,C\,\{Q\}$ to state that the program fragment C has the pre-condition P and post-condition Q; P and Q are the specification of C. If $\{P\}\,C\,\{Q\}$ is interpreted as a "partial correctness" statement then it is true, if whenever C is executed in a state satisfying P and if the execution of C terminates, then it will be in a state which satisfies Q. If $\{P\}\,\texttt{C}\,\{Q\}$ is interpreted as being "totally correct" then it must be partially correct and $\texttt{C}$ must always terminate whenever P is satisfied. The approach often taken to prove that $\{P\}\,\texttt{C}\,\{Q\}$ is partially or totally correct is to reduce the statement to a set of purely logical or mathematical formulae called verification conditions [13] or VC's. This is achieved through the use of proof rules which allow the problem to be broken into smaller fragments. For example, the rule for assignment might be:

$$\frac{P \Rightarrow Q\,[\texttt{e}/\texttt{v}]}{\{P\}\,\texttt{v} := \texttt{e}\,\{Q\}}$$

which states that to prove the partial correctness of $\{P\}\,\texttt{v} := \texttt{e}\,\{Q\}$ we need to prove that $P \Rightarrow Q\,[\texttt{e}/\texttt{v}]$ where $Q\,[\texttt{e}/\texttt{v}]$ represents the formula Q with every occurrence of v replaced with e. For example, the partial correctness proof of $\{x = 0\}\,\texttt{x} := \texttt{x} + \texttt{1}\,\{x = 1\}$ generates the VC $(x = 0) \Rightarrow (x + 1) = 1$; for total correctness we must also show that the evaluation of $\texttt{e}$ terminates.

Our approach to verification condition generation is different—the assignment rule in the previous section is relatively simple but the construction of rules for other features of a programming language such as Aldor is not so easy. In particular, determining the verifications resulting from calling a procedure which mutates the values of its arguments is difficult. In [9] we proposed the use of lightweight formal methods to step around this problem in computer algebra systems. Rather than undertaking long verification proofs, we suggest that the correctness of a procedure may be taken on trust.

Using our notation, $\{P\}\,\texttt{C}\,\{Q\}$ might represent the correctness of a standard library procedure $\texttt{C}$. In any context which executes $\texttt{C}$ we have the verification condition that P is satisfied in this context; we can then assume that Q is satisfied in the new context after $\texttt{C}$ has terminated. Our justification for this is that we believe it is more likely that programming errors will be due incorrect application of functions or procedures than due to mistakes in the the implementation of computer algebra routines. After all the algorithms upon which they are based have almost certainly been well studied.

As an example, consider the 'isqrt' function specified in Section 2.3. With our approach we trust that the implementation of this function satisfies its specification, namely that if $\neg(x < 0)$ then the result r satisfies $r * r \leq x < (r + 1) * (r + 1)$. Now whenever we see a statement such as 'a := isqrt(z)' we can generate the verification condition that $\neg(z < 0)$ holds before the assignment and from the post-condition we infer that $a * a \leq z < (a+1) * (a+1)$ holds afterwards. This inference may help to discharge other verification conditions. Furthermore the user may wish to apply the VC generator to the implementation of 'isqrt' to check that it does indeed satisfy its specification.

4   Case Study

In this section we analyse the behaviour of specific examples of the AXIOM categories and domains described in Section 2.2. We use these examples to illustrate incorrect AXIOM output. In Section 4.1 we provide LSL specifications which provide a formal check on the type-correctness of the example domains. The use of BISL's to provide a complementary methodology for checking type-correctness is described in Section 4.3.

Our case study concerns essential side-conditions for a functor in the AX-IOM library. These conditions are present only as informal comments in the documentation, which are themselves inaccurate. This can result in erroneous AXIOM development in two ways: (i) the library developer may not be aware of the comments and hence the existence of side-conditions, (ii) the library developer may take the side-conditions into account, but be misled by the inaccurate comments. The AXIOM category `ComplexCategory`

- contains domains which represent the Gaussian integers (`Complex Integer`) and Gaussian rationals (`Complex Fraction Integer`)
- contains analogous domains, also obtained by the use of the functor `Complex`
- defines the constants 0, 1, and the square root of -1
- defines multiplication, addition, and subtraction operators
- defines other useful operators, such as norm and conjugate.

The AXIOM functor `Complex`

- takes an AXIOM domain of type `CommutativeRing`, for example `Integer`
- represents ordered pairs as records of two elements
- implements the operators defined in `ComplexCategory` in terms of the record representation and the structure of the argument domain
- returns an AXIOM domain of computation of type `ComplexCategory`.

AXIOM can behave incorrectly when the argument to `Complex` is an integral domain or a field. An integral domain is a commutative ring in which the product of two non-zero elements is always non-zero. This is known as the "no zero divisors" axiom, and can be written as $\forall x, y \ xy = 0 \Rightarrow x = 0 \lor y = 0$. For example, `Integer` is an AXIOM integral domain. A field is an integral domain in which each non-zero element has a multiplicative inverse.

In AXIOM, a domain of type `ComplexCategory(K)` (where K is either an integral domain or a field), is assigned type `IntegralDomain` or `Field` respectively. However, the correctness of this type-assignment is dependent on

(i) $x^2 + y^2 = 0$ having no non-trivial solutions in K when K is an integral domain
(ii) $x^2 + 1 = 0$ having no solutions when K is a field.

These properties do not hold for every integral domain and field. The following AXIOM session demonstrates this: we take the field containing exactly five elements, `PrimeField 5`, and show that `Complex PrimeField 5` is incorrectly given type `Field`, even though $3+i$ and $3-i$ are zero divisors, contradicting one of the field axioms. This behaviour is a consequence of the fact that $x^2 + 1 = 0$ has the solutions 2 and 3 in `PrimeField 5`.

```
(1) → K := PrimeField 5
    (1)  PrimeField 5
                                        Type: Domain

(2) → Complex K has Field
    (2)  true
                                        Type: Boolean

(3) → a := 3 + %i :: Complex K
    (3)  3 + %i
                            Type: Complex PrimeField 5

(4) → b := 3 - %i :: Complex K
    (4)  3 + 4%i
                            Type: Complex PrimeField 5

(5) → a*b
    (5)  0
                            Type: Complex PrimeField 5
```

Our solution to this incorrect type-assignation, presented in the following section, is to (i) specify the AXIOM category, (ii) provide formal axiomatisations and proofs of the conditions for type correctness, and (iii) import these into the specification of the Complex functor. The Aldor library developer is then able to view the conditions in the specification as conditional attributes of the particular argument domain under consideration. Section 4.2 illustrates the verification techniques that we have developed. In Section 4.3 we show how interface specifications can reinforce the properties of the LSL specification of Complex by allowing the generation of VC's.

4.1   LSL Specification of the AXIOM Functor Complex

The LSL trait RequirementsForComplex (given in Section 2.1) defined, at a high level of abstraction, the constructor and observer operations required by an implementation of complex numbers. We specified that elements of sort T have extractable real and imaginary parts, can be obtained only as a result of applying the complex operator, and are equal iff they have equal real and imaginary parts. The trait assumed that the argument domain has AXIOM type CommutativeRing. The ComplexCategory trait below lowers the level of abstraction by the provision of (i) constants of sort T, (ii) the useful shorthand operators conjugate and norm, and (iii) multiplication, addition and subtraction over T. The assertions supply the standard algebraic notions of multiplication, addition and subtraction of complex ring elements represented (in terms of complex) as ordered pairs of elements from the underlying ring. The operators norm, conjugate and imaginary have standard mathematical definitions. The implications of the trait are:

A Larch handbook [16] traits, which combine to require that T is shown to be a commutative ring with unity. Hence Complex (CR) is shown to be a commutative ring whenever CR is.

```
ComplexCategory (CR) : trait
assumes CommRingCat (CR)
includes RequirementsForComplex (CR)
introduces
   imaginary, 0, 1 :  → T
   conjugate : T → T
   norm : T → CR
   __+__, __*__ : T,T → T
   -__ : T → T
asserts ∀ w,z : T
   imaginary == complex(0,1);
   0 == complex(0,0);
   1 == complex(1,0);
   conjugate(z) == complex(real(z),-imag(z));
   norm(z) == (real(z)*real(z)) + (imag(z)*imag(z));
   w + z  == complex(real(w)+real(z),imag(w)+imag(z));
   w*z == complex((real(w)*real(z)) - (imag(w)*imag(z)),
                  (real(w)*imag(z)) + (imag(w)*real(z)));
   -z == complex(-real(z),-imag(z))
implies
   AC (*, T), AC (+, T), Distributive(+, *, T),
   Group(T for T, + for o, 0 for unit, -__ for ⁻¹),          } A
   Monoid(T for T, * for o, 1 for unit)
   ∀ z,w : T
     imaginary*imaginary == -1;                              } B
```

B A check that `imaginary` has been defined correctly as a square root of the additive inverse of the multiplicative unity element of the underlying ring.

4.2 Proving Properties

Proving the implications labelled A and B shows directly that an AXIOM domain of type `ComplexCategory` will have inherited the correct properties asserted informally in the AXIOM documentation. These straightforward proof goals normalise immediately in LP. We now address type correctness in the case that the argument CR is an integral domain or a field.

The following trait provides the necessary conditions for type-correctness of an AXIOM domain of type `ComplexCategory`. The implications are:

A if the argument type is a field in which $x^2 = -y^2 \iff x = 0$, then the resulting complex type will have multiplicative inverses

B if the argument type is a field in which $x^2 = -1$ never holds, then the complex type will have no zero divisors

C if the argument type is an integral domain in which $x^2 = -y^2 \iff x = 0$, then the complex type is an integral domain.

```
TypeConditions (CR,T) : trait
includes
  CommRingCat (CR), ComplexCategory (CR)
introduces
  TypeCondition_1, TypeCondition_2 : → Bool
  InverseExistence : → Bool
asserts ∀ a,b,c : CR
  TypeCondition_1 ⇒ (a ¬= 0 ⇒ a*a ¬= -(b*b));
  TypeCondition_2 ⇒ (a*a ¬= -1);
  InverseExistence ⇒ (a ¬= 0 ⇒ ∃ c (a*c = 1))
implies ∀ v,z,w : T
  TypeCondition_1 ∧ noZeroDivisors ∧ InverseExistence       ⎫
                   ⇒ (w ¬= 0 ⇒ ∃ v (w*v = 1));             ⎬ A
  TypeCondition_2 ∧ noZeroDivisors ∧ InverseExistence       ⎫
                   ⇒ (w*z=0 ⇒ w=0 ∨ z=0);                  ⎬ B
  TypeCondition_1 ∧ noZeroDivisors ⇒ (w*z=0 ⇒ w=0 ∨ z=0) ⎫ C
```

Proof of implication A:

Suppose that the relevant conditions hold, and that $w = (a, b)$ is non-zero. Then $a^2 + b^2 \neq 0$ (by type condition 1), and so there exists a c such that $c(a^2 + b^2) = 1$ (by inverse condition). By setting $v = (ca, c(-b))$ we obtain $vw = (ca, -cb)(a, b) = (ca^2 + cb^2, -cba + cba) = (c(a^2 + b^2), 0) = (1, 0)$ and hence v is the required multiplicative inverse. $\square$

Proof of implications B and C:

Suppose the relevant conditions hold, and that $z * w = 0$ with $z = (a, b)$ and $w = (c, d)$. Then we have

$$\left. \begin{array}{r} ac - bd = 0 \\ ad + bc = 0 \end{array} \right\} \qquad (*)$$

If $a = 0$ and $b \neq 0$, then $bd = 0$ and $bc = 0$, giving $d = c = 0$ and hence $w = (0, 0) = 0$. Similar arguments hold whenever b, c, or d are zero, and the implications are proved for all these cases. If a, b, c, and d are all nonzero then, by equations $(*)$, $ab(ac) = ab(bd)$, or $a^2(bc) = (-bc)b^2$ after substituting for ad. Hence $a^2 = -b^2$ holds for non-zero a and b, immediately contradicting type condition 1 for implication B. When b has the multiplicative inverse c, we have that $a^2 = -b^2$ gives $(ac)^2 = -bcbc = -1$, contradicting type condition 2 for implication C. Hence the result is proved for both implications $\square$

The Aldor library developer, by using this specification, can check the conditions for the particular domain of computation under consideration. For example, neither type condition holds in PrimeField 5, so Complex PrimeField 5 will have type CommutativeRing (justified by the implications of the specification of ComplexCategory) but not type Field. Conversely, since type condition 1 holds in the type Integer, Complex Integer can correctly be assigned type IntegralDomain, with implication C above as formal justification.

```
Complex (CR) : trait
assumes CommRingCat(CR)
includes ComplexCat(CR), TypeConditions (CR,T)
 BiRecord(T, CR, CR, .real for .first, .imag for .second)
introduces
 coerce : CR → T
 __*__ : N,T → T
 isZero, isOne : T → Bool
asserts ∀ x,y : CR, z : T, n : N
 complex(x,y) == [x,y];
 coerce(x) == [x,0];
 n*z == [n*(z.real), n*(z.imag)];
 isZero(z) == z = 0;
 isOne(z) == z = 1
implies
 RequirementsForComplex(CR, __.real for real, __.imag for imag)
 ∀ z, w : T
  norm(z*w) == real((z*w)*conjugate(z*w));
  imag((z*w)*conjugate(z*w)) == 0;
  conjugate(z)*conjugate(w) == conjugate(z*w)
converts complex
```

We now wish to show that the record representation for complex numbers used by AXIOM satisfies our high level requirements. The trait Complex(CR) above is simply a copy of the AXIOM documentation with the element $x + iy$ represented by the record [x,y]. By implying RequirementsForComplex we generate the required proof goal. The proof (although straightforward in LP) is not trivial: we have included the specification of ComplexCategory, which itself includes RequirementsForComplex, but not under the renaming of operators given in the implies clause. Hence we are checking that the record representation is suitable, where suitability was defined in the trait RequirementsForComplex. The same methodology would be used to show that a representation of $x + iy$ as (r, θ) (i.e. the standard modulus/amplitude representation) satisfied our abstract requirements. The remaining implications check that the combined operator definitions satisfy standard results from the abstract theory of complex numbers.

4.3   The Interface Specification

In the previous section we described how the AXIOM functor Complex(CR) allows the user to construct an object which AXIOM considers to be a field even though it is not. Here we show how interface specifications may be used to deal with the problem in a different yet complementary way to that adopted in the previous section. Since functors are functions from types to types, it is quite natural to use interface specifications such as those described earlier to describe their behaviour. In general a functor will not make any modifications to client-visible state which simplifies any reasoning about them. However, since the arguments and return values are types we may need to resort to a higher order logic to capture their meaning. This is not always the case as can be seen here. In the example below we present the skeleton of a Larch/Aldor program which describes the `Complex(CR)` domain.

```
++} requires isIntegralDomain(CR) ∧ ¬(∃ x,y:CR • (x*x + y*y = 0));
++} ensures  isIntegralDomain(%);
++} modifies nothing;
Complex(CR:CommutativeRing):CommutativeRing;
```

The predicate `isIntegralDomain(CR)` in the pre-condition corresponds to a trait in our LSL theory and is true iff the domain `CR` satisfies the properties of a mathematical integral domain; the statement $\neg(\exists x, y : CR \bullet (x^2 + y^2 = 0))$ is intended to capture the notion of type correctness described in the previous section. In the post-condition the concrete instance of `Complex(CR)` is represented by the AXIOM symbol `%`.

If the user instantiates the domain `Complex(Integer)` we can generate the verification condition

$$\texttt{isIntegralDomain(Integer)} \wedge \neg \exists x, y : \texttt{Integer} \bullet (x^2 + y^2 = 0)$$

Since `Integer` is an integral domain `isIntegralDomain(Integer)` holds; in fact the interface specification for `Integer` will state this property as part of its post-condition. This means that the VC can be simplified to

$$\neg \exists x, y : \texttt{Integer} \bullet (x^2 + y^2 = 0)$$

and if the user is familiar with elementary mathematics, they will be able to show that this is true. In doing so they will hopefully gain confidence that the `Complex(Integer)` domain will behave in the way that they expect it to. In addition to the verification condition we infer from the post-condition that

$$\texttt{isIntegralDomain(Complex(Integer))}$$

and as mentioned earlier, this may help to discharge other VC's.

If we repeat the process with `Complex(PrimeField 5)` (which AXIOM considers to be valid even though it isn't an integral domain) we obtain a similar VC to the one above

$$\neg \exists x, y : \texttt{PrimeField 5} \bullet (x^2 + y^2 = 0)$$

since `PrimeField 5` is a finite integral domain (and hence a field). However, this VC can be shown to be false by providing the witnesses $x = 2$ and $y = 4$.

5   Conclusions and Future Work

We have augmented our specification of the AXIOM algebraic category hierarchy with LSL specifications of AXIOM functors. The methodology used allows enhanced type-checking and verification of argument types, as well as proofs of operator properties with respect to value representations. We have implemented a prototype lightweight verification condition generator in Aldor for Larch/Aldor programs. To achieve this the grammar of an Aldor compiler was extended to allow Larch annotations to be recognised. Further modifications to the compiler were made so that it could generate an external representation of the parse tree complete with types and specifications. The prototype analyser uses the parse tree to generate verification conditions and inferences from the user's program. For example, given the annotated Aldor program in Section 2.4 and the program statement "ans := integerDivide(23, 6)" our tool could, in principle, produce the VC $\neg(6 = 0)$ which is obviously true and the inference that:

$$(23 = ((ans.q) * 6 + ans.r)) \wedge (abs(ans.r) < abs(6))$$

The prototype VC generator is by no means completely finished and there is scope for further improvement. Indeed it would be interesting to incorporate it into the compiler itself so that existing control-flow functions and data-structures could be utilised, and so that VC generation could be used to provide additional compiler warnings. In spite of its limitations the authors feel that the prototype is useful as a proof-of-concept and given time it could be extended to analyse functions and domains as well. At present the LP proof assistant is more than capable of discharging the simple verification conditions that it has generated so far. However, we believe that more interesting case studies will probably require the use of a more developed theorem prover such as HOL [14] or PVS [25].

5.1   Related Work

There are a number of other systems which are related to our work and from which we have drawn upon for our ideas. Examples of ways in which CAS and automated theorem proving technology have been used together include work linking HOL and Maple [1] where simplification rules were added to HOL to make selected Maple routines available; the Analytica system which implements automated reasoning techniques in the Mathematica CAS [2]; the Theorema project uses the rewriting engine of Mathematica as a logical system to provide a single framework for both symbolic computation and proof [3]; REDLOG is an extension of the REDUCE to allow symbolic manipulation of first order formulas in a CAS [8]. These approaches differ in the amount of trust given to CAS and ATP results, their overall goals (better ATP, better CAS, or possibly better formalised mathematics), and in the hierarchy of the systems (for example ATP slave to the CAS master or *vice versa*).

Closer to our work is that of [26] where the Aldor type system is being extended to increase the potential of its dependent types. This work can be used to incorporate pre- and post-conditions into type declarations and admit proofs that properties in the documentation also hold at the computational level.

On the Larch side of our work (see Section 2) we are aware that many of the Larch behavioural interface specification languages (BISL's) do not have any program analysis tools associated with them—they are primarily used as clear and concise documentation. One exception is Larch/Ada [15] which uses a syntax-directed editor called Penelope [15] for the interactive development and verification of Larch/Ada programs. Another exception is Larch/C [10] for which the LcLint [10] static program checker has been written. This tool is able to detect violations of subset of Larch/C interface specifications and check other special program annotations. Also in the Larch world, Speckle [29] is an optimising compiler for the CLU language which uses Larch-style interface specifications to select specialised procedure implementations.

The Extended Static Checking (ESC) system [6] provides automatic machine checking of Modula-3 programs to detect violations of array bounds, NIL pointer dereferencing, deadlocks and race conditions through the use of simple yet powerful annotations. ProofPower is a commercial tool developed by the High Assurance Team at ICL [22] based on the HOL theorem prover and the Z notation for a subset of Ada. Programs are prototyped and refined using Compliance Notation into Ada. Verification conditions generated from the Compliance Notation can be discharged via formal or informal arguments as required.

Also of note are the Eiffel [24] and Extended ML [28] programming languages. In Eiffel pre- and post-conditions are an integral part of the language syntax. These annotations can be converted into runtime checks by the compiler and violations may be handled by the programmer via exception handlers. Extended ML also incorporates specifications into its syntax—users can write algebraic specifications describing the properties of functions and use stepwise refinement (*c.f.* reification [20]) to obtain suitable implementations.

Acknowledgements

We acknowledge support of the UK EPSRC under grant number GR/L48256 and of NAG Ltd. We also thank James Davenport of the University of Bath and Mike Dewar from NAG for their interest and suggestions.

References

[1] BALLARIN, C., HOMANN, K., AND CALMET, J. Theorems and algorithms: An interface between Isabelle and Maple. In *Proceedings of International Symposium on Symbolic and Algebraic Computation* (1995), A.H.M.Levelt, Ed., ACM Press, pp. 150–157.

[2] BAUER, A., CLARKE, E., AND ZHAO, X. Analytica—an experiment in combining theorem proving and symbolic computation. *J. Automat. Reason. 21*, 3 (1998), 295–325.

[3] BUCHBERGER, B. Symbolic computation: computer algebra and logic. In *Frontiers of combining systems (Munich, 1996)*. Kluwer Acad. Publ., Dordrecht, 1996, pp. 193–219.

[4] CHAR, B. W. *Maple V language Reference Manual*. Springer-Verlag, 1991.

[5] CHEON, Y., AND LEAVENS, G. T. A gentle introduction to Larch/Smalltalk specification browsers. Tech. Rep. TR 94-01, Department of Computer Science, Iowa State University, 226 Atanasoff Hall, Ames, Iowa 50011-1040, USA, Jan. 1994.

[6] DETLEFS, D. L. An overview of the Extended Static Checking system. In *Proceedings of The First Workshop on Formal Methods in Software Practice* (Jan 1996), ACM (SIGSOFT), pp. 1–9.

[7] DINGLE, A., AND FATEMAN, R. J. Branch cuts in computer algebra. In *Symbolic and Algebraic Computation* (1994), ISSAC, ACM Press.

[8] DOLZMANN, A., AND STURM, T. REDLOG: Computer algebra meets computer logic. *ACM SIGSAM Bulletin 31*, 2 (June 1997), 2–9.

[9] DUNSTAN, M., KELSEY, T., LINTON, S., AND MARTIN, U. Lightweight formal methods for computer algebra systems. In *ISSAC* (1998).

[10] EVANS, D. Using specifications to check source code. Master's thesis, Department of Electrical Engineering and Computer Science, MIT Lab. for Computer Science, 545 Technology Square, Cambridge, MA 02139, June 1994.

[11] FEIT, W., AND THOMPSON, J. G. Solvability of groups of odd order. *Pacific Journal of Mathematics 13* (1963), 775–1029.

[12] THE GAP GROUP. *GAP – Groups, Algorithms, and Programming, Version 4*. Aachen, St Andrews, 1998. (http://www-gap.dcs.st-and.ac.uk/~gap).

[13] GORDON, M. J. C. *Programming language theory and its implementation*. Series in Computer Science. Prentice Hall International, 1988.

[14] GORDON, M. J. C., AND MELHAM, T. F., Eds. *Introduction to HOL*. Cambridge University Press, Cambridge, 1993. A theorem proving environment for higher order logic, Appendix B by R. J. Boulton.

[15] GUASPARI, D., MARCEAU, C., AND POLAK, W. Formal verification of Ada programs. In *First International Workshop on Larch* (July 1992), U. Martin and J. Wing, Eds., Springer-Verlag, pp. 104–141.

[16] GUTTAG, J. V., AND HORNING, J. J. *Larch: Languages and Tools for Formal Specification*, first ed. Texts and Monograps in Computer Science. Springer-Verlag, 1993.

[17] HARRISON, J., AND THÉRY, L. Extending the HOL theorem prover with a computer algebra system to reason about the reals. In *Higher order logic theorem proving and its applications (Vancouver, BC, 1993)*. Springer, Berlin, 1994, pp. 174–184.

[18] JACKSON, P. *Enhancing the NUPRL Proof Development System and Applying it to Computational Abstract Algebra*. PhD thesis, Department of Computer Science, Cornell University, Ithaca, New York, Apr. 1995.

[19] JENKS, R. D., AND SUTOR, R. S. *AXIOM*. Numerical Algorithms Group Ltd., Oxford, 1992. The scientific computation system, With a foreword by David V. Chudnovsky and Gregory V. Chudnovsky.

[20] JONES, C. B. *Systematic Software Development using VDM*, second ed. Computer Science. Prentice Hall International, 1990.

[21] JONES, K. D. LM3: a Larch interface language for Modula-3, a definition and introduction. Tech. Rep. 72, SRC, Digital Equipment Corporation, Palo Alto, California, June 1991.

[22] KING, D. J., AND ARTHAN, R. D. Development of practical verification tools. *The ICL Systems Journal 1* (May 1996).

[23] LEAVENS, G. T., AND CHEON, Y. Preliminary design of Larch/C++. In *First International Workshop on Larch* (July 1992), U. Martin and J. M. Wing, Eds., Workshops in Computing, Springer-Verlag, pp. 159–184.

[24] MEYER, B. *Object-Oriented Software Construction*. Computer Science. Prentice Hall International, 1988.

[25] OWRE, S., SHANKAR, N., AND RUSHBY, J. M. *User Guide for the PVS Specification and Verification System*. Computer Science Laboratory, SRI International, Menlo Park, CA, Feb. 1993.

[26] POLL, E., AND THOMPSON, S. Adding the axioms to Axiom: Towards a system of automated reasoning in aldor. Technical Report 6-98, Computing Laboratory, University of Kent, May 1998.

[27] POTTER, B., SINCLAIR, J., AND TILL, D. *An introduction to formal specification and Z*. Prentice Hall International, 1991.

[28] SANNELLA, D. Formal program development in Extended ML for the working programmer. In *Proceedings of the 3rd BCS/FACS Workshop on Refinement* (1990), Springer Workshops in Computing, pp. 99–130.

[29] VANDEVOORDE, M. T., AND GUTTAG, J. V. Using specialized procedures and specification-based analysis to reduce the runtime costs of modularity. In *Proceedings of the 1994 ACM/SIGSOFT Foundations of Software Engineering Conference* (1994).

[30] WING, J. M. A two-tiered approach to specifying programs. Tech. Rep. LCS/TR–299, Laboratory for Computer Science, MIT, May 1983.

[31] WING, J. M., ROLLINS, E., AND ZAREMSKI, A. M. Thoughts on a Larch/ML and a new application for TP. In *First International Workshop on Larch* (July 1992), U. Martin and J. M. Wing, Eds., Workshops in Computing, Springer-Verlag, pp. 297–312.

[32] WOLFRAM, S. *Mathematica: A system for doing mathematics by computer*, 2 ed. Addison Wesley, 1991.

An Algebraic Framework for Higher-Order Modules

Rosa Jiménez and Fernando Orejas

Dept. Leng. Sist. Inf., Univ. Polit. Catalunya
Barcelona, SPAIN

Abstract. This paper presents a new framework for dealing with higher-order parameterization allowing the use of arbitrary fitting morphisms for parameter passing. In particular, we define a category of higher-order parameterized or module specifications and, then, following the approach started in the ASL specification language, we define a typed λ-calculus, as a formalism for dealing with these specifications, where arbitrary fitting morphisms are allowed. In addition, the approach presented is quite general since all the work is independent of the kind of basic specifications considered and, also, of the kind of operations used for building basic specifications, provided that some conditions hold. In this sense we are not especially bound to any set of basic specification-building operations. We call our parameterized units *modules* to make clear the distinction between the basic specification level that is not fixed a priori and the parameterized units level that is studied in the paper. The kind of calculus presented can be seen as a variation/extension of the simply typed λ-calculus, which means that we do not allow dependent types. This would have been interesting, but it is not possible with the semantics proposed. The main result of the paper shows the adequacy of β-reduction with respect to the semantics given.

1 Introduction

There are two standard approaches for dealing with genericity in specification or programming languages. On the one hand, parametric polymorphism is used, especially, in functional languages like ML or Miranda. On the other, different forms of generic units or modules are used in specification languages like Clear or Act One or programming languages like OBJ or Ada. Each of these approaches has a number advantages and disadvantages of different kind. Actually, some languages like ML provide constructions for both kind of approaches. Among the advantages in favor of generic modules is the additional power provided by allowing modules to have "complex" formal parameters, i.e. parameters need not to be just sorts but may be arbitrary interfaces. In addition, module instantiation is usually defined in a flexible way by means of an arbitrary fitting morphism identifying the "elements" (sorts, functions, predicates,...) in the interface with corresponding elements in the actual parameter. Among the advantages in favour of parametric polymorphism is the additional power provided by allowing to deal with higher-order objects.

J. Wing, J. Woodcock, J. Davies (Eds.): FM'99, Vol. II, LNCS 1709, pp. 1778–1797, 1999.
© Springer-Verlag Berlin Heidelberg 1999

There have been two approaches to provide a higher-order extension of the basic constructions of some specification languages. One approach, consists in extending the logic underlying a given specification language with higher-order sorts (for instance extending first-order equational logic to higher-order equational logic). In this way, the structuring constructions of a specification language remain the same, only the underlying formalism changes. This approach has some disadvantages. The main one is that having a more complex underlying formalism implies a difficulty for building deductive tools. For instance, when going from first-order to higher-order equational logic, unification becomes undecidable. The other approach consists in (without changing the underlying formalism) allowing the interfaces of generic units to be generic or parameterized themselves. A simple way of doing this, which has its origins in the specification language ASL [13], is based on considering that a generic specification is any parameterized λ-expression built over some specification variables. Then, instantiating a parameterization consists in substituting these variables by any (adequate) specification. This can be seen as a form of β-reduction. One of the advantages of this approach, besides its generality, is the simplicity for defining higher-order parameterizations. In particular, given the parameterization:

$$MSP = \lambda X : SP.E(X)$$

where $E(X)$ denotes any expression defined in terms of the specification building operations considered, over a "specification variable" X of "type" (formal parameter specification) SP. If we allow SP or $E(X)$ to be arbitrary λ-expressions then MSP would be a higher-order specification. This kind of typed λ-notation may look a bit awkward since types and objects seem to denote the same thing (specifications). However, the type of a variable and the result of an expression denote different things. Being specific, when declaring $X : SP$, it is considered that the type denoted by SP is the class (or category) of all the specifications that are "more concrete" than SP, i.e. all the admissible actual parameters for SP. Let us see an example of a higher-order parameterization using this approach. Given the specifications:

$ELEM = $ **sorts** $elem$

$PSEQ = \lambda X : ELEM.$ **enrich** X **by**
$\qquad\qquad\qquad$ **sorts** seq
$\qquad\qquad\qquad$ **opns** $\epsilon : \to seq$
$\qquad\qquad\qquad\qquad\quad app : seq\ elem \to seq$

defining a parameterized specification of "linear" structures of a given type of elements, the following specifications :

$ELEM1 = $ **enrich** $BOOL$ **by**
$\qquad\qquad$ **sorts** $elem$
$\qquad\qquad$ **opns** $p : elem \to bool$

$PFILTER = \lambda X : ELEM1.$
  $\lambda Y : PSEQ.$**enrich** $Y[X]_{id}$ **by**
      opns $filter : seq \to seq$
      vars $S : seq;\; V : val$
      axms $filter(\epsilon) = \epsilon$
      $p(V) = true \Rightarrow filter(app(S,V)) = app(filter(S),V)$
      $p(V) = false \Rightarrow filter(app(S,V)) = filter(S)$

define a specification describing how to "filter" the elements of a linear structure satisfying a given property p. Previous work following this approach can be found in [12, 4]. However, in both works this extension is done without allowing the use of arbitrary fitting morphisms in module instantiation. One of the problems with using arbitrary fitting morphisms in this setting is that parameter passing cannot just work as standard β-reduction. The reason can be seen in the following example. Suppose that we have the specification:

$$\lambda X : SP.\textbf{rename } X \textbf{ by } h$$

This specification is considered correct if h is a morphism from the signature of the specification SP into another signature. Now suppose that we apply this parameterization to a specification $SP1$. The result would be:

$$\textbf{rename } SP1 \textbf{ by } h$$

but, if we allow the use of arbitrary fitting morphisms for instantiation, it may happen that the expression is now incorrect because the signatures of $SP1$ and $SP1$ can be different. A second problem is that, if one wants to allow instantiations through arbitrary morphisms one would have to define the adequate notion of morphism between higher-order specifications (and, consequently, the right category of higher-order specifications). In this sense, in [12] actual and formal parameter specifications must share the same signature, which is quite restrictive. Some more flexibility is given in [4],where inclusions of signatures are allowed. However this is done using a quite more complex framework.

The work presented in this paper provides a solution to this problem. Using as a basis [12] and previous work of the authors for the first-order case [10], we define a category of higher-order parameterized or module specifications and, then, we define a typed λ-calculus, as a formalism for dealing with these specifications, where arbitrary fitting morphisms are allowed. In particular, in [12], a detailed study of different semantic issues concerning parameterized units is presented showing, essentially, that two possible meanings can be assigned to parameterizations depending on whether we consider them as parameterized specifications or as specifications of parameterized programs. In this sense, in this paper we consider just the former meaning, although the results could be adapted to deal also with the latter case.

The approach presented is quite general since all the work is independent of the kind of basic specifications considered and, also, of the kind of operations used for building basic specifications, provided that some conditions hold. In this sense we are not especially bound to any set of basic specification-building operations. We call our parameterized units *modules* to make clear the distinction between the basic specification level that is not fixed a priori and the parameterized units level that is studied in the paper. The kind of calculus presented can be seen as a variation/extension of the simply typed λ-calculus, which means that we do not allow dependent types [11]. This would have been interesting, but it is not possible with the semantics proposed. The main result of the paper shows the adequacy of β-reduction with respect to the semantics given. However, it must be pointed out that this is not done for any arbitrary λ-expression but only for expressions in η-long normal form. We do not think that this is a serious limitation, since similar restrictions can be found in related frameworks.

The paper is organized as follows: in section 2, we describe the requirements assumed on the basic specification language. Section 3 defines the category of higher-order modules and a parameter passing operation for the objects in this category. Finally, in section 4 we present the language of λ-expressions, we define β-reduction and we obtain the main results.

2   Preliminaries

In this section we briefly present the abstract framework that we will use along the paper to present all constructions and results. We assume on the reader certain knowledge on the basic algebraic techniques used in the semantics of specification languages. For details see, for instance, [1, 7, 15]. Also, we assume some very basic knowledge on the λ-calculus. For details, see for example [2]. We do not assume much about how basic specifications look like. We just assume that specifications form a category, that we call *Spec*, satisfying certain properties and that we have a specification language to build them. This means that specifications may consist of a signature and a set of axioms [7], or of a signature and a set of models [13, 14] or they may be of any other form. In particular, we do not need to bind them to an arbitrary institution or specification frame [8, 9, 10]. The reason is that, in this work, we are not especially interested with semantical aspects of basic specifications. The only assumption about *Spec* is that it has multiple pushouts. Multiple pushouts were defined in [10] to define parameter passing for arbitrary parameterized expressions, as a slight generalization of the use of pushouts when dealing with parameterizations defined in terms of generic enrichments [3, 5, 6]. The difference with standard pushouts is that two of the arrows of a standard pushout are here a family of morphisms (which we call a multiple morphism). In the following section we will see a couple of examples that show the need of multiple morphisms in this setting.

Definition 1. *A multiple morphism in $\underline{Spec}$ F from $SP0$ to $SP1$, denoted F : $SP0 \Rightarrow SP1$, is a family of morphisms in $\underline{Spec}$, $F = \langle f1, ..., fn : SP0 \rightarrow SP1, (n \geq 0)\rangle$. Multiple morphisms can be composed with standard morphisms: If F is defined as above and $f : SP1 \rightarrow SP2$ then $f \circ F : SP0 \Rightarrow SP2$ is the*

family $\langle f \circ f1, ..., f \circ fn : SP0 \to SP1, (n \geq 0) \rangle$. *Similarly, if* $f : SP2 \to SP0$
then $F \circ f = \langle f1 \circ f, ..., fn \circ f : SP0 \to SP1, (n \geq 0) \rangle$. *Two additional operations
that one can define on multiple morphisms are composition and addition. If*
$F' = \langle f1', ..., fm' : SP1 \to SP2 \rangle$ *then*

$$F \circ F' = \langle f1 \circ f1', ..., f1 \circ fm', ..., fn \circ fm' : SP0 \to SP2 \rangle$$

and if $F' = \langle f1', ..., fm' : SP0 \to SP1 \rangle$ *then*

$$F' + F = \langle f1, ..., fn, f1', ..., fm' : SP0 \to SP1 \rangle$$

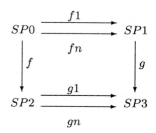

Fig. 1. Multiple pushout

Given a multiple morphism $F : SP0 \Rightarrow SP1$ *as above and given* $f : SP0 \to$
$SP2$ *in* Spec, *the diagram in Figure 1 is called a multiple pushout of* F *and* f *if
we have:*

1. *(Graded Commutativity):* $g \circ fi = gi \circ f$ *(for every* $i \leq n$*)*
2. *(Universal Property): For each object* $SP3'$ *and morphisms* $g', g1, ..., gn$ *with*
   $g' \circ fi = gi' \circ f$ *(for every* $i = n$*) there is a unique morphism* h *such that*
   $h \circ g = g'$ *and* $h \circ gi = gi'$ *(for every* $i \leq n$*)*

Remarks 2

1. *In the case* $n = 1$ *a multiple pushout is a pushout. In the case* $n = 0$ $SP3$ *is
   equal (up to isomorphism) to* $SP1$ *with* $g = 1_{SP1}$.
2. *Multiple pushouts can be defined in terms of pushouts and (finite) coproducts
   or, more generally, finite colimits.*

Example 3. Consider the following specifications and morphisms:

$$SP0 = \textbf{sorts } s0 \qquad\qquad SP1 = \textbf{sorts } s1, s2$$
$$\textbf{opns } f1 : s1 \to s1$$
$$f2 : s2 \to s2$$

$$h1 : SP0 \to SP1 \qquad\qquad h2 : SP0 \to SP1$$
$$\text{with } h1(s0) = s1 \qquad\qquad \text{with } h2(s0) = s2$$

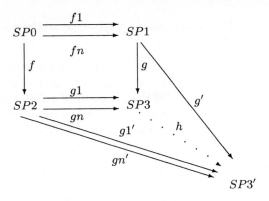

Fig. 2. Universal property of multiple pushouts

Now, if we define:

$$SP2 = \textbf{sorts } s0$$
$$\textbf{opns } a : \rightarrow s0$$
$$c : s0 \rightarrow s0$$

together with the inclusion $i0 : SP0 \rightarrow SP2$, we can "compute" the multiple pushout shown in Figure 3, where $SP3$ would be (up to isomorphism) the specification:

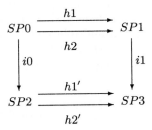

Fig. 3. Multiple pushout

$$SP3 = \textbf{sorts } s1, s2$$
$$\textbf{opns } f1 : s1 \rightarrow s1$$
$$f2 : s2 \rightarrow s2$$
$$a1 : \rightarrow s1$$
$$c1 : s1 \rightarrow s1$$
$$a2 : \rightarrow s2$$
$$c2 : s2 \rightarrow s2$$

and the two morphisms, $h1'$ and $h2'$, would map, respectively, s, a and c to $s1, a1$ and $c1$ and to $s2, a2$ and $c2$.

In addition, we assume that we have a language for building specifications. We may think of this language as a many-sorted signature including, at least, a sort of specifications $SPEC$ and a sort of morphisms $MORPH$ and, as constants of these sorts, all objects and morphisms in $\underline{Spec}$, respectively (or just some distinguished subsets). We will call this signature $\varSigma SPEC$. For example, an operation in this signature may be:

$$combine : SPEC \times SPEC \times SPEC \times MORPH \times MORPH \to SPEC$$

that given specifications $SP0$, $SP1$ and $SP2$ and morphisms $h1 : SP0 \to SP1$ and $h2 : SP0 \to SP2$ is intended to combine the specifications $SP1$ and $SP2$, having a common subspecification $SP0$, where $h1$ and $h2$ make explicit how $SP0$ is included in $SP1$ and $SP2$, respectively. Typically, this combination would be done by means of a pushout.

Hence, $T_{\varSigma SPEC}$ is the class of specification expressions (syntactically) valid in the given specification language. It may be noted that not every term in $T_{\varSigma SPEC}$ may denote a semantically valid construction and, therefore, have a meaning. For instance, $combine(SP0, SP1, SP2, h1, h2)$ would be semantically incorrect if, for instance, $h1$ is not a morphism from $SP0$ into $SP1$. Anyhow, we assume given a semantics for the specification language as a (partial) function, called Sem, mapping (valid) terms in $T_{\varSigma SPEC}$ of sort $SPEC$ (respectively $MORPH$) into objects (respectively morphisms) in $\underline{Spec}$.

We assume that operations in $\varSigma SP\overline{EC}$ are incremental, in the sense that given a variable X of sort $SPEC$ and given a specification term t in $T_{\varSigma SPEC}(\{X\})$ then for any specification SP such that $t[SP/X]$ is valid (i.e. $Sem(t[SP/X])$ is defined) we consider that there is a multiple specification morphism in $\underline{Spec}$ associated to t and SP, denoted $t_{SP} : SP \Rightarrow t([SP/X])$, such that if $h : SP \to SP'$ and $t([SP'/X])$ is valid then the diagram in Figure 4 is a multiple pushout.

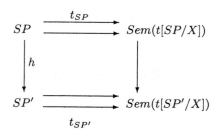

Fig. 4. Incrementality

This means that we are assuming that for every operation op in $\varSigma SPEC$ there is also a morphism between any possible argument for op of sort $SPEC$

and the resulting specification. As a consequence, operations such as derive would not be allowed to be in $\Sigma SPEC$. The reason for this, besides some technical questions, is that we consider that hiding should be considered at the module level. Anyhow, this is not considered in this paper. It could have been done by defining modules with an additional export interface. We believe that the main results would still hold, but at the price of an additional complication.

We also consider that there exists an operation $assign$ that, given t in $T_{\Sigma SPEC}(\{X\}\cup V)$ of sort $SPEC$, where V is a (finite) set of variables, two specifications $SP1$ and $SP2$ and a morphism $h : SP1 \to SP2$, it returns a new term, denoted $assign(t,h)$ such that for every assignment $\sigma : V \to \overline{Spec}$ such that $\sigma^*(t[SP1/X])$ is valid and the diagram in Figure 5 is a multiple pushout, where $\sigma^*(t)$ denotes the term obtained after substituting in t all its variables by the values assigned by σ. Moreover, if $t[SP2/X]$ is valid then $t[SP2/X] = assign(t,h)$.

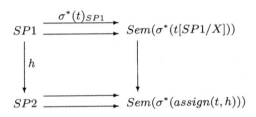

Fig. 5. The operation $assign$

3   The Category of Module Specifications $\underline{MSpec}$

In this section, we introduce $\underline{MSpec}$ a category of module specifications that will be used for giving semantics to module expressions. In particular, this category includes, as a full subcategory, the category of basic specifications, $\underline{Spec}$.

The objects in $\underline{MSpec}$ are either basic specifications, i.e. objects in $\underline{Spec}$, or triples $\langle IMP, R\overline{ES}, F\rangle$ denoting parameterized objects. The intuition is that IMP and RES, which are objects in $\underline{MSpec}$, are, respectively, the imported and the result specification of a module and F is a kind of mapping binding the "elements" (e.g. sorts and operations) in IMP with corresponding elements in RES. For instance, a standard case is when IMP and RES are basic specifications and RES is an enrichment of IMP, i.e. F would be a specification morphism in $\underline{Spec}$. Similarly, when considering modules defining first-order parameterized specifications defined by arbitrary specification expressions, as in [10], F is a multiple specification morphism, $F : IMP \Rightarrow RES$. This is needed, for instance, when dealing with expressions such as:

$$\lambda X : SP.X \sqcup X$$

where $SP1 \sqcup SP2$ denotes the coproduct of $SP1$ and $SP2$. In this case, the relation between the formal parameter and the result specification can be denoted by two morphisms binding the formal parameter SP with the two copies included in $SP \sqcup SP$, as shown in Figure 6. Also, given the parameterization $\lambda X : SP.SP'$,

$$SP \quad \begin{array}{c} \xrightarrow{\ h1\ } \\[-2pt] \xrightarrow[\ h2\ ]{} \end{array} \quad SP \sqcup SP$$

Fig. 6. "Double" morphism

where SP' is a constant specification, then the relation between the formal parameter and the result specification can be denoted by the empty family of morphisms. In the general case, when IMP or RES may be higher-order, the relation between their elements can be established by a multiple morphism between their "ground versions". For instance, consider the module specification $PFILTER$ given in the introduction, its import specification $ELEM1$ is not first-order but its result is the specification denoted by the expression

$\lambda Y : PSEQ.\textbf{enrich } Y[X]_{id} \textbf{ by}$
> **opns** $filter : seq \rightarrow seq$
> **vars** $S : seq;\ V : val$
> **axms** $filter(\epsilon) = \epsilon$
> $\qquad p(V) = true \Rightarrow filter(app(S, V)) = app(filter(S), V)$
> $\qquad p(V) = false \Rightarrow filter(app(S, V)) = filter(S)$

Now, in order to bind the sorts and operations defined in $ELEM1$ with the sorts and operations in the result specification we may, first, define its associated ground specification as the specification denoted by the expression:

enrich $PSEQ[ELEM1]_{id}$ **by**
opns $filter : seq \rightarrow seq$
vars $S : seq;\ V : val$
axms $filter(\epsilon) = \epsilon$
$\qquad p(V) = true \Rightarrow filter(app(S, V)) = app(filter(S), V)$
$\qquad p(V) = false \Rightarrow filter(app(S, V)) = filter(S)$

and, then, establish this binding in terms of a multiple specification morphism (in this case a standard morphism is enough).

To be more precise, we will define a functor $Body : \underline{MSpec} \rightarrow \underline{Spec}$ that associates to every module specification its ground version. Then F is a multiple morphism between $Body(IMP)$ and $Body(RES)$, i.e. $F : Body(IMP) \Rightarrow Body(RES)$. This leads to the following inductive definition:

Definition 4. *The category $\underline{MSpec}$ and the functor $Body : \underline{MSpec} \to \underline{Spec}$ are defined by simultaneous induction as follows:*

- *if SP is in $\underline{Spec}$ then SP is in $\underline{MSpec}$ and $Body(SP) = SP$*
- *if $h : SP1 \to SP2$ is in $\underline{Spec}$ then $h : SP1 \to SP2$ is in $\underline{MSpec}$ and $Body(h) = h$*
- *if $MSP1, MSP2 \in \underline{MSpec}$, and F is a multiple morphism in $\underline{Spec}$, $F : Body(MSP1) \Rightarrow Body(MSP2)$, then $MSP = \langle MSP1, MSP2, F \rangle$ is an object in $\underline{MSpec}$ and $Body(MSP) = Body(MSP2)$.*
- *if $h1 : \overline{MSP21} \to MSP11$ and $h2 : MSP12 \to MSP22$ are in $\underline{MSpec}$ and the diagram in Figure 7 commutes (has graded commutativity) in $\underline{MSpec}$:*

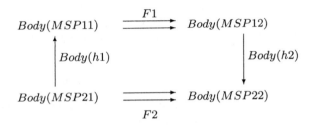

Fig. 7. Morphism in $\underline{MSpec}$

then $h = \langle h1, h2 \rangle : \langle MSP11, MSP12, F1 \rangle \to \langle MSP21, MSP22, F2 \rangle$ is a morphism in $\underline{MSpec}$ and $Body(h) = Body(h2)$.

The morphisms in $\underline{MSpec}$ are defined with the aim of using them as *parameter passing* or *fitting* morphisms. In this sense, morphisms between basic specifications are, as usual, standard specification morphisms. In the case of morphisms between parameterized objects, $\langle h1, h2 \rangle : MSP1 \to MSP2$, where $MSP1 = \langle IMP1, RES1, F1 \rangle, MSP2 = \langle IMP2, RES2, F2 \rangle$, the idea is, as usual, that $MSP2$ should be "less general" than $MSP1$. This means that the result of $MSP2$, $RES2$, should be less general than $RES1$ and that the formal parameter of $MSP2$, $IMP2$, should be more general than $IMP1$. In addition, $h1$ and $h2$ should be coherent with respect to the binding between the elements of $MSP1$ and $MSP2$. This is expressed by the commuting diagram above.

Remarks 5

1. *$\underline{MSpec}$ and Body can be proved to be a category and a functor by defining morphism composition in the most obvious way.*
2. *It may be noted that $\underline{MSpec}$ can not be shown to be a Cartesian Closed Category (CCC) because of the choice of morphisms in its definition. The*

problem is that, as explained above, morphisms in $\underline{MSpec}$ have been defined with the aim of defining instantiation. A different choice would have been defining morphisms in $\underline{MSpec}$ as multiple morphisms in $\underline{Spec}$, i.e. if F : $Body(IMP) \Rightarrow Body(\overline{RES})$ then $F : MSP1 \to MSP2$ is a morphism in $\underline{MSpec}$. This notion of morphism would have allowed the identification between morphisms and functional objects which is the basis for the definition of a CCC. Anyhow, we would have still needed a notion of fitting morphism for parameter passing.

To end this section, we will show how parameter passing or module instantiation can be defined in $\underline{MSpec}$. Suppose that we have specifications $MSP = \langle MSP1, MSP2, F \rangle$ and $\overline{MSP_{act}}$ in $\underline{MSpec}$ and a morphism $h : MSP1 \to MSP_{act}$ in $Mor(\underline{MSpec})$, then the result of *instantiating* MSP over MSP_{act} via h should be the specification obtained by "substituting" $MSP1$ by MSP_{act} in $MSP2$, with respect to the bindings defined by h and F. Now, in general, $MSP2$ will have the form $\langle MSP2_1, \langle MSP2_2, ...\langle MSP2_n, MSP2_{n+1}, F_n \rangle, F_{n-1} \rangle, ..., F_1 \rangle$, where $MSP2_{n+1} = Body(MSP2)$. Then, if we consider that the parameters $MSP2_1, MSP2_2, ...MSP2_n$, are independent of $MSP1$, the result of the instantiation should be a specification

$$MSP_{res} = \langle MSP2_1, \langle MSP2_2, ...\langle MSP2_n, RES, F_n' \rangle, F_{n-1}' \rangle, ..., F_1' \rangle$$

where RES is the result of substituting $Body(MSP1)$ by $Body(MSP_{act})$ in $MSP2_{n+1}$, with respect to the bindings defined by $Body(h)$ and F. This means that RES can be defined in terms of the multiple pushout shown in Figure 8.

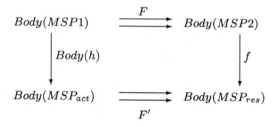

Fig. 8. Multiple Pushout

On the other hand, $F_1', ..., F_n'$ should bind the elements in $MSP2_1,..., MSP2_n$, respectively, to the corresponding elements in RES, i.e. $F_i' = f \circ F_i$. It may be noted that f can be extended into a specification morphism $h' : MSP2 \to RES$ by just defining $h' = \langle Id_1, \langle Id_2, ...\langle Id_n, f \rangle \rangle...\rangle$, where Id_i denotes the identity morphism, $Id_i : MSP2_i \to MSP2_i$. Actually, in what follows we consider h' as part of the result of the operation of instantiation. This means, more precisely:

Definition 6. *Given specifications $MSP = \langle MSP1, MSP2, F \rangle$ and MSP_{act} in $\underline{MSpec}$ and a morphism $h : MSP1 \to MSP_{act}$ in $Mor(\underline{MSpec})$, the re-*

sult of the instantiation of MSP by MSP_{act} via h is a parameterized spec-ification, denoted $MSP_{res} = MSP(MSP_{act})_h$, and a specification morphism $h' : MSP2 \to MSP_{res}$ defined inductively:

- *If $MSP2$ is in $\underline{Spec}$ then MSP_{res} and h' are defined in terms of the multiple pushout shown in Figure 9.*

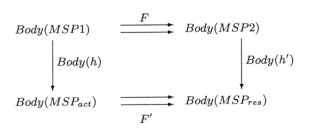

Fig. 9. Multiple Pushout

- *If $MSP2 = \langle MSP2_1, MSP2_2, F2 \rangle$ then $h' = \langle Id : MSP2_1 \to MSP2_1, h'' \rangle$ and $MSP_{res} = \langle MSP2_1, MSP_{res'}, Body(h'') \circ F2 \rangle$, where $MSP_{res'}$ and h'' are the result of the instantiation of $\langle MSP1, MSP2_2, F \rangle$ by MSP_{act} via h.*

This parameter passing construction has the following universal property, which means that h' is unique up to isomorphism:

Proposition 7. *Given $MSP, MSP_{act}, MSP_{res}, h$ and h' as in the previous def-inition and given a specification $MSP3$, a morphism $h3 : MSP2 \to MSP3$ and a multiple morphism $F3 : Body(MSP_{act}) \Rightarrow Body(MSP3)$ such that the dia-gram in Figure 10 commutes, there exist a unique $h3' : MSP_{res} \to MSP3$ such that $h3' \circ h' = h3$ and $Body(h3') \circ F' = F3$.*

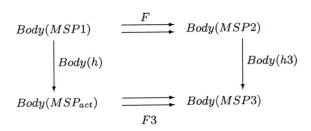

Fig. 10. Multiple diagram

proof sketch The proposition is a consequence of the universal property of multiple pushouts and of the fact that all the component specifications involved as parameters in $MSP2$ and MSP_{res} coincide. $\square$

4   Parameterized Specification Expressions

In this section we define a concrete syntax for module specifications in terms of a language of λ-expressions and we define its semantics in terms of the category defined in the previous section. The class of all specification expressions will be called $\mathcal{SE}$. Since a λ-expression may involve specification morphisms we provide a specific syntax for them in terms of a class of morphism expressions, denoted $\mathcal{ME}$. Finally, we define and study a β-reduction relation between λ-expressions.

Definition 8. *The classes of specification expressions $\mathcal{SE}$ and morphism expressions $\mathcal{ME}$ are defined inductively:*

1. Variable *: any variable X is in $\mathcal{SE}$.*
2. Application *: $E1(E2)_M$ is in $\mathcal{SE}$ if $E1$ and $E2$ are in $\mathcal{SE}$ and M is in $\mathcal{ME}$.*
3. λ-abstraction *: $\lambda X : E1.E2[X]$ is in $\mathcal{SE}$ if $E2[X]$ is an expression over X in $\mathcal{SE}$ and $E1$ is an expression in $\mathcal{SE}$ not including any free variable.*
4. Basic specification expressions *: Any expression $E \in T_{\Sigma SPEC}(\langle \mathcal{SE}, \mathcal{ME} \rangle)$ of sort $SPEC$ is in $\mathcal{SE}$.*
5. Identities *: id_E is in $\mathcal{ME}$ if E is in $\mathcal{SE}$.*
6. Composition *: $M1 \circ M2$ is in $\mathcal{ME}$ if $M1$ and $M2$ are in $\mathcal{ME}$.*
7. Basic morphism expressions *: Any morphism expression $M \in T_{\Sigma SPEC}(\langle \mathcal{SE}, \mathcal{ME} \rangle)$ of sort $MORPH$ is in $\mathcal{ME}$.*
8. Higher-order morphisms *: $\langle M1, M2 \rangle$ is in $\mathcal{ME}$ if $M1$ and $M2$ are in $\mathcal{ME}$.*
9. Subcomponents *: $fst(M)$ and $snd(M)$ are in $\mathcal{ME}$ if M is in $\mathcal{ME}$.*
10. Substitution morphism *: $[E1/E2]_M$ is in $\mathcal{ME}$ if $E1$ and $E2$ are in $\mathcal{SE}$ and M is in $\mathcal{ME}$.*

Remarks 9

1. *The former definition describes the syntactically valid module expressions. However, as before, not every syntactically valid expression can be considered semantically well-formed. Instead, we could have given a definition, in terms of formation rules in order to ensure syntactic and semantic validity.*
2. *Rules 1,2 and 3 are standard for the simply typed λ-calculus. Rule 3 allows the use of expressions such as $\lambda X : E1.\textbf{enrich } X(E2)_M \textbf{ by}...$, where an operation in $\Sigma SPEC$ is used (e.g. an enrichment) over an arbitrary specification expression. As we will see below, this is considered semantically valid only if the parameters of such operation denote basic specifications.*
3. *Rules 5-10 define the morphism expressions considered. In particular, rules 5, 6, 7 and 8 define the most direct ways of denoting morphisms in $MSpec$ i.e. using morphisms from $\underline{Spec}$ (rule 7), using a notation for the identities and for composition or building higher-order morphisms as pairs of lower-order ones. Rule 9 allows one to denote the components of a higher-order morphism. Finally, rule 10 defines a morphism that is defined when performing an operation of substitution and is needed for defining β-reduction.*

In order to cope with expressions that may include free variables we will define semantics with respect to a given environment, where an environment is, as usual, a set of declarations of the form $X : E$ where E is any closed specification expression. The semantics will only be defined for semantically valid expressions.

Definition 10. *Given a specification expression E and an environment Γ, the semantics of E in the environment Γ, denoted $\Gamma \vdash \llbracket E \rrbracket$ (if no specific environment is assumed, e.g. if E is closed, we will just write $\llbracket E \rrbracket$) is defined inductively:*

1. *If $\Gamma \vdash \llbracket E \rrbracket = MSP$ then $\Gamma \cup \{X : E\} \vdash \llbracket X \rrbracket = MSP$*
2. *If $\Gamma \vdash \llbracket E1 \rrbracket = (IMP1, RES1, F1)$, $\Gamma \vdash \llbracket E2 \rrbracket = MSP2$ and $\Gamma \vdash \llbracket M \rrbracket = f$ is a morphism from $IMP1$ to $MSP2$ then*

$$\Gamma \vdash \llbracket E1(E2)_M \rrbracket = (IMP1, RES1, F1)(MSP2)_f$$

3. *If $\Gamma \vdash \llbracket E1 \rrbracket = MSP1$ and $\Gamma \cup \{X : E1\} \vdash \llbracket E2[X] \rrbracket = MSP2$ then*

$$\Gamma \vdash \llbracket \lambda X : E1.E2[X] \rrbracket = \langle MSP1, MSP2, F : Body(MSP1) \Rightarrow Body(MSP2) \rangle$$

where F depends on the form of $E2[X]$. In particular, F is defined as follows:
(a) If $E2[X] = X$, then $F = \langle Id_{Body(MSP1)} \rangle$.
(b) If $E2[X] = E1'(E2')_M$ then $F = (F1'' \circ F2) + (g \circ F1)$, where $\Gamma \vdash \llbracket M \rrbracket = h$, $\Gamma \cup \{X : E1\} \vdash \llbracket E1' \rrbracket = MSP1' = \langle MSP11', MSP12', F1' \rangle$, $\Gamma \cup \{X : E1\} \vdash \llbracket E2' \rrbracket = MSP2'$, $\Gamma \vdash \llbracket \lambda X : E1.E1'[X] \rrbracket = \langle MSP1, MSP1', F1 \rangle$, $\Gamma \vdash \llbracket \lambda X : E1.E2'[X] \rrbracket = \langle MSP1, MSP2', F2 \rangle$ and $MSP2$ is the "result" of the instantiation defined by the multiple pushout in Figure 11.

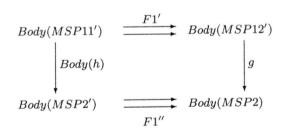

Fig. 11. Multiple Pushout

(c) If $E2[X] = \lambda Y : E1'.E2'$ then F is the multiple morphism defined in $\Gamma \vdash \llbracket \lambda X : E1.E2'[E1'/Y] \rrbracket = \langle MSP1, MSP2', F \rangle$.
(d) If $E2[X] = t[E1'/X1, ..., En'/Xn, M1/Y1, ..., Mm/Ym][X]$, where $t \in T_{\Sigma SPEC}(\{X1, ...Xn, Y1, ...Ym\})$, let us assume that, for each i, $\Gamma \vdash \llbracket \lambda X : E1.Ei' \rrbracket = (MSP1, MSPi', Fi')$ and, for each j, $\Gamma \vdash \llbracket Mj \rrbracket = hj$. In addition, we know (see section 2) that for each i the multiple morphism

$$ti_{MSPi} : MSPi' \Rightarrow t[MSP1'/X1, ..., MSPn'/Xn, h1/Y1, ..., hm/Ym]$$

where

$$ti = t[MSP1'/X1, ..., MSPi-1'/Xi-1, MSPi+1'/Xi+1, ..., Ym/hm]$$

Then

$$F = t1_{MSP1} \circ F1' + ... + tn_{MSPn} \circ Fn'$$

4. *If, for every i,j ($1 \le i \le n$ $1 \le j \le m$), $\Gamma \vdash \llbracket Ei \rrbracket = SPi$, $\Gamma \vdash \llbracket Mj \rrbracket = hj$, with SPi, hj in $\underline{Spec}$ and $t \in T_{\Sigma SPEC}(\langle \{X1, ..., Xn\}, \{Y1, ..., Ym\} \rangle)$ of sort SPEC then*

$$\Gamma \vdash \llbracket t[E1/X1, ..., Ym/Mm] \rrbracket = Sem(t[SP1/X1, ..., hm/Ym])$$

5. *If $\Gamma \vdash \llbracket E \rrbracket = MSP$ then $\Gamma \vdash \llbracket id_E \rrbracket = 1_{MSP}$.*
6. *If $\Gamma \vdash \llbracket M1 \rrbracket = h1 : MSP1 \to MSP2$ and $\Gamma \vdash \llbracket M2 \rrbracket = h2 : MSP2 \to MSP3$ then $\Gamma \vdash \llbracket M2 \circ M1 \rrbracket = h2 \circ h1$.*
7. *If, for every i,j ($1 \le i \le n$ $1 \le j \le m$), $\Gamma \vdash \llbracket Ei \rrbracket = SPi$, $\Gamma \vdash \llbracket Mj \rrbracket = hj$, with SPi, hj in $\underline{Spec}$ and $t \in T_{\Sigma SPEC}(\langle \{X1, ..., Xn\}, \{Y1, ..., Ym\} \rangle)$ of sort MORPH then*

$$\Gamma \vdash \llbracket t[E1/X1, ..., Mm/Ym] \rrbracket = Sem(t[SP1/X1, ..., hm/Ym])$$

8. *If $\Gamma \vdash \llbracket M1 \rrbracket = h1 : MSP1' \to MSP1$, $\Gamma \vdash \llbracket M2 \rrbracket = h2 : MSP2 \to MSP2'$ and $F : Body(MSP1) \Rightarrow Body(MSP2)$, $F' : Body(MSP1') \Rightarrow Body(MSP2')$ are such that the diagram in Figure 12 commutes in $\underline{Spec}$, then $\Gamma \vdash \llbracket \langle M1, M2 \rangle \rrbracket = \langle h1, h2 \rangle$.*

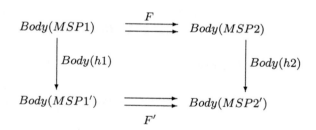

Fig. 12. Semantics of higher-order morphism expressions

9. *If $\Gamma \vdash \llbracket M \rrbracket = \langle h1, h2 \rangle$ then $\Gamma \vdash \llbracket fst(M) \rrbracket = h1$ and $\Gamma \vdash \llbracket snd(M) \rrbracket = h2$*
10. *If $\Gamma \cup \{X : E\} \vdash \llbracket E1 \rrbracket = MSP1$, $\Gamma \vdash \llbracket E \rrbracket = MSP$, $\Gamma \vdash \llbracket E2 \rrbracket = MSP2$ and $\Gamma \vdash \llbracket M \rrbracket = h : MSP \to MSP2$ then $\Gamma \vdash \llbracket [E1/E2]_M \rrbracket = h' : MSP1 \to MSP3$, where $MSP3 = \Gamma \vdash \llbracket (\lambda X : E.E1)(E2)_M \rrbracket$ and h' is the morphism defined by the instantiation operation between $MSP2$ and the result of the instantiation (see def. 6).*

Remark 11. In general, the idea underlying this semantics when dealing with an expression including free variables is that, given an environment, the meaning of the expression is defined as if the variables were substituted by the expressions denoting their type. This is similar to what we explained about obtaining the ground version of a specification in the example in section 3.

Now, once defined the syntax and semantics of module expressions the next step is the definition of a β-reduction relation. Unfortunately, the most obvious candidate does not work, as the following example shows:

Example 12. Consider the following semantically valid module expressions:

$$E = \lambda X : (\lambda Y : SP1.E1).\lambda Z : SP1.X(Z)_{id}$$

$$E' = \lambda Y : SP2.E2$$

where id is the identity morphism, $id : SP1 \to SP1$, $SP1$ and $SP2$ denote two different basic specifications and $E1[SP1/Y]$ and $E2[SP2/Y]$ are semantically valid expressions. Then E and E' are semantically valid and moreover:

$$[\![E]\!] = ((SP1,MSP1,F1),(SP1,MSP1,F1),id : Body(MSP1) \to Body(MSP1))$$

$$[\![E']\!] = (SP2, MSP2, F2)$$

for some multiple morphisms $Fi : SPi \Rightarrow Body(MSPi)(i = 1, 2)$, where $\{Y : SP1\} \vdash [\![E1]\!] = MSP1$ and $\{Y : SP1\} \vdash [\![E2]\!] = MSP2$. Now, suppose that $\langle h1, h2 \rangle$ is a morphism from $(SP1, MSP1, F1)$ to $(SP2, MSP2, F2)$. Then, the expression $E(E')_{\langle h1,h2 \rangle}$ is semantically valid. Actually, $[\![E(E')_{\langle h1,h2 \rangle}]\!] = (SP1, MSP2, h2 \circ F1)$. However, if we β-reduce $E(E')_h$ by substituting in $\lambda Z : SP1.X(Z)_{id}$ all occurrences of X by E' the result is not valid anymore:

$$E(E')_{\langle h1,h2 \rangle} \to_\beta \lambda Z : SP1.(\lambda Y : SP2.E2[Y])(Z)_{id}$$

The problem is that we have assumed that $SP1$ and $SP2$ are different and, as a consequence, we cannot use id in the application $(\lambda Y : SP2.E2[Y])(Z)_{id}$ □

The problem shown by the example above can be avoided by defining β-reduction (or, more precisely, the substitution operation which is the basis of β-reduction) in a slightly more complex way. In particular we need also to change adequately the morphisms involved. In the example above, the right β-reduction would be:

$$E(E')_{\langle h1,h2 \rangle} \to_\beta \lambda Z : SP1.(\lambda Y : SP2.E2[Y])(Z)_{h1}$$

Unfortunately, there is still another, more subtle, problem in this approach as the following example shows:

Example 13. Consider the following semantically valid module expressions:

$$E = \lambda X : (\lambda Y : SP1.E1).X$$

$$E' = \lambda Y : SP2.E2$$

where, as before, $SP1$ and $SP2$ denote two different basic specifications and $E1[SP1/Y]$ and $E2[SP2/Y]$ are semantically valid expressions. Then E and E' are semantically valid and moreover:

$$[\![E]\!] = ((SP1, MSP1, F1), (SP1, MSP1, F1), id : Body(MSP1) \to Body(MSP1))$$

$$[\![E']\!] = (SP2, MSP2, F2)$$

for some multiple morphisms $F1 : SP1 \Rightarrow Body(MSP1)$ and $F2 : SP2 \Rightarrow Body(MSP2)$, where $MSP1 = \{Y : SP1\} \vdash [\![E1]\!]$ and $MSP2 = \{Y : SP1\} \vdash [\![E2]\!]$. Now, suppose as in the previous example that $\langle h1, h2 \rangle$ is a morphism from $(SP1, MSP1, F1)$ to $(SP2, MSP2, F2)$. Then, the expression $E(E')_{\langle h1,h2 \rangle}$ is semantically valid. Actually,

$$[\![E(E')_{\langle h1,h2 \rangle}]\!] = (SP1, MSP2, h2 \circ F1)$$

But, if we β-reduce $E(E')_h$ in the only possible way, by substituting X by E':

$$E(E')_{\langle h1,h2 \rangle} \to_\beta E'$$

we have two not very satisfactory consequences. The first one is that β-reduction does not preserve the semantics since $[\![E(E')_{\langle h1,h2 \rangle}]\!] \neq [\![E']\!]$. The second one is that the most reasonable definition of β-reduction still does not work. The problem is similar to the one shown in the example above but the reasons are slightly different. In particular, consider now the expression:

$$(E(E')_{\langle h1,h2 \rangle})(SP1)_{id}$$

This expression is semantically valid since $[\![E(E')_{\langle h1,h2 \rangle}]\!] = (SP1, MSP2, F2)$ and, thus, it can be applied to $SP1$ via the identity. However, if we consider a standard rule defining β-reduction, ,f $E \to_\beta E'$ then $C[E] \to_\beta C[E']$ for any context C, then we would have that $(E(E')_{\langle h1,h2 \rangle})(SP1)_{id} \to_\beta E'(SP1)_{id}$ Unfortunately, again, $E'(SP1)_{id}$ is not semantically valid. $\square$

One may find the solution to the problem shown in the previous example by making the observation that if we substitute the expression E from example 13 by the expression E of example 12 then the problem disappears, although their meaning is the same (they are η-convertible).That is, if we take the expression

$$E = \lambda X : (\lambda Y : SP1.E1).\lambda Z : SP1.X(Z)_{id}$$

from example 12 and we perform the β-reduction step on the subexpression $E(E')_{\langle h1,h2 \rangle}$ as explained above, we have:

$$(E(E')_{\langle h1,h2 \rangle})(SP1)_{id} \to_\beta (\lambda Z : SP1.E'(Z)_{h1})(SP1)_{id}$$

which is a semantically valid expression. Being specific the problem with the expression E from example 13 is that the information about the "type" is only implicit, i.e. we know that the result of an expression such as $\lambda X : (\lambda Y :$

$SP1.E1).X$ is not a basic specification only by looking to the variable declarations and making some "type inference" (in this case quite trivial). This causes that if we β-reduce the expression and substitute some formal parameters by actual parameters of slightly different type then the type of the result may also change and, as a consequence, it may produce some type mismatches with respect to the context of the expression. This is not the case when considering the expression E in example 12, where the type information about the result $\lambda Z : SP1.X(Z)_{id}$ is included in the result itself. Hence, substituting some external formal parameters by actual parameters of slightly different type will not change the type of the result and will not produce type mismatches. The consequence is that, if we want to avoid this problem, we need to work only with expressions including explicitly all the information necessary about their type. This means that expressions must be "sufficiently" η-*expanded* or, to say it in other words, the expressions must be in η-*long normal form*, as it also happens in some theorem proving tools based on some typed λ-calculus such as Isabelle.

As a consequence, in order to define adequately the β-reduction relation, we first have to define a substitution operation avoiding the problem shown in example 12 and, then, restrict ourselves to η-long λ-expressions. As usual, in the sibstitution operation we assume that there is no problem with clashes of variable names, using α-conversions when needed.

Definition 14. *Given* $E1, E2[X]$ *and* $E3$, *such that* $\Gamma \vdash [\![E1]\!] = MSP1, \Gamma \cup \{X : E1\} \vdash [\![E2[X]]\!] = MSP2$ *and* $\Gamma \vdash [\![E3]\!] = MSP3$ *and given a morphism expression* M, *with* $\Gamma \vdash [\![M]\!] = h : [\![E1]\!] \to [\![E3]\!]$, *the substitution of the expression* $E3$ *through* M *in* $E2[X]$, *written* $Subst(E2[X], E3, M)$, *is the expression:*

1. *If* $E2[X] = X$, *then* $Subst(E2[X], E3, M) = E3$.
2. *If* $E2[X] = E1'[X](E2'[X])_{M1}$, $E5 = Subst(E1'[X], E3, M)$ *and* $E6 = Subst(E2'[X], E3, M)$, *then* $Subst(E2[X], E3, M) = E5(E6)_{M1'}$, *where* $M1' = M6 \circ M1 \circ fst(M5)$ *with* $M6 = [E2'[X]/E3]M$ *and* $M5 = [E1'[X]/E3]M$
3. *If* $E2[X] = \lambda Y : E1'.E2'$, *then* $Subst(E2[X], E3, M) = \lambda Y : E1'.E5$ *where* $E5 = Subst(E2', E3, M)$.
4. *If* $E2[X] = t[E1'/X1, ..., En'/Xn]$, *where* $t \in T_{\Sigma SPEC}(\{X1, ...Xn\})$ *then*

$$Subst(E2[X], E3, M) = assign(...assign(t[X1, ...Xn], M1), ...Mn)$$

where for every i $Mi = [Ei'/E3]M$.

Proposition 15. *Given expressions* $E1, E2[X]$ *and* $E3$ *and a morphism expression* M, *as in the previous definition, if* $Subst(E2[X], E3, M) = E4$ *then* $\Gamma \vdash [\![E4]\!] = MSP4$, *for some* $MSP4$.

proof sketch Cases 1, 3 and 4 are very simple. With respect to case 2, we have to see that if $\Gamma \cup \{X : E1\} \vdash [\![E5]\!] = (IMP5, RES5, F)$ and $\Gamma \cup \{X : E1\} \vdash [\![E6]\!] = MSP6$ then $\Gamma \cup \{X : E1\} \vdash [\![M1']\!] : IMP5 \to MSP6$. We know that $M1' = M6 \circ M1 \circ fst(M5)$, but we also know that: $\Gamma \cup \{X : E1\} \vdash [\![M6]\!] :$

$MSP2' \to MSP6$, where $MSP2' = \Gamma \cup \{X : E1\} \vdash [\![E2'[X]]\!]$, $\Gamma \cup \{X : E1\} \vdash$
$[\![M1]\!] : IMP1' \to MSP2'$, where $(IMP1', RES1', F1') = \Gamma \cup \{X : E1\} \vdash$
$[\![E1'[X]]\!]$, $\Gamma \cup \{X : E1\} \vdash [\![M5]\!] : (IMP1', RES1', F1') \to (IMP5, RES5, F)$,
implying $\Gamma \cup \{X : E1\} \vdash [\![fst(M5)]\!] : IMP5 \to IMP1'$ □

With respect to the second problem described above, we must restrict ourselves to expressions which are "sufficiently" η-expanded, where η-expansion is
the inverse transformation to η-reduction:

$$C[(\lambda X : E1.E2(X)_{id}] \to_\eta C[E2]$$

where C is any arbitrary context. It is clear that, in general, one can η-expand
a term infinitely many times. For instance:

$$C[E2]_\eta \leftarrow C[(\lambda X : E1.E2(X)_{id}]_\eta \leftarrow C[(\lambda X : E1.(\lambda X : E1.E2(X)_{id})(X)_{id}]_\eta \leftarrow ....$$

However, given an arbitrary term it is sufficiently to expand it finitely many
times to make explicit all the necessary information. In particular this leads to
the following notion of η-long normal form:

Definition 16. *Given an expression E and a position p in E we say that E is
η-expanded at p if either the term at p is a λ-abstraction or a basic specification
expression or if the term at position q is an application and $p = q \cdot 1$. An
expression E is in η-long normal form if E is η-expanded at every position.*

As usual, we may see λ-expressions as trees and positions in a term as sequences
of positive integers where the position of the root is the empty string and if
p is a position in E then $p \cdot 1$ is its leftmost son, $p \cdot 2$ is its second son, etc.
For instance, the expression $\lambda X : (\lambda Y : SP1.E1).\lambda Z : SP1.X(Z)_{id}$ is in η-long
normal form, but the expression $\lambda X : (\lambda Y : SP1.E1).X$ is not. The following
proposition shows that if we use the substitution operation defined in 14 for
defining β-reduction the semantics of terms in η-long normal form is preserved.

Proposition 17. *If $E2$ is in η-long normal form, $\Gamma \vdash [\![(\lambda X : E1.E2[X])(E3)_M]\!] =
MSP$ and $Subst(E2[X], E3, M) = \langle E4, h4 \rangle$ then $\Gamma \vdash [\![E4]\!] = MSP$.*

proof sketch By induction on the order of $E2$: If MSP is a basic specification
in $\underline{Spec}$ the result holds by construction since $Body(MSP)$ and $Body(\Gamma \vdash [\![E4]\!])$
always coincide, even if $E2$ is not in η-long normal form. If MSP is higher-order
(and hence $E2$) then $E2$ must be a λ-abstraction. Thus, applying induction, one
would trivially prove the claim. □

Now, we can define the β-reduction relation (almost) as usual:

Definition 18. *β-reduction is the least reflexive and transitive relation satisfying:*

1. *$(\lambda X : E1.E2[X])(E3)_M \to_\beta Subst(E2[X], E3, M)$.*
2. *If $E2[X] \to_\beta E2'[X]$ then $\lambda X : E1.E2[X] \to_\beta \lambda X : E1.E2'[X]$.*
3. *If $E1 \to_\beta E1'$ and $E2 \to_\beta E2'$ then $E1(E2)_M \to_\beta E1'(E2')_M$.*
4. *If $E \to_\beta E'$ and $t[E] \in T_{\Sigma SPEC}(\mathcal{SE})$ then $t[E] \to_\beta t[E']$.*

The following theorem is a direct consequence of proposition 17 and states that β-reduction preserves the semantics of λ−expressions and, in particular, semantic validity. Also, this theorem may be seen as a proof that this calculus satisfies the so-called subject reduction property for expressions in η-long normal form.

Theorem 19. *Let $E1$ and $E1'$ be specification expressions in η-long normal form, if $E1 \rightarrow_\beta E1'$ then $\Gamma \vdash [\![E1]\!] = \Gamma \vdash [\![E1']\!]$ for every Γ such that $\Gamma \vdash [\![E1]\!]$ is defined.*

Acknowledgements This work initially started in cooperation with Hartmut Ehrig. Although he gave it up after some time, afterwards we still had some useful discussions. This work has been partially supported by Spanish CICYT projects COSMOS (ref. TIC95-1016-C02-01) and HEMOSS (ref. TIC98-0949-C02-01).

References

[1] E. Astesiano, H.-J. Kreowski, B. Krieg-Bruckner (eds.) *Algebraic Foundations of System Specification*, Springer-Verlag, To appear.

[2] H. Barendregt: Typed λ-calculi, in *Handbook of Logic in Computer Science* (S. Abramski et. al, eds.), Oxford Univ. Press 1993.

[3] R.M. Burstall, J.A.Goguen. The semantics of Clear, a specification language, *Proc. Copenhagen Winter School on Abstract Software Specification*, LNCS 86, 292–332, Springer 1980

[4] M.V. Cengarle. *Formal Specification with higher order parameterization*, Ph. D. Thesis, Ludwig-Maximilians Universitaet, Muenchen, 1994

[5] H.-D. Ehrich. On the theory of specification, implementation and parameterization of abstract data types. *J. of the ACM* 29, 209–277, (1982)

[6] H. Ehrig, H.-J. Kreowski, J.W. Thatcher, E. Wagner, J. Wright. Parameter passing in algebraic specification languages. *Theor. Comp. Science* 28, 45–81 (1984)

[7] H. Ehrig, B. Mahr. *Fundamentals of Algebraic Specifications 1*, Springer 1985

[8] J.A. Goguen, R.M. Burstall. Introducing institutions. *Proc. Logics of Programming Workshop*, Carnegie-Mellon. LNCS 164, 221–256, Springer 1984

[9] J.A. Goguen, R.M. Burstall. Institutions: Abstract model theory for specification and programming, *J. of the ACM* 39(1), 95–146, (1992)

[10] R. Jiménez, F. Orejas, H. Ehrig. Compositionality and compatibility of parameterization and parameter passing in specification languages, *Math. Structures in Computer Science* 5(2), 283–313 (1995)

[11] B. Krieg-Bruckner, D. Sannella: Structuring specifications in-the-large and in-the-small: higher-order functions, dependent types and inheritance in SPECTRAL, in *TAPSOFT'91 Vol 2*, S. Abramski and T.S.E. Maibaum (eds.), Springer LNCS 494 (1991) pp. 313-336

[12] D. Sannella, S. Sokolowski, A. Tarlecki. Toward formal development of programs from algebraic specifications: parameterisation revisited. *Acta Informatica* 29, 689–736 (1992)

[13] D.T. Sannella, M. Wirsing. A kernel language for algebraic specification and implementation, *Proc. FCT-83*, LNCS 158, 413–427, Springer 1983

[14] M. Wirsing. Structured algebraic specifications: a kernel language. *Theor. Comp. Sc.* 42,123–249 (1986)

[15] M. Wirsing. Algebraic Specification. *Handbook of Theoretical Computer Science, Vol 2: Formal Models and Semantics*, pp. 675 – 788, Elsevier 1991

Applying Formal Proof Techniques to Avionics Software: A Pragmatic Approach

Famantanantsoa Randimbivololona[1] and Jean Souyris[1]
Patrick Baudin[2], Anne Pacalet[2], Jacques Raguideau[2], Dominique Schoen[2]

[1]Aérospatiale Matra Airbus, M8621 - 316, route de Bayonne - 31060 Toulouse cedex, France
[2]CEA Saclay, LETI-DEIN, 91191 Gif-sur-Yvette cedex, France

Abstract. This paper reports an industrial experiment of formal proof techniques applied to avionics software. This application became possible by using Caveat, a tool dedicated to assistance in comprehension and formal verification of safety critical applications written in C. With this approach it is possible to reduce significantly the actual verification effort (based on test) in achieving the verification objectives defined by the DO 178B [4].

1. Introduction

1.1. Purpose

The aim of this paper is to report an industrial experiment of formal verification.

The avionics software verification process must meet the DO 178B [4] requirements. Due to the increasing software size and the hardware technology evolution traditional verification techniques, i.e. the tests, tend to be less and less cost effective in meeting the DO 178B [4] verification requirements.

An alternative and complementary approach consists in using static verification techniques and particularly *formal proof of property*.

The work reported in this paper is a part of a project aiming at the introduction of formal proof in the operational avionics software development. This introduction must be effective in 2001.

All the experiments, and specially the case studies of this paper, have been made by embedded software developers, sometimes with the assistance of formal proof specialists.

1.2. Context

The corresponding applications belong to on-board computers involved in electrical flight control, air/ground communication, alarm and maintenance systems. All these applications have safety, reliability and availability requirements. The consequences of these requirements on the software affect the architecture, fault detection capabilities (functional verifications, asserts, hardware monitoring), recovery from fault detection, etc...

The essential part of the verification cost is due to these features since they require dedicated means.

J. Wing, J. Woodcock, J. Davies (Eds.): FM'99, Vol. II, LNCS 1709, pp. 1798-1815, 1999.
© Springer-Verlag Berlin Heidelberg 1999

1.3. Proof of Property

Property -or program- proof is a well known technique, based on Hoare's [1] or Dijkstra's [2] theories. An interesting characteristic of these theories is that they can be computer aided, i.e. a *tool can be developed to help prove properties*.

In order to meet the objectives defined in section 1.1 the requirements for such a *tool* are listed below.

Ability to prove avionics C code. This is the strongest requirement because formal verification is dedicated to real software products.

Ease of learning and use. The main point, here, is the ability of the tool to be used by "standard" software developers, not only by a team of formal proof specialists.

Early payback. Tool aided formal proof must be used in replacement (not in addition) of the most tedious and expensive phases of the testing process.

Easy integration. The use of the tool should not break down the actual verification process and environment.

A tool which meets this requirement is Caveat, developed by the French Commissariat à l'énergie atomique (CEA). This tool -evaluated by Aerospatiale during the European project LAW [3] - is a "verification assistant" able to perform proof of property.

1.4. Avionics Software Characteristics

Functions. The different classes of functions of an avionics software product are numerical computation, hardware handling, communication protocols, security/protection mechanisms, fault-detection and recovery, Boolean computation.

Properties. An avionics software must have the following types of property : functional, safety, robustness and temporal.

Architecture and sizes. The design and coding rules of an avionics software lead to a modular architecture. They also limit the size and complexity of the individual modules.

The size of an entire avionics software product may be up to 500,000 lines of code.

Algorithms. From that point of view, avionics software is never very complicated. For instance, the loops are very simple (eg : array initialisation, search within an array). So one of the great difficulties of automatic property proof, i.e the analysis of loops, is simplified a lot.

1.5. Development Process of Aerospatiale Matra Airbus Avionics Software

This section gives an overview of the *actual* avionics software development process. It is a typical "V" process.

We will see in section 3.1 how we intend to introduce formal proof in this process.

Specification. There are two families of specifications : *Formal specifications* using the following specification languages : SAO, SCADE, LDS and *textual specifications*, written in natural language.

The formal specifications are most of the time automatically coded.

Design. There is no design activity for the automatically coded pieces of code (from formal specification).

In the case of textual specifications, the design process is based on the HOOD [5] method.

Coding. As stated earlier, the code can be produced automatically when associated with formal specifications (SAO, SCADE, etc) or "intellectually" produced from the HOOD [5] design when the specification is in textual format. Several languages are actually used, e.g. assembly languages, Intel PL/M, C, etc. *Only the C language is considered in this paper.*

Verification process. With the exception of reviews and analyses, all the verifications are performed by *tests* ; the basic principle of the test being the notion of *execution*.

There are three sets of tests : *Unit tests* whose objective is to prove that each module meets its requirements ; *Integration tests* are performed to prove - progressively - that the modules interact correctly, on a host system first and then on the target hardware ; finally, *Validation tests* performed in an environment whose characteristics are very close to the aircraft finally prove that the software meets its customer's requirements.

The typical software properties to be proven during these three verification phases are : functional and safety sequential properties in Unit testing and in Integration testing on the host platform ; real-time and hardware access properties in Integration testing on the final target ; functional, safety and real-time properties in Validation testing.

These properties are not treated as such, they lead to test case generation and test execution.

2. Caveat

Caveat is a tool based on static analysis of source code, for comprehensive analysis and formal verification; it is dedicated to safety critical applications written in C.

Some technical aspects and formalisms used in Caveat and some industrial constraints taken into account in the design of the tool are described below.

2.1. Technical Aspects and Formalisms

The tool is based on the following well-known techniques.

Static analysis of source code. Tables and internal trees coming from compilation, are used to perform detection of anomalies, synthesis of properties and proofs.

A dedicated property language. Based on conventions coming from on Z[9] and VDM[10], it allows properties of the first order logic to be expressed (generated or to be proved).

Models for pointers and arrays are defined to describe such entities in the predicate language; specific operators are added to facilitate the writing of predicates dealing with structures, arrays or pointers of the C language.

Features are added to the property language in order to describe different kinds of property : explicit and implicit operands of a function, class of operands (In , Out, Inout), dependencies of outputs on inputs (From), postcondition (property that must be satisfied at the end of a function : Post), precondition (property that is assumed to be satisfied when the function is called : Pre), local-condition (property that must be verified at a specific location inside a function : Assert).

Some of these properties are automatically computed by the tool during a property synthesis phase. An example of the generated properties is given on figure 1.

Weakest precondition computation. The technique described by Hoare [1] is used to compute the condition that must be satisfied by the inputs of the function to ensure that the given property will be satisfied after execution of the code, if it terminates.

The semantics of each instruction is taken into account, modifying the initial predicate towards the weakest precondition.

An algebraic simplifier. It is used during the weakest precondition computation, to reduce, as soon as possible, the size of the formulae and during the demonstration phase.

It is based on a set of about 2000 re-writing rules of the following shape :

$$\text{left-term [left-proc] --> right-term [right-proc]}$$

where left-proc and right-proc are optional C procedures that may help describe the re-writing.

The tool looks for the matching rules in the initial predicate, computes the substitutions and applies them to obtain the simplified expression.

The simplification strategy of a term proceeds recursively to its sub-terms.

The rules deal with associativity, commutativity, distributivity, equalities, inequalities, arithmetical and boolean operations, numerical constants, and specific notations.

An automatic theorem prover. It is fully integrated ito the tool : it takes, as an input, the predicate coming from the weakest precondition computation (the goal) and the result of the demonstration is expressed in the property language.

The aim of the theorem prover is to demonstrate the goal under some hypotheses. There are two kinds of hypotheses :

. axioms specific to areas and independent from application,

. specific hypotheses in relation with the application : preconditions of the function, postconditions of called functions.

The demonstration is performed by generation of sub-goals using some inference rules. The choice of a rule depends on the syntactic structure of the initial goal. When no decomposition into sub-goals is possible, other inference rules using hypotheses are applied. The algebraic simplifier is also called.

Of course, being fully automatic (as opposed to of the Larch Prover [8]), it may fail. The wish is to avoid asking for assistance from the user for the choice of such or such a strategy during the demonstration phase, because it would suppose a specific skill in that domain.

In case of failure, the result returned by the tool is the remaining part of the initial goal that is not proved. Graphical facilities are provided to understand the structure of the result.

Example and counter-example generation. In case of failure of the demonstration, it is important for the user to know whether the failure comes from the tool or from a real error in the code. The tool offers other possibilities, such as the generation of examples or counter-examples for debugging purposes.

When the user asks the tool to generate counter-examples, the tool computes a predicate giving conditions on inputs which refutes the property. These conditions, after constraint solving, give input values with which the function may be executed to exhibit the problem.

An interactive predicate transformer. Another possibility in case of failure is the re-writing of the remaining predicate resulting from the demonstration. The interactive predicate transfomer offers a list of possibilities to rewrite the remaining formula, in order to facilitate reading, understanding, simplification and even demonstration: the user may introduce "let" notations to reduce the size, break the predicate into cases, rewrite it in a normal disjunctive or conjunctive form, etc. For instance, the disjunctive normal form allows independant proofs to be performed on each member of the disjunction; if only one of the members is proved, the initial property is proved.

Processed Language. Unlike other similar products (see 2.x), caveat performes proofs on the source code, not in an intermediate code, because it is the lowest representation of the executable code easily understandable by the user, on which reasoning can be performed.

The chosen processed language is ANSI C, as defined in the ISO standard, because of its widespread use in industry, but implementation makes it possible to deal with other programming languages without restarting from scratch.

The current version of the tool has some restrictions in the use of ANSI C : features like function pointers, recursive calls, alias are not implemented yet.

2.2. Industrial Constraints

The industrial constraints of the targeted applications match Caveat capabilities.

Suitability for processed language. The features of C language not addressed by Caveat correspond to limitations of critical application coding rules in the aeronautical and nuclear fields.

Size of application. Two other specificities give Caveat the ability to address industrial applications : *iterativity* and *interactivity*. They both make it possible to capture the right level of information from the user and give him back just the necessary information to go further, avoiding getting him bogged down in details due to the size of the application.
Verification work may be performed step by step, in an iterative process: the user asks the tool to verify a property on a function without being obliged to describe anything previously : as an answer, the tool exhibits just the missing information (if any) for performing the proof. Interactivity allows the user to give the missing information and go further in his verification process.

Facility of use. Iterativity and Interactivity are supported by the interface of the tool. It is composed of three main windows (see figure 1) : on the left, the user can read the C source he is working on; the right window displays the C function properties ; the window below shows the result of the last proof done by the tool (if the proof is not established). With a simple selection, it is possible to see the connections between elements of the property or result windows and the source window.
A property file is associated with each C source module. Each function in the C module has its dedicated block of properties. Some of these properties are automatically generated during the initial analysis of sources (prototype of functions, Implicit operands, From, classes of operands In, Out, InOut). During this property

synthesis, anomalies (if any) like uninitialized variables, dead branches are pointed out; the call graph of the application is computed and may be displayed. The result of this initial automatical analysis of sources is displayed in the property window.

The user may then use interactive facilities provided by the interface to add his own properties, either for getting proof, example, counter-example (post, assert), or for detailing the context in which the study is performed (pre), or for analysing the result of failed proof (interactive predicate transformer).

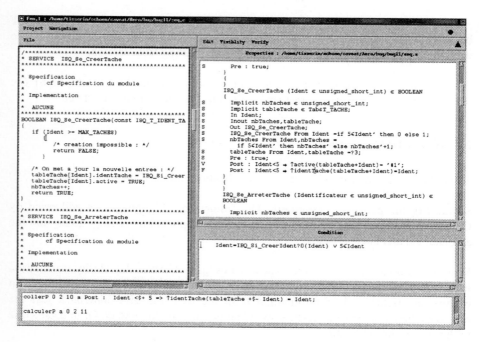

Figure 1.

Figure 1 illustrates the capability of the tool to peerform proofs even if pieces of information are not provided : for instance, a loop invariant is not necessary if the loop does not modify the variables of the property. Figure 1 shows that P1 is satisfied without providing any information about the C function ISQ_SiCreerIdent(). On the other hand, the post property P2 fails : the tool indicates that information on the output of the ISQ_SiCreerIdent() function is missing to perform the proof : this is an example of the iterative work : the user is invited to add this information (and only this) and may remain concentrated on his initial work.

Re-use of previous work. Many applications use identical software components. Validation work performed on these components may be re-used by means of user's libraries in which already demonstrated properties are memorized. This feature is part of the iterative aspect of the proof process defined as a basis of the Caveat tool.

Batch mode. The tool provides the possibility to record commands, and replay them in batch mode. This is very useful when interactivity is no longer needed, for instance for non-regression verification or when results on the verification process have to be given to a licensing authority.

Tracking of dependencies. The tool performs proofs by using the properties of low level components: axioms, semantics of operators, properties of the called functions... The tool manages the links between properties. It is then possible to know the consequences of the modification of low level properties on upper levels, and thus evaluate the work that must be repeated.

2.3. Comparison with Other Tools

A verification tool. Caveat is merely a verification tool. It does not claim to cover the whole software development life-cycle. Is is clearly dedicated to the last development phases, the programmation and verification phases in which it aims to help the user to analyse the code, understand it better and verify it regarding some properties.

Caveat is not a verification system like GVE [7] with a specification language and translators into programming language.

No intermediate language. Unlike tools such as MALPAS[6], *Caveat works directly on the source code*. This provides the advantage of eliminating any translation from source code into an intermediate langage, so that the model on which proofs are performed is as close as possible to the code. Consequently, the results are also as close as possible to the initial source, and are thus easier to analyse.

Interactivity. Caveat seems *much more interactive* than other similar tools. The preference is given to expressivity of properties and readability of results rather than automaticity.

3. Using Caveat on Avionics Software

The main objective of this chapter is to show how the methodolgy being built around Caveat allows the claims made in sections 1.1, i.e. cost reduction, and in section 1.3 to be met.

Three significant examples illustrate the way we will use Caveat and the associated methodology.

3.1. Methodological Approach

In section 1.3, we listed the requirements for a tool (and related methodology) able to perform formal proof.

The following requirements are directly met by Caveat (See chapter 2 for the substanciation of these claims) : *ability to prove avionics C code, ease of learning and use.*

In order to meet the rest of the claims, i.e. cost reduction, early payback and easy integration), a methodology is being developed.

After an analysis of existing avionics software, we defined the following courses for the application of formal proof using Caveat : *algorithm verification* at unit (module) level and *safety* analysis. Both approaches are related to properties which can be expressed in the first order logic.

Algorithm verification at module level takes place in the current unit testing phase. The objective here is to replace this main activity of unit test by formal proof. If achieved, this objective will lead to *spending significantly less time* in verifying a property, *using less expensive specific hardware and related software* (no execution with formal proof) and, finally, *detecting more problems earlier* in the verification process.

The first claim ("spend significantly less time...") is the consequence of the ease of use of Caveat. With this tool, to prove that a C function has a certain property, the user "only" has to express the property in the first order logic language of Caveat, run the tool and analyse the result. To do the same, i.e. prove that a C function has the required property, using unit testing techniques, one has to generate test cases, code a test program, debug it if necessary, execute both test and tested programs linked together and finally analyse the result. This comparison of these techniques allows us to think that formal proof used in module verification is more cost effective than unit testing.

The second claim ("use less expensive hardware") is due to the fact that, currently, the execution of unit tests is performed on a target able to execute the same binary code as the final embedded target (the on-board computer). So, in order to execute unit tests generated with a dedicated commercial tool, we need a run-time per execution hardware type. With formal proof using Caveat, there is no need for test hardware and run-time dedicated to unit verification.

The third claim ("detect problems earlier...") is due to the exhaustivity of formal proof versus tests.

Verification of dependability properties. This is the second application course of the proof of property technique. Critical software have to meet dependability objectives, derived from safety analyses performed at system and equipment levels. Software safety properties concern higher levels of software functions and usually they involve several modules. In this context, Caveat interactivity helps in building a property step by step.

Consequences on the requirements. Using the formal proof technique on software whose specification is textual (not formal) will *improve the quality of the requirements*. They will tend to be more accurate because a lot of them will have to be translated into first order formulae for verification. So, the formulation of these requirements will have to be semantically close to first order logic formulae in order to facilitate the translation into the property language of Caveat. The textual specification will remain in natural language but with a slightly more *logic* form.

3.2. Case Studies

The examples of this section illustrate the use of Caveat on critical embedded software applications and give some methodological indications about the way to use the proof of properties in this industrial context.

They are also representative of the kind of functions and code found in avionics critical embedded software. They reveal the ability of the tool to cope with these sorts of code.

Different types of function. The three examples are functions frequently met in avionics software. The first one belongs to the logic computation family, which can be met in on-board warning or maintenance on-board computers. The second example is representative of the security mechanisms met in several computers into which complex structured data (in a file, for instance) can be entered. The third one represents the hardware interface. Because on-board computer hardware is completely specific ("home made"), avionics software developers have to write hardware interface layers. These layers allow hardware initialisation, input/ouput handling, hardware monitoring, etc.

Coding characteristics. The first example, Boolean computation, shows what we can call "strongly Boolean code" : a lot of boolean operators (AND, OR...), RS flip-flop, confirms, etc. The specificity of the second one is the fact that it involves code running on top of an embedded UNIX-like operating system. There are wo consequences : firstly, the C modules include a lot of system headers defining plenty of data types, constants, etc... ; secondly, the C modules call system or library functions. As explained above, the third example is representative of the pieces of code with inputs coming directly from the hardware. The particularity, here, is the handling of bits present in data words read from hardware registers. The problem is the same when bits are used to compact information into a few data words (in operating systems for instance).

Properties. The examples described below are also representative of different kinds of required properties. For logic computation (first example) it is important to prove that some erroneous outputs or combinations of ouputs which can lead to dangerous behaviours will not be generated. So, the properties for this kind of function are *safety properties*. For the second example, the required properties are clearly *security properties*. But as security is the main function of the family represented by the second example, the properties it requires are also *functional properties*. The properties required by the third example (hardware handling) are *safety properties* because the objective, in that case, is to prove that a logic computation, based on the value of hardware registers (bit-structured), is safe.

3.3.

Making the proof of a property requires the following steps (they are applied to the examples) :

(1)   Identification of the property in the requirements.
(2)   Identification, in the design, of the code modules (C modules) involved in the property.
(3)   Identification, in the design, of the C function on which the property must be verified.
(4)   Creation of the Caveat project, i.e running Caveat on the "project" made of the analysed modules.
(5)   Translation of the property from natural language (the way it is written in the requirements) to the property language of Caveat (based on the first order logic). The property is then given to the tool at the appropriate point of the function identified in step 3.
(6)   Proof of the property by Caveat : Caveat computes the condition (in the first order logic) which has to be TRUE at the beginning of the C function, in order to be sure that the property is verified at the point of the function at which it was introduced.
(7)   Analysis of the result. Two cases :
      Caveat says "V" ("Verified") : the remaining verification condition (See point 6) is TRUE thus the property is verified by the code,
      Caveat says "F" ("Failed") and gives the remaining condition. In this case, there are two potential reasons why Caveat failed :
      - The property is not verified by the code. In this case, it is possible to deduce counter-examples from the remaining condition given by the tool. This can be done with a constraint solver.
      - The property is in fact verified by the code but the tool cannot prove it, i.e. the remaining formula cannot be "simplified" to TRUE. In this case the proof has to be completed "intellectually", aided by the Caveat Interactive Predicate Transformer (IPT). Examples for tests can also be deduced from the remaining verification condition.

3.4. Examples

Safety : Boolean computation.

This case comes from the requirements (in the avionics specification language called SAO) of an on-board computer which performs a lot of logic computation. The analysed SAO sheet produces ten Boolean outputs (out01...out0a) from 32 inputs (In01..In20). It is composed of about 70 logic symbols like Boolean operators (AND, OR) or flip-flop, confirms, etc.

This example is typical of the *dependability verification* course (see section 3.1).

Step 1 : An interesting safety property is : "At any time, at least one output must be set".

Step 2, 3 and 4 have been performed. For the rest of the description, it is not important to know the related names of the modules, functions or tool files.

Step 5 : The ten outputs are declared as an array of unsigned char (out[10]) and only two values can be given to its elements : 0 and 1. An output (eg : out[2]) is "set" when its value is 1. In the property language of Caveat, we obtain :

$$Post :$$
$$\uparrow(out+0) \neq 0 \vee \uparrow(out+1) \neq 0 \vee \uparrow(out+2) \neq 0 \vee \uparrow(out+3) \neq 0$$
$$\vee \uparrow(out+4) \neq 0 \vee \uparrow(out+5) \neq 0 \vee \uparrow(out+6) \neq 0 \vee \uparrow(out+7) \neq 0$$
$$(1)\vee \uparrow(out+8) \neq 0 \vee \uparrow(out+9) \neq 0 ;$$

Note. $\uparrow(out+0)$ in the Caveat property language is equivalent to out[0] in C.

Step 6 : The computation results in "V" ("Verified"). It means that the property is always true, i.e. for all possible input values.

Considering the great number of inputs of the module (32), it is clear that the amount of tests that would be necessary to prove the property leads to a far greater effort than the one needed to perform the mathematical proof.

Security : Uploading checks.

This case study was extracted from another on-board computer. The origin of the analysed piece of code is the uploading facility of this on-board computer. This feature allows avionics applications to be uploaded into the computer, from a floppy disk.
On this floppy disk, there are two sorts of file : a configuration file containing the relevant characteristics of the files to be loaded and the files themselves.
    The main actions of the uploading function are : *loading* the configuration file from the media (using an on-board communication protocol) ; *analysing* the contents of the configuration file in order to identify which files are to be loaded and to verify if their associated characteristics allow them to be loaded ; *loading* the files ; *updating* the internal configuration (internal configuration files).

The case presented here involves the module implementing some of the checks before loading. As these checks are performed by a unique C function, this example illustrates both methodological courses (see sect. 3.1) : algorithm (at module level) and dependability verification.

Step 1 : In the case of software security checks, the interesting properties are "mapped" on the requirements. Checks are there for security, so verifying their code with the "safety point of view" is identical to verifying their function (the requirements).
For this example, twenty properties have been identified. Nineteen of them express reasons for stoping loading and the twentieth says : "If all the checks are OK, the loading can carry on".
    Two examples of properties :
(P1)   "If the name of the file to be loaded exceeds 49 characters then stop loading"

(P2)   "If the application to be loaded is an ABC one and the priority it requires for its
execution is not between 105 and 200 then stop loading".

Step 2, 3 and 4 : same as previous example.

Step 5 : The characteristics of the file to be loaded are read from the configuration file
and loaded in memory via a complex data structure. The checked characteristics are
fields of this complex data structure, called TFC_Ri_FichierConfig in source file.

The translation of both properties into the property language (see step 1) gives the
following post-conditions :

Property P1 :

$$\text{Post P1 :}$$
$$\text{strlen?0}(\uparrow\text{InfoComune(TFC\_Ri\_FichierConfig.Log+num\_elem).NomDest})$$
$$\geq^{333}50$$
$$(1) \Rightarrow \text{TFC\_Si\_VerifElement=0};$$

Let us comment on this formula :

♦ *"TFC_Si_VerifElement"* is the name of the analysed function and
"⇒ TFC_Si_VerifElement=0" means "implies the value returned by
TFC_Si_VerifElement is 0".

♦ *"strlen?0"* in *P1* stands for the return of the function strlen(). This function is
called by the analysed function.

♦ "↑*InfoCommune(TFC_Ri_FichierConfig.Log+num_elem).NomDest*" in *P1*
represents "TFC_Ri_FichierConfig.Log[num_elem].InfoCommune.NomDest" in C
language.

Property P2 :

$$\text{Post P2 :}$$
$$((\uparrow\text{TypeLog(TFC\_Ri\_FichierConfig.Log+num\_elem)=0}$$
$$\wedge (\uparrow\text{InfoCommune(TFC\_Ri\_FichierConfig.Log+num\_elem).Priorite<105}$$
$$\vee$$
$$\uparrow\text{InfoCommune(TFC\_Ri\_FichierConfig.Log+num\_elem).Priorite>2}$$
$$00))$$
$$(2) \Rightarrow \text{TFC\_Si\_VerifElement=0};$$

Step 6 : the computations of P1 and P2 but also the computations of the eighteen other
properties result in "V" ("Verified"). This clearly means that the analysed function
meets its requirements.

Hardware handling. The case study presented here is symptomatic of a logic based on bit-structured data. In this example, such data come from an hardware register (in fact a CPU board status register). The function analysed in this case must convert each configuration of a subset of the register bits into pre-defined integer values. The computed value must be stored in a global resource because the value computed at a given time must be greater than or equal to the one previously stored. *Remark* : the global resource is shared with another piece of code which can reset it. This comparison mechanism is used to set priorities among the actions associated with the computed values.

Applying the method (see section 3.2) to this example, we get :

Step 1. The following property is considered : "If the stored value is the smallest (among the possible ones) and the currently computed value (from the current hardware register value) is not the smallest then the result cannot be the smallest".

Step 2, 3 and 4. Same principles as in previous examples.

Step 5. *Hypotheses for the property* : the current version of the tool does not automatically recognize the values of *const* data. So, because the analysed C function uses a const array to compute the integer value from the register data, the proof can be performed only if we give Caveat the const array values. This is done using a *pre-condition*.

Pre-condition giving Caveat the const array values :

$$\text{Pre :}$$
$$\text{IIS\_Ri\_TabCoupure=Mk\&Tab\&DHT\_T\_TYPE\_COUPURE}$$
$$(4)(@\text{IIS\_Ri\_TabCoupure, } 16, 0, \{0 \rightarrow 17, 1 \rightarrow 0, 2 \rightarrow 33, 3 \rightarrow 66, 4 \rightarrow 0, 5 \rightarrow 0,$$
$$6 \rightarrow 0, 7 \rightarrow 0, 8 \rightarrow 0, 9 \rightarrow 0, 10 \rightarrow 33, 11 \rightarrow 66, 12 \rightarrow 0, 13 \rightarrow 0, 14 \rightarrow 0, 15 \rightarrow 66\},);$$

Remark. With this property, Caveat considers that the array IIS_Ri_TabCoupure[16] (used by the analysed function) has the values 17, 0, 33, ..., 66.
Another pre-condition Caveat has to know is the set of possible values of the global resource used to store the previous computed value.

$$\text{Pre :}$$
$$(5)\text{Stocke\_dem}=0 \lor \text{Stocke\_dem}=17 \lor \text{Stocke\_dem}=33 \lor$$
$$\text{Stocke\_dem}=50 \lor \text{Stocke\_dem}=66 \lor \text{Stocke\_dem}=81;$$

The property : Writing a property containing a lot of operands and/or operators in Caveat property language can be very difficult, because it leads to a very complicated formula. It is not due to the tool but to the fact of expressing the property by a mathematical formula. To solve this problem, the best way is to use Caveat incrementally. The purpose here is to let Caveat generate a part of the formula. This can be done using an Assert property. To introduce such a property into a C function, it is necessary to put a label in the code at which the Assert property must be true. Then Caveat can compute the condition on the function input operands that leads to verifying the property.

Applying this method to the current example, an Assert is used to determine the mathematical predicate equivalent to the proposition (which belongs to the property to be verified) "the currently computed value (from the current hardware register value) is not the smallest" (in the code, the smallest value is 17).

The assert property is :

$$(6)\text{Assert : At label1 } \uparrow(\text{IIS\_Ri\_TabCoupure'}+\text{val}) \neq 17;$$

With this property, Caveat will compute the condition for obtaining a value not equal to 17 from the const array IIS_Ri_TabCoupure.

Let C2 be the condition Caveat computed.

The result is :
C2 :
¬ (((if bit&32($\uparrow$(@ad12345678), 12)
then (if bit&32($\uparrow$(@ad12345678), 11)
then (if bit&32($\uparrow$(@ad12345678), 10)
then 17=$\uparrow$(IIS_Ri_TabCoupure+~14)else
else 17=$\uparrow$(IIS_Ri_TabCoupure+~6))
                else (if bit&32($\uparrow$(@ad12345678), 10)
                then 17=$\uparrow$(IIS_Ri_TabCoupure+~10)
                else 17=$\uparrow$IIS_Ri_TabCoupure+~2)))
            else (if bit&32($\uparrow$(@ad12345678), 11)
            then (if bit&32($\uparrow$(@ad12345678), 10)
                then 17=$\uparrow$(IIS_Ri_TabCoupure+~12)
                else 17=$\uparrow$(IIS_Ri_TabCoupure+~4))
            else (if bit&32(-(@ad12345678), 10)
                then 17=$\uparrow$(IIS_Ri_TabCoupure+~8)
                else 17=$\uparrow$(IIS_Ri_TabCoupure)))
⇒ bit&32($\uparrow$(@ad12345678), 13))
⇒ bit&32($\uparrow$(@ad12345678), 13)
            ∧ (if bit&32($\uparrow$(@ad12345678), 12)
            then (if bit&32($\uparrow$(@ad12345678), 11)
                then (if bit&32($\uparrow$(@ad12345678), 10)
                then 17=$\uparrow$(IIS_Ri_TabCoupure+~15)
                else 17=$\uparrow$(IIS_Ri_TabCoupure+~7))
            else (if bit&32($\uparrow$(@ad12345678), 10)
                then 17=$\uparrow$(IIS_Ri_TabCoupure+~11)
                else 17=$\uparrow$(IIS_Ri_TabCoupure+~3)))
            else (if bit&32($\uparrow$(@ad12345678), 11)

```
        then (if bit&32(↑(@ad12345678), 10)
          then 17=↑(IIS_Ri_TabCoupure+~13)
          else 17=↑(IIS_Ri_TabCoupure+~5))
        else (if bit&32(↑(@ad12345678), 10)
          then 17=↑(IIS_Ri_TabCoupure+~9)
          else 17=↑(IIS_Ri_TabCoupure+~1))))
   ∨ bit&32(↑(@ad12345678), 17)
   ∨ bit&32(↑(@ad12345678), 22))
```

Notes. eg : the predicate "bit&32(↑(@ad12345678), 13)", in Caveat property language, is TRUE if the bit 13 of the data stored at address 12345678 is set (=1).

As we can see, it is better to let Caveat provide the formula.

The property, as written in step 1, is composed of three propositions : "the stored value is the smallest (among the possible ones) ", "the currently computed value (from the current hardware register value) is not the smallest" and "the result cannot be the smallest". With the Assert property computation, the second proposition has just been computed. The other two are quite simple, they do not need any intermediary computation.

So, the property is :

(7)Post : Stocke_dem'=17 ∧ C2 ⇒ TypeDemarrage ≠ 17;

where C2 is the condition computed by Caveat using the Assert property.
Step 6. Caveat proves this post-condition ("V").

This example shows that a logic based on bit-structured data coming from the hardware can be efficiently verified without having to use real or even simulated hardware. Again it allows a gain in terms of verification cost.

4. Conclusion

4.1. Lessons Learnt

Caveat and the way we have used it on these examples shows its ability to meet the requirements stated in section 1.3 : (1) ability to prove avionics C code, (2) ease of learning and use, (3) early payback, (4) easy integration.

Requirements 1 and 2 are directly met by Caveat, as explained in chapter 2. Practical examples did not reveal any major difficulty around the C language used.

This examples also revealed that the initial training effort that a "standard" software engineer needs to produce is not greater than for another industrial software verification technique : one week's training is enough to be able to perform formal proofs with Caveat.

Requirement 3 should be met if we consider that a lot of tests (mainly unit tests) will be simply replaced by formal proof, and that each formal proof can be performed in significantly less time and with less hardware than the corresponding tests. The ease of learning and use will also help to meet this requirement.

Requirement 4 is met by the fact that the introduction of the formal proof technique in our development methodology (see sect. 1.5 and 3.1) does not change it fundamentally.

These examples also reveal the necessity for some enhancements of Caveat. They will be implemented soon. The main point is the improvement to automaticity in theorem proving.

4.2. Qualitative/Quantitative Results

Qualitative results.

♦ The good level of maturity of Caveat plus the enhancements planned for this year (better automaticity in theorem proving) confirm its ability to improve the verification of avionics applications significantly.

♦ The property language of Caveat can easily be used by a software developer.

♦ The incremental way to use Caveat helps manage the complexity of the mathematical representation of the source code (see example 3 in section 3.3).

♦ The tool and the method for using it make it possible to detect software faults and find counter-examples which can be used in debug sessions.

Quantitative results.

♦ The computation time of Caveat is compatible with an industrial usage.

♦ In terms of cost effectiveness the examples described in this document reveal the three types of gain stated in section 3.1.

Example 1 is very expensive in terms of testing effort in the sense that the required property depends on thirty-two inputs. So, by using the property proof technique, it is no longer necessary to generate and execute a large amount of test cases (first type of gain).

Example 2. In this case (and for this type of code, i.e. checks implemented by "if..else.."), the gain, in terms of time spent, is around 20 %. If we consider that a lot of avionics functions are similar, in terms of implementation, to example 2, it is possible to replace unit testing on these functions and so, the gain on a quite large part of an avionics software product would be about 20 %.

Example 3 : in this case, the cost is reduced because less hardware is needed to perform the verification. In a classical approach, the kind of verification of example 3 is performed during the integration phase, on the real hardware. So the third reason why cost can be reduced is also true in this example.

After these experiments, and the finalisation of the formal proof methodology, it will also be necessary, for the overall verification process (not only unit tests and safety verification) to define a methodology which combines classical tests with property proof.

References

1. C.A.R Hoare : An axiomatic basis for computer programming, Comm. ACM 12 (10), 576-580, 583 (Oct. 1969).
2. Dijkstra BW 1976, A discipline of programming, in *Series Automatic Computation,* Prentice Hall.
3. Pavey D et al. 1997, LAW : Legacy Assessment Workbench, in the UK *Reliability and Metrics Club's news letter.*
4. A joint RTCA-EUROCAE achievement : DO-178B / ED-12B, Software considerations in airborne systems and equipment certification (Dec. 1992).
5. HOOD Technical Group, Jean-Pierre Rosen : HOOD - An industrial approach for software design (1997).
6. A. Smith - MALPAS Userguide. *Technical Report*, Rex, Thomson & partners Limited, 1991.
7. R. Cohen - Proving Gypsy Programs, in *CLI Technical Reports*, 1989.
8. Sj. Garland & Jv. Guttag - A guide to LP, the Larch Prover, MIT Laboratory for Computer Science, 1991.
9. JM. Spivey - The Z Notation, A Reference manual. University of Oxford, 1988.
10. CB. Jones - Systematic Software Development Using VDM. Prentice Hall Int., 1986.

Secure Synthesis of Code: A Process Improvement Experiment

P. Garbett[1], J.P. Parkes[1], M. Shackleton[1]*, and S. Anderson[2]

[1] Lucas Aerospace, York Road, Hall Green, Birmingham B28 8LN, UK,
shacklm@liyorkrd.li.co.uk,
Tel: +44 121 627 6600, Fax: +44 121 607 3619
[2] Division of Informatics, University of Edinburgh, Edinburgh EH9 3JZ, UK,
soa@dcs.ed.ac.uk,
Tel: +44 131 650 5191, Fax: +44 131 667 7209

Abstract. Arguments for and against the deployment of formal methods in system design are rarely supported by evidence derived from experiments that compare a particular formal approach with conventional methods [2]. We illustrate an approach to the use of formal methods for secure code synthesis in safety-critical Avionics applications. The technique makes use of code components and uses sound introduction rules for the components to ensure constraints on their use are enforced. The approach we describe is the subject of a controlled experiment where it is running in parallel with the conventional approach. We describe the experiment and report some preliminary findings.

1 Introduction

Lucas Aerospace[1] develop safety-critical avionics software. In particular, we have a long history of constructing Full Authority Digital Engine Controllers (FADECs) that control the fuel supply to aircraft engines. "Full Authority" means that there is no reversionary (backup) control. This means the digital control system is a critical function. In an earlier paper [8] we described Lucas Aerospace's overall approach to process improvement. Process improvement is necessary in highly critical software production because we would like to see a reduction in life-cycle costs for new, more sophisticated designs while maintaining or improving on the safety integrity of the product.

In mature development processes it is necessary to innovate in the process to achieve significant improvements. Because untried techniques carry implementation risk we have developed an approach to process innovation based on

---

* Partially supported by the EU ESSI programme projects, no. 23743, *Proof by Construct using Formal Methods* and no.27825, *Implementing Design Execution using Ada*.
[1] Lucas Aerospace is a TRW company.

J. Wing, J. Woodcock, J. Davies (Eds.): FM'99, Vol. II, LNCS 1709, pp. 1816–1835, 1999.

experimentation with new techniques. This paper describes our approach to process innovation in one facet of our current process and the ongoing experiment to assess the effectiveness of the approach.

The aspect of our development process we consider here is the generation of code from a specification. We use formal development to synthesise code from the specification. The aim of the experiment is to see the extent to which using formal methods can control errors arising in code production. We believe there will be a measurable difference between our formal approach and the existing approach.

1.1 Safety Critical Avionics Software

The main characteristics of safety-critical avionics software are: A *high reliability requirement*, typically the required system reliability of software components is better than one failure in 10^6 flying hours. The controller and equipment under control are *co-engineered*, this leads to much greater variability of requirements through the lifetime of the system. As aircraft employ more digital systems the *size and complexity* of individual sub-systems tends to grow. Software produced by Lucas Aerospace must *certified* to comply with Level A of DO178B [14]. Developing software that complies to such exacting standards take a great deal of effort — safety critical software is expensive to produce.

In justifying any claim of high-reliability the producer of the system needs to (explicitly or implicitly) make a safety case for the system. The safety case must be: *a demonstrable and valid argument that a system is adequately safe over its entire lifetime* [1]. Any safety case will deploy three different kinds of argument in its support: *Deterministic* rule-based, logical arguments that are used to argue that some state of affairs is certainly true. The current Lucas Aerospace process rests to some extent on such elements[12]. *Probabilistic* arguments based on data drawn from testing, field experience etc. *Qualitative* arguments based on showing good practice or conformance to DO178B, and ISO 9000-3.

Generally a well-balanced safety case will involve diverse arguments of all types. In the case of high-reliability systems diversity is essential. Lucas Aerospace already have some experience in the use of formal verification to move the burden of evidence in the safety case from test to proof. This experiment aims to move the demonstration of the absence of certain classes of coding error from testing to the point at which code is synthesised. We believe this could result in significant cost reductions without compromising the safety and reliability of the products. Earlier discovery of errors in requirements and development rather than waiting until test is often claimed to be one of the principal benefits of formal methods [5, 9]

The seeds of the applicability of formal methods lie in the restrictions inherent in the approach to coding and design embodied in the current development process. In the next section we highlight those aspects of the current process that facilitate the use of formal methods.

1.2   The Current Approach

The current development process used by Lucas Aerospace has been refined for over a decade. It produces highly reliable systems and is stable and well understood. We are therefore keen that any proposed change retains the best features of existing processes whilst gaining the benefits of greater formality.

In the current approach, project staff implement requirements by composition of highly verified microprocessor specific elements [3]. This is codified in the domain specific language LUCOL[2] [12].

LUCOL elements are developed by specialists. The development of these elements is via a process which is mature, monitored by metrics which are used for feedback, and supported by highly developed verification processes, including formal verification [12]. That is, it satisfies many of the properties required to achieve the higher levels of the Capability Maturity Model (CMM) [17].

The LUCOL language embodies many constraints that facilitate informal validation and verification processes:

- Design is carried out at the level of combining LUCOL modules to provide high-level functionality.
- Individual LUCOL modules consist of up to around 100 lines of assembler. These are formally verified using the SPADE tool [3]. Loops can occur within these modules and formal verification guarantees their partial correctness. Confidence of termination derives from design guidelines, informal reasoning and extensive test. These modules are also reused across projects and have considerable operational evidence for correctness and reliability.
- LUCOL modules have determinate space, time and functional characteristics and this is inherited by programs constructed from LUCOL modules.
- LUCOL programs are loop-free. The acyclic structure guarantees termination provided each module terminates. The acyclic structure is iterated by a single control loop containing a cyclic executive that controls lower level functions.
- LUCOL programs are executed cyclically. The program is similar to a large filter that is executed at discrete time intervals (frequently enough to ensure adequate control).
- Coding conventions ensure each variable is defined once and there are strong controls over "non-functional" interactions between modules.
- Diagrammatic output can be generated from the code, and then compared to the requirements, which are very often of a similar form.

Taken together, these constraints make the code very amenable to dynamic test. This is particularly true if no historic data sources are kept. These amount to the introduction of feedback loops in the LUCOL program. The absence of loops means that there is no dependence on sequences of events or values, so the function mapping inputs to outputs is time independent. This feature also eases formal proof. Unfortunately it is impossible to eliminate feedback completely so

---

[2] LUCOL is a trademark of Lucas Aerospace.

we need good tools to analyse programs with feedback. We believe that formal approaches provide such tools to control and analyse these feature of programs.

These considerations mean that LUCOL programs exhibit many of the characteristics of circuits. This suggested that, in addition to considering formal methods tools that support software development, we should consider formal methods tools for hardware development. The resulting approach is aimed at supporting the development of software whose structure is constrained in a manner similar to LUCOL. The approach is language independent and the work is intended to target either LUCOL or Ada.

2   Formal Code Synthesis

2.1   Choice of Formal Methods Tool

The following considerations shaped our choice of formal methods tool. The final decision to choose LAMBDA[3] [16, 15, 11, 7, 6] was taken because it appears to be the most mature industrial-strength tool that matches most of these requirements.

- The core functionality of controllers is specified as a control law expressing the relationship between input and output over time. *Signals* varying over time are conveniently expressed as functions from time to data values. Thus a language with conveniently expressible functional forms is attractive because it is natural to describe our systems as functionals over a set of input and output signals.
- Because we want to reason about functionals it is desirable to use some form of higher logic or type theory.
- The cyclic nature of the system suggests that in most circumstances a loop invariant is the most natural statement of the functional requirements.
- An assumption of the development process is that a top level decomposition of the software into components would split this large invariant into sub-pieces which apply to sub-components.
- The actual implementations we have, which have had exposure to millions of hours of in-service life, show that it is possible to build extremely effective systems given highly restricted means of altering the flow of control, in particular loopless construction. These structures are particularly easy to formalise in higher-order logic.
- The majority (all but one) of loops can be placed in reusable components, these can be modelled functionally using recursion. These are the most difficult of the specifications to construct (especially given that they are ideally primitive recursive) so are best left to specialists. Ideally we would like to make the internal structure of components (e.g. LUCOL modules) invisible to designers who use the components to construct programs. The method should support the factoring of proof effort between specialist and the development team.

---

[3] LAMBDA is a trade mark of Abstract Hardware Limited

– An important aspect of any controller design is the control of when a component is active. This is important both for scheduling activity and for sequencing of control modes of the system. An important requirement was a simple method to specify activation/deactivation of components. This is an essential prerequisite to allow the development of any part of a realistic control system.

LAMBDA using poly/ML and the L2 logic was chosen as a vehicle for implementing the functionally based specifications of the components and programs. Although targeted at hardware techniques the method of specification is very similar to that used for controllers. In choosing LAMBDA we felt that it fitted our needs particularly well.

The LAMBDA hardware synthesis method is predicated on the approach that formal techniques could be made as transparent as possible to the project user. This therefore both technically and otherwise supports the factoring of expertise which is a positive attribute of the existing development process. This division of activity between formal methods experts and developers is reflected in the following two sections. In Section 2.3 we consider the activity of developing a formally verified "library" of code components along with formally defined rules for their use. In Section 2.4 we consider using the predefined rules to structure code synthesis.

In our preliminary investigations of the feasibility of the approach, software involving reactive control components was used as a test case for the method. The original motivation for this work was to capture control diagrams, and this is where it is most effective. The essentially discrete switching logic controlling these functional programs has been targeted by other formal methods, e.g. they could be approached using formalisms based on state machine diagrams.

2.2   An Overview of LAMBDA

This section is intended to provide enough background to LAMBDA to allow the reader to understand the notation used in the technical sections of the paper. We split the account into three sections dealing with the things one can define and manipulate in LAMBDA, how to express goals and theorems in LAMBDA and how to represent the current state of a proof.

LAMBDA Terms The L2 logic used in LAMBDA is a type theory with higher order objects. The language used to define terms in the logic is very similar to the purely functional fragment of the Standard ML programming language [10]. This provides a convenient means to define the behaviour of code components used in the synthesis of controllers. The higher order features of the term language are particularly useful in defining functions that have *signals* as inputs and generate a signal as output. For example the function:

```
fun x ladd y = fn t => wrange(x t ++ y t) ;
```

defines an infix operation ladd that takes two signals x and y as input and has the signal whose value at time t is the sum of the values of signals x and y at time t.

LAMBDA Sequents The truth of any proposition in the LAMBDA logic is always relative to a context that defines the terms used in the proposition. The context may have dependencies within it so the order of terms in the context is important. For example the axiom asserting reflexivity is given by:

```
G // P $ H |- P
```

The context to the left of the turnstile is called the *assumptions* and the proposition to the right of the turnstile is called the *assertion*. Often we want to think of sequents as *schematic*. In the reflexivity axiom the P stands for an arbitrary proposition and the G and H stand for the rest of the context to the left and right of the assumption P.

LAMBDA Rules LAMBDA represents the state of an incomplete proof using the notion of a derived rule in the LAMBDA logic. This notion was first introduced by Paulson [13] in his proof assistant Isabelle. The mechanism of constructing new schematic rules from the basic set of rules in the logic is fundamental to LAMBDA. A typical rule is the and introduction rule:

```
G//H |- P
G//H |-    Q
---------------
G//H |- P/\Q
```

This has the usual interpretation that if the two *premises* above the line are true then the *conclusion* below the line is true. New derived rules are constructed by unifying the conclusion of some rule with one of the premises of another rule. The process of proving some theorem then proceeds by repeatedly carrying out this procedure until the required rule is derived (provided it is derivable). For more details we refer the reader to the references on LAMBDA.

2.3 Reduction of Code to Component Form

In this section we consider the activity of developing the basic library of components from which programs will be synthesised and establishing sound introduction rules in the LAMBDA logic that admit the use of the components in synthesising code. This work requires detailed knowledge of the LAMBDA logic and is usually carried out by formal methods experts.

The code synthesis technique can target either the LUCOL or Ada language. Since Ada is the more generally known, the discussion will here be restricted to Ada. It is worth mentioning in passing that because Ada is compiled language, even if the Ada source is formally synthesised from its specification there is no guarantee that the machine code emitted by the compiler will in turn conform

to that specification. In contrast, no machine code is generated when targeting
to the LUCOL language; all of the code resides within the hand-coded modules
which are proved to conform to their pre- and postconditions. The LUCOL
approach eliminates the need to depend on a large and complex tool.

```
fun x ladd y = fn t => wrange(x t ++ y t) ;

function add (input1 : short_integer;
              input2 : short_integer) return short_integer
--# pre   true;
--# post add = wrange (input1 + input2);
is
    outval : integer;
    output : short_integer;
begin
    outval := integer (input1) + integer (input2);
    if outval < integer (short_integer'first) then
        output := short_integer'first;
    elsif integer (short_integer'last) < outval then
        output := short_integer'last;
    else
        output := short_integer (outval);
    end if;
    return output;
end add;
```

Fig. 1. Specification of Protected Addition

Whilst functional programming languages possess many attractive qualities,
for the foreseeable future imperative languages will continue to be used in embedded systems. Imperative functions without side effects or pre-conditions match
the semantics of their functional counterparts fairly closely. Figure 1 shows an example of an L2 specification of a "protected addition" and a counterpart written
in Ada. In this context protected means that overflows are mitigated by clamp-
ing at the appropriate extreme of the 16 bit two's complement integer range.
The L2 specification takes two *signals* as arguments and generates a signal as
result. Recall that a signal is a map from time (here modelled by the natural
numbers) to data values. Despite the simplicity of the function, it is not immediately obvious that the imperative code and the applicative specification perform
the same operation. The formal comments (introduced by --#) in the Ada code
giving the precondition and postcondition for the add function are more useful in
this respect than the code itself, provided that they have been formally verified.
Having conducted such a proof, one might feel justified in believing that the Ada
function add implements the L2 "software component" whose specification is

```
val ADD#(input1 : int, input2 : int, output int) =
                output == wrange(input1 ++ input2);
```

More will be said about this correspondence later when modelling the code in L2 is considered. For the moment the point is that one can replace a sub-expression of the form

```
x ladd y
```

with the output z of the software component[4]

```
ADD#(x t, y t, z t)
```

knowing that there is some code available which corresponds to it.

Our approach is: To construct a detailed low-level specification of the required functions in L2. This specification is type correct and is close in form to the informal requirements for the system. Then replace each subexpression in the L2 specification by a software component which has an imperative implementation. This is carried out under the control of LAMBDA and so each replacement must be justified in the logic. Finally during code generation each software component is replaced by the corresponding implementation to derive the code for the system.

Because the limitations on what can be done efficiently in imperative code, notably the limited integer word length, are captured accurately in LAMBDA's logic the specifier must take account of all boundary conditions and other implementation constraints as they synthesise the component form from the L2 specification.

The replacement of subexpressions by software components is a process of replacing L2 by L2 which is performed formally. Such replacements are achieved by an "introduction rule". An introduction rule for the ADD# component might be of the form

```
G // H |- P#(o)
-----------------------------------------------------------
G // forall t. ADD#(x t, y t, o t) $ H |- P#(x ladd y)
```

This rule says that if we connect up an ADD with inputs x and y and output o then any occurrence of a sub-expression of the form x ladd y may be replaced by o. In this instance we are committed to calling our ADD component for all time ie. on every cycle of the program, which is not always what is required. Other forms of introduction rules only require output from a component at times when a given set of conditions holds.

Introduction rules are proved to be sound. This guarantees that a component cannot be used incorrectly. The introduction rule for the ADD component is very

---

[4] Note that we are being a little imprecise here. Strictly we would need to be replacing (x ladd y) in a context where it is applied to t or the ADD# relation would have to hold for all times t.

easily proved since the component definition differs little from the L2 function it replaces. In some cases the proof can be quite complex.

The simplicity of the ADD example suggests two things; firstly that this is not getting us very far, and secondly that every sub-expression of the L2 specification is going to end up as a subprogram. To illustrate that the former is not necessarily the case we consider a slightly more interesting function. A major strength of an L2 functional specification is that it is free of the state which exists in an imperative program. Thus a simple rectangular integrator may be specified as

```
fun intgr x gain init 0   = init ++ gain ** x 0
  | intgr x gain init 1't = intgr x gain init t ++ gain ** x 1't;
```

The corresponding software component might be

```
val INTGR#(input:int,gain:int,store:int signal,output:int,t:time)=
        output == store t ++ gain ** input /\ store 1't == output;
```

This is not easily implementable as imperative code, of course, because it requires unbounded integer arithmetic and a practical definition of the L2 function intgr would restrict word lengths, but it does illustrate the introduction of state into the software component. The introduced state here is the integer signal store. Whereas the L2 function is defined recursively, the software component introduces a state variable to eliminate the recursion. The corresponding imperative code would have the (infeasible due to limited length arithmetic) specification

```
procedure intgr(input: in short_integer; gain: in short_integer;
          store: inout short_integer; output: out short_integer)
--# pre true;
--# post output = store~ + gain * input and store = output;
```

In order for the imperative code to be able to implement the requirement of the software component that store 1't == output, each use of the integrator function must have associated with it a separate statically allocated state variable which preserves its value between successive calls to the procedure, recording the value of output on the last iteration. Furthermore, the output of the L2 specification of intgr at time 0 requires that the state variable is initialised at time 0. An introduction rule for this component might be

```
G // H |- P#(o) /\ store 0 == init
-----------------------------------------------------------
G // forall t. INTGR#(i t,gain,store,o t,t) $ H |-
                              P#(intgr x gain init)
```

This rule could not be proved without the extra condition that store is initialised at time 0, and ensures that this initialisation constraint is introduced at the same time as the software component. As development proceeds the formal structure of LAMBDA gathers all such constraints and maintains them so the developer has a clear statement of the constraints under which the code can implement the L2 specification.

When the target language is Ada, software components can be implemented by inline code. For instance, the code fragment

```
--# pre divisor <> 0
output := input / divisor;
--# post output = input div divisor
```

can straightforwardly be used to implement integer division, assuming the parameters have the correct Ada types. Where preconditions are other than true, as here, they appear as a side-condition in the corresponding introduction rule, requiring their discharge as part of the code synthesis process.

So far, only component replacements for all time instants have been considered. For instance, when we compute

```
out1 t = if select t then fn1 in1 t else fn2 in1 t
```

it is certainly possible to compute the value of both `fn1` and `fn2` on all cycles and then to discard the value which is not required according to the value of boolean `select t`. This does not make for very efficient code. To avoid this we need a nested introduction rule. For example, such a rule for the `ADD` component is

```
G // H |- if select1 t then P#(o t) else Q
------------------------------------------------------------
G // forall t. select1 t == true ->> ADD#(i1 t,i2 t, o t) $ H |-
                    if select1 t then P#((i1 ladd i2) t) else Q
```

Then we only have to "run" our `ADD` component at times when `select1 t`, or rather when whatever variable it unifies with when the introduction rule is used, is `true`. There are however a whole family of such rules catering for each conceivable nesting of if .. then .. else statements, each of which requires to be proved. The approach to this is to prove a base rule of a particular form and from this base rule to sequentially prove the rules required for successive nesting depths. An ML function

```
mkCond : rule->int->rule
```

has been developed which will generate introduction rules for any given nesting depth when supplied with the base rule for the component and the required depth. Whilst this is not totally general - a completely general function would require not just an integer nesting depth but, say, a sequence of booleans to steer to either the if or the else part of each successive nesting - it served its purpose in our original small example of code synthesis.

The base rule for the `ADD` component is

```
G // H |- P#(o t)
------------------------------------------------------------
G // ADD#(i1 t,i2 t,o t) $ H |- P#((i1 ladd i2) t)
```

Whilst this works well for simple components, the technique falls down for components such as the integrator. In this case a nested introduction of the component is not possible; the component must be run on every cycle. To see this, suppose select 1't is true then if t <> 0, for the component to function correctly at time 1't we must have

```
store 1't == intgr x gain init t
```

which implies that the component was run on the previous iteration which in turn assumes it was run on the iteration previous to that ....

If an integrator (or any component with introduced state) is not to be run on all cycles then this must be reflected in its L2 functional specification. Adding the boolean signal active to the function and changing the initialisation value to a signal gives

```
fun intgr active x gain init 0   = init 0 ++ gain ** x 0
 |  intgr active x gain init 1't =
          if active 1't then
            let val ynm1 = if active t
                           then intgr active x gain init t
                           else init 1't
            in
               ynm1 ++ gain ** x 1't
            end
          else
               intgr active x gain init t;
```

Here provision is made to re-initialise the integrator value whenever a state transition occurs from inactive to active. The function, being total, also specifies the output from the integrator when active is false. Here it holds to the output value which obtained the last time active was true. Figure 2 shows two possible implementations. Both introduce another state variable active_last which keeps track of the last cycle's value of active. This is used to determine when a transition from inactive to active has occurred. The first of these implementations is suitable for replacing an integrator for all time and respects the requirement that the integrator hold its value when active is false. The second implementation is suitable for a limited form of nested introduction rule applicable only when the integrator is active. In this case the value output from the component when the integrator is inactive is irrelevant and could equally well be specified in the L2 component as any x:int.TRUE.

Proving introduction rules and verifying that code conforms to its stated precondition and postcondition requires certain skills. Once a library of proven software components is available however, the process of actually generating code is quite straightforward (with the possible exception of proving the preconditions) as will be explained in the Section 2.4. Thus this approach serves to separate concerns between the formal methods analysts and the control systems analysts.

```
type time = natural;
type ''a signal = time -> ''a;

fun unchanged signal init 0   = signal 0      == init
  | unchanged signal init 1't = signal 1't == signal t;

val INTGR1#(input:int signal,gain:int,store:int signal,output:int signal,
             active:bool signal,active_last:bool signal,init:int signal) =
forall t:time. (if active t then
                     (active_last t == false ->> store t == init t) /\
                     INTGR#(input t,gain,store,output t, t)
                else
                     unchanged output (init 0) t) /\
                     active_last 1't == active t;

val INTGR2#(input:int signal,gain:int,store:int signal,output:int signal,
             active:bool signal,active_last:bool signal,init:int signal) =
forall t:time. (active t == true ->>
                     (active_last t == false ->> store t == init t) /\
                     INTGR#(input t,gain,store,output t, t)) /\
                     active_last 1't == active t;
```

Fig. 2. Two Integrator Implementations

2.4   Code Synthesis

Our method of specification differs from other model based systems (eg. Z, VDM, AMN) in that it does not use a predicate-transformer style but specifies the behaviour for all time. This approach is suited to the loopless, cyclic nature of our software. In effect, the specification is a loop invariant.

To specify, a library of L2 functions which have corresponding software components is required. Each of the functions must be implementable; they respect the limited word length integer arithmetic available, and if they involve the introduction of state variables then they must make suitable initialisations when transitions from inactive to active occur. Whilst the first proviso may be regarded as a nuisance, the second can be a positive benefit in ensuring that such initialisations are not forgotten; each component takes care of itself, helping to ensure that state transitions are seamless. More complex functions are constructed from these components.

The result of applying component introduction to a simple PID[5] controller, the subject of the initial HOLD II[6] study, is shown in Figure 3. The conclusion of the rule gives the initial starting point. It merely specifies a single output as a function of time. Above the line, the first premiss is the result of expanding the

---

[5] PID stands for Proportional Integrator and Differentiator
[6] *Higher Order Language Demonstrator*, contract ref. FSIA/420, supported by the UK Ministry of Defence.

```
2: G // H |- active 0 == false
1: G // H
  |- forall t.
          (if active t
          then
            (if active_last t
            then
                SCALE#(fmvpe t,dfmvgi t,+1250,o13 t)
                /\ SCALE#(fmvpv t,dfmvgf t,+500,o12 t)
                /\ ADD#(o12 t,dfm2mn t,o11 t)
                /\ ADD#(o12 t,dfm2mx t,o10 t)
                /\ INTGR#(o13 t,store1,+2048,o10 t,o11 t,o1 t,t)
            else
                store t == difinit t /\ (o1 t == upper (intinit t)
            /\ store1 (1't) == intinit t))
            /\ INLINE_DIV#(fmvpe t,+25,o9 t)
            /\ DIFR#(o9 t,store,+25,o t,t)
          else
              unchanged o1 (upper (intinit 0)) t /\ unchanged o +0 t)
          /\ SCALE#(fmvpv t,dfmvgf t,+500,o2 t) /\ SUB#(o1 t,o2 t,o3 t)
          /\ INLINE_DIV#(fmvpe t,+500,o4 t) /\ ADD#(o3 t,o4 t,o5 t)
          /\ ADD#(o5 t,o t,o6 t) /\ SCALE#(o6 t,+2,+1,o7 t)
          /\ LIMIT#(o7 t,cfmcmx t,cfmcmn t,o8 t)
          /\ active_last (1't) == active t /\ output t == o8 t
----------------------------------------------------------------------
G // H
  |- forall t. output t == pid active difinit intinit fmvpe fmvpv
                          dfmvgf dfm2mn dfm2mx dfmvgi cfmcmx cfmcmn t
```

Fig. 3. Simple PID Controller

function definition and introducing the appropriate software component for each of the sub-functions in the specification. The only software components which have been discussed so far are the ADD and INLINE_DIV components, the latter corresponding to an inlined divide with the simple preconditions here of 25 <> 0 and 500 <> 0.

Arithmetic is generally protected against overflow in the sense discussed earlier and the SCALE component is useful in this respect in multiplying its input by its second parameter to produce a double length result, then dividing by its third parameter to produce a single length result with suitable adjustment for any overflow. The integrator is similar to the one discussed, but has extra parameters and a somewhat more complicated specification to make it practical.

Since they introduce state, the integrator and the differentiator (DIFR) both introduce state variables active and active_last to determine when a state transition occurs, as well as their individual storage locations. The functionality of both of these components becomes distributed throughout the "code". Thus the two `if` expressions at the start of the component form are attributable jointly to these components (there are no conditional expressions in the specification of function `pid`, and both the integrator and the differentiator have been replaced for all time).

Re-initialisation of the stores occurs when a transition from inactive to active occurs - the update of the the integrator output `o1` here is a consequence of the way the integrator is specified. And, because the integrator and differentiator are active for all time, their outputs are held unchanged when `active` is `false`. The updating of `active_last` with the value of `active` also derives from these two components.

The signals `o`, `o1` to `o13` which connect the software components together are just a consequence of the usage of `o` as an output in the introduction rules. They could be instantiated with more meaningful names, but this would not alter the meaning of the premiss.

The second premiss, that at time 0 the function is inactive, is an artifice to get round the problem of a lack of support for the integers in the LAMBDA rule base. It enabled the introduction rules for the integrator and differentiator to be proved with a dearth of rule support. A useful theory of the integers has subsequently been put in place. This premiss will not be mentioned further.

The associated code which has been automatically generated from the first premiss after reduction to software components is shown in Figure 4. The state variables have been allocated statically. The requirement that the outputs of the differentiator and integrator be unchanging when these components are inactive leads to the static allocation of their outputs and their initialisation at time 0. Since the initial value of the integrator, `o1`, depends on an input variable, it is gated in on the first iteration. In other respects the Ada code matches the software component form fairly closely.

There are, however, significant differences between the Ada code and the software component form. The most obvious is that, whilst the order of the Ada code statements leaves little scope for permutation if the meaning of the program is to be preserved, conjunction is commutative and only the if expressions impose any ordering at all on the component form. The other major difference is that the variables in the component form are integers (and booleans), whereas the Ada variables are signed two's complement with a limited number of bits. One, not completely satisfactory, way of dealing with this semantic gap is to model the generated code in L2. Figure 5 shows an extract of a model of our generated code. The code is thus a function which takes two labelled records one of which contains the inputs, the other the state. The labelled record for the state contains both the statically and dynamically allocated variables, but the latter are undefined on input. The words and longwords in the state are modelled as (isomorphic to) subtypes of the integers satisfying their range constraints. Applying function code with its inputs to the state represents one cycle of execution of procedure `pid`. Functions used in the modelled code consist of the basic software components, and functions which access and update the fields of the labelled records. For example, the latter are of the form

```
with modules ;
package body pid
is

active_last : boolean ;    gate_at_time0 : boolean := true ;
o : short_integer := 0 ;   o1 : short_integer ;
store : short_integer ;    store1 : integer ;

procedure pid (active : boolean ;       difinit : short_integer ;
               intinit : integer ;      fmvpe : short_integer ;
               fmvpv : short_integer ;  dfmvgf : short_integer ;
               dfm2mn : short_integer ; dfm2mx : short_integer ;
               dfmvgi : short_integer ; cfmcmx : short_integer ;
               cfmcmn : short_integer ; output : out short_integer)
is
    o2 : short_integer ; (* declaration of o3 - o12 omitted *)
begin
    if gate_at_time0 then
        o1 := modules.highw(intinit) ; gate_at_time0 := false ;
    end if ;
    if active then
        if active_last then
            o13 := modules.scale (fmvpe, dfmvgi, 1250) ;
            o12 := modules.scale (fmvpv, dfmvgf, 500) ;
            o11 := modules.add (o12, dfm2mn) ;
            o10 := modules.add (o12, dfm2mx) ;
            modules.intgr (o13, store1, 2048, o10, o11, o1) ;
        else
            store := difinit ; o1 := modules.highw(intinit) ;
            store1 := intinit ;
        end if ;
        o9 := fmvpe / 25 ;  modules.difr (o9, store, 25, o) ;
    end if ;

    o2 := modules.scale (fmvpv, dfmvgf, 500); o3 := modules.sub (o1, o2);
    o4 := fmvpe / 500 ;  o5 := modules.add (o3, o4) ;
    o6 := modules.add (o5, o) ;  o7 := modules.scale (o6, 2, 1) ;
    o8 := modules.limit (o7, cfmcmx, cfmcmn) ; active_last := active ;
    output := o8 ;
end pid ;

end pid ;
```

Fig. 4. Code Synthesis Example

```
fun code (input:inrec) (st:state) : state =
let val st =
    if state'gate_at_time0 st then
        let val st = state'o1'up st (highw (inrec'intinit input))
            val st = state'gate_at_time0'up st false
        in
            st
        end
    else [ ... ]
in
    st
end;
```

Fig. 5. Code Modelled in L2

```
state'o12 st   (* Access field o12 of labelled record st:state *)
state'o12'up st value   (* Update field o12 of st with 'value' *)
```

The starting state at each iteration is then modelled. At time 0 all variables in the state are undefined other than those which are explicitly initialised. At times other than 0, the defined variables in the starting state are just those that are statically allocated each of which have the value generated by the previous execution of function code. The state at any time is then given by the function

```
fun st inp t = code (inp t) (start inp t);
```

Having got a model of the code and the state, the proof proceeds by replacing the software components, which are expressed in integers, by even lower level components which work with restricted word lengths. Thus the ADD component has the rewrite rule

```
------------------------------------------------------------
G // is_sw i1 /\ is_sw i2 $ H |-
    ADD#(i1,i2,o) == (o == wordRep (add (wordAbs i1,wordAbs i2))
```

Here is_sw i1 declares i1 to be within the signed word range, and wordRep and wordAbs convert from subtype word to integer and vice versa. The lower level function add is given by

```
fun add (input1,input2) =
    wordAbs (wrange (wordRep input1 ++ wordRep input2)) ;
```

The variables in the component form are instantiated with their values in the state, e.g. variable o becomes: fn t => wordRep (state'o (st inp t)).

Following a case analysis on whether or not t == 0 and a path analysis of the if expressions, our original rule is reducible to the form shown in Figure 6. This says that if the output takes its value in the state, the inputs supply the appropriate fields of the input record inp, and the inputs are range restricted to

```
val INP#(inp : inrec signal, active : bool signal, difinit : int signal,
         intinit : int signal, fmvpe  : int signal, fmvpv  : int signal,
         dfmvgf : int signal, dfm2mn : int signal, dfm2mx : int signal,
         dfmvgi : int signal, cfmcmx : int signal, cfmcmn : int signal)
 = forall t. inp t ==
     {active = active t, difinit = wordAbs (difinit t),
      intinit = longAbs (intinit t), fmvpe = wordAbs (fmvpe t),
      fmvpv = wordAbs (fmvpv t), dfmvgf = wordAbs (dfmvgf t),
      dfm2mn = wordAbs (dfm2mn t), dfm2mx = wordAbs (dfm2mx t),
      dfmvgi = wordAbs (dfmvgi t), cfmcmx = wordAbs (cfmcmx t),
      cfmcmn = wordAbs (cfmcmn t)} /\
    is_sw (difinit t) /\ is_sl (intinit t) /\ is_sw (fmvpe t) /\
    is_sw (fmvpv t) /\ is_sw (dfmvgf t) /\ is_sw (dfm2mn t) /\
    is_sw (dfm2mx t) /\ is_sw (dfmvgi t) /\ is_sw (cfmcmx t) /\
    is_sw (cfmcmn t) ;

3: G // H |- forall t. output t == wordRep (state'output (st inp t))
2: G // H |- INP#(inp,active,difinit,intinit,fmvpe,fmvpv,dfmvgf,dfm2mn,
                  dfm2mx,dfmvgi,cfmcmx,cfmcmn)
1: G // H |- active 0 == false
------------------------------------------------------------------------
   G // H
   |- forall t. output t ==
      pid active difinit intinit fmvpe fmvpv dfmvgf dfm2mn dfm2mx dfmvgi
      cfmcmx cfmcmn t
```

Fig. 6. Verification conditions for the synthesised code

values representable by signed words and signed longwords as appropriate, then the code implements the specification. One should add the proviso: provided the low level software components are implemented by the code.

2.5 Preliminary Experience

The preliminary work detailed in this section was carried out entirely by formal methods specialists. The work addresses a particular class of errors, namely initialisation errors, arithmetic overflow/underflow, type mismatch and the control of activation of components. On the basis of experience we believe that better control of this class of errors has significant cost implications for the Lucas Aerospace development process.

The approach provides very strong guarantees that these errors will not arise in programs that are subjected to test after formal synthesis. This suggests that test effort could either be redirected to providing improved testing of other parts of the program or if that is shown to be unnecessary this could save on development costs.

The approach seems to provide good partitioning between the specialist work involved in building component libraries and proving introduction rules for the components. This requires specialist work and is time-consuming, however it appears that components are reused in this approach and the cost of verification of the introduction rules can be amortised across a number of projects.

The use of this approach will also change the balance of evidence in the safety case. Formally developed systems will have significantly more deductive evidence of the absence of errors this will lead to a more balanced case.

3   The Experiment

The preliminary case studies have demonstrated that this approach could reap benefits and can be integrated into the existing development process. The next stage in the process of introducing this innovation is a controlled experiment in circumstances that are close to the "real world" situation. To be useful the method must be usable by normal project staff given appropriate training.

Currently we are running a large scale process improvement experiment to assess the utility of the approach. This is funded by the EU ESSI programme. We anticipate the experiment will be complete by the autumn of 1999. This project, known as PCFM, involves collection of metrics from both conventional and formal development processes. The metrics are defined and collected in a controlled manner, so that the two processes can be compared. Our aim is to assess the new process objectively and in a way which de-risks the introduction of new technology.

At the time of writing the project is incomplete. At the moment data is being collected and we are beginning to have enough data to allow comparisons to be made. By the time of the FM99 conference we will have a substantial body of data.

3.1   The Problem

The system being developed is the signal selection and control laws for the *Fuel Metering Unit Smart Electronics Module (FMM SEM)* on the HiPECS project. This project is a demonstrator programme on distributed processing being undertaken in collaboration with the UK Ministry of Defence. The FMM SEM controls the fuel flow and shutoff valve positions to demands received from the core electronics unit. The system is similar to the PID system described in detail earlier but it includes more logic elements that accommodate for errors in sensors and software. This is an interesting extension of the PID case study because it explores the interface between control and logic elements.

3.2   Experimental Setup

The experiment is set up in parallel with a normal project team working to develop a software component. Each project is well instrumented. Data are being collected on where and when faults are uncovered and metrics are being gathered to help compare progress in the two project teams. Data being gathered falls into two broad categories: Effort data measures developer time through each of the stages of the development process. We believe we will see significant redistribution of effort over the development process (in particular a move away from test effort towards specification and design). The other broad category of data being collected is on product quality. This includes error frequencies and classification. We believe that the formal approach has the potential to greatly reduce the incidence of the errors it is targeting.

3.3   Current Status

At the time of writing the development team have had formal methods training in the use of LAMBDA and have begun to explore the formal specification of the components using LAMBDA to provide simulation facilities and to informally validate the specification against the requirement.

The formal methods experts have constructed a suitable library of formally verified components and introduction rules. These are complete and are currently under review. Once this is complete work on formal code synthesis will commence.

3.4   Preliminary Experience

At this time our experience with the approach in this experiment can only be impressionistic. However we have seen some results that are worth recording:

Difficulties encountered by project staff in forming specifications show we have some usability problems. Despite the similarities, pure functional forms are based on such a different paradigm. Project staff find it hard to adjust to this change. In a small number of cases (e.g. initialisation of historic stores) the imperative model is deeply ingrained. The method being superficially so similar to the conventional approach may paradoxically make it harder for staff to identify and adjust to the differences. One possible line of attack for this problem would be by use of a diagrammatic interface followed by generation of the appropriate L2. DERA Malvern are pursuing some work in this direction [4].

The formal specification gives enhanced visibility of transfer functions. The functional form of the specification means it can be animated to some extent and this has raised some early validation issues.

The code generation method can be expanded to remove some routine calculations (e.g. iteration rates to time constants) which are a potential source of error and/or inconsistency. When available, a secure process should have an easily justifiable business case simply in terms of the amount of reviewing costs one could avoid because informal approach to identifying these inconsistencies is very time consuming.

Being originally targeted at hardware, the LAMBDA environment lacks some features which are essential for this work, but fortunately can be added in (e.g. enhanced rules for manipulation of integers).

References

[1] Adelard. *ASCAD - Adelard Safety Case Development Manual*. Adelard, 1998. ISBN 0 9533771 0 5.

[2] Geoff Barrett. Formal methods applied to a floating-point number systems. *IEEE Transactions on Software Engineering*, 15(5):611–621, May 1989.

[3] B. A. Carre, D. L. Clutterbuck, C. W. Debney, and I. M. O'Neill. SPADE - the thampton Program Analysis and Development Environment. In *Software Engineering Environments*, pages 129–134. Peter Peregrinus, 1986.

[4] P. Caseley, C. O'Halloran, and A. Smith. Explaining code with pictures – a case study. Technical Report DERA/CIS/CIS3/TR990083/1.0 (DRAFT), DERA, 1997.

[5] S. Easterbrook, R Lutz, R. Covington, J. Kelly, Y. Ampo, and D. Hamilton. Experiences using lightweight formal methods for requirements modeling. *IEEE Transactions on Software Engineering*, 24(1), Jan 1998.

[6] E.M. Mayger and M.P. Fourman. Integration of formal methods with system design. In A. Halaas and P.B. Denyer, editors, *International Conference on Very Large Scale Integration*, pages 59–70, Edinburgh, Scotland, August 1991. IFIP Transactions, North-Holland.

[7] M. P. Fourman. *Formal System Design*, chapter 5, pages 191–236. North-Holland, 1990.

[8] P. Garbett, J. Parkes, M. Shackleton, and S. Anderson. A case study in innovative process improvement: Code synthesis from formal specifications. In *Avionics 98*, 1998.

[9] R. Lutz. Targeting safety-related errors during software requirements analysis. *The Journal of Systems and Software*, 34:223–230, Sept 1996.

[10] Robin Milner, Mads Tofte, and Robert Harper. *The Definition of Standard ML*. MIT Press, Cambridge, MA, 1989.

[11] M.P. Fourman and E.M. Mayger. Formally Based System Design - Interactive hardware scheduling. In G. Musgrave and U. Lauther, editors, *Very Large Scale Integration*, pages 101–112, Munich, Federal Republic of Germany, August 1989. IFIP TC 10/WG10.5 International Conference, North-Holland.

[12] I.M. O'Neill, D.L. Clutterbuck, P.F. Farrow, P.G. Summers, and W.C. Dolman. The formal verification of safety critical assembly code. In *Safety of Computer Control Systems*, pages 115–120. Pergammon Press, 1988.

[13] L. C. Paulson. Isabelle: A generic theorem prover. *Lecture Notes in Computer Science*, 828:xvii + 321, 1994.

[14] Requirements and Technical Concepts for Aviation. *Software Considerations in Airborne Systems and Equipment Certification*, Dec 1992. (document RTCA SC167/DO-178B).

[15] S. Finn, M.P. Fourman, and G. Musgrave. Interactive synthesis in HOL-abstract. In M. Archer, J.J. Joyce, K.N. Levitt, and P.J. Windley, editors, *International Workshop on Higher Order Logic Theorem Proving and its Applications*, Davis, California, August 1991. IEEE Computer Society, ACM SIGDA, IEEE Computer Society Press.

[16] S. Finn, M.P. Fourman, M.D. Francis, and B. Harris. Formal system design - interactive synthesis based on computer assisted formal reasoning. In Luc J. M. Claesen, editor, *Applied Formal Methods For Correct VLSI Design*, volume 1, pages 97–110. IMEC-IFIP, Elsevier Science Publishers, 1989.

[17] H. Saiedan and L. M. Mc Clanahan. Frameworks for quality software process: SEI capability maturity model. *Software Quality Journal*, 5(1):1, 1996.

Cronos: A Separate Compilation Toolset for Modular Esterel Applications

Olivier Hainque[1]*, Laurent Pautet[1], Yann Le Biannic[2], and Éric Nassor[2]

[1] École Nationale Supérieure des Télécommunications
46, rue Barrault - F-75013, Paris - France
hainque@inf.enst.fr - pautet@inf.enst.fr
[2] Dassault-Aviation
78, quai Marcel Dassault - F-92214, Saint-Cloud Cedex - France
eric.nassor@dassault-aviation.fr - yann.lebiannic@dassault-aviation.fr

Abstract. ESTEREL is an imperative synchronous language designed for the specification and the development of reactive systems. Recent studies pointed out that its use for the development of avionics software can yield great benefits but that the lack of support for separate compilation in the current toolset may be an obstacle to the development of large systems. This paper presents the CRONOS framework which provides such support for some specific cases of ESTEREL programs.

Technical Paper related to Industrial Applications

Keywords :
Esterel, Compilation, Synchronous Reactive Systems, Avionics Software

1 Introduction

Dassault-Aviation is a French aircraft manufacturer which has been studying the industrial applicability of the ESTEREL synchronous language in the development process of avionics software since 1989. Some recent experiments [4], [5] showed that using ESTEREL in this context can actually yield great benefits but that the current toolset is missing some separate compilation capabilities to be applicable to large industrial systems. This paper presents the CRONOS framework developed by Dassault-Aviation to deal with this issue for some specific cases of ESTEREL programs.

Sections 2 and 3 provide a short background about ESTEREL and a basic example which will be used as an illustrative support for the following sections. Section 4 describes the current compilation process and points out its major weaknesses regarding its applicability to large systems. Sections 5 and 6 explains how the CRONOS toolset balances these weaknesses and details the kind of applications it can handle. Finally, sections 7 and 8 summarize the major advantages of the approach and present the results of experiments conducted to evaluate it.

---

* Contact author : O. Hainque - Tel : (+33) 1 47 11 36 94, Fax : (+33) 1 47 11 52 83

J. Wing, J. Woodcock, J. Davies (Eds.): FM'99, Vol. II, LNCS 1709, pp. 1836–1853, 1999.
© Springer-Verlag Berlin Heidelberg 1999

2   Basic Esterel Background

ESTEREL is an imperative synchronous language designed for the specification and the development of reactive systems [1].

A reactive system is an entity which produces output signals and updates its internal state when triggered by input events coming from its environment. The environment generates the events at its own rate and each handling of an event by the system is called a reaction.

In this context, the synchronous approach first makes the assumption that the reaction execution time is null and defines a discrete logical time scale from instants corresponding to each reaction (Fig. 1). Reactions are then said to be instantaneous and all the associated triggering inputs can be considered as strictly simultaneous. This strict characterization of the notions of instantaneity and simultaneity allows the definition of very precise semantics from which highly deterministic behaviors can be derived. Naturally, the actual execution time of a reaction is never null, but in practice the results are applicable as soon as it is possible to ensure that a reaction is always complete before the occurrence of the next event.

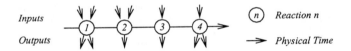

Fig. 1. Synchronous Reactive Systems : a discrete logical time scale

ESTEREL allows the description of a synchronous system as a set of interconnected modules. Inter-modules and system-environment communications are achieved through signal based interfaces, with pure signals simply indicating individual events and valued signals able to carry additional data. The modules behavior is specified thanks to a rich set of imperative constructs, including support for exceptions, preemptions and parallelism. The full description of the language and of its semantics is beyond the scope of this article but can be found in [2], [3], and in the documentation distributed with the compiler.

3   A Simple Example

As an illustrative support for the following sections, we shall consider the case of a simple system called COMCTL with a controller CTL and a controlled component COM (Fig. 2). At the environment level, a Switch signal alternatively activates or deactivates the component and a Status_Rq signal requests the controller to emit a COM_Is_Active or COM_Is_Inactive indication corresponding to the current component state.

1838   Olivier Hainque et al.

We have specified this with three modules : one for COM, one for CTL and one to combine them and build the system using a couple of internal signals, `Activity_Rq` and `Activity`. Every time CTL receives `Status_Rq`, it emits `Activity_Rq` to which COM instantaneously replies by an `Activity` indication if the component is currently active. CTL then tests the presence of this indication to emit one of the two expected system outputs.

With `run`, `;` and `||` as respectively the module instantiation, sequencing and parallelism operators, we obtain the organization and code on Fig. 2 :

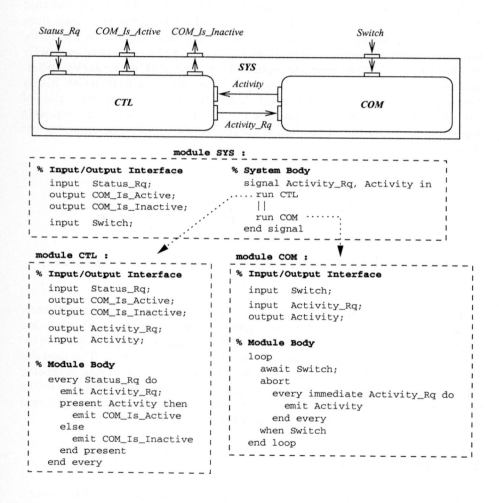

Fig. 2. General organization of COMCTL

Fig. 3 shows an example sequence of reactions of this system, each represented by a circle with the triggering inputs above and the emitted outputs below.

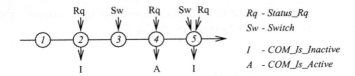

Rq - *Status_Rq*
Sw - *Switch*

I - *COM_Is_Inactive*
A - *COM_Is_Active*

Fig. 3. An example sequence of reactions for COMCTL

4 The Esterel Compilation Process

4.1 General Description

From a given specification, the latest V5 release of the ESTEREL compiler generates a boolean sequential circuit equivalent to a finite state machine for the control aspects. The system inputs/outputs are connected to input/output wires and a set of boolean latches encodes the state between two consecutive reactions (Fig. 4). Data handling, such as if statements or variable assignments, is operated outside the circuit by operations called actions, triggered by wires evaluated to true and possibly returning information back into the circuit through another wire. The execution of a reaction basically consists in computing the status (emitted or not) of every output and the next system state from the provided status (present or not) of all the inputs combined with the current state. In this context, every signal which status is known (provided or computed) is said to be determined.

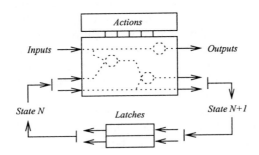

Fig. 4. General form of a circuit generated by ESTEREL

This approach has two interesting advantages :

– The logical part of the circuit can be submitted to very efficient specialized optimization tools,
– The state encoding enables to handle pretty huge state spaces (up to 10^{14} states reached in Dassault-Aviation applications).

If we consider the CTL module as an independent system and submit it to the ESTEREL toolset, we get an example on Fig. 5 :

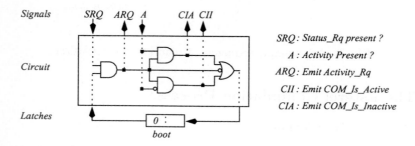

Signals   SRQ ARQ A   CIA CII

Circuit

SRQ : Status_Rq present ?
A : Activity Present ?
ARQ : Emit Activity_Rq
CII : Emit COM_Is_Active
CIA : Emit COM_Is_Inactive

Latches

0 :
boot

Fig. 5. Circuit translation for CTL

The corresponding generated C code includes one function for each input signal and one function to request a reaction. This function executes considering as present only the input signals which associated function has been called at least once since the previous reaction. It evaluates the gates in topological order, calls a user provided function for every emitted output, updates the registers and resets the inputs status to `false` (absent) before returning.

The boot register visible on the figure has a 0 initial value and is subsequently always set to 1. As its name suggests, it provides an indication of whether or not we are running the very first reaction. It is there due to a specificity of the ESTEREL `every` construct which starts looking at the condition only one instant after its own activation, unless the condition is prepended by `immediate`. Thus, our CTL module actually never emits anything at the first instant, even if `Status_Rq` is present, as ensured by the leftmost **and** gate in the circuit layout. This is not a serious problem and provides a nice simple example of the use of registers to encode the system state.

A very important point about this general scheme is that a reaction always leads to the evaluation of all the gates. This approach significantly differs from the one adopted for other synchronous languages such as LUSTRE or SIGNAL which only evaluate parts of an overall dataflow graph depending on the status the system inputs ([12], [11], [10]).

4.2   Major Translation Steps

The ESTEREL compilation environment achieves the translation of a specification through various intermediate tools and formats. It is not possible to precisely describe them in this article, but some key points are important to understand what the issues addressed by CRONOS are and how the solutions will take advantage of the existing toolset.

Fig. 6 below shows the most important steps for our example and purpose of presentation :

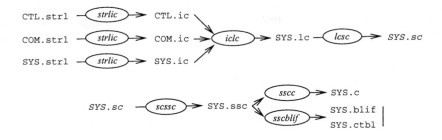

Fig. 6. ESTEREL to circuit translation for COMCTL

The first format (`ic` for Intermediate Code) enables the internal representation of all the necessary modules. The resulting files are linked together by `iclc` to build a `lc` (Linked Code) representation of the entire system. `lcsc` then transforms this representation into a boolean equation system associated with a set of tables describing the actions and their relations with the equations (Software Code). A topological sort of the equations by `scssc` yields a `ssc` file (Sorted sc), from which `sscc` can directly produce a C emulation of the circuit.

Starting from a `ssc` file, it is also possible to get a pure description of the circuit in the standard `blif` format (Berkeley Logic Interchange Format) associated with a `ctbl` file (Common Tables) for the tables. `blif` level optimizers are then usable together with a `blifssc` processor to build a `ssc` file from which a much more efficient C code can be obtained.

4.3   Weaknesses When Applied to Large Systems

As illustrated by Fig. 6, a representation of the entire system is built very early during the translation process and is then submitted to a significant number of operations. An immediate consequence is that any modification to any module imposes to apply again almost the whole translation process to the entire system, which is not reasonable when hundreds or thousands of modules are concerned.

Moreover, some compilation steps sometimes require the execution of costly algorithms which should only be applied to a specific part of the system. For instance, if the combinational part of the circuit contains cycles despite a semantically correct specification, producing the `ssc` file requires the use of a causality analyzer to compute an equivalent acyclic circuit (SCCAUSAL : [8], [9]). The involved analysis is complex and performed at the `sc` level, that is for the whole system, even if only one specific module is the source of the anomaly.

Finally, the optimization processes we have mentioned are often necessary to reach acceptable reaction execution times, but are sometimes computationally not tractable when the system is too large.

5   Separate Compilation with Cronos

5.1   Basic Assumptions and Ideas

CRONOS basically consists in a set of code generation tools for ESTEREL which enable to delay the modules assembly step until the very end the overall compilation process. To achieve this goal at a reasonable cost, we first consider the following restriction :

The root level description of the system only contains parallel module instantiations with possible local signals for their interconnection. [1]

This allows to consider the whole system circuit as a simple signal-level interconnection of the circuits for each module and to bind the separate compilation issue to a two steps process :

1. Generating the code for each module from the representation of its circuit which is trivially obtainable with the existing ESTEREL tools;
2. Generating the code for the interconnection of these circuits as it is specified by the root level description of the system.

This may seem pretty simple at first sight but the possible occurrence of instantaneous bidirectional communications between modules raises a critical problem. As described in section 4.1, a full reaction of any module corresponds to the evaluation of the whole associated circuit and requires all the module inputs to be determined. Thus, instantaneous bidirectional communications prevent to simply build a global system reaction from a sequence of module reactions because no execution order satisfies all the signal determination precedence constraints. In the COMCTL case, for instance, the `Activity/Activity_Rq` loop would require each module to react before the other (CTL before COM to determine `Activity_Rq` and COM before CTL to determine `Activity`).

This problem has already been mentioned in [13] which proposed to reject the interconnection if it does not include at least one logical delay to break the instantaneity of the communications. We observed through several experiments that this solution imposes serious restrictions upon applications structure. Indeed, true causality problems come from instantaneous cyclic dependencies between signals, which are not implied by such dependencies between modules. An alternative is to build a consistent system reaction from an ordered sequence of partial evaluations of each module circuit, which is possible as soon as the combinational part of the overall system circuit is acyclic. This requires a deep analysis of the module circuits and a careful integration but greatly relaxes the final constraints. We decided to support this in CRONOS with a couple of tools implementing the generation steps mentioned above and presented in the following sections. The first one is called `mgen` and generates the code enabling the part by part evaluation of one module circuit as its inputs get determined. The second one is called `mbind` and generates the code for a specific composition of parallel modules previously submitted to `mgen`. It also checks for the overall acyclicity constraint that will be further discussed.

---

[1] We will now denote by "modules" the modules instantiated at the root level.

5.2   Individual Modules Analysis

This step consists in generating for each module the code that enables to evaluate its associated circuit incrementally as its inputs get determined. Such a
generation is the result of an analysis explained in this section and from which
is also produced an information file required to allow the further integration of
the modules into a system parallel composition.

The natural starting point for the generation of a circuit evaluation is the
description of the circuit itself, that is the blif/ctbl representation of the module which can easily be obtained with the existing ESTEREL tools. The blif file
contains the description of the logical part of the circuit, including the boolean
registers. The ctbl file contains the description of the actions, of their connections with the circuit wires, and of some ordering constraints which have to
be enforced but which were only implicit at the ssc level. mgen analyzes them
and builds an internal representation of the circuit as a partially ordered graph
of evaluation nodes for gates and actions, with arcs expressing precedence constraints. Fig. 7 below provides an example of such graph for the CTL module.

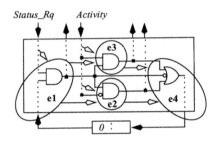

Status_Rq   Activity

Fig. 7. CRONOS evaluation splitting for the CTL module

The figure shows four evaluation nodes for CTL, symbolized by the e1 to e4
ovals. e1 and e4 are a bit larger because they respectively perform latch reading
and latch update operations. The arrows inside the circuit box represent the
precedence constraints which determine the graph partial order. Arrows which
do not have their origin on a node but on an input wire indicate a precedence
constraint between the determination of this input and the possibility to evaluate
the node to which the arrow points.

In this specific case, e1 can be evaluated as soon as Status_Rq is determined,
but not before because the gate it computes uses the corresponding wire. e2 and
e3 can only be evaluated once Activity is determined and after e1 for similar
reasons. Finally, because the rightmost or gate uses the wires computed by all the
others, the node which computes it shall only be evaluated after all the others.
The e1 to e4 precedence constraint is not on the figure and is actually removed by
mgen since it is trivially enforced by transitivity. The latches update corresponds
to an actual state transition and is always performed after everything else.

The context into which a module will be instantiated is not known a-priori. The order of its inputs determination is then undefined and some triggering mechanism is required to schedule the nodes execution at run-time. This becomes costly as the graph gets larger and it is clear that one node for each gate and action will easily yield a huge number of nodes. To deal with this, mgen executes a graph compression algorithm which preserves all the dependencies as well as the possibility to evaluate parts of the circuit progressively with input determinations. In the CTL example, e2, e3 and e4 can be safely merged into an evaluation group eg1 linked after e1 and the determination of Activity. This does not change the basic principles regarding the separate compilation issue but helps a lot in getting an industrially usable result in terms of memory footprints and efficiency. For illustration purposes, we will keep considering the CTL graph before the compression step because it is clearly closer to the structure of the underlying circuit.

mgen first produces code which reflects this structure. Its detailed architecture is not useful at this point of the paper and is presented in 5.4.

It also generates a textual representation of the module evaluation graph and of all the related dependencies, as summarized by Fig. 8 for CTL. This description additionally includes what we call output supports, which express for each output signal of the module the inputs on which it depends via some path in the graph.

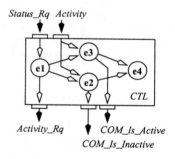

Fig. 8. CRONOS evaluation graph for the CTL module

All these information will be the base of the mbind processing to integrate instances of the module into an outer parallel composition, as explained in the following section.

One important aspect is that we actually achieve true separate compilation since the code for each module is produced without any information about the context into which it will be instantiated. This prevents from performing some optimizations but allows to use the generated binaries in different contexts, which is crucial when such binaries are involved in certification processes.

5.3   Binding the Modules Together

After the analysis of each module by mgen, the CRONOS mbind tool enables to bind them together accordingly with a purely parallel composition specification. Since this specification is also an ESTEREL module, the basic goal is to generate code with the same interface as the one produced by mgen and possibly integrable into a still outer purely parallel system.

The starting point is the ESTEREL source file of the composition module, which specifies the interconnection of all the instance interface signals. mbind builds an internal representation of the whole system based on an analysis of this specification and of the graph description files associated with each instantiated module. At this stage, the only information used from these files is the list of signals attached to each module.

Signal interconnections are represented with entities called nets, which ensure the propagation of the status and possible value of signals as they are determined. Fig. 9 below shows the result for COMCTL with circles to symbolize the nets :

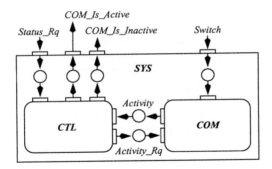

Fig. 9. CRONOS global representation of COMCTL

The figure shows three kinds of nets : input nets which link a system input to an instance input, output nets which link an instance output to a system output, and internal nets which link an instance output to an instance input. They all represent an information flow between some producer and some consumer to which mbind associates an evaluation node performing the necessary propagation operations.

mbind then uses for each module the dependencies between its inputs/outputs and its partial evaluations to merge the evaluation graphs of all the instances via the net evaluation nodes. Fig. 10 shows the result of this operation for the COMCTL example, also indicating that the mgen compression produced a graph with only one evaluation node.

As mgen, mbind finally performs a graph compression, generates a description file of the result and produces the corresponding code.

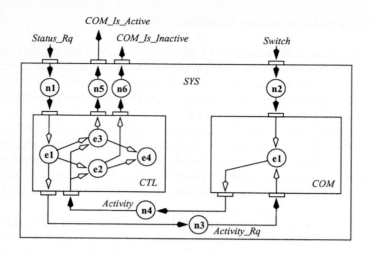

Fig. 10. CRONOS graph integration for COMCTL

As already mentioned in 5.1, such a binding operation is only possible if the overall circuit is acyclic. To ensure this, `mbind` checks that the system evaluation graph is acyclic and indicates an error if it fails. In such cases, the cycles are exhibited in terms of signal dependencies and their resolution is left to the user.

The following sections describe the overall architecture of the generated code to provide a more concrete view of the process. The chosen target language is Ada because of its numerous good properties for the real-time domain and since its integration with other classical languages is easy anyway.

5.4   Module Code Architecture

From any ESTEREL module, `mgen` produces an Ada package which enables the exploitation of the corresponding circuit through a simple interface.

This interface includes one accessor (`Set_I`) for each input signal `I`, one accessor (`O`) for each output signal `O`, one accessor for each partial evaluation node and four module-level entry points (`Initialize`, `Reset`, `Run` and `Clear`).

`Initialize` performs some internal initializations and shall be called once before anything else. `Clear` sets to `Absent` the status of all the module inputs and shall be called at least once before the beginning of any reaction. `Reset` sets the circuit registers to their initial value and shall be called at least once before the first reaction. `Run` triggers a one step complete reaction by calling all the evaluation procedures in topological order.

For any reaction in the context of which an input `I` should be considered present, `Set_I` shall be called before all the evaluation procedures accessing its status. The emission status of any output `O` can be retrieved via the corresponding accessor, which should only be called once it is sure that `O` is determined.

Fig. 11 below shows the specification obtained for CTL :

```
package CTL is

    type CTL_T is limited private;

    -- General entry points
    procedure Initialize (M : in out CTL_T);
    procedure Reset      (M : in out CTL_T);
    procedure Clear      (M : in out CTL_T);
    procedure Run        (M : in out CTL_T);

    -- Accessors for input signals
    procedure Set_Status_Rq    (M : in out CTL_T);
    procedure Set_Activity     (M : in out CTL_T);

    -- Accessors for output signals
    function COM_Is_Active   (M : in CTL_T) return Boolean;
    function COM_Is_Inactive (M : in CTL_T) return Boolean;
    function Activity_Rq     (M : in CTL_T) return Boolean;

    -- Accessors for partial evaluations
    procedure Evaluation_1 (M : in out CTL_T);
    procedure Evaluation_2 (M : in out CTL_T);
    procedure Evaluation_3 (M : in out CTL_T);
    procedure Evaluation_4 (M : in out CTL_T);

private
    -- Circuit internal representation
    subtype Wires_Range is 0 .. 6;
    type Wires_Array is array (Wires_Range) of Boolean;

    subtype Latches_Range is Natural range 0 .. 0;
    type Latches_Array is array (Latches_Range) of Boolean;

    type CTL_T is limited record
       Wires   : Wires_Array;   -- Circuit Wires
       Latches : Latches_Array; -- Circuit Latches
    end record;

end CTL;
```

Fig. 11. CRONOS Ada specification for the CTL module

The abstraction of the module circuit is provided through a private record type which contains all the circuit components and offers the possibility to safely instantiate the same module several times when necessary.

The first possible use of such a package is the instantiation of the corresponding module as an independent system. After a simple variable declaration with the provided type, the instance has to be initialized with Initialize and Reset. A sequence of reactions can then be triggered, each as a set of calls to Clear, to Set for every input to be considered present, and to Run to process the complete circuit evaluation. After every reaction the status of any output can be retrieved with the provided accessors.

Thus, **mgen** does not only allow the separate compilation of a module to be integrated into an outer pure parallel system, but also provides an Ada code generation alternative for any ESTEREL specification. Section 8 provides some experiment results intended to evaluate its efficiency.

Fig. 12 below provides an overview of the package body for CTL :

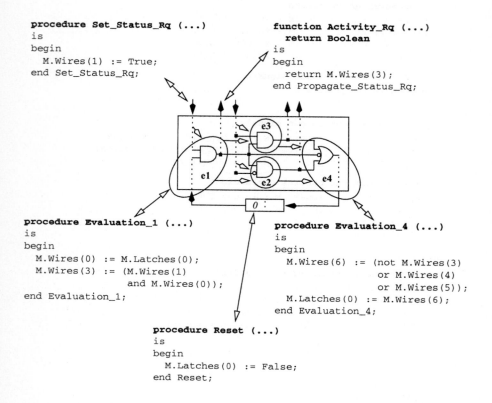

```
procedure Set_Status_Rq (...)
is
begin
   M.Wires(1) := True;
end Set_Status_Rq;
```

```
function Activity_Rq (...)
   return Boolean
is
begin
   return M.Wires(3);
end Propagate_Status_Rq;
```

```
procedure Evaluation_1 (...)
is
begin
   M.Wires(0) := M.Latches(0);
   M.Wires(3) := (M.Wires(1)
          and M.Wires(0));
end Evaluation_1;
```

```
procedure Evaluation_4 (...)
is
begin
   M.Wires(6) := (not M.Wires(3)
            or M.Wires(4)
            or M.Wires(5));
   M.Latches(0) := M.Wires(6);
end Evaluation_4;
```

```
procedure Reset (...)
is
begin
   M.Latches(0) := False;
end Reset;
```

Fig. 12. CRONOS evaluation splitting for the CTL module

In case instances of the module are integrated into a parallel composition, it is the responsibility of the code produced by **mbind** for this composition to use the services offered by the package in a consistent way.

5.5 System Code Architecture

mbind generates an Ada package which offers exactly the same kind of interface as the one provided by **mgen** for individual modules. The very detail of the system record is not important, but it is interesting to notice that it contains a set of fields for the instances from which the system is built and a set of variables for the status/value of the system interface signals.

Initialize and Reset are propagated to each instance, as well as Clear which additionally resets the status of the system interface signals. Fig. 13 shows the sequence of reactions of Fig. 3 with the simplified code for the initialization of the system and using Run for the logical instants 3 and 4.

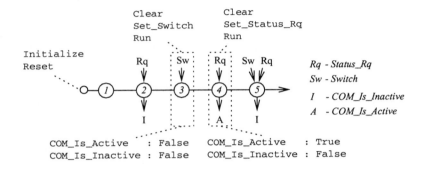

Fig. 13. Example sequence of reactions for COMCTL

As previously described, the system evaluation nodes are a combination of net evaluation nodes and integrated instance nodes, possibly grouped by a compression algorithm. Evaluation of instance nodes are translated into calls to the corresponding evaluation procedure and Fig. 14 shows the translation for internal nets achieving the signal propagations between modules.

Each system node is supported by an evaluation procedure and Run contains a topologically ordered sequence of calls to these procedures which ensures the respect of all the precedence constraints.

```
if (Activity (M.Instances.COM))
then
   Set_Activity (M.Instances.CTL);
end if;
```

CTL.Activity   COM.Activity
(Input)   (Output)

Activity

Fig. 14. An example of CRONOS net evaluation node

The processing for input or output nets is similar, but uses the internal record variables storing the status of the system interface signals. Handling valued signals and signals with multiple producers and/or consumers, allowed by ESTEREL, requires a little more processing, both at the mgen and mbind levels. Such processing is available in CRONOS but does not change any fundamental aspect of our solution regarding the separate compilation issue, so we will not provide information about it.

6   Integration within the Esterel Toolset

Fig. 15 provides a user-level overview of the whole separate compilation process for COMCTL. The .ads and .adb files are respectively Ada package specifications and Ada package bodies. The .dep files are the graph description files produced by mgen from its analysis of each module (dep stands for dependencies).

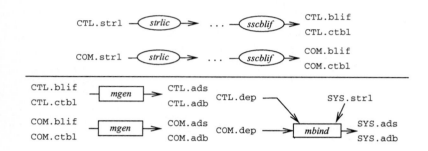

Fig. 15. ESTEREL/CRONOS integration for separate compilation

This process clearly delays the modules assembly step and still uses the vast majority of the existing tools, so CRONOS will benefit from all their possible future enhancements.

7   Major Advantages

CRONOS both provides an Ada alternative to the existing C code production from ESTEREL and separate compilation framework for specifications with pure parallelism at the root level. CRONOS also supports hierarchically organized systems, where the highest level modules are themselves written as pure parallel module instantiations, and so possibly recursively.

The first benefits are classical regarding separate compilation in general : the code for an unchanged module can be used directly in different contexts and does not have to be generated again when a system is rebuilt. The operations applied to a global representation of a system to rebuild it after a local modification are minimized, and in case of a "from scratch" build, most of the translation steps are only applied to one module at a time. The latter point is very strong because algorithms such as the causality analysis mentioned in 4.3 are sometimes too time and memory demanding for a large system as a whole. In such cases, CRONOS offers an alternative to succeed in obtaining a final result.

Moreover, since CRONOS uses the blif representation of each module as a starting point, it is possible to build a system from an optimized version of each of its components. This may enable the production of a system of acceptable size and performance when a global optimization is not possible.

Finally, the requirements about the root-level parallelism and the global graph acyclicity seem to be reasonable in the case of carefully designed modular applications. Several large projects have actually been developed this way by Dassault-Aviation and respecting these constraints has never been considered as a true obstacle. Actually, some rare global cycles appeared, but always corresponded to design flaws and have been easily solved thanks to their expression in terms of interface signal dependencies without intra-module paths.

8   Experiments and Results

Two significant prototype applications have been developed in the context of our studies. The first one handles a small part of the specification for the computing system of one aircraft model. The second one is a model of fuel management used in a more general simulation environment. They will be denoted by ACS for the Aircraft Computing Subsystem and FMS for the Fuel Management Simulation. Table 1 provides general information about their source :

Table 1. Source characteristics for ACS and FMS

System	Lines	Modules	Instances
ACS	4500	14	14
FMS	4560	7	14

"Lines" indicates the number of ESTEREL lines involved, "Modules" the number of separately compiled modules, and "Instances" the number of instances of such modules in the system. The ESTEREL code has been generated from SYNC-CHARTS [7] graphical specifications.

The next table is intended to compare the efficiency of the generated code for four different compilation processes. The first one (further denoted by "C-Mono") is the standard ESTEREL scheme producing monolithic C code without intermediary `blif` optimizations. The second one ("Ada-Mono") produces monolithic Ada code via `mgen` without prior `blif` optimization by considering the main ESTEREL source itself as a single module. The third one ("Ada-Modular") is a CRONOS separate compilation without `blif` optimization. The last one ("Ada-Opt-Modular") is a CRONOS separate compilation after some optimizations performed on the `blif` representation of each module. In every case, the system has first been submitted to a simulation test to ensure that its behavior corresponds to a validation reference (what output sequence from a set of reactions with predefined inputs). Then a simple main procedure has been written for the target language to trigger 10000 reactions. Executables have been generated with the same class of compiler/options and run several times on the same machine (RS6000/41T-PowerPC-AIX 4.2.1) with no other user logged in.

Table 2 below provides the mean per-reaction execution times observed :

Table 2. Mean reaction execution times for ACS and FMS

System	C-Mono	Ada-Mono	Ada-Modular	Ada-Opt-Modular
ACS	1.01 ms	0.93 ms	1.32 ms	0.41 ms
FMS	1.58 ms	1.36 ms	1.28 ms	0.35 ms

The comparison of the "C-Mono" and "Ada-Mono" columns shows that the Ada code generation is efficient by itself since it yields slightly better results starting from the same ssc representation of the entire system.

Comparing "Ada-Mono" and "Ada-Modular" requires a careful look at the statistics from Table 1 : ACS instantiates each module only once whereas FMS instantiates some modules several times. In the monolithic case, the instantiation of the parallel modules is performed by the ESTEREL compiler which basically expands the code for each instance. In the modular case, these instantiations are translated into variable declarations, but the code for different instances of the same module is not duplicated. Some portions of code are then shared in FMS and not in ACS. The execution time increase between Mono and Modular for ACS is due to the addition of the net evaluation nodes for inter-module communications. Such nodes are naturally also present for FMS, but it seems that the code sharing balances the overhead, probably because it results in a better cache utilization.

Finally, the last column clearly demonstrates the interest of the possibility to bind optimized modules, especially when a global optimization is not tractable (which was indeed the case for these applications on our machine).

9   Conclusion and Work in Progress

CRONOS both provides an efficient Ada alternative to the existing C code production from ESTEREL and separate code generation schemes for modular specifications. This greatly increases the maximum size of systems for which runnable code can be obtained and provides a code production process more suitable to large industrial applications. This enables to take advantage of the ESTEREL determinism and formal verification features in the context of large avionics software developments such as the ones Dassault-Aviation leads.

Much related work is still in progress in the company. The most important activities are the development of an integrated graphical environment, a PhD thesis about the distributed execution of separately compiled modules, and studies about a model of asynchronous interconnection of synchronous systems.

All of these projects are conducted in cooperation with the ESTEREL team of École des Mines de Paris and Centre de Mathématiques Appliquées at Sophia Antipolis, constantly improving the ESTEREL technology.

References

[1] Berry, G., The Foundations of Esterel, École des Mines de Paris (1998) [1]
[2] Berry, G., The constructive semantics of pure Esterel - Draft V2.0, École des Mines de Paris (May, 1996) [1]
[3] Berry, G., The Esterel v5 Language Primer, École des Mines de Paris (1997) [1]
[4] Berry, G., Bouali, A., Fornari, X., Ledinot, E., Nassor, E., and De Simone, R., Esterel : A Formal Method Applied to Avionic Software Development, To appear in Journal of Science of Computer Programming (1998)
[5] Hainque, O., Pautet, L., Le Biannic, Y., and Nassor, E., Using Esterel for Avionics Software Development : Motivation, Experiments and Work in progress, In Proc. of the 1998 Workshop on Programming Languages for Real-Time Industrial Applications, (December, 1998), 9–18
[6] E.M. Sentovic, K.J. Singh and L. Lavagno, C. Moon , R. Murgai,A. Saldanha, H. Savoj , P.R. Stephan, R.K. Brayton , andA.L. Sangiovanni-Vincentelli SIS : A System for Sequential Circuit Synthesis, University of California Berkeley : UCB/ERL M92/41 (1992)
[7] C. André, M. Bourdellès and S. Dissoubray SyncCharts/Esterel : Un environnement graphique pour la spécification et la programmation d'applications réactives complexes, In Revue du Génie Logiciel (46) (1997)
[8] G. Berry, T.R. Shiple, H. Touati, Constructive Analysis of Cyclic Circuits, (March, 1996), ED-TC 328–333
[9] H.A. Toma, Analyse constructive et optimisation séquentielle des circuits générés à partir du langage synchrone réactif ESTEREL, PhD thesis, École des Mines de Paris (September, 1997) [1]
[10] Amagbegnon, T.P., Forme canonique arborescente des horloges de SIGNAL, PhD thesis, Université de Rennes I (December, 1995)
[11] Beneviste, A., Le Guernic, P., and Jacquemot, C. Synchronous programming with events and relations : the SIGNAL language and its semantics, In Science of Computer Programming, v.16, (1991)
[12] Halbwachs, N., Caspi, P., Raymond, P., and Pilaud, D. The Synchronous dataflow programming language LUSTRE, Proceedings of the IEEE, 79(9):1305-1320, (September, 1991)
[13] André, C., Boulanger, F., Péraldi, M.-A., Rigault, J.P., and Vidal-Naquet, G. Objects and Synchronous Programming, In European Journal on Automated Systems, v.31(3), 417–432, Hermes (1997)

---

[1] Available at `http://www.inria.fr/meije/esterel`

Tool Support for Production Use of Formal Techniques

John C. Knight, P. Thomas Fletcher, and Brian R. Hicks

Department of Computer Science
University of Virginia, Charlottesville, VA 22903, USA

Abstract. Despite their popularity in academia and many claimed benefits, formal techniques are still not widely used in commercial software development. We claim that lack of effective tools is a major factor limiting the adoption of formal techniques.

Tools supporting formal techniques must integrate smoothly into the overall software development process. To be accepted for regular use in engineering development, innovative tool ideas must be combined with a multitude of essential though routine facilities. Formal specifications using notations like Z include both formal and informal content, and developers of such specifications appreciate the value of innovative analysis but must be able to perform routine manipulations conveniently. However, implementing these routine facilities requires very extensive resources. This has led to valuable tools being developed with very restricted routine facilities thereby limiting the exploitation of their innovation in commercial software development.

To test the idea that high performance tools will promote the use of formal techniques, we have developed a toolset (named Zeus) for the manipulation of Z specifications. Recent experience has shown that large package programs can be reused to provide convenient access to routine facilities. Zeus is based on FrameMaker, a commercial desktop publishing system, and as a result it provides all the document-processing features that FrameMaker provides including WYSIWYG editing using the Z character set and a wealth of formatting features, such as controlling page layouts. It also provides the standard look and feel of Microsoft Windows applications and access to all operating-system services and supported applications. Supplementing these basic features, Zeus provides many Z-specific facilities. Graphic structures are inserted automatically using a menu selection, move with the text to which they are anchored, are resized as their contents change, and can be cut, copied and pasted as desired. Zeus also provides convenient access to Z/EVES, a widely-used, high-performance system for the analysis of Z specifications. Formal text from a FrameMaker document can be selected and sent to Z/EVES for analysis, and the document is annotated to show which text has been checked. The interface seen by a Zeus user is a desktop publishing system that permits convenient manipulation of Z text together with a relatively seamless connection to a powerful analysis capability and access to all the other services supporting software development that are present on the development platform, such as configuration management tools. Whether such a system will promote the wider use of formal techniques in industry is the subject of ongoing experimentation.

Information about Zeus is available at http://www.cs.virginia.edu/zeus. This work was supported in part by the National Science Foundation under grant number CCR-9213427, and in part by NASA under grant number NAG1-1123-FDP.

J. Wing, J. Woodcock, J. Davies (Eds.): FM'99, Vol. II, LNCS 1709, pp. 1854-1854, 1999.
© Springer-Verlag Berlin Heidelberg 1999

Modeling Aircraft Mission Computer Task Rates

Jin Song Dong[1], Brendan P. Mahony[2], and Neale Fulton[3]

[1] School of Computing, National University of Singapore
[2] Defence Science and Technology Organisation (DSTO), Australia
[3] Commonwealth Science and Industrial Research Organisation (CSIRO), Australia

Recently the Royal Australian Air Force (RAAF) has been considering an upgrade to the F/A-18 aircraft in Australia. This upgrade may well involve the modification of Mission Computer (MC) systems. Maintaining correct functionality for the upgraded F/A-18 is therefore a major concern for the RAAF. This particular problem received interest from CSIRO and DSTO to support a joint Research Fellowship to investigate specification of hard real-time characteristics by formal method approaches.

Our initial approach [1] used Object-Z to model an aircraft MC Operational Flight Program (OFP) pre-run time scheduler. However, the treatment of timing issues in this approach is cumbersome and it is not well suited for modeling the OFP process concurrent interactions. From this experience, we realised that the state-based Object-Z notation lacks adequate mechanisms for treating real-time and concurrency. Therefore we have developed a notation called Timed Communicating Object Z (TCOZ) [2, 3, 4] which integrates Object-Z with Timed CSP. The MC process definitions, concurrent interactions, and task rate sequences have been effectively formalised in TCOZ. The benefits of the TCOZ model have included consistent use of terminology, a well-defined collection of synchronisation and concurrency primitives, and the ability to apply object abstraction techniques to structure and simplify the description.

During the formalisation process, we also identified a number of ambiguities in the original requirement documentation regarding the synchronisation relationships between the MC processes. Understanding those critical inter-process synchronisations required painstaking reading of different text sections with many clarifications from our local aviation domain expert. Whence we precisely understand those critical inter-process synchronisations differences, in the TCOZ model these differences are clearly captured by using differing communication mechanisms, sensor/actuators or channels as appropriate. We also believe our approach to be complementary to the original requirement documentation, in as much as the tables and diagrams provide a valuable visualisation and comprehension aid to the formal TCOZ model.

References

[1] J.S. Dong, N. Fulton, L. Zucconi, and J. Colton. Formalising Process Scheduling Requirements for an Aircraft Operational Flight Program. ICFEM'97, November 1997. IEEE Press.
[2] J.S. Dong and B. Mahony. Active Objects in TCOZ. ICFEM'98, IEEE Press, December 1998.
[3] B. Mahony and J.S. Dong. Network Topology and a Case Study in TCOZ. ZUM'98, *LNCS*, September 1998. Springer-Verlag.
[4] B. P. Mahony and J.S. Dong. Blending Object-Z and Timed CSP: An introduction to TCOZ. ICSE'98, April 1998. IEEE Press.

J. Wing, J. Woodcock, J. Davies (Eds.): FM'99, Vol. II, LNCS 1709, pp. 1855–1855, 1999.
© Springer-Verlag Berlin Heidelberg 1999

A Study of Collaborative Work: Answers to a Test on Formal Specification in B

Henri Habrias[1], Pascal Poizat[1], and Jean-Yves Lafaye[2]

[1] IRIN, Université de Nantes & École Centrale
2 rue de la Houssinière, B.P. 92208, F-44322 Nantes cedex 3, France
`Henri.Habrias,Pascal.Poizat@irin.univ-nantes.fr`
`http://www.sciences.univ-nantes.fr/info/perso/permanents/poizat`
[2] L3I, Université de la Rochelle, France
avenue Marillac, F-17042, La Rochelle cedex 1, France
`jylafaye@iut-univ-lr.fr`

Objective It is commonly admitted that strength comes through unity. The point we address here, is to discuss to what extent this applies to a pair of students facing a test in formal specification (B notation). More precisely, we aim at deciding whether collaborative work is of benefit for one, other, or both of the collaborating students. We use data analysis to examine a sample of students and derive some qualitative and quantitative information. What follows is a seminal work: i.e., the sample is small. Here follow the main points of our contribution:

- Identification of a strategy to design a formal specification test and collect data
- Proposal of a statistical approach to exploratory data analysis
- Application of graphical analysis and statistical hypothesis testing procedures

Further analysis carried out in the same manner on larger samples may be of interest and would provide for more accurate conclusions.

Sampling 26 students involved in the first year of a course (IUT[1]) in computer science were first presented with a test in formal specification. The test was made of incomplete source text for three B machines, and students were asked to fill in the missing parts. Time for answering was limited but amply sufficient. Individual results ranging between 0 and 20 were recorded.

Independently from these results, students were asked to discuss the previous examination and the answers they provided. Each student was allowed to revise his work and give an individual corrected final version. Once again, copies were corrected and given a mark between 0 and 20. Individual and collective results have been confronted and analysed.

---

[1] Institut Universitaire de Technologie: two years study that trains computer science technicians

J. Wing, J. Woodcock, J. Davies (Eds.): FM'99, Vol. II, LNCS 1709, pp. 1856–1857, 1999.
© Springer-Verlag Berlin Heidelberg 1999

Statistical Analysis In brief, our main conclusions are the following:

- Collaborative work never is prejudicial except for one student in the sample. The overall average mark is 8.5 without collaboration and around 13 after collaboration. All pairs gained on average. According to Student's means comparison test procedure, all effects are significant (5%). One could advance that better results might be assigned to more time for answering the test, independently of any collaboration effect. This seems not to be sound since time was not an actual constraint during the individual examination.
- We applied a linear regression model $M2 = a_0 + a_1 M! + \epsilon$ to capture the relation between the independent variable (individual result before collaboration: $M1$) and the dependent variable (individual result after collaboration: $M2$). Doing so, we could compute an estimate for the general effect of collaboration ($a_0 \approx 7$) and one for an extra bonus related to the initial level of the student ($a_1 \approx 0.7$). It is worth discussing the meaning of $a1$ which is significantly not null and less than unity.
- Graphical plots suggest that heterogeneity of results within pairs of students increased after collaboration. This intuition is not confirmed by a statistical analysis (T test). More precisely, we concluded that collaborative work has a consensus effect for groups over 8, while collaboration widens the gap for groups under 8.
- Lastly, a correlation analysis showed that no significant relation existed between the difference within groups and the score of groups.

Archived Design Steps in Temporal Logic

Pertti Kellomäki[1] and Tommi Mikkonen[2]

[1] Tampere University of Technology, Finland, pk@cs.tut.fi,
[2] Nokia Telecommunications, Finland, Tommi.Mikkonen@nokia.com

We demonstrate how solutions to recurring problems in the design of nonterminating reactive systems can be archived and verified in an abstract form using the DisCo specification method [1, 3].

DisCo is based on incremental development of temporal logic specifications using *superposition*. Superposition is a form of refinement in which new state variables and operations on them are added layerwise to a specification.

An archived specification $\mathcal{L}_1 + \mathcal{L}_2$ is applied to a specification S as depicted in Fig. 1. The "+" symbol denotes superposition, and "$\leq$" denotes refinement.

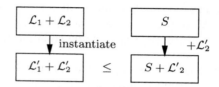

Fig. 1. Applying an archived step.

The archived specification is first instantiated with concrete classes, types and functions, yielding the specification $\mathcal{L}'_1 + \mathcal{L}'_2$. The layer $\mathcal{L}'_2$ is then superimposed on S, yielding the specification $S + \mathcal{L}'_2$. Establishing that $S + \mathcal{L}_2$ is a refinement of $\mathcal{L}_1 + \mathcal{L}_2$ also establishes that $S + \mathcal{L}_2$ has the safety properties verified for the archived specification. Establishing the refinement incurs proof obligations, but these are relatively trivial because of the superposition methodology.

In an archived specification, $\mathcal{L}_1$ represents a problem and its context, and $\mathcal{L}_2$ a solution to the problem. They thus embody formally some of the information contained in behavioral *design patterns* [2]. Assumptions about the behavior of the context are formalized in an operational manner using the same formalism used for specifying the solution.

This research was supported by the Academy of Finland, project 757473.

References

[1] The DisCo project WWW page. http://www.cs.tut.fi/ohj/DisCo/.
[2] Erich Gamma, Richard Helm, Ralph Johnson, and John Vlissides. *Design Patterns*. Addison Wesley, Reading, MA, 1995.
[3] Reino Kurki-Suonio. Fundamentals of object-oriented specification and modeling of collective behaviors. In H. Kilov and W. Harvey, editors, *Object-Oriented Behavioral Specifications*, pages 101–120. Kluwer Academic Publishers, 1996.

A PVS-Based Approach for Teaching Constructing Correct Iterations

Michel Lévy and Laurent Trilling

Laboratoire IMAG-LSR
B.P. 72, 38041 St Martin d'Hères, France
Michel.Levy@imag.fr, Laurent.Trilling@imag.fr

Just claiming the importance of formal methods is not enough, it is necessary to teach programming using formal methods. Also, we have to convince students to use them in their programming. To fill this goal, two points seem necessary: a no-fault approach combined with (apparently) affordable proofs and the use of automatic provers.

More than twenty years ago, David Gries and others said that the goal should be to forbid the construction of incorrect programs by teaching constructions of correct programs using a no-fault approach. This point of view appears to us to be both simple and challenging for students, because teaching correct program construction means teaching methodologies based on a process with well-defined steps which decomposes into sub-tasks, each of which is human in scope. Human scope means the sub-tasks are considered obvious or easy to prove by humans; for example, easy to prove sub-tasks preferably do not require inductive proof.

Formal pen and paper teaching of program construction methodologies using formal methods is not enough, since proofs by hand sometimes contain over-looked errors and, by not facing this reality, students do not develop the conviction to use these methods systematically. What is needed here are computer systems to check proof automatically. Using such systems challenges students to write correct proofs, and, in turn, motivates students to employ formal methods in their programming.

Our first objective relates to designing a system called CIA-PVS (for Constructions d'Itérations Assistées par PVS). This system is used in teaching a long known and well known methodology for constructing simple programs, i.e. loops. CIA-PVS is based on a well known proof-checker, PVS (for Prototype Verification System), which was developed at SRI (Stanford Research Institute). What is expected from the CIA-PVS system is that it reacts quasi-automatically to prove the lemmas necessary for the construction of programs which are traditional exercises such as the Dutch National Flag and the dichotomic research in an ordered list. What should be noted here is the simplicity of the lemmas to be proved. The real difficulty in constructing the program should not be the proof of these lemmas but the formalisation of the problem as the definition of the formulas expressing the result of the program, the invariants and the termination function of the iteration.

Our second objective relates to evaluating CIA-PVS for teaching programming via a methodology employing formal methods. In particular, the evaluation

J. Wing, J. Woodcock, J. Davies (Eds.): FM'99, Vol. II, LNCS 1709, pp. 1859–1860, 1999.
© Springer-Verlag Berlin Heidelberg 1999

will be based on two criteria: automatic proof power and modelisation. Modelisation refers to the capacity to model easily the formal methods methodology so as to reduce as much as possible the gap between the formal teaching of the methodology and the concrete use of it in programming.

Our work began by constructing a PVS theory, called CIA-PVS, which proves the methodology itself. We need to prove it because, even if a methodology is, like this one, very well-known and appears to everybody correct, it is still possible that an error will arise as we attempt to formalise it precisely. Moreover, the use of this theory reduces the proving task of students, as desired, because the proof of the well-foundedness of the methodology is done once and for all. The use of subtypes provided by PVS to construct CIA-PVS has been very useful for reaching this goal. First experimentation on simple yet not trivial problems is encouraging. Once CIA-PVS is proved, power is clearly impressive in many cases and that is clearly positive. The remaining sensitive points are (1) some proofs may become easier or more difficult depending the chosen modelisation and (2) some proofs require a significant know-how level in PVS. The challenge for teaching remains both to define a starting knowledge of PVS to be taught to students and to extend CIA-PVS to deal with more sophisticated exchanges with students.

A Minimal Framework for Specification Theory

Bernd Baumgarten

German National Research Center for Information Technology (GMD)
Rheinstr. 75, D-64295 Darmstadt, Germany
baumgart@darmstadt.gmd.de
http://www.darmstadt.gmd.de/~baumgart/aspekte.html

Abstract. Notions concerning the specification, implementation, verification and testing of systems are ordinarily defined within a given context. We discuss what could and should belong to such a specification context. We obtain a unique practice-oriented specification semantics resp. conformance relation. We expect our framework to permit the definition of a general vocabulary for specification, verification and testing, independent of specific models or languages.

Overview

When dealing with specifications, we are usually doing so within some context. In the full paper we argue that a *specification context* should comprise some or all of the following components:

- a set *Systs* of systems of interest,
- a set *Obs* of possible observations to be made of these systems,
- a set *Props* of potentially relevant system properties,
- a set *Specs* of specification terms (or specifications),
- a relation *permits* between systems and observations,
- a relation *has_property* between systems and properties, and
- a function *obs_sem* mapping each specification to a set of (permitted) observations.

In the full paper, we discuss in which regards these components form a useful framework covering more aspects than might be suspected at first sight, as well as special topics, for example why time is such an essential ingredient in observations.
Specification contexts have been used successfully

- to assess the significance of system requirements, and
- to give a formal meaning to formerly vague notions of testability.

We intend to use this framework to formalize a multitude of practically motivated concepts in testing (for a typical list, cf. ISO 9646 Part 1), as a contribution towards reliable and formally founded test generation procedures. We also plan to extend our concepts to aspects of concurrency, probability, and security.
For the full paper and related information, see the web page given above.

J. Wing, J. Woodcock, J. Davies (Eds.): FM'99, Vol. II, LNCS 1709, pp. 1861-1861, 1999.
© Springer-Verlag Berlin Heidelberg 1999

A Model of Specification-Based Testing of Interactive Systems

Ian MacColl and David Carrington

Software Verification Research Centre,
Department of Computer Science and Electrical Engineering,
The University of Queensland, Brisbane QLD 4072, Australia
ianm@csee.uq.edu.au
http://www.csee.uq.edu.au/~ianm/

In this paper we present a model of specification-based testing of interactive systems. This model provides the basis for a framework to guide such testing.

Interactive systems are traditionally decomposed into a functionality component and a user interface component; this distinction is termed dialogue separation and is the underlying basis for conceptual and architectural models of such systems. Correctness involves both proper behaviour of the user interface and proper computation by the underlying functionality. Specification-based testing is one method used to increase confidence in correctness, but it has had limited application to interactive system development to date.

Our starting point is the York model of interactors in which an interactive system (or component) is described in terms of functionality, presentation and interaction viewpoints, with the first two specified in a model-based notation and the last in a behaviour-based notation. Model-based specifications are represented as a state transition relation and behaviour-based specifications are represented as event sequences.

For a model-based notation, such as Z or Object-Z, specification-based testing is concerned with dividing the state transition relation, typically forming a partition of the input space of each operation. A single point in each equivalence class is used as a test input, and its projection onto the output space is a test oracle, used to determine the result of the test.

The state transition relation of a model-based specification (or testing information derived from it) can be interpreted as an implicit behavior-based specification. This is useful for test sequencing and to relate the testing information for each of the operations.

For a behaviour-based notation, testing information is derived from the specification to show an implementation conforms to the specification in terms of some relation, such as equivalence, quasi-equivalence or reduction for nondeterministic finite state machines, or equivalences based on trace or failure semantics for notations based on labelled transition systems (such as CCS and CSP).

We are using the model presented in this paper to develop a framework for specification-based testing of interactive systems. The framework aims to relate the model-based testing information, which is useful for unit testing, and the behaviour-based information, which is useful for system and usability testing. The paper is available at http://www.csee.uq.edu.au/~ianm/model.ps.gz.

J. Wing, J. Woodcock, J. Davies (Eds.): FM'99, Vol. II, LNCS 1709, pp. 1862–1862, 1999.
© Springer-Verlag Berlin Heidelberg 1999

Algebraic Aspects of the Mapping between Abstract Syntax Notation One and CORBA IDL

Radu Ocică[1] and Dan Ionescu[1]

School of Information Technology and Engineering
University of Ottawa, Ottawa, Ontario

With the advent of network computing, a distributed program computation is a product of computations of single programs running on heterogeneous platforms, written in different programming languages, and exchanging messages. In this context, the need of a uniform abstract notation, machine and platform independent, to be used for the message exchange between communicating software entities, has given birth to ASN.1. This notation is a data type specification beyond the scope of any programming language. In the same context, the need of an environment to program distributed applications at a high level of abstraction with respect to communication protocols and operating systems architectures has led to the emergence of the Common Object Request Broker Architecture (CORBA). The core of CORBA is represented by the Interface Description Language (IDL). IDL is used to define objects which can be accessed via the Object Request Broker (ORB). Similar to the case of ASN.1, IDL has its own mechanisms to build complex data types, which can be mapped partially to those of ASN.1. Such a mapping makes the subject of this paper. It allows building applications that bridge the field of ASN.1 based communication protocols and that of CORBA based distributed applications.

In the present work a high level formal specification in Z of both the ASN.1 and IDL syntax notations is given. Syntactic aspects of the two notations are expressed in Z using free type definitions, while for the semantic features of the two notations invariants are used. This framework is used for analyzing the ambiguities of ASN.1 definitions as well as for finding the extent to which the mapping between the two notations is possible. The target of the present research is to formulate the ASN.1 - IDL translation rules, such that the diagram (1) below commutes and to set the mechanisms for gateways between CORBA based network management applications and agents using SNMP or CMIP; both network management protocols relying on the ASN.1 notation. The mapping is analyzed both at a high level, that of the abstract syntax as well as at a low level, the one of the transfer syntax. So far these aspects have been investigated for small isomorphic subsets of ASN.1 and IDL. The Z notation and the Z-EVES theorem prover have been successfully used to prove that the diagram (1) commutes.

$$
\begin{array}{ccc}
ASNType & \xrightarrow{\;RelationalMap\;} & IDLType \\
\scriptstyle ASNImageOfType \downarrow & & \downarrow \scriptstyle IDLImageOfType \\
ASNValue & \longrightarrow & IDLValue
\end{array}
\qquad (1)
$$

J. Wing, J. Woodcock, J. Davies (Eds.): FM'99, Vol. II, LNCS 1709, pp. 1863–1863, 1999.
© Springer-Verlag Berlin Heidelberg 1999

Retrenchment

R. Banach[1] and M. Poppleton[1,2]

[1] Computer Science Dept., Manchester University, Manchester, M13 9PL, U.K.
[2] School of Mathl. and Inf. Sciences, Coventry University, Coventry, CV1 5FB, U.K.
banach@cs.man.ac.uk , m.r.poppleton@coventry.ac.uk

It has been noticed for some time, that when refinement is used as the sole means of progressing from an abstract model to a concrete one, then certain difficulties plague the development process due to the unforgiving nature of the usual refinement proof obligations. In its familiar downward simulation setting, refinement implies two things. Firstly that whenever the abstract model is able to make a step, the concrete model must also be able to make some step. And secondly that whenever the concrete model actually makes a step, there must be an abstract step that simulates it, in order to preserve the user's fiction, that it is the abstract model that is doing the work. The abstract model says *when* a step must be possible, while the concrete model dictates *how* the outcome may appear. This close link may be counterproductive in certain situations.

Consider natural number arithmetic. Suppose the abstract model contains some numerical state variables, modelled using Peano naturals. The concrete model must reflect the finite nature of real resources, so that concrete variables are finite naturals. Now there is no sensible refinement relation between these models. For consider what happens when the values of some variables are at their bounds. At the abstract level there is no problem as we can always do a calculation. However the concrete model will throw some exception because of the finite bounds. The POs of refinement require that a concrete calculation takes place (because the abstract level can perform a step), but even if there is a concrete calculation, its result will not correspond to the abstract result (by the concrete finiteness assumption).

Refinement works fine in textbook examples, small enough that eg. awkward limits can be captured at the abstract level without pain. In industrial scale situations though, the complexity of the resulting descriptions diminishes their usefulness, and makes refinement applicable close to code only — the bulk of the development effort must remain informal. Retrenchment avoids these problems by loosening the tight correspondence between abstract and concrete enforced by the refinement POs. As well as the usual initialisation and internal consistency POs, retrenchment demands:

$$G(u,v) \land P(i,j,u,v) \land Op_C(v,j,v',p) \Rightarrow$$
$$\exists u',o \bullet Op_A(u,i,u',o) \land (G(u',v') \lor C(u',v',o,p,\ldots))$$

where i,j are abstract/concrete inputs, u,v are state values, o,p are outputs, Op_A, Op_C are operations, G is the retrieve relation, and P and C are the within and concedes relations. P strengthens G, while C weakens G; '...' allows before values to be refered to. (In total correctness, concrete termination is additionally assumed, and abstract termination is derived.) Arbitrary I/O and state mixing

J. Wing, J. Woodcock, J. Davies (Eds.): FM'99, Vol. II, LNCS 1709, pp. 1864–1865, 1999.
© Springer-Verlag Berlin Heidelberg 1999

between levels facilitates specification evolution. P limits contact between levels, allowing maximum simplicity in the abstract level. C allows exceptions and non-refinement properties to be captured. The added flexibility allows radically different models to be related, eg. a continuous abstract model and a discrete concrete model, as is needed in the development of embedded systems, which usually need to interface to continuous physical models. Retrenchment allows formal techniques and mechanical checkability, to migrate higher into the development process than refinement alone reaches. Contradicting previous properties via C, allows high degrees of complexity to be introduced gradually, stepwise.

Banach R., Poppleton M.; Retrenchment: An Engineering Variation on Refinement. *in*: Proc. B-98, Bert (ed.), Springer, 1998, 129-147, LNCS **1393**.
Also: UMCS Tech. Rep. UMCS-99-3-2, http://www.cs.man.ac.uk/cstechrep
See also: http://www.cs.man.ac.uk/~banach/Recent. publications.html

Proof Preservation in Component Generalization

Anamaria Martins Moreira

Universidade Federal do Rio Grande do Norte (UFRN) — DIMAp
59078-970 Natal, RN, Brazil
http://www.dimap.ufrn.br/~anamaria

Abstract. Formal specifications can provide significant support for software component reuse, as they allow tools to "understand" the semantics of the components they are manipulating. For instance, they can be of great help on the generation of reusable components through the parameterization of more specific ones, supporting the process of creation and maintenance of libraries of reusable components.
In this work[1], we concentrate on the generalization of algebraic specification components by their parameterization. Knowing that highly specific components have small chances of being reused, but that, on the other hand, if a component is too general, its reuse will often be useless; we try to preserve some set of semantic properties of a component that are considered "important" somehow. So, we propose means to identify the requirements that a formal parameter should satisfy in order to preserve part of the original component semantics in the generalization. To reach this goal, we may (or may not) consider proofs for these properties in the original context and identify the conditions under which these proofs are reproducible after generalization. In our PhD Thesis, we considered both cases; here, we concentrate in the case of known proofs. When these known proofs are rewrite proofs, a set of equations can be extracted from them and added to the formal parameter so that they are preserved in the process. This simple technique provides sufficient conditions for the validity of the considered properties in the models of the more general specification, with the advantage of being easily computed by a simple algorithm that we propose. This algorithm is to be applied in conjunction with a generalization operator that safely effectivates the generalization transformations in the component. This combination provides the means to obtain a more general specification component from which the original one is a specialization and that still satisfies a given set of equational properties with their rewrite proofs.
We have also shown that more complex proofs can benefit from this result, although only partially. One of the next steps in this work is to improve the treatement of these other kinds of proofs.

Keywords. algebraic specifications, component parameterization and reuse, proof generalization.

---

[1] A full version of this article may be found in the author's URL.

J. Wing, J. Woodcock, J. Davies (Eds.): FM'99, Vol. II, LNCS 1709, pp. 1866–1866, 1999.
© Springer-Verlag Berlin Heidelberg 1999

Formal Modelling and Simulation of Train Control Systems Using Petri Nets

Michael Meyer zu Hörste[1] and Eckehard Schnieder[1]

Institut für Regelungs- und Automatisierungstechnik, Technische Universität
Braunschweig, Langer Kamp 8, D-38106 Braunschweig, Germany
{meyer|schnieder}@ifra.ing.tu-bs.de

Abstract. A formal model was prepared on behalf of the German railways (Deutsche Bahn AG) starting from an informal (natural language) specifications of the European Train Control System (ETCS) system. Proceeding from the existing models of the system design - the waterfall and the spiral model - a model for the system design was developed so as to use Petri nets as a universal means of description for all the phases of the ETCS. Following a thorough and detailed comparison, it was decided to use Petri nets as a means of description for this procedure, as they permit universal application, the use of different methods and formal analysis. The method developed is an integrated event- and data-oriented approach, which shows the different aspects of the system on their own net levels. The model comprises three sub-models with a model of the environment developed next to the onboard and trackside systems. This environment model covers all the additional systems connected through the system interfaces, examples of which are interlocking or regulation. Starting from a net representing the system context, the process of the onboard and trackside sub-systems was modelled. Here, the different operations and processes are visualized in the form of scenarios, which in turn have access to additional refinements representing specific functions. System modelling was supported by the tool Design/CPN. It was chosen after a careful evaluation of several Petri net tools. ETCS system modelling was taken to a point permitting partial model simulation. On the basis of these models, additional options of the spiral model of the system design now appear: the train and trackside models may expand into specific visualizations, the algorithms can be further refined and compared, the models can be used for different kinds of tests and also for purposes of system quality assurance, which may go as far as furnishing proof of safety standards. Additional phases of system development may now be elaborated on the basis of the spiral model. Our experience has shown that it is possible to take real-life and operational systems specifications written in a natural language and express their content as a formal specification. Our experience has also demonstrated that it is possible to incorporate real life practices of software development cycles (spiral model, waterfall model) into formal models. The paper makes an overview of our experiences and highlights the various problems which were encountered and solved.

References can be found at: www.ifra.ing.tu-bs.de/~m31/etcsrefs.html

J. Wing, J. Woodcock, J. Davies (Eds.): FM'99, Vol. II, LNCS 1709, pp. 1867–1867, 1999.
© Springer-Verlag Berlin Heidelberg 1999

Formal Specification of a Voice Communication System Used in Air Traffic Control

An Industrial Application of Light-Weight Formal Methods Using VDM++

Johann Hörl and Bernhard K. Aichernig

Technical University Graz, Institute for Software Technology (IST),
Münzgrabenstr. 11/II, A-8010 Graz, Austria
{jhoerl|aichernig}@ist.tu-graz.ac.at

A joint project of the Austrian company Frequentis[1] and the Technical University Graz demonstrates the applicability of executable formal models[2]. The formal method VDM++ has been applied to specify a safety critical voice communication system (VCS) for air-traffic control. Besides the expected improvement of the informal specification documents, 64 defects have been found, the efficiency of the system test-cases to cover the functionality of the VCS has been analyzed. In order to get a test-coverage measure, the formal specification has been animated with existing system test-cases using IFAD's VDMTools. A

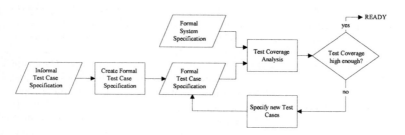

main result of this work was the realization that only 80% of the system's radio functionality had been covered by the former existing test cases. Consequently, additional test cases have been derived from the formal specification. In addition, the specification high-lighted how much more economic test cases could be designed, in order to cover more system functionality in a single run. Furthermore, an existing change request has been chosen in order to investigate the role of an explicit model in the modification process. It turned out that the low abstraction level of an executable specification is certainly an advantage in analysing the impacts of change-requests: Since the object-oriented VDM++ model reflected the system's architecture, the impacts on the different components could be analyzed in the model. A further experience is that VDM's well-known refinement concepts, such as retrieve functions, are well suited to design the modifications.

---

[1] http://www.frequentis.co.at/

[2] See also ftp://www.ist.tu-graz.ac.at/pub/publications/IST-TEC-99-03.ps.gz

J. Wing, J. Woodcock, J. Davies (Eds.): FM'99, Vol. II, LNCS 1709, pp. 1868–1868, 1999.
© Springer-Verlag Berlin Heidelberg 1999

Model-Checking the Architectural Design of a Fail-Safe Communication System for Railway Interlocking Systems

Bettina Buth[1] and Mike Schrönen[2]

[1] BISS, Bremen Institute for Safe Systems,
bb@informatik.uni-bremen.de
[2] Department of Electrical Engineering, University of Cape Town,
mschronen@eleceng.uct.ac.za

The design and development of safety-critical systems requires particular care in order to ensure the highest level of confidence in the systems. A variety of life-cycle models and development standards have evolved in various areas. Formal methods are touted to be the best approach for the development on all levels. Up to now, the lack of adequate tools, the lack of knowlegde on the developers side, and the well-known problems of scalability have prevented a migration of these methods into industries.

Schrönen proposes a methodology for the development of microprocessor based safety-critical systems which takes into account the state-of-the-art methods and guidelines for this specific field. The use of formal methods for the verification of the overall design as well as the specification of tests is proposed and demonstrated, using the development of a fail-safe data transceiver (FSDT) for Transnet, South Africa, as a case study. Here we report on the validation of the system architecture based on CSP specification and refinement. The model-checker FDR2 was used as a tool for this task.

The validation was a joint effort of the two authors, the one being the developer of the transceiver, the other an experienced user of FDR2 and thus a prototypical setting for industrial projects: formal methods specialists take part in the system development by supporting the modelling and validation process. Experiences are positive in this respect, but also support the claim that it is not possible in general to perform this kind of validation without cooperation with the developer of a system.

On the technical side, experiences show that while it is possible to use FDR2 as a validation tool, there are some aspects of the case study which are not easily captured in the CSP model. This is true for timing properties both for the environment and internal actions as well as for the atomicity of internal actions. In both cases, semaphores and flags were used for modelling on the CSP side.

The overall result of the work so far is positive even with the problems mentioned above. We plan to continue the cooperation for further investigation of the FSDT, starting with investigations related to exceptional behaviour such as corrupted and lost data. In general it would be interesting to investigate how far other model-checking tools as for example the SPIN tool, allow an easier approach to modelling the system and formulating the desired properties.

J. Wing, J. Woodcock, J. Davies (Eds.): FM'99, Vol. II, LNCS 1709, pp. 1869–1869, 1999.
© Springer-Verlag Berlin Heidelberg 1999

Analyzing the Requirements of an Access Control Using VDMTools and PVS

Georg Droschl

IST – Technical University of Graz, Austria *and*
Austrian Research Center Seibersdorf (ARCS).
droschl@ist.tu-graz.ac.at, http://www.ist.tu-graz.ac.at

SSD is an access control, which is part of a comprehensive security system developed by the Austrian Research Center Seibersdorf. SSD is being re-developed in a formal methods case study(cf Fig. 1). Since executable code has to be de-

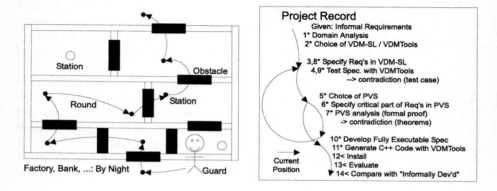

Fig. 1. The Access Control and the Project Record of the Case Study.

veloped, a tool with an automatic code generator had to be chosen. VDMTools for VDM-SL is such a tool. When testing the specification, a test case indicating a contradiction in the requirements has been found. In order to achieve a better understanding of the nature of the contradiction, the theorem prover PVS has been used to formally prove properties of a certain aspect described by the requirements[1]. The benefits of the PVS analysis include theorems which indicate inconsistencies in the requirements. Subsequently, linking VDM and PVS has been further investigated[2]. There are VDM and PVS specifications which share the concept of events. However, they are used in a different manner in the two formalisms. Another aspect is using VDM for event-based systems.

---

[1] Droschl G. Using PVS for requirements analysis of an access control. Technical Report IST-TEC-99-05, IST, TU-Graz, Austria, February 1999. Available at http://www.ist.tu-graz.ac.at/Publications
[2] Droschl G. Events and Scenarios in VDM and PVS. To appear in the proceedings of 3rd Irish Workshop in Formal Methods, Juli 1–2, Galway, Ireland, 1999.

J. Wing, J. Woodcock, J. Davies (Eds.): FM'99, Vol. II, LNCS 1709, pp. 1870–1870, 1999.
© Springer-Verlag Berlin Heidelberg 1999

Cache Coherence Verification with TLA+

Homayoon Akhiani, Damien Doligez, Paul Harter, Leslie Lamport,
Joshua Scheid, Mark Tuttle*, and Yuan Yu

Compaq Computer Corporation

We used the specification language TLA+ to analyze the correctness of two cache-coherence protocols for shared-memory multiprocessors based on two generations (EV6 and EV7) of the Alpha processor. A *memory model* defines the relationship between the values written by one processor and the values read by another, and a *cache-coherence protocol* manipulates the caches to preserve this relationship. The cache-coherence protocol is a fundamental component of any shared-memory multiprocessor design. Proving that the coherence protocol implements the memory model is a high-leverage application of formal methods. The analysis of the first protocol was largely a research project, but the analysis of the second protocol was a part of the engineers' own verification process.

The EV6-based multiprocessor uses a highly-optimized, very complicated cache-coherence protocol. The protocol uses about sixty different types of messages, and the documentation for the protocol consists of a stack of twenty documents about four inches tall, none of it complete or precise enough to be the basis of a proof. After more than two man-years of effort, four of us were able to write a 1900-line specification of the algorithm, a 200-line specification of the Alpha memory model, and about 3000 lines of proof that the algorithm implements the memory model. This was far from a complete proof, but enough of a proof to subject the algorithm to a rigorous analysis, and to discover one bug in the protocol and one bug in the memory model.

The cache-coherence protocol for EV7-based multiprocessors is dramatically simpler, bringing a complete correctness proof within the realm of possibility. A new tool, a model checker for TLA+ called TLC, increased the odds of success. TLC enumerates the reachable states in a finite-state model of a specification written in an expressive subset of TLA+, and it checks that an invariant written in TLA+ holds in each of these states. When TLC discovers an error, a minimal-length sequence of states leading from an initial state to a bad state is reported. One of us wrote an 1800-line specification of the algorithm. Using TLC to check multiple invariants uncovered about 66 errors of various kinds. The engineers were also able to use state sequences output by TLC as input to their own RTL-verification tools, an interesting case of formal methods helping engineers use their own tools more efficiently.

We were pleased to see that the basic verification methodology, refined through years of research, works pretty much as expected, although the proofs were hard. The engineers had little difficulty learning to read and write TLA+ specifications. We hope TLA+ will play a role in other projects in the near future.

---

* Mark Tuttle, Cambridge Research Lab, Compaq Computer Corporation, One Kendall Square, Building 700, Cambridge, MA 02139, mark.tuttle@compaq.com.

J. Wing, J. Woodcock, J. Davies (Eds.): FM'99, Vol. II, LNCS 1709, pp. 1871–1871, 1999.
© Springer-Verlag Berlin Heidelberg 1999

Author Index

Lecture Notes in Computer Science

For information about Vols. 1–1619
please contact your bookseller or Springer-Verlag

Vol. 1663: F. Dehne, A. Gupta. J.-R. Sack, R. Tamassia (Eds.), Algorithms and Data Structures. Proceedings, 1999. IX, 366 pages. 1999.

Vol. 1664: J.C.M. Baeten, S. Mauw (Eds.), CONCUR'99. Concurrency Theory. Proceedings, 1999. XI, 573 pages. 1999.

Vol. 1666: M. Wiener (Ed.), Advances in Cryptology – CRYPTO '99. Proceedings, 1999. XII, 639 pages. 1999.

Vol. 1667: J. Hlavička, E. Maehle, A. Pataricza (Eds.), Dependable Computing – EDCC-3. Proceedings, 1999. XVIII, 455 pages. 1999.

Vol. 1668: J.S. Vitter, C.D. Zaroliagis (Eds.), Algorithm Engineering. Proceedings, 1999. VIII, 361 pages. 1999.

Vol. 1671: D. Hochbaum, K. Jansen, J.D.P. Rolim, A. Sinclair (Eds.), Randomization, Approximation, and Combinatorial Optimization. Proceedings, 1999. IX, 289 pages. 1999.

Vol. 1672: M. Kutylowski, L. Pacholski, T. Wierzbicki (Eds.), Mathematical Foundations of Computer Science 1999. Proceedings, 1999. XII, 455 pages. 1999.

Vol. 1673: P. Lysaght, J. Irvine, R. Hartenstein (Eds.), Field Programmable Logic and Applications. Proceedings, 1999. XI, 541 pages. 1999.

Vol. 1674: D. Floreano, J.-D. Nicoud, F. Mondada (Eds.), Advances in Artificial Life. Proceedings, 1999. XVI, 737 pages. 1999. (Subseries LNAI).

Vol. 1675: J. Estublier (Ed.), System Configuration Management. Proceedings, 1999. VIII, 255 pages. 1999.

Vol. 1976: M. Mohania, A M. Tjoa (Eds.), Data Warehousing and Knowledge Discovery. Proceedings, 1999. XII, 400 pages. 1999.

Vol. 1677: T. Bench-Capon, G. Soda, A M. Tjoa (Eds.), Database and Expert Systems Applications. Proceedings, 1999. XVIII, 1105 pages. 1999.

Vol. 1678: M.H. Böhlen, C.S. Jensen, M.O. Scholl (Eds.), Spatio-Temporal Database Management. Proceedings, 1999. X, 243 pages. 1999.

Vol. 1679: C. Taylor, A. Colchester (Eds.), Medical Image Computing and Computer-Assisted Intervention – MICCAI'99. Proceedings, 1999. XXI, 1240 pages. 1999.

Vol. 1680: D. Dams, R. Gerth, S. Leue, M. Massink (Eds.), Theoretical and Practical Aspects of SPIN Model Checking. Proceedings, 1999. X, 277 pages. 1999.

Vol. 1682: M. Nielsen, P. Johansen, O.F. Olsen, J. Weickert (Eds.), Scale-Space Theories in Computer Vision. Proceedings, 1999. XII, 532 pages. 1999.

Vol. 1683: J. Flum, M. Rodríguez-Artalejo (Eds.), Computer Science Logic. Proceedings, 1999. XI, 580 pages. 1999.

Vol. 1684: G. Ciobanu, G. Păun (Eds.), Fundamentals of Computation Theory. Proceedings, 1999. XI, 570 pages. 1999.

Vol. 1685: P. Amestoy, P. Berger, M. Daydé, I. Duff, V. Frayssé, L. Giraud, D. Ruiz (Eds.), Euro-Par'99. Parallel Processing. Proceedings, 1999. XXXII, 1503 pages. 1999.

Vol. 1687: O. Nierstrasz, M. Lemoine (Eds.), Software Engineering – ESEC/FSE '99. Proceedings, 1999. XII, 529 pages. 1999.

Vol. 1688: P. Bouquet, L. Serafini, P. Brézillon, M. Benerecetti, F. Castellani (Eds.), Modeling and Using Context. Proceedings, 1999. XII, 528 pages. 1999. (Subseries LNAI).

Vol. 1689: F. Solina, A. Leonardis (Eds.), Computer Analysis of Images and Patterns. Proceedings, 1999. XIV, 650 pages. 1999.

Vol. 1690: Y. Bertot, G. Dowek, A. Hirschowitz, C. Paulin, L. Théry (Eds.), Theorem Proving in Higher Order Logics. Proceedings, 1999. VIII, 359 pages. 1999.

Vol. 1691: J. Eder, I. Rozman, T. Welzer (Eds.), Advances in Databases and Information Systems. Proceedings, 1999. XIII, 383 pages. 1999.

Vol. 1692: V. Matoušek, P. Mautner, J. Ocelíková, P. Sojka (Eds.), Text, Speech and Dialogue. Proceedings, 1999. XI, 396 pages. 1999. (Subseries LNAI).

Vol. 1693: P. Jayanti (Ed.), Distributed Computing. Proceedings, 1999. X, 357 pages. 1999.

Vol. 1694: A. Cortesi, G. Filé (Eds.), Static Analysis. Proceedings, 1999. VIII, 357 pages. 1999.

Vol. 1695: P. Barahona, J.J. Alferes (Eds.), Progress in Artificial Intelligence. Proceedings, 1999. XI, 385 pages. 1999. (Subseries LNAI).

Vol. 1696: S. Abiteboul, A.-M. Vercoustre (Eds.), Research and Advanced Technology for Digital Libraries. Proceedings, 1999. XII, 497 pages. 1999.

Vol. 1697: J. Dongarra, E. Luque, T. Margalef (Eds.), Recent Advances in Parallel Virtual Machine and Message Passing Interface. Proceedings, 1999. XVII, 551 pages. 1999.

Vol. 1698: M. Felici, K. Kanoun, A. Pasquini (Eds.), Computer Safety, Reliability and Security. Proceedings, 1999. XVIII, 482 pages. 1999.

Vol. 1699: S. Albayrak (Ed.), Intelligent Agents for Telecommunication Applications. Proceedings, 1999. IX, 191 pages. 1999. (Subseries LNAI).

Vol. 1701: W. Burgard, T. Christaller, A.B. Cremers (Eds.), KI-99: Advances in Artificial Intelligence. Proceedings, 1999. XI, 311 pages. 1999. (Subseries LNAI).

Vol. 1702: G. Nadathur (Ed.), Principles and Practice of Declarative Programming. Proceedings, 1999. X, 434 pages. 1999.

Vol. 1703: P. Laurence, T. Kropf (Eds.), Correct Hardware Design and Verification Methods. Proceedings, 1999. XI, 366 pages. 1999.

Vol. 1704: Jan M. Żytkow, J. Rauch (Eds.), Principles of Data Mining and Knowledge Discovery. Proceedings, 1999. XIV, 593 pages. 1999. (Subseries LNAI).

Vol. 1705: H. Ganzinger, D. McAllester, A. Voronkov (Eds.), Logic for Programming and Automated Reasoning. Proceedings, 1999. XII, 397 pages. 1999. (Subseries LNAI).

Vol. 1707: H.-W. Gellersen (Ed.), Handheld and Ubiquitous Computing. Proceedings, 1999. XII, 390 pages. 1999.

Vol. 1708: J.M. Wing, J. Woodcock, J. Davies (Eds.), FM'99 – Formal Methods. Proceedings Vol. I, 1999. XVIII, 937 pages. 1999.

Vol. 1709: J.M. Wing, J. Woodcock, J. Davies (Eds.), FM'99 – Formal Methods. Proceedings Vol. II, 1999. XVIII, 937 pages. 1999.